Alaster Crowley

# THE WORKS

OF

# ALEISTER CROWLEY

*WITH PORTRAITS*

VOLUME I

Martino Publishing
Mansfield Centre, CT
2012

*Martino Publishing*
*P.O. Box 373,*
*Mansfield Centre, CT 06250 USA*

www.martinopublishing.com

ISBN   978-1-61427-279-3

© *2012  Martino Publishing*

Cover design by T. Matarazzo

*Printed in the United States of America On 100% Acid-Free Paper*

# THE WORKS

OF

# ALEISTER CROWLEY

*WITH PORTRAITS*

VOLUME I

FOYERS
SOCIETY FOR THE PROPAGATION OF
RELIGIOUS TRUTH
1905

# PREFACE

IT is not without some misgiving that I have undertaken to edit the collected writings of Aleister Crowley. The task has been no easy one. His numerous references to the obscurer bypaths of classical mythology, and his not less frequent allusions to the works of Qabalistic writers, have demanded much elucidation. In making the explanatory notes, I have endeavoured to strike a golden mean between the attitude of Browning, when he published "Sordello," and that of Huxley, who took it for granted that his readers were entirely ignorant: and only such passages or phrases have been annotated as were thought likely to present any difficulty to the student of ordinary intelligence.

It is no part of the duty of an editor to assume the rôle of critic. But I must explain that I am conscious of Crowley's weaknesses. They are in the main the outcome of his astonishing perversity; nowhere more strikingly demonstrated than in "The Poem," throughout which there is a struggle for the supremacy between his sense of the ridiculous and his sense of the sublime.

I am also aware that his views on religious matters will be found unpalatable in some quarters. But it should be remembered that these writings represent the ideas of a man of an unconventional mind brought up in conventional surroundings. When he came to man's estate he not unnaturally revolted: and the result has been, as in many such cases, that his search for the truth has led him to investigate the religious beliefs of many nations; nor have those investigations tended to lessen the gulf which separates him from the orthodox point of view.

The edition is authorised, and, as such, complete: therein are contained all the important works of Aleister Crowley.

I. B.

LONDON, *March* 1905.

# CONTENTS OF VOLUME I.

# ACELDAMA,

## A PLACE TO BURY STRANGERS IN.

### A Philosophical Poem.

### 1898.

[The poems collected in Volume I. comprise the whole of the first period of Crowley's life; namely, that of spiritual and mystic enthusiasm. The poet himself would be inclined to class them as Juvenilia. A few other early poems appear in "Oracles," Vol. II., chosen as illustrative of the progress of his art. The great bulk of the early MSS. from 1887 to 1897 have been sedulously sought out and destroyed. They were very voluminous.]

## ACELDAMA.

"I contemplate myself in that dim sphere
Whose hollow centre I am standing at
With burning eyes intent to penetrate
The black circumference, and find out God."

"Except a corn of wheat fall into the ground and die, it abideth alone; but if it die, it bringeth forth much fruit. He that loveth his life shall lose it; and he that hateth his life in this world shall keep it unto life eternal."—ST. JOHN xii. 24, 25.

IT was a windy night, that memorable seventh night of December, when this philosophy was born in me. How the grave old Professor[1] wondered at my ravings! I had called at his house, for he was a valued friend of mine, and I felt strange thoughts and emotions shake within me. Ah! how I raved! I called to him to trample me, he would not. We passed together into the stormy night. I was on horseback, how I galloped round him in my phrenzy, till he became the prey of a real physical fear! How I shrieked out I know not what strange words! And the poor good old man tried all he could to calm me; he thought I was mad! The fool! I was in the death struggle with self: God and Satan fought for my soul those three long hours. God conquered—now I have only one doubt left—which of the twain was God? Howbeit, I aspire!

"And falling headlong, he burst asunder in the midst, and all his bowels gushed out. . . . Insomuch as that field is called in their proper tongue, Aceldama, that is to say—the field of blood."—ACTS i. 18, 19.

[1] C. G. Lamb, Demonstrator of Engineering at Cambridge.

## DEDICATION.

DIVINE PHILOSOPHER![1] Dear Friend![2]
Lover and Lord![3] accept the verse
That marches like a sombre hearse,
Bearing Truth's coffin, to the end.

Let man's distorted worships blend
In this, the worthier and the worse,
And penetrate the primal curse.
Alas! They will not comprehend.

Accept this gospel of disease
In wanton words proclaimed, receive
The blood-wrought chaplet that I weave.

Take me, and with thine infamies
Mingle my shame, and on my breast
Let thy desire achieve the rest.

## ACELDAMA.

"Six months and I sit still and hold
In two cold palms her cold two feet;
Her hair, half grey half ruined gold,
Thrills me and burns me in kissing it.

Love bites and stings me through to see
Her keen face made of sunken bones.
Her worn-out eyelids madden me,
That were shot through with purple once."
SWINBURNE, "The Leper,"
*Poems and Ballads*, 1866.

[1] Von Eckartshausen.
[2] An adept who was in correspondence with the author.
[3] Christ.

## ACELDAMA.

DARK night, red night.   This lupanar [1]
Has rosy flames that dip, that shake,
Faint phantoms that disturb the lake
Of magic mirror-land.   A star
Like to a beryl, with a flake
        Of olive light
Struck through its dull profound, is steadfast
    in the night.

### I.

I AM quite sane, quite quiet.   Sober thought
Is as a woof to my mad dreams.   My brain
Beats to the double stroke ; the double
    strain
Warps its gray fibres ; all the dream is
    wrought
A spider-tapestry ; the old blood-stain
        Spreads through the air
Some hot contagious growth to slay men
    unaware.

### II.

I have discovered God !   His ghastly way
Of burning ploughshares for my naked
    feet
Lies open to me—shall I find it sweet
To give up sunlight for that mystic day
    That beams its torture, whose red banners
    beat
        Their radiant fire
Into my shrivelled head, to wither Love's
    desire ?

### III.

I was a child long years ago, it seems,
    Or months it may be—I am still a child !
They pictured me the stars as wheeling
    wild
In a huge bowl of water ; but my dreams
    Built it of Titan oak, its sides were piled
        Of fearful wood
Hewn from God's forests, paid with sweat
    and tears and blood.

[1] Brothel.

### IV.

I crept, a stealthy, hungry soul, to grasp
    Its vast edge, to look out to the beyond ;
To know.   My eyes strained out, there
    was no bond,
No continuity, no bridge to clasp,
    No pillars for the universe.   Immond,[1]
        Shapeless, unstayed,
Nothing, Nothing, Nothing, Nothing !   I
    was afraid.

### V.

That was my sanity.   Brought face to face
    Suddenly with the infinite, I feared.
My brain snapped, broke ; white oarage-
    wings [2] appeared
On stronger shoulders set, a carapace,
    A chariot.   I did essay that weird
        Unmeasured dome ;
Found in its balance, peace ; found in its
    silence, home.

### VI.

That was my madness.   On bright plumage
    poised
    I soared, I hovered in the infinite ;
Nothing was everything ; the day was
    night,
Dark and deep light together, that rejoiced
    In their strange wedlock.   Marvellously
    white
        All rainbows kissed
Into one sphere that stood, a circumambient
    mist.

### VII.

I climbed still inwards.   At the moveless point
    Where all power, light, life, motion con-
    centrate,
I found God dwelling.   Strong, immaculate,
He knew me and he loved !   His lips anoint
    My lips with love ; with thirst insatiate
        He drank my breath,
Absorbed my life in His, dispersed me, gave
    me death.

[1] Unclean—from the French *immonde.*
[2] *Cf.* Virgil, *Aeneid*, vi. 20.

### VIII.

This is release, is freedom, is desire ;
  This is the one hope that a man may gain ;
  This is the lasting ecstasy of pain
That fools reject, the dread, the searching
     fire
    That quivers in the marrow, that in vain
      Burns secretly
The unconsuméd bush where God lurks
    privily.

### IX.

This was a dream—and how may I attain?
  How make myself a worthy acolyte?
  How from my body shall my soul take
     flight,
Being constrained in this devouring chain
    Of selfishness? How purge the spirit quite
      Of gross desires
That eat into the heart with their corrupting
    fires ?

### X.

Old Buddha gave command ; Jehovah spake ;
  Strange distant gods that are not dead to-
    day
Added their voices ; Heaven's desart way
Man wins not but by sorrow—let him break
  The golden image with the feet of clay ![1]
      Let him despise
That earthen vessel which the potter marred [2]
  —and rise !

### XI.

As life burns strong, the spirit's flame grows
    dull ;
  The ruddy-cheeked sea-breezes shame its
     spark ;
  Wan rainy winds of autumn on the dark
Leafless and purple moors, that rage and lull
  With a damned soul's despair, these leave
    their mark,
      Their brand of fire
That burns the dross, that wings the heart to
    its desire.

[1] Vide Daniel ii.
[2] Oriental symbol for the body.

### XII.

No prostitution may be shunned by him
  Who would achieve this Heaven.  No
    satyr-song,
  No maniac dance shall ply so fast the thong
Of lust's imagining perversely dim
    That no man's spirit may keep pace, so
    strong
      Its pang must pierce;
Nor all the pains of hell may be one tithe as
    fierce.

### XIII.

All degradation, all sheer infamy,
  Thou shalt endure.  Thy head beneath the
    mire
  And dung of worthless women shall desire
As in some hateful dream, at last to lie ;
    Woman must trample thee till thou respire
      That deadliest fume ;[1]
The vilest worms must crawl, the loathliest
    vampires gloom.[2]

### XIV.

Thou must breathe in all poisons ; for thy
    meat,
  Poison ; for drink, still poison ; for thy
    kiss,
  A serpent's lips !  An agony is this
That sweats out venom ; thy clenched hands,
    thy feet
  Ooze blood, thine eyes weep blood ; thine
    anguish is
      More keen than death.
At last—there is no deeper vault of hell
    beneath !

### XV.

Then thine abasement bringeth back the
    sheaves
  Of golden corn of exaltation,
  Ripened and sweetened by the very sun

[1] The concrete expression of the horror of
the individual.
[2] Morbid imaginations, which ever torment
the traveller upon the path of asceticism.

Whose far-off fragrance steals between the
leaves
Of the cool forest, filling every one
    That reaps yon gold
With strange intoxications mad and manifold.

### XVI.

Only beware gross pleasure—the delight
  Of fools : the ecstasy, the trance of love—
Life's atom-bonds must strain—aye, and
  must move,
And all the body be forgotten quite,
  And the pure soul flame forth, a deathless
  dove,
    Where all worlds end !
If thou art worthy God shall greet thee for a
friend.

### XVII.

I am unworthy.  In the House of Pain
  There are ten thousand shrines.  Each one
  enfolds
  A lesser, inner, more divine, that holds
A sin less palpable and less profane.
  The inmost is the home of God.  He
  moulds
    Infinity,
The great within the small, one stainless
unity !

### XVIII.

I dare not to the greater sins aspire ;
  I might—so gross am I—take pleasure in
  These filthy holocausts, that burn to sin
A damnéd incense in the hellish fire
  Of human lust—earth's joys no heaven may
  win ;
    Pain holds the prize
In blood-stained hands ; Love laughs, with
anguish in His eyes.

### XIX.

These little common sins may lead my lust
  To more deceitful vices, to the deeds
  At whose sweet name the side of Jesus
  bleeds

In sympathy new-nurtured by the trust
  Of man's forgiveness that his passion
  breeds—
    These petty crimes !
God grant they grow intense in newer,
worthier times !

### XX.

Yet—shall I make me subject to a pang
  So horrible ?  O God, abase me still !
  Break with Thy rod my unrepentant will,
Lest Hell entrap me with an iron fang !
  Grind me, most high Jehovah, in the mill
    That grinds so small !
Grind down to dust and powder Pride of
  Life—and all !

### XXI.

In every ecstasy exalt my heart ;
  Let every trance make loose and light the
  wings
  My soul must shake, ere her pure fabric
  springs
Clothed in the secret dream-delights of Art
  Transcendant into air, the tomb of Things ;
    Let every kiss
Melt on my lips to flame, fling back the gates
  of Dis ! [1]

### XXII.

Give me a master !  not some learned priest
  Who by long toil and anguish has devised
  A train of mysteries, but some despised
Young king of men, whose spirit is released
  From all the weariness, whose lips are
  prized
    By men not much—
Ah ! let them only once grow warm, my lips
  to touch.

### XXIII.

Ah ! under his protection, in his love,
  With my abasements emulating his,
  We surely should attain to That which Is,

[1] A name contracted from Dives, sometimes
given to Pluto and hence also to the lower
world.  But *vide* Dante, *Inferno*, Canto xxxiv.

And lose ourselves, together, far above
  The highest heaven, in one sweet lover's
    kiss,
        So sweet, so strong,
That with it all my soul should unto him
  belong.

### XXIV.

An ecstasy to which no life responds,
  Is the enormous secret I have learned :
  When self-denial's furnace-flame has
    burned
Through love, and all the agonising bonds
  That hold the soul within its shell are
    turned
        To water weak ;
Then may desires obtain the cypress crown
  they seek.

### XXV.

Browning attained, I think, when Evelyn
  Hope
  Gave no response to his requickening kiss ;
  In the brief moment when exceeding bliss
Joined to her sweet passed soul his soul, its
  scope
  Grew infinite for ever.   So in this
        Profane desire
I too may join my song unto his quenchless
  quire.

### XXVI.

When Hallam died, did Tennyson attain
  When his warm kisses drew no answering
    sigh
  From that poor corpse corrupted utterly,
When four diverse sweet dews exude to stain
  With chaste foul fervour the cold canopy ?
        Proud Reason's sheath
He cast away ; the sword of Madness flames
  beneath !

### XXVII.

Read his mad rhymes ; their sickening savour
  taste ;
  Bathe in their carnal and depraving stream :
  Rise, glittering with the dew-drops of his
    dream,

And glow with exaltation ; to thy waist
  Gird his gold belt ; the diamond settings
    gleam
        With fire drawn far
Through the blue shuddering vault from some
  amazing star.

### XXVIII.

Aubrey[1] attained in sleep when he dreamt
  this
  Wonderful dream of women, tender child
  And harlot, naked all, in thousands piled
On one hot writhing heap, his shameful
  kiss
  To shudder through them, with lithe limbs
    defiled
        To wade, to dip
Down through the mass, caressed by every
  purple lip.

### XXIX.

Choked with their reek and fume and bitter
  sweat
  His body perishes ; his life is drained ;
  The last sweet drop of nectar has not
    stained
Another life ; his lips and limbs are wet
  With death-dews !  Ha !  The painter has
    attained
        As high a meed
As his who first begot sweet music on a reed.

### XXX.

And O ! my music is so poor and thin !
  I am poor Marsyas[2] ; where shall I find
  A wise Olympas and a lover kind
To teach my mouth to sing some secret sin,
  Faint, fierce, and horrible ; to tune my
    mind,
        And on a reed
Better beloved to bid me discourse at his
  need ?

[1] Aubrey Beardsley.   The dream is authentic.
[2] Marsyas, a Satyr, inventor of the pastoral flute ; Olympas, his favourite pupil.   It will be seen that the names are carelessly transposed.

## XXXI.

Master !¹ I think that I have found thee
  now :
  Deceive me not, I trust thee, I am sure
  Thy love will stand while ocean winds
    endure.
Our quest shall be our quest till either brow
  Radiate light, till death himself allure
        Our love to him
When life's desires are filled beyond the
  silver brim.

## XXXII.

Here I abandon all myself to thee,
  Slip into thy caresses as of right,
  Live in thy kisses as in living light,
Clothed in thy love, enthronéd lazily
  In thine embrace, as naked as the night,
        As love and lover
More pure, more keen, more strong than all
  my dreams discover.

¹ Christ.

## EPILOGUE.

My heavy hair upon my olive skin
  (*Baise la lourde crinière !*)
Frames with its ebony a face like sin.
  My heavy hair !

You touched my lips and told me I was fair ;
  It was your wickedness my love to win.
(*Baise la lourde crinière !*)
Your passion has destroyed my soul—what
    care
  If you desire me, and I hold you in
My arms a little, and you love for lair
    My heavy hair !

It is a fatal web your fingers spin.
  (*Baise la lourde crinière !*)
Let our love end as other loves begin,
  Or, slay me in a moment, unaware !
Nay ? Kiss in double death-pang, if you
    dare !
Or one day I will strangle you within
    My heavy hair !

# THE TALE OF ARCHAIS.

## A ROMANCE IN VERSE.

### 1898.

TO

## THE WHITE MAIDENS OF ENGLAND

THIS TALE OF GREECE IS DEDICATED.

## THE AUTHOR'S BALLADE OF HIS TALE.

Go to the woodlands, English maid,
　Or where the downs to seaward bend,
When autumn is in gold arrayed,
　Or spring is green, or winters send
A frosty sun, or summers blend
Their flowers in every dainty dye,
　And take, as you would take a friend,
This pleasant tale of Thessaly.

Lie on the greensward, while the shade
　Shortens as morning doth ascend
The gates of Heaven, and bud and blade
　Laugh at the dawn, while breezes lend
Their music, till you comprehend
The meaning of the world, and sigh—
　Yet love makes happy in the end
This pleasant tale of Thessaly.

Turn from my book, the poet prayed,
　And look to Heaven, an hour to spend
Before His throne who spake and bade
　The fountains of the deep descend,
And bade the earth uproot and rend
To pitch like tents the mountains high,
　And gave him language who hath penned
This pleasant tale of Thessaly.

### ENVOI.

Fair maiden, who hast rightly weighed
　The message of the morning sky,
Think kindly of the man who made
　This pleasant tale of Thessaly.

## THE TALE OF ARCHAIS.

### PART I.

SHE lay within the water, and the sun
Made golden with his pleasure every one
Of small cool ripples that surround her
　throat,
Mix with her curls, and catch the hands that
　float
Like water-lilies on the wave ; she lay
And watched the silver fishes leap and play,
And almost slept upon the soughing breast
That murmured gentle melodies of rest,
And touched her tiny ear, and made her
　dream
Of sunny woods above the sacred stream
Where she abode (her home was cool and
　dark
That no small glow-worm with his tender
　spark
Might lighten till the moon was down, a nook
Far from the cool enticements of the brook,
And hidden in the boskage close and green.)
So dreamed she, smiling like a faëry queen ;
So the bright feet and forehead of the breeze
Lured her to sleep, and shook the morning
　trees
Clear of the dewfall, and disturbed the grass,
So that no rustle, should a serpent pass,
Might rouse her reverie.   So then, behold,
Chance leant from Heaven with feet and face
　of gold,
And hid the iron of her body bare
With such warm cloudlets as the morning air

7

Makes to conceal the fading of the stars :
Chance bowed herself across the sunny bars,
And watched where through the silence of
　　the lawn
Came Charicles, the darling of the dawn,
Slowly, and to his steps took little heed ;
He came towards the pool, his god-wrought
　　reed
Shrilling dim visions of things glorious,
And saw the maiden, that disported thus,
And worshipped.   Then in doubt he stood,
　　grown white
And wonderful, with passion's perfect might
Firing his veins and tingling in his brain,
He stood and whitened, and waxed red
　　again.
His oat[1] unheeded glanced beneath the
　　wave,
His eyes grew bright and burning, his lips
　　clave—
A sudden cry broke from him : from the
　　height
His swift young body, like a ray of light,
Divides the air, a moment, and the pool
Flings up the spray like dew, divinely cool :
A moment, and he flashed towards her side
And caught her trembling, as a tender bride
At the first kiss ; he caught her, and compelled
Her answer, in his arms securely held.
And she no word might say ; her red lips
　　quailed,
Her perfect eyelids drooped, her warm cheek
　　paled,
A tear stole over it.   His lips repent
With vain weak words—O iron firmament !
How vain, how cold are words !—his lips
　　repeat
Their faint sweet savour, but her rosy feet
Held in his hands and touched with reverent
　　lips
Revived her soul more perfectly.   Soon slips
Her gentle answer ; now her timid eyes
So tender with the lifted lashes rise
To meet his gaze.
　　　　　　He spoke : " Have pity on me
Who wronged thee for my perfect love of thee,

[1] Panpipe.

My perfect love, O love ! for strange and
　　dread
Delights consume me ; I am as one dead
Beating at Heaven's gate with nerveless
　　wing,
Wailing because the song the immortals sing
Is so fast barred behind the iron sky.
Speak but thine anger quickly ; let me
　　die ! "
" But I forgive thee, thou art good and
　　kind."
" O love ! O love ! O mistress of my
　　mind,
You love me ! " " Nay, I was awhile afraid,
Being so white and tender ; for a maid
I lived alone with flower and brook, nor
　　guessed
Another dwelt within the quiet nest
That these woods build me ; hold my tremb-
　　ling hand,
Teach me to love ; I do not understand."
He clasped her to him, but no word might
　　say,
And led her from the pool a little way,
And there he laid her on the flowery mead,
And watched her weeping.   His forgotten
　　reed
Floated away, a ship for fairy folk,
Along the limpid rivulet.   Then broke
From smitten heart and ravished lips the
　　tongue
Of fire that clad its essence with the robe of
　　song.

### SONG OF CHARICLES.

MAN's days are dim, his deeds are dust,
　　His span is but a little space,
He lusts to live, he lives to lust,
His soul is barren of love or trust,
His heart is hopeless, seeing he must
　　Perish, and leave no trace :
With impious rage he mocks the bounds
　　Of earth, albeit so wholly base ;
His ears are dead to subtle sounds,
His eyes are blind, for Zeus confounds
His vain irreverence, and astounds
　　High Heaven with wrathful face.

But I am born of gods, and turn
  My eyes to thee, thyself divine.
My vigorous heart and spirit yearn
With love, my cheeks with passion burn—
As thy clear eyes may well discern
  By gazing into mine.
Thy heart is cool, thy cheeks are pale,
  Nor blush with shame like winter wine
To understand my amorous tale,
For words and looks of Love must fail
To touch thee, since a snowy veil
  Is 'twixt my mind and thine.

Dear goddess, at whose early breast
  I drank in all desires and woes;
Most reverend god, who oft caressed
Her pale chaste wifehood, and who pressed
Upon my forehead kisses blest;
  Bid blossom out this rose,
This fair white bud whose heart is pure,
  Whose bosom fears not, neither knows
The long vague mysteries that endure
Of life uncertain, of love sure.
Teach her the mystic overture
  To Love's transcendant throes.

He ceased : but out of Heaven no sound of
  might,
No tongue of flame gave answer.  Still as
  night,
Silence and sunlight, stream and mead, pos-
  sessed
The whole wide world.   The maid's re-
  luctant breast
Heaved with soft passion nowise under-
  stood,
And her pulse quickened.   Through the
  quiet wood
Her answer rang: " My voice with thine
  shall break
The woodland stillness, for the fountain's
  sake.
I'll sing thee—Lamia ! mother, I obey !"
In vain the desperate boy pursued the way
With awful eyes ; no bruiséd flower betrayed
The tender footsteps of a goddess maid ;
No butterfly flew frightened ; on the pool
No ripple spoke of her; the streamlet cool

Had no small wreath of amber mist to mark
Her flight ; she was not there, the silver
  spark
Had flashed and faded ; all the field was bare,
No wave of wing bestirred the sultry air,
Save only where the noontide lark rose high
To chant his liberty.   The vaulted sky
Was one blue cupola of rare turquoise
That shimmered with the heat.
                His pulses pause
For his despair ineffable.   Her name
He called; she was not, and the piercing
  flame
Of love struck through him, till his tortured
  mind
Drove his young limbs, the wolf that hunts
  the hind,
Far through the forest.   Lastly sleep, like
  death,
With strong compulsion of his labouring
  breath
Came on him dreamless.
            When he woke, the day
Stooped toward the splendour of the western
  bay,
And he remembered.   Like a wild bird's cry
The song within him flamed, a melody
Dreadful and beautiful.   The sad sea heard
And echoed over earth its bitter word.

### SONG.

Ere the grape of joy is golden
  With the summer and the sun,
Ere the maidens unbeholden
  Gather one by one,
To the vineyard comes the shower,
No sweet rain to fresh the flower,
  But the thunder rain that cleaves,
  Rends and ruins tender leaves.

Ere the wine of perfect pleasure
  From a perfect chalice poured,
Swells the veins with such a measure
  As the garden's lord
Makes his votaries dance to, death
Draws with soft delicious breath
  To the maiden and the man.
  Love and life are both a span.

Ere the crimson lips have planted
  Paler roses, warmer grapes,
Ere the maiden breasts have panted,
  And the sunny shapes
Flit around to bless the hour,
Comes men know not what false flower:
  Ere the cup is drained, the wine
  Grows unsweet, that was divine.

All the subtle airs are proven
  False at dewfall, at the dawn
Sin and sorrow, interwoven,
  Like a veil are drawn
Over love and all delight;
Grey desires invade the white.
  Love and life are but a span;
  Woe is me! and woe is man!

The sound stood trembling in the forest dim
Lingering a little, yet there taketh him
A strong man's one short moment of despair.
He fell, the last of Titans, his loose hair
Tangled in roses; while his heart and mind
Broken and yet imperishable, blind,
Hateful, desire they know not what, and turn
Lastly to pray for death; his wild eyes burn,
And bitter tears divide his doubtful breath.
So grew his anguish to accomplish death,
Had not the goddess with the rosy shoon
Stoop'd o'er the silver surface of the moon
To touch his brow with slumber, like a kiss
Whose dreams perfused the name of Archais,
Till the sweet odour dulled his brain, and
  sleep
Loosened his limbs, most dreamless and most
  deep.
The mosses serve him for a bed; the trees
Wave in the moonlight, daughters of the
  breeze;
Hardly the pleasant waters seem to shake,
And only nightingales, for slumber's sake,
Lull the soft stars and seas, and matchless
  music make.

And now the sun is risen above the deep;
The mists pass slowly on the uplands steep;
Far snows are luminous with rosy flecks
Of lambent light, and shadow tints and decks
Their distant hollows with black radiance,
While the delivered fountains flash and
  glance
Adown the hills and through the woods of
  pine
And stately larch, with cadences divine
And trills and melodies instinct with light
  and wine.

The sun, arising, sees the sleeping youth
And lumes his locks with evanescent gold,
While birds and breezes, watching, hold them
  mute,
And light and silence, the twin-born of truth,
Reign o'er the meadow, and possess the wold.
The poet bows his head, and lays aside his
  lute.

## PART II.

WHEN God bethought Him, and the world
  began,
He made moist clay, and breathed on it, that
  man
Might be most frail and feeble, and like earth
Shrink at Death's finger from the hour of
  birth;
And like the sea by limits of pale sand
Be utterly confined; but so He planned
To vivify the body with the soul,
That fire and air were wedded to control
The heavy bulk beneath them, so His breath
Touched the warm clay and violated death,
Gave to the spirit wings and bade it rise
To seek its Maker with aspiring eyes,
Gave to the body strength to hold awhile
The spirit, till the passions that defile
Should waste and wither, and the free soul
  soar.
But evil lusted with the soul, and bore
A thousand children deadlier than death;
The sin that enters with the eager breath
Of perfect love; the sin that seeks its home
In lights and longings frailer than the foam;
The sin that loves the hollows of the night,
The sin that fears; the sin that hates the
  light;
The sin that looks with wistful eyes; the sin
That trembles on the olive of the skin;

The sin that slumbers; these divide the day
And all the darkness, and deceive, and slay.
And these regather in the womb of hell
To marry and increase, and by the spell
Of their own wickedness discover sin
Unguessed at, by slow treason creeping in,
To spread corruption, and destroy the earth.
But in the holy hour and happy birth
That swam through stars propitious, meadows white,
And fresh with newer flowers of the night
In the pale fields supernal, when his sire
Took from the nurse the child of his desire,
A man, the prayers of many maidens sent
So sweet a savour through the firmament
That no false spirit might draw nigh. And still
His angel ministers defend from ill
The head they nurtured. Evil dreams and spells,
Cast at the dimmest hour, the sword repels
And drives them down the steep of Hell. But dim
Sweet faces of dead maidens drew to him;
Quiet woods and streams and all the mountains tall,
Cool valleys, silver-streaked with waterfall,
Came in his slumbers, chaste and musical,
While through their maze his mind beheld afar
Dim and divine, Archais, like a star.

It was no dream, or else the growing dawn
Deepened the glory of the misted lawn,
For to his eyes, half open now, there seems
A figure, fairer than his dearest dreams.
He sprang, he caught her to his breast, the maid
Smiled and lay back to look at him. He laid
Her tender body on the sloping field,
And felt her sighs in his embraces yield
A sweeter music than all birds. But she,
Lost in the love she might not know, may see
No further than his face, and yet, aware
Of her own fate, resisted like a snare

Her own soft wishes. As she looked and saw
His eager face, the iron rod of law
Grew like a misty pillar in the sky.
In all her veins the blood's desires die,
And then—O sudden ardour!—all her mind
And memory faded, and looked outward, blind,
Beyond their bitterness. Her arms she flung
Around him, and with amorous lips and tongue
Tortured his palate with extreme desire,
And like a Mænad maddened; equal fire
Leapt in his veins; locked close for love they lie,
The heart's dumb word exprest without a sigh
In the strong magic of a lover's kiss,
And the twin light of love; but Archais
Felt through her blood a sudden chill; her face
Blanched and besought a moment's breathing space;
Her heart's desire welled up, and then again
Whitened her cheeks with the exceeding pain
Of uttermost despair. At last her strength
Failed, and she flung her weary body at length
Amid the bruiséd flowers; while from her eyes
Surged the salt tears; low moans she multiplies
Because her love is blasphemous; the wind
Sighs for all answer, sobs and wails behind
Among the trees; the stream grows deadly pale
Hearing her weep, and like a silver sail
The fading moon drifts sorrowful above.
Then Charicles must ask his weeping love
To lead him to the fountain of her tears.
But she, possessed by vague and violent fears,
Spake not a little while, and then began:
"O thou, a child of Heaven, and a man,
Even so my lover, shall my woeful song
So move thy spirit for my bitter wrong
(God-nurtured though thou be) against the rods
Laid on me by my mother, whom the gods

Righteous in anger, doomed, for fiery sin
Kindled by hell-flames, cherishéd within
Her lustful heart, for sin most damnable,
To suffer torment in remotest hell,
Where the grim fiend grinds down with fiery
    stones
The unrepentant marrow of men's bones,
Or chills their blood with poisonous vials of
    death,
Or dooms them to the tooth and venomous
    breath
Of foul black worms; and on the earth to
    dwell
For a long space, and there (most terrible!)
To change her shape at times, and on her
    take
The fierce presentment of a loathly snake
To wander curst and lonely through the dire
    black brake.
And this thing is my mother, whose foul
    tomb
Is a black serpent, spotted with the gloom
Of venomous red flecks, and poisonous
    sweat,
While on her flat lewd head the mark is set
Of utter loathsomeness; and I, her child
Born of incestuous lust, and sore defiled
With evil parentage, am now (Most just
Unpitying Zeus!) condemned with her, I
    must
The hated semblance of a serpent wear
When noon rides forth upon the crystal air."
While yet she spake, the dwindling shadow
    ran
Beneath the feet of Charicles, the wan
Waste water glinted free, and to the deep
Cool pebbles did the kiss of sunshine creep;
The busy lark forgot for joy to sing,
And all the woods with fairy voices ring;
The hills in dreamy languor seem to swoon
Through the blue haze! behold, the hour
    of noon!

And lo! there came to pass the dreadful fate
Her lips had shuddered out; her pulses bate
Their quick sweet movement; on the ground
    she lies
Struggling, and rending Heaven with her cries.

Like light, in one convulsive pang the snake
Leapt in the sunlight, and its body brake
With glistening scales that golden skin of
    hers,
And writhing with pure shame, the long
    grass whirrs
With her sharp flight of fury and despair.
Then Charicles at last became aware
Of the fell death that had him by the throat
To mar his music; like one blind he smote
The quivering air with cries of sorrow; then,
Disdaining fear and sorrow, cried to men
And gods to help him; then, resolved to dare
All wrath and justice, he rose up to swear
(Lifting his right hand to the sky, that glowed
Deadly vermilion, like the poisonous toad
That darts an angry red from out its eye,)
By sword and spear, by maze and mystery,
By Zeus' high house, and by his godhead
    great,
By his own soul, no ardour to abate
Until he freed Archais. Like a star
Rebellious, thrust beyond the morning's bar,
Erect, sublime, he swore so fierce an oath
That the sea flashed with blasphemy, and
    loath
Black thunder broke from out the shudder-
    ing deep.
He swore again, and from its century's sleep
Earthquake arose, and rocked and raved
    and roared.
He swore the third time. But that Heaven's
    Lord
Curbed their black wrath, the stars of
    Heaven's vault
Had rushed to whelm the sun with vehement
    assault.

The heavens stood still, but o'er the quaking
    earth,
That groaned and shrank with the untimely
    birth
Of fury and freedom, Charicles strode on
With fervid foot, to Aphrodite's throne
In seagirt Paphos, to exact her aid—
The sun stood still, creation grew afraid
At his firm step and mien erect and un-
    dismayed.

Strident the godlike hero called aloud
Blaspheming, while that sombre bank of
    cloud
Witnessed the wrath of Zeus; the thunder
    broke
From purple flashes vanished into smoke
That rolled unceasingly through heaven;
    the youth
Cried out against high Zeus, "The cause of
    Truth,
Freedom, and Justice!" and withal strode on
To the vast margin of the waters wan
That barred him from his goal; his cloak he
    stripped,
Then in the waves his sudden body dipped
And with his strenuous hands the emerald
    water gripped.

Long had he struggled (for Poseidon's hand
Heaped foam against him) toward the
    seemly strand,
But that Love's Mother,[1] journeying from
    Rome,
Passed in her car the swimmer, while her
    home
Scarce yet was glimmering o'er the waste
    wide sea
Against whose wrath he strove so silently;
Whom now beholding, checked her eager
    team,
Dipped to the foam from which she sprang.
    whose gleam
Bore the sweet mirage of her eyes, and
    bent
Over the weary Charicles. Content
With him she spake, and he, still buffeting
The waves, looked never up, but with the
    swing
Of strong fierce limbs, clove through the
    water gray.
Hearing her voice, he answered, "Ere the
    day
Has fallen from his pinnacle must I
Reach sea-girt Paphos, with a bitter cry
To clasp the knees of Cytherea, and pray
That she will aid me." Then the billows
    lay

[1] Aphrodite.

Fondly quiescent while she answered him:
"Yea, are thine eyes with weeping grown
    so dim
Thou canst not see who hovers over thee?
For I am she thou seekest. Come with me,
And tell me all thy grief; thy prayer is
    heard
Before thy spirit clothes in wintry word
The fire it throbs with." So her eager
    doves
Waited. From seas grown calm the wanton
    loves
Lifted the hero to the pearly car,
Whose floor was azure and whose front a
    star
Set in seven jewels girt with ivory.

Then the light rein the goddess left to lie
Unheeded, and the birds flew on apace,
Until the glint and glory of the place
Grew o'er the blue dim line of ocean.
It was a temple never built of man,
Being of marble white, and all unhewn,
Above a cliff, about whose base were strewn
Boulders of amethyst or malachite.
Save these the cliffs rose sheer, a dazzling
    white,
Six hundred feet from ocean; so divine
Was the tall precipice, that from the shrine
A child might fling a stone and splash it in
    the brine.
Within whose silver courts and lily bowers
The Queen of Love led Charicles; white
    flowers
Blushed everywhere to scarlet, as her feet,
Themselves more white, did touch them.
    On a seat,
White with strewn rose, and leaves of silver
    birch,
Remote from courts profane, and vulgar
    search,
They rested, till the hero's tale was told.
Then Aphrodite loosed a snake of gold
From her arm's whiteness, and upon his
    wrist
Clasped it. Its glittering eyes of amethyst
Fascinate him. "Even so," the goddess cried,
"I will bind on thy arm the serpent bride

Free from her fate, and promise by this kiss
The warmer kisses of thy Archais."
She spake, and on his brow, betwixt her
    hands
Pressed softly, as a maid in bridal bands,
Kissed him a mother's kiss.   Then Charicles
Gave her due thanks, and bent his ear to
    seize
Her further words.  And she: "Not many
    days
Shall flame and flicker into darkened ways
Before the wings of night, ere Hermes fly
Hither, the messenger of Zeus.   But I
Bid thee remain beneath the temple gate
While I consider of our war on Fate.
Till then, and I will tell thee everything
That thou must do; but now let song take
    wing
Till the pale air swoon with the deep delight
That makes cool noontide from the sultry
    night.
What are your dreams, my maidens?   Your
    young dreams?
Are they of passion, or of rocks and streams,
Of purple mountains, clad about with green,
Or do their lamps grow dim in the unseen?
Sing to this hero; sing, lure slumber to your
    queen."

## SONG OF APHRODITE'S HANDMAIDENS.

My dreams are sweet, because my heart is
    free,
    Because our locks still mingle and lips
    meet,
Because thine arms still hold me tenderly,
    My dreams are sweet.

Visions of waters rippling by my feet,
    Trees that re-weave their branches lovingly,
Birds that pass passionate on pinions fleet :

Such quiet joys my eyes in slumber see—
    Let death's keen sickle wander through
    the wheat !
I love not life o'ermuch; since loving thee
    My dreams are sweet.

Sing, little bird, it is dawn ;
    Cry ! with the day the woods ring ;
Now in the blush of the morn
    Sing !

Love doth enchain me and cling,
    Love, of the breeze that is born,
Love, with the breeze that takes wing.

Love that is lighter than scorn,
    Love, that is strong as a king,
Love, through the gate that is horn, [1]
    Sing !

Then Charicles rejoicing quickly ran
And chose a lyre, and thus his song began
Rippling through melodies unheard of man.

## SONG OF CHARICLES.

Wake, fairy maid, for the day
    Blushes our curtain to shake ;
Summer and blossoms of May
    Wake !

Lilies drink light on the lake,
    Laughter drives dreamland away,
Kisses shall woo thee, and slake

Passion with amorous play,
    Clip thee and love, for Love's sake.
Wake and caress me, I pray,
    Wake !

Snow-hills and streams, dew-diamonded,
    Call us from silvery dreams
To where the morning kindles red
    Snow-hills and streams.

See, breezes whisper, sunlight gleams
    With gentle kissings; flowers shed
Pale scents, the whole sweet meadow steams.

Forth, glittering shoulders, golden head,
    And tune our lutes to tender themes
Among the lost loves of the dead,
    Snow-hills and streams.

[1] The gate through which true dreams are
perceived.

The queen clapped dainty hands, caressed of dew,
And bade the love-lorn wanderer sing anew.
His muse came trembling, soon through starry air it flew.

SONG OF CHARICLES.

Within the forest gloom
 There lies a lover's bower,
  A lotus-flower
   In bloom.

O lotus-flower too white,
 Starred purple, round and sweet,
  Rich golden wheat
   Of night !

I'll kiss thee, lotus-flower,
 I'll pluck thee, yellow grain,
  Once and again
   This hour.

There coos a dove to me
 Across the waves of space ;
  O passionate face
   To see !

I'll woo thee, silver dove,
 Caress thee, lotus-flower ;
  It is the hour
   Of Love.

Cypris blushed deep ; albeit for love did swoon
At the song's sweetness, while the cold dead moon
Was still and pale ; her nymphs are fain to sigh
With sudden longing filled, and like to die
For vain delight, for still across the sea
Stole sensuous breaths of Sapphic melody
From the far strand of Lesbos ; then there came
Into their eyes a new and awful flame
Suddenly burning ; now upon the beach
The waves kept tune in unexpressive speech
As the sad voice drew nigh ; the hero shrank
Like one in awe ; the flame shot up and sank

From the crimson-vestured altar ; then the song
Found in the wavering breeze from over sea a tongue.

Here, on the crimson strand of blood-red waters,
 We, Cypris, not thy daughters,
Clad in bright flame, filled with unholy wine,
 O Cypris, none of thine !—

Here, kissing in the dim red dusk, we linger,
 Striking with amorous finger
Our lyres, whose fierce delights are all divine—
 O Cypris, none of thine !

Quenchless, insatiable, the unholy fire
 Floods our red lips' desire ;
Our kisses sting, as barren as the brine—
 O Cypris, none of thine !

Our songs are awful, that the heavens shrink back
 Into their void of black.
We worship at a sad insatiate shrine—
 O Cypris, none of thine !

Scarcely the song did cease when out of heaven
A little cloud grew near, all thunder-riven,
Scarred by the lightning, torn of ravaging wind ;
Upon it sate the herald, who should find
The home of Aphrodite, and should bring
A message from high Zeus. The mighty king
Had bidden him to speed. His wings drew nigh
And hushed the last faint echoed melody
With silver waving. As the messenger
Of mighty Zeus descending unto her
He stood before her, and called loud her name,
Wrapped in a cloud of amber-scented flame
Befitting his high office ; but his word,
Too terrible for mortals, passed unheard

To Cypris' ear alone.  She bowed her head
And bade her nymphs prepare a royal bed
Where he should rest awhile ; and, being
   gone,
Cypris and Charicles were left alone.
An aureole of purple round her brow
Flames love no more ; but fierce defiance now
Knotted the veins, suffused them with rich
   blood,
And wrath restrained from sight the torrid
   flood
Of tears; her eyes were terrible; she spake:
" Rise for thy life, and flee.  Arise, awake,
And hide thee in the temple; Zeus hath
   spoken
To me—me, Queen of Love—O sceptre
   broken !—
O vainest of all realms ! that thou must die.
This only chance is left thee yet, to fly
Within that sanctity even he not dares
To touch with impious hand ; thus un-
   awares
Creep in among the columns to a gate
My hand shall show thee; it will open
   straight
And thou must lie forgotten till his rage
Have lost its first excess—then may we wage
A more successful war against his power."
But Charicles : " Shall I for one short hour
Fly from his tyranny?  Am I such man
As should flee from him ?  Let the pale and
   wan
Women have fear—in strength of justice, I
His vain fierce fury do this hour defy !"
There shot through Heaven an awful tongue
   of fire,
Attended by its minister, the dire
Black thunder.  In clear accents, cold and
   chill,
There sounded : " Boldest mortal, have thy
   will !
I do reverse the doom of Archais
And lay it on thyself; nor ever this
Shall lift its curse from off thee, this I swear."
And Cypris looked upon him and was ware
His form did change, and, writhing from her
   clasp,
Fled hissing outward, a more hateful asp

Than India breeds to-day, so terrible
Was his despair, so venomous as hell
The sudden hate that filled him.  So away,
Knowing not whither, did he flee, till day
Dropped her blue pinions, and the night
   drew on,
And sable clouds banked out the weary sun.

### PART III

LONG days and nights succeeded in despair.
Each noon beheld his doom—too proud for
   prayer,
And scorning Aphrodite's help—he strayed
Through swamps and weary bogs, nor yet
   betrayed
His anguished countenance to mortal men.
There was so keen an hour of sorrow, when
He had destroyed himself; but Heaven's
   hand,
Stretched out in vengeance, held him back.
   The land,
Where rest is made eternal, slipped his
   clutch ;
He wandered through the world and might
   not touch
The sceptre of King Death.  In vain he
   sought
Those fierce embraces, nor availed him aught
To numb the aching of his breast.  The
   maid
He loved, now freed from doom, no longer
   prayed
For anything but to discover him,
And her large eyes with weeping grew more
   dim
Than are the mists of Autumn on the hills.
She sought him far and near ; the rocks and
   rills
Could tell her nought; the murmur of the
   trees
Told her their pity and no more ; the breeze
That cooled its burning locks within the sea,
And dared not pass o'er the dank swamps
   where he
Was hid, knew nothing ; nor the soughing
   waves,
Through all the desolation of those caves

The sea-nymphs haunt, could say a word of
him;
No stars, to whom she looked, had seen the
grim
Abodes of Charicles, for deadly shade
Lowered o'er their top, nor any light be-
trayed
The horror of their core. Despairing then
Of nature's prophets, and of gods and men,
She cast her arms wide open to the sky,
Cried loud, and wept, and girt herself to die.

It was a pinnacle of ivory
Whereon she stood, the loftiest of three
fangs
Thrust up by magic, in the direst pangs
Of Earth, when Earth was yet a whirling
cloud
Of fire and adamant, a ceaseless crowd
Of rushing atoms roaring into space,
Driven by demons from before the Face.
And these gleamed white, while Helios lit
the heaven,
Like tusks; but at the coming of the even
Were visions wonderful with indigo;
And in the glory of the afterglow
Were rosy with its kiss; and in the night
Were crowned with that unutterable light
That is a brilliance of solemn black,
Glistening wide across the ocean track
Of white-sailed ships and many mariners.
So, on the tallest spire, where wakes and
whirrs
The eagle when dawn strikes his eyrie, came
The maiden, clad in the abundant flame
Of setting sun, with shapely shoulders bare,
And even the glory of her midday hair
Was bound above her head; so, naked pure,
Fixed in that purpose, which the gods endure
With calm despair, the purpose to be passed
Into the circle, that, serene and vast,
Girds all, and is itself the All—to die—
So stood she there, with eyes of victory
Fixed on the sun, about to sink his rays
Beneath the ocean, that the pallid bays
Fringed with white foam. But, as in pity,
yet
The sun forgot his chariot, nor would set,

VOL. I.

Since as he sank the maiden thought to leap
Within the bosom of the vaulted deep
From that high pedestal. And seeing this,
That yet an hour was left her, Archais
Lift up her voice and prayed with zeal divine
To Aphrodite, who from her far shrine
Heard and flew fast to aid over the night-clad
brine.

PRAYER OF ARCHAIS.

O Mother of Love,
By whom the earth and all its fountains move
In harmony,
Hear thou the bitter overwhelming cry
Of me, who love, who am about to die
Because of love.

O Queenliest Shrine,
Keeper of keys of heaven, most divine
Yet Queen of Pain,
Since Hell's gates open, and close fast again
Behind some servants of thy barren and vain
Though queenliest shrine.

I am of those
Who hear their brazen clanging as they close
Fastward on life.
I wane to-night, wearied with endless strife,
A lover alway, never yet a wife,
Lost in love's woes.

Not unperceived of Cypris did her song
Die fitfully upon her tremulous tongue,
Nor fell the melody on cruel ears:
The bright-throat goddess sped through
many spheres
Of sight, beyond the world, and flamed
across
All space, on wings that not the albatross
Might match for splendour, stretch, or airy
speed,
From cluster unto cluster at her need
Of stars, wide waving, and from star to star
Extended, in whose span the heavens are.
So came she to the maiden, and unseen
Gazed on her rapt. So sighed the amorous
queen

B

"For her indeed might Charicles despair!"
Yet of her presence was the maiden 'ware,
Although her mortal eyes might see her not;
So she knelt down upon that holy spot
And greeted her with tears; for now at
    last
The fountains of her sorrow, vague and vast,
Burst from the strong inexorable chain
Of too great passion, and a mortal pain
Beyond belief, and so in sudden waves
Tears welled impatient from their crystal
    caves.
(Men say those barren pinnacles are set
Since then with jewels; the white violet
Was born of those pure tears; the snowdrop
    grew
Where wakening hope her agony shot through,
And where the Queen of Love had touched
    her tears,
The new-born lily evermore appears.)
So Cypris comforts her with tender words
That pierce her bosom, like dividing swords,
With hopes and loves requickened, and her
    breath
Grew calm as worship's, though as dark as
    death
Her soul had been for weary days no few;
Now, lightened by the spirit thrust anew
As into a dead body breath of life,
She gave sweet thanks with gentle lips that
    ope,
Like buds of roses on the sunny slope
Of lily gardens falling toward a stream
That flashes back the intolerable beam
Of sunlight with light heart.

                    They fled away
At Cypris' word, beyond the bounds of day
Into the awful caverns of the night,
Eerie with ghosts imagined, and the might
Of strange spells cast upon them by the dead.
So, ere the dying autumn-tide was fled,
There, in a lonely cleft of riven rock,
Whose iron fastnesses disdain and mock
Fury and fire with impassivity,
Archais rested, there alone must she
Wait the event of Aphrodite's wiles.
There, like a statue, 'mid the massy piles

Of thunder-smitten stone, as motionless
As Fate she sat, in manifold distress,
Awaiting and awaiting aye the same
One strong desire of life, that never came.

For Aphrodite sought in vain the woods,
The silent mountains, and impetuous floods
In all the world, nor had she knowledge of
Such dens as him concealed; (for what should
    Love
Know of such vile morasses?) in despair
Waved angry wings, and, floating through
    the air,
Came unto Aphaca, lewd citadel
Of strange new lusts and devilries of hell,
Where god Priapus dwelt; to him she
    came—
She, Love!—and, hiding her fair face for
    shame,
Nor showing aught the quivering scorn that
    glowed
Through all her body, her desire showed
In brief sharp words, and the lewd god gave
    ear
(For he shook terribly with bastard fear
Of being cast beneath the hoof of Time)
And answered her: "O mightiest, O sublime
White deity of heaven, a swamp is known
To me, so vile, so more than venomous
    grown
With filthy weeds; yea, all lewd creatures
    swarm
Its airless desolation through; and warm
Sick vapours of disease do putrefy
Its feverish exhalations; yet do I
With some fond band of loyal worshippers
Often draw thither; and black ministers
Of mine therein do office; I have seen
This being cursed of Zeus, a snake unclean
With its unholy neighbourhood; at morn
A fair bright youth, whose large eyes well
    might scorn
The wanton eyes of Ganymede, whose tongue
Reiterates ill curses idly strung
In circles meaningless high Zeus to move,
Yet has twain other cries; the one is 'Love!'
The other 'Archais!'" The Paphian lips
Smiled with a splendour potent to eclipse

The large-lipped drawn-out grinning of that
    court
That mouthed and gibbered in their swinish
    sport.
So with meet words of gratitude the dame
That rules our lives withdrew, triumphant
    flame
Kindling in her bright eyes and sunwarmed
    hair,
Burning in dawny cheeks as the fresh air
Kissed, cleansing them from that infested den
Of obscene deities and apish men,
Rivalling their gods in petty filthiness.
So Love's white-bosomed Queen gat full
    success
In the first season of her sojourning.

Then, on the verge of night, she went a-wing
To that most damned pestilence-rid marsh,
And, changing her bright shape, she donned
    the harsh
Vile form of woman past the middle age,
Who hath not virtue that may charm the sage
When the desire of folly is gone by,
And wrinkles yield to no false alchemy.
So, lewd of countenance, dressed all in rags,
She waited, fit mate of hell's filthiest hags,
Within a little hut upon the marge
Extreme of that bad swamp, whereby a
    barge,
Rotted with years and pestilence, lay moored.
The rusty chain men meant to have secured
Its most unwieldy hulk was eaten through
Of sharp-tongued serpents, and the poisonous
    dew
That the foul damp let fall at evening
Rotted it even to its core.    A ring
Of silver girt it to the landing-stage,
Yet brimstone joined in wedlock with foul age
To burn into its vitals; thus the breath
Of Satyrs wantoning at noon with Death
Strained it, and all but cast it loose; the
    night
Drew on the outer world; no change of light
Was known within those depths, but vermin
    knew
By some strange instinct; forth the unholy
    crew

Of vampires and swamp-adders drew them
    out.
Alone amid the pestilential rout
Charicles' crest did glimmer red with wrath,
And, stealing from the barge, he drew him
    forth
And writhed into the hut, for latterly
So dark his soul had grown that never he
For shame and sorrow wore the form of man.
So to the hut on writhing coils he ran
With angry head erect, and passed within
Its rotten doorway.   Then the thing of Sin
That mocked the name of woman fondled
    him,
Stroked his flat head, his body curved and
    slim,
And from the fire brought milk.   He drank
    it up
From the coarse pewter of the borrowed cup
And cried: "In eating, swear.    I have
    vowed to make
The gods infernal on their couches quake
With fear before I die; I have vowed to live
With one aim only; never to forgive
The wrong the gods do me, and in my
    form
Love his high self, by whom the earth is
    warm
To-day, by whose defiance the universe
Would crash in one inextricable curse
To primal chaos.   Hear me, I have sworn."
Then, suddenly, more glorious than the morn
Tipping the golden tops of autumn hills
With light, more countless than the myriad
    rills
Of bright dew running off the bracken leaves,
With gold more saturated than the sheaves
In the red glow that promises the day
Shall glory when the night is fled away
In bonds, a captive; so more glorious
Than the supreme ideal dreams of us
Mortals, he sprang forth suddenly a man.
Wherefore the hag, triumphant, then began
Likewise to change.    The writhled visage
    grew
Fouler and fiercer, blacker in its hue;
The skewed deformities became more vile,
The rags more rotten, till a little while,

And all was changed to a putrescent heap
Of oily liquid on the floor asleep,
Like poisonous potency of mandragore
Ready to strike.   And then a change came
    o'er
Its turbid mass, that shook, and grew divine,
A million-twinkling ocean of bright brine
That seemed to spread beyond the horizon,
Whence, stirred by strange emotions of the
    sun,
Waves rolled upon it, and a wind arose
And lashed it with insatiable blows
Into a surging labyrinth of foam,
Boiling up into heaven's unchanging dome
Of brightest æther; then, its womb uncloses
To bring to birth a garden of white roses,
Whence, on a mystic shell of pearl, is borne
A goddess, bosomed like the sea at morn,
Glittering in all the goodlihead and grace
Of maiden magic; her delicious face
Grew more and more upon the hero's sight,
Till all the hut was filled with rosy light,
And Charicles' grey eyes were luminous
With love-reflections multitudinous
As lilies in the spring.   Again was seen
As in a mirror, like the ocean green,
The admirable birth of Love's eternal Queen.

So Charicles a moment was amazed.
A moment; then, contemptuous, he gazed
With curling lip on her, and sourly scorns
Her petty miracle: "The deed adorns
Too well a queen whose promises are foam."
And she, indignant, would have hied her
    home
And left him to despair, but pitying
His soul struck through with darts: "A
    bitter thing"
(She cried) "thou sayest, yet perchance my
    power
Is not as great as thine, for while I cower
Under the lash of Zeus, stand thou upright,
And laugh him to his beard for all his spite."
"I, even now beneath his doom?"   "Even
    thou!
For learn this law, writ large upon the brow
Of white Olympus, writ by him who made
Thee, yea and Zeus, of whom is Zeus afraid,

Graven by Him with an eternal pen,
The first law in the destiny of men :
**He whom Zeus wrongfully once injures may
    not be
Hurt by his power again in the most small
    degree.**
Thus, thy Archais"—"Mine! ah never-
    more!"
"Peace, doubter!—is made free from all
    the sore
Oppressions of the past, nor may again
Zeus lay on her the shadow of a pain."
"But I, but I"—"Yea, verily, fear not
But stratagem may lift thy bitter lot
From thy worn shoulders.   Thus for half
    the day
Thou art as free as air, as woodland fay
Treading the circle of unearthly green,
By maiden eyes at summer midnight seen.
These hours of freedom thou may'st use to free
Love from his toils, and joy and goodly gree [1]
Shall be thy guerdon.   Listen! I have power
To change thy semblance in thy happier
    hour;
Thou shalt assume the countenance of Love's
Divinest maiden in the darkling groves
Of Ida.   There shalt thou meet happily
With Zeus himself.   I leave the scheme to
    thee."

The flash of her desire within his brain
Came as a meteor through the wildered train
Of solemn spheres of night's majestic court.
He kissed the extended hand, and lastly
    sought
A blessing from the kindly Queen of Love.
Then, smiling, she was bountiful thereof,
And bade him haste away, when at the
    gate—
Twin witch-oaks that presided o'er the state
Of that detested realm—he felt a change,
Half pleasant, only beyond wonder strange,
A change as from a joy to a delight,
As from broad sunshine to the fall of night,
As from strong action to endurance strong,
As from desire to the power to long,

[1] Gladness.

From man to woman with a strange swift
   motion,
Like tide and ebb upon a summer ocean.
Thus he went forth a girl; his steps he
   presses
Through sickly wastes and burning wildernesses
To the lascivious shade of Ida's deep recesses.

## PART IV.

FAIRER than woman blushing at the kiss
Of young keen Phoibos, whose lips' nectar is
More fresh than lilies, whose divine embrace
Flushes the creamy pallor of her face,
And, even in those depths of azure sea
Where her eyes dwell, bids them glint
   amorously,
While the intense hushed music of his breath
Sighs, till her longing grows divine as death—
The young far, drew dawn on Ida's grove.
The young sun rose, whose burning lips of
   love
Kissed the green steeps, whose royal locks
   of flame
Brushed o'er the dewy pastures, with acclaim
Of tuneful thrushes shrill with mountain song,
And noise of nightingales, and murmur long—
A sigh half-sad, as if remembering earth
And all the massy pillars of her girth;
Half-jubilant, as if foreseeing a world
Fresher with starlight and with waters
   pearled,
Sunnier days and rivers calm and clear,
And music for four seasons of the year,
And pleasant peoples with glad throat and
   voice
Too wise to grieve, too happy to rejoice.
So came the dawn on Ida to disclose
Within her confines a delicious rose
Lying asleep, a-dreaming, white of brow,
Stainless and splendid.   Yea, and fair enow
To tempt the lips of Death to kiss her eyes
And bid her waken in the sad surprise
Of seeing round her the iron gates of hell
In gloomy strength: so sweet, so terrible,
So fair, her image in the brook might make
A passionless old god his hunger slake

By plunging in the waters, though he knew
His drowning body drowned her image too.
Yet she seemed gentle.   Never thorn assailed
The tender finger that would touch, nor
   failed
The strong desire of Zeus, who wisely went,
As was his wont, with amorous intent
Among those pastures, and fresh fragrant
   lawns,
And dewy wonder of new woods, where
   dawns
A new flower every day, a perfect flower,
Each queenlier than her sister, though the
   shower
Of early dew begemmed them all with stars,
Diamond and pearl, between the pleasant bars
Of cool green trees that avenued the grove.
Zeus wandered through their bounds, and
   dreamt of love.
Weary of women's old lascivious breed,
The large luxurious lips of Ganymede,
He, weary of tainted kiss and feverish lust,
Esteeming love a desert of dry dust
Because he found no freshness, no restraint,
No virgin bosom, lips without a taint
Of lewd imagining, yet passed not by
With scorn of curled lip and contempt of eye
The chaste abandon of the sleeping maid,
But looked upon her lips, checked course,
   and stayed,
And noted all the virginal fresh air
Of Chariclès, the maiden head half bare
To Phoibos' kiss, half veiled by dimpled
   arms
Within whose love it rested, all her charms
Half-shown, half-hidden, amorous but chaste.
And so, between the branches interlaced
And all the purple white-starred under-
   growth,
Zeus crept beside the maiden, little loath
To waken her caresses, and let noon
Fade into midnight in the amorous swoon
Of long delight, and so with gentle kiss
Touched the maid's cheek, and broke her
   dream of bliss.
And she, more startled than the yearling
   fawn
As the rude sun breaks golden out of dawn,

One swift sharp beam of glory, leapt aside
And made as if to flee, but vainly plied
Her tender feet amid the tangled flowers.
For Zeus, enraptured, put forth all his powers,
And caught her panting, timid, tremulous.
And he with open lips voluptuous
Closed her sweet mouth with kisses, and so
    pressed
Her sobbing bosom with a manlier breast
That she was silent ; next, with sudden
    force,
Implacable, unshamed, without remorse,
Would urge his further suit ; but so she strove
That even the power of Zeus, made weak for
    love,
Found its last limit, and, releasing her,
Prayed for her grace, a raptured worshipper,
Where but a moment earlier had he striven
A sacrilegious robber. And all heaven
Seemed open to his eyes as she looked down
Into their love, half smiling, with a frown
Coquetting with her forehead. Then a
    change,
Angry and wonderful, began to range
Over her cheeks ; she bitterly began :
" I will not yield to thee—a mortal man
Alone shall know my love. No God shall
    come
From his high place and far immortal home
To bend my will by force. Freeborn, I live
In freedom, and the love that maidens give
To men I give to one, but thou, most high,
(For woman's wits through your deceptions
    spy
And know ye for Olympians) shalt know
A maiden's heart no lover may win so.
Farewell, and find a fairer maid to love !
Farewell ! " But he : " Through all the
    silent grove
I sought thee sighing—for thy love would I
Consent to be a man, consent to die,
Put off my godhead." " If thou sayest sooth,
And thy fair words bedew the flowers of
    truth
Nor wander in the mazy groves of lying,
I will be thine—speak not to me of dying
Or abdication, sith I deem so far
To tempt thee were unwise—we mortals are

Chary to ask too much—didst thou refuse
Either my honour or thy love to lose
Were a hard portion, for in sooth I love."
" Ah happy hour, sweet moment ! Fairest
    grove
Of all fair Ida, thou hast sealed my bliss ! "
Then with one long intense unpitying kiss
Pressed on her bosom, he arose and swore
By heaven and earth and all the seas that
    roar
And stars that sing, by rivers and fresh
    flood,
By his own essence, by his body and blood,
To lay his godhead down, till night drew
    nigh,
To be a mortal till the vesper cry
Of dying breezes. So the morning past
And found them linked inexorably fast
Each in the other's arms. Their lips are
    wed
To drink the breezes from the fountain-
    head
Of lovers' breath. Now Zeus half rises up,
Sips once again from that moon-curvéd
    cup,
And, in his passion gazing on the flower,
Darker and riper for Love's perfect hour,
His clear voice through the silent atmosphere
Burst rich and musical upon her ear.


### SONG OF ZEUS.

O rosy star
Within thy sky of ebony shot through
    With hints of blue
    More golden and more far
Than earthly stars and flowers
That beam lasciviously through night's em-
    purpled hours !

O well of fire !
O fountain of delicious spurting flame
    Grown sad with shame,
    Whose imminent desire
Drinks in the dew of earth,
Gives its own limpid streams to quench
    man's deathly dearth.

O gardened rose !
The fern-fronds gird thy fragrant beauty
round.
    Thy ways are bound
    With petals that unclose
When the sun seeks his way
Through night and sleep and love to all the
dreams of day.

    Love, sleep, and death !
The three that melt together, mingle so
    Man may not know
    The little change of breath
(Caught sigh that love desires,)
When love grows sleep, and sleep at last in
death expires.

    O lamp of love !
The hissing spray shall jet thee with desire
    And foaming fire,
    And fire from thee shall move
Her spirit to devour,
And fuse and mingle us in one transcendent
hour.

    Godhead is less
Than mortal love, the garland of the spheres,
    Than those sweet tears
    That yield no bitterness
To the luxurious cries
That love shrills out in death, that murmur
when love dies.

    Love dies in vain.
For breezes hasten from the summer south
    To touch his mouth
    And bid him rise again,
Till, ere the dawn-star's breath,
Love kisses into sleep, Sleep swoons away
to Death.

So Zeus in her sweet arms slept daintily
Till the sun crept into the midmost sky,
And his own curse came back to sleep with
him.
Through the noon's haze the world was vast
and dim,
The streams and trees and air were
shimmering
With summer heat and earth's cool vapouring,
When, round his limbs entwined, a fiery
snake
Hissed in his frightened ear the call "Awake."
And Zeus arisen strives vainly to release
His valiant body from the coils, nor cease
His angry struggles in their cruel hold.
But all implacable, unyielding, cold,
Their sinuous pressure on his breast and
thighs,
The white teeth sharp and ready otherwise
In one fierce snap to slay. There hissed
"Beware !
Fear Charicles avenging, and despair !"

And Zeus beheld the springe his foot was in,
And, once more wise, being out of love,
would win
His freedom on good terms. His liberty
For Charicles' he bartered. Willingly
The boy accepts, yet in his eye remains
A tender woman-feeling, and his pains,
And even Archais' woes he did forget
In the sweet Lethe, that his lips had set
To their ripe brim, that he had drained.
But now,
Freedom regained, more manly grows the
brow ;
He is again the free, the bold, the lover !
Far o'er the green his new-starred eyes dis-
cover
A kirtle glancing in the breeze, a foot
That lightly dances, though the skies be
mute
Of music. Forth she flies, the distant dove,
And calls the woodland birds to sing of love ;
Forth leaps the stag and calls his mates ; the
stream
Flashes a silver sunbeam, a gold gleam
Of leaping laughter, that the fish may know
The goodly tidings ; all the woodlands
glow
With olive and pure silver and red gold,
And all sweet nature's marvels manifold
Combine together in the twilight dim
To harmonise in the thalamic hymn.

## HYMN.

O Lord our God !
O woodland king ! O thou most dreadful
    God !
Who chasest thieves and smitest with thy
    rod,
    That fearful rod, too sharp, too strong
For thy weak worshippers to bear !
    Hear thou their murmured song
Who cry for pardon ; pity, and prepare
For pain's delight thy votaries who kiss thy
    rod,
        O high Lord God !

O Lord our God !
God of green gardens ! O imperious god !
Who as a father smitest with thy rod
    Thine erring children who aspire
In vain to the high mysteries
    Of thy most secret fire.
Beat us and burn with nameless infamies !
We suffer, and are proud and glad, and kiss
    thy rod,
        O high Lord God !

O Lord our God !
O despot of the fields ! O silent god !
Who hidest visions underneath thy rod,
    And hast all dreams and all desires and
        fears,
All secrets and all loves and joys
    Of all the long vague years
For lightsome maidens and desire-pale boys
Within thy worship. We desire thy bitter
    rod,
        O high Lord God !

Thus that most reverend sound through all
    the vale
Pealed in low cadences that rise and fail,
And all the augurs promise happy days,
And all the men for Archais have praise,
And all maids' eyes are fixed on Charicles.
Then, to the tune of musical slow seas,
The wind began to murmur on the mead,
And he, unconscious, drew his eager reed

From the loose tunic ; now they seat them-
    selves
On moss worn smooth by feet of many elves
Dancing at midnight through them, and their
    voice
Bids all the woodland echoes to rejoice
Because the lovers are made one at last.
Then Charicles began to play ; they cast
Tunic and snood and sandal, and began
To foot a happy measure for a span,
While still Archais at his feet would sit,
Gaze in his eyes, by love and triumph lit,
And listen to the music. And the fire
Of his light reed so kindled her desire
That she with new glad confidence would
    quire
A new song exquisite, whose tender tune
Was nurtured at the bosom of the moon
And kissed on either cheek by sun and
    rain.
She trembled and began. The troop was
    fain
To keep pure silence while her notes resound
Over the forest and the marshy ground.

## ARCHAIS.

Green and gold the meadows lie
    In the sunset's eye.
Green and silver the woods glow
    When the sun is low,
And the moon sails up like music on a sea
    of breathing snow.

Chain and curse are passed away ;
    Love proclaims the day.
Dawned his sunrise o'er the sea,
    Changing olive waves to be
Founts of emerald and sapphire ; he is risen,
    we are free.

Light and dark are wed together
    Into golden weather ;
Sun and moon have kissed, and built
    Palaces star-gilt
Whence a crystal stream of joy, love's eternal
    wine, is spilt.

CHARICLES.

Join our chorus, tread the turf
    To the beating of the surf.
Dance together, ere we part,
    And Selene's dart
Give the signal for your slumber and the
    rapture of our heart.

*Semi-Chorus of Men.*

Exalted with immeasurable gladness;
    Bonds touched with tears and melted like
        the snow :—
Wake the song loudly; loose the leash of
    madness,
    Beat the loud drum, and bid the trumpet
        blow !

*Semi-Chorus of Women.*

Let the lute thrill divinely low,
    Let the harp strike a tender note of sad-
        ness;
Louder and louder, till the full song flow,
    One earth-dissolving stream of utter glad-
        ness !

CHORUS.

Free ! ye are free !   Delight, thou Moon, to
    hear us !
    Smile, Artemis, thy virgin leaves thy fold !
Star of the morning, fling thy blossom near
    us !
    Phoibos, re-kindle us with molten gold !
Starbeams and woven tresses of the ocean,
    Flowers of the rolling mountains and the
        lea,
        Trees, and innumerable flocks and herds,
        Wild cattle and bright birds,
    Tremble above the sea
With song more noble, the divinest potion
    Of poet's wonder and bard's melody.

ARCHAIS.

Cold is the kiss of the stars to the sea,
    The kiss of the earth to the orient grey
    That heralds the day;
Warmer the kiss of a love that is free
    As the wind of the sea,
Quick and resurgent and splendid.

CHARICLES.

Night her bright bow-string has bended;
    Fast flies her arrow unsparing
        Through the beech-leaves,
        Æther it cleaves
    Rapid and daring.
Ah ! how it strikes as with silver ! how the
    sun's laughter is ended !

ARCHAIS.

How the moon's arms are extended !

*Semi-Chorus of Men.*

Rejoicing, inarticulate with pleasure,
    Joy streams a comet in the strong con-
        trol
Of the sun's love ; weave, weave the eager
    measure,
    Fill the sea's brim from pleasure's foaming
        bowl !

*Semi-Chorus of Women.*

Weave, weave the dance ; the stars are not
    your goal.
    Freed slaves of Fortune, love's your only
        treasure.
While the gold planets toward the sunlight
    roll,
    Weave, weave the dance !   Weave, weave
        the eager measure !

CHARICLES.

Of your revels I'll be king,

ARCHAIS.

I the queen of your array.
Foot it nimbly in the ring,

CHARICLES.

Strewn with violet and may.

ARCHAIS.

Apple-blossom pile on high,
    Till the bridal bed is duly
Panoplied with blooms that sigh.

CHARICLES.

Not a flower of them shall die,
  Every one shall blossom newly ;
Stars shall lend them of their beauty,
Rain and sunshine know their duty.

ARCHAIS.

Not a flower of them shall die
  That compose our canopy ;
Beech and chestnut, poplar tall,
Birch and elm shall flourish all
  Dewed with ever-living spring.
Song and dance shall close the day,

CHORUS.

Close this happy, happy day.

CHARICLES.

Of your revels I'll be king,

ARCHAIS.

I the queen of your array.

*Both.*

Foot it nimbly in the ring !

CHORUS.

Stay, stars, and dance with us !  Our songs
  compel
The very gods to tremble,
Banish the ill ghosts of hell,
  Make fiends their shape dissemble.
Freedom forbids their tyrannous reign here,
  Flee to their prison must they, nor deceive ;
Love has a lightning that shall strip them
  clear,
    Truth through the curtain of the dark shall
      reave.
    Ye love, O happy ones and chaste,
      Ye love, and light indwells your eyes ;
    Truth is the girdle of your waist,
      Ye play before the gates of pearl of
        Paradise.
Happy lovers, dwell together
In the isles of golden weather,
Free of tyranny and tether,
  Roam the world, linked hand in hand,

Moonlight for your sleep, and breezes
Fresh from where the Ocean freezes,
  And the cold Aurora stands
  With new lilies in her hands.
Happy lovers, twilight falls.
  Let us leave you for awhile,
Guarding all the golden walls
  With the weapon of a smile.
Silver arrows from the maiden
  With new labours laden
Shall be shot at bold intruders who would
  violate your peace ;
Lightning shall keep watch and warden
  through the sea-born isles of Greece.
    Sleep ! Sleep !
Sleep, ye happy lovers, sleep,
Soft and dreamless, sweet and deep,
    Sleep ! Sleep !

    We will steal away
    Till the break of day.

ARCHAIS.

In the arms of love at last
  Love is anchored fast,
Firm beyond the rage of Heaven, safe be-
  yond the ocean blast.

CHARICLES.

  In the arms of love close prest !
  O thy tender breast
Pillows now my happy head ; softly breezes
  from the west

*Both.*

  Stir the ring-dove's nest.
  In the arms of love we lie ;
  Music from the sky
Tunes the hymeneal lyre that will echo till
  we die.
  God we feel is very nigh ;
  Soft, breeze, sigh
While we kiss at last to slumber,
  And the varied number
  Of the forest songsters cry :
This is immortality ; this is happiness for
  aye.

Hush ! the music swells apace,
　Rolls its silver billows up
Through the void demesnè of space
　To the heavens' azure cup !
Hush, my love, and sleep shall sigh
　This is immortality !


## EPILOGUE.

### IN HOLLOW STONES, SCAWFELL.

BLIND the iron pinnacles edge the twilight ;
Blind and black the ghylls of the mountain
　clefted,
Crag and snow - clad slope in a distant
　vision
　　Rise as before me.

Here (it seems) my feet by a tiny torrent
Press the moss with a glad delight of
　being :
Here my eyes look up to the riven moun-
　tain
　　Split by the thunder.

Rent and rifted, shattered of wind and
　lightning,
Smitten, scarred, and stricken of sun and
　tempest,
Seamed with wounds, like adamant, shod
　with iron,
　　Torn by the earthquake.

Still through all the stresses of doubtful
　weather
Hold the firm old pinnacles, sky-defying ;
Still the icy feet of the wind relentless
　　Walk in their meadows.

Fields that flower not, blossom in no new
　spring-tide ;
Fields where grass nor herb nor abounding
　darnel
Flourish ; fields more barren, devoid, than
　ocean's
　　Pasture ungarnered.

Deserts, stone as arid as sand, savannahs [1]
Black with wrecks, a wilderness evil,
　fruitless ;
Still, to me, a land of the bluest heaven
　　Studded with silver.

Castles bleak and bare as the wrath of ocean,
Wasted wall and tower, as the blast had risen,
Taken keep and donjon, and hurled them
　earthward,
　　Rent and uprooted.

Such rock-ruins people me tribes and nations,
Kings and queens and princes as pure as
　dawning,
Brave as day and true ; and a happy people
　　Lulled into freedom ;

Nations past the stormier times of tyrants,
Past the sudden spark of a great rebellion,
Past the iron gates that are thrust asunder
　　Not without bloodshed :

Past the rule of might and the rule of lying,
Free from gold's illusion, and free to
　cherish
Joys of life diviner than war and passion—
　　Falsest of phantoms.

Only now true love, like a sun of molten
Glory, surging up from a sea of liquid
Silver, golden, exquisite, overflowing,
　　Soars into starland.

Sphere on sphere unite in the chant of wonder ;
Star to star must add to the glowing chorus ;
Sun and moon must mingle and speed the
　echo
　　Flaming through heaven.

Night and day divide, and the music
　strengthens,
Gathers roar of seas and the dirge of moor-
　lands ;
Tempest, thunder, birds, and the breeze of
　summer
　　Join to augment it.

[1] Spanish term for wide, grassy plains.

So the sound-world, filled of the fire of all things,
Rolls majestic torrents of mighty music
Through the stars where dwell the avenging spirits
  Bound in the whirlwind . . .

So the cliffs their Song . . . For the mist regathers,
Girds them bride-like, fit for the sun to kiss them ;
Darkness falls like dewfall about the hill-sides ;
  Night is upon me.

Now to me remain in the doubtful twilight
Stretches bare of flower, but touched with whispers,
Grey with huddled rocks, and a space of woodland,
  Pine-tree and poplar.

Now a stream to ford and a stile to clamber ;
Last the inn, a book, and a quiet corner . . .
Fresh as Spring, there kisses me on the forehead
  Sleep, like a sister.

NOTE.—With the exception of this epilogue, and one or two of the lyrics, Crowley wished to suppress the whole of " The Tale of Archais." But it was thought inadvisable to form a precedent of this kind, as the book was regularly published. On the other hand, by adhering to this rule any poem not appearing in this edition may be definitely discarded as spurious.

# SONGS OF THE SPIRIT.*

## 1898.

### SONGS OF THE SPIRIT.

> " A fool also is full of words."
> *Ecclesiastes.*

### DEDICATION

#### To J. L. BAKER.

THE vault of purple that I strove
To pierce, and find unchanging love,
Or some vast countenance [1] above
    All glory of the soul of man,
Baffled my blind aspiring gaze
With sunlight's melancholy rays,
And closed with iron hand the ways
That sunder space, divide the days with fiery
    fan.

Thine was the forehead mild and grave
That shone throughout the azure nave
Where Monte Rosa's silence gave
    The starry organ's measured sound.
Where for an altar stood the bare
Mass of Mont Cervin,[2] towering there;
And angels dwelt upon the stair,
And all the mountains were aware that stood
    around.

Thine was the passionless divine
High hope, and the pure purpose thine,
Higher and purer than stars shine,
    And thine the unexpressed delight
To hold high commune with the wind
That sings, in midnight black and blind,
Strange chants, the murmurs of the mind,
To grasp the hands of heaven and find the
    lords of light.

[1] The supreme Deity is shadowed by Qabalists in this glyph. See Appendix, " Qabalistic
dogma," for a synthesized explanation of this
entire philosophy.
[2] Commonly known as the Matterhorn.

Mine was the holy fire that drew
Its perfect passion from the dew,
And all the flowers that blushed and blew
    On sunny slopes by little brooks.
Mine the desire that brushed aside
The thorns, and would not be denied,
And sought, more eager than a bride,
The cold grey secrets wan and wide of sacred
    books.

Thine was the hand that guided me
By moor and mountain, vale and lea,
And led me to the sudden sea
    That lies superb, remote, and deep,
Showed me things wonderful, unbound
The fetters that beset me round,
Opened my waking ear to sound
That may not by a man be found, except in
    ' sleep.

Thy presence was as subtle flame
Burning in dawny groves ; thy name
Like dew upon the hills became,
    And all thy mind a star most bright ;
And, following with wakeful eyes
The strait meridian of the wise,
My feet tread under stars and skies ;
My spirit soars and seeks and flies, a child of
    light.

Thus eager, may my purpose stand
Firm as the faith of honest hand,
Nor change like castles built of sand
    Until the sweet unchanging end.
Happy not only that my eye
Single and strong may win the sky,
But that one day the birds that fly
Heard your fair friendship call me by the name
    of friend.

* In this volume and throughout Crowley's works the visions, ordeals, etc., are, as a rule,
not efforts of imagination, but records of (subjective) fact.

## THE GOAD.

ἀν' ὑγρὸν ἀμπταίην
αἰθέρα πόρσω γαίας Ἑλλανίας
ἀστέρας ἑσπέρους
οἶον, οἶον ἄλγος ἔπαθον, φίλαι.
EURIPIDES.

AMSTERDAM, *December 23rd*, 1897.

LET me pass out beyond the city gate.
  All day I loitered in the little streets
Of black worn houses tottering, like the fate
  That hangs above my head even now, and
    meets
Prayer and defiance as not hearing it.
  They lean, these old black streets ! a little
    sky
Peeps through the gap, the rough stone path
  is lit
Just for a little by the sun, and I
Watch his red face pass over, fade away
  To other streets, and other passengers,
See him take pleasure where the heathen
  pray,
  See him relieve the hunter of his furs,
All the wide world awaiting him, all folk
  Glad at his coming, only I must weep :
Rise he or sink, my weary eyes invoke
  Only the respite of a little sleep ;
Sleep, just a little space of sleep, to rest
  The fevered head and cool the aching eyes ;
Sleep for a space, to fall upon the breast
  Of the dear God, that He may sympathise.
Long has the day drawn out ; a bitter frost
  Sparkles along the streets ; the shipping
    heaves
With the slow murmur of the sea, half lost
  In the last rustle of forgotten leaves.
Over the bridges pass the throngs ; the sound,
  Deep and insistent, penetrates the mist—
I hear it not, I contemplate the wound
  Stabbed in the flanks of my dear silver
    Christ.
He hangs in anguish there ; the crown of
  thorns
  Pierces that palest brow ; the nails drip
    blood ;

There is the wound ; no Mary by Him
  mourns,
  There is no John beside the cruel wood ;
I am alone to kiss the silver lips ;
  I rend my clothing for the temple veil ;
My heart's black night must act the sun's
  eclipse ;
  My groans must play the earthquake, till
    I quail
At my own dark imagining ; and now
  The wind is bitterer ; the air breeds snow ;
I put my Christ away ; I turn my brow
  Towards the south stedfastly ; my feet must
    go
Some journey of despair.  I dare not turn
  To meet the sun ; I will not follow him :
Better to pass where sand and sulphur burn,
  And days are hazed with heat, and nights
    are dim
With some malarial poison.  Better lie
  Far and forgotten on some desert isle,
Where I may watch the silent ships go by,
  And let them share my burden for awhile.
Let me pass out beyond the city gate
  Where I may wander by the water still,
And see the faint few stars immaculate
  Watch their own beauty in its depth, and
    chill
Their own desire within its icy stream.
  Let me move on with vacant eyes, as one
Lost in the labyrinth of some ill dream,
  Move and move on, and never see the
    sun
Lap all the mist with orange and red gold,
  Throw some lank windmill into iron shade,
And stir the chill canal with manifold
  Rays of clear morning ; never grow afraid
When he dips down beyond the far flat
  land,
  Know never more the day and night
    apart,
Know not where frost has laid his iron
  hand
  Save only that it fastens on my heart ;
Save only that it grips with icy fire
  These veins no fire of hell could satiate ;
Save only that it quenches this desire.
  Let me pass out beyond the city gate.

## IN MEMORIAM A. J. B.[1]

THE life (by angels' touch divinely lifted
  From our dim space-bounds to a vaster
    sphere),
The spirit, through the vision of clouds rifted,
  Soars quick and clear.

Even so, the mists that roll o'er earth are
    riven,
  The spirit flashes forth from mortal sight,
And, flaming through the viewless space, is
    given
  A robe of light.

As when the conqueror Christ burst forth of
    prison,
  And triumph woke the thunder of the
    spheres,
So brake the soul, as newly re-arisen
  Beyond the years.

Far above Space and Time, that earth environ
  With bands and bars we strive against in
    vain,
Far o'er the world, and all its triple iron
  And brazen chain,

Far from the change that men call life fled
    higher
  Into the world immutable of sleep,
We see our loved one, and vain eyes desire
  In vain to weep.

Woeful our gaze, if on lone Earth descendent,
  To view the absence of yon flame afar—
Yet in the Heavens, anew, divine, resplendent,
  Behold a star !

One light the less, that steady flamed and
    even
  Amid the dusk of Earth's uncertain shore ;
One light the less, but in Jehovah's Heaven
  One star the more !

  [1] A maternal aunt of the poet.

## THE QUEST.

APART, immutable, unseen,
Being, before itself had been,
Became.   Like dew a triple queen
  Shone as the void uncovered :
The silence of deep height was drawn
A veil across the silver dawn
  On holy wings that hovered.[1]

The music of three thoughts became
The beauty, that is one white flame,
The justice that surpasses shame,
  The victory, the splendour,
The sacred fountain that is whirled
From depths beyond that older world
  A new world to engender.[2]

The kingdom is extended.[3]   Night
Dwells, and I contemplate the sight
That is not seeing, but the light
  That secretly is kindled,
Though oft time its most holy fire
Lacks oil, whene'er my own Desire
  Before desire has dwindled.

I see the thin web binding me
With thirteen cords of unity [4]
Toward the calm centre of the sea.
  (O thou supernal mother !) [5]
The triple light my path divides
To twain and fifty sudden sides [6]
  Each perfect as each other.

  [1] A qabalistic description of Macroprosopus.
" Dew," " Deep Height," etc., are his titles.
  [2] Microprosopus.
  [3] Malkuth, the Bride.   In its darkness the
Light may yet be found.
  [4] The Hebrew characters composing the
name Achd, Unity, add up to 13.
  [5] Binah, the Great Deep : the offended
Mother who shall be reconciled to her
daughter by Bn, the Son.
  [6] Bn adds to 52.

Now backwards, inwards still my mind
Must track the intangible and blind,
And seeking, shall securely find
   Hidden in secret places
Fresh feasts for every soul that strives,
New life for many mystic lives,
   And strange new forms and faces.

My mind still searches, and attains
By many days and many pains
To That which Is and Was and reigns
   Shadowed in four and ten,[1]
And loses self in sacred lands,
And cries and quickens, and understands
   Beyond the first Amen.[2]


## THE ALCHEMIST.

THIS POEM WAS INTENDED AS THE PRO-
   LOGUE TO A PLAY—AT PRESENT UN-
   FINISHED.[3]

*An old tower, very lofty, on a small and
rocky islet. In the highest chamber a man
of some forty years, but silver-haired, looks
out of the window. Clear starry night,
no moon. Chamber furnished with books,
alchemic instruments, etc. He gazes some
minutes, sighs deeply, but at last speaks.*

THE world moves not. I gaze upon the
   abyss,
Look down into the black unfathomed vault
Of starland and behold—myself.
               The sea
To give a sense of motion or of sound
Washes the walls of this grey tower in vain ;
I contemplate myself in that dim sphere
Whose hollow centre I am standing at
With burning eyes intent to penetrate
The black circumference, and find out God—

[1] Jehovah, the name of 4 letters. $1+2+3+4=10$.
[2] The first Amen is $=91$ or $7 \times 13$. The second is the Inscrutable Amoun.
[3] "The Poisoners," finished later, but discarded as over-Tourneuresque.

And only see myself. The walls of Space
Mock me with silence. What is Life ? The
   stars
Are silent. O ye matchless ministers
That daily pass in your appointed ways
To reach—we know not what ! How mean-
   ingless
Your bright assemblage and your steady task
Of doubtful motion. And the soul of man
Grapples in death-pangs with your mystery,
And fails to wrestle down the hard embrace
That grips the thighs of thought. And so he
   dies
To pass beyond ye—whither ? To find God ?
All my life long I have gazed, and dreamed,
   and thought,
Unless my thought itself were but a dream,
A little, troubled dream, a dream of death
Whence I may wake—ah, where? In some
   new world
Where Consciousness doth touch the Infinite,
And all the strivings of the soul be found
Sufficient to beat back the waves of doubt,
To pierce the void, and grasp the glorious,
To find out Truth ? Would God it might be
   so,
Since here is nothing for the soul to love
Or cling to beyond self. My chamberlain
Once showed me a pet slave, dwarf, savage,
   black,
A vile, lewd creature, who would cast a staff[1]
Far wheeling through the air :—'twould
   suddenly
Break its swift course, and curving rapidly
Come hard upon himself who threw. Even so
These vile deformities—our souls—cast forth
Missiles of thought, and seek to reach some
   end
With swift imagining—and end in self.
What sage[2] called God the image of man's
   self
He sees cast dimly on a bank of cloud,
Thrice his own size ? And I whose life has
   been
               [*Cry without.*

[1] A boomerang.
[2] The image is Crowley's own, drawn from the Spectre of the Brocken.

One bitter fight with nature and myself
To find Him out, turn, terrible, to-night
                              [*Cry without.*
To see myself—myself—myself.
                              [*Cry without.*
                              Hush ! Hark !
Methought I heard a cry.  The seamew
    wails
Less humanly than that—I will go down
And seek the stranger.
              [*Making as to leave room.*
                  E'en this rocky isle
Shall prove a friend——
    *A Voice.*[1]          Stand still.
    *Philosopher.*              Again !  Is this
The warning of a mind o'er-strained ?
                      [*Moving towards door.*
    *Voice.*                      Stand still
And see salvation in Jehovah's hands.
    *Ph.* Is this the end of life ?
    *Voice.*                  Thy Life begins.
    *Ph.* Strange Voice, I hear thee, and obey.
    Perchance
I have not lived so far.  Perchance to-day,
Like a spring-flower that slowly opens out
Its willing petals to the tender dawn,
My soul may open to the knowledge of
A dawn of new thought that may lead——
    *Voice.*                      To God.
    *Ph.* Hope hardly dared to name it !


              *Enter* Messenger.

    *Mess.* My lord, the king's command !
    *Ph.*                    I heed it not.
See thou disturb not my high meditation.
Away !
    *Voice.* With meditations centred in thyself.
    *Mess.* Who spoke ?
    *Ph.*          Speak thou.  I obey the king.
    *Mess.*                      My lord,
He bids thee to his court, to hold the reins
Tight on the fretful horses of the state
Whose weary burden makes them slip—nay,
    fall
On the stern hill of war.  Thou art appointed,

[1] This voice is again heard, using the identical words, at the last great crisis of his life.
VOL. I.

Being the wisest man in all the realm,
(So spake the king) the second to him-
    self——
    *Ph.* Thy vessel waits ?
    *Mess.*                  For dawn.
    *Ph.*                    Then hasten thee
To tell them I am ready.  The meanwhile
I will devote to prayer.
    *Mess.*              At dawn, my lord.
                      [*Exit* Messenger.
    *Ph.* [*Turns to window.*]  O Maker and O
    Ruler of all worlds,
Illimitable power, immortal God,
Vague, vast, unknown, dim-looking, scarcely
    spied
Through doubtful crannies of the Universe,
Unseen, intangible, eluding sense
And poor conception, halting for a phrase
Of weak mind-language, O Eternity,
Hear thou the feeble word, the lame
    desire,
The dubious crying of the pinioned dove,
The wordless eloquent emotion
That speaks within a man, despite his
    mind !
Hear, who can pray for naught, unknowing
    aught
Whereof, for what to pray.  But hear me,
    thou !
Hear me, thou God, who fettered the bleak
    winds
Of North and East, and held in silken rein
The golden steeds of West and South, who
    bade
The tireless sea respect its narrow bounds,
And fixed the mountains, that eternal ice
Might be thy chiefest witness, and who wove
The myriad atoms of Infinitude
Into the solid tapestry of night,
And gave the sun his heat, and bade him
    kiss
The lips of Death upon the moon's dark
    face,
So that her silver lustre might rejoice
The fiery lover, the sharp nightingale,
And those pale mortals whom the day be-
    holds
Asleep, because the many bid them slave
                                          C

From dusk to dawn, being poor ; and braided up
The loose hair of all trees and flowers, and made
Their one white light divide to red and green
And violet [1] and the hues innumerable
Lesser than these, and gave man hope at last
With the invariable law of death
Abundant in new life, and having filled
The world with music, dost demand of us
"Is my work meaningless?" O thou, supreme,
Thou, First and Last, most inconceivable
All-radiating Unity, thou sphere
All-comprehensive, all-mysterious,
Spirit of Life and Death, bow down and hear !

[*Bends deeper and prays silently.
The flame grows duller, and
finally leaves the room in absolute darkness. Curtain.*

## SONNETS TO NIGHT.

### I.

O NIGHT ! the very mother of us all,
For from thy hollow womb we children came,
A little space to flicker as a flame,
And then within thy tender arms to fall
Tired, fain of nothing but to lie at last
Upon thy bosom, and gaze in thine eyes
Clear, calm, dispassionate, supremely wise,
And pass with thee the gates that must be passed.[2]

O Night, on thee is set our only hope,
Because our eyes, too tender for the day,
Are dazed with sunlight, and poor fingers grope
For those far truths that mock our vague endeavour,

[1] Chosen in accordance with the theory of Young and Helmholz.
[2] Compare this octet with that of the "Sonnet to Sleep" of P. B. Marston, which Crowley had not at this time read.

Whilst we may find in thee the secrets grey
Of all things God would fain have hid for ever.

### II.

All things grow still before thine awful face.
Now fails the lover's sigh; Sleep's angel clings
About the children with her dreamy wings,
And all the world is silent for a space.
The waving of thy dusky plumes in heaven
Alone breathes gentle music to mine ears,
So that despair is fain to flee, and fear
Cowers far away amid the shades of even.

"Hope," is thy whisper, "hope, and trust in Night ;
My realm is the eternal, and my power
The absolute.  My child, gird on thy strength ;
Clothe limbs with lustiness, and mind·with might,
That, communing with me, though for an hour,
Thou mayest conquer when day comes at length."

## THE PHILOSOPHER'S PROGRESS.

*That which is above, is like that which is
below ; and that which is below, is like that
which is above.*

HERMES TRISMEGISTUS.

THAT which is highest as the deep
Is fixed, the depth as that above :
Death's face is as the face of Sleep ;
And Lust is likest Love.

So stand the angels one by one
Higher and higher with lamps of gold :
So stand the shining devils ; none
Their brightness may behold.

I took my life, as one who takes
Young gold to ruin and to spend ;
I sought their gulfs and fiery lakes,
And sought no happy end.

I said : the height is as the deep,
Twin breasts of one white dove ;
Death's face is as the face of Sleep,
And Lust is likest Love.

And with my blood I forced the door
That guards the palaces of sin ;
I reached the lake's cinereous [1] shore ;
I passed those groves within.

My blood was wasted in her veins,
To freshen them, who stood like death,
Our Lady of ten thousand Pains
With heavy kissing breath.

I said : Our Lady is as God,
Her hell of pain as heaven above ;
Death's feet, like Sleep's, with fire are shod,
And Lust is likest Love.

Our Lady crushed me in her bed ;
Between her breasts my life was wet ;
My lips from that sweet death were fed ;
I died, and would forget.

But so God would not have me die ;
Her deadly lips relax and fade,
Her body slackens with a sigh
Reluctant, like a maid.

I said : O vampire [2] Lover, weep,
Who cannot follow me above,
Though Death may masquerade as Sleep,
And Lust laugh out like Love.

But God's strong arms set under me
Lifted my spirit through the air
Beyond the wide supernal sea,[3]
Beyond the veil of vair.

[1] Ash-covered.
[2] Any being who, under the guise of love,
draws the strength from another.
[3] Binah.

God said : My ways are sweet and deep :
The sceptres and the swords thereof
Change : for Death's face is fair as Sleep ;
And Lust is clean as Love.

I slept upon His breast ; and Death
Came like Sleep's angel, and I died,
And tasted the Lethean breath.
There was a voice that cried :

Behold, I stand above His head
With feet made white with whitest fire,
Above His forehead, that is red
As blood with His Desire.

I knew that Voice was more than God,
And echo trembled for its trust :
Sleep's feet, like Death's, with fire are shod,
And Love is likest Lust.

So I returned and sought her breast,
Our Lady of ten thousand Pains ;
I drank her kisses, and possessed
Her pale maternal veins.

I said : Drain hard my sudden breath,
Be cruel for the vampire thrust !
Let Sleep's desire be sweet as Death,
And Love be clean as Lust !

I died amid her kisses : so
This last time I would not forget—
So I attained The Life ;[1] and know
Her lips and God's have met.

For in Those Hands [2] above His head
The Depth is one with That Above,
And Sleep and Death and Life are dead,
And Lust is One with Love.

[1] *I.e.*, that state of mind which perceives the
hidden unity.
[2] A hand is here used as a symbol of the
Infinite Point because Yod—the Greek Iota—
means a hand.

## SONNET.

THE woods are very quiet, and the stream
Hardly awakes the stilled ear with its word ;
The voice of wind above like dawn is heard,
And all the air moves up, a sultry steam,
Here in the flower-land, where I lie and
    dream
And understand the silence of the bird ;
My sorrow and my weakness are interred
In the deep water where the pebbles gleam.

I rouse the force persistent of my will
To compel matter to the soul's desire,
To make Heaven aid the mind that would
    aspire
To touch its borders, and to drink their fill
At those far fountains whence one drop of
    dew [1]
Descends upon my head from yonder blue.

## AN ILL DREAM.

IN the grim woods when all the bare black
    branches
  Creak out their curses like a gallows-tree,
When the miasmal pestilence-light dances,
  A spectre-flame, through midnight's in-
    famy,
My blood grows chill and stagnant with my
    shame,
      O Love, to speak thy name !

O Life ! O Heaven ! O dreams long dead !
    Ye Spirits
  Rising unbidden from Hope's cobwebbed [2]
    door,
Ye quick desires that every soul inherits,
  Leave me to weep, and torture me no
    more !
My face grows grey with sheer despair ; I
    shrink
      From dreams ; I dare not think.

[1] The Amrita, or Elixir of Immortality.
[2] Because long shut, as in the story of Bruce
and the spider.

I had a poet's dreams.  My soul was yearn-
    ing
  To grasp the firmament and hold it fast,
To reach toward God, and, from His shrine
    returning,
  To sing in magic melodies the vast
Desires of God towards man—O dreams ! O
    years
      Drowned in these bitter tears !

I felt the springs of youth within me leap-
    ing,
  Let loose my pleasure, never guessed that
    pain
Was worth the holding—now, my life is
    weeping
  Itself away, those agonies to gain
Which are my one last hope. that by some
    cross
      Eld may avenge youth's loss !

Yet still youth burns !  The hours its pleasure
    wasted
  Compel their bitter memories to grow
    sweet ;
Like some warm-perfumed poison if I tasted,
  Felt its fierce savour pulse, and burn, and
    beat ;
Yet in my veins its sleepy fire might bring
      Strange dreams of some sweet thing.

Half a regret and half a shuddering terror,
  The past lies desolate and yet is here,
Half guide, half tempter toward the stream
    of error,
  On whose fresh bosom many a mariner
Puts out with silken sail—to find his grave
      In its voluptuous wave.

Here are few rocks whereon a ship hath
    peril ;
  No storms may ruffle its insidious stream ;
Only, no fish invade its waters sterile,
  No white-winged birds above it glance and
    gleam,
Only, it hath no shore, no wave, but gloom
      Wraps it within her womb.

No sun is mirrored in its treacherous water,
Only the false moon flickers and flits by
Like to the bloodless phantom shape of
   slaughter
Laughing a lipless laugh—a mockery,
A ghastly memory to wake and weep
   —Should Sorrow let me sleep.

No current draws a man, to his fair seem-
   ing,
Yet all the while he whirls a stealthy sweep
Narrower, nearer, where the wave is steam-
   ing
With the slight spray tossed from that funnel
   deep
Which dips, one wide black shaft, most
   horrible,
   Down to the nether Hell.

Yet there seems time.  God's grief has not
   forgotten
   His mighty arm, and with His pitying
   breath
A strong wind woke me ere my boat grew
   rotten
With venom of the stream, that quivereth
Now as He blew upon it—fish and bird
   Live at that silent word !

And I arose to seek the oars of Lying
   Wherewith I had embarked—the wind had
   torn
Their wood to splinters—"Jesus !  I am
   dying !
   Send me Thy cross to fashion some un-
   born
Oarage of Truth to quit this stream of Death !"
   O vain, O wasted breath !

I have no strength.  Upright I kneel, lament-
   ing
   The days when Love seemed fair, the bitter
   years
When pain might have found truth, ere un-
   relenting
   I shipwrecked Life !  O agony of tears !
Vain tears !  In silence, with abated breath
   I drift, drift on to Death !

## THE PRIEST SPEAKS.

*(Boccaccio.  Day IV.  Tale VIII.)*

LAY them together for the sake of Love
Within a little plot of piteous earth,
When life's last flower is faded in the sun.
Lay them together in the tender ground
That summer showers may shed a trembling
   tear,
And summer breezes whisper melodies
Of pity.  Lay them there, and when the sky
Opens a lingering eyelash of deep cloud,
And the sea sparkles out from under it
To kiss the earth into awakening
From the dream-slumbers that its fancies
   weave—
Fancies of starlight on the lucent sea
Gleaming from wide horizon to the feet
Of Cynthia's bow, all silver-shot with fire,
That virgin flame that lingers evermore
In the sweet phantasies of subtle sleep—
Fancies of lonely shadows darkly strewn
About the leaves of autumn in the woods,
Where the small floweret, hidden by the
   maze
Of the dying children of the copper-beech,
Lifts a blue forehead to the sun to kiss—
Fancies of old romance too pitiful
For any delicate quill to light upon—
Yes, when the sky from stainless ebony
Merges in azure, like as if the light
Of stars had melted into all the black
To gladden it, O then the solemn hush
Of morning shall behold the silent grave,
And wait a moment in rich worshipping
Of Love, creator of the world's delight,
Till the full chorus of the spirits of fire
(Whose mighty shoulders and wide-flashing
   wings
Bear the proud sun from his luxurious bed
Of rosy fleeces in the West low lying
Into the staircase of the jealous day)
Burst on the silence of the world beyond
And bid the listening poet catch the strain
Of their half-echoed hymn.  But come, my
   friends,

Lay them together, breast to maiden breast,
Limb linked with limb, and lips to pallid lips,
So beautiful in death—the moth o' th' mind
Tells the grief-numbèd senses "'Tis but sleep.
See ! the pale glimmer of a ghostly arm
Flashes a spot of light !"   Ah ! weary day !
'Tis but the flickering of the candle-light
And the unmanning sorrow of the heart
That lends the reins to fancy's charioteer.
Lay them together, let us leave them there !
There comes a vision to my mortal eyes
Of things immortal.   Hark ! the growing
   swell
Of some wild clarion through the dazzling
   night,
Whose fairy æther suddenly illumes
With silver meteors innumerable
And golden showers of stars—lost worlds of
   thought
And poets' dreams, and jewels of virgin sighs.
Hark ! the broad rings of sound go wavering
   on
Eddying and rippling through the desart sky
That now is peopled with the diamond wings
That float through all the palaces of God.
O now to join them rise the armies vast
Of the lone spirits of the empty tomb,
And there I see the lovers piteous
Splendidly flash within the silver sphere
Of light, and there I lose them at the last
Most wonderfully passed within the veil
Of Time ; caught up into the Infinite.
Lay them together.   And the hollow hill
Shall echo me " together," and the sky,
And the wide sea, and all the fragrant air,
Shall linger in the tumult of the dawn.
Lay them together.   And the still small voice
Shall whisper " Peace," and in the evening
   " Peace."


## THE VIOLET'S LOVE-STORY.

AMONG the lilies of the sacred stream
There grew a violet, like a maiden's dream,
And when the wind passed over them, it
   stirred
Their white soft petals with its quiet word.

The sun looked on them and their leaves were
   glad ;
Only the purple blossom there, that had
No kindred by the stream, let fall a tear,
Half wishing for the autumn of the year.

But when the summer came, the violet
   guessed
By some slow dream that thrilled her gentle
   breast,
That some sweet thing might come to her ;
   she thought
Through the long days of how her dream was
   wrought :

She guessed it woven of the spider's thread,
And coloured like the river's changing bed
Where polished pebbles shine ; she guessed
   it frail
And perfect, with pure wings, like silver
   pale.

So there, behind the leaves and stems, her
   lids
Grew deep with veins of love, and Bassarids [1]
Racing the dim woods through, beheld her
   face,
Whispered together, and desired the place.

The grey was blushing in the Eastern sky
When there drew near a child of poesy
With full lips very tender, and grave eyes
Where deep thoughts dwelt in some delicious
   wise.

He looked upon the lilies, and a tear
Dropped on their blossom ; but a little fear
Came to the bosom of the violet
Lest he see not, or see her, and forget.

But he did see her, and drew close, and
   said :
" O perfect passion of my soul, O dead
Living desire, O sweet unspoken sin,
Leave thou the lilies ; they are not thy kin.

[1] Votaries of Bacchus, so called from the
Bassara, or long mantle, which they wore.

"Within my heart one slow sweet whisper
     stole
Consuming and destroying all my soul
Lest, if the pure cold mind should conquer it,
I might not know, although it still were
     sweet.

"My pure desires arose and cast out love
That flew away, most like a wounded
     dove,
Only the drops were mine its bosom bled.
Now the last time it hovers by my head:

"Now the last time I turn and go to her."
The violet smiled at him; his fingers fair
Plucked the sweet blossom to his breast;
     his eyes
Mused like delight, and like desire were
     wise.

There was a maiden like the sun, to whom
His footsteps turned amid the myriad bloom
Of flowers and leafy pathways of the wood,
Where, in a dell of roses white, she stood.

He came to her and looked so dear and deep
Into her eyes, the wells and woods of sleep,
And took the violet from his breast, and
     stood
A glad young god within the golden wood.

He kissed the blossom, and bent very low,
And put it to her lips—and even so
His lips were set on them; the flower sighed
For deep delight, and in the long kiss died.

Years fled and faded, yet a flower was seen
Gracious and comely in its nest of green,
And tender hands would water it and say:
"O happy sister, she that went away!

"For she brought back my lover to my
     heart,
And knew her work was perfect, and her
     part
Most perfect when she died between the
     breath,
And in the bridal kisses kissed to death."

So grew the newer blossom and was glad:
Sweet little hopes her faint fair forehead had
That one day such a death might crown her
     days.
And so God too was glad, the story says.


## THE FAREWELL OF PARACELSUS TO APRILE.[1]

THOU Sun, whose swift desire to-day is
     dull,
   And all ye hosts of heaven, whose lips
     are mute,
And trees and flowers and oceans beautiful
   Among whose murmurs I have struck this
     lute
With joy supreme or agony acute,
And love transcending everything alway,
   Pity me, pity, since the poisonous root
Of parting strikes the beauty of the day;
We meet for the last time beside the ocean
     gray.

Soul of my soul, we never can forget—
   But, is our parting burnt across the skies?
Is the last word said?   Must our lips be
     set
   Not to new song, but to the bitter sighs
   As of a child whose flower-garden dies,
Who knows no hope of some enduring
     spring?
   Is the last song made, whose faint melodies
Brushed the pale air with an archangel's wing?
Is Hope divorced, our queen?  Is Love dis-
     crowned, our King?

Far o'er the Ocean sets a fiery star
   And meteors cross the angry horizon;
A comet blazes, reddening the bar
   Of silver water where the moonlight shone,
   And, as I stand upon the cliff like one

1 *Paracelsus.*  I am he that aspired to
KNOW: and thou?
   *Aprile.* I would LOVE infinitely, and be loved.
               BROWNING, *Paracelsus.*

But Crowley here opposes Browning.

Amazed, a shape seems always at my back
 To whisper wickedness, o'erheard of
  none,
And stealthily to follow on my track,
And cloke my lifted eyes with suffocating
 black.

Vainly I turn to seek him, for my eyes
 Are dimmed with saltness never born of
  brine ;
Vainly I fight the air ; he sneers, and lies.
 He laughs at all this agony of mine.
 He chills my heart, and desecrates the
  shrine
Where Love his holy incense used to burn.
 He mocks those thoughts, those songs,
  those looks divine
While his lewd visage no man may dis-
 cern,
And baffling darkness hides his terror if I
 turn.

Fighting and falling ever, weariest
 Even of beating off the tempter's blows,
Struggling in vain to what one hopes the
 best,
 A distant river over many snows,
 On whose green bank the purple iris
  glows,
And the anemone in some wild cleft,
 With the white violet, and the briar rose,
And the blue gentian from the heavens reft—
Lo ! 'Twas that golden bank but yester
 morn I left.

O river where we dwelt ! Yon summer sward
 Whereon we lay, two kings of earth and
  air ;
For whom ten thousand angels had drawn
 sword
 At our light bidding. Surely, surely,
  there
We might float ever to the sea, and spare
The dainty plumage of that perfect place.
 O God ! O Life ! O Death, thou
  would'st not wear
Such evil mask upon thy golden face—
O Mary, pity me of thine abounding grace.

Those days are dead, and hope no newer
 birth.
 I left thy shores, blue stream, at His com-
  mand
Who reared the mountains from the shaken
 earth ;
 Who holds the lightning in His holy hand,
 And binds the stars in adamantine band,
And yearns towards the children of His mind.
 I left their summer and their dewy strand
To pass a life of work, alone, unkind,
To fight a way toward heaven, mute, deso-
 late, and blind.

The dusty desert glimmers in the night ;
 A solitary palm-tree shades the well ;
I am alone, a weary eremite
 Striving the secrets of the stars to tell,
 And every blade of grass that makes the
  dell
Is counted and divined by me, who stare
 With eyes half blinded by the fires of Hell
That my wild brain imagines everywhere,
Roaring and raging round with red infernal
 glare.

The yellow sand toward the deep sky extends:
 A dusky mirage would confuse my view ;
Far, far away, where desolation ends,
 There is a water of serenest blue ;
 And by it stands, as patient and as true
As in the past, his form to whom I turn,
 And break my bondage and would touch
  anew
His holy lips ; my body and spirit yearn ;
He fades away, and fires of Hell within me
 burn.

Still, as I journey through the waste, I see
 A silver figure more divine arise ;
The Christ usurps the horizon for me.
 And He requickens the forgotten skies ;
 His golden locks are burning on my eyes,
And He with rosy finger points the way,
 The blood-wrought mystic path of Paradise
That leads at last through yonder icy spray
Of Death to the blue vaults of the undying
 day.

But oh ! this desert is a weary land !
  Poisons alone their prickly heads lift high ;
The sun, a globe of fury, still doth stand
  In the dark basin of the burning sky.
There is no water, no, nor herb, and I
Faint at his anger who compels the herd
  To fall upon the waste, so fierce and dry
That none may pass it, not the very bird.
Throughout the vast expanse no single sound
    is heard.

Only the moaning of the dying ox,
  And my parched cry for water from cracked
    lips ;
In vain the stern impenetrable rocks
  Mock my complaint : the empty pitcher
    dips
  Into the empty well ; the water drips,
Oozing in tiny drops caught up again
  By the sun's heat, that brooks not his
    eclipse
And dissipates the welcome clouds of rain.
God ! have Thou pity soon on this amazing
    pain.

If but a lion stirred with distant roar
  The silence of the world, perchance at last
I might find honey in his mouth, and store
  His tawny flanks until the sand were past.[1]
  Nay, but these wastes intolerably vast,
Like glowing copper raging for the heat,
  Stretch and stretch on and leave me all
    aghast
Straining my eyes in horror and defeat
Toward the long vista seen where rescue
    seems to greet.

The vessel fills with brackish foam.  I drink,
  Drink to the end, and stagger on alone
Without a staff to hold me if I sink
  In the hot quagmires of untrusty stone.
  Foodless and beastless, so despairing grown,
I know not, care not, only trust that soon
  The sun's dominion may be overthrown,
And o'er the wilderness appear the moon
With cold lips to bestow the inestimable
    boon.

        [1] See the story of Samson.

Still I have never prayed for death, but
    rather
  Would be found fighting toward the goal
    I seek,
Stretching both hands toward a loving
    father,
  And struggling toward some barren voice-
    less peak
With feet made stedfast, if God made them
    weak ;
So, on the journey, in the hottest fight
  I would be found by Death, whose palace
    bleak
Should be a resting-place until the night
Broke, and I met my God, and stood within
    His sight.

Only my brain grows feebler with the
    toil,
  And clearer runs the river I forsook ;
Now in clear pools its myriad fountains
    boil,
  Now there runs singing to its breast a
    brook ;
  Now it flows gently to a little nook
Where I once rested—Ah ! I clench my
    hand
  And turn away with yet undaunted look,
Setting my face toward the distant land
That must lie somewhere far beyond this
    world of sand.

About me are the bones of many men
  Who turned to God their rapt adoring
    eyes,
And cast away the love within their ken
  For this vague treasure-house beyond the
    skies—
Whither I turn, like a dumb beast that
    dies,
A wistful look, and breathe a dumb com-
    plaint.
  Lo ! they have cast away the mask of
    lies
And not found Truth.  So he would be a
    saint
Whose skeleton lies here because his soul
    did faint !

I will not turn toward Sodom any more,
  Lest its ripe glades of fruit waft up their
    scent,
And draw me to them, what time heavens
    pour
  Brimstone and fire from out the firma-
    ment,
  And all my substance in its fall be spent ;
Lest I lie there beneath a barren sea
Forgotten of high God, until there went
The final trumpet of the dead, who flee
Vainly that fearful blast of judgment.  Woe
    is me !

My feet, in spite of me, in circles bend ;
  I meet my own tracks often, all in vain
I seek some tower or cliff to make an end,[1]
  I find no object on the distant plain ;
  Misty distortions crowd upon my brain,
And spectre fountains gurgle on the ground ;
  I drop to drink, and hear the horrid strain
Of chuckling devils, that grimace around,
And think I catch the note of Hell's three-
    headed Hound.

Up still and staggering to the doubtful goal,
  Feet dragging horribly behind, I move
Deathlike for dearth and for despair of soul ;
  At last I drop.  From Heaven there comes
    a Dove
  Bearing the semblance of the Man I love,
And fountains and fresh grass by magic
    spell
  Are suddenly around me.  And above
I hear the voice my visions know so well :
" Well striven all this day against the power
    of Hell !"

I know these mercies still diviner grow
  Each day I strive.  But should I sit and
    rest
One hour of dawn, and cry, " I will not go
  Another step without more sleep," that
    blest
  Dove flies away, the fountains are re-
    pressed,

  [1] I.e., to serve as a direction.

The grass is withered, and the angry sky
  Rages more fierce that day, and from the
    crest
Of black foul mountains comes a bitter cry :
" He that returneth now shall in destruction
    die."

So I press on.  Fresh strength from day to
    day
  Girds up my loins and beckons me on
    high.
So I depart upon the desert way,
  So I strive ever toward the copper sky,
  With lips burnt black and blind in either
    eye.
I move for ever to my mystic goal
  Where I may drain a fountain never dry,
And of Life's guerdon gather in the whole,
And on celestial manna satisfy my soul.

Each night new failure and each day fresh
    strength,
  A sense of something nearer day by day ;
Though the ill road's intolerable length,
  League upon league, fling back the torrid
    ray
Of the fierce sunlight night can scarce allay
With the incessant beating of cool wings,
  And men's bleached skeletons infest the
    way ;
Yet Hope her passion like a flower brings,
And Courage ranks me with unconquerable
    kings.

So, in the power of these who guard my path,
  I hope one day to earn a loftier crown
Than that pale garland fresh from summer
    scath
That I called Love, and lie delighted down
  Beside the fountains, fled the roaring town,
Where we were happy all the summer
    through,
  And merry when the autumn tinged with
    brown
The glades, and in the winter thought we
    knew
Behind the cloudy weather some far sky was
    blue.

That crown I hope for shall be garlanded
  Of deathless flowers of equal bloom.   And
    thou,
O thou true lover, thou belovéd head
  And marble pallor of a prince's brow,
  At the cliff's edge we stand together now ;
The parting of our ways has come at last.
  Mine is the bitterest journey, as I trow,
A man may take, so solitary, so vast,
It binds the future now, and stultifies the
    past.

Only the hope that God may reunite
  Our ways diverging, and make one again
The deathless love that burns a beacon bright
  On the black deeps, the irremeable main,
  That men must launch on, the exalted plain
Of Life.   We sever, and our tears are few,
  Knowing perchance beyond the moment's
    pain
We shall regather where the skies are blue,
And live and love for aye, pure, passionate,
    and true.

Also before my eyes there gleams from
    Heaven
  The likeness of a Man in glory set ;
The sun is blotted, and the skies are riven—
  A God flames forth my spirit to beget ;
  And where my body and his love are met
A new desire possesses altogether
  My whole new self as in a golden net
Of transcendental love one fiery tether,
Dissolving all my woe into one sea of
    weather.

So I am ready to assume the Cross,
  Start on my journey with the last word
    said ;
Turn my back resolute on dung and dross,
  And face the future with no twitch of
    dread,
  But dare to converse with the holy dead,
And taste the earnest of the church's bliss.
  Love, God be with you !   He is overhead
And watches us, that nothing be amiss—
Love ! our hearts bleed as one in the last
    lingering kiss.

Good-bye, good-bye, good-bye ! the echo
    rings
A harsh, jarred sound in my self-tortured
    ears,
And agony, a fount of blood, upsprings
  And tears our bosoms with dividing fears.
  The cruel sea its final billow rears
And I must pass to seek an unknown sky ;
  We dare not see each other's face for tears,
And the last kisses—Did we only die !
Love ! Ah ! One kiss ! One kiss ! One kiss !
    Good-bye, Good-bye !


## A SPRING SNOWSTORM IN WASTDALE.[1]

On rocky mountain bare
  Of grass, and meadows fair,
Angels their trumpets blow upon the night.
  While o'er the shrinking dale
  The insatiable gale
Roars with unconquered and impassive might.
  Their robes of snow they rend,
  And their deep voices blend
With tempest, like that angry Amphitrite,[2]
  Her hair blown wild and loose
  On windy Syracuse,
Lashing the waves with words of wrath, a
    terror of bright light.

  Here the thick snowflakes fall,
  Till mountain in their pall,
And stream beneath their curtain are em-
    braced ;
  They drive and beat and hiss,
  Till their cold maiden kiss
Touches the lake's intolerable waste,
  And from the wave is born
  A maiden like the morn,
In sudden foam, an Aphrodite chaste,
  Clean as the cold wind blown
  From each abyss of stone,
Where the north whirlpool rushes down with
    wreckage interlaced.

1 Crowley was one of the pioneers of rock-
climbing among the Cumbrian fells.
2 Goddess of the Mediterranean Sea.

Here on the bank I stand
In this grey barren land
Of winter, and the doubtful glint of spring
If on the hills there glow
Through the thick mist of snow
Sunshine from westward in the evening ;
While in a dell appear
Violets and snowdrops clear,
Buds of the larch, and swallows on the
    wing,
Ere once again the storm
Lofty and multiform
Close the bright glimpse of summer and the
    hope of everything.


Silence her throne assumes,
Stars mount the sky, and looms
The misty monarch of the dale on high :
About the silver feet
I worship, as is meet,
The warrior God that fixed the curvéd
    sky,
Rent the cavernous earth,
Moulded in awful birth
The terror of the cloudy canopy,
And tore from underground
The lake's immense profound,
And clad the mountains now with this faint
    snow embroidery.


Now the white flakes decrease.
Wastwater lies in peace,
Kissed by the breezes where the wind once
    bit ;
Gable alone doth stand,
A Pyrámid more grand
Than Pharaoh's pride exalted, or the wit
Of magian shepherds built
Who sought his land and spilt
Blood of ten million slaves to conquer it.[1]
Clad in sparse robes of white
The mountain beckons Night
Her tracery of azure with the cold moon-rays
    to knit.

[1] The reference is to the "Shepherd Kings"
of Abydos, who, says one theory, built Ghizeh.

Armoured with secret might
I stand on earth upright,
Strong in the power of Him who welded
    earth,
Barred in the sky with steel,
And breathed upon the wheel
Of this vast scheme of stars, and made Him
    mirth
In the poor dreams of us
Who strive mysterious
To pierce the bands of sense, and break the
    girth
Of our own minds' desire,
Till He relume the fire
Lost at our fall, not kindled fresh till that
    diviner birth.


## IN NEVILLE'S COURT, TRINITY COLLEGE, CAMBRIDGE.[1]

I THINK the souls of many men are here
Among these cloisters, underneath the
    spire
That the moon silvers with magnetic
    fire ;
But not a moon-ray is it, that so clear
Shines on the pavement, for a voice of
    fear
It hath, unless it be the breeze that
    mocks
My ear, and waves his old majestic locks
About his head.   There fell upon my ear :

"O soul contemplative of distant things,
Who hast a poet's heart, even if thy
    pen
Be dry and barren, who dost hold Love
    dear,
Speed forth this message on the fiery
    wings
Of stinging song to all the race of men :
That they have hope ; for we are happy
    here."

[1] The "Voice" is that of Lord Tennyson,
whose rooms were in this court.

## SUCCUBUS.[1]

WHO is Love, that he should find me as I
   strive,
Pale and weary, dumb and blind, where
   curses thrive,
Fold my sleep within his wings, and lead
   my dreams
Through a land of pleasant things, of woods
   and streams,
Bind my slumber with a chain of pure delight,
Though the canker of it stain at death of
   night,
Fill with passion and distaste and wakened
   pleasure
All the moments run to waste that else were
   treasure ?
Who is Love ? a fury red with all men's blood
On his cruel altars shed, a deadly flood ?
Or a veiléd vision black with shame and fear,
Whose most loathliest attack at night is near,
When the gates of spirit tense with angel's
   tread
Close, and all the gates of sense swing wide
   instead,
When the will of men is sleeping, and when
   the mind
Hears no sobs of spirits weeping above the
   wind,
All the subtle paths are clear for wicked
   breath,
And no angel warns the ear that this is
   death ?
Is this fiend the Love that came when youth
   rose up
Purple with its holy flame, and flower-fair
   cup,
Gave me of his burning wine to fire my heart,
Filled me with desires divine toward my art ?
Is he then the Love who robs me of my aim,
Doubts me if my heart still throbs with that
   cold flame,

[1] The Succubus, and its male counterpart
the Incubus, bulk largely in mediæval literature and philosophy.   The poem explains
itself.

Calm and eager purpose yet to reach the
   goal
That high hopes have sternly set before my
   soul,
To know, will, dare for man's sake if man
   may,
Grasp the secret of the plans that rule the
   way
Of stars and suns, that shape the tiniest
   blade
Of grass whose frailties 'scape the passing
   maid,
Whose light foot brushes fern and moss ?
   But Love
Comes a thief to men who turn toward things
   above
To set snares, by night, and makes afraid
The spirit's holy might with one slight
   maid
Visioned and unsubsisting save in foreign
   thought,
To its own strength a slave by witchcraft
   brought !
This is not Love but Lust, not Life but Death
   is found :—
All the halls of sense with strife cry and re-
   sound.
The Brain awakes in wrath ; behold ! the
   foemen flee,
All the earth is clad with gold, and all the
   sea ;
Driven back the demons yield, falter and
   cease ;
For a little while the shield of sleep is peace.
Clear and bright the lamp burns ; clean and
   sharp the sword,[1]
While I watch their paths between before
   the Lord.

## A RONDEL.

REST, like a star at sea
   Thrice loved, thrice blest,
Burns.   Will there come to me
   Rest ?

[1] Common magical implements.   The lamp
signifies Illumination and the sword Will.

By these suppressed
  Desires my soul must flee,
By heaven's crest,

I pray that secretly
  Toward God's breast
I draw, to find, maybe,
  Rest !


## NIGHTFALL.

THE seas that lap the sand
Where lilies fill the land
Are silent, while the moon ascends to span
    the curvéd leaves.
The lordly stars arise
With pity in their eyes
So large and clear and wise,
And angels yearn toward the world that
    wonders, wakes, and grieves.

Sleep holds the hand of life,
And, as a loving wife
Moves not for fear the sufferer should wake
    before his hour,
So sleep is deadly calm,
And fills with perfect balm
The night's unquiet psalm
That wanders all too trembling up, and
    quivers as a flower.

The wise man opens wide
His casement, as a bride
Flings her bright arms to meet her spouse
    homeward who hasteneth ;
He trims his lamp, and brings
The books of many kings
To spread their holy wings
About his head, and sing to him the secret
    ways of death.

He knows, and doth not fear ;
His will is keen and clear ;
His lips are silent to protect the secret
    mysteries.

No tempter spreads his net
So that his thoughts forget
The glory they have set
Before their face, nor loose their hold upon
    the perfect prize.

My hands no longer write :
Communion with the night
Is built, a bridge of fiery truth across the
    subtle mind.
God's angels, and His fire,
Consume the soul's desire,
And strike a lighter lyre.
I seek ; the angels lead me on, all light and
    truth to find.


## THE INITIATION.

THERE is a bare bleak headland which the
    sea
Incessantly devours,
A rock impregnable, where herb and tree
Are not.   A vision of it came to me
In night's most ghastly hours.

I who desire, beyond all named desire,
To pass the envious bounds of air and fire,
And penetrate the bosom of the night,
Saw in a vision such a neophyte
Stand on the forehead of the rock ; I saw
The armies of unalterable law
Shudder within their spheres, as to him came
His master's spirit, like a tongue of flame,
To touch his lips and ears and eyes and hands
With that pale amber that divides the lands
Of sense and spirit, and beheld him quail
As fell from all his shaken soul the veil.
Then on the night began the awful gale
That did assume a voice
Whereat the air was peopled with such forms
As ride abroad upon the path of storms,
And in the awe rejoice.
They gather, chanting, round that noble head.
The master of the prisons of the dead
Loosens the bonds and bids the furies spring
For their last struggle ere they own a king.
This pæan of the sky they sing.

*We ride upon the fury of the blast,*
*Fast, fast.*
*We race upon the horses of the wind:*
*The tameless thunder follows hard behind,*
*Fast, and too fast.*
*The lightning heralds us; the iron blast*
*Lends us its splendour for a steed fire-shod,*
*The steed of God!*

From all the caverns of the hollow sea,
And all the fortresses that guard the air,
And all the fearful palaces of fire,
And all the earth's dwarf-ridden secrecy,
They come, they gather, and they ride, to
    bear
Destruction and disorder and desire;
They cling to him who braves the gale of
    night,
And mock his might.
They rush upon him like a wave, and break
In fiery foam against him, and they shake
Life in its citadel.
They open Hell
To let the Furies and the Fates spring forth
On their wild chargers of the icy North
To quench the holy lamp.
His spirit and his life within him quail,
And all the armaments of sin assail
With deadly tramp
And swordless fury. Hell devours and tears
The heart of any a man, whom heavenly airs
Shield and lead on afar,
Where beyond storm and passion is the
    sky,
And where the sacred hand of the Most High
Holds out a star.
He stands amid the storm, a mighty rock;
His long hair blows about, the demons
    mock
His entry to their kingdom, and despair.
Groans in the blackness, infamous and bare,
And hateful shapes and eyes surround his
    head—
O for the magic of those mightier dead
To scatter them, and utterly destroy
Their likeness, and to penetrate the joy
Of yonder places past the realm of fear!
O that some mighty seer

Came to avenge, that might deliver him
From this grim fight, whose horrid ranks
    are dim
With mist of spuméd blood, whose long chill
    hour
Beats out each second with the ghastly
    power,
Reluctant till the morning. Shall they cease,
These black battalions, and the dawn bring
    peace
To a head holier? Or shall he succumb,
Fight through long agonies and perish dumb,
Sword gripped hard to the last? or shall he
    fall
Recreant, coward, and no more at all
Reach the dim martyr-hall of heroes? Yet
The surging shapes gape hideous, to beget
Fresh arméd foemen to destroy the king.
And first, on black imperishable wing,
    That Nameless Thing.

Darkness, a dragon, now devours
The vision of those deadly powers,
The legions of the lords of sin.
It is an hour ere dawn begin.

## ISAIAH.

### A SONNET.

THE world is dusk, expectant of its doom.
Foulness is rampant; purity is dumb;
Despair stalks terrible. But I am come,
God-nurtured, in the void abyss of gloom;
The Spirit of my God is set on me;
He hath anointed me to preach glad news
Unto the meek; the broken heart to loose,
To utter to the captive liberty,
The prison's opening to all the bound,
And unto all men to proclaim aloud
The year acceptable before the Lord.
Therefore He fills my voice with silvery
    sound,
And by His spirit, a pillar of fire and cloud,
My eyes are lightning, and my tongue a
    sword.

## THE STORM.

IN the storm that divides the wild night
    from the passionate kiss of the morn-
    ing
   Stands there a tower by the sea un-
    shaken by wave and by wind ;
Lightning assails, and the sea breaks vain on
    the battlements, scorning
   Even to fling back the foam shattered
    before and behind ;
   Save for one window its height rears up
    unbroken and blind.
Here may a man gaze out to the night by the
    stars of it stricken,
   Out to the blind black air that the lightning
    divides, and is dumb ;
Here, and look back in the tower where
    pallid shades murmur and quicken :
   Low laughs leap in the silence, sink to a
    sigh ere there come,
   Far from the feet of the storm, a pulse like
    the beat of a drum.
Throbs the wild sound through the storm,
    and the wings of it waken and quiver,
   Only the watcher, unmoved, looks on the
    face of the night ;
Sees the strong hosts that unite, a fervent
    implacable river
   Foaming from heaven and hell, two armies
    of crimson and white ;
   Flecked is the sky with their blood shed
    as by sabres of light.
Now they are clutching his arms, the
    phantoms that throng there behind
    him,
   Foul and distorted, whose sight may not
    on men ever dawn ;
Now they entice and entreat, now strive with
    fresh fury to bind him,
   Cords that are cut by an angel whose
    sword is unceasingly drawn,
   Glitters, and bids them fall back as if
    struck by the eye of the morn.
Would he but turn he should see a woman
    laid naked before him,

Stretching her arms to his breast, reach-
    ing her lips to his face,
   Lips that should grant but one kiss ere the
    demons descended and tore him
Limb from wet limb, and devoured, and bore
    his stained soul into space
   Far from the regions of hope and the lands
    that are holy with grace.
Alway the battle proceeds and alway the
    tempest re-quickens,
   Pregnant with thunder, delivered when the
    swift knife is let flash ;
Alway the wind has its will and the slaughter-
    steam rises and thickens ;
   Alway the sea is a lion, enraged by the
    wind and its lash ;
   Alway the heavens resound with the
    thunder's reverberate crash.
Heaven has conquered, behold ! and the
    hosts of the demons are fleeing ;
   Dawn drives before her fair feet the feather-
    light wings of the gale ;
Silent the tower rears aloft its front into
    beauty and seeing.
   Only the window is dark ; only there
    hangs like a veil
Sleep on the chamber and clings. Heard
    I a woman-fiend wail?
Heard I the sound of a kiss? Has man
    been destroyed in the daylight,
   Man whom the night could not quell?
    What angel fled weeping away?
There in the East there extends a white
    light devouring the grey light,
   There the sun rises and brings hope with
    the dawn of the day.
Silence hides certainty—surely voices of
    angels that pray,
Surely the sound of delight, and of praise,
    and unspeakable glory
   Rings in the wind like a bell, and wakes
    the white air of the lea ;
All the bright sea is aflame, and the caps of
    it, golden or hoary,
   Leap in the light of the sun, in the light
    of the eyes of the sea.
   Triumph is born like a flower, and the
    soul of the adept is free.

## WHEAT AND WINE.

CLEAR, deep, and blue, the sky
  Is silvered by the morn,
And where the dewdrop's eye
Catches its brilliancy
  Strange lights and hues are born :
I have seen twelve colours hover on a single
  spray of thorn.

There is a great grey tower [1]
  Cut clear against the deep ;
In the sun's wakening hour
I think it has the power
  To touch the soul of sleep
With its tender thought, and bid me to awake
  for joy—and weep.

This night I am earlier.
  No drowsy thoughts drew nigh
At eve to make demur
That I be minister
  To Cynthia maidenly :
All night I have watched her sail through a
  black and silver sky.

Within my soul there fight
  Two full and urgent streams,
Work's woe and dream's delight :
Like snow and sun they smite,
  Days battle hard with dreams :
On a world of misty beauty the Aurora
  clearly beams.

So labour fought with pride,
  And love with idleness,
My soul was torn and tried
With the impassioned tide
  Of storm and deathly stress—
I had never dreamed a lily should arise amid
  the press.

[1] St. John's Chapel, Cambridge, which
Crowley's rooms in 16 St. John's Street overlooked. It was his habit to work from midnight to dawn, when he could no longer be
disturbed by visits from friends.

Yet such a flower sprang here
  Within this soul of mine,
When foemen bade good cheer
To foemen, grew one clear
  Concept, ideal, divine,
Of a god of light and laughter, of a god of
  wheat and wine.

Work on, strong mind, devise
  The outer life aright !
Dream, subtle soul, and arise
To noblest litanies
  That pierce the mask of night—
In a man work lifts his eyelids, but his dreams
  lend eyes their light.

So dreams and days are wed,
  And soul and body lie
Ambrosial in Love's bed.
See, heaven with stars is spread—
  So glad of life am I
If an angel came to call me I am sure I
  would not die.

## A RONDEL.

THE wail of the wind in the desolate land
  Lifts voice where the heaven lies pallid and
  blind ;
Sweeps over the hills from the sea and the
  sand
    The wail of the wind.

The earth gives a bleak echo back, and
  behind
  Lurk sorrows and sins in the grasp of a
  hand,
And love and despair are the lords of mankind.

The mountains are steadfast ; immutably
  grand,
  Bid me to their bosom the chain to unbind :
At peace and at pity I now understand
    The wail of the wind.

## THE VISIONS OF THE ORDEAL.

THE mind with visions clouded,
  (Asleep? Awake?)
By bloodless shades enshrouded,
  (By whom, and for whose sake?)
With visions dimly lighted,
By its own shade affrighted,
In its own light benighted,
  The doors of hell may shake.

Unbidden spring the spectres
  (Whence come, where bound?)
To baffle those protectors
  Whose wings are broad around.
Uprise they and upbraid,
Till life shrinks back afraid,
And death itself dismayed
  Sinks back to the profound.

Unholy phantom faces
  (Of self? Of sin?)
Grin wild in all the places
  Where blood is trodden in :
The ground of night enchanted
With deadly blooms is planted,
Where evil beasts have panted
  And snakes have shed their skin.

With poison steams the air,
  And evil scent
Is potent everywhere ;
  Creation waits the event :
In silence, without sighing,
The living and the dying,
Oppressed and putrefying,
  Curse earth and firmament.

What dreams disturb my slumber,
  Or what sights seen?
Foul orgies without number
  In dens and caves obscene,
Accurst, detestable,
In which I laugh with hell,
And furies chant the knell
  Of all things clean.

Ah God ! the shapes that throng !
Ah God ! what eyes !
The souls grown sharp and strong
  That my lips made their prize,
The ruined souls, the wrecks
Of bodies fair of flecks
Long since, ere God did vex
  My soul with sacrifice.

These press upon my lips
  What lips of flame
To burn me, unless slips
  Some cooler kiss, from shame
Washed clean by God's desire,
To save me from their fire—
Those kiss me and respire
  The perfume of the Name.[1]

Remorse and terror banished
  By pitying lovers,
Who from my eyes have vanished,
  (The Lidless Eye[2] discovers),
Repenting souls that turn,
Whose hearts with pity burn
For me, who now discern
  Their love around me hovers.

Their love wards from my head
  The furious hate
Of those loves doubly dead
  That may not pass the gate :
By their entreating prayer
The angels fill the air
To guard my steps, to bare
  The veil inviolate.

The visions leave me now ;
  I sink to sleep ;
Calm and content my brow ;
  My eyes are large and deep.
The morning shall behold
On feet and plumes of gold
My spirit soon enfold
  The flocks on heaven's steep.

[1] Jehovah, here and throughout, unless expressly stated to the contrary.
[2] That of Macroprosopus, who "neither slumbers nor sleeps."

Refreshed, encouraged, lightened,
    Sent on the Way
Whose Sun and Star have brightened
    From dawning into day,
I set my face, a flint,
Toward where the holy glint
Of lamps affords the hint
    That leads me—where it may.

## POWER.

THE mighty sound of forests murmuring
In answer to the dread command ;
The stars that shudder when their king[1]
Extends his hand,

His awful hand to bless, to curse ; or moves
Toward the dimmest den
In the thick leaves, not known of loves
Or nymphs or men ;

(Only the sylph's frail gossamer may wave
Their quiet frondage yet,
Only her dewy tears may lave
The violet ;)

The mighty answer of the shaken sky
To his supreme behest ; the call
Of ibex that behold on high
Night's funeral,

And see the pale moon quiver and depart
Far beyond space, the sun ascend
And draw earth's globe unto his heart
To make an end ;

The shriek of startled birds ; the sobs that tear
With sudden terror the sharp sea
That slept, and wove its golden hair
Most mournfully ;

The rending of the earth at his command
Who wields the wrath of heaven, and is
    dumb ;
Hell starts up—and before his hand
Is overcome.

1. G. C. Jones, then of Basingstoke, a profound mystic.

I heard these voices, and beheld afar
These dread works wrought at his behest :
And on his forehead, lo ! a star,
And on his breast.

And on his feet I knew the sandals were
More beautiful than flame, and white,
And on the glory of his hair
The crown of night.

And I beheld his robe, and on its hem
Were writ unlawful words to say,
Broidered like lilies, with a gem
More clear than day.

And round him shone so wonderful a light
As when on Galilee
Jesus once walked, and clove the night,
And calmed the sea.

I scarce could see his features for the fire
That dwelt about his brow,
Yet, for the whiteness of my own desire,
I see him now ;

Because my footsteps follow his, and tread
The awful bounds of heaven, and make
The very graves yield up their dead,
And high thrones shake ;

Because my eyes still steadily behold,
And dazzle not, nor shun the night,
The foam-born lamp of beaten gold
And secret might ;

Because my forehead bears the sacred Name,
And my lips bear the brand
Of Him[1] whose heaven is one flame,
Whose holy hand

Gathers this earth, who built the vaults of
    space,
Moulded the stars, and fixed the iron sea,
Because His[1] love lights through my face
And all of me.

1. Jehovah.

Because my hand may fasten on the sword
If my heart falter not, and smite
Those lampless limits most abhorred
Of iron night,

And pass beyond their horror to attack
Fresh foemen, light and truth to bring
Through their untrodden fields of black,
A victor king.

I know all must be well, all must be free;
I know God as I know a friend;
I conquer, and most silently
Await the end.


## VESPERS.

THE incense steams before the Christ;
    It wraps His feet with grey,
A perfumed melancholy mist,
    Tears sacred from the day;
An awe, a holiness, I wist,
    More sweet than man may say.

I bend my head to kiss the brow,
    Scarred and serene and wide,
The bosom and the loin-cloth now
    And where the blood has dried,
The blood whose purple tide doth flow
    From out the smitten side.

The fragrance of his skin begets
    Desire of holy things;
Through the dim air a spirit frets
    His closely woven wings;
Like love, upon my brow he sets
    The crowns of many kings.

(The trembling demons of the sea
    Before the poet bend;
He greets the angels quietly
    As one who greets a friend;
He waiteth, passionless, to be
    A witness of the end.)

I chant in low sweet verses still
    A mystic song of dread,
As one imposing all his will
    Upon the expectant dead;
And lights dip down, and shadows fill
    The dreams that haunt my head.

I sing strange stories of that world
    No man may ever see;
My lips with strong delight are curled
    To kiss the sacred knee,
And all my soul is dewed and pearled
    With tears of poetry.

The strong mysterious spell is cast
    To bind and to release;
To give the devils hope at last,
    To the unburied peace;
To gladden the reluctant past
    With silent harmonies.

The song grows wilder now and strives
    All heaven to enchain,
As who should grasp a thousand lives,
    And draw their breath again
Into some cavern where he dives,
    A hell of grisly pain.

And now behold! the barren Cross
    Bursts out in vernal flowers;
The music weeps, as on the moss
    The summer's kissing showers,
And there sweep, as sweeps an albatross,
    The happy-hearted hours.

My rapt eyes grow more eager now,
    God smites within the host,
White fires illuminate my brow
    Lit of the Holy Ghost;
I see the angel figures bow
    On Heaven's silent coast.

Eternity, a wheel of light,
    And Time, a fleece of snow,
I saw, and deep beyond the night,
    The steady mystic glow
Of that lamp's flame unearthly bright
    That watches Earth below.

Long avenues of sleepy trees
  And bowers arched with love,
And kisses woven for a breeze,
  And lips that scarcely move,
Save as long ripples on the seas,
  That murmur like a dove.

I saw the burning lips of God
  Set fast on Mary's face,
I saw the Christ, with fire shod,
  Walk through the holy place,
And the lilies rosier where he trod
  Blushed for a little space.

I saw myself, and still I sang
  With lips in clearer tune,
Like to the nightingale's that rang
  Through all those nights of June ;
Such nights when stars in slumber hang
  Beneath the quiet moon.

Still, in those avenues of light,
  No maid, with golden zone,
And lily garment that from sight
  Half hides the ivory throne,
Lay in my arms the livelong night
  To call my soul her own.

The Christ's cold lips my lips did taste
  On Time's disastrous tide ;
His bruiséd arms my soul embraced,
  My soul twice crucified ;
And always then the thin blood raced
  From out the stricken side.

The incense fumes, the chant is low,
  Perfume around is shed ;
I am as one of Them who know
  The secrets of the dead :
The sorrows that walk to and fro,
  The love that hides his head.

O living Head ! whose thorns are keen
  To bruise and pierce and slay ;
O Christ ! whose eyes have always been
  Fixed fast upon the way,
Where dim Jerusalem was seen
  A city cold and grey !

The flowers of fire that grow beneath
  And blossom on the Tree
Are fed from his despair and death
  Who sings of land and sea,
And all those mountains where thy breath,
  Jehovah, still must be.

The censer swings to slower time ;
  The darkness falleth deep :
My eyes, so solemn and sublime,
  Relent, and close, and weep :
And on the silence, like a chime,
  I heard the wings of Sleep.


## BY THE CAM

TWILIGHT is over, and the noon of night
  Draws to its zenith.  Here beyond the
    stream
  Dance the wild witches that dispel my dream
Of gardens naked in Diana's sight.
Foul censers, altars desecrated, blight
  The corpse-lit river, whose dank vapours
    teem
  Heavy and horrible, a deadly steam
Of murder's black intolerable might.

The stagnant pools rejoice ; the human feast
  Revels at height ; the sacrament is come ;
God wakes no lightning in the broken East ;
  His awful thunders listen and are dumb ;
Earth gapes not for that sin ; the skies renew
At break of day their vestiture of blue.


## ASTROLOGY.

A LONELY spirit seeks the midnight hour,
  When souls have power
To cast away one moment bonds of clay,
  And touch the day
With pallid wistful lips beyond the earth,
  And bring to birth
New thoughts with which life  long  has
    travailed ;
  As if one dead

Should rise and utter secrets of the tomb,
  And from hell's womb
Or heaven's breast bring all the load of fears,
  Toils of long years,
Sorrows of life and agonies of death,
  Hard caught-up breath,
The labouring hands of love, the cheeks of
    shame,
  The gloomy flame
Of lust, the cruel torment of desire
  More than hell fire,
And bid them fade, as if the bryony
  Let her flower die,
And banished them through space, as if a
    star
  Dropped through the far
Vault of the sky, and, as a lamp extinct
  With blood-red tinct,
Went out.  So lonely in mysterious night
  A wild, strange light
Flickers around the sacred head of man,
  And bids him scan
The scroll of heaven, and see if there be not,
  Black with no blot
Of cloud, but golden lettered on the blue
  That mothers dew,
This message of good hope, good trust, good
    fate
  And good estate :
" Work on, hope ever, let your faith be built
  Of gold ungilt ;
Your love exceed the starry vault for height,
  The heaven for might ;
Your faith wax firmer than a ship at sleep
  On the grey deep,
Anchored in some most certain anchorage
  From ocean's rage ;
Your patience stand when mountains shake
    and quail
  Before the gale
Of God's great tribulation.   Make thee sure
  Thou canst endure !
And work, work ever, sleep not, gird thy
    head
  With garlands red
Of blood from swollen veins forced in bitter
    toil
  To win some spoil

Of knowledge from the caverns of the deep !
  So shall the steep
Pathways of heaven gleam with loftier fires
  Than earth's desires.
So shalt thou conquer Space, and lastly
    climb
  The walls of Time,
And by the golden path the great have trod
  Reach up to God ! "


## DÆDALUS.

THE scorpion kisses and the stings of sin
  Cling hard within
The heart whose fibres, like a slender
    vine,
  Earth's hopes entwine,
And all the furies of the air caress
  The sorceress
Whose bosom beats in unison with shame,
  A flower of flame
Whose root most secretly made fast in hell
Is watered by the seraphim that fell.


The heart wherein is lit the sacred fire
  Of high desire,
Burnt clean from all untruth and sacrilege,
  Her wings may fledge,
And fly a little in the broad sweet air,
  Till unaware
The Spirit of Jehovah, like a dove
  On wings of love,
Breathe the sweet kiss, a sacrament un-
    told,
And clothe the heart's desire with flames of
    gold.


No rash Icarian wing this passion plies,
  But sanctifies,
As if a censer (that a cherub swings)
  Blossomed with wings
And floated up, an incense-breathing bird,
  With songs half heard

Before the throne of God.   Even so this life
  Of sordid strife
Is made most holy, beautiful, and pure,
  By this desire, if this desire endure.

So to the altar of the Highest aspire
  Those souls whose fire
Has on it cast one grain of pure incense,
  (Who guesses—whence?)
Those souls that cast their trammels off, and
    spring
  On eager wing,
Immaculate, new-born, toward the sky,
  And shall not die
Until they cleave at last the lampless dome,
And lose their tent because they find their
    home.


### EPILOGUE.

LIKE snows on the mountain, uplifted
  By weather or wind as it blows,
In hollows the heaps of it drifted,
  The splendour of fathomless snows;
So measure and meaning are shifted to
    fashion a rose.

The garland I made in my sorrow
  Was woven of infinite peace;
The joy that was white on the morrow
  Made music of viols at ease;
The thoughts of the Highest would borrow
    the roar of the seas.

This pastime of hope and of labour
  Fled singing through bountiful hours,
With sleep for a bride, for a neighbour
  With Death in the blossoming bowers
That slays with his merciless sabre the
    passion of flowers.

This pastime had hope for its metre,
  And trust in high God for the tune,
And passion of sorrow made sweeter
  Than loves of the leafiest June,
When Artemis' arrows are fleeter than rays
  of the moon.

My hope in the ocean was founded,
  Nor changed for the wind and the tide;
My love by the heaven was bounded,
  And knew not a barrier beside;
My faith beyond heaven was grounded, as
    God to abide.

Though death be the stain on our roses,
  The roses of heaven are white;
Though day on the world of us closes
  The stars only dream of the night
As of music that roars and reposes and dies
    in delight.

Dead stars in the season of sighing,
  Lost worlds of unspeakable pain,
White winds in the winter-tide dying,
  Or pestilence risen from rain;
So thoughts are that perish for lying and
    rise not again.

Blue waves in the summer uncrested,
  New homes for the fair and the free,
Bright breezes in forest-leaves nested,
  Sweet birds in the flowering tree;
So thoughts that by truth have been tested
    sing down to the sea.

But weak as the flowers of summer
  Are the flowers that float on my stream;
My song-birds to others are dumber
  Than voices half heard in a dream;
My muse, louder gods overcome her, the
    eyes of them gleam.

The sorrow that woke me to singing
  Is deeper than songs that I sing;
The birds that fresh music are bringing
  No chords for my memory bring;
Those lips like a soul that are clinging most
    silently cling.

Take thought for these verses, though time be
  So sure and so swift for thy feet,
Though far from this England thy clime be [1]
  In years that sway slow as the wheat,
Take thought, for an hour let my rhyme be
    not wholly unsweet.

[1] Julian Baker expected at this time to be
abroad for some years.

For truth and desire and devotion
  May lend through the verses a voice,
They tremble with violent motion,
  They yearn to be fair for thy choice
As billows and winds of the ocean that roar
  and rejoice.

For winds that are shaken and riven
  I bound by my power unto me;
For these have I battled and striven
  With winds that are rapid and free;
With weapons of words I have driven the
  pulse of the sea.

There steals through my coldness a fire,
  Between my slow words is a sword,
One lit by the heart of desire,
  One sharp in the hand of the Lord;
To these that sink, sleep, and expire, your
  welcome accord.

With wrath or repose for its raiment
  Your power, like a pyramid, stands;
My love, with no claim, as a claimant
  Came seeking out truth in the sands,
Found truth, and must place in poor payment
  this book in your hands.

# THE POEM.

## A LITTLE DRAMA IN FOUR SCENES.

### 1898.

I dedicate this play * to the gentleman who, on the evening of June 24th, 1898, turned back in Shaftesbury Avenue to give a halfpenny to a little girl, and thereby suggested to me the idea here rendered.

### SCENES.

I. THE ANGEL OF PITY.
II. THE ANGEL OF LOVE.
III. THE ANGEL OF DEATH.
IV. THE FORM OF THE FOURTH WAS LIKE
    THE SON OF GOD.[1]

### PERSONS.

PERCY BRANDON (*a Poet*).
ESMÉ VAUGHAN.
MR. VAUGHAN (*her Father*).
MR. BRANDON (*Father of Percy*).
A FRIEND TO VAUGHAN.
Butler, Footmen, etc., etc.

### SCENE I.

*Shaftesbury Avenue, 8.30 p.m. A gentleman walking with a friend, both in evening dress. A little ragged girl. A young man. The gentleman stops and gives the little girl a halfpenny. The young man smiles.*
*The gentleman notices the smile, and sees how great a sadness underlies it.*

#### VAUGHAN.

[*Turning to the young man.*]
AND you — what are you doing here? Excuse my rudeness—you seem so sad.

[1] See Daniel iii. 25.

#### PERCY.

I am sad to-night. I am very lonely in this place.

#### VAUGHAN.

There are plenty of people about.

#### PERCY.

People—mere shells, husks of the golden wheat that might grow even here.

#### VAUGHAN.

Why do you stay here?

#### PERCY.

I cannot think at home.

#### VAUGHAN.

Why think, if thinking makes you sad?

#### PERCY.

That I may write. I have not long to live, and I must write, write always.

#### FRIEND [*aside to Vaughan*].

Il me semble qu'il a faim.

#### PERCY.

I am hungry for a little love, a little pity. To-night you have shown me your soul, and I am not hungry any more.

* Like all plays of this form, it may be read as a delicate idyll or a screaming parody, according to the nature and mood of the reader.

VAUGHAN.

But, boy, you are starving physically. Come home with me and have some dinner. Only my daughter will be there.

PERCY.

You are very kind. Thank you.

FRIEND [aside].

He is a gentleman.

VAUGHAN.

But what are you doing to be alone in London?

PERCY.

Where should I go?

VAUGHAN.

Your father—

PERCY.

Has shown me the door.

VAUGHAN.

How have you quarrelled?

PERCY.

Because I must write.

VAUGHAN.

What do you write about that he dislikes?

PERCY.

He calls it waste of time.

VAUGHAN.

He may be right. What do you write about?

PERCY.

I write about all the horrible things I see, and try to find beauty in them, or to make beauty; and I write about all the beautiful things I only dream of. I love them all; yes, even that woman yonder.

VAUGHAN.

Do you find beauty in her?

PERCY.

No, but I see in her history a poem, to which I trust that God will write an end.

VAUGHAN.

What end can come but evil?

PERCY.

O! if I had no hope for her I should have none for myself.

VAUGHAN.

How? Have you then fallen?

PERCY.

Oh, yes, I have fallen. I am older every hour. I have wasted time, I have wasted love.

VAUGHAN.

Perhaps it is not all waste after all. There is a use for everything, nothing is destroyed —believe so, anyhow!

FRIEND.

What about this dinner of yours, Vaughan? Esmé will think us a long while gone.

VAUGHAN.

Hansom!                    [Exeunt.

## SCENE II.

*A year later.* VAUGHAN's *house in Mayfair.* PERCY's *bedroom. Moonlight streams through an open window in the corridor.* PERCY *asleep. He dreams uneasily, and after a little wakes up with a start and a cry.*

PERCY.

OH! I had such a bad dream. I dreamt I was straining out after a beautiful bird, and suddenly it stopped, and then I held it in my hands, and it was happy, and then I dropped down somehow into the darkness and the bird had gone—only it got so confused, and I woke up. I hear steps!

ESMÉ [*in corridor*].

Did you call, Percy? I heard a cry as if you were in pain.

PERCY.

Esmé, I will come and talk to you in the moonlight. I want to say something that I couldn't say before, because my heart choked me.

ESMÉ.

Come out, Percy, the moon is so white, looking out of the black sky. The sky is quite black near the moon; only far down where there are no more bright stars it is a deep, deep blue. It is bluer and deeper than the sea.

PERCY.

It is like your eyes. [*Comes out into corridor.*] Esmé! I have looked into your eyes as your eyes look into Heaven, and there I have found my Heaven. O serene depths! O faultless face of my desire! O white brow too clear! I sin against your holiness by my presence. Only the moon should see you, Esmé.

ESMÉ [*half in tears*].

You don't mean like that, Percy, quite. Why do you say that?

*Enter* VAUGHAN *in shadow. He draws back and stands watching.*

PERCY.

Oh, you are crying, my heart! Do you cry because I have spoken and touched with fire the sweet child-love we have lived in all this year? Or is it that you do not understand? Or are you sorry? Or are you glad?

ESMÉ.

I am very, very glad. [*They kiss. A little cloud passes across the moon without dimming its brightness.*] Percy! Percy!

PERCY.

My wife, my own wife, will you kiss me?

ESMÉ.

I am too happy to kiss you!

PERCY.

Esmé, my Esmé. And we will write our poem now together.

ESMÉ.

I cannot write; we will live our poem now together.

PERCY.

Dear heart, dear heart! And she will give us light, our dear moon out yonder, always a pure cold light: and our life shall answer a purer, warmer flame. She is like a maiden covered with lilies; your lilies have kissed roses.

ESMÉ.

And when the moon's light fails, the light of your song.

PERCY.

Let that light be drawn from Heaven too!

ESMÉ.

Oh, Percy, I am so glad, so glad!

PERCY.

Esmé!

ESMÉ.

When will you begin your great poem—now?

PERCY [*as if in pain*].

Ah! my poem. I am in despair! It is so great, and I am so little; it is so pure, and I am so dull of understanding. When I write I feel as it were the breath of an angel covering me with holiness, and I know —then! But now—I only write mechanically. I force myself. To-day I tore up all I wrote last night.

ESMÉ.

Let us ask God to send you the angel, shall we?

[*They kneel, with arms intertwined; at the open window, and bow their heads silently.* VAUGHAN *also prays, with arms outspread in blessing. Curtain.*

SCENE III.

*Six months later.*

*The dining-room.* PERCY, VAUGHAN, ESMÉ *at dinner.*

*Enter* BUTLER.

BUTLER.

IF you please, sir, a gentleman has called; he says he must see you at once.

VAUGHAN.

Have you told him we are at dinner?

BUTLER.

Yes, sir; but he would not take that; begging your pardon, sir, he said it was only an excuse, and he wouldn't stand any nonsense.

VAUGHAN.

An excuse! Who is the fellow?

BUTLER.

I think he is a friend of Mr. Percy's, sir.

PERCY [*alarmed*].

It might be my father. [*Aside.*] And I could have finished to-night—the very last word. Something has been singing in me all day.

VAUGHAN.

I will come and speak to him.
[*Exit. The voices are heard outside.*

BRANDON [*stout, purple, "knobbed," and ill-tempered*].

Yes, sir. Either I see my son now, or I fetch in a policeman. Kidnapper! Yes, sir, that's what I call you! Yes, sir! my name *is* Brandon. And your damned name is Vaughan, sir! And I'll drag your damned name through a police-court, sir, as soon as —as—Where's my son?
[*Is heard to move towards dining-room.*

VAUGHAN.

John! shut that door. Mr. Brandon, my daughter is at dinner in that room. I cannot allow you to enter.

BRANDON.

That's where he is, you scoundrel. Out of the way, fool! [*Knocking* JOHN *over, bursts the door open and enters.*] There you are, you snivelling little swine. My God! to think that damned puppy's my son! Come out of it!

VAUGHAN. [*who has entered and rung the bell for the servants*].

I shall have you locked up for assaulting my servant.

BRANDON.

And you for abducting my son. He's coming with me now or there'll be a fuss. Mark my words, you rascal!

[*Enter two Footmen.*

VAUGHAN.

Seize that man. [*They seize and hold him after a struggle.*] Esmé! go away to your room; this is no place for you. Now, sir, say all you have to say!

[ESMÉ *waits in the doorway.*

BRANDON.

Give me my son, and be damned to you! That's all; and it's plain enough, I hope.

PERCY.

Father, I am leaving Mr. Vaughan's house, as I shall only get him into trouble if I stay. But I will not come home with you, you who broke my mother's heart, and turned me from your doors penniless.

BRANDON.

Unnatural puppy!

PERCY.

My mother's spirit forgives you, and in my heart is no longer the desire for vengeance. So far have I risen, but not far enough to forget that you are the most abominable villain that plagues God's beautiful world with his infesting life.

BRANDON [*with sudden calmness*].

This to his father! What does the Bible say, you wretch?

PERCY [*to* VAUGHAN].

I will go, my true new father. Kiss Esmé for me a hundred times!

BRANDON [*breaking from the Footmen*].

Damn you; that's your game, is it? No, you go with me, Sir Poet.

[*Rushing at his son, strikes.* PERCY, *warding off the unexpected blow, staggers.* BRANDON, *maddened by the idea of fighting, snatches up a knife and drives it into his heart. He falls with a low cry.* VAUGHAN *dashes forward and strikes* BRANDON *heavily. He falls; footmen drag him off insensible.*

VAUGHAN [*bending over* PERCY].

Are you hurt?

PERCY.

Oh, hardly hurt at all! Only my head a little, and I wanted so to finish the poem to-night.

ESMÉ.

Let me come to him, father. Oh, Percy, Percy, look at me, look at me; you're not hurt, are you?

PERCY.

Am I ever hurt with your arms round me?

ESMÉ.

Oh, but you grow whiter; you must be hurt.

VAUGHAN.

A knife! He must have stabbed him. Fetch a doctor, one of you, sharp!

[*Exit a man.*

## ESMÉ.

It is his heart ; see, my hand is all covered with blood. Give me a handkerchief. Here, I will staunch the wound. [*She attempts to prevent the bleeding with her handkerchief.*] Oh ! Percy ! [*A pause.*] Oh ! Percy !

## PERCY.

I am going away, Esmé. I shall see you often. When you think of me I shall always be with you. One day you will come to me, Esmé ! Kiss me ! Your kisses must finish my poem. One day your pen must finish it.

## ESMÉ.

You know I cannot write a line. Oh, how sorry I am for that !

## PERCY [*to* VAUGHAN].

Good-bye, my dear, dear friend. Take care of Esmé for me. I shall watch over her myself, I and God together. She is so frail and white, and she understands. She sees my soul, and Heaven is always open to her eyes when she looks up, and she is so beautiful. Will it seem long, Esmé, till we kiss again beyond the moon there—it is the moon, isn't it, come to see that Esmé is not too sad about my dying ? Be kind to her always, moon, when I am gone beyond you ! You must finish my poem, Esmé ; there is only a little to do. Kiss me the last time ! Good-bye, my dear friends. I wish I could take your hands, but I am so weak. Kiss me, Esmé, quickly. I feel the voice of God come like a shudder in my blood ; I must go to Him. Esmé ! Esmé ! Esmé ! I am so happy !                                [*Dies.*
  [ESMÉ *flings herself passionately on to the body, weeping and kissing the dead face. Curtain.*

## SCENE IV.

*The next morning.* ESMÉ *in bed asleep.*

### *Enter* VAUGHAN.

#### VAUGHAN.

POOR child, poor child, how are you ? You have not slept, I know. Why, she is still asleep ! Hush ! How calmly and regularly she breathes ! How fresh she looks ! How she smiles ! It is wonderful ! It is impossible ! Esmé ! Esmé ! it is a pity you cannot always sleep so, and never wake up to the cruel sorrow of yesterday. Ah me ! When we all thought to be so happy. And in a month he would have married her : in a day he would have finished the poem. What a wonderful poem it was ! One could hear, above the angels that sang, the voice of God in that awful music that made his lines quiver and shimmer like live coals. And the end was to have been so perfect: there was on the last passage of his work a hush, a silence almost as if the world—his world—awaited the voice of some great one. And now the silence is not broken. Perhaps men were not ready for those final chords. Perhaps to hear them would be to pass where he has passed ! But oh ! the pity ! To leave his greatest task undone ! To be stricken down in the last charge, a good soldier to the end ! Would God he could come back only for an hour to put the keystone to his palace that he built of running brooks and trees and buds and the sound of the sea, and all the lights of heaven to window it. [ESMÉ'S *eyes open.*] Esmé ! you must wake up and kiss father !

#### ESMÉ [*half awake*].

He sang to me all night, not his voice only, but a deeper voice that I understood so well as I never understood, a voice like his poem, only more beautiful even than that, and I can't remember one word, only that he kissed me all the night ; and there was as it were a vapour, an incense-cloud, about me, and I could not see—and I am so happy.

VAUGHAN.

Esmé, I am here, your father.

ESMÉ.

Ah! it comes back. He is dead. Oh, God! Oh, God! And we were to have been married a month to-day.

VAUGHAN.

And he left the poem and could not finish it.

ESMÉ [*pointing to scattered papers on a table*].

What have you been doing with those papers, father?

VAUGHAN [*astonished*].

They are not mine, child. I did not see them till you showed me. [*Taking papers.*] Why, they are in your handwriting; what are they? [*Reading, gradually becomes aware that something strange has happened.*] It is finished—it is finished! [*Curtain.*

# JEPHTHAH.

## 1899.

TO

GERALD KELLY,

POET AND PAINTER,

I DEDICATE THIS TRAGEDY.

CAMBRIDGE, *November*, 1898.

## JEPHTHAH.

"Let my Lamp, at midnight hour,
Be seen in some high lonely Tower,
Where I may oft outwatch the Bear,
With thrice-great Hermes, or unsphear
The spirit of Plato, to unfold
What Worlds, or what vast Regions hold
The immortal mind that hath forsook
Her mansion in this fleshly nook ;
And of those Dæmons that are found
In fire, air, flood, or under ground,
Whose power hath a true consent
With Planet, or with Element.
Some time let Gorgeous Tragedy
In Sceptr'd Pall come sweeping by."
                              *Il Penseroso.*

Τάδε νῦν ἐταίραις
Ταῖς ἔμαισι τέρπνα κάλως ἀείσω.
                              SAPPHO.

"It need not appear strange unto you that
this Book is not at all like unto so many others
which I have, and which are composed in a
lofty and subtle style."—*The Book of the Sacred
Magic of Abra-Melin the Mage.*

## PRELIMINARY INVOCATION.
### TO A. C. S.

IN the blind hour of madness, in its might,
  When the red star of tyranny was highest ;
When baleful watchfires scared the witless
    night,
  And kings mocked Freedom, as she wept :
    "Thou diest !"

When priestcraft snarled at Thought : "I
    crush thee quite !"
  Then rose the splendid song of thee,
    "Thou liest !"
Out of the darkness, in the death of hope,
Thy white star flamed in Europe's horoscope.

The coffin-nails were driven home : the curse
  Of mockery's blessing flung the dust upon
    her :
The horses of Destruction dragged the hearse
  Over besmirchéd roads of Truth and
    Honour :
The obscene God spat on the universe :
  The sods of Destiny were spattered on her :—
Then rose thy spirit through the shaken skies :
"Child of the Dawn, I say to thee, arise !"

Through the ancestral shame and feudal
    gloom,
  Through mediæval blackness rung thy
    pæan :
Let there be light !—the desecrated tomb
  Gaped as thy fury smote the Galilean.
Let there be light ! and there was light : the
    womb
  Of Earth resounded, and the empyréan
Roared : and the thunder of the seas averred
The presence of thy recreating word.

The stone rolls back : the charioted night,
  Stricken, swings backwards on her broken
    pinions :
Faith sickens, drunken tyranny reels, the spite
  Of monarchs, ruinous of their chained
    dominions :

The splendid forehead, crowned with Love
and Light,
Flames in the starry air : the fallen minions
Drop like lost souls through horrid emptinesses
To their own black unfathomable abysses !

Now Freedom, flower and star and wind and
wave
And spirit of the unimagined fire,
Begotten on the dishonourable grave
Of fallen tyranny, may seek her sire
In the pure soul. of Man, her lips may lave
In the pure waters of her soul's desire,
Truth : and deep eyes behold thine eyes as
deep,
Fresh lips kiss thine that kissed her soul
from sleep.

See Italy, the eagle of all time,
Triumphant, from her coffin's leaden prison,
Soar into freedom, seek the heights sublime
Of self-reliance, from those depths new-
risen,
Stirred by the passion of thy mighty rhyme :
Eagle, and phœnix : shrill, sharp flames
bedizen
The burning citadel, where crested Man
Leaps sword in hand upon the Vatican.

Those dire words spoken, that thine hammer
beat,
Of fire and steel and music, wrath god-
worded,
Consuming with immeasurable heat
The sties and kennels of priest and king,
that girded
The loins of many peoples, till the seat
Of Hell was shaken to its deep, and herded
Hosts of the tyrant trembled, faltered, fled,
When none pursued but curses of men
dead :—

See, from the Calvary of the Son of Man,[1]
Where all the hopes of France were trodden
under ;
See, from the crucifixion of Sedan
Thy thought the lightning, and thy word
the thunder !
See her supreme, kingly, republican,
New France arisen, with her heart in
sunder—
Yet throned in Heaven on ever-burning
wheels,
Freedom resurgent, sealed with seven seals.

[1] Napoleon III.

The seal of Reason, made impregnable :
The seal of Truth, immeasurably splendid :
The seal of Brotherhood, man's miracle :
The seal of Peace, and Wisdom heaven-
descended :
The seal of Bitterness, cast down to Hell :
The seal of Love, secure, not-to-be-rended :
The seventh seal, Equality : that, broken,
God sets His thunder and earthquake for a
token.

Now if on France the iron clangours close,
Corruption's desperate hand, and lurking
treason,[1]
Or alien craft,[2] or menace of strange blows
Wrought of her own sons,[3] in this bitter
season :
Lift up thy voice, breathe fury on her foes,
Smite bigots yet again, and call on Reason,
Reason that must awake, and sternly grip
The unhooded serpent of dictatorship ![4]

Or, if thou have laid aside the starry brand,
And scourge, whose knots with their foul
blood are rotten
Whom thou didst smite ; if thine unweary
hand
Sicken of slaughter ; if thy soul have gotten
Its throne in so sublime a fatherland,
Above these miscreants and misbegotten ;
If even already thy spirit have found peace,
Among the thronged immortal secrecies ;

If with the soul of Æschylus thy soul
Talk, and with Sappho's if thy music
mingle ;
If with the spirit infinite and whole
Of Shakespeare thou commune ; if thy
brows tingle
With Dante's kiss ; if Milton's thunders roll
Amid thy skies ; if thou, supreme and single,
Be made as Shelley or as Hugo now,
And all their laurels mingle on thy brow—

Then (as Elijah, when the whirling fire
Caught him) stoop not thy spiritual
splendour,
And sacred-seeking eyes to our desire,
But mould one memory yet, divinely tender,

[1] Ultramontanism.
[2] Dreyfusardism.
[3] Militarism.
[4] At the time this poem was written, French
patriots looked with a distrustful eye on General
de Gallifet.

E

Of earth, and leave thy mantle, and thy lyre,
　A double portion of thy spirit to render,
That yet the banner may fling out on high,
And yet the lyre teach freemen how to die !

Master, the night is falling yet again.
　I hear dim tramplings of unholy forces :
I see the assembly of the foully slain :
　The scent of murder steams : riderless
　　horses
Gallop across the earth, and seek the inane :
　The sun and moon are shaken in their
　　courses :
The kings are gathered, and the vultures fall
Screaming, to hold their ghastly festival.

Master, the sons of Freedom are but few—
　Yea, but as strong as the storm-smitten sea,
Their forehead consecrated with the dew,
　Their heart made mighty : let my voice
　　decree,
My spirit lift their standard : clear and true
　Bid my trump sound, "Let all the earth
　　be free !"
With thine own strength and melody made
　strong,
And filled with fire and light of thine own
　song.

Only a boy's wild songs, a boy's desire,
　I bring with reverent hands.　The task is
　　ended—
The twilight draws on me : the sacred fire
　Sleeps : I have sheathed my sword, my
　　bow unbended :
So for one hour I lay aside the lyre,
　And come, alone, unholpen, unbefriended,
As streams get water of the sun-smit sea,
Seeking my ocean and my sun in thee.

Yea, with thy whirling clouds of fiery light
　Involve my music, gyring fuller and faster !
Yea, to my sword lend majesty and might
　To dominate all tumult and disaster,
That even my song may pierce the iron night,
　Invoking dawn in thy great name, O
　　Master !
Till to the stainless heaven of the soul
Even my chariot-wheels on thunder roll.

And so, most sacred soul, most reverend head,
　The silence of deep midnight shall be bound;
And with the mighty concourse of the dead
　That live, that contemplate, my place be
　　found,

Even mine, through all the seasons that are shed
　Like leaves upon the darkness, where the
　　sound
Of all high song through calm eternity
Shall beat and boom, thine own maternal sea.

For in the formless world, so swift a fire
　Shall burn, that fire shall not be com-
　　prehended ;
So deep a music roll, that our desire
　Shall hear no sound ; shall beam a light
　　so splendid
That darkness shall be infinite : the lyre
　Fashioned of truth, strung with men's
　　heart-strings blended,
Shall sound as silence : and all souls be still
In wisdom's high communion with will.


# JEPHTHAH.

## A TRAGEDY.

"O Jephthah ! judge of Israel !"—HAMLET.


## *CHARACTERS.*

JEPHTHAH.
ADULAH, *his Daughter.*
JARED, *A Gileadite, cousin to* Jephthah.
A Prophet of the Lord.
ELEAZAR, *Chief of the Elders of Israel.*
AHINOAM, *an aged Priest.*
First Messenger.
Second Messenger.
First Herald.
Second Herald.
Soldiers of Jephthah.
Soldiers of Israel.
Chorus of Elders of Israel.
Maidens of Israel.

SCENE :—*An Open Place before Mizpeh.　In
　　the midst an Altar.*

TIME :—*The duration of the play is from noon
　of the first day to dawn of the third.*


## JEPHTHAH.

*Eleazar.　Prophet.　Chorus.*

CHORUS.

Now is our sin requited of the Lord.
For, scorning Jephthah for an harlot's son,
We cast him forth from us, and said : Begone,
Thou shalt not enter in with us ; thy throat

Shall thirst for our inheritance in vain ;
Thou hast no lot nor part in Gilead.
And now, he gathers to himself vain men,
Violent folk, and breakers of the law,
And holds aloof in rocky deserts, where
The land, accurst of God, is barren still
Of any herb, or flower, or any tree,
And has no shelter, nor sweet watersprings,
Save where a lonely cave is hollow, and where
A meagre fountain sucks the sand. Our folk
Are naked of his counsel and defence
Against the tribe of Ammon, and stand aghast ;
Our feeble arms sway doubtfully long swords,
And spears are flung half-heartedly ; and he
With warlike garrison and stronger arms
Who might have helped us, laughs, and violence
Threatens the white flower of our homes : our wives,
Daughters, and sons are as a prey to them,
And where the children of the Ammonites
Throng not swift hoofs for murder, Jephthah's men
Blaspheme our sanctuaries inviolate,
And rob us of our dearest. Woe on woe
Hangs imminent to crush the slender sides
And battered bulwarks of our state. O thou
Whose hoary locks and sightless eyes compel
Our pity and our reverence, and whose mouth
Foams with the presence of some nearer god
Insatiate of thy body frail, give tongue,
If tongue may so far master deity
As give his fury speech, or shape thy words
From the blind auguries of madness.

### PROPHET.

Ha !
The rose has washed its petals, and the blood
Pours through its burning centre from my heart.
The fire consumes the light ; and rosy flame
Leaps through the veins of blue, and tinges them
With such a purple as incarnadines

The western sky when storms are amorous
And lie upon the breast of toiling ocean,
Such billows to beget as earth devours
In ravening whirlpool gulphs. My veins are full,
Throbbing with fire more potent than all wine,
All sting of fleshly pangs and pleasures. Oh !
The god is fast upon my back ; he rides
My spirit like a stallion ; for I hate
The awful thong his hand is heavy with.

### ELEAZAR.

Speak, for the god compels, and we behold.

### PROPHET.

A harlot shall be mother of Israel.

### CHORUS.

He speaks of her who sighed for Gilead.

### PROPHET.

A maiden shall be slain for many men.

### CHORUS.

A doubtful word, and who shall fathom it ?

### PROPHET.

Thy help is from the hills and desert lands.

### CHORUS.

Our help is from the hills : we know the Lord.

### PROPHET.

Death rides most violently against the sun.

### CHORUS.

And who shall bridle him, or turn his way ?
For Fate alone of gods, inflexible,
And careless of men's deeds, is firm in heaven.

### PROPHET.

I see a sword whose hilt is to thy hand.

### CHORUS.

But which of us shall wield the shining blade ?

PROPHET.

I see a dove departing to the hills;

CHORUS.

I pray it bring an olive-branch to us.

PROPHET.

The god has overcome me ; I am silent.

CHORUS.

He lies as one lies dead; none wakens
him..
Nor life nor death must touch him now:
beware !

ELEAZAR.

Beware now, all ye old wise men, of this.
For high things spoken and unjustly heard,
Or heard and turned aside, are fruitless
words,
Or bear a blossom evil and abhorred,
Lest God be mocked.  Consider well of this.

CHORUS.

A sword, a sword, to smite our foes withal !

ELEAZAR.

A help shall come from desert lands to us.

CHORUS.

Toward what end?   For present help is
much,
But uttermost destruction more, for we
Have no strong hope in any hand of man :
God is our refuge and our tower of strength.
In Him if any man abide—But if
He put his faith in horsemen, or the sword,
The sword he trusted shall be for an end.

ELEAZAR.

But evils fall like rain upon the land.

CHORUS.

Let us not call the hail to give us peace.

ELEAZAR.

Nor on the sun, lest he too eat us up.

CHORUS.

The heart of a man as the sea
   Beats hither and thither to find
Ease for the limbs long free,
   Light for the stormy mind,
A way for the soul to flee,
   A charm for the lips to bind ;
And the struggle is keen as the strife to be,
   And the heart is tossed by the thankless
   wind.

ELEAZAR.

Nay, for a man's sure purpose is of God.

CHORUS.

The large pale limbs of the earth are tanned
With the sun and the sea and the yellow
   sand ;
And the face of earth is dark with love
Of the lords of hell and the spirits above
That move in the foggy air of night,
And the spirit of God, most like a dove,
Hovers, and lingers, and wings his flight,
Spurned and rejected and lost to sight ;
But we desire him, a holy bird,
And we turn eyes to the hollow hills ;
For God is strong, and His iron word
Mocks at the gods of the woods and rills.

For our God is as a fire
That consumeth every one
That is underneath the sun.
We, for uttermost desire,
Must abase, with rent attire,
Souls and bodies to His throne,
Where above the starry choir
Stands the jasper, where alone
Vivid seraphim respire
Perfumes of a precious stone,
Where beneath His feet the dire
World of shells is pashed with mire,
And the evil spirits' ire
Steams and fumes within the zone
Girt with minaret and spire
Broken, burst, and overthrown,
Dusty, and defiled, and dun,
Palled with smoke of fruitless altars

Cast beneath the ocean now,
Ruined symbols, changéd psalters,
Where no lip no longer falters,
And the priest's deep brow
Pales not, flushes not for passion,
Clouds not with concealéd thought,
And the worshipper's eye, wrought
To the stars in subtle fashion,
By no magic is distraught.

Ay! our hope is in His holy
Places, and our prayers ascend
Fervent, and may sunder slowly
The blue darkness at the end.
For we know not where to send
For a sword to cleanse the land,
For a sharp two-edgéd brand,
All our homesteads to defend.
Now amid the desert sand
Lives an outcast of our race,
Strong, immutable, and grand,
And his mighty hand
Grips a mighty mace.
He would shatter, did we call,
Sons of Ammon one and all,
Did we fear not lest his eye
Turn back covetous to try
For our pleasances, to rule
Where the far blue Syrian sky
Stretches, where the clouds as wool
Mark the white Arabian border,
To become a tyrant king
Where his sword came conquering.
Out of chaos rises order
On her wide unwearying wing,
But the desolate marauder
Never over us shall swing
Such a sceptre as should bring
Sorrow to one home of ours.
Better bear the heavy hours
Under God's avenging breath,
Better brave the horrid powers,
Better taste the foreign death,
Humbling all our pride before
God's most holy throne, abasing
Every man's strong soul, and facing
All the heathen Ammon bore
On the angry shore,

Trusting to the mercy rare
Of Jehovah, than to bare
Hearts and bosoms to a friend
Who high truth and faith may swear,
And betray us at the end
To his robber bands.
So we clasp our humble hands,
Praying God to lift His sword
From our bleeding state, that stands
Tottering to its fall.
Though we call not Jephthah back
To repel the harsh attack,
Nor his followers call,
Hear thou, O Most High, give ear
To our pitiful complaint :
Under woes of war we faint.
Pity, Lord of Hosts, our fear !
Hear, Most High, oh, hear !

*Enter* Messenger.

MESSENGER.

My lords, take heed now, prayer is good to
    save
While yet the foemen are far off; but now
They howl and clamour at our very gates.

ELEAZAR.

Blaspheme not God, but tell thy woeful news.

CHORUS.

I fear me for the sorrow that he speaks.

MESSENGER.

The tribe of Ephraim went forth to fight
Armed, and with bows, and turned them
    back to-day.
For in the South a cloud of many men,
And desert horsemen fiery as the sun,
Swarmed on the plains, a crescent from the
    hills
That girdle Mahanaim : and behold !
Our men were hemmed before the city gates,
The elders having fortified them : so
They fled about the city, and the horsemen,
Dashing, destroyed them as the wind that
    sweeps

Sere leaves before its fury : then the city
With arrows darkened all the air ; and luck
Smote down some few pursuing ; but their
    captain,
Riding his horse against the gate, drove in
His spear, and cried to them that followed
    him :
Who plucks my spear out shall be chief
    of all
That ply the short spear : and who breaks
    the gate
Shall lead my horsemen into Mizpeh :
    then,
Rushing, their spearmen battered in the
    gate
And overpowered the youths and agéd
    men,
That put up trembling spears, and drew
    slack bows,
And flung weak stones that struck for
    laughter's sake.
So now the city is the spoil of them,
And all our women-folk are slain or violate,
And all our young men murderously slain,
And children spitted on their coward spears.

### CHORUS.

How heavy is Thy hand upon us, Lord !

### MESSENGER.

Nor stayed they there ; but, firing Mahanaim,
Sweep toward Mizpeh like a locust-cloud.

### ELEAZAR.

Get thee to horse and carry me this message :
The Elders unto Jephthah, greeting : Help !
No single cry beyond that Help ! Be gone !
                    [*Exit* Messenger.

### CHORUS.

I fear me our necessity is sure.
But they come hither.   Shall we rather flee ?

### ELEAZAR.

I stand here manly, and will die a man.

### CHORUS.

For cowardice not pleases God, nor fear.
Shall we not take up weapons ?   Or shall He
Rather defend us with His Holy Arm,
We not presuming in our arrogance
To come with cunning, and defend ourselves ?

### ELEAZAR.

Nay, but God smites with sharpness of our
    swords.

### CHORUS.

The sword is made sharp in our hands, but
    the point He shall guide ;
We grasp the tough ash of the spear, but
    His hand is beside ;
We drive in a cloud at the foe, but His
    chariots ride
Before us to sunder the spears.

We trust in His arms, and His prowess shall
    fledge our song's wing ;
Our triumph we give to His glory, our spoil
    to the King ;
Our battles He fights as we fight them, our
    victories bring
For His temple a tribute of tears.

*Enter* JEPHTHAH *amid his Soldiers, with
    many young men of Israel.*

### JEPHTHAH.

Yea, for a man's sword should not turn again
To his own bosom, and the sword of fear
Smites not in vain the heart of cowardice.
But who hath called me hither to what end ?

### ELEAZAR.

For these, and for the sake of Israel.

### JEPHTHAH.

And who are these ?   And who are Israel ?

### CHORUS.

Turn not thy face from us in wrath, for we
Are thine own father's children, and his loins
With double fervour gat a double flower ;
And we indeed were born of drudging wives,

Pale spouses whom his heart despised, but
thou
Wast of a fairer face and brighter eyes,
And limbs more amorous assuaged thy sire;
And fuller blood of his is tingling thus
Now in thy veins indignant at our sin.
But thou art strong and we are weak indeed,
Nor can we bear the burden, nor sustain
The fury of the Children of the East
That ride against us, and bright victory
Is throned in their banners, while on ours
Perches the hideous nightbird of defeat.
Mourn, mourn and cry; bow down unto the
dust
O Israel, and O Gilead, for your son
Comes with unpitying eyes and lips com-
pressed
To watch the desecration of thy shrine,
Jehovah, and the ruin of our hearth.

### JEPHTHAH.

I am your outcast brother. At my birth
My father did not smile, nor she who bore
These limbs dishonourable did not smile,
Nor did my kisses soothe a mother's woe,
Because my thews grown strong were im-
potent
To reign or be a captain any more,
Though I might serve the children who had
grown
Less godlike from his loins who made me
god.
So when the day was ripe, my brethren
turned
And gnashed upon me, mocking, with their
teeth:
Thou art the son of a strange woman, thou!
Begone from honest folk!—and I in wrath
Smote once or twice with naked hand, and
slew
Two gibing cowards, and went forth an
outcast,
And gathered faithful servitors, and ruled
Mightiest in the desert, and was lord
Of all the marches where my spear might
throw
Its ominous shadow between night and noon.
Yet always I considered my revenge,

And purposed, seeking out those kin of mine,
To make them as those kings that Gideon
slew
Hard by the bloody waters of a brook.
And now ye call me to your help, forsooth!

### CHORUS.

Let no ill memory of an ancient wrong,
Most mighty, edge thy sword
Against the prayer of this repentant song.
Dire sorrow of the Lord
Consumes our vital breath, and smites us
down,
And desecrates the crown.
For we have sinned against thee, and our
souls
Scathe and devour as coals,
And God is wroth because of thee, to break
The spirit of our pride, our lips to make
Reverent toward thee, as of men ashamed.
And now we pray thee for our children's
sake,
And thine own pity's sake, to come untamed,
And furiously to ride against our foes,
To be our leader, till one sanguine rose
Spread from thy standard awful leaves of
blood,
And thy swords pour their long insatiate
flood
Through ranks of many dead! then, then to
close
The wounds of all the land, and bid it bud
And blossom; as when two-and-thirty men,
The sons of Jair, on milk-white asses rode,
And judged us righteously, and each abode
Safe in the shadow of his vine; as when
The peace of Joshua lay upon the land,
And God turned not away His piteous eyes,
Nor smote us with the fury of His hand,
Nor clouded over His mysterious skies.
Then storm and wind had no more might
at all,
And death and pestilence forgotten were;
Then angels came to holy men that call,
And gracious spirits thronged the happy air;
Then God was very gracious to all folk;
He lifted from us the Philistian yoke,
And all the iron power of Edom broke:—

Ah ! all the Earth was fair !
Now, seeing that we are sinners, wilt not
    thou
Relent thy hateful brow,
Bend down on us a forehead full of peace,
Bidding thine anger cease,
Speaking sweet words most comfortable.  O
    lose
The bitter memory of the wrong long dead !
O be the lord and prince we gladly choose
And crown the mercy of thy royal head !
Be thou the chief, and rule upon thy kin,
And be not wroth for sin.
For surely in the dusty days and years
There is a little river flowing still
That brings forgetfulness of woes and fears
And drinks up all the memory of ill.
Wherefore our tribute to thy feet we bring ;
Conquer our foes, and reign our king !

### JEPHTHAH.

Ye have no king but God : see ye to that !

### ELEAZAR.

Behold, these people are as children, hiding
Thoughts beautiful and true in profuse words,
Not meaning all the lofty flight that fancy
And the strong urgement of a tune dis-
    cover.
Be thou our judge, as Joshua long ago.

### JEPHTHAH.

Swear by the Name unspoken that the truth
Flashes between the lips that tremble thus !
Ye love me not ; ye fear me ; ye might thrust
Some petty obstacle before my hands
When I would grasp your promise, and
    betray
Your faith for fear of me.  I read thy
    thoughts,
Old man ; I trust no word of thine ; but
    these
Full-hearted mourners, them will I believe
Upon their oath most solemn and secure.
But take thou warning now !  I shall not
    spare
Grey hairs or faltering limbs for treachery.

### ELEAZAR.

Lift up your hands, all people of this land,
And swear with me this oath my lips pro-
    nounce :
By Wisdom, father of the world, we swear ;
By Understanding, mother of the sea,
By Strength and Mercy, that support the
    throne,
By Beauty, Splendour, Victory, we swear,
And by the strong foundations, and the
    Kingdom,
Flower of all kingdoms, and by the holy
    Crown
Concealed with all concealments, highest
    of all,
We swear to be true men to thee and thine.

### JEPHTHAH.

I thank you, people.  Let the younger men
Gather their swords and spears, and pass
    before
This spear I strike into the earth, that so
I see how many fight for Israel.

### CHORUS.

The young men are girded with swords ;
    The spears flash on high, and each shield
Gleams bright like the fury of lords
    Through the steam of the well-foughten
    field.
The children of Ammon are broken, their
    princes and warriors yield.

The captain is chosen for fight ;
    The light of his eye is as fire,
His hand is hardy of might
    And heavy as dead desire ;
The sword of the Lord and of Jephthah shall
    build our dead women a pyre.

The people were sad for his wrath ;
    The elders were bowed with despair,
And death was the piteous path ;
    With ashes we covered our hair ;
The voice of the singer was dumb, the voice
    of the triumph of prayer.

But God had pity upon us,
  Our evil and fallen way ;
His mercy was mighty on us ;
  His lips are as rosy as day
Broken out of the sea at the sunrise, as
  fragrant as flowers in May.

Our sin was great in His sight :
  We chased from our gates our brother,
We shamed his father's might,
  We spat on the grave of his mother,
We laughed in his face and mocked, look-
  ing slyly one to another.

But God beheld, and His hand
  Was heavy to bring us grief ;
He brought down fire on the land,
  And withered us root and leaf
Until we were utterly broken, lost men,
  without a chief.

But whom we scorned we have set
  A leader and judge over all ;
His wrong he may not forget,
  But he pitieth men that call
From the heart that is broken with fear and
  the noise of funeral.

### JEPHTHAH.

Are all these ready for their hearth and altars
To perish suddenly upon the field,
Pavilioned with the little tents at noon,
And ere the nightfall tented with the dead,
And every hollow made a sepulchre,
And every hill a vantage ground whereon
Hard-breathing fighting men get scanty
  sleep,
Till the dawn lift his eyebrows, and the day
Renew the battle? Will ye follow me
Through slippery ways of blood to Ephraim
To beat with sturdy swords unwearying
Our foemen to their Ammon, and to grapple
With red death clutching at the throat of us,
With famine and with pestilence, at last
To reach a barren vengeance, and per-
  chance
An hundred of your thousands to return

Victors—so best God speed us—and for
  worst
Death round our cities horrible and vast,
And rape and murder mocking at our
  ghosts?

### A SOLDIER.

Better they taunt our ghosts than us for
  cowards !
Live through or die, I will have my sword
  speak plain
To these damned massacring invaders. Say,
My fellows, will ye follow Jephthah? Hail !

### SOLDIERS.

We follow Jephthah to the death. All
  hail !

### JEPHTHAH.

Go then, refresh yourselves. Sleep well
  to-night !
I will send messages to their dread lord
                    [Enter a Herald.
Demanding his fell purpose, threatening
My present aid to you with men of valour
Chosen of all your tribes, and charging
  him
As he loves life, and victory, to content
His army with their present brief success,
Lest he pass by the barrier of our suffer-
  ing,
And find our wrath no broken sword, and
  find
Despair more terrible than hope. Go now !

### A SOLDIER.

We go, my lord, less readily to sleep
Than if you bade us march. No man of us
But stirs a little, I warrant, in his dreams,
And reaches out for sword-hilt. All hail,
  Jephthah !

### SOLDIERS.

Jephthah ! a leader, a deliverer. Hail !
                [Exeunt Soldiers and Young Men.

### JEPHTHAH.

Hearken, Jehovah, to thy servant now ;
Fill Thou my voice with thine own thunders ;
 fill
My swift sharp words with such a lightning-
 fork
As shall fall venomous upon the host
Of these idolatrous that thus invade
Our fencéd cities, these that put to sword
Our helpless.   Hear the cry of widowed
 men !
Of young men fatherless !   Of old men reft
Of children !   Grant us victory to avenge
Their innocent shed blood, and ruined land.
So, to gain time for prayer and penitence
For grievous trespass of idolatry
Done to the accurséd Baalim (aside)—and
 time
To gather fugitives, and make them men,
And straggling herdsmen for our arma-
 ment !—(aloud)
We send thee, herald, to the furious king
Who lies with all his power encamped some-
 where
Hence southward toward Mahanaim.   Say
Unto the king of Ammon: Thus saith
 Jephthah :
Why hast thou come with bloody hands
 against us?
Our holy God, that bound the iron sea
With pale frail limits of white sand, and
 said :
Thus far, and not one billowy step beyond !
Saith unto thee in like commandment : Thou
Who hast destroyed my people from the land
So far, shalt not encroach upon their places
One furlong more, lest quickly I destroy
Thee and thy host from off the earth.   Say
 thus ;
Ride for thy life, and bring me speedy word.
                                    [Exit Herald.

### CHORUS.

Not wingéd forms, nor powers of air,
Nor sundered spirits pale and fair,
Nor glittering sides and scales, did bring
The knowledge of this happy thing

That is befallen us unaware.
In likeness to the lips that sing
Ring out your frosty peal, and smite
Loud fingers on the harp, and touch
Lutes, and clear psalteries musical,
And all stringed instruments, to indite
A noble song of triumph, such
As men may go to fight withal.
For now a captain brave and strong
Shall break the fury of the thong
Wherewith the sons of Ammon scourge
Our country ; and his war shall urge
Long columns of victorious men
To blackest wood and dimmest den,
Wherever fugitive and slave
Shall seek a refuge, find a grave ;
And so pursue the shattered legions
Through dusty ways and desert regions
Back to the cities whence they came
With iron, massacre, and flame,
And turn their own devouring blade
On city fired and violate maid,
That Israel conquer, and men know
God is our God against a foe.

For the web of the battle is woven
 Of men that are strong as the sea,
When the rocks by its tempest are cloven,
 And waves wander wild to the lee ;
When ships are in travail forsaken,
 And tempest and tumult awaken ;
When foam by fresh foam overtaken
 Boils sanguine and fervent and free.

The sword is like lightning in battle,
 The spear like the light of a star ;
It strikes on the shield, and the rattle
 Of arrows is hail from afar.
For the ways of the anger of lords
Are bloody with widowing swords,
And the roar of contention of chords
 Rolls back from the heart of the war.

The fighters slip down on the dying,
 And flying folk stumble on dead,
And the sound of the pitiless crying
 Of slaughter is heavy and red,

The sound of the lust of the slayer
As fierce as a Persian's prayer,
And the sound of the loud harp-player
  Like the wind beats to their tread.

A royal triumph is waiting
  For the captain of Heaven's choice,
A noise as of eagles mating,
  A cry as of men that rejoice.
For victory crowns with garlands
Of fame his valour in far lands,
And suns sing back to the starlands
  His praise with a perfect voice.

JEPHTHAH.

Leave prophecy until I come again !

CHORUS.

A prophet told us thou shouldst fight for us
And save thy people from the Ammonites.

JEPHTHAH.

Why look you so ?  He told you other thing.

CHORUS.

Nay, lord, no saying that we understood.

JEPHTHAH.

Speak thou its purport ; I may understand.
For, know you, in the desert where I dwelt
I had strange store of books obscure ; books
    written
Not openly for fools, but inwardly
Toward the heart of wise men.  And myself
Studied no little while upon these things,
And, seeking ever solitude, I went
Nightly upon a rock that stood alone
Threatening the sandy wilderness, and
    prayed
Where many visions came before mine eyes
So strange—these eyes have started from my
    head,
And every hair, grown fearful, like a steed
Reared in its frenzy : see, these lips of mine
Have blanched, these nails have bitten
    through my flesh

For sundry things I saw—and these in-
    formed
My open spirit by their influence,
And taught mine ears to catch no doubtful
    sound
Of prophecy, but fix it in my mind,
A lambent liquid fire of poetry
Full of all meaning as the very stars.
Yet of my own life they have never breathed
One chilly word of fear, or one divine
Roseate syllable of hope and joy.
Still less of love.  For no sweet life of love
Lies to my hand, but I am bound by Fate
To the strong compulsion of the sword ; my
    lips
Shall fasten on my wife's not much ; nor
    those
Pure lips of innocent girlhood that call me
Father ; but my lips must wreathe smiles no
    more,
But set in fearful strength of purpose toward
The blood of enemies, in horrid gouts
And hideous fountains leaping from great
    gashes,
Rather than that belovéd blood that wells
Fervent and red-rose-wise in loving breasts,
And little veins of purple in the arms,
Or cheeks that are already flushed with it,
To crimson them with the intense delight
Of eyes that meet and know the spirit dwells
Beyond their profound depth in sympathy.
Nay, my delight must find some dearest foe,
And cleave his body with a lusty stroke
That sets the blood sharp tingling in my
    arm.
Yet tell me if perchance I lay aside
One day the harness of cold iron, bind on
The lighter reins of roses deftly twined
By children loving me, to be a harness
To drive me on the road of happiness
To the far goal of heaven.  Would to God
It might be so a little ere I die !

CHORUS OF ELDERS.

This doubtful word his fuming lips gave
    forth :
A maiden shall be slain for many men.
This only of his fury seemed obscure.

### JEPHTHAH.

A maiden shall be slain for many men.
Surely, O people, and men of Israel,
The prophecy is happy to the end.
For see yon moon that creeps inviolate
Against the corner of the mountains so,
Slowly and gracefully to lighten us.
So, ere three nights be gone, the course of
heaven
Shall be most monstrously o'erwhelmed
for us
Ere sundown, as for Joshua, and the moon,
The maiden moon, be slain that we may see
By the large moveless sun to strike and slay,
More utterly proud Ammon to consume.
This is the omen. Shout for joy, my friends!
But who comes whirling in yon dusty cloud,
His eager charger dimly urging him
Toward our conclave? 'Tis our messenger.

*Re-enter Herald.*

Sir, you ride well. I pray your news be
good.

### HERALD.

So spake the haughty and rebellious Ammon
Defying your most gentle words with scorn:
Tell Jephthah: Israel took away my land
When they came out of Egypt from the
river
Of Ammon unto Jabbok, and unto Jordan.
Wherefore, I pray thee, sheathe thy sword,
restore
Peaceably these my lands, and go in peace,
Lest wrath, being kindled, consume thee
utterly.

### JEPHTHAH.

Let yet another herald stand before me
[*Enter Second Herald.*
Fresh, and go thou, swiftest of messengers,
And sleep and eat a little, and to-morrow
Thou shalt have guerdon of thy faithfulness.
[*Exit Herald.*
But now, sir, go to this rebellious king

And say to him: Thus Jephthah, judge of
Israel,
With gentle words answers thy greediness:
Israel took not thy land, nor that of Moab:
But, coming out of Egypt, through the sea
And over wilderness, to Kadesh came.
Our people sent a message unto Edom
Unto the king thereof, and prayed his grace,
To let them pass through his dominions
And unto Moab: and they answered Nay.
So Israel abode in Kadesh: then
Passing through all the desert round about
Edom and Moab, pitched their weary tent
Beyond the bank of Ammon; and they sent
Messengers thence to Sihon, Heshbon's
king,
The lord of Amorites, and said to him:
I prithee, let us pass to our own place
Through thy dominions: but his crafty
mind,
Fearing some treachery, that was not, save
In his ill mind that thought it, did determine
To gather all his people, and to pitch
Tents hostile in the plains before Jahaz.
And there he fought with Israel; but God
Delivered Sihon to our hands, and all
That followed him: whom therefore we
destroyed
With many slaughters: so we dispossessed
The envious Amorites, and had their land,
A land whose borders were the Ammon
brook
On the one hand, and on the other Jabbok
And Jordan: we, who slew the Amorites.
What hast thou, king of Ammon, here to
do?
How thinkst thou to inherit their posses-
sions
That the Lord God hath given us? Go to!
Chemosh your god hath given you your
land;
Possess that peaceably; but whomsoever
The Lord our God shall drive before our
spears,
His lands we will possess. And thou, O
king,
Art thou now better than that bloody Balak
Whose iron hand was upon Moab? He,

Fought he against us, while three hundred years
We dwelt in Heshbon and her towns, and Aroer
And her white cities, and by Ammon's coast?
Why therefore did ye not recover them
Then and not now? I have not sinned against thee;
But thou dost me foul wrong to bring thy sword
And torch of rapine in my pleasant land.
Between the folk of Ammon and the folk
Of Israel this day be God the judge.

[*Exit Second Herald.*

### ELEAZAR.

Well spoken: but the ear that will not hear
Is deafer than the adder none may charm.

### JEPHTHAH.

I know it, and will not await the answer.
But dawn shall see a solemn sacrifice,
And solemn vows, and long swords glittering,
And moving columns that shall shake the earth
With firm and manly stride; and victory
Most like a dove amid the altar-smoke.

### CHORUS.

We, passing here the night in prayer, will wait
And with thee offer up propitious doves,
And firstling males of all the flocks of us.

### JEPHTHAH.

Not so: but I will have you hence in haste
To gather food and arms and carriages,
That all our soldiers may have sustenance,
And fresher weapons. I alone will spend
The long hours with Jehovah, at His throne,
And wrestle with the accuser. So, depart!

### CHORUS.

When the countenance fair of the morning
And the lusty bright limbs of the day
Race far through the west for a warning
Of night that is evil and gray;
When the light by the southward is dwindled,
And the clouds as for sleep are unfurled,
The moon in the east is rekindled,
The hope of the passionate world.
The stars for a token of glory
Flash fire in the eyes of the night,
And the holy immaculate story
Of Heaven is flushed into light.
For the night has a whisper to wake us,
And the sunset a blossom to kiss,
And the silences secretly take us
To the well of the water that is [1];
For the darkness is pregnant with being,
As earth that is glad of the rain,
And the eyes [2] that are silent and seeing
Are free of the trammels of pain.
Like light through the portals they [3] bounded,
Their lithe limbs with cruelty curled,
And the noise of their crying resounded
To kindle the death of the world.
For the heaven at sunset is sundered;
Its gates to the sages unclose,
And through waters that foamed and that wondered
There flashes the heart of a rose;
In its petals are beauty and passion,
In its stem the foundation of earth,
Its bloom the incarnadine fashion
Of blessings that roar into birth;
And the gates [4] that roll back on their hinges
The soul of the sage may discern,
Till the water [5] with crimson that tinges
Beyond them miraculous burn;
And the presence of God to the senses
Is the passion of God in the mind,
As the string of a harp that intenses
The note that its fire may not find.
For here in the tumult and labour
And blindness of cowering man,

---

[1] This emphatic use of "to be" as a principal verb is very common with Crowley, who thereby wishes to distinguish between the noumenon and the phenomenon.
[2] The eyes of Jehovah: they are 700,000 spirits. See Idra Rabba Qadishah, xxxi.
[3] The eyes.
[4] The gates of Binah—understanding.
[5] Binah, the great Sea. The colour of crimson is attributed to it by certain Qabalists.

The spirit has God for a neighbour,
　And the wheels unreturning that ran
Return to the heart of the roses,
　And curl in the new blossom now,
As the holiest fire that encloses
　Gray flame [1] on the holiest brow.
So midnight with magic reposes,
　And slumbers to visions bow.
For the soul of man, being free, shall pass
　the gates of God,
And the spirit find the Sea by the feet of
　Him [2] untrod,
And the flesh, a lifeless ember, in ashen fear
　grow cold,
As the lives before remember the perished
　hours of gold.

　　　　　[*Exeunt all but* JEPHTHAH.


### JEPHTHAH.

Surely, my God, now I am left alone
　Kneeling before Thy throne,
I may grow beautiful, even I, to see
　Thy beauty fair and free.
For on the vast expanses of the wold
　I hear the feet of gold,
And over all the skies I see a flame
　That flickers with Thy Name.
Therefore, because Thou hast hid Thy face,
　and yet
　Given me not to forget
The foaming cloud that shaped itself a rose,
　Whose steady passion glows
Within the secretest fortress of my heart,
　Because, my God, Thou Art,
And I am chosen of Thee for this folk
　To break the foreign yoke,
Therefore, Existence of Existence, hear !
　Bend low Thine holy ear,
And make Thyself, unseen, most terrible
　To these fierce fiends of hell
That torture holiest ears with false com-
　plaint :
　Bend down, and bid me faint

Into the arms of night, to see Thine hosts
　March past the holy coasts,
A wall of golden weapons for the land,
　And let me touch Thy hand,
And feel Thy presence very near to-night !
　I sink as with delight
Through places numberless with fervid
　fires
　Of holiest desires
Into I know not what a cradle, made
　Of subtle-shapéd shade,
And arms most perdurable.[1]　I am lost
　In thought beyond all cost—
Nay, but my spirit breaks the slender
　chain
That held it down.　The pain
Of death is past and I am free.　Nay, I,
　This body, dead, must lie
Till Thou come home again, O soaring
　Soul.
　The gates supernal roll !
Flash through them, O white-winged, white-
　blossom ghost !
Ah, God ! for I am lost.

　　　　　[ JEPHTHAH *remains motionless.*[2]
　　　　　　　　　[*Morning dawns.*


*Enter* JARED, *Soldiers, Prophet.*


### SOLDIERS.

Hail, captain !　We are ready now for
　death,
Or victory, if shining wings are fain
To hover over dauntless hearts.　Behold
Our ready bands to follow to the fray.


### JEPHTHAH.

Welcome !　hail ye this happy dawn as
　one
That shall see freedom smile on us, and
　peace,
And victory, and new hours of happiness.

---

[1] The flame of Chokmah—wisdom—which is gray in colour.　*Cf.* the Hindu Ajna.
[2] Microprosopus, who reacheth not so high as Understanding.

[1] Able to endure *to the end.*
[2] The description is of a certain spiritual exercise familiar to mystics.

CHORUS OF SOLDIERS.

Out of the waters of the sea
  Our father Abraham beheld
The lamp of heaven arise to be
  The monarch quenchless and unquelled ;
But we on this far Syrian shore
See dawn upon the mountains pour.[1]

The limit of the snows is bright ;
  As spears that glitter shine the hills ;
The foaming forehead of the light
  All air with cloudy fragrance fills ;
And, born of desolation blind,
The young sweet summer burns behind.

The Altar of the Lord is set
  With salt and fire and fervid wine,
And toward the east the light is let
  For shadow for the holiest shrine :
One moment hangs the fire of dawn
Until the sacrament be sworn.

Behold, the priest, our captain, takes
  The sacred robes, the crown of gold,
The light of other sunlight [2] breaks
  Upon his forehead calm and cold ;
And other dawns more deep and wise
Burn awful in his holy eyes.

A moment, and the fire is low
  Upon the black stone of the altar,
The spilt blood eagerly doth glow,
  And lightnings lick the light, and falter,
Feeling the vast Shekinah [3] shine
Above their excellence divine.

The Lord is gracious to His own,
  And hides with glory as a mist
The sacrifice and smitten stone,
  And on the lips His presence kissed
Burn the high vows with ample flame
That He shall swear to by the Name.

[1] Abraham before his migration saw dawn rise over the Persian Gulf; but to the east of Palestine are mountains.
[2] *i.e.* the light of the Divine Presence.
[3] The presence of God.

JEPHTHAH.

Highest of Highest, most Concealed of all,
Most Holy Ancient One, Unnamable,
Receive for these Thy servants this our oath
To serve none other gods but Thee alone.
And for my own part who am judge of these
I vow beyond obedience sacrifice,
And for the victory Thou shalt give, I vow
To sacrifice the first of living things
That with due welcome shall divide the doors
Of my house, meeting me, an offering
Burnt before Thee with ceremony meet
To give Thee thanks, nor take ungratefully
This first of favours from the Hand Divine.

SOLDIERS.

A noble vow : and God is glad thereat.

PROPHET.

I charge you in the name of God, go not !
I see a mischief fallen on your souls
Most bitter.   Aye ! an evil day is this
If ye go forth with such a sacrifice,
And vows most hideous in their consequence.

SOLDIERS.

It is the prophet of the Lord.

JEPHTHAH.

               Possessed
By Baal ; scourge him hence ; he lies, for God
With powerful proof and many lightnings came
Devouring up the offering at the altar.

PROPHET.

O Jephthah, it is thou on whom it falls,
The sorrow grievous as thy life is dear.

A SOLDIER.

He is the prophet of the Baalim.
We have enough of such : in God's name,
  home !             [*Stabbing him.*

PROPHET.

Thy spear shall turn against thyself, alas !
But welcome, death, thou looked-for spouse
    of mine !
Thy kiss is pleasant as the shaded well
That looks through palm leaves to the quiet
    sky.                                      [*Dies.*

JEPHTHAH.

Thou didst no evil in the slaying him,
For God is a consuming fire ; high zeal
Against idolatry lacks not reward.
And now the sun is up : for Israel, march !

JARED.

Good luck be with your spears ; and home-
    coming
Gladden victorious eyes ere set of sun.
                [*Exeunt* JEPHTHAH *and Soldiers.*

*Enter* ELEAZAR, AHINOAM, *Chorus of
            Elders.*

CHORUS.

The sun is past meridian.   No sound
Of trampling hoofs assails the unquiet wind,
Nor trembles in the pillared echo-places,
And windy corridors of pathless snow.
But let us wait, expecting victory.
No fugitive returns, nor messenger :
They have not shocked together, or perchance
The grim fight rolls its sickening tide along
Homeward or southward, undecided yet ;
Or victory made certain but an hour
Lends no such wings to jaded horses as
May bear a jaded rider to our gates.
Wait only, friends, and calm our troubled
    mind,
Nor stir the languid sails of our desire
With breath of expectation or despair.
Rather give place to those untroubled thoughts
That sit like stars immobile in the sky
To fathom all the desolate winds of ocean,
And draw their secrets from the hidden mines
Whose gold and silver are but wisdom,
    seeking
Rather things incorruptible above

Than sordid hopes and fears.   But look you,
    friends,
Where in the sun's eye rolls a speck of cloud
Lesser than the ephemeral gnat may make
Riding for sport upon a little whirl
Of moving breezes, so it glows and rolls,
Caught in the furnace of the sun, opaque
To eyes that seek its depth, but penetrable
By those long filaments of light beyond.
See, the spot darkens, and a horseman spurs
A flagging steed with bloody flanks, and
    waves
A cloudy sword to heaven—I am sure
He brings us eagle wingéd victory,
And tiding of no battle lost for Israel.
Yes, he grows great before the sun, and
    stands
Now in his stirrups, and shouts loud, and
    waves
A blade triumphant.   Now the weary horse
Stumbles with thundering strides along the
    last
Furlong, and greets us with a joyous neigh
As if he understood the victory.

*Enter Second Messenger.*

SECOND MESSENGER.

Rejoice, O Israel, for this day hath seen
Utter destruction overtake, and death
Ride furious over, trampled necks of men
Desperate in vain ; hath seen red hell gape
    wide
To swallow up the heathen.   Victory
Swells the red-gleaming torrent of pursuit,
And Israel shakes her lazy flanks at last
A lion famished, and is greedy of death.

CHORUS.

O joyful day !   And where is Jephthah now ?

MESSENGER.

Faint with the heat of a hard battle fought,
But following hard after with the horse.
For from Aroer even unto Minnith
He smote them with a slaughter most un-
    heard,
And twenty cities saw from trembling walls

Twice twenty thousand corpses; stragglers
few
Call to the rocks and woods, whose dens
refuse
Shelter and refuge to the fugitives,
But, in revolt against the natural order,
Gape like the ravening jaws of any beast
To let the furious invaders down
Into the bowels of the earth, and close
Upon those grisly men of war, whose life
Groans from the prison that shall crush it
out.

CHORUS.

Be thou most blessed of the Lord for ever !

FIRST ELDER.

But what shall he that hath delivered us
Have for his guerdon when he comes in
triumph ?

SECOND ELDER.

A milk-white ass shall bear him through
the city.

THIRD ELDER.

And wreaths of roses be instead of dust.

FOURTH ELDER.

And dancing girls—

FIFTH ELDER.

And feet of maidens most
Shall strike a measure of delight.

SIXTH ELDER.

And boys
With bright unsullied curls shall minister
Before him all the days of life God grants.

SEVENTH ELDER.

And all his platters shall be made of gold.

EIGHTH ELDER.

And jewels beyond price shall stud them all.
VOL. I.

ELEAZAR.

What sayest thou, O wisest of our race,
Ahinoam, the aged priest of God,
Who weighest out the stars with balances,
And knowest best of men the heart of man ?

AHINOAM.

Ye are as children, and nowise your tongues
Speak sense. I never hear your voice but
know
Some geese are gabbling. Sing to him
perchance !
The voice of old men is a pleasant thing.

CHORUS.

What say ye, brethren ? Shall we sing to
him
Some sweet low ditty, or the louder pæan ?

AHINOAM.

They verily think I speak, not mocking them.

CHORUS.

Who shall uncover such a tongue for wiles,
And pluck his meaning from his subtle words ?

AHINOAM.

Who shall speak plain enough for such as
these
To understand ? Or so debase his thought
As meet their minds, and seem as wisdom's
self ?

CHORUS.

Leave now thy gibing in the hour of joy,
And lend sweet wisdom to awaiting ears.
Thy voice shall carry it, thy words shall bear
Full fruit to-day. Speak only, it is done.

AHINOAM.

I am grown old, and go not out to wars.
But in the lusty days of youth my face
Turned from the battle and pursuit and spoil
Only to one face dearer than my soul.

F

And my wife's eyes were welcome more desired
Than chains of roses, and the song of children,
And swinging palm branches, and milk-white
—elders.

CHORUS.

Fie on thy railing! But his wife is sick,
And cannot leave the borders of her house.

AHINOAM.

But he hath one fair only daughter! Friends,
With maidens bearing trimbrels, and with
dances,
Let her go forth and bring her father home.

JARED [aside].

Horrible! I must speak and silence this
Monstrous impossible villainy of fate.

CHORUS.

O wise old man, thou speakest cleverly.

AHINOAM.

So do, and praise be given you from God.

ELEAZAR.

God, Who this day has slumbered not, nor
slept;
He only keepeth Israel: He is God!

CHORUS.

When God uplifted hands to smite,
    And earth from chaos was unrolled;
When skies and seas from blackest night
    Unfurled, twin sapphires set with gold;
When tumult of the boisterous deep
Roared from its slow ungainly sleep,
    And flocks of heaven were driven to fold;
Then rose the walls of Israel steep,
    For in His promise we behold
The sworded Sons of glory leap
Our tribes in peace to keep.

Deep graven in the rocky girth
    Of Israel's mountains, in the sky,
In all the waters of the earth,
    In all the fiery steeds that ply

Their champing harness, and excel
The charioteers of heaven and hell,
    In all the Names writ secretly
And sacred songs ineffable;
    In all the words of power that fly
About the world, this song they spell
He keepeth Israel.

AHINOAM.

Ye praise God of full heart: I would to God
Your minds were somewhat fuller, and could
    keep
Discretion seated on her ivory throne.
What folly is it they will now be at,
Gray beards, and goatish manners? Hark to
    them!

CHORUS.

In the brave old days ere men began
    To bind young hearts with an iron tether,
Ere love was brief as life, a span,
    Ere love was light as life, a feather,
    Earth was free as the glad wild weather,
God was father and friend to man.


AHINOAM.

Then when with mildness and much joy our
    judge
Draw hither, let us send to meet his steps
In sackcloth clad, with ashes on their heads,
His cruel brethren, that he spare their lives.


CHORUS.

In the heart of a conqueror mercy sits
    A brighter jewel than vengeance wroken.
Grace is the web that his people knits,
    And love is the balm for the hearts nigh
    broken.
    Peace is arisen, a dove for token;
Righteousness, bright as the swallow flits.


JARED [aside].

So, in his victory is our disgrace.

CHORUS.

Fair as the dawn is the maiden wise ;
  Pale as the poppies by still white water !
Sunlight burns in her pure deep eyes ;
  Love lights the tresses of Jephthah's
    daughter.
  Kissing rays of the moon have caught her,
Rays of the moon that sleeps and sighs.

JARED [*aside*].

In our disgrace, behold ! our vengeance
  strikes.
I am inspired with so profound a hate—
He shall not triumph : in the very hour
When his o'ermastering forehead tops the
  sky
I strike him to the earth.  I need not move.
Silence—no more—and all accomplishes.
Leviathan, how subtle is thy path !

CHORUS.

Not now may the hour of gladness fade,
  The wheel of our fate spins bright and
    beaming.
God has fashioned a sun from shade.
  Mercy and joy in one tide are streaming.
  Fortune is powerless, to all good seeming.
Fate is stricken, and flees afraid.

JARED.

Bring me the sackcloth and the ashes now !

ELEAZAR.

Behold ! the crown of all our maiden wreath,
Adulah, white and lissome, with the flames
Of dawn forth blushing through her flower-
  crowned hair.

CHORUS.

Behold a virgin to the Lord !
  Behold a maiden pale as death,
Whose glance is silver as a sword,
  And flowers of Kedar fill her breath,
  Whose fragrance saturates the sward,
    Whose sunny perfume floating saith :
From my ineffable desire is drawn
The awful glory of the golden dawn.

Behold her bosom bare and bold
  Whose billows like the ocean swing !
The painted palaces of gold
  Where shell-born maidens laugh and sing
Are mirrored in those breasts that hold
  Sweet odours of the sunny spring.
Behold the rising swell of perfect calm
In breezy dells adorable of balm !

Behold the tender rosy feet
  Made bare for holiness, that move
Like doves amid the waving wheat,
  Or swallows silver in the grove
Where sylph and salamander meet,
  And gnome and undine swoon for love !
Her feet that flit upon the windy way
Twin fawns, the daughters of the rosy day.

Behold, the arms of her desire
  Wave, weave, and wander in the air,
Vines life-endued by subtle fire
  So quick and comely, curving bare.
The white diaphanous attire
  Floats like a spirit pale and fair.
The dance is woven of the breeze ; the tune
Is like the ocean silvered by the moon.

Behold the maidens following !
  O every one is like a flower,
Or like an ewe lamb of the king
  That comes from water at the hour
Of even.  See, the dancers swing
  Their censers ; see, their tresses shower
Descending flames, and perfumes teem divine,
And all the air grows one pale fume of wine.

Their songs, their purity, their peace,
  Glide slowly in the arms of God ;
His lips assume their sanctities,
  His eyes perceive the period
Of woven webs of lutes at ease,
  And measures by pure maidens trod,
Till, like the smoke of mountains risen at
  dawn,
The cloud-veils of the Ain [1] are withdrawn.

[1] The Negative, surrounded by a triple veil
in the Theogony of the Qabalists, from which
all things spring and to which all shall return.
See " Berashith " in a subsequent volume.

Pure spirits rise to heaven, the bride.
  Pure bodies are as lamps below.
The shining essence, glorified
  With fire more cold than fresh-fallen
    snow,
And influences, white and wide,
  Descend, re-gather, kindle, grow,
Till from one virgin bosom flows a river
Of white devotion adamant for ever.

*Enter* ADULAH *and her Maidens.*

#### ADULAH.

Fathers of Israel, we are come to you
With many maidens praising God, for
  this
The victory of my father.   Happy girls!
Whose brothers struck to-day for Israel,
Whose fathers smote the heathen; happiest,
Ye blushing flowers, beyond your younger
  spring
That bends in you toward summer, faint and
  fair,
Whose lovers bared their swords to-day;
  and ye,
O reverend heads, most beautiful for gray,
The comely crown of age, that doth be-
  seem
Your wise sweet beauty, as the ivy wreathes
The rugged glory of the sycamore,
Have ye heard aught of Jephthah's home-
  coming?
For our cheeks tingle with the expected
  kiss
Of hardy warriors dear to us, and now
By double kinship rendered doubly dear.
For O! my father comes to gladden me
With those enduring kisses that endow
Heart, hope, and life with gladness.   Comes
  he soon?

#### ELEAZAR.

Maiden most perfect, daughter of our lord,
And ye, most fairest branches of our tree,
Maidens of Israel, we await you here
That ye, no other, may go forth to meet
The chief victorious.   And after you

Those villains that once cast him out shall
  forth
In sackcloth to his feet, if haply so
He spare their vagabond and worthless lives.

#### ADULAH.

Not so, my father.   In my father's name
I promise unto all great happiness,
And vengeance clean forgotten in the land;
"Vengeance is mine, Jehovah will repay."
My father shall not frown on any man.

#### JARED [*aside*].

She is most gracious: I must speak and
  save.
[*Aloud.*] Friends!  [*Aside.*] Stay—Is this a
  tempter voice that soothes
My consciehce?   Art thou that Leviathan,
Thou lipless monster, gnashing at my soul
Abominable teeth?   Art thou the fiend
Whom I have seen in sleep, and waking
  served?
O horrible distortion of all truth
That I must serve thee still!
                    Yet—dare I speak,
Those eyes upon me, torturing my soul
And threatening revenge?   Those fingers
  gross,
Purple, and horrible, to blister me
With infamous tearing at my throat.   O
  Hell!
Vomit thy monsters forth in myriads
To putrefy this fair green earth with blood,
But make not me the devilish minister
Of such a deed as this!   No respite?—
  Must?
Irrevocable?   I dare not call on God.
Thou, thou wilt serve me if I do this thing?
Oh, if this be a snare thou settest now,
Who hast once already mocked our pact, I
  swear
By God, I cast thee off.   Leviathan!
Accept the bargain.   And I seal it—thus.
                    [*Writing in the air.*
I will keep silence, though they tear my
  tongue
Blaspheming from my throat.   My servant
  now!

#### ELEAZAR.

Mingled emotions quickly following
Fear upon fear, and joy and hope at last
Crowning, have maddened Jephthah's kins-
 man here.
Mark his lips muttering, and his meaningless
Furious gestures, and indignant eyes
Starting, and hard-drawn breath! Him lead
 away
Tenderly, as beseems the mercy shown
To his repentance by this maiden queen.
The Lord is merciful to them that show
Mercy, and all such as are pure of heart;
Thy crown, Adulah, wears a double flower
Of these fair blossoms wreathed in one device
Of perfect love in perfect maidenhood.

#### JARED [*recovering himself*].

Nay, but my voice must fill the song of joy
With gratitude, and meet thanksgiving. Me
More than these others it beseems, who love
Less dearly for their innocence than I,
Pardoned of my unpardonable sin.

#### ADULAH.

The flowers turn westerward; the sun is
 down
Almost among those clouds that kiss the sea
With heavy lashes drooping over it,
A mother watching her own daughter swoon
To sleep. But look toward the southern
 sky;
It is my father. Let us go to him,
Maidens, with song and gladness of full
 hearts.

#### SEMICHORUS OF MAIDENS I.

The conqueror rides at last
 To home, to love;
The victory is past,
 The white-wing dove
Sails through the crystal air of eve with a
 pæan deep and vast.
 Jephthah!

#### SEMICHORUS OF MAIDENS II.

Forth, maidens, with your hands
 White with new lilies!
Forth, maidens, in bright bands,
 Virgins whose one sweet will is
To sing the victory of our God in all sky-
 girdled lands!
Jahveh!

#### SEMICHORUS I.

With dancing feet, and noise
 Of timbrels smitten,
With tears and tender joys,
 With songs unwritten,
With music many-mouthed, with robes in
 snowy equipoise.
Jephthah!

#### SEMICHORUS II.

With hearts infused of fire,
 Eyes clear with many waters,
With lips to air that quire,
 We, earth's desirous daughters,
Lift up the song of triumph, sound the lutes
 of our desire!
Jahveh!

#### SEMICHORUS I.

With branches strewn before us,
 And roses flung
In all the ways, we chorus
 With throat and tongue
The glory of our warrior sires whose victor
 swords restore us
Jephthah!

#### SEMICHORUS II.

With angels vast and calm
 That keep his way,
With streams of holy balm,
 The prayers of them that pray,
We go to bring him home and raise to Thee
 our holy psalm,
Jahveh!

ELEAZAR.

Go ye, make ready for the happy march.
[*Exeunt* ADULAH *and Maidens.*
And we too, changing these funereal vest-
    ments
Will clothe in moonlike splendour, candid
    robes
Of priestly purity, our joyous selves.
O fortunate day! O measured steps of
    noon,
Quicken, if once ye stayed for Joshua,
To keep sweet music to our hearts.   Away!
                      [*Exeunt all but* JARED.


JARED.

I will await, and hide myself away
Behind yon bushes, to behold the plot
Bud to fulfilment.   Then, Leviathan,
I am thy master.   Mockery of a God
That seest this thing prosper—Ha! thine
    altar!
Let me give thanks, Jehovah! O thou
    God
That rulest Israel as sheep and slaves,
But over me no ruler; thou proud God
That marshallest these petty thunder-clouds
That blacken over the inane abyss
But canst not tame one fierce desire of
    mine,
Nor satiate my hatred, nor destroy
This power of mine over thy devil-brood,
The hatchment of thine incest, O thou
    God
Who knowest me, me, mortal me, thy master,
Thy master—and I laugh at thee, the
    slave!
Down from Thy throne, impostor, down,
    down, down
To thine own Hell, immeasurable—


A VOICE.

                            Strike!
[*The storm, gathering to a climax,
    bursts in a tremendous flash of
    lightning, and* JARED *is killed.*


*Enter* JEPHTHAH *and Soldiers.*

JEPHTHAH.

A terrible peal of thunder!   And the sky
Seems for an hour past to have been in
    labour
And, safely now delivered, smiles again.
For see, the sun!   O happy sunlight hours—
What is this blackened and distorted thing?


A SOLDIER.

Some fellow by the altar that kept watch,
Some faithful fellow—he is gone to God.


JEPHTHAH.

How is't the cattle have been driven home?
I trusted we had found a tender lamb,
A lamb of the first year, unblemished, white,
To greet me, that we do meet sacrifice,
Fulfilling thus my vow, and all our duty.
              [*A noise of timbrels and singing.*
Surely some merriment—our news hath
    reached.
Glad news and welcome: God is very good.


*Enter* ADULAH, *running, followed by
    singing Maidens.*

ADULAH.

Father!

JEPHTHAH.

My daughter!
            [*He suddenly stops, and
            blanches, understanding.*
                      Alas my daughter!
    [*He continues in a dazed, toneless voice.*
Thou hast brought me very low, and thou
art one of them that trouble me; for I have
opened my mouth unto the Lord, and I
cannot go back.


ADULAH.

My father, O my father!

*Enter* ELEAZAR *and Chorus.*

ELEAZAR.

Most welcome, conqueror !
[JEPHTHAH *waves him aside.*
What is this ?  What is this ?

CHORUS.

Speak, Jephthah, speak !  What ill has
fallen ?  Speak !
[*Silence.  After a little the Chorus of
Maidens understand, and break into
wailing.  The old men gradually
understand and fill the air with
incoherent lamentations.  Behind
JEPHTHAH the soldiers, with white
lips, have assumed their military
formation, and stand at attention
by a visible effort of self-control.*

ADULAH.

My father, if thou hast openéd thy mouth
Unto the Lord, fulfil the oath to me,
Because the Lord hath taken vengeance
for thee
Of all thine enemies, the Ammonites.
Let this be done for me, that I may go
Two months upon the mountains, and bewail,
I and my fellows, my virginity !

JEPHTHAH.

Go !

CHORUS OF MAIDENS.

O the time of dule and teen !
O the dove the hawk has snared !
Would to God we had not been,
We, who see our maiden queen,
Love has slain whom hate had spared.
Sorrow for our sister sways
All our maiden bosoms, bared
To the dying vesper rays,
Where the sun below the bays
Of the West is stooping ;
All our hearts together drooping,
Flowers the ocean bears.
All the garb that gladness wears

To a rent uncouth attire
Changed with cares ;
Happy songs our love had made
Ere the sun had sunk his fire,
In the moonrise fall and fade,
And the dregs of our desire
Fall away to death ;
Tears divide our labouring breath
That our sister—O our sister !
Moon and sun and stars have kissed her !
She must touch the lips of death,
Touch the lips whose coldness saith :
Thou art clay.
Let us fare away, away
To the ice whose ocean gray
Tumbles on the beach of rock,
Where the wheeling vultures mock
Our distress with horrid cries ;
Where the flower relenting dies,
And the sun is sharp to slay ;
Where the ivory dome above
Glimmers like the dawn of love
On the weary way ;
Where the ibex chant and call
Over tempest's funeral ;
Where the hornéd beast is shrill,
And the eagle hath his will,
And the shadows fall
Sharp and black, till day is passed
Over to the ocean vast ;
Where the barren rocks resound
Only to the rending roar
Of the shattering streams that pour
Rocks by ice eternal bound,
Myriad cascades that crowned
Once the far resounding thróne
Of the mountain spirits strong,
All the treacherous souls that throng
Desolate abodes of stone,
Barren of all comely things,
Given to the splendid kings,
Gloomy state, and glamour dark,
Swooping jewel-feathered wings,
Eyes translucent with a spark
Of the world of fire, that swings
Gates of adamant below
Lofty minarets of snow.
Thence the towering flames arise,

Where the flashes white and wise
Find their mortal foe.
Let us thither, caring not
Anything, or any more,
Since the sorrow of our lot
Craves to pass the abysmal door.
Never more for us shall twine
Rosy fingers on the vine.
Never maiden lips shall cull
Myriad blossoms beautiful.
Never cheeks shall dimple over
At the perfume of the clover.
Never bosoms bright and round
Shall be garlanded and bound
With the chain of myrtle, wreathed
By the fingers of the maid
Each has chosen for a mate,
When the west wind lately breathed
Murmurs in the wanton glade
Of the day that dawneth late
In a maiden's horoscope,
Dawning faith and fire and hope
On the spring that only knew
Flowers and butterflies and dew,
Skies and seas and mountains blue,
On the spring that wot not of
Fruit and falling leaves and love.
Never dew-dashed foreheads fair
Shall salute the idle air.
Never shall we wander deep
Where the fronds of fern, asleep,
Kiss her rosy feet that pass
On the spangled summer grass,
Half awake, and drowse again.
Never more our feet shall stain
Purple with the joyous grape,
Whence there rose a fairy shape
In the fume and must and juice,
Singing lest our eyes escape
All his tunic wried and loose
With the feet that softly trod
In the vat the fairy god.
Never more our eyes shall swim,
Looking for the love of him
In the magic moon that bent
Over maidens moon-content,
When the summer woods were wet
With our dewy songs, that set

Quivering all seas and snows,
Stars and tender winds that fret
Lily, lily, laughing rose,
Sighing, sighing violet,
Dusky pansy, swaying rush,
And the stream that flows
Singing, ringing softly : Hush !
Listen to the bird that goes
Wooing to the brown mate's bough ;
Listen to the breeze that blows
Over cape and valley now
At the silence of the noon,
Or the slumber-hour
Of the white delicious moon
Like a lotus-flower !
Let us sadly, slowly, go
To the silence of the snow !


ADULAH [*embracing* JEPHTHAH].

Whose crystal fastnesses shall echo back
The lamentations of these friends of mine,
But not my tears.   For I will fit myself
By solitude and fasting and much prayer
For his most holy ceremony, to be
A perfect, pure, accepted sacrifice.
Only this sorrow—O father, father, speak !


JEPHTHAH.

Go !


ADULAH.

        Most unblamable, we come again.
I would not weep with these ; I dare not
        stay,
Lest I weep louder than them all.   Fare
        well,
My father, O my father !   I am passing
Into the night.   Remember me as drawn
Into the night toward the golden dawn.[1]
                [*Exeunt* ADULAH *and Maidens.*

[1] The "Golden Dawn" meant at this time
to Crowley all that "Christ" means to an
Evangelical, and more.   The symbol constantly recurs in this and many other poems,
and always in the sense of a rescuing force.

## CHORUS.

Toward the mountains and the night
  The fruitless flowers of Gilead go ;
Toward the hollows weird and white,
  Toward the sorrow of the snow ;
To desolation black and blind
They move, and leave us death behind.

The Lord is great : the Lord is wise
  Within His temple to foresee
With calm impenetrable eyes
  The after glory that shall be ;
But we, of mortal bodies born,
Laugh lies consoling unto scorn.

The God of Israel is strong ;
  His mighty arm hath wrought this day
A victory and a triumph-song—
  And now He breathes upon His clay,
And we, who were as idols crowned,
Lie dust upon the empty ground.

She goes, our sorrow's sacrifice,
  Our lamb, our firstling, frail and white,
With large sweet love-illumined eyes
  Into the night, into the night.
The throne of night shall be withdrawn ;
So moveth she toward the dawn.

All peoples and all kings that move
  By love and sacrifice inspired
In light and holiness and love,
  And seek some end of God desired,
Pass, though they seem to sink in night,
To dawns more perdurably bright.

So priest and people join to praise
  The secret wisdom of the Lord,
Awaiting the arisen rays
  That smite through heaven as a sword ;
Remembering He hath surely sworn :
Toward the night, toward the dawn !

Behold the moon that fails above,
  The stars that pale before the sun !
How far, those figures light as love
  That laughing to the mountains run !
Behold the flames of hair that leap
Above her forehead mild and deep !

She turns to bless her people still :
  So, passes to the golden gate
Where snow burns fragrant on the hill,
  Where for her step those fountains wait
Of light and brilliance that shall rise
To greet her beauty lover-wise.

The silver west fades fast, the skies
  Are blue and silver overhead ;
She stands upon the snow, her eyes
  Fixed fast upon the fountain-head
Whence from Eternity is drawn
The awful glory of the dawn !

## ELEAZAR.

Let every man depart unto his house.

## CHORUS.

He hath made His face as a fire ; His wrath
  as a sword ;
He hath smitten our soul's desire ; He is the
  Lord.
He hath given and taken away, hath made
  us and broken ;
He hath made the blue and the gray, the sea
  for a token ;
He hath made to-day and to-morrow ; the
  winter, the spring ;
He bringeth us joy out of sorrow ; Jehovah
  is King.

  [*Exeunt.* JEPHTHAH *is left standing
    with white set face. Presently tears
    come into his eyes, and he advances,
    and kneels at the altar.*

# MYSTERIES:

## LYRICAL AND DRAMATIC.

### 1898.

## THE FIVE KISSES.[1]

### I.

### AFTER CONFESSION.

DAY startles the fawn from the avenues deep
that look to the east in the heart of the
wood :
Light touches the trees of the hill with its
lips, and God is above them and sees
they are good :
Night flings from her forehead the purple-
black hood.

The thicket is sweet with the breath of the
breeze made soft by the kisses of slumbering maids ;
The nymph and the satyr, the fair and the
faulty alike are the guests of these
amorous shades ;
The hour of Love flickers and falters and
fades.

Oh, listen, my love, to the song of the brook,
its murmurs and cadences, trills and low
chords ;
Hark to its silence, that prelude of wonder
ringing at last like the clamour of swords
That clash in the wrath of the warring
of lords.

Listen, oh, listen ! the nightingale near us
swoons a farewell to the blossoming brake ;
Listen, the thrush in the meadow is singing
notes that move sinuous, lithe as a
snake ;
The cushats are cooing, the world is awake.

[1] Crowley's biographer will note the astonishing coincidences of scene and incident between
this poem and the events of 1903-4.

Only one hour since you whispered the story
out of your heart to my tremulous ear ;
Only one hour since the light of your eyes
was the victor of violent sorrow and fear ;
Your lips were so set to the lips of me here.

Surely the victory ripens to perfect conquest
of everything set in our way.
We must be free as our hearts are, and gather
strength for our limbs for the heat of
the fray :
The battle is ours if you say me not nay.

Fly with me far, where the ocean is bounded
white by the walls of the northernmost
shore,
Where on a lone rocky island a castle laughs
in its pride at the billows that roar,
My home where our love may have peace
evermore.

Yes, on one whisper the other is waiting
patient to catch the low tone of delight.
Kiss me again for the amorous answer ; close
your dear eyelids and think it is night,
The hour of the even we fix for the flight.

### II.

### THE FLIGHT.

LIFT up thine eyes ! for night is shed around,
As light profound,
And visible as snow on steepled hills,
Where silence fills
The shaded hollows : night, a royal queen
Most dimly seen

90

Through silken curtains that bedeck the bed.
    Lift up thine head !
For night is here, a dragon, to devour
    The slow sweet hour
Filled with all smoke of incense, and the
    praise
    More loud than day's
That swings its barren censer in the sky
    And asks to die
Because the sea will hear no hollow moan
    Beyond its own,
Because the sea that kissed dead Sappho[1]
    sings
    Of strange dark things—
Shapes of bright breasts that purple as the
    sun
    Grows dark and dun,
Of pallid lips more haggard for the kiss
    Of Salmacis,[2]
Of eager eyes that startle for the fear
    Too dimly dear
Lest there come death, like passion, and
    fulfil
    Their dreams of ill !
Oh ! lift thy forehead to the night's cool
    wind !
    The meekest hind
That fears the noonday in her grove is bold
    To seek the gold
So pale and perfect as the moon puts on :
    The light is gone.
Hardly as yet one sees the crescent maid
    Move, half afraid,
Into the swarthy forest of the air
    And, breast made bare,
Gather her limbs about her for the chase
    Through starry space,
And, while the lilies sway their heads, to
    bend
    Her bow, to send

[1] Sappho, the great lyric poet of Greece, plunged from a rock into the sea, according to later tradition.
[2] A stream into which a man plunged, and was united, as a Hermaphrodite, with its attendant nymph. The reference is connected with Sappho's loves. See her Ode to Aphrodite and Swinburne's Anactoria and Hermaphroditus.

A swift white arrow at some recreant
    star.
    The sea is far
Dropped in the hollows of the swooning
    land.
    Oh ! hold my hand !
Lift up thy deep eyes to my face, and let
    Our lips forget
The dumb dead hours before they met to-
    gether !
    The snowbright weather
Calls us beyond the grassy downs, to be
    Beside the sea,
The slowly-breathing ocean of the south.
    Oh, make thy mouth
A rosy flame like that most perfect star
    Whose kisses are
So red and ripe ! Oh, let thy limbs entwine
    Like love with mine !
Oh, bend thy gracious body to my breast
    To sleep, to rest !
But chiefly let thine eyes be set on me,
    As when the sea
Lay like a mirror to reflect the shape
    Of yonder cape
Where Sappho stood and touched the lips
    of death !
    Thy subtle breath
Shall flow like incense in between our cheeks,
    Where pleasure seeks
In vain a wiser happiness. And so
    Our whispers low
Shall dim the utmost beauty of thy gaze
    Through moveless days
And long nights equable with trancéd
    pleasure :
    So love at leisure
Shall make his model of our clinging looks,
    And burn his books
To write a new sweet volume deeper much,
    And frail to touch,
Being the mirror of a gossamer
    Too soft and fair.
This is the hour when all the world is
    sleeping ;
    The winds are keeping
A lulling music on the frosty sea.
    The air is free,

As free as summer-time, to sound or cease :
    God's utmost peace
Lies like a cloud upon the quiet land.
    O little hand !
White hand with rose leaves shed about the
    tips,
    As if my lips
Had left their bloom upon it when they
    kissed,
    As if a mist
Of God's delicious dawn had overspread
    Their face, and fled !
O wonderful fresh blossom of the wood !
    O purpling blood !
O azure veins as clear as all the skies !
    O longing eyes
That look upon me fondly to beget
    Two faces, set
Either like flowers upon their laughing blue,
    Where morning dew
Sparkles with all the passion of the dawn !
    The happy lawn
Leads, by the stillest avenues, to groves
    Made soft by loves ;
And all the nymphs have made a mossy dell
    Hard by the well
Where even a Satyr might behold the grace
    Of such a face
As his [1] who perished for his own delights,
    So well requites
That witching fountain his desire that looks.
    Two slow bright brooks
Encircle it with silver, and the moon
    Strikes into tune
The ripples as they break.   For here it was
    Their steps did pass,
Dreamy Endymion's and Artemis', [2]
    Who bent to kiss
Across the moss-grown rocks that build the
    well :
    And here the  tell

[1] Narcissus, a beautiful youth, inaccessible
to love.   Echo, a nymph enamoured of him,
died of neglect.   To punish him, Nemesis
caused him to behold his image in a pool; he
pined of love for the reflection, and was changed
into the flower which still bears his name.
[2] The reader may consult Keats's poem of
"Endymion."

Of one [1] beneath the hoary stone who hid
    And watched unbid
When one most holy came across the glade,
    Who saw a maid
So bright that mists were dim upon his eyes,
    And yet he spies
So sweet a vision that his gentle breath
    Sighed into death :
And others say that here the fairies bring
    The fairy king, [2]
And crown him with a flower of eglantine,
    And of the vine
Twist him a throne made perfect with wild
    roses,
    And gathered posies
From all the streams that wander through
    the vale,
    And crying, " Hail !
All hail, most beautiful of all our race ! "
    Cover his face
With blossoms gathered from a fairy tree
    Like foam from sea,
So delicate that mortal eyes behold
    Ephemeral gold
Flash, and not see a flower, but say the moon
    Has shone too soon
Anxious to greet Endymion ; and this
    Most dainty kiss
They cover him withal, and Dian sees
    Through all the trees
No pink pale blossom of his tender lips.
    The little ships
Of silver leaf and briar-bloom sail here,
    No storm to fear,
Though butterflies be all their mariners.
    The whitethroat stirs
The beech-leaves to awake the tiny breeze
    That soothes the seas,
And yet gives breath to shake their fairy
    sails ;
    Young nightingales,
Far through the golden plumage of the night,
    With strong delight

[1] A gentle sophistication of the story of
Actaeon who beheld Artemis at the bath, and
being changed into a stag, was torn to pieces
by her hounds.
[2] From sophistication Crowley proceeds to
pure invention.

Purple the evening with amazing song ;
　　The moonbeams throng
In shining clusters to the fairy throat,
　　Whose clear trills float
And dive and run about the crystal deep
　　As sweet as sleep.
Only, fall love of this full heart of mine,
　　There lacks the wine
Our kisses might pour out for them ; they
　　wait,
　　And we are late ;
Only, my flower of all the world, the thrush
　　(You hear him ?　Hush !)
Lingers, and sings not to his fullest yet :
　　Our love shall get
Such woodland welcome as none ever had
　　To make it glad.
Come, it is time, cling closer to my hand.
　　We understand.
We must go forth together, not to part.
　　O perfect heart !
O little heart that beats to mine, away
　　Before the day
Ring out the tocsin for our flight !　My ship
　　Is keen to dip
Her plunging forehead in the silvering sea.
　　To-morrow we
Shall be so far away, and then to-morrow
　　Shall shake off sorrow
And be to-morrow and not change for ever :
　　No dawn shall sever
The sleepy eyelids of the night, no eve
　　Shall fall and cleave
The blue deep eyes of day.　Your hand, my
　　queen !
　　Look down and lean
Your whole weight on me, then leap out, as
　　light
　　As swallow's flight,
And race across the shadows of the moon,
　　And keep the tune
With ringing hoofs across the fiery way.
　　Your eyes betray
How eager is your heart, and yet—O dare
　　To fashion fair
A whole long life of love !　Leap high, laugh
　　low !
　　I love you—so !—

One kiss—and then to freedom !　See the
　　bay
　　So far away,
But not too far for love !　Ring out, sharp
　　hoof,
　　And put to proof
The skill of him that steeled thee !　Freedom !
　　Set
　　As never yet
Thy straining sides for freedom !　Gallant
　　mare !
　　The frosty air
Kindles the blood within us as we race.
　　O love !　Thy face
Flames with the passion of our happy speed !
　　The noble steed
Pashes the first gold limit of the sand.
　　Ah love, thy hand !
We win, no foot pursuing spans the brow !
　　Yes, kiss me now !


III.

THE SPRING AFTER.

NORTH, by the ice-belt, where the cliffs
　　appease
Innumerable clamour of sundering seas,
And garlands of ungatherable foam
Wild as the horses maddening toward home,
Where through the thunderous burden of the
　　thaw
Rings the sharp fury of the breaking flaw,
Where summer's hand is heavy on the snow,
And springtide bursts the insuperable floe,
North, by the limit of the ocean, stands
A castle, lord of those far footless lands
That are the wall of that most monstrous
　　world
About whose pillars Behemoth is curled,
About whose gates Leviathan is strong,
Whose secret terror sweetens not for song.
The hoarse loud roar of gulphs of raging
　　brine
That break in foam and fire on that divine
Cliff-base, is smothered in the misty air,
And no sound penetrates them, save a rare

Music of sombre motion, swaying slow.
The sky above is one dark indigo
Voiceless and deep, no light is hard within
To shame love's lips and rouse the silky skin
From its dull olive to a perfect white.
For scarce an hour the golden rim of light
Tinges the southward bergs; for scarce an hour
The sun puts forth his seasonable flower,
And only for a little while the wind
Wakes at his coming, and beats cold and blind
On the wild sea that struggles to release
The hard grip from its throat, and lie at ease
Lapped in the eternal summer. But its waves
Roam through the solitude of empty caves
In vain; no faster wheels the moon above;
And still reluctant fly the hours of love.
It is so peaceful in the castle: here
The night of winter never froze a tear
On my love's cheek or mine; no sorrow came
To track our vessel by its wake of flame
Wherein the dolphin bathed his shining side;
No smallest cloud between me and my bride
Came like a little mist; one tender fear,
Too sweet to speak of, closed the dying year
With love more perfect, for its purple root
Might blossom outward to the snowy fruit
Whose bloom to-night lay sleeping on her breast,
As if a touch might stir the sunny nest,
Break the spell's power, and bid the spirit fly
Who had come near to dwell with us. But I
Bend through long hours above the dear twin life,
Look from love's guerdon to the lover-wife,
And back again to that small face so sweet,
And downwards to the little rosy feet,
And see myself no longer in her eyes
So perfectly as here, where passion lies
Buried and re-arisen and complete.
O happy life too sweet, too perfect sweet,
O happy love too perfectly made one
Not to arouse the envy of the sun

Who sulks six months[1] for spite of it! O love,
Too pure and fond for those pale gods above,
Too perfect for their iron rods to break,
Arise, awake, and die for death's own sake!
That one forgetfulness may take us three,
Still three, still one, to the Lethean sea;
That all its waters may be sweet as those
We wandered by, sweet sisters of the rose,
That perfect night before we fled, we two
Who were so silent down that avenue
Grown golden with the moonlight, who should be
No longer two, but one; nor one, but three.
And now it is the spring; the ice is breaking;
The waters roar; the winds their wings are shaking
To sweep upon the northland; we shall sail
Under the summer perfume of the gale
To some old valley where the altars steam
Before the gods, and where the maidens dream
Their little lives away, and where the trees
Shake laughing tresses at the rising breeze,
And where the wells of water lie profound,
And not unfrequent is the silver sound
Of shepherds tuneful as the leaves are green,
Whose reedy music echoes, clear and clean,
From rocky palaces where gnomes delight
To sport all springtime, where the brooding night
With cataract is musical, and thrushes
Throb their young love beside the stream that rushes
Headlong to beat its foamheads into snow,
Where the sad swallow calls, and pale songs flow
To match the music of the nightingale.
There, when the pulses of the summer fail,
The fiery flakes of autumn fall, and there
Some warm perfection of the lazy air
Swims through the purpling veins of lovers.
    Hark!
A faint bird's note, as if a silver spark

---

[1] In Arctic latitudes the sun hardly rises at all from September to March, and is only visible in the south.

Struck from a diamond ; listen, wife, and
    know
How perfectly I love to watch you so.
Wake, lover, wake, but stir not yet the
    child :
Wake, and thy brow serene and low and
    mild
Shall take my kisses, and my lips shall
    seek
The pallid roses on thy perfect cheek,
And kiss them into poppies, and thy mouth
Shall lastly close to mine, as in the south
We see the sun close fast upon the sea ;
So, my own heart, thy mouth must close on
    me.
Art thou awake ?   Those eyes of wondering
    love,
Sweet as the dawn and softer than the
    dove,
Seek no quick vision—yet they move to
    me
And, slowly, to the child.   How still are
    we !
Yes, and a smile betokens that they wake
Or dream a waking dream for kisses' sake ;
Yes, I will touch thee, O my low sweet
    brow !
My wife, thy lips to mine—yes, kiss me
    now !

## IV.

## THE VOYAGE SOUTHWARD.

HOLY as heaven, the home
Of winds, the land of foam,
The palace of the waves, the house of rain,
    Deeper than ocean, dark
    As dawn before the lark
Flings his sharp song to skyward, and is fain
    To light his lampless eyes
    At the flower-folded skies
Where stars are hidden in the blue, to fill
    His beak with star-dropt dew,
    His little heart anew
With love and song to swell it to his will ;
    Holy as heaven, the place
    Before the golden face

Of God is very silent at the dawn.
    The even keel is keen
    To flash the waves between,
But no soft moving current is withdrawn :
    We float upon the blue
    Like sunlight specks in dew,
And like the moonlight on the lake we
    lie :
    The northern gates are past,
    And, following fair and fast,
The north wind drove us under such a
    sky,
    Faint with the sun's desire,
    And clad in fair attire
Of many driving cloudlets ; and we flew
    Like swallows to the South.
    The ocean's curving mouth
Smiled day by day and nights of starry
    blue ;
    Nights when the sea would shake
    Like sunlight where the wake
Was wonderful with flakes of living things
    That leapt for joy to feel
    The cold exultant keel
Flash, and the white ship dip her woven
    wings ;
    Nights when the moon would hold
    Her lamp of whitest gold
To see us on the poop together set
    With one desire, to be
    Alone upon the sea
And touch soft hands, and hold white bosoms
    yet,
    And see in silent eyes
    More stars than all the skies
Together hold within their limits gray,
    To watch the red lips move
    For slow delight of love
Till the moon sigh and sink, and yield her
    sway
    Unto the eastern lord
    That draws a sanguine sword
And starts up eager in the dawn, to see
    Bright eyes grow dim for sleep,
    And lazy bosoms keep
Their slumber perfect and their sorcery,
    While dawny winds arise,
    And fast the white ship flies

To those young groves of olive by the shore,
   The spring-clad shore we seek
   That slopes to yonder peak
Snow-clad, bright-gleaming, as the silver ore
   Plucked [1] by pale fingers slow
   In balmy Mexico,
A king on thunder throned, his diadem
   The ruby rocks that flash
   The sunlight like a lash
When sunlight touches, and sweeps over
   them
   A crown of light ! Behold !
   The white seas touch the gold,
And flame like flowers of fire about the
   prow.
   It is the hour for sleep :—
   Lulled by the moveless deep
To sleep, sweet wife, to sleep ! Yes, kiss
   me now !

## V.

## THE ULTIMATE VOYAGE.[2]

THE wandering waters move about the world,
And lap the sand, with quietest complaint
Borne on the wings of dying breezes up,
To where we make toward the wooded top
Of yonder menacing hill.   The night is fallen
Starless and moonless, black beyond belief,
Tremendous, only just the ripple keeps
Our souls from perishing in the inane,
With music borrowed from the soul of God.
We twain go thither, knowing no desire
To lead us ; but some strong necessity
Urges, as lightning thunder, our slow steps
Upward.   For on the pleasant meadow-land
That slopes to sunny bays, and limpid seas
(That breathe like maidens sleeping, for their
   breast
Is silver with the sand that lies below,)
Where our storm-strengthened dragon rests
   at last,

---

[1] Referring to the story of the accidental
discovery of the mine of Potosi by a man who,
plucking a plant, found its roots shining with
silver.
[2] The Spiritual Journey towards the Supreme
Knowledge which is life and bliss.

---

And by whose borders we have made a home,
More like a squirrel's bower than a house.
For in this blue Sicilian summertime
The trees arch tenderly for lovers' sleep,
And all the interwoven leaves are fine
To freshen us with dewdrops at the dawn,
Or let the summer shower sing through to us,
And welcome kisses of the silver rain
That raps and rustles in the solitude.
But in the night there came to us a cry :
" The mountains are your portion, and the
   hills
Your temple, and you are chosen." Then I
   woke
Pondering, and my lover woke and said :
" I heard a voice of one majestical
With waving beard, most ancient, beautiful,
Concealed and not concealed ; [1] and I awoke,
Feeling a strong compulsion on my soul
To go some whither." And the dreams were
   one
(We somehow knew), and, looking such a
   kiss
As lovers' eyes can interchange, our lips
Met in the mute agreement to obey.
So, girding on our raiment, as to pass
Some whither of long doubtful journeying,
We went forth blindly to the horrible
Damp darkness of the pines above.   And
   there
Strange beasts crossed path of ours, such
   beasts as earth
Bears not, distorted, tortured, loathable,
Mouthing with hateful lips some recent blood,
Or snarling at our feet.   But these attacked
No courage of our hearts, we faltered not,
And they fell back, snake's mouth and
   leopard's throat,
Afraid.   But others fawning came behind
With clumsy leapings as in friendliness,
Dogs with men's faces, and we beat them off
With scabbard, and the hideous path wound
   on.
And these perplexed our goings, for no light
Gleamed through the bare pine-ruins lava-
   struck,

---

[1] Macroprosopus.

Nor even the hellish fire of Etna's maw.
But lucklessly we came upon a pool
Dank, dark, and stagnant, evil to the touch,
Oozing towards us, but sucked suddenly,
Silently, horribly, by slow compulsion
Into the slipping sand, and vanishing,
Whereon we saw a little boat appear,
And in it such a figure as we knew
Was Death.   But she, intolerant of delay,
Hailed him.   The vessel floated to our feet,
And Death was not.   She leapt within, and
    bent
Her own white shoulders to the thwart, and
    bade
Me steer, and keep stern watch with sword
    unsheathed
For fear of something that her soul had
    seen
Above.   And thus upon the oily black
Silent swift river we sailed out to reach
Its source, no longer feeling as compelled,
But led by some incomprehensible
Passion.   And here lewd fishes snapped
    at us,
And watersnakes writhed silently toward
Our craft.   But these I fought against, and
    smote
Head from foul body, to our further ill,
For frightful jelly-monsters grew apace,
And all the water grew one slimy mass
Of crawling tentacles.   My sword was swift
That slashed and slew them, chiefly to protect
The toiling woman, and assure our path
Through this foul hell.   And now the very
    air
Is thick with cold wet horrors.   With my
    sword
Trenchant, that tore their scaly essences—
Like Lucian's sailor writhing in the clutch
Of those witch-vines—I slashed about like
    light,
And noises horrible of death devoured
The hateful suction of their clinging arms
And wash of slipping bellies.   Presently
Sense failed, and—Nothing !
                    By-and-by we woke
In a most beautiful canoe of pearl
Lucent on lucent water, in a sun

That was the heart of spring.   But the green
    land
Seemed distant, with a sense of aery height ;
As if it were below us far, that seemed
Around.   And as we gazed the water grew
Ethereal, thin, most delicately hued,
Misty, as if its substance were dissolved
In some more subtle element.   We heard
" O passers over water, do ye dare
To tread the deadlier kingdoms of the air ? "
Whereat I cried : Arise !   And then the pearl
Budded with nautilus-wings, and upward now
Soared.   And our souls began to know the
    death
That was about to take us.   All our veins
Boiled with tumultuous and bursting blood ;
Our flesh broke bounds, and all our bones
    grew fierce,
As if some poison ate us up.   And lo !
The air is peopled with a devil-tribe
Born of our own selves.   These, grown
    furious
At dispossession by the subtle air,
Contend with us, who know the agony
Of half life drawn out lingering, who groan
Eaten as if by worms, who dash ourselves
Vainly against the ethereal essences
That make our boat, who vainly strive to
    cast
Our stricken bodies over the pale edge
And drop and end it all.   No nerve obeys ;
But in the torn web of our brains is born
The knowledge that release is higher yet.
So, lightened of the devils that possessed
In myriad hideousness our earthier lives,
With one swift impulse, we ourselves shake
    off
The clinging fiends, and shaking even the
    boat
As dust beneath our feet, leap up and run
Upward, and flash, and suddenly sigh back
Happy, and rest with limbs entwined at last
On pale blue air, the empyreal floor,
As on a bank of flowers in the old days
Before this journey.   So I think we slept.
But now, awaking, suddenly we feel
A sound as if within us, and without,
So penetrating and so self-inspired
                                    G

Sounded the voice we knew as God's.  The words
Were not a question any more, but said :
" The last and greatest is within you now."
Then fire too subtle and omniscient
Devoured our substance, and we moved again
Not down, not up, but inwards mystically
Involving self in self, and light in light.
And this was not a pain, but peaceable
Like young-eyed love, reviving ; it consumed
And consecrated and made savour sweet
To our changed senses.   And the dual self
Of love grew less distinct and I began
To feel her heart in mine, her lips in mine. . . .
Then mistier grew the sense of God without,
And God was I, and nothing might exist,
Subsist, or be at all, outside of Me,
Myself Existence of Existences.

.      .      .      .      .

We had passed unknowing to the woody crown
Of the little hill.   There was a secret Vault.
We entered.   All without the walls appeared
As fire, and all within as icy light ;
The altar was of gold, and on it burnt
Some ancient perfume.   Then I saw myself
And her together, as a priest, whose robe
Was white and frail, and covered with a cope
Of scarlet bound with gold : upon the head
A golden crown, wherein a diamond shone ;
Within which diamond we beheld our self
The higher priest, not clothed, but clothed upon
With the white brilliance of high nakedness
As with a garment.[1]   Then of our self there came
A voice : " Ye have attained to That which Is ;
Kiss, and the vision is fulfilled."   And so
Our bodies met, and, meeting, did not touch
But interpenetrated in the kiss.

.      .      .      .      .

This writing is engraved on lamina
Of silver, found by me, the trusted friend

[1] See the description of the robes and crown of the Magus in the "Book of the Sacred Magic of Abramelin the Mage."

And loving servant of my lady and lord,
In that abandoned Vault, of late destroyed
By Etna's fury.   Nothing else remained
(Save in the ante-room the sword we knew
So often flashing at the column-head)
Within.   I think my lord has written this.
Now for the child, whose rearing is my care,
And in whose life is left my single hope,
This writing shall conclude the book of song
His father made in worship and true love
Of his fair lady, and these songs shall be
His hope, and his tradition, and his pride.
Thus have I written for the sake of truth,
And for his sake who bears his father's sword—
I pray God under my fond guardianship
As worthily.   Thus far, and so—the end.


## THE HONOURABLE ADULTERERS

### I.

I LOOKED beneath her eyelids, where her eyes
Like stars were deep, and dim like summer skies ;
    I looked beneath their lashes ; and behold !
    My own thought mirrored in their maiden gold.
Shame drew to them to cloud their light with lies,
    And shrank back shamed ; but Love waxed bright and bold.

The devilish circle of the fiery ring[1]
Became one moment like a little thing,
    And Truth and God were near us to withdraw
    The veil of Love's unalterable law.
We feared no fury of the jealous King,
    But, lest in honour love should find a flaw.

[1] i e. the wedding ring.

Only our looks and trembling lips we dread,
And the dear nimbus of a lover's head,
   The dreamy splendour and the dim-delight
   That feels the fragrance fallen from the
     night,
When soul to soul is locked, and eyes are wed,
   And lips not touched kiss secretly by sight.

These things we fear, and move as in a mist
One from the other, and we had not kissed.
   Only the perfume of her lips and hair
   Love's angel wafted slowly to me there,
And as I went like death away I wist
   Its savour faded, nor my soul aware.

I turned and went away, away, away,
Out of the night that was to me the day,
   And rode to meet the sun to hide in light
   The sorrow of the day that was the night.
So I rode slowly in the morning gray,
   And all the meadows with the frost were
     white.

And lo ! between the mountains there uprose
The winter sun ; and all the forest glows,
   And the frost burns like fire before my
     eyes,
   While the white breeze awoke with slum-
     berous sighs
And stirred the branches of the pine ; it
     knows,
   It surely knows how weary are the wise !

Even my horse my sorrow understands,
Would turn and bear me to those western
     lands ;
   In love would turn me back ; in love would
     bring
   My thirsty lips to the one perfect spring—
My iron soul upon my trembling hands
   Had its harsh will ; my bitterness was king.

So verily long time I rode afar.
My course was lighted by some gloomy star
   That boded evil, that I would not shun,
   But rather welcome, as the storm the sun,
Lowering and red, a hurtful avatar,
   Whose fatal forehead like itself is dun

It was no wonder when the second day
Showed me a city on the desert way,
   Whose brazen gates were open, where
     within
   I saw a statue for a sign of sin,
And saw the people come to it and pray,
   Before its mouth set open for a gin.

And seeing me, a clamour rose among
Their dwarfish crowds, whose barbarous
     harsh tongue
   Grated, a hateful sound ; they plucked me
     down,
   And mocked me through the highways of
     the town,
And brought me where they sang to censers
     swung
   A grotesque hymn before her body brown.

For Sin was like a woman, and her feet
Shone, and her face was like the windy
     wheat ;
   Her eyes were keen and horrible and
     cold,
   Her bronze loins girdled with the sacred
     gold ;
Her lips were large, and from afar how
     sweet !
   How fierce and purple for a kiss to hold !

But somehow blood was black upon them ;
     blood
In stains and clots and splashes ; and the
     mud
   Trampled around her by the souls that
     knelt,
   Worshipping where her false lewd body
     dwelt,
Was dark and hateful ; and a sleepy flood
   Trickled therefrom as magic gums that
     melt.

I had no care that hour for anything :
Not for my love, not for myself ; I cling
   Desperate to despair, as some to hope,
   Unheeding Saturn in their horoscope ;
But I, despair is lord of me and king ;
   But I, my thoughts tend ever to the rope.

But I, unknightly, recreant, a coward,
Dare not release my soul from fate untoward
  By such a craven's cunning. Nay, my soul
  Must move unflinching to what bitter goal
The angry gods design—if gods be froward
I am a man, nor fear to drain the bowl.

Now some old devil, dead no doubt and damned,
But living in her life, had wisely crammed
  Her fierce bronze throat with such a foul device
  As made her belly yearn for sacrifice.
She leered like love on me, and smiled, and shammed,
  And did not pity for all her breast of spice.

They thrust me in her hateful jaws, and I
Even then resisted not, so fain to die
  Was my desire, so weary of the fight
  With my own love, so willing to be quite
Sure of my strength by death ; and eagerly
  Almost I crossed the barrier keen and white.

When lo ! a miracle ! Her carven hand
Is lifted, and the little space is spanned,
  And I am plucked from out her maw, and set
  Down on the pedestal, whose polished jet
Shone like a mirror out of hell—I stand
  Free, where the blood of other men is wet.

So slowly, while the mob stood back, I went
Out of the city, with no life content,
  And certain I should meet no death at least.
  Soon, riding ever to the stubborn east,
I came upon a shore whose ocean bent
  In one long curve, where folk were making feast.

So with no heart to feast, I joined the mirth,
Mingled the dances that delight the earth,
  And laughing looked in every face of guile.
  Quick was my glance and subtle was my smile ;
Ten thousand little loves were brought to birth,
  Ten thousand loves that laughed a little while.

No ; for one woman did not laugh, too wise !
But came so close, and looked within my eyes
  So deeply that I saw not anything.
  Only her eyes grew, as a purple ring
Shielding the sun. They grew ; they uttered lies—
  They fascinate and cleave to me and cling.

Then in their uttermost profound I saw
The veil of Love's unalterable law
  Lifted, and in the shadow far behind
  Dim and divine, within the shadow blind
My own love's face most amorously draw
  Out of the deep toward my cloudy mind.

O suddenly I felt a kiss enclose
My whole live body, as a rich red rose
  Folding its sweetness round the honey-bee !
  I felt a perfect soul embracing me,
And in my spirit like a river flows
  A passion like the passion of the sea.

## II.

He did not kiss me with his mouth ; his eyes
Kissed mine, and mine kissed back ; it was not wise,
But yet he had the strength to leave me ; so
I was so glad he loved enough to go.

My arms could never have released his neck ;
He saved our honour from a single speck.
And so he went away ; and fate inwove
The bitterest of treason for our love.

For scarce two days when sickness took the
    King,
And death dissolved the violence of the ring.
I ruled alone ; I left my palace gate
To see if Love should have the laugh at
    Fat .

And so I violated Death, and died ;
But in the other land my spirit cried
For incarnation ; conquering I came
Within my soulless body as a flame.

Endowing which with sacred power I sought
A little while, as thought that seeks for
    thought.
I found his changeless love endure as mine,
His passion curl around me as a vine.

So clinging fibres of desire control
My perfect body, and my perfect soul
Shot flakes of light toward him.   So my eyes,
Seeking his face, were made divinely wise.

So, solemn, silent, 'mid a merry folk
I bound him by my forehead's silver yoke,
And grew immense about him and within,
And so possessed him wholly, without sin.

For I had crossed the barrier and knew
There was no sin.   His lips reluctant grew
Ardent at last as recognising me,
And love's wild tempest sweeps upon his sea.

And I ? I knew not anything, but know
We are still silent, and united so,
And all our being spells one vast To Be,
A passion like the passion of the sea.


## THE LEGEND OF BEN LEDI.[1]

ON his couch Imperial Alpin[2]
    In majestic grandeur lay,
Dying with the sun that faded
    O'er the plain of granite gray.

[1] The " Hill of God."
[2] The first King of all Scotland.

Snowy white his beard descended,
    Flecked with foeman's crimson gore,
And he rose and grasped his broadsword,
    And he prayed to mighty Thor :

" God of thunder, god of battle,
    God of pillage and of war,
Hear the King of Scotland dying
    On the Leny's thundrous shore !

" Thrice three hundred have I smitten
    With my single arm this day ;
Now of life my soul is weary,
    I am old, I pass away.

" Grant me this, immortal monarch,
    Such a tomb as ne'er before,
Such a tomb as never after
    Monarch thought or monarch saw."

Then he called his sons around him,
    And he spake again and cried :
" Seven times a clansman's bowshot
    Lay me from the Leny's side.

" Where the plain to westward sinketh,
    Lay me in my tartan plaid,
All uncovered to the tempest,
    In my hand my trusty blade."

Hardly had he spake the order,
    When his spirit passed away ;
And his sons their heads uncovered
    As they bore him o'er the brae.

Seven times did Phail McAlpine
    Bend his mighty bow of yew ;
Seven times with lightning swiftness
    West the wingèd arrow flew.

Seven times a clansman's bowshot
    From the Leny's western shore,
Laid they him where on to Achray
    Spread the plain of Ian Vohr.

Hard by Teith's tumultuous waters
    Camped his sons throughout the night,
Till the rosy blush of morning
    Showed a vast majestic sight

Where of late the plain extended
  Rose a mighty mass of stone,
Pierced the clouds, and sprang unmeasured
  In magnificence—alone !

There the clansmen stood and wondered,
  As the rock, supremely dire,
Split and trembled, cracked and thundered,
  Lit with living flecks of fire.

Spake the chief : " My trusty clansmen,
  This is not the day of doom ;
This is honour to the mighty ;
  Clansmen, this is Alpin's tomb."

NYMPSFIELD RECTORY,
  *December* 1893.

## A DESCENT OF THE MOENCH.[1]
### JULY 14, 1896.

AN island of the mist.   White companies
Of clouds thronged wondrously against the
    hills,
And in the east a darkening of the winds
That held awhile their breath for very rage,
Too wild for aught but vaporous quivering
Of melting fleeces, while the sudden sun
Fled to his home.   Afar the Matterhorn
Reared a gaunt pinnacle athwart the bank,
Where towered behind it one vast pillar of
    cloud
To thrice its height.   **Behold** the ice-clad
    dome
On which we stood, all **weary of the way,**
And marked the east awaken into scorn,
And rush upon us.   Then we set our teeth
To force a dangerous passage, and essayed
The steep slope not in vain.   **We pushed our**
    way
Slowly and careworn down the **icy ridge,**
Hewing with ponderous strokes the **riven** ice
In little flakes and chips, and now **again**
Encountered strange and fearsome sentinels,

[1] The first guideless traverse of this mountain,
one of the peaks of the Bernese Oberland.

Gray pinnacles of lightning-riven rock
Fashioned of fire and night.   We clomb
    adown
Fantastic cliffs of gnarlèd stone, and saw
The vivid lightning flare in purple robes
Of flame along the ridge, and even heard
Its terrible crackle, 'mid the sullen roar
Of answering thunder.   Now the driven hail
Beat on our faces, while we strove to fling
Aloft the axe of forgèd steel, encased
In glittering ice, and smite unceasingly
On the unyielding slope of ice, as black
As those most imminent ghosts of Satan's
    frown
That shut us out from heaven, while the
    snow
Froze on our cheeks.   Thus then we gained
    the field
Where precipice and overwhelming rock,
Avalanche, crag, leap through the dazzled air
To pile their mass in one Lethean plain
Of undulations of rolled billowy snow
Rent, seamed, and scarred with wound on
    jagged wound,
Blue-rushing to the vague expanse below
Of the unknown secrecies of mountain song.
Dragging behind us beautiful weary limbs,
We turned snow-blinded eyes towards the
    pass [1]
That shot a jasper wall above the mist
Into the lightning-kindled firmament,
Behind whose battlements a shelter [2] lay,
Rude-built of pine, whose parents in the
    storm
Of some vast avalanche were swept away
Into the valley.   Thither we hasted on,
And there, as night stretched out a broken
    wing
Torn by the thunder and the bitter strife
Of warring flames and tempest's wrath, we
    came
And flung ourselves within, and laid us down
At last to sleep ; and Sleep, a veinèd shape
Of naked stateliness, came down to us,
And tenderly stooped down, and kissed our
    brows.

[1] The Mönchjoch.
[2] The Berglihütte.

## IN A CORNFIELD.

O VOICE of sightless magic
  Clear through day's crystal sky,
Blithe, contemplative, tragic,
  As men may laugh or sigh ;
As men may love or sorrow,
  Their moods thy music borrow
    To bid them live or die.
So sweet, so sad, so lonely,
In silent noontide only
  Thy song-wings float and lie
On cloud-foam scarred and riven,
By God's red lightnings shriven,
And quiet hours are given
  To him that lingers nigh.

Fain would I linger near thee
  Amid the poppies red,
Forget this world, and hear thee
  As one among the dead ;
Amid the daffadillies,
Red tulips and white lilies,
  Where daisies' tears are shed ;
Where larkspur and cornflower
Are blue with sunlight's hour,
  And all the earth is spread
As in a dream before me ;
While steals divinely o'er me
Love's scented spring to draw me
  From moods of dreamy dread.

O wingèd passion ! traveller
  Too near to God to see !
O lyrical unraveller
  Of knotted life to me !
O song ! O shining river
Of thought and sound ! O giver
  Of goodly words of glee !
Like to a star that singeth,
A flower that incense bringeth,
  A love-song of the free !
Oh ! let me sing thy glories
While spring winds whisper stories
Of winter past, whose shore is
  Beyond a shoreless sea.

Sing on, thou lyric lover !
  Sing on, and thrill me long
With such delights as cover
  The days and deeds of wrong !
Live lyre of songs immortal
That pierce Heaven's fiery portal
  With shafts of splendour strong,
Winged with thought's sharpest fires,
Arrowed with soul's desires
  And sped from thunder's thong ;
Heaven's gates rock, rage, and quiver,
Earth's walls gape wide and shiver,
While Freedom doth deliver
  Men's spirits with thy song.

Ah, chainless, distant, fleeting,
  To lands that know no sea,
Where ocean's stormy greeting
  Fills no man's heart with glee ;
Where lovers die or sever, .
And death destroys for ever,
  And God bears slavery :—
Fly thither, so thou leave us
That no man's hand may reave us
  Of this—that we are free.
Free all men that may heed thee,
On freemen's praises feed thee,
Who chorus full, " God speed thee,
  Live lyre of Liberty !"

## DREAMS.

WHAT words are these that shudder through
    my sleep,
  Changing from silver into crimson flakes,
    And molten into gold
Like the pale opal through whose gray may
    sweep
  A scarlet flame, like eyes of crested snakes,
    Keen, furious, and too cold.

What words are these ?  The pall of slumber
    lifts ;
  The veil of finiteness withdraws.   The
    night
    Is heavier, life burns low :

Yet to the quivering brain three goodly
    gifts
  The cruelty of Pluto and his might
    In the abyss bestow:

Change, foresight, fear.   The pageant whirls
    and boils;
  Restricted not by space and time, my
    dream
  Foresees the doom of Fate ;
My spirit wrestles in the Dream-King's toils
  Always in vain, and Hope's forerunners
    gleam
  Alway one step too late.

Not as when sunlight strikes the counter-
    pane ;
  Half wakening, sleep rolls back her iron
    wave,
  And dawn brings blithesomeness ;
Not as when opiates lull the tortured brain
  And sprinkle lotus on the drowsy grave
  Of earth's old bitterness ;

But as when consciousness half rouses up
  And hurls back all the gibbering harpy
    crowd ;
  And sleep's draught deepeneth,
And all the furies of hell's belly sup
  In the brain's palaces, and chant aloud
  Songs that foretaste of Death.

Maddened, the brain breaks from beneath
    the goad,
  Flings off again the foe, and from its
    hell
  Brings for a moment peace,
Till weariness and her infernal load
  Of phantom memory-shapes return to quell
  The shaken fortresses.

Till nature reassert her empery,
  And the full tide of wakefulness at last
  Foam on the shore of sleep
To beat the white cliffs of reality
  In vain, because their windy strength is
    past,
  And only memories weep.

Why is the Finite real ?   And that world
  So larger, so more beautiful and fleet,
    So free, so exquisite,
The world of dreams and shadows, not
    impearled
  With solitary shaft of Truth?   Too sweet,
    O children of the Night,

Are your wide realms for our philoso-
    phers,
  Who must in hard gray balance-shackles
    bind
    The essence of all thought :
No sorrier sexton in a grave inters
  The nobler children of a poet's mind
    Of wine and gold well wrought.

By the poor sense of touch they judge that
    this
  Or that is real or not.   Have they divined
    This simplest spirit-bond,
The joy of some bad woman's deadly
    kiss ;
  The thought-flash that well tunes a lover's
    mind
    Seas and gray gulfs beyond ?

So that which is impalpable to touch,
  They judge by touch; the viewless they
    decide
    By sight ; their logic fails,
Their jarring jargon jingles—even such
  An empty brazen pot—wise men deride
    The clouds that mimic whales.

My world shall be my dreams.   Religion
    there
  And duty may disturb me not at all ;
    Nor doubts, nor fear of death.
I straddle on no haggard ghostly mare ;
  Yea, through my God, I have leapt o'er a
    wall !
    (As poet David saith.)

The wall that ever girds Earth's thought with
    brass
  Is all a silver path my feet beneath,
    And o'er its level sward

Of sea-reflecting white flowers and fresh
    grass
  I walk.   Man's darkness is a leathern
    sheath,
    Myself the sun-bright sword !

I have no fear, nor doubt, nor sorrow now,
  For I give Self to God—I give my best
    Of soul and blood and brain
To my poor Art—there comes to me some-
    how
    This fact : Man's work is God made mani-
      fest ;
      Life is all Peace again.

And Dreams are beyond life.   Their wider
    scope,
    Limitless Empire o'er the world of thought,
    Help my desires to press
Beyond all stars toward God and Heaven
    and Hope ;
    And in the world-amazing chase is wrought
      Somehow—all Happiness.


## THE TRIUMPH OF MAN.

BEFORE the darkness, earlier than being,
When yet thought was not, shapeless and
    unseeing,
Made misbegotten of deity on death,
There brooded on the waters the strange
    breath
Of an incarnate hatred.   Darkness fell
And chaos, from prodigious gulphs of hell.
Life, that rejoiced to travail with a man,
Looked where the cohorts of destruction ran,
Saw darkness visible, and was afraid,
Seeing.   There grew like Death a monster
    shade,
Blind as the coffin, as the covering sod
Damp, as the corpse obscene, the Christian
    God.
So to the agony dirges of despair
Man cleft the womb, and shook the icy air
With bitter cries for light and life and love.
But these, begotten of the world above,

Withdrew their glory, and the iron world
Rolled on its cruel way, and passion furled
Its pure wings, and abased itself, and bore
Fetters impure, and stooped, and was no
    more.
But resurrection's ghastly power grew strong,
And Lust was born, adulterous with Wrong,
The Child of Lies ; so man was blinded still,
Garnered the harvest of abortive ill,
For wheat reaped thistles, and for worship
    wrought
A fouler idol of his meanest thought :
A monster, vengeful, cruel, traitor, slave,
Lord of disease and father of the grave,
A treacherous bully, feeble as malign,
Intolerable, inhuman, undivine,
With spite close girded and with hatred shod,
A snarling cur, the Christian's Christless God.
Out ! misbegotten monster ! with thy brood,
The obscene offspring of thy pigritude,
Incestuous wedlock with the Pharisees
That hail the Christ a son of thee !   Our
    knees
Bend not before thee, and our earth-bowed
    brows
Shake off their worship, and reject thy
    spouse,
The harlot of the world !   For, proud and
    free,
We stand beyond thy hatred, even we :
We broken in spirit beneath bitter years,
Branded with the burnt-offering of tears,
Spit out upon the lie, and in thy face
Cast back the slimy falsehood ; to your place,
Ye Gadarean swine, too foul to fling
Into the waters that abound and spring !
Back, to your mother filth !   With hope, and
    youth,
Love, light, and power, and mastery of truth
Armed, we reject you ; the bright scourge we
    ply,
Your howling spirits stumble to your sty :
The worm that was your lie—our heel its
    head
Bruises, that bruised us once ; the snake is
    dead.
Who of mankind that honours man discerns
That man of all men, whose high spirit burns,

Crowned over life, and conqueror of death,
The godhood that was Christ of Nazareth—
Who of all men, that will not gird his brand
And purge from priestcraft the uxorious land?
Christ, who lived, died, and lived, that man
    might be
Tameless and tranquil as the summer sea,
That laughs with love of the broad skies of
    noon,
And dreams of lazy kissings of the moon,
But listens for the summons of the wind,
Shakes its white mane, and hurls its fury
    blind
Against oppression, gathers its steep side,
Rears as a springing tiger, flings its tide
Tremendous on the barriers, smites the sand,
And gluts its hunger on the breaking land;
Engulphing waters fall and overwhelm:—
Christ, who stood dauntless at the shaken
    helm
On Galilee, who quelled the wrath of God,
And rose triumphant over faith, and trod
With calm victorious feet the icy way
When springtide burgeoned, and the rosy
    day
Leapt from beneath the splendours of the
    snow:—
Christ, ultimate master of man's hateful foe,
And lord of his own soul and fate, strikes
    still
From man's own heaven, against the lord of
    ill;
Stage thunders mock the once terrific nod
That spoke the fury of the Christian God,
Whose slaves deny, too cowardly to abjure,
Their desecrated Moloch. The impure
Godhead is powerless, even on the slave,
Who once could scar the forehead of the
    brave,
Break love's heart pitiful, and reach the
    strong
Through stricken children, and a mother's
    wrong.
Day after darkness, life beyond the tomb!
Manhood reluctant from religion's womb
Leaps, and sweet laughters flash for freedom's
    birth
That thrills the old bosom of maternal earth.

The dawn has broken; yet the impure fierce
    fire
Kindles the grievous furnace of desire
Still for the harpy brood of king and priest,
Slave, harlot, coward, that make human feast
Before the desecrated god, in hells
Of darkness, where the mitred vampire
    dwells,
Where still death reigns, and God and priests
    are fed,
Man's blood for wine, man's flesh for meat
    and bread,
The lands of murder, of the obscene things
That snarl at freedom, broken by her wings,
That prop the abomination, cringe and smile,
Caressing the dead fetich, that defile
With hideous sacraments the happy land.
Destruction claims its own; the hero's hand
Grips the snake's throat; yea, on its head
    is set
The heel that crushes it, the serpent wet
With that foul blood, from human vitals
    drained,
From tears of broken women, and sweat
    stained
From torturers' cloths; the sickly tide is
    poured,
And all the earth is blasted; the green
    sward
Burns where it touches, and the barren sod
Rejects the poison of the blood of God.
Yet, through the foam of waters that enclose
Their sweet salt bosoms, through the summer
    rose,
Through flowers of fatal fire, through fields
    of air
That summer squanders, ere the bright moon
    bare
Her maiden bosom, through the kissing gold
Where lovers' lips are molten, and breasts
    hold
Their sister bodies, and deep eyes are wed,
And fire of fire enflowers the sacred head
Of mingling passion, through the silent sleep
Where love sobs out its life, and new loves
    leap
To being, through the dawn of all new things,
There burns an angel whose amazing wings

Wave in the sunbright air, whose lips of
    flame
Chant the almighty music of One Name
Whose perfume fills the silent atmosphere,
Whose passionate melodies caress the ear ;
An angel, strong and eloquent, aloud
Cries to the earth to lift the final shroud,
And, having burst Faith's coffin, to lay by
The winding-sheet of Infidelity,
And rise up naked, as a god, to hear
This message from the reawakened sphere ;
Words with love clothed, with life immortal
    shod :—
" Mankind is made a little part of God." [1]
Till the response, full chorus of the earth,
Flash through the splendid portals of re-
    birth,
Completing Truth in its amazing span :—
" Godhead is made the Spirit that is Man."
To whose white mountains, and their arduous
    ways,
Turn we our purpose, till the faith that
    slays
Yield up its place to faith that gives us
    life,
The faith to conquer in the higher strife ;
Our single purpose, and sublime intent,
With their spilt blood to seal our sacra-
    ment,
Who stand among the martyrs of the
    Light ;
Our single purpose, by incarnate might
Begotten after travail unto death,
To live within the light that quickeneth ;
To tread base thoughts as our high thoughts
    have trod,
Deep in the dust, the carrion that was God ;
Conquer our hatreds as the dawn of love
Conquered that fiend whose ruinous throne
    above
Broke lofty spirits once, now falls with Fate,
At last through his own violence violate ;

[1] *i.e.* the idea of God, dissociated from the
legends of priests, and assimilated to the
impersonal Parabrahma of the Hindu. This
dual use of the word is common throughout
Crowley : the context is everywhere sufficient
to decide. In the play " Jephthah," however,
conventional ideas are followed.

To live in life, breathe freedom with each
    breath,
As God breathed tyranny and died in
    death ;
Secure the sacred fastness of the soul,
Uniting self to the absolute, the whole,
The universal marriage of mankind,
Free, perfect, broken from the chains that
    bind,
Force infinite, love pure, desire untold,
And mutual raptures of the age of gold,
The child of freedom ! So the moulder,
    man,
Shakes his grim shoulders, and the shadows
    wan
Fall to forgetfulness ; so life revives
And new sweet loves beget diviner lives,
And Freedom stands, re-risen from the
    rod,
A goodlier godhead than the broken God ;
Uniting all the universe in this
Music more musical than breezes' kiss,
A song more potent than the sullen sea,
The triumph of the freedom of the free ;
One stronger song than thrilled the rapturous
    birth
Of stars and planets and the mother, earth ;
As lovers, calling lovers when they die,
Strangle death's torture in love's agony ;
As waters, shaken by the storm, that roar,
Sea unto sea ; as stars that burn before
The blackness ; as the mighty cry of swords
Raging through battle, for its stronger chords ;
And for its low entrancing music, made
As waters lambent in the listening glade ;
As Sappho's yearning to the amorous sea ;
As Man's Prometheus, in captivity
Master and freeman ; as the holy tune
All birds, all lovers, whisper to the moon.
So, passionate and pure, the strong chant
    rolls,
Queen of the mystic unity of souls ;
So from eternity its glory springs
King of the magical brotherhood of kings ;
The absolute crown and kingdom of desire,
Earth's virgin chaplet, molten in the fire,
Sealed in the sea, betokened by the wind :
" There is one God, the Spirit of Mankind ! "

## THE DREAMING DEATH.[1]

MY beauty in thy deep pure love
Anchors its homage far above
All lights of heaven.   The stars awake ;
The very stars bend down to take
From its fresh fragrance for the sake
Of their own cloud-compelling peace.
On earth there lies a silver fleece
Of new-fallen snow, secure from sun,
In alleys, leafy every one
This year already with the spring.
The breeze blows freshly, thrushes sing,
And all the woods are burgeoning
With quick new buds ; across the snow
The scent of violets to and fro
Wafts at the hour of dawn.   Alone
I wait, a figure turned to stone
(Or salt for pain).   A week ago
Thine arms embraced me ; now I know
Far off they clasp the empty air :
Thy lips seek home, and in despair
Lament aloud over the frosted moor.
Sad am I, sad, albeit sure
There is no change of God above
And no abatement of our love.
For still, though thou be gone, I see
In the glad mirror secretly
That I am beautiful in thee.
Thy love irradiates my eyes,
Tints my skin gold ; its melodies
Of music run over my face ;
Smiles envy kisses in the race
To bathe beneath my eyelids.   Light
Clothes me and circles with the might
Of warmer rosier suns.   Thy kiss
Dwells on my bosom, and it is
A glittering mount of fire, that burns
Incense unnamed to heaven, and yearns
In smoke toward thy home.   Desire
Bellies the sails of molten fire
Upon the ship of Youth with wind
Urgently panting out behind,
Impatient till the strand appear

[1] The scene of this poem is a little spinney
near the wooden bridge in Love Lane, Cambridge.—A. C.

And the blue sea have ceased to rear
Fountains of foam against the prow.
Hail !   I can vision even now
That golden shore.   A lake of light
Burns to the sky ; above, the night
Hovers, her wings grown luminous.
(I think she dearly loveth us.)
The sand along the glittering shore
Is all of diamond ; rivers pour
Unceasing floods of light along,
Whose virtue is so bitter strong
That he who bathes within them straight
Rises an angel to the gate
Of heaven and enters as a king.
Birds people it on varied wing
Of rainbow ; fishes gold and fine
Dart like bright stars through fount and brine,
And all the sea about our wake
Foams with the silver water-snake.
There is a palace veiled in mist.
A single magic amethyst
Built it ; the incense soothly sighs ;
So the light steam upon it lies.
There thou art dwelling.   I am ware
The music of thine eyes and hair
Calls to the wind to chase our ship
Faster toward ; the waters slip
Smoothly and swift beneath the keel.
The pulses of the vessel feel
I draw toward thee ; now the sails
'Hang idly, for the golden gales
Drop as the vessel grates the sand.
Come, thou true love, and hold my hand !
I tremble (for my love) to land.
I feel thy arms around me steal ;
Thy breath upon my cheeks I feel ;
Thy lips draw out to mine : the breath
Of ocean grows as still as death ;
The breezes swoon for very bliss.
The sacrament of true love's kiss
Accomplishes : I feel a pain
Stab my heart through and sleep again,
And I am in thine arms for ever.

.      .      .      .      .      .

There came a tutor, who had never
Known the response of love to love ;
He wandered through the woods above
The river, and came suddenly

Where he lay sleeping.   Purity
And joy beyond the speech of man
Dwelt on his face, divinely wan.
" How beautiful is sleep ! " he saith,
Bends over him.   There is no breath,
No sound, no motion : it is death.
And gazing on the happy head
" How beautiful is Death ! " he said.

## A SONNET IN SPRING.

O CHAINLESS Love, the frost is in my brain,
   Whose swift desires and swift intelligence
   Are dull and numb to-day ; because the
      sense
Only responds to the sharp key of pain.
O free fair Love, as welcome as the rain
   On thirsty fallows, come, and let us hence
   Far where the veil of Summer lies immense,
A haze of heat on ocean's purple plain.

O wingless Love, let us away together
   Where the sure surf rings round the beaten
      strand ;
Where the sky stands, a dome of flawless
   weather,
And the stars join in one triumphal band,
Because we broke the inexorable tether
   That bound our passion with an iron hand.

## DE PROFUNDIS.[1]

BLOOD, mist, and foamy then darkness.   On
   my eyes
Sits heaviness, the poor worn body lies
   Devoid of nerve and muscle ; it were death
Save for the heart that throbs, the breast
   that sighs.

The brain reels drowsily, the mind is dulled,
Deadened and drowned by noises that are
   lulled
By the harsh poison of the hateful breath.
All sense and sound and seeing is annulled.

[1] Composed while walking home through
the starry streets from an evil evening in St.
Petersburg. Vv. 1–3 are the feelings, vv. *sqq.*,
the reflections thus engendered.

Within a body dead a deadened brain
Beats with the burden of a shameful pain,
   The sullen agony that dares to think,
And think through sleep, and wake to think
   again.

Fools ! bitter fools !   Our breaths and kisses
   seem
Constrained in devilry, debauch, and dream :
   Lives logged in the morass of meat and
   drink,
Loves dipped in Phlegethon,[1] the perjured
   stream.

Behold we would that hours and minutes
   pass,
Watch the sands falling in the eager glass ;
   To wile their weariness is pleasure's bliss ;
But ah ! the years ! like smoke They fade,
   alas !

We weep them as they slip away ;  we gaze
Back on the likeness of the former days—
   The hair we fondle and the lips we kiss—
Roses grow yellow and no purple stays.

Ah ! the old years !  Come back, ye vanished
   hours
We wasted ;  come, grow red, ye faded
   flowers !
   What boots the weariness of olden time
Now, when old age, a tempest-fury, lowers ?

Up to high God beyond the weary land
The days drift mournfully ;  His hoary hand
   Gathers them.   Is it so ?   My foolish
   rhyme
Dreams they are links upon an endless band.

The planets draw in endless orbits round
The sun ;  itself revolves in the profound
   Deep wells of space ;  the comet's mystic
   track
By the strong rule of a closed curve is bound.

[1] The fiery river of Hades.

Why not with time ?   To-morrow we may see
The circle ended—if to-morrow be—
    And gaze on chaos, and a week bring back
Adam and Eve beneath the apple tree.

Or, like the comet, the wild race may end
Out into darkness, and our circle bend
    Round to all glory in a sudden sweep,
And speed triumphant with the sun to friend.

Love will not leave my home.   She knows
    my tears,
My angers and caprices ; still my ears
    Listen to singing voices, till I weep
Once more, less sadly, and set hounds on fears.

She will not leave me comfortless.   And
    why ?
Through the dimmed glory of my clouded
    eye
    She catches one sharp glint of love for
    her :
She will not leave me ever till I die :—

Nay, though I die !   Beyond the distant gloom
Heaven springs, a fountain, out of Change's
    womb !
    Time would all men within the grave
    inter :—
For Time himself shall no god find a tomb?

Glory and love and work precipitate
The end of man's desire—so sayeth Fate.
    Man answers : Love is stronger, work more
    sure,
Glory more fadeless than her shafts abate.

Though all worlds fail, the pulse of Life be
    still,
God fall, all darken, she hath not her will
    Of deeds beyond recall, that shall endure :
For us, these three divinest glasses fill,

Fill to the brim with lustrous dew, nor fail
To leave the blossom and the nightingale,
    Love's earlier kiss, and manhood's glowing
    prime,
These us suffice.   Shall man or Fate prevail ?

Lo, we are blind, and dubious fingers grope
In Despair's dungeon for the key of Hope ; [1]
    Lo, we are chained, and with a broken
    rhyme
Would file our fetters and enlarge our scope.

Yet ants may move the mountain ; none is
    small
But he who stretches out no arm at all ;
    Toadstools have wrecked fair cities in a
    night,
One poet's song may bid a kingdom fall.

Add to thy fellow-men one ounce of aid—
The block begins to shift, the start is made :
    The rest is thine ; with overwhelming might
The balance changes, and the task is paid.

Join'st thou thy feeble hands in foolish prayer
To him thy brain hath moulded and set there
    In thy brain's heaven ?   Such a god replies
As thy fears move.   So men pray everywhere.

What God there be, is real.   By His might
Begot the universe within the night ;
    If he had prayed to His own mind's weak
    lies
Think'st thou the heaven and earth had stood
    upright ?

Remember Him, but smite !   No workman
    hews
His stone aright whose nervy arms refuse
    To ply the chisel, but are raised to ask
A visionary foreman he may choose

From the distortions of a sodden mind.
God did first w o r k on earth when woman-
    kind
    He chipped from Adam's rib—a thankless
    task
I wot His wisdom has long since repined.

[1] See Bunyan's Pilgrim's Progress, where
Hope unlocks the dungeon of Giant Despair.
Crowley more wisely would use the key of
Work.

Christ t o u c h e d the leper and the widow's
  son ;
And thou wouldst serve the work the Perfect
  One
Began, by folding arms and gazing up
To heaven, as if thy work were rightly done.

I tell thee, He should say, if ye were met :
" Thou hadst a talent—ah, thou hast it yet
  Wrapped in a napkin ! thou shalt drain
    the cup
Of that damnation that may not forget

" The wasted hours ! "  Ah, bitter interest
Of our youth's capital—forgotten zest
  In all the pleasures of o'erflowing life,
Wine tasteless, tired the brain, and cold the
    breast !

Ah ! but if with it is one good deed wrought,
One kind word spoken, one immortal thought
  Born in thee, all is paid ; the weary strife
Grows victory.  " Love is all and Death is
    nought."

Such an one wrote that word[1] as I would meet,
Lay my life's burden at his silver feet,
  Have him give ear if I say " Master." Yea !
I know no heaven, no honour, half so sweet !

He passed before me on the wheel of Time,
He who knows no Time—the intense sublime
  Master of all philosophy and play,
Lord of all love and music and sweet rhyme.

Follow thou him !  Work ever, if thy heart
Be fervent with one hope, thy brain with art,
  Thy lips with song, thine arm with strength
    to smite :
Achieve some act ; its name shall not depart.

Christ laid Love's corner-stone, and Cæsar
    built
The tower of glory ; Sappho's life was spilt
  From fervent lips the torch of song to
    ignite :
Thou mayst add yet a stone—if but thou wilt.

  [1] Browning, in " The Householder."

And yet the days stream by ; night shakes
    the day
From his pale throne of purple, to allay
  The tremors of the earth ; day smiteth dark
With the swift poignard dipped in Helios' ray.

The days stream by ; with lips and cheeks
    grown pale
On their indomitable breast we sail.
  There is a favouring wind ; our idle bark
Lingers, we raise no silk to meet the gale.

The bank slips by, we gather not its fruit,
We plant no seed, we irrigate no root
  True men have planted ; and the tare and
    thorn
Spring to rank weedy vigour ; poisons shoot

Into the overspreading foliage ;
So as days darken into weary age
  The  flowers  are  fewer ;  the  weeds  are
    stronger born
And hands are grown too feeble to assuage

Their venom ; then, the unutterable sea !
Is she green-cinctured with the earlier tree
  Of Life ?  Do blossoms blow, or weeds
    create
A foul rank undergrowth of misery ?

From the deep water of the bitterest brine
Drowned children raise their arms ; their lips
    combine
  To force a shriek ; bid them go con-
    template
The cold philosophy of Zeno's[1] shrine ?

Nay, stretch a hand !  Although their eagle
    clutch
O'erturn thy skiff, yet it is overmuch
  To grieve for that : life is not so divine—
I count it little grief to part with such !

  [1] The Stoic.  To be distinguished from the
Eleatic and the Epicurean of the same name.
He was born at Citium in Cyprus in 340 B.C.
He preached ἀπάθεια, happiness in oneself in-
dependent of all circumstance, as the highest
good.

We are wild serpents in a ring of fire ;
Our necks stretch out, our haggard eyes
    aspire
In desperation ; from the fearful line
Our coils revulse in impotence and ire.

An idle song it was the poet sang,
A quavering note—no brazen kettle's clang,
    But gentle, drooping, tearful.    Nay,
    achieve !
I can remember how the finish rang

Clear, sharp, and loud ; the harp is glad to
    die
And give the clarion one note silver-high.
    It was too sweet for music, and I weave
In vain the tattered woof of memory.

Ashes and dust !
    Cold cinders dead !
Our swords are rust ;
    Our lives are fled
Like dew on glass.
    In vain we lust ;
Our hopes are sped,
    Alas ! alas !
From heaven we are thrust, we have no more
    trust.
    Alas !

Gold hairs and gray !
    Red lips and white !
Warm hearts, cold clay !
    Bright day, dim night !
Our spirits pass
    Like the hours away.
We have no light,
    Alas ! alas !
We have no more day, we are fain to say
    Alas !

In Love's a cure
    For Fortune's hate ;
In Love's a lure
    Shall laugh at Fate ;
We have tolled Death's knell ;
    All streams are pure ;

We are new-create ;
    All's well, all's well !
We have God to endure, we are very sure
    All's well !

In such wise rang the challenge unto Death
With  clear  high  eloquence  and  happy
    breath ;
    So did a brave sad heart grow glad again
And mock the riddle that the dead Sphinx
    saith.

When I am dead, remember me for this
That I bade workers work, and lovers kiss ;
    Laughed with the Stoic at the dream of
    pain,
And preached with Jesus [1] the evangel—bliss.

When I am dead, think kindly.    Frail my
    song ?
'Twas the poor utterance of an eager tongue ;
    I stutter in my rhyme ? my heart was full
Of greater longings, more divinely wrung

By love and pity and regret and trust,
High  hope  from heaven that God will be
    just,
    Spurn not the child because his mind was
    dull,
Still less condemn him for his father's lust.

Yet I think priests shall answer Him in vain :
Their gospel of disgrace, disease, and pain,
    Shall  move  His heart of Love to such a
    wrath—
O Heart !   Turn back and look on Love
    again !

Behold, I have seen visions, and dreamed
    dreams !
My verses eddy in slow wandering streams,
    Veer like the wind, and know no certain
    path—
Yet their worst shades are tinged with dawn-
    ing beams !

[1] The all sion betrays Crowley's ignorance
(at this time) of the results of modern criticism
of the New Testament.

I have dreamed life a circle or a line,
Called God, and Fate, and Chance, and Man,
      divine.
   I know not all I say, but through it all
Mark the dim hint of ultimate sunshine !

Remember me for this !  And when I go
To sleep the last sleep in the slumberous snow,
   Let child and man and woman yet re-
      call
One little moment that I loved you so !

Let some high pinnacle my tombstone be,
My epitaph the murmur of the sea,
   The clouds of heaven be fleeces for my
      pall,
My unknown grave the cradle of the free.


## TWO SONNETS

ON HEARING THE MUSIC OF BRAHMS
AND TSCHAIKOWSKY.

*To* C. G. LAMB.

### I.

MY soul is aching with the sense of sound
   Whose angels trumpet in the angry air ;
Wild mænads with their fiery snakes en-
      wound
In the black waves of my abundant hair.
Now hath my life a little respite found
   In the brief pauses exquisite and rare ;
In the strong chain of music I am bound,
   And all myself before myself lies bare.

Drown me, oh, drown me in your fiery
      stream !
   Wing me new visions, fierce enchanting
      birds !
      Peace is less dear than this delirious
         fight !
For all the glowing fragrance of a dream
   And all the sudden ecstasy of words
      Deluge my spirit with a lake of light.

### II.

The constant ripple of your long white hands,
   The soul-tormenting violin that speaks
Truth, and enunciates all my soul seeks,
That binds my love in its desirous bands,
And clutches at my heart, until there stands
   No fibre yet unshaken, while it wreaks
   In one sharp song the agony of weeks,
And all my soul and body understands.

The music changes, and I know that here,
   In these new melodies, a tongue of fire
Leaps at each waving of the silver spear ;
   And all my sorrow dons delight's attire
Because the gate of Heaven is so near,
   And I have comprehended my desire.


## A VALENTINE.

(FEB. 14, 1897.)

WHY did you smile when the summer was
      dying
   If it were not that the hours
Might bring in winter, while sad winds are
      sighing,
   Some of Love's flowers ?

Now is beginning of spring, and I ask not
   Roses to flame o'er the lawn—
Who should know better that peonies bask
      not
   In the sun's dawn ?

Still, through the snow, it may be there is
      peeping
   Veiled from the kiss of the sun
One lone white violet, daintily sleeping,
   Hard to be won.

So with my fairy white maiden (you hear
      me ?)
   Winter may yet pass away ;
Spring may arrive, (will it find your heart
      near me ?)
   Summer may stay.

H

Passionate roses I seek not, whose glories
  Now are too fierce for the spring,
While the white flames of the frost flake that
    hoar is
  Flicker, on wing.

Only a primrose, a violet laden
  With the pale perfume of dawn ;
Only a snowdrop, my delicate maiden ;
  These have no thorn.

Old-fashioned love, yet you feel it a fountain
  Springing for ever, most pure ;
Old-fashioned love, yet as adamant mountain
  Solid and sure.

Yes, tender thoughts on your lips will be
    breaking
  By-and-by into a smile ;
Love, ere he springs up divine at his waking,
  Slumbers awhile.

So, my kissed snowdrop, you took its white
    blossom
  Tenderly into your hand,
Kissed it three times, wear it yet in your
    bosom—
  I understand.

## ODE TO POESY.

UNTO what likeness shall I liken thee,
O moon-wrought maiden of my dewy sleep?
For thou art Queen of Thoughts, and unto me
  Sister and Bride ; the worn earth's echoes
    leap
Because thy holy name is Poesy.
  Whereto art thou most like?
Thou art a Dian, crescent o'er the sea
  That beats sonorous on the craggy shore,
  Or shakes the frail earth-dyke.
  So calm and still and far, that never more
Thy silken song shall quiver through the
    land ;
Only by coral isle, by lonely strand
Where no man dwells, thy voice re-wakens
  wild and grand.

Thou art an Aphrodite.  From the foam
  Of golden grape and red thou risest up
Immaculate ; thou hast an ebon comb
  Of shade and silence, and a jasper cup
Wherein are mingled all desires.  Thine home
  Is in the forest shade.
Thy pale feet kiss the daffodils ; they roam
  By moss-grown springs, and shake the
    bluebell tips.
  Each flower of the deep glade
  Has whispered kisses for thy listening lips,
While Eos blushes in the sky, to find
A fairer, queenlier maiden, and as kind
To man and maid, whose eyes are lit by the
  same mind.

Thou hast, as Pallas hath, a polished shield,
  Whose Gorgon-head is Hatred, and a sword
Sharper than Love's.  Thy wisdom is revealed
  To them who love, but thou hast aye ab-
    horred
The children of revenge ; to them is sealed
  Thy book, so clear to me.
Thy book where seven sins their sceptres
    wield,
  And seven sorrows track them, and one joy
  Cancels their infamy ;
Shame and regret are fused to an alloy,
Whose drossy weight sinks down and is
  consumed,
While o'er the ruddy metal is relumed
A purer flame of peace, with knowledge now
  perfumed.

Thy ways are very bitter.  Not one rose
  Twines in the crown of thorns thy spouse
    must wear ;
There is no Lethe for the scoffs, the blows,
  Nor find they a Cyrenian [1] anywhere
  Amid the mob, to lift my cross, to share
    Its burden : not one friend
Whose love were silence, whose affection
  knows
  To press my hand and close my dying eyes
    There, at the endless end.
I am alone on earth, and from the skies

[1] Simon the Cyrenian, who bore the cross
of Christ.

Sometimes I seem so far—and yet, thy kiss
Re-quickens Hope ; through æther's emptiness
Thou guidest me to touch the Hand of Him
who Is.

Thou hadst a torch to lume my lips to song ;
Thou hast a cooler fountain for my thirst,
Lest my young love should work thy fame
a wrong ;
So the grape's veins in purple ardour burst,
And opiates in bloomless gardens throng,
And Life, a moon, wanes fast ;
But to thy garden richer buds belong
And hardier flowers, and Love, a death-
less sun,
Flames eager to the last,
And young desires in fleeter revels run,
And Life revives, and all the flowers rejoice,
Bird and light butterfly have made their choice,
Creation hymns its God with an united voice.

There is a storm without.  The hoary trees
Stagger ; the foam is angry on the sea :
I know the secret mountains are at ease,
And in the deepest ice-embroidery
Where great men's spirits linger there is
peace.
Heed not the unquiet wind !
Dawn's finger shall be raised, its wrath shall
cease,
The sun shall rouse us whom the tempest
lulled,
And thy poor poet's mind
For respite by its own deep anguish dulled
Shall wake again to watch the cruel day
Drift slowly on its chill and wasted way
With but thy smile to inspire some sad
melodious lay.

From whose rude caverns sweep these gusty
wings
That shake the steeples as they mock at
God ?
Who reared the stallion wind ?  Whose foal-
ing flings
The billows starward ?  Whose the steeds
fire-shod

That sweep throughout the world ?    What
spearman sings
The fearful chant of war
That fires, and spurs, and maddens all the
kings
That rule o'er earth, and air, and ocean ?
Whose hand excites the star
To shatter into fiery flakes ?  No man,
No petty god, but One who governs all,
Slips the sun's leash, perceives the sparrow's
fall,
Too high for man to fear, too near for man
to call.

## SONNETS.[1]

TO THE AUTHOR OF THE PHRASE : "I AM
NOT A GENTLEMAN AND I HAVE NO
FRIENDS."

### I.

SELF-DAMNED, the leprous moisture of thy
veins
Sickens the sunshine, and thine haggard
eyes,
Bleared with their own corrupting infamies,
Glare through the charnel-house of earthly
pains,
Horrible as already in hell.   There reigns
The terror of the knowledge of the lies
That mock thee ; thy death's double
desti..ies
Clutch at the throat that 'sobs, and chokes,
and strains.

Self-damned on earth, live out thy tortured
days,
That men may look upon thy face, and see
How vile a thing of woman born may be.
Then, we are done with thee ; go, go thy
ways

[1] The virulence of these sonnets is excusable
when it is known that their aim was to destroy
the influence in Cambridge of a man who
headed in that University a movement parallel
to that which at Oxford was associated with
the name of Oscar Wilde.  They had their
effect.

To other hells, thou damned of God hereafter,
  'Mid men's contempt and hate and pitiless
laughter.

## II.

Lust, impotence, and knowledge of thy soul,
  And that foreknowledge, fill the fiery lake
  Of lava where thy lazar corpse shall break
The burning surface to seek out a goal
More horrible, unspeakable. The scroll
  Opens, and "coward, liar, monster" shake
  Those other names of "goat" and "swine"
    and "snake"
Wherewith Hell's worms caress thee and
control.

Nay, but alone, intolerably alone,
  Alone, as here, thy carrion soul shall
    swelter,
  Yearning in vain for sleep, or death, or
    shelter;
No release possible, no respite known!
  Self-damned, without a friend, thy eternal
    place
  Sweats through the painting of thy harlot's
    face.

*At the hour of the eclipse,*
*Wednesday, Dec. 28.*

### BESIDE THE RIVER.

RAIN, rain in May. The river sadly flows,
  A sullen silver crossed with sable bars,
  Damp, gloomy, shivering, while reluctant
    stars,
Between swart masses of thick clouds that
    close,
  Drive with drooped plumes their wingéd
    cars
Toward sleep, the scythe of woes.

Woes,  woes  in  Spring.  Ere  summer
    deepeneth
  The pink of roses to a purpler tint;
  Ere ripening corn shafts back the sudden
    glint

Of sunshine that brings healing with the
    breath
  Of western winds that sigh, they hint
Of sleep, twin soul with death.

Death, death ere dawn. The night is over
    dark;
  Trees are grown terrible; the shadows
    wan
  Make shudder all the tense desires of
    man;
No gleam of moonlight bears the golden
    mark
  Of sunny lips, nor shines upon
Our sleep—Love's birchen bark.

Love, love to-night. To-night is all we know,
  Is all our care; lips joined to lips we lie,
  Tender hands touching, hearts in tune to
    die,
With willing kiss reluctant to let go;
  So sweet love's last enduring sigh
For sleep, so sure, so slow.

Sleep, sleep to-night. Our arms are inter-
    twined;
  Breath desires breath and hand imprisons
    hand;
  Breezes cool faces, rosy with the brand
Of long sweet kisses; sun shall dawn and
    find
  Two lovers who have passed the land
Of sleep—and found Death kind.

### MAN'S HOPE.

ERE fades the last red glimmer of the sun;
  Ere day is night, when on the glittering
    bar
  The waves are foaming rubies, and afar
Streaks of red water, gold on the horizon,
On summer ripples rhythmically run;
  Ere dusk is weaned, there sails on silver
    car
  From the expectant East, the evening Star;
And all the threads of sorrow are unspun.

So He who ordered this shall still work thus,
  And ere life's lamp shall flicker into death,
And Time lose all his empire over us,
  A gleam of Hope, of Knowledge, shall arise,
  A star to silver o'er Death's glooming skies,
And gladden the last labouring torch of breath.

## SONNET

FOR G. F. KELLY'S DRAWING OF AN HERMAPHRODITE.

O BODY pale and beautiful with sin !
  O breasts with venom swollen by the snakes
  Of passion, whose cold slaver slimes and slakes
The soul-consuming fevers that within
Thy heart the fires of hell on earth begin !
  O heart whose yearning after truth forsakes
  The law of love ! O heart whose ocean breaks
In sterile foam against some golden skin !

O thou whose body is one perfect prayer,
  One long regret, one agony of shame,
Lost in the fragrance, speeding, subtle and rare,
  Up to the sky, an avenue of flame !
My soul, thy body, in the same sin curled,
With vivid lust annihilate the world.

## A WOODLAND IDYLL.

FRESH breath from the woodland blows sweet
  O'er the flowery path we are roaming,
On the dimples of light lover's feet
  In the mystical charm of the gloaming,
      Yvonne !
On the buds that blush bright as we meet
  In the mystical charm of the gloaming !

A tear for the stars of the night,
  And a smile for the avenue shady,
A kiss for the eyelashes bright,
  And a blush for the cheek of my lady,
      Yvonne !
A laugh for the moon and her spite,
  And a blush for the cheek of my lady !

We'll tread where the daffodils shake
  And the primrose smiles up through her weeping,
Where the daisies dip down to the lake,
  Where the wonderful thrushes are sleeping,
      Yvonne !
By the marge of the maze of the brake
  Where the wonderful thrushes are sleeping.

Where the brook trickles clear to the eye
  Below dew-spangled frondlets of willow
We will wander to find by-and-by
  The sward of our delicate pillow,
      Yvonne !
Where the mosses so lusciously lie
  For the sward of our delicate pillow.

For a bride fairer far than the flower
  Is the couch spread by fingers of even,
The blossom of apples for bower,
  Its roof-tree the sapphires of heaven,
      Yvonne !
For the bride of the mystical hour,
  Its roof-tree the sapphires of heaven !

With songsters the heavy sweet air
  Is trembling and sighing and sobbing,
With meteors magically fair
  The sky is deliciously throbbing,
      Yvonne !
With splendour and subtlety rare
  The sky is deliciously throbbing.

Sweet bride to fond arms with a sigh,
  Strong arms to fond bosom, are curling ;
The winds breathe more musically by ;
  The moon has a rosier pearling,
      Yvonne !
The stars grow more dim in the sky,
  The moon has a rosier pearling.

So, birds, are you shy to awake
Your voices to laughter-tuned numbers?
So, sun, do you tremble to shake
The dews of the night from our slumbers?
                                    Yvonne!
So, breeze, too reluctant to take
The dews of the night from our slumbers?

Light breaks, and the breezes caress
Cool limbs and soft eyes and fair faces;
The nightingales carol to bless
The dawn of our maiden embraces,
                                    Yvonne!
The woods wear a lovelier dress
In the dawn of our maiden embraces!


## PERDURABO.[1]

EXILE from humankind! The snow's fresh
flakes
Are warmer than men's hearts.  My mind is
wrought
Into dark shapes of solitary thought
That loves and sympathises, but awakes
No answering love or pity.  What a pang
Hath this strange solitude to aggravate
The self-abasement and the blows of Fate!
No snake of hell hath so severe a fang!

I am not lower than all men—I feel
Too keenly.  Yet my place is not above,
Though I have this—unalterable Love
In every fibre.  I am crucified
Apart on a lone burning crag of steel,
Tortured, cast out; and yet—I shall abide.


## ON GARRET HOSTEL BRIDGE.[2]

HERE in the evening curl white mists and
wreathe in their vapour
All the gray spires of stone, all the immobile towers;

[1] "I shall endure to the end." This was
the mystic title taken by Crowley at his first
initiation.
[2] A bridge on the "Backs" at Cambridge.

Here in the twilight gloom dim trees and
sleepier rivers,
Here where the bridge is thrown over the
amber stream.
Chill is the ray that steals from the moon to
the stream that whispers
Secret tales of its source, songs of its
fountain-head.
Here do I stand in the dusk; like spectres
mournfully moving
Wisps of the cloud-wreaths form, dissipate
into the mist,
Wrap me in shrouds of gray, chill me and
make me shiver,
Not with the Night alone, not with the
sound of her wing,
Yet with a sense of something vague and
unearthly stalking
(Step after step as I move) me, to annul
me, quell
Hope and desire and life, bid light die
under my eyelids,
Bid the strong heart despair, quench the
desire of Heaven.
So I shudder a little; and my heart goes out
to the mountain,
Rock upon rock for a crown, snow like an
ermine robe;
Thunder and lightning free fashioned for
speech and seeing,
Pinnacles royal and steep, queen of the
arduous breast!
Ye on whose icy bosom, passionate, at the
sunrise,
Ye in whose wind-swept hollows, lulled in
the moonrise clear,
Often and oft I struggled, a child with an
angry mother,
Often and oft I slept, maid in a lover's
arms.
Back to ye, back, wild towers, from this flat
and desolate fenland,
Back to ye yet will I flee, swallow on wing
to the south;
Move in your purple cloud-banks and leap
your far-swelling torrents,
Bathe in the pools below, laugh with the
winds above,

Battle and strive and climb in the teeth of
the glad wild weather,
Flash on the slopes of ice, dance on the
spires of rock,
Run like a glad young panther over the
stony high-lands,
Shout with the joy of living, race to the
rugged cairn,
Feel the breath of your freedom burn in my
veins, and Freedom !
Freedom ! echoes adown cliff and pre-
cipitous ghyll.
Down by the cold gray lake the sun descends
from his hunting,
Shadow and silence steals over the frozen
fells.
Oh, to be there, my heart ! And the vesper
bells awaken ;
Colleges call their children ; Lakeland
fades from the sight.
Only the sad slow Cam like a sire with age
grown heavy
Wearily moves to the sea, to quicken to
life at last.
Blithelier I depart, to a sea of sunnier kindness ;
Hours of waiting are past ; I re-quicken to
love.


## ASTRAY IN HER PATHS.[1]

COPENHAGEN, *January,* '97.

I FEEL thee shudder, clinging to my arm,
Before the battlements of the salt sea,
Black billows tipped with phosphorescent
light,
Towering from where we stand to yonder
shore
That is no earthly shore, but guards the coast
Of that which is from that which is to be ;
Wherefore it kindles no evasive fire
Nor blazes through the night, but lies for-
gotten
Gray in the twilight ; never a star is out

[1] This satirical title is from Proverbs vii. 25.
A poet's nature is to refine to purest gold even
the sordidest of dross.

To light the broad horizon ; only here
Behind us cluster lamps, and busy sounds
Of men proclaim a city ; but to us
They are not here ; for we, because we love,
Are not of earth, but, as the immortals, stand
With eyes immutable ; our souls are fed
On a strange new nepenthe from the cup
Of the vast firmament. Nor do we dream,
Nor think we aught of the transient world,
But are absorbed in our own deity :
And our clear eyes reflect—(who dares to
gaze
Shall see and die !)—the changeless empyrèan
Eternity, the concentrated void
Of space, for being the centre of all things,
Time is to us the Now, and Space the Here ;
From us all Matter radiates, is a part
Of our own thoughts and souls ; because we
love.
Thou shudderest, clinging to me ; though
the night
Jewels her empire with the frosty crown
Of thousand-twinkling stars, whose hoary
crests
Burn where light touches them, with diamond
points
Of infinite far fire, save where the sea
Is ebony with sleep, and though the wind
Pierces the marrow, since it is the word
Of the Almighty, and cuts through the air
That may not stay its fury, with a cold
Nipping and chill, it is not in the wind ;
Nor though the thunder broke, or flashed
the fire
From all the circle of eternity,
Were that the reason ; for thou shudderest
To hear the Voice of Love ; it is no voice
That men may hear, but an intensest rich
Silence, that silence when man waits to hear
Some faint vibration in the smitten air,
And, if he hear not, die ; but we who love
Are beyond death, and therefore may
commune
In that still tongue ; it is the only speech
And song of stars and sun ; nor is it marred
By one dissentient tremor of the air
That girds the earth, but in lone æther
spreads

Its song.   But now I turn to thee, whose
    eyes
Blaze on me with such look as flesh and blood
May never see and live; for so it burns
Into the innest being of the spirit
And stains its vital essence with a brand
Of fire that shall not change; and shudder-
    ing I
Gaze back, spirit to spirit, with the like
Insatiable desire, that never quenched,
Nor lessened by sublime satiety,
But rather crescent, hotter with the flame
Of its own burning, that consumes it not,
Because it is the pure white flame of God.
I shudder, holding thee to me; thy gaze
Is still on me; a thousand years have passed,
And yet a thousand thousand; years they are
As men count years, and yet we stand and
    gaze
With touching hands and lips immutable
As mortals stand a moment; . . .
The universe is One: One Soul, One Spirit,
One Flame, One infinite God, One infinite
    Love.


### SONNET TO CLYTIE.

CLYTIE, beyond all praise, thou goodliest
    Of queens, thou royal woman, crowned
        with tears,
    That could not move the dull stars from
        their spheres
To kiss thee.   For the sun would fainer rest
In the gold chambers of the glowing west
    Than answer thy love, thine, whose soul
        endears
All souls but his, whose slow desire fears
The fierce embraces of thine olive breast.

O Queen, sun-lover, we are wed with thee
    In changeless love, in passion for a fire
        Whose lips bind all men in their bitter
            spell;
A love whose first caress, hard won, would
    be
    The final dissolution of desire,
        A flame to shrivel us with fire of hell.


### A VALENTINE, '98.[1]

Now on the land the woods are green;
    A wild bird's note
Shrills till the air trembles between
    His beak and throat.

And up through blue and gold and black
    The shivering sound
Rushes; no echo murmurs back
    From sky or ground.

In the loud agony of song
    The moon is still;
The wind drops down the shore along;
    Night hath her will.

The bird becomes a dancing flame
    In leaf and bower.
The forest trembles; loves reclaim
    Their own still hour.

The dawn is here, and on the sands
    Where sun first flames,
I gather lilies from all lands
    Of sad sweet names.

The Lesbian lily is of white
    Stained through with blood,
Swayed with the stream, a wayward light
    Upon the flood.

The Spartan lily is of blue,
    With green leaves fresh;
Apollo glints his crimson through
    The azure mesh.

The English lily is of white,
    All white and clean;
There plays a tender flame of light
    Her flowers between.

The English lily is a bloom
    Too cold and sweet;
One might say—in the twilight gloom
    A maiden's feet.

[1] Nothing more; be it well remembered!—
A. C.

Silent and slim and delicate
  The flower shall spring,
Till there be born immaculate
  A fair new thing.

Tall as the mother-lily, still
  By faint winds swayed ;
Tender and pure, without a will—
  An English maid.

No tree of poison, at whose feet
  All men lie dead ;
No well of death, whose waters sweet
  Are tinged with red.

No hideous impassioned queen
  For whom love dies ;
No warm imperious Messaline
  That slew with sighs.

Fiercer desires may cast away
  All things most good ;
A people may forget to-day
  Their motherhood.

She will remain, unshaken yet
  By storm and sun ;
She will remain, when years forget
  That fierier one.

A race of clean strong men shall spring
  From her pure life.
Men shall be happy ; bards shall sing
  The English wife.

And thou, forget thou that my mouth
  Has ever clung
To flame of hell ; that of the south
  The songs I sung.

Forget that I have trampled flowers,
  And worn the crown
Of thorns of roses in the hours
  So long dropped drown.

Forget, O white-faced maid, that I
  Have dallied long
In classic bowers and mystery
  Of classic song.

Eros and Aphrodite now
  I can forget,
Placing upon thy maiden brow
  Love's coronet.

Wake from the innocent dear sleep
  Of childhood's life :
An English maiden must not weep
  To be a wife.

So shall our love bridge space, and bring
  The tender breath
Of sun and moon and stars that sing
  To gladden Death.

I see your cheek grow pale and cold,
  Then flush above.
Kiss me ; I know that I behold
  The birth of Love.

## PENELOPE.

ULYSSES 'scaped the sorceries of that queen
  That turned to swine his goodly company,
And came with sails broad-burgeoning and clean
  Over the ripples of his native sea.
Yet for the shores his eyes had lately seen,
  He kept a half-regretful memory ;
And thought, when all the flower-strewn ways were green,
  " Better love Circe than Penelope ! "

Yes. A good woman's love will forge a chain
  To break the spirit of the bravest Greek ;
While with an harlot one may leap again
Free as the waters of the western main,
  And turn with no heart-pang the vessel's beak
  Out to the oceans that all seamen seek.

## A SONNET OF BLASPHEMY.

EXALTED over earth, from hell arisen,
There sits a woman, ruddy with the flame
Of men's blood spilt, and her uncleanly
    shame,
And the thrice-venomous vomit of her prison.

She sits as one long dead : infernal calm,
Chill hatred, wrap her in their poisonous
    cold.
She careth not, but doth disdainly hold
Three scourges for man's soul, that know no
    balm.

They know not any cure.  The first is Life,
A well of poison.  Sowing dust and dung
Over men's hearts, the second scourge, above
All shameful deeds, is Lying, from whose
    tongue
Drops Envy, wed with Hatred, to sow
    Strife.

These twain are bitter ; but the last is Love.


## THE RAPE OF DEATH.

ARGUMENT.—Sir Godfrey, a knight of Normandy, leapeth into a light vessel of Jarl
Hungard, while they sit at feast, and, slaying the crew, seeketh the high seas with the
Lady Thurla.  He slayeth the swiftest pursuers, and escapeth in a great tempest ; which
on the second day abating, he maketh the
inside of a bar, and must await the breeze.
Jarl Hungard coming with his men and two
dragons, is wrecked, but a knave shooting,
slayeth the Lady Thurla.  Sir Godfrey forthwith sinketh the other dragon, and saileth
forth into the ocean, and is not heard of ever
after.[1]

PALE vapours lie like phantoms on the sea,
    The tide swells slumberous beneath our
        keel,
The pulses of our canvas fail ; and we

[1] The argument is not founded on tradition.

No faint sweet summons from the south wind
    feel :
The crimson waters of the west are pale,
And bloodless arrows like a stream of steel

Flash from the moon, that rises where the
    gale
    Only a day past raged ; the clouds are lost
In pleasant rains that ripple on the sail.

The sudden fascination of the frost
    Touches the heavy canvas ; now there
        form
Reluctant crystals, and the vessel, tossed

The wild night through in the devouring
    storm,
    Glistens with dew made sharp and bright
        with cold.
For no north wind may drive us to the warm

Long-looked-for lands where day, with
    plumes of gold,
    Flaps like a lazy eagle in the air ;
Where night, a bird of prey divinely bold,

Wings through the sky, intangible but fair,
    And pale with subtle passion ; and no
        wind
Turns our prow southward, till the canvas
    bear

No more up into it, but still behind
    Follow like flame, and lead our love along
Into the valleys of the ocean, blind,

But seeing all the world awake with song
    Of many lyres and lutes and reeds of straw,
And all the rivers musical that throng

In bright assemblage of unchanging law,
    Like many flute-players ; and seeing this,
(That all the mountains looked upon and
    saw)

The sweetness of the savour of a kiss,
    And all its perfume wafted to the sky.
Nay, but no wind will drive our fortalice

(So strong against the sun) to where they ply
    Those pallid wings, or turn our vessel's
        beak
With utmost fury to the North, to dye

Our prows with seaweed, such as wise men
        seek
    For cleansing of their altars with slow
        blood
Wrenched from the long dark leaves, with
        fingers weak

With age and toil ; to stem the restless flood
    That boils between the islands ; to attain
The ultimate ice, where some calm hero stood

And looked one last time for a sail in vain,
    And looking upward not in vain, lay down
And died, to pass where cold and any pain

Are not.  So still the night is, like the crown
    Most white of the high God that glittereth !
The stars surround the moon, and Nereids
        drown

Their rippled tresses in her golden breath.
    Let us keep watch, my true love, caught
        at last
Between my hands, and not remember death.

Only bethink us of the daylight past,
    The long chase oversea, the storm, the
        speed
Whereby we ran before the leaping blast,

And left the swift pursuers at our need
    With one wrecked dragon and one
        shattered ; yea !
And on their swiftest many warriors bleed,

Having beheld, above the gray seaway
    Between them and the sun, my sword arise,
Like the first dagger flashing for the day,

My sword, that darts among them serpent-
        wise—
    And all their warriors fell back a space,
    And all the air rang out with sudden cries,

Seeing the death and fury of my face,
    And feeling the long sword sweep out
        and kill,
Till there was won the slippery path, the
        place

Whence I might sever the white cords, and
        fill
    The ship with tangled wreckage of the
        sail.
All this I did, and bore the blade of ill

Back, dripping blood, to thee most firm and
        pale
    Who held our rudder, all alone, and stood
Fierce and triumphant in the rising gale,

Bent to my sword, and kissed the stinging
        blood,
    While the good ship leapt free upon the
        deep,
And felt the feet of the resistless flood

Run, and the fervour of the billows sweep
    Under our keel—and we were clean away,
Laughing to see the foamheads sough and
        sleep,

As we kept pace with ocean all the day
    And one long night of toil ; until the sun
Lit on these cliffs his morning beams that
        play

With our sails rent and rifted white, and
        run
    Like summer lightning all about the deck,
And laugh upon the work my sword had
        done

When the feast turned to death for us ; we
        reck
    Nothing to-night of all that past despair :
Only to-night I watch your curving neck,

And play with all the kisses of your hair,
    And feel your weight, as if you were
        to be
Always and always—O my queen, how rare

Your lips' perfume ; like lilies on the sea
  Your white breasts glimmer ; let us wait
  awhile.
There is no breeze to drive us down to lee

On the cold rocks of yonder icy isle,
  And your sire's passion must forget the
  chase
As I forget, the moment that you smile,

And sea and sky are brighter for your face—
  I hear the sound of many oars ; perchance
Your father's, but within this iron place

The heavy dragons will not dare advance
  Where our light vessel barely skimmed the
  rock :
Their anger may grow cool, the while they
  dance

Like fools before the bar we crossed, and
  mock
  Pursuit.   Behold ! one dragon strikes the
  reef,
Breaks in the midst before the dreadful shock,

Shattered and stricken by the rousing sheaf
  Of wild intolerable foam that breaks
Full on their stem : she sinks.   One fierce
  foul thief

Springs desperate upon her poop ; she shakes ;
  He strings a sudden arrow.   Ocean sweeps
Over his cursèd craft.   The arrow takes

The straight swift road—Ah God !—to her
  who sleeps,
  To her bright bosom as at peace she lies.
She is dead quickly, and the ocean keeps

The secret of my sorrow from her eyes.
  I will not weep ; I cannot weep ; I turn
And watch the sail fill with the wind that
  sighs

A little for pure pity—I discern
  The cowards shake with fear ; the vessel
  springs
Light to the breezes, as the golden erne

That seeks a prey on its impetuous wings :
  The reef is past ; I crash upon the foe,
And all the fury of my weapon rings

On armour temperless ; the waters flow
  Through the dark rent within the side ; I
  leap
Back to my dead love ; back, desiring so

That they had killed me, for I cannot weep.
  They killed her, and a mist of blood
  consumes
My sight ; they killed my lover in her sleep.

The breeze has freshened, and the water
  fumes,
  The vessel races on beneath the sky ;
Beneath her bows the eager billow spumes.

I wonder whither, and I wonder why.
  No ray of light this sea of blood illumes.
I wonder whether God will let me die.

## IN THE WOODS WITH SHELLEY.

SING, happy nightingale, sing ;
  Past is the season of weeping ;
Birds in the wood are on wing,
  Lambs in the meadow are leaping.
Can there be any delight still in the butter-
  cups sleeping ?

Dawn, paler daffodil, dawn ;
  Smile, for the winter is over ;
Sunlight makes golden the lawn,
  Spring comes and kisses the clover ;
All the wild woodlands await poet and
  songster and lover.

Linger, dew, linger and gem
  All the fresh flowers in the garland ;
Blossom, leaf, bud and green stem
  Flash with your light to some far land,
Where men shall wonder if you be not a
  newly-born starland.

Ah ! the sweet scents of the woods !
  Ah ! the sweet sounds of the heaven !
Sights of impetuous floods,
  Foam like the daisy at even,
Folding o'er passionate gold petals that sun-
  rise had riven !

See, like my life is the stream
  Now its desire is grown quiet ;
Life was a passionate dream
  Once, when light fancy ran riot,
Now, ere youth fades, flows in peace past
  woody bank and green eyot.

Highest, white heather and rock,
  Mountain and pine, with young laughter,
Breezes that murmur and mock
  Duller delights to come after,
Wild as a swallow that dives whither the sea
  wind would waft her.

Lower, an ocean of flowers,
  Trees that are warmer and leafier,
Starrier, sunnier hours
  Spurning the stain of all grief here,
Bringing a quiet delight to us, beyond our
  belief, here.

Lastly, the uttermost sea,
  Starred with the flakes of spray sunlit,
Blue as its caverns that be
  Crystal, resplendent, yet unlit ;
So like a mother receives the kiss of the
  dainty-lip runlet.

Here the green moss is my seat,
  Beech is a canopy o'er me,
Calm and content the retreat ;
  Man, my worst foe, cannot bore me ;
Life is a closed book behind—Shelley an
  open before me.

Shelley's own birds are above
  Close to me (why should they fear me ?)
May I believe it—that love
  Brings his bright spirit so near me
That, should I whisper one word—Shelley's
  swift spirit would hear me.

Heaven is not very far ;
  Soul unto soul may be calling
When a swift meteor star
  Through the quick vista is falling.
Loose but your soul—shall its wings find the
  white way so appalling ?

Heaven, as I understand,
  Nearer than some folk would make it ;
God—should you stretch out a hand,
  Who can be quicker to take it ?
Then you have pacted an oath—judge you
  if He will forsake it !

I have had hope in the spring —
  Trust that the God who has given
Flowers, and the thrushes that sing
  Dawnwards all night, and at even
Year after year, will be true now we are
  speaking of heaven.

Breezes caress me and creep
  Over the world to admire it ;
Sweet air shall sigh me to sleep,
  Softly my lips shall respire it,
Lying half-closed with a kiss ready for who
  shall desire it.


A VISION UPON USHBA.[1]

HERE in the wild Caucasian night,
  The sleepless years
Seem to pass by in garments white,
  Made white with tears,
A pageant of intolerable light
  Across the sombre spheres,
And, mingling with the tumult of the morn,
Methought a single rose of blood was born.

[1] A mountain in the Caucasus.  Crowley
never visited this district.

Far on the iron peaks a voice
   Crystal and cold,
Sharper than sounds the aurochs' [1] choice
   O'er wood and wold,
A summons as of angels that rejoice,
   A pæan glad and bold,
A mighty shout of infinite acclaim
Shrieks through the sky some dread forgqtten
   Name.

Trembles the demon on his perch
   Of crags ice-bound ;
Tremble near forest and far church
   At that quick sound ;
The silver arrows that bedeck the birch
   Shiver along the ground :
Priest, fiend, and harpy answer to the call,
And hasten to their ghastly festival.

There in the vale below my feet
   I see the crew
Gather, blaspheming God, and greet
   Their shame anew.
A feast is spread of some unholy meat ;
   Ofttimes there murmurs through
Their horrid ranks a cry of pain, as God
Bids them keep memory of His iron rod.

The vale is black with priests.  They fight,
   Wild beasts, for food,
The orphan's gold, the widow's right,
   The virgin's snood.
All in their maws are crammed within the
      night
   That hides their chosen wood,
Where through the blackness sounds the
      sickening noise
Of cannibals that gloat on monstrous joys.

The valley steams with slaughter.  Here
   Shall the pure snow
The bloody reek of murder rear
   To crush the foe ?
In Titan fury shall the rocks spring clear,
   And smite the fiends below ?
Shall poisonous wind and avalanche combine
To wreck swift justice, human and divine ?

   [1] The extinct Wild Bull of Europe.

Priests thrive on poison.   Carrion
   Their eager teeth
Tear, till the sacramental sun
   Its sword unsheath,
And bid their horrid carnival be done,
   And smite beneath
In their cold gasping valleys, and bid light
Break the battalions of the angry night.

That sword that smote from Heaven was so
      keen,
   Its silver blade
No angel's sight, no fairy's eye hath seen,
   No tender maid
With subtle insight may behold its sheen
   With light inlaid ;
But God, who forged it, breathed upon its
      point,
And His pure unction did the hilt anoint.

Within the poet's hand he laid the sword :
   With reverent ear
The poet listened to His word
   Cleansed through of fear.
The brightness of the glory of the Lord
   Grew adamant, a spear !
And when he took the falchion in his hand
Lo ! kings and princes bowed to his command.

Then shall the flag of England flaunt
   In peaceful might,
The sceptred isle of dying Gaunt [1]
   Shall rule by right.
The sons of England shall bid Hell avaunt
   And priest and harlot smite.
Then all the forces of the earth shall be
Untamable, a shield of Liberty.

Freedom shall burgeon like a rose,
   While in the sky
A new white sun with ardour glows
   On liberty.
Men shall sing merrily at work as those
   Who fear no more to die—
Ay ! and who fear no more at last to live
Since man can love and worship and forgive.

   [1] See *Richard II.*, ii. 1.

Then on these heights of Caucasus
  A fire shall dwell,
Pure as the dawn, and odorous
  Of bud and bell ;
A flower of fire, a flame from Heaven to us
  All triumph to foretell,
A glory of unspeakable delight,
A flower like lightning, adamant and white.

There needs no more or sun or sea
  Or any light ;
On golden wheels Eternity
  Revolves in Night.
The island peoples are too proud and free
  And full of might
To care for time or space, but glorious wend
A royal path of flowers to the end.

I pray thee, God, to weapon me
  With this keen fire,
That I may set this people free
  As my desire ;
That the white lilies of our liberty
  Grow on Life's crags still higher,
Till on the loftiest peaks their blossom flower,
The rampart of a people and their power.


ELEGY, *August 27th, 1898.*[1]

So have the days departed, as the leaves
  Smitten by wrath of Autumn blast ;
So the year, fallen from delight, still grieves
  Over the happy past.

The year of barren summer, when the wind
  Blew from the south unlooked-for snow,
The year when Collon,[2] desolate and blind,
  Gloomed on the vale below,

When logs of pinewood lit the little room,
  And friendship ventured in to sit
Beside their blaze, to listen in the gloom
  To wisdom and to wit ;

[1] When Dr. John Hopkinson and three of his children perished on the Petite Dent de Veisivi.
[2] A mountain at the head of the Val d'Hérens.

When we discussed our hopes, and told the stories
  Of happy climbing days gone by ;
The stubborn battle with the cliffs, the glories
  Of the blue Alpine sky.

The keen delight of paths untrodden yet,
  And new steep ice and rocky ways
Too dangerous and splendid to forget.
  Those dear strong happy days !

And now what happier fate to your brave souls
  Than so to strive and fighting fall ?
Think you that He who sees you, and controls,
  Did not devise it all ?

The mountains that you loved have taken you,
  And we who love you will not weep.
Shall we begrudge ? Your last look saw sky blue ;
  You will be glad to sleep.

Your pure names (thine renowned, yours fresh with youth
  And full of promise) shall be kept
Still in our hearts for monuments of truth,
  As if you had not slept.


EPILOGUE.

HORACE, in the fruitful Sabine country,
Where the wheat and vine are most abundant,
Where the olive ripens in the sunshine,
Where the streams are voiced with Dian's whispers,
Lived in quiet, with a woman's passion
To inspire his lute and bring contentment
In the gray still days of early winter.
I, remote from cities, like the poet,

Tune my lesser lyre with other fingers,
Yet am not a whit the less belovéd.
Unto me the stars are never silent,
Nor do sea and storm deny their music,
Nor do flower and breeze refuse their
    kisses :
So my soul is flooded with their magic;
So my love completes the joy of living.
I am like the earth, to whom there gather
Rays of gold to bid the gray horizon
Melt, recede, and brighten into azure.
Let me sing, O holy one, Apollo !
Sing as Horace sang, and flood the ocean
With a living ecstasy of music
Till the whole creation echo, echo,
Echo till the tune dissolve the heavens ?

Still song lingers ; lamely from the lute-
    string
Steals a breath of melody ; the forest
Treasures in its glades the sighs I utter.
Yet may I be happy, storing honey
Lover's lips hold, gathering the sunlight
Eyes and hair have kept for me, delighting
In the bells far-off, in yonder thrushes,
In the tawny songster of the forest,
In the stream's song, all the words of passion,
Echoes of the deeper words unspoken
In thy breast and mine, O heart of silence !
Will they pierce one day to other nations
Clear and strong and triumphing?
                                    It may be.
Then we shall not envy you, my Horace !

# JEZEBEL;

## AND OTHER TRAGIC POEMS.

### By COUNT VLADIMIR SVAREFF.*

Edited, with an Introduction and Epilogue, by ALEISTER CROWLEY.

1899.

## DÉDICACE.

LONDRES, *Juin* 1898.

PEINTRE, que ton amour inspire
  Des chansons toujours plus sublimes,
Malgré qu'aujourd'hui ma mauvaise lyre
      Chante l'abîme.

Nos espoirs, nos desirs nous rendent
  Des amis chers aux dieux ;
Demain, ma voix, plus haute et plus profonde,
      Chante les cieux.
              À GERALD.[1]

## PERDITA.

LIKE leaves that fall before the sullen wind
  At summer's parting kiss and autumn's call,
Lost thoughts fly half-forgotten from my mind,
  Like leaves that fall.

They shall not come again ; the wintry pall
  Of consciousness clouds o'er them ; they shall find
No rest, no hope, no tear, no funeral.

Into the night, despairing, bleeding, blind,
  They pass, nor know their former place at all,
Lost to my soul, to God, to all mankind,
  Like leaves that fall.

[1] Gerald Kelly, the eminent painter.

## JEZEBEL.

### PART I.

A LION'S mane, a leopard's skin
  Across my dusty shoulders thrown;
A swart fierce face, with eyes where sin ·
  Lurks like a serpent by a stone.
A man driven forth by lust to seek
Rest from himself on Carmel's peak.

A prophet [1] with wild hair behind,
  Streaming in fiery clusters !  Yea,
Tangled with vehemence of the wind,
  And knotted with the tears that slay ;
And all my face parched up and dried,
And all my body crucified.

Ofttimes the Spirit of the Lord
  Descends and floods me with his breath ;
My words are fashioned as a sword,
  My voice is like the voice of death.
The thunder of the Spirit's wings
Brings terror to the hearts of kings.

Anon, and I am driven out
  In desert places by desire ;
My mouth is salt and dry ; I doubt
  If hell hath such another fire ;
If God's damnation can devise
A lust to match these agonies.

[1] Not Elijah, as the sequel shows.  Foolish contemporary reviews, however, made this silly blunder.

* Under this name the poet lay perdu in the heart of London, prosecuting, under circumstances of romantic and savage interest, his first occult studies.

The desert wind my body burns,
  The voice of flesh consumes my soul;
My body towards the city turns,
  My spirit seeks its fierier goal;
In wells of heaven to quench my thirst,
And take God's hand among the first.

I conquered self; I grew at last
  A prophet chosen of the Lord;
I blew the trumpet's iron blast
  That called on Zimri Omri's sword;
My voice inflamed the fiery steel
That was to smite upon Jezreel.

And now, I haste from yonder sands,
  With fervour filled, to say God's doom
To Ahab of the bloody hands,
  The spoiler of his father's tomb,
The slayer of the vineyard king.
God's judgment, and his fate, I bring.

The city gleams afar; I see
  Samaria's white walls on high;
The mountains echo back to me
  The vengeful murmur of the sky;
All heaven and earth on me attend
To prophesy the tyrant's end.

The gates are closed because of night
  Whose heavy breath infects the air;
The dog-star gleams, a devilish light:
  I thought I saw behind me glare
The eyes of fiends.  I thought I heard
An evil laugh, a mocking word.

The gates swing open at the Name,
  Without a warder roused from sleep;
I pass, with face of burning flame,
  That is not quenched, although I weep.
(For even my tears are tears of fire,
For loathing, madness, and desire.)

Ah God! the traps for fervent feet!
  The morrow beaconed, and I came
By where the golden groves of wheat
  In summer glories fiercely flame;
To those white courts, by princes trod,
Where Ahab sat, and mocked at God.

Where Ahab sat:—but lo! I saw
  No king, no tyrant to be curst;
But she, who filled me with blind awe,
  She, for whose blood my thin veins
    thirst;
The blossom of a painted mouth
And bare breasts tinctured with the south.

For lo! the harlot Jezebel!
  Her hands dropped perfume, and her
    tongue
(A flame from the dark heart of hell,
  The ivory-barred mouth, that stung
With unimaginable pangs)
Shot out at me, and Hell fixed fangs.

Her purple robes, her royal crown,
  The jewelled girdle of her waist,
Her feet with murder splashed, and brown
  With the sharp lips that fawn and taste,
The crimson snakes that minister
To those unwearying lusts of her.

And all her woman's scent did drift
  A steam of poison through the air;
The haze of sunshine seems to lift
  And toil in tangles of black hair,
The hair that waves, and winds, and bites,
And glistens with unholy lights.

For lo! she saw me, and beheld
  My trembling lips curled back to curse,
Laughed with strong scorn, whose music
  knelled
  The empire of God's universe.
And on my haggard face upturned
She spat! Ah God! how my cheek
  burned!

Then, as a man betrayed, and doomed
  Already, I arose and went,
And wrestled with myself, consumed
  With passion for that sacrament
Of shame.  From that day unto this
My cheek desires that hideous kiss.

Her hate, her scorn, her cruel blows,
  Fill my whole life, consume my breath ;
Her red-fanged hatred in me glows,
  I lust for her, and hell, and death.
I see that ghastly look, and yearn
Toward the brands of her that burn.


Sleep shuns me; dreams divide the night,
  (My parched throat thirsty for her veins)
That she and I with deep delight
  Suck from death's womb infernal pains,
Whose fire consumes, destroys, devours
Through night's insatiable hours.


And altogether filled with love,
  And altogether filled with sin,
The little sparks and noises move
  About the softness of her skin.
Her pleasures and her passions purr
For the delight I have of her.


Aching with all the pangs of night
  My shuddering body swoons ; my eyes
Absorb her eyelids' lazy light,
  And read her bosom to devise
Fresh blossoms of the heart of hell
And secret joys of Jezebel.


Her lips are fastened to my breast
  To suck out blood in feverish tides ;
The token of her I possessed,
  Still on my withered cheek abides.
Thus slowly the desire grows
To kill and have her yet—who knows?


### PART II.

I know.  When Ramoth-Gilead's field
  Grew bloody with hot ranks of dead,
I smote amain with sword and shield ;
  My brows with mingled blood were
    red ;
And on my cheek the kiss of hell,
The hatred of my Jezebel.

I waited many days.  At last
  The rushing of a chariot grew
Frightful through all the city vast :
  Men were afraid.  But I—I knew
Jehu was here, whose sword should dip
Deep in my love's adulterous lip.

The spirit filled me.  *And behold !*
  *I saw her dead stare to the skies:*
*I came to her ; she was not cold,*
  *But burning with old infamies.*
*On her incestuous mouth I fell,*
*And lost my soul for Jezebel.*

I followed him afoot, afire ;
  Beneath her window he drew rein ;
She looked forth, clad in glad attire,
  Haggard and hateful, once again ;
And taunted him.  His bastard blood
Quailed, but his violent soul withstood.

He blenched, and then with eyes of flame,
  "Who is on my side?  Who?" he said.
Three eunuchs, passionless, grown tame,
  Grinned from behind her laughing head.
"Throw down that woman !"  And my
    breath
Caught as they flung her out to death.

I think I died that moment.  He,
  Foaming for vengeance and blood-lust,
Laughed his coarse laugh of hideous glee.
  Her sweet bad body in the dust
He trampled.  Royal from the womb
A martyred murderess lacks a tomb !

A tigress woman, clad with sin,
  And shod with infamy, who pressed
The bloody winepress of my skin,
  And plucked the purple of my breast—
Her lovers in their hearts shall keep
Her memory passionate and deep.

They cast her forth on Naboth's field
  Still living, in her harlot's dress ;
Her belly stript, her thighs concealed,
  For shame's sake and for love's no less.
Night falls; the gaping crowds abide
No longer by her stiffening side.

I crept like sleep toward the place
  That held for me her evil head;
I bent like sin above her face
  That dying she might kiss me dead.
I whispered "Jezebel!"  She turned,
And her deep eyes with hatred burned.

"Ah! prophet, come to mock at me
  And gloat on mine exceeding pain?"
"Nay, but to give my soul to thee,
  And have thee spit at me again!"
She smiled—I know she smiled—she sighed,
Bit my lips through, and drank, and died!

Her murders and her blasphemies,
  Her whoredoms, God has paid at last;
Upon my bosom close she lies;
  Her carnal spirit holds me fast.
My blood, my infamy, my pain,
Seal my subjection and her reign.

My veins poured out her marriage cup,
  For holy water her cruel tongue;
For blessing of white hands raised up,
  These perfumed infamies unsung;
For God's breath, her sharp tainted breath;
For marriage bed, the bed of death.

The hounds that scavenge, fierce and lean,
  Snarl in the moonlight; in the sky
The vulture hangs, a ghost unclean;
  The lewd hyæna's sleepless eye
Darts through the distance; these admit
My lordship over her—and it.

The host is lifted up.  Behold
  The vintage spilt, the broken bread!
I feast upon the cruel cold
  Pale body that was ripe and red.
Only, her head, her palms, her feet,
I kissed all night, and did not eat.

So, and not otherwise, the word
  Of God was utterly fulfilled.
So, and not otherwise.  I heard
  Her spirit cry, by death not stilled:
"My sin is perfect in thy blood,
And thou and I have conquered God."

Now let me die, at last desired,
  At last beloved of thee my queen;
Now let me die, with blood attired,
  Thy servant naked and obscene;
To thy white skull, thy palms, thy feet,
Clinging, dead, infamous, complete.

Now let me die, to mix my soul
  With thy red soul, to join our hands,
To weld us in one perfect whole,
  To link us with desirous bands.
Now let me die, to mate in hell
With thee, O harlot Jezebel.

## CONCERNING CERTAIN SINS.

SOME sins assume a garb so fine and white
  That the blue veil of Heaven seems to
    shade
  Their purity.  They are winged so wide and
    bright
  That even angels' pinions seem to fade,
And the archangel's wing recedes in night:—
  Ay! even God seems perturbed and afraid
Because it wears so holy a garb of light
  Of perfumed fire immaculately made.

These sins are deadly.  God is merciless
  For Love that joins Man's passion with
    His power,
  And makes to bloom on earth a fairer flower
Than heaven bears.  Our token of success
  Is that displeasure toward our sin unnamed
Of a fierce demon jealous and ashamed.

## A SAINT'S DAMNATION.

YOU buy my spirit with those peerless eyes
  That burn my soul; you loose the torrent
    stream
Of my desire; you make my lips your prize,

And on them burns the whole life's hope:
    you deem
  You buy a heart; but I am well aware
How my damnation dwells in that supreme

Passion to feed upon your shoulders bare,
And pass the dewy twilight of our sin
In the intolerable flames of hair

That clothe my body from your head; you
win
The devil's bargain; I am yours to kill,
Yours, for one kiss; my spirit for your skin!

O bitter love, consuming all my will!
O love destroying, that hast drained my
life
Of all those fountains of dear blood that fill

My heart! O woman, would I call you
wife?
Would I content you with one touch divine
To flood your spirit with the clinging strife

Of perfect passionate joy, the joy of wine,
The drunkenness of extreme pleasure, filled
From sin's amazing cup? Oh, mine, mine,
mine,

Mine, if your kisses maddened me or killed,
Mine, at the price of my damnation deep,
Mine, if you will, as once your glances
willed!

Take me, or break me, slay or soothe to
sleep,
If only yours one hour, one perfect hour,
Remembrance and despair and hope to steep

In the infernal potion of that flower,
My poisonous passion for your blood!
Behold!
How utterly I yield, how gladly dower

Our sin with my own spirit's quenchéd
gold,
Clothe love with my own soul's immortal
power,
Give thee my body as a fire to hold—
O love, no words, no songs—your breast
my bower!

## LOT.

"And while he lingered . . . they brought
him forth, and set him without the city."—
GEN. xix. 16.

TURN back from safety: in my love abide,
Whose lips are warm as when, a virgin bride,
I clung to thee ashamed and very glad,
Whose breasts are lordlier for the pain they
had,
Whose arms cleave closer than thy spouse's
own,
Thy spouse—O lover, kiss me, and atone!
All my veins bleed for love, my ripe breasts
beat
And lay their bleeding blossoms at thy feet!
Spurn me no more! O bid these strangers
go;
Turn to my lips till their cup overflow;
Hurt me with kisses, kill me with desire,
Consume me and destroy me with the fire
Of bleeding passion straining at the heart,
Touched to the core by sweetnesses that
smart;
Bitten by fiery snakes, whose poisonous
breath
Swoons in the midnight, and dissolves to
death!
Ah! let me perish so, and not endure
Thy falsehood who have known thy love was
sure,
Built up by sighs a palace of long years—
Lo! it was faery, and the spell of tears
Dissolves it utterly. O bid them go,
These white-faced boys, where calmer rivers
flow
And birds less passionate invoke the spring
Or seek their loves with weaker, wearier
wing.
Turn back from safety! Let God's rivers
pour
Brimstone and fire, and all his fountains roar
Lava and hail of hell upon my head,
So be he leave us altogether dead,
Burnt in that shameful whirlwind of his ire,
Consumed in one tall pyramid of fire

Whose bowers of flame shall tell the sky of
  God
How we despised his feet with thunder
  shod,
And conquered, clasping, all the host of
  death.
Turn to me, touch me, mix thy very breath
With mine to mingle floods of fiery dew
With flames of purple, like the sea shot
  through
With golden glances of a fiercer star.
Turn to me, bend above me, you may char
These olive shoulders with an old-time kiss,
And fix thy mouth upon me for such bliss
Of sudden rage rekindled.    Turn again,
And make delight the minister of pain,
And pain the father of a new delight,
And light a lamp of torture for the night
Too grievous to be borne without a cry
To rend the very bowels of the sky
And make the archangel gasp—a sudden
  pang,
Most like a traveller stricken by the fang
Of the black adder whose squat head
  springs up,
A flash of death, beneath a cactus cup.
Ah turn! my bosom for thy love is cold;
My arms are empty, and my lips can hold
No converse with thee far away like this.
O for that communing pregnant with a kiss
That is reborn when lips are set together
To link our souls in one desirous tether,
And weld our very bodies into one.
Ah fiend Jehovah, what then have we done
To earn thy curse—is love like ours too
  strong
To dwell before thee, and do thy throne
  no wrong?
Art thou grown jealous of the fiery band?
Lo! thou hast spoken, and thy strong com-
  mand
Bade earth and air divide, and on the sea
Thy spirit moved—and thou must envy me!
Gird all thy godhead to destroy a man
Whose little moment is a single span,
Whose small desire is nothing—and thy
  power
Must root from out his bosom the fair flower

Of passion!    Listen to thine own voice yet:
" A rich man many flocks and herds did get
And took the poor man's lamb."    Thou
  art the man!
Our love must lie beneath thy bitter ban!
Thou petty, envious God!    My king, be
  sure
His brute force shall not to the end endure;
Some stronger soul than thine shall wrest
  his crown
And thrust him from his own high heaven
  down
To some obscure forgetful hell.    For me
Forsake thy hopes in him!    We worship,
  we,
Rather the dear delights we know and hold;
The first cool kiss, within the water cold
That draws its music from some bubbling
  well,
Looks long, looks deadly, looks desirable,
The touch that fires, the next kiss, and the
  whole
Body embracing, symbol of the soul,
And all the perfect passion of an hour.
Turn to me, pluck that amaranthine flower,
And leave the doubtful blossoms of the sky!
You dare not kiss me! dare not draw you
  nigh
Lest I should lure you to remain! nor speak
Lest you should catch the blood within your
  cheek
Mantling.    You dared enough—so long
  ago!—
When to my blossom body clean as snow
You pressed your bosom till desire was pain,
And—then—that midnight—you did dare
  remain
Though all my limbs were bloody with your
  mouth
That tore their flesh to satiate its drouth,
That was not thereby satisfied!    And now
A pallid coward, with sly, skulking brow,
You must leave Sodom for your spouse's
  sake.
Coward and coward and coward! who would
  take
The best flower of my life and leave me so,
Still loving you—Ah! weak—and turn to go

For fear of such a God! O blind! O
    fool!
To heed these strangers, and to be the tool
Of their smooth lies and monstrous miracles!
O break this bondage and cast off their
    spells!
Five righteous! Thou a righteous man! A
    jest!
A righteous man—you always loved me best,
And even when lured by lips of wanton girls
Would turn away and sigh and touch my
    curls
And slip half-conscious to the old em-
    brace :—
And now you will not let me see your face
Or hear your voice or touch you. Ah! the
    hour!
He moves. Come back, come back, my
    life's one flower!
Come back. One kiss before you leave
    me. So!
Stop—turn—one little kiss before you go ;
It is my right—you must. Oh no! Oh no!

## EPILOGUE.

To die amid the blossoms of the frost
  On far fair heights; to sleep the quiet
    sleep
  Of dead men underneath the snowy steep
Of many mountains ; ever to have lost
These cares and these distrusts; to lie alone,
  Watched by the distant eagle's drowsy
    wing,
  Stars and grey summits, and the winds
    that sing
Slow dirges in eternal monotone.

Such is my soul's desire, being weary of
  This vain eternity of sleepless dreams
  That is my life ; withal there still may be
In other worlds, the hope of other love
  Than this that floods my veins with
    poisonous streams,
  And wastes with wan desire the soul
    of me.

# AN APPEAL TO THE AMERICAN REPUBLIC.

## 1899.

THOU fair Republic oversea afar,
 Where long blue ripples lap the fertile
land,
Whose manifest dominion, like a star,
Fixed by the iron hands and swords of
 war,[1]
 Now must for aye, a constellation, stand—
Thou new strong nation! as the eagle
 aspires
  To match the sun's own fires,
Children of our land, hear the children of
 your sires.

We stretch out hands to-day when the white
 wings
 Of Peace are spread beneath you and your
 foe.
O race of men that slay the slaves of
 kings !
We, whom the foam-crowned ocean still
 enrings,
 We, whose strong freedom never brooked
 a blow,
Hail you now victors, hail you of the sword
  Proved in the west the lord,
Hail you, and bid you sound quick friend-
ship and accord.

The eagle of your emblem would not stoop
 To the proud vaunts of that outrageous
 wing
That Bismarck reared, and strengthened,
 and bade swoop
Fierce upon France, whose pallid pinions
 droop
 To own an Emperor where she mocked a
 king :

[1] This poem was written shortly after the
Spanish war.

Their challenge you hurled back across the
 foam :
  Vienna and tall Rome
Trembled for their ally : you stirred our
 hearts at home.

The fire of love no waters shall devour;
 The faith of friendship stands the shocks
 of time ;
Seal with your voice the triumph of this hour,
Your glory to our glory and our power,
 Alliance of one tongue, one faith, one
 clime !
Seal and clasp hands ; and let the sea pro-
 claim
  Friendship of righteous fame,
And lordship of two worlds that time can
 never tame.

Stoop not and tender not an hour's regret
 For those wild words in trivial anger
 passed :
Forget your fools, as we their words forget,
And join our worlds in one amazing net
 Of empire and dominion, till aghast
The lying Russian cloke his traitor head
  More close, since Spain has bled
To wake in us the love that lay a century
 dead.

Let all the world keep silence at our peace ;
 Let France retreat and Russia step aside
From their encroachments, bid their envy
 cease
Stricken by Fear, who see our strength in-
 crease
 By comradeship that quickens to abide,
A bond of justice, light, and liberty,
  To make the wide earth free
As the wild waves that slake the passion of
 the sea.

Let all the world keep silence and behold
   The wrath of two great nations that are
     friends
Against who bartered Poland, and who sold
Italy, weighed out Hungary for gold,
   And shattered Greece to serve no noble
     ends.
The traitors and the peoples and the kings
     That love not righteous things ;
They shall behold our wrath, and find our
   anger stings.

White slaves shall look up and behold a light
   Grow in the islands of the sacred sea,
And on the land whose forehead kisses night
And has the dawn upon its wings, whose
   might
Is mightier for the lips of Liberty
Pressed on its new-born cheek, when Church
   and State
     Drove forth to baffle Fate
Our sires and yours, whose fame is grown
   this year so great.

That morning of deliverance is at hand ;
   The world requickens, and all folk rejoice,
Seeing our kingdom look toward your land,
And both catch hands, indissolubly grand
   In the proud friendship of a better choice.
Your winds that wrought wild wreckage on
   our shore
     Shall sink and be no more,
Or waft your barks, with wheat gold-laden,
   swiftly o'er.

Our foamcaps, that your rocks disdainful
   flung
     Back to the waves that left our beaten
     coast,
Shall be like echoes of sweet songs unsung,
And all the ocean noises find a tongue
   To voice the clamour of a righteous
     boast—
That friendship and dominion shall be
   wrought
     Out of the womb of thought,
And all the bygone days be held for things
   of nought.

What matter though our fathers did you
   wrong ?
   Though brave sons brake our bitter yoke ?
     Though we
Strove to compel you to a cruel thong?
What, though the stronger did defeat the
   strong?
   Both, wild and patient as the steep strong
     sea ?
What matter that some strive to waken hate,
     Traitors to either state,
Hang them in chains !  Our way to Freedom
   cannot wait !

The petty partisans of party war,
   The hireling quillmen, and the jingo crowd,
The well-paid patriots, scenting from afar
Silence, their doom—shall they eclipse the
   star
Now crescent in the sky, whose music loud
Rejoices humble hearts and true men all,
     And sounds the funeral
Dirge of slave, tyrant, priest, that snarl, and
   snarling fall ?

These we forget—remembering only this :
   Ye are blood-brothers, and our tongues
     are one ;
Our hopes and conquests in one splendid
   kiss
Unite and struggle not for empire.   Is
   Our land and yours too little for the sun
To gladden, to illume, to bid increase,
     Bound by two mighty seas
In one fraternal clasp of admirable peace ?

Ye are our brothers ; ye have spurned the
   power
   That bound the islands of your eastern
     shore ;
Ye have restored to freedom that fair flower,
Cuba, in her most agonising hour,
   And east and west have thundered with
     red war.
We freed us from the slavery of Spain,
     And laid upon the main
Our hand three centuries back — and ye
   have struck again.

Priestcraft and tyranny in this defeat
  Shake, and the walls of hell with fear re-
    sound ;
The sun laughs gladlier on the heavier wheat,
  Because the fates must weave a winding-
    sheet
  At last for Fear.   Deliverers are found
Who will deliver.   Mountain, stream, and
    brake,
        Lone wood, and sleepy lake,
Are peopled with bright shapes that sing for
  freedom's sake.


Rocks, and pale fountains, and tall trees
    that quiver,
  And all the clouds that deck the sunset
    sky
Move like the music of a mighty river
Where ripples break, and rapids gleam and
    shiver,
  And calm rebuilds her empire by-and-
    by.
For joy of this alliance all the earth
        Forgets her day of dearth,
In her new birth forgets, and maddens into
  mirth.

The stars swing censers of pale gold to God,
  Whose incense is the love-song of the
    free ;
Angels with mercy and with beauty shod
Move in the mazes of an Eden, trod
  Not by the seemly spirits of the sea,
But by brave men built wholly of desire
        And freedom's mystic fire,
To clothe its habitants with glorious attire.


Clasp hands, O fair republic of the west,
  And leave the kingdoms to their sudden
    fate.
With new-born love and ardour unrepressed,
Let Lethe steep in its unquiet rest
  The old years whose red hands have made
    us great.
O fair republic, strong and swift, unbind
        The shackles of thy mind :
More than our kin ye are ; henceforth not
  less than kind.

Bind on the splendid sandals, and unloose
  The burning horses, and fling wide the reins !
From cold Archangel unto Syracuse
Europe shall see and tremble and ask truce,
  And new blood pour through Asia's wasted
    veins.
Our Empire from Guiana to Hong Kong,
        In your new love made strong,
Shall last while earth is glad because of sun
  and song.


And O ! ye desert places of the sea,
  Ye plains and mountains rugged with the
    wind,
And all ye hollow caverns whence there flee
Foam-heads and blusterous waves, give ear
  to me,
  And O thou thunder, follow hard behind !
O womb of night, reverberate these chords,
        Ye clouds, ye stormy lords,
With clamour and shrill voice as of ten
  thousand swords.


Swords that clang sharp on heaven's anvil,
    white
  With heat of God's own forehead that be-
    holds
The building broken that is made of might,
Nor builded firm on justice' iron height,
  Nor is not cast in mercy's silver mould :—
Swords sharp to slay, when vengeance must
    its fill
        Drink of the bloody rill
Wherein men lave their mouths, arise and
  smite and kill.


Listen, all lands, and wonder !   For the night
  Rolls back her beaten iron, and the day
Breaks, and the passionate heralds of the
    light,
Armoured with love for panoply of might,
  Rush on the portals of the falling way.
The lamps of heaven are dim while swords
    strike fire
        From   rocks   whose   crests   burn
          higher :—
At their assault hell's dogs gasp, totter, and
  expire.

All the gold gates are open of the East ;
  The rugged columns of the hills uphold
A dome of changeless turquoise, and they
    feast,
The sun's lips, on the woods that have in-
    creased
Since dawn with store of unimagined gold.
The steam of many exhalations fair
        Sweetens the midday air ;
Echo and tree and bud chant and give birth
    and bear.

The broad Pacific brightens into blue,
  And coral isles are white with beating
    flame
Of living water on their strand, live through
With million flames candescent as the dew,
  Red flowers too queenly for a mortal name !
The sea is pregnant with green stars ; the
    land,
        The sky, like lovers stand
With kiss half-consciously exchanged, hand
    fast in hand.

O lovers fair and free, the wings of peace
  Bear this voice onward ; linger as you will
By moon-wrought glades, and softly mur-
    muring seas,
Lands white with summer, and the quiet
    leas !
  Linger, and let no word of music thrill
Your hearts ; young love is all the harp ye
    need :
        Your kiss in very deed
Is keen to echo song well tuned from
    Milton's reed.

O lovers, and ye happy groves that hear
  Their whispers, and ye vales that know
    their feet,
And all ye mountains that incline your ear
To the still murmur of the love-lorn sphere,
  And all ye caves their murmurs who
    repeat ;
Your music throbs in unison with mine ;
        The world is flushed with wine
Bubbling from Freedom's well, warm,
    luminous, divine.

Burn, changeful purple of the vine's cool
    stream !
  Burn, like the sunset of a stormy sky
When white winds gather, and white horses
    gleam
Upon the ocean, and the meadows steam
  With haze of thunder, when the crimson
    eye
Dips, and deep darkness falls and lies, and
    breaks
        In lightning's awful flakes,
When thunder unto thunder calls and the
    storm awakes.

With maddening hoofs, ye coursers of the
    sun,
  Spurn the reverberant air and paw the day,
Make east and west indissolubly one,
And night fall beaten, for its day is spun,
  And bid light gird its sword to thigh, dis-
    play
The shield of heaven's blue, and call the deep
        To watch the warrior sleep
Of two fast friends that wake only if brave
    men weep.

Wake, western land so fair, and this shall be !
  Speak and accomplish, let no ardour slip,
A sullen hound, and be brought shamefully
Back, and resurge the tremor of the sea,
  And spoil a perfect kiss from free land's lip.
O fair free sister country, for our sake,
        Who at thy side would break
All bars, all bonds, and bid the very dead
    awake.

Are not your veins made purple with our
    blood,
  And our dominions touch they not afield ?
Pours not the sea its long exultant flood
On either's coast ?  The rose has one same
    bud,
  And the vine's heart one purple pledge
    doth yield.
Are we not weary of the fangéd pen ?
        Are we not friends, and men ?
Le us look frankly face to face—and quarrel
    then !

For by the groves of green and quiet ways,
  And on the windy reaches of the river,
In moonlit night and blue unbroken days,
And where the cold ice breaks in pallid bays,
  And where dim dawns in frosty forest
    shiver ;
Where India burns and far Australia glows ;
    Where cactus blooms, where rose,
Let our hearts' beat be heard, to lighten
  many woes.

Sister and daughter of our loyal isle,
  Our hands reach out to you, our lips
    are fain
To wreathe with yours in one delicious smile
Of budding love, to grow a kiss awhile,
  And laugh like bride and groom, and
    kiss again !
Let our alliance like a marriage stand,
    Supreme from strand to strand,
The likeness of our love, the clasp of hand
  in hand.

And men who come behind us yet unborn,
  Nor dimly guessed at down the brook of
    time,
Shall celebrate the brave undying morn
When the free nations put aside their scorn
  For friendship, rock no sundering surge
    may climb,

When their strong hands gripped hard across
  the sea,
    Flushed with fresh victory,
Lands royal, leal, and great, vast, beautiful,
  and free.

Our children's children shall unsheathe the
  sword
  Against the envy of some tyrant power :
The leader of your people and our lord
Shall join to wrest from slavery abhorred
  Some other race, a fair storm-ruined
    flower !
O fair republic, lover and sweet friend,
    Your loyal hand extend,
Let freedom, peace and faith grow stronger
  to the end !

O child of freedom, thou art very fair !
  Thou hast white roses on thy eager
    breast,
The scent of all the South is in thy hair,
Thy lips are fragrant with the blossoms
  rare
  Blown under sea waves when the white
    wings rest !
Come to our warrior breast, where victory
    Sits passionate and free—
Ring out the wild salute !  Our sister over
  sea !

# THE FATAL FORCE.*

1899.

"She
In the habiliments of the goddess Isis
That day appeared."—*Antony and Cleopatra*, iii. 6, 16.

"Stoop not down, for a precipice lieth beneath the earth, reached by a descending ladder which hath Seven Steps, and therein is established the throne of an evil and fatal force."—ZOROASTER.

*PEOPLE.*

RATOUM, *Queen of Egypt.*
THE LEPER, *her divorced husband.*
KHOMSU, *their son* (dead).
S'AFI, *son of* KHOMSU *and* RATOUM.
THE KING OF SYRIA.
AMENHATEP, *High Priest.*
Chorus of Priests.
Soldiers of Egypt.
Syrian Troops.

### S'AFI.

WHY is thy back made stiff, unrighteous
   priest,
Thy knee reluctant? Thine old eyes, grown
   blind,
Stare into silence, and behold no god
Longer. Thy forehead knows no reverence
Nor sign of worship. Or sits mutiny
Blasphemous on thy brows? For in thine
   eyes
I see full knowledge, and some glittering fire
Lurks in the rheumy corners; yea, some fire
Malignant, terrible—nay, pitiable,
Thou poor fool stricken with senility,
How spurred to passion? Yet behold thy
   god,

Horus, lest anger take benignancy
From his left hand and smite thee with his
   strength.
Thou hearest? Nay, thou pitiful old man,
For I have loved thee. Yet my godhead
   must
Get worship. Anger not the god, but stoop,
My faithful priest, and worship at my feet.

### AMENHATEP.

I am most miserable. But truth must leap
In this tremendous moment from my lips,
Its long-shut barrier. For I pity thee
With my old heart's whole pity. Thou art
   young,
And beautiful, and proud, and dear to me,
Whom I have served thy life through. Now
   that love
Demands a deadlier service—to speak truth.
Thou art not Horus, but a man as I.

### CHORUS.

Thou art not Horus, but a man. Thy life
Is not of the immortals, but, as ours,
Stands at the summons of the hooded death.

* This play deals with the effect of shattering all the solid bases of a young man's mind. Here we find him strong enough to win through. In the "Mother's Tragedy" is a similar case with a weaker nature. It is well to note that in the former play the mother is evil; in the latter good. Hence also in part of tragedy. For a good mother is an affliction against which none but the strongest may stare. It is fortunately rare.

141

### S'AFI.

Speak ! I have this much of a god in me—
I am not shaken at your cries ; my lips
Are silent at your blasphemy ; my ears
Are strong to hear if there be truth at all
In your mixed murmurs : I command you,
        speak !

### AMENHATEP.

The burden of the madness of the Queen
Lies on the land : the Syrian is near ;
And she, believing that her godhead guards
Her people, sleeps.    The altars are thrown
    down ;
The people murmur.    She hath done thee
    wrong,
But be thou mighty to avenge !

### S'AFI.

                        To-day
I, Horus, shall become Osiris.    Yea,
Strange secret dreams of some mysterious
    fate
Godlike have come upon me, and the throne
Totters for your disloyalty.

### AMENHATEP.

                        Beware !
How died thy father?

### S'AFI.

                    That amazing god
Incarnate in him chose a nobler form,
And in my mother's body sought his home,
Whose double incarnation is divine
Beyond the old stories.    Yes, I am a god.

### AMENHATEP.

Beware the fatal magic of her heart !
For she is great and evil, and her voice
Howls blasphemy against yet living gods.
Thou knowest not the story of thy birth,
The truth.

### S'AFI.

        Then speak the truth, if so a priest
May tune his tongue to anything but lies.

### AMENHATEP.

Sixteen strange seasons mingle gold and grey
Since in this very temple she, the Queen,
Spake, and threw open to our reverent gaze
A royal womb made pregnant with that seed
Of which thou art the harvest.    She spake
    thus :
" Princes, and people of the Egyptian land,
And broken priests of broken deities
Discrowned this hour, look up, behold your
        god !
For I am pregnant with my own son's child,
The fruit of my desire's desire.    Most pure,
The single spirit of my godhead yearned
From death to reap dominion, and from birth
To pluck the blossom of its fruitful love,
And be the sun to ripen and the rain
To water it.    My soul became the bride
To its own body, and my body leapt
With passion from mine own imperial loins
Begotten, and made strong from my own
        soul
To answer it.    I hail thee, son of mine,
Thou royal offspring of a kingly sire,
Less kingly for the single flower of love !
I hail thee, son, the secret spouse of me,
King of my body and this realm to-day !
For lo ! the child leapt up within my womb,
Hailing me mother, and my spirit leapt,
Hailing him brother !    Son and spouse and
        king,
Exulting father of the royal soul
That lies here, loving me, assume thy crown
And sit beside me, equal to thy queen.
For look ye to the burning south, and see
The sun grown amorous, and behold his fire
Leap to my godhead.    For without a man
I single, I the mother, have conceived
Of my own loins, and made me no less god
Than all your gods !    Ye people and ye
        priests,
Behold the burden of my life, and fear,

And know me Isis. Worship me, and praise
The goodliest ruler of the world, the queen
Of all the white immeasurable seas,
And that vast river of our sowing-time,
And of your Sun. Behold me made a god
Of my own godhead, and adore the sun
Of my queen's face, and worship ye the fount
And fertile river of my life. Bow down,
Ye people and ye priests, and worship me,
And him co-equal. I am very god !"
So spake the Queen ; but I arose and said :

"Queen and our lord, we worship ! Let
  the smoke
Of this divinest incense be a smell
Sweet to thy nostrils ! For three times I
  cast
Its faint dust in the tripod, and three times
The smoke of adoration has gone up
To greet our gods ; for the old gods are
  dead."

Then there came forth a leper in the hall,
In the most holy temple. So amazed
All shrank. And he made prophecy and
  said:
"The child that shall be born of thee is
  called
Fear.[1] He shall save a people from their
  sin ;
For the old gods indeed go down to death,
But the new gods arise from rottenness."
Then said the goddess : "I indeed am pure
In my impurity ; immaculate
In misconception ; maiden in my whoredom ;
Chaste in my incest, being made a god
Through my own strength." The leper with
  smooth words
Turned, and went laughingly towards the
  west,
And took of his own leprosy and threw
Its foul flakes in the censer. So he passed,
Laughing, and on the altar the flame fell,
Till a great darkness was upon the room,
And only the Queen's eyes blazed out. So
  all

[1] S'afi is the Egyptian for fear.

Silently went, and left her naked there,
Crowned, sceptred, and exultant, till a chant
Rolled from her moving lips ; and great fear
  fell
Upon us, and the flame leapt, and we fled,
Worshipping. But the mood passed, and
  we see
A lecherous woman whose magician power
Is broken, and the balance of her mind
Made one with the fool's bauble, and her
  wand,
That was of steel and fire, like a reed,
  snapped !

### S'AFI.

So lived my father. Tell me of his death.

### AMENHATEP.

At thy first breath the gods were patient
  still,
Till the abomination filled its cup,
And hatred took her heart. She slew thy
  sire,
And made his body the banquet of her sin
In the infernal temple. "So," she said,
"I reap the incarnation of the god."
So, gloomy and hideous, she would prowl
  about
Seeking fresh human feasts, and bloody rites
Stained the white altar of the world. And
  yet
Her power is gone, and we behold her go,
Haggard and weary, through the palace
  courts
And through the temple, lusting for strange
  loves
And horrible things, and thirsting for new
  steam
Of thickening blood upon her altar steps.
Her body wearies of desire, and fails
To satisfy the fury of her spirit ;
The blood-feasts sicken her and yield no
  strength ;
She is made one with hell, and violent force
Slips and is weakness, and extreme desire
Spends supple.

S'AFI.

I have heard you as a god
Immutable.

CHORUS.

Thou art as proud and calm
As statued Memnon.  Thou art more than
    god
And less than man.  Thine eyelids tremble
    not.

S'AFI.

I shall avenge it as a god.  The land
Shall be made free.

AMENHATEP.

And the old gods have sway,
Re-born from incorruption.

S'AFI.

The old gods !
I must muse deeply.  Keep your ancient
    ways
A little.  I must play the part through so.

CHORUS.

In the ways of the North and the South
    Whence the dark and the dayspring are
        drawn,
We pass with the song of the mouth
    Of the notable Lord of the Dawn.
Unto Ra, the desire of the East, let the
    clamour of singing proclaim
    The fire of his name !

In the ways of the East and the West
    Whence the night and the day are dis-
        crowned,
We pass with the beat of his breast,
    And the breath of his crying is bound.
Unto Toum, the low Lord of the West, let
    the noise of our chant be the breath
    Proclaiming him Death !

In the ways of the depth and the height,
    Where the multitude stars are at ease,
There is music and terrible light,
    And the violent song of the seas.
Unto Mou, the most powerful Lord of the
    South, let our worship declare
    Him Lord of the Air !

In the mutable fields that are sown
    Of a seed that is whiter than noon,
Whose harvest is beaten and blown
    By the magical rays of the moon,
In the caverns and wharves of the wind, in
    the desolate seas of the air,
    Revolveth our prayer !

In the sands and the desert of death,
    In the horrible flowerless lands,
In the fields that the rain and the breath
    Of the sun make as gold as the sands
With ripening wheat, in the earth, in the
    infinite realm of its seed,
    The hearts of us bleed !

In the wonderful flowers of the foam,
    Blue billows and breakers grown grey,
When the storm sweeps triumphantly home
    From the bed of the violate day,
In the furious waves of the sea, wild world
    of tempestuous night,
    Our song is as light !

In the tumult of manifold fire,
    Multitudinous mutable feet
That dance to an infinite lyre
    On the heart of the world as they beat,
In the flowers of the bride of the flame, in
    the warrior Lord of the Fire,
    There burns our desire !

AMENHATEP.

Cry now, bewail the broken house, be-
    wail
The ruin of the land ; cry out on Fate !

## CHORUS.

Slow wheels of unbegotten hate
And changeless circles of desire,
Formless creations uncreate,
Swift fountains of ungathered fire,
The misty counterpoise of time,
Dim winds of ocean and sublime
Pyramids of forgotten foam
Whirling, vague cones of shapeless sleep
And infinite dreams, and stars that roam,
And comets moving through the deep
Unfathomable skies,
Darker for moonlight, and the glow-worm
     eyes
Of dusky women that were stars,
And paler curves of the immutable bars
That line the universe with light,
Great eagle-flights of mystic moons
That dip, while the dull midnight swoons
About the skirts of Night :
These bowed and shaped themselves and
     said :
" It shall be thus ! "
And the intolerable luminous
Death that is god bent down his head
And answered : " Thus, immutably,
Above all days and deeds, shall be ! "
And the great Light that is above all gods
Lifted his calm brow, spake, and all the
     seas,
And all the air, and all the periods
Of seasons and of stars gave ear, and these
Vaults of the heaven heard
The great white Light that shaped its secrecies
Into one holy terrible word,
Higher than all words spoken ; for He said :
" Death is made change, and only change
     is dead."
For the most holy spirit of a man
Burns through the limit of the wheels that
     ran
Through all the unrelenting skies
When Icarus died,
And leaps, the flight of wise omnipotent eyes,
When Dædalus espied
An holy habitation for the shrine
Solitary, 'mid the night of broken brine
VOL. I.

That foamed like starlight round the desolate
     shore.[1]
So to the mine of that crystalline ore
Golden, the electric spark of man is drawn
Deep in the bosom of the world, to soar
New-fledged, an eagle to the dazzling dawn
With lidless eyes undazzled, to arise,
Son of the morning, to the Southern skies ;
And fling its wild chant higher at the fall
Of even, and of bright Hyperion ;
To mix its fire with dew, to call
The spirit of the limitless air, made one
In the amazing essence of all light
Limitless, emanation of the migh'
Of the great Light above all gods, the fire
Of our supreme desire.
So out of grievous labyrinths of the mind
The soul's desire may find
Some passionate thread, the clear note of a
     bird,
To make the dark ways of the gods as light,
And bring forth music from slow chants un-
     heard,
And visions from the fathomless night.
So is the spirit of the loftier man
Made holy and most strong against his fate ;
So is the desolate visage of the wan
Lord of Amenti[2] covered, and the gate
Of Ra made perfect.  So the waters flow
Over the earth, throughout the sea,
Till all its deserts glow,
And all its salt springs vanish, and night flee
The pinions of the day wide-spread, and pure
Fresh fountains of sweet water that endure
Assume the crown of the wide world, and
     lend
A star of many summits to his head
That rules his fate and compasses his end,
And seeks the holy mountain of the dead
To draw dead fire, and breathe, and give it
     life !

But thou, be strong for strife,
And, as a god, cry out, and let there be
The mark of many footsteps on the sea

[1] See Vergil, *Aen.* vi. ll. 14-19.
[2] The West : the Egyptian Land of the
Dead.
                                                    K

Of angels hastening to fulfil
Thy supreme, single will !
Alone, intense, unmoved, not made for
　　change,
Let thy one godhead rise
To move like morning, and like day to range,
A furnace for the skies,
That all men cry: "The uncreated God !
Formless, ineffable, just, whose period
Is as his name, Eternity !"　So bear
The sceptre of the air !
So mayest thou avenge, all-seeing, blind,
The wrath of this consuming fire, that licks
The rafters and the portals of the house,
The gateways of the kingdom, where behind
Lurk ruinous fates and consequence ; where
　　fix
Their fangs the scorpions ; where hide their
　　brows
The shamed protectors of the Egyptian land.
Go forth avenging ; men shall understand
And worship, seeing justice as a spouse
Lean on thine iron hand.

For Murder walks by night, and hides her
　　face,
But righteous Wrath in the light, and knows
　　his place ;
For hate of a mother is ill, and the lightning
　　flashes
But foil a harlot's will, burn the earth to
　　ashes,
Cleanse the incestuous sty of a whore's desire,
Scatter the dung to the sky, and burn her
　　with fire !
So the avenging master shall cleanse his fate
　　of shame,
Set his seal of disaster, a royal seal to his
　　name.　　　　　　　　　　[*Exeunt.*

S'AFI.

I am not Horus, but I shall be king.


Enter THE LEPER.

THE LEPER.

I am a leper, but I am the king.

S'AFI.

Monstrous illegible horror, let thy mouth
Frame from its charnel-house some pregnant
　　word
Intelligible.

THE LEPER.

　　　　　　I am king ; thy mother's limbs
Clung fast to mine when I begot thy father.

S'AFI.

He died in battle ; thou art not the king.

THE LEPER.

I did not fall in battle ; but my queen
Saw on my breast the livid mark of sin
That was the leprosy of her own soul,
And drove me forth to compass my disgrace
With infamies ineffable.

S'AFI.

　　　　　　　　I know ;
I shall avenge.　The old gods come again.

THE LEPER.

Nay ! I have lived through all these barren
　　years,
Discrowned, diseased, abominable, cast out,
And meditating on the event of life,
And that initiated Hope that we,
Royal, inherit, of the final life,
Nor newer incarnation, and possessed
Of strange powers, who have moved about
　　this court
Loathed, and unrecognised, and shunned,
　　have thought
That the old bondage was as terrible
As thine incestuous mother's iron hand,
Rending the entrails of her growing realm
To seek her bloody fate, whose violence
Even now makes the abyss of wrath divine
Boil in the deep.　Thou mayest be that great
Osiris, bidding man's high soul be free,
Justified in its own higher self, made pure
And perfect in its own eyes, being a god.

Destroy this priestcraft! We are priests
indeed,
Highest among the secret ones ; and we—
See where our heritage is made ; I, king,
A leper, and thyself, the hideous fruit
Of what strange poisons? But in mine own
self
I am the king and chief of all the priests ;
And thou, in thine own eyes, art a young
god,
Strong, beautiful, and lithe, a leaping fawn
Upon the mountains.

S'AFI.

Yea, I am a god.
I am fire against the fountain of my birth,
The storm upon the earth that nurtured me ![1]
Leave me : we twain have no more words to
speak.

THE LEPER.

Neither in heaven nor in hell. I go,
The dead king, worshipping the living man.
[*Exit.*

S'AFI.

I have been a god so long, my thoughts run
halt
From many contemplations. Like the flow
Of a slow river deep and beautiful,
My even life moved onward to full scope,
The ocean of profounder deity,
And—suddenly—the cataract ! My soul,
Centred eternally upon itself,
Comprehends hardly all this violence
Of wayward men intemperate. I am calm,
And contemplate, without a muscle moved
Or nerve set shrieking, all these ruinous
deeds
And dissolution of the royal house.
I see this grey unnatural mother of mine
Now, as she is, disrobed of deity,
And like some reeling procuress grown wolf
By infamous bewitchment, haunt the stairs,

And pluck the young men by the robe, and
take
The maidens for her sacrifice, and burn
With great unquenchable dead lustrous eyes
Toward impossible things grown possible
In Egypt. I will cleanse the land of this.
Let me remember I am yet a god !

*Re-enter* THE LEPER.

THE LEPER.

Thou must be brought before her presently
Borne in a coffin. See thou fill it not,
But take the lion's mask and play his part
Before the throne. Be ready, and be strong.

S'AFI.

I shall do so. Come, let us go together
In hateful love and sacrilegious hate,
Disease and godhead. I am still the god.
[*Exeunt.*

*Enter* RATOUM.

RATOUM.

I stood upon the desert, and my eyes
Beheld the splendid and supernal dawn
Flame underneath the single star that burns
Within the gateway of the golden East
To rule my fate ; but I have conquered Fate
Thus far, that I am perfect in myself,
The absolute unity and triple power
Engrafted. For the foolish people see
An old grey woman, wicked, not divine,
Who[1] shall this hour assume the royal self
And the old godhead, and the lithe strong
limbs
And supple loins and splendid bosom bare
Full of bright milk, the breast of all the
world.
This lesser mastery I have made mine own
By strange devices, by unheard-of ways
Of wisdom, by strong sins, and magical
Rituals made righteous of their own excess
Of horror ; but I have not made myself

---

[1] Fire and Water, Air and Earth, are the
" antagonisms " of the " elements."

[1] This antithetical use of the relative is
uncommon.

So absolute as I shall do to-day
In this new infamy.  For I must pass
Desolate into the dusk of things again,
Having risen so far to fall to the abyss,
Deeper for exaltation ; I must go
Wailing and naked into the inane
Cavernous shrineless place of misery,
Forgetful, hateful, impotent, except
The last initiation seize my soul,
And fling me into Isis' very self,
The immortal, mortal.  Let me know this
    night
Whether my place is found among the stars
That wander in the deep, or made secure
As the high throne of her that dwells in
    heaven,
Fruitful for life and death, Wisdom her name !
This hour the foolish ones shall see their souls
Shrink at my manifest deity.  This night
My spirit on my spirit shall beget
Myself for my own child.  Behold ! they
    come,
Fantastically moving through the dance,
The many mourners, and the fatal bier
Looms in the dimness of the anteroom.
It is enough.  My hour is at hand !

CHORUS *enter and circumambulate.*

Even as the traitor's breath
Goeth forth, he perisheth
By the secret sibilant word that is spoken
    unto death.

Even as the profane hand
Reacheth to the sacred sand,
Fire consumes him that his name be forgotten
    in the land.

Even as the wicked eye
Seeks the mysteries to spy,
So the blindness of the gods takes his spirit :
    he shall die.

Even as the evil priest,
Poisoned by the sacred feast,
Changes by its seven powers to the misbe-
    gotten beast :

Even as the powers of ill,
Broken by the wanded will,
Shriek about the holy place, vain and vague
    and terrible :

Even as the lords of hell,
Chained in fires before the spell,
Strain upon the sightless steel, break not
    fetters nor compel :

So be distant, O profane !
Children of the hurricane !
Lest the sword of fire destroy, lest the ways
    of death be plain !

So depart, and so be wise,
Lest your perishable eyes
Look upon the formless fire, see the maiden
    sacrifice !

So depart, and secret flame
Burn upon the stone of shame,
That the holy ones may hear music of the
    sleepless Name !

Now the sacred and obscene
Kiss, the pure and the unclean,
Mingle in the incense steaming up before the
    goddess queen.

Holy, holy, holy spouse
Of the sun-engirdled house,
With the secret symbol burning on thy mul-
    tiscient brows !

Hear, O hear the mystic song
Of the serpent-moving throng,
Isis mother, Isis maiden, Isis beautiful and
    strong !

Even as the traitor's breath
Goeth forth, he perisheth
By the secret sibilant word that is spoken
    unto death.

RATOUM.

The hour is given unto death.  Bring in
Dead Horus, for the night is shed above.
                    [*Coffin brought in.*

CHORUS.

The noise of the wind of the winter; the
    sound
Of the wings of the charioted night;
The song of the sons of the seas profound;
The thunder of death; the might
Of the eloquent silence of black light!

RATOUM.

The noise of many planets fallen far!

CHORUS.

Death listens for the voice of life; night
    waits
The dawn of wisdom: winter seeks the
    spring!

RATOUM.

The music of all stars arisen; the breath
Of God upon the valley of the dead!

CHORUS.

The silence of the awaiting soul asleep!

RATOUM.

The murmur of the fountain of my life!

CHORUS.

The whole dead universe awaits the Word.

RATOUM.

Now is the hour of life; my voice leaps up
In the dim halls of death, and kindling flame
Roars like the tempest through forgetfulness.
This is my son, whose father is my son,
From my own womb complete and absolute,
And in this strong perfection of myself
Stands the triumphant power of my desire,
Manifest over self, and man, and god!
For in the sacred coffin lies his corpse
Who shall arise at the enormous word
Of my creating deity; his life
Shall quicken in him, and the dead man
    rise,

Osiris; and all power be manifest
In our supreme reunion; let the priest
Cast incense on the fire, upon the ground
Let water of the fertilising Nile
Be spilt, because these dark maternal breasts
That gave their milk to that divinest child
Are not yet full of the transcending stream
That knows its fountain in my deity.
The incense fumes before me: I am come,
Isis, within this body that ye know,
Transmuting! Look upon me, ye blind
    eyes!
Behold, dull souls and ignorant desires!
See if I be not altogether god!
    [*She assumes the appearance of her
      mature beauty, standing before them
      with the wand upraised.*
Wonder and worship! Sing to me the song
Of the extreme spring! Rejoice in my great
    strength
And infinite youth and new fertility,
And lave your foreheads in this holy milk
That springs, the fountain of humanity,
Luminous in the temple! Raise the hymn.

CHORUS.

Through fields of foam ungarnered sweeps
    The fury of the wind of dawn;
Through fiery desolation creeps
    The water of the wind withdrawn.
With fire and water consecrate
The foam and fire are recreate.
    With air uniting fire and water,
    The springtide's unbegotten daughter
Blossoms in oceans of blue air,
Flowers of new spring to bear.

The sorrowful twin fishes glide
    Silent and sacred into sleep;
The joyful Ram exalts his pride,
    Seeing the forehead of the deep
Glow from his palace, as the sun
Leaps to the spring, whose coursers run
    Flaming before their golden master,
    As death and winter and disaster
Fall from the Archer's bitter kiss
Fast to their mute abyss.

The pale sweet blooms of lotus burn;
  The scent of spring is in the soul;
Men's spirits to the loftiest turn;
  Light is extended and made whole.
The waters of the whispering Nile
Lisp of their loves a little while,
  Then break, like songsters, into sighing,
  Because the lazy days are dying;
And swift and tawny streams must rise
World's world to fertilise.

The lotus is afire for love,
  Its yearnings are immortal still;
But in its bosom, fed thereof,
  Lust, like a child, will have his will.
Immortal fervour, strangely blent
With mystic sensual sacrament,
  Fills up its cup; its petals tremble
  With faint desires that dissemble
The fierce intention to be wed
One with the spring sun's head.

The fountains of the river yearn
  Toward the sacred temple-walls,
They foam upon the sands that burn
  With spring's delirious festivals.
They flash upon the gleaming ways,
They cry, they chant aloud the praise
  Of Isis, and our temple kisses
  Their flowery water-wildernesses,
Whose foamheads nestle to the stones
With slumberous antiphones.

All birds and beasts and fish are fain
  To mingle passion with the hope
All creatures hold, that cycled pain
  May make its stream the wider scope
Of many lives and changing law,
  Till to the sacred fountains draw
  Essences of dim being, mated
  With lofty substance uncreated,
Concluding the full period
That makes all being God.

S'AFI (*disguised in the mask of a lion*).

I lift the censer. Hail, immortal queen,
From the vast hall of death! Dead Horus
  cries

Towards the dawn.    Bid me awake, O
  mother!
O mother! from the darkness of the tomb,
That live Osiris may cry back to thee,
O spouse! O sister! from the halls of life,
The profound lake, the immeasurable depth,
The sea of the three Loves! O mother,
  mother!
Isis, the voice that even Amenti hears,
Speak, that I rise from chaos, from the world
Of shapeless and illusionary forms,
Of dead men's husks, and unsubstantial
  things.
O mother, mother, mother! I arise!

RATOUM.

Horus, dread godhead, child of me, arise!
Arise Osiris, to the sacred rites
And marriage-bed of fuller deity.
Now, at the serpent-motion of this wand,
Rise from the dead! Arise, dead Horus,
  rise
To be Osiris. Isis speaks! Arise!
  [*The coffin is opened.* THE LEPER *is
    raised out of it swathed in bandages.*
Out of the sleep of ages wake and live!
                [*The wrappings fall off.*

THE LEPER.

I am the resurrection and the death!
  [RATOUM *falls back shrieking. The
    priests raise a chant to stifle the
    sound.*

S'AFI (*tearing off his mask*).

I am the hideous poison of thy veins
And foulest fruit of thy incestuous womb.

RATOUM.

I am thy mother! I have nurtured thee
With woman's tenderness and godhead's
  strength.

S'AFI.

I am the avenger of my own false birth.

RATOUM.

I have loved thee ever; I have made thee god.

S'AFI.

I hate myself, and therefore I hate thee.

RATOUM.

I am still goddess, still desire thy love.
That leper lies : thou art indeed a god.

S'AFI.

I am a god to execute my will.
    [*Threatens her with his dagger.*

RATOUM.

Mercy ! Thou canst not strike a woman down !

S'AFI.

So ! The thin casing of the godhead rots,
Mere mummy-cloth: the rotten corpse within,
Dust and corruption ! I am still the god,
And gods slay women : therefore I slay thee.

RATOUM.

Then thou shalt see me once again a god !
    [*By a tremendous effort she towers
    before him. Silently they gaze at
    one another for a while, he vainly
    endeavouring to force himself to
    strike. At last she collapses into the
    throne; he springs forward and
    drives his knife into her.*

THE LEPER.

It is finished ! The sacrament is made !
The god
Has flamed within the altar-cake : 'tis done !
    [*Silence: presently* THE LEPER *breaks
    into a horrible, silent, smooth
    laughter. Again silence.*

S'AFI.

I am done with godhead: let me be a man.

CHORUS.

Hail, S'afi, king of Egypt and the Nile !
Hail, S'afi, Lord of the two lands,[1] all hail !

S'AFI.

King of himself and lord of life and death,
No lesser throne ! I have borne me as a god,
Avenging on my nearest blood the sin
That brought me shameful to the shameless
    light.
I have not faltered nor turned back at all,
Nor moved my purpose for a moment's
    thought.
Nor will I now. The god is gone from me,
And as a man I feel the living shame
Of my existence, and the biting brand
Of murder set upon me, and the sting
Of my discrownèd forehead. I shall die
Having this proof of my own nobleness
To soothe the rancour of my stricken soul
In the abodes of night, that I have dared,
With the first knowledge to make good my
    spirit
Against its fate, to steel my flinching heart
Against all men, dominions, shapes, and
    powers,
Seen and unseen, to justice and to truth,
Sought out by desolate ways of hateful deeds,
And so set free myself from my own fate,
Whom I will smite to end the coil of things
Here, to begin—what life ? For Life I know
Stands like a living sentinel behind
The rugged barrier of death, the gates
Where the rude valley narrows, and man
    hears
The steep and terrible cataract of time
Break, and lose shape and substance in the
    foam
And spray of an eternity of air !
My death, and not my life, may crown me
    king !

    [1] Upper and Lower Egypt.

So let me not be buried in that state
Due to the hateful rank that I abjure
By this proud act, but let my monument
Say to succeeding peoples and dim tribes
Unthought of: "This was born a living man
Bound, and he cut the chain of circumstance,
And spat on Fate." And all the priests shall
    say
And all the people: "Verily and Amen."
                              [*Stabs himself.*

### CHORUS.

Spirit of the Gods! O single,
Sacred, secret, let the length
East and west, the depth and height,
North and south, with music tingle,
Ring with battled clarion choirs of the far-
    resounding light!
Let the might
Of Osirian sacrifice
Dwell upon the self-slain king!
Spirit of the Gods! Unite
Streams of sacramental light
In the soul, thrice purified,
Consecrated thrice,
Till Osiris justified
In the supreme sacrifice
Take his kingdom. Hear the cry
That the wailing vultures make,
Circling in the blackening sky
Over the abysmal lake.
Spirit, for our spirit's sake
Give the token of thy fire
Trident in the lambent air,
Till our spirits unaware
Worship and aspire!
Hear, beyond all periods,
Timeless, formless, multiform,
Thou, supreme above the storm,
Spirit of the Holy Ones, Spirit of the
    Gods!

*Enter* MESSENGER.

### MESSENGER.

The battle rages: even now the shock
Of hostile spears makes the loud earth re-
    sound,
The wide sky tremble.

### AMENHATEP.

                    Here lies Horus dead,
There Isis slain. We have no leader left.

### MESSENGER.

The fight is doubtful. We may conquer still.

### AMENHATEP.

By this shed blood and desecrated shrine
And horrible hour of madness, may it be
That all the evil fortune of the land,
Created of these dead iniquities,
Burn its foul flame out. Are ye not appeased,
Even ye, O Powers of Evil, at this shame
And sacrilege? And ye, Great Powers of
    Good,
Hath not enough of misery been wrought,
Enough of expiation? We have sinned,
But our iniquity he purged away,
Who as avenger hath denied his life,
To be made one with ye. O by his blood
And strong desire of holiness, and might
And justice, let him mediate between
And mitigate your anger, that the name
Of Egypt may not perish utterly.
Make, make an end!

### THE LEPER.

                    All things must work themselves
To their own end. Created sin grown strong
Must claim its guerdon. Ye abase your-
    selves
Well for repentance; but ye shall not ward
With tears and prayers the ruin ye have made,
Nor banish the enormous deities
Of judgment so invoked by any prayers,
Or perfumes or libations. What must be
Will be. Material succour ye demand
In vain. But ye may purify yourselves.

### AMENHATEP.

Knows then thy prophecy our final doom?

THE LEPER.

Inquire not of your fate ! Myself do know,
Mayhap. Ye shall know. I await the event.


AMENHATEP.

We shall be patient, and we shall be strong.


THE LEPER.

The noise of rushing feet ! The corridor
Rings with their scurrying fear. This is the
end.
[*Enter a flying soldier, crying aloud,
and seeks a hiding-place.*
Speak not, thou trembling slave : we understand !
[*The soldier slips on the marble floor,
and lies groaning.*


AMENHATEP.

See that due silence greets catastrophe !
No word from now without command of
mine.
[*Silence. Then grows a noise of men
fighting, &c. ; above this after a
while rises a shrill laughter, terrifying to hear. Then cries of victory
and the triumphant laugh of a great
conqueror. His heavy step, and that
of his staff, &c., is next heard coming masterfully down the corridor.
The soldier gives a shriek.*


THE LEPER.

The Syrian must not see a cur like this
Cower at death. For Egypt's honour,
then !

Give me that spear. [*Aside.*] That royalty's
own hand
Should send this thing to his long misery !
[*Taking a spear, he runs through the
soldier.*

*The* KING OF SYRIA, *attended, enters.*

KING OF SYRIA.

Your armies beaten back before my face,
Your weapons broken, I am come to take
The crown from her pale brows that sitteth
there.

THE LEPER.

The Queen is dead : I am the King of Egypt.
To-day I saved the house from its own shame
By strange ways : I will strike one blow to
save
The land from its invaders. In the name
Of all our gods, I here invoke on thee
The spirit of my leprosy. Have at you !
[*Springs at the* KING OF SYRIA, *only
to be transfixed on his drawn
sword ; but he succeeds in clasping
the King, who staggers. His soldiers, with a shout, rush forward,
drag down* THE LEPER *and attack
the priests. All are slain. Silence :
then a shield drops, clanging on the
ground.*

KING OF SYRIA (*assuming crown and
sitting on throne*).

Salute the conqueror of the Egyptian land !
[*The soldiers salute and cheer.*
I am a leper : get ye hence !
[*Exeunt soldiers.*
Unclean ! [*Silence.*
This was the hour that my ambitious hopes
Centred upon : and now I grasp the hour—
So fares mortality. [*Silence.*
Unclean ! unclean !


CURTAIN.

# THE MOTHER'S TRAGEDY.*

## 1899.

SCENE.—*The room is furnished with comfort as well as luxury. A crucifix is in the window to the East, and the room is flooded with a ray of sunlight.*

CORA VAVASOUR (*late of the Halls*).
ULRIC, *illegitimate son of* CORA, *ignorant of his parentage.*
MADELINE, *girl in love with* ULRIC.
THE SPIRIT OF TRAGEDY, *as Chorus, sits in the back, crouched, brooding over the scene. It is veiled and throned.*

### SPIRIT OF TRAGEDY.

HERE, in the home of a friend,
Here, in the mist of a lie,
The pageant moves on to the desolate end
Under a sultry sky.
Noon is upon us, and Night,
Spreading her wings unto flight,
Visits the lands that lie far in the West,
Where the bright East is at peace on her
    breast :
Opposite quarters unite.
Soon is the nightfall of Destiny here ;
Nature's must pass as her hour is gone by.
Only another than she is too near,
Gloom in the sky.
One who can never pass over shall sever
Links that were forged of Love's hand ;
Love that was strong die away as a song,
Melt as a cable of sand.
But I am watching, with unwearied eye,
The wayfare of the tragedy.

I see the brightness of the home ; I see
The grisly phantom of despair to be.
I see the miserable past redeemed,
(Intolerable as its purpose seemed,)
Redeemed by love : I see the jealous days
Pass into sunshine, and youth-beaming rays
Quicken the soul's elixir.   Let me show
How these air-castles tumble into woe.
    [*Raises sceptre as if to start action of
    play.*

### CORA.

Why did your eyelids quiver as I spoke ?
A smile, a tear ? that trembling, in their
    deep
Violet passion, of the beautiful
Eyes that they half discover ?   Speak to
    me.
I have long thought a secret was your spouse,
Shared your deep fancies and your lightest
    word,
Partook your maiden bed, and gave you
    dreams
Somewhat too troublous to be virginal.

### MADELINE.

My dear kind Cora, do they lie to you,
These fancies of my idle hours ?   Believe,
I seem to tremble at my inward thought ;
My heart is full of wonder.   When I go
Nightward beneath the moon, and take my
    thoughts
Past her pale beauty through some glowing
    skies

---

* The justification of this play, both in subject and construction, is to be found in the Introduction to the "Ion" of Euripides. [Verrall, Camb. Univ. Press, 1890.] The chief of its many morals is that sin must reap its harvest in spite of repentance, prayer, and the other dodges by which men seek to elude Fate.

Not unfamiliar, through exulting gates—
"Lift up your heads," I hear the angels cry ;
"Be ye lift up, ye everlasting doors.
A child-heart seeks the Lover of the Child !"
O meek and holy Jesus, hath Thy heart
Yearned unto me, Thy maiden ?  For I knew
A bliss so pregnant with the unforeseen
As brought me to the very feet of Christ,
Weeping.  How clouded that mysterious
Passion !  I fell a-weeping in my bed,
Forgetting, or not knowing.  For a fire
Too perfect for my sinful soul to touch
Gathered me closely in itself, to hide
Its utter glory from me.  Now I feel
Swift troubled tremblings in myself : I seek
Again those visionary skies.  Alas !
That angel chorus swells another note
I cannot understand.

CORA.
                    I am so moved,
I cannot find it in my heart to say
The words I purposed.  Let my folly pass
As an old worldly woman's talk.

MADELINE.
                              O no !
You bear the sainted fragrance of your love
Higher than even my dreams.  In earthly
    life
You are not earthly.  I have often thought
The Virgin has some special care for you,
And given of her beauty and her peace
A special dower.  Your thoughts are ever
    pure ;
Your soul in sweet communion with God !
Why, you are crying ?

CORA.
                    You say this to me ?
O could you look within a magic glass,
Holding my hand, such sights would come
    to you
Beyond your knowledge—ay, beyond belief !
I am no saintly virgin wrapped in prayer,

Nor is my life one river of clear water
Drawn from the wells of God.  You foolish
    child !
My love for you you cannot understand,
Nor the low motive—you have shown it me—
Of this beginning of our talk.

MADELINE.
                              Say on !

CORA (meaningly).
Much less you understand the love I bear
To Ulric !

MADELINE gives a little cry.
                    Heart of Christ ! it cannot be !

CORA.
No, child ; I tricked you.  Is your secret
    out ?

MADELINE.
I am dismayed at my discovery.
(Slowly.)  I never guessed my own poor silli-
    ness
Until that moment when you frightened me.

CORA.
And now you know how dear he is to you !
Come, child, I love you both.  Your happi-
    ness
Is my life's purpose.  I have seen the truth
Of this in you ; it comes to every one.
I know that he is half in love with you.
Look once again as you did look just now,
And he would die for you.  O foolish girl !
        [MADELINE weeps quietly for a little,
            CORA caressing her.

MADELINE.
Please let me go : you are too kind to me !

## Cora.

Rest, sunny head ! A little while to sleep,
And then—perhaps the Mother in a dream
May comfort you. A woman's love is this
To have one heart, an undivided love ;
But Hers—division in the universe
Makes multiple each part. Sweet Madeline,
Believe me, She will come to maiden dreams,
Bestow Her peace, and so direct the life
That is not unto God unconsecrate
For being dedicated unto love !

[*Exit* Madeline.

### Cora *remains thinking.*

I was no bolder twenty years ago !
Time, Time, thou maker and destroyer both,
Only in resurrection hast no part !

[*Broods.*

### Spirit of Tragedy (*with light enjoyment*).

How light and how agreeable,
Paved pathway to the gate of hell !
See how all virtues, graces, shin
Till woman half appears divine !
But I am waiting, watching still
The treason of the powers of ill.
Soft, moveless, as a tigress glides,
Strange laughing devilry abides
Its hour to poison. How they gloat,
The fiends, upon her lips and throat !
They touch her heart, they speer [1] her eyes,
They linger on the lovely prize !
O dead she thought them ! It is written :
" Eve's heel is by the serpent bitten,
His head she bruises." No indeed !
Not woman, but the woman's seed !
Hark ! in the cloak of " Love of Truth "
They whisper " Memory of Youth " ;
And, mindful of the deadliest sin,
Hint : " Sinful woman, look within ! "

[1] To search, with the idea of looking more deeply. The grotesque word is used to suggest the quaint inspection of the malicious goblins.

## Cora.

Ah me ! if she could look within a glass [1]
With spells and pantacles [2] well fortified !
I have a glass whose bitter destiny
No wizard may conjure. Arise ye there,
Old hours of horror, clear by one and one,
In the confused and tossing ocean,
Where memory picks spar and spar from out
The dreadful whirlpool hardly yet appeased,
To join together in imagination
The ship—the wreck ! And yet I stand at last
Secure in my unselfish love to them,
Repaid in mine own currency. I trust
God hath made smooth the road beneath the hearse
Of my forgetful age. All must be well.

### Spirit of Tragedy (*with sombre joy*).

Mortals never learn from stories
How catastrophe becomes ;
How above the victor's glories
In the trumpets and the drums,
And the cry of millions " Master ! "
Looms the shadow of disaster.
Every hour a man hath said
" That at least is scotched and dead."
Some one circumstance : " At last
That, and its effects, are past."
Some one terror—subtle foe !—
" I have laid that spectre low ! "
They know not, learn not, cannot calculate
How subtly Fate

[1] The crystal sphere is habitually used by clairvoyants and others for purposes of divination. Such a globe should be ceremonially consecrated and vitalised.

[2] From παν, all, a diminutive. The word thus means "a universe in little." It is usually a square or circle of vellum or other material, designed and painted appropriately to its purpose ; a spirit is then evoked and commanded to dwell therein, that it may do the required office.

Weaves its fine mesh, perceiving how to
    wait ;
Or how accumulate
The trifles that shall make it master yet
Of the strong soul that bade itself forget.


CORA.

Let me not shrink ! Truth always purifies.
I will go through those two impossible
Actual years.  The city was itself ;
Hard  thinking  if  hard  drinking — sober-
    sides !
One night I stepped up tremulous on the
    stage,
Sang something, found my senses afterward
Only to that intolerable sound
Of terrible applause.  They shook the sky
With calling me to answer.  And I lay—
A  storm  of  weeping  swept  across  my
    frame—
Till the polite, the hateful manager
Led me to face a nation's lunatic
Roar of delight.  I soon got over that,
And over--yes, the other thing.   Three
    months—
They used to quote me on the Stock Ex-
    change !
I will say this to me, I will not shrink :
Look up, you coward, Cora Vavasour !
Which fathered me the bastard ?   Every
    rag,[1]
Prurient licksores of society,
Gave it a different father.  Am I sure
Myself ?  The shameful Mammon was his
    name,
Glittering gold !  I loved my opulence,
Cursed    my   " misfortune."    Childbirth
    sobered me.
I loved the child, the only human love
I ever tasted, and I sacrificed
The popularity, the infamy,
Of my old life ; I sought another world.
I  " got  religion " — how   I   hate   the
    phrase !—
So jest the matron newspapers.  The end.

              [1] Society papers.

Since then I lived, as I am living still,
Wrapped in the all-absorbing love of him
My child, my child !  And now my selfishness
Is shamed, and I have made the sacrifice
To give this pure heart to that maidenly,
And let mine old age grow upon my hair,
Finding my happiness in seeing him
The all-devoted, and in God's good pleasur
Have little children playing at my knees,
That I may listen, in their innocent prayers,
For Jesus' voice.  And I will never break
The secret of his being to my boy
Lest he despise me.  This one reticence
I think my long-drawn agony may earn.
For I will do without a mother's name
If only I may keep a son's love still !
                                        [Exit.


SPIRIT OF TRAGEDY (with sarcastic verve).

She will not break an oath so wisely sworn,
Unlock her secret to disdain.
Wisdom is hers—what angel need to warn ?
Since angels only seek to gain
That wisdom of the unprofane.
All future happiness I surely see.
I am the Soul of Tragedy !


Enter ULRIC (musing, with love-light
              in his eyes).

          [At his entrance, SPIRIT OF
          TRAGEDY changes to a shape
          of incarnate Horror, and
          continues :

Naked as dawn, the purpose of the hour
Grows on my vision, and my cynic laughter
Chills in my veins : the old avenging power
Shows me the thing that is to be hereafter.
I gloated on the coming of the curse—
I did create an hearse,
Black plumes and solemn mourners ; and I
    saw
The triumph of some natural law
Fit for a poet's verse.
I saw some common fate to lure, to tempt ;
(No mortal of the ages is exempt)

Some notable disaster to the house
Wherein such piety and love abide ;
I saw some hateful spouse
Carry away the bride.
That feeble prescience of events to come,
That stultified imagining, hath lied ;
And I can see, though all the signs be
    dumb
And auguries unfruitful—I can see,
Now, some intolerable tragedy
Fit for a god to picture, not a man !
I see the breaking of the rosary,
And Fate's cold fingers snap the span
Of three most innocent and pleasant lives.
So terrible a happening dives
Swift from God's hand to the abyss of
    hell,
And in its torment thrives,
Gathering curses from the darkest cave,
Calling corruption from the grave
To form one shape of aspect multiple
Divided in its single spell ;
One spectre smooth and suave,
More horrible than any fear or active doom,
Beckoning with its lewd malignant finger,
Beckoning, beckoning, to no pious tomb
Where pitiable memory might linger.
A creeping, living horror hems me in,
A masterpiece of sin !
Even my soul, inured to contemplate
The dreadful, the perverse design of Fate,
In many stories never meant to win
Applause of mortals or of gods, but made
To choke man's spirit in its shade,
And make him, in his pride and happiness,
In virtue's mantle and love's seemly dress,
Immeasurably afraid.
The hour is on them—let its weight express
All blood, all life, from the disastrous grape !
In God, in mercy, there is no escape,
No anchor for distress.
The hour strikes mournfully upon the bell
Of the most awful precipice
That merges hell in hell.
There is deep silence in that dread abyss ;
There is deep silence in the sphered sun ;
There is deep silence where the planets
    run,

Majestic fires !  Before the throne of God
Deep silence waits the lifting of the rod,
The moving nod.
Silence, reflected thence, still and intense,
    into the firmament ;
Such silence as befits the event.

*Re-enter* CORA.

CORA.

This is the hour, O child whom I have loved
With love more tender than a mother's love
Being thy friend ; this moment have I sough
Awaiting always the propitious time,
To speak some purpose grown more definite
Than is our wont.  We spend the honey days
In gentle intercourse : high souls have stood
Watching us drink from their crystalline
    stream
Meandering through language : mighty kings
Have listened as we read of their dead
    pomp ;
Fair women blushed as their imagined shapes
Flitted before us in the tender page.
We too have followed every curve and line
In fairy fancies on our canvas drawn
Of stately people, and the changing rhyme
Of virgins dancing before Artemis ;
In all the pleasures that delight the mind
Invigorate the soul, lend favour to
The body of the youth—for I am old—

ULRIC.

My Cora ! old !  But urgently a word
Came of some purpose.  I am half afraid
To hear it—and yourself !  Reluctance sits
Dogg èd against the will to speak.  Dear
    friend,
Let us sit close and whisper.

CORA.

                          Listen, then !
You are grown man : young men seek
    happiness.
Is there one joy your soul hath never felt ?
One pure sweet passion ?

ULRIC (*surprised*).

Sweet ! you speak of love !
You must have guessed I meant to question you,
And smoothed the passage to my modesty.

CORA (*with bitter sorrow at her heart*).

You make me very glad. Yes, yes, indeed,
Love is my meaning. Does it shame me much
To talk so openly of love to you?
But I am old enough to be—to be——

ULRIC (*breaking right out*).

My wife ! O Cora, I have loved you so !
My heart is like a fountain of the sea.
I burn, I tremble ; in my veins there swims
A torrid ecstasy of madness. Ah !
Ah God ! I kiss you, kiss you ! O you faint !
Sweetheart, my passion overwhelms your soul.
Your virginal sweet spirit cannot reach
My fury. You are silent. Yet you love !
I read it in the terror of your eyes,
The crimson of your burning face. I know,
I know you love me ! Cora, Cora, tell me!
O she will die ! I would not—I was rough—
My overmastering desire to you—
My queen, my wife, this maddens me.

CORA (*recovering*).

You fool !
You beast ! I hate you for your stupid self !
I am defiled ! Go ! Touch me not ! Speak not !
I am accursed of the Lord my God.
[*Shrieks.*

ULRIC (*still passionate, yet full of tender concern*).

Darling ! my darling ! How have I done this?

CORA.

Fool ! It is madness ! Yes, and punishment.
O God, that all my love should come to this !
You, you are mad ! I speak of love, and you,
You—you are acting ! I was taken in !
Let's laugh about it !
[*Tries to laugh, sinks back.*
It was not well done.
[ULRIC *is silent, and, puzzled, waits for her to go on.*
Surely you knew that it was Madeline !

ULRIC.

What ! I should wed that pretty Puritan ?
The downcast eyes and delicate white throat,
The lily, when I saw the rose before me ?
Your full delicious beauty was as God !
You are a bunch of admirable grapes
Fit to intoxicate my being ! Yes !
I would not give that sunny fruit of yours
For twenty such frail flowers as Madeline.
I am a man—you mate me with a girl !

CORA.

Stop ! not a word ! My blasphemy to hear,
Yours to speak out—when you are told the truth !

ULRIC.

What truth? This word hath first an ugly sound.
The truth ! God curse it to His blackest hell
If but it stand between us and our love !

CORA.

O Ulric, Ulric ! bear with me awhile !
Speak no more words—each syllable strikes
    here,            [*Hand to heart.*
A cloud of wingèd scorpions, that rage
In mine own deepest self; for there I
    know
Tame harpies that had ceased to torture
    me ;
And this more ghastly brood renews their
    sting,
Adding a triple poison !   O my soul
Is torn with pangs more horrible than
    hell,
Scorching the very marrow of my bones,
Corrupting me—corrupting me, I say—
O God ! is any safety at Thy feet ?
Be silent, O be silent for awhile,
And I will shrivel up thy wretched ears,
Give thee to curse the hour that saw thee
    first,
To curse thy parents and thine own young
    head.
May God forbid that thou should rail on
    Him !
Leave me a little to my torment yet,
That I may quell the host of devil forms
That eat my soul up, many torturing,
And one—ah ! one accursed beyond all—
Soothing !   O heart of Jesus, bleed with
    mine !        [*Kneels towards East.*
See, see ! I seek Thee on maternal knees !
Conceive Her pangs that bore Thee, when
    her shame
Devoured Her, with no memory of love—
As mine, as mine !   O bitter memories !
                   [*A pause.*

ULRIC.

Tell me, dear friend ! anxiety and love
Are like to kill me.   Tell me in three words.

CORA (*slowly and deliberately*).

I am a dancer and a prostitute !

ULRIC *smiles contemptuously.*

Why trick me with so pitiful a lie?
Were you the vilest woman on the earth,
Mere scum of filth shed off the city's dregs—
Were you the meanest and most treacher-
    ous—
Were you the sordid soul that most con-
    trasts
With your true, noble, and unselfish self—
Were you the synthesis of all I hate,
In mind and body leprous and deformed—
Did every word and gesture fill my soul
With hatred and its parody, disgust—
It touches not my question !   This one
    fact
O'ermasters all eccentric circumstance :
I love you—you, and not your attributes !

CORA.

Great noble soul ! I hate myself the more
That I must wound you further with the
    truth.
A double prong this poisoned poniard
Snaps in our hearts.   I kept the secret
    long.
Your breath, that burns upon me, wraps
    me round
With whirling passion, pierces through my
    veins
With its unhallowed fire, constrains, com-
    pels,
Drags out the corpse of twenty years ago
From the untrusty coffin of my mind,
To poison, to corrupt, to strike you there
Blind with its horror.

ULRIC.

            Leave these bitter words !
They torture me with terrible suspense,
And you with fear.   I see by these dread
    looks,
Tedious prologues, that there is a truth
You are afraid to speak.

CORA (*aside*).

What subterfuge?
What shield against the lightning of his love?
(*Hastily.*) I have a husband living.

ULRIC.

Think you, then,
I have lived so long and looked into you eyes
To listen to so hastily disgorged
A prentice falsehood not grown journeyman?
Then, had you fifty husbands, am I one,
Reared in the faith of high philosophy,
Schooled from my childhood in the brotherhood
Of poets, to descend to this absurd
Quibble of tedious morality?
Shame not your truth with that ignoble thought!
And also—tell me, once for all, the truth!
[*Bitterly.*
Say that you love him—it is on your tongue

CORA.

Learn the momentous horror of thy birth!
[*A pause.*

ULRIC.

I would not urge my suit against that plea,
But—I have known you, and your own pure soul
Should cast no doubt against me—you have said
" Rather we love such as the child of love ;
And pity—he is not unpitiful
In this vile system ; and respect him too—
He stands alone, the evidence of Strength ! "
You move your purpose with no bastardy !
Only you claim to speak the generous thought :
For you I wait, for you, to offer love !
VOL. I.

CORA.

All is too true—my own philosophy
Mars my world's wisdom. (*Suddenly.*) Can you tell me why
I loved you as a child, and why I dare
Now take your head between my hands and kiss
Your forehead with these shameful lips of mine,
These harlot lips, and kiss you unashamed?

ULRIC.

Strange are these words, and this emotion strange !

CORA.

Strange is the truth, and deadly as an asp.

ULRIC.

Wear me no more with this anxiety.

CORA.

How can I speak? For this will ruin us.

ULRIC.

Unspoken, I demand thy heart of thee.

CORA.

My heart is broken. This will murder thine.

ULRIC.

Kill, but not torture ! Let me know the truth.

CORA.

This shaft is aimed even against thy life. L

ULRIC.

What is my life without the love of thee?

CORA.

I hate each word as I do hate the devil.

ULRIC.

I, each evasion.  I am bound a slave
To this wild passion.  It will eat me up.

CORA.

You cannot guess the horror that you speak.
I tell you, if I know your golden heart,
This detestation of yourself shall cry
The cry of Œdipus—" I have profaned——— "

ULRIC.

What sphinx more cruel?  What new
    Œdipus?
You riddle, Cora, and it breaks my heart.
                        [*He sinks exhausted.*

(*Rallying.*)  By God, I swear to you no lie
    shall keep
Its Dead Sea bar against our marrying.

CORA.

The truth!  The truth!  The truth!  I am
    indeed
That whore I told you.  That makes nothing
    here.
I am the mother of thy bastard birth!

ULRIC (*the conventional criticism is
    nearest the surface.*)

Stop! stop!  I did not hear you.  O my
    God !
What agony is this?  What have I done
To earn this infamy?  Or rather, Thou,
What have I not done?  Have Thou pity
    yet ;
Sustain me in this vile extremity !
                        [*He prays silently.*

CORA (*watching him*).

How wonderful !  He will abide the shock.
Death and mute horror fight within his face
Against a will made masterful to Fate.

ULRIC (*raises his eyes and lifts his arm in
    act to strike*).

Then I detest you !  Mother !  Treacher-
    ous !
Vile as the worm that battens on the dead !

CORA.

Ulric !  He's mad !  Sweet heaven !  what is
    this?
        [CORA *is now hysterical.*  ULRIC
        *does not notice.  She shrieks at each
        new insult.*

ULRIC.

Say rather, what are you?  I loved you
    once
Childlike ;  then came the power of reason-
    ing,
And I beheld you, the unselfish one,
Befriending me, the angel of my life.
See what it rested on, my happiness !
Your sacrifice is utter selfishness ;
Me, the sole pledge of your debaucheries
You keep—your love, the mere maternity
You share with swine and cattle !  All your
    care
Is duty : let the harlot cleanse herself—
Tardy repentance !—In the name of God !
Worse, you have lied, and built me up a
    house
Of trust in you as being truth and love,
Who are in truth all lies, all treachery !
You made me love you as an honest man !
You watched this passion, this intolerable
Desire, this flame of hell ; you fed it full,
Sunned it and watered—O my brain will
    snap !—
Only to blast it.  Take your story back ;

Be what you will except that infamous !
For as my mother—I should spit on you !
  [CORA *is at his feet grovelling.  She*
    *half rises to listen.*
Ignoble is your foul maternity,
The cattle-kinship.   But the other crime
Is viler than the first one.   "Look !" you
    say :
"His passion threatens to defile my bed !"
And put a hideous abiding curse
On both our lives to save your modesty
From my incestuous embrace !   O God !
My love is nobler—to defy the past,
Deny !—your love is merely natural ;
Mine, against Nature, is the love Divine !
What   crime   is   this ?     Thy   pale   Son's
    martyrdom
Cleansed earth from no such vile hypocrisy
As this my mother's.    And I call thee,
    God,
To witness ; and I call mankind to hear ;
This is my faith : I live and die by it.
I, nobler, cast away the infamy,
Break  with  my  hands  these  rotten  barri-
    cades,
    [*He picks up his mother's Bible, tears*
      *it, and casts it into the fire.*
And swear before the Spirit of the World,
In  sight  of  God,  this  day :  I  love  you
    still
With carnal love and spiritual love !
And I will have you, by the living God,
To be my mistress.   If I fail in this,
Or falter in this counsel of despair,
May God's own curses dog me into hell,
And mine own life perpetuate itself
Through all the ages of eternity.
Amen ! Amen !  Come, Cora, to my heart !
    [*He stoops to embrace her.  Horror*
      *and madness catch him, and he runs*
      *about the room wildly, crying for*
      CORA, *whom he cannot see.  MA-*
      DELINE *enters.*

### MADELINE.

O  Cora !   Cora !   Ulric !   Help !   Help !
Help !

ULRIC (*regains his self-control*).

Hush !   All  is  well !   I  cannot  tell  you
    now.
Some news—a letter—it has frightened her.

### MADELINE.

But you were crying as a madman would.

### ULRIC.

Believe me, I am nervous and distraught.
You know me, how excitable I am.
A moment, and you see me calm again.
Come, Cora, do not frighten Madeline !
    [*He raises her to lead her from the room.*

### CORA.

Where  would  you  lead  me ?   I  am  blind
    with tears.

### ULRIC.

I have no tears.   Mine eyes are hard and
    cold
As my intention.   Help me, Madeline !

### CORA.

God will avenge me bitterly on you
If you stretch hand to aid this infamy.

### ULRIC.

You  shall  not  wreck  her  life.   Be  silent
    now !
Believe me, it is nothing, Madeline !
She often falls into a fit like this.
Excess is danger, equally in prayer
(Her vice is prayer) as in debauchery.
    [*He is again going mad.  He drags*
      CORA *from the room.*

MADELINE.

[MADELINE *is uncertain what to do
during this scene : so fidgets about
and does nothing.*
It is not illness that hath made them mad.
I cannot guess what storm has lashed itself
Thus in one hour from peace and happiness
To such a fury that the very room
Seems to my fancy to be tossed about,
Rocking and whirling on some dizzy sea.
There is a horrible feeling in the air.
[*She shudders*


SPIRIT OF TRAGEDY.

[*During this speech sighs, cries, voices
from without indicate the action.*
The keystone of this arch of misery
Is set by the unfaltering hands
Of Fate.   How desperate the anarchy
Wrought in one hour !
The fickle sands
Run through the glass, and all the light is
    gone.
Abysses without name the mighty power
Spans with spread fingers ; on the horizon
Blood stains the setting sun,
The shattered sun ; it shall not rise again !
No resurrection to the trampled flower,
No hope to angels watching as in vain
Love—lies—slain !
Madness and Terror and the deadly mood of
    Fortitude,
A misbegotten brood
Of all things shameful—O the desolate eyes
Of the cold Christ enthroned !   The weep-
    ing heaven
Answers for angels : the oppressive skies
See them dislink from bodily form and shape,
Unloved and unforgiven,
Unwept, unpenitent, unshriven !
Their hell of horror knows no gate of any
    escape.
This tragedy is terrible to me.
Even I, its spirit, shudder as I see ;
I, passionless, the moulder of men's hope,
The slayer of them, cast no horoscope

Divining what befell.   And I am moved :
Both love, and both are worthy to be loved.
Ah Fate ! if thou hadst cast the dies
Whence no appeal, in any other wise !
I am the soul of the grim face of things :
Mine are the Sphinx's wings ;
Mine own life lives with this event !
Yet even I, its very self, lament
The execrable tyranny,
The rayless misery
Of this wild whirlpool sea of circumstance.
Mine old eyes look askance :
It is my punishment to dwell
In mine own self-created hell.
[CORA *rushes in.*


MADELINE.

What curse of God hath smitten you ?   I see
Exceeding horror in abiding shape
Blasting the countenance of peace and love
With some distortion.   O your mouth's awry !


CORA (*in a hoarse, horrible voice*).

You cannot tell !   I cannot tell myself.
Some vital mist of blood is shrouding sight
From all but my corruption's self.   Come here
And look within mine eyes, if you can see
Remembrance that there was a God !   I say
I see the whole bright universe a tomb,
With creeping spectres moving in the mist,
Some suffocating poison that was air.
O Phædra ![1] lend me of thy wickedness,
Lest I go mad to contemplate myself !
I choke—I grope—I fall !
                    What name is this
That strikes my spirit as a broken bell
Struck by some devilish hammer ?   In my
    brain
Reverberates some word impossible.
O I am broken on the wheel of death ;
My bones are ground in some infernal mill ;
My blood is as the venom of a snake,
Striking each vessel with unwonted pangs,
Killing all good within me.   I am—Ah !

[1] Wife of Theseus, in love with his son
Hippolytus, by whom she was repulsed.

MADELINE.

Dear friend, dear friend, seek comfort in my
   arms !
Look to Our Lady of the Seven Stars !

CORA.

Can you not see ?   I am cut off from God !
Loathsome bull-men in their corruption
   linked
Whisper lewd fancies in my ear.   Great fish,
Monstrous and flat, with vile malignant eyes,
And crawling beetles of gigantic strength,
Crushed, mangled, moving,[1] are about me.
   Go !
Go ! do not touch the carcase of myself
That is abased, defiled, abominable.

MADELINE.

O Heart of Jesus ! Thou art bleeding still !
This was Thy true disciple.   Leave her not,
Sweet Jesus, in this madness.   Who is this ?

*Enter* ULRIC ; *he carries a razor.*

ULRIC.[2]

I have a lovely bride at last, my dear !
A phantom with intolerable eyes
Came close and whispered : I am Wisdom's
   self,
Thy spouse from everlasting.   Mortal king
Of my immortal self, I claim thy love !
So, we are wedded close.   Justice demands
The punishment of this accursèd one,
Originator of the cruel crimes
My mother-mistress carried to their close.
It was your vile affection, Madeline,
And your perverted hankering for me

[1] The descriptions of demons are from a
little-known Rabbinical MS. on the "Qliphoth,"
or shells (larvae) of the dead.   They are known
also as the " cut off from God."
[2] *Cf.* the speech of the Dweller of the
Threshold in Lytton's " Zanoni."

That caused this thing abominable.   Come !
I will not hurt you in the killing you !
   [*He catches* MADELINE *gently by the
    hair, bending back her head.*   CORA
    sits thunderstruck, unable to move
    or speak.*)

MADELINE.

Help, Cora, help ! he means to murder me !
Jesus, my Saviour, save them from this deed !
Help !         [ULRIC *cuts her throat.*

ULRIC.

   So perish the Queen's enemies !
Well, little lover, have I done it well ?
Cora, my sweetheart, we are happy now
To think our troubles should be ended so
In perfect love and—I am feeling ill——
   [CORA *recovers her mental balance.*

CORA.

A blood-grey vapour and a scorpion steam
To poison the unrighteous life of God !
   [ULRIC *looks on in a completely dazed
    manner, uncomprehending.*

CORA (*takes razor and puts it in his hand*).
          Kill yourself.

ULRIC (*smiling, as if with some divine
    and ineffable joy, draws the razor
    across his throat, cutting in deeply.
    He falls bleeding.*)
          My dear !

CORA.

That is my duty to my motherhood.
Let me now think of all this happening.
   [*She sinks slowly into a chair tremb-
    ling.   She puts her hand to her
    throat as if choking.   She bites her
    lip and sits easily back, looking
    straight before her with uncompre-
    hending eyes.*

CURTAIN.

# THE TEMPLE OF THE HOLY GHOST.*

## 1901.

## I. THE COURT OF THE PROFANE.

### PROLOGUE.

### OBSESSION.

TO CHARLES BAUDELAIRE.

"Car ce que ta bouche cruelle
  Eparpille en l'air,
Monstre assassin, c'est ma cervelle,
  Mon sang et ma chair !"

THY brazen forehead, and its lustre gloom,
  Great angel of Night's legion chosen
    chief,
Beam on me like the hideous-fronted tomb,
  Whereon are graven strange words of mis-
    belief ;
Thy brazen forehead, and its lustre gloom !

Sinister eyes, you burn into my breast,
  Creating an infernal cavern of woe,
Where strange sleek leopards lash them in
    unrest,
  And furtive serpents crawling to and
    fro—
Sinister eyes, you burn into my breast !

All hell, all destinies of death are written
  Like litanies blaspheming in those eyes ;
And where the lightning of high God hath
    smitten
  Lie the charred brands of monstrous in-
    famies,
Wherein all destinies of death are written.

Thou cam'st to obsess me first that Easter
    Eve,
  When, from the contemplation of His
    pain,
I turned to look into my own heart's heave,
  And saw the bloody nails made fast again.
Thou cam'st to obsess me first that Easter
    Eve !

The lustre of old jet was over thee,
  And through thy body coursed the scented
    blood ;
Thy flesh was full of amorous ecstasy :
  Polished, and gloomier than some black
    full flood,
The lustre of old jet was over thee !

In thy great brazen blackness I am bathed ;
  Through all thy veins, like curses, my
    blood runs ;
In all thy flesh my naked bones are swathed,
  My womb is pregnant with mad moons
    and suns.
In thy great brazen blackness I am bathed !

Imminent over me thy hatred hangs ;
  Thy slow blood trickles on my swollen
    sides,
The curdling purple where those poison-
    fangs
  Struck, slays desire ; and only death abides.
Imminent over me thy hatred hangs !

* At the publisher's suggestion, this volume was split up into "The Soul of Osiris" and "The Mother's Tragedy." The original design of the poet is now restored.

Thy jet smooth body clung to mine awhile,
Descending like the thunder-pregnant
night.
Ominous, black, thy secret cruel smile
Lured me. We lay like death; until the
light
Thy jet smooth body clung to mine awhile!

Thou wast a lion as an angel then,
In copper-glowing lands that gnaws the
prey
He has regotten from the tribes of men.
We lay like passion all that deadly day—
Thou wast a lion as an angel then!

Great angel of the brazen brows, great lover,
Great hater of my body as my soul,
To whom I gave my life and love thrice
over,
Fill me one last caress—the poison-bowl!
Great angel of the brazen brows, great
lover!

### FAME.

O IF these words were swords, and I had
might
From some old prophet in whose tawny
hair
The very breath of the Jehovah were
To smite the Syrian, and to smite, and
smite,
And splash the sun's face with the blood, for
spite
Of his downgoing, till I had made fair
All glories of my master, I could bear
To sink myself in the abundant night.

O if these words were lightnings, and their
flame
Deluged the world, and drowned the seed of
shame
In these ill waters where alone Truth's
ark
May float, where only lovers may embark,
I were contented to abandon fame
And live with love for ever in the dark.

### THE MOTHER AT THE SABBATH.[1]

COME, child of wonder! it is Sabbath
Night,
The speckled twilight and the sombre
singing!
Listen and come: the owl's disastrous flight
Points out the road! Hail, O propitious
sight!
See! the black gibbet and the murderer
swinging!

Come, child of wonder and the innocent
eyes!
Come where the toad his stealthy way is
taking.
Flaps the bat's wing upon thy cheek? How
wise,
How wicked are those faces! And the skies
Are muffled, and the firmament is quaking.

Spectres of cats misshapen nestle close,
And rub their phantom sides against our
dresses.
Come, child of wonder! in these souls
morose
Keen joys may shudder—how the daylight
goes!—
Night shall betray thee to the cold caresses!

Yes; it is nigh the hour of subtlety
And strange looks meaning more than Hell
can utter:—
Come, child of wonder! watch the woman's
eye
Who lurks toward us through the stagnant
sky.
Hark to the words her serpents hiss or
mutter!

[1] The Sabbath of the Witches. The reader should consult Payne Knight, "Two Essays on the Worship of Priapus"; Eliphaz Levi, "Histoire de la Magie" and "Dogme et Rituel de la Haute Magie"; P. Christian, "Histoire de la Magie"; and Goethe, "Faust." Also J. Glanvil, "Saducismus Triumphatus."

Close we are come ; before us is the Cross
To trample and defile : the bones shall
    shudder
Of many a self-slain darling.    From the
    moss
Swamp-adders greet us.    How the dancers
    toss
The frantic limb, the unreluctant udder !

See, how their frenzy peoples all the ground !
Strange demon-shapes take up the unholy
    measure,
Strange beast and worm and crab : the un-
    couth sound
Of the unheard-of kisses : the profound
Gasps of the maniac, the devouring pleasure !

A curse of God is on them !—ha ! the curse,
The curse that locks them in obscene em-
    braces !
See how love mocks the melancholy hearse
Dressed as an altar : is she nun or nurse,
The priestess chosen of the half-formed faces ?

An abbess, child of the unsullied eyes !
Why ?  To blaspheme !  Sweet child, the
    dance grows madder.
O I am faint with pleasure !   Ah ! be wise ;
One measure more, and then—the sacrifice ?
What victim ?   Guess — a woman or an
    adder ?

Nay, fear not, baby !   In your mother's
    hand
You must be safe ?   You trust the womb
    that bare you !
Who comes toward us ?   Why, our God, the
    Grand !
Our Baphomet ! [1]   Come, baby, to the
    band :
Our God may kiss you—yes, he will not
    spare you !

[1] Supposed to be the abbreviation of the
Templar's Order spelt backwards : Tem. o. h.
p. ab. = Templi omnium hominum pacis pater
(Heb. Ab, father).   Some assert the word to be
really a synthesis of a great body of secret
doctrine, discoverable by any one who knows
the Qabalistic meaning of each letter.

Fall down, my baby ; worship him with me.
There, go ; I give you to his monster kisses !
Take her, my God, my God, my infamy,
My love, my master ! take the fruit of me !
— Shrieks every soul and every demon
    hisses !

Out ! out ! the ghastly torches of the feast !
Let darkness hide us and the night discover
The shameless mysteries of God grown
    beast,
The nameless blasphemy, the slimèd East—
Sin incarnatéd with a leprous lover !

" Hoc est enim " [1]—the victim ! ah ! my
    womb,
My womb has borne the victim !  Now I
    queen it
To-night upon the damned—thy love makes
    room,
My goat-head godhead, for my hecatomb !
I am thy mistress, and thy slaves have seen
    it !

Even as thy cold devouring kisses roll
Over my corpse ; I hear its death-cry thrill
    me !
Thine !—O my God ! I render thee the
    whole,
My broken body and my accursèd soul !
Come, come, come, come !  Ah ! conquer
    me and kill me !


THE BRIDEGROOM.

No passion stirs the cool white throat of
    her ;
No living glory fills the deep dead eyes ;
    No sleep that breaks her Southern
    indolence ;
Not all the breezes out of heaven, that stir
    The sleepy wells and woodlands, bid her
    rise ;
    Nor all a godhead's amorous violence.
    She is at peace ; we will go hence.

[1] " Hoc est enim corpus meum," the words
used in the Mass at the elevation of the Host.

Warm wealth of draperies, the broidered
  room,
    And delicate tissues of pale silk that shine
      About her bed : all kiss the dead girl's
      face
With shadowy reluctances that gloom
  Over and under, and the cold divine
    Presence of Death bedews the quiet
    place.
    She was so gracious ; she w a s grace.

Once, in the long insidious hours that steal
  Through summer's pleasant kingdom, she
    would weave
    Such songs, such murmurs of the dusky
    breeze
That passed, like silken tapestries that feel
  The silkier cheeks of maidens as they
    cleave
    Tender to patient lovers, for the ease
    Of lips fulfilled of harmonies.

Such songs were hers.  What song is hers
  to-night
When she is smitten in her bridal bed,
    Because I would not trust the God that
    gave
Her smooth virginity to godlier might,
  My glory?  There she lies divine and
  dead
    Because I would not trust the sullen
    wave
    Of time ; and chose this way—her grave.

I had not thought the poison left her so—
  Smiling, enticing, exquisite.  I meant
    Rather that beauty to destroy, to leave
No subtle languors on that breast of snow,
  No curves by God's caressing finger bent,
    To bid me think of her : I would de-
    ceive
    My memory—now I can but grieve.

Perhaps our happiness, despite of all,
  Would have grown comelier and never
    tired ;
    Perhaps the pitiful pale face had been

Alway my true wife's ; let me not recall
  Her first shy glance !  This woman I desired,
    And sealed my own for ever by this
    keen
    Death that crowns her Death's queen.

Death's and not mine : I was a fool to kiss
  Her dead lips—ay, her living lips for
  that !
    I cannot bid her rise and live again.
I would not.   Nay, I know not ; for is this
  My triumph or my ruin, satiate
    Of death, insatiate alway of pain?
    What have I done ?   In vain, in vain !

I will not look at her ; I dare not stay.
  I will go down and mingle with the
    throng,
    Find some debasing dulling sacrifice,
Some shameless harlot with thin lips grown
  grey
  In desperate desire, and so with song
    And wine fling hellward.   Yes, she
    does not rise—

    O if she opened once her eyes !


## THE ALTAR OF ARTEMIS.

WHERE, in the coppice, oak and pine
  With mystic yew and elm are found,
Sweeping the skies, that grow divine
  With the dark wind's despairing sound,
  The wind that roars from the profound,
And smites the mountain-tops, and calls
Mute spirits to black festivals,
  And feasts in valleys iron-bound,
  Desolate crags, and barren ground ;—
There in the strong storm-shaken grove
Swings the pale censer-fire for love.

The foursquare altar, rightly hewn,
  And overlaid with beaten gold,
Stands in the gloom ; the stealthy tune
  Of singing maidens overbold
  Desires mad mysteries untold,

With strange eyes kindling, as the fleet
Implacable untiring feet
  Weave mystic figures manifold
  That draw down angels to behold
The moving music, and the fire
Of their intolerable desire.

For, maddening to fiercer thought,
  The fiery limbs requicken, wheel
In formless furies, subtly wrought
  Of swifter melodies than steel
  That flashes in the fight : the peal
Of amorous laughters choking sense,
And madness kissing violence,
  Rings like dead horsemen ; bodies reel
  Drunken with motion ; spirits feel
The strange constraint of gods that dip
From Heaven to mingle lip and lip.

The gods descend to dance ; the noise
  Of hungry kissings, as a swoon,
Faints for excess of its own joys,
  And mystic beams assail the moon,
  With flames of their infernal noon ;
While the smooth incense, without breath,
Spreads like some scented flower of death,
  Over the grove ; the lover's boon
  Of sleep shall steal upon them soon,
And lovers' lips, from lips withdrawn,
Seek dimmer bosoms till the dawn.

Yet on the central altar lies
  The sacrament of kneaded bread
With blood made one, the sacrifice
  To those, the living, who are dead—
  Strange gods and goddesses, that shed
Monstrous desires of secret things
Upon their worshippers, from wings
  One lucent web of light, from head
  One labyrinthine passion-fed
Palace of love, from breathing rife
With secrets of forbidden life.

But not the sunlight, nor the stars,
  Nor any light but theirs alone,
Nor iron masteries of Mars,
  Nor Saturn's misconceiving zone,
  Nor any planet's may be shown,

Within the circle of the grove,
Where burn the sanctities of love :
  Nor may the foot of man be known,
  Nor evil eyes of mothers thrown
On maidens that desire the kiss
Only of maiden Artemis.

But horned and huntress from the skies,
  She bends her lips upon the breeze,
And pure and perfect in her eyes,
  Burn magical virginity's
  Sweet intermittent sorceries.
When the slow wind from her sweet word
In all their conchéd ears is heard.
  And like the slumber of the seas,
  There murmur through the holy trees
The kisses of the goddess keen,
And sighs and laughters caught between.

For, swooning at the fervid lips
  Of Artemis, the maiden kisses
Sob, and the languid body slips
  Down to enamelled wildernesses.
  Fallen and loose the shaken tresses ;
Fallen the sandal and girdling gold,
Fallen the music manifold
  Of moving limbs and strange caresses,
  And deadly passion that possesses
The magic ecstasy of these
Mad maidens, tender as blue seas.

Night spreads her yearning pinions ;
  The baffled day sinks blind to sleep ;
The evening breeze outswoons the sun's
  Dead kisses to the swooning deep.
  Upsoars the moon ; the flashing steep
Of Heaven is fragrant for her feet ;
The perfume of the grove is sweet
  As slumbering women furtive creep
  To bosoms where small kisses weep,
And find in fervent dreams the kiss
Most memoried of Artemis.

Impenetrable pleasure dies
  Beneath the madness of new dreams ;
The slow sweet breath is turned to sighs
  More musical than many streams
  Under the moving silver beams,

Fretted with stars, thrice woven across.
White limbs in amorous slumber toss
  Like sleeping foam, whose silver gleams
  On motionless dark seas ; it seems
As if some gentle spirit stirred
Their lazy brows with some swift word.


So, in the secret of the shrine,
  Night keeps them nestled ; so the gloom
Laps them in waves as smooth as wine,
  As glowing as the fiery womb
Of some young tigress, dark as doom,
And swift as sunrise.   Love's content
Builds its own mystic monument,
  And carves above its vaulted tomb
  The Phœnix on her fiery plume,
To their own souls to testify
Their kisses' immortality.



### THE COURSE OF TRUE LOVE.

O CRIMSON cheeks of love's fierce fever !
  O amber skin, electric to the kiss !
  O eyes of sin ! O bosom of my bliss !
Sorrow, the web, is spun of Love the
  weaver.


Twelve moons have circled in their seasons ;
  The earth has swept, exultant, round the
  sun ;
  Our love has slept, and, sleeping, made
  us one.
The thirteenth moon, be sure, the time or
  treasons !


Another spirit waves its pinions.
  Love vanishes : we hate each other's sight.
  In sullen seas sinks our sun-flaming light,
Darkness is master of the dream-dominions.


Lo ! in thy womb a child !  How rotten
  Seems love to me who love it as my soul !
  The love of thee hath broken its control,
The misconceived become the misbegotten.

In thee the love of me is broken.
  Fear, hatred, pain, discomfort mock thy
  days ;
  Thou canst disdain ; these solitary bays
Twine with decaying myrtles for a token.


Dislike, disgust (you say repulsers)
  Link me to thee despite—because of—
  this
  Skeleton key to charnel-house.   My kiss
Is the dog's kiss to Lazarus his ulcers !


Mock me, ye clinging lovers, at your peril !
  God turns to dust the blossom of your
  youth.
  The fruit of lust is poisonous with—truth !
Its immortality is—to be sterile !


This lie of Love hath no abiding :
  " Two loves are ended ; one, the infant
  band,
  Rises more splendid."  Spin the rope of
  sand !
Two loves are one ; but O to their dividing !


Fertility—distaste's adoption !
  Her body's growth—desire's mortality !
  I look and loathe.   Behold how lovers die,
And immortality puts on corruption !



### ASMODEL.[1]

CALL down that star whose tender eyes
  Were on thy bosom at thy birth !
Call, one long passionate note that sighs !
  Call, till its beauty bend to earth,
Meet thee and lift thee and devise
  Strange loves within the gleaming girth,
And kisses underneath the star
Where on her brows its seven rays are.

Call her, the maiden of thy sleep,
  And fashion into human shape
The whirling fountains fiery and deep,
  The incense-columns that bedrape

[1] One of the " Intelligences " of the Planet
Venus.

Her glimmering limbs, when shadows creep
 Among blue tresses that escape
The golden torque that binds her hair,
Whose swarthy splendours drench the air.

She comes ! she comes ! The spirit glances
 In quick delight to hold her kiss ;
The fuming air shimmers and dances ;
 The moonlight's trembling ecstasies
Swoon ; and her soul, as my soul, trances,
 Knowing no longer aught that is ;
Only united, moving, mixed,
A music infinitely fixed.

Music that throbs, and soars, and burns,
 And breaks the possible, to dwell
One moving monotone, nor turns,
 Making hell heaven, and heaven hell,
The steady impossible song that yearns
 And brooks no mortal in its swell—
This monotone immortal lips
Make in our infinite eclipse !

Formless, above all shape and shade ;
 Lampless, beyond all light and flame ;
Timeless, above all age and grade ;
 Moveless, beyond the mighty name ;
A mystic mortal and a maid,
 Filled with all things to fill the same,
To overflow the shores of God,
Mingling our proper period.

The agony is passed : behold
 How shape and light are born again ;
How emerald and starry gold
 Burn in the midnight ; how the pain
Of our incredible marriage-fold
 And bed of birthless travail wane ;
And how our molten limbs divide,
And self and self again abide.

The agony of extreme joy,
 And horror of the infinite blind
Passions that sear us and destroy,
 Rebuilding for the deathless mind

A deathless body, whose alloy
 Is gold and fire, whose passions find
The tears of their caress a dew,
Fiery, to make creation new.

This agony and bloody sweat,
 This scarring torture of desire,
Refine us, madden us, and set
 The feast of unbegotten fire
Before our mouths, that mingle yet
 In this ; the mighty-moulded lyre
Of many stars still strikes above
Chords of the mastery of love.

This subtle fire, this secret flame,
 Flashes between us as she goes
Beyond the night, beyond the Name,
 Back to her unsubstantial snows ;
Cold, glittering, intense, the same
 Now, yesterday, for aye ! she glows
No woman of my mystic bed ;
A star, far off, forgotten, dead.

Only to me looks out for ever
 From her cold eyes a fire like death ;
Only to me her breasts can never
 Lose the red brand that quickeneth ;
Only to me her eyelids sever
 And lips respire her equal breath ;
Still in the unknown star I see
The very god that is of me.

The day's pale countenance is lifted,
 The rude sun's forehead he uncovers ;
No soft delicious clouds have drifted,
 No wing of midnight's bird that hovers ;
Yet still the hard blind blue is rifted,
 And still my star and I as lovers
Yearn to each other through the sky
With eyes half closed in ecstasy.

Night, Night, O mother Night, descend !
 O daughter of the sleeping sea !
O dusk, O sister-spirit, lend
 Thy wings, thy shadows, unto me !

O mother, mother, mother, bend
  And shroud the world in mystery
That secrets of our bed forbidden
Cover their faces, and be hidden !

O steadfast, O mysterious bride !
  O woman, O divine and dead !
O wings immeasurably wide !
  O star, O sister of my bed !
O living lover, at my side
  Clinging, the spring, the fountain-head
Of musical slow waters, white
With thousand-folded rays of light !

Come !  Once again I call, I call,
  I call, O perfect soul, to thee,
With chants, and murmurs mystical,
  And whispers wiser than the sea :
O lover, come to me !  The pall
  Of night is woven : fair and free,
Draw to my kisses ; let thy breath
Mingle for love the wine of death !

## MADONNA OF THE GOLDEN EYES.

NIGHT brings madness ; moonlight dips her
    throat to madden us ;
Love's swift purpose darts, the flash of a
    striking adder.
Love that kills and kisses dwells above to
    sadden us ;
Dawn brings reason back and the violet
    eyes grows sadder.
      O Madonna of the Golden Eyes !

Swooned the deep sunlight above the summer
    stream ;
Droned the sleepy dragon-fly by the water
    spring ;
Stood we in the noontide in a misty
    dream,
Fearful of our voices, of some sudden
    thing.
      O Madonna of the Golden Eyes !

Dared we whisper ?  Dared we lift our eyes
    to see there
In their desperate depth some mutual flame
    of treason ?
Dared we move apart ?  So glad were we
    to be there,
Nothing in the world might change the
    constant season.
      O Madonna of the Golden Eyes !

Did a breath of wind disturb the lazy day ?
Did a soul of fear flit phantom-wise across ?
Suddenly we clasped and clave as spirit unto
    clay ;
Suddenly love swooped to us as swoops the
    albatross.
      O Madonna of the Golden Eyes !

Did thy husband's venom breathe on the
    trembling scale ?
Did that voice corrupting cry across the
    midnight air ?
What decided ?  Gabriel may spin the
    foolish tale.
What decided ?  We were lovers — who
    should care ?
      O Madonna of the Golden Eyes !

How we clave together !  How we strained
    caresses !
How the swooning limbs sank fainting on
    the sward !
For the fiery dart raged fiercer ; in excesses
Long restrained, it cried, " Behold ! I am
    the Lord ! "
      O Madonna of the Golden Eyes !

Yes, we sat with modest eyes and murmur-
    ing lips
Downcast at the table, while the husband
    drank his wine.
So thy sly, slow hand stretched furtively ;
    there slips
Deadly in his throat the poison draught
    divine !
      O Madonna of the Golden Eyes !

Then we left his carcase with the stealthy
   tread
Reverent, in presence of the silent place;
Then you burned, afire, caught up the
   ghastly head,
Looked like Hell right into it, and spat
   upon the face!
      O Madonna of the Golden Eyes!


"Come with me," you whispered, "come,
   and let the moon
Lend her light to madden us through the
   hours of pleasure;
Let the dayspring pass and brighten into noon!
Yet no limit find our love, nor passion find
   a measure!"
      O Madonna of the Golden Eyes!


Dawn brought reason back, and the violet
   eyes are sadder :—
O they were golden once, and I call them
   golden still!
Dawn has brought remorse, the sting of a
   foul swamp-adder—
I hate you! beast of Hell! I have snapped
   Love's manacle!
      O Murderess of the hateful eyes!


O and you fix them on me! your lips curse
   now—'tis fitter!
Snarl on! eat out your heart with the poison
   that is its blood.
Speak! and her lips move now with
   blasphemies cruel and bitter.
Slow the words creep forth as a sleepy
   and deadly flood.
      They glitter, those Satanic eyes!


"Beast! I gave you my soul and my body
   to, all your lust!
Beast! I am damned in Hell for the kisses
   we sucked from death!
Now remorse is yours, and love is fallen
   in dust—
I shall seek Him again for its sacramental
   breath!
      Yes, fear the gold that glitters from
      these eyes!"

She took a dagger, and I could not stir.
She pierced my silent fascinated breast.
She held me with the deadly look of her.
I cried to Mary in the House of Rest:
      "O Madonna of the Virgin eyes!"

     *     *     *

I pierced him to the very soul: I took
His whole life's love to me before he died:
Mad kisses mingled that enduring look
Of death-caught passion: in his death he
   cried,
      "O Madonna of the Golden Eyes!"


## LOVE AT PEACE.

THE valleys, that are splendid
With sun ere day is ended
   And love-lutes take to tune,
See joyless and unfriended
The perfect bowstring bended,
   Whose bow is called the moon.
They see the waters slacken
And all the sky's blue blacken,
While in the yellow bracken
   Love lies in death or swoon.

The stars arise and brighten;
The summer lightnings lighten,
   Faint and as midnight mute.
Afar the snowfields tighten
The iron bands that frighten
   No fairy's tender foot.
Across the stiller river
Stray flowers of ice may shiver,
Before the day deliver
   The murmur of its lute.

The sleep of bird and flower
Proclaims that Heaven has power
   To guard its gentlest child.
The lover knows the hour,
And goes with dew for dower
   To wed in woodland wild.
The silvern grasses shake,
And through the startled brake
Glides the awakened snake,
   Untamable and mild.

The song of stars ; the wail
Of women wild and pale,
　　Forlorn and not forsaken ;
The tremulous nightingale ;
The waters wan that fail
　　By frost-love overtaken,
Make sacred all the valley ;
And softly, musically,
The breezes lull and rally ;
　　The pine stirs and is shaken.


Beneath whose sombre shade
I hold a lazy maid
　　In chaste arms and too tender.
Lo ! she is fair ! God said ;
And saw through the deep glade
　　How sweet she was and slender.
But I—could I behold her
Curved shapeliness of shoulder ?
I, whose strong arms enfold her
　　Immaculate surrender.


Pure as the dawns that quicken
On snow-topped mountains stricken
　　By first gray light that grows,
By beams that gather, thicken,
A web of fairy ticken [1]
　　To make a fairy rose :
Pure as the seas that lave
With phosphorescent wave
The sombre architrave
　　Of Castle No-man-knows.


Pure as the dreams, undreamt
(That men have in contempt,
　　That wise men yearn to see),
Of angel forms exempt
From mockeries that tempt
　　Who fly about the lea ;
proclaiming things unheard,
unknown to brightest bird,
things, whose unspoken word
　　Is utmost secrecy.

　　　　[1] A closely woven fabric.


So pure, so pale we lie,
Like angels eye to eye,
　　Like lovers lip to lip.
So, the elect knight, I
Keep vigil to the sky,
　　While the dumb moments slip.
So she, my bride, my queen,
So virginal, so keen,
Swoons, while the moon-rays lean
　　To fan their silver ship.


No sleep, but precious kisses
In those pale wildernesses,
　　Mark the dead hours of night,
No sleep so sweet as this is,
Whose pulse of purple blisses
　　Beats calm and cool and light.
No life so fair with roses,
No day so swift to close is ;
No cushion so reposes
　　Fair love so sweet and slight.


MORS JANUA AMORIS.

" None but the dead can know the worth of
love."—KELLY.

IN the night my passion fancies
　　That an incense vapour whirls,
That a cloud of perfume trances
　　With its dreamy vapour-curls
All my soul, with whom their dances
　　The one girl of mortal girls.
The one girl whose wanton glances
　　Soften into living pearls
Comes, a fatal, fleeting vision,
Turns my kisses to derision,
Smiles upon my breast, and sighs,
Flits, and laughs, and fades, and dies.


By the potent starry speeches ;
　　By the spells of mystic kings ;
By the magic passion teaches ;
　　By the strange and sacred things

By whose power the master reaches
 To the stubborn fiery springs ;
By the mystery of the beaches
 Where the siren Sibyl sings ;
I will hold her, live and bleeding ;
Clasp her to me, pale and pleading ;
Hold her in a human shape ;
Hold her safe without escape !


So I put my spells about her
 As she flew into my dreams ;
So I drew her to the outer
 Land of unforgetful streams ;
So I laid her (who should doubt her?)
 Where enamelled verdure gleams,
Drew her spirit from without her !
 In her eyelids stellar beams
Glow renascent, now I hold her
Breast to breast, and shining shoulder
Laid to shoulder, in the bliss
Of the uncreated kiss.


Lips to lips beget for daughters
 Little kisses of the breeze ;
Limbs entwined with limbs, the waters
 Of incredible blue seas ;
Eyes that understand, the slaughters
 Of a thousand ecstasies
Re-embodied, as they wrought us
 Garlands of strange sorceries ;
New desires and mystic passion
Infinite, of starry fashion ;
The mysterious desire
Of the subtle formless fire.


Vainly may the Tyanæan [1]
 Throw his misconceiving eye
To bewitch our empyrean
 Splendours of the under sky !
If the loud infernal pæan
 Be our marriage-melody,
We are careless, we Achæan
 Moulders of our destiny.

Hell, it may be, for his playing,
Renders Orpheus the decaying
Love—in Hell, if Hell there be,
I would seek Eurydice !


If she be the demon sister
 Of my brain's mysterious womb ;
If she brand my soul and blister
 Me with kisses of the tomb ;
If she drag me where the bistre
 Vaults of Hell gape wide in gloom ;
Little matter ! I have kissed her !
 Little matter ! as a loom
She has woven love around me,
As with burning silver bound me,
Held me to her scented skin
For an age of deadly sin !


So I fasten to me tighter
 Fetters on her limbs that fret ;
So my kisses kindle brighter,
 Fiercer, flames of Hell, and set
Single, silent, as a mitre
 Blasphemous, a crown of jet
On our foreheads, paler, whiter
 Than the snowiest violet.
So I forge the chains of fire
Round our single-souled desire.
Heaven and Hell we reck not of,
Being infinite in love.


Come, my demon-spouse, to fashion
 The fantastic marriage-bed !
Let the starry billows splash on
 Both our bodies, let them shed
Dewfall, as the streams Thalassian
 On Selene's fallen head !
Let us mingle magic passion,
 Interpenetrating, dead,
Deathless, O my dead sweet maiden !
Lifeless, in the secret Aidenn ! [1]
Let our bodies meet and mix
On the spirit's crucifix !

[1] Apollonius of Tyana, the sage whose glance dissolved the illusion which Lamia had cast about herself.  See Keats's poem.

[1] This word is taken direct from Poe's "Raven" in the sense in which it is used by him.

## THE MAY QUEEN.[1]

### (OLD STYLE.)

It is summer and sun on the sea,
  The twilight is drawn to the world :
We linger and laugh on the lea,
The light of my spirit with me,
  Sharp limbs in close agony curled.

The noise of the music of sleep,
  The breath of the wings of the night,
The song of the magical deep,
The sighs of the spirits that weep,
  Make murmur to tune our delight.

Slow feet are our measures that move ;
  Swift songs are more soft than the breeze ;
Our mouths are made mute for our love ;
Our eyes are made soft as the dove ;
  We mingle and move as the seas.

The light of the passionate dawn
  That kissed us, and would not awaken,
Grew golden and bold on the lawn ;
The rays of the sun are withdrawn
  At last, and the blossoms are shaken.

Oh, fragrant the breeze is that stirs
  The grasses around us that lean !
Oh, sweet is the whisper that purrs
From those wonderful lips that are hers,
  From the passionate lips of a queen.

A queen is my lover, I say,
  With a crown of the lilies of light—
For a maiden they crowned her in May,
For the Queen of the Daughters of Day
  That are flowers of the forest of Night.

They crowned her with lilies and blue,
  They crowned her with yellow and roses ;
They gave her a sceptre of rue,
And a girdle of laurel and yew,
  And a basket of pansies in posies.

[1] See Frazer, "The Golden Bough," for proof of the universality of the ritual described. The parallelism is accidental, Crowley having read no sociology at this time.

They led her with songs by the stream ;
  They brought her with tears to the river ;
They danced as the maze of a dream ;
They kissed her to roses and cream,
  And they cried, " Let the queen live for
    ever ! "

They took her, with all of the flowers
  They had girded her with for God's
    daughter ;
They cast her from amorous bowers
To the river, the horrible powers
  Of the Beast that lurks down by the Water !

My way was more swift than a bow
  That flings out its barb to the night :
My sword struck the infinite blow
That smote him, and blackened the flow
  Of the amorous river of light.

I plunged in the stream, and I drew
  My queen from the clasp of the water ;
I crowned her with roses and blue,
With yellow and lilies anew ;
  I called her my love and God's daughter !

I gave her a sceptre of may ;
  I gave her a girdle of green ;
I drew her to music and day ;
I led her the beautiful way
  To the land where the Winds lie between.

So still lingers sun upon sea ;
  Still twilight draws down to the world ;
The light of my spirit is she ;
The soul of her love is in me ;
  Lithe kisses with music are curled.

Like light on the meadows we dwell ;
  Like twilight clings heart unto heart ;
Like midnight the depth of the spell
Our love weaves, and stronger than hell
  The guards of our palace of art.

We are one as the dew that is drawn
  By the sun from the sea : we are curled
In curves of delight and of dawn,
On the lone, the immaculate lawn,
  Beyond the wild way of the world.

M

## SIDONIA THE SORCERESS.[1]

SIDONIA the Sorceress ! I revel in her amber
    skin,
    Dream in her eyes and die in her caress.
She is for me the avatar of sin,
    Sidonia the Sorceress.

The one unpardonable wickedness,
    Strange serpent-blasphemies, are curled
    within
The heart of her Hell gives me to possess.

Her hair is fastened with a dagger thin ;
    A dead man's heart is woven with each
    tress.
I murdered Christ before my lips could win
    Sidonia the Sorceress.


## THE GROWTH OF GOD.

### (AS DEVELOPED ON A MOONLESS NIGHT
### IN THE TROPICS.) [2]

EVEN as beasts, where the sepulchral ocean
    Sobs, and their fins and feet keep Runic
    pace,
Treading in water mysteries of motion,
    Witch-dances : where the ghastly carapace
Of the blind sky hangs on the monstrous
    verge :
    Even as serpents, wallowing in the slime ;
So my thoughts raise misshapen heads, and
    urge
    Horrible visions of decaying Time.

For in the fiery dusk arise distorted
    Grey shapes in moonless phosphorus glow
    of death ;
The keen light of the eyes thrust back and
    thwarted,
    The quick scent stabbed by the miasma
    breath.

[1] For her history see Wilhelm Meinhold.
[2] When Crowley was benighted on the way
from Iguala to Mexico City, whither he was
riding unattended.

The day is over, when the lizard darted,
    A flash of green, the emerald outclassed ;
Night is collapsed upon the vale : departed
    All but the Close, suggestive of the Vast.

The heavy tropic scent-inspiring gloom
    Clothes the wide air, the circumambient
    æther.
The earth grins open, as it were a tomb,
    And struggling earthquakes gnash their
    teeth beneath her.
The night is monstrous : in the flickering fire
    Strange faces gibber as the brands burn
    low ;
Old shapes of hate, young phantoms of desire
    More hateful yet, shatter and change and
    grow.

There is a sense of terror in the air,
    And dreadful stories catch my breath and
    bind me,
Soft noises as of breathing : unaware
    What devils or what ghosts may lurk
    behind me !
Even my horse is troubled : vain it is
    Invoking memory for sweet sound of
    youth ;
The song, the day, the cup, the shot, the kiss !
    This night begets illusion—ay ! the truth.

I know the deep emotion of that birth,
    When chaos rolled in terror and in
    thunder ;
The abortion of the infancy of earth ;
    The monsters moving in a world of
    wonder ;
The Shapeless, racked with agony, that
    grew
    Into these phantom forms that change and
    shatter ;
The falling of the first toad-spotted dew ;
    The first lewd heaving ecstasy of matter.

I see all Nature claw and tear and bite,
    All hateful love and hideous : and the
    brood
Misshapen, misbegotten out of spite ;
    Lust after death ; love in decrepitude.

Thus, till the monster-birth of serpent-man
  Linked in corruption with the serpent-
    woman,
Slavering in lust and pain—creation's ban.
The horrible beginning of the human.

The savage monkey leaping on his mate ;
  The upright posture for sure murder taken ;
The gibberings modified to spit out hate :
  Struggle to manhood—surely God-for-
    saken.
The bestial cause of Morals—fear and hate.
  At last the anguish-vomit of despair,
The growth of reason—and its pangs abate
  No whit : the knife replaces the arm bare.

Fear grows, and torment ; and distracted
    pain
  Must from sheer agony some respite find ;
When some half-maddened miserable brain
  Projects a God in his detesting mind.
A God who made him—to the core all
    evil,
  In his own image—and a God of Terror ;
A vast foul nightmare, an impending devil ;
  Compact of darkness, infamy, and error.

Some bestial woman, beaten by her mates,
  In utter fear broke down the bar of
    reason ;
Shrieked, crawled to die ; delirium abates
  By some good chance her terror in its
    season.
Her ravings picture the cessation of
  Such life as she had known: her mind
    conceives
A God of Mercy, Happiness, and Love ;
  Reverses life and fact : and so believes.

So man grew up ; and so religion grew.
  Now in the æons shall not truth dissever
The man and maker, smite the old lie
    through,
  Cast God to black oblivion for ever ?
Picture no longer in fallacious thought
  A doer for each deed ! the real lurks
Nowhere thus hidden : there is truly nought
  Substantial in these unsubstantial works.

But work thou ever ! Thou who art or art not,
  Work that the fever of thy life abate ;
Work ! though for weary ages thou depart
    not,
  At last abideth the sequestered state.
Sure is the search ! O seeker, as the bird,
  Homing through distant skies toward its
    rest,
Shall surely find—and thou shalt speak the
    word
  At last that shall dissolve thee into rest.


## TO RICHARD WAGNER.

O MASTER of the ring of love, O lord
  Of all desires, and king of all the stars,
  O strong magician, who with locks and bars
Dost seal that kingdom silent and abhorred
That stretches out and binds with iron cord
    The hopes and lives of men, and makes
      and mars !
  O thou thrice noble for the deadly scars
That answered vainly thy victorious sword !

Wagner ! creator of a world of light
  As beautiful as God's, bend down to me,
    And whisper me the secrets of thy
      heart,
That I may follow and dispel the night,
    And fight life through, a comrade unto
      thee,
      Under Love's banner with the sword of
        Art !


## THE TWO EMOTIONS.

How barren is the Valley of Delight !
Swift the gaunt hounds that nose the warm
    close trail
Of all my love's content ; in vain I veil
My secret of remorse ; from their keen sight
And scent my poor deception takes to flight.
I borrow perfume from young loves waxed
    pale ;
I borrow music from the nightingale.
In vain : she knows me, that I hate her
    quite.

Not altogether : in my patchwork brain
Some rag of passion tears its woof asunder.
Strange, that its own insatiable pain
Should find an opiate in her eyes of wonder !
Yes, though I hate her well enough to kill,
I know that then my soul would love her
    still.

## THE SONNET.

### I.

THE solemn hour, and the magnetic swoon
    Of midnight in a poet's lonely hall !
    Grave spirits answer (angels if he call)
The invocations of his lofty tune.
Thus in his measures nature craves the boon
    To be reflected ; and his rhymes appal
    Or charm mankind as tides that flow or
        fall,
Waxes or wanes the tempestival moon.

Her course is measured in the sonnet's
        tether.
    Waxes the eightfold ecstasy ; exceeds
    The minor sestet, where some passion bleeds
    Or truth discourses : or eclipse may
        end,
    Proof against thought ; but if man com-
        prehend
The stars in all their stations sing together.

### II.

What power or fascination can there lie
    In this fair garden of the straight-kept
        rows,
    The sonnet ?   Surely some archangel
        knows
Why, having written in mere ecstasy
One sonnet-thought, the metre cannot die
    But urges, but compels me to compose
    More and still more,[1] and still my spirit
        goes
Striving up glittering steeps of symphony.

    [1] This is a singular psychological fact.

There is an angel who is guardian.
    Surely her wings are rosy, and her feet
        Black as the wind of frost ; but oh ! her
            face !
Whoso may know it is no more a man,
    But walks with God, and sees the Lady
        sweet
        Whose body was the vehicle of grace.

## WEDLOCK.

### A SONNET.

I SAW the Russian peasants [1] build a ring
    Of glowing embers of the bubbling pine.
    In the green heart o' the salamander line
They scatter roses.    Now the youngsters
        spring
Within, who with hard-shut eyes hope to bring
    From out the fiery circle one divine
    Blossom of rose, as from a poisonous mine
Gold comes to gird the palace of a king.

Envious I sprang—and found the last rose
        gone.
    So in the fiery ring of wedlock, blind,
    Mad, one may leap, no rose perhaps to
        find
(Or, if no rose, good fortune finds no thorn),
    But—mark the difference—palpable and
        plain :
    Rose or no rose, one leaps not out again.

## SONNET FOR GERALD KELLY'S DRAWING OF JEZEBEL.

LIFT up thine head, disastrous Jezebel !
    Fire and black stars are melted in thine
        hair
    That curls to Hell, as in Satanic prayer ;
Thy mouth is heavy with its riper smell
Than clustered pomegranates beside a well ;
    The cruel savour of thy lust lies there,
    That blood may tinge thy kisses unaware
To fill thy children with the hope of Hell.

    [1] In my mind's eye, Horatio.  The story
is a pretty fiction.

O evil beauty ! Heart of mystery
  Wherein my being toils, and in the blood
  Mixed with thy poison finds its subtle
    food,
Intoxicating my divinity !
  Disdainful hands behind thee, I may take
  What joys I will — but thou wilt not
    awake.

## MANY WATERS CANNOT QUENCH LOVE.[1]

In my distress I made complaint to Death :
  Thy shadow strides across the starry air ;
  Thou comest as a serpent unaware,
Striking love's heart and crushing out man's
    breath :
Thy destiny is even as God saith
  To mark the impotence of human prayer,
  Choke hope, sting all but Love ; and
    never care
If man or flower or sparrow perisheth.

Thee, I invoke thee, though no mercy move
  Thy heart !  No power is to thy hate
    assigned
    On love (sing, poets ! shrill, Pandean
      reeds !).
  But me, look on me, how my bosom
    bleeds—
Invoke new power of cruelty ; be kind,
And ask authority to quench my love !

## COENUM FATALE.

" La cour d'appel de la volonté de l'homme—
C'est le ventre ! "—*Old proverb.*

The worst of meals is that we have to meet.
  They trick my purpose and evade my will,
  Remind my conscience that I love her still,
And pull my spirit from its lofty seat.
For I withdraw myself : my stealthy feet
  Seek half-ashamed the alembic which I fill
  To the epic-mark—one sonnet to distil,
In this poor miracle—my love to cheat.

[1] Canticles viii. 6, 7.

Dinner clangs cheerily from my lady's gong.
A man must eat in intervals of song !
  Swift feet run back to hide my hate of her.
And then — that hate flies truant, as my
    thought
Rests (surely it beseems the overwrought)
And I am left her slave and minister.

## THE SUMMIT OF THE AMOROUS MOUNTAIN.

To love you, Love, is all my happiness ;
  To kill you with my kisses ; to devour
  Your whole ripe beauty in the perfect hour
That mingles us in one supreme caress ;
To drink the purple of your thighs ; to press
  Your beating bosom like a living flower ;
  To die in your embraces, in the shower
That dews like death your swooning loveliness

To know you love me ; that your body leaps
  With the quick passion of your soul ; to
    know
  Your fragrant kisses sting my spirit so ;
To be one soul where Satan smiles and
    sleeps ;—
Ah ! in the very triumph-hour of Hell
Satan himself remembers whence he fell !

## CONVENTIONAL WICKEDNESS.

Before the altar of Famine and Desire
  The Two in One, a golden woman stands
  Holding a heart in her ensanguine hands,
The nightly victim of her whore's attire.
Quick sobs of lust instead of prayers inspire
  Some oracle of Death.  From many lands
  Come many worshippers.  Their fading
    brands
Rekindle from the sacrificial fire.

Before the altar of Plenty, Love, and Peace,
  Stand purer priests in bloodless sacrifice,
    And quiet hymns of happiness are heard.
Here sound no hatreds and no ecstasies ;
  Here no polluted sacrament of Vice
    Unveiled !  I chose the first without
      a word !

## LOVE'S WISDOM.

THERE is a sense of passion after death.
  Passion for death, desire to kiss the scythe,
  All know, whose limbs in envious glory
      writhe,
And lie exhausted, mingling happy breath.
"Could I end so—this moment !" Lingereth
The lazy gaze half mournful and half blithe.
But there's another, when the body dieth—
Hast thou no knowledge what the carcase
      saith ?

I watched all night by my dead lover's bed.
  I saw the spirit ; heard the motionless
  Lips part in uttering a supreme caress :
" I care not or for life or death ;" they said,
  "Only for love." "What difference ?"
      said I,
  "Dead or alive, I love thee utterly."


## THE PESSIMIST'S PROGRESS.[1]

MORTAL distrust of mortal happiness
  Is born of madness and of impotence ;
  A miserable and distorted sense,
Defiant in its hatred of success.
Even where love's banners flame, and flowers
      bless
  The happy head ; all faith and hope
      immense
  Fly, for possession dwells supreme, intense ;
And to possess is only—to possess.

But, as the night draws snailwise to its end,
  And sleep invades the obstinate desire,
    And lovers sigh—but not for kisses'
      sake—
  There comes this misery, as half awake
  I watch the embers of my passion-fire,
And see love dwindled in my—call her
      friend !

[1] The obscurity of this poem demands ex
planation. Its thesis is the fact that human
happiness is only found in strife and aspiration.
Victory and achievement inevitably lead to
discontent, because only the impossible is
truly desirable.


## NEPHTHYS.

" There is no light, nor wisdom, nor knowledge in the grave, whither thou goest."—
SOLOMON.

A FOOLISH and a cruel thing is said
  By the Most High that mocks man's
      empty breast,
  As if the grave were mere eternal rest,
Or merest resurrection of the dead.
All petty wishes : at the fountain-head,
  A dead girl's whisper—I have stooped
      and pressed
  My ear unto her heart—her soul confessed
That none of life her joy relinquishéd.

" I died the moment when you tore away
  The bleeding veil of my virginity.
    The pain was sudden—and the joy was
      long.
  Persists that triumph, keenly, utterly !
    Write, then, in thy mysterious book of
      song :
' Death chisels marble where life moulded
      clay.' "


## AGAINST THE TIDE.

I KILLED my wife—not meaning to, indeed—
Yet knew myself the sheer necessity :
For I too died that miracle-hour—and she,
She also knew the immedicable need.
She sighed, and laughed, and died. How
      loves exceed
In that strange fact ! Yet robbed (you say)
      are we
Of God's own purpose of fecundity.
Exactly ! You have read the golden rede.

That is the pity of all things on earth :
That all must have its consequence again.
Life ends in death and loving ends in birth.
  All's made for pleasure : man's device is
      pain.
And in that pain and barrenness men find
Triumph on God ; and glory of the mind.

## STYX.

### (TO M. M. M.)

" The number nine is sacred, as the Oracles inform us, and attaineth the summits of philosophy."—ZOROASTER.

NINE times I kissed my lover in her sleep:
The first time, to make sure that she was there ;
The second, as a sleepy sort of prayer ;
The third, because I wished that she should weep ;
The fourth, to draw her kisses and to keep ;
The fifth, for love ; the sixth, in sweet despair ;
The seventh, to destroy us unaware ;
The eighth, to dive within the infernal deep.

The last, to kill her—and myself as well !
Ah ! joy of sweet annihilation,
The blackness that invades the burning sun,
My swart limbs and her limbs adorable !
So nine times dead before the night is done,
Even as Styx nine times embraces Hell.

## LOVE, MELANCHOLY, DESPAIR.[1]

DEEP melancholy—O, the child of folly !—
Looms on my brow, a perched ancestral bird ;
Black are its plumes, its eyes melancholy,
It speaks no word.

Like to a star, deep beauty's avatar [2]
Pales in the dusky skies so far above :
Seven rays of gladness crown its passionate star,
One heart of love.

[1] This poem is partially composed on Mr. Poe's scheme of verse—*vide* " The Philosophy of Composition."—A. C.
[2] Incarnation.

The fringing trees, marge of deep-throated seas,
Move as I walk : like spectres whispering
The spaces of them : let me leave the trees—
It is not spring !

Spring — no ! but dying autumn fast and flying,
Sere leaves and frozen robins in my breast !
There is the winter—were I sure in dying
To find some rest !

There is a shallop—how the breakers gallop,
Grinding to dust the unresisting shore,
A moon-mad thought to wander in the shallop !
Act—think no more !

Pale as a ghost I leave the sounding coast,
The waters white with moonrise. I embark,
Float on to the horizon as a ghost,
Confront the dark.

The cadent curve of Dian seems to swerve,
Eluding helmcraft : let me drift away
Where sea and sky unite their clamorous curve
In praise of Day.

Is it an edge ? Some spray-bechiselled ledge ?
Some sentry platform to an under sky ?
Let me drift onward to the azure edge—
I can but die !

The moon hath seen ! An arrow cold and keen
Brings some cold being from the water chill,
Rising between me and the world—unseen,
Most terrible.

Dawns that unheard-of terror ! Never a word of
The spells that chain ill spirits I remember.
And oh ! my soul ! What hands of ice unheard-of
Disturb, dismember !

It hath no shape; and I have no escape!
  It wraps around me, as a mist, despair.
Fear without sense and horror without
    shape
  Most surely there!

O melancholy! charming child of folly,
  Where is thy comfort told without a
    word?
Where are thy plumes, beloved melan-
    choly,
  Familiar bird?

O emerald star, deep beauty's avatar,
  Are thy skies dim? What throne is thine
    above?
Where is the crown of thee—thy sevenfold star,
  My heart of love?

Then from the clinging mist there came a
    singing;
  A dirge re-echoes to the poet prayer:
"I am their child to whom thy soul is
    clinging,
  I am Despair!"

## II. THE GATE OF THE SANCTUARY.

### TO LAURA.

MISTRESS, I pray thee, when the wind
  Exults upon the roaring sea,
Come to my bosom, kissed and kind
  And sleep upon the lips of me!

Dream on my breast of quiet days,
  Kindled of slow absorbing fire!
Sleep, while I ponder on the ways
  And secret paths of my desire!

Dream, while my restless brain probes deep
  The mysteries of its magic power,
The secrets of forgotten sleep,
  The birth of knowledge as a flower!

Slow and divine thy gentle breath
  Woos my warm throat: my spirit flies
Beyond the iron walls of death,
  And seeks strange portals, pale and wise.

My lips are fervent, as in prayer,
  Thy lips are parted, as to kiss:
My hand is clenched upon the air,
  Thy hand's soft touch, how sweet it is!

The wind is amorous of the sea;
  The sea's large limbs to its embrace
Curl, and thy perfume curls round me,
  An incense on my eager face.

I see, beyond all seas and stars,
  The gates of hell, the paths of death
Open: unclasp the surly bars
  Before the voice of him that saith:

"I will!" Droop lower to my knees!
  Sink gently to the leopard's skin![1]
I must not stoop and take my ease,
  Or touch the body lithe and thin.

Bright body of the myriad smiles,
  Sweet serpent of the lower life,
The smooth silk touch of thee defiles,
  The lures and languors of a wife.

Slip to the floor, I must not turn:
  There is a lion in the way![2]
The stars of morning rise and burn:
  I seek the dim supernal day!

Sleep there, nor know me gone: sleep there
  And never wake, although God's breath
Catch thee at midmost of the prayer
  Of sleep—that so dream turns to death!

Pass, be no more! The beckoning dawn
  Woos the white ocean: I must go
Whither my soul's desire is drawn.
  Whither? I know not. Even so.

[1] An actual rug: not a symbol.
[2] Tennyson: the Holy Grail. The phrase
is, however, much older.

## THE LESBIAN HELL.

THE unutterable void of Hell is stirred
  By gusts of sad wind moaning ; the inane
Quivers with melancholy sounds unheard,
  Unpastured woes, and unimagined pain,
    And kisses flung in vain.

Pale women fleet around, whose infinite
  Long sorrow and desire have torn their
    wombs,
Whose empty fruitlessness assails the night
  With hollow repercussion, like dim tombs
    Wherein some vampire glooms.

Pale women sickening for some sister
    breast ;
  Lone sisterhood of voiceless melancholy
That wanders in this Hell, desiring rest
  From that desire that dwells for ever free,
    Monstrous, a storm, a sea.

In that desire their hands are strained and
    wrung ;
  In that most infinite passion beats the
    blood,
And bursting chants of amorous agony flung
  To the void Hell, are lost, not understood,
    Unheard by evil or good.

Their sighs attract the unsubstantial shapes
  Of other women, and their kisses burn
Cold on the lips whose purple blood escapes,
  A thin chill stream ; they feel not nor
    discern,
    Nor love's low laugh return.

They kiss the spiritual dead, they pass
  Like mists uprisen from the frosty moon,
Like shadows fleeting in a seer's glass,
  Beckoning, yearning, amorous of the noon
    When earth dreams on in swoon.

They are so sick for sorrow, that my eyes
  Are moist because their passion was so fair,
So pure and comely that no sacrifice
  Seems to waft up a sweeter savour there,
    Where God's grave ear takes prayer.

O desecrated lovers ! O divine
  Passionate martyrs, virgin unto death !
O kissing daughters of the unfed brine !
  O sisters of the west wind's pitiful breath,
    There is One that pitieth !

One far above the heavens crowned alone,
  Immitigable, intangible, a maid,
Incomprehensible, divine, unknown,
  Who loves your love, and to high God
    hath said :
  " To me these songs are made ! "

So in a little from the silent Hell
  Rises a spectre, disanointed now,
Who bears a cup of poison terrible,
  The seal of God upon his blasted brow,
    To whom His angels bow.

Rise, Phantom disanointed, and proclaim
  Thine own destruction, and the sleepy
    death
Of those material essences that flame
  A little moment for a little breath,
    The love that perisheth !

Rise, sisters, who have ignorantly striven
  On pale pure limbs to pasture your desire,
Who should have fixed your souls on highest
    Heaven,
  And satiated your longings in that fire,
    And struck that mightier lyre !

Let the ripe kisses of your thirsty throats
  And beating blossoms of your breath, and
    flowers
Of swart illimitable hair that floats
  Vague and caressing, and the amorous
    powers
  Of your unceasing hours,

The rich hot fragrance of your dewy skins,
  The eyes that yearn, the breasts that bleed,
    the thighs
That cling and cluster to these infinite sins,
  Forget the earthlier pleasures of the prize,
    And raise diviner sighs ;

Cling to the white and bloody feet that hang,
  And drink the purple of a God's pure side;
With your wild hair assuage His deadliest
    pang,
And on His broken bosom still abide
  His virginal white bride.

So, in the dawn of skies unseen above,
  Your passion's fiercest flakes shall catch
    new gold,
The sun of an immeasurable love
  More beautiful shall touch the chaos cold
  Of earth that is grown old.

Then, shameful sisterhood of earth's disdain,
  Your lips shall speak your hearts, and
    understand;
Your lovers shall assuage the amorous pain
  With spiritual lips more keen and bland,
  And ye shall take God's hand.


### THE NAMELESS QUEST.[1]

THE king was silent.  In the blazoned hall
Shadows, more mute than at a funeral
True mourners, waited, waited in the
    gloom;
Waited to hear what child was in the womb
Of his high thoughts.  As dead men were
    we all;
As dead men wait the trumpet in the tomb.

The king was silent.  Tense the high-strung
    air [2]
Must save itself by trembling—if it dare.
Then a long shudder ran across the space;
Each man ashamed to see his fellow's face,
Each troubled and confused.  He did not
    spare
Our fear—he spake not yet a little space.

  [1] This poem has no foundation in tradition.
  [2] Here and in several other passages intense
energy of will, or importance of situation, is
represented as producing an actual condition
of strain in the air or the ether.  The fact
observed is at least subjectively true to many
people.

After a while he took the word again:
"Go thou then moonwards [1] on the great
    salt plain;
So to a pillar.  Adamant, alone,
It stands.  Around it see them overthrown,
King, earl, and knight.  There lie the quest-
    ing slain,
A thousand years forgotten—bone by bone.

"No more is spoken—the tradition goes:
'There learns the seeker what he seeks or
    knows.'
Thence—none have passed.  The desert
    leagues may keep
Some other secret—some profounder deep
Than this one echoed fear: the desert shows
Its ghastly triumph—silence.  There they
    sleep.

"There, brave and pure, there, true and
    strong, they stay
Bleached in the desert, till the solemn day
Of God's revenge — none knoweth them:
    they rest
Unburied, unremembered, unconfessed.
What names of strength, of majesty, had they?
What suns are these gone down into the
    West?

"Even I myself—my youth within me said:
Go, seek this folly; fear not for the dead,
And God is with thine arm!  I reached the
    ridge,
And saw the river and the ghastly bridge
I told you of.  Even then, even there, I fled.
Nor knight, nor king—a miserable midge!

"Yet from my shame I dare not turn and
    run.
My oath grows urgent as my days are done.
Almost mine hour is on me: for its sake
I tell you this, as if my heart should break :—
The infinite desire—a burning sun!
The listening fear — the sun-devouring
    snake!"

  [1] The moon here symbolises the path of ℷ,
which leads from Tiphereth, the human will,
to Kether, the divine Will.

The king was silent.   None of us would stir.
I sat, struck dumb, a living sepulchre.
For—hear me! in my heart this thing be-
came
My sacrament, my pentecostal flame.
And with it grew a fear—a fear of Her.
What Her?  Shame had not found itself a
name.

Simply I knew it in myself.   I brood
Ten years—so seemed it—O! the bitter
food
In my mouth nauseate!   In the silent hall
One might have heard God's sparrow in its
fall.
But I was lost in mine own solitude—
I should not hear Mikhael's[1] trumpet-call.

Yet there did grow a clamour shrill and
loud:
One cursed, one crossed himself, another
vowed
His soul against the quest; the tumult ran
Indecorous in that presence, man to man.
Stilled suddenly, beholding how I bowed
My soul in thought: another cry began.

"Gereth the dauntless! Gereth of the Sea!
Gereth the loyal! Child of royalty!
Witch-mothered Gereth! Sword above the
strong,
Heart pure, head many-wiled!"   The
knightly throng
Clamour my name, and flattering words, to
me—
If they may 'scape the quest—I do them
wrong;

They are my friends!   Yet something
terrible
Rings in the manly music that they swell.
They are all caught in this immense desire
Deeper than heaven, tameless as the fire.
All catch the fear—the fear of Her—as well,
And dare not—even afraid, I must aspire.

[1] Correct for "Michael."   A piece of
pedantry pardonable in a youth of 25.

A spirit walking in a dream, I went
To the high throne—they shook the firma-
ment
With foolish cheers.   I knelt before the
queen
And wept in silence.   Then, as it had been
An angel's voice and touch, her face she
bent,
Lifted and kissed me—oh! her lips were
keen!

Her voice was softer than a virgin's eyes:
"Go! my true knight: for thither, thither
lies
The only road for thee; thou hast a prayer
Wafted each hour—my spirit will be there!"
Too late I knew what subtle Paradise
Her dreams and prayers portend: too fresh,
too fair!

I turned more wretched than myself knew
yet.
I told my nameless pain I should forget
Its shadow as it passed.   The king did start,
Gripped my strong hands, and held me to
his heart,
And could not speak a moment.   Then he
set
A curb on sorrow and subdued its dart.

"Go! and the blessing of high God attend
Thy path, and lead thee to the doubtful end.
No tongue that secret ever may reveal.
Thy soul is God-like and thy frame is steel;
Thou mayst win the quest—the king, thy
friend,
Gives thee his sword to keep thee—Gereth,
kneel!

"I dub thee Earl; arise!"   And then there
rings
The queen's voice:  "Shall my love not
match the king's?
Here, from my finger drawn, this gem of
power
Shall guard thee in some unimagined hour.
It hath strange virtue over mortal things.
I freely give it for thy stirrup's dower."

I left the presence.  Now the buffeting wind
Gladdens my face—I leave the court be-
   hind.
Am I stark mad?  My face grows grim and
   grave ;
I see—O Mary Mother, speak and save !
I stare and stare until mine eyes are blind—
There was no jewel in the ring she gave ! [1]

Oh !  my pure heart !     Adulterous love
   began
So subtly to identify the man
With its own perfumed thoughts.  So steals
   the grape
Into the furtive brain—a spirit shape
Kisses my spirit as no woman can.
I love her—yes ; and I have no escape.

I never spoke, I never looked !  But she
Saw through the curtains of the soul of me,
And loved me also !  It is very well.
I am well started on the road to Hell.
Loved, and no sin done !  Ay, the world
   shall see
The quest is first—a love less terrible.

Yet, as I ride toward the edge of snow
That cuts the blue, I think.  For even so
Comes reason to me : " Oh, return, return !
What folly is it for two souls to burn
With hell's own fire !  What is this quest
   of woe ?
What is the end ?  Consider and discern ! "

Banish the thought !  My working reason
   still
Is the rebellious vassal to my will,
Because I will it.  That is God's own mind.
I cast all thought and prudence to the
   wind :
On, to the quest !  The cursed parrot hill
Mocks on, on, on !  The thought is left
   behind.

[1] The gift of a wedding ring is of course
typical of the supreme surrender on the part
of a married woman.

Night came upon me thus—a wizard hand
Grasping with silence the reluctant land.
Through night I clomb—behind me grew
   the light
Reflected in the portal of the night.
I reach the crest at dawn—pallid I stand,
Uncomprehending of the sudden sight.

The river and the bridge !  The river flows,
Tears of young orphans for its limpid woes.
The red bridge quivers — how my spirit
   starts,
Its seeming glory built of widows' hearts !
And yet I could disdain it—heaven knows
I had no dear ones for their counterparts.

Yet the thought chilled me as I touched the
   reins.
Ah !  the poor horse, he will not.  So re-
   mains,
Divided in his love.  With mastered tears
I stride toward the parapet.  My ears
Catch his low call ; and now a song com-
   plains.
The bridge is bleeding and the river hears.

Ah !  God !  I cannot live for pity deep
Of that heart-quelling chant—I could not
   sleep
Ever again to think of it.  I close
My hearing with my fingers.  Gently goes
A quivering foot above them as they weep—
I weep, I also, as the river flows.

Slowly the bridge subsides, and I am flung
Deep in the tears and terrors never sung.
I swim with sorrow bursting at my breast.
Yet I am cleansed, and find some little rest.
Still from my agonised unspeaking tongue
Breaks : I must go, go onward to the quest.

Again the cursed cry : " What quest is this ?
Is it worth heaven in thy lover's kiss ?
A queen, a queen, to kiss and never tire !
Thy queen, quick-breathing for your twin
   desire ! "
I shudder, for the mystery of bliss ;
I go, heart crying and a soul on fire !

"Resolve all question by a moonward
    tread.
Follow the moon!" Even so the king had
    said.
My thought had thanked him for the generous
    breath
Wherewith he warned us: for delay were
    death.
And now, too late! no moon is overhead—
Some other meaning in the words he saith?

Or, am I tricked in such a little snare?
I lifted up my eyes. What soul stood there,
Fronting my path? Tall, stately, delicate,
A woman fairer than a pomegranate.
A silver spear her hands of lotus bear,
One shaft of moonlight quivering and
    straight.

She pointed to the East with flashing eyes:
"Thou canst not see her—but my Queen
    shall rise."
Bowed head and beating heart, with feet
    unsure
I passed her, trembling, for she was too pure.
I could have loved her. No: she was too
    wise.
Her presence was too gracious to endure.

"She did not bid me go and chain me to
    her,"
I cried, comparing. Then, my spirit knew
    her
For One beyond all song [1]—my poor heart
    turned:
Then, 'tis no wonder. And my passion
    burned
Mightier yet than ever. To renew her
Venom from those pure eyes? And yet I
    yearned.

Still, I stepped onward. Credit me so far!
The harlot had my soul: my will, the star!
Thus I went onward, as a man goes blind,
Into a torrent crowd of mine own kind;
Jostlers and hurried folk and mad they are,
A million actions and a single mind.

       [1] The "Higher Self."

"What is thy purpose, sweet my lord?" I
    pressed
One stalwart. "Ah! the quest," he cried,
    "the quest."
God's heart! the antics, as they toil and
    shove!
One grabs a coin, one life, another love.
All shriek, "The prize is mine!" as men
    possessed.
I was not fooled at anything thereof.

Rather I hated them, and scorned for
    slaves;
"Fools! all your treasure is at last the
    grave's!"
Mine eyes had fixed them on the sphinx,
    the sky.
"Is then this quest of immortality?"
And echo answered from some unseen caves:
Mortality! I shrink, and wonder why.

Strange I am nothing tainted with this fear
Now, that had touched me first. For I am
    here
Half-way I reckon to the field of salt,
The pillar, and the bones—it was a fault
I am cured of! praise to God! What meets
    mine ear,
That every nerve and bone of me cries halt?

What is this cold that nips me at the throat?
This shiver in my blood? this icy note
Of awe within my agonising brain?
Neither of shame, nor love, nor fear, nor
    pain,
Nor anything? Has love no antidote,
Courage no buckler? Hark! it comes
    again.

Friend, hast thou heard the wailing of the
    damned?
Friend, hast thou listened when a murderer
    shammed
Pale smiles amid his fellows as they spoke
Low of his crime: his fear is like to choke
His palsied throat. How, if Hell's gate
    were slammed
This very hour upon thy womanfolk?

Conceive, I charge thee !  Brace thy spirit
     up
To drink at that imagination's cup !
Then, shriek, and pass !  For thou shalt
     understand
A little of the pressure of the hand
That crushed me now.  Yes, yes ! let fancy
     sup
That grislier banquet than old Atreus[1]
     planned !

mind cannot fathom, nor the brain conceive,
Nor soul assimilate, nor heart believe
The horror of that Thing without a Name.
Full on me, boasting, like Death's hand
     it came,
And struck me headlong.    Linger, while
     I weave
The web of mine old agony and shame.

A little shadow of that hour of mine
Touches thy heart ?  Fill up the foaming
     wine,
And listen for a little !  How profound
Strikes memory keen-fanged ; memory, the
     hound
That tracks me yet ! a shiver takes my spine
At one half-hint, the shadow of that sound.

Where am I ?  Seven days my spirit fell,
Down, down the whirlpools and the gulfs
     of hell :
Seven days a corpse lay desolate—at last
Back drew the spirit and the soul aghast
To animate that clay—O horrible !
The resurrection pang is hardly past.

Yet in awhile I stumbled to my feet
To flee—no nightmare could be worse to
     meet.
And, spite of that, I knew some deadlier
     trap
Some worm more poisonous would set—
     mayhap !

[1] Atreus, King of Mycenae, gave a banquet
of pretended reconciliation to his half-brother
Thyestes, at which the two sons of Thyestes
were served up.

I turned—the path ?  My horror was com-
     plete—
A flaming sword across the earthquake gap.

I cried aloud to God in my despair.
"The quest of quests !  I seek it, for I
     dare !
Moonward ! on, moonward !"  And the full
     moon shone,
A glory for God's eyes to dwell upon,
A path of silver furrowed in the air,
A gateway where an angel might have gone.

And forward gleamed a narrow way of
     earth
Crusted with salt : I watch the fairy birth
Of countless flashes on the crystal flakes,
Forgetting it is only death that makes
Its home the centre of that starry girth.
Yet, what is life ?  The manhood in me
     wakes.

The absolute desire hath hold of me.
Death were most welcome in that solemn
     sea ;
So bitter is my life.  But carelessness
Of life and death and love is on me—yes !
Only the quest ! if any quest there be !
What is my purpose ?  Could the Godhead
     guess ?

So the long way seemed moving as I went,
Flashing beneath me ; and the firmament
Moving with quicker robes that swept the
     air.
Still Dian drew me to her bosom bare,
And madness more than will was my con-
     tent.
I moved, and as I moved I was aware !

The plain is covered with a many dead.
Glisten white bone and salt-encrusted head,
Glazed eye imagined, of a crystal built.
And see ! dark patches, as of murder spilt.
Ugh !  "So thy fellows of the quest are
     sped !
Thou shalt be with them : onward, if thou
     wilt !"

So was the chilling whisper at my side,
Or in my brain.  Then surged the madden-
    ing tide
Of my intention.  Onward !  Let me run !
Thy steed, O Moon !  Thy chariot, O Sun !
Lend me fierce feet, winged sandals, wings
    as wide
As thine, O East wind !  And the goal is
    won !

Was ever such a cruel solitude ?
Up rears the pillar.  Quaintly shaped and
    hued,
It focussed all the sky and all the plain
To its own ugliness.  I looked again,
And saw its magic in another mood.
A shapeless truth took image in my brain.

A hollow voice from every quarter cries :
"O thou, zelator of this Paradise,
Tell thou the secret of the pillar !  None
Can hear thee, of the souls beneath the sun.
Speak, or the very Godhead in thee dies.
For we are many and thy name is One."

The Godhead in me !  As a flash there
    came
The jealous secret and the guarded name.
The quest was mine !  And yet my thoughts
    confute
My intuition ; and my will was mute.
My voice—ah ! flashes out the word of
    flame :
"Eternal Beauty, One and absolute !"

The overwhelming sweetness of a voice
Filled me with Godhead.  "Still remains
    the choice !
Thou knowest me for Beauty !  Canst thou
    bear
The fuller vision, the abundant air ?"
I only wept.  The elements rejoice ;
No tear before had ever fallen there.

I thought within myself a bitter thing,
Standing abased.  The golden marriage ring
The queen had given—how her beauty
    stank

Now in mine eyes, where once their passion
    drank
Its secret sweets of poison.  Let the spring
Of love once dawn—all else hath little
    thank !

Yet resolute I put my love away.
It could not live in this amazing day.
Love is the lotus that is sickly sweet,
That makes men drunken, and betrays their
    feet :
Beauty, the sacred lotus : let me say
The word, and make my purity complete.

The whole is mine, and shall I keep a
    part ?
O Beauty, I must see thee as thou art !
Then on my withered gaze that Beauty
    grew—
Rosy quintessence of alchemic dew !
The Self-informing Beauty !  In my heart
The many were united : and I knew.

Smitten by Beauty down I fell as dead—
So strikes the sunlight on a miner's head.
Blind, stricken, crushed !  That vast efful-
    gence stole,
Flooded the caverns of my secret soul,
And gushed in waves of weeping.  I was
    wed
Unto a part, and could not grasp the whole.

Thus, I was broken on the wheel of Truth.
Fled all the hope and purpose of my youth,
The high desire, the secret joy, the sin
That coiled its rainbow dragon scales within.
Hope's being, life's delight, time's eager
    tooth ;
All, all are gone ; the serpent sloughs his
    skin !

The quest is mine !  Here ends mortality
In contemplating the eternal Thee.
Here, She is willing.  Stands the Absolute
Reaching its arms toward me.  I am mute,
I draw toward.  Oh, suddenly I see
The treason-pledge, the royal prostitute.

One moment, and I should have passed be-
    yond
Linked unto Spirit by the fourfold bond.
Not dead to earth, but living as divine,
A priest, a king, an oracle, a shrine,
A saviour! Yet my misty spirit conned
The secret murmur: "Gereth, I am thine!"

I must have listened to the voice of hell.
The earthly horror wove its serpent spell
Against the Beauty of the World: I heard
Desolate voices cry the doleful word
"Unready!" All the soul invisible
Of that vast desert echoed, and concurred.

The voices died in mystery away.
I passed, confounded, lifeless as the clay,
Somewhere I knew not. Many a dismal
    league
Of various terror wove me its intrigue,
And many a demon daunted: day by day
Death dogged despair, and misery fatigue.

Behold! I came with haggard mien again
Into the hall, and mingled with the train,
A corpse amid the dancers. Then the king
Saw me, and knew me—and he knew the ring!
He did not ask me how I sped: disdain
Curled his old lips: he said one bitter thing.

"You crossed the bridge—no man's heart
    trod you there?"
Then crossed his breast in uttering some
    prayer:
"I pray you follow of your courtesy,
My lord!" I followed very bitterly.
"Likes you the sword I gave?" I did not
    dare
Answer one word. My soul was hating me.

He bade me draw. I silently obeyed.
My eye shirked his as blade encountered
    blade.
I was determined he should take my life.
"Went your glance back—encountering my
    wife?"
"Taunt me!" I cried; "I will not be
    afraid!"
My whole soul weary of the coward strife.

He seemed to see no opening I gave,
But hated me the more. Serene and suave,
He fenced with deep contempt. I stumble,
    slip,
Guard wide—and only move his upper lip.
"You know I will not strike, Sir pure and
    brave!
Fight me your best—or I shall find a whip!"

That stung me, even me. He wronged me,
    so:
Therefore some shame and hate informed
    the blow;
Some coward's courage pointed me the steel;
Some strength of Hell: we lunge, and leap,
    and wheel;
Hard breath and laboured hands—the flashes
    grow
Swifter and cruel—this court hath no appeal!

He gladdened then. I would not slip again,
And baulk the death of half its shame and
    pain.
I, his best sword, must fall, in earnest fight.
The old despair was coward—he was right.
Now, king, I pay your debt. A purple stain
Hides his laced throat—I sober at the sight.

"King, you are touched!" "Fight on,
    Earl Lecherer!"
I cursed him to his face—the added spur
Sticks venom in my lunge—a sudden thrust!
No cry, no gasp; but he is in the dust,
Stark dead. The queen—I hate the name
    of her!
So grew the mustard-seed, one moment's lust.

I too was wounded: shameful runs the song.
She nursed me through that melancholy long
Month of despair: she won my life from
    death.
Ah God! she won that most reluctant breath
Out of corruption: love! ah! love is strong!
What waters quench it? King Shalomeh [1]
    saith.

[1] Hebrew form of Solomon. See Canticles
viii. 6, 7.

I am the king: you know it, friend! We
   wed.
That is the tale of how my wooing sped.
And oh! the quest: half won—incredible?
I am so brave, and pure—folk love me well.
But oh! my life, my being! That is dead,
And my whole soul—a whirlwind out of hell!


## THE REAPER.

IN middle music of Apollo's corn
   She stood, the reaper, challenging a kiss;
The lips of her were fresher than the morn,
   The perfume of her skin was ambergris;
The sun had kissed her body into brown;
   Ripe breasts thrown forward to the
      summer breeze;
Warm tints of red lead fancy to the crown,
   Her coils of chestnut, in abundant ease,
That bound the stately head. What joy
   of youth
Lifted her nostril to respire the wind?
What pride of being? What triumphal
   truth
Acclaimed her queen to her imperial mind?

I watched, a leopard, stealthy in the corn,
   As if a tigress held herself above;
My body quivered, eager to be torn,
   Stung by the snake of some convulsive
      love!
The leopard changed his spots; for in me
   leapt
   The mate, the tiger. Murderous I sprang
Across the mellow earth: my senses swept,
· One torrent flame, one soul-dissolving pang.
How queenly bent her body to the grip!
   How lithe it slips, her bosom to my own!
The throat leans back, to tantalise the lip :—
   The sudden shame of her is overthrown!
O maiden of the spirit of the wheat,
   One ripening sunbeam thrills thee to the
      soul,
Electric from red mane to amber feet!
   The blue skies focus, as a burning bowl,
The restless passion of the universe
   Into our mutual anger and distress,
VOL. I.

To be forbidden (the Creator's curse)
   To comprehend the other's loveliness.
We cannot grasp the ecstasy of this;
   Only we strain and struggle and renew
The utter bliss of the unending kiss,
   The mutual pang that shudders through
      and through,
Repeated and repeated, as the light
   Can build a partial palace of the day,
So, in our anguish for the infinite,
   One moment gives, the other takes away.
(I, the mere rhymer, she, the queen of rhyme,
   As sweeps her sickle in the falling wheat,
Her body's sleek intoxicating time,
   The music of the motion of her feet!)

I swoon in that imperial embrace—
   Lay we asleep till evening, or dead?
I knew not, but the wonder of her face
   Grew as the dawn and never satiated.
She knew not in her strong imperial soul
   How hopeless was the slavery of life,
How by the part man learns to love the
      whole,
   How each man's mistress calls herself a
      wife.
I tired not of the tigress limbs and lips—
   Only, my soul was weary of itself,
Being so impotent, who only sips
   The dewdrops from the flower-cup of an elf,
Not comprehending the mysterious sea
   Of black swift waters that can drink it up,
Not trusting life to its own ecstasy,
   Not mixing poison with the loving-cup.
I, maker of mad rhymes, the reaper she!
   We lingered but a day upon the lawn.
O Thou, the other Reaper! come to me!
   Thy dark embraces have a germ of Dawn!


## THE TWO MINDS.

"THEY SHALL BE NO MORE TWAIN, BUT
      ONE FLESH."

WELL have I said, "O God, Thou art, alone,
   In many forms and faces manifest!
Thou, stronger than the universe, Thy throne!
   Thou, calm in strength as the sea's heart
   at rest!"

N

But I have also answered : "Let the groan
　Of this Thy world reach up to Thee, and
　　wrest
Thy bloody sceptre : let the wild winds own
　Man's lordship, and obey at his behest ! "

Man has two minds : the first beholding all,
　As from a centre to the endless end :
The second reaches from the outer wall,
　And seeks the centre. This I comprehend.
But in the first : "I can — but what is
　　worth ? "
　　And in the second : "I am dust and
　　earth ! "

## THE TWO WISDOMS.

SOPHIE ! I loved her, tenderly at worst.
　Yet in my passion's highest ecstasy,
　When life lost pleasure in desire to die
And never taste again the deadly thirst
For those caresses ; even then a curst
　Sick pang shot through me : looking far
　　on high,
Beyond, I see Σοφια in the sky.
The petty bubble of Love's pipe is burst !

Yea ! through the portals of the dusky dawn
　I see the nameless Rose of Heaven un-
　　fold !
Yea ! through rent passion and desire with-
　　drawn
Burns in the East the far ephemeral gold.
O Wisdom ! Mother of my sorrow ! Rise !
And lift my love to thine immortal eyes !

## THE TWO LOVES.

WHAT is my soul ? The shadow of my will.
　What is my will ? The sleeper's sigh at
　　waking.
Osiris ! Orient godhead ! let me still
　Rest in the dawn of knowledge, ever slaking
My lips and throat where yon rose-glimmer-
　　ing hill,
　The Mountain of the East, its lips is taking

To Thy life-lips : I hear Thy keen voice thrill ;
　Arise and shine ! the clouds of earth are
　　breaking !

The clouds are parted : yes ! And there above
　I bathe in ether and self-shining light ;
My soul is filled with the eternal love ;
　I am the brother of the Day and Night.
I AM ! my spirit, and perhaps my mind !
But O my heart ! I left thy love behind !

## A RELIGIOUS BRINGING-UP.

WITH this our "Christian" parents marred
　　our youth :
　"One thing is certain of our origin.
　We are born Adam's bastards into sin,
Servants to Death and Time's devouring
　　tooth.
God, damning most, had this one thought
　　of ruth
　To save some dozens—Us : and by the skin
　Of teeth to save us from the devil's gin—
Repentance ! Blood ! Prayer ! Sackcloth !
　This is truth."

Our parents answer jesting Pilate so.[1]
　I am the meanest servant of the Christ :
But, were I heathen, cannibal, profane,
　My cruel spirit had not sacrificed
My children to this Moloch. I am plain ?
"Blasphemer ! Damned ! " ? Undoubtedly
　—I know !

## THE LAW OF CHANGE.

SOME lives complain of their own happiness.
　In perfect love no sure abiding stands ;
　In perfect faith are no immortal bands
Of God and man. This passion we possess
Necessitous ; insistent none the less
　Because we know not how its purpose
　　brands
　Our lives. Even on God's knees and in
　　His hands :
　　The Law of Change. "Out, out,
　　adulteress !" ?

　　[1] See Bacon's Essay on Truth.

These be the furies, and the harpies these?
  That discontent should sum the happiest
    sky?
  That of all boons man lacks the greatest
    —rest?
Nay! But the promise of the centuries,
  The certain pledge of immortality,
    Child-cry of Man at the eternal Breast.


## SYNTHESIS.

WHEN I think of the hundreds of women I
  have loved from time to time,
White throats and living bosoms where a
  kiss might creep or climb,
Smooth eyes and trembling fingers, faint
  lips or murderous hair,
All tunes of love's own music, most various
  and rare ;
When I look back on life, as a mariner on
  the deep
Sees, tranced, the white wake foaming,
  fancies the nereids weep ;
As, on a mountain summit in the thunders
  and the snow,
I look to the shimmering valley and weep:
  I loved you so !
For a moment cease the winds of God upon
  the reverent head ;
I lose the life of the mountain, and my soul
  is with the dead ;
Yet am I not unaware of the splendour of the
  height,
Yet am I lapped in the glory of the Sun of
  Life and Light :—
Even so my heart looks out from the harbour
  of God's breast,
Out from the shining stars where it entered
  into rest—
Once more it seeks in memory for reverence,
  not regret,
And it loves you still, my sisters ! as God
  shall not forget.
It is ill to blaspheme the silence with a
  wicked whispered thought—
How still they were, those nights ! when this
  web of things was wrought !

How still, how terrible ! O my dolorous
  tender brides,
As I lay and dreamt in the dark by your
  shameful beautiful sides !
And now you are mine no more, I know;
  but I cannot bear
The curse—that another is drunk on the life
  that stirs your hair :
Every hair was alive with a spark of mid-
  night's delicate flame,
Or a glow of the nether fire, or an old
  illustrious shame.
Many, so many, were ye to make one
  Womanhood—
A thing of fire and flesh, of wine and glory
  and blood,
In whose rose-orient texture a golden light
  is spun,
A gossamer scheme of love, as water in the
  sun
Flecked by wonderful bars, most delicately
  crossed,
Worked into wedded beauties, flickering,
  never lost—
That is the spirit of love, incarnate in your
  flesh !
Your bodies had wearied me, but your passion
  was ever fresh :
You were many indeed, but your love for
  me was one.
Then I perceived the stars to reflect a single
  sun—
Not burning suns themselves, in furious
  regular race,
But mirrors of midnight, lit to remind us of
  His face.
Thus I beheld the truth : ye are stars that
  give me light ;
But I read you aright and learn I am walk-
  ing in the night.
Then I turned mine eyes away to the Light
  that is above you :
The answering splendid Dawn arose, and I
  did not love you.
I saw the breaking light, and the clouds fled
  far away :
It was the resurrection of the Golden Star
  of Day.

And now I live in Him ; my heart may trace
the years
In drops of virginal blood and springs of
virginal tears.
I love you now again with an undivided
song.
Because I can never love you, I cannot do
you wrong.
I saw in your dying embraces the birth of a
new embrace ;
In the tears of your pitiful faces, another
Holier Face.
Unknowing it, undesiring, your lips have led
me higher ;
You have taught me purer songs that your
souls did not desire ;
You have led me through your chambers,
where the secret bolt was drawn,
To the chambers of the Highest and the
secrets of the Dawn !
You have brought me to command you, and
not to be denied ;

You have taught me in perfection to be
unsatisfied ;
You have taught me midnight vigils, when
you smiled in amorous sleep ;
You have even taught a man the woman's
way to weep.
So, even as you helped me, blindly, against
your will,
So shall the angel faces watch for your own
souls still.
A little pain and pleasure, a little touch of
time,
And you shall blindly reach to the subtle and
sublime ;
You shall gather up your girdles to make
ready for the way,
And by the Cross of Suffering climb seeing
to the Day.
Then we shall meet again in the Presence of
the Throne,
Not knowing ; yet in Him ! O Thou ! knowing as we are known.

## III. THE HOLY PLACE

### THE NEOPHYTE.[1]

TO-NIGHT I tread the unsubstantial way
That looms before me, as the thundering night
Falls on the ocean : I must stop, and pray
One little prayer, and then—what bitter fight
Flames at the end beyond the darkling goal?
These are my passions that my feet must
tread ;
This is my sword, the fervour of my soul ;
This is my Will, the crown upon my head.
For see ! the darkness beckons : I have gone,
Before this terrible hour, towards the gloom,
Braved the wild dragon, called the tiger on
With whirling cries of pride, sought out the
tomb
Where lurking vampires battened, and my
steel

[1] This poem describes the Initiation of the
*true* " Hermetic Order of the Golden Dawn "
in its spiritual aspect.

Has wrought its splendour through the gates
of death.
My courage did not falter : now I feel
My heart beat wave-wise, and my throat
catch breath
As if I choked ; some horror creeps between
The spirit of my will and its desire,
Some just reluctance to the Great Unseen
That coils its nameless terrors, and its dire
Fear round my heart ; a devil cold as ice
Breathes somewhere, for I feel his shudder
take
My veins : some deadlier asp or cockatrice
Slimes in my senses : I am half awake,
Half automatic, as I move along
Wrapped in a cloud of blackness deep as
hell,
Hearing afar some half-forgotten song
As of disruption ; yet strange glories dwell
Above my head, as if a sword of light,
Rayed of the very Dawn, would strike within

The limitations of this deadly night
That folds me for the sign of death and sin—
O Light ! descend !  My feet move vaguely on
In this amazing darkness, in the gloom
That I can touch with trembling sense. There shone
Once, in my misty memory, in the womb
Of some unformulated thought, the flame
And smoke of mighty pillars ; yet my mind
Is clouded with the horror of this same
Path of the wise men : for my soul is blind
Yet : and the foemen I have never feared
I could not see (if such should cross the way),
And therefore I am strange : my soul is seared
With desolation of the blinding day
I have come out from: yes, that fearful light
Was not the Sun: my life has been the death,
This death may be the life : my spirit sight
Knows that at last, at least.  My doubtful breath
Is breathing in a nobler air ; I know,
I know it in my soul, despite of this,
The clinging darkness of the Long Ago,
Cruel as death, and closer than a kiss,
This horror of great darkness.  I am come
Into this darkness to attain the light :
To gain my voice I make myself as dumb :
That I may see I close my outer sight :
So, I am here.  My brows are bent in prayer ;
I kneel already in the Gates of Dawn ;
And I am come, albeit unaware,
To the deep sanctuary : my hope is drawn
From wells profounder than the very sea.
Yea, I am come, where least I guessed it so,
Into the very Presence of the Three
That Are beyond all Gods.  And now I know
What spiritual Light is drawing me
Up to its stooping splendour.  In my soul
I feel the Spring, the all-devouring Dawn,
Rush with my Rising.  There, beyond the goal,
The Veil is rent !
   Yes: let the veil be drawn.

## SIN.

YE rivers, and ye elemental caves,
 Above the fountains of the broken ice,
Know ye what dragon lurks within your waves ?
 Know ye the secret of the cockatrice?
  The basilisk whose shapeless brood
  Take blood and muck for food ?
The sexless passion, the foul scorpion spawn ?
  The witches and the evil-chanting ones
  Who strangle stars and suns,
Eclipse the moon, and curse against the dawn ?
  Know ye the haunts of death ?
  The hole that harboureth
  The sickening breath,
Whence all disease is bred, and all corruption drawn ?

Nay, these ye know not, or your waters cold
 Would stagnate, shudder, putrefy for fear ;
Your echoes hate existence, and be rolled
 Into the silent, desolate, dead sphere.
  For in those sightless lairs
  No living spirit fares :—
Caught in a chain, linked corpses for a lure !
  Shall human senses feel
  Or human tongue reveal ?
Nay, shall the mortal know them and endure
  Whose little period
  Is limited by God ;
  Whose poor abode
Is the mean body, prey to all distemperature ?

Yet, mortal, in the Light and Way Divine,
 Gird on the armour of the Holy One :
Seek out the secret of the inmost shrine,
 Strong in the might and spirit of the sun.
  Arise, arise, arise,
  Give passage to mine eyes,

Ye airs, ye veils; ye bucklers of the
    Snake !
  I knew the deepest cells,
  Where the foul spirit dwells ;
Called to the dead, the drowsed, arise !
    awake !
    Their dark profoundest thought
    Was less than She I sought,
    It was as nought !
I drew my soul, I dived beneath the burning
    lake.


Thrice, in the vault of Hell, my Word was
    born,
Abortive, in the empty wilderness.
False echoes, made malicious, turn to scorn
  The awful accents, the Supreme address.
    The Fourth, the final word !
    All chaos shrank and heard
  The terror that vibrated in the breath.
    Hell, Death, and Sin must hear,
    Tremble and visibly fear,
  Shake the intangible chain that hungereth.
    That Mother of Mankind
    Sprang in the thunder-wind !
    The strong words bind
For evermore, Amen ! the keys of Hell and
    Death.[1]


Central, supreme, most formidable, Night
  Gathered its garments, drew itself apart ;
Gaunt limbs appear athwart the coprolite
  Veil of deep agony, display the heart ;
    Even as a gloomy sea,
    Wherein dead fishes be,
  Poisonous things, nameless ; the eightfold
    Fear,
    Misshapen crab and worm,
    The intolerable sperm,
  Lewd dragons slime-built.    Stagnant, the
    foul mere
  Crawled, moved, gave tongue,
    The essential soul of dung
    That lived and stung ;
That spoke : no word that living head may
    hear !

[1] Rev. i. 18.

Even as a veil imaging Beauty's eyes
  Behind, lifted, lets flash the maiden face ;
So that dead putrefying sea supplies
  A veil to the unfathomable Place.
    Behind it grew a form,
    Wrapped in its own dire storm,
  Dark fires of horror about it and within,
    A changing, dreadful Shape :
    Now a distorted ape ;
  Now an impending vampire, vast and
    lean ;
    Last, a dark woman pressed
    The world unto her breast,
    Soothed and caressed
With evil words and kisses of the mouth
    of Sin.


The Breath of men adoring.  "Worship
    we !
  "The mighty Wisdom, the astounding
    power,
 "The Horror, the immense profundity,
    "The stealthy, secret paces of thy Bower !
    "Thee we adore and praise
    "Whose breast is broad as day's ;
   "Thee, thee, the mistress of the barren
    sea,
    "Deep, deadly, poisonous ;
    "Accept the life of us,
   "Dwell in our midst; yea, show thy
    cruelty !
    "Suck out the life and breath
    "From breast that quickeneth !
    "Such pain is death,
  "Such terror, such delight—all, all is unto
    thee !"


I too, I also, I have known thy kiss.
I also drank the milk that poisons man,
Sought to assume the impenetrable bliss
    By spells profound and draughts Canidian.[1]
    One lifted me : and, lo !
    Thalassian,[2] white as snow,

[1] Canidia, a sorceress of Rome in the time of
Horace, who attacked her.
[2] From Θαλασσα, the sea. But Crowley
always uses the word as exalting, idealising,
personifying the idea.

The scarlet vesture and the crimson skin !
  As Aphrodite clove
  The foam, incarnate Love,
Maiden ; as light leaps the dawn-gardens in,
  So in the Love and Light,
  Life slain, yet infinite,
  The God-Man's night,
Leaps pure the Soul re-arisen from the
    embrace of Sin.

Yet, in the terror of that Breast, abides
  So sweet and deadly a device, a lure
Deep in the blood and poison of her sides,
  Swart, lean, and leprous, that her stings
    endure.
    Even the soul of grace
    Abideth not her face
Without vague longing, infinite desire,
    Stronger because suppressed,
    Unto the wide black breast,
The lips incarnate of blood, flesh, and fire,
    So to slip down between
    Thighs vast and epicene,
    Morose and lean,
To that unnameable morass, the ultimate mire.

Wherefore behoves the Soul that leaps divine,
  Even beholding, darkly in a mirror,
The face of God, to sink before His Shrine,
  Weeping : O Beauty, Majesty, and Terror,
    Wisdom and Mind and Soul,
    Crown simplex, Mighty Whole,
Lord of the Gods ! O Thou, the King of
    Kings !
    To me a sinner, me,
    Lowest of all that be,
  Be merciful, O Master Soul of things !
    Show me thy face of ruth,
    And in thy way of truth
    Guide my weak youth,
That stumbles while it walks, makes discord
    when it sings !

So, Mighty Mother ! Pure, Eternal Spouse,
  Isis, thou Star, thou Moon, thou Mightiest,
Lead my weak steps to thine Eternal House !
  Rest my vain head on thine Eternal
    Breast !

Spread wide the wings divine
Over this shadowy shrine,
Where in my heart their hovering lendeth
  Light !
Bend down the amazing Face
Of sorrow and of grace,
Share the deep vigil of thine eremite !
  So let the sighing breath
  Draw on the Hour of Death,
  Whence wakeneth
The Spirit of the Dawn, begotten of the
  night.

## THE NAME.

SACRED, between the serpent fangs of pain,
Ringed by the vortex of the hurricane,
Lurks the abyss of fate : the gloomy cave,
Sullen as night, and sleepy as a wave
When tempest lowers and dare not strike,
  gapes wide,
Vomiting pestilence ; the deadly bride
Of death, Despair, grins charnel-wise : the
  gate
Of Hope clangs resonant : and starless Fate
Glowers like a demon brooding over death.
Monstrous and mute, the slow resurgent breath
Spreads forth its poison : the pale child at
  play
Coughs in his gutter ; the hard slave of day
Groans once and dies : the sickly spouse can
  feel
Some cold touch kill the unborn child, and
  steal
Up to her broken heart : the pale hours hang
Like death upon the agéd : the days clang
Like prison portals on the folk of day.
Yet for the children of the night they play
Like fountains in the moonlight : for the few,
The sorrowful, sweet faces of the dew,
The laughter-loving daughters of the dawn,
Whose moving feet make tremble all the
  lawn
From Hesper to the break of rose and gold,
Where Heaven's petals in the East unfold
The awful flower of morning : for the folk
Bound in one single patient love, a yoke

Too light for fairy fingers to have woven,
  oo strong for mere archangels to have cloven
With adamantine blades from the armoury
Of the amazing forges of the sea :
The folk that follow with undaunted mien
The utmost beauty that their eyes have
  seen—
O patient sufferers ! yet your storm-scarred
  brows
Burn with the star of majesty : your vows
Have given you the wisdom and the power
To weld eternities within one hour,
To bind and braid the North wind's serpent
  hair,
And track the East wind to his mighty lair
Even in the caverns of the womb of dawn ;
To take the South wind and his fire with-
  drawn
And clothe him with your kiss ; to seize the
  West
In his gold palace where the sea-winds rest,
And hurl him ravening on the breaking foam ;
To find the Spirit in his glimmering home
And draw his secret from unwilling lips ;
To master earthquake, and the dread eclipse ;
To dominate the red volcanic rage ;
To quench the whirlpool, conquering war to
  wage
Against all gods not wholly made as ye,
O patient, and O marvellous !  I see,
I see before me an archangel stand,
Whose flaming scimitar, a triple brand,
Quivers before him, whose vast eyebrows
  bend,
A million comets: for his locks extend
A million flashing terrors : on his breast
He bears a mightier cuirass : for his vest
All heaven blazes : for his brows a crown
Roars into the abyss: his mighty frown
Quells many an universe and many an age—
Yea, many eternities !  His nostrils rage
With fire and fury, and his feet are shod
With all the splendours of the avenging God.
I see him and I tremble !  But my hand
Still flings its gesture of supreme command
Upwards ; my voice still dares to tongue the
  word
That hell and chaos and destruction heard

And ruined, shrieking ! yea, my strong voice
  rolls,
That martyr-cry of many slaughtered souls,
Utterly potent both to bless and ban—
I, I command thee in the name of Man !
He trembled then.  And far in thunder rolled
Through countless ages, through the infinite
  gold
Beyond existence, grew that master-sound
Into the rent and agonized profound,
Till even the Highest heard me: and He said,
As one who speaks alone among men dead :
"Behold, he rules as I the abyss of flame.
For lo ! he knoweth, and hath said, My Name !"

## THE EVOCATION.

FROM the abyss, the horrible lone world
  Of agony, more sharp than moonbeams
    strike
The shaken glacier, my cry is hurled,
As the avenger lightning.  Swiftly whirled,
  It flings in circles closing serpent-like
On the abominable devil-horde
I summon to the mastery of the sword.

In my white palace, where the flashing dawn
  Leaps from the girdling bastions, where
    the light
Flames from the talisman as if a fawn
Glode through the thickets, where the soul,
  withdrawn
    From every element, gleams through the
    night
Into that darkness palpable, where They
Lurk from the torment of the light of day.

Swings the swift sword in paths of vivid blue ;
  Rings the sharp summons in the halls of
    fear ;
Flames the great lamen [1]; as a fiery dew
Falls the keen chanted music ; fierce and true
  Beams the bright diamond of the crowning
    sphere.

[1] A plate bearing the Names of God appropriate to the work in hand, with other symbols
of power, worn by the exorciser upon his breast.

None may withstand the summons: like
    dead flame
Flares darkness deeper, and demands its name.

Mine eyes peer deeper in the quivering
    gloom—
    What horrors crowd upon the aching sight !
Behold ! the phantom ! Icy as the tomb,
His head of writhing scorpions in the womb
    Of deadlier terrors : how a charnel-light
Gleams on his beetle frame ! What poison
    drips
Of slime and blood from his disastrous lips !

What oceans of decaying water steam
    For his vast essence ! And a voice rolls
    forth
With miserable fury from that stream
Of horror : " Thou hast called me by the
    beam
    Of glory, by the devastating wrath
Of thine accursèd godhead : tell me then
My Name ! Thou hardiest of the Sons of
    Men ! "

" Thy name is—stay ! thou liest ! I discern
    In Thee no terror that my spells evoke.
Begone, thou wandering corpse of night !
    return
Into thy shadowy world ! My symbols burn
    Against thee, shade of terror ! Go ! " It
    spoke :
" Yea ! I am human. Know my actual
    truth :
I am that ghost, the father of thy youth ! "

" Poor wandering phantom ! "—the exultant
    yell
    And wolfish howling of all damnèd souls
Peals from the ravening jaws and gulfs of hell:
Leaps that foul horror through the terrible
    Extinguished circle of the burning bowls.
Then I remember, fling the gleaming rod
Against him : " Liar, back ! For I am God ! "

Back flung the baffled corpse. But through
    the air
    Looms the more startling vision in the
    night ;

The actual demon of my work is there !
Where is the glittering circle ? Where, ah,
    where
    The radiant bowls whose flame rose fiery
    bright ?
I am alone in the absolute abyss ;
No aid ; no helper ; no defence—but this !

My left hand seeks the lamen. Once again
    Fearless I front the awful shape before me,
Fearless I speak his Name. My trembling
    brain
Vibrates that Word of Power. I cry amain :
    " Down, Dweller of the Darkness, and
    adore me !
I am thy Master, and thy God ! Behold
The Rose of Ruby and the Cross of Gold ! "[1]

" I am thy Saviour ! " At the kindling word
    Up springs the dawn-light in the broken
    bowls ;
Up leaps the glittering circle. Then I heard
A hoarse shrill voice, as if some carrion bird
    Shrieked, mightier than the storm that
    rocks and rolls
Through desolation : " Thou hast known
    my Name.
What is thy purpose, Master of the Flame ? "

I made demand : through long appalling hours
    Stayed he to tempt and try my adamant
Purpose : at last the legionary powers
Behind him sank affrayed ; his visage lowers
    Less menacing : his head is turned aslant
In vain : I bid him kneel and swear : the earth
Rocked with the terror of that deadlier birth.

He swore : he vanished : the wide sky resounds
    With echoing thunders : through the
    blinding night
The stars resume their courses : at the bounds
Of the four watch-towers cry the waking
    hounds :
    " The night is well ": slow steals the
    ambient light
Through all the borders of the universe
At that last lifting of my strenuous curse.

[1] " Ave Frater ! " " Rosae Rubeae." " Et
Aureae Crucis." Greeting of Rosicrucians.

Slow steals the ambient light ; white peace
  resumes
In planet, element, and sign, her sway.
The twisted ether shapes itself : relumes
The benediction all the faded fumes
  With holier incense : in the fervid way
All nature rests : .with holy calm I blend
Blessing and prayer at the appointed end.


## THE ROSE AND THE CROSS.[1]

OUT of the seething cauldron of my woes,
  Where sweets and salt and bitterness I
    flung ;
  Where charméd music gathered from my
    tongue,
And where I chained strange archipelagoes
Of fallen stars ; where fiery passion flows
  A curious bitumen ; where among
  The glowing medley moved the tune
    unsung
Of perfect love : thence grew the Mystic Rose.

Its myriad petals of divided light ;
  Its leaves of the most radiant emerald ;
Its heart of fire like rubies.  At the sight
  I lifted up my heart to God and called :
How shall I pluck this dream of my desire?
And lo ! there shaped itself the Cross of Fire !


## HAPPINESS.

IT is the seasonable sun of spring
  That gilds the all-rejuvenescent air—
New buds, young birds, so happy in the rare
Fresh life of earth : myself am bound to sing,
Feeling the resurrection crown me king.
  I am so happy as men never were.
Of sorrow much, of suffering a share,
Leave me unmoved, or leave me conquering.

---

[1] The.symbol of the " Rose and Cross " now
replaces that of the "Golden Dawn."  We
may suppose from this that Crowley was about
this time received into the former fraternity.

---

O miserable ! that it should be so !
  Lord Jesus, Sufferer for the sins of man,
    Thou didst invite me to Thy shame and
      loss.
And I am happy !  Pity me !  Bestow
  The right to work in the eternal Plan,
    The right to hang on the eternal Cross !


## THE LORD'S DAY.

THE foolish bells with their discordant clang
  Summon the harlot-ridden Hell to pray :
  The vicar's snout is tuned, the curates bray
Long gabbled lessons, and their noisy twang
Fills the foul worshippers with hate ; the fang
  Of boredom crushes out the holy day,
  Where whore and jobber sit and gloom,
    grown grey
For hating of each other ; the hours hang.

But where cliffs tremble, and the wind and sea
  Clamour, night thunders from the roaring
    West ;
I worship in the storm, and fires flee
  From my gripped lightnings and my burn-
    ing crest ;
And when my voice rolls, master of the
    weather,
A thousand mighty angels cry together !

BRIGHTON, *January* 1899.


## CERBERUS.

I STOOD within Death's gate,
  And blew the horn of Hell :
Mad laughters echoing against Fate,
  Harsh groans less terrible,
Howled from beneath the vault ; in night the
  avenging thunders swell.

The guardian stood aloof,
  A monster multiform.
His armour was of triple proof,
  His voice out-shrilled the storm.
Behind him all the Furies whirl and all the
  Harpies swarm.

The first face spake and said :
  "Welcome, O King, art thou !
Await thy throne a thousand dead ;
  A crown awaits thy brow,
A seven-sting scorpion ; for thy rod thou
    hast a bauble now."

The next face spake and said :
  "Welcome, O Priest, to me !
Red blood shall dye thee robes of red,
  Hell's cries thy litany !
Thy mitre sits, divided strength, to end thy
    church and thee ! "

The third face spake and said :
  "Welcome, O Man, to Death !
Thy little span of life is sped,
  Sighed out thy little breath.
The worm that never dies is thine ; the fire
    that lingereth ! "

"Three voices has thy frame,
  Their music is but one.
Fool-demon, slave of night and shame,
  That canst not see the sun !
I am the Lord thy God :[1] make thou homage
    and orison ! "

The wild heads sank in fear :
  Then, troubled, to those eyes
Remembrance crept of many a year,
  Barred gates of Paradise.
Again the Voice rolled in the deep, mingled
    with murmuring sighs :

"I mind me of the day
  One [2] came from Death to me ;
His soul was weary of the day,
  His look was melancholy ;
He bade me open in the Name that binds
    Eternity.

"Yet though He passed within
  And plunged within the deep,

[1] The assumption of the form of the God of
the Force whom one addresses is the Egyptian
magical spell to subdue it.
  [2] Ieheshua, or " Jesus."

The seven palaces of sin,
  And slept the lonely sleep,
Yet came He out alone: but then I thought
  I heard Them weep.

"He passed alone, above,
  Out of the Gates of Night ;
Angels of Purity and Love
  Drew to my sound and sight.
I heard Them cry that even there He fixed
  the eternal Light.

"I think beneath these groans,
  And laughters madness-born,
Tears fell that might dissolve the stones
  That grind the accursèd corn.
Beneath the deep, beneath the deep, may
  dwell the star of morn !

"Therefore, O God, I pray
  Redemption for the folk
That dread the scourging light of day,
  That bear the midnight yoke.
The Chaos was no less than this—and there
  the light awoke."

"O Dog of Evil, yea !
  Thou hast in wisdom said.
The glory of the living day
  Shall shine among the dead.
Thy faith shall have a holier task, thy
  strength a goodlier stead."

Then I withdrew the light
  Of mine own Godhead up,
As stars that close with broken night
  Their adamantine cup.
I sought the solar airs: my soul on its own
  tears might sup.

For in the vast profound
  Still burns the rescuing sign ;[1]
Beyond all sight and sense and sound
  The symbol flames divine.
For He shall make all life, all death, His
  solitary shrine.

[1] The Triangle surmounted by the Cross.
This was the symbol of the " Golden Dawn."

## THE HOLY OF HOLIES

### THE PALACE OF THE WORLD.[1]

THE fragrant gateways of the dawn [2]
Teem with the scent of flowers.
The mother, Midnight, has withdrawn
Her slumberous kissing hours :
Day springs, with footsteps as a fawn,
Into her rosy bowers.

The pale and holy maiden horn [3]
In highest heaven is set.

[1] Describes the spiritual aspect of the "Lesser Ritual of the Pentagram," which we append, with its explanation. The abstruse nature of many of these poems is well reflected in this one.
(i.) Touching the forehead, say Ateh (Unto Thee).
(ii.) Touching the breast, say Malkuth (the Kingdom).
(iii.) Touching the right shoulder, say ve-Geburah (and the Power).
(iv.) Touching the left shoulder, say ve-Gedulah (and the Glory).
(v.) Clasping the hands upon the breast, say le-Olahm, Amen (to the Ages, Amen).
(vi.) Turning to the East, make a pentagram with the proper weapon. Say יהוה.
(vii.) Turning to the South, the same, but say אדני.
(viii.) Turning to the West, the same, but say אהיה.
(ix.) Turning to the North, the same, but say אגלא.
(x.) Extending the arms in the form of a cross, say—
(xi.) Before me Raphael,
(xii.) Behind me Gabriel,
(xiii.) On my right hand Michael,
(xiv.) On my left hand Auriel,
(xv.) for about me flames the Pentagram,
(xvi.) and in the Column stands the six-rayed Star.
(xvii.–xxi.) Repeat (i.) to (v.), the "Qabalistic Cross."
Those who regard this ritual as a mere device to invoke or banish spirits, are unworthy to possess it. Properly understood, it is the Medicine of Metals and the Stone of the Wise. [Author's Note.]
[2] This ritual was given to Neophytes of the Order of the Golden Dawn.
[3] The moon, as before, signifies Aspiration to the Highest.

My forehead, bathed in her forlorn
Light, with her lips is met ;
My lips, that murmur in the morn,
With lustrous dew are wet.

My prayer is mighty with my will ;
My purpose as a sword [1]
Flames through the adamant, to fill
The gardens of the Lord
With music, that the air be still,
Dumb to its mighty chord.

I stand above the tides of time
And elemental strife ;
My figure stands above, sublime,
Shadowing the Key of Life,[2]
And the passion of my mighty rhyme
Divides me as a knife.

For secret symbols on my brow,
And secret thoughts within,
Compel eternity to Now,
Draw the Infinite within.
Light is extended.[3] I and Thou
Are as they had not been.[4]

So on my head the light is one,
Unity manifest ;
A star more splendid than the sun
Burns for my crownéd crest ;
Burns, as the murmuring orison
Of waters in the west.

What angel from the silver gate
Flames to my fierier face?
What angel, as I contemplate
The unsubstantial space?
Move with my lips the laws of Fate
That bind earth's carapace?

[1] For the " Flaming Sword " is the " Pentagram unwound."
[2] The arms being extended, and the magus being clad in a Tau-shaped robe and a nemmes, the sacred Egyptian headdress, his figure would cast a shadow resembling the Ankh, or " Key of Life."
[3] Khabs am Pekht. Konx om Pax. Light in Extension. The mystic words which seal the current of light in the sphere of the aspirant.
[4] Cf. Omar Khayyam the Sufi.

No angel, but the very light
And fire and spirit of Her,
Unmitigated, eremite,
The unmanifested myrrh,
Ocean, and night that is not night,
The mother-mediator.[1]

O sacred spirit of the Gods ![2]
O triple tongue ![3] Descend,
Lapping the answering flame that nods,
Kissing the brows that bend,
Uniting all earth's periods
To one exalted end.

Still on the mystic Tree of Life
My soul is crucified ;[4]
Still strikes the sacrificial knife
Where lurks some serpent-eyed
Fear, passion, or man's deadly wife
Desire, the suicide !

Before me dwells the Holy One
Anointed Beauty's King ;[5]
Behind me, mightier than the Sun,
To whom the cherubs sing,
A strong archangel,[6] known of none,
Comes crowned and conquering.

An angel stands on my right hand
With strength of ocean's wrath ;[7]
Upon my left the fiery brand,
Charioted fire smites forth :[8]
Four great archangels to withstand
The furies of the path.[9]

[1] Binah, the revealer of the Triad of Light.
[2] Ruach Elohim (see Genesis i.) adds up to 300=שׁ=Fire.
[3] שׁ by shape hath a triple tongue.
[4] These archangels are at points on the "Tree of Life" which cause them to surround as described one who is "crucified" thereon.
[5] Raphael dwells in Tiphereth, Beauty.
[6] Gabriel, dweller in Yesod, where are the Kerubim.
[7] Michael, lord of Hod, an Emanation of a watery nature.
[8] Auriel, archangel of Netzach, to which Fire is attributed.
[9] The path of ת, or Saturn and Earth, which leads from Malkuth to Yesod indeed, but is dark and illusory. This first step upward attracts the bitterest opposition of all the Enemies of the Human Soul.

Flames on my front the fiery star,
About me and around.[1]
Pillared, the sacred sun, afar,
Six symphonies of sound ;
Flames, as the Gods themselves that are ;
Flames, in the abyss profound.[2]

The spread arms drop like thunder ! So
Rings out the lordlier cry,
Vibrating through the streams that flow
In ether to the sky,
The moving archipelago,
Stars in their seigneury.

Thine be the kingdom ! Thine the power !
The glory triply thine ![3]
Thine, through Eternity's swift hour,
Eternity, thy shrine—
Yea, by the holy lotus-flower,
Even mine ![4]

## THE MOUNTAIN CHRIST.[5]

O WORLD of moonlight ! Visionary vale
Of ocean-sleeping mountains ! Mighty chasm
Within whose wild abyss there chants the pale,
The dolorous phantasm
Of wrecked white womanhood ! The wizard cold
Grips the mute valley in his grasp of gold !

[1] As asserted in the ritual.
[2] It flames both above and beneath the magus, who is thus in a cube of 4 pentagrams and 2 hexagrams, 32 points in all. And 32 is אהיהוה, the sacred word that expresses the Unity of the Highest and the Human.
[3] As in ritual.
[4] Supreme affirmation of Unity with the Highest in the Lotus, the universal symbol of Attainment.
[5] Composed during a solitary ramble across the Col du Géant.

Yonder the hatred of the dismal steep
  Sweeps up to wrathful thunders, that are
    curled
In billowy menace, as the deadlier deep
  That menaces the world
With breaking foam : so hangs the glacier,
    rent
By giant sunrays, in the frost-grip pent.

Yonder again rears up the craggy wall
  Its cleaving head to heaven : thither I
Clomb the vast terrors, where the echoing
    fall
*Roars* stony from the sky.
Thither I pressed at midnight, and the dawn
Saw my swift feet move faster than the fawn.

Pale seas of blue soft azure lie beyond,
  Far o'er the gleaming green : the smoke
    is risen
Out of the cloudy north ; the incense-wand
  That binds dead souls in prison,
That prison of the day, when sleepless dead
Rest for awhile from agony and dread.

Strange ! how a certain fear possesses me
  Alone amid their crag-bound solitude.
Even beyond the keen delight—to Be—
  Steals that diviner mood
Of wonder at the miracle—the plan
Of Nature crowned by the astounding Man !

The secret of the Lord is set with him
  That wonders at His majesty :[1] his praise
Wells from no trembler's misery : his hymn
  Swells the exultant day's.
His psalm wings upward, and reflected down
Even in Hell makes music and renown.

Yea ! for the echo of the anthem rolls
  Down to the lost unfathomable deep.
Down, to the darkness of all shades and souls,
  The founts of music sweep.
Even the devils in the utter night
Feel it the saving, not the avenging light.

[1] See the Psalms of David. "Wonders" is
a correcter rendering than "fears."

Yea ! for the worship of my secret song
  Vibrates through every chasm of the world :
Its sound is caught by angels, and made
    strong !
By sylphs, and dewed, and pearled
With fairy melodies, and borne, alone,
Aloft, to the immeasurable throne.

O mighty palace of immortal stone !
  O glamour of the fathomless gray snow !
O clouds ! O whirlwinds of my mountain
    throne !
I charge your souls to go
Unto the souls of men, and bid them rise
Toward redemption, and the unsullied eyes.

I charge you go and whisper unto men
  The solemn glories of your secret mind,
Making them pure, and wise ; return ye then
  Unto your proper kind,
Having thus offered water, blood, and tears,
For the remission of our carrion years.[1]

So deepen all the mountains : even so
  The wandering shadows close upon the day ;
The sunlight burns its fading ruby glow
  On the chaotic way.
Night falls, and I must tread the dizzy steep
Again, to plunge to the devouring deep.

The blessing of the Highest shall be set
  On your white heads, O monarchs of the
    snow !
The blessing of the Highest, lightening yet
  The burdens that ye know.
So, as three golden arrows of the sun
Strike, may the threefold sacrament be One !

O visionary valley of my Soul !
  When shall thy beauty, even thine, be
    made
As pure and mighty as these hills that roll
  In mist and sun and shade ?
O thou ! the Highest ! make my will as
    thine,
My consciousness, the consciousness divine !

[1] See the Prayer of the Undines, given by
Eliphaz Levi and some other writers on occult
subjects.

## TO ALLAN BENNETT MACGREGOR.[1]

O MAN of Sorrows: brother unto Grief!
  O pale with suffering, and dumb hours of
    pain!
  O worn with Thought! thy purpose
    springs again
The Soul of Resurrection: thou art chief
And lord of all thy mind: O patient thief
  Of God's own fire! What mysteries find
    fane
  In the white shrine of thy white spirit's
    reign,
Thou man of Sorrows: O, beyond belief!

Let perfect Peace be with thee: let thy days
  Prosper in spite of thine unselfish soul;
    And as thou lovest, so let Love increase
Upon thee and about thee: till thy ways
  Gleam with the splendour of that secret
    goal
    Whose long war grows the great abiding
      peace.


## THE ROSICRUCIAN.

À SA MAJESTÉ JACQUES IV D'ÉCOSSE.[2]

I SEE the centuries wax and wane.
I know their mystery of pain,
  The secrets of the living fire,
The key of life: I live: I reign:
  For I am master of desire.

Silent, I pass amid the folk
Caught in its mesh, slaves to its yoke.
  Silent, unknown, I work and will
Redemption, godhead's master-stroke,
  And breaking of the wands of ill.

[1] Now a Buddhist recluse in Burma. In
England he was a martyr to spasmodic
asthma, which, however, could not quench,
could hardly dull even, the fire of his soul.
[2] Supposed to have escaped from Flodden,
and become an Adept: to have reappeared as
the "Comte de St. Germain," and later (so
hinted Mr. S. L. Mathers) as Mr. S. L.
Mathers.

No man hath seen beneath my brows
Eternity's exultant house.
  No man hath noted in my brain
The knowledge of my mystic spouse.
  I watch the centuries wax and wane.

Poor, in the kingdom of strong gold,
My power is swift and uncontrolled.
  Simple, amid the maze of lies;
A child, among the cruel old,
  I plot their stealthy destinies.

So patient, in the breathless strife;
So silent, under scourge and knife;
  So tranquil, in the surge of things;
I bring them from the well of Life,
  Love, from celestial water-springs!

From the shrill fountain-head of God
I draw out water with the rod
  Made luminous with light of power.
I seal each æon's period,
  And wait the moment and the hour.

Aloof, alone, unloved, I stand
With love and worship in my hand.
  I commune with the Gods: I wait
Their summons, and I fire the brand.
  I speak their Word: and there is Fate.

I know no happiness, no pain,
No swift emotion, no disdain,
  No pity: but the boundless light
Of the Eternal Love, unslain,
  Flows through me to redeem the night.

Mine is a sad slow life: but I,
I would not gain release, and die
  A moment ere my task be done.
To falter now were treachery—
  I should not dare to greet the sun!

Yet, in one hour I dare not hope,
The mighty gate of Life may ope,
  And call me upwards to unite
(Even my soul within the scope)
  With That Unutterable Light.

Steady of purpose, girt with Truth,
I pass, in my eternal youth,
  And watch the centuries wax and wane:
Untouched by Time's corroding tooth,
  Silent, immortal, unprofane!

My empire changes not with time.
Men's kingdoms cadent as a rhyme
  Move me as waves that rise and fall.
They are the parts, that crash or climb;
  I only comprehend the All.

I sit, as God must sit; I reign.
Redemption from the threads of pain
  I weave, until the veil be drawn.
I burn the chaff, I glean the grain;
  In silence I await the dawn.

### THE ATHANOR.

LIBERTINE touches of small fingers creep
  Among my curls to-night: pale ghastly
    kisses,
Like mournful ghosts roused from their
    ruined sleep
  By clamorous cries of murder. Strange
    abysses
Loom in the vista keen eyes penetrate,
Vague forecasts of immeasurable fate.

O thou belovéd blood, that wells and weeps!
  O thou belovéd mouth, that beats and
    bleeds!
O mystic bosom where some serpent sleeps,
  Sweet mockery of a thousand saintlier
    creeds!
Even I, that breathe your perfume, taste
    your breath,
Know, even this hour, ye are not life, but
    death!

No death ye bring more godlike than de-
    sire,
  When seas roar tempest-lashed, and foam
    is flung

Raging on pitiless crags, and gloomy fire
  Lurks in the master-cloud; corpses are
    swung
Helpless and horrible in trough and crest—
That death were music, and the lord of
    rest.

No death ye bring as when the storm is
    rolled,
  An imminent giant on the sun-ripped
    snows,
Where icy fingers grip the overbold
  Son of their secrets, and like springes
    close
On his choked throat and frozen body—
    Nay!
That death were twilight, and the gate of
    Day!

No death ye bring as his, that grips the flag
  In desperate fingers, and with bloody
    sword
Flames up the thundering breach, while
    bastioned crag,
  Glacis, and pent-house belch their mon-
    strous horde
Of hideous engines shattering—this strife
Clears the straight road of Glory and of
    Life!

Nay: but the hateful death that stings the
    soul
  Into rebellion; the insensate death
That chokes its own delight with words that
    roll
  Mightier-mouthed than the archangel's
    breath;
The death that murders courage ere it drink
The soul's own life-blood on the desperate
    brink!

So, from the languid fingers in my curls
  And dreamy worship of a woman's eyes,
I look beyond the miserable whirls
  Of foolish measures woven in the skies;
Beyond the thoughtless stars: beyond God's
    sleep:
Beyond the deep: beneath the deadly deep!

Infinite rings of luminous ether move
   At first amid the blackness that I seek:
Infinite motion and amazing love
   Deaden the lustre of the night.   I speak
The cry of silence, that is heard unspoken ;
That, being heard, rings evermore unbroken.

Silence, deep silence.   Not a shudder stirs
   The vast demesne of unforgetful space,
No comet's lunatic rush: no meteor whirs,
   No star dares breathe, no planet knows
      his place
In that supreme unquiet quietude.
I am the master of my own deep mood.

I am the master.   Yea, no doubt I rule
   The whole mad universe by will extended[1]—
Who whispers then, " O miserable fool !
   This night thy might and majesty are
      ended ;
Thy soul shall be required of thee " ?   I heard
This voice, and knew it for my proper word !

Yea, mine own voice : the higher spirit speaks,
   Stemming the hands that guide, the arms
      that hold,
Even the infinite brain : that spirit seeks
   A loftier dawn of more ephemeral gold—
Ephemeral, and eternal: droop thine head,
O God ! for thou must suffer this : I said !

Droop thy wide pinions, O thou mortal God !
   Sink thy vast forehead, and let Life con-
      sume
The miserable life thy feet have trod
   Beneath them, that thine own life in its
      doom
Fall, in its resurrection to arise ;
Stoop, that its holier hope may cleave the skies.

Power, power, and power !   O single sacrifice
   On thine own altar : let thy savour steam
Up, through the domes of broken Paradise ;
   Up, by Euphrates'[2] unimagined stream ;
Up, by strange river and mysterious lawn
To some impossible diadem of dawn !

[1] Cf. Fichte.
[2] Or Phrath, the Fourth River of the Mystic
Eden, flowing from Tiphereth to Yesod.
   VOL. I.

So the mere orderly ruling of events
   Shall change and blossom to a finer flower
Until it serve to worlds and elements
   For aspiration in the nobler hour—
Not mere repression, but the hope and crown
Of fallen hierarchies no more cast down.

O misery of triple love and grief
   And hope !   O joy of hatred and despair
And happiness !   The little hour is brief,
   And the lithe fingers soothe the listless hair
Less, and the kisses swoon to tenderer sighs
And little sobs of sleeping ecstasies.

No ! for the envy of the infinite
   Crushes the juice from out the poppy's
      stem,
And brown-stained fingers wring the petals
      white,
   And weary lips seek lotus-life in them
Vainly : the lotus burns above the tomb—
Yea, but in thought's unfathomable womb !

For spiritual life and love and light
   Climb the swayed ladder of our various
      fate ;
The steep rude stair that mocks the hero's
      might,
   Casts off the wise, and crumbles with the
      great.
Yet from the highest crown no blossom fell,
Save one, to bring salvation unto Hell.

O angel of my spiritual desire ![1]
   O luminous master of the silver feet !
O passionate rose of infinite white fire !
   O cross of sacrifice made bitter-sweet !
O wide-wing, star-brow, veritable lord !
O mystic bearer of the flaming sword !

O brows half seen, O visionary star
   Seen in the fragrant breezes of the East !
O lover of my love, O avatar
   Of the All-One, O mystical High Priest !
O thou before whose eyes my weak eyes fail,
Wonderful warden of the Holy Grail !

[1] The " Genius " of Socrates ; the " Holy
Guardian Angel " of Abramelin the Mage ; or
the " Higher Self " of the Theosophists.
                                    O

O thou, mine angel, whom these eyes have seen,
  These hands have handled, and this mouth has kissed !
O thou, the very tongue of fire, the clean
  Sweet-scented presence of a holier Christ !
Listen, and answer, and behold ! My wings
Droop, O thou stronger than the immortal kings !

My flame burns dim ! O bring the broken jar
And alabaster casket, and dispense
The oil that flows from that supernal star,
  And holy fountains of the Influence.[1]
Bring peace, and strength, and quicken in my heart
Mastery of night-fear and the day-flung dart.

Yea ! from the limit of the fallen day,
  And barren ocean of ungathered Time,
Bring Night, and bring Eternity, and stay
  With white wings pointing where tired feet may climb :
Even the pathway where shed blood ran deep
To build red roses in the land of Sleep.

O guardian of the pallid hours of night !
  O tireless watcher of the smitten noon !
O sworded with the majesty of light,
  O girded with the glory of the moon !
Angel of absolute splendour ! Link of mine
Old weary spirit with the All-Divine !

Ship that shalt carry me by many winds
  Driven on the limitless ocean ! Mighty sword,
By which I force that barrier of the mind's
  Miscomprehension of its own true lord !
Listen, and answer, and behold my brow
Fiery with hope ! Bend down, and touch it now !

[1] From Kether, the Vast Countenance, are said to flow " 13 fountains of magnificent oil " through Mezla, the Influence, upon Tiphereth, the Lesser Countenance.

Press the twin dawn of thy desirous lips
  In the swart masses of my hair ; bend close,
And shroud all earth in masterless eclipse,
  While my heart's murmur through thy being flows,
To carry up the prayer, as incense teems
Skyward, to those immeasurable streams !

Breathe the creative Sigh upon my mouth
  That even the body may become the soul :
Cry, as the chainéd Eagle of the South,
  " A house of death,"[1] and make my spirit whole !
Touch with pure balm the five mysterious wounds !
Come ! come away ! but not your mighty sounds ![1]

O wind of all the world ! O silent river !
  O sea of seas ! O flower of all the flowers
O fire ! O spirit ! Beam thou on for ever
  Through æons of illimitable hours !
Kiss thou my forehead, let thy tender breath
Woo me to life, and my desire to death !

I shall be ready for it by-and-by,
  That sharp initiation, when the whole
Body is torn with sundering pangs, and I,
  The very conscious essence of the soul,
Am rent with agony, as when the pale
Christ heard the shriek of the dividing veil.

That awful mystery, its heart torn out,
  Palpitates on the altar-stone of life :
That broken self, that hears the triumph-shout
  Of its own voice beneath the falling knife,
When, like a bad dream changing, swiftly grows
A new soul's joy, a fuller-petalled rose.

Many the spirits broken for one man ;
  Many the men that perish to create
One God the more ; many the weary and wan
  Old Gods that die to constitute a Fate :
How many Fates then, think you, must control
The stainless aspiration of the soul ?

[1] See the " 48 Calls or Keys " of Dr. Dee, from which this is quoted.

Not one.  I tell you, destiny is sure,
  Yet moves no finger: though it tune my
    tongue,
My tongue shall tune it too : my words
    endure
  As destiny decays : my hands are flung
In prayer to Heaven   nay, to mine own
    crown,
To raise myself, and not to drag it down ! [1]

O holiest Lord of the divine white flame
  Of brilliance sworded in the temple sky !
O thou who knowest my most secret name,
  Who whisperest when only thou and I
Make up our universe : bestow thy kiss :
Arise !   Come, let us pierce the old abyss !

Rise !  Move !  Appear !  Let us go forth
    together,
  Into the solemn passionless profound,
Into the darkness, and the thrilling weather,
  Into the silence louder than all sound,
Into the vast implacable inane !
Come, let us journey thither once again !


## THE CHANT TO BE SAID OR SUNG UNTO OUR LADY ISIS.

ROLL through the caverns of matter, the
  world's irremovable bounds !
Roll, ye wild billows of ether ! the Sistron [2]
  is shaken and sounds !
Wild and sonorous the clamour, vast in the
  region of death,
Live with the fire of the Spirit, the essence
  and flame of the breath !
    Sound, O sound !

[1] An allusion to the sign called " Enterer of
the Threshold," in which the Egyptian Gods
often stand.   It is a sign of high initiation (if
you know the rest !) and implies the gathering
of force from the Gods and its projection as
will toward any object.
[2] A musical instrument used for religious
purposes by the Egyptians.   It consisted of an
oval framework (with a handle) crossed by
four wires loosely fixed, which on being shaken
gave forth a musical sound.

Gleam in the world of the dark, where the
  chained ones shall tremble and flee !
Gleam in the skies of the dusk, for the Light
  of the Dawn is in me !
Light on the forehead, and life in the nostrils,
  and love in the breast,
Shine, O thou Star of the Dawning, thou
  Sun of the Radiant Crest !
    Shine, O shine !


Flame through the sky in the strength of
  the chariot-wheels of the Sun !
Flame, ye young fingers of light, on the
  West of the morning that run !
Flame, O thou Meteor Car, for my fire is
  exalted in thee !
Lighten the darkness and herald the day-
  light, and waken the sea !
    Flame, O flame !


Crown Her, O crown Her with stars as with
  flowers for a virginal gaud !
Crown Her, O crown Her with Light and
  the flame of the down-rushing Sword !
Crown Her, O crown Her with Love for
  maiden and mother and wife !
Hail unto Isis !   Hail !  For She is the
  Lady of Life !
    Isis crowned !


## A LITANY.

THE ghosts of abject days flit by ;
  The bloated goblins of the past ;
  Dim ghouls in soulless apathy ;
    Fates imminent, and dooms aghast !
O Mother Mout,[1] O Mother Night,
Give me the Sun of Life and Light ! [2]

[1] Mout, the Vulture Goddess of The Womb
of Years.
[2] " Mother, give me the Sun ! "   This, the
tragedy-word of Ibsen's " Ghosts," served as
inception—by reversal—of this poem.

The shadows of my hopes devoured,
  The crowns of my intent cast down,
The hate that shone, the love that lowered,
  Make up God's universal frown.
O Lord, O Hormakhou,[1] display
The rosy earnest of the day !

The mighty pomp of desolate
  Dead kings, a pageant, moves along ;
Dead queens unite in desperate,
  Unsatisfied, unholy song.
O Khephra,[2] manifest in flesh,
Arise, create the world afresh !

The silence of my heart is one
  With memory's insatiate night ;
I hardly dare to hope the sun.
  I seek the darkness, not the light.
O Lord Harpocrates,[3] be still
The moveless centre of my will !

My sorrows are more manifold
  Than His that bore the sins of man.
My sins are like the starry fold,
  My hopes their desolation wan.
O Nuit,[4] the starry one, arise,
And set thy starlight in my skies !

In darkness, in the void abyss,
  I grope with vain despairing arms.
The silence as a serpent is,
  The rustle of the world alarms.
O Horus,[5] Light in Darkness, bless
My failure with thine own success !

My suffering is keen as theirs
  That in Amenti taste of death ;

---

[1] The Dawn-God.
[2] The Beetle-Headed God, who brings light out of darkness, for He is the Sun at Midnight.
[3] God of Silence. Usually shown as a child.
[4] The bowed Goddess of the Stars. Shown as a naked woman, her hands and feet on the earth, the arms and legs much elongated, so that her body arches the firmament.
[5] The Hawk-headed Lord of Strength, the Avenger of Osiris' death.

Not mine own pains create these prayers :
  For them I claim the living Breath.
O Lord Osiris,[1] bend and bring
All winters to thy sign of Spring !

Poor folly mine : I cannot see
  Save from one corner of one star !
So many millions over me ;
  So many, and the next, how far !
O Wisdom-crowned Ta-hu-ti,[2] lend
Thy magic : let my light extend ![3]

I cannot comprehend one truth.
  My sight is biassed, and my mind—
One snake-skin thought is of its youth ;
  Grows old, and casts the slough behind.
O Themis,[4] Lady of the plume,
Shed thy twin godhead in the gloom !

How ugly is this life of mine !
  How slimes it in the terrene mud !
Clouds hide the beauty all-divine,
  The moonlight has a mist of blood.
O Hathoor,[5] Lady of the West,
Take thy sad lover to thy breast !

Even the perfumes of the dawn
  Intoxicate, deceive the soul.
Let every shadow be withdrawn !
  Let there be Light, supreme and whole !
O Ra,[6] thou golden Lord of Day,
The Sun of Righteousness display !

The burden is so hard to bear.
  I took too adamant a cross ;
This sackcloth rends my soul to wear ;
  My self-denial is as dross !
O Shu,[7] that holdest up the sky,
Hold thou thy servant, lest he die !

---

[1] The Redeemer by His suffering.
[2] Thoth, the Ibis God. Equivalent to the higher Hermes.
[3] Khabs am Pekht again.
[4] Goddess of Justice.
[5] Goddess of Beauty and Love.
[6] The Hawk-headed God, the Sun in his strength.
[7] The Egyptian Atlas—à rebours.

Nature is one with my distress.
  The flowers are dull, the stars are pale.
I am the Soul of Nothingness.
  I cannot lift the golden veil.
O Mother Isis,[1] let thine eyes
Behold my grief, and sympathise !

I cannot round the perfect wheel,
  Attain not to the fuller end.
In part I love, in part I feel,
  Know, worship, will, and comprehend.
O Mother Nephthys,[2] fill me up
Thine own perfection's deadly cup !

My aspiration quails within me ;
  " My heart is fixed," in vain I cry ;
The little loves and whispers win me :—
  " Eli, lama sabacthani ! "

    [1] Nature : the beginning.
    [2] Perfection : the end.

O Chomse,[1] moon-god, grant thy boon,
The silver pathway of the moon !

Beyond the Glory of the Dawn,
  Beyond the Splendour of the Sun,
Thy secret Spirit is withdrawn,
  The plumes of the Concealed One.
Amoun ![2] upon the Cross I cry,
  " I am Osiris, even I ! "

O Thou ! the All, the many-named,
  The One in many manifest :
Let not my spirit be ashamed,
  But win to its eternal rest !
Thou Self from Nothing ! bring Thou me
  Unto that Self which is in Thee !

### AMEN.

  [1] See previous explanations of moon-symbolism.
  [2] The Supreme and Concealed One. Osiris, justified by trial, purified through suffering, can at the moment of his crucifixion—which is also his equilibration—attain to him.

## THE EPILOGUE IS SILENCE

# CARMEN SAECULARE *

1900

## PROLOGUE.

### THE EXILE.

" The Sun, surmounted by a red rose, shining on a mossy bank." [1]

OVER the western water lies a solar fire,
Rapt lives and drunken ecstasies of sad
  desire ;
Poppies and lonely flag-flowers haunt the
  desolate
Marsh-strand : the herons gaunt still contemplate
What was delight, is ruin, may breed love
  again,
Even as darkness breeds the day : when life
  is slain.

.    .    .    .    .

O who will hear my chant, my cry ; my
  voice who hear,
Even in this weary misery, this danker mere,
Me, in mine exile, who am driven from
  yonder mountains
Blue-gray, and highland airs of heaven, and
  moving fountains?
Me, who shall hear me? Am I lost, a
  broken vessel,
Caught in the storm of lies and tossed,
  forbid to wrestle?
Shall not the sun rise lively yet, the rose
  yet bloom,
The crown yet lift me, life beget flowers on
  the tomb?
I was born fighter. Think you then my task
  is done,
My work, my Father's work for men, the
  rising sun ?

[1] This is the heraldic description of Crowley's crest.

Who calls me coward? Let them wait
  awhile ! Shall I
Bow down a loyal head to fate : despair and
  die?
I hear the sea roll strong and pure that bore
  me far
From Méalfourvónie's [1] scalp, gray moor and
  lonely scaur ;
I hear the waves together mutter in counsel
  deep ;
I hear the thunder the winds utter in broken
  sleep ;
I hear the voices of four rivers crying
  aloud ;
Four angels trumpet, and earth shivers : the
  heavens shroud
Their faces in blank terror for the sound of
  them :
The mountains are disturbed and roar : the
  azure hem
That laps all lands is broken, lashed in fiery
  foam,
And all God's thunderbolts are crashed—
  against my home.
Written in heaven, written on earth, written
  in the deep,
Written by God's own finger-birth ; the stars
  may weep,
The sun rejoice, that see at last His vengeance strike ;
The fury of destruction's blast ; the fiery
  spike
As of an arrow of adamant, comet or
  meteor :
" The dog returneth to his vomit : the ancient
  whore [2]

[1] A mountain on Loch Ness, opposite the poet's home.
[2] England.

* Crowley, an Irishman, was passionately attached to the Celtic movement, and only abandoned it when he found that it was a mere mask for the hideous features of Roman Catholicism.

That sitteth upon many waters, even she
That called together all her daughters upon
    the sea ;
That clad herself in crimson silk and robes
    of black
And gave men blood instead of milk ; and
    made a track
Of lives and gold and dust and death on
    land and sea,
She is fallen, is fallen ! Her breath I take
    to me.
That which I gave I take, and that she
    thought to build,
I, even I, will break it flat : my curse ful-
    filled.
No stone of London soon shall stand upon
    another,
No son of her throughout the land shall
    know his brother.
I will destroy her who is rotten : from the
    face
Of earth shall fail the misbegotten, root and
    race ;
And the fair country unto them again I give,
Whom in long exile men contemn : for they
    shall live."
Yea, they shall live ! The Celtic race !
    Amen ! And I
Give praise, and close mine eyes, cover my
    face, and laugh—and die.


"CARMEN SAECULARE."

" I prophesy, with feet upon a grave,
    Of death cast out, and life devouring death.
    .    .    .    .    .
Of freedom, though all manhood were one
    slave ;
    Of truth, though all the world were liar ;
    of love,
    That time nor hate can raze the witness of."
            SWINBURNE, *Tiresias.*

NINE voices that raise high the eternal hymn !
    Nine faces that ring round the rainbow sky.!
Hear me ! The century's lamp is growing
    dim ;
    Saturnian gloom descends and it must die.
Fill, fill my spirit to the utter brim
    With fire and melody !

O nine sweet sisters ! I have heard your song
    In blue soft waters and in stern grey seas ;
I listen for your voices in the throng ;
    I languish for your deadly melodies !
Yet, when I hear the sound for which I
    long,
    My soul is not at ease.

There rings an iron music in my ears ;
    A Martial cadence, chorus of the Hours :
The years of plenty, the abundant years
    Flee, as the halcyon from the dying flowers.
The chariot of Miseries and Fears
    Marshals its sombre powers.

Take up thy pen and write ! I must obey.
    No shrinking at that terrible command !
Their voices mingle in the feeble lay,
    Their fire impulses the reluctant hand.
My words must prophesy the avenging day
    And curse my native land.

How have I loved thee in thy faithlessness
    Beneath the rule of those unspeakable ! [1]
How would I shield thee from this sorceress
    That holds my words imprisoned in her
    spell !
I would be silent. And the words obsess
    My spirit. It is well.

O England ! England, mighty England,
    falls !
    None shall lament her lamentable end !
The Voice of Justice thunders at her walls.
    She would not hear. She shall not com-
    prehend !
The nations keep their mocking carnivals :
    She hath not left a friend !

The harlot that men called great Babylon,
    In crimson raiment and in smooth attire,
The scarlet leprosy that shamed the sun,
    The gilded goat that plied the world for
    hire ;—
Her days of wealth and majesty are done :
    Men trample her for mire !

[1] The House of Hanover.

The temple of their God is broken down ;
  Yea, Mammon's shrine is cleansed ! The
    house of her
That cowed the world with her malignant
  frown,
  And drove the Celt to exile and despair,
Is battered now—God's fire destroys the
  town ;
  London admits God's air.

They scorned the God that made them ; yea,
  they said :
  "Lords of this globe, the Saxon race,
  are we.
" Europe before us lies, as men lie d  .;
  "Britannia—ho ! Britannia rules the sea !"
This night thy kingdom shall be finishèd,
  Thy soul required of thee.

Hail ! France ! Because thy freedom hath
  rebelled
  Against the alien, and the golden yoke ;[1]
Because thy justice lives and reigns, un-
  quelled,
  Unbribed ;[2] because thy head above the
  smoke
Soars, eagle ! Tribulation hath not felled
  Thy freedom's ancient oak !

Therefore, this message of the Gods to
  thee !
  What banner floats above thy bastions ?
The oriflamme, the golden fleur-de-lys ?
  The eagle, or the tricolour ? Thy sons
Choose their own flag, contented to be
  free,
  With freemen's orisons.

The mist is gathering on the seer's sight—
  I cannot see the future of thy state.
Or, am I dazzled by resounding light ?
  I know this thing—thy future shall be
  great !
Come war, come revolution ! In their spite
  Thou mayst compel thy Fate.

      [1] The Jews.
      [2] The verdict of Rennes.

O German Empire ! Let thy sons beware,
  Not crowding sordid towns for lust of
  gold,
Not all forgetful of the herdsman's care,
  Not arming all men in an iron mould.
Peaceful be thou : with watching and with
  prayer.
  But be not overbold.

Fall, Austria ! In the very day and hour
  That reverend head that holds thee in its
  awe
Shall sink in peace, I see thy rotten power
  Break as the crumbling ice-floe in the
  thaw.
Destruction shatters thy blood-builded tower.
  Death has thee in his maw.

Stand, Russia ! Let thy freedom grow in
  peace,
  Beneath the constant rule, the changing
  Czar.
Thy many, thine inhospitable seas
  Shall ring thee round, a zodiac to thy
  star,
And Frost, the rampart of thine iron ease,
  Laugh at the shock of war.

Turn, Italy ! The Voice is unto Thee !
  Return, poor wounded maiden, to thy
  home !
Thou hast well tried a spurious liberty :
  Thou art made captive ; let thy fancy
  roam
To the great Mother, deeper than the sea,
  And fairer than the foam.

O Gateway of the admirable East !
  Hold fast thy Faith ! Let no man take
  thy Crown !
The Birds of Evil, that were keen to
  feast,
  (Fools cried) but herald thy renewed re-
  nown.
Mad Christians see in thee the Second
  Beast,
  But shall not shake thee down.

Therefore reign thou, saith God, august,
   alone,
  White - winged to East and West, an
    albatross,
"Abdul the Damned, on thy infernal
    throne ! " [1]
Allah can wed the Crescent and the Cross !
According to the wisdom thou hast shown
  Mete thou thy gain and loss !

O melancholy ruin, that wert Greece !
  What little comfort canst thou take from
    time ?
Years pass, in shameful war or sordid peace—
  What god can recreate thee, the sublime ?
Alas ! let Lethe roll her sleepy seas
  Over thy ruined clime.

O piteous fallen tyranny of Spain !
  What dogs are tearing at thy bowels yet ?
Let thine own King,[2] saith God, resume his
    reign !
Loyal and happy seasons may forget
The ancient scars.   Thy moon is on the
    wane ?
Thy sun may never set !

And thou, foul oligarchy of the West,
  Thou, soiled with bribes and stained with
    treason's stain,
Thou, heart of coin beneath a brazen breast,
  Rotten republic, prostitute of gain !
Thou, murderer of the bravest and the best
  That fringed thy southern main ! [3]

The doom is spoken.   Thine own children
    tear
  Thy cruel heart and thy corrupted tongue ;
Thy toilers snare thee in thine own foul
    snare,
  And sting thee where thy gilded worms
    had stung.
The politician and the millionaire
  Regain maternal dung.

[1] A notorious phrase, from the hysterical
sonnets of a poetaster of the period.
[2] Don Carlos.
[3] In the Civil War, 1861–1864.

Then only shall thy liberty arise ;
  Then only shall thine eagle shake his
    wings,
And sunward soar through the unsullied
    skies,
  And careless watch the destiny of kings.
Then only shall truth's angel in thine eyes
  Perceive eternal things.

The oracle is suddenly grown still.
  Only, mine eyes, unweary of the sight,
Pierce through the dawn-mist of the sacred
    hill
  And yearn toward the rose of love and
    light.
My lips, that drank the Heliconian rill,
  Murmur with slow delight.

I see the faces of the lyric Nine !
  The Rose of God its petals will unfold !
I madden with the ecstasy divine !
  My soul leaps sunwards, shrieking—and
    behold !
Out of the ocean and the kindling brine
  Apollo's face of gold !

What music, what delirium, what delight !
  What dancing madness catches at my
    feet !
A tongue of fresh, impossible, keen light
  Burns on my brow—a silver stream of
    heat.
I am constrained : The Awful Word I write
  From the one Paraclete.

The Reign of Darkness hath an end.
    Behold !
  Eight stars are gathered in one fiery
    sign.[1]
This is the birth-hour of the Age of Gold ;
  The false gold pales before the Gold
    divine.
The Christ is calling to the starry fold
  Of Souls—Arise and shine !

[1] Eight planets were together in the "fiery"
sign, Sagittarius, towards the close of the year
1899.

The Isis of the World hath raised her veil
  One moment, that fresh glory of the stars
May glow through winter, where the sun
    is pale;
  Melt snow-bound lilies; bid the prison
    bars,
Wherein men bow their heads and women
    wail,
  Blossom to nenuphars.

The sacred lotus of the universe
  Blossoms this century—a million tears
Melted the ice of Eve's accursèd curse:
  A million more have watered it—it peers,
A resurrection fragrance, to disperse
  Men's folly and their fears.

The contemplation of those awful eyes,
  The flaming void, the godhead of the light,
The abyss of these unfathomable skies,
  Exhaust my being; I desire the night.
Lo! I have written all the destinies
  Thy spirit bade me write.

The noise of rushing water! And the sound
  Of tenfold thunder! Mighty a flame of fire
Roars downward: as a maiden from a swound
  My spirit answers to its own desire.
My feet are firm again upon the ground—
  Yea! but my head is higher.

My face is shining with the fire of heaven.
  I move among my fellows as a ghost.
With thought for bread and memory for
    leaven
  My life is nourished, yet my life is lost.
I live and move among the starry seven,
  Nor count the deadly cost.

Only I see the century as a child
  Call Truth and Justice, Light and Peace,
    to guide;
Wisdom and Joy, and Love the undefiled,
  Lead up true worship, its eternal bride.
Stormy its birth; its youth, how fierce and
    wild!
  Its end, how glorified!

O Spirit of Illimitable Light!
  O Thou with style and tablet![1] Answer me
In that dread pomp of Triumph and of Right,
  The awful day: my witnesses are Ye
That I have said in all men's sound and sight
  The things that are to be.


## IN THE HOUR BEFORE REVOLT.

". . . the green paradise which western waves
  Embosom in their ever-wailing sweep,
Talking of freedom to their tongueless caves,
  Or to the spirits which within them keep
A record of the wrongs which, though they
    sleep,
  Die not, but dream of retribution."
                *Adonais* [*cancelled passage*].

WILD pennons of sunrise the splendid,
  And scarlet of clustering flowers
Cry aloud that the Winter is ended,
  Claim place for the re-risen hours.
The Ram in the Heavens exalted[2]
  Calls War to uncover her wing;
Through skies that be hollow and vaulted
  Exulting the shouts of him ring:
    The Sign of the Spring.

How hollows the heart of the heaven!
  How light swells his voice for a cry!
The winter is shaken and riven,
  And death and the fruits of him die.
The billow roars back to its tyrant,
  The wind; the red thunderbolts roar;
The flame and the earthquake aspirant
  Leap forth as an herald before
    The trumpet of war.

In crimson he robes him for raiment,
  In armour all rusted and red:
Spear shakes and sword flashes, exclaimant
  To share in the spoil of the dead.

[1] Thoth, the Scribe of the Gods.
[2] Aries, the sign which the Sun enters at the Vernal Equinox, is "ruled" by Mars, the planet of War.

A helmet flames forth on his forehead,
  Gold sparks from the forge of the stars,
His shield with the Gorgon made horrid
  Hath blood on its bull-battled bars—
    Thou God of me, Mars !

He strides through the vibrating aether ;
  Spurns earth from His warrior feet ;
Shakes fire from the forges beneath her ;
  His glances are fervid and fleet.
With a cry that makes tremble the thunder,
  Light-speared, with a sword that is flame,
He bursts the vast spaces asunder.
  His angels arise and proclaim :
    The Lord is His Name !

O Lord ! Thou didst march out of Edom !
  Thou leapedst from the Mountains of Seir !
The breath of Thy voice was as Freedom !
  The nations did tremble with fear.
The heathen, their fury forsook them ;
  The Moabites trembled and fled.
O Lord, when Thy countenance shook them,
  Thy voice in the House of the Dead.
    O Lord ! Thou hast said !

The lightnings were kindled and lightened,
  Thy thunder was heard on the deep ;
The stars with Thy Fear shook and whitened,
  The sun and the moon in the steep.
The sea rose in tumult and clamour,
  The earth also shook with Thee then,
As Thor had uplifted his hammer,
  And smitten the mutinous men.
    O ! rise Thou again !

The voice of the Lord is uplifted ;
  The wilderness also obeys ;
The flames of the fire they are rifted ;
  The waves of the sea know His ways.
The cedars of Lebanon hear Thee,
  The desert of Kadesh hath known ;
The Sons of Men know Thee and fear Thee,
  Flee far from the Light of Thy Throne.
    For Thou art alone.

O Lord ! Is Thy path in the Water,
  The marvellous ways of the Deep ?
Not there, O not there ! Wilt Thou slaughter
  Oblivion's sons in their sleep ?
Hath the deep disobeyed Thee or risen
  In wrath and revolt to Thy sky,
Broken loose from the bands of her prison ?
  Held counsel against the Most High ?
    Yea, even as I !

But I, O Most Mighty, invoke Thee,
  Whose footsteps are in the Unknown.
My cries were the cries that awoke Thee,
  Upstarting in arms from Thy Throne !
I call Thee, I pray Thee, I chide Thee,
  Whose glory my foes have abhorred.
My spirit is fixed, may abide Thee,
  Awake the Invisible Sword.
    For Thou art the Lord !

Look down upon earth and behold us
  Few folk who have sworn to be free.
Past days, when the traitors had sold us,
  We trample ; we call upon Thee !
Look Thou on the armed ones, the furious,
  The Saxons ! they brandish the steel ;
Heaven rings with their insults injurious ;
  Earth moans for their harrow and wheel.
    To Thee we appeal.

They boast, though their triumph Hell's
    gift is,
  On Africa's desperate sons :
"Our thousands have conquered their fifties ;
  Our twenties have murdered their ones."
That glory—that shame—let them trumpet
  To Europe's unquickening ear.
List Thou to the boast of the strumpet !
  Lend Thou, Thou indignant, an ear !
    Then—shall they not fear ?

O Lord, to Thy strength in the thunder,
  Thy chariot-wheels in the war,
We, Ireland, look upward and wonder,
  The Sword of Thee smiting before.

In the hour of Revolt that burns nigher
  Each hour as it leaps to the sky,
We look to Thee, Lord, for Thy Fire ;
  We look—shall Thy Justice deny?
    Well, can we not die?

But Thou, Thou shalt fall from the heaven
  As hail on the furious host.
I see them : their legions are driven ;
  Their cohorts are broken and lost.
Thy fire hath dispersed them and shattered !
  They hesitate, waver, and flee !
The tyrant is shaken and scattered,
    And Ireland is clear to the Sea !
      Green Erin is free !

Hail ! Hail to Thee, Lord of us, Horus ![1]
  All hail to the warrior name !
Thy chariots shall drive them before us,
  Thy sword sweep them forth as a flame.
Rise ! Move ! and descend ! I behold Thee,
  Heaven cloven of fieriest bars,
Armed Light ; and they follow and fold Thee,
  Thine armies of terrible stars.
    The Powers of Mars !

At the brightness that leapeth before Thee,
  The heavens bow down at Thine ire ;
Thick clouds pass to death and adore Thee,
  Wild hailstones and flashings of fire.
The mountains of Ages are shattered ;
  Perpetual hills are bowed down ;
The Winds of the Heaven are scattered,
  Borne back from Thy furious frown,
    O Lord of Renown !

In terror and tumult and battle
  Thy breath smiteth forth as a sword ;
The Saxons are driven as cattle ;
  We know Thee, that Thou art the Lord !
Forth Freedom flings skyward, a maiden
  Rejoicing, upsprung from the sea,
And the wild lyre of Erin is laden
  At last with the songs of the free !
    Hail ! Hail unto Thee !

[1] Egyptian God of the Sun, and of War. Cf.
p. 212, note 5.

## EPILOGUE.

TO  THE  AMERICAN  PEOPLE  ON  THE
ANNIVERSARY OF THEIR INDEPENDENCE.

THE ship to the breezes is bended ;
  The wind whistles off to the lee ;
The sun is arisen, the splendid !
  The sun on the marvellous sea !
And the feast of your freedom is ended,
    O sons of the free !

Your shouts have gone up to remember
  The day of your oath to the world.
Is its flame dwindled down to an ember?
  The flag of your liberty furled?
Your limbs are too strong to dismember—
    In sloth are they curled?

The price of your freedom—I claim it !
  Your aid to make other men free !
Your strength—I defy you to shame it !
  Your peace—I defy it to be
Dishonoured !  Arise and proclaim it
    From sea unto sea !

From Ireland the voice of the dying,
  The murdered, the starved, the exiled,
In hope to your freedom is crying
  A dolorous note and a wild :
" Your star-bestrewn banner is flying,
    And ours—is defiled."

From Ind—shall her summons awaken ?
  Her voices are those of the dead !
By famine and cholera shaken,
  By taxes and usury bled,
In the hour of her torture forsaken,
    Stones given for bread !

In Africa women are fighting
  Their homes and their freedom to hold
Young children and graybeards, delighting
  To die for their country of old !
For the ravenous lion is smiting
    A stroke for their gold.

They fall in the shelterless hollow ;
  They sleep in the cold and the sun ;
They fight, and the Englishmen follow—
  The odds are as twenty to one !
Hide, hide thy bright eyes, O Apollo !
    The murder is done.[1]

The stones should arise to declare it,
  Their terror and tyrannous reign !
The earth be unable to bear it,
  Gape wide, for her motherly pain !
Shalt thou, O Columbia, share it,
    The shame and the stain ?

Your stripes are the stripes of dishonour ;
  Your stars are cast down from the sky ;

[1] Kruger, however, fulfilled his threat to
drive the English into the sea. Only Jews and
Chinamen have survived the struggle ; as the
fox in the contest between the lion and the
bear, recorded by Aesop.—A. C.
  Time will show whether Crowley's cynicism
is justified.

While earth has this burden upon her,
  Your eagle unwilling to fly !
Loose, loose the wide wings ! For your
    honour !
    Let tyranny die !

Remember, this day of your glory,
  Your fight for the freedom you own.
Those years—is their memory hoary ?
  Your chains—is their memory flown ?
Your triumph is famous in story,
    But yours is alone.

In the name of your Freedom I claim it,
  Your power in the cause of the free !
In the name of our God as I name it,
  AMEN ! I demand it of ye,
Man's freedom ! Arise and proclaim it,
    The song of the sea !

S.S. PENNSYLVANIA,
  *July 4, 1900.*

# TANNHÄUSER

## A STORY OF ALL TIME

### TANNHÄUSER.

#### XVI

One is incisive, corrosive ;
  Two retorts, nettled, curt, crepitant ;
Three makes rejoinder, expansive, explosive ;
  Four overbears them all, strident and
    strepitant :
Five [1] . . . O Danaides, O Sieve !

#### XVII

Now, they ply axes and crowbars ;
  Now, they prick pins at a tissue
Fine as a skein of the casuist Escobar's
  Worked on the bone of a lie.  To what
    issue ?
Where is our gain at the Two-bars ?

#### XVIII

*Est fuga, volvitur rota.*
  On we drift : where looms the dim port ?
One, Two, Three, Four, Five, contribute
    their quota ;
  Something is gained, if one caught but
    the import—
Show it us, Hugues of Saxe-Gotha !

—R. BROWNING, *Master Hugues of
  Saxe-Gotha.*

### DEDICATION.

I SHALL not tell thee that I love thee !
  Nay ! by the Star in Heaven burning,
  Its ray to me at midnight turning
To tell me that it beams above thee—
  Nay ! though thou wert, as I am, yearning,
I should not tell thee that I love thee !

[1] The reference is to the five acts of the play.

I know what secret thought once blossomed
  Into a blush that seemed a kiss,
  Some swift suppressed extreme of bliss
In thy most fearful sigh embosomed.
  What oracle should prate of this ?
I know the secret thought that blossomed !

Extol the truth of love's disdain !
  Love, daring by no glance to gladden
  A heart that waits but that to madden
In purple pleasure plucked of pain.
  Nay ! let our tears, that fail to sadden,
Extol the truth of love's disdain !

.     .     .     .     .

Let deeper silence shield the deeper rapture !
  Hardly our eyes reveal the inward bliss,
  Sealed by no speech and shadowed by no
    kiss.
Love is no wizard to elude recapture
  In the strong prison of his silences !
Let deeper silence shield the deeper rapture !

Twin souls are we, to one Star bound in
    Heaven !
  Twin souls on earth by earthly bars
    divided !
  But, did thy spirit glide as mine has glided
Straight to That Star—no rose-leaves ask to
    leaven
  The manna that the Moon of Love pro-
    vided !
Twin souls are we, to one Star bound in
    Heaven !

Not to thy presence in the veil and vision
  Of solemn lies that men miscall the world ;
  Not to thy mind the lightnings truthward
    hurled
I turn.  I laugh dead distance to derision !—
  Spirit to spirit : there our loves are curled,
Not to thy presence in the veil and vision !

222

Beyond the gold and glamour of Life's lotus,
The flower that falls from this our stronger
sight,
We dwell, eternal shapes of shadowy light.
Only the love on earth that shook and smote
us
Begets new stars—truth's flowers fallen
through night
Beyond the gold and glamour of Life's lotus !

Eternal bliss of Love in birthless bowers !
Light, the gemmed robes of Love ! Life,
lifted breath,
Ageless existence deifying death !
Love, the sole flower beyond these lesser
flowers !—
In thee at last the live fruit quickeneth ?
Eternal bliss of Love in birthless bowers !

.    .    .    .    .

There, secret ! Know it ! Now forget !
Betray not Wisdom unto Folly !
Less sweet is Joy than Melancholy !—
Why should our eyes for this be wet?
Enough : be silent and be holy !
There, secret ! Know it ! Now forget !

Now I have told thee that I love thee !
To me our Star in Heaven burning
Tells me thy heart as mine is yearning ;
Tells me Love's fragrance stolen above thee
Thy soul to mine at last is turning
Now I have told thee that I love thee !

## PREFACE.

As, after long observation and careful study,
the biologist sees that what at first seemed
isolated and arbitrary acts are really part of
a series of regular changes, and presently
has the life-history of the being that he is
examining clear from Alpha to Omega in
his mind ; as, during a battle, the relative
importance of its various incidents is lost,
the more so owing to the excitement and
activity of the combatant, and to the fact
that he is himself involved in the vicissitudes
which he may have set himself to observe ;
while even for the commander, though the
smoke-pall may lift now and again to show
some brilliant charge or desperate hand-to-
hand struggle, he may fail to grasp its
significance in his dispositions ; or indeed
find it to be quite unexpected and foreign
to his calculations ; yet a few years or months

later the same battle may be lucidly, tersely,
and connectedly described, so that a child
is able to follow its varying fortunes with
delight and comprehension : just so has my
own observation of a life-history more subtle,
a battle more terrible, been at last co-ordinated : I can view the long struggle from a
standpoint altogether complete, calm, and
philosophical ; and the result of this review
is the present story of Tannhäuser, just as
the isolated and often apparently contra-
dictory incidents of the fight were recorded
in that jungle of chaotic emotions which I
printed under the title of "The Soul of
Osiris,"[1] calling it a history so that my
readers might discover for themselves (if
they chose to take the trouble) the real
continuity in the apparent disjointedness.

The history of any man who seriously and
desperately dares to force a passage into the
penetralia[2] of nature ; not with the calm
philosophy of the scientist, but with the
burning conviction that his immortal destiny
is at stake ; must be a strange one : to me
at least strangely attractive. The constant
illusions ; the many disappointments ; the
bitter earnestness of the man amid the grim
humour, or more often sheer cacchination
of his surroundings ; all the bestial mockery
of the baffling fiends ; the still more hideous
mockery in which the Powers of Good themselves seem to indulge ; doubt of the reality
of that which he seeks ; doubt even of the
seeker ; the irony of the whole strife : are
fascinating to me as they are, I make no
doubt, to the majority of mankind.

This is the subtler form of that mental
bewilderment which the Greek Tragedians
were so fond of depicting ; as subtle in effect,
yet grosser in its determining factors. For
we are thus changed from the times of
Sophocles and Euripides ; that the fixed
ideas of morality and religion which they
employed as the motives of pathos or of
horror are now shattered. Ibsen, otherwise
in spirit and style purely Greek, and dealing
as the Greeks did with the emotions of the
soul, has realised the changed and infinitely
more complex conditions of life ; our self-
appointed spiritual guides notwithstanding,
or, rather, withstanding in vain. Consequently it is impossible any more to divine
whether virtue or vice (as understood of old)

[1] Now " The Temple of the Holy Ghost."
[2] Hidden places.

will cause the irreparable catastrophe which is the one element of drama which we may still (in the work of a modern dramatist) await with any degree of confidence.

I trust that I may be forgiven for adopting the idea that Tannhäuser was one of those mysterious Germans whose reputed existence so perturbed the Middle Ages; in short, a Rosicrucian.[1] Some people may be surprised that a Member of that illustrious but unhappy fraternity should take cognizance of what my friend Bhikku Ananda Maitriya calls "hog-nosed Egyptian deities," still more that he should show reverence to symbols like the B. V. M. and the Holy Grail. But the most learned and profound students of the Mysteries of the Rosy Cross assure me that it was the special excellence of these mystics that they declined to be bound down by any particular system in their sublime search for the Eternal and the Real.

Under these circumstances I have not scrupled to subvert anything that appeared to me to need subverting in the interests, always identical, of beauty and of truth. Anachronism may be found piled upon anachronism, and symbolism mixed with symbolism.

In one direction I have restrained myself. Nowhere does Tannhäuser refer to the Vedas and Shastras[2] or to the Dhamma[3] of that blameless hypochondriac, Gotama Buddha. I take all the blame for so important an omission, not without a shrewd suspicion that the commination will take the form of "For this relief much thanks!"

The particular object that I have in view in speaking both in Hebrew and Egypto-Christian symbolism is that by this means I may familiarise my readers with the one thing of any importance that life, travel, and study have taught me, to wit: the Origin of Religions.

I take it that there have always, or nearly always, been on the earth those whom Councillor von Eckartshäusen,[4] the Svámi Vivekananda[5] and their like, call

"great spiritual giants" (can there be any etymological link between "yogi"[1] and "ogre"?) and that such persons, themselves perceiving Truth, have tried to "diminish the message to the dog"[2] for the benefit of less exalted minds, and hidden that Truth (which, unveiled, would but blind men with its glory) in a mass of symbols often perverted or grotesque, yet to the proper man transparent; a "bait of falsehood to catch the carp of truth." Now, regarded in this light, all religions, quâ religions, are equally contemptible. The Hindu Gnanis[3] say "That which can be thought is not true." As machineries for the exercise of spiritual and intellectual powers innate or developed, certain sets of symbols may be more or less convenient to a special trend of mind, reason, or imagination; no more: I deny to any one religion the possession of any essential truth which is not also formulated (though in a different language) in every other. To this rule Buddhism appears a solitary exception. Whether it is truly so I have hardly yet decided: the answer depends upon certain recondite mathematical considerations, to discuss which would be foreign to the scope of my present purpose, but which I hope to advance in a subsequent volume.[4]

If you do not accept my conclusion that all religions are the expression of truth under different aspects, facets of the same intolerable gem, you are forced back on the conclusions of those unpleasing persons the Phallicists. But should you travel to the East, and tell a Lingam-worshipping Sivite that his is a phallic worship he will not be pleased with you. Compare on this point Arnold, "India Revisited," 1886, p. 112.

So much for the symbolology of this, I fear, much-mangled drama. Drama indeed is an altogether misleading term; monodrama is perhaps better. It is really a series of introspective studies; not necessarily a series in time, but in psychology, and that rather the morbid psychology of the Adept than the gross mentality of the ordinary man.

It may help some of my readers if I say that my Tannhäuser is nearly identical in

---

[1] See their original documents, fairly enough translated in "Real History of the Rosicrucians," by A. E. Waite.
[2] Hindu sacred books.
[3] The law.
[4] Author of the "Cloud upon the Sanctuary," a profound mystical treatise.
[5] A well-known Indian mystic, author of "Raja Yoga."

[1] "Yogi" is "one who seeks union," i.e. with the Supreme.
[2] Browning, "Mr. Sludge the Medium."
[3] Philosophers.
[4] Berashith, q.v. infra, vol. ii.

scheme with the "Pilgrim's Progress." Literary and spiritual experts will however readily detect minor differences in the treatment. It will be sufficient if I state that "the Unknown," whether minstrel, pilgrim, or Egyptian sage, represents Tannhäuser in his true Self,—the "Only Being in an Abyss of Light!" The Tannhäuser who talks is the "Only Being in an Abyss of Darkness," the natural man ignorant of his identity with the Supreme Being. The various other characters are all little parts of Tannhäuser's own consciousness and not real persons at all: whether good or bad, all alike hinder and help (and there is not one whose function is not thus double) the realisation of his true unity with all life. This circumstance serves to explain, though perhaps not to excuse, the lack of dramatic action in the story. Love being throughout the symbol of his method, as Beauty of its object, it is through Love, refined into Pity, that he at last attains the Supreme Knowledge, or at least sufficient of it to put the last straw on the back of his corporeal camel, and bring the story to a fitting end.

To pass to more mundane affairs. I may mention for the benefit of those who may not be read in certain classes of literature, and so think me original when I am hardly even paraphrasing, that Tannhäuser's songs in Act IV. are partly adapted from the so-called "Oracles of Zoroaster," partly from the mysterious utterances of the great angel Avé,[1] perhaps equally spurious. Of course Bertram's song is merely a rather free adaptation of the two principal fragments of Sappho, which so many people have failed to translate that one can feel no shame in making yet another attempt. There may be one or two conscious plagiarisms besides, for which I do not apologise. For any unconscious ones which may have crept in owing to my prolonged absence from civilised parts, and the consequent lack of opportunity for reference and comparison, I emphatically do.

One word to the reviewers. It must not be taken as ungracious if I so speak. From nearly all I have received the utmost justice, kindness, and consideration: two or three only seem to take delight in deliberately perverting the sense of my remarks: and to them, for their own sake, I now address

these words of elementary instruction. You are perfectly welcome to do with my work in its entirety what Laertes did with his allegiance and his vows: but do not pick out and gloat over a few isolated passages from the Venusberg scenes and call me a sensualist, nor from the Fourth Act and groan "Mysticism!"; do not quote "Two is by shape the Coptic Aspirate" as a sample of my utmost in lyrics; do not take the song of Wolfram as my best work in either sentiment or melody. As a *quid pro quo* I give you all full permission to conclude your review of this book by quoting from Act III. "Forget this nightmare!"

I must express my great sense of gratitude to Oscar Eckenstein,[1] Gerald Kelly, and Allan MacGregor, who have severally helped me in the work of revision, which has extended over more than a year of time and nearly twenty thousand miles of space. Some few of the very best lines were partially or wholly suggested by themselves, and I have not scrupled to incorporate these: if the book be but a Book, the actual authorship seems to me immaterial.

I have written this preface in lighter vein, but I hope that no one will be led to suppose that my purpose is anything but deadly serious. This poem has been written in the blood of slain faith and hope; each foolish utterance of Tannhäuser stings me with shame and memory of old agony; each Ignis Fatuus that he so readily pursues, reminds me of my own delusions. But, these follies and delusions being the common property of mankind, I have thought them of sufficient interest, dramatic and philosophical, to form the basis of a poem. Let no man dare to reproach me with posing as the hero of my tale. I fall back on the last utterance of Tannhäuser himself: "I say, then, 'I': and yet it is not 'I' Distinct, but 'I' incorporate in All." Above all, pray understand that I do not pose as a teacher. I am but an asker of questions, such as may be found confronting those who have indeed freed their minds from the conventional commonplaces of the platitudinous, but have not yet dared to uproot the mass of their convictions, and to examine the whole question of religion from its most fundamental source in the consciousness of mankind. Such persons may find the reason-

---

[1] In "Dr. Dee."

[1] The famous mountaineer.

ing of Tannhäuser useful, if only to brace them to a more courageous attempt to understand the "Great Arcanum," and to attain at last, no matter at what cost, to "true Wisdom and perfect Happiness." So may all happen !

KANDY, CEYLON, *Sept.* 1901.

### PERSONS CONCERNED.

*THE WORLD OF GODS.*

ISIS.
HATHOÖR.

*THE WORLD OF MEN.*

TANNHÄUSER.
ELIZABETH.
AN UNKNOWN MINSTREL.
THE LANDGRAVE.
WOLFRAM,
BERTRAM, } *At the Court of the Landgrave.*
HEINRICH,
A SHEPHERD BOY.
PILGRIMS, FORESTERS, COURTIERS, ETC.

*THE WORLD OF DEMONS.*

THE EVIL AND AVERSE HATHOÖR, CALLED VENUS.

## TANNHÄUSER.

### ACT I.

"Therefore we are carefully to proceed in Magic, lest that Syrens and other monsters deceive us, which likewise do desire the society of the human soul."
*Arbatel of Magic. Aphorism* 35.

*A lonely and desolate plain.* TANNHÄUSER *riding towards a great mountain.*

#### TANNHÄUSER.

SIX days. Creation took no longer ! Yet
I wander eastward, and no light is found.
The stars their motion shirk, or else forget.
The sun—the moon ? Imprisoned under-
 ground
Where gnomes disport, and devils do
 abound.

Six days. I journey to the black unknown,
 Always in hope the Infinite may rise
Some unexpected instant, as 'twere grown
 A magic palace to enchanted eyes ;
 A wizard guerdon for a minstrel wise.

Perhaps I am a fool to think that here,
 Merely by rending Nature's hollow veil,
I may attain the Solitary Sphere,
 Achieve the Path ; or, haply, if I fail,
 Gain the Elixir, or behold the Grail.[1]

I seek the mystery of Life and Time,
 The Key of all that is not and that is,
And that which — climb, imagination !
 climb !—
Transcends them both—the mystical abyss
Where Mind and Being marry, and are
 Bliss.[2]

So have I journeyed—like a fool ! Ah, well !
 Let pass self-scorn, as love of self is
 past !
But—am I further forward ? Who can tell ?
 God is the Complex as the Protoplast :
 He is the First (not "was"), and is the
 Last

(Not "will be"). Then why travel ? To
 what end ?
What is the symbol I am set to find ?
What is that burning heart of blood to
 spend
Caught in a sunset with the night behind,
The Grail of God ? I would that I were
 blind !

I would that I were desolate and dumb,
 Naked and poor ! That He might mani-
 fest
A crimson glory subtly caught and come,
 An opal crucible of Alkahest ![3]
 And yet—what gain of vital gold expressed ?

---

[1] A vessel containing the blood of Jesus. See Malory, "Morte d'Arthur."
[2] Sat-Chit-Ananda, the qualities of Atman, the Soul.
[3] See Eirenaeus Philalethes, his treatise.

This were my guerdon : to fade utterly
  Into the rose-heart of that sanguine vase,
And lose my purpose in its silent sea,
  And lose my life, and find my life, and
    pass
  Up to the sea that is as molten glass.

I mind me of that old Egyptian,
  Met where Aurora streamed her rainbow
    hair,
Who called me from the quest.   An holy
    man !
  A crown of light scintillant in the air
  Shone over him : he bade me not despair.

"The Blood of the Osiris !" was his word :
  (Meaning the Christ ?) "The life, the
    tears, the tomb !
"The Love of Isis is its name !"   (I heard
  This for the love of Mary.)   In her womb
  Brews the Elixir, and the roses bloom.

For the Three Maries (so he said) were One :
  Three aspects of the mystic spouse of God,
Isis !   This pagan !   "Look towards the
    Sun "[1]
  (Quoth he), "and seek a winepress to be
    trod ;
  "With Beauty girdled, garlanded, and
    shod.

"Thus," riddled he, "thy heart shall know
    its Peace !"
  Let be !   I ride upon the sand instead,
Look to the Cross, whereon I take mine ease !
  Let be !   Just so the Roman soldier said.
  Esaias ?[2]   He is dead—as I am dead !

What was his symbol and his riddle's key ?
  Go, seek the stars and count them and
    explore !
Go, sift the sands beyond a starless sea !
  So, find an answer where the dismal shore
  Of time beats back eternity !   No more !

1 _i.e._, Tiphereth, the Sphere of Beauty.
2 See Mark xv. 35, 36 for the obscure allusions.

Let me ride on more hastily than this,
  That so my body may be tired of me,
And fling me to the old forgetful kiss,
  Sleep's, when my mind goes, riderless and
    free,
  Into some corner of eternity.

Alas ! that mind returns from its abode
  With newer problems, fiercer thoughts !
    But stay !
Suppose it came not?   It must be with
    God !—
  Then this dull house of gold and iron and
    clay
  Is happy also—'tis an easy way !

So easy, I am fearful of mishap.
  Some fatal argument the God must find
That linked us first.   The dice are in His
    lap—
  Let Him decide in His imperial mind !
  My choice ; to see entirely—and be blind !

Yet I bethink me of that holy man,
  (Pagan albeit) my stirrup's wisdom-share :
"Learn this from Thothmes the Egyptian.
  "Use only in thine uttermost despair !"
  He whispered me a Word.[1]   "Beware !
    Beware !

"Two voices are there in the sullen sea ;
  "Two functions hath the inevitable fire ;
"Earthquake hath earth, and yet fertility :
  "See to thy purpose, and thy set desire !
  "Else, dire the fate—the ultimation dire !"

Vague threats and foolish words !   Quite
    meaningless
  The empty sounds he muttered in mine ear.
Why should their silly mystery impress
  My thoughtful forehead with the lines of
    fear ?
  (This riding saps my courage as my cheer.)

1 It is a tradition of magic that all words
have a double effect ; an upright, and an-averse.
See the shadow of a devil's head cast by the
fingers raised in blessing as figured in Eliphaz
Levi's "Dogme et Rituel de la Haute Magie"
and elsewhere.   Upon this tradition the whole
play hangs.

Still, I must see his symbol of the Sun,
  The Winepress, and the Beauty!  Puerile
And pagan to that old mysterious one,
  The awful Light and the anointed Vial,
  The Dawning of the Blood, even as a
    smile :—

Even as a smile on Beauty's burning cheek—
Ha!  In a circle?  As this journey is?
How vain is man's imagining and weak!
Begod [1] my lady, and my lady's kiss?
Back swing we to the pitiful abyss,

Liken God's being to the life of man.
  So reason staggers.   Angels, answer me!
Ye who have watched the far unfolding
    plan—
  How is time shorter than eternity?
  Prove it and weigh!   By mind it cannot be.

All our divisions spring in our own brain.
  See!   As upsprings on the horizon there
A clefted hill contemptuous of the plain.
  (Why, which is higher?)  I am in despair.
Let me essay the Pharaoh and his prayer!
  [TANNHÄUSER *speaks the Word of
  Double Power.*

Oh God, Thy blinding beauty, and the light
Shed from Thy shoulders, and the golden
    night
Of mingling fire and stars and roses swart
In the long flame of hair that leaps athwart,
Live in each tingling gossamer!   Dread
    eyes!
Each flings its arrow of sharp sacrifice,
Eating me up with poison!   I am hurled
Far through the vaporous confines of the
    world
With agony of sundering sense, beholding
Thy mighty flower, blood-coloured death,
    unfolding!
Lithe limbs and supple shoulders and lips
    curled,
Curled out to draw me to their monstrous
    world!

  [1] To invest with divine attributes.

Warm breasts that glow with light ephemeral
And move with passionate music to en-
    thral,
To charm, to enchant, to seal the entrancing
    breath.
I fall!   Stop!   Spare me!—Slay me!
  [TANNHÄUSER *enters into an ecstasy.*
                                This is death.
  [*The evil and averse* HATHOÖR, *or*
  VENUS, *who hath arisen in the place
  of the Great Goddess, lifteth up her
  voice and chanteth* :—

VENUS.

Isis am I, and from my life are fed
  All showers and suns, all moons that
    wax and wane,
All stars and streams, the living and the
    dead,
  The mystery of pleasure and of pain.
I am the mother!   I the speaking sea!
I am the earth and its fertility!
Life, death, love, hatred, light, darkness,
    return to me—
To me!

Hathoör am I, and to my beauty drawn
  All glories of the Universe bow down,
The blossom and the mountain and the
    dawn,
  Fruit's blush, and woman, our creation's
    crown.
I am the priest, the sacrifice, the shrine,
I am the love and life of the divine!
Life, death, love, hatred, light, darkness, are
    surely mine—
Are mine!

Venus am I, the love and light of earth,
  The wealth of kisses, the delight of tears,
The barren pleasure never come to birth,
  The endless, infinite desire of years.
I am the shrine at which thy long desire
Devoured thee with intolerable fire.
I was song, music, passion, death, upon thy
    lyre—
Thy lyre!

I am the Grail and I the Glory now :
  I am the flame and fuel of thy breast ;
I am the star of God upon thy brow ;
  I am thy queen, enraptured and possessed.
Hide thee, sweet river ; welcome to the
    sea,
Ocean of love that shall encompass thee !
Life, death, love, hatred, light, darkness,
    return to me—
To me !
    [TANNHÄUSER *perceives that he is in*
    *the palace of a Great Queen.*

Rise, rise, my knight ! My king ! My
    love, arise !
See the grave avenues of Paradise,
The dewy larches bending at my breath,
Portentous cedars prophesying death ! ʻ
See the long vistas and the dancing sea,
The measured motion of fecundity !
Bright winds set swaying the soft-sounding
    flowers
(Here flowers have music) in my woven
    bowers,
Where sweet birds blossom, and in chorus
    quire
The rapt beginnings of immense desire.
Here is the light and rapture of the will :
We touch the stars—and they are tiny
    still !
O mighty thews ! O godlike face and hair !
Rise up and take me ; ay, and keep me
    there,
One tingle at thy touch from head to
    feet ;
Lips that cling close, and never seem to
    meet,
Melting as sunlight melts in wine ! Arise !
Shame ! Has thy learning left thee over-
    wise ?
Thy lips sing fondly—to another tune.
Nay ! 'twas my breathing beauty made
    thee swoon,
Dread forkéd fire across the cloven sky ;
Stripped off thy body of mortality—
Nay, but on steeper slopes my love shall
    strive !
Our bodies perish and our hearts revive

Vainly, unless the shaking sense beware
The crested snakes shot trembling through
    our hair,
Their wisdom ! But our souls leap, flash,
    unite,
One crownéd column of avenging light,
Fixed and yet floating, infinite, immense,
Caught in the meshes of the cruel sense,
Two kissing breaths of agony and pleasure,
Mixed, crowned, divided. beyond age or
    measure,
Time, thought, or being ! Now thine eyes
    awake,
Droop at my kisses ; the long lashes slake
Their sleek and silky thirst in tears of
    light !
Thine eyes ! They burn me, even me !
    They smite
Me who am scatheless, and a flame of fire.
See, in our sorrow and intense desire
All worlds are caught and sealed ! The
    stars are taken
In love's weak web, and gathered up, and
    shaken !
Our word is mighty on the magic moon !
The sun resurges to our triple tune !
(See, it is done !) O chosen of the Christ !
My knight, and king, and lover, wast thou
    priced,
A portion in the all-pervading bliss,
Thou, whom I value at my ageless kiss ?
Chosen of Me ! Thou heart of hearts,
    thou mine,
Man ! Stamping into dust the Soul Divine
By might of that mere Manhood ! Sense
    and thought
Reel for the glory of thee kissed and caught
In the eternal circle of my arms !
Woven in vain are the mysterious charms
Endymion taught Diana ! For one gaze ;
One word of my unutterable praise ;
And I was utterly and ever lost,
Lost in the whirlwind of thy love, and
    tossed
A wreck on its irremeable sea !
Life ! Life ! This kiss ! Draw in thy
    breath ! To me !
To me !             [TANNHÄUSER *is lost.*

## ACT II.

"But a moment's thought is passion s passing
bell."—KEATS, *Lamia.*

*In Venusberg.*

VENUS.

SWEET, sweet are May and June, dear,
  The loves of lambent spring,
Our lamp the drooping moon, dear,
  Our roof, the stars that sing ;
The bed, of moss and roses ;
  The night, as long as death !
  Still, breath !
Life wakens and reposes,
  Love ever quickeneth !

Sweet, sweet, when Lion and Maiden,[1]
  The motley months of gold,
Swoop down with sunlight laden,
  And eyes are bright and bold.
Life-swelling breasts uncover
  Their warm involving deep—
  Love, sleep !—
And lover lies with lover
  On air's substantial steep.

TANNHÄUSER.

Ah !· sweeter was September—
  The amber rain of leaves,
The harvest to remember,
  The load of sunny sheaves.
In gardens deeply scented,
  In orchards heavily hung,
  Love flung
Away the days demented
  With lips that curled and clung.

Ah ! sweeter still October,
  When russet leaves go grey,
And sombre loves and sober
  Make twilight of the day.

[1] Leo and Virgo, in which the Sun is during
July and August.

Dark dreams and shadows tenser
  Throb through the vital scroll,
  Man's soul.
Lift, shake the subtle censer
  That hides the cruel coal !

Still sweeter when the Bowman [1]
  His silky shaft of frost
Lets loose on earth, that no man
  May linger nor be lost.
The barren woods, deserted,
  Lose echo of our sighs—
  Love—dies ?—
Love lives—in granite skirted,
  And under oaken skies.

But best is grim December,
 ' The Goatish God [1] his power ;
The Satyr blows the ember,
  And pain is passion's flower ;
When blood drips over kisses,
  And madness sobs through wine :—
  Ah, mine !—
The snake starts up and hisses
  And strikes and—I am thine !

VENUS.

Those are thy true joys ?   Cruelty for love ?

TANNHÄUSER.

And death in kissing.  How I have despised,
Riding  through  meadows  of  the  rushing
    Rhine,
To watch the gentle foresters of spring
Crush dainty violets in their dalliance,
Laughing in chorus with the birds ; and then
(Coming at harvest time upon my tracks)
See these same lovers in the golden sheaves
Under the sun.   The same, the fuller fruit,
Say you ?   But somehow, nearer to the end.
Lost the old sense of mystery, and lost
That curious reverence in sacrilege
With Wonder—the child's faculty !  Less joy,
Less laughter, yes ! that symptom I approve ;
Yet is that subtle fading-out of smiles

[1] Sagittarius, Capricornus, in which is the
Sun during November and December.

Rather the coming of a dull despair,
And not at all that keen despair, that sharp
Maddening pain that should torment a man
With deadliest delight, the self-same hour
That he unveils the Isis of desire.
These little lovers strip their maidens bare,
And find them—naked ! Poor and pitiful !
Look at our love instead ! I raised Thy veil,
Nay, tore Thy vesture from Thee, and
  behold !
Then only did I see what mystery,
What ninefold forest, shade impassible,
Surrounds Thy heart, as with a core of light
Shut in the mystery of a dead world.
Thou formless sense of gloom and terror !
  Thou
Upas,[1] new tree of life—by sinister
Cherubim with averted faces kept !
Nay ! This one secret I suspect, and gloat
Over the solemn purport of the dream
With subtle shuddering of joy,—and that
Keener delight, a sense of deadly fear !
This secret : Thou art darkness in Thyself,
And evil wrapped in light, and ugliness
Vested in beauty ! Therefore is my love
No petty passion like these country-folk's :
No fertile glory (as the Love of God) :
But vast and barren as the winter sea,
Holding I know not what enormous soul
In its salt bitter bosom, underneath
The iron waters and the serpent foam ;
Below, where sight and sound are set no
  more,
But only the intolerable weight
Of its own gloomy selfhood. This am I :
This passion, lion-mouthed and adder-eyed.
A mass compressed, a glowing central core,
Like molten metal in the crucible !
Death's secret is some sweetness ultimate,
Sweeter than poison. Ah ! My very words,
Chance phrases, ravel out the tale for me—
Sweetness and death — poison and love.
    Consider
How this same striving to the Infinite,
Which I intend by "love," is likest to

[1] A legendary tree in Java, which had the property of poisoning any one who rested in its shade.

That journey's wonder to the womb of death :
Because no soul of man has ever crossed
Again that River—the old fable's wrong ;
Æneas came never to the ghostly side !
Was not the boat weighed with his body still ?
Felt he the keen emotions of the dead ?
Could he, the mortal and the warrior,
Converse with Them, and understand ? Be-
  lieve !
No soul has crossed in utter sympathy
And yet returned ; because of this decree :
No man can look upon the face of God !
Yet Moses looked upon His hinder parts,[1]
And I—yes, goddess ! in this passionate
Life in our secret mountain, well I know
Thy beauty, and Thy love (although they be
Infinite, far beyond the mortal mind,
Body, or soul to touch, to comprehend,
And dwell in), that the utter intimate
Knowledge of Thee, if once I ravelled out
Thy secret, laid Thee naked to the bone—
Nay, to the marrow ! were to come, aware,
Face to face full with deity itself.
And this I strive at ! Therefore is my love
Wholly in tune with that concealed desire
Bred in each mortal, though he never know
(Few do know), to transcend the bound of
  things,
And find in Death the purpose of this life.

#### VENUS.

Yes, there you tear one veil away from me !
Yet, am not I the willing one ? Indeed
I feel the wonder of that same desire
From mine own side of the Impassible.
See then how equal God and man are made !
For I have clothed me in the veil of flesh,
And strive toward thy finite consciousness
As thou art reaching to my infinite,
Nurturing my Godhead at the breast of Sin
With milk of fleshly stings—even to pain :—

#### TANNHÄUSER.

I see, I see the Christian mystery !
That was the purpose of High God Himself

[1] See Exodus xxxiii. 18 to end.

Clothed in the Christ ! Ah ! Triumphed He
at last ?
Nay, not in death ! The slave—He rose
again !
Alas ! Alas !

VENUS.

Alas indeed, my knight !
We love not ! Being both enamoured of
Just the one thing that is impossible.
But in this carnal strife the Intimate
Achieves for one snatched swiftness. Kiss
me, love !

TANNHÄUSER.

Ah, but the waking ! As I sink to sleep
Pillowed in nuptial arms — so fresh and
cool—
(Yet in their veins I know the fire that runs
Racing and maddening from the crown of
flame,
The monolithic core of mystical
Red fury that is called a woman's heart)
Sinking, I say, from the supreme embrace,
The Good-night kisses ; sinking into sleep—
What dreams betoken the dread solitude ?

VENUS.

What dreams ? Ah, dreamest not of me, my
knight ?
Of vast caresses that include all worlds ?
Of transmutation into molten steel
Fusing with my intolerable gold
In the red crucible of alchemy,
That is—of clay ?

TANNHÄUSER.

I dream of no such thing.
But of Thy likeness have I often seen
The vast presentment—formless, palpable,
Breathing. Not breathing as we use the
word,
When life and spirit mingle in one breath,
Slay passion in one kiss—breathing, I say,
Differently from Thee !

VENUS.
Explain, explain !

TANNHÄUSER.
As if were kindled into gold and fire
The East !

VENUS.
The East !

TANNHÄUSER.
As if a flowerless moss
Suddenly broke in passionate primroses ! [1]

VENUS.
Violets, violets !

TANNHÄUSER.
Or as if a man
Lay in the fairest garden of the world,
In the beginning : and grew suddenly
A living soul at that caressing wind !

VENUS.
A living soul !

TANNHÄUSER.
So is Thy shade to me
When sleep takes shape.

VENUS.
She is mine enemy.
Hate her, O hate her, she will slay thy soul !

TANNHÄUSER.
And is my soul not slain within me now ?
Yet, I do hate her—in these waking hours.
But in my sleep she grows upon the sense,
A solitary lotus that pales forth
In the wide seas of space and separateness.
That radiance !—Amber-scented voice of
light,
Calling my name, ever, ever calling—

[1] Taken as symbols of bright and open joys :
violets as soft and sombre.

VENUS.

Answer that call—and thou art lost indeed!
Wake thou thy spirit in this hateful sleep,
Keeping the vision, rise, and spit on her!

TANNHÄUSER.

Spit on Thy likeness? I who love Thee so?

VENUS.

Yes, yes: obey me! She will leave thee
then.
She hath assumed mine image!
[*Thunder.*

TANNHÄUSER.

What is that?

VENUS.

Mere thunder on the mountain top. Do
this,
And I will come in sleep, in sleep renew
The carnal joys of day.

TANNHÄUSER.

Hast Thou forgot?
It is the fleshly I would flee!

VENUS.

Forget?
But I strive fleshwards. Let our sleep renew
The endless struggle—and perhaps, for thee,
For thee!—the veil may lift another fold.

TANNHÄUSER.

Why dost Thou hate this vision?

VENUS.

She would take
Thee from these arms!

TANNHÄUSER.

But she is beautiful
With Thine own beauty: yet as if the God
Cancelled its mortal comeliness, and came
More intimate than matter, closing in

Keen on my spirit; as if all I sought
In Thine own symbol, Beauty, were con-
cealed
Under her brows—how wider than the air!
How deeper than the sea! How radiant
Beyond the fire!

VENUS.

O shun her devilish lures!
That Beauty is the sole detested fear
That can annul our conquests, and arouse
Our rapt dream-kisses.

TANNHÄUSER.

That is my intent.
It is the spiritual life of things
I seek—Thou knowest!

VENUS.

Oh, I did not mean!
Remember my dilemma! Hear me speak
The story of her. She is a wicked witch
That seeketh to delude thy sleepy sense
In vicious purpose and malignant hope
To ape my Godhead.
[*Thunder.*

TANNHÄUSER.

Thunder rolls again.
I am uneasy.

VENUS.

Heed it not at all!
May not my servants of the elements
Play children's gambols on the mountain
crest
About our fortress? Leave this idle talk!
Come, in this sweet abandonment of self—
Come, with this kiss I seal thy loyal oath
To spit upon her!

TANNHÄUSER.

Ah, you murder me!
[*Sings.*
Come, love, and kiss my shoulders! Sleepy
lies
The tinted bosom whence its fire flies,

The breathing life of thee, and swoons, and
  sighs,
And dies !
None but the dead can know the worth of
  love !

Come, love, thy bosom to my heart recalls
Strange festivals and subtle funerals.
Soft passion rises in the amber walls,
And falls !
None but the dead can breathe the life of
  love !

Come, love, thy lips, curved hollow as the
  moon's !
Bring me thy kisses, for the seawind tunes,
The song that soars, and reads the starry
  runes,
And swoons !
None but the dead can tune the lyre of love !

Come, love, thy body serpentine and bright !
What love is this, the heart of sombre light,
Impossible, and therefore infinite ?
Sheer height !
None but the dead can twine the limbs of
  love !

Come, love ! My body in thy passion weeps
Tears keen as dewfall's, salter than the
  deep's.
My bosom ! How its fortress wakes, and
  leaps,
And sleeps !
None but the dead can sleep the sleep of love !

Come, love, caress me with endearing eyes !
Light the long rapture that nor fades nor flies !
Love laughs and lingers, frenzies, stabs, and
  sighs,
And dies !
None but the dead can know the worth of
  love !

[TANNHÄUSER *sleeps.*

VENUS.

Sleep on, poor fool, and in thy sleep deceived
Defy the very beauty that thou seekest !

Now is the solemn portal of the dusk
Lifted ; and in the gleaming silver-gray,
The eastern sky, steps out the single One,
Hathoör and Aphrodite—whom I mock !
I may not follow in the dimness—I
Chained unto matter by my evil will,
Delight of death and carnal life.   But see !
He stirs, as one beholding in a dream
Some deadly serpent or foul basilisk
Sunning its scales, called kingly, in the mire.
Strike, O my lover !   I will drag thee down
Into mine own unending pain and hate
To be one devil more upon the earth. —
Come !  ye my serpents, wrap his bosom
  round
With your entangling leprosy !   And me,
Let me assume the belovéd limber shape,
The crested head, the jewelled eyes of death,
And sinuous sinewy glitter of serpenthood,
That I may look once more into his face,
And, kissing, kill him !   Thus to hold him
  fast,
Drawing his human spirit into mine
For strength, for life, for poison !   Ah, my
  God !
These pangs, these torments !   See !   the
  sleeper wakes !
I am triumphant !   For he reaches out
The sleepy arms, and turns the drowsy head
To catch the dew dissolving of my lip.
Wake, lover, wake !   Thy Venus waits for
  thee !
Draw back, look, hunger !—and thy mouth
  is mine !

TANNHÄUSER.

" Once I will shew Me waking.   Destiny
 " Adds one illusion to thee.   Yet, Oh child !
" Yet will I not forsake thee ; for thy soul,
" Its splendid self, hath known Me.   Fare
  thee well."

VENUS.

What are these strange and silly words ?
  Awake !
Wake and devour me with the dawn of love,
The dragon to eclipse this moon of mine !

TANNHÄUSER.

I sleep not.   Those were Her mysterious
    words
As faded the great vision.   And I knew
In some forgotten corner of my brain
Some desperate truth.

VENUS.

            Forget this foolishness !
            [*There cometh a shadow.*
I am afraid, even I !   What moves me thus?

TANNHÄUSER.

I saw the mighty vision as before
Forming in front of the awakening east,
All permeated with the rose of dawn,
And pale with delicate green light and shade,
Marvellous !   So, you say, she is a witch
Seeking to rob or trick you of your power ?

VENUS.

I say so?   No !   I dare not !   Oh forbear !

TANNHÄUSER (*starts up*).

There, there She comes in waking !   Hail
    to Thee !
I am afraid, I also, I myself !
Help !  lover, Venus, mistress of my life !
I cannot bear the glory of the gaze.
No man shall look upon the face of God !
Where   art   thou?    Save   me   from   the
    scorpion ![1]
I am—alone !

HATHOÖR.

    Light, Truth, arise, arise !

TANNHÄUSER.

I see—I see !   All blinded by the Light—
Thou art the Way, the Truth, and Life, the
    Love !
Thou, Whom I sought through ages of deep
    sleep

---

[1] Lilith, among other shapes, can assume
that of a scorpion.

Forgotten when I died.   There is no death :
Change alternating ; and forgetfulness
Of one state in the other—easy truth
I could not understand !   Oh hear me, hear !
Spare me the last illusion !—She is gone !

VENUS.

Save me, my knight !   To thy sufficing arms
I cling in this distress of womanhood !

TANNHÄUSER.

Kiss me the last time.

VENUS.

            Whom have I but thee,
Thee in the ages ?   Barren were my bliss
And shorn my Godhead of eternal joy,
Barred from thy kiss.

TANNHÄUSER.

            Call not thyself again
Goddess.   I saw thee in the Presence there.
The scales are fallen, and mine eyes see clear.

VENUS.

Then you would leave me !   Serpent if I were,
My coils should press in dolorous delight
Thy straining bosom, and my kiss were death !
Death !   Dost thou live, Tannhäuser?   Sayest
    thou still :
"None but the dead can know the worth of
    love ! " ?

TANNHÄUSER.

Still. ·  I am not in any sense estranged.
I yearn for thee in the first hour of spring,
As in the dying days of autumn.   I
Would clasp thee, as a child its mother's
    throat,
Drinking celestial wine from that dear mouth,
Or with goodwill see poison in thy smile,
And die, still kissing thee, and kissed again !
This, though I saw thee crawl upon the earth,
Howl at Her presence Whom thou wouldest
    ape,
Thy tale reversed.   I read that thunder now !

This, though I know thee.  Aphrodite, no !
Nor Anael,[1] nor Eva !  Rather thou
Lilith, the woman-serpent, she who sucks
The breath of little children in their sleep,
Strangles young maidens, and presides upon
Sterile debauchery and unnatural loves.

### VENUS.

Lilith !  Ah, lover !  Thou hast known my
   name !

### TANNHÄUSER.

So ; yet I love thee !  Rended is the veil !
Calling thee Ugliness, I guessed aright,
Who saw, and see, all Beauty in thee still.
Only, a beauty risen out of Hell ;
Death and delusion—ay, corruption's self,
Wickedness sliming into impotence,
Pleasure in putrefaction.  But, in sleep,
I will put off that evil as a clout
Cast by a beggar.

### VENUS.

      And the sore is left.

### TANNHÄUSER.

Oh, but this body, very consciousness !
I banish both.  I cross the crimson wall—
My spirit shall reach up to and attain
That other.

### VENUS.

      So Persephone must hold
Thy life divided in Her dark domain.[2]

### TANNHÄUSER.

Already I have tasted once of this
In its own lesser way.  Ten years ago
I loved a maiden called Elizabeth.
A child she was, so delicate and frail,
Far, white, and lonely as the coldest star
Set beyond gaze of any eye but God's ;

[1] The semi-divine woman, between Aphrodite the divine, and Eve the human.
[2] Persephone was compelled to spend six months of the year in Hades.

And, to forget her, found due somnolence
In such a warm brown bosom as thine own
Is fire and amber.  Then I came away :—
I heard of knights no better horsed than I,
No better sworded, with no gift of song,
Who, caught by one ineffable desire,
Rode on by old mysterious watersheds,
Traversed strange seas, or battled with strange
   folk,
Held vigil in wild forests, all to seek
The vision of the Holy Grail.  And I
Rode forth on that same foolish wandering,
And found a-many ventures on the way ;
At last an old Egyptian ; who bestowed
The magic word, which, when I had pro-
   nounced,
Called up thine evil corpse-light in the sky.
He riddled me—ah God !  I see it now !
The bloody winepress ?  The ascending sun ?
Thy dawning beauty and thine evil bed !
The double meaning !  I had evil thoughts
When I pronounced it—else had She Herself,
Hathoör or Mary, risen.  Misery !
Incessant mystery of the search for Truth !

### VENUS.

Search out my mystery a little while !

### TANNHÄUSER.

There is a flush of passion in thine eyes,
An hunger in them ; fascinate me now,
My serpent-woman, drawing out my breath
Into thy life, and mingling that in mine !
See the rich blood that mantles to my touch,
Invites the tooth to bite the shimmering skin,
Till I could watch the ripe red venom flow
Slow on the hills of amber, staining them
Its own warm purple.  Look, the tender
   stream !

### VENUS.

Let its old sleepy fragrance lull thee now,
Yet madden thee in brain and sense and soul,
Mixing success with infinite despair.
So ; take our secret back to sleep with us :—
And in that sleep I know that thou wilt
   choose

The fact, and leave the dream, and so disdain
These far-off splendours, catch the nearer joy,
Take squalid kisses, banish crested love
Intangible.  Delights it thee, my friend,
To reach the summits unattained before,
And stumble on their snows?  Thine old
    desire
Was just to touch the mere impalpable,
To formulate the formless.  Otherwise
Christ did as well—thine own words turn
    again !

### TANNHÄUSER.

Ah, if pure love could grow material !
There are pure women !

### VENUS.

                There you make me laugh !
Remember—I have known such.  But besides
You ask hot snow and leaden feather-flights !

### TANNHÄUSER.

And you—you keep me worrying, fair queen,
In logic and its meshes, when to-day
I rather would be caught in other nets,
The burning gold and glory of your hair,
Lightning and sunshine, storm and radiance,
Your flaming pell ! [1]

### VENUS.

            Come, sing to me again !
That we may watch each other as you sing ;
Feel how it overmasters and o'erwhelms,
The growing pang of hunger for a kiss !

### TANNHÄUSER

Brood evil, then, in your amazing eyes,
That I may see the serpent grow in you ;
As I were just the bird upon the bough—
So let the twittering grow faint and still,
And let me fall, fall into the abyss,
Your arms—a culminating ecstasy,
Darkness and death and rapture.  Sing to
    you ?

[1] From Latin *pellis*, skin.

What song ?  My tunes are played upon
    too oft
My first great cry of love inaudible
Sapped me of music.

### VENUS.

            Sing me that again !

### TANNHÄUSER.

Who is this maiden robéd for a bride,
    White shoulders and bright brows adorable,
The flaming locks that clothe her, and abide,
    As God were bathing in the fire of Hell ?
        They change, they grow, they shake
        As sunlight on the lake :
    They hiss, they glisten on her bosom bare.
        O maiden, maiden queen !
        The lightning flows between
    Thy mounting breasts, too magically fair.
        Draw me, O draw me to a dreaming
            death !
        Send out thine opiate breath,
    And lull me to the everlasting sleep,
        That, closing from the kisses of disdain
        To ecstasy of pain,
    I may sob out my life into their dangerous
        deep.

Who cometh from the mountain as a tower
    Stalwart and set against the fiery foes ?
Who, breathing as a jasmine-laden bower ?
    Who, crowned and lissome as a living rose ?
        Sharp thorns in thee are set ;
        In me, in me beget
    The dolorous despair of this desire.
        Thy body sways and swings
        Above the tide of things,
    Laps me as ocean, wraps me round as fire !
        Ye elemental sorceries of song,
        Surge, strenuous and strong,
    Seeking dead dreams, the secret of the shrine ;
        So that she drain my life and being up
        As from a golden cup,
    To mingle in her blood, death's kiss incarna-
        dine.

Who cometh from the ocean as a flower?
 Who blossometh above the barren sea?
Thy lotus set beneath thee for a bower,
 Thine eyes awakened, lightened, fallen
  on me?
  O Goddess, queen, and wife!
  O Lady of my life!
Who set thy stature as a wood to wave?
 Whose love begat thy limbs?
 Whose wave-washed body swims
That nurtured thee, and found herself a grave?
 But thou, O thou, hast risen from the
  deep!
 All mortals mourn and weep
To see thee, seeing that all love must die
 Beside thy beauty, see thee and despair!
 Deadly as thou art fair,
I cry for all mankind—they are slain, even
 as I!
   [TANNHÄUSER *pauses, bends eagerly
   towards* VENUS. *She smiling luxu-
   riously, he continues.*

Who cometh wanton, with long arms out-
  spread?
 Who cometh with lascivious lips aflame?
Whose eyes invite me to the naked bed
 Stark open to the sun, dear pride of shame?
 Whose face draws close and near,
 Filling the soul with fear,
Till nameless shudders course in every limb?
 Whose breath is quick and fierce?
 Whose teeth are keen to pierce
The arms that clasp her? Whose the eyes
  that swim
 For dear and delicate delight? And
  whose
 The lips that halt and choose
The very centre of my mouth, and meet
 In one supreme and conquering kiss,
  and cleave
 Unto the wound they leave,
Bringing all heart's blood to one house, too
  sore and sweet?

Who rageth as a lioness bereaved,
 If, for a moment's breathing space, I move

Back from the purple where her bosom
  heaved,
 Back from the chosen body that I love?
 Whose lips cling faster still
 In desperate sweet will?
Whose body melts as fire caught in wine
 Into the clasping soul?
 Whose breathing breasts control
Her heart's quick pulsing, and the sob of
  mine?
 O Venus, lady Venus, thou it is
 Whose fierce immortal kiss
Abides upon me, about me, and within:
 Thou, lady of the secret of the Sea,
 Made one for love with me,
Love and desire and dream, a sense of
  mortal sin!

Who cometh as a visionary shape
 Within my soul and spirit to abide,
Mysterious labyrinth without escape,
 Magical lover, and enchanted bride?
 O Mother of my will!
 Set thy live body still
Unto my heart, that even Eternity
 Roll by our barren bed—
 That even the quick and dead,
Being mortal, mix in our eternal sea!
 Distil we love from all the universe!
 Defy the early curse!
Bid thorns and thistles mingle in delight!
 And from the athanor of death and
  pain
 Bring golden showers of rain
To crown our bed withal, the empire of the
  Night!

O Wife! Incarnate Beauty self-create!
 O Life! O Death! Love unimaginable!
Despair grows hope, as hope grows despe-
  rate;
 And Heaven bridges the great gulf of
  Hell.
 Thy life is met with mine,
 Transmuted, grown divine,
Even in this, the evil of the world!
 What agony is this,
 The first undying kiss

From jewelled eyes and lips in passion
   curled ?
  O sister and O serpent and O mate,
  Strike the red fang of hate
Steady and strong, persistent to the heart !
  So shall this song be made more ter-
   rible
  With the soul-mastering spell,
Choke, stagger, know the Evil, Beauty's
   counterpart !

Whose long-drawn curse runs venom in my
   veins ?
  What dragon spouse consumes me with
   her breath ?
What passionate hatred, what infernal pains,
  Mixed with thy being in the womb of
   Death ?
  Blistering fire runs,
  Scorching, terrific suns,
Through body and soul in this abominable
  Marriage of demon power
  Subtle and strong and sour,
A draught of ichor of the veins of Hell!
  Curses leap leprous, epicene, unclean,
  The soul of the Obscene
Incarnate in the spirit : and above
  Hangs Sin, vast vampire, the corrupt,
   that swings
  Her unredeeming wings
Over the world, and flaps for lust of Death
  —and Love !

### VENUS.

This man was drained of music ! Five new
  songs
Chase the three ancient to oblivion ! Oh !
Love is grown fury !

### TANNHÄUSER.

Kill me !

### VENUS.

          In the kiss.
    [TANNHÄUSER *sleeps.*

## ACT III.

For Love is lord of truth and loyalty,
Lifting himself out of the lowly dust
On golden plumes up to the purest sky,
Above the reach of loathly sinful lust,
Whose base affect through cowardly distrust
Of his weak wings dare not to heaven fly,
But like a moldwarp in the earth doth lie.

His dunghill thoughts, which do themselves
  enure
To dirty dross, no higher dare aspire,
Nor can his feeble earthly eyes endure
The flaming light of that celestial fire
Which kindleth love in generous desire,
And makes him mount above the native might
Of heavy earth, up to the heaven's height.
    SPENSER, *Hymn in Honour of Love.*

*In Venusberg: changing afterward to
    a woodland crossway.*

### VENUS.

GONE to his Goddess ! the poor worm's
  asleep.
And yet—I cannot follow him. Not even
Into the dreamland that these mortals use.
There, I am barred. The flaming sword of
  Light
Is set against me, and new pangs consume
This nest of scorpions where my heart once
  was.
Yet to my fearful task of hate I set
No faltering bosom. I will have this man,
His life, his strength ; and live a little more.
Life—shall I ever reach the splendid sword
Of womanhood, and gird it, gain my will,
A human soul, and from that altitude
Renew the terrible war against the Gods?
I have called Chronos the devouring God
My father—shall his desolating reign
Never return ? Ay me ! this heart of hate,
Loathing the man, takes comfort in the beast,
And gloats on the new garbage for an hour.
So, Sin, embrace me ! Watch ; he moves
  again,
Transfigured by the dream : slow rapture
  steals
Over his face. Mere godhead could not
  bring

That human light and living ! I shall win.
He must have banished Her—and dreams
    of me.

TANNHÄUSER (*in sleep*).
Elizabeth !

VENUS.
            His far-off baby-love !
I triumph, then ! The Goddess hath with-
drawn.
His mind works back to childhood, babydom;
Will grow to manhood and remember me.

TANNHÄUSER (*awaking, leaps to his feet*).

Freedom ! Elizabeth ! All hail to Her !
Radiant Goddess ! Liberty and love !

VENUS.
What sayest thou ? Curse Her !

TANNHÄUSER.
                    My Elizabeth !

VENUS.
What ? Art thou mad ? Come close to me
    again.
Forget this nightmare. Rather, tell me it,
And I will soothe thee. Have I not a balm,
A sovereign comfort in my old caress ?

TANNHÄUSER.
I must begone. She waits.

VENUS.
            Who waits ? Come here !
Let us talk fondly, set together still,
Not with these shouts and wavings of the
    arms,
Struts and unseemly gestures. Tannhäuser !

TANNHÄUSER.
She waits for me, my sweet Elizabeth !
Venus or Lilith, I have loved thee well !
Now, to my freedom !

VENUS.
            Your Elizabeth !

TANNHÄUSER.
Ay, to those pure and alabaster brows,
The tender fingers, and the maiden smile.
Burn the whore's bed ! Unpaint the cruel
    lips !
Cover the shameless belly, and forget
The cunning attitudes and aptitudes !
Unlearn the mowings, the lascivious grins !
I perceive purity.

VENUS.
            Nay, I have loved thee !
Fresh pleasure hourly filled the crystal cup.
Shalt thou find wine so comely and so keen,
So fresh with life to fill each aching vein
With new electric fervour ? Will she be
My equal ? She is mortal and a child.
Her arms are frail and white. Her lily
    cheeks
Could never take thy kiss. Thy love would
    shock,
Repel. I scorn to say her love were less
Than mine : I tell thee that she could not
    love
Thee even at all as thou wouldst understand.

TANNHÄUSER.
So certain art thou ? Let me go to her,
Try, and come back !

VENUS.
            No doubt of that success !
A child is easy to degrade !

TANNHÄUSER.
                    Vile thing !
I will try otherwise—to raise myself :
But if I fail, I will not drag her down ;
I will return.

VENUS.
            To lose thee for one hour
Is my swift death—so desolate am I !
I have not got one lover in the world,
Save only Tannhäuser. And he will go.

TANNHÄUSER.

One lover ! Who makes up the equal soul
Of all the wickedness beneath the sun ?
Lilith ! Seek out thy children to devour !
Leave me. I go to my Elizabeth.

VENUS.

O no ! It kills me ! That is naked truth.
I am the soul and symbol of desire,
Yet individual to thy love. Stay ! Stay !
One last caress, and then I let thee go,
And—die. I fear, and I detest, this death.
I am not mortal, doomed to it ! I slip
Into mere slime ; no resurrection waits
Me, made the vilest of the stars that fell.
I must not die. I dare not. But for thee,
Thy love, one last extreme delirium !—
Take thou this dagger ! At the miracle
Of a moment when our lips are fastened close
Once more, in the unutterable kiss,
Drive its sharp spirit to my heart !

TANNHÄUSER.

Not I !
I know the spell.[1] I am warned. I will
begone.

VENUS.

I swear I will not let thee ! Thinkest thou
So long I have held thee not to have the
power
To hold thee still by charm, or love, or force?
Fool, for I hate thee ! I will have thy life !

TANNHÄUSER.

Where is the cavern in the mountain side,
The accurséd gateway of this house of Hell ?

VENUS.

Thou canst not find it ! Fool !

TANNHAUSER.

And yet I will.

[1] Which would have given her power to use
his body as an habitation, according to legend.
VOL. I.

VENUS.

Meanwhile my chant shall tremble in the air,
And rack thy limbs with poison, wither up
The fine full blood, breed serpents in thy
heart,
And worms to eat thee. Living thou shalt
be
A sensible corpse, a walking sepulchre.
Come, come, Apollyon ! Come, my
Aggereth ![1]
Belial, cheat his ears and blind his eyes !
Come, all ye tribes of serpents and foul fish !
Beetle and worm, I have a feast for you !

TANNHÄUSER.

The palace staggers. I can hardly see—
Only these writhing horrors. I am blind !

VENUS.

Ha ! My true knight ! I ask thee once again,
Once more invoke the epithets of love,
Suspend my powers—constrain thee on my
knees
For thine old kisses. See, I am all thine !
All thine the splendid body, and the shape
Of mighty breasts, and supple limbs, and wide
Lips, and slow almond eyes ! Adorable,
Seductive, sombre, moving amorously,
Droop the long eyelids, purple with young
blood,
The lazy lashes and the flowing mane,
The flame of fire from head to feet of me !
The subtle fervours, drunken heats and ways,
And perfumes maddening from the soul of
spring !
The little nipples, and the dangerous pit
Set smiling in the alabaster ; thine,
The glowing arms are thine, the desperate
Fresh kisses, and the gold that lurks upon
The sunny skin, the marble of these brows,
The roses, and the poppies, and the scent
Subtle and sinful—thine, all thine, are these,
What with my heart that only beats for thee,
The many-throned and many-minded soul
Centred to do thee worship. Hither, hither !

[1] A female demon. She rides in a chariot
drawn by an ox and an ass. See Deut. xxii. 10.

Q

TANNHÄUSER.

This shakes my spirit as a winnower
Whose fan is the eternal breath of God ;
Yet on my forehead I perceive a Star
That shames thy beauties and thy manifold
Mind with Its tiny triple flame.   I go !

VENUS.

Try not the impossible.   Thou knowest my
    power.
I shall renew the charm.

TANNHÄUSER.

                              I see a Power
Above thy mockery of witchcraft.   Work
Thy devilish lusts on me unfortunate !
There is no gateway to this fortalice ?
Thy fiends surround me ?   Hein !   their pangs
    begin !
I have one word, one cry, one exorcism :
Avé Maria !

VENUS.

          Mercy !   Mercy, God !
[*Thunder rolls in the lightning-riven
sky.   All the illusion vanishes, and
TANNHÄUSER finds himself in a
cross-way of the forest, where is a
Crucifix.   He is kneeling at the foot,
amazed, as one awakening from a
dream, or from a vision of mysterious
power.*

TANNHÄUSER.

I am escapéd as a little bird
Out of the fowler's net.   I thank Thee, God !
For in the pit of horror, and the clay
Of death I cried, and Thou hast holpen me,
Set me upon a rock, established me,
And filled my mouth, and tuned mine
    ancient lyre
With a new song—praise, praise to God
    above,[1]
And to Our Lady of the Smitten Heart,

[1] Psalm xl.

That David never knew : my pettiness
Exceeding through Her mercy and Her
    might
The King and Priest of Israel ; for I know
Her love, and She hath shewn to me Her
    face,
And given me a magic star to stand
Over the house that hides Elizabeth.
          [*A shepherd-boy is discovered upon a
          rock hard by.*

SHEPHERD-BOY.

Ta-lirra-lirra !   Hillo ho!   The morning !
          [*He plays upon his flute.*

TANNHÄUSER.

These were the melodies that I despised !
Oh God !   Be merciful to sinful me,
And keep me in the Way of Truth.   But
    Thou !
Forgive, forgive !   Lead, lead me to Thy
    Light !

SHEPHERD-BOY (*sings*).

Light in the sky
    Dawns to the East !
    Song-bird and beast
Wake and reply.
Let me not die,
    Now, at the least !
Lord of the Light !
    Queen of the dawn !
Soul of the Night
    Hid and withdrawn !
Voice of the thunder !
    Light of the levin !
I worship and wonder,
    O maker of Heaven !
The night falls asunder ;
    The darkness is riven !

Light, O eternal !
Life, O diurnal !
    Love, O withdrawn !
Heart of my May, spring
    Far to Thy dawn !
God of the dayspring !
    Sun on the lawn !

Hail to Thy splendour,
   Holy, I cry !
Mary shall bend her
   Face from the sky,
Subtle and tender—
   Then I can die !

TANNHÄUSER.

The simple love of life and gladness there !
Merely to be, and worship at the heart.
How complex, the machinery of me !
Better ? I doubt it.   Hark ! he tunes again.

SHEPHERD-BOY (sings).

O Gretchen, when the morn is gray,
Forsake thy flocks and steal away
To that low bank where, shepherds say,
   The flowers eternal are.
Thine eyes should gleam to see me there,
   As fixed upon a star.
And yet thy lips should take a tune,
   And match me unaware—
So steals the sun beside the moon
   And hides her lustre rare.
The bloom upon the peach is fine ;
The blossom on thy cheek is mine !
   O kiss me—if you dare !
I called thee by the name of love
That mothers fear and gods approve,
   And maidens blush to say—
O Gretchen, meet me in the dell
We know and love, who love so well,
   While morn is cold and gray !
So, match thy blushes to the dawn ;
   Thy bosom to the rising moon,
Until our loves to earth have drawn
   Some new bewitching tune.
Come, Gretchen, in the dusk of day,
Where nymphs and dryads creep away
Beneath the oaks, to laugh and play
   And sink in lover's swoon.
We'll sing them sister songs, and show
What secrets mortal lovers know.

TANNHÄUSER.

The simple life of love and joy therein !
Merely to love—to take such pride in it

Gods must behold !   The childish easiness,
Impossible to me, who am become
Perhaps the subtlest mind of men.   Alas !
Maybe in this I still am self-deceived,
Merely the fool swelled up with bitter words,
Imagination, and the toadstool growth,
Thought, wounded ; as a scorpion to sting
Its own bruised life out.   This is Tannhäuser !
How long ago since he took pleasure in
Such love—                          [A horn winds.
   such music as yon horn below—
                  [A chant is heard.
Such worship as the simple chant that steals
Calm and majestic in the solitude
Up from the valley.   Pilgrims, by my fay !
                  [Enter PILGRIMS.

PILGRIMS (sing).

Hail to Thee, Lady bright,
Queen of the stars of night !
   Avé Maria !
Spouse of the Breath divine,
Hail to Thee, shrouded shrine,
Whence our Redeemer came !
Hail to Thy holy name !
   Avé Maria !

TANNHÄUSER.

Those words that saved me !

SHEPHERD-BOY.

          Pray, your blessing, sirs !
I worship Mary in my simple way,
And see Her name in all the starry host,
And Jesus crucified on every tree
For me !   God speed you to the House of
   God !

THE ELDEST PILGRIM.

The Blessing of the Virgin on your head !

THE YOUNGEST PILGRIM.

What make you, sir, so downcast ?   Come
   with us
Who taste all happiness in uneasiness,
Hunger and thirst, in His sweet Name—

#### TANNHÄUSER.

Ah no!
I have been shown another way than yours!
I am too old in this world's weariness,
Too hungry in its hunger unto God,
Too foolish-wise, too passionate-cynical,
To seek your royal road to Deity!

#### ANOTHER PILGRIM.

Leave him! Belike 'tis some philosopher
With words too big to understand himself.

#### TANNHÄUSER.

With heart too seared to understand himself!
With mind too wise to understand himself!
With soul too small to understand himself!

#### ELDEST PILGRIM.

Cling to the Cross, sir, there is hope in that!

#### TANNHÄUSER.

You know not, friend, the man to whom
  you speak.
I have lived long in miracles enough,
Myself the crowning miracle of all,
That I am merely here.  God speed you, sirs!
I ask your blessing, not to stay therewith
My soul's own need (though that is dire
  enough)
But—he that blesseth shall himself be
  blessed!
My blessing were small help to you, my
  friends.

#### AN INTELLIGENT PILGRIM.

For your own reason, give it to us, then!

#### TANNHÄUSER.

The Blessing of the Lord!  May Mary's self
Be with you and defend you evermore,
Most from the fearful destiny of him
Men used to call the minstrel Tannhäuser!

#### ELDEST PILGRIM.

A sombre blessing!  May God's mercy fall
On you and yours!

#### TANNHÄUSER.

On mine, ah mine!  Amen,
Amen to that!

#### ELDEST PILGRIM (*smiles*).

On her you love, my friend!
We will pass onward, by your honour's leave!

#### PILGRIMS (*sing*).

Hail, hail, O Queen, to Thee,
Spouse of Eternity!
  Avé Maria!
Mother in Maidenhood!
Saintly Beatitude!
Queen of the Angel Host!
Bride of the Holy Ghost!
  Avé Maria!

[*Exeunt Pilgrims.*

#### TANNHÄUSER.

The love of Isis!  No mere love to Her
That is inborn in every soul of us!
It is Her love to Christ that we must taste,
Uniting us with Her eternal sigh.
There is a problem infinite again.
I have not gained one jot since first I saw
The stately bosom of the Venusberg,
Save that mine eyes have seen a little truth,
My body found a little weariness.
I am very feeble!  Hither comes the hunt!
[*A horn winds quite close by.*
The noble, doomed, swift beauty!  Closer
  yet
Pant the long hounds!  What heart he has!
  One, two!
See the brach [1] dying by his bloody flank!
So could not Tannhäuser awhile ago.
My help lay outside and above myself.
What skills him he is brave?  He ends the
  same.
Poor stag!  Here sweep the foremost
  hunters up.
My very kinsmen!  There rides Wolfram
  too!

[1] Feminine of hound.

The proper minstrel! The ideal lover!
The pure, unsullied soul. Even so, forsooth!
They tell no secrets in the scullery.
And there is Heinrich, wastrel of the Court,
Yet hides a heart beneath the foolish face.
And lo! The Landgrave! Flushed, undignified!
The chase was long—if he could see himself!
Wind, wind the mort! What call will answer me
When I step forward? Am I dead, I wonder,
Or merely on my hare-brain quest? Three years
Since I was seen in Germany!
                [*He descends the hill and enters the company.*
                                    Hail, friends!
Good cousin Landgrave, merry be the meet!

LANDGRAVE.

Hands off me, fellow! Who are you?

TANNHÄUSER.
                                    My lord,
Your cousin. Is my face so changed with care,
My body shrunken with my suffering
(That was not ever of the body) so?

WOLFRAM.

I know you, my old friend! Our chiefest bird!
Sweetest of singers!

TANNHÄUSER.
                    No, the naughty one!

HEINRICH.

Tannhäuser! Yes! And we have thought you dead.

LANDGRAVE.

Friends, will you swear to him?

HEINRICH.
                            Yes, yes, 'tis he!

WOLFRAM.

I know the blithe look in the sober eyes!

LANDGRAVE.

Changed verily. It was most urgent, cousin,
I were assured of your identity.
Three weeks the couriers scour the land for you,
Urgent demands:—how came you here at last?
Your horse? Your arms? Three years since Germany
Saw the brave eyes and kindly face of you!
Where have you been? Upon the sacred quest
Still riding?

TANNHÄUSER.
            Ay, my lord, upon the quest.

LANDGRAVE.

You travelled in far lands?

TANNHÄUSER.
                        Far, very far!

LANDGRAVE.

You fought with Turks?

TANNHÄUSER.
                    I fought within myself.

LANDGRAVE.

Why is such suffering written in dark lines,
And painted in the greyness of your hair?

TANNHÄUSER.

I had an evil dream.

LANDGRAVE.
                    You saw the Grail?

TANNHÄUSER.

I saw—strange things.

WOLFRAM.

           For very feebleness
Your limbs shake under you.    How hither,
   friend ?
Your horse and arms?    Your squire?

TANNHÄUSER.

           My squire is dead.
      [*With sudden passion.*
I am no weakling that I need a knave
Hanging upon me—'tis an incubus.

LANDGRAVE.

And then your horse ?

TANNHÄUSER.

          I know not ; possibly
Kept as an hostage.    I was prisoner once.

WOLFRAM.

Prisoner?    By here?

TANNHÄUSER.

         A-many castles, sir,
Held by old ogres—and not all of them
Stand in the mid-day, front the sober sun,
Answer the slug-horn.[1]

LANDGRAVE.

         You are pleased to riddle.
Ever the poet !

TANNHÄUSER (*aside*).

         Let me try the truth
For certitude of incredulity !
(*Aloud, laughing*) I was in Venusberg !

ALL (*except* HEINRICH, *who laughs*).

           Save us, Maria !
   [*They look about them fearfully and
    cross themselves.*

[1] I prefer to follow Browning in his " absurd
blunder" than to imitate the alleged correctness
of our critics.—A. C.

LANDGRAVE.

Even in jest, such words !—Most dangerous
Even to think of !—but to speak !

HEINRICH (*aside*).

           These fools !
  [*He remains, thoughtfully regarding
  TANNHÄUSER.*

LANDGRAVE.

God avert omens !    Soft you, Tannhäuser,
You heard the heralds ?

TANNHÄUSER.

         Never a word of them !

LANDGRAVE.

You must remember my Elizabeth,
My daughter—I designed to marry her
To a most noble youth—

TANNHÄUSER.

         Von Aschenheim ?

LANDGRAVE.

The same.    I would have wed her, but ('tis
   strange !)
The lady had a purpose of her own,
And swore by all the Virgins in the Book
She would wed nobody but—Tannhäuser.
So, like the foolish, doting sire I am,
I gave her thirty days to find you.    This
Must dumb you with astonishment.

TANNHÄUSER.

           Well, no !
The details, unfamiliar !    But the theme
I knew.    And therefore leaps my bosom up :
I rob your verderer of his nag, and ho !
Low the long gallop to Elizabeth !

WOLFRAM.

Lucky and brave.    How we all envy you !

HEINRICH.

Envy? This day when he comes back to us!
Why, we are lucky too! We thought you
  dead!

WOLFRAM.

Begrudge you, no! But—wish our luck
  were yours?
Yes! Come, Tannhäuser, there's my hand
  on it!
Luck, love, and loyalty—the triple toast!

FORESTERS.

Tannhäuser! Luck, and love, and loyalty!

TANNHÄUSER.

I thank you, loving kinsmen and my friends.
But see, I am impatient to be gone!
(*To the verderer.*) Your horse—that favour
  I shall not forget,
Nor linger to repay. Good morrow then!
Good sport all day!

LANDGRAVE.

God speed thee, Tannhäuser!
                  [*Exit* TANNHÄUSER.
Am I still dreaming? It was surely he.
But such an one, compact of suffering,
Of joy, of love, of pity, of despair;
Half senseless, half too subtle for my sense.

WOLFRAM.

He has passed through some unimagined test,
Or undergone some sorrow. Leave it so!
I saw high grief upon him, and new love!

HEINRICH.

You are the poet! To your instinct then!
Here's to the insight given us by God!

LANDGRAVE.

Wolfram is right; a truce to jest to-day.
The dogs are loose. Ride forward, gentle-
  men!
  [*Amid the winding of horns and cries of
    the huntsmen the company moves off.*

HEINRICH.

They hate his very name! Dear Tannhäuser!
                  [*Exit.*

ACT IV.

" So, force is sorrow, and each sorrow, force:
    What then? since Swiftness gives the
      charioteer
The palm, his hope be in the vivid horse
    Whose neck God clothed with thunder,
      not the steer
Sluggish and safe! Yoke Hatred, Crime,
      Remorse,
    Despair: but ever mid the whirling fear,
Let, through the tumult, break the poet's face
    Radiant, assured his wild slaves win the
      race!"
                  *Two Poets of Croisic.*

SCENE I.

*A room in the palace of the* LANDGRAVE.

ELIZABETH.

I AM ashamed to look upon thy face!

TANNHÄUSER.

O Love! Pure mystery of life!

ELIZABETH.
                        Not so.
Learn how this came. My father would
      have made
A match of lands and titles. I declined,
Minded to keep my high virginity.
He laughed, was cruel. So I said at last:
" Tannhäuser only!" Was this modesty?
Listen. You loved me when I was a child;
And, in my childish way, I looked to you,
Loved sitting at your knee and toying with
The great cross-hilt, or watching how the
      steel
Outshone the jewelled scabbard when you
      drew
(You would not let me touch) the delicate
      blade
Half out: and also fingering your harp,
Picking child's tunes out, while you curled
      my hair
Between two fingers, dreamily enough!
Then, too, you went away out of my life!
You see the symbol you have been to me?
The swift high mind, the heart of gold and
      fire,

The living purpose and the mystic life
Of lonely seeking for the Grail of God !
I—call you husband ?   When I said your
   name,
It was to set the task impossible,
Had they but known it—just as one should
   say :
"Bring down St. Michael : let me marry
   him !"
They knew the angels were too pure ; but
   you,
They guessed not how exalted were your
   hopes ;
How utterly unselfish, pure, and true,
Your great heart beat !

TANNHÄUSER (*with bitterness*).
                        I hardly knew, myself !
(*Aside.*)  Here is the virgin insight of the
   truth !
Or—cannot purity be brought to know
Aught but itself ?   Some poets tell us that !
(*Aloud.*)  I am unworthy even to speak to
you.

ELIZABETH.
The proof !  The proof !  Dear God, how
   true it is
That such high worthiness sees nothing there
In his own heart (save what is very Christ)
But wickedness !

TANNHÄUSER (*aside*).
                        This is my punishment !
This faith, this hope, this love—to me—to
me !

ELIZABETH.
Yet, once my word went forth into the world,
Suddenly came the fear that you were still
Accessible to men—might hear, might come !
The kind, grave face of you—that light out-
   shone
The mystical ideal.   Therefore too
I minded me of our old baby-love,

And—marriages are made in heaven, you
   know !
Besides—Our Lady showed me in a dream
How you would come.

TANNHÄUSER.
                        And now ?  So sure are you
The loving word you spoke an hour ago
Came from the heart—who called me by
   mistake ?

ELIZABETH.
So sure ?  You want me to confess again
The deep pure love, the love indicible.

TANNHÄUSER (*to himself*).
Words, thoughts, that fail her ?  How should
   acts exceed ?
(*Aloud.*)  Better sit thus and read each
   other's thoughts—
I in the blue eyes, in the hazel you !
Then, bending, I may touch my lips upon
Sweet thoughtful brows.

ELIZABETH.
                        Your kisses move my soul.
Strange thoughts and unimagined destinies
Take ship, and harbour in the heart of me.

TANNHÄUSER.
Words mean too much, and never mean
   enough.
Look, only look !

ELIZABETH.
                        I am so happy—so !

SCENE II.

*The Court assembled in the Great Hall.
LANDGRAVE enthroned, ELIZABETH by
his side.  Facing them are the competing
minstrels.  Around, courtiers and fair
ladies.*

LANDGRAVE.
Welcome all minstrels !  Let us celebrate
In the old fashion, dear to Germany,
My child's betrothal to this noble youth,

Great lord, true knight, and honest gentle-
   man,
So long who journeyed on the holy quest
Forgotten of these younger days, and now
Come back among us to receive reward
For those long sufferings ; in days of peace,
In fruitful love, and marriage happiness.
So, to the poet's tourney.

HERALD.
           Sire, Lord Heinrich
Craves your high pardon.

LANDGRAVE.
       Ha ! He is not here !

WOLFRAM.
Our sturdy lover will not be consoled
For losing, as he phrases it, his friend.

LANDGRAVE.
Well, we forgive him the more readily
Because of the occasion.  One alone
Of all themes possible may grace this hour ; —
Love !  Let the lots of precedence be drawn.
Tannhäuser, you will string us once again
Your harp forgotten ?

TANNHÄUSER.
         That will I, my lord.

HERALD.
On the Lord Wolfram falls it first to sing.

WOLFRAM (sings).
Tender the smile, and faint the lover's sigh,
When first love dawns in the blue maiden sky,
Where happy peace is linked with purity.

As sad spring's sun starts on his daily race,
Reddens the east, as if in sad disgrace ;
So love first blushes on true maiden's face.

Soft, soft, the gaze of married folk, I think,
Limpid and calm as pools where cattle drink ;
And, when they kiss, most discontentments
    shrink !

Even as the stars together sing (we hear)
So sings the married life, a tuneful sphere.
Husband is he, and she is very dear.

How truly beautiful it is to see
Old age in perfect unanimity,
Affections smooth, and buzzing like a bee.

The sun sets, in conjunction with the moon.
Death comes at last, a pleasure and a boon,
And they arrive in heaven very soon.
    [*Immense, spontaneous, uncontrollable
       applause sweeps like a whirlwind
       through the court.*

AN UNKNOWN MINSTREL (*breaking in
       unheralded*).
Tender the phrase, and faint the melody,
When poets praise a maiden's purity ;
Platitude linked to imbecility.
         [*Murmurs of surprise.*

As 'mongst spring's sprigs sprouts sunshine's
    constant face ;
Or as a mill grinds on, with steady pace ;
So sprouts, so grinds, the unblushing
    commonplace.

Soft, soft the brain—
    [*The murmurs break into an indig-
       nant uproar.*

HERALD.
Silence !

LANDGRAVE.
      Sir Minstrel, you are insolent !
We do not know you, yet have borne with
    you,
Rudely uprising ere your turn was come :—
And you abuse our patience to insult
The noble minstrel whose impassioned song
Touched every heart.  Sing in your turn
    you may.
Love is the theme, not imbecility !

WOLFRAM.

That is the subject next his heart, no doubt !
[*Laughter.*

HERALD.

Lord Bertram !

BERTRAM.

I shall sing in other key.
[*Sings.*
He is the equal of the gods, my queen,
He crowned and chosen out of men,
Who sits beside thee, sees
Love's laughing ecstasies
Flame in thy face, and alter then
To the low light of passion dimly seen
In shaded woods and dells, Love's wide
demesne.

But me ! I burn with love ! My lips are
wan !
Thy face is turned—I flame ! I melt ! I
fall !
My heart is chilled and dark ;
My soul's ethereal spark
Is dulled for sorrow ; my despairs recall
At last Thy name, O gracious Paphian,
Lady of Mercy to the love of man !

Come, come, immortal, of the many thrones !
Sparrows and doves in chariot diamonded
Drawn through the midmost air !
O Lady of despair,
Who bound the golden helmet of Thine
head ?
Whose voice rings out the pitiful low tones :
" Who, who hath wronged thee ? And my
power atones.

" She who now doth flee, shall soon pursue
thee ;
" She who spurns thy gifts, with gifts shall
woo thee ;
" She who loves not, she shall cleave unto
thee,
    " Thou the unwilling ! "

Peer of Gods is he, equal soul to theirs,
    Who lingers in thy passionate embrace :
        Whose languor-laden kiss
        Cleaves where thy bosom is
A throne of beauty for thy throat and face !
In these dark joys and exquisite despairs,
O Love, let Death lay finger unawares !

LANDGRAVE.

Passion and music—but no Principle !
How different is Tannhäuser !
(*To the unknown minstrel*) You, sir, next !
Sing of pure love and noble womanhood.
Our court loves not these wastrel troubadours,
Loose locks, flushed faces, soul's unseemli-
ness.

THE UNKNOWN MINSTREL (*sings*).

Amid earth's motley, Gaia's cap and bells,
    This too material, too unreal life,
Sing, sing the crown of tender miracles,
    The pure true wife !

Sing not of love, the unutterable one,
    The love divine that Mary has to men.
Seek not the winepress and the rising sun
    Beyond thy ken !

TANNHÄUSER (*aside*).

Who is this man that reads my inmost
thoughts ?

THE UNKNOWN MINSTREL.

I sing of love, most delicate and pure,
    Surely the crown of life ! How slow
    and sweet
Its music ! Shall the ecstasy endure,
    Sunshine on wheat ?

Where leads this gentle love ? I see you
sigh !
    The scythe is laid unto the golden grain :
A note of utter unreality
    Usurps the strain.

I sing not of that other flame of hell
  Wrapping with torture the delighted
    brow—
But thou ! who knowest, and hast known,
    so well,
  Sing thou !
    [TANNHÄUSER, *entranced, imagines*
      *himself to be still in Venusberg.*


        TANNHÄUSER (*aside*).

I have been dreaming that I left this place,
Escaped with life, wooed my Elizabeth ;
My dreams are always strange in Venusberg.
                        [*Taking his harp.*
Sing thee again, dear lady, of our joy ?
Listen, then, listen ! For some sombre finger,
Other than mine, impulses on the string.
This tune I knew not ! See, the strings are
    moved
Subtly as if by witchcraft—or by God !
                              [*Sings.*
In the Beginning God began,
And saw the Night of Time begin ;
Chaos, a speck ; and space, a span ;
Ruinous cycles fallen in,
And Darkness on the Deep of Time.
Murmurous voices call and climb ;
Faces, half-formed, arise ; and He
Looked from the shadow of His throne,
The curtain of Eternity ;
He looked—and saw Himself alone,
And on the sombre sea, the primal one,
Faint faces, that might not abide ;
Flicker, and are fordone.
So were they caught within the spacious tide,
The sleepy waters that encased the world.
Monsters rose up, and turned themselves,
    and curled
Into the deep again.


The darkness brooded, and the bitter pain
Of chaos twisted the vast limbs of time
In horrid rackings : then the spasm came :
The Serpent rose, the servant of the slime,
In one dark miracle of flame
Unluminous and void : the silent claim
Of that which was, to be : the cry to climb,

The bitter birth of Nature : uttermost Night
Dwelt, inaccessible to sound and sight ;
Shielded from Voice, impervious to Light.


Lo ! on the barren bosom, on the brine,
The spirit of the Mighty One arose,
A flickering light, a formless triple flame,
The self-begotten, the impassive shrine,
The seat of Heaven's archipelagoes ;
Yet lighted not the glory whence it came,
Nor shone upon the surface of the sea.
Time, and the Great One, and the Nameless
    Name,
Held in their grip the child, Eternity.
Silence and Darkness in their womb with-
    held
That spiritual fire, and brooded still :
Nature and Time, their soleness undispelled,
Ever awaiting the eternal Will.
And Law was unbegotten : uttermost Night
Dwelt, inaccessible to sound and sight ;
Shielded from Voice, impervious to Light.


Then grew within the barren womb of this
The Breath of the Eternal and the Vast,
Softer than dawn, and closer than a kiss—
And lo ! the chaos and the darkness passed !
At the creative sigh the Light became.
Chaos rolled back in the abundant flame.
The vast and mystic Soul,
The Firmament, a living coal,
Flamed 'twixt the glory and the sea below.
The whirling force began.   The atom whirled
In vortices of flashing matter : wild as snow
On mountain tops by the wind-spirits hurled,
Blinding and blind, the sparks of spirit curled
Each to its proper soul ; the wide wheels flow,
Orderly streams, and lose the rushing speed,
Meet, mingle, marry.   Fire and air express
Their dews and winds of molten loveliness,
Fine flakes of arrowy light, the dawn's first
    deed,
Metallic showers and smoke self-glittering
For many an aeon.   Wild the pennons spring
Of streaming flame !   Then, surging from
    the tide,

Grew the desirable, the golden one,
Separate from the sun.
Now fire and air no more exult, exceed,
Are balanced in the sphere. The waters wide
Glow on the bosom of fixed earth ; and Need,
The Lady of Beginning, also was.
Thus was the firmament a vital glass,
The waters as the vessel of the soul ;
Thus earth, the mystic basis of the whole,
Was smitten through with fire, as chrysopras,
Blending, uniting, and dividing it,
Volcanic, airy, and celestial.

I rose within the elemental ball,
And lo ! the Ancient One of Days did sit !
His head and hair were white as wool, His
    eyes
A flaming fire : and from the splendid mouth
Flashed the Eternal Sword ! [1]
Lo ! Lying at his feet as dead, I saw
The leaping-forth of Law :
Division of the North wind and the South,
The lightning of the armies of the Lord ;
East rolled asunder from the rended West ;
Height clove the depth : the Voice begotten
    said :
" Divided be thy ways and limited ! "
Answered the reflux and the indrawn breath :
" Let there be Life, and Death ! "

" The Earth, she shall be governed by her
    parts : [2]
Division be upon her ! Let her glory
From crown to valley, source and spring to
    mouth,
North unto South,
Smooth gulf and sea to rugged promontory,
Always be vexed and drunken, that the
    hearts
Ruling her course round alway in the sky ;
And as an handmaid let her serve and die !
One season, let it still confound another ;
No man behold his brother ;
No creature in it or upon, the same !

[1] See Daniel vii. 9.
[2] This passage is a paraphrase of the 19th
" call " in Dr. Dee's book, referred to above.

Her members, let them differ ; be no soul
Equal ! Let thought, let reasonable things,
Bow to thy wings,
Thy manifest control,
Vexation ! weeding out of one another.
Their dwelling-places, let them lose their
    name !
The work of man, and all his pomp and power,
Deface them : shatter the aspiring tower !
Let all his houses be as caves and holes,
Unto the Beast I give them. And their
    souls—
Lift up the shadowy hand !—
Confound with darkness them that under-
    stand !
For why ?
Me, the Most High,
It doth repent Me, having made mankind !
Let her be known a little while, and then
A little while a stranger. Dumb and blind,
Deaf to the Light and Breath of Me be men !
She is become an harlot's bed, the home
And dwelling of the fallen one ! Arise !
Ye heavens, ye lower serving skies !
Beneath My dome
Serve ye the lofty ones. The Governors,
Them shall ye govern. Cast the fallen down !
Bring forth with them that are Fertility's !
Destroy the rotten ! Let no shores
Remain in any number ! Add and crown,
Diminish and discrown, until the stars
Be numbered ! Rise, ye adamantine bars !
Let pass your Masters ! Move ye and
    appear !
Execute judgment and eternal ill,
The law of justice, and the law of fear.
It is my Will ! "

So shed the primal curse
Its dreadful stature, its appalling shape.
In giant horror the clouds rolling drape
Earth, like a pluméd pall upon an hearse,
Till God looms up, half devil and half ape,
Heaven exulting in the hateful rape ;
And still the strong curse rolls
Over accurséd and immortal souls,
Covering the corners of the universe
Without escape.

This is the evil destiny of man :
The desperate plan
Made by the Ancient One, to keep His
   power.
Limits He set, made space unsearchable
Yet bounded, made time endless to transcend
Man's thought to comprehend :
Builded the Tower
Of life, and girded it with walls of hell,
The name of Death.   This limit in all things
Baffles the spirit wings,
Chains the swift soul ; for even Death is
   bound.
In its apparent amplitude I saw,
I, who have slept through death, have surely
   found
The old accursèd law,
And death has changed to life.   This task
   alone
Shoots to the starry throne :
That if man lack not purpose, but succeed,
Reaching in very deed
Impersonal existence ;—Lo !
Man is made one with God, an equal soul.
For he shall know
The harmony, the oneness of the Whole.

This was my purpose.   Vain,
Ah vain !   The Star of the Unconquered
   Will
Centred its vehemence and light, to stain
In one successful strain
The stainless sphere of the unchangeable,
With its own passionate, desperate breath
Ever confronting the dark gate of Death.
I passed that gate !   O pitiful !   The same
Mystery holds me, and the flame
Of Life stands up, unbroken citadel,
Beyond my sight, vague, far, intangible.
Broken are will, and witchery, and prayer.
Remains the life of earth, which is but hell,
Destiny's web, and my immense despair.

### LANDGRAVE.

Your words are terrible !   We knew them
   true
Even while you sang.   But see ! the light
   of day !

Beauty in all things and—for you—true love !
All the blind horror of the song recedes.
There is a sequel ; is there not, my friend ?
Of love, your theme, we have not heard a
   note.

### TANNHÄUSER.

That is a question.   I am not so sure
My song was not entirely to that end.

### WOLFRAM.

Yes, poet, true one that you are indeed !
You show us the dilemma of the soul,
The Gordian knot Love only hews asunder.

### TANNHÄUSER.

Or—shall I say ?—soothes only, bandages,
Not heals the sore of Destiny ?

### WOLFRAM.
                                   No, certes,
But substitutes for one reality
Another—and a lovely pleasant one.

### TANNHÄUSER.

Existence is illusion after all ;
Man, a bad joke ; and God, mere epigram !
If we must come to that.   And likewise love.

### LANDGRAVE.

You have dipped somewhat in philosophy
Of a too cynical and wordy sort.

### TANNHÄUSER.

To logic there is one reality,
Words.   But the commonsense of humankind
By logic baffles logic, chains with Deed
The lion Thought.   It is a circle, friends !
All life and death and mystery ravel out
Into one argument—the rounded one.

### THE UNKNOWN MINSTREL.

Count me your children their arithmetic !
Zero, the circle, grows to one, the line :
Both limitless in their own way.   Proceed.

Two is by shape the Coptic aspirate,[1]
Life breathed, and death indrawn.  And so
Rounds you at last the ten, completion's self,
The circle and the line.  Why stick at
   nought?

#### BERTRAM.

Only a donkey fastened to a post
Moves in a circle.

#### LANDGRAVE.

                 This is noble talk !

#### THE UNKNOWN MINSTREL.

Leave the wide circle—word and argument !
Move to the line—the steady will of man,
That shall attract the Two, the Breath of
   Life,
The Holy Spirit : land you in the Three,
Where form is perfect—in the triangle.

#### TANNHÄUSER.

My friend, the Three is infinitely small,
Mere surface.  And I seek the Depth divine !

#### THE UNKNOWN MINSTREL.

The solid !  But the triangle aspires
To that same unity that you despise,
And lo ! the Pyramid !  The Sages say :
Unite that to the Sphinx, and all is done,
Completion of the Magnum Opus.

#### TANNHÄUSER.

                 No !
Each new dimension lands me farther yet
In the morass of limit.

#### THE UNKNOWN MINSTREL.

               Be it so !
But follow me through all the labyrinth,
And ten rewards us.  And your Zero's found
To have an actual value and effect
On unity—your Will.

     [1]

#### TANNHÄUSER.

              What's then to seek ?

#### THE UNKNOWN MINSTREL.

The fourth dimension, for the early step.

#### LANDGRAVE.

It seems this talk is merely mystical.
This is no College of the Holy Ghost
For Rosencreutz his mystifying crew ![1]

#### A COURTIER.

A Poet's tourney, and the theme is Love !

#### THE UNKNOWN MINSTREL.

There is a sequel to our poet's song,
And he will sing it.

#### TANNHÄUSER.

            No ! I know it not !

#### THE UNKNOWN MINSTREL.

The winepress and the sun !

#### TANNHÄUSER (*again in Venusberg*).

            My spouse and Queen !
Bright Goddess of the amber limbs, the lips
Redder than poppies in the golden corn
That is your mane !  Listen, the after-song !
               [*Taking his harp.*

#### LANDGRAVE.

What are these words?

#### THE UNKNOWN MINSTREL.

            Let silence now abide :
Disturb not the impassioned utterance !

#### TANNHÄUSER.       [*Sings.*

Can you believe the deadly will's decree,
The bitter earnestness of this desire,
The deep intention, the solemnity,
Profound as night and penetrant as fire,

[1] The secret headquarters of the Rosicrucians was named by them Collegium Spiritus
Sancti.

The awful grasping at the Infinite,
Even as I grapple at the breasts of thee,
The seeking and the striving to the light
Deep in thine eyes, where Hell flames
    steadily?
I am not clinging thus
Despairing to the body of thy sin
For mere delight—Ah, deadly is to us
The pleasure wrapping us, and holding in
All love, all hate—the miserable way!
Dawns no devouring day
Still on the infinite slow tune of limbs
Moving in rapture; sleepy echo swims
In the dissolving brain,
Love conquering lassitude at last to win
Pain out of peace, and pleasure from a pang;
Then, scorpion-stung of its own terrible tang,
Burnt of its own fire, soiled of its own stain,
Falls conquered as a bird
Bolt-stricken through the brain,
To the resounding plain:
The double word,
The seesaw of all misery—begin
The alluring mysteries of lust and sin;
Ends their delight!—and are they clear to
    sight?
Or mixed with death, compact of night?
Begin—the bitter tears of impotence,
The sad permuted sense
Of this despair—what would you? and re-
    new
The long soft warfare—the enchanted arms, .
The silken body's charms,
The lips that murmur and the breasts that
    sting;
The eyes that sink so deep
Beyond the steeps and avenues of sleep,
And of their wonder bring
No ultimation from the halls of night,
The slippery staircase, and the Fatal Throne,
The Evil House, the Fugitive of Light,
The great Unluminous, the Formless One!
Stoop not! Beneath, a precipice is set,
The Seven Steps. Stoop not, forget
Never the Splendid Image, and the realm
Where lightnings overwhelm
The evil, and the barren, and the vile,
In God's undying smile!

Stoop not, O stoop not, to yon splendid
    world,
Yon darkly-splendid, airless, void, inane,
Blind confines in stupendous horror curled,
The sleepless place of Terror and distress,
Luring damned souls with lying loveliness,
The Habitation and the House of Pain.
For that is their abode, the Wretched Ones,
Of all unhappiness the sons!

And when, invoking often, thou shalt see
That formless Fire; when all the earth is
    shaken,
The stars abide not, and the moon is gone,
All Time crushed back into Eternity,
The Universe by earthquake overtaken;
Light is not, and the thunders roll,
The World is done:
When in the darkness Chaos rolls again
In the excited brain:
Then, O then call not to thy view that visible
Image of Nature; fatal is her name!
It fitteth not thy body to behold
That living light of Hell,
The unluminous, dead flame,
Until that body from the crucible
Hath passed, pure gold!
For, from the confines of material space,
The twilight-moving place,
The gates of matter, and the dark threshold,
Before the faces of the Things that dwell
In the Abodes of Night,
Spring into sight
Demons dog-faced, that show no mortal sign
Of Truth, but desecrate the Light Divine,
Seducing from the sacred mysteries.

But, after all these Folk of Fear are driven
Before the avenging levin
That rives the opening skies,
Behold that Formless and that Holy Flame
That hath no name;
That Fire that darts and flashes, writhes and
    creeps
Snake-wise in royal robe,
Wound round that vanished glory of the
    globe,
Unto that sky beyond the starry deeps,

Beyond the Toils of Time—then formulate
In thine own mind, luminous, concentrate,
The Lion of the Light, a child that stands
On the vast shoulders of the Steed of God :
Or winged, or shooting flying shafts, or shod
With the flame-sandals.    Then, lift up thine
    hands !
Centre thee in thine heart one scarlet thought
Limpid with brilliance of the Light above !
Draw into nought
All life, death, hatred, love :
All self concentred in the sole desire—
Hear thou the Voice of Fire !

This hope was Zoroaster's—this is mine !
Not one but many splendours hath the Shrine :
Not one but many paths approach the gate
That guards the Adytum, fortifying Fate !
Mine was, by weariness of blood and brain,
Mere bitter fruit of pain
Sought in the darkness of an harlot's bed,
To make me as one dead :
To loose the girders of the soul, and gain
Breathing and life for the Intelligible ;
Find death, yet find it living.   Deep as Hell
I plunged the soul ; by all blind Heaven
    unbound
The spirit, freed, pierced through the maze
    profound,
And knew Itself, an eagle for a dove.
So in one man the height and deep of love
Joined, in two states alternate (even so
Are life and death)—shall one unite the
    two,
My long impulsive strife ?
Did I find life ?
The real life—to know
The ways of God.   Alas ! I never knew.
Then came our Lady of the Sevenfold Light,
Showed me a distant plan, distinct and clear,
As twilight to the dayspring and the night,
Dividing and uniting even here :
The middle path—life interfused with death—
Pure love ; the secret of Elizabeth !
This is my secret—in the man's delight
To lose that stubborn ecstasy for God !
To this clear knowledge hath my path been
    trod

In deepest hell—in the profoundest sky !
This knowledge, the true immortality,
I came unto through pain and tears,
Tigerish hopes, and serpent loves, and dragon
    fears,
Most bitter kisses, salted springs and dry ;
In those deep caverns and slow-moving years,
When dwelt I, in the Mount of Venus, even I !
    [*The spell is broken, and uproar
    ensues.*

LANDGRAVE.

The fiend !   The atheist !   Devil that you
    are !

VOICES.

Kill him, ay, kill him !

TANNHÄUSER.

                    Crucify him, say !
    [TANNHÄUSER *extends his arms as
    on a cross.*

LANDGRAVE.

Blaspheme not !   Dare not to insult the sign
Of our Redemption !   Gentlemen and peers,
What say you ?  shall he live to boast himself,
The abandoned, perjured, the apostate soul,
Daring to come to our pure court to brag
Of his incredible vileness ?   To link up
The saintly purity of this my child
With his seducer's heart of hell !   My voice !
Death !   Your cry echoes me ?

VOICES.

                    Death !   Death !

TANNHÄUSER.

                    Leap out,
Sword of my fathers !  You have heard my
    harp !
Its music stings your vile hypocrisy
Into mere hatred.   Truth is terrible !
You, cousin, taken in adultery !
You, Wolfram, lover of the kitchen maids !
You, Jerome—yes, I know your secret deeds !

You, ladies ! Are your faces painted thus
Not to hide wrinkles of debauchery ?
To catch new lovers ?

LANDGRAVE.

Stop the lying mouth !
Friends, your sword-service !

TANNHÄUSER.

Will they answer you ?
My arm is weary as your souls are not
Of beastliness: I have drawn my father's
sword,
Hard as your virtue is the easy sort,
Heavy to handle as your loves are light,
Smooth as your lies, and sharper than your
hates !
I know you ! Cowards to the very bone !
[Driving them out.
Who fights me, of this sworded company ?
Cannot my words have sting in them enough,
Now, to make one of you turn suddenly
And stab me from behind ? Out, out with
you !
Fling-to the doors ! A murrain on the curs!
So, I am master !

THE UNKNOWN MINSTREL.

Well and merrily done !
But look you to the lady ; she has swooned.

TANNHÄUSER.

Who are you, sir, stood smiling, nonchalant,
At all the turmoil, ridiculing it ?
You knew the secret symbol of my life,
You forced me to that miserable song.

THE UNKNOWN MINSTREL.

My name, sir, at your service, is Geſchiſt.

TANNHÄUSER.

Sent ? And the purpose of your coming
here ?
You must wield power to keep them silent so,
When the first word had culminated else
In twice the tempest echoed to the last !
VOL. I.

THE UNKNOWN MINSTREL.

It was most necessary for yourself
To formulate your thought in word.
Enough—
The thought transmuted in the very act.

TANNHÄUSER.

You know ? You know ! The new illusion
gone !
Bitter, O bitter will it be to say !

THE UNKNOWN MINSTREL.

Due grace and courage will be found for you.
Farewell, Tannhäuser !

TANNHÄUSER.

Shall we meet again ?

THE UNKNOWN MINSTREL.

There is one glamour you must wreathe in
gloom
Before you come to the dark hill of dreams.

TANNHÄUSER.

My soul is sick of riddling. Fare you well !
[Exit THE UNKNOWN MINSTREL.
Wake, wake, poor child, poor child, Eliza-
beth !

ELIZABETH.

What says my dear one? I have been with
God.

TANNHÄUSER (aside).

How shall I speak ? A violent good-bye,
As one distraught, ashamed ? I had unbared
My bosom to these folk, but the sole pride,
My father's gift—to be a gentleman—
Forbade the dying, welcome otherwise,
At any despicable hands as theirs.
They, they might boast—*we hundred swords
or so
Set on the mighty Tannhäuser, and slew him.
We, scarce an hundred ! Yes, believe it, sirs*

R

*We are not so feeble !*—But death anyhow
Cuts and not loosens the entangled life.
Be mine the harder and the better way,
The single chance : not hope ; appeal no
  more ;
Hardly the arrowy wisdom of despair ;
Hardly the cowardice or courage yet
To drift, nor cursing nor invoking God.

ELIZABETH.

I heard, I pure, I virginal, your song ;
The shameful story of your intercourse
With—fiend or woman ?  And your burning
  will,
Even in that horror, to the Highest ; at last
Your choice of me—the middle course of
  them,
Pure human love ?  And, if your song be true,
As I, who heard the voice, the earnestness,
Saw the deep eyes, and truth aflame in them,
Know—then the choice be Mary's and not
  mine !
I love you better, were that possible ;
Will make you a true wife, and lead your
  hand,
Or be led by you, in the pleasant path.
For me, I enter not—Blessèd be God !—
In those dark problems that disturb your soul.
Mine is the simple nature.  Look at me !

TANNHÄUSER.

O Lady pure, miracle of true love,
I have a bitter word and harsh to say.
This is my curse—no sooner do I speak,
Or formulate my mind in iron words,
Than my mind grows, o'erleaps the limit set,
And I perceive the truth that lies beyond—
One further step into a new-fallen night.
Hear then—I hate to hurt your perfect soul ;
I hate myself because I love you still
In that strange intermediate consciousness,
The reason and the mind !  This middle way
Ancients called safe [1]—that damns it in-
  stantly !
Without some danger nothing great is done !
Let me be God !  Or, failing of that task,

[1] " In medio tutissimus ibis."—OVID.

Were it but by an unit, let me fall !
And, falling, be it from so great a height
That I may reach some uttermost Abyss,
Inhabit it and reign, most evil one
Of all the Horrors there—and in that path
Seem, even deluded, to approach once more
Infinity.  For all the limitless
Hath no distinction—evil is no more,
And good no more.

ELIZABETH.

  But God is absolute Good !

TANNHÄUSER.

No ! He is Not !  That negative alone
Shadows His shadow to our mortal mind.

ELIZABETH.

That is too deep ; I cannot fathom you.

TANNHÄUSER.

Define, give utterance to this "Good."  You
  see
God slips you, He the Undefinable !
Not good ! Not wise ! Not anything at all
That heart can grasp, or reason frame, or soul
Shadow the sense of !

ELIZABETH.

  He is far too great !
I see !

TANNHÄUSER.

  Not great !  The consciousness of man
Their many generations moulded so
To fix in definite ideas, and clothe
Their Maker in the rags.  If skies are vast,
So gems are tiny : who shall choose between?
Who reads the riddle of the Universe?
All words !  Thus, from his rock-wrought
  peeking-point
Out speers the hermit : " See, the sun is
  dead ! "
It shines elsewhere.  You from your tiny
  perch,
The corner of the corner of the earth,

Itself a speck in solar life ; the sun,
For all I know, a speck among the stars,
Themselves one corporate molecule of
    space !—
You from your perch judge, label, limit Him !
Not that your corner is not equally
The centre and the whole. Fool's talk it is !
Consider the futility of mind !
Realise utterly how mean, how dull,
How fruitless is Philosophy !

ELIZABETH.
                  Indeed
My brain is baffled. But I see your point.
Talking of God, even imagining,
Insane ! But for aspiring—that I will !

TANNHÄUSER.
That is true marriage, in my estimate.
Aspire together to one Deity ?
Yes ! But to love thee otherwise than that ?

ELIZABETH.
This one thing clearly do I understand :
We shall not marry. It is well, my lord.

TANNHÄUSER.
Miserable, miserable me ! I bring
Hate and disruption and unhappiness
Unto all purity I chance to touch.
I have no hope but I am fallen now ;
So journey, in this purpose of despair,
To Lilith and the Venusberg.

ELIZABETH.
               Oh no !
Grant me one boon—the one that I shall
    ask
Ever in this world ! Promise me !

TANNHÄUSER.
                Alas !
One promise gave I once to woman—that
Drove me to this illusion of your love,
And broke your heart.

ELIZABETH.
          Oh no, I shall not die.
Have I not Mary and the angels yet ?

TANNHÄUSER.
You are so pure, so pitiful—your word
Cannot bring evil. Yes, I promise you !

ELIZABETH.
Go then the bitter pilgrimage to Rome,
Gain absolution for this piteous past
From him that owns the twin all-opening keys
That bar your infinite on either side.
Then ! look with freshness, hope, and fortitude
Still to the summit—the ideal God.

TANNHÄUSER.
I have no hope nor trust in man at all ;
But I will go. Fare well, Elizabeth !
    [*Going, returns and kneels before her.*
Dare you once kiss these gray and withered
    brows?
As 'twere some flower that fell amid my hair.
The lotus of eternal hope and life.

ELIZABETH.
Dare I ? I kiss you once upon the brow,
Praying that God will make the purpose clear,
And on the eyes—that He may lend them light.
    [TANNHÄUSER *rises, and silently de-*
        *parts.*
Oh God! Oh God! That I have loved him so !
Be merciful ! Be merciful ! to him,
The great high soul, bound in the lofty sin ;
To me, the little soul, the little sin !

## ACT V.

  " One birth of my bosom ;
     One beam of mine eye ;
    One topmost blossom
      That scales the sky.
Man, equal and one with me, man that is
    made of me, man that is I."
                   *Hertha.*

*A desolate and melancholy wood.*   *Nightfall.*

HEINRICH.
WELL, I am lost ! The whistle brings no
    hound,
The horn no hunter ! North and South are
    mixed

In this low twilight and the hanging boughs.
I have slept worse than this.  Poor Tann-
  häuser !
I met him walking, as in dream, across
The courtyard, while behind him skulked
  that crew
That lurked, and itched to kill him, him
  unarmed,
Not daring !  But he reached his hand to me!
"Good luck, old friend ! " and, smiling, he
  was gone.
Gone to the Pope—great soul to mounte-
  bank !
It was her wish, they whisper.  Well-a-day !
He's gone, and not a friend have I again.
This bank is soft with delicate white moss,
No pillow better in broad Germany.
Were Madeline but here !  What rustle stirs
These leaves?  A strong man sobbing !  The
  earth quakes
Responsive.    Hillo-ho !    Who comes by
  there ?

  [TANNHÄUSER *enters.  He appears
  old and worn ; but from his whole
  body radiates a dazzling light, and
  his face is that of the Christ crucified.*

Save us, Saints, save us !  I have looked on
  God !

### TANNHÄUSER.

Heinrich !  my friend, my old true-hearted
  friend !
Fear not !  I am not ghost, but living man !
Ah me, ah me, the sorrow of the world !

### HEINRICH.

Thou, Tannhäuser !  what miracle is this ?
Your body glows—with what unearthly light ?

### TANNHÄUSER.

I did not know.  Ah ! sorrow of this earth !
What tears are falling from the Pleiades !
What sobs tear out Orion's jewelled heart !
Ah me !  As these, as these !

### HEINRICH.

              Speak, speak to me !
Else, I am feared.   Why run these tears to
  earth ?
Why shakes your bosom ?   Why does glory
  flame
A crown, a cincture ?   What befell you there ?

### TANNHÄUSER.

I came to Rome across the winter snows
Barefoot, and through the lovely watered
  land
Rich in the sunshine—even unto Rome.
There knelt I with the other sinful folk
At the great chair of Peter.   Sobbed they
  out
From full repentant hearts their menial sins,
And got them peace.   But I told brutally
(Cynical phrase, contempt of self and him)
My sojourn in the Venusberg ; then he
Rose in his wrath, and shook the barren staff
Over my head, and cried—I heard his voice
Most like the dweller of the hurricane
Calm, small, and still, directing desolation ;
Death to the world athwart its path.—So he
Cried out upon me, " Till this barren staff
Take life, and bud, and blossom, and bear
  fruit,
And shed sweet scent—so long God casteth
  thee
Out from His glory ! "   Stricken, smitten,
  slain—
When—one unknown, a pilgrim with the rest,
Darting long rugged fingers and deep eyes,
Reached to the sceptre with his word and
  will—
Buds, roses, blossoms !   Lilies of the Light !
Bloom, bloom, the fragrance shed upon the
  air !
Out flames the miracle of life and love !
Out, out the lights !  Flame, flame, the rushing
  storm !
Darkness and death, and glory in my soul !
Swept, swept away are pope and cardinal,
Palace and city !   There I lay beneath
The golden roof of the eternal stars,
Borne up on some irremeable sea

That glowed with most internal brilliance ;
Borne up, borne up by hands invisible
Into a firmament of secret light
Manifest, open, permeating me !
Then, then, I cried upon the mystic Word !
(That once begot in me the Venusberg)
And lo ! that light was darkness—in the face
Of That which gleamed above.   And verily
My life was borne on the dark stream of death
Down whirling aeons, linked abysses, columns
Built of essential time.   And lo ! the light
Shed from Her shoulders whom I dimly saw ;
Crowned with twelve stars and hornéd as the moon ;
Clothed with a sun to which the sun of earth
Were tinsel ; and the moon was at Her feet [1]—
A moon whose brilliance breaks the sword of song
Into a million fragments ; so transcends
Music, that starlight-sandalled majesty !
Then—shall I contemplate the face of Her ?
O Nature !   Self-begotten !   Spouse of God,
The Glory of thy Countenance unveiled !
Thy face, O mother !   Splendour of the Gods !
Behold ! amid the glory of her hair
And light shed over from the crown thereof,
Wonderful eyes less passionate than Peace
That wept !   That wept !   O mystery of Love !
Clasping my hands upon the scarlet rose
That flamed upon my bosom, the keen thorns
Pierced me and slew !   My spirit was withdrawn
Into Her godhead, and my soul made One
With the Great Sorrow of the Universe,
The Love of Isis !   Then I fell away
Into some old mysterious abyss
Rolling between the heights of starry space ;
Flaming above, beyond the Tomb of Time,
Blending the darkness into the profound
Chasms of matter—so I fell away
Through many strange eternities of Space,

[1] Revelations xii. 1.

Limitless fields of Time.   I knew in me
That I must fall into the ground and die ;
Dwell in the deep a-many years, at last
To rise again—Osiris, slain and risen !
Light of the Cross, I see Thee in the sky,
My future !   I must perish from the earth,
Abide in desolate halls, until the hour
When a new Christ must needs be crucified.—
So weep I ever with Our Lady's tears,
Weep for the pain, the travail, the old curse ;
Weep, weep, and die.   So dawns at last the Grail,
The Glory of the Crucified !   Dear friend,
Be happy, for my heart goes out to you,
And most to that poor pale Elizabeth—
Were it not only that the selflessness
That fills me now, forbids the personal,
Casts out the individual, and weeps on
For the united sorrow of all things.
For if I die, it is not Tannhäuser,
Rather a spark of the supreme white light
That dwelt and flickered in him in old time ;
That Light, I say, that hides its flame awhile
To shine more fully—to redeem the world !
I say, then, " I " ; and yet it is not " I "
Distinct, but " I " incorporate in All.
I am the Resurrection and the Life !
The Work is finished, and the Night rolled back !
I am the Rising Sun of Life and Light,
The Glory of the Shining of the Dawn !
I am Osiris !   I the Lord of Life
Triumphant over death—
O Sorrow, Sorrow, Sorrow of the World !


HEINRICH.

This was my friend.   Deep night descends, perfused
With unsubstantial glory from beyond.
The stars are buried in the mist of light.
Beyond the hill the world is, and laments
Existence—the wide firmament of woe !

And he--his heart was great enough for
    all,
The fall of sparrows as the crash of stars.
The tears of lonely forests, and the pain
Of the least atom—all were in his heart.
Was that indeed the truth? that he should
    come
At last a Christ upon the waiting world,
Redeem it to more purpose than the
    last!
So fills his sorrow, and Her sympathy,
My common soul, that I am fain to fall
Upon my face, and cry aloud to God:
"O Thou, Sole Wise, Sole Pure, Sole
    Merciful,
Who hast thus shown Thy mystery to
    man:
Grant that his coming may be very soon!"
See, the sobs shake me like a little child.

The moon is crescent, waxing in the West.
Take the last kiss, dear.
                  What is the strange song?
[*The great Goddess ariseth, weeping
for the slain Osiris* TANNHÄUSER,
*the perfected through suffering.*

ISIS.

Isis am I, and from my life are fed
    All stars and suns, all moons that wax and
    wane,
Create and uncreate, living and dead,
    The Mystery of Pain.
I am the Mother, I the silent Sea,
    The Earth, its travail, its fertility.
Life, death, love, hatred, light, darkness,
    return to me—
    To Me!

# EPILOGUE

## A DEATH IN THESSALY.[1]

*Μόνος Θεῶν γὰρ θάνατος οὐ δώρων ἐρᾷ.*
—ÆSCH., *Fr. Niobe.*

FAREWELL! O Light of day, O torch
    Althæan!
The strange fruits lure me of Persephone;
I raise the last, the memorable pæan,
    Storm-throated, mouthed as the cave-roll-
      ing sea;
I lift the cup: deep draughts of blue Lethean!
    My wine to me.

O lamentable season of Apollo,
    When swoops his glory to the golden
      wave!
As all his children, so their lord shall follow!
    The flower he slew, the maiden he would
      save,[2]
As Itylus,[2] light woven, tuned! Oh swallow,
      Bewail their grave!

The gracious breast of Artemis may light me
    To men—yet loved I ever Artemis?
Surely the vine-song and the dance delight
    me,
    The sea-blue bowers where Aphrodite is.
Terrible gods and destinies excite me,
      The strange sad kiss.

Thus may no moon tell Earth my story after,
    No virgin sing my fame as virginal.

---

[1] The northern portion of Greece. It was
renowned for wizard rites.
[2] See Swinburne, Poems and Ballads, 1st
Series.

Yet some night-leaves the southern stream
    may waft her,
    Some amorous nymph across the wood
    may call
A loud mad chant; love, tears, harsh sombre
    laughter.
      No more at all.

Oh, mother, Oh, Demeter, in my burthen
    Let me assume thy sorrow singular;
A branching temple and an altar earthen,
    A fire of herbs, a clayen water-jar;
An olive grove to bind the sacred girth in
      Lone woods afar.

Let life burn gently thence, as when the
    ember
    In one faint incense-puff to shrineward
    dies.
No care, no pain, no craving to remember,
    One leap toward the knees and destinies,
Where shine Her lips like flames, Her
    breasts like amber,
      Like moons Her eyes.

For my heart turns—ah still!—in Sorrow's
    traces,
    Where sad chill footprints pash the sodden
    leaves;
Where ranged around me are the cold, gray
    faces;
    Fallen on the stubble are the rotten sheaves;
The vicious ghosts abound; and Chronos'
    paces
      No soul deceives.

Yet my heart looks to Madness as its mother,
  Remembering Who once caught me by
    the well;
And the strange loves of that misshapen Other,
  The feast of blood, the cold enchanted dell,
Where fire was filtered up through earth to
  smother
            Sick scents of hell.

And that wild night when vine-leaves wooed
    and clustered
  Round my wild limbs, and like a woman
    I went
Over the mountains—how the Northwind
  blustered !—
  And slew with them the beast, and was
    content.
The madness :—Oh ! the dreadful light that
  lustred
            The main event.

Ay ! the wild whirlings in the woodland
  reaches ;
The ghastly smile upon the Stone God's[1] lip;
The rigid tremors, anguish that beseeches
  From eye to eye fresh fervours of the whip ;
The mounded moss below the swaying
  beeches—
            Kiss me and clip !

Why ! the old madness grows !—how feebly
  lying
  Smooth by this bay where waves are
    tender flowers.
Winds, soft as the old kisses were, are sighing.
  Clouds drift across the sun for silken
    bowers.
The moon is up—an hastening nymph ! I,
  dying,
            Await the Hours.

[1] Priapus, like Jehovah, is the phallic god of
generation. It is to be remarked that Crowley
never uses Jehovah in this sense, but in the
later spiritualised sense of the Qabalists.

And thou, Persephone, I know thy story,
  That I must taste the terror of thy wrong :
How Hades ride across the promontory,
  Snatch my pale body in mid over-song ;
Drag me from sight of my Apollo's glory
            With horses strong.

Nay ! as Apollo half the day is shrouded,
  As Artemis twice seven nights is dark ;
Surely he shines in other lands unclouded,
  Surely her shaft shall find another mark.
So dawns the day on Acheron ghost-crowded,
            And on my bark.

I know not how yon world may prove, nor
  whither
  Hermes conduct me to what farther end.
Yet if these bays abide, this heart not
  wither,
  It cannot be I shall not find a friend.
Some pale immortal lover draw me thither !
            To kiss me bend !

Moreover, as Apollo re-arisen
  Flames, with a roaring of the morning
    sea,
Up from the stricken gray, the iron-barred
  prison,
Flashes his face again upon the lea,
And diamond dews the woodland ones
  bedizen ;
            So—so for me !

Some forty years this earth knew song and
  passion
  Pour from my lips, saw gladness in mine
    eyes !
Some forty shall I sing some other fashion,
  Dance in strange measures, change the
    key of sighs.
Then rise in Thessaly again, Thalassian !
            Only, more wise.

# APPENDIX

## QABALISTIC DOGMA

[This short explanatory article has been specially contributed by an Adept, revered alike for his intellectual gifts and his spiritual attainments by the few to whom he permits himself to be known. Thanks to him would be impossible, but the Editor wishes to express his gratitude to the student who kindly obtained for him the introduction. No liberties have been taken with the MS., even to the retention of the capitals, but the spelling of some Eastern names has been assimilated to the universal alphabet—*e.g.* Qabalah for Kabbala—with the permission of the author.]

THE Evolution of Things is thus described by the Qabalists.

First is Nothing, or the Absence of Things, אין, which does not and cannot mean Negatively Existing (if such an Idea can be said to mean anything), as S. Liddell Macgregor Mathers, who misread the Text and stultified the Commentary by he Light of his own Ignorance of Hebrew and Philosophy, pretends in his Translation of v. Rosenroth.

Second is Without Limit אין סוף, *i.e.*, Infinite Space.

This is the primal Dualism of Infinity; the infinitely small and the infinitely great. The Clash of these produces a finite positive Idea which happens (see בראשית, *infra*, vol. ii., for a more careful study, though I must not be understood to indorse every Word in our Poet-Philosopher's Thesis) to be Light, אור. This word אור is most important. It symbolises the Universe immediately after Chaos, the Confusion or Clash of the infinite Opposites. א is the Egg of Matter; ו is ט, the Bull, or Energy-Motion; and ר is the Sun, or organised and moving System of Orbs. The three Letters of אור thus repeat the three Ideas. The Nature of אור is thus analysed, under the figure of the ten Numbers and the 22 Letters which together compose what the Rosicrucians have diagrammatised under the name of Minutum Mundum. (See Table of Correspondences.) It will be noticed that every Number and Letter has its " Correspondence " in Ideas of every Sort; so that any given Object can be analysed in Terms of the 32. If I see a blue Star, I should regard it as a Manifestation of Chesed, Water, the Moon, Salt the Alchemical Principle, Sagittarius or What not, in respect of its Blueness—one would have to decide which from other Data—and refer it to the XVIIth Key of the Taro in Respect of its Starriness.

The Use of these Attributions is lengthy and various: I cannot dwell upon it: but I will give one Example.

If I wish to visit the Sphere of Geburah, I use the Colours and Forces appropriate: I go there: if the Objects which then appear to my spiritual Vision are harmonious therewith, it is one Test of their Truth.

So also, to construct a Talisman, or to invoke a Spirit.

The methods of discovering Dogma from sacred Words are also numerous and important: I may mention :—

(*a*) The Doctrine of Sympathies : drawn from the total Numeration of a Word, when identical with, or a Multiple or Submultiple of, or a Metathesis of, that of another Word.

(*b*) The Method of finding the Least Number of a Word, by adding (and re-adding) the Digits of its total Number, and taking the corresponding Key of the Taro as a Key to the Meaning of the Word.

(*c*) The Method of Analogies drawn from the Shape of the Letters.

(*d*) The Method of Deductions drawn from the Meanings and Correspondences of the Letters.

(*e*) The Method of Acrostics drawn from the Letters. This Mode is only valid for Adepts of the highest Grades, and then under quite exceptional and rare Conditions.

(*f*) The Method of Transpositions and Transmutations of the Letters, which suggest Analogies, even when they fail to explain in direct Fashion.

All these and their Varieties and Combinations, with some other more abstruse or less important Methods, may be used to unlock the Secret of a Word.

Of course with Powers so wide it is easy for the Partisan to find his favourite Meaning in any Word. Even the formal Proof $0 = 1 = 2 = 3 = 4 = 5 = \ldots \ldots = n$ is possible.

But the Adept who worked out this Theorem, with the very Intent to discredit the Qabalistic Mode of Research, was suddenly dumbfounded by the Fact that he had actually stumbled upon the Qabalistic Proof of Pantheism or Monism.

What really happens is that the Adept sits down and performs many useless Tricks with the Figures, without Result.

Suddenly the Lux dawns, and the Problem is solved.

The Rationalist explains this by Inspiration, the superstitious Man by Mathematics.

I give an Example of the Way in which one works. Let us take IAO, one of the "Barbarous Names of Evocation," of which those who have wished to conceal their own Glory by adopting the Authority of Zarathustra have said that in the holy Ceremonies it has an ineffable Power.

But what Kind of Power? By the Qabalah we can find out the Force of the Name IAO.

We can spell it in Hebrew יאו or יאע. The Qabalah will even tell us which is the true Way. Let us however suppose that it is spelt יאו. This adds up to 17.

But first of all it strikes us that I, A, and O are the three Letters associated with the three Letters ה in the great Name of Six Letters, אהיהוה, which combines אהיה and יהוה, Macroprosopus and Microprosopus. Now these feminine Letters ה conceal the "Three Mothers" of the Alphabet, א, מ, and ש. Replace these, and we get אשימוא, which adds up to 358, the Number alike of נחש, the Serpent of Genesis, and the Messiah. We thus look for redeeming Power in IAO, and for the Masculine Aspect of that Power.

Now we will see how that Power works. We have a curious Dictionary, which was made by a very learned Man, in which the Numbers from 1 to 10,000 fill the left hand Column, in Order, and opposite them are written all the sacred or important Words which add up to each Number.

We take this Book, and look at 17. We find that 17 is the number of Squares in the Swastika, which is the Whirling Disc or Thunderbolt. Also there is חון, a Circle or Orbit ; זור, to seethe or boil ; and some other Words, which we will neglect in this Example, though we should not dare to do so if we were really trying to find out a Thing we none of us knew.  To help our Deduction about Redemption, too, we find חדה, to brighten or make glad.

We also work in another Way.  I is the Straight Line or Central Pillar of the Temple of Life ; also it stands for Unity, and for the Generative Force.  A is the Pentagram, which means the Will of Man working Redemption.  O is the Circle from which everything came, also Nothingness, and the Female, who absorbs the Male.  The Progress of the Name shows then the Way from Life to Nirvana by means of the Will : and is a Hieroglyph of the Great Work.

Look at all our Meanings !  Every one shows that the Name, if it has any Power at all, and that we must try, has the Power to redeem us from the Love of Life which is the Cause of Life, by its masculine Whirlings, and to gladden us and to bring us to the Bosom of the Great Mother, Death.

Before what is known as the Equinox of the Gods, a little while ago, there was an initiated Formula which expressed these Ideas to the Wise.  As these Formulas are done with, it is of no Consequence if I reveal them.  Truth is not eternal, any more than God ; and it would be but a poor God that could not and did not alter his Ways at his Pleasure.

This Formula was used to open the Vault of the Mystic Mountain of Abiegnus, within which lay (so the Ceremony of Initiation supposed) the Body of our Father Christian Rosen Creutz, to be discovered by the Brethren with the Postulant as said in the Book called Fama Fraternitatis.

There are three Officers, and they repeat the Analysis of the Word as follows :—

Chief.  Let us analyse the Key Word—I.
2nd.   N.
3rd.   R.
All.   I.
Chief.  Yod. י
2nd.   Nun. נ
3rd.   Resh. ר
All.   Yod. י
Chief.  Virgo (♍) Isis, Mighty Mother.
2nd.   Scorpio (♏) Apophis, Destroyer.
3rd.   Sol (☉) Osiris, slain and risen.
All.   Isis, Apophis, Osiris, IAO.

All spread Arms as if on a Cross, and say :—

The Sign of Osiris slain !

Chief bows his Head to the Left, raises his Right Arm, and lowers his Left, keeping the Elbow at right Angles, thus forming the Letter L (also the Swastika).

The Sign of the Mourning of Isis.

2nd.  With erect Head, raises his Arms to form a V (but really to form the triple Tongue of Flame, the Spirit), and says :—

The Sign of Apophis and Typhon.

3rd. Bows his Head and crosses his Arms on his Breast (to form the Penta-gram).

The Sign of Osiris risen.

All give the Sign of the Cross, and say :—

L. V. X.

Then the Sign of Osiris risen, and say :—

Lux, the Light of the Cross.

This Formula, on which one may meditate for Years without exhausting its wonderful Harmonies, gives an excellent Idea of the Way in which Qabalistic Analysis is conducted.

First, the Letters have been written in Hebrew Characters.

Then the Attributions of them to the Zodiac and to Planets are substituted, and the Names of Egyptian Gods belonging to these are invoked.

The Christian Idea of I.N.R.I. is confirmed by these, while their Initials form the sacred Word of the Gnostics. That is, IAO. From the Character of the Deities and their Functions are deduced their Signs, and these are found to signal (as it were) the Word Lux (אור), which itself is contained in the Cross.

A careful Study of these Ideas, and of the Table of Correspondences, which one of our English Brethren is making, will enable him to discover a very great Deal of Matter for Thought in these Poems which an untutored Person would pass by.

To return to the general Dogma of the Qabalists.

The Figure of Minutum Mundum will show how they suppose one Quality to proceed from the last, first in the pure God-World Atziluth, then in the Angel-World Briah, and so on down to the Demon-Worlds, which are however not thus organised. They are rather Material that was shed off in the Course of Evolution, like the Sloughs of a Serpent, from which comes their Name of Shells, or Husks.

Apart from silly Questions as to whether the Order of the Emanations is con-firmed by Palæontology, a Question it is quite incompetent to discuss, there is no Doubt the Sephiroth are types of Evolution as opposed to Catastrophe and Creation.

The great Charge against this Philosophy is founded on its alleged Affinities with Scholastic Realism. But the Charge is not very true. No Doubt but they did suppose vast Storehouses of "Things of one Kind" from which, pure or mingled, all other Things did proceed.

Since ג, a Camel, refers to the Moon, they did say that a Camel and the Moon were sympathetic, and came, that Part of them, from a common Principle: and that a Camel being yellow brown, it partook of the Earth Nature, to which that Colour is given.

Thence they said that by taking all the Natures involved, and by blending them in the just Proportions, one might have a Camel.

But this is no more than is said by the Upholders of the Atomic Theory.

They have their Storehouses of Carbon, Oxygen, and such (not in one Place, but no more is Geburah in one Place), and what is Organic Chemistry but the Production of useful Compounds whose Nature is deduced absolutely from theoretical Considera-tions long before it is ever produced in the Laboratory?

The difference, you will say, is that the Qabalists maintain a Mind of each Kind behind each Class of Things of one Kind ; but so did Berkeley, and his Argument in that Respect is, as the great Huxley showed, irrefragable.   For by the Universe I mean the Sensible ; any other is Not to be Known ; and the Sensible is dependent upon Mind.   Nay, though the Sensible is said to be an Argument of an Universe Insensible, the latter becomes sensible to Mind as soon as the Argument is accepted, and disappears with its Rejection.

Nor is the Qabalah dependent upon its Realism, and its Application to the Works magical—but I am defending a Philosophy which I was asked to describe, and this is not lawful.

A great Deal may be learned from the Translation of the Zohar by S. Liddell Macgregor Mathers, and his Introduction thereto, though for those who have Latin and some acquaintance with Hebrew it is better to study the Kabbala Denudata of Knorr von Rosenroth, in Despite of the heavy Price ; for the Translator has distorted the Text and its Comment to suit his belief in a supreme Personal God, and in that degraded Form of the Doctrine of Feminism which is so popular with the Emasculate.

The Sephiroth are grouped in various Ways.   There is a Superior Triad or Trinity ; a Hexad ; and Malkuth : the Crown, the Father, and the Mother ; the Son or King ; and the Bride.

Also, a Division into seven Palaces, seven Planes, three Pillars or Columns : and the like.

The Flashing Sword follows the Course of the Numbers and the Serpent Nechushtan or of Wisdom crawls up the Paths which join them upon the Tree of Life, namely the Letters.

It is important to explain the Position of Daath or Knowledge upon the Tree. It is called the Child of Chokmah and Binah, but it hath no Place.   But it is really the Apex of a Pyramid of which the three first Numbers form the Base.

Now the Tree, or Minutum Mundum, is a Figure in a Plane of a solid Universe. Daath, being above the Plane, is therefore a Figure of a Force in four Dimensions, and thus it is the Object of the Magnum Opus.   The three Paths which connect it with the First Trinity are the three lost Letters or Fathers of the Hebrew Alphabet.

In Daath is said to be the Head of the great Serpent Nechesh or Leviathan, called Evil to conceal its Holiness.   (נחש = 358 = משיח, the Messiah or Redeemer, and מלכות = 496 = ליתך, the Bride.)   It is identical with the Kundalini of the Hindu Philosophy, the Kwan-se-on of the Mongolian Peoples, and means the magical Force in Man, which is the sexual Force applied to the Brain, Heart, and other Organs, and redeemeth him.

The gradual Disclosure of these magical Secrets to the Poet may be traced in these Volumes, which it has been my Privilege to be asked to explain.   It has been impossible to do more than place in the Hands of any intelligent Person the Keys which will permit him to unlock the many Beautiful Chambers of Holiness in these Palaces and Gardens of Beauty and Pleasure.

# THE WORKS

OF

# ALEISTER CROWLEY

*WITH PORTRAITS*

VOLUME II

Martino Publishing
Mansfield Centre, CT
2012

*Martino Publishing*
*P.O. Box 373,*
*Mansfield Centre, CT 06250 USA*

www.martinopublishing.com


ISBN   978-1-61427-279-3


© *2012  Martino Publishing*

Cover design by T. Matarazzo

*Printed in the United States of America On 100% Acid-Free Paper*

# THE WORKS

OF

# ALEISTER CROWLEY

*WITH PORTRAITS*

VOLUME II

FOYERS
SOCIETY FOR THE PROPAGATION OF
RELIGIOUS TRUTH
1906

# CONTENTS OF VOLUME II

# ORACLES

## THE AUTOBIOGRAPHY OF AN ART *

### 1905

### THE DEATH OF THE DRUNKARD.[1]

#### I.

TERROR, and darkness, and horrid despair!
Agony painted upon the once fair
Brow of the man who refused to give up
The love of the wine-filled, the o'erflowing
    cup.
"Wine is a mocker, strong drink is raging."
No wine in death is his torment assuaging.

#### II.

.    .    .    .    .

.    .    .    .    .

Just what the parson had told me when
    young:
Just what the people in chapel have sung:
"Wine is a mocker, strong drink is raging."

.    .    .    .

*Desunt cetera.*

### A PEEP BEHIND THE SCENES.

IN the hospital bed she lay,
    Rotting away!
Cursing by night and cursing by day,
    Rotting away!

[1] This, the earliest poem ever written by me,
has perished save the above fragment. Its
date is 1886.—A. C.
    It should be noted that this fragment is of a
wildly revolutionary tendency. It made him
the Ibsen of a school where a parson and a
chapel were considered with the rest of the
non-Plymouth-Brethren world as so many
devils let loose from hell.

The lupus is over her face and head,
Filthy and foul and horrid and dread,
And her shrieks they would almost wake the
    dead;
    Rotting away!

In her horrible grave she lay,
    Rotting away!
Rotting by night, and rotting by day,
    Rotting away!
In the place of her face is a gory hole,
And the worms are gnawing the tissues foul,
And the devil is gloating over her soul,
    Rotting away!

### LINES ON BEING INVITED TO MEET THE PREMIER IN WALES, SEPTEMBER 1892.

I WILL not shake thy hand, old man,
    I will not shake thy hand;
You bear a traitor's brand, old man,
    You bear a liar's brand.
Thy talents are profound and wide,
    Apparent power to win;
It is not everyone has lied
    A nation into sin.

And look thou not so black, my friend,
    Nor seam that hoary brow;
Thy deeds are seamier, my friend,
    Thy record blacker now.

* This volume consists of unpublished poems dating from 1886-1903. Concerning the title
Crowley writes, "The sense is of dead leaves drifting in the dusty cave of my mind." He
does not seem to have been aware that Coleridge gave the title "Sibylline Leaves" to a similar
collection.

Your age and sex forbid, old man,
　I need not tell you how,
Or else I'd knock you down, old man,
　Like that extremist cow.[1]

You've gained your every seat, my friend,
　By perjuring your soul ;
You've climbed to Downing Street, my friend,
　A very greasy poll.
You bear a traitor's brand, old man,
　You bear a liar's brand ;
I will *not* shake thy hand, old man,
　I will *not* shake thy hand.

　　　　　　[*And I didn't.*

## THE BALLOON.

*Written (at the age of fifteen, and still unsur-
passed) while in bed with measles at Ton-
bridge in Kent.*

　FLOATING in the summer air,
　　What is that for men to see?
　Anywhere and everywhere,
　　Now a bullet, now a tree—
　Till we all begin to swear :
　　What the devil can it be?

　See its disproportioned head,
　　Tiny trunk and limbs lopped bare,
　Hydrocephalus the dread
　　With a surgeon chopping there ;
　Chopping legs and arms all red
　　With the sticky lumps of hair.

　Like a man in this complaint
　　Floats this creature in the sky,
　Till the gaping rustics faint
　　And the smirking milkmaids cry,
　As the cord and silk and paint,
　　Wood and iron drifteth by.

　Floating in the summer sky
　　Like a model of the moon :—
　How supreme to be so high
　　In a treacherous balloon,
　Like the Kings of Destiny,
　　All the earth for their spittoon.

[1] Mr. Gladstone was attacked by a cow in
Hawarden Park in 1891.

Toads are gnawing at my feet.
　Take them off me quick, I pray !
Worms my juicy liver eat.
　Take the awful beasts away !
Vipers make my bowels their meat.
　Fetch a cunning knife and slay !

Kill the tadpoles in my lung,
　And the woodlice in my spine,
And the beast that gnaws my tongue,
　And the weasel at my chine,
And the horde of adders young
　That around mine entrails twine !

Come, dissect me !　Rip the skin !
　Tear the bleeding flesh apart !
See ye all my hellish grin
　While the straining vitals smart.
Never mind !　Go in and win,
　Till you reach my gory heart !

While my heart's soft pulse did go,
　Devils had it in their bands.
Doctors keep it in a row,
　Now, on varnished wooden stands :
And I really do not know
　If it is in different hands.

## SPOLIA OPIMA.

MY home is set between two ivory towers,
Fresh with the fragrance of a thousand flowers.
And the twin portals of a ruby door,
Portcullissed with the pearls of India's shore,
Loosed with a smile and opened with a kiss,
Bid me a joyous welcome there, I wis.
My home is on the brink of heaven's delight,
But for that endless day a lovelier night
Is in my home, that sunset's arms enfold,
Lit with the mellowness of autumn gold.

　　　．　　　．　　　．　　　．　　　．

Pillowed on linen of the purest white,
Half-hidden by her locks' luxurious night,
Maddened by those soft eyes of melting glow,
Enamoured of that breast of breathing snow,
Caught in the meshes of her fine-spun hair,
Rocked by the beating of her bosom fair,

Held by her lips too tempting and too warm,
Bewitched by every beauty of her form,
The blush upon her cheek is deeper red,
Half glad, and half repenting what she said.
A moment's struggle, as her form I press :—
One soft sad sigh. Love conquers. I possess.

## A WELCOME TO JABEZ.[1]

*Reprinted from the " Eastbourne Chronicle."*

GREAT Liberator, come again,
  Thy country needs thee sadly ;
In Scotland Yard they all complain
  They "want" thee, oh ! so badly.

Thou canst not tell the sighs and sobs
  That for thy presence yearn ;
And the great heart of England throbs
  With joy at thy return.

For many a year prolong thy stay
  By Portland's shady harbour ;
And all expenses we will pay—
  Especially the barber.

A change of work is rest, they say,
  So honest toil shall rest thee ;
No fears that thou must go away
  Need haunt thee and molest thee.

We pray a level-headed set
  Of fellow men, who know thee,
In some small measure grateful yet,
  May pay thee what is owed thee.

The joys of single blessedness,
  And undisturbed seclusion,
We envy for thee, we confess,
  Until thy final fusion.

## ELVINA.

*Written at Eastbourne.*

*Tune*—" German Evening Hymn."

WAS thy fault to be too tender ?
Was thine error to be weak ?
Was my kiss the chief offender
Pressed upon thy blushing cheek ?

[1] Jabez Balfour, author of the "Liberator" frauds.

Was it sin to press and press thee
  Till thy burning lips at last
Madly kissed me ? How I bless thee,
  Now, for that superb repast !

All-consuming, all-devouring,
  All-absorbing, burnt the flame ;
Burnt unchecked till, hotly showering,
  Passion disregarded Shame !

Was it sin—that moonlight madness?
  Was our passion so accurst ?
Sweetness damned to mother Sadness?
  Satisfaction to bring Thirst ?

Was our love to bring division?
  Nay ! ten thousand devils ! nay !
And a devil in a vision
  Hisses as I slumber, " Yea !

" Heaven of your accurst creation
  Shall become a hell of fire ;
Death for kisses, and damnation
  For your love shall God require."

## ADAPTATION OF "ONWARD, CHRISTIAN SOLDIERS" TO THE NEEDS OF BRETHREN.[1]

### PREFACE.

IN response to many suggestions from dear Brethren, I have adapted a hymn to the wants of the Church. In view of the grossly unscriptural nature of the original hymn (so-called) many changes have been rendered necessary, but I hope and trust that this has been effected without losing the grandeur of the original.[2] To this effort of mine certain "false brethren unawares brought in" have objected, saying, "Touch not the accursed thing." I pass over the blasphemy of their thus adapting verses of Scripture to their own vile ends.
  Let me, however, tell these "wolves in

[1] This astonishing piece of satire was composed after some weeks in the house of a Plymouth Brother. Almost every phrase used therein is a quotation, not a parody.
[2] See preface to "Hymns for the Little Flock," 1856, from which this stupefying sentence has been bodily taken.

sheep's clothing," these "clouds without water, carried about of winds; trees whose fruit withereth, without fruit, twice dead, plucked up by the roots; raging waves of the sea, foaming out their own shame; wandering stars, to whom is reserved the blackness of darkness for ever (Jude 12, 13), that they are "dogs, and sorcerers, and whoremongers, and murderers, and idolaters" (Rev. xxii. 15), and again, that they are "fearful and unbelieving, and abominable, and murderers, and whoremongers, and idolaters, and all liars" (Rev. xxi. 8), and that they "shall have their part in the lake which burneth with fire and brimstone, which is the second death" (Rev. xxi. 8), "where their worm dieth not, and the fire is not quenched" (Mark. ix. 44).

Let me only add that they are "a herd of many swine feeding" (Matt. viii. 30).

"Ye serpents, ye generation of vipers, how can ye escape the damnation of hell?" (Matt. xxiii. 33).

And now, belovèd brethren, with every prayer that this adaptation may prove of lasting blessing to You all, bringing forth "the fruits of the Spirit" (Gal. v. 22), especially "faith, hope and charity." "But the greatest of these is charity" (1 Cor. xiii. 13).

## "ONWARD, PLYMOUTH BRETHREN."

### Chorus.

ONWARD, Plymouth Brethren, marching
    as to war,
With the cross of jesus trampled on the
    floor;
Kelly, Lowe or Jewell [1] lead against the
    foe,
Forward into battle, see their followers
    go.
Onward, Plymouth Brethren, marching
    as to war,
With the cross of jesus trampled on the
    floor.

At the name of Barton, Raven's host doth flee,
On, M'Arthy's following, on to victory,

[1] These and others mentioned are or were great names among the contending "Brethren."

Stoney's scoundrels shiver at Our howls of
    rage,
Brothers, lift Your voices, Shriek aloud, Rampage!

Like a mighty army moves the Church of
    god.
Brothers, We are treading where the saints
    have trod.
We are all divided, fifty bodies We,
Fifty hopes and doctrines, nary charity.

Church and chapel perish! Open Plyms to
    hell!
But Our kind of Brethren still in safety
    dwell.
Raven's lot can never 'gainst the lord
    prevail,
We are his brave followers, you are Satan's
    tail.

Come then, outside peoples, join Our noble
    throng!
Blend with Ours your voices in the triumph
    song!
Glory, praise and honour unto Us alone!
Christians' necks our footstool, Heaven itself
    Our throne!

*P.S.*—BELOVED BRETHREN,—The spirit indeed is willing, but the flesh is weak. For I, like Balaam (in the old legend), was compelled to express our real feelings and not our pretended ones. This, of course, absolutely ruins the adaptation. In fact, I am not certain as to whether it does not rather give us away! Alas! we are only poor, weak, failing creatures! Your broken-hearted, broken-winded, broken-kneed brother,

      JUDAS CAIAPHAS TRUELOVE.

[The man Truelove was at once put out of fellowship. He will be certainly damned. —PILATE CROSSPATCH.]

## TO MRS O . . . . . N C . . . T.

*Written during the first session of the Licensing Committee of the London County Council.*

I WILL not bring abuse to point my pen,
  Nor a sarcastic tongue.
Think only what you might be, before men,
  If you were young.

What fierce temptations might not lovers
    bring
  In London's wicked city?
Perhaps you might yourself have one wee
    fling,
  If you were pretty.

What might not hard starvation drive you to,
  With Death so near and sure?
Perhaps it might drive even virtuous you,
  If you were poor.

But is it just, or grateful to the One
  That keeps even you from wrong,
Or even humble to shriek, " Get you gone,
  For I am strong " ?

Temptation has not touched you, Mrs. C . . . t !
  Forsooth, I do not lie there,
For you are only not the thing you aren't
  Through being neither.

And since some fall in Life's tremendous
    storm,
  And you are on your feet,
Were it not better with a bosom warm
  And accents sweet

To help to raise (and no man will upbraid
    you)
  Your sisters fallen far?
'Tis vain ! God's worst omission—Heart—
    has made you
  The thing you are !

## THE LITTLE HALF-SOVEREIGN.[1]

RED is the angry sunset,
  Murk is the even grey,
Heavy the clouds that hover
  Over our Hell to-day.

" Say, in our dark Gomorrah,
  Lord, can an angel find
Fifty, but fifty, righteous—
  Body—I say not Mind."

Sadly the angel turneth—
  " Stay, ere thou fleest, stay ;
Canst thou not find me twenty?"
  " Nay " is the answer, " nay."

" Are there not ten, bright spirit,
  Hidden, nor quickly seen,
Somewhere in Hell's dark alleys,
  Somewhere in Walham Green?

" Speak, for I see thy forehead
  Sadden in dark denial,
Is there not one that standeth
  Tempter and longsome trial?

" Is not a candle burning
  Somewhere amid the flame
Scorching the smoke of London
  With its eternal shame?

" Is there no gate so stubborn
  That shall not find a key,
That with our Sovereign's image
  Graven in majesty?"

[1] The occasion of this poem was the meeting of the author with a fair and virtuous damsel of pleasant address and conversation. She politely asked him to call at her residence on the following Sunday : but, on his doing so, she straightway demanded half-a-sovereign, and proffered a shameful equivalent. The indignant boy went off and gave vent to his feelings in the above rhymes.

Why not the Devil's portrait
  Graven in Walham Green?
Why with the bare suggestion
  Dare we insult our Queen?

Give me the golden trumpet
  Blown at the judgment-day,
Closing the gate of mercy
  Over the Cast Away.

Melt me its gold to money,
  Coin me that small, small ring
Stamped with the Hoof of Satan,
  Bearing the name of King.

Then, in the murky midnight,
  Silently lead me down,
Down into Hell's dark portals,
  Far in the West of Town.

Then to the shrieks of devils
  Writhing in torments keen,
Sing me the song that tells me
  Ever of Walham Green.

Sing of the little half-sovereign
  Dancing in golden sheen;
Leave me in Hell—or, better,
  Leave me in Walham Green.

### ODE TO SAPPHO.

O LESBIAN maiden!
  O plumèd and snowlike in glory of white-
    ness!
  O mystical brightness
With love-lyrics laden!
  Joy's fulness is fainting for passion and
    sorrow.
To-night melts divine to the dawn of
    to-morrow,
O Lesbian maiden!

The flame-tongue of passion
  Is lambent and strong;
In mystical fashion
  Sucks sweetness from shade,
  As the voice of thy song
    In the halls of the dead,
    Breaking fitful and wild,
    Weird waking the slumber of Venus,
      the sleep of her child,
O Lesbian maiden!

Thy tongue reaches red
  On that pillar of might!
Flaming gold from thy head
  Is a garland of light
  On the forehead of night,
As we lie and behold
All the wonders untold
  That the joys of desire
In their secrets enfold,
  As the pillars of fire
On the ocean of old!
O Lesbian maiden!

The delight of thy lips
  Is the voice of the Spring
  That the nightingales sing
Over Winter's eclipse,
  While my fingers enring
    The white limbs of thy sleep
And my lips suck the lips
  Of the house of my dream,
  And press daintily deep,
  Till the joys are supreme
That thine amorous mouth
  On the home of thy love
Would exhaust the fierce drouth
  Of the rivers thereof,
Till thy white body quiver
  With mystic emotion
As the star-blossoms shiver
On silvery river
  Rushed into the ocean!
O Lesbian maiden!

## IN A LESBIAN MEADOW.

### I.

UNDER the summer leaves
  In the half-light
Love his old story weaves
  Far out of sight.
Here we are lone, at last.
Heaven is overcast
  Yet with no night.
Ere her immortal wings
Gather the thread of things
  Into her might,
Up will the moon arise
Through the black-azure skies :
Birds shall sing litanies
  Still of delight.

### II.

Let my lips wander where
  Tender moss grows,
Where through their dusky air
  Beams a red rose.
Where the bee honey sips
Let my desirous lips,
  Kissing, unclose
Delicate lips and chaste,
Sweetness divine to taste
  While the sun glows ;
There in the dusk to dwell
By the sweet water-well
In the wood's deepest dell
  Where—my love knows.

### III.

Skies are grown redder far ;
  Tempest draws nigher ;
Dark lowers a single star ;
  Mars, like the fire !
Fiercer our lips engage ;
Limbs, eyes, ears, gather rage ;
  Sharp grows desire.

Hear thy short bitter cries?
Pity thine agonies?
  Loose, though love tire?
Nay, neither hear nor spare ;
Frenzy shall mock at prayer ;
Torture's red torch shall flare
  Till thou expire.

### IV.

Stars stud a cloudless sky ;
  Moon silvers blue ;
Breeze is content to die ;
  Lightly falls dew.
Calm after strain and stress
Now to our weariness
  Brings love anew.
Peace brings her balm to us,
Lying as amorous
  Still, and as true,
Linked by new mystery,
Lovers confessed.   A sigh
Sobs to the happy sky,
  " Sorrow, go to !"

## " 'TIS PITY——"
—FORD.[1]

BLOW on the flame !
  The charcoal's vaporous fume
Shall hide our shame !
  Come, love, within the gloom !
For one last night, sweet sister, be the same ;
  Come, nestle with me in sweet Death's
    hot womb !

Two sunny eyes !
  And this is all my ruin !
Two gleaming thighs !
  And all to my undoing !
Far-swelling curves in ivory rapture rise
  Warm and too white—bethink you of the
    wooing !

[1] John Ford, author of " 'Tis Pity she s a
Whore," a drama of fraternal incest, and other
well-known plays.

A kiss of fire ;
  A touch of passionate yearning
Steals higher and higher—
  And kisses are returning !
The strong white grasp draws me still nigher
    and nigher,
  Our fusing forms in one fierce furnace
    burning !

Fails to us speech
  In Love's exultant leaping !
Each merged in each
  The golden fruit is reaping !

.     .     .     .     .

Wilt slumber, dear ?  One last kiss, I beseech !

.     .     .     .     .

  Come to us, Death !  My love and I are
    sleeping !


## EPILOGUE TO "GREEN ALPS."[1]

FAREWELL, my book, whose words I have
    not given
  One tithe of those fierce fires that in me
    dwell !
Now, after these long nights that I have
    striven,
  Farewell !

My spirit burns to know, but may not
    tell,
  Whether thy leaves, by autumn breezes
    driven,
Fly far away beyond the immutable ;

Whether thy soul shall find its home in
    heaven,
  Or dart far-flaming through the vaults of
    hell—
To him that loveth much is much for-
    given.
  Farewell !

[1] A volume which was never issued. MSS.
and proofs have been carefully destroyed.
Several of the poems in this volume are taken
from that, viz. pp. 6–19.


## TWO SONNETS IN PRAISE OF
## A PUBLISHER,

WHO SOUGHT TO INFECT OUR YOUTH
WITH HIS NOXIOUS WARES.

The ordure of this goat, who is called
" Master Leonard."—ELIPHAZ LEVI.
He's the man for muck.—BROWNING.

### I.

SMALL coffin-worms that burrow in thy brain
Writhe with delight ; thy rotten body teems
With all infesting vermin, as beseems
The mirror of an obscene mind.  In vain
Thy misbegotten brutehood shirks the pain
Of its avenging leprosies : death steams
In all thy rank foul atmosphere : the gleams
Of phosphorescent putrefaction wane.

Thy sordid hands reach through the filth to
    snatch
The offal money of a prurient swarm.
Thy liar's tongue licks liquid dung to hatch
From fetid ulcers with its slimy warm
Venom some fouler vermin, in their nest
Thy rotten heart and thy polluting breast !

### II.

Egg of the Slime !  Thy loose abortive lips
Mouth hateful things : thy shifty bloodshot eyes
Lurk craftily to snare some carrion prize,
The dainty morsel whence the poison drips
Unmarked : the maskèd infamy that slips
Into an innocent maw : corrupter wise !
Sly worm of hell ! that close and cunning lies
With sucking tentacles for finger-tips.

Earth spits on thee, contagious Caliban !
Hell spits on thee ; her sin is spiritual.
Only the awful slime and excrement
That sin sheds off will own thee for a man.
Only the worms in dead men's bowels that
    crawl
To lick a loathlier brother are content.

## MY WIFE DIES.

THE sun of love shone through my love's
  deep eyes
  And made a rainbow of her tender tears,
And on her cheeks I saw a blush arise
When her lips opened to say, loverwise,
  "I love"—and light broke through the
    cloud of fears
That hid her eyes.

The storm of passion woke in her red lips,
  When first they clung to mine and rested
    there ;
Lightnings of love were eager to eclipse
That earlier sunshine, and her whole soul
  clips
My soul—I kissed out life within her hair
Upon her lips.

We parted lips from lips and soul from soul
  To new strange passions in unholy lands,
Where love's breath chars and scorches like
  a coal.
So she is dead to-day—the sweet bells toll
  A lost, lost soul, a soul in Satan's bands,
A lost, lost soul !


## ODE TO VENUS CALLIPYGE.[1]

WHERE was light when thy body came
  Out of the womb of a perished prayer ?
  Where was life when the sultry air,
Hot with the lust of night and shame,
  Brooded on dust, when thy shoulders bare
Shone on the sea with a sudden flame
Into all Time to abundant fame ?

  *Daughter of Lust by the foam of the sea !*
    *Mother of flame ! Sister of shame !*
    *Tiger that Sin nor her son cannot tame !*
  *Worship to thee ! Glory to thee !*
  *Venus Callipyge, mother of me.*

[1] A statue in Naples. Callipyge means
"having beautiful buttocks."

Fruitless foam of a sterile sea,
  Wanton waves of a vain desire,
  Maddening billows flecked with fire,
Storms that lash on the brine, and flee,
  Dead delights, insatiate ire
Broke like a flower to the birth of thee,
Venus Callipyge, mother of me !


Deep wet eyes that are violet-blue !
  Haggard cheeks that may blush no more !
  Body bruised daintily, touched of gore
Where the sharp fierce teeth have bitten
  through
  The olive skin that thy sons adore,
That they die for daily, are slain anew
By manifold hate ; for their tale is few.


Few are thy sons, but as fierce as dawn.
  Sweet are the seconds, weary the days.
  Nights ? Ah ! thine image a thousand ways
Is smitten and kissed on the fiery lawn
  Where the wash of the waves of thy native
    bays
Laps weary limbs, that of thee have drawn
Laughter and fire for their souls in pawn.


O thy strong sons ! they are dark as night,
  Cruel and barren and false as the sea.
  They have cherishèd Hell for the love of
    thee,
Filled with thy lust and abundant might,
  Filled with the phantom desire to free
Body and soul from the sound and sight
Of a world and a God that doth not right.


O thy dark daughters ! their breasts are
  slack,
  Their lips so large and as poppies red ;
  They lie in a furious barren bed ;
They lie on their faces ; their eyelids lack
  Tears, and their cheeks are as roses
    dead ;
White are their throats, but upon the back
Red blood is clotted in gouts of black.

All on their sides are the wounds of lust
  Wet, from the home of their auburn hair
  Down to the feet that we find so fair;
Where the red sword has a secret thrust,
  Pain, and delight, and desire they share.
Verily pain! and thy daughters trust
Thou canst bid roses spring out of dust.


Mingle, ye children of such a queen,
  Mingle, and meet, and sow never a seed!
  Mingle, and tingle, and kiss, and bleed
With the blood of the life of the Lampsa-
  cene,[1]
  With the teeth that know never a pitiful
  deed
But fret and foam over with kisses obscene—
Mingle and weep for what years have been.


Never a son nor a daughter grow
  From your waste limbs, lest the goddess
  weep;
  Fill up the ranks from the babes that
  sleep
Far in the arms of a god of snow.
  Conquer the world, that her throne may
  keep
More of its pride, and its secret woe
Flow through all earth as the rivers flow.


Which of the gods is like thee, our queen?
  Venus Callipyge, nameless, nude,
  Thou with the knowledge of all indued,
Secrets of life and the dreams that mean
  Loves that are not, as are mortals', hued
All rose and lily, but linger unseen,
Passion-flowers purpled, garlands of green!


Who like thyself shall command our ways?
  Who has such pleasures and pains for hire?
  Who can awake such a mortal fire
In the veins of a man, that deathly days
  Have robbed of the masteries of desire?
Who can give garlands of fadeless bays
Unto the sorrow and pain we praise?


[1] Priapus.

Yea, we must praise, though the deadly
  shade
  Fall on the morrow, though fires of hell
  Harrow our vitals; a miracle
Springs at thy kisses, for thou hast made
  Anguish and sorrow desirable;
Torment of hell as the leaves that fade
Quickly forgotten, despised, decayed.


They are decayed, but thou springest again,
  Mother of mystery, barren, who bearest
  Flowers of most comeliest children, who
  wearest
Wounds for delight, whose desire shall stain
  Star-space with blood as the price thou
  sharest
Sweet with thy lovers, whose passing pain
Ripens to marvellous after-gain.


Thou art the fair, the wise, the divine!
  Thou art our mother, our goddess, our
  life!
  Thou art our passion, our sorrow, our
  strife!
Thou, on whose forehead no lights ever
  shine,
  Thou, our redeemer, our mistress, our
  wife,
Thou, barren sister of deathlier brine,
Venus Callipyge, mother of mine!


  *Daughter of Lust by the foam of the sea!*
    *Mother of flame! Sister of shame!*
    *Tiger that Sin nor her son cannot tame!*
  *Worship to thee! Glory to thee!*
  *Venus Callipyge, mother of me.*


## THE CANNIBALS.

ALL night no change, no whisper. Scarce
  a breath,
But lips closed hard upon the cup of death
To drain its sweetest poison. Scarce a sigh
Beats the dead hours out; scarce a melody

Of measured pulses quickened with the blood
Of that desire which pours its deadly flood
Through soul and shaken body; scarce a
    thought,
But sense through spirit most divinely wrought
To perfect feeling; only through the lips
Electric ardour kindles, flashes, slips
Through all the circle to her lips again,
And thence, unwavering, flies to mine, to
    drain
All pleasure in one draught. No whispered
    sigh;
No change of breast; love's posture perfectly
Once gained, we change no more. The
    fever grows
Hotter or cooler, as the night wind blows
Fresh gusts of passion on the outer gate.
But we, in waves of frenzy, concentrate
Our thirsty mouths on that hot drinking cup,
Whence we may never suck the nectar up
Too often or too hard; fresh fire invades
Our furious veins, and the unquiet shades
Of night make noises in the darkened room.
Yet, did I raise my head, throughout the
    gloom
I might behold thine eyes as red as fire
A tigress maddened with supreme desire;
White arms that clasp me; fervent breast
    that glides
An eager snake, about my breast and sides;
Teeth keen to bite, red tongue that never tires,
And lips ensanguine with unfed desires,
A very beast of prey; hot hands caress,
And violent breath that surfeits not excess.
But raise no head! I know thee, breast and
    thigh,
Lips, hair, and eyes, and mouth: I will not
    die
But thou come with me o'er the gate of death.
So, blood and body furious with breath
That pants through foaming kisses, let us stay
Gripped hard together to kiss life away,
Mouths drowned in murder, never satiate,
Kissing away the hard decrees of Fate,
Kissing insatiable in mad desire,
Kisses whose agony may never tire,
Kissing the gates of hell, the sword of God,
Each unto each a serpent or a rod,

A well of wine and fire, each unto each,
Whose lips are fain convulsively to reach
A higher heaven, a deeper hell. Ah! day
So soon to dawn, delight to snatch away!
Damned day, whose sunlight finds us as with
    wine
Drunken, with lust made manifest divine
Devils of darkness, servants unto hell—
Yea, king and queen of Sheol, terrible
Above all fiends and furies, hating more
The high Jehovah, loving Baal Peor,
Our father and our lover and our god!
Yea, though he lift his adamantine rod
And pierce us through, how shall his anger
    tame
Fire that glows fiercer for the brand of shame
Thrust in it; so, we who are all of fire,
One dull red flare of devilish desire,
The God of Israel shall not quench with tears,
Nor blood of martyrs drawn from myriad
    spheres,
Nor watery blood of Christ; that blood shall
    boil
With all the fury of our hellish toil;
His veins shall dry with heat; his bones
    shall bleach
Cold and detested, picked of dogs, on each
Dry separate dunghill of burnt Golgotha.
But we will wrest from heaven a little star,
The Star of Bethlehem, a lying light
Fit for our candle, and by devils' might
Fix in the vast concave of hell for us
To lume its ghastly shadows murderous,
That in the mirror of the lake of fire
We may behold the image of Desire
Stretching broad wings upon us, and may leap
Each upon other, till our bodies weep
Thick sweet salt tears, till, perfected of
    shames,
They burn to one another as the flames
Of our hell fuse us into one wild soul:
Then, one immaculate divinest whole,
Plunge, fire, within all fire, dive far to death;
Till, like king Satan's sympathetic breath,
Burn on us as a voice from far above
Strange nameless elements of fire and love;
And we, one mouth to kiss, one soul to lure,
For ever wedded, one, divine, endure

Far from sun, sea, and spring, from love or
    light,
Imbedded in impenetrable night ;
Deeper than ocean, higher than the sky,
Vaster than petty loves that dream and die,
Insatiate, angry, terrible for lust,
Who shrivel God to adamantine dust
By our fierce gaze upon him, who would strive
Under our wrath, to flee away, to dive
Into the deep recesses of his heaven.
But we, one joy, one love, one shame for
    leaven,
Quit hope and life, quit fear and death and
    love,
Implacable as God, desired above
All loves of hell or heaven, supremely wed,
Knit in one soul in one delicious bed
More hot than hell, more wicked than all
    things,
Vast in our sin, whose unredeeming wings
Rise o'er the world, and flap for lust of death,
Eager as any one that travaileth ;
So in our lust, the monstrous burden borne
Heavy within the womb, we wait the morn
Of its fulfilment.   Thus eternity
Wheels vain wings round us, who may never
    die
But cling as hard as serpent's wedlock is,
One writhing glory, an immortal kiss.


### THE BLOOD-LOTUS.

THE ashen sky, too sick for sleep, makes my
    face grey ; my senses swoon.
Here, in the glamour of the moon, will not
    some pitying godhead weep

For cold grey anguish of her eyes, that look
    to God, and look in vain,
For death, the anodyne of pain, for sleep,
    earth's trivial paradise ?

Sleep I forget.   Her silky breath no longer
    fans my ears ; I dream
I float on some forgotten stream that hath
    a savour still of death,

A sweet warm smell of hidden flowers whose
    heavy petals kiss the sun,
Fierce tropic poisons every one that fume
    and sweat through forest hours.

They grow in darkness ; heat beguiles their
    sluggish kisses ; in the wood
They breathe no murmur that is good, and
    Satan in their blossom smiles.

They murder with the old perfume that
    maddens all men's blood ; we die
Fresh from some corpse-clothed memory,
    some secret redolence of gloom,

Some darkling murmurous song of lust quite
    strange to man and beast and bird,
Silent in power, not overheard by any snake
    that eats the dust.

No crimson-hooded viper knows ; no silver-
    crested asp has guessed
The strange soft secrets of my breast ; no
    leprous cobra shall disclose

The many-seated, multiform, divine, essential
    joys that these
Dank odours bring, that starry seas wash
    white in vain ; intense and warm

The scents fulfil ; they permeate all lips, all
    arteries, and fire
New murmured music on the lyre that throbs
    the horrors they create.

Omniscient blossom !  Is thy red slack bosom
    fresher for my kiss ?
Are thy loves sharper ?  Hast thou bliss in
    all the sorrow of the dead ?

Why art thou paler when the moon grows
    loftier in the troublous sky ?
Why dost thou beat and heave when I press
    lips of fire, hell's princeliest boon,

To thy mad petals, green and gold like angels'
    wings, when as a flood
God's essence fills them, and the blood
    throughout their web grows icy cold ?

To thy red centre are my eyes held fast and
  fervent, as at night
Some sad miasma lends a light of strange and
  silent blasphemies

To lure a soul to hell, to draw some saint's
  charred lust, to tempt, to win
Another sacrifice to sin, another poet's heart
  to gnaw

With dubious remorse. Oh! flame of torturing flower-love! sacrament
Of Satan, triple element of mystery and love
  and shame,

Green, gold, and crimson, in my heart you
  strive with Jesus for its realm,
While Sorrow's tears would overwhelm the
  warriors of either part.

Jesus would lure me: from His side the
  gleaming torrent of the spear
Withdraws, my soul with joy and fear waits
  for sweet blood to pour its tide

Of warm delight—in vain! so cold, so
  watery, so slack it flows,
It leaves me moveless as a rose, albeit her
  flakes are manifold.

He hath no scent to drive men mad; no
  mystic fragrance from his skin
Sheds a loose hint of subtle sin such as the
  queen Faustina had.

Thou drawest me.   Thy golden lips are
  carven Cleopatra wise.
Large, full, and moist, within them lies the
  silver rampart, whence there slips

That rosy flame of love, the spring of blood
  at my light bidding spilt ;
And thy desires, if aught thou wilt, are softer
  at my suffering.

Fill up with Death Life's loving-cup!  Give
  me the knowledge, me the power
For some new sin one little hour, provoking
  Hell to belch us up.

So in some damned abyss of woe thy chant
  should dazzle as of old,
Thy kisses burn like molten gold, thy visions
  swing me to and fro.

Strange fascinations whirl and wind about
  my spirit lying coils ;
Thy charm enticeth, for the spoils of victory,
  all an evil mind.

Thy perfume doth confound my thought, new
  longings echo, and I crave
Doubtful liaisons with the grave and loves of
  Parthia for sport.

I think perhaps no longer yet, but dream and
  lust for stranger things
Than ever sucked the lips of kings, or fed
  the tears of Mahomet.

Quaint carven vampire bats, unseen in curious
  hollows of the trees,
Or deadlier serpents coiled at ease round
  carcases of birds unclean ;

All wandering changeful spectre shapes that
  dance in slow sweet measure round
And merge themselves in the profound, nude
  women and distorted apes

Grotesque and hairy, in their rage more
  rampant than the stallion steed ;
There is no help : their horrid need on these
  pale women they assuage.

Wan breasts too pendulous, thin hands
  waving so aimlessly, they breathe
Faint sickly kisses, and inweave my head in
  quiet burial-bands.

The silent troops recede ; within the fiery
  circle of their glance
Warm writhing woman - horses dance a
  shameless Bacchanal of sin ;

Foam whips their reeking lips, and still the
  flower-witch nestles to my lips,
Twines her swart lissome legs and hips, half
  serpent and half devil, till

My whole self seems to lie in her ; her kisses
  draw my breath ; my face
Loses its lustre in the grace of her quick
  bosom ; sinister

The raving spectres reel ; I see beyond my
  Circe's eyes no shape
Save vague cloud-measures that escape the
  dance's whirling witchery.

Their song is in my ears, that burn with their
  melodious wickedness ;
But in her heart my sorceress has songs more
  sinful, that I learn

As she sings slowly all their shame, and
  makes me tingle with delight
At new debaucheries, whose might rekindles
  blood and bone to flame.

The circle gathers. Negresses howl in the
  naked dance, and wheel
On poniard-blades of poisoned steel, and
  weep out blood in agonies ;

Strange beast and reptile writhe ; the song
  grows high and melancholy now ;
The perfume savours every brow with lust
  unutterable of wrong.

Clothed with my flower-bride I sit, a harlot
  in a harlot's dress,
And laugh with careless wickedness that
  strews the broad road of the Pit

With vine and myrtle and thy flower, my
  harlot-maiden, who for man
Now first forsakest thy leman, thy Eve, my
  Lilith, in this bower

Which we indwell, a deathless three, changeless and changing, as the pyre
Of earthly love becomes a fire to heat us
  through eternity.

I have forgotten Christ at last ; he may look
  back, grown amorous,
And call across the gulf to us, and signal
  kisses through the vast :

We shall disdain, clasp faster yet, and mock
  his newer pangs, and call
With stars and voices musical, jeers his
  touched heart shall not forget.

I would have pitied him. This flower spits
  blood upon him ; so must I
Cast ashes through the misty sky to mock
  his faded crown of power,

And with our laughter's nails refix his torn
  flesh faster to the wood,
And with more cruel zest make good the
  shackles of the Crucifix.

So be it ! In thy arms I rest, lulled into
  silence by the strain
Of sweet love-whispers, while I drain damnation from thy tawny breast :

Nor heed the haggard sun's eclipse, feeling
  thy perfume fill my hair,
And all thy dark caresses wear sin's raiment
  on thy melting lips—

Nay, by the witchcraft of thy charms to sleep,
  nor dream that God survive ;
To wake, this only to contrive—fresh passions
  in thy naked arms ;

And, at that moment when thy breath mixes
  with mine, like wine, to call
Each memory, one merged into all, to kiss,
  to sleep, to mate with death !

## THE NATIVITY.

### CHRISTMAS 1897.

THE Virgin lies at Bethlehem.
  (Bring gold and frankincense and myrrh !)
The root of David shoots a stem.
  (O Holy Spirit, pity her !)

She lies alone amid the kine.
  (Bring gold and frankincense and myrrh !)
The straw is fragrant as with wine.
  (O Holy Spirit, pity her !)

Mine host protects an honest roof.
 (Bring gold and frankincense and myrrh !)
His spouse sniffs loud and holds aloof.
 (O Holy Spirit, pity her !)

The Angel has not come again.
 (Bring gold and frankincense and myrrh !)
Why did God deal her out such pain?
 (O Holy Spirit, pity her !)

Her love-hours held the Holy Ghost.
 (Bring gold and frankincense and myrrh !)
Where is he now she needs him most?
 (O Holy Spirit, pity her !)

Joseph drinks deep outside the inn.
 (Bring gold and frankincense and myrrh !)
She is half hated by her kin.
 (O Holy Spirit, pity her !)

The agony increases fast.
 (Bring gold and frankincense and myrrh !)
Each spasm is a holocaust.
 (O Holy Spirit, pity her !)

There are three kings upon the road.
 (Bring gold and frankincense and myrrh !)
She hath thrice cursed the name of God.
 (O Holy Spirit, pity her !)

There stands her star above the sky.
 (Bring gold and frankincense and myrrh !)
She hath thrice prayed that she may die.
 (O Holy Spirit, pity her !)

Her bitter anguish hath sufficed.
 (Bring gold and frankincense and myrrh !)
She is delivered of the Christ.
 (The angels come to worship her.)

## TRANSLATIONS FROM BAUDE-
### LAIRE.[1]

#### CAIN ET ABEL.

##### I.

SEED of Abel, eat, drink, sleep !
 God shall smile complaisantly.
Seed of Cain, in the muck-heap
 Crawl and miserably die !

[1] The original metres are in all cases closely
imitated.

Seed of Abel, thine oblation
 Sweet to Seraphim doth smell :
Seed of Cain, shall thy damnation
 Ever find the bounds of Hell?

Race of Abel, see thy seed
 And thy cattle flourish more !
Race of Cain, for hunger's need,
 Like a dog thy bowels roar.

Seed of Abel, warm thy paunch
 At thy patriarchal hall !
Seed of Cain, on shivering haunch
 Squat in cave, despised jackal !

Seed of Abel, love and swarm !
 So thy gold shall also grow.
Seed of Cain, heart over-warm,
 Guard thy lust and crush it low !

Seed of Abel, grow, well-faring
 Like the bugs in forest beats !
Seed of Cain, at bay, despairing,
 Throw thy children on the streets !

##### II.

Seed of Abel, carrion
 Shall make fat the smoking soil.
Seed of Cain, on thee has none
 Laid sufficient woes of toil.

Seed of Abel, this thy shame—
 To the boar-spear yields the sword.
Seed of Cain, to heaven flame,
 And to earth cast Heaven's Lord !

#### THE LITANY OF SATAN.

O thou, of Angels fairest and most wise,
God by Fate's treachery shorn of liturgies !
O Satan, have pity of my long misery !

O Prince of Exile, Sufferer of wrong,
Whose vengeance, conquered, rises triply
 strong !
O Satan, have pity of my long misery !

Who knowest all, of under earth the king,
Familiar healer of man's suffering !
O Satan, have pity of my long misery !

Who to the leper, even the cursed pariah,
Hast taught by love the taste of heavenly fire !
O Satan, have pity of my long misery !

Thou who on Death, thine old and strong
    leman,
Begottest Hope—a charming madwoman !
O Satan, have pity of my long misery !

Who knowest in which caves of envious lands
God has hid precious stones with jealous
    hands !
O Satan, have pity of my long misery !

Thou whose clear eye discerns the arsenals
    deep,
Where the small folk of buried metals sleep !
O Satan, have pity of my long misery !

Whose broad hand hides the giddy precipice
From sleepers straying about some edifice !
O Satan, have pity of my long misery !

Whose skill makes supple the old bones, at
    needs,
Of the belated sot, 'mid surging steeds !
O Satan, have pity of my long misery !

Who taught frail man, to make his suffering
    lighter,
Consoling, to mix sulphur with salt nitre !
O Satan, have pity of my long misery !

O subtle complice, who as blatant Beast
Brandest vile Crœsus, him that pities least !
O Satan, have pity of my long misery !

Who in girls' eyes and hearts implantest deep
Lust for the wound, the twain that wound
    bids weep !
O Satan, have pity of my long misery !

Staff of the exiled, the inventor's spark,
Confessor of hanged men and plotters dark !
O Satan, have pity of my long misery !

Adopted sire of whom black wrath and power
Of God the Father chased from Eden Bower !
O Satan, have pity of my long misery !


FEMMES DAMNÉES.

Like pensive cattle couched upon the sand
    They turn their eyes to ocean's distant ring ;
Feet seek each other, hand desires hand,
    With languor sweet and bitter shuddering.

Some, hearts love-captured with long
    whispering,
    Spell out the love of timorous childhood,
Where babbles in deep dell the gentle spring,
    And dive among the young trees of the
        green wood.

Others, like sisters, slowly, with grave eyes,
    Cross the rocks filled with apparitions dim,
Where Antony beheld, like lavers, rise
    The nude empurpled breasts that tempted
        him.

Some, by the dying torch-light, call thy name,
    In the dumb hollow of old pagan fanes,
To succour feverish shriekings of fierce flame,
    O Bacchus, soother of men's ancient pains.

Others, whose throat is thirsty for breast-
    blood,
    To hide a whip 'neath flowing robes are
        fain,
Mingling in lonely night and darksome wood
    The foam of pleasure and the tears of pain.

O virgins, demons, monsters, O martyrs !
    Great souls contemptuous of reality !
Seekers for the Infinite, satyrs, worshippers,
    Now mad with cries, now torn with agony !

You whom my soul has followed to your hell,
    Poor sisters, more beloved than wept by
        me,
For your fierce woes, your lusts insatiable,
    And the urns of love that fill the hearts
        of ye !

### CARRION.

Recall, my soul, the sight we twain have
    looked upon
This summer morning soft and sweet,
Beside the path, an infamous foul carrion,
    Stones for its couch a fitting sheet.

Its legs stretched in the air, like wanton
    whores
    Burning with lust, and reeking venom
    sweated,
Laid open, carelessly and cynically, the doors
    Of belly rank with exhalations fœtid.

Upon this rottenness the sun shone deadly
    straight
    As if to cook it to a turn,
And give back to great Nature hundredfold
    the debt
    That, joining it together, she did earn.

The sky beheld this carcase most superb out-
    spread
    As spreads a flower, itself, whose taint
Stank so supremely strong, that on the grass
    your head
    You thought to lay, in sudden faint.

The flies swarmed numberless on this putres-
    cent belly,
    Whence issued a battalion
Of larvæ, black, that flowed, a sluggish liquid
    jelly,
    Along this living carrion.

All this was falling, rising as the eager seas,
    Or heaving with strange crepitation—
Was't that the corpse, swollen out with a
    lascivious breeze,
    Was yet alive by copulation?

And all the carcase now sounded strange
    symphonies
    Like wind, or running water wan,
Or grain that winnower shakes and turns,
    whene'er he plies
    With motion rhythmical his fan.

The shapes effaced themselves; no more
    their images
    Were aught but dreams, a sketch too slow
To tint the canvas, that the artist finishes
    By memory that does not go.

Behind the rocks a bitch unquietly gazed on
    Ourselves with eye of wrathful woe,
Watching her time to return unto the skeleton
    For tit-bits that she had let go.

Yet you are like to it, this dung, this carrion,
    To this infection doubly dire,
Star of my eyes that are, and still my nature's
    sun,
    You, O my angel! You, my own desire!

Yes! such will you be, queen, in graces that
    surpass,
    Once the last sacraments are said;
When you depart beneath wide-spreading
    blooms and grass
    To rot amid the bones of many dead.

Then, O my beauty! tell the worms, who
    will devour
    With kisses all of you to dust;
That I have kept the form and the essential
    power
    Divine of my distorted lust.

### THE DENIAL OF ST. PETER.

#### I.

WHAT makes God then of all the curses deep
    That daily reach his Seraphim divine?
    Like to a tyrant gorged with meat and wine,
Our blasphemous music lulleth him to sleep.

#### II.

Tears of the martyrs, and saints tortured,
    Must prove intoxicating symphonies,
    Since, spite of blood-price paid to gain
    them ease,
The heavens therewith are not yet satiated.

### III.

Jesus ! recall Gethsemane afresh,
  Where thy simplicity his pity sought
  Who in his heaven heard, and mocked for
    nought,
Coarse hangmen pierce with nails thy living
  flesh.

### IV.

When on thy godhead spat the virulence
  Of scum of soldiery and kitchen-knaves ;
  When thou didst feel the thorns pierce
    bloody graves
Within thy brain where Manhood burnt in-
  tense ;

### V.

When thy bruised broken body's horrid weight
  Racked thy stretched arms, that sweat and
    blood enow
    Coursed down the marble paleness of thy
      brow,
Lift up on high, a butt for all men's hate :—

### VI.

Dreamedst thou then of those triumphant
  hours
  When, that the eternal promise might
    abide,
  Thy steed a mild she-ass, thou once didst
    ride
On roads o'erstrewn with branches and fresh
  flowers ;

### VII.

When, thy heart beating high with hope and
  pride,
  Thou didst whip out those merchants vile
    with force,
  At last the master ?  Did not keen remorse
Bite thy soul ere the spear had pierced thy
  side ?

### VIII.

I, certes, I shall gladly quit this hell
  Where dream and action walk not hand-
    in-hand !
  May I use the brand and perish by the
    brand !
Saint Peter denied Jesus.  He did well.

### GLOIRE ET LOUANGE.

GLORY and praise to thee, O Satan, in the
  height
Of Heaven, where thou didst rule, and in
  the night
Of Hell, where conquered, dost dream
  silently !
Grant that one day my soul 'neath Know-
  ledge-Tree
Rest near thine own soul, when from thy
  forehead
Like a new temple all its branches spread.

### THE FOUNT OF BLOOD.

SOMETIMES I think my blood in waves ap-
  pears,
Springs as a fount with music in its tears ;
I hear it trickling with long murmuring sound,
But search myself in vain to find the wound.

Across the city, as in closèd meres,
Making the pavements isles, it disappears ;
In it all creatures' thirst relief hath found ;
All nature in its scarlet hue is drowned.

I have often prayed these fickle wines to weep
For one day Lethe on my threatening fear—
Wine makes the ear more sharp, the eye more
  clear.

I have sought in Love forgetfulness and
  sleep—
My love's a bed of needles made to pierce,
That drink be given to these women fierce !

### LA BEATRICE.

As I one day to nature made lament
In burnt-up lands, calcined of nutriment,
As in my musing thought's vague random dart
I slowly poised my dagger o'er my heart,
I saw in full noon o'er my forehead form
A deathly cloud far pregnant with the storm,
That bore a flock of devils vicious
Most like to dwarfs cruel and curious.

Coldly they set themselves to gaze on me,
Like passers-by a madman that they see—
I heard them laugh and chuckle, as I think,
Now interchange a signal, now a wink.
" Let us at leisure view this caricature,
This shade of Hamlet mimicking his posture,
The doubting look and hair flung wide to
wind !
A pity, eh ? to see this merry hind,
This beggar, actor out of work, this droll,
Because he plays artistically his rôle,
Wishing to interest in his chanted woes
Brooks, eagles, crickets, every flower that
blows,
And even to us the rubric old who made
To howl out publicly his wild tirade ? "
I could have (for my pride is mountains high,
And dominates cloud tops or demon's cry)—
I could have simply turned my sovereign
head,
Had I not seen, 'mid their obscene herd led,
Crime, that the sun has not yet brought to
book,
Queen of my spirit with the peerless look.
And she laughed with them at my dark
distress,
And turned them oft some dirtiest caress.

## LE VIN DU SOLITAIRE.

THE strange look of a woman of the town,
Who glides toward us like the rays that slake
The wave-wrought moon within the trembling
lake,
Where she would dip her careless beauty
down ;
The last crowns unto which a gambler's
fingers cling ;
A libertine caress from hungry Adeline ;
The sound of music, lulling, silver, clean,
Like the far cry of human suffering :

All these, deep bottle ! are of little worth
Beside the piercing balm thy fertile girth
Holds in the reverent poet's lifted soul ;
To him thou givest youth, and hope, and life,
And pride, this treasure of all beggar's strife
That gives us triumph, Godhead, for its dole.

## CHALDEAN FOOLS.

CHALDEAN fools, who prayed to stars and
fires,
Believed there was a God who punished liars.
These gods of theirs they often would
invoke,
Apparently with excellent effect :
They trusted to escape the penal smoke
By making Truth the trade-mark of their
sect.

How fortunate that we are Christian Folk,
And know these notions to be incorrect !

## CALL OF THE SYLPHS.[1]

BEHOLD, I am ; a circle on whose hands
The twelvefold Kingdom of my Godhead
stands.
Six are the mighty seats of living breath,
The rest sharp sickles, or the horns of death,
Which are, and are not, save in mine own
power.
Sleep they ? They rise at mine appointed
hour.
I made ye stewards in the primal day,
And set your thrones in my celestial way.
I gave ye power above the moving time
That all your vessels to my crown might climb.
From all the corners of your fortress caves
Ye might invoke me, and your wise conclaves
Should pour the fires of increase, life and
birth,
Continual dewfall to the thirsty earth.
Thus are ye made of Justice and of Truth,
The Souls of Fury, and the Lords of Ruth.
In His great Name, your God's, I say, arise !
Behold ! His mercies murmur in the skies.
His Name is mighty in us to the end.
In Him we cry : Move, answer, and descend !
Apply yourselves to us ; arise ! For why ?
We are the Wisdom of your God most high !

[1] This Fragment is a paraphrase of one of
the elemental invocations given in Dr. Dee's
famous record of magical working.—A. C.

## INVOCATION.[1]

O SELF Divine !  O Living Lord of Me !
Self-shining flame, begotten of Beyond !
Godhead immaculate !  Swift tongue of fire,
Kindled from that immeasurable light
The boundless, the immutable.  Come forth,
My God, my lover, spirit of my heart,
Heart of my soul, white virgin of the Dawn,
My Queen of all perfection, come thou forth
From thine abode beyond the Silences
To me the prisoner, me the mortal man,
Shrined in this clay : come forth, I say, to me,
Initiate my quickened soul ; draw near,
And let the glory of thy Godhead shine
Through all the luminous aethers of the air
Even to earth, thy footstool ; unto me
Who by these sacred invocations draw
The holy influence within myself,
To strengthen and to purify my will
And holy aspiration to thy Life.
Purge me and consecrate until my heart
Burn through the very limits of the veil,
And rend it at the hour of sacrifice
That even the secret pillar in the midst
May be made manifest to mortal eyes.
Behold upon my right hand and my left
The mighty pillars of amazing fire,
And terrible cloud.  Their tops in Heaven
    are veiled,
Whereon the everlasting lamps rejoice.
Their pedestals upon the Universe
Are set in rolling clouds, in thunder-gusts,
In vivid flame, and tempest : but to me,
Balanced between them, burns the holy light
Veilless, one liquid wheel of sacred fire,
Whirling immutably within itself
And formulating in the splendid sun
Of its white moony radiance, in the light
Of its immaculate eternity,
Thy glorious vision !  O thou Starlight face,
And crownèd diamond of my self and soul,

---

[1] Versified from the Manuscript called "ϟ"
of ϟ in Za."—A. C.
  Za was a MS. of magical formulæ given to
advanced members of the Zelator Adeptus
Minor grade in the Hermetic Order of the
Golden Dawn.

---

Thou Queenly Angel of my Higher Will,
Form in my spirit a more subtle fire
Of God, that I may comprehend the more
The sacred purity of thy divine
Essence !  O Queen, O Goddess of my life,
Light unbegotten, Scintillating spark
Of the All-Self !  O holy, holy Spouse
Of my most godlike thought, come forth !  I
    say,
And manifest unto thy worshipper
In more candescent fulgours !  Let the air
Ring with the passion of my holy cry
Unto the Highest.  For persistent will
And the continual fervour of my soul
Have led me to this hour of victory,
This throne of splendour.  O thou Beauty's
    Self,
Thou holiest Crown thus manifest to me,
Come forth, I say, come forth !  With
    mightier cries
Than Jesus uttered on the quivering cross :
" Eli, Eli, lama sabachthani,"
Thee, thee, thee only I invoke !  O Soul
Of my own spirit, let thy fervid eyes
Give me their light : for thou dost stand, as
    God
Among the Holy Ones.  Before the gods
Thy music moves, coequal, coeterne,
Thou, Lord of Light and Life and Love !
    Come forth !
I call thee in the holiest name of Him
Lord of the Universe, and by His Name,
Osiris perfected through suffering,
Glorious in trial : by His Holy Name,
Jesus, the Godhead passing through the gates
Of Hell, that even there the rescuers
Might find the darkness, and proclaim the
    light ;
For I invoke thee by the sacred rites
And secret words of everlasting power :
By the swift symbol of the Golden Dawn
And all its promise, by the Cross of Fire,
And by the Gleaming Symbol : by the Rose
And Cross of Light and Life : the holy Ankh,
The Rose of Ruby and the Cross of Gold.
By these I say, Come forth !  my holy
    Spouse,
And make me one with thine abundant ray

Of the vast ocean of the unmanifest
Limitless Negativity of Light
Flowing, in Jesus manifest, through space,
In equilibrium, upon the world
Illumined by the White Supernal Gleam
Through the red Cross of Calvary : Come
 forth,
My actual Self! Come forth, O dazzling one,
Wrapped in the glory of the Holy Place
Whence I have called thee : Come thou forth
 to me,
And permeate my being, till my face
Shine with thy light reflected, till my brows
Gleam with thy starry symbol, till my voice
Reach the Ineffable : Come forth, I say,
And make me one with thee : that all my
 ways
May glitter with the holy influence,
That I may be found worthy at the end
To sacrifice before the Holy Ones :
That in thy Glory, Strength, and Majesty,
And by the Beauty and Harmony of Heaven
That fills its fountains at the Well of Life,
I may be mighty in the Universe.
Yea, come thou forth, I mightily conjure
Thy radiant Perfection, to compel
All Spirits to be subject unto Me,
That every spirit of the Firmament
And of the Ether, and upon the Earth
And under Earth, and of the stable land,
Of water, of the whirling of the air,
Of the all-rushing fire ; and every Spell
And scourge of God the Vast One may be
 made
Obedient unto me, to the All-Good
And ultimate Redemption : Hear me, thou !

> Eca, zodacare, Iad, goho,
> Torzodu odo kikale qaa !
> Zodacare od zodameranu !
> Zodorje, lape zodiredo Ol
> Noco Mada, das Iadapiel !
> Ilas ! hoatahe Iaida ! [1]

O crowned with starlight ! Winged with
 emerald

[1] This conjuration is in the "angelic" language of Dr. Dee. See the edition of Goetia published by the S.P.R.T.

Wider than Heaven ! O profounder blue
Of the abyss of water ! O thou flame
Flashing through all the caverns of the night,
Tongues leaping from the immeasurable
Up through the glittering Steeps unmanifest
To the ineffable ! O Golden Sun !
Vibrating glory of my higher self !
I heard thy voice resounding in the Abyss :
" I am the only being in the deep
Of Darkness : let me rise and gird myself
To tread the path of Darkness : even so
I may attain the light. For from the Abyss
I came before my birth : from those dim halls
And silence of a primal sleep ! And He,
The Voice of Ages, answered me and said :
Behold ! for I am He that formulates
In darkness ! Child of Earth ! the Light
 doth shine
In darkness, but the darkness understands
No ray of that initiating light ! "
Now, by Initiation's dangerous path
And groping aspiration, came I forth
Where the White Splendour shone upon the
 Throne,
Even to the Temple of the Holy Ones :
Now, by that Light, come forth, I say, to me,
My Lady of the Starlight and the Moon !
Come and be absolute within my mind,
That I may take no dim remembrance back
To drown this glory with earth's quivering
 gloom.
But, O abide within Me ! Every hour
I need the lofty and the limpid stream
Of that White Brilliance : Leave me not alone,
O Holy Spirit ! Come to comfort me,
To draw me, and to make me manifest,
Osiris to the weeping world ; that I
Be lifted up upon the Cross of Pain
And Sacrifice, to draw all human kind
And every germ of matter that hath life,
Even after me, to the ineffable
Kingdom of Light ! O holy, holy Queen !
Let thy wide pinions overshadow me !

I am, the Resurrection and the Life !
The Reconciler of the Light and Dark.
I am the Rescuer of mortal things.
I am the Force in Matter manifest.

I am the Godhead manifest in flesh.
I stand above, among the Holy Ones.
I am all-purified through suffering,
All-perfect in the mystic sacrifice,
And in the knowledge of my Selfhood
    made
One with the Everlasting Lords of Life.
The Glorified through Trial is My Name.
The Rescuer of Matter is My Name.
I am the Heart of Jesus girt about
With the Swift Serpent !  I, Osirified,
Stand in this Hall of Twofold Truth and
    say :
Holy art Thou, Lord of the Universe !
Holy art Thou, whom Nature hath not formed !
Holy art Thou, O Vast and Mighty One !
O Lord of Darkness and O Lord of Light !
Holy art Thou, O Light above all Gods !
O Holy, Holy, Holy, Holy King
Ineffable, O Consciousness Divine
In whose white Presence, even I, a god,
A god of gods, prostrate myself and say :
I am the spark of Thine abundant flame.
I am the flower, and Thou the splendid
    Sun
Wherefrom my Life is drawn !  All hail to
    Thee,
For Holy, Holy, Holy, is Thy Name !
Holy art Thou, O Universal Lord !
Holy art Thou, whom Nature hath not formed !
Holy art Thou, the Vast and Mighty
    One !
O Lord of Darkness and O Lord of Light !


I see the Darkness fall as lightning falls !
I watch the Ages like a torrent roll
Past Me : and as a garment I shake off
The clinging skirts of Time.  My place is
    fixed
In the abyss beyond all Stars and Suns.
I AM, the Resurrection and the Life !


Holy art Thou, Lord of the Universe !
Holy art Thou, whom Nature hath not formed !
Holy art Thou, the Vast and Mighty One !
O Lord of Darkness and O Lord of Light !

## HYMN TO APOLLO.

*Written in the Temple of Apollo.*

GOD of the golden face and fiery forehead !
Lord of the Lion's house of strength, exalted
In the Ram's horns !  O ruler of the vaulted
        Heavenly hollow !
Send out thy rays majestic, and the torrid
Light of thy song ! thy countenance most
    splendid
Bend to the suppliant on his face extended !
        Hear me, Apollo !

Let thy fierce fingers sweep the lyre forgotten !
Recall the ancient glory of thy chanted
Music that thrilled the hearts of men, and
    haunted
        Life to adore thee !
Cleanse thou our market-places misbegotten !
Fire in my heart and music to my pæan
Lend, that my song bow, past the empyrean,
        Phœbus, before thee !

All the old worship in this land is broken ;
Yet on my altar burns the ancient censer,
Frankincense, saffron, galbanum, intenser !
        Ornaments glisten.
Robes of thy colour bind me for thy token.
My voice is fuller in thine adoration.
Thine image holds its god-appointed station.
        Lycian, listen !

My prayers more eloquent than olden chants
Long since grown dumb on the soft forgetful
    airs—
My lips are loud to herald thee : my prayers
        Keener to follow.
I do aspire, as thy long sunbeam slants
Upon my crown ; I do aspire to thee
As no man yet—I am in ecstasy !
        Hear me, Apollo !

My chant wakes elemental flakes of light
Flashing along the sandal-footed [1] floor.
All listening spirits answer and adore
        Thee, the amazing !

[1] Strewn with sandalwood (?)

I follow to the eagle-baffling sight,
Limitless oceans of abounding space ;
Purposed to blind myself, but know thy face,
    Phœbus, in gazing.

O hear me ! hear me ! hear me ! for my hands,
Dews deathly bathe them ; sinks the stricken
    song ;
Eyes that were feeble have become the strong,
    See thee and glisten.

Blindness is mine ; my spirit understands,
Weighs out the offering, accepts the pain,
Hearing the pæan of the unprofane !
    Lycian, listen !

God of the fiery face, the eyes inviolate !
Lord of soundless thunders, lightnings light-
    less !
Hear me now, for joy that I see thee sightless,
    Fervent to follow.
Grant one boon ; destroy me, let me die
    elate,
Blasted with light intolerant of a mortal,
That the undying in me pass thy portal !
    Hear me, Apollo.

Hear me, or if about thy courts be girded
Paler some purple softening the sunlight
Merciful, mighty, O divide the one light
    Into a million
Shattered gems, that I mingle in my worded
Measures some woven filament of passion
Caught, Phœbus, from thy star-girt crown, to
    fashion
    Poet's pavilion.

Let me build for thee an abiding palace
Rainbow-hued to affirm thy light divided,
Yet where starry words, by thy soul guided,
    Sing as they glisten,
Dew-drops diamonded from the abundant
    chalice !
Swoons the prayer to silence ; pale the altar
Glows at thy presence as the last words
    falter—
    Lycian, listen !

## THE HERMIT'S HYMN TO SOLITUDE.

Namo Tassa Bhagavato Arahato Sammasambuddhasa.

Venerable Lord and Best of Friends,
  We, seeing the cycle in which Maha Brahma
is perhaps more a drifting buoy than ourselves,
knowing that it is called the walking in delusion,
the puppet show of delusion, the writhing of
delusion, the fetter of delusion, are aware that
the way out of the desert is found by going
into the desert. Will you, in your lonely
lamaserai, accept this hymn from me, who,
in the centre of civilisation, am perhaps more
isolated than you in your craggy fastness among
the trackless steppes of your Untrodden Land?
              ALEISTER CROWLEY.

PARIS, A.B. 2446.

### I.

MIGHTIEST Self ! Supreme in Self-Con-
    tentment !
Sole Spirit gyring in its own ellipse ;
Palpable, formless, infinite presentment
Of thine own light in thine own soul's eclipse !
Let thy chaste lips
Sweep through the empty aethers guarding
    thee
(As in a fortress girded by the sea
The raging winds and wings of air
Lift the wild waves and bear
Innavigable foam to seaward), bend thee
    down,
Touch, draw me with thy kiss
Into thine own deep bliss,
Into thy sleep, thy life, thy imperishable
    crown !
Let that young godhead in thine eyes
Pierce mine, fulfil me of their secrecies,
Thy peace, thy purity, thy soul impenetrably
    wise.

### II.

All things which are complete are solitary ;
The circling moon, the inconscient drift of
    stars,
The central systems. Burn they, change
    they, vary ?
Theirs is no motion beyond the eternal bars.
Seasons and scars

Stain not the planets, the unfathomed home,
The spaceless, unformed faces in the dome
Brighter and blacker than all things,
Borne under the eternal wings
No whither: solitary are the winter woods
And caves not habited,
And that supreme grey head
Watching the groves: single the foaming
    amber floods,
And O ! most lone
The melancholy mountain shrine and throne,
While far above all things God sits, the
    ultimate alone !

### III.

I sate upon the mossy promontory
Where the cascade cleft not his mother rock,
But swept in whirlwind lightning foam and
    glory,
Vast circling with unwearying luminous shock
To lure and lock
Marvellous eddies in its wild caress ;
And there the solemn echoes caught the stress,
The strain of that impassive tide,
Shook it and flung it high and wide,
Till all the air took fire from that melodious
    roar ;
All the mute mountains heard,
Bowed, laughed aloud, concurred,
And passed the word along, the signal of
    wide war.
All earth took up the sound,
And, being in one tune securely bound,
Even as a star became the soul of silence
    most profound.

### IV.

Thus there, the centre of that death that
    darkened,
I sat and listened, if God's voice should
    break
And pierce the hollow of my ear that
    hearkened,
Lest God should speak and find me not
    awake—
For his own sake.

No voice, no song might pierce or penetrate
That enviable universal state.
The sun and moon beheld, stood still.
Only the spirit's axis, will,
Considered its own soul and sought a deadlier
    deep,
And in its monotone mood
Of supreme solitude
Was neither glad nor sad because it did not
    sleep ;
But with calm eyes abode
Patient, its leisure the galactic load,[1]
Abode alone, nor even rejoiced to know that
    it was God.

### V.

All change, all motion, and all sound, are
    weakness !
Man cannot bear the darkness which is death.
Even that calm Christ, manifest in meekness,
Cried on the cross and gave his ghostly breath,
On the prick of death,
Voice, for his passion could not bear nor dare
The interlunar, the abundant air
Darkened, and silence on the shuddering
Hill, and the unbeating wing
Of the legions of His Father, and so died.
But I, should I be still
Poised between fear and will ?
Should I be silent, I, and be unsatisfied ?
For solitude shall bend
Self to all selffulness, and have one friend,
Self, and behold one God, and be, and look
    beyond the End.

### VI.

O Solitude ! how many have mistaken
Thy name for Sorrow's, or for Death's or
    Fear's !
Only thy children lie at night and waken—
How shouldst thou speak and say that no
    man hears ?
O Soul of Tears !
For never hath fallen as dew thy word,
Nor is thy shape showed, nor as Wisdom's
    heard

[1] Via Lactea, the "Milky Way."

Thy crying about the city
In the house where is no pity,
But in the desolate halls and lonely vales of
sand :
Not in the laughter loud,
Nor crying of the crowd,
But in the farthest sea, the yet untravelled
land.
Where thou hast trodden, I have trod ;
Thy folk have been my folk, and thine abode
Mine, and thy life my life, and thou, who
art thy God, my God.

### VII.

Draw me with cords that are not ; witch me
chanted
Spells never heard nor open to the ear,
Woven of silence, moulded in the haunted
Houses where dead men linger year by year.
I have no fear
To tread thy far irremeable way
Beyond the paths and palaces of day,
Beyond the night, beyond the skies,
Beyond eternity's
Tremendous gate ; beyond the immanent
miracle.[1]
O secret self of things !
I have nor feet nor wings
Except to follow far beyond Heaven and
Earth and Hell,
Until I mix my mood
And being in thee, as in my hermit's hood
I grow the thing I contemplate—that selfless
solitude !

### THE STORM.

*Written on the North Atlantic Ocean.*

IN the sorrow of the silence of the sunset,
when the world's heart sinks to sleep,
And the waking wind arises from the wedding
of the aether and the deep,
There are perfumes through the saltness of
the even ; there are hints of flowers afar;
And the God goes down lamented by the
lonely vesper star.

[1] The universe.

The monsters rise around us as we move in
moving mist,
Slow whales that swim as musing, and lo !
or ever we wist,
Looms northward in the grey, mysterious ice,
cathedral high,
Clad in transparent clouds of cold, as a ghost
in drapery.

The solemn dusk descending creeps around
us from the East ;
Clouded as with the ungainly head of a
mysterious beast.
Long wisps of darkness (even as fingers)
reach and hold
The sobbing West toward them, clasp the
barred Hesperian gold.

Still pale a rose reflection lingers, in pure
soft blue ;
Even above the tempest, where a lonely
avenue
Leads from the wan moon's image, shadowy
in the air,
Waning, half hidden from the sun—and yet
her soul is there.

So stand I looking ever down to the rolling
sea,
Breast-heaves of a sleeping mother, spouse of
Eternity :
The dark deep ocean mother, that another[1]
hath reviled,
Calling her bitter and barren—and am I not
her child ?

O mother sea, O beautiful, more excellent
than earth,
How is thy travail understood, except thou
give me birth ?
O waves of death, O saltness, O sorrow
manifold !
I see beneath thy darkness azure ; deeper
still, the heart of gold.

[1] It is not known to whom Crowley refers.

Am I not true, O mother, who hast held the
  lives of men
Sucked down to thy swart bosom—O render
  not again !
Keep thou our life and mix it with thine
  eternal sleep :
Rest, let us rest from passion there, deep !
  O how deep !

Deep calleth unto deep, Amen ! hast thou no
  passion, thou ?
Even now the white flames kindle on thy
  universal brow.
I hear white serpents hiss and wild black
  dragons roll ;
And the storm of love is on thee—ah ! shall
  it touch thy soul ?

Nay, O my mother, in eternal calm thy
  virginal depths lie.
The peace of God, that passeth understanding,
  that am I !
Even I, perceiving deeply beneath the eyes
  of flame
The soul that, kindling, is not kindled : I
  have known thy Name.

Awake, O soaring billows ! Lighten the
  raging dome,
Wrap the wide horizon in a single cloak of
  flaming foam,
Leap in your fury ! Beat upon the shores
  unseen ! Devour your food,
The broken cliff, the crumbled bank, the
  bar. I know the mood.

Even so I see the terror of universal strife :
Murderous war, and murderous peace, and
  miserable life :
The pang of childbirth, and the pain of
  youth, and the fear of age,
Life tossed and broken into dust in the
  elemental rage.

Is not God part of every the tiniest spark
  of man ?
Is He not moulded also in His own eternal
  plan ?

Even so ; as the woes of earth is the angry
  crested sea.
Even so ; as Her great peace abideth in the
  deep—so He !

What wreck floats by us ? What pale corpse
  rolls horribly above,
Tossed on the unbewailing foam, cast out of
  light and life and love ?
The sea shall draw thee down, O brother, to
  her breast of peace,
Her unimaginable springs, her bridal secrecies.

Even so draw me in life, O Mother, to thy
  breast !
Below the storm, below the wind, to the
  abiding rest !
That I may know thy purpose and understand
  thy ways :
So, weeping always for the woe, also the love
  to praise !

The darkness falls intensely : no light invades
  the gloom.
Stillness drops dew-like from the heaven's
  unreverberant womb.
Westward the ship is riding on the sable
  wings of night,
I understand the darkness—why should I
  seek the light ?


## ASSUMPTA CANIDIA.

*Written in Mexico City.*

WATERS that weep upon the barren shore
  Where some lone mystery of man abides ;
  As if the wailing of forsaken brides,
Rapt from the kiss of love for evermore,
Impressed its memory on the desolate
  Sounds at its edge ; on such a strand of
    tears
  I linger through the long forgetful years,
My sin for mother, and my woe for mate.
  I am a soul lost utterly—forbear !
  I am unworthy both of tear and prayer.

The mystic slumber of my sense forlorn
　Stirs only now and then ; some deeper
　　pang
　Reminds despair there is a sharper fang,
Reminds my night of a tempestuous morn.
For I am lost and lonely : in the skies
　I see no hope of any sun or star ;
　On earth there blooms no rose, no nenu-
　　phar ;
No cross is set for hope of sacrifice.
　I cannot sleep, I cannot wake ; and death
　Passes me by with his desirèd breath.


No shadow in my mind to prove a sun ;
　No sorrow to declare that joy exists ;
　A cycle of dim spectres in the mists
Moves just a little ; lastly there is One,
One central Being, one elusive shape,
　Not to aspire to, not to love ; alas !
　Only a memory in the agèd mass
Of chained ones bound to me without escape !
　Oh, doom of God ! Oh, brand how worse
　　than Cain's !
　Divided being, undivided pains !


What is this life ? (To call it life that grows
　No inch throughout all time.) This bitter-
　　ness
Too weak and hateful to be called distress ?
Slow memory working backward only knows
There was some horror grown to it for kin ;
　Some final leprous growth that took my
　　brain,
　Weaving a labyrinth of dullest pain
From the sweet scarlet thread I thought was
　　sin.
　I cannot sin ! Alas, one sin were sweet !
　But sin is living—and we cannot meet !


So long ago, so miserably long !
　I was a maiden—oh how rich and rare
　Seemed the soft sunshine woven in my hair !
How keen the music of my body's song !
How white the blossom of my body's light !
　How red the lips, how languorous the eyes,
　How made for pleasure, for the sleepy
　　sighs

Softer than sleep ; amorous dew-dreams of
　night
That draw out night in kisses to the day !
So was I to my seeming as I lay.

That soft smooth-moving ocean of the west
　Under the palm and cactus as it rolled,
　Immortal blue, fixed with immortal gold,
Moving in rapture with my sleeping breast !
The young delicious green, the drunken smell
　Of the fresh earth, the luxury of the glow
　Where many colours mingled into snow,
Song-marvels in the air desirable.
　So lazily I lay, and watched my eyes
　In the deep fountain's sun-stirred har-
　　monies.

I loved myself ! O Thou ! (I cried) divine
　Woman more lovely than the flowers of
　　earth !
O Self-hood softer than the babe at birth,
Sweeter than love, more amorous than wine,
Where is thy peer upon the face of life ?
　I love myself, the daughter of the dawn.
　Come, silken night, in your deep wings
　　withdrawn
Let me be folded, as a tender wife
　In my own arms imagined ! Let me sleep,
　Unwaking from the admirable deep !

My arms fell lazily about the bed.
　I lay in some delicious trance. I fell
　Deep through sleep's chambers to the gate
　　of Hell,
And on that flaming portalice I read
The legend, " Here is beauty, here delight,
　Here love made more desirable than thine,
　Fiercer than light, more dolorous than wine.
Here the embraces of the Sons of Night !
　Come, sister, come ; come, lonely queen
　　of breath !
　Here are the lustres and the flames of
　　death."

Hence I was whirled, as in a wind of light,
　Out to the fragrance of a loftier air,
　A keener scent, and rising unaware
Out of the Palace of Luxurious Night,

I came to where the Gate of Heaven shone,
  Battled with comet and with meteor.
  Behold within that crested House of War,
One central glory of a sapphire stone,
  Whereon there breathed a sense, a mist,
    a sun !
  I stood and laughed upon the Ancient One.

For He was silent as my body's kiss,
  , And sleeping as my many-coloured hair,
  And living as my eyes and lips ; and where
The vast creation round him cried " He Is !",
No murmur reached Him ; He was set alone,
  Alone and central. Ah ! my eyes were dim.
  I worshipped even ; for I envied Him.
So, moving upward to the azure throne,
  I spread my arms unto that ambient mist ;
  Lifted my life and soul up to be kissed !

A million million voices roared aloud !
  A million million sabres flashed between !
  Flamed the vast falchion ! Fiery Cherubin
Flung me astounded to the mist and cloud.
A stone, flung downward through eternal
    space,
  I dropped. What bitter curses and despair
  Rang through wide aether ! How the
    trumpet blare
Cursed back at me ! Thou canst not see His
    Face !
  Equal and Spouse ? Bring forth the Virgin
    Dower,
  Eternal Wisdom and Eternal Power !

I woke ! and in a well's untroubled pool
  I saw my face—and I was ugly now !
  Blood-spattered ebony eyelash and white
    brow !
Blood on my lips, and hair, and breast !
    " Thou fool ! "
A horrid torture in my heart—and then
  I licked my lips : the tigress tasted blood.
  My changèd features—wash them in the
    flood
Of murder ! This is power over men
  And angels. I will lift the twisted rod,
  And make my power as the power of God !

I made my beauty as it was before.
  I learned strange secrets ; by my love and
    skill
  I bent creation to my wanded will.
I tuned the stars, I bound the bitter shore
Beyond the Pleiads : until the Universe
  Moved at my mantra [1] : Heaven and Hell
    obeyed ;
  Creation at my orders stayed or swayed.
" Take back," I cried, " the mockery of a
    curse ! "
  " I wield Thy Power." With my magic rod
  Again I strode before the Throne of God.

" Forgone my Virgin Splendour ! I aspire
  No longer as a maiden to thy Love.
  We twain are set in majesty above :
My cloud is mighty as thy mystic Fire."
Vanished the mist, the light, the sense, the
    throne !
  Vanished the written horror of the curse ;
  Vanished the stars, the sun, the Universe.
I was in Heaven, lost, alone. Alone !
  A new curse gathered as a sombre breath :
  " Power without Wisdom is the Name of
    Death ! "

And therefore from my devastating hand
  (For I was then unwilling to be dead)
  I loosed the lightning, and in hate and
    dread
Despairing, did I break the royal wand.
Mortal, a plaything for a thousand fears,
  I found the earth ; I found a lonely place
  To gaze for ever on the ocean's face,
Lamenting through the lamentable years ;
  Without a god, deprived of life and death,
  Sensible only to that sombre breath.

Thus wait I on the spring-forgotten shore ;
  Looking with vain unweeping eyes, for aye
  Into the wedding of the sea and sky,
(That do not wed, ay me !) for evermore
Hopeless, forgetting even to aspire
  Unto that Wisdom ; miserably dumb ;
  Waiting for the Impossible to come,
Whether in mercy or damnation dire—

  [1] The Hindu equivalent for " spell."

I who have been all Beauty and all
    Power !—
This is thine hour, Apollyon, thine Hour !

I, who have twice beheld the awful throne ;
    And, as it were the vision of a glass,
    Beheld the Mist be born thereon, and pass ;
I, who have stood upon the four-square stone !
I, who have twice been One——! Woe,
    woe is me !
    Lost, lost, upon the lifeless, deathless plane,
    The desert desolate, the air inane ;
Fallen, O fallen to eternity !
    I, who have looked upon the Lord of Light ;
    I, I am Nothing, and dissolved in Night !

(THE SPIRIT OF GOD, DESCENDING,
    ASSUMETH HER INTO THE GLORY
    OF GOD.)


## VENUS.

*Written in the temple of the L.I.L.,* [1] *No. 9,
Central America.*

MISTRESS and maiden and mother, im-
    mutable mutable soul !
Love, shalt thou turn to another ? Surely
    I give thee the whole !
Light, shalt thou flicker or darken ? Thou
    and thy lover are met.
Bend from thy heaven and hearken ! Life,
    shalt thou fade or forget ?

Surely my songs are gone down as leaves
    in the dark that are blown ; .
Surely the laurel and crown have faded and
    left me alone.
Vainly I cry in the sunlight ; moon pities
    my passion in vain.
Dark to my eyes is the one light, aching in
    bosom and brain.

Surely, O Mother, thou knowest ! Have I
    not followed thy star ?
I have gone whither thou goest, bitterly
    followed afar,

[1] A secret Order, probably established by
Crowley himself.

Buried my heart in thy sorrow, cast down
    my soul at thy knees.
Thou, thou hast left me no morrow. Days
    and desires, what are these ?

Nay, I have torn from my breast passion and
    love and despair :
Sought in thy palaces rest, sleep that awaited
    me there ;
Sleep that awaits me in vain : I have done
    with the hope of things ;
Passion and pleasure and pain have stung
    me, and lost their stings.

Only abides there a hollow, void as the
    heart of the earth.
Echo may find it and follow, dead from the
    day of her birth.
Life, of itself not insatiate ; death, not pre-
    suming to be ;
Share me intense and emaciate, waste me,
    are nothing to me.

Still in the desolate place, still in the bosom
    that was
Even as a veil for thy face, thy face in a
    breathed-on glass,
Hangs there a vulture, and tears with a beak
    of iron and fire.
I know not his name, for he wears no
    feathers of my desire.

It is thou, it is thou, lone maiden ! My heart
    is a bird that flies
Far into the azure laden with love-lorn songs
    and cries.
O Goddess of Nature and Love ! Thyself
    is the lover I see.
But thou art in the above, and thy kiss is
    not for me.

Thou art all too far for my kiss ; thou art
    hidden past my prayer.
Thy wing too wide, and the bliss too sweet
    for me to share.
Thou art Nature and God ! I am broken in
    the wheelings of thy car ;
Thy love-song unheard or unspoken, and I
    cannot see thy star.

Thou art not cold, but bitter is thy burning
   cry to me.
My tiny heart were fitter for a mortal than
   for thee.
But I cast away the mortal, and I choose the
   tortured way,
And I stand before thy portal, and my face
   is cold and grey.

Thou lovest me with a love more terrible
   than death;
But thou art in the above, and my wings feel
   no wind's breath.
Thou art all too fierce and calm, too bitter
   and sweet, alas!
Thou weavest a cruel charm on my soul that
   is as glass.

I know thee not, who art naked; I lie beneath thy feet
Who hast called till my spirit achèd with a
   pang too deathly sweet.
Thou hast given thee to me dying, and made
   thy bed to me.
I shiver, I shrink, and, sighing, lament it
   cannot be.

I have no limbs as a God's to close thee in
   and hold :
Too brief are my periods, and my hours are
   barren of gold.
I am not thewed as Jove to kill thee in one
   caress!
Not a golden shower is my love, but a child's
   tear of distress.

Give me the strength of a panther, the tiger's
   strenuous sides,
The lion's limbs that span there some thrice
   the turn of the tides,
The mutinous frame, the terror of the royal
   Minotaur,
That our loves may make a mirror of the
   dreadful soul of war!

For love is an equal soul, and shares an
   equal breath.
I am nought—and thou the whole? It were
   not love, but Death.

Give me thy life and strength, let us struggle
   for mastery,
As the long shore's rugged length that battles
   with the sea.

I am thine, I am thine indeed! My form
   is vaster grown,
And our limbs and lips shall bleed on the
   starry solar throne.
My life is made as thine; my blessing and
   thy curse
Beget, as foam on wine, a different universe.

I foam and live and leap: thou laughest,
   fightest, diest!
In agony swift as sleep thou hangest as the
   Christ.
My nails are in thy flesh; my sweat is on thy
   brow;
We are one, we are made afresh, we are
   Love and Nature now.

I am swifter than the wind: I am wider
   than the sea :
I am one with all mankind: and the earth
   is made as we.
The stars are spangles bright on the canopy
   of our bed,
And the sun is a veil of light for my lover's
   golden head.

O Goddess, maiden, and wife! Is the
   marriage bed in vain?
Shall my heart and soul and life shrink back
   to themselves again?
Be thou my one desire, my soul in day as in
   night!
My mind the home of the Higher! My
   heart the centre of Light!

## A LITANY.[1]

### I.

BLACK thine abyss of noon
Flings forth the thunder-swoon.
Smite us, and slay, Amoun,
   Amoun, Achiha!

[1] The Table of Correspondences will elucidate any doubtful point in this poem.

### II.

Thoth, from the starry space
Flash out the splendid face !
Wisdom, immortal grace,
 Thoth, turn to usward !

### III.

Deep, deep thy sombre Sea,
Spouse of eternity !
Mother, we cry to Thee :
 Hear us, Maut, Mother !

### IV.

Sound, sistron, sound afar !
Shine, shine, O dawning Star !
Flame, flame, O meteor Car !
 Isis, Our Lady !

### V.

Strike, strike the louder chord !
Draw, draw the flaming sword,
Crowned child and conquering Lord :
 Horus, avenger.

### VI.

Dawn-star of flaming light,
Five rays in one unite,
Light, Life, Love, Mercy, Might,
 Star of the Magi.

### VII.

Lift, lift the Cross of Light,
Rose, golden, green, and white,
Rise, rise athwart the night !
 Mighty Aeshuri !

### VIII.

Flame, flame, thou Blazoned Sun !
Seal-Star of Solomon !
Seven Mysteries in One !
 Godhead and Mankind !

### IX.

Beauty and life and love !
Let fly thy darling dove !
Bend to us from above,
 Lady Ahathor !

### X.

Where light and darkness meet,
There shine thy flaming feet,
There is thy splendid seat ;
 Mighty Anubi !

### XI.

Swift-winged Stability,
Lifting the earth and sky,
Hold me up utterly,
 Keep me, O Shuwe !

### XII.

Virginal Queen of Earth,
Late love, and last of birth,
Loose, loose the golden girth,
 Nephthys, the crowned one !

### XIII.

Hail, crowned Harpocrates,
Show, show thy secrecies,
Lotus-throned silences,
 Typhon's replacer !

## MARCH IN THE TROPICS.

### *Written near Manzanillo.*

WHAT ails thee, earth ?  Is not the breath
 of Spring
Exultant on thy breast ?  What aileth thee,
O many-mooded melancholy sea ?
Hear the swift rush of that triumphant wing !
Listen ! the world's whole heart is listening !
In England now the leaf leaps, and the tree
Gleams dewy, and the bird woos noisily.
Here in the tropics now is no such thing.

Dull heavy heat burns through the clouded
 sky,
And yet no promise of the latter rains.
Earth bears her fruit, but unrefreshed of
 death.
In winter is no sorrow, in the dry
Harsh spring no joy, while pestilence and
 pains
Hover like wolves behind the summer's breath.

## NIGHT IN THE VALLEY.

*Written at the foot of Citlaltepetl.*

I LAY within the forest's virgin womb
  Tranced in the sweetness, nuptial, indolent,
Of the faint breeze and tropical perfume,
  And all the music far lone waters lent
Unto the masses of magnolia bloom,
  Tall scarlet lilies, and the golden scent
Shed by strange clusters of more pallid flowers,
And purple lustre strewn amid the twilight
  bowers.

Far, far the pastureless, the unquiet sea
  Moaned ; far the stately pyramid of cold
Shrouding the stars, arose : sweet witchery
  That brought them in the drowsing eye,
  to fold
The picture in : the wingèd imagery
  That Hermes gathers with that floral gold
Whose triple flower or flame or pinioned light
Lends life to death, and love and colour unto
  light.

How flames that scarlet stronger than Apollo,
  Too swift and warm to know itself a bird !
How the light winds and waves of moonlight
  follow,
  Shot from the West, cadence of Daylight's
  word !
How flock the tribes of wings within the
  hollow,
  Even as darkness summons home the herd !
The still slow water slackens into sleep.
The rose-glow dies, leaves cold Citlaltepetl's [1]
  steep.

The chattering voices of the day depart.
  Earth folds her limbs and leans her loving
  breast
Even to all her children : the great heart
  Beats solemnly the requiem of rest.
The sea keeps tune ; the silent stars upstart
  Seeming to sentinel that sombre crest
Where of old time burst out the vulture fire
Cyclopean, that is dead, now, as a man's
  desire.

[1] Called by the Spaniards Orizaba.

The drowsy cries of night birds, then the
  song
  Lovely and lovelorn in the listening vale,
So wild and tender, swooping down in long
  Notes of despair, then lifting the low tale
In golden notes to skyward in one throng
  Of clustered silver, so the nightingale
Tunes the wild flute, as dryads he would
  gather
To roof with music in the palace of the
  weather,

With love despairing, dying as music dies ;
  With lost souls' weeping, and the bitter
  muse
Of such as lift their hearts in sacrifice
  On some strange cross, or shed Sicilian
  dews
Over a sadder lake than Sicily's—
  Hark ! they are leaping from the valley
  views
Into the light and laughter and deep grief
Of that immortal heart that sings beyond
  belief.

How pitiful, how beautiful, the faces !
  The long hair shed on shoulders ivory
  white !
Each note shoots down the dim arboreal
  spaces
  Like amber or like hyaline lit with light.
Each spirit glimmers in the shadowy places
  Like hyacinths or emeralds : or the night
Shows them as shadows of some antique
  gem
Where moonlight fills its cup and flashes into
  them.

So, in the moony twilight and the splendour
  Of music's light, the desolate nightingale
Fills all the interlunar air with tender
  Kisses like song, or shrills upon the scale,
Till quivering moonrays shake again, to send
  her
  Luminous tunes through every sleepy vale,
While the slow dancers rhythmically reap
The fairy amaranth, and silver wheat of
  sleep.

Now over all that scythe of sleep impending
  Mows the pale flowers of vision following ;
Dryad and bird and fount and valley blending
  Into one dreamy consciousness of spring ;
And all the night and all the world is ending,
    And all the souls that weep and hearts
      that sing !
So, as the dew hides in the lotus blossom,
Sleep draws me with her kiss into her bridal
  bosom.

## METEMPSYCHOSIS.

### *Written at Vera Cruz.*

DIM goes the sun down there behind the tall
And mighty crest of Orizaba's snow :
Here, gathering at the nightfall, to and fro,
Fat vultures, foul and carrion, flap, and call
Their ghastly comrades to the domèd wall
That crowns the grey cathedral.  There they
      go—
The parasites of death, decay and woe,
Gorged with the day's indecent festival.

I think these birds were once the souls of
    priests.
They haunt by ancient habit the old home
Wherein they held high mass in days of old.
But now they soar above it—for behold !
God hath looked mercifully down on Rome,
Promoting thus her children to be beasts.

## ADVICE OF A LETTER.[1]

THE Wingèd Bull that dwellèd in the north
Hath flown into the West, and uttered forth
His thunders in the Mountains.  He shall
  come
Where blooms the sempiterne chrysanthe-
  mum.
The wingèd Lion, that wrought dire amaze
In the Dark Place, where Light was, did his
  ways

[1] With a letter to Ceylon, sent from Mexico
in duplicate for certainty by way both of England and Japan.  The allusions are Hermetic
or Alchemical.
VOL. II.

Take fiery to enkindle a new flame :
The Eagle of the High Lands yet that came
By the red sunset to an eastern sky
Shall  plume  himself  and  gather  him  and
  fly
Even as a Man that rideth on a Beast
Trained, to the Golden Dawn-sky of the
  East.
Therefore  his  word  shall  seek  the  Ivory
  Isle
By double winds and by the double Style,
Twin doorways of the Sunset and the Dawn.
And thou who tak'st it, shalt be subtly drawn
Into strange vigils, and shalt surely see
The ancient form and memory of me,
Nor me distinct, but shining with that Light
Wherein the Sphinx and Pyramid unite.

## ON WAIKIKI BEACH.[1]

UPHEAVED from Chaos, through the dark
      sea hurled,
    Through the cleft heart of the amazèd sea,
    Sprang, 'mid deep thunderous throats of
      majesty,
Titanic, in the waking of the world ;
    Sprang, one vast mass of spume and
      molten fire,
    Lava, tremendous waves of earth ; sprang
      higher
      Than the sea's crest volcano-torn, to be
      Written in Cyclopean charactery,
      Hawaii.   Here she stands
      Queen of all laughter's lands
    That  dance  for  dawn,  lie  tranced  in
      leisured noon,
      Dreaming  through  day  towards
        night,
      Craving the perfumed light
Of the stars lustrous, and the gem-born
      moon.
      Dewy with clustered diamond,
The long land swoons to sleep ; the sea
      sleeps and yet wakes beyond.

      [1] Near Honolulu.                    C

Here, in the crescent beach and bay, the sea,
  Curven and carven in warm shapes of
      dream,
  Answers the love-song of the lilied
      stream,
And moves to bridal music.  Stern and free,
  The lion-shapen headland guards the
      shore ;
  The ocean, the bull-throated, evermore
    Roars ; the vast wheel of heaven turns
      above,
    Its rim of pain, its jewelled heart of
      love ;
      Sun-waved, the eagle wing
      Of the air of feathered spring
Royally sweeps, and on the musical marge
    Watches alone the man.
    O silvern shape and span
  Of moonlight, reaching over the grey,
      large
    Breast of the surf-bound strand,
Life of the earth, God's child, Man's bride,
    the light of the sweet land !


Are emeralds ever a spark of this clear green,
  Or sapphires hints of this diviner blue,
  Or rubies shadows of this rosy hue,
Or light itself elsewhere so clear and clean ?
  For all the sparkling dews of heaven
      fallen far
  Crystalline, fixed, forgotten (as a star
    Forgets its nebulous virginity)
  Are set in all the sky and earth and sea.
    Shining with solar fire,
    The single-eyed desire
Of scent and sound and sight and sense
      perfuses
    The still and lambent light
    Of the essential night ;
And all the heart of me is fain, and muses,
    As if for ever doomed to dream
Or pass in peace Lethean adown the grey
    Lethean stream.


So deep the sense of beauty, and so keen !
  The calm abiding holiness of love
  Reigns ; and so fallen from the heights
    above

Immeasurable, the influence unseen
  Of music and of spiritual fire,
  That the soul sleeps, forgotten of desire,
  Only remembering its God-like birth
    Reflected in the deity of earth,
    Becometh even as God.
    The pensive period
  Of night and day beats like a waving fan
    No more, no more : the years,
    Reft of their joys and fears,
  Pass like pale faces, leave the life of man
    Untroubled of their destinies,
Leave him forgotten of life and time, im-
    mortal, calm and wise.


Only the ceaseless surf on coral towers,
  The changeless change of the unchanging
    ocean,
  Laps the bright night, with unsubstantial
    motion
Winnowing the starlight, plumed with
    feathery flowers
  Of foam and phosphor glory, the strange
    glow
  Of the day's amber fallen to indigo,
    Lit of its own depth in some subtle
      wise,
  A pavement for the footsteps from
    the skies
    Of angels walking thus
    Not all unseen of us,
Nor all unknown, nor unintelligible,
    When with souls lifted up
    In the Cadmean cup, [1]
As incense lifted in the thurible,
  We know that God is even as we,
Light from the sky, and life on earth, and
    love beneath the sea.


## THE TRIADS OF DESPAIR.

*Written off the Coast of Japan.*

I.

I LIE in liquid moonlight poured from the
  exalted orb.
Orion waves his jewelled sword ; the tingling
  waves absorb

    [1] See Euripides, *Bacchae.*

Into their lustre as they move the light of
    all the sky.
I am so faint for utter love I sigh and long
    to die.
Far on the misty ocean's verge flares out the
    Southern Cross,
And the long billows on the marge of coral
    idly toss,
This night of nights! The stars disdain a
    lustre dusk or dim.
Twin love-birds on the land complain, a
    wistful happy hymn.
I turn my face toward the main: I laugh
    and dive and swim.

Now fronts me foaming all the light of surf-
    bound waters pent;
Now from the black breast of the night the
    Southern Cross is rent.
I top the mighty wall of fears; the dark
    wave rolls below.
A tall swift ship on wings appears, a cataract
    of snow
Plunging before the white east wind; she
    meets the eager sea
As forest green by thunder thinned meets
    fire's emblazonry.
Then I sink back upon the breast of mighty-
    flinging foam,
Ride like a ghost upon the crest, the silver-
    rolling comb;
Float like a warrior to his rest, majestically
    home.

But oh! my soul, what seest thou, whose
    eyes are open wide?
What thoughts inspire me idling now, lone
    on the lonely tide?
Here in the beauty of the place, hope laughs
    and says me nay;
In nature's bosom, in God's face, I read
    *Decay, Decay.*
Here in the splendour of the Law that built
    the eternal sphere,
Beauty and majesty and awe, I fail of any
    cheer.
Here, in caprice, in will divine, I see no
    perfect peace;

Here, in the Law's impassive shrine, no hope
    is of release.
All things escape me, all repine, all alter,
    ruin, cease.

## II.

But thou, O Lord, O Apollo,
Must thou utterly change and pass?
Thy light be lost in the hollow?
Thy face as a maid's in a glass
Go out and be lost and be broken
As the face of the maid is withdrawn,
And thy people with sorrow unspoken
Wait, wait for the dawn?

But thou, O Diana, our Lady,
Shall it be as if never had been?
The vales of the sea grown shady
And silver and amber and green
As thy light passed over and kissed them?
Shall thy people lament thee and swoon,
And we miss thee if thy love missed them,
Awaiting the moon?

But thou, who art Light, and above them,
Who art fire and above them as fire,
Shall thy sightless eyes not love them
Who are all of thine own desire?
Immaculate daughters of passion,
Shalt thou as they pass be past?
And thy people bewail thee, Thalassian,
Lost, lost at the last?

## III.

Nay, ere ye pass your people pass,
As snow on summer hills,
As dew upon the grass,
As one that love fulfils,
If he in folly wills
Love a lass.

Yet on this night of smiles and tears
A maiden is the theme.
The universe appears
An idle summer dream
Lost in the grey supreme
Mist of years.

For she is all the self I own,
And all I want of will.
She speaks not, and is known.
Her window shining chill
Whispers "He lingers still.
I am alone."

### IV.

But to-night the lamp must be wasted,
And the delicate hurt must ache,
And the sweet lips moan untasted,
My lady lie lonely awake.
The night is taken from love, and love's
    guerdon
Is life and its burden.

To-night if I turn to my lover
I must ask : If she be? who am I?
To-night if her heart I uncover
No heart in the night I espy.
I am grips with the question of eld, and the
    sphinx holds fast
My eyes to the past.

Who am I, when I say I languish?
Who is she, if I call her mine?
And the fool's and the wise man's anguish
Are burnt in the bitter shrine.
The god is far as the stars, and the wine and
    fire
Salt with desire.

*Desunt cetera.*

He danced the measure golden
    On dead men . . .
His Saints and Rishis[1] olden,
    The yogins that . . .
He trampled them to dust-and they
Were sparks and no more clay.

The dust thrown up around Him
    In cycles whirled and twined,
Dim sparks that fled and found Him
    Like mist beyond the mind.
The universe was peopled then
With little gods, and men.

In that ecstatic whirling
    He saw not nor . . .

He knew not in His fervour
    Creation's sated sigh ;
The groan of the Preserver,
    Life's miserable lie.
I broke that silence, and afraid
I knew not what I prayed.

   .     .     .     .

Let peace awaken for an hour
And manifest as power.

   .     .     .     .

Cease not the dance unceasing,
    The glance nor swerve nor cease,
Thy peace by power increasing
    In me by power to peace.

*Desunt cetera.*

## THE DANCE OF SHIVA.[1]

*Written at the House of Sri Parananda
Swami, Ceylon.*

WITH feet set terribly dancing,
    With eyelids filled of flame,
Wild lightnings from Him glancing,
    Lord Shiva went and came.
The dancing of His feet was heard
And was the final word.

[1] The MS. of this Hymn most mysteriously
(for I am very careful) disappeared two days
after being written. I can remember no more
of it than the above ; nor will inspiration return.
--A. C.

## SONNET FOR A PICTURE.

*Written in the woods above Kandy. Inscribed
to T. Davidson.*

LURED by the loud big-breasted courtesan
    That plies trained lechery of obedient eyes,
He sits, holds bed's last slattern-sweet
    surprise,
Late plucked from gutter to grace groves
    of Pan.

[1] The seven Rishis are the great Sages of
India. They received from the Gods the
sacred Books.

The third one, ruddy as they twain are wan,
  Hungrily gazes, sees her tower of lies
  Blasted that instant in some wizard wise—
The frozen look—the miserable man !

What sudden barb of what detested dart
Springs from Apollo's bowstring to his
  heart ?
On sense-dulled ears what Voice rings the
  decree ?
  " For thee the women burn : the wine is
  cool :
  For thee the fresco and the fruit—thou
  fool !
This night thy soul shall be required of thee.!"


### THE HOUSE.

#### A NIGHTMARE.[1]

*Written at Anuradhapura.*

I MUST be ready for my friend to-night.
  So, such pale flowers as winter bears
  bedeck
The old oak walls: the wood-fire's cheerful
  light
Flashes upon the fire-dogs silver-bright.
  Wood? why, the jetsam of yon broken
  wreck
  Where the white sea runs o'er the sandy
  neck

That joins my island to the land when tides
  Run low.  What curious fancies through
  my brain
Run, all so wild and all so pleasant !  Glides
No phantom creeping from the under sides
  Of the grey globe : no avatar of pain
  Gathering a body from the wind and rain.

[1] This, with slight variations, was one of the
regular dreams of Allen Bennett Macgregor,
just as the "flying" dream, the "naked in
church" dream, the "taken in adultery"
dream, the "lost tooth" dream, the "being
shaved" dream, and many others of specific
type recur from time to time in the life of most
people.—A. C.

So the night fell, and gently grew the
  shades
  In firelight fancies taking idle form ;
Often a flashing May-day ring of maids,
Or like an army through resounding glades
  Glittering, with martial music, trumpet,
  shawm,
  Drum—so I build the echoes of the storm

Into a pageant of triumphant shapes.
  So, as the night grows deeper, and no
  moon
Stirs the black heaven, no star its cloud
  escapes,
I sit and watch the fire : my musing drapes
  My soul in darker dreams ; the storm's
  wild tune
  Rolls ever deeper in my shuddering swoon :

Whereat I start, shudder, and pull together
  My mind.  Why, surely it must be the
  hour !
My friend is coming through the wet wild
  weather
Across the moor's inhospitable heather
  To the old stately tower—my own dear
  tower.
  He will not fail me for a sudden shower !

My friend !  How often have I longed to
  see
  Again his gallant figure and that face
Radiant—how long ago we parted !—we
The dearest friends that ever were !  Ah me !
  I curse even now that hateful parting-
  place.
  But now—he comes !  How glad I am !
  Apace

Fly the glad minutes—There he is at last !
  I know the firm foot on the marble floor.
The hour-glass turns !  What miseries to cast
For ever to the limbo of the past !
  He knocks—he comes—my friend !  O joy for ever-
  more !
  He calls !  " Open the door !  Open the
  door !"

You guess how gladly to the door I rushed
And flung it wide. Why ! no one's there !
   Arouse !
I am asleep. What horror came and crushed
My whole soul's life out as some shadow
   brushed
   My body and passed in ? All sense allows
At last the fearful truth—This is the house !

This is my old house on the marsh, and here,
   Here is the terror of the distant sea
Moaning, and here the wind that wails, the
   drear
Groans like a ghost's, the desolate house of
   fear
   Whence I fled once from my great enemy—
This is the house ! O speechless misery !

Here the great silver candlesticks illume
   The agèd book, the blackness blazoned o'er
With golden characters and scarlet bloom
Twined in the blue-tinged sigils wrought for
   doom,
   And dreadful names of necromancer's lore
Written therein : so stood my room before

When the hissed whisper came, " Beware !
   Beware !
They're coming !" and " They're coming !"
   when the wind
Bore the blank echoes of their stealthy care
To creep up silently and find me there,
   Hid in the windowless old house, stark
   blind
   For fear—and then—what horrors lurked
   behind

The door firm barred !—and thus they cried
   in vain :
" Open the door !" Then crouched I mad
   with fear
Till at the dawn their footsteps died again.
They can do nothing to me—that is plain—
   While the door bars them ! What is it
   runs clear
   Truth in my mind ? Once more they may
   be near ?

And then came memory. Wide the portal
   stood
And—what had brushed me as it passed ?
   What froze
My dream to this awakening—fearful flood
Of horror loosed, loosing a sweat of blood,
   An agony of terror on these brows?
   God ! God ! Indeed, indeed this is the
   house !

The candles sputtered and went out. I stood
   Fettered by fear, and heard the lonely wind
Lament across the marsh. A frenzied flood
Of hate and loathing swept across my mood,
   And with a shudder I flung the door to.
   Mind
And body sank a huddled wreck behind.

Nought stirred. Draws hither the grim doom
   of Fate ?

A long, long while.

            Now—in the central core
Of my own room what accent of keen hate,
Triumphant malice, mockery satiate,
   Rings in the voice above the storm's wild
   roar ?
   It cries " Open the door ! Open the door !"

## ANIMA LUNAE.

*Written partly under the great rock Sigiri, in
Ceylon, partly in Arabia, near Aden.*

ZôHRA the king by feathered fans
Slept lightly through the mid-day heat.
Swart giants with drawn yataghans
Guard, standing at his head and feet,
Zôhra, the mightiest of the khans !

Each slave Circassian like a moon
Sits smiling, burning with young bloom
Of dawn, and weaves an airy tune
Like a white bird's song bright and bold
That dips a fiery plume.
So the song lulled, lazily rolled
In tubes of silver, lutes of gold ;

And all the palace drowsed away
The hours that fanned with silken fold
The progress of the Lord of Day.
Yet, as he slept, a grey
Shadow of dream drew near, and stooped
And glided through the ranks of slaves,
Leaving no shadow where they drooped,
No echo in the architraves
As silent as the grave's.
That shape vibrated to the tune
Of thought lulled low ; the stirless swoon
Half felt its fellow gather close,
Yet stirred not : now the intruder moves,
Turns the tune slowlier to grave rows
Of palm trees, losing life in loves
Less turbid than the mildest dream
That ever stirred the stream
Whereon night floats, a shallop faint,
Ivory and silver bow and beam,
Dim-figured with the images
Divinely quaint
Of gold engraved, forth shadowing sorceries.
So the king dreamed of love : and passing on
The shape moved quicker, winnowing with
    faint fans
The soundless air of thought : the noonday sun
Seemed to the mightiest of a thousand khans
Like to a man's
Brief life—a thousand such dream spans !—
And so he dreamed of life : and failing
    plumes
Wrought through ancestral looms
In the man's brain : and so he dreamed of
    death.
And slower still the grey God wrought
Dividing consciousness from breath,
And life and death from thought.
So the king dreamed of Nought.

Yet subtly-shapen was this Nothingness,
Not mere negation, as before that dream
Drew back the veil of sleep ;
But strange : the king turned idly, sought to
    press
The bosom where love lately burnt supreme,
And found no ivory deep.
He turned and sought out life ; and nothing
    lived :

Death, and nought died.  The king's brow
    fell.  Sore grieved
He rose, not knowing : and before his will
Swan's throat, dove's eyes, moon's breast,
    and woman's mouth,
And form desirable
Of all the clustered love drew back : grew
    still
" O turn, my lover, turn thee to the South ! "
The girl's warm song of the Siesta's hour.
Heedless of all that flower,
Eager to feel the strong brown fingers close
On the unshrinking rose
And pluck it to his breast to perish there ;
With neither thought nor care
Nor knowledge he went forth : none stay,
    none dare
Proffer a pavid prayer.

There was a pavement bright with emerald
Glittering on malachite
Clear to the Sun : low battlements enwalled
With gold the ground enthralled,
Sheer to the sight
Of sun and city : thither in his trance
The king's slow steps advance.
There stood he, and with eyes unfolded far
(Clouds shadowing a star
Or moonlight seen through trees—so came
    the lashes
Over—and strong sight flashes !)
Travelled in thought to life, and in its gleam
Saw but a doubtful dream.

His was a city crescent-shaped whose wall
Was brass and iron : in the thrall
Of the superb concave
Lay orbed a waveless wave.
Four moons of liquid light revolved and threw
Their silvery fountains forth, whose fruitful
    dew
Turned all the plain to one enamelled vale
Green as the serpent's glory, and—how still !
—To where the distant hill
Shaped like an Oread's [1] breast arose beyond,
Across the starless pond

[1] Mountain nymph.

Silent and sleeping—O the waters wan
That seem the soul of man !—
Suddenly darkness strikes the horizon round
With an abyss profound
That blots the half-moon ere the sun be set.
A mountain of pure jet
Rears its sheer bulk to heaven ; and no snows
Tinge evening with rose.
No blaze of noon invades those rocks of night,
Nor moon's benignant might.
And looking downward he beheld his folk
Bound in no tyrant's yoke ;
Knowing no God, nor fearing any man ;
Life's enviable span
Free from disease and vice, sorrow and age.
Only death's joys assuage
A gathering gladness at the thought of sleep.
Never in all the archives, scroll on scroll,
Reaching from aeons wrote they " Women
    weep,
Men hate, the children suffer." In the place
Where men most walked a tablet of fine brass
Was set on marble, with an iron style
That all might carve within that golden space
If one grief came—and still the people pass,
And since the city first began
None wrote one word thereon till one—a man
Witty in spite of happiness—wrote there :
" I grieve because the tablet is so fair
And still stands bare,
There being none to beautify the same
With the moon-curved Arabian character."
Whereat the king, " Thy grief itself removes
In its own cry its cause." And thence there
    came
Soft laughter that may hardly stir
The flowers that shake not in the City of
    Loves.
(For so men called the city's name
Because the people were more mild than
    doves,
More beautiful than Gods of wood or river ;
And so the city should endure for ever.)

But the king's mood was otherwise this day.
Along time's river, fifty years away,
There was a young man once
Ruddier than autumn suns

With gold hair curling like the spring sun's
    gold,
And blue eyes where stars lurked for happi-
    ness,
And lithe with all a young fawn's loveliness.
Such are the dwellers of the fire that fold
Fine wings in wanton ecstasy, and sleep
Where the thin tongues of glory leap
Up from the brazen hold
And far majestic keep
Of Djinn, the Lord of elemental light.
But he beheld some sight
Beyond that city's joy : his gentle word
The old king gently heard.
(This king was Zôhra's father) " Lord and
    king
Of love's own city, give me leave to wing
A fervid flight to yonder hills of night.
Not that my soul is weary of the light
And lordship of thy presence ; but in tender
    dream
I saw myself on the still stream
Where the lake goes toward the mountain wall.
These little lives and loves ephemeral
Seemed in that dream still sweet : yet even
    now
I turned the shallop's prow
With gathering joy toward the lampless
    mountains.
I heard the four bright fountains
Gathering joy of music—verily
I cannot understand
How this can be,
Yet—I would travel to that land."
So all they kissed him—and the boy was gone.
But when the full moon shone
A child cried out that he had seen that face
Limned with incomparable grace
Even in the shape of splendour as she passed.
The king's thought turned at last
To that forgotten story : and desire
Filled all his heart with aureate fire
Whose texture was a woman's hair ; so fine
Bloomed the fair flower of pleasure :
Not the wild solar treasure
Of gleaming light, but the moon's shadowy
    pearl,
The love of a young girl

Before she knows that love : so mused the king ;
" I am not weary of the soul of spring,"
He said, "none happier in this causeless chain
Of life that bears no fruit of pain,
No seed of sorrow," yet his heart was stirred,
And, wasting no weak word
On the invulnerable air, that had
No soul of memories sad,
He passed through all the palace : in his bowers
He stooped and kissed the flowers ;
And in his hall of audience stayed awhile,
And with a glad strange smile
Bade a farewell to all those lords of his ;
And greeted with a kiss
The virgins clustered in his halls of bliss.
Next, passing through the city, gave his hand
To many a joyous band
Flower-decked that wandered through the wanton ways
Through summer's idle days.
Last, passing through the city wall, he came
Out to the living flame
Of lambent water and the carven quay,
Stone, like embroidery !
All the dear beauty of art's soul sublime
He looked on the last time,
And trod the figured steps, and found the ledge
At the white water's edge
Where the king's pinnace lodged ; but he put by
That shell of ivory,
And chose a pearl-inwoven canoe, whose prow
Bore the moon's own bright brow
In grace of silver sculptured ; and therein
He stepped ; and all the water thin
Laughed to receive him ; now the city faded
Little by little into many-shaded
Clusters of colour.   So his boat was drawn
Subtly toward the dawn
With little labour ; and the lake dropped down
From the orb's utter crown
O'er the horizon ; and the narrowing sides
Showed him the moving tides

And pearling waters of a tinier stream
Than in a maiden's dream
She laves her silken limbs in, and is glad.
Then did indeed the fountains change their tune,
Sliding from gold sun-clad
To silver filigree wherethrough the moon
Shines—for the subtle soul
Of music takes on shape, and we compare
The cedar's branching hair,
The comet's glory, and the woman's smile,
To strange devices otherwise not heard
Without the lute's own word.

So on the soul of Zôhra grew
A fashioned orb of fiery dew :
Yet (as cool water on a leaf)
It touched his spirit not with grief,
Although its name was sorrow.
" O for a name to borrow "
(He mused) " some semblance for this subtle sense
Of new experience !
For on my heart, untouched, my mind not used
To any metre mused,
Save the one tranquil and continuous rhyme
Of joy exceeding time,
Here the joy changes, but abides for ever,
Here on the shining river
Where the dusk gathers, and tall trees begin
To wrap the shallop in,
Sweet shade not cast of sun or moon or star,
But of some light afar
Softer and sweeter than all these—what light
Burns past the wondrous night
Of yonder crags ?—what riven chasm hides
In those mysterious sides ?
Somewhere this stream must leap
Down vales divinely steep
Into some vain unprofitable deep ! "

So mused the king.   Mark you, the full moon shone !
Nay, but a little past the full, she rose
An hour past sunset : as some laughter gone,
After the bride's night, lost in subtler snows

Rosy with wifehood.   Now the shallop glides
On gloomier shadier tides,
While the long hair of willows bent and kissed
The stream, and drew its mist
Up through their silent atmosphere.
Some sorrow drawing near
That slow, dark river would for sympathy
Have found its home and never wandered out
Into the sunlight any more.   A sigh
Stirred the pale waters where the moonlight
    stood
Upon the sleepy flood
In certain bough-wrought shapes of mystic
    meaning,
As if the moon were weaning
The king her babe from milk of life and love
To milk new-dropped above
From her sweet breast in vaporous light
Into the willowy night
That lay upon the river.   So the king
Heard a strange chant—the woods began to
    sing ;
The river took the tune ; the willows kept
Time ; and the black skies wept
Those tears, those blossoms, those pearl drops
    of milk
That the moon shed : and looking up he saw
As if the willows were but robes of silk,
The moon's face stoop and draw
Close to his forehead : at the tears she shed
He knew that he was dead !
Thus he feared not, nor wondered, as the
    stream
Grew darker, as a dream
Fades to the utter deep
Of dreamless sleep.
The stream grew darker, and the willows
    cover
(As lover from a lover
Even for love's sake all the wealth of love)
The whole light of the skies : there came to
    him
Sense of some being dim
Bent over him, one colour and one form
With the dark leaves ; but warm
And capable of some diviner air.
Her limbs were bare, her face supremely
    fair,

Her soul one shapely splendour,
Her voice indeed as tender
As very silence : so he would not speak,
But let his being fade : that all the past
Grew shadowy and weak,
And lost its life at last,
Being mere dream to this that was indeed
Life : and some utter need
Of this one's love grew up in him : he knew
The spirit of that dew
In his own soul ; and this indeed was love.
The faint girl bent above
With fixed eyes close upon him ; oh ! her face
Burned in the rapturous grace
Feeding on his ; and subtly, without touch,
Grew as a flower that opens at the dawn
Their kiss : for touch of lips is death to love.
Even as the gentle plant one finger presses,
However soft the tress is
Of even the air's profane caresses,
It closes, all its joy of light withdrawn ;
The sun feels sadness in his skies above,
Because one flower is folded.   Thus they
    floated
Most deathlessly devoted
Beyond the trees, and where the hills divide
To take the nighted tide
Into a darker, deeper, greener breast,
Maybe to find—what rest ?
Now to those girdling mountains moon-exalted
Came through the hills deep-vaulted
That pearly shallop : there the rocks were
    rent,
And the pale element
Flowed idly in their gorges : there the night
Admits no beam of light ;
Nor can the poet's eye
One ray espy.
Therefore I saw not how the voyage ended,
Only wherethrough those cliffs were rended
I saw them pass : and ever closer bent
The lady and the lover ; ever slower
Moved the light craft, and lower
Murmured the waters and the wind com-
    plained ;
And ever the moon waned ;
Not wheeling round the world,
But subtly curved and curled

In shapes not seen of men, abiding ever
Above the lonely river
Aloft : no more I saw than this,
The shadowy bending to the first sweet kiss
That surely could not end, though earth
    should end.
Therefore my shut eyes blend
With sleep's own secret eyes and eyelashes,
Long and deep ecstasies,
Knowing as now I know—at last—how this
Foreshadows my own bliss
Of falling into death when life is tired.
For of all things desired
Not one as death is so desirable,
Seeing all sorrows pass, all joys endure,
All lessons last.   Not heaven and not hell
(My spirit is grown sure)
Await the lover
But death's veil draws, life's mother to dis-
    cover,
Nature ; no longer mother, but a bride !
Ay ! there is none beside.

O brothers mightier than my mightiest word
In the least sob that stirred
Your lyres, bring me, me also to the end !
Be near to me, befriend
Me in the moonlit, moonless deeps of death,
And with exalted breath
Breathe some few flames into the embers dull
Of these poor rhymes and leave them
    beautiful.


## "SABBÉ PI DUKKHAM."

(*Everything is Sorrow.*)

A LESSON FROM EURIPIDES.

*Written in Lamma Sayadaw Kyoung, Akyab.*

LAUGHTER in the faces of the people
Running round the theatre of music
When the cunning actors play the Bacchae,
Greets the gay attire and gait of Pentheus,
Pentheus by his blasphemy deluded,
Pentheus caught already in the meshes
Of the fate that means to catch and crush him,
Pentheus going forth with dance and revel,
Soon by Bassarids (wild joys of Nature)
To be hunted.   Ai ! the body mangled
By the fatal fury of the Maenads
Led by Agave his maddened mother
(Nature's self).   But this the people guess not,
Only see the youth in woman's raiment,
Feignèd tresses drooping from his forehead,
Awkward with unwonted dress, rude waving
Aye the light spear tipped with mystic pine-
    cone ;
Hear his boast who lifts the slender thyrsus :
" I could bear the mass of swart Cithaeron,
And themselves the Maenads on my shoul-
    ders."
So the self-willed's folly lights the laughter
Rippling round the theatre.   But horror
Seizes on the heart of the judicious.
They see only madness and destruction
In the mockery's self innate, implicit.
Horror, deeper grief, most dreadful musings
Theirs who penetrate the poet's purpose !
So in all the passing joys of nature,
Joys of birth, and joys of life, in pleasures
Beautiful or innocent or stately,
May the wise discern the fact of being—
Change and death, the tragedy deep-lurking
Hidden in the laughter of the people,
So that laughter's self grows gross and hateful.
Then the Noble Truth of Sorrow quickens
Every heart, and, seeking out its causes,
Still the one task of the wise, their wisdom
Finds desire, and, seeking out its medicine,
Finds cessation of desire, and, seeking
How so fierce a feat may be accomplished,
Finds at first in Truth a right foundation,
Builds the walls of Rightful Life upon it,
Four-square, Word and Act and Aspiration
Folded mystically across each other,
Crowns that palace of enduring marble
With sky-piercing pinnacles of Will-power
Rightly carven, rightly pointed ; strengthens
[Mind sole centred on the single object]
All against the lightning, earthquake, thunder,
Meteor, cyclone with strong Meditation.
There, the sacred spot from wind well-
    guarded,
May the lamp, the golden lamp, be lighted

To illume the whole with final Rapture
And destroy the House of pain for ever,
Leave its laughter and its tears, and shatter
All the causes of its mockery, master
All the workings of its will, and vanish
Into peace and light and bliss, whose nature
Baffles so the little tongues of mortals
That we name it not, but from its threshold,
From the golden word upon its gateway,
Style "Cessation"; that whose self we guess
　　not.
Thus the wise most mystically interpret
Into wisdom the worst folly spoken
By the mortal of a god deluded.
So, the last wise word rejected, Pentheus
Cries, "ἄγ' ὡς τάχιστα, τοῦ χρόνου δέ
σοι φθονῶ?" — "Why waste we time in
　　talking?
Let us now away unto the mountains!"
So the wise, enlightened by compassion,
Seeks that bliss for all the world of sorrow,
Swears the bitter oath of Vajrapani:
"Ere the cycle rush to utter darkness
Work I so that every living being
Pass beyond this constant chain of causes.
If I fail, may all my being shatter
Into millions of far-whirling pieces!"
Swears that oath, and works, and studies
　　silence,
Takes his refuge in the triple jewel,
Strangles all desires in their beginning,
Leaves no egg of thought to hatch its serpent
Thrice detested for unnatural breeding—
Basilisk, to slay the maddened gazer.
Thus the wise man, for no glory-guerdon,
Hope of life or joy in earth or heaven,
Works, rejecting all the flowers of promise
Dew-lit that surround his path; but keepeth
Steady all his will to one endeavour,
Till the light, the might, the joy, the sorrow,
Life and death and love and hate are broken:
Work effaces work, avails the worker.
Strength, speed, ardour, courage and endur-
　　ance
(Needed never more) depart for ever.
All dissolves, an unsubstantial phantom,
Ghost of morning seen before the sunrise,
Ghost of daylight seen beyond the sunset.

All hath past beyond the soul's delusion.
All hath changèd to the ever changeless.
Name and form in nameless and in formless
Vanish, vanish and are lost for ever.

## DHAMMAPADA.[1]

### I.

#### ANTITHESES. (THE TWINS.)

ALL that we are from mind results, on mind
　　is founded, built of mind.
Who acts or speaks with evil thought, him
　　doth pain follow sure and blind:[2]
So the ox plants his foot and so the car-wheel
　　follows hard behind.

All that we are from mind results, on mind
　　is founded, built of mind.
Who acts or speaks with righteous thought,
　　him happiness doth surely find.
So failing not, the shadow falls for ever in
　　its place assigned.

"Me he abused and me he beat, he robbed
　　me, he defeated me."
In whom such thoughts find harbourage
　　hatred will never cease to be.

"Me he abused and me he beat, he robbed
　　me, he defeated me."
In whom such thoughts no harbourage may
　　find, will hatred cease to be.

"The state of hate doth not abate by hate in
　　any clime or time,
But hate will cease if love increase,"[3] so
　　soothly runs the ancient rhyme.

[1] An attempt to translate this noblest of the
Buddhist books into the original metres. The
task soon tired.—A. C.
[2] Blind, i.e., operated by law, not by caprice
of a deity.
[3] Crowley has imitated the punning of the
Pali by the repeated rhymes, which further
gives the flavour of the Old English proverbial
saw.

The truth that "here we all must die" those
others do not comprehend ;
But some perceiving it, for them all discords
find an utter end.


Sodden [1] with passion, unrestrained his senses
(such an one we see),
Immoderate in the food of sense, idle and
void of energy :
Him surely Mara [2] overcomes, as wind throws
down the feeble tree.


Careless of passion, well restrained his senses,
such an one we find
Moderate in pleasure, faithful, great in mighty
energy of mind :
Him Mara shakes not ; are the hills thrown
down by fury of the wind ?


He, void of temperance and truth, from
guilt, impurity, and sin
Not free, the poor and golden robe he hath
no worth to clothe therein. [3]


Regarding temperance and truth, from guilt,
impurity, and sin
Freed, he the poor and golden robe indeed
hath worth to clothe therein.


They who see falsehood in the Truth,
imagine Truth to lurk in lies,
Never arrive to know the Truth, but follow
eager vanities.


To whom in Truth the Truth is known,
Falsehood in Falsehood doth appear,
To them the Path of Truth is shown ; right
aspirations are their sphere !

[1] Sodden — the habitual — who *lives* unrestrained, etc.
[2] The Indian power of evil.
[3] Alternative reading !—
　　Who is not free from dirty taint, and tem-
　　　perate and truthful ain't,
　　He should not wear the garment quaint
　　　that marks the Arahat or Saint.—A. C.

An ill-thatched house is open to the mercy
of the rain and wind.
So passion hath the power to break into an
unreflecting mind.

A well-thatched house is proof against the
fury of the rain and wind.
So passion hath no power to break into a
rightly-ordered mind.

Here and hereafter doth he mourn, him
suffering doth doubly irk,
Who doeth evil, seeing now at last how evil
was his work.

The virtuous man rejoices here, hereafter
doth he take delight,
Both ways rejoices, both delights, as seeing
that his work was right.

Here and hereafter suffers he : the pains of
shame his bosom fill
Who thinks " I did the wrong," laments his
going on the Path of Ill.

Here and hereafter hath he joy : in both the
joy of rectitude
Who thinks "I did the right" and goes
rejoicing on the Path of Good.

A-many verses though he can recite of Law,
the idle man who doth it not
Is like an herd who numbereth cows of
others, Priesthood him allows nor part
nor lot.

Who little of the Law can cite, yet knows
and walks therein aright, and shuns the
snare
Of passion, folly, hate entwined : Right
Effort liberates his mind, he doth not
care
For this course done or that to run : surely in
Priesthood such an one hath earned a
share.

## II.

### EARNESTNESS.

Amata's[1] path is Earnestness, Dispersion
   Death's disciples tread :
The earnest never die, the vain are even as
   already dead.

Who understand, have travelled far on con-
   centration's path, delight
In concentration, have their joy, knowing the
   Noble Ones aright.

In meditation firmly fixed, by constant strenuous effort high,
They to Nibbana[2] come at last, the incomparable security.

Whose mind is strenuous and reflects ; whose
   deeds are circumspect and pure,
His thoughts aye fixed on Law, the fame of
   that concentred shall endure.

By Earnestness, by centred thought, by self-
   restraint, by suffering long,
Let the wise man an island build against the
   fatal current strong.

Fools follow after vanity, those men of evil
   wisdom's sect ;
But the wise man doth earnestness, a precious
   talisman, protect.

Follow not vanity, nor seek the transient
   pleasures of the sense :
The earnest one who meditates derives the
   highest rapture thence.

When the wise man by Earnestness hath
   Vanity to chaos hurled
He mounts to wisdom's palace, looks serene
   upon the sorrowing world.

   [1] Sanskrit, Amrita, the "Elixir of Life"
and food of the gods.
   [2] Sanskrit, Nirvana. See Childers' Pali
Dictionary for etymological discussion. The
signification is too difficult a question to settle
offhand in a note.

Mighty is wisdom : as a man climbs high
   upon the hills ice-crowned,
Surveys, aloof, the toiling folk far distant
   on the dusty ground.

Among the sleepers vigilant, among the
   thoughtless eager-eyed
The wise speeds on ; the racer so passes the
   hack with vigorous stride.

By earnestness did Maghava[1] attain of Gods
   to be the Lord.
Praise is one-pointed thought's reward ; Dispersion is a thing abhorred.

The Bhikkhu who in Earnestness delights,
   who fears dispersions dire,
His fetters all, both great and small, burning
   he moves about the fire.

The Bhikkhu who in Earnestness delights,
   Dispersion sees with fear,
He goes not to Destruction ; he unto Nibbana
   draweth near.

## III.

### THE ARROW.

Just as the fletcher shapes his shaft straightly,
   so shapes his thought the saint,
For that is trembling, weak, impatient of
   direction or restraint.

Mara's dominion to escape if thought im-
   petuously tries
Like to a fish from water snatched thrown on
   the ground it trembling lies.

Where'er it listeth runneth thought, the tameless trembling consciousness.
Well is it to restrain :—a mind so stilled and
   tamed brings happiness.

Hard to perceive, all-wandering, subtle and
   eager do they press,
Thoughts ; let the wise man guard his
   thoughts ; well guarded thoughts bring
   happiness.

   [1] Indra, the Indian Zeus.

Moving alone, far-travelling, bodiless, hidden
   i' th' heart, who trains
His thought and binds it by his will shall be
   released from Mara's chains.

Who stills not thought, nor knows true laws;
   in whom distraction is not dumb,
Troubling his peace of mind; he shall to
   perfect knowledge never come.

His thoughts concentred, unperplexed his
   mind renouncing good and ill
Alike, for him there is no fear if only he
   be watchful still.

Knowing this body to be frail, making this
   thought a fortalice, do thou aright
Mara with wisdom's shaft assail! Watch
   him when conquered. Never cease thou
   from the fight.

Alas! ere long a useless log, this body on
   the earth will lie
Contemned of all, and void of sense and
   understanding's unity.

What foe may wreak on foe, or hate work
   on the hated from the hater,
Surely an ill directed mind on us will do
   a mischief greater.

Father and mother, kith and kin, of these
   can none do service kind
So great to us, as to ourselves the good
   direction of the mind.

IV.

FLOWERS.

O who shall overcome this earth, the world
   of God's and Yama's [1] power!
Who find the well taught Path as skill of
   herbist finds the proper flower?

[1] Hades plus Minos; he both rules and
judges the dead, according to Hindu mythology.

The seeker shall subdue this earth, the world
   of God's and Yama's power;
The seeker find that Path as skill of herbist
   finds the proper flower.

Like unto foam this body whoso sees, its
   mirage-nature comprehends aright,
Breaking dread Mara's flower-pointed shaft
   he goes, Death's monarch shall not meet
   his sight.

Like one who strayeth gathering flowers, is
   he who Pleasure lusteth on;
As the flood whelms the sleeping village, so
   Death snaps him—he is gone.

Like one who strayeth gathering flowers is
   he whose thoughts to Pleasure cling;
While yet unsatisfied with lusts, there con-
   quereth him the Iron King.

As the bee gathers nectar, hurts not the
   flower's colour, its sweet smell
In no wise injureth, so let the Sage within
   his hamlet dwell.

To others' failures, others' sins done or good
   deeds undone let swerve
Never the thought; thine own misdeeds,
   omissions,—these alone observe.

Like to a lovely flower of hue bright, that
   hath yet no odour sweet,
So are his words who speaketh well, fruitless,
   by action incomplete.

Like to a lovely flower of hue delightful and
   of odour sweet
So are his words who speaketh well, fruitful,
   by action made complete.

As from a heap of flowers can men make
   many garlands, so, once born,
A man a-many noble deeds by doing may
   his life adorn.

Travels the scent of flowers against the wind ?
Not Sandal, Taggara, nor Jasmine scent !
But the odour of the good doth so, the good
pervadeth unto every element.

When Sandal, Lotus, Taggara and Vassiki
their odour rare
Shed forth, their fragrant excellence is verily
beyond compare.

Yet little is this fragrance found of Taggara
and Sandal wood :
Mounts to the Gods, the highest, the scent of
those whose deeds are right and good.

Perfect in virtue, living lives of Earnestness,
Right Knowledge hath
Brought into liberty their minds, that Mara
findeth not their path.

As on a heap of rubbish thrown by the way-
side the Lotus flower
Will bloom sweet scented, delicate and ex-
cellent to think upon ;
So 'mid the slothful worthless ones, the
Walkers in Delusion's power,
In glory of Wisdom, light of Buddh forth
hath the True Disciple shone.

*Desunt cetera.*[1]


## ST. PATRICK'S DAY, 1902.

*Written at Delhi.*

O GOOD St. Patrick, turn again
Thy mild eyes to the Western main !
Shalt thou be silent ? thou forget ?
Are there no snakes in Ireland yet ?

*Death to the Saxon ! Slay nor spare !*
*O God of Justice, hear us swear !*

[1] The reader will kindly note such important
changes of metre as occur in the two last verses
of " The Twins " and elsewhere. The careless
might suppose that these do not scan ; they do,
following directly or by analogy a similar
change in the Pali.

The iron Saxon's bloody hand
Metes out his murder on the land.
The light of Erin is forlorn.
The country fades : the people mourn.

Of land bereft, of right beguiled,
Starved, tortured, murdered, or exiled ;
Of freedom robbed, of faith cajoled,
In secret councils bought and sold !

Their weapons are the cell, the law,
The gallows, and the scourge, to awe
Brave Irish hearts : their hates deny
The right to live—the right to die.

Our weapons—be they fire and cord,
The shell, the rifle, and the sword !
Without a helper or a friend
All means be righteous to the End !

Look not for help to wordy strife !
This battle is for death or life.
Melt mountains with a word—and then
The colder hearts of Englishmen !

Look not to Europe in your need !
Columbia's but a broken reed !
Your own good hearts, your own strong hand
Win back at last the Irish land.

Won by the strength of cold despair
Our chance is near us—slay nor spare !
Open to fate the Saxons lie :—
Up ! Ireland ! ere the good hour fly !

Stand all our fortunes on one cast !
Arise ! the hour is come at last.
One torch may fire the ungodly shrine—
O God ! and may that torch be mine !

But, even when victory is assured,
Forget not all ye have endured !
Of native mercy dam the dyke,
And leave the snake no fang to strike !

They slew our women : let us then
At least annihilate their men !
Lest the ill race from faithless graves
Arise again to make us slaves.

Arise, O God, and stand, and smite
For Ireland's wrong, for Ireland's right !
Our Lady, stay the pitying tear !
There is no room for pity here !

What pity knew the Saxon e'er ?
Arise, O God, and slay nor spare,
Until full vengeance rightly wrought
Bring all their house of wrong to nought !

Scorn, the catastrophe of crime,
These be their monuments through time !
And Ireland, green once more and fresh,
Draw life from their dissolving flesh !

By Saxon carcases renewed,
Spring up, O Shamrock virgin-hued !
And in the glory of thy leaf
Let all forget the ancient grief !

Now is the hour !   The drink is poured !
Wake ! fatal and avenging sword !
Brave men of Erin, hand in hand,
Arise and free the lovely land !

> *Death to the Saxon !   Slay nor spare !*
> *O God of Justice, hear us swear !*


## THE EARL'S QUEST.

*Written at Camp Despair, 20,000 ft., Chogo*
*Ri Lungma, Baltistan.*

So now the Earl was well a-weary of
The grievous folly of this wandering.
Had he been able to have counted Love

Or Power, or Knowledge as the sole strong
   thing
Fit to suffice his quest, his eyes had gleamed
With the success already grasped.   The sting

Of all he suffered, was that he esteemed
His quest partook of all and yet of none.
So as he rode the woodlands out there beamed

The dull large spectre of a grim flat sun,
Red and obscure upon the leaden haze
That lapped and wrapped and rode the
   horizon.

The Earl rode steadily on.   A crest caught
   rays
Of that abominable sunset, sharp
With needles of young pines, their tips ablaze,

Their feet dead black ; the wind's dark
   fingers warp
To its own time their strings, a sombre mode
Found by a ghost on a forgotten harp

Or (still more terrible !) the lost dread ode
That used to call the dead knights to their
   chief
To the lone waters from the shadowy road.

So deemed the weary Earl of the wind's grief,
And seemed to see about him form by form
Like mighty wrecks, wave-shattered on a reef,

Moulded and mastered by the shapeless storm
A thousand figures of himself the mist
Enlarged, distorted : yet without a qualm

(So sad was he) he mounted the last
   twist
Of the path's hate, and faced the wind, and
   saw
The lead gleam to a surly amethyst

As the sun dipped, and Night put forth a paw
Like a black panther's, and efface the East.
Then, with a sudden inward catch of awe

As if behind him sprang some silent beast,
So shuddered he, and spurred his horse, and
   found
A black path towards the water ; he released

The bridle ; so the way went steep, ill bound
On an accursed task, so dark it loomed
Amid its yews and cypresses, each mound

About each root, a grave, where Hell en-
tombed
A vampire till the night broke sepulchre
And all its phantoms desperate and doomed

Began to gather flesh, to breathe, to stir.
Such was the path, yet hard should find the
work
Glamour, to weave her web of gossamer

Over such eyesight as the Earl's for murk.
He had watched for larvæ by the midnight
roads,
The stake-transpiercèd corpse, the caves
where lurk

The demon spiders, and the shapeless toads
Fed by their lovers duly on the draught
That bloats and blisters, blackens and cor-
rodes.

These had he seen of old ; so now he laughed,
Not without bitterness deep-lying, that erst
He had esteemed such foolish devil's craft

Part of his quest, his quest when fair and first
He flung the last, the strongest horseman back
With such a buffet that no skill amerced

Its debt but headlong in his charger's track
He must be hurled, rib-shattered by the shock ;
And the loud populace exclaimed " Alack ! ",

Their favourite foiled. But oh ! the royal
stock
Of holy kings from Christ to Charlemagne
Hailed him, anointed him, fair lock by lock,

With oil that drew incalculable gain
From those six olives in the midst whereof
Christ prayed the last time, ere the fatal Wain [1]

Stood in the sky reversed, and utmost Love
Entered the sadness of Gethsemane.
So did the king ; so did the priest above

[1] Charles' Wain—Ursa Major. There is a
silly legend to this effect.

Place his old hands upon the Earl's, decree
The splendid and the solemn accolade
That he should go forth to the world and be

Knight-errant ; so did then the fairest maid
Of all that noble company keep hid
The love that melted her ; she took the blade

Blessed by a mage, who slew the harmless kid
With solemn rite and water poured athwart
In stars and sigils,—fire leapt out amid,

And blazed upon the blade ; and stark cold
swart
Demons came hurtling to enforce the spell,
Until the exorcisms duly wrought

Fixed in the living steel so terrible
A force nor man nor devil might assail,
Nay— might approach the wary warrior well,

So long as he was clothed in silver mail
Of purity, and iron-helmeted
With ignorance of fear : so through the hail

Of flowers, of cries, of looks, of white and red,
Fear, hatred, envy, love—nay, self-conceit
Of girls that preened itself and masqued in-
stead

Of love—he rode with head deep bowed—
too sweet,
Too solemn at that moment to respond,
Or even to lift his evening eyes to greet

The one he knew was nearest—too, too fond !
He dared not—not for his sake but for hers.
So he bent down, and passed away beyond

In space, in time. [The myriad ministers
Of God, seeing her soul, prayed God to send
One spirit yet to turn him—subtly stirs

The eternal glory of God's mouth ; " The end
Is not, nor the beginning." Such the speech
Our language fashions down — to compre-
hend.]

The wood broke suddenly upon the beach,
Curved, flat ; the water oozing on the sand
Stretched waveless out beyond where eye
    might reach,

A grey and shapeless place, a hopeless land !
Yet in that vast, that weary sad expanse
The Earl saw three strange objects on the
    strand

His keen eye noted at the firstborn glance,
And recognised as pointers for his soul ;
So that his soul was fervid in the dance,

Knowing itself one step more near the goal,
Should he but make the perfect choice of
    these.
Farthest, loose tethered, at a stake's control,

A shallop rocked before the sullen breeze.
Midway, a hermit's hut stood solitary,
A dim light set therein.   Near and at ease

A jolly well-lit inn—no phantom airy !
Solid and warm, short snatches of light song
Issuing cheery now and then.   " Be wary ! "

Quoth the wise Earl, " I wander very long
Far from my quest, assuredly to fall
Sideways each step towards the House of
    Wrong,

" Were but one choice demented.   Choice
    is small
Here though.   (A flash of insight in his mind)
Which of these three gets answer to its call ?

" Yon shallop?—leave to Galahad !   Re-
    signed
Yon hermit be to welcome Lancelot !
For me—the inn—what fate am I to find ?

" Who cares ?   Shall I seek ever—do ye
    wot ?—
But in the outré, the obscure, the occult ?
My Master is of might to lift me what

" Hangs, veil of glamour, on my ' Quisque
    vult,'
The morion's motto : to exhaust the cross,
Bidding it glow with roses—the result

" What way he will : may be adventure's loss
Is gain to common sense ; whereby I guess
Wise men have hidden Mount Biagenos[1]

" And all its height from fools who looked no
    less
For snows to lurk beneath the roots of yew,
Or in the caverns grim with gloominess

" Hid deep i' the forests they would wander
    through,
Instead of travelling the straightforward road.
I call them fools—well, I have been one too.

" Now then at least for the secure abode
And way of luck — knight-errantry once
    doffed,
The ox set kicking at his self-set goad,

" Here's for the hostel and the light aloft !
Roderic, my lad ! there's pelf to pay the score
For ale and cakes and venison and a soft

" Bed we have missed this three months—
    now no more
Of folly !  Avaunt, old Merlin's nonsense
    lore !
Ho there ! Travellers ! Mine host ! Open the
    door ! "

*Desunt cetera.*

In the second part—a joyous inn fireside
—the Earl refuses power, knowledge, and
love (offered him by a guest) by the symbolic
drink of ale and the cherry cheeks of the
maid.

In part three she, coming secretly to him,
warns him he must destroy the three vices,
faith, hope, and charity.   This he does
easily, save the love of the figure of the
Crucified ; but at last conquering this, he
attains.   [These were never written.]

[1] The mystic mountain of the Rosicrucians.

## EVE.

*Written in the Mosque of Omar.*

HERS was the first sufficient sacrifice
  That won us freedom, hers the generous
    gift
  That turned herself upon the curse adrift
Sailless and rudderless, to pay the price
Of permanence with pain, of love with vice,
  Like a tall ship swan-lovely, swallow-swift,
  That makes upon the breakers. So the rift
Sprang and the flame roared.   Farewell,
    Paradise !

How shall a man that is a man reward
Her priceless sacrifice, rebuke the Lord?
  Why, there's Convention's corral ; ring her
    round !
Here's shame's barbed wire ; push out the
    unclean thing !
Here's freedom's falconry ; quick, clip her
    wing !
There, labour's danger—thrust her under-
    ground !

## THE SIBYL.

CROUCHED o'er the tripod the pale priestess
    moans
  Ambiguous destiny, divided fate.
  Sibylline oracles of woe create
Roars as of beasts, majestic monotones
Of wind, strong cries of elemental thrones,
  All sounds of mystery of the Pythian state !
  O woman without change or joy or date
I await thy oracle as the Delphian stone's !

*Desunt cetera.*

## LA COUREUSE.

*Written in the Quartier Latin, Paris.*

A FADED skirt, a silken petticoat,
  A little jacket, a small shapely shoe,
  A toque.   A symphony in gray and blue,
The child ripples, the conquering master-note

Subtlety.  Faint, stray showers of twilight float
  In shadows round the well-poised head ;
    dark, true,
  Joyous the eyes laugh—and are weeping
    too,
For all the victory of her royal throat.

She showed her purse with tantalising grace :
  Some sous, a franc, a key, some stuff, soft
    grey.
The mocking laughter trills upon her tongue :
  " There's all my fortune."    " And your
    pretty face !
What do you do ?"  Wearily, " I am gay."
" What do you hope for ?"  Simply, " To
    die young."

## SONNET FOR A PICTURE.[1]

*" ποικιλόθρον', ἀθάνατ' 'Αφροδιτα."*
                  *Σαπφω.*

    " ——We have seen
Gold tarnished, and the gray above——"
                —SWINBURNE.

As some lone mountebank of the stage may
    tweak
  The noses of his fellows, so Gavin [2]
Tweaks with her brush-work the absurd
    obscene
Academicians.   How her pictures speak !
Chiaroscuro Rembrandtesque, form Greek !
  What values !  What a composition clean !
  Breadth shaming broadness !   Manner
    epicene !
Texture superb !  Magnificent technique !

Raphael, Velasquez, Michael Angelo,
  Stare, gape, and splutter when they see
    thy colour,
  Reds killing roses, greens blaspheming
    grass.
O thou art simply perfect, don't you know ?
  Than thee all masters of old time are duller,
  O artiste of the Quartier Montparnasse !

[1] A parody on his own appreciations of
Rodin's sculpture.
[2] An art student in Paris at this time.

## TO "ELIZABETH."

WITH A COPY OF TANNHÄUSER.

*Written in the Akasa.*[1]

THE story of a fool. From love and death
Emancipate, he stands above. The goal
Is in the shrines of misty air: there roll
The voices and the songs of One who saith:
"There is no peace for him who lingereth."
Love is a cinder now that was a coal:
Either were vain. The great magician's soul
Is far too weak to risk Elizabeth.

All this is past and under me. Above,
Around, the magian tree of knowledge waves
Its rosy flowers and golden fruit. I know
Indeed that he is caught therein who craves;
But I, desiring not, accept the glow
And blossom of that Knowledge that is Love.

## RONDELS (AT MONTE CARLO).

*Written in the Casino, Monte Carlo.*

### I.

THERE is no hell but earth: O coil of fate
  Binding us surely in the Halls of Birth,
The unsubstantial, the dissolving state!
  There is no hell but earth.

Vain are the falsehoods that subserve to mirth.
  Dust is to dust, create or uncreate.
The wheel is bounded by the world's great
    girth.

By prayer and penance unregenerate,
  Redeemed by no man's sacrifice or worth,
We swing: no mortal knows his ultimate.
  There is no hell but earth.

### II.

In all the skies the planets and the stars
  Receive us, where our fate in order plies.
Somewhere we live between the savage bars
    In all the skies.

[1] Space or Ether. The Hindus say that all
actions, especially important (*i.e.* spiritual)
ones, are written therein. It is an Automatic
Recording Angel.

Let God's highest heaven receive the man
    who dies—
All hath an end: he falls: the stains and
    scars
Are his throughout unwatched eternities.

The roses and the scented nenuphars
  Give hope—oh! monolith! oh house of
    lies!
We change and change and fade, strange
    avatars
    In all the skies.

### III.

One way sets free. That way is not to tread
  Through fire or earth or spirit, air or sea.
That secret is not gathered of the dead.
    One way sets free.

*Not to desire* shall lead to *not to be.*
  There is no hope within, none overhead,
None by the chance of fate's august decree.

It is a path where tears are ever shed.
  There is no joy—is that a path for me?
Yea! though I track the ways of utmost dread,
    One way sets free.

## IN THE GREAT PYRAMID OF GHIZEH.[1]

I SAW in a trance or a vision the web of the
ages unfurled, flung wide with a scream of
derision, a mockery mute of the world. As
it spread over sky I mapped it fair on a
sheet of blue air with a hurricane pen. I
copy it here for men. First on the ghostly
adytum of pale mist that was the abyss of
time and space (the stars all blotted out,
poor faded nenuphars on the storm-sea of
the infinite:) I wist a shapeless figure arise
and cover all, its cloak an ancient pall,
vaster and older than the skies of night,
and blacker than all broken years—aye!
but it grew and held me in its grasp so that

[1] If this poem be repeatedly read through,
it falls into a subtly rhymed and metrical form.

I felt its flesh, not clean sweet flesh of man but leprous white, and crawling with innumerable tears like worms, and pains like a sword-severed asp, twitching, and loathlier than all mesh of hates and lusts, defiling; nor any voice it had, nor any motion, it was infinite in its own world of horror, irredeemably bad as everywhere sunlit, being this world, forget not! being this world, this universe, the sum of all existence; so that opposing fierce resistance to the all-law, stood loves and joys, delicate girls, and beautiful strong boys, and bearded men like gods, and golden things, and bright desires with wings, all beauties, and all truths of life poets have ever prized. So showed the microscope, this agèd strife between all forms; but seen afar, seen well drawn in a focus, synthesised, the whole was sorrow and despair; agony biting through the fair; meanness, contemptibility, enthroned; all purposeless, all unatoned; all putrid of an hope, all vacant of a soul. I called upon its master, as who should call on God. Instead, arose a shining form, sweet as a whisper of soft air kissing the brows of a great storm; his face with light was molten, musical with waves of his delight moving across: his countenance utterly fair! then was my philosophic vision shamed: conjecture at a loss; and my whole mind revolted; then I blamed the vision as a lie; yet bid that vision speak how he was named, being so wonderfully desirable. Whereat he smiled upon me merrily, answering that whoso named him well, being a poet, called him Love; or else being a lover of wisdom, called him Force; or being a cynic, called him Lust; or being a pietist, called him God. The last—thou seest!—(he said), a lie of Hell's, and all a partial course of the great circle of whirling dust (stirred by the iron rod of thought) that men call wisdom. So I looked deep in his beauty, and beheld its truth. The life of that fair youth was as a whiz of violent little whirls, helical coils of emptiness, grey curls of misty and impalpable stuff, torn, crooked, all ways

and none at once, but ever pressed in idiot circles; and one thing he lacked, now I looked from afar again, was rest. Thence I withdrew my sight, the eyeballs cracked with strain of my endeavour, and my will struck up with subtler skill than any man's that in fair Crete tracked through the labyrinth of Minos, and awoke the cry to call his master; grew a monster whirlwind of revolving smoke and then, mere nothing. But in me arose a peace profounder than Himalayan snows cooped in their crystalline ravines. I saw the ultimation of the one wise law. I stood in the King's Chamber, by the tomb of slain Osiris, in the Pyramid and looked down the Great Gallery, deep, deep into the hollow of earth; grand gloom burned royally therein; I was well hid in the shadow; here I realised myself to be in that sepulchral sleep wherein were mirrored all these things of mystery. So the long passage steeply sliding ever up to my feet where I stood in the emptiness; at last a sure abiding only in absolute ceasing of all sense, and all perceived or understood or knowable; thus, purple and intense, I beheld the past that leads to peace, from royal heights of mastery to sleep, from self-control imperial to an end, therefore I shaped the seven tiers of the ascending corridor into seven strokes of wisdom, seven harvests fair to reap from seven bitter sowings.[1] Here ascend the armies of life's universal war chasing the pious pilgrim. First, his sight grew adamant, sun-bright, so that he saw aright. Second, his heart was noble, that he would live ever unto good. Third, in his speech stood tokens of this will, so pitiful and pure he spake, nor ever from him brake woe-wingèd words, nor slaver of the snake. Fourth, in each noble act of life he taught crystalline vigour of thought, so in each deed he was aright; well-wrought all the man's work; and fifth, this hero strife grew one with his whole life, so harmonised to the one after-end his every

[1] Compare the Noble Eightfold Path, as described in "Science and Buddhism," *infra*.

conscious and unconscious strain, his peace and pleasure and pain, his reflex life, his deepest-seated deed of mere brute muscle and nerve ! Thence, by great Will new-freed, the ardent life leaps, sixth, to Effort's tower, invoking the occult, the secret power, found in the void when all but Will is lost ; so, seventh, he bends it from its bodily station into the great abyss of Meditation, whence the firm level is at last his own and Rapture's royal throne is more than throne, sarcophagus ! an end ! an end ! Resounds the echo in the stone, incalculable myriads of tons poised in gigantic balance overhead, about, beneath. O blend your voices, angels of the awful earth ! dogs ! demons leaping into hideous birth from the imprisoned deserts of the Nile ! And thou, O habitant most dread, disastrous crocodile, hear thou the Law, and live, and win to peace !

## THE HILLS.

### TO OSCAR ECKENSTEIN.

WHENCE the black lands shudder and darken,
    Whence the sea birds have empire to
    range,
Whence the moon and the meteor hearken
    The perpetual rhythm of change,
On earth and in heaven deluded
    With time, that the soul of us kills,
I have passed.   I have brooded, fled far to
    the wooded
    And desolate hills.


Not there is the changing of voices
    That lament or regret or are sad,
But the sun in his strength rejoices,
    The moon in her beauty is glad.
As timeless and deathless time passes,
    And death is a hermit that dwells
By the imminent masses of ice, where the
    grasses
    Abandon the fells.

There silence, arrayed as a spectre,
    Is visible, tangible, near,
To the cup of the man pours nectar,
    To the heart of the coward is fear :
Though the desolate waste be enchaunted
    By a spell that bewilders and chills,
To me it is granted to worship the haunted
    Delight of the hills.


To me all the blossoms are seedless,
    Yet big with all manner of fruit :
And a voice in the waste is needless
    Since my soul in its splendour is mute.
Though the height of the hill be deserted,
    The soul of a man has its mate ;
With the wide sky skirted his heart is reverted
    To commune with Fate.


Far flings out the spur to the sunset ;
    Its help to the hope of the sun
That all be unfolded if one set,
    That none be apart from the One ;
And the sweep of the wings of the weather,
    Marked bright with the silvery ghylls
For flickering feather, brings all things
    together
    To nest in the hills.


Like a great bird poised in the æther,
    The mountain keeps watch over earth,
On the child that lies sleeping beneath her
    Wild-eyed from a terrible birth.
But by noise of the world unshaken,
    By dance of the world not bedinned,
The hill bides forsaken, yet only to waken
    Her lover, the wind.


Like a lion asleep in his fastness,
    Or a warrior leant on his spear,
The hill stands up in the vastness,
    And the stars grow strangely near ;
For the secret of life and its gladness
    Are hidden in strength that distils
A potion of madness from berries of sadness
    Grown wild in the hills.

Though the earth be disparted and rended,
  Thus only the great peaks change
That their image is moulded and blended
  Into all that a fancy may range ;
And the silence my song could refigure
  To the note of a bird did I will,
Of glory or rigour, of passion or vigour—
  The change were to ill !

For silence is better than singing
  Though a Shelley wove songs in the sky,
And hovering is sweeter than winging ;
  To live is less good than to die.
The secret of secrets is hidden
  Not in lives nor in loves, but in wills
That are free and unchidden, that wander
    unbidden
  To home in the hills.

A strength that is more than the summer
  Is firm in that silence and rest,
Though stiller the rocks be and dumber
  That the soul of its slumber oppressed.
For stronger control is than urging,
  And mightier the heart of the sea
Than her waves deep-merging and striving
    and surging
  That deem they are free.

In spirit I stand on the mountain,
  My soul into God's withdrawn,
And look to the East like a fountain
  That shoots up the spray of the dawn.
And the life of the mountain swims through
    me
  (So the song of a thrush in me thrills)
And the dawn speaks to me, of old for it
    knew me
  The soul of the hills.

I stand on the mountain in wonder
  As the splendour springs up in the East,
As the cloud banks are rended asunder,
  And the wings of the Night are released.
As in travail a maiden demented,
  Afraid of the deed she hath done,
By no man lamented, springs up the sweet-
    scented
  Pale flower of the sun.

So change not the heights and the hollows ;
  The hollows are one with the heights
In that pallid grave dawn of Apollo's
  Confusion of shadows and lights.
Unreal save to sense that can sense her
  That maiden of sunrise refills
The air's grey censer with perfumes intenser
  The higher the hills.

So, vague as a ghost swift faded,
  Steals dawn, and so sunset may see
How her long long locks deep-braided
  Fall down to her breast and her knee.
So night and so sunrise discover
  No light and no darkness to heed.
Night is above her, and brings her no lover ;
  And day, but no deed.

Such a sense is up and within me,
  A tongue as of mystical fire !
Love, beauty, and holiness win me
  To the end of the great desire,
Where I cease from the thirst and the labour,
  As the land that no ploughman tills
Lest the robber his neighbour unloosen the
    sabre
  From holds in the hills.

From love of my life and its burden
  Set free in the silence remote,
Grows a sorrow divine for my guerdon,
  A peace in my struggling note.
Compassion for earth far extended
  Beneath me, the swords and the rods,
My Spirit hath bended, bowed me and
    blended
  My self into God's.

But God—what divinity rises
  To me in the mountainous place ?
What sun beyond suns, and surprises
  Mine eyes at the dawn of His face ?
No God in this silence existing,
  No heaven and no earth of Him skills,
Save the blizzards unresting, whirling and
    twisting
  Adrift on the hills.

So witless and aimless and formless
  I count the Creator to be ;
Not strong as who rides on the stormless
  And tames the untamable sea.
But motion and action distorted
  Are marks of the paths He hath trod.
Hated or courted, aided or thwarted :—
  Lo, He is your God !


But mine in the silence abideth ;
  Her strength is the strength of rest ;
Not on thunders or clouds She rideth
  But draweth me down to Her breast :
No maker of men, but dissolving
  Their life from its burden of ills,
Ever resolving the circle revolving
  To peace of the hills.


And dark is Her breast and unlighted ;
  But a warm sweet scent is expressed,
And a rose as of sunset excited
  In the strength of Her sunless breast.
Her love is like pain, but enchanted :
  Her kiss is an opiate breath
Amorously panted : Her fervours last granted
  Are sorrow, and death.

Nor death as ye name in derision
  The change to a cycle of pain,
To a cycle of joy as a vision
  Ye chase, and may capture in vain.
Endeth you peace, and your change is
  Like the change in a measure that shrills
And slackens and ranges ; your passion
    estranges
  The love of the hills !


Nay ! death is a portal of passing
  To miseries other but sure.
Yet the snow on the hills amassing
  The wind of an hour may endure ;
But as day after day grows the summer
  The crystals melt one after one.
The hill—shall they numb her?   Their frost
    overcome her ?
  Demand of the sun !


That uttermost death of my lady
  Revealed in the heart of the range
Is as light in the groves long shady
  As peace in the halls of change.
The web of the world is rended ;
  Stayed are the causal mills ;
Time is ended ; space unextended.
  An end of the hills !

# ALICE: AN ADULTERY

## 1903

INTRODUCTION[1] BY THE EDITOR.

YOKOHAMA, *April, 1901.*

IT has often been pointed out how strange are the prophecies made from time to time by writers of what purports to be merely fiction.

Of all the remarkable tales with which Mr. R. Kipling has delighted the world, none is more striking than that of McIntosh Jellaludin[2] and his mysterious manuscript. And now, only a few years after reading that incredible tale, I myself, at Yokohama, come across a series of circumstances wonderfully analogous. But I will truthfully set down this history just as it all happened.

I went one memorable Wednesday night to No. 29.[3] For my advent in this most reputable quarter of the city, which is, after all, Yama,[4] and equally handy for the consul, the chaplain, and the doctor, readers of Rossetti will expect no excuse; for their sakes I may frankly admit that I was actuated by other motives than interest and solicitude for my companion, a youth still blindly groping for Romance beneath the skirts of tawdry and painted Vice. Perhaps I may have hoped to save him from what men call the graver and angels the lesser consequences of his folly. This for the others.

As to the character of the mansion at which we arrived, after a journey no less dubious than winding, I will say that, despite its outward seeming, it was, in reality, a most respectable place; the main occupation of its inhabitants seemed to be the sale of as much "champagne" as possible; in which inspiring preface my friend was soon deeply immersed. . . .

Golden-haired, a profound linguist, swearing in five Western and three Oriental languages, and comparable rather to the accomplished courtesans of old-time Athens than to the Imperial Peripatetics of the *Daily Telegraph* and Mr. Raven-Hill,[1] her looks of fire turned my friend's silky and insipid moustache into a veritable Burning Bush. But puppy endearments are of little interest to one who has just done his duty by No. 9[2] in distant Yoshiwara; so turned to the conversation of our dirty old Irish hostess, who, being drunk, grew more so, and exceedingly entertaining.

Of the central forces which sway mankind, her knowledge was more comprehensive than conventional. For thirty years she had earned her bread in the capacity of a Japanese Mrs. Warren;[3] but having played with fire in many lands, the knowledge she had of her own subject, based on indefatigable personal research, was as accurate in detail as it was cosmopolitan in character. Yet she had not lost her ideals; she was a devout Catholic, and her opinion of the human understanding, despite her virginal innocence of Greek, was identical with that of Mr. Locke.[4]

On occasions I am as sensitive to inexplic-

---

[1] This and the "Critical Essay" (now omitted) were the result of collaboration. Some omissions, &c., in the text of the First Edition were intended to aid the illusion of this introduction.

[2] A dissipated but gifted European who became unified with the Indian native, and wrote a book about him.

[3] Disinclination to marry is congenital in the elect: the Pauline alternative is discountenanced by my doctor.—ED.

[4] The Bluff, or European quarter.

[1] A talented artist, who published a book of amusing sketches of the loose women who promenaded the "Empire" Music Hall.

[2] Called "Nectarine," a famous brothel.

[3] A bawd. From Shaw's play, "Mrs. Warren's Profession."

[4] The philosopher.

able interruption as Mr. Shandy,[1] and from behind the hideous yellow partition came sounds as of the constant babbling of a human voice. Repeated glances in this direction drew from my entertainer the information that it was "only her husband," indicating the yellow-haired girl with the stem of her short clay pipe. She added that he was dying.

Curiosity, Compassion's Siamese twin, prompted a desire to see the sufferer.

The old lady rose, not without difficulty, lifted the curtain, and let it fall behind me as I entered the gloom which lay beyond. On a bed, in that half-fathomed twilight, big with the scent of joss-sticks smouldering in a saucer before a little bronze Buddha-rupa,[2] lay a man, still young, the traces of rare beauty in his face, though worn with suffering and horrid with a week's growth of beard.

He was murmuring over to himself some words which I could not catch, but my entrance, though he did not notice me, seemed to rouse him a little.

I distinctly heard—

" These are the spells by which to re-assume An empire o'er the disentangled doom."

He paused, sighing, then continued—

" To suffer woes which hope thinks infinite;
To forgive wrongs darker than death or night ;
To defy power which seems omnipotent ;
To love, and bear ; to hope till hope creates From its own wreck the thing it contemplates ;
Neither to change, nor falter, nor repent :
This, like thy glory, Titan, is to be Good, great, and joyous, beautiful, and free ;
This is alone Life, Joy, Empire, and Victory."[3]

The last phrase pealed trumpet-wise : he sank back into thought. "Yes," he said slowly, " neither to change, nor falter, nor repent." I moved forward, and he saw me. " Who are you ? " he asked.

" I am travelling in the East," I said. " I love Man also ; I have come to see you. Who are you ? "

[1] See "Tristam Shandy," by Laurence Sterne, Chap. I.
[2] Image of Buddha.
[3] Shelley, " Prometheus Unbound," iv.

He laughed pleasantly. " I am the child of many prayers."

There was a pause.

I stood still, thinking.

Here was surely the very strangest outcast of Society. What uncouth bypaths of human experience, across what mapless tracks beyond the social pale, must have led hither—hither to death in this Anglo-Saxon-blasted corner of Japan, here, at the very outpost of the East. He spoke my thought.

" Here I lie," he said, " east of all things. All my life I have been travelling eastward, and now there is now no further east to go."

" There is America," I said. I had to say something.

" Where the disappearance of man has followed that of manners : the exit of God has not wished to lag behind that of grammar. I have no use for American men, and only one use for American women."

" Of a truth," I said, " the continent is accursed—a very limbo."

" It is the counterfoil of evolution," said the man wearily. There was silence.

" What can I do for you ? " I asked. " Are you indeed ill ? "

" Four days more," he answered, thrilling with excitement, " and all my dreams will come true—until I wake. But you can serve me, if indeed— Did you hear me spouting poetry ? "

I nodded, and lit my pipe. He watched me narrowly while the match illuminated my face. " What poetry ? "

I told him Shelley.

" Do you read Ibsen ? " he queried, keening visibly. After a moment's pause : " He is the Sophocles of manners," I said, rewarded royally for months of weary waiting. My strange companion sat up transfigured. " The Hour," he murmured, " and the Man ! . . . What of Tennyson ? "

" Which Tennyson ? " I asked.

The answer seemed to please him.

" In Memoriam ? " he replied.

" He is a neurasthenic counter-jumper."

" And of the Idylls ? "

" Sir Thomas[1] did no wrong ; can impotence excuse his posthumous emasculation ? "[2]

[1] Sir T. Malory : author of the true " Morte d' Arthur."
[2] See A. C. Swinburne, " Under the Microscope."

He sank back contented. "I have prayed to my God for many days," he said, "and by one of the least of my life's miracles you are here; worthy to receive my trust. For when I knew that I was to die, I destroyed all the papers which held the story of my life—all save one. That I saved; the only noble passage, perhaps—among the many notable. Men will say that it is stained; you, I think, should be wiser. It is the story of how the Israelites crossed the Red Sea. They were not drowned, you know (he seemed to lapse into a day-dream), and they came out on the Land of Promise side. But they had to descend therein."

"They all died in the wilderness," I said, feeling as if I understood this mystical talk, which, indeed, I did not. But I felt inspired.

"Ay me, they died—as I am dying now."

He turned to the wall and sought a bundle of old writing on a shelf. "Take this," he said. "Edit it as if it were your own: let the world know how wonderful it was." I took the manuscript from the frail, white hand.

He seemed to forget me altogether.

"Namo tassa Bhagavato arahato samma-sambuddhasa,"[1] he murmured, turning to his little black Buddha-rupa.

There was a calm like unto—might I say, an afterwards?

"There is an end of joy and sorrow,
Peace all day long, all night, all morrow,"

he began drowsily.

A shrill voice rose in a great curse. The hoarse anger of drunken harlotry snarled back. "Not a drop more," shouted my friend, adding many things. It was time for my return.

"I will let them know," I whispered. "Good-bye."

"'There is not one thing with another;
But Evil saith to Good: "My brother—"'"[2]

he went on unheeding.

I left him to his peace.

My re-appearance restored harmony. The

[1] "Glory to the Blessed One, the Perfected One, the Enlightened One." It is the common Buddhist salute to their Master.
[2] These quotations are from Swinburne's "Ilicet."

fulvous and fulgurous lady grew comparatively tranquil; the pair withdrew. The old woman lay sprawled along the divan sunk in a drunken torpor.

I unrolled the manuscript and read.

Brutal truth-telling humour, at times perhaps too Rabelaisian; lyrics, some of enchanting beauty, others painfully imitative; sonnets of exceedingly unequal power, a perfectly heartless introduction (some fools would call it pathetic),[1] and, as a synthesis of the whole, an impression of profound sadness and, perhaps, still deeper joy, were my reward. Together with a feeling that the writer must have been a philosopher of the widest and deepest learning and penetration, and a regret that he showed no more of it in his poetry. First and last, I stood amazed, stupefied: so stand I still.

Dramatic propriety forbade me seeing him again; he was alone when he started.

Let us not too bitterly lament! He would hate him who would "upon the rack of this tough world stretch him out longer."

To the best of my poor ability I have executed his wishes, omitting, however, his name and all references sufficiently precise to give pain to any person still living.[2] His handwriting was abominably difficult, some words quite indecipherable. I have spent long and laborious hours in conjecture, and have, I hope, restored his meaning in almost every case. But in the Sonnets of the 12th, 18th, 23rd, 24th, 29th, 35th, 41st, 43rd, and 48th days, also in "At Last," "Love and Fear," and "Lethe," one or more whole lines have been almost impossible to read. The literary student will be able readily to detect my patchwork emendations. These I have dared to make because his whole pattern (may I use the word?) is so elaborate and perfect that I fear to annoy the reader by leaving any blanks, feeling that my own poverty of diction will be less noticeable than any actual hiatus in the sense or rhythm. I attempt neither eulogy nor criticism here. Indeed, it seems to me entirely uncalled for. His words were: "Let the world know how wonderful it was," that is, his love and hers; not "how wonderful it is," that is, his poem.

The poem is simple, understandable, direct, not verbose. More I demand not,

[1] The MS. has been lost.—ED.
[2] The *essential* facts are, of course, imaginary.

seeing it is written (almost literally so) in blood; for I am sure that he was dying of that love for Alice, whose marvellous beauty it was his mission (who may doubt it?) to reveal. For the burning torch of truth may smoke, but it is our one sure light in passion and distress. *The jewelled silence of the stars* is, indeed, the light of a serener art; but love is human, and I give nothing for the tawdry gems of style when the breast they would adorn is that of a breathing, living beauty of man's love, the heart of all the world. Nor let us taint one sympathy with even a shadow of regret. Let us leave him where

" Sight nor sound shall war against him more,
   For whom all winds are quiet as the sun,
      All waters as the shore." [1]

NOTE.—The sudden and tragic death of the Editor has necessitated the completion of his task by another hand. The introduction was, however, in practically its present form.

## WHAT LAY BEFORE.

### WHITE POPPY.

AMID the drowsy dream,
Lit by some fitful beam
   Of other light
Than the mere sun, supreme
On all the glint and gleam
   Shooting through night,
Above the water-way
Where my poor corpse must stay,
I bend and float away
   From human sight.

Unto the floral face,
Carven in ancient grace
   Of Gods or Greeks,
The whole sky's way gives place :
Open the walls of space,
   And silence speaks.

1 Swinburne. " Ave atque Vale."

See ! I am floating far
Beyond space and sun and star,
As drifts a nenuphar
   Down lilied creeks.

Beyond the heavens I see
The pale embroidery
   Of some wan child
Wasted by earth and sea,
Whose kisses were too free,
   Too swift and wild ;
A Maenad's floating tress
Lost in the wilderness
Of death's or my caress,
   Discrowned, defiled.

Clad in pale green and rose,
Her thin face flickers, glows,
   Tempestuous flame.
Horrid and harsh she goes,
Speaks, trembles, wakes and knows
   How frail is shame !
Grows vast and cloudy and is
The whole mouth's sobbing kiss,
And crushes me with bliss
   Beyond a name.

Then fall I from excess
Of bitter ecstasies,
   Pale ghosts of blood,
To worlds where palaces
Shine through dim memories
   Of flower and flood,
Shine in pale opal and pearl,
Void of bright boy or girl,
Desolate halls that furl
   Their shapes subdued.

And wide they sunder, wide
They fall into the tide
   Of fallen things.
Me, me, O meek-browed bride,
Horrible faces hide
   And devilish wings.

Me the grim harpies hold
In kisses slaver-cold,
Mute serpent-shapes of gold
    With serpent stings.

The dreadful bridal won,
The demon banquet done,
    My flesh let loose :—
Rises a strange red sun,
A sight to slay or stun ;
    Sepulchral dews
Fall from the rayless globe,
Whose sightless fingers probe
My golden-folded robe,
    My soul's misuse.

And in that thankless shape
Vines grow without a grape,
    Thorns roseless spring.
Nay ! There is no escape :—
The yawning portals gape,
    The orbèd ring
As by a whirlpool drawn
Into that devil-dawn :—
I sink and shriek and fawn
    Upon the thing.

Ha ! in the desperate pang
And subtle stroke and fang
    Of hateful kisses
Whence devilish laughter sprang,
Close on me with a clang
    The brazen abysses.
The leopard-coloured paw
Strikes, and the cruel jaw
Hides me in the glutless maw—
    Crown of ten blisses !

For all the vision world
Is closed on me and curled
    Into the deep
Of my slow soul, and hurled
Through lampless lands, and furled,
    Sharp folds and steep :
Till all unite in one,
Seven planets in the sun,
And I am deeplier done
    Into full sleep.

## MESSALINE.

BENEATH the living cross I lie
And swoon towards eternity :
Prodigious sinewy shapes, and lean
And curving limbs of Messaline.
    The deep arched eyes, the floating mane,—
One pierces, one wraps-in my brain.
A crown of thorn, a spear of clean
Cold fire of dying Messaline.
    Swart tangles of devouring hair,
The scorpion labyrinth and snare,
Leprous entanglements of sense,
The Imminence of the Immense.
And in the deep hard breath I draw
Kissed from her strangling mouth and maw,
I feel the floating deaths that dwell
About that citadel of hell ;
A soft lewd flavour, an obscene
Mysterious self of Messaline.
    Or, in the kisses that swoop low
To catch my breath and kill me so,
I feel the ghostliness of this
Unreal shuttle-game—the kiss !
Her moving body sobs above,
And calls its lechery true love.
Out from the flame of heart she plucks
One flower of fiery light, and sucks
Its essence up within her lips,
And flings it into mine, and dips
And bends her body, writhes and swims
To link the velvet of our limbs,
My drouthy passion worn and keen,
And lusty life of Messaline.
    The heart's blood in her boiling over
She sucked from many a dying lover :
The purple of her racing veins
Leapt from some soul's despairing pains ;
She drinks up life as from a cup ;
She drains our health and builds it up
Into her body ; takes our breath,
And we—we dream not it is death !
Arm unto arm and eye to eye,
Breast to great breast and thigh to thigh,
We look, and strain, and laugh, and die.
I see the head hovering above
To swoop for cruelty or love ;

I feel the swollen veins below
The knotted throat; the ebb and flow
Of blood, not milk, in breasts of fire;
Of deaths, not fluctuants, of desire;
Of molten lava that abides
Deep in the vast volcanic sides;
Deep scars where kisses once bit in
Below young mountains that be twin,
Stigmata cruciform of sin,
The diary of Messaline.

The moving mountains crater-crowned;
The valleys deep and silver-bound;
The girdle treacherously wound;
One violet-crested mounded mole,
Some blood-stain filtered from the soul;
The light and shadow shed between
My soul and God from Messaline.

And even as a dark and hidden
Furnace roars out in woods forbidden,
A sullen tide of molten steel
Runs from deep furrows in the wheel;
So from afar one central heat
Sends the loud pulse to fever beat;
So from one crown and heart of fire
Spring the vast phantoms of desire,
Impossible and epicene,
Familiar souls of Messaline.

And as, when thunder broods afar
Imperial destinies of war,
Men see the haze and heat, and feel
The sun's rays like a shaft of steel,
Seeing no sun; even so the night
Clouds that deep miracle from sight:
Until this destiny be done
Hangs the corona on the sun;
And I absorbed in those unclean
Ghost-haunted veins of Messaline.

## CALIFORNIA.

FORGED by God's fingers in His furnace,
    Fate,
My destiny drew near the glowing shore
Where California hides her golden ore,
Her rubies and her beryls; gross and great,

Her varied fruits and flowers alike create
    Glories most unimaginable, more
    Than Heaven's own meadows match; yet
        this is sore,
    A stain; not one of these is delicate.

Save only the clear green within the sea—
    Because that rolls all landless from Japan.
    I did not know until I missed it here
How beautiful that beauty is to me,
    That life that bears Death's sigil[1] traced
        too clear,
    Blue lines within the beauty that is man.

## MARGARET.

THE moon spans Heaven's architrave;
    Stars in the deep are set;
Written in gold on the day's grave,
    "To love, and to forget;"
And sea-winds whisper o'er the wave
    The name of Margaret.

A heart of gold, a flower of white,
    A blushing flame of snow,
She moves like latticed moons of light—
    And O! her voice is low,
Shell-murmurs borne to Amphitrite,
    Exulting as they go.

Her stature waves, as if a flower
    Forgot the evening breeze,
But heard the charioted hour
    Sweep from the farther seas,
And kept sweet time within her bower,
    And hushed mild melodies.

So grave and delicate and tall—
    Shall laughter never sweep
Like a moss-guarded waterfall
    Across her ivory sleep?
A tender laugh most musical?
    A sigh serenely deep?

[1] Signature, usually applied to the supposed signatures of divine beings.

She laughs in wordless swift desire
  A soft Thalassian tune ;
Her eyelids glimmer with the fire
  That animates the moon ;
Her chaste lips flame, as flames aspire
  Of poppies in mid-June.

She lifts the eyelids amethyst,
  And looks from half-shut eyes,
Gleaming with miracles of mist,
  Gray shadows on blue skies ;
And on her whole face sunrise-kissed,
  Child-wonderment most wise.

The whitest arms in all the earth
  Blush from the lilac bed.
Like a young star even at its birth
  Shines out the golden head.
Sad violets are the maiden girth,
  Pale flames night-canopied.

O gentlest lady ! Lift those eyes,
  And curl those lips to kiss !
Melt my young boyhood in thy sighs,
  A subtler Salmacis !
Hide, in that peace, these ecstasies ;
  In that fair fountain, this !

She fades as starlight on the stream,
  As dewfall in the dell ;
All life and love, one ravishing gleam
  Stolen from sleep's crucible ;
That kiss, that vision is a dream :—
  And I—most miserable !

Still Echo wails upon the steep,
  "To love—and to forget !"
Still sombre whispers from the deep
  Sob through Night's golden net,
And waft upon the wings of sleep
  The name of Margaret.

---

## ALICE: AN ADULTERY.

"Commit not with man's sworn spouse."
          *King Lear.*

AGAINST the fiat of that God discrowned,
  Unseated by Man's justice, and replaced,
By Law most bountiful and maiden-faced
  And mother-minded : passing the low
      bound

Of man's poor law we leapt at last and
    found
Passion ; and passing the dim halls dis-
    graced
Found higher love and larger and more
    chaste,
A calm sphinx waiting in secluded ground.

Hear the sad rhyme of how love turned to
    lust,
  And lust invigorated love, and love
  Shone brighter for the stain it rose above,
Gathering roses from the quickening dust ;
  And faith despoiled and desecrated trust
  Wore pearlier plumes of a diviner dove.

## THE FIRST DAY.

"Who ever loved that loved not at first sight ?"
          *As You Like It.*

THE waving surf shone from the Peaceful
    Sea.[1]
Young palms embowered the house
    where Beauty sate
Still but exultant, silent but elate
In its own happiness and majesty
Of a mild soul unstirred by rivalry
  Of any life beyond its own sweet state.
I looked around me, wondered whether
    Fate
Had found at last a woman's love for me.

I had no hope : she was so grave and
    calm,
  So shining with the dew-light of her
    soul,
  So beautiful beyond a woman's share.
Yet—here ! Soft airs, and perfume through
    the palm,
  And moonlight in the groves of spice,
    control
  The life that would not love and yet be
    fair.

[1] *I.e.* the Pacific.

## THE SECOND DAY.

"Keep you in the rear of your affection
Out of the shot and danger of desire."
                                    *Hamlet.*

I WAS so hopeless that I turned away
    And gave my love to foul oblivion,
    Shuttered my bosom's window from the
        sun,
    Kindled a corpse-light and proclaimed
        "The day!";
Lurked in Aeaean [1] fens to elude the ray
    Whose beauty might disturb me: I did
        shun
    The onyx eyes that saw me not as one
    Possible even for a moment's play.

Thus I was tangled in some house of hell,
    Giving mine own soul's beauty up to lust,
    Hoping to build some fort impregnable
Against my love: instead the deep disgust
    Of my own beasthood crushed it into
        dust,
    And left my manhood twisted in her
        spell.

## THE THIRD DAY.

"My love is most immaculate white and red."
                            *Love's Labour's Lost.*

SHE was more graceful than the royal palm;
    Tall, with imperial looks, and excellence
    Most simply swathed in spotless ele-
        gance,
    And holy and tuneful like some stately
        psalm.
Her breath was like a grove of myrrh and
        balm,
    And all the sight grew dim before the
        sense
    Of blind attraction toward; an influence
    Not incompatible with her own calm.

1. Circe, who dwelt on the island of Aeaea,
transformed men into swine.
VOL. II.

All the red roses of the world were blended
    To give the lively colour of her face;
    All the white lilies of the sea shone
        splendid
Where the blue veins afforded them a space;
    Like to the shapely fragrance of dawn's
        shrine
    She gleamed through mist, enchanting,
        Erycine.[1]

## THE FOURTH DAY.

"Amen, if you love her; for the lady is very
    well worthy."
                    *Much Ado about Nothing.*

I TOOK another way to shield my love.
    I turned my thoughts to the abyss of sky,
    Pierced the frail veil, and sought Eter-
        nity;
    Where the Gods reign most passionless
        above
All foolish loves of men, and weary of
    The slow procession of Earth's mystery;
    Where worlds, not men, are born and
        live and die,
    And aeons flit unnoticed as a dove.

Thither I fled, busied myself with these;
    When—lo! I saw her shadow following!
    In every cosmic season-tide of spring
She rose, being the spring: in utter peace
    She was with me and in me: thus I saw
    Ours was not love, but destiny, and law.

## REINCARNATION.

IN Life what hope is always unto men?
    Stories of Arthur that shall come again
    To cleanse the Earth of her eternal stain,
    Elias, Charlemagne, Christ. What
        matter then?

1 At Eryx, in Sicily, was a famous temple of
Venus.
                                    E

What matter who, or how, or even when?
  If we but look beyond the primal pain,
  And trust the Future to write all things
    plain,
  Graven on brass with the predestined pen.

This is the doom.   Upon the blind blue sky
  A little cloud, no larger than an hand !
  Whether I live and love, or love and die,
I care not : either way I understand.
  To me—to live is Christ ; to die is gain :
  For I, I also, I shall come again.


### THE FIFTH DAY.

"Thine eyes, sweet lady, have infected mine."
                                  *Richard III.*

ALL thought of work is almost cast aside.
  I followed like a dog the way she went,
  Speaking but seldom, very well content
  To day-dream, oft imagining a bride,
A wife, a lover, even a sister, tied
  By some soft bond of twinning : thus
    I blent
  A real joy with a brighter element
  Of fancy free to wander far and wide.

For as I followed by the shore and bended
  Over her footsteps in the wood, my will
  Rose to high strength assertive and
    transcended
The petty forms of the seducer's skill.
  Chaste love strode forth, a warrior's
    stern and splendid
  Determined footsteps on the Arcadian
    Hill.


### THE SIXTH DAY.

            "Are there not charms
By which the property of youth and maidhood
May be abusèd?"
                                  *Othello.*

I DREW a hideous talisman of lust
  In many colours where strong sigils
    shone ;
  Crook'd mystic language of oblivion,
  Fitted to crack and scorch the terrene
    crust

And bring the sulphur steaming from the
    thrust
  Of Satan's winepress, was ill written on
  The accursèd margin, and the orison
  Scrawled backwards, as a bad magician
    must.

By these vile tricks, abominable spells,
  I drew foul horrors from a many hells—
  Though I had fathomed Fate ; though
    I had seen
Chastity charm-proof arm the sea-gray eyes
  And sweet clean body of my spirit's
    queen,
  Where nothing dwells that God did not
    devise.


### THE SEVENTH DAY.

"This word 'love,' which greybeards call
    divine,
  Be resident in men like one another
  And not in me : I am myself alone."
                                  *3 Henry VI.*

THEREFORE I burnt the wicked pantacle,
  And cast my love behind me once
    again.
  I mused upon the mystery of pain,
  Where the Gods taught me by another
    spell
Not chosen from the armoury of Hell,
  But given of Mercury to cleanse the
    stain
  Of the old planet : thus I wrote me
    plain
  Secrets divine—tremendous, terrible !

Thus I forgot my soul and dwelt alone
  In the strong fortress of the active
    mind
  Whose steady flame burned eager in the
    night ;
Yet was some shadow on the starry throne,
  Some imperfection playing hoodman-
    blind
  So that I saw not perfectly aright.

## THE EIGHTH DAY.

> "A certain aim he took
> At a fair Vestal thronèd by the West."
> *Midsummer Night's Dream.*

HERE in the extreme west of all the earth
  This Vestal sate ; and I from Cupid's
    bow
Loosed a fair shaft of verses shapen so
As to fling love through the chaste girdle's
    girth,
And show my love how meek was my love's
    birth,
  How innocent its being : thus arow
  Stood the mild lines, immaculate, to
    show
  My harmless passion and her own great
    worth.

She could not be offended : and moreover—
  When at the nightfall I sought Heaven's
    light,
  All my work grew unspotted, done
    aright !
The high Gods came above my head to hover,
  Because I worked with a diviner might,
  The perfect sage being the perfect lover.

## THE NINTH DAY.

> " How canst thou tell she will deny thy suit
> Before thou make a trial of her love?"
> *1 Henry VI.*

I WAS most weary of my work : the mind
  Shuddered at all the wonders it had
    written,
  And the whole body by the spirit smitten
  Groaned : so I went and left my love
    behind,
Danced the gross "hula,"[1] hardly disinclined,
  By a new lust emphatically bitten ;
  And so in flames at harlot glances litten
  I sought that solace I shall never find.

[1] The indecent dance of the South Sea
Islands.

Fool ! not to tell her. Triple fool to fly
  The sunny glance, the moonlight medi-
    tation,
  For even the light of heaven. How
    much worse
The dark antithesis, the coarser curse
  Of Eden ! Pass, O shadows of crea-
    tion,
  Into the daybreak of Eternity !

## THE TENTH DAY.

> " O God ! I could be bounded in a nutshell,
> and count myself king of infinite space, were
> it not that I have bad dreams."
> *Hamlet.*

THE mere result of all this was a dream.
  The day passed damned, void of my
    love's dear light,
  And stole accursèd to the endless night,
  Forgotten (as I trust) by God : no
    beam
Of memory lighting it down Time's dark
    stream.
  I dreamt : my shrine was broken and
    my might
  Defiled, and all my Gods abased, in
    sight
  Of all blind Heaven exenterate[1] and
    extreme.[2]

The foulest traitor of all womankind
  I ever knew, became my friend :[3] un-
    clean
  Sexual abominations floated through,
More foul because a golden cord did wind
  Unspotted through that revel epicene,
  The pure faith of one woman that was
    true.

[1] Disembowelled.
[2] Used here to mean "at the last gasp."
[3] This circumstance was later fulfilled : I
having judged her actions on insufficient evidence.—AUTHOR.

## THE ELEVENTH DAY.

"What win I if I gain the thing I seek?"
*Rape of Lucrece.*

THERE is much sorcery in the word eleven.
　I took my lover's image pale and clear,
　Fixed in my mind; I saw her standing
　　near,
　Wooed her, conjured her by the power
　　of heaven,
Of my own mind, the Genii of the Seven,
　To come and live with me and be my
　　dear,
　To love me in the spirit without fear;—
　Leaving the body's love to follow at
　　even.

Seemeth it not absurd? to use the thought,
　The utterly divine impersonal
　Mind of a man, the pure, the spiritual,
To such a purpose rather less than nought,
　A woman's love—considering that all
　Wise men assure us that it may be
　　bought!

## THE TWELFTH DAY.

"I grant thou wert not married to my Muse
And therefore mayst without attaint o'erlook
The dedicated words which writers use
Of their fair subjects."
　　　　　　　*The Sonnets.*

I LEARNT at last some sort of confidence,
　Called me the fool I was, knowing my
　　skill
　Proven of old, all women's native will
　To do all things soever that lack sense,
Especially if evil: thoughts immense
　Like this I thought: plumes of my
　　amorous quill
　I tickled her withal: then grave and still
　Waited secure: the silence grew intense.

She read—and saw me but a beardless boy,
　Too young to fear, too gentle not to pity,
　Not overbold; quite powerless to destroy
Her life's long peace, the ten-year-wallèd city.[1]
　Why be too cruel, check such baby joy?
　She said "I think the poem very pretty."

## RED POPPY.[2]

I HAVE no heart to sing.
What offering may I bring,
　Alice, to thee?
My great love's lifted wing
Weakens, unwearying,
　And droops with me,
Seeing the sun-kindled hair
Close in the face more fair,
The sweet soul shining there
　For God to see.

Surely some angel shed
Flowers for the maiden head,
　Ephemeral flowers!
I yearn, not comforted.
My heart has vainly bled
　Through age-long hours.
To thee my spirit turns;
My bright soul aches and burns,
As a dry valley yearns
　For spring and showers.

Splendid, remote, a fane
Alone and unprofane,
　I know thy breast.
These bitter tears of pain
Flood me, and fall again
　Not into rest.
Me, whose sole purpose is
To gain one gainless kiss,
And make a bird's my bliss,
　Shrined in that nest.

[1] She had been married ten years.
[2] The poem in question.

O fearful firstling dove !
My dawn and spring of love,
    Love's light and lure !
Look (as I bend above)
Through bright lids filled thereof
    Perfect and pure,
Thy bloom of maidenhood.
I could not : if I could,
I would not : being good,
    Also endure !

Cruel, to tear or mar
The chaliced nenuphar ;
    Cruel to press
The rosebud ; cruel to scar
Or stain the flower-star
    With mad caress.
But crueller to destroy
The leaping life and joy
Born in a careless boy
    From lone distress.

More cruel then art thou
The calm and chaste of brow,
    If thou dost this.
Forget the feeble vow
Ill sworn : all laws allow
    Pity, that is
Kin unto love, and mild.
List to the sad and wild
Crying of the lonely child
    Who asks a kiss.

One kiss, like snow, to slip,
Cool fragrance from thy lip
    To melt on mine ;
One kiss, a white-sail ship
To laugh and leap and dip
    Her brows divine ;
One kiss, a starbeam faint
With love of a sweet saint,
Stolen like a sacrament
    In the night's shrine !

One kiss, like moonlight cold
Lighting with floral gold
    The lake's low tune ;
One kiss, one flower to fold,

On its own calyx rolled
    At night, in June !
One kiss, like dewfall, drawn
A veil o'er leaf and lawn—
Mix night, and noon, and dawn,
    Dew, flower, and moon !

One kiss, intense, supreme !
The sense of Nature's dream
    And scent of Heaven
Shown in the glint and gleam
Of the pure dawn's first beam,
    With earth for leaven ;
Moulded of fire and gold,
Water and wine to fold
Me in its life, and hold !—
    In all but seven !

I would not kiss thee, I !
Lest my lip's charactery
    Ruin thy flower.
Curve thou one maidenly
Kiss, stooping from thy sky
    Of peace and power !
Thine only be the embrace !—
I move not from my place,
Feel the exultant face
    Mine for an hour !

## THE THIRTEENTH DAY.

"If it be a sin to make a true election, she is
    damned."
                                    *Cymbeline.*

IN the dim porchway where the sea's deep
    boom
Under our very feet made ceaseless song,
We sate, remote, the lone lanai[1] along
Sequestered from the young moon in
    the gloom

[1] The South Sea word for balcony, or rather
verandah.

Of early even: then the tender bloom
  Shone on her cheek and deepened as
    the strong
  Arms gathered round her, more than
    shame or wrong,
  And the soft question murmured " Love
    you—whom ? "


The deepening rose ; the heart's pulse
    quickening ;
  The fear ; the increasing ecstasy of this—
A little cloud lifted a sombre wing
Shadowing our secret breath from Artemis—
  Breasts met and arms enclosed, and all
    the spring
  Grew into summer with the first long
    kiss.


## THE FOURTEENTH DAY.

  " Some there be that shadows kiss;
    Such have but a shadow's bliss;
    There be fools alive, I wis."
             *Merchant of Venice.*

ALL day we chose each moment possible
  When to the other's face each face
    might cling,
  Each kiss burn forth, a double fiery
    sting
  Exalting us in joy foreseen to swell
A mighty exultation ; it befell,
  However, that I saw the shadowy thing
  Lurk behind love, and flap a scornful
    wing,
  Seeing our honour stood a citadel.


I saw the foolishness of love that saith :
  " I am exalted over shame and death,
  But will not take my fill of death and
    shame."
For each kiss leaps, a more insistent breath,
  And adds fresh fuel to the amorous
    flame,
  Not quells it—Is not honour but a name?

## THE FIFTEENTH DAY.

  " Were kisses all the joys in bed,
    One woman would another wed."
       *Sonnets to Sundry Notes of Music.*

ANOTHER day rose of unceasing fire:
  Kisses made monstrous for their sterile
    storm
  Maddening with sea-sounds, as of lute
    or shawm
  Fluting and clashing in extreme desire ;
The silly " Thus far and no farther," nigher
  Each hour to break (poor arbitrary
    form !)
  As each kiss bade our bodies wed and
    warm
  Give love one chance before its wave
    retire.

Not so : this trial was the tiniest
  Man ever knew, confronted afterward
  With giant fears and passions ;—long to
    fight
And last to yield a Maenad-swelling breast
  Unto a furious Dionysian horde
  Drunk not with wine, but with aveng-
    ing night.


## THE SIXTEENTH DAY.

" My chastity's the jewel of our house
  Bequeathèd down from many ancestors,
  Which were the greatest obloquy i' th' world
  For me to lose."
                    *All's Well.*

THERE was no secret cave of the wood's
    womb
  Where we might kiss all day without a
    start
  Of fear that meant to stay and must
    depart,
  Nor any corner where the sea's perfume

Might shelter love in some wave-carven tomb.
   But Maytime shone in us ; with words
      of art
I drew her down reluctant to my heart,
When night was silence and my bed
      the gloom.

So without sin we took strange sacrament,
   Whose wine was kisses, and whose bread
      the flower
   Of fast and fervent cleaving breast to
      breast.
As lily bends to lily we were bent,
   Not as mere man to woman : all the
      dower
   Of martyred Virgins crowned our dan-
      gerous quest.

## ALICE.

THE roses of the world are sad,
   The water-lilies pale,
Because my lover takes her lad
   Beneath the moonlight veil.
No flower may bloom this happy hour—
Unless my Alice be the flower.

The stars are hidden in dark and mist,
   The moon and sun are dead,
Because my love has caught and kissed
   My body in her bed.
No light may shine this happy night—
Unless my Alice be the light.

So silent are the thrush, the lark !
   The nightingale's at rest,
Because my lover loves the dark,
   And has me in her breast.
No song this happy night be heard !—
Unless my Alice be the bird.

The sea that roared around the house
   Is fallen from alarms,
Because my lover calls me spouse,
   And takes me to her arms.
This night no sound of breakers be !—
Unless my Alice be the sea.

Of man and maid in all the world
   Is stilled the swift caress,
Because my lover has me curled
   In her own loveliness.
No kiss be such a night as this !—
Unless my Alice be the kiss.

No blade of grass awaiting takes
   The dew fresh-fallen above,
Because my lover swoons, and slakes
   Her body's thirst of love.
This night no dewfall from the blue !—
Unless my Alice be the dew.

This night—O never dawn shall crest
   The world of wakening,
Because my lover has my breast
   On hers for dawn and spring.
This night shall never be withdrawn—
Unless my Alice be the dawn.

## THE SEVENTEENTH DAY.

         " Now I want
   Spirits to enforce, art to enchant."
                *Tempest.*

LAST night—but the boy shrieked in's sleep
     —then, there
   I had ended all !  Having ingressed the
     track
   That leads from green or white-crowned
     hours to black,
   The pleasant portals of the scorpion
     snare,
First gleaming toils of an enchantress' hair
   That afterward shall change their fer-
     vours slack
   To strong gripe of a devil-fish : go back ?
   The hand is put forth to the plough—
     beware !

I took my shrine down : [1] at the night we lay
   Four hours debating between fear and sin:
   Whether our love went deeper than the
     skin,

[1] Meaning that spiritual work was abandoned for the moment, and that he wished to
use the room for a profane purpose.

Or lower than the lips : love won the day.
 We nestled like young turtles that be
  twin
 Close till the morn-star chased the moon
  away.


## LOVE AND FEAR.

THE rose of the springtime that bended
 Its delicate head to the breeze
Is crimson and stately and splendid
 Now summer is here and at ease ;
Love risen as the sun hath transcended its
 passion and peace.

In a garden of dark foliage that clusters
 Round your face as a rosebud withdrawn,
New splendour springs carmine and
  lustres
 Your cheeks with the coming of
  dawn,
Love's light as an army that musters its
 plumes—and is gone.

For fear as a fountain, that trembles
 With wind, is arisen, and hides
The light of your love, and dissembles
 The roar of the passionate tides ;
Though a flickering flame it resembles, love
 is, and abides.

I see through the moonlight that covers
 (As a mist on the mountain) your
  head
The flame of your heart as a lover's
 Shine out in your face and be shed,
A ruby that flashes and hovers and droops
 and is dead.

As a saint in a vision half hidden
 I see the sweet face in a mist,
A nimbus of glory unbidden
 That shades you or shows as you
  list.
But I, as a bridegroom, unchidden, may
 kiss—and am kissed.

In the light and the manifest splendour
 That shows you in darkness a bride,
Pale blossom of moonlight and slender,
 A lily that sways in the tide,
A star that falls earthward to bend her sweet
 breast to my side :—

No depth of the darkness may shield you
 From eyes that with love are aflame,
No darkness, but light, as you yield you
 To love that is stronger than shame,
No music but kisses, that pealed you their
 pæan, proclaim :

That the light of the heaven is shaded,
 The sound of the sea is made still,
The climax shall come unupbraided
 Obedient alone to our will,
And the flowers that were fallen and faded
 drink dew to their fill :

Dew filling your eyes and their lashes
 With tender mirage of a tear ;
Dew fallen on the mouth as it flashes,
 The kiss that is master of fear ;
Dew covering the body that dashes and
 clings to me here.

O fairest, O rose among roses !
 O flower of the innermost fire !
O tune of my soul that encloses
 All life, the tempestuous lyre !
O dawn of my dawn that reposes and darts
 in desire !

And death and its portals are rifted,
 Life listens our kisses that weep ;
Love hears, and his measure is shifted,
 Grows solemn and deadly and deep ;
Love's ship droops its sails and is drifted in
 silence to sleep.

And soft as a seal on our slumber
 Dreams drift of Aurorean dew ;
Dreams shapen of flames that encumber
 The shrine of the morn in the blue ;
Flames shapen of lips that outnumber our
 kisses anew.

## THE EIGHTEENTH DAY.

" Touches so soft still conquer chastity."
*Passionate Pilgrim.*

SHE grew most fearful, starting at slight noise ;
    As knowing that the sting of shame was
        hers
    Worse than a guilty love administers,
    Since our pure shame unworthily destroys
The love of all she had, her girls and boys,
    Her home, their lives : and yet my
        whisper stirs
    Into live flame her passion, and deters
    Her fear from spurning all the day's
        due joys.

She had not dared to speak one word, to tell
    How deep and pure a fountain sunward
        leapt
    In her life's garden : but to-night she lay
In my intense embraces : so the spell
    Moved her : " I love you," said she. So
        we kept,
    Remurmuring that one phrase until the
        day.

## THE NINETEENTH DAY.

" The boy is foolish, and I fear not him."
*Richard III.*

SHE dared not come into my room to-night.
    So ? I was acquiescent, sharp despair
    And nervous purpose mixing in me there
    The while I waited : then I glided light
(Clad in the swart robe of an eremite) [1]
    Across the passage.  Now, all unaware
    My kisses underneath the veil of vair
    Woke her : she turned and sighed and
        held me tight.

Her child slept gently on the farther side.
    But we took danger by the throat, de-
        spised
    All but the one sole splendour that we
        prized ;

[1] Crowley was accustomed to wear a black robe of a magical pattern as a *robe de chambre.*

And she, whose robe was far too slight to hide
    The babe-smooth breasts, was far too
        frail to cover
    Her heart's true fire and music from her
        lover.

## THE TWENTIETH DAY.

" *Val.* How long hath she been deformed ?
*Speed.* Ever since you loved her."
*Two Gentlemen of Verona.*

AGAIN the unveiled goddess of delight
    Watched us at midnight : there my
        lover lay
    Child-breasted, maiden as the rose of day
    Dawning on snowy mountains : through
        deep night
Her body gleamed self-luminously white
    With the sweet soul that sundered the
        quick clay,
    And all her being was a sense of May ;—
    Scent conquering colour, soul out-
        running sight.

Not with the Lysian,[1] nor Iacchian dew
    Of frenzy covered, but with warmer
        flakes
    Of Aphrodite shed upon our life,
We clung still closer, till the soul ran through
    Body to body, twined like sunny snakes,
    Sinlessly knowing we were man and wife.

## THE TWENTY-FIRST DAY.

" *Mal.* Dispute it like a man.
    *Macd.*                    I shall do so.
    But I must also feel it as a man."
*Macbeth.*

I HAD a fearful dream (on going away)
    Of scorpion women curled in my caress,
    And twenty days they closed on my
        distress
    Not giving me relief, but gold and gray,

[1] Cornelius Agrippa distinguishes three frenzies ; of Apollo, Dionysus, and Aphrodite ; song, wine, and love.

Cold and inténse ; the one-and-twentieth day
    They drew my life out, one exceeding
        stress,
    Volcanic anguish !—Here's the strange
        excess :
    I called, ere waking, on the name
        *Eheieh !*

Solve me the riddle of the dream who can !
    That night I sought a new toy for a lure,
    And she would not : but knew how hard
        to endure
Is love like ours, the love of purity.
    So she : " Dispute it like a man !" and I :
    " But I must also feel it as a man ! "

    Note.   Eheieh is the Hebrew for "I am that
I am."   Its numerical value is 21.   I was not
aware at the time that this was the 21st day.—
AUTHOR.[1]


## THE TWENTY-SECOND DAY.

" I'll have her : but I will not keep her long."
                    *Richard III.*

IT was impossible that she should come
    Over the leagues of summer-coloured sea
    Alone with love and laughter and tears
        and me
    To the toy land [2] of the chrysanthemum,
Where all the flowers lack scent, the birds
        are dumb,
    The fruits are tasteless : where the
        jewelled lea
    And all the many-leavèd greenery
    Is dwarf : French gem-work on a baby's
        thumb.

The Yankee God [3] frowned also on the plan.
    We had enough, no more. But I insist,
    Still thinking I was master of my heart :
Saying, " Another month to be a man,
    Another month to kiss her and be kissed,
    And then—all time to Magic and to
        Art ! "

    [1] That is, the imaginary author.
    [2] Japan.        [3] The dollar.

## THE TWENTY-THIRD DAY.

    " He has strangled
    His language in his tears."
                    *K. Hen. VIII.*

MY comedy has changed its blithe aspect
    To bitterest face of tragedy ; she said :
    "Alas ! O soul of mine ! I am surely
        dead,
    Seeing my life is by a serpent wrecked
Of sore disease : but spare me, and reflect
    That in few months I die : but were I
        wed—
    O lover ! O desire discomfited !
    I die at once : consider, and elect."

How could I otherwise than spare my wife ?
    With tender lips and fingers one strong
        kiss
    Swooned slave-wise even before the gate
        of bliss,
No more : for I rose up and cursed my life,
    Hating the God that made us to dissever
So soon so sweet a love, and that for ever.

    *Ut. Canc.* sublatum iri dixisse.   Vae Capri-
corno ![1]   (Author's Note.)


## THE TWENTY-FOURTH DAY.

    " She having the truth of honour in her, hath
made him that gracious denial which he is
most glad to receive."
                *Measure for Measure.*

OF course I might have known it was a lie.
    Nathless, I wept all morning and de-
        spaired.
    Nothing for any life of earth I cared,
    Neither for heaven : I railed against the
        sky,

    [1] This intentionally obscure note means that
she said she had cancer.   Now Capricorn, the
opposite to Cancer in the Zodiac, is called " the
symbol of gross passion."

Hating the earth, the sea, the witchery
   Of all the universe : my breast I bared
   And cursed God, hoping lightning ; and
      I dared
   Not ask my love " In very truth—you
      die ! "

I could not bear it longer ; then she
      spake :
   " I lied indeed, love, for mine honour's
      sake,"
   And I reproached her for her love's dis-
      trust,
Saying " I would not so in any wise
   Have lowered love unto the level of lust
   But now—" I hid my thought in tears
      and sighs.


## THE TWENTY-FIFTH DAY.

" I am in health, I breathe, and see thee ill."
                        *Richard II.*

ALICE was desperately ill at morn.
   Hour by sweet hour I watched her
      sorrowing,
   While the strong fever fought uncon-
      quering
   With native coolness of her life, o'er-
      worn
Or poisoned ; thus I fought the long forlorn
   Battle all day, until the evening
   Brought back sweet health on sleep
      and noiseless wing :
   Strong love of the long battle was re-
      born.

The child slept elsewhere that she might
      sleep well.
   Therefore, not fearing anything, I came ;
   Lit my love's candle at her body's flame,
And fought not with the fevers now that
      swell
   Our burning lips and bosoms, until
      shame
   Nearly surrendered the sweet citadel.


## THE TWENTY-SIXTH DAY.

" I think the devil will not have me damned
. . . he would never else cross me thus."
             *Merry Wives of Windsor.*

THIS time she set her will against my will ;
   Swore that she would not come : in my
      despair
   I half believed her an enchantress fair
   Cruel as hell and dowered with subtle
      skill
To strain my life out with her love, and kill
   My soul with misery : suddenly a rare
   Swift smile set shimmering all the am-
      bient air,
   And then I knew she was my true love
      still.

She would not come ? Why, were Hell's
      portals fast
   Shut, as to Orpheus on Eurydice,
   Their brass would break before love's
      gold and steel,
The sharpness inlaid with sweet tracery
   Of talismans of virtue : she is leal
   To come and live and be my love at
      last.


## UNDER THE PALMS.

THE woodland hollows know us, bird-
      enchanted,
   Likewise the spaces of the ghostly sea,
The lake's abundant lilies, the pale slanted
   Moonlight on flowers, the wind's low
      minstrelsy ;
For all the tropic greenery is haunted
   By you and me. . . . . . . .

The tall palms bend and catch love's tender
      ditty
   To learn a sweeter song to lure their
      mate.
The soft wind sighs in amorous self-pity,
   Having no love wherein to laugh elate,
And turns to the cold harbour and the city,
   Wailing its fate . . . . . . . .

Two faces and two bosoms, breathing slowly
   In tune and time with the sea's hymn
     below,
Breathing in peace of love, mighty and holy,
   Fearing to fuse, and longing—be it so !
And the world's pulse stops, as God bends
   him lowly
     To hear and know. . . . . . . .

For not the heights of heaven shall exalt her
   Whose heart is full of love's dumb deity,
Nor harp-strings lift me, nor the sound of
     psalter,
   Whose love is merged and molten into
     thee,
Nor incense sweeter be by shrine or altar
     For you and me. . . . . . . . .

But like dove's eyes where glamour lies
   a-dwelling,
   Like sweet well-water rising in the well,
Strong steep black currents thrust up,
   flooding, welling,
   Into the moonlight, swift, adorable, —
So kisses cluster, so our bosoms swelling
     Abide and dwell. . . . . . . .

Yet the twin faces, like Madonnas, meeting,
   Fear and draw back and gaze a little
     space ;
Fear, lest they lose the moonlight frail and
   fleeting,
   Lose their own beauty in their own
     embrace,
But feel how gladdening hearts and bosoms
   beating
     Kindle the face . . . . . . . . .

But not for long shall lilies strive with roses,
   Nor fear be fearful, nor delight repose,
Nor love retire ; the woodland cleaves and
   closes
   Round heads an aureole hides, a rainbow
     shows.
A swifter shape of fire cleaves us, encloses
     Rosebud and rose. . . . . . . .

Mouth unto mouth ! O fairest ! Mutely lying,
   Fire lambent laid on water,—O ! the
     pain !
Kiss me, O heart, as if we both were dying !
   Kiss, as we could not ever kiss again !
Kiss me, between the music of our sighing,
     Lightning and rain !

Not only as the kiss of tender lovers—
   Let mingle also the sun's kiss to sea,
Also the wind's kiss to the bird that hovers,
   The flower's kiss to the earth's deep
     greenery.
All elemental love closes and covers
     Both you and me.

All shapes of silence and of sound and seeing,
   All lives of Nature molten into this,
The moonlight waking and the shadows
   fleeing,
   Strange sorcery of unimagined bliss,
All breath breathing in ours ; mingled all
   being
     Into the kiss.

## THE TWENTY-SEVENTH DAY.

" The ship is in her trim ; the merry wind
   Blows fair from land."
               *Comedy of Errors.*

QUITE careless whether golden gales of wind
   Fling our boat forward, or the storm
    and spark
   Of lightning lamp or shroud us in the
    dark,
Careless if ever land again we find,
Careless of all things (this love being blind),
   We put to sea. O gladly stand and mark
   The diamond headland fall behind our
    barque,
   Wrapped in shrine - shadow of love's
    central mind !

We are alone to-day on the strange sea,
   Divider of the dawn's divinity
   From sunset's splendour : our eternal
    noon

Of love recks little of eternity—
　　And though the moon is dying, ourselves
　　　may swoon,
　　One deathless shape of the large-
　　　breasted moon.


## THE TWENTY-EIGHTH DAY.

　"But I perceive in you so excellent a touch
of modesty that you will not extort from me
what I am willing to keep in."
　　　　　　　　　　　　　*Twelfth-Night.*

A CURIOUS conflict this of love and fear,
　　Honour and lust, and truth and trust
　　　beguiled;
　　One in the semblance of a rose-bright
　　　child :—
　　The other in a shape more gross and
　　　clear,
A fiercer woman-figure crowned severe
　　With garlands woven of scourges, but
　　　whose wild
　　Breast beat with splendour of sin, whose
　　　looks were mild,
　　Hiding the cruel smile behind a tear.

So she: "I know you never would ; " yet did
　　Such acts that no end otherwise might be.
　　So I : "I will not ever pluck the
　　　flower ; "
Yet strayed enchanted on the lawns forbid,
　　And bathed enamoured in the secret sea,
　　Both knowing our words were spoken—
　　　for an hour.


## THE TWENTY-NINTH DAY.

　"Persever in that clear way thou goest,
　And the gods strengthen thee."
　　　　　　　　　　　　　*Pericles.*

LINKED in the tiny shelf upon the ship,
　　My blind eyes burned into her mild
　　　ones : limbs
　　Twined to each other while fine dew
　　　bedims
　　Their quivering skins: lip fastened unto
　　　lip :

Whole soul and body frenzied meet and clip ;
　　And the breath staggers, and the life-
　　　blood swims !
　　Terrible gods chant black demoniac
　　　hymns
　　As the frail cords of honour strain and
　　　slip.

For in the midst of that tremendous tide
　　The mighty vigour of a god was mine !
　　Drunk with desire, her lamentations
　　　died.
The dove gave place a moment to the swine !
　　Rapturous draughts of madness ! Out
　　　she sighed
　　Uttermost life's love, and became a
　　　bride.


## THE THIRTIETH DAY.

　"For God's sake, lords, convey my tristful
　　Queen,
　For tears do stop the floodgates of her eyes."
　　　　　　　　　　　　　*King Henry IV.*

BITTER reproaches passed between us twain,
　　Hers real, mine with sneering logic sewn
　　Proving my trespass hardly half her own,
　　Its cause; I proved her how she made
　　　me fain
And left me mad, and led through joy and
　　pain
　　To that unthinkable thing: I might atone
　　No whit in this way: then that stubborn
　　　stone
　　My heart grew tears: we were good
　　　friends again.

Therefore at night I added nothing new :
　　Only a little while I lay with her
　　And with mere kisses sucked her soul
　　　away,
And made my banquet of immortal dew,
　　Demanding nothing but to minister
　　To her desire until the dawn grew grey.

## THE DAY WITHOUT A NUMBER.

*" O never shall the sun that morrow see."*
*Macbeth.*

WE lost a day ! [1]  Nor kisses, nor regret,
   Nor fear, nor pain, nor anything at all !
   The day was lost, evanished past recall,
   That saw no sunrise, never saw sun set—
For East and West invisibly were met
   In gateways neither glad nor musical
   Nor melancholy nor funereal.
Nought is there to remember nor forget.

Yet in my westward journey many hours
   I stole, and now must pay them back
     again.
   I plucked not one flower, but an hundred
     flowers ;
I bore an hundred passions in my brain—
   King Solomon had three hundred para-
     mours.
   I quite agree that everything is vain.

## THE THIRTY-FIRST DAY.

*" You whoreson villain ! will you let it fall?"*
*Taming of the Shrew.*

THE inexpiable fate whose shuddering wing
   Fear fled from, changed the native deed
     of sin
   Into a spasmic kiss too salt and keen,
   Windless, that ended with a sterile sting
The earlier hour whose heart was full of
     spring ;
   And the large love grew piteously lean ;
   Dreadful, like death ; withdrawn and
     epicene
At the mad crisis of the eventful thing.

O that such tender fondness like a flower's
   Should take such nameless infamy !
     That we
   Should pluck such bitter bloom, rooted
     in fear,

[1] On the westward voyage across the Pacific
a day is " lost " on the 180th degree.

Salt with the scurf of some diseasèd sea,
   Foul with the curse of God: that we
     are here,
   Hating the night's inexorable hours.

## THE THIRTY-SECOND DAY.

*" Me of my lawful pleasure she restrained*
*And prayed me oft forbearance."*
*Cymbeline.*

HOW sweet the soft looks shot, endearing
     shame
   With their warm fragrance of love's
     modest eyes !
   The secret knowledge of our secrecies
Shone from their distance with a subtle
     flame,
And gave to pudency a rosier name
   When the long lashes drooped, and
     saintlier sighs
   Took softer meanings, till my arteries
Throbbed with the glad desire that went
     and came.

" I charge you in the very name of love."
   Quoth she : " We have all day to steal
     below
   And snatch short kisses out of danger's
     throat.
Why beg you night : is not the day enough?"
   But I : " The night is panting and aglow
   To feel our hair distraught and limbs
     afloat."

## THE THIRTY-THIRD DAY.

*"Clubs, clubs ! These lovers will not keep the*
*peace."*
*Titus Andronicus.*

NATHLESS she locked her cabin-door to me.
   All lovers guess the piteous night I
     passed—
   Shuddering phantoms, hideous and
     aghast,
Loomed, lust of hate ! toward me: how
     did she?

She never told : but I might surely see
   In the drawn face and haggard eyes
      what vast
   Voices of misery had held her fast,
   And made her curse her own lock's
      cruelty.

So by her beauty and my love we swore,
   And by the light within mine eyes, by
      her
   Sweet shame : that never so we sunder
      again.
But she : " You swear ' by thy bright face '
      in vain ;
   ' By thy sweet self ' you grow a perjurer;
   Who have shamed my face and made
      me but an whore."


## THE THIRTY-FOURTH DAY.

" *Ben.* Stop there, stop there.
  *Mer.* Thou desirest me to stop in my tale
     against the hair."
              *Romeo and Juliet.*

SWEET are the swift hard struggles ere the
   kiss,
   When the frail body blushes into tears,
   And short breaths cancel the long sighs,
     and fears
   Constrain delight, until their import is
Made foolish when the struggle's synthesis
   Leads to hot armistice, as dewy spheres
   Glow, and increase the fury that reveres
   No God, no heaven but its own hell's
     bliss.

So after desperate shifts of modesty
   We could no more ; loosened and lax
     we lay
   Breathing and holding : then in amorous
     play
She laughed and left her body's love to me,
   And kissed one kiss holding the heart
     of May,
   And kissed again, and kissed our lives
     away.


## THE THIRTY-FIFTH DAY.

" I cannot kiss, that is the humour of it, but
  adieu."
              *King Henry V.*

THE third time bitterly came reason back.
   Is it a fault in love when mornings find
   The soul grown sober and rethroned the
     mind ?
   Or is it mere necessity to track
The candid chequer cross-wise to the black,
   And love, not mutable, yet well inclined
   To take his pleasure in becoming blind
   After such sight mere day is wont to lack?

So we were angry with ourselves and said
   We would not kiss—two days, and we
     would part.
   And she prayed heaven that she might
     be dead,
And I cursed heaven and my foolish head.
   I strove to turn towards old shapes of
     Art ;
   She, to some phantom faded from her
     heart.


## THE THIRTY-SIXTH DAY.

  " 'Twas not their infirmity,
    It was married chastity."
          *Phœnix and Turtle.*

YET ere the stars paled slowly in the east
   I could not sleep : and she—how else ?
     What rest
   May a man know until his quiet breast
   Beats to her tune ? I garbed me as a
     priest
And moved towards my Host—on God I
     feast !
   We lay in naked chastity, caressed
   Child-like or dreaming, till the dawn
     repressed
   Our sighs : that nuptial yet hath never
     ceased.

That was the best : far sundered by the tide
    Dolorous, endless as Oceanus,[1]
    A serpent-river girdling the large earth,
Still in that pure embrace we bring to birth
    A thousand pleasant children born of us,
    Sacred and sinless, if unsanctified.


## LETHE.

WE have forgotten all the days of fear,
    The nights of torment when the kiss
        expired,
    Lost upon lips with love not overtired,
But fearing many things—the after year,
The end, the man—O no, not him ! the
        tear,
    The children's sorrow, and our own
        shame fired
    Not less in doing all that love desired :
We have forgotten, surely—being here !

We have forgotten every shape of sorrow,
    Knowing no end to one night's ecstasy
    In the night's kiss from morning that
        we borrow,
From the hard usurer, Eternity—
    Seeing we have it in our power to die
    Before the new kiss kindle for the
        morrow.


## THE THIRTY-SEVENTH DAY.

" By long and vehement suit I was seduced
    To make room for him in my husband's
        bed."
                                King John.

MORTALS are not for nectar all the time :
    Ambrosia feeds not men ; nepenthe's sip
    Is only for a moment : then we dip
    Back to the earth and leave the bed
        sublime,

[1] The imaginary river of the Ancients, which
formed the circumference of the world-disk.

And tune our kisses to a terrene rhyme.
    So, once again before we left the ship
    With right good will our bodies cling
        and slip,
    And the life's flame sinks as the kisses
        climb.

There never has been such a supreme kiss
    Since heaven and earth began to be as
        this !
    Doubt nothing of it ! yet our spirits
        knew
Its savour was as roses fallen to dust :
    Our proper food was of Selenian dew,
    And love without a battle conquered lust.


## THE THIRTY-EIGHTH DAY.

" The carcass of a beauty spent and done."
                        Lover's Complaint.

ONE day from landing.  Kamakura sees
    Pass to the mighty shrine and shape of
        bronze[1]
    Me, pilgrim, murmuring pious orisons,
    Taking my refuge in that House of
        Peace,
And after, sees my love, and doth not please.
    She was too young to know that shrine
        the Son's,
    Or see the Virgin's House in Kwan-
        se-on's ;[1]
    And when I told her, flushed, and bade
        me cease.

I ceased indeed !  All hope of mental flower
    She shattered in five minutes : following
        lust,
    All intellectual communing did pass,
And all respect of mind : but love's high
        tower,
    Stricken of lightning, stood : not fallen
        in dust,
    Beautiful fragments as of a Greek vase.

[1] The Dai-Butsu, a vast statue of Buddha.
[2] The Goddess.  Her function is variously
identified with that of Isis, Bhavani, or the
Kundalini.

## THE THIRTY-NINTH DAY.

" Had I no eyes but ears, my ears would love
  That inward beauty and invisible."
                    *Venus and Adonis.*

NOTE from this day no possible event.
  All secrets told, and all desires fulfilled
  Primitive passion of our soul have killed.
  We dwell within a calmer element
Perfectly pure and perfectly content.
  The subtler splendour of our love has
    stilled
  Those sombre glories that it never willed,
  Those giant meanings that it never
    meant.

Fire only is our substance ; there we dwell,
  The Salamandrine with the Salamander.
  No fuel to crack, no water to make
    tunes,
No air to blow us hither and thither ; well !
  At our own will through cosmic space
    we wander
  Alive, the sun's beam mixing with the
    moon's.

## THE FORTIETH DAY.

" Away, you rascally Althea's dream, away ! "
                    *2 King Henry IV.*

MERE terror struck into our souls, one shaft
  Sudden and swift ; our punishment was
    here.
  The shapeless form of an avenging fear
  Shuddered within her ; from the deep
    rich draught
Of lively labour that her nights had quaffed
  Rises a serpent : prescience of next year,
  The springtide ; may the Minotaur[1]
    appear,
  Prodigious offspring of the fatal graft ?

[1] The offspring of Europa and of Jupiter
under the form of a bull.

The worst has happened.   Time must now
    discover
  What love had hidden from the wittol's[1]
    eyes
  (What hate may tell him if he read my
    song,
If he be subtle : not if he be wise).
  In our despair came laughter to my
    lover :
  " All's well as yet.   I calculated wrong."

## THE FORTY-FIRST DAY.

" I am sick."
                *Antony and Cleopatra.*

How things are changed since Alice was so
    ill !
  I, being in high fever, lay in bed,
  While my love smoothed the pillows
    for my head :
  Her calm looks christened me with dew
    to still
All chance of fever to the soul, and fill
  My heart with pure love like a snowfall
    shed
  Meekly, a blossom where frail white and
    red
  Were never frenzied at some mad god's
    will.

She sat and gazed upon me all day long.
  Sometimes she held my hands ; then
    she would weep,
  And then stoop tenderly and kiss my
    lips,
Or lull me with some chaste and gentle
    song
  Of angel love.   Night's plume its dew
    fall drips
  As she still sits and watches me to sleep.

[1] Cuckold.
                                        F

## THE FORTY-SECOND DAY.

" *Pol.* No longer stay.
*Leon.* One seven-night longer.
*Pol.* Very sooth, to-morrow."
*Winter's Tale.*

I COULD not let her leave me the day after.
　　Also we *must* wait till the month decide
　　Whether the mother stood behind the
　　　bride.
　　In any other case what love and laughter
Such tidings of an angel's birth would waft
　　　her ;
　　Now, what a fear !   And  so  she  would
　　　abide
　　Another vessel and another tide,
　　Until we held the key of the hereafter.

But this sad spectre could not change our
　　　calm.
　　The day went by more peaceful than a
　　　dream
　　Dreamt by a maiden in pure winds of
　　　balm ;
Love's sweet still music like a far-off psalm
　　Thrilled our quiet pulses : with the in-
　　　tent supreme :
　　" This one week more a century shall
　　　seem."

## AT LAST.

O TEARLESS sorrow of long years, depart !
　　O joy of minutes that be ages long,
　　Come !  Let the  choral  pulse  and
　　　strength of song
Quicken, and the fire of lute and lyre dart,
An arrow red with blood and bright with
　　　art,
　　And cover all the fiery bloom of wrong
　　With blossoms blacker where the blood
　　　runs strong
As our lips pale, their life fled to the heart.

Surely we are as dead, we loving so,
　　So bitterly, so keenly : let no breath
　　Persuade us we are living and must die !

Better believe eternal kisses flow
　　Under the strong rude current miscalled
　　　death,
　　The lotus-river where our bodies lie !

## THE FORTY-THIRD DAY.

" O theft most base
That we have stolen what we do fear to keep."
*Troilus and Cressida.*

IMPOSSIBLE that we shall ever part !
　　The heart shrinks back from thinking it,
　　　the mind
　　Hates it, and prays as love is to be blind.
　　Yet we know well that no magician's art
Can keep our two selves near their single
　　　heart.
　　Self-mocked I urged her " Come and
　　　leave behind
　　All fear and friends and children : we
　　　shall find
　　Love risen sole without a counterpart."

Even while I begged her, I well knew she
　　　must.
　　We could not, loving to see her children
　　　laugh,
　　Let cowards twit them with their
　　　mother's lust.
Even our own purity confirmed the trust.
　　How long, O Lord, how long?  Too
　　　long by half
　　Till men read, wondering, wedlock's
　　　epitaph.

## THE FORTY-FOURTH DAY.

" lips, O you
The doors of breath, seal with a righteous kiss
A dateless bargain to engrossing death."
*Romeo and Juliet.*

SLEEP, O deep splendour of disastrous years,
　　Gone like a star fallen at the fall of night !
　　Wake, O mute mouth and majesty of
　　　light,
　　Made of no sound that even silence
　　　hears,

But born of strings intangible, of spheres
  Shaken of love, a mightier music's might
  Frailer to sound than dewfall is to sight !
  Wake, O sweet soul incorporate of tears !

Or else dream on and let no tears begem
  Love's crown of thorns, ensanguine
    diadem,
  But let pale kisses blossom, starry shrine
Of lips most deathlike, that endure divine
  Past sleep's, or parting's, or death's spoil
    of them
  In the pomegranate walks of Proser-
    pine !¹

### THE FORTY-FIFTH DAY.

"Peace, fool ! I have not done."
*Troilus and Cressida.*

THOU knowest, O Love, how tired our
    bodies grow
  Forgotten in quick converse, love to
    love ;
  How the flame flickers of the ghost
    above,
  The spirit's kiss ; the sleepless to-and-fro
Movement of love's desire too strong to know
  Or care for that it takes its substance
    of—
  As if life's burden were not drear enough
  Or death's deliverance not so far and
    slow.

Our bodies almost perish, with one thought
  Crowned and completed, consecrate and
    shrined :
  A perfect temple of fine amber wrought,
Whose shrine's the body and whose lamp
    the mind.
  The heart is priest and sacrifice in one ;
  And, where it sinned or sorrowed, shall
    atone.

¹ Proserpine, ravished by Hades, was sought
by her mother Demeter. But as she had eaten
(a pomegranate) in Hell, Hades retained a
claim upon her for half the year. See Forty-
eighth Day.

### THE FORTY-SIXTH DAY.

" Because I love you, I will let you know
  . . . . . . . my wife . . . . . . .
  . . . like a fountain with a hundred spouts
  Did run pure blood."
*Julius Cæsar.*

WAS it a sense of uttermost relief
  We gladdened with, and bade our fears
    forget ?
  Was there no subtle fragrance of regret ?
  For me, at least, a pang of perfect grief ?
Had it been otherwise, I would be chief
  And drive her to abandon all things yet
  In mere despair, that by-and-by shall
    get
  Young comfort in a babe beyond belief.

God would not curse and bless us to such
    measure ;
  We were not sad enough nor glad
    enough !
  A little time of misery and pleasure ;
Pain strangling half the ecstasy thereof—
  Such all our gain, who gained the
    utmost treasure,
  Gift of the wizard wand and cup of love.

### THE FORTY-SEVENTH DAY.

"Thou ever young, fresh, lov'd, and delicate
    wooer."
*Timon of Athens.*

THE little money that we had to spend
  Was gone long since : the little more I
    stole
  Followed : I pledged then all things but
    my soul
  (On which the usurers refused to lend)
To raise our utmost, till a ship should send
  Much plenty from the Sunset : to control
  And stop her yet a little while, the whole
  I meant to waste before the week should
    end.

Thus we went Northward to the capital,
  Desolate huts and ways funereal,
  An hateful town; earthquake and heat
    and rain
Made the place wretched, did not love enchain
  There even as here : what mattered
    aught at all
  While love was hovering and our lips
    were fain?

## THE FORTY-EIGHTH DAY.

      " Let us return
And strain what other means is left to us
In our dear peril."
              *Timon of Athens.*

OUR love takes on a tinge of melancholy,
  The six months glory of life past on earth
  About to yield to Hades' bridal birth,
  The world's sad sympathy with Perse-
    phone.
Yet I myself, while tuning to her key
  My sighs of sorrow, mused in secret mirth:
  " I am convinced at last of money's
    worth,
  For lack of which she cannot cross the
    sea."

I told her, like a fool, a day too soon.
  She went and told her story to the priest ;
  She wept, and borrowed money of the
    beast.
She told me she would go: June fell from June.
  I, left in limbo ; she, to front the elate
  Cuckoldy lawyer in the Lone Star State.

## THE FORTY-NINTH DAY.

      " Let me twine
Mine arms about that body."
              *Coriolanus.*

I STOLE her money, even then to prove
  She had no wings to fly with: but I
    knew
  What to her hateful duty there was due,
  And how the hateful system stank there-
    of:

I let her go, both weeping, both enough
  Heart-broken: no farewell went ever
    through—
  Words came not : only ever : " I love
    you !"
  With broken kisses and stained cheeks
    of love.

So all day long and half the night we wan-
    dered
  Down deep lanes and in gardens, like
    lost souls.
  Strong kisses that had surfeited a score
Of earthly bridals in an hour we squandered ;
  And tears like fire, and looks like burn-
    ing coals,
  Without a word passed on for evermore.

## THE FIFTIETH DAY.

*Suffolk.*  " If I depart from thee I cannot live."
*Margaret.*        " let me hear from thee,
    For whereso'er thou art in this world's
      globe
    I have an Iris that shall find thee
      out."
              *2 King Henry VI.*

### I.

AT noon she sailed for home, a weeping
    bride
  Widowed before the honeymoon was
    done.
  Always before the rising of the sun
  I swore to come in spirit to her side
And lie like love; and she at eventide
  Swore to seek me and gather one by one
  The threads of labyrinthine love new
    spun,
  Cretan[1] for monstrous shadows serpent-
    eyed.

So the last kiss passed like a poison-pain,
  Knowing we might not ever kiss again.
  Mad tears fell fast: " Next year !" in
    cruel distress

---

[1] The reference is still to the Minotaur, who
dwelt in a labyrinth in Crete.

We sobbed, and stretched our arms out, and
    despaired,
  And—parted.   Out the brute-side of
    truth flared ;
  " Thank God I've finished with that
    foolishness ! "


## II.

AH ! there be two sides to all shapes of
    truth !
  I might indeed go back to bitter toil,
  Prune the mind's vine, and gather in the
    spoil
  Rough-conquered from books, men,
    fields, without ruth
Pillaging Nature, pawning strength and
    youth
  For some strange guerdon (or its counter-
    foil)
  Gainless or not-to-be-gained, priestly or
    royal,
  Profane, canaille—I know not, in good
    sooth !

I might do this : or else I might repose
  Wrapped in the urned leaves of my
    love's blown rose,
  Seek her in spirit, and commune, and
    wait
Her freedom and the rapture to enclose
  In my own house her beauty intimate.
  I am a fool, tossing a coin with Fate.


## III.

Is love indeed eternal ?   Otherwise
  Is evolution an eternal plan ?
  Must I move upward in the stream of
    Man,
  God-ward : my life as Christ to sacrifice,

As Buddha to repress : to grow so wise,
  Space, time shall lie within my finger-
    span ?
  I know not which I wish : either I can ;
  Not both, unless all meditation lies.

I am not sure : if love as great as ours
  May not be God to part of us at least,
  Leaving the rest to find its heights and
    powers
In other spheres ; that, night's enamoured
    priest ;
  This, on the lake the dewy lotus-flowers
  That lift their jewelled hearts toward
    the East.


## AFTER.

Now, when the sun falls in the dismal sky
  And no light leaps beneath the plunging
    prow,
  I know the fulness of my sorrow now :—
  That all my talk and laughter was a lie ;
That as each hour widens the gulfs that sigh
  Between us ; the truth scores upon my
    brow
  Sigils of silence, burns in me the vow
  " I love you, and shall love you till I
    die."

Whether next year, as fondly we made oath,
  Shall see us meet at least, whether as
    wife
  I shall at last gather the whole vow's
    breath—
Not heaven nor hell shall break our solemn
    troth.
  I love you, and shall love you all my
    life,
  I love you, and shall love you after
    death.

# THE ARGONAUTS *

## 1904

## ARGONAUTAE.

### *ACTUS PRIMUS.*

### JASON.

PELIAS.  JASON.  *Semi-chorus of Iolchian*
Men.  *Semi-chorus of Iolchian* Women.

SCENE: *The Throne-chamber of* KING
PELIAS.

#### SEMI-CHORUS OF MEN.

THE prophecies are spoken in vain,
  The auguries vainly cast,
Since twenty years of joyous reign
  In peace are overpast ;
And those who cursed our King's desires
Are branded in the brow for liars.

#### SEMI-CHORUS OF WOMEN.

We heard the aged prophet speak
  The doom of woe and fear.
We wait with blanched and icy cheek
  The one-and-twentieth year :
For Justice lies, as seeds lie, dead,
But lifts at last a Gorgon head !

#### MEN.

What fear can reach our Thessaly?
  What war disturb our peace?
Long stablished is young amity
  Maid-blushing over Greece :
And fair Iolchus stands sublime,
A monument to lesson time.

#### WOMEN.

But if such fear were come indeed,
  Who reads the riddle dread
Spoken in frenzy by the seer
  Against the royal head ?
We know the Rhyme's involving spell—
Its purport ?  Irresolvable !

#### MEN.

We heard his foolish maundering :
  But, bred in wiser ways,
We have forgotten : do ye sing
  The rune of ancient days !
To-day his curse cacophonous
Shall earn at least a laugh from us !

#### WOMEN.

"O ! when the armèd hand is nigh,
  Iolchus shall not see
Peace shining from Athena's sky
  Until the Fleece be free ;
Until the God of War shall scorn
The sting, and trust him to the horn.

" Until the Sun of Spring forsake
  His eastern home, and rise
Within our temple-walls and make
  One glory of the skies—
Until the King shall die and live,
Athena never shall forgive."

#### MEN.

Surely, O friends, at last 'tis clear
  The man was mad indeed !
Such nonsense we did never hear
  As this prophetic screed !
More, as 'tis never like this land
Should ever see an armèd hand.

---

* This play, written when Crowley was studying Hindu religion, derives much of its colour
and philosophical import from Pataiyali, the Upanishads and Sankarachariya's commentary,
Shaivite mysticism, the Bhagavat Purana, Bhagavat Gita, and Vedantist literature in general.

JASON.

Where is the son of Tyro and Poseidon?

MEN.

Iolchus' King has here a dwelling-place.

WOMEN.

See you the sword shake—and the iron
    hand
Not shaking? The man's mood is full of
    wrath.

MEN.

Peace, foolish! Were it so, we would not
    see.

WOMEN.

Ay me! this stranger seems most ominous.

JASON.

Where is the son of Tyro and Poseidon?

MEN.

This is the Palace-place of Pelias,
Son of Poseidon, of Iolchus King.

JASON.

Iolchus' King is here, in very truth.
Where is the son of Tyro?

MEN.
                    Who art thou?

JASON.

Know me for Jason and great Aeson's heir.

MEN.

We learn good news, most enviable sir;
That Aeson hath such grand inheritance.

JASON.

You have grown fat beneath an evil rule.
Your period is at hand. Go, one of you,
And drag the impious wretch before my
    sight!

MEN.

Aeson? Thy father?

JASON.
        Play not with my wrath!
My mood is something dangerous.

MEN.
                    Dangerous sir,
I go indeed, to bring some danger more
Hither.

JASON.
        Poltroonery dislikes the wise.
Fair maidens, I salute you pleasantly.

WOMEN.

Welcome, O welcome to the land,
    Young heir of prophecy!
The armèd hand, the glittering brand,
    The scabbard's jewellery!
That wealth avails not: cast it down!
The sword alone may win the crown!

JASON.

Ye languish wretched in the tyrant's rule?

WOMEN.

Most happy are we, King. But change is
    sweet.

JASON.

A short-lived omen of success to me.

WOMEN.

Nay, but adventure and the prophecy!

JASON.

I see I have but small support in you.

WOMEN.

Not so, great Jason! Had I suffered much,
My spirit had been broken to the scourge.
Now, being strong and happy, with what
    joy
I cry: Evohe! Revolution!
I have grown weary of this tiresome peace.

JASON.

I promise you intense unhappiness.

WOMEN.

Here is the ugly monster!  Out!  To think
We once believed him reverend and refined,
Saw majesty in all that tottering gait,
And honour in the goat-like beard of him !

FIRST WOMAN.

A week ago your blue eyes were in tears,
Sidelong regarding the old mountebank.

SECOND WOMAN.

To-day I would not be his concubine
For all Iolchus—for all Thessaly !

THIRD WOMAN.

I see the same glance seek out Jason now.

SECOND WOMAN.

Ay, there's a man !  What muscles !  What
    fine fire
In the quick eye !  What vigour and warm
    strength !

FIRST WOMAN.

Yes, in your wishes.  But indeed he is
A proper man.  Away, you ancient egg !

PELIAS.

With what audacious foot and impious voice
Strides this young man and talks?  Let him
    advance,
Trembling at our offended majesty.
Who art thou whose rude summons startles us
From work of state to listen a young mouth
Beardless?  Speak, man, for shortly thou
    shalt die.

JASON.

Athena speaks.

WOMEN.

Ah, there's a fine retort !

PELIAS.

Goddesses speak and men list reverently.
Could he not find a fitter messenger ?

JASON.

Her cause is Jason's.  Jason therefore
speaks.

PELIAS.

Aha !  A suppliant to our clemency !
I did mistake the gesture and the sword
Angrily gripped, the foot flung terribly
Foremost, the fierce, constrainèd attitude.
But—as a suppliant !  Tell thy woeful tale,
Sad youth !  Some woman thou hast loved
    and lost ?

JASON.

Thou hast robbed me of this kingdom.
    Thou hast kept
My father (poor half-witted man !) a slave
And parasite about thy court (one grief
The more I add to this account of thine !)
Myself a babe thou didst seek out to slay,
And, I being hid, with fish-hooks bent with
    lies
And gilded with most spacious promises,
Cunningly angled for old Chiron's [1] grace
To catch me yet.  Athena hears me swear
To right all this—nay, answer me before
Anger get all the spoil of me, and drink
Thy life-blood in one gulp !  Descend that
    daïs !
Bend thou a suppliant at my awful knee,
And thus—perhaps—at least get grace of life.

PELIAS.

And if I say I will not yield the throne ?

JASON.

I am of force to take it.

PELIAS.

                    Are my friends
Not faithful ?  Who draws sword for Pelias ?

MEN.

Shall we not slay thee this presumptuous
fool ?

[1] A Centaur who hid the child Jason.

JASON.

I am of force, I say.  I wrestled once
From sunrise to sunset with Heracles,
Great Heracles !  Not till the full moon
    rose
Availed his might to lay me prone.  Be-
    ware !
Ye weakling knaves !  I am of force, I say.

PELIAS.

Rebellious youth, the justice of thy cause
And force I will admit—where force goes
    far.
But think'st thou wait no wild Erinyes
For thee a guest in these my halls, for thee
Whose hands are dipped not yet in blood
    so deep
As to have murdered an old man, and him
Thy father's brother ?

JASON.

             Justice covers all.
The Furies cannot follow if a man
To his own heart be reconciled.  They feed
On his own bosom, nay ! are born thereof.
An alien clan he might elude, but these,
Blood of his blood, he shall nor slay nor
    'scape.
My heart hath never pastured on regret
Or pang for thee.  My justice covers all.

PELIAS.

That one word " justice " covers all indeed
To thine own self.  But think'st thou for a
    word
To ruin many years of commonweal,
And poison in an hour the politics
Of states and thrones for—justice ?  Thou
    art just ;
But wisdom, but the life of innocents,
The happiness of all, are better served
By solemn thought and weighty counsel
    held.

JASON.

This is more simple.  I abolish thee—
One sword-sweep—and assume thy "politics."

PELIAS.

Thou art this " simple " !  Will my liege
    allies
(Willing with age and wisdom to accord)
Not tremble at thy firebrand breed, not
    think
Who hath in blood, an old man's blood,
    made fast
A perilous footing, may betimes discover
More " justice "—and invasion footing it
Hard after ?  Wilt thou plunge all Thessaly,
All Greece, in haste and sudden armament,
Fury of thought and frenzy of deed, at once
For justice ?  Wouldst thou be so violent
For justice, save in thine own cause, O boy ?
And wilt thou pity not the happy days
And storm-unshatterèd abodes of Greece ?

JASON.

Athena, who is Justice, also is
Wisdom : and also " She who buildeth
    towns."

PELIAS.

Think also, I am born of deity.
I am inured to majesty ; I know
How venerable is the sight of kings,
And how the serpent Treason writhes
    beneath
The royal foot, conscious of its own shame,
And how the lion of Rebellion cowers
Before the presence of a king unarmed,
Quelled by one mild glance of authority.

JASON.

A king unjust is shorn of majesty.

PELIAS.

Still the one fool's word—justice—answers
    all.
Would thou wert older and more politic !

JASON.

Would I were liar with thine own foul
    brand !
The gods are weary of thy cozening.

PELIAS.

To proof, then, boy. I lay my sceptre by,
Put off my crown, descend the steps to thee.
Here is my breast.    Look firmly in my
    face,
And slay me.   Is there fear writ large and
    deep
In mine old eyes?   Or shudderest thou
    with fear?

JASON.

More hate than fear.  In sooth, I cannot
strike.

PELIAS.

A king is not so slain—except a madman
May fall upon him with averted head.[1]
Indeed, I conquer.     [Aside.]       Even so,
    beware !
Victory ill-nurtured breeds the babe defeat.
[Aloud.] Listen, my brother's son ! Nay,
    stoop not so,
Bending ashamèd brows upon the earth !
I am well weary of the world of men.
I grow both old and hateful to myself,
Most on the throne : power which to youth
    is sweet
To age looks fearful.   Also I have wept—
Alas ! how often !—and repented me
Of those unkingly deeds whereby I gained
This throne whose joy is turned to bitterness.
I will make peace with thee, and justice
    still
Shall have a home and shrine in Thessaly.
Be patient notwithstanding ! Prove thyself
Valiant and wise—and reign here ! If in
    sooth
An aged counsellor, whose reverend hair
Commands a hearing, may assist at all,
Wisdom to wisdom added, I am here.
Yet would I rather slide into my grave,
Untroubled with the destinies of states,
Even of such an one so dear to me
Who thus a score of years have nurtured it.

[1] These two lines are directly taken from
Eliphaz Levi.

JASON.

I hear thee.   Thou art grown like royal
    wine
Better with age.   Forgive my violence !

PELIAS.

[Aside.] The fish bites hard. [Aloud.] There
    is a prophecy :
" Once stirred, Iolchus never shall know
    peace
Till in its temple hangs the Golden Fleece."
Now thou hast so disquieted our days,
The time is come : seek thou Aea's[1] isle,
And hang this trophy on our temple walls !

JASON.

Tell me what is this fleece.

PELIAS.

            Let women sing.

WOMEN.

In Ares' grove, the sworded trees,
    The world's heart wondering,
Hangs evermore the Golden Fleece,[2]
    The glory of the spring,
The light of far Aea's coast.
Such glamour as befits a ghost.

Before that glittering woof the Sun
    Shrinks back abashed in shame,
The splendour of the shining one,
    One torrent-fleece of flame !
What heart may think, what tongue may
    sing
The glory of the golden thing?

[1] Colchis, a county of Asia, bounded on the
W. by the Euxine, on the N. by the Caucasus,
and on the E. by the Iberia.   Distinguish from
Aeaea.
[2] The symbolism of the Fleece and its
guardians is curious.  The Fleece is of ($\Upsilon$) Aries
the Ram, the sign of the spring.   The sun
being exalted in this sign, the fleece is called
golden.   Ares or Mars ($\delta$) is in Astrology
the ruler of this sign.   His other house is
Scorpio ($\mathrm{m}$) the Dragon.   The whole legend is
thus a glyph of the Magnum Opus.   That
Crowley neglects this is a significant mark of
the change to his maturer manner.

About the grove the scorpion coils
   Inextricably wind
Within the wood's exceeding toils,
   The shadow hot and blind ;
There lurk his serpent sorceries,
The guardian of the Golden Fleece.

The dragon lifts his nostrils wide
   And jets a spout of fire ;
The warrior questing turns aside,
   Not daring to desire ;
And Madness born of Ares lurks
Behind the wonder of his works.

Be sure that were the woodland way
   Tracked snakewise to the core,
The dragon slain or driven away,
   The good Fleece won by war,
Not yet should Ares sink his spear,
Or fail of flinging forth a fear.

The torch of Madness should be lit,
   And follow him afar :
Upon his prow should Madness sit,
   A baleful beacon-star ;
And in his home Despair and Strife
Lie in his bosom for a wife !

But oh, the glory of the quest,
   The gainless goodly prize !
The fairest form man e'er caressed,
   The word he heard most wise ;—
All lures of life avoid and cease
Before the winning of the Fleece !

O nameless splendour of the Gods,
   Begotten hardly of Heaven !
Unspoken treasure of the abodes
   Beyond the lightning levin !
No misery, no despair may pay
The joy to hold thee for a day !

JASON.

Athena's servant recks not much of Ares.

PELIAS.

Are thine eyes kindled at the golden
   thought ?

JASON.

Mine eyes see farther than the Fleece of
   Gold.

PELIAS.

What heroes can attain so fair a thing ?

JASON.

I have some friends who would esteem this
   quest
Lightly—a maiden's pleasure-wandering
Through lilied fields a summer's afternoon.

PELIAS.

The Gods give strength ! I pray them send
   thee back
Safe to this throne.

JASON.

           I will not see thy face
Ever again until the quest be won.
Rule thou with justice in my sacred seat
Until I come again.

PELIAS.

           The Gods thy speed.

MEN.

The hardy hero goes to find
   The living Fleece of Gold ;
Or else, some death may chance to bind
   Those limbs of manly mould.
In sooth, I doubt if I shall earn
The singer's fee for his return.

PELIAS.

Think now—I feared that fool. It must be
   true
That guilt is timorous. Ay ! when danger's
   none !
Let but swords flash—and guilt grows God
   for might !
Indeed I rule—until he come again.
Ay, when the stars fall, Jason shall be king !

EXPLICIT ACTUS PRIMUS.

## ARGONAUTAE.

### *ACTUS SECUNDUS.*

### ARGO.

ARGUS *the son of* PHRIXUS, JASON, HERACLES, CASTOR, POLLUX, THE- SEUS, ORPHEUS. *Chorus of* Heroes. *Chorus of* Shipbuilders.

SCENE : *An open place near Iolchus.*

#### CHORUS OF SHIPBUILDERS.

THE sound of the hammer and steel !
  The song of the level and line !
The whirr of the whistling wheel !
  The ring of the axe on the pine !

The joy of the ended labour,
  As the good ship plunges free
By sound of pipe and tabor
  To front the sparkling sea !

The mystery-woven spell !
  The voyage of golden gain !
The free full sails that swell
  On the swell of the splendid main !

The song of the axe and the wedge !
  The clang of the hammer and chain !
Keen whistle of chisel and edge !
  Smooth swish of the sliding plane !

Hail to the honour of toil !
  Hail ! to the ship flown free !
Hail ! to the golden spoil,
  And the glamour of all the sea !

#### HERACLES.

A good stout song, friend Argus, matching well
The mighty blows thou strikest : yet me-thinks
One blow should serve to drive yon nail well home
Where thou with tenfold stroke—

#### THESEUS.
            Good Heracles !
Not all men owe thy strength——

#### ARGUS.
                  Nay, let him try !
Take my toy hammer !

#### HERACLES.
            I have split the wood !

#### THESEUS.
Vexation sits tremendous on his brow.
Beware a hero's fury !   Thou art mad,
Argus, to play so dangerous a trick.

#### ARGUS.
True, Theseus—if he had but hit his thumb !

#### CASTOR.
Cease this fool's talk.   The moon waits not
  the work.

#### POLLUX.
The sun will sink no later for your pleasure.
On to thy work, man.

#### THESEUS.
            He that traps a lion
And baits him for an hour, and lets him go,
Does well to think before he tempt again
The forest paths.

#### HERACLES.
            The wise man wisely thinks
That nothing is but wisdom—and myself
Think strongly that no other thing exists
But strength : so with his subtleties of mind
He baffles me ; and I lift up my club,
And with one blow bespatter his wise brains.

#### JASON.
Ay, not for nothing did the darkness reign
Those eight-and-forty hours,[1] O Zeus-begot !

[1] Zeus caused a night to extend to this length, that he might efficiently beget Hercules.

THESEUS.

Tell me, friend master, how the work goes
on.
When shall our gallant vessel breast the
deep?
When shall we see the sun sink o'er the
poop,
And look toward moonrise, and the land
be lost,
And the perched watcher on the mast
behold
The melting mirror of the ocean meet
The crystallising concave of the sky?

ARGUS.

All this shall happen when the work is done.

JASON.

How many moons, friend fool, before that
day?

ARGUS.

These things are known not even to the
Gods,
Except the Father only.[1]

HERACLES.

Fools must talk.

ARGUS.

I talk, divulging nothing.

HERACLES.

I strike thee,
Yet act not.

ARGUS.

Hero, stay that heavy hand!
The ship shall sail ere spring.

THESEUS.

But now you talk
More as befits a workman to a king.

[1] The satire is on Matthew xxiv. 36.

JASON.

Be gentle now, my friends! These ship-
builders,
Reared in the rugged borders of the North,[1]
Have northern manners; surly if attacked,
But genial when——

ARGUS.

The proper treatment is
Kindness—like lions whom Demeter tamed.

THESEUS.

I promise thee, the next time thou art
wroth,
A second kindness from Alcides' hand.

ARGUS.

Spare me that, King, and take, thyself, a
club.

JASON.

King Theseus, thou art far reputed wise.
Hast thou not learnt a lesson from the hap
Of Heracles supreme in—shipbuilding?
I by my meekness will abash thy strength.
Good Argus, thou art unsurpassed in art
To curve the rougher timbers, to make
smooth
The joints and girders, and to plane and
work
The iron and the nailheads, and to lift
Row after row the tiers of benches thrice
In triple beauty, and to shape the oars,
To raise the mast——

ARGUS.

Thy knowledge staggers me!
How wast thou thus instructed?

JASON.

By much thought.
To clamp the decks——

[1] Argus is wittily characterised as a Scottish
shipbuilder.

ARGUS.

I stand with brows abashed.
Thou art the master—build the ship thyself.

JASON.

Nay, but my knowledge is of mind alone.
I cannot so apply it as to build
An Argo.

ARGUS.

Yet I verily believe
Such mind must pierce far deeper than these
    names,
Seeking the very nature of the things
Thou namest thus so pat. Perchance to
    thee
These logs, nails, bolts, tools, have some
    life of sense,
Some subtle language. Tell us what they
    say![1]

THESEUS.

'Tis but a giber—leave the churl alone.

JASON.

Indeed I spake of things I knew not of.

ARGUS.

You speak more wisely when you float away
Into pure dream, and talk of mystic things
That no man born of woman understands,
And therefore does not dare to contradict.

JASON.

He who speaks much and bitterly at last
Lays himself open to retort. I think
I never heard such contradictions fly
As when men talk of gods—that never
    were!

ARGUS.

Thou wouldst do better to leave men alone.
The wisest talk is folly when work waits.
Look! how these sturdy villains gape around,
Fling down their task, and hang upon the
    words
That flow like nectar from your majesty.

[1] The gibe in these twenty lines is against
Rudyard Kipling's silly vitalisation of machinery,
and his ignorance even of the correct terms.

CASTOR.

In truth, my friend, if you would wear your
    crown
This side of Orcus, you should go away.

POLLUX.

Ay! let the men work! For a mind as yours
Is good, and skill as theirs is also good.

CASTOR.

But mix the manual and the mental—well,
No ship was built by pure philosophy.

POLLUX.

Nor yet designed by artisans.

JASON.

Enough!
Come, great Alcides, it is time to go.

ARGUS.

A fool allows a moment's irritation
To move the purpose of a thousand years.
Go, go!

HERACLES.

Remember! We are met this day
To call upon the name with praise and
    prayer
Of great Athena, since our ship is built
With sculptured olive pregnant in the prow,
And all the length of pine is coiled and
    curled
With the swift serpent's beauty, and the owl
Sits in huge state upon the midmost bench.
Thus, therefore, by the manifest design,
Joining the wisdom to the power and will,
We build the Argo.

ARGUS.

What a heavy club
We carry! And how well becomes our figure
The lion's skin!

HERACLES.

Be still, thou art an ass!

ARGUS.

The fabled ass, O Zeus-descended one?

HERACLES.

What ass?

ARGUS.

The one that wore the lion's skin!

THESEUS.

This fellow were beneath a man's contempt.
How should a God-born heed him?

JASON.

We are here,
Then, to invoke Athena, immolate
The sacred cock upon her altar-stone,
That She, who sprang in armour from the
brain
Of the All-Father, may descend to bless
Our labours, since delay grows dangerous,
If haply by Her power and subtlety
She please to aid the work, and to perform
A prodigy to save us! Mighty Queen,
That art the balance and the sword alike
In cunning Argus' brain——

HERACLES.

Ay! Mighty Wisdom,
Who thus can overshadow such a fool,
And make him capable to build a ship.

ARGUS.

O Thou! Athena, whose bright wisdom
shone
In this beef-witted fellow, making him
Competent even to sweep a stable out!
Glorious task!—I shall return anon.

JASON.

Nay, follow not! The Goddess were dis-
pleased,
Coming, to find our greatest hero gone.

THESEUS.

This is the midmost hour of day.

JASON.

Arise,
All heroes, circling round the sacred stone
In beautiful order and procession grave,
While our chief priest, our mightiest in song,
The dowered of Phoebus, great Oeager's
heir,
Invokes that glory on the sacrifice
That kindles all its slumber into life
And vivid flame descending on the wheel
And chariot of lightning, licking up
The water of the loud-resounding sea
Lustral, poured seven times upon the earth,
And in one flash consuming wood and stone
And the sweet savour of the sacrifice.

ORPHEUS.

But when the flame hath darted from the
eye
Of my divine existence, and hath left
Nothing, where was the altar and the earth,
The water and the incense and the victim—
Nothing of all remains! Then look to it
That ye invoke not Wisdom by the Name
Of bright Athena!

JASON.

We are here to call
Upon that Wisdom by that mighty Name!

ORPHEUS.

Who calleth upon Wisdom is not wise.
Is it not written in the Sibyl's book [1]
That Wisdom crieth in the streets aloud
And none regardeth her? Obey my voice.

JASON.

O master of Apollo's lyre and light!
We are not wise—and for that very cause
We meet to-day to call on Wisdom.

ORPHEUS.

Well!
The altar stands, shadowing the Universe
That with my fire of Knowledge I destroy—
And there is Wisdom—but invoke Her not,
Friends, Who is only when none other is.

[1] Actually Proverbs i. 20.

JASON.

Let us begin: the hour draws on apace.
Drive off the demons from the sacrifice!

ORPHEUS.

Let all the demons enter and dwell therein!
My friends, ye are as ignorant as priests!
Let there be silence while the sleeper[1]
wakes!

O coiled and constricted and chosen!
O tortured and twisted and twined!
Deep spring of my soul deep frozen,
The sleep of the truth of the mind!
As a bright snake curled
Round the vine of the World!

O sleeper through dawn and through day-
light,
O sleeper through dusk and through
night!
O shifted from white light to gray light,
From gray to the one black light!
O silence and sound
In the far profound!

O serpent of scales as an armour
To bind on the breast of a lord!
Not deaf to the Voice of the Charmer,
Not blind to the sweep of the sword!
I strike to the deep
That thou stir in thy sleep!

Rise up from mine innermost being!
Lift up the gemmed head to the heart!
Lift up till the eyes that were seeing
Be blind, and their life depart!
Till the Eye that was blind[2]
Be a lamp to my mind!

[1] The Hindus hold that the Kundalini, the
spring of spiritual power, lies coiled and sleeping upon a lotus-flower at the base of the spine.
She may be aroused by various methods.
[2] The "third eye," that rudimentary eye
called the pineal gland.

Coil fast all thy coils on me, dying,
Absorbed in the sense of the Snake!
Stir, leave the flower-throne, and up-
flying
Hiss once, and hiss thrice, and awake!
Then crown me and cling!
Flash forward—and spring!

Flash forth on the fire of the altar,
The stones, and the sacrifice shed;
Till the Three Worlds[1] flicker and falter,
And life and her love be dead!
In mysterious joy
Awake—and destroy!

JASON.

It is enough!

HERACLES.

Too great for a god's strength!

THESEUS.

Speak!

CASTOR.

Change! Not to be borne!

POLLUX.

But this is death!

ORPHEUS.

Let the light fade. The oracle is past.

JASON.

The Voice is past. We are alive again.

ORPHEUS.

What spake That Silence?

HERACLES.

"This is not a quest
Where strength availeth aught." I shall not
go.

[1] Of gods, men, and demons.

JASON.

Nay, brother. The voice was: "The end
is sorrow!"

THESEUS.

Ye heard not, O dull-witted! Unto me
(Alone of all ye wise) the great voice
came,
"The Gates of Hell shall not in all
prevail."

CASTOR.

I heard, "Regret not thy mortality!
Love conquers death!"

POLLUX.

But I, "Regret not thou
Thine immortality! Love conquers life!"[1]

ORPHEUS.

A partial wisdom to a partial ear.

JASON.

But what speech came to thee?

ORPHEUS.

I heard no voice.

ARGUS.

What means this? Here's my labour thrown
away,
My skill made jest of, all my wage destroyed
At one fell stroke.

JASON.

What? Is the Argo burnt?

[1] Pollux being immortal, and Castor mortal,
at the former's request Zeus allowed them to
pool their fates, and live alternate days in
Hades and Olympus.

ARGUS.

Burnt! Should I then complain? The
ship is finished.

JASON.

The Goddess, furious at thine absence,
Argus,
Hath frenzied thee with some delusion.

HERACLES.

Calm!

Control thy madness! I am sorry now
My pungent wit so shamed his arrogance
As made him seem to scorn Athena.

ARGUS.

Thou!

But see me, I am ruined. The good ship
Is finished! Where's my daily wage?

JASON.

Be sure

I pay thee treble if thy tale be true.

ARGUS.

Ay! treble nothing! I shall buy a palace.

JASON.

Treble thine utmost wish.

ARGUS.

Two evils then

Thou pilest on one good! But come and
see!

[*The Argo is discovered.*

CHORUS OF HEROES.

By Wisdom framed from ancient days
    The stately Argo stands above;
Too firm to fear, too great to praise,
    The might of bright Athena's love!
Oh! ship of glory! tread the foam,
And bring our guerdon from its home!

The silent thought, the hand unseen,
The rayless majesty of light
Shed from the splendour of our Queen
Athena! mystery and might;
These worked invisibly to bring
The end of triumph to our King.

Great Jason, wronged by hate of man,
Shall pass the portals of the deep;
Shall seek the waters wide and wan;
Shall pass within the land of sleep;
And there the guardians of the soil
Shall rest at last from pain and toil.

O ruler of the empyréan,
Behold his fervour conquering
The fury of the breed Cadmean,
The dragons of the Theban king;
And armèd men shall spring from earth
In vain to ward the gloomy girth!

But thou, Athena, didst devise
Some end beyond our mortal ken,
Thy soul impenetrably wise
Shines not to us unthinking men.
O guard the warrior band of Greece,
And win for us the Golden Fleece!

By miracle this happy day
The ship is finished for our quest.
Bring thou the glory from the gray!
Bring thou our spirits into rest!
O Wisdom, that hast helped so far,
Sink never thou thy guiding star!

CHORUS OF WORKMEN.

Then let us gather one and all,
And launch our dragon on the main
With paeans raised most musical,
Until our heroes come again.
With watching and with prayer we wait
The imperious Destinies of Fate!

EXPLICIT ACTUS SECUNDUS.

ARGONAUTAE.

*ACTUS TERTIUS.*

MEDEA.

AEETES, JASON, MEDEA, Messengers,
*Chorus of* Heroes.

SCENE: *The Palace of* AEETES.

AEETES.
Were this man son of Zeus, beloved of Heaven,
And skilled with very craft of Maia's son,
Stronger than Phoebus, subtler than the Sphinx,
This plague should catch him, nor my wisdom spare.

CHORUS OF HEROES.
Thus hast thou sent him unto Hades, king.

AEETES.
Not otherwise were such gain possible.
Ye are the witnesses that with much skill,
And eloquence of shining words, and thought
Darkling behind their measured melody,
I did dissuade him.

CHORUS.
                    Such an enterprise
After such toils no man should lightly leave.
Remember all the tasks impossible
This hero hath already done, before
He ever touched this sounding coast of thine.

AEETES.
Alas! but now his weird is loneliness!

CHORUS.
Was that from Destiny, or will of thine?

AEETES.

I love him little.  Yet my words were true,
Nor would it skill him aught if myriad men
Bucklered his back and breast.  For when
    a man
Batters with sword-hilt at the frowning
    gates
That lead to the Beyond, not human force—
Hardly the favour of the gods themselves—
Shall stead him in that peril.

CHORUS.
                  Yet we know
Courage may conquer all things.

AEETES.
                  Such a man
Is greater than the gods!

CHORUS.
                  If only he
Know who he is—that all these gods and
    men
And things are but the shadows of himself!

AEETES.

I cannot give you hope.  Await the end.

CHORUS.

We fear indeed that in the trap
    Of wiles our king is taken.
Lachesis shakes a careless lap
    And dooms divine awaken!
A desolate and cruel hap
    In this sad hour is shaken.

The desperate son and violent
    Of Helios hath designed
A fate more hard than Pelias meant,
    Revolving in his mind
Mischief to catch the coiled ascent
    Of groaning humankind.

O bright Athena, hitherto
    Protectress of the quest,
Divide the deep descending blue!
    Be present, ever-blest!
Bring thou the hero Jason through
    To victory—and rest!

MEDEA.

Not by Athena's calm omnipotence,
O heroes, look for safety!  Little men,
Looking to God, are blinded; mighty ones,
Seeking His presence, reel before the glance;
And They, the greatest that may be of men,
Become that Light, and care no whit for
    earth.
But all your prayers are answered by your-
    selves,
As I myself achieve this thought of mine.

CHORUS.

To me thou seemest to blaspheme the gods.

MEDEA.

Belike I seem, O ye of little wit.

CHORUS.

Surely thy tender years and gentle looks
Belie such hatred to our king!  I scorn
To triumph on an enemy once fallen.

MEDEA.

Fools always!  I am tenderer than my years,
And gentler than my glances

CHORUS.
              Sayst thou—what?

MEDEA.

Ye know me a most powerful sorceress.

CHORUS.

So I have heard, O lotus-footed[1] one!
Nathless I see not any miracle.

MEDEA.

Last night the heavy-hearted audience
Broke up, and Jason wended wearily
His way, oppressed by direful bodements of
The fate of this forenoon.  I saw him go
Sad, and remembered how sublime he stood,

    [1] An epithet common in the East, conveying
a great compliment.

Bronzed with a ruder sun than ours, and
     scarred
(Rough tokens of old battles) yet so calm
And mild (with all that vigour) that to me
Came a swift pity—the enchanter's bane.
That I flung from me.   But my subtle soul
Struck its own bosom with the sword of
     thought,
So that I saw not pity, but desire !

CHORUS.

Surely a bane more potent than the first.

MEDEA.

Love is itself enchantment !

CHORUS.
                         Some kind god
Whispers from this a little light of hope.

MEDEA.

Only the hopeless are the happy ones.[1]

CHORUS.

But didst thou turn him from his gleaming
     goal ?
Cover that shame with sweeter shame than
     this ?

MEDEA.

Thou knowest that his vigil was to keep,
Invoking all Olympus all the night,
And then to yoke the oxen, and to plough
The fearful furrow, sow the dreadful seed,
Smite down the armies, and assuage the
     pest
Of slime thrice coiled about the sacred grove.

CHORUS.

Thy bitter love disturbed that solitude ?

MEDEA.

Not bitter, heroes.   See ye yet the end ?

[1] "The hopeless are happy, like the girl
Pingala" (Buddhist Proverb).   Pingala waited
for her lover, and mourned because he came
not.   But, giving up hope at last, she regained
her cheerfulness.   Cf. 2 Samuel xii. 15-23.

CHORUS.

Our good quest ended by thy father's hate,
And by thy own hour's madness !   This I
see.

MEDEA.

But if he gain the Fleece ?

CHORUS.
                         A blissful end.

MEDEA.

This end and that are moulded diversely.

CHORUS.

Riddle no more, nor ply with doubtful hope
Hearts ready to rejoice and to despair
Equally minded.

MEDEA.
                    At the midmost hour,
His mind given up to sleepless muttering
Of charms not mine—decrees Olympian—
All on a sudden he felt fervent arms
Flung round him, and a hot sweet body's
     rush
Lithe to embrace him, and a cataract
Of amber-scented hair hissing about
His head, and in the darkness two great
     eyes
Flaming above him, and the whole face filled
With fire and shapen as kisses.   And those
     arms
And kisses and mad movements of quick
     love
Burnt up his being, and his life was lost
In woman's love at last !

CHORUS.
                    Unseemly act !
Who dared thus break on meditation ?

MEDEA.
                                        I.

CHORUS.

Surely thy passion mastered thee, O queen !

MEDEA.

I tell you—thus the night passed.

CHORUS.

Verily,

The woman raves.

MEDEA.

Such victory as this
Outsails all shame. Before the dawn was up
I bound such talismans about his breast
That fire and steel grow dew and flowery
    wreaths
For all their power to hurt him. Presently
I made a posset, drugged with somnolence,
Sleepy with poppy and white hellebore,
Fit for the dragon. This was my design.

CHORUS.

Beware thy father's anger when he finds
His plans thus baffled ! He will murder us.

MEDEA.

Heroes indeed ye are, and lion hearts.

CHORUS.

No woman need school me in bravery.

MEDEA.

Rather a hare.

CHORUS.

Most impudent of whores !

MEDEA.

But when my husband comes victorious
Fleece-laden, he will rather——

CHORUS.

Wilt thou then
Further my ruin, making known this shame !

MEDEA.

Here is the Argive sense of gratitude.
Let me stir up its subtler thought, and show
What favours ye may gather afterward
From hands and lips ye scorn—not courte-
    ously.

CHORUS.

What ? Canst thou save us from this newer
    doom ?

MEDEA.

I love your leader with no mortal love,
But with the whole strength of a sorceress.

CHORUS.

It seems indeed thy hot will can bewitch
Our chaste one with one action impudent.

MEDEA.

I will not leave him ever in the world.

CHORUS.

Persistence in these ills—will cure them not.
" Worst " is the hunter, " worse " the hound,
    when " bad "
Is the stag's name.

MEDEA.

We rule Iolchus' land.

CHORUS.

Indeed the hunter follows. I despise
Lewd conduct in the lowest, and detest
Spells hurtful to the head, when ancient
    hags
Brew their bad liquors at the waning moon,
Barking their chants of murder. But to rule
A land, and wive a king, and breed to him
Kings—then such persons are unsuitable.

MEDEA.

Unless these words were well repented of
I might transform ye into——

CHORUS.

Stay, great queen !

MEDEA.

Well for your respite comes this messenger.

MESSENGER.

Queen and fair mother of great kings un-
born,
And mighty chosen of the land of Greece,
A tidings of deep bliss is born to you.

CHORUS.

Tell me that Jason has achieved the quest.

MESSENGER.

Truth is no handmaid unto happiness.

CHORUS.

What terror dost thou fill my heart withal?

MEDEA.

O timorous heroes! Let the herald speak!
Who meets fear drives her back; who flees
from fear
Stumbles; who cares not, sees her not.
Speak on!

THE MESSENGER.

Terrible bellowings as of angry bulls
Broke from the stable as the first swift shaft
Of dawn smote into it: and stampings fierce
Resounded, shaking the all-mother earth.
Whereunto came the calm and kingly man,
Smiling as if a sweet dream still beguiled
His waking brows; not caring any more
For spring or summer; heeding least of all
That tumult of ox-fury. Suddenly
A light sprang in his face; the great hand shot
Forth, and broke in the brass-bound door;
the day
Passed with him inwards; then the brazen
hoofs
Beat with a tenfold fury on the stone.
But Jason, swiftly turned, evaded these,
And chose two oxen from that monstrous herd
To whose vast heads he strode, and by the
horns
Plucked them. Then fire, devouring, sprang
at him
From furious nostrils: and indignant breath,
Fountains of seething smoke, spat forth at him.

But with no tremor of aught that seemed like
fear
Drew them by sheer strength from their
place, and yoked
Their frenzy to his plough, and with the goad
Urged them, thrice trampling the accursèd field
Until the furrows flamed across the sun,
Treading whose glory stood Apollo's self
As witness of the deed. Then a last thrust
Savage, drove them less savage to their stalls,
And Jason turned and laughed. Then drew
he out
The dreadful teeth of woe, Cadmean stock
Of Thebes' old misery, and presently
Pacing the furrowed field, he scattered them
With muttered words of power athwart the
course
Of the bright moon, due path of pestilence
And terror. Ere the last bone fell to earth
The accursèd harvest sprang to life. Armed
men,
Fiery with anger, rose upon the earth
While Jason stood, one witnessing a dream,
Not one who lives his life. The sword and
spear
Turn not to him, but mutual madness strikes
The warriors witless, and fierce wrath invades
Their hearts of fury, and with arms engaged
They fell upon each other silently
And slew, and slew. As in the middle seas
A mirage flashes out and passes, so
The phantoms faded, and the way was clear.
Thus, stepping ever proud and calm, he went
Unto the grove of Ares, where the worm,
Huge in his hatred, guarded all. But now
Sunk in some stupor, surely sent of Zeus,
He stirred not. Stepping delicately past
The dragon, then came Jason to the grove
And saw what tree umbrageous bore the fruit
That he had saddened for so long. And he,
Rending the branches of that wizard Oak,
With a strong grasp tore down the Fleece of
Gold.
Then came a voice: "Woe, woe! Aea's isle!
The glory is departed!" And a voice
Answered it "Woe!" Then Jason seemed
to see
Some Fear behind the little former fears;

And his face blanched a moment, as behold-
ing
Some Fate, some distant grief.   Then,
catching sight
Now of the glory of his gain, he seemed
Caught in an ecstasy, treading the earth
As in a brighter dream than Aphrodite
Sent ever to a man, he turned himself
(We could not see him for the golden flame
Burning about him !) moving hitherward.
But I took horse and hasted, since reward
May greet such tidings, and for joy to see
Your joy exceed my joy.

MEDEA.

Reward indeed
Awaits thee from such folk as us, who stand
In fear of life, when great Aeetes hears
This news, and how all came.

MESSENGER.

My lady's smile
Is the reward I sought, not place nor gold.

MEDEA.
Thou hast it, child.

SECOND MESSENGER.
The hero is at hand.

CHORUS.
O happy of mortals !
O fronter of fear,
The impassable portals !
Ye heavens, give ear !
Our song shall be rolled in the praise of the
gold, and its glory be told where the
heavenly fold rejoices to hold the stars
in its sphere.

O hero Iolchian !
Warrior king !
From the kingdom Colchian
The Fleece dose bring !
Our song shall be sung and its melody flung
where the Lyre and the Tongue are
fervid and young, all islands among
where the Sirens sing.

Thou bearest, strong shoulder,
The sunbright fleece !
Glow swifter and bolder
And brighter—and cease !
O glory of light !  O woven of night !  O
shining and bright !  O dream of de-
light !  How splendid the sight for the
dwellers of Greece !

Gained is the guerdon !
The prize is won.
The fleecy burden,
The soul of the sun !
The toil is over ; the days discover high joys
that hover of lover and lover, and fates
above her are fallen and done.

JASON.
Queen of this people !  O my heart's desire
Spotless, the Lady of my love, and friends
By whose heroic ardours I am found
Victor at last, well girded with the spoil
Of life in gleaming beauty, and this prize
Thrice precious, my Medea—all is won !
Needs only now the favouring kiss of Eurus,
Bright-born of Eos, to fulfil for us
The last of all the labours, to inspire
The quick-raised sail, and fill that flushing
gold
With thrice desirèd breath, that once again
Our prow plunge solemn in the Argive waters
To strains of music—victory at peace
Mingling with sweeter epithalamy—
To tell our friends how happy was the quest.

MEDEA.
But not those strains of music, though divine
From Orpheus' wingèd lyre, exalt at all
Our joy to joy, beyond all music's power !

CHORUS.
I fear Aeetes, and the Pelian guile.

JASON.
Fear is but failure, herald of distress !

MEDEA
What virtue lives there in the coward's hrate ?

CHORUS.

In sooth, I have no fear at all—to flee.

JASON.

Night, like a mist, steals softly from the East.
The hand of darkness gathers up the folds
Of day's gold garment, and the valleys sink
Into slow sadness, though the hills retain
That brilliance for a little.

CHORUS.

Let us go!
Methinks that under cover of the night
I may escape Aeetes.

JASON.

If he chase,
Our Argo is not battered by rough winds
So far but what some fight were possible.

MEDEA. [Leads forward ABSYRTUS.]

I know a better way than that, my lord.
This boy shall come with us.

JASON.

Ah, not to Greece!
Aea needs to-morrow's king.

MEDEA.

" With us "
I said. " To Greece "—I said not.

CHORUS.

What is this?
Thou hintest at some dangerous destiny.

MEDEA.

Come love, to the long years of love with
me!

JASON.

Form, heroes, and in solemn order stride;
The body-guardians of the Golden Fleece!

MEDEA.

Guarding your king and queen on every
side—

CHORUS.

We sail triumphant to the land of Greece.

MEDEA.

A woman's love, a woman's power be told
Through ages, gainers of the Fleece of Gold.

EXPLICIT ACTUS TERTIUS.

## ARGONAUTAE.

### ACTUS QUARTUS.

### SIRENAE.

JASON, MEDEA, ORPHEUS, THESEUS, HER-
ACLES, Chorus of Heroes, the Sirens.

SCENE: The Argo.

MEDEA.

Ay! I would murder not my brother only,
But tear my own limbs, strew them on the
sea,[1]
To keep one fury from the man I love!

CHORUS.

This act and speech are much akin to madness.

MEDEA.

Remember that your own skins pay the price.

CHORUS.

I now remember somewhat of the voice
Of the oracle, that Madness should hunt hard
On the thief's furtive track, upon the prow
Brooding, and at the table president,
And spouse-like in the bed.

[1] The Argonauts being pursued by Aeetes,
Medea threw the severed limbs and trunk of
Absyrtus upon the sea, so that the father, stop-
ping to perform the sacred duties of burial, was
left behind.

MEDEA.

But this is like
That Indian fable[1] of a king : how he,
Taking some woman—an indecent act
Not proper to be done !—against the will
Of priests or princes, sought the nuptial bed
And
    " Climbed the bed's disastrous side,
    He found a serpent, not a bride ;
    And scarcely daring to draw breath,
    He passed the dumb night-hours with
        death,
    Till in the morning cold and gray
    The hooded fear glided away.
    Which morning saw ten thousand pay
    The price of jesting with a king ! "—

JASON.

Indeed these toils and dangerous pursuits,
Labours and journeys, go to make one
    mad.
Well were it to beguile our weariness
With song.

MEDEA.

And here is the sole king of song.

ORPHEUS.

My song breaks baffled on the rocks of
    time
If thy bewitching beauty be the theme.

MEDEA.

Sing me thy song, sweet poet, of the sea,
That song of swimming when thy love lost
    sense
Before the passion of the Infinite.

JASON.

The more so as my master warns me oft
Of late how near that island is, where dwell
The alluring daughters of Melpomene.

    [1] The " fable " is Crowley's own.

ORPHEUS.[1]

Light shed from seaward over breakers bend-
    ing
    Kiss-wise to the emerald hollows : light
    divine
    Whereof the sun is God, the sea his
    shrine ;
Light in vibrations rhythmic ; light unending ;
    Light sideways from the girdling crags
    extending
    Unto this lone and languid head of
    mine ;
    Light, that fulfils creation as with wine,
Flows in the channels of the deep : light,
    rending
    The adamantine columns of the night,
    Is laden with the love-song of the light.

Light, pearly-glimmering through dim gulf
    and hollow,
    Below the foam-kissed lips of all the sea ;
    Light shines from all the sky and up to
    me
From the amber floors of sand : Light calls
    Apollo !
The shafts of fire fledged of the eagle follow
    The crested surf, and strike the shore,
    and flee
    Far from green cover, nymph-enchanted
    lea,
Fountain, and plume them white as the sea-
    swallow,
    And turn and quiver in the ocean, seem-
    ing
    The glances of a maiden kissed, or
    dreaming.

Light, as I swim through rollers green and
    gleaming,
    Sheds its most subtle sense to penetrate
    This heart I thought impervious to Fate.
Now the sweet light, the full delight, is
    beaming

    [1] The song describes Waikiki Beach, near
Honolulu.

Through me and burns me : all my flesh is
   teeming
   With the live kisses of the sea, my mate,
   My mistress, till the fires of life abate
And leave me languid, man-forgotten, deem-
   ing
   I see in sleep, in many-coloured night,
   More hope than in the flame-waves of
   the light.

Light ! ever light ! I swim far out and follow
   The footsteps of the wind, and light in-
   vades
   My desolate soul, and all the cypress
   shades
Glow with transparent lustre, and the hollow
I thought I had hidden in my heart must
   swallow
   The bitter draught of Truth ; no Nereid
   maids
   Even in my sea are mine ; the whole
   sea's glades
And hills and springs are void of my Apollo—
   The Sea herself my tune and my desire !
   The Sun himself my lover and my lyre !


                     CHORUS.
This song is sweeter than the honeycomb.


                      MEDEA.
Nearly as sweet as good friends quarrelling.


                      JASON.
Look, friends, methinks I see a silvern shape
Like faint mist floating on the farthest sea.


                      MEDEA.
I see a barren rock above the tides.


                      JASON.
I hear a sound like water whispering.


                      MEDEA.
I hear a harsh noise like some ancient crone
Muttering curses.

                      JASON.
            Now I hear a song.
'Tis like some shape of sleep that moans for
   joy,
Some bridal sob of love !


                      MEDEA.
                     O Son of God !
My poet, swiftly leap the live lyre forth !
Else we are all enchanted—yet to me
This song is nowise lovely.   But in him
I note the live look of the eyes leap up,
And all his love for me forgotten straight
At the mere echo of that tune.


                     ORPHEUS.
                         Hark, friends !
Aea's tune—my Colchian harbour-song ! [1]

I hear the waters faint and far,
And look to where the Polar Star,
Half hidden in the haze, divides
The double chanting of the tides ;
But, where the harbour's gloomy mouth
Welcomes the stranger to the south,
The water shakes, and all the sea
Grows silver suddenly.

As one who standing on the moon
Sees the vast horns in silver hewn,
Himself in darkness, and beholds
How silently all space unfolds
Into her shapeless breast the spark
And sacred phantom of the dark ;
So in the harbour-horns I stand
Till I forget the land.

Who sails through all that solemn space
Out to the twilight's secret place,
The sleepy waters move below
His ship's imaginary flow.
No song, no lute, so lowly chaunts
In woods where still Arisbe haunts,
Wrapping the wanderer with her tresses
Into untold caresses.

[1] The harbour in which this lyric was written
was that of Vera Cruz.

For none of all the sons of men
That hath known Artemis, again
Turns to the warmer earth, or vows
His secrets to another spouse.
The moon resolves her beauty in
The sea's deep kisses salt and keen ;
The sea assumes the lunar light,
And he—their eremite !

In their calm intercourse and kiss
Even hell itself no longer is ;
For nothing in their love abides
That passes not beneath their tides,
And whoso bathes in light of theirs,
And water, changes unawares
To be no separate soul, but be
Himself the moon and sea.

Not all the wealth that flowers shed,
And sacred streams, on that calm head ;
Not all the earth's spell-weaving dream
And scent of new-turned earth shall seem
Again indeed his mother's breast
To breathe like sleep and give him rest ;
He lives or dies in subtler swoon
Between the sea and moon.

So standing, gliding, undeterred
By any her alluring word
That calls from older forest glades,
My soul forgets the gentle maids
That wooed me in the scarlet bowers,
And golden cluster-woof of flowers ;
Forgets itself, content to be
Between the moon and sea.

No passion stirs their depth, nor moves ;
No life disturbs their sweet dead loves ;
No being holds a crown or throne ;
They are, and I in them, alone :
Only some lute-player grown star
Is heard like whispering flowers afar ;
And some divided, single tune
Sobs from the sea and moon.

Amid thy mountains shall I rise,
O moon, and float about thy skies?
Beneath thy waters shall I roam,
O sea, and call thy valleys home ?

Or on Daedalian oarage fare
Forth in the interlunar air ?
Imageless mirror-life ! to be
Sole between moon and sea.

CHORUS.

No song can lure us while he sings so well.

JASON.

But look ! I see entrancing woman-forms
That beckon—fairy-like and not of earth.
So, fitter than the bed of this my queen
To rest heroic limbs !

MEDEA.

The wretched one !
Thou knowest that their kiss is death !

JASON.

Perhaps.
It were their kiss.

MEDEA.

Are not my kisses sweet ?

JASON.

Listen, they sing. This time the words ring
true,
Sailing across that blue abyss between.
Like young birds winging their bright flight
the notes
Glimmer across the sea.

MEDEA.

They sing, they sing !

PARTHENOPE.

O mortal, tossed on life's unceasing ocean,
Whose waves of joy and sorrow never
cease,
Eternal change—one changeless thing,
commotion !
Even in death no hint of calm and
peace !—

Here is the charm, the life-assuaging
    potion,
  Here is a better home for thee than
    Greece !
Come, lover, to my deep, soft, sleepy
    breast !
      Here is thy rest !

O mortal, sad is life !  But in my kisses
  Thou may'st forget its fever-parchèd
    thirst.
Age, death, and sorrow fade in slender
    blisses :
  My swoon of love drinks up the draught
    accurst.
And all thy seasons grow as sweet as this
    is,
  One constant summer in sleep's bosom
    nursed.
All storm and sunlight, star and season,
    cease,
      Here is thy peace.

O mortal, sad is love!  But my dominion
  Extends beyond love's ultimate abode.
Eternity itself is but a minion,
  Lighting my way on the untravelled
    road.
Gods shelter 'neath one shadow of my
    pinion.
  Thou only tread the path none else hath
    trode !
Come, lover, in my breast all blooms
    above,
      Here is thy love !

#### MEDEA.

My poet, now !  The one song in the world !

#### ORPHEUS.

Above us on the mast is spread
  The splendour of the fleece !
Before us, Argive maidens tread
  The glowing isles of Greece !
Behind us, fear and toil are dead :
  Below, the breakers cease !
The Holy Light is on my head—
  My very name is Peace !

The water's music moves ; and swings
  The sea's eternal breast.
The wind above us whistles, rings,
  And wafts us to the West.
Greece lures us on with beckonings
  And sighs of slumber blest.
I am not counted with the kings—
  My very name is Rest !

Medea shoots her sweetest glance
  And Jason bends above—
Young virgins in Iolchus dance,
  Hearing the news thereof.
The heroes—see their glad advance !
  Hath Greece not maids enough ?
I lie in love's ecstatic trance.
  My very name is Love !

#### LIGIA.

Come over the water, love, to me !
  Come over the little space !
Come over, my lover, and thou shalt see
  The beauty of my face !
Come over the water ! I will be
A bride and a queen and a lover to thee !

Come over the water, love, and lie !
  All day and all night to kiss !
Come over, my lover, an hour to die
  In the language-baffling bliss !
Come over the water !  Must I sigh ?
Thy lover and bride and queen am I !

Come over the water, love, and bide
  An hour in my swift caress !
So short is the space, and so smooth the
    tide—
  More smooth is my loveliness !
Come over the water, love, to my side !
I am thy lover and queen and bride !

#### MEDEA.

Sing, poet, ere the rash fool leap !

#### JASON.

          Ah, Zeus !

ORPHEUS.

The hearts of Greeks with sharper flames
  Burn than with one fire of all fire,
We have the Races and the Games,
  The song, the chisel, and the lyre ;
We have the altar, we the shrine,
And ours the joy of love and wine.

Why take one pleasure, put aside
  The myriad bliss of life diverse ?
Unchanging joy will soon divide
  Into the likeness of a curse.
Have we no maidens, slender, strong,
Daughters of tender-throated song ?

I swear by Aphrodite's eyes
  Our Grecian maids are fairer far !
What love as sweet as theirs is lies
  In Sun or planet, moon or star ?
What nymphs as sweet as ours are dwell
By foreign grove and alien well ?

With every watchman's cheery cry,
  "Land ho ! " through all the journeying
      years
Our ever-hoping hearts reply,
  "A land of bliss at last appears."
But what land laps a foreign foam
So sweet as is the hero's home ?

At every port the novel sights
  Charm for an hour—delusive bliss.
On every shore the false delights
  Of maidens ply the barbarous kiss.
But where did hero think to stay
Lulled in their love beyond a day ?

No shoreland whistles to the wind
  So musically as Thrace : no town
So gladdens the toil-weary mind
  As brave Athenae : no renown
Stands so divine in war and peace
As the illustrious name of Greece.

This island of the subtle song
  Shall vanish as the shaken spray
Tossed by the billow far and strong
  On marble coasts : we will not stay !
Dreams lure not those who ply the sail
Before, the home ! behind, the gale !

JASON.

Ah ! I am torn, I am torn !

MEDEA.

                    God's poet, hail !
Help us, Apollo !   Light of Sun, awake !
This is the desperate hour.

JASON.

                  I have no strength.

MEDEA.

Beware the third, the awful ecstasy !

ORPHEUS.

A higher spell controls a lower song.
Listen, they sing !

JASON.

    Joy ! Joy ! they sing, they sing !

LEUCOSIA.

O lover, I am lonely here !
  O lover, I am weeping !
Each pearl of ocean is a tear
  Let fall while love was sleeping.

A tear is made of fire and dew
  And saddened with a smile ;
The sun's laugh in the curving blue
  Lasts but a little while.

The night-winds kiss the deep : the stars
  Shed laughter from above ;
But night must pass dawn's prison bars :
  Night hath not tasted love.

With me the night is fallen in day ;
　　The day swoons back to night ;
The white and black are woven in gray,
　　Faint sleep of silken light.

A strange soft light about me shed
　　Devours the sense of time :
Hovers about my sleepy head
　　Some sweet persistent rhyme.

Beneath my breast my love may hear
　　Deep murmur of the billows—
O gather me to thee, my dear,
　　On soft forgetful pillows !

O gather me in arms of love
　　As maidens plucking posies,
Or mists that fold about a dove,
　　Or valleys full of roses !

O let me fade and fall away
　　From waking into sleep,
From sleep to death, from gold to gray,
　　Deep as the skies are deep !

O let me fall from death to dream,
　　Eternal monotone ;
Faint eventide of sleep supreme
　　With thee and love alone !

A jewelled night of star and moon
　　Shall watch our bridal chamber,
Bending the blue rays to the tune
　　Of softly-sliding amber.

Dim winds shall whisper echoes of
　　Our slow ecstatic breath,
Telling all worlds how sweet is love,
　　How beautiful is death.

#### MEDEA.

Sing, Orpheus, this doth madden them the
　　most.
Should one man leap—This tune is terrible !

#### ORPHEUS.

I am not moved, although I am a man.
So strong a safeguard is cool chastity.

#### MEDEA.

But love thou me ! My husband is distraught.

#### ORPHEUS.

Madness is on him for thy punishment.

#### MEDEA.

Sing, therefore !

#### ORPHEUS.

　　　　This last song of theirs was sweet.

#### MEDEA.

Thine therefore should be sweeter.

#### ORPHEUS.

　　　　　　The Gods grant it !

Lift up this love of peace and bliss,
　　The starry soul of wine,
Destruction's formidable kiss,
　　The lamp of the divine :
This shadow of a nobler name
Whose life is strife, whose soul is fame !

I rather will exalt the soul
　　Of man to loftier height,
And kindle at a livelier coal
　　The subtler soul of Light.
From these soft splendours of a dream
I turn, and seek the Self supreme.

This world is shadow-shapen of
　　The bitterness of pain.
Vain are the little lamps of love !
　　The light of life is vain !
Life, death, joy, sorrow, age and youth
Are phantoms of a further truth.

Beyond the splendour of the world,[1]
　　False glittering of the gold,
A Serpent is in slumber curled
　　In wisdom's sacred cold.
Life is the flaming of that flame.
Death is the naming of that name.

[1] The theory of these verses is that of certain
esoteric schools among the Hindus.

The forehead of the snake is bright
  With one immortal star,
Lighting her coils with living light
  To where the nenuphar
Sleeps for her couch.   All darkness dreams
The thing that is not, only seems.

That star upon the serpent's head
  Is called the soul of man :
That light in shadows subtly shed
  The glamour of life's plan.
The sea whereon that lotus grows
Is thought's abyss of tears and woes.

Leave Sirenusa !  Even Greece
  Forget ! they are not there !
By worship cometh not the Peace,
  The Silence not by prayer !
Leave the illusions, life and time
And death, and seek that star sublime—

Until the lotus and the sea
  And snake no longer are,
And single through eternity
  Exists alone the Star,
And utter Knowledge rise and cease
In that which is beyond the Peace !

JASON.
Those isles have faded : was this vision true ?

HERACLES.
I know not what hath passed : I seem asleep
Still, with the dream yet racing in my brain.

THESEUS.
There was a sweetness : whether sight or
    song
I know not.

JASON.
  But my veins grew strong and swollen
And madness came upon me.

MEDEA.
                You are here,
Let that suffice.  Remember not !

ORPHEUS.
            But now
I see the haze lift on the water-way,
And hidden headlands loom again.

JASON.
               I know
The pleasant portals.

CHORUS.
      Here is home at last.

ORPHEUS.
The sunset comes : the mist is lifted now
To let the last kiss of the daylight fall
Once ere night whisper "Sleep !"

JASON.
           And see ! the ship
Glides between walls of purple.

MEDEA.
           The green land
Cools the tired eyes.

CHORUS.
      The rocks stand sentinel.

MEDEA.
Let still the song that saved us gladden us.
Lift up thy lyre, sweet Orpheus, on the sea.

ORPHEUS.[1]

Over a sea like stainèd glass
At sunset like a chrysopras :—
  Our smooth-oared vessel over-rides
  Crimson and green and purple tides.
Between the rocky isles we pass;
And greener islets gay with grass ;
  Between the over-arching sides
  Our pinnace glides.

[1] The song describes the approach to Hong
Kong Harbour.

Just by the Maenad-haunted hill
Songs rise into the air, and thrill,
　　Like clustered birds at evening
　　When love outlingers rain and spring.
Faint faces of strange dancers spill
Their dewy scent ; and sweet and chill
　　The wind comes faintly whispering
　　　　On wanton wing.

Between the islands sheer and steep
Our craft treads noiseless o'er the deep,
　　Turned to the gold heart of the west,
　　The sun's last sigh of love expressed
Ere the lake glimmer, borrow sleep
From clouds and tinge their edges ; weep
　　That night brings love not to his breast,
　　　　But only rest.

We move toward the golden track
Shed in the water : we look back
　　Eastward, where rose is set to warn
　　Promise and prophecy of dawn
Reflected, lest the ocean lack
In any space serene or slack
　　Some colour, blushing o'er the fawn
　　　　Dim-lighted lawn.

And under all the shadowy shapes
Of steep and silent bays and capes
　　The water takes its darkest hue ;
　　Catches no laughter from the blue ;
No purple ray or gold escapes,
But dim green shadow comes and drapes
　　Its lustre : thus the night burns through
　　　　Tall groves of yew.

Thither, ah thither ! Hollow vales
Trembling with early nightingales !
　　Languish, O sea of sleep ! Young moon !
　　Dream on above in maiden swoon !
None daring to invoke the gales
To shake our sea, and swell our sails.
　　Not song, but silence, were a boon—
　　　　Save for this tune.

Round capes grown darker as night falls,
We see at last the splendid walls
　　That ridge the bay ; the town lies there
　　Lighted (the temple's hour for prayer)

At grave harmonious intervals.
The grand voice of some seaman calls,
　　Just as the picture fades, aware
　　　　How it was fair.

#### JASON.

A thousand victories bring us to the shore
Whence we set out : look forth ! The people
　　come
Moving with lights about the anchorage
To greet the heroes of the Golden Fleece.
My Queen ! Medea ! Welcome unto Greece !

EXPLICIT ACTUS QUARTUS.

## ARGONAUTAE.

### ACTUS QUINTUS.[1]

#### ARES.

JASON, MEDEA, PELIAS, ACASTUS, AL-
CESTIS *and her* Sisters, MADNESS.

SCENE : *The Palace at Iolchus.*

#### MADNESS.

Black Ares hath called
　　Me forth from the deep !
Blind and appalled,
　　Shall the palace high-walled
　　Shake as I leap
Over the granite,
　　The marble over,
One step to span it,
　　One flight to hover,
Like a moon round a planet,
　　A dream round a lover !

---

[1] The legend is grotesque, and the poet's
power is strained—perhaps overstrained—to
be faithful without being ridiculous. Only the
tragic necessity of avenging the indignity done
to Ares compelled this conclusion of the
drama, and the somewhat fantastic and unreal
machinery of the catastrophe.

How shall I come?
Shrieking and yelling?
Or quiet and dumb
To the heart of the dwelling?
Silently striding,
Whispering terror
Into their ears;
Watching, abiding,
Madness and error,
Brooder of fears!

Thus will I bring
Black Ares to honour,
Draw the black sting
Of the serpent upon her!
How foolish to fight
With the warrior God
Who brings victory bright
Or defeat with a nod,
Who standeth to smite
With a spear and a rod!
Here is the woman,
Thinking no evil,
Wielding the human
By might of a devil!
But I will mock her
With cunning design,
In my malice lock her.
The doom is divine!

MEDEA.

Ai! Ai! This rankles sorely in my mind
That Pelias should wander, free to slide
His sidelong looks among our courtiers
Ripe ever for some mischief. Yet methinks
There is a wandering other than this present—
Say, by the Stygian waves, unburied corpse!—
But, for the means? It ill befits our power
And grace—my husband's honour—to stretch
forth
The arm of murder o'er the head of age.
But surely must be means——

MADNESS.

The prophecy!

MEDEA.

Happy my thought be! I have found it.
Ha!
"Athena shall relent not till the king
Shall die and live." Vainly the prophet
meant
Mere transference of the crown. I'll twist
his saying
To daze the children—fools they are! So mask
Evil beneath the waxen face of Good,
Trick out Calamity in robes of Luck—
Come, children! Is the sun bright? And
your eyes?

ALCESTIS.

Dear queen, all's well with us. Such happiness
Crowds daylight—even sleep seems sorrowful,
Though bright with dainty dreams!

FIRST DANAID.
But you are sad!

MEDEA.

I meditate the ancient prophecy.
Thus a foreboding is upon my heart,
Seeing some danger follow yet, o'erhang
Our heads, poised gaily in incertitude!

SECOND DANAID.

Nay, grieve not, dear Medea! All men say
The prophecy is well fulfilled.

MEDEA.
Ay me!
"Until the king shall die and live again."

ALCESTIS.

What means that?

MEDEA.
I have meditated long.

SECOND DANAID.
To what sad end?

MEDEA.

At the full end I see
Allusion to my magic—to that spell
Whereby an old man may renew his youth.

ALCESTIS.
Our father!

MEDEA.

You have guessed aright, my child.
Your father must abandon his old age
And—by my magic—find sweet youth again !

DANAIDES.
But this is very difficult to do.

MEDEA.

For me such miracles are merely play,
Serving to while away the idle hours
While Jason hunts——

ALCESTIS.

How grand it were to see
Our aged father rival the strong youths
In feats of great agility !

MEDEA.

Agreed !
But surely you should work the charm your-
selves.
For children magic is a blithesome game !

DANAIDES.
Dear lady ! teach us how to say the spell !

MEDEA.
Words must be aided by appalling deeds !

ALCESTIS.
O ! O ! you frighten us.

MEDEA.

Be brave, my child !
I too passed through unutterable things !

ALCESTIS.
Let me fetch father !

MEDEA.

Nay, consider first.
Would he consent ?   The process is severe !

DANAIDES.
We know the sire is not exactly brave,
Though very wise and good.

MEDEA.

'Tis clear to me ;
Without his knowledge we must do the deed.

ALCESTIS.
What is this " deed " ?

MEDEA.

A caldron is prepared ;
And, having hewn your father limb from
limb,
We seethe him in a broth of magic herbs.

ALCESTIS.
And then ?

MEDEA.

The proper incantations said,
There rises from the steam a youthful shape
More godlike than like man.   And he will
fall
In kind embraces on his children's necks.

ALCESTIS.
O queen, this process seems indeed severe.

MEDEA.
Without his knowledge must the thing be
done.

DANAIDES.
This also seems to us no easy task.

MEDEA.
He sleeps through noon, while others are
abroad.

ALCESTIS.
Let us make haste !   Dear queen, how good
you are !

MEDEA.

One thing remember! While you say the
spell—
Here is the parchment!—let no thought arise
In any of your minds![1]

ALCESTIS. [*To her Sisters.*]
Remember that!

MEDEA.

Else—Otototototoi!

FIRST DANAID.
What woe is this?

MEDEA.

The charm is broken.

SECOND DANAID.
And our father——

MEDEA.
Lost!

DANAIDES.

Ai Ai! Ai Ai! Ai Ai!

MEDEA.
Ai Ai! Ai Ai!

ALCESTIS.

Be brave, dear sisters, pluck your courage up!
Easy this one condition! All is safe.

MEDEA.

Haste then! Good luck attend you! When
the hunt
Returns, how joyful——

[1] It is a common jest among the Hindus to
play this trick on a pupil, *i.e.*, to promise him
magical powers on condition that during a
given ceremonial he abstains from thinking of
a certain object (*e.g.*, a horse). He fails, because only the training of years can enable a
student so to control his mind as to accomplish
this feat of suppressing involuntary thought.

FIRST DANAID.

Striding vigorous,
The man renewed grasps Jason in embrace
Worthy of Heracles.

ALCESTIS.
Thanks, thanks, dear queen!
We go, we go!

MEDEA.
The Goddess be your speed!
Thus will the danger pass! That vicious fool
Shall cease his plots against my best beloved.
No taint of fell complicity shall touch
My honour in this matter. I will sleep
Through the delicious hours of breezy noon,
Lulled by sweet voices of my singing maids;
Secure at least that no one will attempt
To wreck my virtue or—restore my youth!

CHORUS.

O sleep of lazy love, be near
In dreams to lift the veil,
And silence from the shadowy sphere
To conjure in our lady's ear!—
The voices fall and fail;
The light is lowered. O dim sleep,
Over her eyelids creep!

The world of dreams is shapen fair
Beyond a mortal's nod:
A fragrant and a sunny air
Smiles: a man's kisses vanish there,
Grow kisses of a god;
And in dreams' darkness subtly grows
No Earth-flowered bloom of rose.

O dreams of love and peace, draw nigh,
Hover with shadowy wings!
Let shining shapes of ecstasy
Cover the frail blue veil of sky,
And speak immortal things!
Dream, lady, dream through summer noon,
Lulled by the sleepy tune!

The sense is riven, and the soul
  Goes glimmering to the abode,
Where aeons in one moment roll,
And one thought shapes to its control
  Body's forgotten load.
Our lady sleeps !  Our lady smiles
In far Elysian isles !

FIRST WOMAN.

Thrice have I crept towards the bed, and
  thrice
An unseen hand has caught the uplifted knife,
A grinning face lurked out from the blank
  air
Between me and that filthy sorceress.

SECOND WOMAN.

Daily I poison the she-devil's drink,
And nothing harms her !

THIRD WOMAN.

            I have a toad whose breath
Destroys all life——

CHORUS.

        Thou dealest in such arts?

THIRD WOMAN.

Ay ! for this hate's sake.   Are we sisters all
Herein?

CHORUS.

    True sisters !

THIRD WOMAN.

            The familiar soul
Sucks at her mouth—She sickens not nor
  dies ;
More poisonous than he.

FIRST WOMAN.

            Ah ! beast of hell !
What may avail us ?

SECOND WOMAN.

            Jason is quite lost
In her black sorceries.

FOURTH WOMAN.
    Our chance gone !

FIRST WOMAN.
                        Our life
Degraded to her service.

SECOND WOMAN.
                We, who are
Born nobly, are become her minions.

THIRD WOMAN.
Slaves, not handmaidens !

ALCESTIS.
                Otototoi !
Ai Ai !  What misery !

FIRST WOMAN.
            See ! the lady weeps !

ALCESTIS.
Ai Ai ! the black fiend, how he dogs my
  feet !
The fatal day !  Ai ! Ai !

CHORUS.
            What sorrow thus,
Maiden, removes the feet of fortitude ?

ALCESTIS.
Who shall arouse him ?

CHORUS.
            Peace, our lady sleeps.

ALCESTIS.
Ah me ! but she must wake !  A black, black
  deed
Hangs on the house.

MEDEA.
    What meets my waking ear ?
Alcestis !

ALCESTIS.
Ah, dear queen, lament, lament!
I am undone by my own——

MEDEA.
What! the work?

ALCESTIS.
Alas! Alas! the work!

MEDEA.
Thy father?

ALCESTIS.
Slain!

CHORUS.
Ai Ai! the old man slain!

MEDEA.
Ai Ai!

ALCESTIS.
Ai Ai!

MEDEA.
The strong spell broken?

ALCESTIS.
Nay, but thoughts arose,
So many thoughts—or ever I was ware—
And he—the caldron seethes——

MEDEA.
He rises not?

ALCESTIS.
Nought but moist smoke springs up.

MEDEA.
Alas! for me!
All is but lost.

ALCESTIS.
Canst thou do anything?

MEDEA.
Nothing.   Ai Ai!

ALCESTIS.
Ai Ai!

CHORUS.
Ai Ai! Ai Ai!

JASON.
What! Shall the hunter find his joy abroad,
And sorrow in his house?

MEDEA.
Thy very hearth
Polluted with the old man's blood!

ACASTUS.
What blood?
Answer me, woman!

MEDEA.
To thy knees, false hound,
Fawning to snap!

ACASTUS.
What misery, pale slaves,
Lament ye?

CHORUS.
Ah! the ill omen!   Ah, the day!
Alcestis hath her sire in error slain.

ACASTUS.
Sister!

ALCESTIS.
O brother, bear thine anger back!

ACASTUS.
Speak!

ALCESTIS.
Ah, the prophecy!   Ai Ai!

CHORUS.
Ai Ai!

ACASTUS.

What folly masks what wickedness? Speak
on!

ALCESTIS.

I cannot speak.

JASON.

Speak thou, Medea!

MEDEA.

The child
Hath hewn her sire asunder, seething him
In herbs of sacred power.

ACASTUS.

By thy decree?

MEDEA.

Nay!

MADNESS.

Safer is it to admit to these
Fools—charge the child with lack of fortune!

MEDEA.

Yea!
I bade her take a waxen shape, carved well
To look like the old man——

ALCESTIS.

Nay! nay! the Sire
Himself we stole on sleeping——

CHORUS.

Hewn apart!
Ai Ai!

MEDEA.

I said not thus!

ALCESTIS.

I am so wild,
Bewildered with these tears.

ACASTUS.

Enough of this!
It is the malice of that sorceress
Disguised —she well knows how.

CHORUS.

Thus, thus it is!
We know the witch's cunning.

JASON.

Dogs and fools!
For this ye die.

MADNESS.

Nobility and love
Urge my own sanction to support the wife!

JASON.

I bade my queen prepare this spell. Disputes
Your arrogance my kingship?

ACASTUS.

Ay, indeed!
Now justice turns against thee, fickle jade
As fortune. Mine is a boy's arm, but I
Advance against thee an impervious blade,
And give thee in thy throat and teeth the
lie!

JASON.

Boy's bluster!

MADNESS.

Justice will be satisfied.
It will be best to flee!

JASON.

But what is this?
A sword? I scorn a sword. I scorn a boy.
Let none suppose me fearful!

MEDEA.

Give not back!

MADNESS.

It will be finer far to go away
As those disdaining aught but their own love.

MEDEA.

Ay! let us leave these folk's ingratitude,
My husband! in thy love alone I rest.
This splendour and this toil alike resume
Our life from the long honeymoon of love
We wish at heart.

JASON.

To Corinth !

MEDEA.
                          Creon bears
The name of favourable to suppliants.

ACASTUS.

How virtue tames these tameless ones !
  To-day
I am indeed a man.

MEDEA.
                      Thou brainless boy !
Thus, thus, and thus I smite thee on the
  cheek—
Thus, thus I spit upon thy face.   Out, dog !

SEMICHORUS 1.

His patience shows as something marvellous.

SEMICHORUS 2.

Virtue takes insult from the fortuneless.

MEDEA.

The curse of Ares dog you into Hades !
I have my reasons [*doubtfully*], ay, my reasons
  plain !
Going, not forced.

CHORUS.
                  Yet going—that is good !

JASON.

To Corinth !   Bride of my own heart, Medea,
Well hast thou put thy power off for the
  time
Preferring love to pomp, and peace to revel—

MEDEA.

And the soft cushions of the moss-grown
  trees
To royal pillows, and the moon's young light
To gaudy lamps of antique workmanship—

JASON.

And music of the birds to harps of gold
Struck by unwilling fingers for gold coin.

MEDEA.

Come ! lest the curse I call upon this house
Eat us up also !   May the red plague rot
Their bones !   I lift my voice and prophesy :
The curse shall never leave this house of
  fear ;
But one by treachery shall slay another,
And vengeance shall smite one, and one
  lay bare
Her breasts in vain for love : until the
  house
Perish in uttermost red ruin.

CHORUS.
                        Bah !
Speared wild-cats bravely spit !

JASON.
                        To Creon, come !

MADNESS.
        Black Ares hath chosen
          Me wisely, to send
        A doom deep-frozen
          From now to the end.
        Never the curse
          Shall pass from the house,
        But gather a worse
          Hate for a spouse.
        The lovers are better
          Escaped from my toils
        Than these in the fetter
          Of the golden spoils.

        Yet still lies a doom
          For the royal lovers.
        Time bears in her womb
          That darkness covers
        A terror, and waits
          The hour that is Fate's.

The work is done.   Let miracle inspire
Iolchian voices to the holy hymn,
Praise to black Ares, echo of this doom.

CHORUS.

So fearful is the wrath divine,
  That once aroused it shall not sleep,
Though prostrate slaves before the shrine
  Pray, praise. do sacrifice, and weep.
Ten generations following past
Shall not exhaust the curse at last.

From father unto son it flees,
  An awful heritage of woe.
Wives feel its cancerous prodigies
  Invade their wombs ; the children know
The inexpiable word, exhaust
Not by a tenfold holocaust.

Thus let mankind abase in fear
  Their hearts, nor sacrilege profane
The awful slumber of the seer,
  The dread adytum of the fane ;
Nor gain the mockery of a fleece,
Losing reality of peace.

Hail to wild Ares !  Men, rejoice
  That He can thus avenge his shrine !
One solemn cadence of that voice
  Peal through the ages, shake the spine
Of very Time, and plunge success
False-winged into sure-foot distress !

Hail to black Ares !  Warrior, hail !
  Thou glory of the shining sword !
What proven armour may avail
  Against the vengeance of the Lord ?
Athena's favour must withdraw
Before the justice of thy law !

Hail to the Lord of glittering spears,
  The monarch of the mighty name,
The Master of ten thousand Fears
  Whose sword is as a scarlet flame !
Hail to black Ares !  Wild and pale
The echo answers me : All Hail !

EXPLICIT ACTUS QUINTUS.

# AHAB

## AND OTHER POEMS

### DEDICACE.

#### TO G. C. J.

PILGRIM of the sun, be this thy scrip!
 The severing lightnings of the mind
Avail where soul and spirit slip,
 And the Eye is blind.

PARIS, *December* 9, 1902.

### RONDEL.

BY palm and pagoda enchaunted o'er-
 shadowed, I lie in the light
Of stars that are bright beyond suns that
 all poets have vaunted
In the deep-breathing amorous bosom of
 forests of amazon might
By palm and pagoda enchaunted.

By spells that are murmured and rays of my
 soul strongly flung, never daunted;
 By gesture of tracery traced with a wand
 dappled white;
I summon the spirits of earth from the gloom
 they for ages have haunted.

O woman of deep-red skin! Carved hair
 like the teak! O delight
Of my soul in the hollows of earth—how
 my spirit hath taunted—
Away! I am here, I am laid to the breast of
 the earth in the dusk of the night,
 By palm and pagoda enchaunted.

### AHAB.

#### PART I.

THE polished silver flings me back
 Dominant brows and eyes of bronze,
A curling beard of vigorous black,
 And dusky red of desert suns
Burnt in my cheeks. Who saith me Nay?
Who reigns in Israel to-day?

Samaria in well-ordered ranks
 Of houses stands in honoured peace:
Sweet nourishment from Kenah's banks
 Flows, and the corn and vine increase.
In two pitched fields the Syrian hordes
Fled broken from our stallion swords.

Ay me! But that was life! I see
 Now, from that hill, the ordered plain;
The serried ranks like foam flung free,
 Long billows, flashing on the main.
Past the eye's grip their legions roll—
Anguish of death upon my soul!

For, sheltered by the quiet hill,
 Like two small flocks of kids that wait,
Going to water, ere the chill
 Blow from the East's forsaken gate,
Lie my weak spears: O trembling tide
Of fear false-faced and shifty-eyed!

God! how we smote them in the morn!
 Their ravening tides rolled back anon,
As if the cedared crest uptorn
 Roared from uprooted Lebanon
Down to the sea, its billows hurled
Back, past the pillars of the world!

Ah, that was life !  I feel my sword
  Live, bite, and shudder in my hand,
Smite, drink, the spirit of its lord
  Exulting through the infinite brand !
My chariot dyed with Syrian blood !
My footmen wading through the flood !

Ay ! that was life !  Before the night
  Dipped its cool wings, their hosts were
    stricken
Like night itself before the light.
  An hundred thousand corpses sicken
The air of heaven.  Yet some by speed
Escape our vengeance—ours, indeed !

Fate, the red hound, to Aphek followed.
  Some seven and twenty thousand died
When the great wall uprising hollowed
  Its terror, crashed upon its side,
And whelmed them in the ruin.  Strife,
Strength, courage, victory—that is Life !

Then—by my father's beard !  What seer
  Promised me victory?  What sage
Now in my triumph hour severe
  Spits out red oracles of rage?
Jehovah's.  The fanatic churl
Stands—see his thin lips writhe and curl !

" Because thou hast loosed the kingly man,
  To uttermost destruction's dread
In my almighty power and plan
  Appointed, I will have thy head
For his, thy life for his make mine,
And for his folk thou hast spared, slay thine."

But surely I was just and wise !
  Mercy is God's own attribute !
Mercy to noble enemies
  Marks man from baser mould of brute.
To fight their swordsmen—who would shirk ?
To slay a captive—coward's work !

" I have loved mercy," that He said ;
  Nor bade me slay the Syrian Chief.
Yet my head answers for his head ;
  My people take his people's grief.
Sin, troth, to spare one harmless breath,
Sith all my innocents earn death !

By timely mercy peace becomes,
  And kindly love, and intercourse
Of goodly merchandise, that sums
  Contention in united force.
" Praise who, relenting, showeth pity ;
Not him who captureth a city !"

A wild strong life I've made of mine.
  Not till my one good deed is done—
Ay ! for that very deed divine—
  Comes the fierce mouth of malison.
So grows my doubt again, so swell
My ancient fears for Israel.

I hurled Jehovah's altars down ;
  I slew and I pursued his priests ;
I took a wife from Zidon Town ;
  I gave his temples to the beasts ;
I set up gods and graven shapes
Of calves and crocodiles and apes.

Myself to sorceries I betook ;
  All sins that are did I contrive,
Sealed in the Thora's dreadful book—
  I live, and like my life, and thrive !
Doth God not see?  His ear is dull ?
Or His speech strangled, His force null ?

Nay, verily !  These petty sins
  His mercy and long-suffering pardon.
What final crime of horror wins
  At last His gracious heart to harden ?
What one last infamy shall wake
His anger, for His great Name's sake?

Is there one sin so horrible
  That no forgiveness can obtain,
That flings apart the bars of hell,
  For which repentance shall be vain ?
Ay ! but there is !  One act of ruth
Done in my rash unthinking youth !

Who wonders if I hold the scale
  Poised in my deep deliberate mind,
Between the weight of Zidon's Baal
  And Judah's God—each in his kind
A god of power—each in his fashion
The hideous foeman of compassion ?

The blood alike of man and beast
  The worship of each God demands.
All priests are greedy—gold and feast
  Pour from the poor folk to their hands.
The doubtful power from heaven to strike
The levin bolt they claim alike.

I take no heed of trickery played
  By cunning mad Elijah's skill,
When the great test of strength was made
  On Carmel's melancholy hill,
And on the altar-stone the liar
Cried "Water," and poured forth Greek fire !

Then while the fools peer heavenward,
  Even as he prays, to see the skies
Vomit the flash, his furtive sword
  Fast to the flinty altar flies.
Whoof ! the wild blaze assures the clods
Jehovah is the God of gods !

Nor do I set peculiar store
  By tricks twin-born to this they show
When, with well-simulated lore
  Of learning, Baal's great hierarchs go
Into the gold god's graven shell
And moan the ambiguous oracle.

In my own inmost heart I feel,
  Deep as a pearl in seas of Ind,
A vision, keen as tempered steel,
  Lofty and holy as the wind,
And brighter than the living sun :
If these be gods, then there is none !

Baal and Jehovah, Ashtoreth
  And Chemosh and these Elohim,
Life's pandars in the brothel, Death !
  Cloudy imaginings, a dream
Built up of fear and words and woe.
All, all my soul must overthrow.

For these are devils, nothing doubt !
  Yet nought should trouble me : I see
My folk secure from foes without,
  Worship in peace and amity
Baal and Jehovah, sects appeased
By peace assured and wealth increased.

Yet am I troubled.   Doubt exists
  And absolute proof recoils before me.
Truth veils herself in awful mists,
  And darkness wakens, rolling o'er me
When I approach the dreadful shrine,
In my own soul, of the divine.

And what cries laughing Jezebel ?
  Golden and fragrant as the morn,
Painted like flames adorning Hell,
  Passions and mysteries outworn,
Ever enchanting, ever wise,
And terror in her wondrous eyes !

Her fascination steals my strength,
  Her luxury lures me as she comes ;
Reaches her length against my length,
  And breaks my spirit ; life succumbs—
A nameless avatar of death
Incarnate in her burning breath.

I know her gorgeous raiment folded
  In snaky subtle draperies,
All stalwart captains mighty-moulded
  To lure within her sorceries,
Within her bed—and I, who love,
See, and am silent, and approve !

Strange !   Who shall call the potter knave
  Who moulds a vessel to his will ?
One, if he choose, a black-browed slave :
  One, if he choose, a thing of ill,
Writhing, misshapen, footless, cruel :
One, like a carved Assyrian jewel ?

Shame on the potter heavy sit,
  If he revenge his own poor skill
That marred a work by lack of wit,
  By heaping infamy and ill
On the already ruined clay.
Shame on the potter, then, I say !

But what cries laughing Jezebel ?
  Scornful of me as all her lovers,
More scornful as we love her well !
  "Good king, this rage of doubt discovers
The long-hid secret !   All thy mind
A little shadow lurks behind."

Hers are the delicate sorceries
  In black groves: hers the obscure, obscene
Rites in dim moonlight courts; the wise
  Dreadful occasions when the queen
Like to a bat, flits, flits, to gloat
Blood-drunk upon a baby's throat !


Therefore : all doubt, this fierce unrest
  Between that knowledge self bestows
And leaves of palm, and palimpsest,
  Scrawled sacred scrolls, whose legend goes
Beyond recorded time, and founds
Its age beyond all history's bounds ;


Therefore : all search for truth beyond
  The doubtful canon of the law,
The bitter letter of the bond
  Given when Sinai shook with awe,
They swear ; all wit that looks aslant
Shamed at the shameful covenant ;[1]


Therefore : this brooding over truth
  She much avers cuts short my day,
Steals love and laughter from my youth,
  Will dye my beard in early grey.
" Go forth to war !  Shall Judah still
Set mockery to thy kingly will ?"


May be.   I often feel a ghost
  Creeping like darkness through my brain ;
Sensed like uncertainty at most,
  Nowise akin to fear or pain.
Yet it is there.   To yield to such
And brood, will not avail me much.


Ho ! harness me my chariot straight,
  My white-maned horses fleet and strong !
Call forth the trumpeters of state !
  Proclaim to all Samaria's throng :
The  King  rides  forth !   Hence,  slaves !
    Away !
Haste ye !   The King rides forth to-day.


[1] Circumcision, medically commendable, is
both ridiculous and obscene if considered as a
religious rite. Gen. xvii. 9-14.

## PART II.

WOULD God that I were dead !  Like Cain,
  My punishment I cannot bear.
There is a deep corrosive pain
  Invades my being everywhere.
Sprung from a seed too small to see,
A monster spawns and strangles me.

'Tis scarce a week !  In power and pride
  I rode in state about the city ;
Took pleasure in the eager ride,
  Saw grief, took pleasure in my pity ;
Saw joy, took pleasure in the seeing,
And the full rapture of well-being.

Would God that I had stayed, and smote
  My favourite captain through the heart,
Caught my young daughter by the throat,
  And torn her life and limbs apart,
Stabbed my queen dead : remorse for these
Might ape, not match, these miseries.

For, hard behind the palace gate,
  I spied a vineyard fair and fine,
Hanging with purple joy, and weight
  Of golden rapture of the vine :
And there I bade my charioteer
Stay, and bid Naboth to appear.

The beast !  A gray, deceitful man,
  With twisted mouth the beard would hide,
Evil yet strong : the scurril clan
  Exaggerate for its greed and pride,
The scum of Israel !  At one look
I read my foe as in a book.

The beast !  He grovelled in the dust.
  I heard the teeth gride as he bowed
His forehead to the earth.   Still just,
  Still patient, passionless, and proud,
I ruled my heavy wrath.   I passed
That hidden insult : spake at last.

I spake him fair.   My memory held
  Him still a member of my folk ;
A warrior might be bold of eld,
  My hardy spearman when we broke
The flashing lines of Syrians.   Yea !
I spake him fair.   Alas the day !

" Friend, by my palace lies thy field
    Fruitful and pleasant to the sight.
Therefore I pray thee that thou yield
    Thy heritage for my delight.
Wilt thou its better ? Or its fee
In gold, as seemeth good to thee ?

" Content thyself ! " As by a spell
    He rears his bulk in surly rage.
" The Lord forbid that I should sell
    To thee my father's heritage ! "
No other word. Dismissal craves ?[1]
Nay, scowls and slinks among his slaves.

Hath ever a slave in story dared
    Thus to beard openly his lord ?
My chariot men leapt forth and flared
    Against him with indignant sword.
Why wait for king's word to expunge
Life so detested with one lunge ?

" Cease ! " My strong word flamed out.
        The men
    Shook with dead fear. They jumped and
        caught
With savage instinct, brutal ken,
    At what should be my crueller thought :
Torture ! And trembled lest their haste
Had let a dear life run to waste.

They argued after their brute kind.
    I have two prides ; in justice, one :
In mercy, one : " No ill I find
    In this just man," I cried ; " the sun
Is not defiled, and takes no hurt
When the worm builds his house of dirt.

" Curse ye Jehovah ! He abides,
    Hears not, nor smites ; the curse is pent
Close with the speaker ; ill betides
    When on himself the curve is bent,
And like the wild man's ill-aimed blow,[2]
Hits nought, swerves, swoops, and strikes
        him low.

[1] In the East the inferior dare not leave the presence of his superior without permission.
[2] Another reference to the boomerang.

" Let the man go ! " The short surprise
    Sinks in long wonder : angrily
Yet awed they spurn him forth. " Arise !
    O swine, and wallow in thy sty !
The King hath said it." Thus the men
Turned the beast free—to goad again.

For now the little shadow shapes
    An image ever in my brain ;
Across my field of sight there gapes
    Ever a gulf, and draws the pain
Of the whole knowledge of the man
Into its vague and shifting span.

Moreover, in that gulf I see
    Now the bright vineyard sweet and clean,
Now the dog Naboth mocking me
    With rude curt word and mouth obscene
Wried in derision—well relied
Dog's insolence on monarch's pride.

Ah, friend ! Some winds may shake a city !
    Some dogs may creep too near a feast !
Thou, reckoning on my scorn, my pity,
    Thine own uncleanness as a beast :
Wilt thou not take thy count again ?
Seest thou the shadow on my brain ?

It grows, it grows. Seven days slide past :
    I groan upon an empty bed :
I turn my face away : I fast :
    There cometh in my mouth no bread.
No man dare venture near to say :
" Why turns the King his face away ? "

It grows. Ah me ! the long days slide ;
    I brood ; due justice to the man
Dogging desire. A monarch's pride
    Outweighs his will : yet slowlier ran
To-day the thought : " I will no wrong : "
" The vines are cool," more sweet and strong

There is no sleep. All natural laws
    Suspend their function : strange effects
And mighty for so slight a cause !
    What whim of weakling strength protects
This dog of Satan at my gate
From the full whirlwind of my hate ?

What mighty weakness stays the king
  If he arise, and cast desire
Far from its seat and seed and spring
  To Hinnom the detested fire?
Ay! both were wise.  Madness alone
Sits throned on the king's vacant throne.


Dogs!  Who dares break on me?  "Dread
    lord!
  Mightiest of monarchs!"—"Cease, thou
    crow!
Thine errand! ere the eunuch's sword
  Snatch thy bald head off at a blow."
" Mercy, World's Light!"  Swings clear and
    clean
The call " Room for the Queen! The Queen!"


Strong as a man, the Queen strides in.
  Even she shrank frighted!—my aspect
More dreadful than all shapes of sin
  Her dreams might shape or recollect',
Hideous with fasting, madness, grief,
Beyond all speaking or belief.


But the first glance at those bold eyes!
  Ah! let me fling me at her feet!
Take me, O love!  Thy terror flies.
  Kiss me again, again, O sweet!
O honeyed queen, old paramour,
So keen our joy be and so sure!


" The king would be alone!"  Fast fly
  The trembling lackeys at her voice.
Lapped in her billowy breasts I lie,
  And love, and languish, and rejoice,
And—ah—forget!  The ecstatic hour
Bursts like a poppy into flower.


Back! thou black spectre!  In her arms
  Devouring and devoured of love,
Feeding my face in myriad charms,
  As on a mountain feeds a dove,
Starred with fresh flowers, dew-bright, and
    pearled
With all the light of all the world :

Back !  With the kisses ravening fast
  Upon my panting mouth, the eyes
Darting hot showers of light, the vast
  And vicious writhings, the caught sighs
Drunk with delight, on love's own throne,
The moment where all time lies prone :


Back !  At the very central shrine,
  Pinnacled moment of excess
Of immolation's blood divine :
  Back ! from the fleshly loveliness:
Back ! loved and loathed !  O face concealed !
Back !  One hath whispered " Naboth's
    field."


I am slain.  Her body passion-pearled
  Dreams her luxurious lips have drawn
My spirit, as the dust wind-whirled
  Sucks up the radiance of the dawn
In rainbow beauty[1]—yet remains
Mere dust upon the barren plains.


Reluctance to reveal my grief
  Is of my sickness a strange feature.
Yea, verily ! beyond belief
  Is the machinery of man's nature !
If thus spake Solomon in kind
Of body, I of soul and mind !


The lazy accents stir at last
  The scented air : " Oh, wherefore, lord,
Is thy soul sad ?  This weary fast
  Strikes to my heart a lonely sword !"
In brief words stammered forth I spoke
My secret ; and the long spell broke.


And now the gilded sin of her
  Leapt and was lambent in a smile :
" Give me but leave to minister
  This kingdom for a little while !
The vineyard shall be thine.  O king,
This trouble is a little thing !"

---

[1] " Dust-devils " show opalescence in certain
aspects of light.

I gave to her the signet's gold
  Carved in the secret charactery,
Whose flowers of writing bend and fold
  The star of Solomon, the eye
Whence four rays run—the Name ! the seal
Written within the burning wheel.

And now I lean with fevered will
  Across the carven screen of palm.
All nature holds its function still ;
  The sun is mild ; the wind is calm ;
But on my ear the voices fall
Distant, and irk me, and appal.

Two men have sworn the solemn oath :
  " God and the king this dog blasphemed,"
Two judges, just, though little loth,
  Weigh, answer.  As on one who dreamed
Comes waking—in my soul there groaned :
" Carry forth Naboth to be stoned ! "

Nine days !  And still the king is sad,
  And hides his face, and is not seen.
The tenth ! the king is gaily clad ;
  The king will banquet with the queen ;
And, ere the west be waste of sun,
Enjoy the vineyard he hath won.

All this I hear as one entranced.
  The king and I are friend and friend,
As if a cloud of maidens danced
  Between my vision and the end.
I see the king as one afeared,
Hiding his anguish in his beard.

I laugh in secret, knowing well
  What waits him in the field of blood ;
What message hath the seer to tell ;
  What bitter Jordan holds its flood
Only for Ahab, sore afraid
What lurks behind the vine's cool shade.

Yet—well I see—the fates are sure,
  And Ahab will descend, possess
The enchanting green, the purple lure,
  The globes of nectared loveliness,
And, as he turns ! who wonders now
The grim laugh wrinkles on my brow ?

I see him, a fantastic ghost,
  The vineyard smiling white and plain,
And hiding ever innermost
  The little shadow on his brain ;
I laugh again with mirthless glee,
As knowing also I am he.

A fool in gorgeous attire !
  An ox decked bravely for his doom !
So step I to the great desire.
  Sweet winds upon the gathering gloom
Bend like a mother, as I go,
Foreknowing, to my overthrow.

## NEW YEAR, 1903.

O FRIENDS and brothers !  Hath the year
  deceased,
And ye await the bidding to fare well ?
How shall ye fare, thus bound of fate in hell ?
How, whom no light hath smitten, and
  released ?
Ye trust perchance in God, or man, or priest ?
Ay !  Let them serve you, let them save you !
  Spell
The name that guards the human citadel,
And answer if your course hath checked or
  ceased.

Path of the eightfold star !  Be thou revealed !
Isle of Nirvana, be the currents curled
About thee, that the swimmer touch thy
  shore !
Thought be your sword, and virtue be your
  shield !
Press on !  Who conquers shall for evermore
Pass from the fatal mischief of the world.

## MELUSINE.

### TO M. M. M.

HANGS over me the fine false gold
  Above the bosom epicene
    That hides my head that hungereth.
The steady eyes of steel behold,
  When on a sudden the fierce and thin
    Curled subtle mouth swoops on my breath,

And like a serpent's mouth is cold,
  And like a serpent's mouth is keen,
  And like a serpent's mouth is death.

Lithe arms, wan with love's mysteries,
  Creep round and close me in, as Thule
    Wraps Arctic oceans ultimate ;
Some deathly swoon or sacrifice,
  This love—a red hypnotic jewel
    Worn in the forehead of a Fate !
And like a devil-fish is ice,
  And like a devil-fish is cruel,
    And like a devil-fish is hate.

Beneath those kisses songs of sadness
  Sob, in the pulses of desire,
    Seeking some secret in the deep ;
Low melodies of stolen gladness,
  The bitterness of death ; the lyre
    Broken to bid the viol weep :
And like a Maenad's chants are madness,
  And like a Maenad's chants are fire,
    And like a Maenad's chants are sleep.

A house of pain is her bedchamber.
  Her skin electric clings to mine,
    Shakes for pure passion, moves and
      hisses ;
Whose subtle perfumes half remember
  Old loves, and desolate divine
    Wailings among the wildernesses ;
And like a Hathor's skin is amber,
  And like a Hathor's skin is wine,
    And like a Hathor's skin is kisses.

Gray steel self-kindled shine her eyes.
  They rede strange runes of time defiled,
    And ruined souls, and Satan's kin.
I see their veiled impurities,
  An harlot hidden in a child,
    Through all their love and laughter lean ;
And like a witch's eyes are wise,
  And like a witch's eyes are wild,
    And like a witch's eyes are Sin.

She moves her breasts in Bacchanal
  Rhymes to that music manifold
    That pulses in the golden head,

Seductive phrase perpetual,
  Terrible both to change or hold ;
    They move, but all their light is fled ;
And like a dead girl's breasts are small,
  And like a dead girl's breasts are cold,
    And like a dead girl's breasts are dead.

Forests and ancient haunts of sleep
  See dawn's intolerable spark
    While yet fierce darkness lingereth.
So I, their traveller, sunward creep,
  Hail Ra uprising in his bark,
    And feel the dawn-wind's sombre breath.
Strange loves rise up, and turn, and weep !
  Our warm wet bodies may not mark
    How these spell Satan's shibboleth
And like a devil's loves are deep,
  And like a devil's loves are dark,
    And like a devil's loves are death.

## THE DREAM.

BEND down in dream the shadow-shape
  Of tender breasts and bare !
Let the long locks of gold escape
And cover me and fall and drape,
  A pall of whispering hair !
And let the starry eyes look through
  That mist of silken light,
And lips drop forth their honey-dew
And gentle sighs of sleep renew
  The scented winds of night !
As purple clusters of pure grapes
  Distil their dreamy wine
Whose fragrance from warm fields escapes
On shadowy hills and sunny capes
  In lands of jessamine !
So let thy figure faintly lined
  In pallid flame of sleep
With love inspire the dreamer's mind,
Young love most delicate and kind,
  With love—how calm and deep !
Let hardly half a smile revive
  The thoughts of waking hours.
How sad it is to be alive !
How well the happy dead must thrive
  In green Elysian bowers !

A sleep as deep as theirs bestow,
　　Dear angel of my dreams !
Bid time now cease its to-and-fro
That I may dwell with thee, and know
　　The soul from that which seems !
The long hair sobs in closer fold
　　And deeper curves of dawn ;
The arms bend closer, and the gold
Burns brighter, and the eyes are cold
　　With life at last withdrawn.
And all the spirit passing down
　　Involves my heart with gray :
So the pale stars of even crown
The glow of twilight ; dip and drown
　　The last despairs of day.
Oh ! closer yet and closer yet
　　The pearl of faces grows.
The hair is woven like a net
Of moonlight round me : sweet is set
　　The mouth's unbudded rose.
Oh never ! did our lips once meet
　　The dream were done for ever,
And death should dawn, supremely sweet,
One flash of knowledge subtle and fleet
　　Borne on the waveless river.

And therefore in the quiet hour
　　I rose from lily pillows
And swiftly sought the jasmine bower
Still sleeping, moonlight for a dower,
　　And bridal wreaths of willows.
And there I laid me down again :
　　The stream flowed softly by :
And thought the last time upon pain,
Earth's joy—the sad permuted strain
　　Of tears and ecstasy.
And there the dream came floating past
　　Borne in an ivory boat,
And all the world sighed low " At last."
The shallop waited while I cast
　　My languid limbs afloat
To drift with eyelids skyward turned
　　Up to the shadowy dream
Shaped like a lover's face, that burned ;
To drift toward the soul that yearned
　　For this—the hour supreme !
So drifting I resigned the sleep
　　For death's diviner bliss ;
As mists in rain of springtide weep,
Life melted in the dewfall deep
　　Of death's kiss in a kiss.

# THE GOD-EATER *

## A TRAGEDY OF SATIRE

### 1903

[The idea of this obscure and fantastic play is as follows :—

By a glorious act human misery is secured (History of Christianity).

Hence, appreciation of the personality of Jesus is no excuse for being a Christian.

Inversely, by a vile and irrational series of acts human happiness is secured (Story of the play).

Hence, attacks on the Mystics of History need not cause us to condemn Mysticism.

Also, the Knowledge of Good and Evil is a Tree whose fruit Man has not yet tasted : so that the Devil cheated Eve indeed ; or (more probably) Eve cheated Adam. Unless (most probable of all) God cheated the Devil, and the fruit was a common apple after all. Cf. H. Maudsley, " Life in Mind and Conduct."]

## PERSONS.

CRIOSDA, aged 33.

MAURYA, his sister, aged 16.

RUPHA, the Hag of Eternity.

*The scene of the Tragedy is laid in an ancient Scottish Hall, very remote.*

*The time is the One-and-Twentieth Century after Christ.*

*The action of the play occupies many years.*

## THE GOD-EATER.

### ACT I.

#### CRIOSDA, MAURYA.

[*The Scene is an old Baronial Hall, elaborately, yet somewhat grotesquely (from the incongruity), fitted up as an antique Egyptian temple. Centre : an altar between two obelisks ; on it a censer vomits smoke in great volumes. Above at back of stage is a stately throne, square and simple, on steps. In it sits* MAURYA, *quiet and silent. She is dressed in sombre green robes, lightened with old rose facings. She is heavily braceleted and ankleted with gold, and her crown is a gold disc, supported in silver horns, rising from her forehead. Above her is a rude painted board, representing the Winged Globe in many colours. Before the altar* CRIOSDA *is kneeling ; he is dressed in a white robe fastened by a blue sash. A leopard's skin is over his shoulders, clasped with a golden clasp about his neck. He bears an " ankh " in his left hand, in his right a caduceus [1] wand. On his head is the winged helmet of Mercury, and his sandals are winged also. He is muttering low some fervent prayer, and anon casts incense upon the censer. The low muttering continues for a considerable time,* MAURYA *remaining quite still, as one rapt in her own thoughts. Suddenly, with startling vehemence, the song breaks out.*

CRIOSDA.

HAIL ! HAIL ! HAIL !

[MAURYA, *startled, looks up and half rises. Then sits again, with a strange sweet smile of innocence and tenderness.*

CRIOSDA. [*Lower.*]

The world is borne upon thy breast
Even as the rose.

[1] The wand of Mercury.

* For the foundations of this play the student may consult any modern treatises on Sociology.

130

Wilt thou not lull it into rest,
  Some strong repose
More satisfying than pale sleep ;
Than death more long, more deep?

Hail ! at the twilight as at dawn !
  The sunset close
Even on the lake as on the lawn !
  The red ray glows
Across the woven stardrift's ways
In mystery of Maurya's praise.

Hear me, thy priest, at eventide !
  These subtler throes
Than love's or life's, invade, divide
  The world of woes.
Thy smile, thy murmur of delight, be enough
To fill the world with life and love !

[*He bends over into deep reverence,
yet with the air of one expecting
a grace.*

[MAURYA, *like one in trance, rises
slowly, gathers her robes about her,
and descends to the altar. Reaching
over it, she bends and lifts him by
his outstretched arms. She puts
her lips to his forehead, and he,
with a deep gasp, as of one in ecstasy
not to be borne, drops back, breathing deeply. She lifts her hands,
and brings them slowly, very forcibly, forward, and says solemnly :*

The Blessing of Maurya.
Blessed be the House of the Servants of
Maurya.
Blessed be the Stones of the House.
Blessed be the Tree of the House.
Blessed be the Food of the House.
Blessed be the Men of the House.
Blessed be all the Universe for their sakes.
The Blessing of Maurya.

[*A short silence.*

[MAURYA *goes back and lays her
crown and robes on the throne.
She is now dressed in wonderful
close-fitting crimson silk, trimmed
with ermine. Her bronze-gold hair
is coiled wonderfully about her head.*

*She comes down stage to* CRIOSDA,
*who rises on one knee and takes
her thereon. She removes his
helmet and strokes gently his hair.*

Criosda, my brother !
CRIOSDA. Maurya, little sister !
[*He smiles with deep tenderness ;
suddenly a pang catches him ; he
strikes at his throat, and cries
sharply :*
Ah !        [*Shivers with terrible emotion.*
MAURYA. Criosda, ever the same ! The
  old world runs
On wheels of laughter for us little ones ;
To you, whose shoulders strain, the chariot
  seems
A poised fiend flogging you to hell.
CRIOSDA.          These thoughts,
Maurya,—Maurya ! they become you not.
Child, to see sorrow is to taste it.
MAURYA.          No ;
For such a sorrow is its own calm joy.
But—share me now your pain.
CRIOSDA. [*In agony.*] No ! no ! not that !
MAURYA. [*Smiling.*] The priest has
  secrets from the goddess ?
CRIOSDA.
[*With a cry as of physical pain, deadly sharp.*
          Stop !
No jesting there.
MAURYA.      I did not mean to jest.
As brother to sister ?
CRIOSDA.      Ah ! that hurts, that hurts.
MAURYA. I am heavy ?
CRIOSDA.  Heavy as my own heart's fear.
MAURYA. You fear? Am I in fault? Is
  Maurya maid
The foe to Maurya goddess ?
CRIOSDA.          Ah, indeed !
MAURYA. Is not the work nigh ready ?
[CRIOSDA *grips his caduceus, which
he has dropped, and presses it
savagely to his breast. Then, with
a mingled burst of ferocity and joy,
dashes* MAURYA *aside to the ground,
reaches his hand towards the empty
throne, apostrophising it, and cries
with a strident laugh :*

CRIOSDA.　　　　　　　　　Ay, to-night!
[*A spasm overcomes him and he falls prone.*
MAURYA. Criosda! You are ill, ill!
Help!
　　[*He is silent; she unclasps the
　　leopard's skin, and busies herself
　　in trying to restore him.*
Janet! Angus! Angus!
　　　　　　　　　　[*Under her breath.*
Angus is the man—he saved poor Kenneth!
　　　　　　　　　　[*Aloud.*
Angus! Oh, miserable! No help comes
here.
Criosda! wake! wake!—
Oh, I must take him out—no man may enter
here!—It is ill luck. Old Andrew found
the passage! and the next day he was dead
—murdered, murdered! Oh, how horrible!
—what a horrible place this is with all its
beauty and love! and my worship—oh, how
strange it all is. Criosda! come!
　　[*She begins to carry him to the great
　　door, then notices his white robe.*
This must come off: they must not see the
holy robes.
Criosda! my darling dear brother, do look
at me!
　　[*She has removed the robes.* CRIOSDA
　　*is now seen to be dressed in a dark-
　　green tartan kilt and quasi-military
　　tunic with silver buttons. A dirk
　　hangs at his side. Its hilt is of
　　unusual shape, being surmounted
　　by the circle and cross familiar to
　　visitors to Iona.*
Criosda! Ah yes, look up, look up!
How pale you are! There is no blood in
your lips.
CRIOSDA.
　　[*Starting violently from her arms.*
　　　Blood! Blood!
MAURYA. Lie still, dear, you are ill.
Now! That is better. Come—can you
walk a little?—we will get Angus to help.
CRIOSDA. No! No! I am well! I am
well! Go, go!
If you love me, go. I cannot bear it
longer.

Your presence is my pain. There is nothing
here.
Nothing—leave me!
MAURYA.　　　　Criosda, my own brother!
CRIOSDA. Go! O devil! Devil! Maurya!
　　[*He reaches out a threatening arm
　　against the empty throne. Sud-
　　denly, with an inarticulate noise
　　in his throat, he again collapses.*
MAURYA. Oh! Oh! he must come out
and be tended. Where is the lever? Here—
　　[*Still supporting him on one arm,
　　she raises a ponderous knocker and
　　lets it fall. A clang, sombre, and
　　of surprising volume, resounds.
　　The door slowly opens of itself.*
CRIOSDA. [*Recovering.*] Who is at the
door? Back, back. It is ill luck, ill luck,
I say. Where is old Andrew? The faithful
fool—Oh, the last dreadful look of his glazed
eyes! What am I saying? Maurya, girl,
go! I must tend the temple. I must be
alone. It is not fitting—
MAURYA. You are ill; come and be
tended yourself, first.
CRIOSDA. No! I am well. You are a
girl, not a God.
MAURYA. Oh! Oh! Have I done amiss?
Am I not——
CRIOSDA. Stop, don't!
[*Aside.*] I must be man—tut! tut!—
[*Aloud.*] Why, little sister, know
Those whom we worship as our gods are
gods.
The power is mine: that art no skill resists.
No God dethrones himself; none can.
Will he, nill he, God must be God: it is a
luckless fate for a girl's dower, a thank-
less way for a maiden's feet.
MAURYA. Why, then, am I not the
Goddess Maurya?
CRIOSDA. Yes! yes! of course, but only
by my making.
MAURYA. Was not my birth miraculous?
and strange
The death of the old people of this house
That left you guardian?
CRIOSDA.　　　　Yes, girl, that was strange

MAURYA. Then, is the power that makes
   me in the end
True Goddess Maurya, yours, yours only?
   CRIOSDA. [*Solemnly.*] No!
Stop! ask no more! There lies the awful crux.
Blind are fate's eyes, and pinioned are will's
   wings.
In you the whole chance lies.
   MAURYA.                    In me?
   CRIOSDA.                          In you.
   MAURYA. I will do all to win!
   CRIOSDA.                       Do all?
   MAURYA.                        Do all.
   CRIOSDA. Ah then! No, no, it is not yet
   enough.
Not definite yet. Stop! fool, shall I hint
   and ruin all with a word? Backwards
   or forwards, the blow goes home either
   way. [*Looks at her with keen fierce eyes.*]
   Ah!
   MAURYA. [*A little frightened.*] Come,
   O my brother!
It is time to go.
   CRIOSDA. No! leave me. It is but an hour.
     [MAURYA *smiles; leaves her hand a*
      *little in his, and so passes out*
      *slowly through the open door with*
      *her eyes fixed in love and trust on*
      *him.* CRIOSDA *starts up and pulls*
      *fiercely at a second lever, and the*
      *door clangs to with the same nerve-*
      *shattering shock.* CRIOSDA *staggers*
      *to altar; and, with his hand on it,*
      *turns towards door.*
Mouths of God's mercy! I would her eyes
Were bleeding wounds in my heart! Ah
though! If she were a dog I could not do
it. She is my sister——
     [*Turns with a cry to throne and*
      *flings up his hands.*
and I will!
Death! Death!
It is a year to-night. I arrayed her first
In yon gold ornaments—My brain is sick!
I want coffee—or hashish—No! That is for
   her!
I must be very clear and calm, very clear,
   very calm,

How I must be ill—
   [*Correcting himself with effort.*] Ill I
   must be. Ha!
   [*Goes to altar, opens it, takes out a*
     *flask filled with a clear pale blue*
     *liquor with rosy stars of light in*
     *it, pours it into a long vial, and*
     *holds it to the light. The room*
     *is lighted by electricity, the globes*
     *being the eyes of strange sculpturea*
     *stone beasts on the walls.*
So far the story is true.
                [*Drinks a little.*
Why, that is better already. I am again
the priest of Maurya—who is the brother
of Maurya? A trivial ape o' the time!—
cold, logical to a fault!—Ay! and a crime,
a crime at which the stars shake in the
heaven, men might think. Yet the stars,
I will wager, are indifferent. True, the
news has not reached them: true, that star
I see is not a star; it was so six, ten, twenty
thousand years ago—logical, I say!—and I
will drink, for parenthetical is a poor
substitute--
                   [*Drinks.*
Why, how thou fir'st me! with that icy fire
Of adamant thought. It well befits this hour
If I recoil the chain whose last smooth link
Slides o'er Time's cogwheel. In the be-
   ginning then
The vastness of the heavens and the earth
Created the idea of God. So Levi once
Sarcastic in apostasy; à rebours.
So Müller, mythopoeic in his mood
Of the unmasking mythopoeia. Now
Profounder science, Spencer's amplitude,
Allen's too shallow erudition, Frazer's
Research, find men have made—since men
   made aught—
Their Gods, and slain, and eaten. Sur-
   face! I,
Criosda of the Mist, see truth in all
Rather than truth in none. Below the rite,
The sight! Beyond the priest, the power!
   Above
The sense, the soul! So men who made
   their gods

Did make in very deed : so I will make
In uttermost truth a new god, since the old
Are dead, or drunk with wine, and soma-
    juice
And hemp and opium ! Maurya, thou shalt be!
So for long years I have dared.  First the
    twin death
Of the dotards, slow constraint of Maurya's
    mind
To the one end.  Next, study : next, research
In places long-forgotten of the West,
Deep hidden of the East : the perfect rite
Dragged by laborious hand and brain to shape
And this [*Raises glass*] the first fruits ! Hail,
    thou fount of wit,
Light liquor, child of cares how heavy! Drink!
The peace of the Priest !
                    [*He drinks up the liquor.*
                    Be thou my light !
Uncloud the misty channels of the mind !
Off, horror !  Off, compassion !  Be the brain
The almighty engine of the Will—and those
Subtler and deeper forces grimly guessed,
Terribly proven—be they strong thereby !
Awake, O sleeping serpent of the soul,
Unhinted skills, and unimagined powers,
And purposes undreamed of !
        [*He goes now calmly about the temple,
        arranging all the ornaments.  He
        empties the censer.*
                    Shadowy influence
Of smoke !  Where lies its physiologic act ?
What drug conceals the portent ?  Mystery !
Mystery ninefold closed upon itself
That matter should move mind—Ay ! darker
    yet
That mind should work on matter ?  And
    the proof
Extant, implicit in the thought thereof !
Else all our work were vain.  These twain
    be one ;
And in their essence ?  Deeper, deeper yet
I dive.
        [*He draws the dirk and tests the point.*
        And will to-morrow show me aught ?
        [*He extinguishes the lamps, goes to
        the door and opens it.  The clang
        startles him.*

I hate that door !  Strange that the outer
    air
Should bring back manhood !  Man, thou
    pitiest her !
Man, thou art whelmed in that red tide of
    lust
That rolls over strong loathing by vast will,
Hideous rapture of death.  That's for thee
    man !
Thine are the scalding tears of sympathy,
The tender love for the young flower.  And
    these
Are none of the priest's.  Enough !
        [*Exit.  The door clangs again.  The
        curtain falls ;  a scene drops.
        RUPHA, an aged and wizened hag,
        of gigantic stature, is discovered
        seated, C.  The scene represents a
        lonely hill-top covered with stones.
        A little coarse grass grows in places.
        Three great menhirs stand up, C.
        Moonlight.*
RUPHA.  The rune of the breath.
        The saga of death.
        The secret of earth.
        The beginning of birth.
        The speech of woe.
        Ho ! Ho !

        I scent the prey.
        I sniff the air.
        The dawn of day
        Makes Maurya May
        The Goddess rare.
        The light of the stars
        Be hers ;  go, go,
        Ye silent folk,
        Harness your cars !
        Brace the yoke !
        It is time to Know.
        Ho ! Ho !

        Desolate deeds !
        She bleeds, she bleeds.
        The golden head
        Is drooped for aye.
        She is dead, she is dead.
        She is God, and I ?

I am might.
I am power.
I am light
For an hour.
I am strong, I grow.
Ho! Ho!


I taught Criosda
The evil runes.
Mine were the tunes
His passion sang.
Mine is the clang
Of the olden door.
Half the secret
I gave: no more!
Half the secret
Hidden I keep.
Hide it deep!
That is mine!
I will work.
He is nought.
The runes divine
Awry be wrought.
Hail to the murk!
                [*A distant whine is heard.*
Cover me! Lurk,
Rupha, lurk!
'Tis a foe.
Ho! Ho!
[*Clouds have been obscuring the moon;*
*it is now dark. A fox passes over*
*the stage.*
Crafty! Crafty!
That is the omen.
Fear not the foemen!
                [*She rises up.*
Mine is the spoil
Of the grimly toil.
Gloomy, gloomy!
Ah! but I laugh.
He is but a fool.
He has lost!
He is lost!
Take the staff!
Trace the rule
Of the circle crossed!
[*She makes a circle and a cross therein.*

No light therein!
Mother of sin,
Thou hast won!
Death to the sun!
Hail to the glow
Of the corpse decayed!
Hail to the maid!
Ho! Ho!
[*She rambles about the stage, mutter-*
*ing savage runes with dismal*
*laughter. Her words are inarticu-*
*late, when with a last* Ho! Ho!
*the curtain falls.*
[*The scene rises, and we again see*
*the stage as in* Scene I. MAURYA
*and* CRIOSDA *as in the opening.*
CRIOSDA *is, however, absolutely*
*calm.*
MAURYA. Criosda, answer!
CRIOSDA.            I obey, having heard.
MAURYA. This dawn shall see me take
    the final flight?
CRIOSDA.            It shall.
MAURYA. I shall be taken utterly from
    earth?
CRIOSDA.   So.
MAURYA. Yet abide with thee, my priest.
CRIOSDA.                    Ay! Ay!
MAURYA. I feel no early prompting thither.
CRIOSDA.                            No.
It is sudden.
MAURYA. What then lacks?
CRIOSDA.            A draught: a word.
MAURYA. Where is the draught?
CRIOSDA.        This incense in my hand.
MAURYA. What is the word?
                [CRIOSDA *is silent.*
                Criosda, answer me.
CRIOSDA. To invoke death it were to
    answer this.
MAURYA. Ah, then, forbear!
                [CRIOSDA *is silent.*
                How shall I know the word?
CRIOSDA. Good luck may bring it to the
    light.
MAURYA.   Ill luck?
CRIOSDA. A year's delay.
MAURYA.            Ah, let me gain one gift

Whose sweet reversion hangs above me now :
To order luck !
  CRIOSDA. Skill orders luck !
  MAURYA.       The draught !
  CRIOSDA. Hither, O Maurya !
  MAURYA.      I will come to thee.
    [CRIOSDA, *taking hashish, throws it upon the glowing censer.* MAURYA *comes down stage and bends over it.* CRIOSDA *lifts it up and offers it reverently.*
  MAURYA. Methinks anticipation o' the event
Shoots in my veins, darting delight.
Why, this is strange !
I am losing myself. Criosda !
The walls of the world fall back with a crash.
Where is all this? I am out of myself: I expand
O Maurya, where art thou, little phantom
  of myriads of ages ago ? What a
  memory ! Ah ! Ah ! She is falling.
    [MAURYA *staggers.* CRIOSDA, *who has been watching her narrowly, catches her and lays her tenderly on the altar.*
Oh, what happiness, what happiness ! Criosda, dear brother, how I love you !
I wish to sleep for ever—I wish to die !
    [CRIOSDA, *who has been bending over her, leaps up, shrieks.*
  CRIOSDA. The luck of Maurya !
    [*He draws quickly his dirk ; it flashes on high, he leaps on to the body of* MAURYA, *and plunges it into her heart.*

CURTAIN.

ACT II.

FORTY YEARS AFTERWARDS.

*The scene is an open and stormy sea.* RUPHA, *with her staff, wave-riding in a cockleshell.*

  RUPHA.     Ha ! Ha !
    In the storm
    I ride.

The winds bear me.
The waves fear me.
I appal ; I inform
Their pride.
Let him hither,
Drifting ever
Wrecked and lost !
His life shall wither.
The dirk shall sever
His rune ill-crossed.

I hear him come
Across the foam
With a bang and a boom.
The winds, hum, hum.
The billows comb.
Ho ! Ho ! the doom !
Ho ! Ho ! I have won.
I shall win.
Death to the sun !
Life to sin !
They reap who sow.
Ho ! Ho !
    [*A boat drifts in, L. In it the aged* CRIOSDA, *his white hair afloat in the storm, is standing with folded arms. His eyes are dull, as seeing inward.*
  RUPHA. Ha ! Ha !
    'Tis the priest.
    Dost think
    O' the feast ?
    Criosda, shrink !
    The rune is woe.
    Ho ! Ho !
  CRIOSDA. Mother of Sin !
  RUPHA.       Ho ! Ho !
  CRIOSDA. Thus then at last the Luck of Maurya throws
A double-six to lost Criosda.
  RUPHA. Ho !
    The Luck of Maurya !
    The power of the deed.
  CRIOSDA. I find thee, mother, at last.
    Life's final flash
Gleams through the storm.
  RUPHA. I am found !
    Ho ! Ho !

CRIOSDA. What of the power? I bid
these waves be calm
In Maurya's name.
[*The storm increases momently in vio-
lence.* RUPHA *mutters on.* CRIOSDA
*shows with a gesture that he knows
his words avail nothing.*
RUPHA. Ho! Ho!
CRIOSDA. I wittingly and well resumed
the rite
Learnt at thy breast, old wolf!
RUPHA. Ho! Ho!
    The might is mine
    O' the rune divine.
    Silence, winds!
    Peace, ye waves!
    The spell binds
    Their wrath
    In the graves
    Below ocean.
    Clear the path!
    Cease your motion?
    Swift, be slow!
    Ho! Ho!
        [*The storm ceases.*
CRIOSDA. *Thy* words avail then?
RUPHA. Ha! Ha!
    They avail.
    I avail.
    Did Rupha fail,
    All would be done.
    Death to the sun!
    I know.
    Ho! Ho!
CRIOSDA. All this I did for thee?
RUPHA. Ha! Ha!
    What didst thou do?
    Ha! Ha!
    Ha! Ha!
CRIOSDA. What did I not do? All!
RUPHA. Tell! Tell!
    'Tis a spell.
CRIOSDA. I will tell all. O sea, swallow
me up
With the last word!
RUPHA. It obeys?
    No! No!
    Ho! Ho!

CRIOSDA. Thou sinister one! Thy rite
I duly did;
That drugged (and dancing with delight
thereof
The maiden's mind) the maiden's body prone
Lay on her altar. Then she gave consent,
And I smote once.
RUPHA. Ha! Ha!
    What came then?
CRIOSDA. I tore out her heart,
And held its flame aloft. The blackening
blood
Gushed on my arms—and then—
RUPHA. Ho! Ho!
CRIOSDA. With red lips reeking from the
sweet foul feast,
I sang in tuneless agony the spell;
Rolled athwart space the black words: then
some force
Tore me: I heard the tears drop in my
heart.
I heard the laughter of some utmost God
Hid in the middle of matter. That was I,
The hideous laugher of the maniac laugh
When loathing makes the bed to lust, and
twine
The limbs of agony about the trunk
Of torture — rapture stabbing through—
Maurya!
Ay, that was I; and I the weeping wolf
That howls about this hell that is my heart;
And I the icy and intangible
That beholds all, and is not.
RUPHA. Three in one!
    One in three!
    Death to the sun!
    Glory to thee!
    Thou wast there!
    Enough!
    It will grow.
    Ho! Ho!
CRIOSDA. In English, I was mad. But
no new portents
Confound the course of the sun. I left my
home
To seek thee out. When skill availed me
not,
I put to sea to try the Luck of Maurya.

RUPHA. Thou shouldst have tried that
first of all.
CRIOSDA.            Why then
The Luck may avail if that wried tongue
can speak
Straight! Hast thou aught to bid me do?
To me naught matters more. My life I cast
On the one throw; and, having lost, I have
lost.
I am indifferent to my fate as the stars
Are to my curses, were I fool enough
To curse.
RUPHA. Destiny has strange ways.
CRIOSDA.                I care not.
RUPHA. How long hast thou left home?
CRIOSDA.              Seven years.
RUPHA.                Return!
CRIOSDA.             How can I?
RUPHA. Stamp the boat beneath thy feet
Down wallowing in the trough!
CRIOSDA.              It is done!
    [*The boat sinks from under* CRIOSDA.
    *He would sink did he not grasp the
    staff extended to him.*
RUPHA. Now, stand alone!
CRIOSDA.                 I stand.
RUPHA.          Then break, O vision
Of sea; awake, O vision of the shrine!
CRIOSDA. All is illusion?
RUPHA.               All. Murder a mode
And love a mode of the unknown that is,
That nor thyself nor I can ever see.
Yet, so far as may be, awake, O shrine!
    [*She strikes the sea with her staff;
    the storm rises; it grows bitter
    dark; only their shapes are dimly
    seen against the dark background
    of cloud. The scene rises.*
RUPHA. Break, break, O mist of morning!
    [*The stage, which is full of mist,
    gradually clears. It shows the
    Temple as in* Scene I. *On the
    throne the embalmed body of*
    MAURYA *is seated. The altar
    flames with glowing charcoal, and
    a thin steam of incense arises.*
    RUPHA *and* CRIOSDA *are in front,
    R. Two priests minister; a goodly*

*crew of choristers intone low litanies.
A few young folk are at a barrier
by the footlights (centre) in prayer.
An old woman enters and brings
an offering of flowers, which the
priests receive and cast before the
throne.* RUPHA *motions* CRIOSDA
*to be silent.*
1st PRIEST. Glory unto thee, Maurya,
secret Lady of the Stars!
CHORISTERS. Who wast born on earth!
2nd PRIEST. Glory unto thee, Maurya,
Lady of Life!
CHORISTERS. Who didst die for us!
ALL. Glory for ever unto Maurya!
THE WORSHIPPING FOLK. Maurya, hear
us!
    [*All bend deeper and deeper in adora-
    tion. Silence awhile. They rise,
    and the priests see* RUPHA *and*
    CRIOSDA.
1st PRIEST. [*Whispers.*] It is the Mother
of our Lady.
2nd PRIEST. [*Whispers.*] Who is with her?
1st PRIEST. [*Whispers.*] The first disciple.
2nd PRIEST. [*Whispers.*] Blessed is this
day, O brother!
1st PRIEST. [*Whispers.*] Let us go and
do them reverence.
    [*They approach* RUPHA *and* CRIOSDA,
    *and bend low before them.*
RUPHA. Criosda! Of one act the ultimation
Rings through eternity past the poles of space.
Choose then what spangle on the robe of time
Shall glitter in thine eyes: for the hour
strikes.
CRIOSDA. Mother! I would see the Luck
of Maurya stand
Two thousand years from now.
RUPHA. Good priest, bring forth
The globe of crystal.
1st PRIEST.            Hearing is enough.
    [*The priest takes a crystal from out
    the altar, and places it thereupon.*
    RUPHA *and* CRIOSDA *advance.*
RUPHA. Look! I uplift the veil.
    [*She unveils the crystal.*

CRIOSDA. I see a lofty pyramid sun-white
Blaze in immaculate glory to the stars ;
Its splendour of itself, since all is dark
About, above.    Thereon a countless folk,
Multitudes many-coloured, grave and tall,
Beautiful, make a beautiful murmur, move,
In infinite musical labyrinths about.
Them doth the soul of love inhabit, them
The light of wisdom doth inform, them
    peace
Hath marked and sealed her own.   But on
    their lips
Is one imagined silence like a sigh.
Unanimous the hushèd harmony
Flows forth from heart to mouth ; and
    mouths bloom red
With ripe and royal repetition ; kisses
Flow like thick honey-drops in honeysuckle.
That is their worship.
    RUPHA. Whom then worship they ?

CRIOSDA.                               Maurya !
    [*Recalled to himself, he perceives the
    meaning of this ; with a great cry
    breaks forward and stands before
    the throne, raises himself up and
    says in triumph and knowledge of
    peace :*
Then—I have lived !
    [*Reaches out his hand towards the
    enthroned mummy.*
                                    Maurya !
    [*With the last terrible cry he collapses,
    and falls dead with his head on
    MAURYA'S knees.*
RUPHA. As it was in the beginning, is
now, and ever shall be : world without end.
    [*She deliberately breaks her staff in
    her hands.   The report is sharp
    and very loud, like a pistol shot.*

CURTAIN.

# THE SWORD OF SONG

CALLED BY CHRISTIANS

## THE BOOK OF THE BEAST

1904

TO MY OLD FRIEND AND COMRADE IN THE ART

### BHIKKHU ANANDA METTEYA

AND TO THOSE

### FOOLS

WHO BY THEIR SHORT-SIGHTED STUPIDITY IN
ATTEMPTING TO BOYCOTT THIS BOOK
HAVE WITLESSLY AIDED THE
CAUSE OF TRUTH

I DEDICATE THESE MY BEST WORDS

[This book is so full of recondite knowledge of various kinds that it seems quite ineffective to annotate every obscure passage. Where references and explanations can be concisely given, this has been done.]

"You are sad!" the Knight said, in an anxious tone; "let me sing you a song to comfort you." *

"Is it very long?" Alice asked.

"It's long," said the Knight, "but it's *very very* beautiful. The name of the song is called 'The Book of the Beast.'"

"Oh! how ugly!" cried Alice.

"Never mind," said the mild creature. "*Some* people call it 'Reason in Rhyme.'"

"But which *is* the name of the song?" Alice said, trying not to seem too interested.

"Ah, you don't understand," the Knight said, looking a little vexed. "That's what the name is *called*. The name really *is* 'Ascension Day and Pentecost; with some Prose Essays and an Epilogue,' just as the title is 'The Sword of Song' you know, just in the same way, just in the same way, just in the same way . . ."

Alice put her fingers in her ears and gave a little scream. "Oh, dear me! That's

harder than ever!" she said to herself, and then, looking determinedly intelligent: "So *that's* what the song is called. I see. But what *is* the song?"

"You must be a perfect fool," said the Knight, irritably. "The song is called 'Stout Doubt; or the Agnostic's Anthology,' by the author of 'Gas Manipulation,' 'Solutions,' 'The Management of Retorts,' and other physical works of the first order—but that's only what it's *called*, you know."

"Well, what *is* the song then?" said Alice, who was by this time completely bewildered.

"If I wished to be obscure, child," said the Knight, rather contemptuously, "I should tell you that the Name of the Title was 'What a man of 95 ought to know,' as endorsed by eminent divines, and that . . ." Seeing that she only began to cry, he broke off and continued in a gentler tone: "it *means*, my dear . . ." He stopped short, for she was taking no notice; but as her figure was bent by sobs into something very like a note of interrogation: "You want to know what it *is*,

* This passage is a parody on one in "Alice through the Looking-Glass."

140

I suppose!" continued the Knight, in a superior, but rather offended voice.

"If you would, please, sir!"

"Well, *that*," pronounced the Knight, with the air of having thoroughly studied the question and reached a conclusion absolutely final and irreversible, "*that*, Goodness only knows. But I will sing it to you."

## PRELIMINARY INVOCATION.

### NOTHUNG.*

THE crowns of Gods and mortals wither;
  Moons fade where constellations shone;
Numberless aeons brought us hither;
  Numberless aeons beckon us on.
The world is old, and I am strong—
Awake, awake, O Sword of Song!

Here, in the Dusk of Gods, I linger;
  The world awaits a Word of Truth.
Kindle, O lyre, beneath my finger!
  Evoke the age's awful youth!
To arms against the inveterate wrong!
Awake, awake, O Sword of Song!

Sand-founded reels the House of Faith;
  Up screams the howl of ruining sect;
Out from the shrine flits the lost Wraith;
  "God hath forsaken His elect!"
Confusion sweeps upon the throng—
Awake, awake, O Sword of Song!

Awake to wound, awake to heal
  By wounding, thou resistless sword!
Raise the prone priestcrafts that appeal
  In agony to their prostrate Lord!
Raise the duped herd—they have suffered long!
Awake, awake, O Sword of Song!

My strength this agony of the age
  Win through; my music charm the old
Sorrow of years: my warfare wage
  By iron to an age of gold:—
The world is old, and I am strong—
Awake, awake, O Sword of Song!

  * The name of Siegfried's sword.

## INTRODUCTION TO "ASCENSION DAY AND PENTECOST."

NOT a word to introduce my introduction! Let me instantly launch the Boat of Discourse on the Sea of Religious Speculation, in danger of the Rocks of Authority and the Quicksands of Private Interpretation, Scylla and Charybdis. Here is the strait; what God shall save us from shipwreck? If we choose to understand the Christian (or any other) religion literally, we are at once overwhelmed by its inherent impossibility. Our credulity is outraged, our moral sense shocked, the holiest foundations of our inmost selves assailed by no ardent warrior in triple steel, but by a loathly and disgusting worm. That this is so, the apologists for the religion in question, whichever it may be, sufficiently indicate (as a rule) by the very method of their apology. The alternative is to take the religion symbolically, esoterically; but to move one step in this direction is to start on a journey whose end cannot be determined. The religion, ceasing to be a tangible thing, an object uniform for all sane eyes, becomes rather that mist whereon the sun of the soul casts up, like Brocken spectre, certain vast and vague images of the beholder himself, with or without a glory encompassing them. The function of the facts is then quite passive: it matters little or nothing whether the cloud be the red mist of Christianity, or the glimmering silver-white of Celtic Paganism; the hard grey dim-gilded of Buddhism, the fleecy opacity of Islam, or the mysterious medium of those ancient faiths which come up in as many colours as their investigator has moods.*

  * "In order to get over the ethical difficulties presented by the naïve naturalism of many parts of those Scriptures, in the divine authority of which he firmly believed, Philo borrowed from the Stoics (who had been in like straits in respect of Greek mythology) that great Excalibur which they had forged with infinite pains and skill—the method of allegorical interpretation. This mighty 'two-handed engine at the door' of the theologian is warranted to make a speedy end of any and every moral or intellectual difficulty, by showing that, taken allegorically, or, as it is otherwise said, 'poetically' or 'in a spiritual sense,' the plainest words mean whatever a pious interpreter desires they should mean" (Huxley, "Evolution of Theology").—A. C.

If the student has advanced spiritually so that he can internally, infallibly perceive what is Truth, he will find it equally well symbolised in most external faiths.

It is curious that Browning never turns his wonderful faculty of analysis upon the fundamental problems of religion, as it were an axe laid to the root of the Tree of Life. It seems quite clear that he knew what would result if he did so. We cannot help fancying that he was unwilling to do this. The proof of his knowledge I find in the following lines :—

"I have read much, thought much, experi-
   enced much,
Yet would die rather than avow my fear
The Naples' liquefaction may be false . . .
I hear you recommend, I might at least
Eliminate, decrassify my faith
Since I adopt it : keeping what I must
And leaving what I can ; such points as this . . .
Still, when you bid me purify the same,
To such a process I discern no end . . .
First cut the liquefaction, what comes last
But Fichte's clever cut at God himself? . . .
I trust nor hand, nor eye, nor heart, nor brain
To stop betimes : they all get drunk alike.
The first step, I am master not to take."

This is surely the apotheosis of wilful ignorance ! We may think, perhaps, that Browning is "hedging" when, in the last paragraph, he says : " For Blougram, he believed, say, half he spoke," * and hints at some deeper ground. It is useless to say, "This is Blougram and not Browning." Browning could hardly have described the dilemma without seeing it. What he really believes is, perhaps, a mystery.

That Browning, however, believes in universal salvation, though he nowhere (so far as I know) gives his reasons, save as they are summarised in the last lines of the below-quoted passage, is evident from the last stanza of "Apparent Failure," and from his final pronouncement of the Pope on Guido, represented in Browning's master-piece as a Judas without the decency to hang himself.

" So (i.e., by suddenness of fate) may the
   truth be flashed out by one blow,
And Guido see one instant and be saved.
Else I avert my face nor follow him
Into that sad obscure sequestered state
Where God unmakes but to remake the soul
He else made first in vain : which must not be."

* Probably a record for a bishop.—A. C.

This may be purgatory, but it sounds not unlike reincarnation.

It is at least a denial of the doctrine of eternal punishment.

As for myself, I took the first step years ago, quite in ignorance of what the last would lead to. God is indeed cut away— a cancer from the breast of truth.

Of those philosophers, who from unassailable premisses draw by righteous deduction a conclusion against God, and then for His sake overturn their whole structure by an act of will, like a child breaking an ingenious toy, I take Mansel as my type. *

Now, however, let us consider the esoteric idea-mongers of Christianity, Swedenborg, Anna Kingsford, Deussen and the like, of whom I have taken Caird as my example. I wish to unmask these people : I perfectly agree with nearly everything they say, but their claim to be Christians is utterly confusing, and lends a lustre to Christianity which is quite foreign. Deussen, for example, coolly discards nearly all the Old Testament, and, picking a few New Testament passages, often out of their context, claims his system as Christianity. Luther discards James. Kingsford calls Paul the Arch Heretic. My friend the " Christian Clergyman " accepted Mark and Acts—until pushed. Yet Deussen is honest enough to admit that Vedanta teaching is identical, but clearer ! and he quite clearly and sensibly defines Faith — surely the most essential quality for the adherent to Christian dogma —as " being convinced on insufficient evidence." Similarly the dying-to-live idea of Hegel (and Schopenhauer) claimed by Caird as the central spirit of Christianity is far older, in the Osiris Myth of the Egyptians. These ideas are all right, but they have no more to do with Christianity than the Metric System with the Great Pyramid. But see Piazzi Smyth ! † Henry Morley has even the audacity to claim Shelley—Shelley !—as a Christian " in spirit."

Talking of Shelley :—With regard to my open denial of the personal Christian God, may it not be laid to my charge that I have dared to voice in bald language what Shelley

* As represented by his Encyclopædia article; not in such works as " Limits of Religious Thought."—A. C.

† An astronomer whose brain gave way. He prophesied the end of the world in 1881, from measurements made in the Great Pyramid.

sang in words of surpassing beauty: for of course the thought in one or two passages of this poem is practically identical with that in certain parts of " Queen Mab " and " Prometheus Unbound." But the very beauty of these poems (especially the latter) is its weakness: it is possible that the mind of the reader, lost in the sensuous, nay ! even in the moral beauty of the words, may fail to be impressed by their most important meaning. Shelley himself recognised this later : hence the direct and simple vigour of the " Masque of Anarchy."

It has often puzzled atheists how a man of Milton's genius could have written as he did of Christianity. But we must not forget that Milton lived immediately after the most important Revolution in Religion and Politics of modern times : Shelley on the brink of such another Political upheaval. Shakespeare alone sat enthroned above it all like a god, and is not lost in the mire of controversy.* This also, though " I'm no Shakespeare, as too probable," I have endeavoured to avoid : yet I cannot but express the hope that my own enquiries into religion may be the reflection of the spirit of the age ; and that plunged as we are in the midst of jingoism and religious revival, we may be standing on the edge of some gigantic precipice, over which we may cast all our impedimenta of lies and trickeries, political, social, moral, and religious, and (ourselves) take wings and fly. The comparison between myself and the masters of English thought I have named is unintentional, though perhaps unavoidable ; and though the presumption is, of course, absurd, yet a straw will show which way the wind blows as well as the most beautiful and elaborate vane : and in this sense it is my most eager hope that I may not unjustly draw a comparison between myself and the great reformers of eighty years ago.

* So it is usually supposed. Maybe I shall one day find words to combat, perhaps to overthrow, this position. P.S. As, for example, page 185. As a promise-keeper I am the original eleven stone three Peacherine.—A. C.

I must apologise (perhaps) for the new note of frivolity in my work : due doubtless to the frivolity of my subject : these poems being written when I was an Advaitist and could not see why—everything being an illusion—there should be any particular object in doing or thinking anything. How I have found the answer will be evident from my essay on this subject.* I must indeed apologise to the illustrious Shade of Robert Browning for my audacious parody in title, style, and matter of his " Christmas Eve and Easter Day." The more I read it the eventual anticlimax of that wonderful poem irritated me only the more. But there is hardly any poet living or dead who so commands alike my personal affection and moral admiration. My desire to find the Truth will be my pardon with him, whose whole life was spent in admiration of Truth, though he never turned its formidable engines against the Citadel of the Almighty.

If I be appealed of blasphemy or irreverence in my treatment of these subjects, I will take refuge in Browning's own apology, from the very poem I am attacking :

" I have done : and if any blames me,
Thinking that merely to touch in brevity
  The topics I dwell on were unlawful—
Or worse, that I trench with undue levity
On the bounds of the holy and the awful—
I praise the heart and pity the head of him,
  And refer myself to Thee, instead of him,
Who head and heart alike discernest,
  Looking below light speech we utter
Where frothy spume and frequent splutter
  Prove that the soul's depths boil in earnest ! "

But I have after all little fear that I am seriously wrong. That I show to my critics the open door of the above city of refuge may be taken as merely another gesture of contemptuous pity, the last insult which may lead my antagonists to that surrender which is the truest victory.

PEACE TO ALL BEINGS.

* Vide infra, " Berashith."

# ASCENSION DAY

Curious posi-
tion of poet.

I FLUNG out of chapel [1] * and church,
   Temple and hall and meeting-room,
   Venus' Bower and Osiris' Tomb,[2]
And left the devil in the lurch,
   While God [3] got lost in the crowd of gods,[4]      5
And soul went down [5] in the turbid tide
Of the metaphysical lotus-eyed,[6]
   And I was—anyhow, what's the odds?

What is Truth?
said jesting
Pilate: but
Crowley waits
for an answer.†

The life to live? The thought to think? Shall I take refuge
In a tower like once Childe Roland ‡ [7] found, blind, deaf, huge, 10
Or in that forest of two hundred thousand
Trees,[8] fit alike to shelter man and mouse, and—
Shall I say God? Be patient, your Reverence,[9]
I warrant you'll journey a wiser man ever hence !
Let's tap (like the negro who gets a good juice of it,      15
Cares nought if that be, or be not, God's right use of it),[10]
In all that forest of verses one tree [11]
Yclept " Red Cotton Nightcap Country " :
How a goldsmith, between the Ravishing Virgin
And a leman too rotten to put a purge in,      20
Day by day and hour by hour,
In a Browningesque forest of thoughts having lost himself,
Expecting a miracle, solemnly tossed himself
Off from the top of a tower.
Moral : don't spoil such an excellent sport as an      25
Ample estate with a church and a courtesan !

Alternative
theories of
Greek authors.
Browning's
summary.

" Truth, that's the gold ! " [12] But don't worry about it !
I, you, or Simpkin [13] can get on without it !
If life's task be work and love's (the soft-lippèd) ease,
Death's be God's glory ? discuss with Euripides !      30

* The numbered notes are given at p. 190.
† Bacon, " Essay on Truth," line 1.
‡ " Childe Roland to the dark Tower came."—BROWNING.

Or, cradle be hardship, and finally coffin, ease,
Love being filth? let us ask Aristophanes!
Or, heaven's sun bake us, while Earth's bugs and fleas kill us,
Love the God's scourge?   I refer you to Aeschylus!
5       (Nay! that's a slip!   Say we "Earth's grim device, cool
        loss!—"
Better the old Greek orthography!—Aischulos![14])
Or, love be God's champagne's foam; death in man's
        trough, hock lees,
Pathos our port's beeswing? what answers Sophocles?
Brief, with love's medicine let's draught, bolus, globule us!
10     Wise and succinct bids, I think, Aristobulus.[15]
Whether my Muse be Euterpe or Clio,
Life, Death, and Love are all Batrachomyo[16]—
Machia, what? ho! old extinct Alcibiades?
For me, do ut—God true, be mannikin liar!—des!

45     It's rather hard, isn't it, sir, to make sense of it?
Mine of so many pounds—pouch even pence of it?[17]
Try something easier,[18] where the bard seems to me
Seeking that light, which I find come in dreams to me.
Even as he takes two feasts to enlarge upon,
50     So will I do too to launch my old barge upon.
Analyse, get hints from Newton[19] or Faraday,[20]
Use every weapon—love, scorn, reason, parody!
Just where he worships?   Ah me! shall his soul,
Far in some glory, take hurt from a mole
55     Grubbing i' th' ground?   Shall his spirit not see,
Lightning to lightning, the spirit in me?
Parody?   Shall not his spirit forgive
Me, who shall love him as long as I live?
Love's at its height in pure love?   Nay, but after
60     When the song's light dissolves gently in laughter!
Then and then only the lovers may know
Nothing can part them for ever.   And so,
Muse, hover o'er me!   Apollo, above her!

I, of the Moderns, have let alone Greek.[21]
65     Out of the way Intuition shall shove her.
Spirit and Truth in my darkness I seek.
Little by little they bubble and leak;
Such as I have to the world I discover.
Words—are they weak ones at best?   They shall speak!

*Margin notes:*

Apology of poet. Skeleton of poem. Valuable fact for use of lovers. Invocation.

Imperfect scholastic attainments of author remedied by his great spiritual insight. His intention.

| | |
|---|---|

His achieve-
ment.
Plan of poem
"Conspuez
Dieu!"

Shields?  Be they paper, paint, lath?  They shall cover          70
Well as they may, the big heart of a lover !
Swords?   Let the lightning of Truth strike the fortress
Frowning of God !  I will sever one more tress
Off the White Beard [22] with his son's blood besprinkled,
Carve one more gash in the forehead [23] hate-wrinkled :—          75
So, using little arms, earn one day better ones ;
Cutting the small chains,[24] learn soon to unfetter one's
Limbs from the large ones, walk forth and be free !—
So much for Browning ! and so much for me !

Apology for
manner of
poem.
A chance for
Tibet.

Pray do not ask me where I stand !          80
"Who asks, doth err." [25]   At least demand
No folly such as answer means !
" But if " (you [26] say) "your spirit weans
Itself of milk-and-water pap,
And one religion as another          85
O'erleaps itself and falls on the other ; [27]
You'll tell me why at least, mayhap,
Our Christianity excites
Especially such petty spites
As these you strew throughout your verse."          90
The chance of birth !  I choose to curse
(Writing in English [28]) just the yoke
Of faith that tortures English folk.
I cannot write [29] a poem yet
To please the people in Tibet ;          95
But when I can, Christ shall not lack
Peace, while their Buddha I attack.[30]

Hopes.   Iden-
tity of poet.
Attention
drawn to my
highly decora-
tive cover.

Yet by-and-by I hope to weave
A song of Anti-Christmas Eve
And First- and Second-Beast-er Day.          100
There's one *[31] who loves me dearly (vrai!)
Who yet believes me sprung from Tophet,
Either the Beast or the False Prophet ;
And by all sorts of monkey tricks
Adds up my name to Six Six Six.          105
Retire, good Gallup ![32]  In such strife her
Superior skill makes *you* a cipher !

* Crowley's mother.

Ho ! I adopt the number.  Look
At the quaint wrapper of this book ! *
10    I will deserve it if I can :
It is the number of a Man.[33]

So since in England Christ still stands          Necessity of
With iron nails in bloody hands                  poem.
Not pierced, but grasping ! to hoist high
15    Children on cross of agony,
I find him real for English lives.
Up with my pretty pair of fives ![34]
I fight no ghosts.

                          " But why revile "      Mysticism *v.*
20    (You urge me) " in that vicious style        literal interpre-
The very faith whose truths you seem             tation.  Former
(Elsewhere) [35] to hold, to hymn supreme        excused.
In your own soul ? "  Perhaps you know
How mystic doctrines melt the snow
25    Of any faith : redeem it to
A fountain of reviving dew.
So I with Christ : but few receive
The Qabalistic Balm,[36] believe
Nothing—and choose to know instead.
30    But, to that terror vague and dread,
External worship ; all my life—
War to the knife !  War to the knife !

No ! on the other hand the Buddha              Buddha re-
Says : " I'm surprised at you !  How could a    bukes poet.
                                                Detailed
35    Person accept my law and still             scheme of
Use hatred, the sole means of ill,             modified poem.
In Truth's defence ?  In praise of light ? "
Well !  Well !  I guess Brer Buddha's right !
I am no brutal Cain [37] to smash an Abel ;
40    I hear that blasphemy's unfashionable :
So in the quietest way we'll chat about it ;
No need to show teeth, claws of cat about it !
With gentle words—fiat exordium ;
Exeat dolor, intret gaudium !

* It had a design of 666 and Crowley's name in Hebrew (which, like
nost names, adds up to that figure) on the reverse.

We'll have the ham to logic's sandwich                     145
Of indignation : last bread bland, which
After our scorn of God's lust, terror, hate,
Prometheus-fired, we'll butter, perorate
With oiled indifference, laughter's silver :
" Omne hoc verbum    let nil, vir " !                      150

Let me help Babu Chander Grish up !
As by a posset of Hunyadi [38]
Clear mind !  Was Soudan of the Mahdi
Not cleared by Kitchener ?  Ah, Tchhup !
Such nonsense for sound truth you dish up,    155
Were I magician, no mere cadi,
Not Samuel's ghost you'd make me wish up,
Nor Saul's (the mighty son of Kish) up,
But Ingersoll's or Bradlaugh's, pardie !
By spells and caldron stews that squish up,   160
Or purifying of the Nadi,[39]
Till Stradivarius or Amati
Shriek in my stomach !  Sarasate,
Such strains !  Such music as once Sadi
Made.Persia ring with !  I who fish up        165
No such from soul may yet cry : Vade
Retro, Satanas !  Tom Bond Bishop ! [40]

You old screw, Pegasus !  Gee (Swish !) up !
(To any who correctly rhymes [41]
With Bishop more than seven times           170
I hereby offer as emolum-
Ent, a bound copy of this volume.)

These strictures must include the liar
Copleston,[42] Reverend F. B. Meyer,
(The cock of the Dissenter's midden, he !)   175
And others of the self-same kidney :—
How different from Sir Philip Sidney !
But " cave os, et claude id, ne
Vituperasse inventus sim."
In English let me render him !               180
'Ware mug, and snap potato-trap !
Or elsely it may haply hap

Panel * in libel I bewail me !
(Funny how English seems to fail me !)
85   So, as a surgeon to a man, sir,
Let me excise your Christian cancer
Impersonally, without vanity,
Just in pure love of poor humanity !

Here's just the chance you'd have !   Behold     Ascension Day.
190   The warm sun tint with early gold               Moral aspect
Yon spire : to-day's event provide               of Christianity
                                                  to be discussed
My text of wrath—Ascension-tide !                to prejudice of
Oh ! 'tis a worthy day to wrest                  the metaphysi-
Hate's diadem from Jesus' Crest !                cal.
195   Ascends he ?  'Tis the very test
By which we men may fairly judge,
From the rough roads we mortals trudge
Or God's paths paved with heliotrope,
The morals of the crucified.
200   (Both standpoints join in one, I hope,
In metaphysic's stereoscope !)
But for the moment be denied
A metaphysical inspection—
Bring out the antiseptic soap !—
205   We'll judge the Christ by simple section,
And strictly on the moral side.

But first ; I must insist on taking          Orthodoxy to
The ordinary substantial creed               be our doxy.†
                                             Gipsies barred.
Your clergy preach from desk and pulpit      Henrik Ibsen
210   Each Sunday ; all the Bible, shaking     and H. G.
Its boards with laughter, as you read        Wells
Each Sunday.   Ibsen [43] to a full pit
May play in the moon.   If (lunars they)
They thought themselves to be the play,
215   It's little the applause he'd get.

I met a Christian clergyman, ‡               Parson and
The nicest man I ever met.                   poet.  Fugitive
                                             nature of
We argued of the Cosmic plan.                dogma in these
I was Lord Roberts, he De Wet.[44]           latter days.
                                             The Higher
                                             Criticism.

* Scots legal term for defendant.
† A Romany word for woman.
‡ The Rev. J. Bowley.   The conversation described actually occurred
in Mr. Gerald Kelly's studio in Paris.

He tells me when I cite the " Fall "                        220
" But those are legends, after all."
He has a hundred hills [46] to lie in,
But finds no final ditch [46] to die in.
" Samuel was man ; the Holy Spook
Did not dictate the Pentateuch."                           225
With cunning feint he lures me on
To loose my pompoms on Saint John ;
And, that hill being shelled, doth swear
His forces never had been there.
I got disgusted, called a parley,                          230
(Here comes a white-flag treachery !)
Asked : " Is there anything you value,
Will hold to ? "   He laughed, " Chase me, Charlie ! "
But seeing in his mind that I
Would not be so converted, " Shall you,"                   235
He added, " grope in utter dark ?
The Book of Acts and that of Mark
Are now considered genuine."
I snatch a Testament, begin
Reading at random the first page ;—                        240
He stops me with a gesture sage :
" You must not think, because I say
St. Mark is genuine, I would lay
Such stress unjust upon its text,
As base thereon opinion.   Next ? "                        245
I gave it up.   He escaped.   Ah me !
But so did Christianity.


Lord George          As for a quiet talk on physics sane ac
Sanger * on the      Lente, I hear the British Don
Unknowable.          Spout sentiments more bovine than a sane yak    250
How the crea-        Ever would ruminate upon,
tures talk.          Half Sabbatarian and half Khakimaniac,
                     Built up from Paul and John,
With not a little tincture of Leviticus
Gabbled pro formâ, jaldi,† à la Psittacus                  255
To aid the appalling hotch-potch ; lyre and lute
Replaced by liar and loot, the harp and flute

* Proprietor of a circus and menagerie.
† Hindustani : quickly.

Are dumb, the drum doth come and make us mute :
The Englishman, half huckster and half brute,
260   Raves through his silk hat of the Absolute.
The British Don, half pedant and half hermit,
Begins : "The Ding an sich *—as Germans term it—"
We stop him short ; he readjusts his glasses,
Turns to his folio—'twill eclipse all precedent,
265   Reveal God's nature, every dent a blessed dent !
The Donkey : written by an ass, for asses.

So, with permission, let us be
Orthodox to our finger-ends ;
What the bulk hold, High Church or Friends,
270   Or Hard-shell Baptists—and we'll see.

*Basis of poem to be that of the Compromise of 1870.*

I will not now invite attack
By proving white a shade of black,
Or Christ (as some [47] have lately tried)
An epileptic maniac,
275   Citing some cases, " where a dose
Of Bromide duly given in time
Drags a distemper so morose
At last to visions less sublime ;
Soft breezes stir the lyre Aeolian,
280   No more the equinoctial gales ;
The patient reefs his mental sails ;
His Panic din that shocked the Tmolian [48]
Admits a softer run of scales—
Seems no more God, but mere Napoleon
285   Or possibly the Prince of Wales " :—
Concluding such a half-cured case
With the remark " where Bromide fails !—
But Bromide people did not know
Those 1900 years ago."
290   I think we may concede to Crowley an
Impartial attitude.

*Non-medical nature of poem. Crowley J.*

And so
I scorn the thousand subtle points
Wherein a man might find a fulcrum
295   (Ex utero Matris ad sepulcrum,

*No mention will be made of the Figs and the Pigs.*

* *Vide infra*, Science and Buddhism, and the writings of Immanuel Kant
and his successors.

Et præter—such as Huxley tells)
I'll pierce your rotten harness-joints,
Dissolve your diabolic spells,
With the quick truth and nothing else.

Christian pre-
misses ac-
cepted. Severe
mental strain
involved in
reading poem.

So not one word derogatory                                    300
To your own version of the story !
I take your Christ, your God's creation,
Just at their own sweet valuation.
For by this culminating scene,
Close of that wondrous life of woe                            305
Before and after death, we know
How to esteem the Nazarene.
Where's the wet towel ?

                    Let us first

The Ascension
at last !  This
is a common
feat.  Prana-
yama.

Destroy the argument of fools,                                310
From Paul right downward to the Schools,
That the Ascension's self rehearsed
Christ's Godhead by its miracle.
Grand !—but the power is mine as well !
In India levitation counts                                    315
No tithe of the immense amounts
Of powers demanded by the wise
From Chela ere the Chela rise
To Knowledge.  Fairy-tales ?  Well, first,
Sit down a week and hold your breath                          320
As masters teach [49]—until you burst,
Or nearly—in a week, one saith,
A month, perchance a year for you,
Hard practice, and yourself may fly—
Yes !  I have done it ! you may too !                         325

Difference be-
tween David
Douglas
Home, Sri
Swami
Sabapati
Vamadeva
Bhaskara-
nanda Saras-
wati and the
Christ.
Latter com-
pared to
Madame Hum-
bert.

Thus, in Ascension, you and I
Stand as Christ's peers and therefore fit
To judge him—" Stay, friend, wait a bit ! "
(You cry) " Your Indian Yogis fall
Back to the planet after all,                                 330
Never attain to heaven and stand
(Stephen) or sit (Paul) [50] at the hand
Of the Most High !—And that alone,
That question of the Great White Throne,
Is the sole point that we debate."                            335
I answer, Here in India wait

Samadhi-Dak,[51] convenient
To travel to Maha Meru,[52]
Or Gaurisankar's [53] keen white wedge
340    Spearing the splendid dome of blue,
Or Chogo's [54] mighty flying edge
Shearing across the firmament,—
But, first, to that exact event
You Christians celebrate to-day.
345    We stand where the disciples stood
And see the Master float away
Into that cloudlet heavenly-hued
Receiving him from mortal sight.
Which of his sayings prove the true,
350    Lightning-bescrawled athwart the blue?
I say not, Which in hearts aright
Are treasured? but, What àfter ages
Engrave on history's iron pages?
This is the one word of " Our Lord " ;
355    " I bring not peace ; I bring a sword."
In this the history of the West [55]
Bears him out well.   How stands the test?
One-third a century's life of pain—
He lives, he dies, he lives again,
360    And rises to eternal rest
Of bliss with Saints—an endless reign !
Leaving the world to centuries torn
By every agony and scorn,
And every wickedness and shame
365    Taking their refuge in his Name.
*No Yogi shot his Chandra [56] so.*
**Will Christ return ?  What ho ?  What ho !**
What?   What?   " He mediates above
Still with His Sire for mercy, love,—"
370    And other trifles !  Far enough
That Father's purpose from such stuff !


You see, when I was young, they said :
" Whate'er you ponder in your head,
Or make the rest of Scripture mean,
375    You can't evade John iii. 16."

* " For God so loved the world, that he gave his only begotten Son, that
whosoever believeth in him should not perish, but have everlasting life."

*Side notes:*

Former compared to Kerubim ; as it is written, Running and Returning.

Shri Parananda applauds Yogi. Gerald jeers at Jesus.

John iii. 16.* Its importance. Its implied meaning.

Exactly !   Grown my mental stature,
I ponder much : but never yet
Can I get over or forget
That bitter text's accursed nature,
The subtle devilish omission,[57]     380
The cruel antithesis implied,
The irony, the curse-fruition,
The calm assumption of Hell's fevers
As fit, as just, for unbelievers—
These are the things that stick beside     385
And hamper my quite serious wish
To harbour kind thoughts of the " Fish." [58]

My own vague
optimism. Im-
possibility of
tracing cause
back or effect
forward to the
ultimate.
Ethics
individual.

Here goes my arrow to the gold !
I'll make no magpies !   Though I hold
Your Christianity a lie,     390
Abortion and iniquity,
The most immoral and absurd
—(A priest's invention, in a word)—
Of all religions, I have hope
In the good Dhamma's [59] wider scope,     395
Nay, certainty ! that all at last,
However came they in the past,
Move, up or down—who knows, my friend ?—
But yet with no uncertain trend
Unto Nibbana in the end.     400
I do not even dare despise
Your doctrines, prayers, and ceremonies !
Far from the word ".you'll go to hell !"
I dare not say " you do not well ! "
I must obey my own mind's laws,     405
Accept its limits, seek its cause :
My meat may be your poison !   I
Hope to convert you by-and-by ?
Never !   I cannot trace the chain [60]
That brought us here, shall part again     410
Our lives—perchance for aye !   I bring
My hand down on this table-thing,[61]
And that commotion widens thus
And shakes the nerves of Sirius !
To calculate one hour's result     415
I find surpassing difficult ;

One year's effect, one moment's cause ;
What mind could estimate such laws ?
Who then (much more !) may act aright
420  Judged by and in ten centuries' sight ?
(Yet I believe, whate'er we do
Is best for me and best for you
And best for all : I line no brow
With wrinkles, meditating how.)


425  Well, but another way remains.
Shall we expound the cosmic plan
By symbolising God and man
And nature thus ?  As man contains
Cells, nerves, grey matter in his brains,
430  Each cell a life, self-centred, free
Yet self-subordinate to the whole
For its own sake—expand !—so we
Molecules of a central soul,
Time's sons, judged by Eternity.
435  Nature is gone—our joys, our pains,
Our little lives—and God remains.
Were this the truth—why ! worship then
Were not so imbecile for men!
But that's no Christian faith !   For where
440  Enters the dogma of despair ?
Despite his logic's silver flow
I must count Caird [62] a mystic !  No !
You Christians shall not mask me so
The plain words of your sacred books
445  Behind friend Swedenborg his spooks !
Says Huxley [63] in his works (q. v.)
" The microcosmic lives change daily
In state or body "—yet you gaily
Arm a false Hegel cap-à-pie—
450  Your self, his weapons—make him wear
False favours of a ladye fayre,
(The scarlet woman !) bray and blare
A false note on the trumpet, shout :
"A champion ?  Faith's defender !  Out !
455  Sceptic and sinner !  See me !  Quail I ?"
I cite the Little-go.   You stare,
And have no further use for Paley !

Caird's inter-
pretation of
Hegel.  His
identification
of it with Chris-
tianity proved
to be mystical.
His interpreta-
tion false.

Mysticism does not need Christ. Krishna will serve, or the Carpenter. The Sacred Walrus. God, some Vestments, and Lady Wimborne.

But if you drink your mystic fill
Under the good tree Igdrasil [64]
Where is at all your use for Christ?       460
Hath Krishna not at all sufficed?
I hereby guarantee to pull
A faith as quaint and beautiful
As much attractive to an ass,
And setting reason at defiance,       465
As Zionism, Christian Science,
Or Ladies' League, [65] " Keep off the Grass ! "
From " Alice through the Looking-Glass."

Fearful aspect of John iii. 16.

Hence I account no promise worse,
Fail to conceive a fiercer curse       470
Than John's third chapter (sixteenth verse).

Universalism. Will God get the bara * slam?

But now (you say) broad-minded folk
Think that those words the Master spoke
Should save all men at last.  But mind !
The text says nothing of the kind !       475
Read the next verses ! †

Eternal life. Divergent views of its desirability. Buddhist idea.

                          Then—one-third
Of all humanity are steady
In a belief in Buddha's word,
Possess eternal life already,       480
And shun delights, laborious days
Of labour living (Milton's phrase)
In strenuous purpose to—? to cease !
" A fig for God's eternal peace !
True peace is to annihilate       485
The chain of causes men call Fate,
So that no Sattva [66] may renew
Once death has run life's shuttle through."
(Their sages put it somewhat thus)
What's fun to them is death to us !       490
That's clear at least.

Dogma of Belief.

                   But never mind !
Call them idolaters and blind !
We'll talk of Christ.  As Shelley sang,
" Shall an eternal issue hang       495

* Great slam—a term of Bridge-Whist.  Bara is Hindustani for great.
† John iii. 18, " He that believeth not is condemned already."

On just belief or unbelief;
And an involuntary act
Make difference infinite in fact
Between the right and left-hand thief?
Belief is not an act of will!"

I think, Sir, that I have you still,
Even allowing (much indeed!)
That any will at all is freed,
And is not merely the result
Of sex, environment, and cult,
Habit and climate, health and mind,
And twenty thousand other things!
So many a metaphysic sings.
(I wish they did indeed: I find
Their prose the hardest of hard reading!)

"But if," you cry, "the world's designed
As a mere mirage in the mind,
Up jumps free will." But all I'm pleading
Is against pain and hell. Freewill
Then can damn man? No fearful mill,
Grinding catastrophe, is speeding
Outside—some whence, some whither? And
I think we easier understand
Where Schelling (to the Buddha leading)
Calls real not-self. In any case
There is not, there can never be
A soul, or sword or armour needing,
Incapable in time or space
Or to inflict or suffer. We
I think are gradually weeding
The soil of dualism. Pheugh!
Drop to the common Christian's view!

This is my point; the world lies bleeding:—
(Result of sin?)—I do not care;
I will admit you anywhere!
I take your premisses themselves
And, like the droll despiteful elves
They are, they yet outwit your plan.
I will prove Christ a wicked man

Side notes:

500

505

510

515

520

525

530

Free will.
Herbert
Spencer.

If there is free
will how can
there be pain
or damnation?
not-Self being
an illusion.
Self or not-Self
real? Chute
d'Icare.

I have pity:
had Christ
any? The
Sheep and the
Goats.

(Granting him Godhead) merciless                              535
To all the anguish and distress
About him—save to him it clung
And prayed.  Give me omnipotence?
I am no fool that I should fence
That power, demanding every tongue                           540
To call me God—I would exert
That power to heal creation's hurt ;
Not to divide my devotees
From those who scorned me to the close :
A worm, a fire, a thirst for these ;                         545
A harp-resounding heaven for those !

**Will Satan be saved?  Who pardons Judas?**

And though you claim Salvation sure
For all the heathen⁶⁸—·there again
New Christians give the lie to plain
Scripture, those words which must endure !                   550
(The Vedas say the same !) and though
His mercy widens ever so,
I never met a man (this shocks,
What I now press) so heterodox,
Anglican, Roman, Methodist,                                  555
Peculiar Person--- all the list !—
I never met a man who called
Himself a Christian, but appalled
Shrank when I dared suggest the hope
God's mercy could expand its scope,                          560
Extend, or bend, or spread, or straighten
So far as to encompass Satan
Or even poor Iscariot.

**God's fore-knowledge of Satan's fall and eternal misery makes him re-sponsible for it.  If he and Judas are finally re-deemed, we might perhaps look over the matter this once.  Poet books his seat.  Creator in**

Yet God created (did he not ?)
Both these.  Omnisciently, we know !                         565
Benevolently?  Even so !
Created from Himself distinct
(Note that !—it is not meet for you
To plead me Schelling and his crew)
These souls, foreknowing how were linked                     570
The chains in either's Destiny.
"You pose me the eternal Why?"
Not I?  Again, "Who asks doth err."
But this one thing I say.  Perchance
There lies a purpose in advance                              575

Tending to final bliss—to stir
Some life to better life, this pain
Is needful : that I grant again.
Did they at last in glory live,
680    Satan and Judas [69] might forgive
The middle time of misery,
Forgive the wrong creation first
Or evolution's iron key
Did them—provided they are passed
685    Beyond all change and pain at last
Out of this universe accurst.
But otherwise !   I lift my voice,
Deliberately take my choice
Promethean, eager to rejoice,
690    In the grim protest's joy to revel
Betwixt Iscariot and the Devil,
Throned in their midst !   No pain to feel,
Tossed on some burning bed of steel,
But theirs : My soul of love should swell
695    And, on those piteous floors they trod,
Feel, and make God feel, out of Hell,
Across the gulf impassable,
That He was damned and I was God !

Ay !   Let him rise and answer me
600    That false creative Deity,
Whence came his right to rack the Earth
With pangs of death,[70] disease, and birth :
No joy unmarred by pain and grief :
Insult on injury heaped high
605    In that quack-doctor infamy
The Panacea of—Belief !
Only the selfish soul of man
Could ever have conceived a plan
Man only of all life to embrace,
610    One planet of all stars to place
Alone before the Father's face ;
Forgetful of creation's stain,
Forgetful of creation's pain,
Not dumb !—forgetful of the pangs
615    Whereby each life laments and hangs,
(Now as I speak a lizard [71] lies
In wait for light-bewildered flies)

*heaven suffers Hell's pangs, owing to reproaches of bard.*

*Ethical and eloquent denunciation of Christian Cosmogony.*

Each life bound ever to the wheel [72]
Ay, and each being—we may guess
Now that the very crystals feel!—                        620
For them no harp-resounding court,
No palm, no crown, but none the less
A cross, be sure! The worst man's thought
In hell itself, bereft of bliss,
Were less unmerciful than this!                          625
No! for material things, I hear,
Will burn away, and cease to be—
(Nibbana! Ah! Thou shoreless Sea!)
Man, man alone, is doomed to fear,
To suffer the eternal woe,                               630
Or else, to meet man's subtle foe,
God—and oh! infamy of terror!
Be like him—like him! And for ever!
At least I make not such an error:
My soul must utterly dissever                            635
Its very silliest thought, belief,
From such a God as possible,
Its vilest from his worship. Never!
Avaunt, abominable chief
Of Hate's grim legions; let me well                      640
Gird up my loins and make endeavour,
And seek a refuge from my grief,
O never in Heaven—but in Hell!

Death-bed of
poet. Effect
of body on
mind.

"Oh, very well!" I think you say,
"Wait only till your dying day!                          645
See whether then you kiss the rod,
And bow that proud soul down to God!"
I perfectly admit the fact;
Quite likely that I so shall act!
Here's why Creation jumps at prayer.                     650
You Christians quote me in a breath
This, that, the other atheist's death; [73]
How they sought God! Of course! Impair
By just a touch of fever, chill,
My health—where flies my vivid will?                    655
My carcase with quinine is crammed;
I wish South India were damned;
I wish I had my mother's nursing,
Find precious little use in cursing,

680     And slide to leaning on another,
       God, or the doctor, or my mother.
       But dare you quote my fevered word
       For better than my health averred?
       The brainish fancies of a man
       Hovering on delirium's brink :
665     *Shall these be classed his utmost span ?*
       All that he can or ought to think ?
       No ! the strong man and self-reliant
       Is the true spiritual giant.
670     I blame no weaklings, but decline
       To take their maunderings for mine.


       You see I do not base my thesis
       On your Book's being torn in pieces
       By knowledge ; nor invoke the shade
675     Of my own boyhood's agony.
       Soul, shudder not !  Advance the blade
       Of fearless fact and probe the scar !
       You know my first-class memory ?
       Well, in my life two years there are
680     Twelve years back—not so very far !
       Two years whereof no memory stays.
       One ageless anguish filled my days
       So that no item, like a star
       Sole in the supreme night, above
685     Stands up for hope, or joy, or love.
       Nay, not one ignis fatuus glides
       Sole in that marsh, one agony
       To make the rest look light.  Abides
       The thick sepulchral changeless shape
690     Shapeless, continuous misery
       Whereof no smoke-wreaths might escape
       To show me whither lay the end,
       Whence the beginning.  All is black,
       Void of all cause, all aim ; unkenned,
695     As if I had been dead indeed—
       All in Christ's name !  And I look back,
       And then and long time after lack
       Courage or strength to hurl the creed
       Down to the heaven it sprang from !  No !
700     Not this inspires the indignant blow

*Poem does not treat of Palæontology : nor of poet's youth : nor of Christian infamies. Poet forced to mystic position.*

At the whole fabric—nor the seas
Filled with those innocent agonies
Of Pagan Martyrs that once bled,
Of Christian Martyrs damned and dead
In inter-Christian bickerings,                              705
Where hate exults and torture springs,
A lion on anguished flesh and blood,
A vulture on ill-omen wings,
A cannibal [74] on human food.
Nor do I cry the scoffer's cry,                             710
That Christians live and look the lie
Their faith has taught them : none of these
Inspire my life, disturb my peace.
I go beneath the outward faith
Find it a devil or a wraith,                                715
Just as my mood or temper tends !

Mystical mean-
ing of "Ascen-
sion Day."
Futility of
whole discus-
sion, in view of
facts.

And thus to-day that "Christ ascends,"
I take the symbol, leave the fact,
Decline to make the smallest pact
With your creative Deity,                                   720
And say : The Christhood-soul in me,
Risen of late, is now quite clear
Even of the smallest taint of Earth.
Supplanting God, the Man has birth
("New Birth" you'll call the same, I fear,)                725
Transcends the ordinary sphere
And flies in the direction "x."
(There lies the fourth dimension.)   Vex
My soul no more with mistranslations
From Genesis to Revelations,                               730
But leave me with the Flaming Star,[75]
Jeheshua (See thou Zohar !) [76]
And thus our formidable Pigeon- [77]
Lamb-and-Old-Gentleman religion
Fizzles in smoke, and I am found                           735
Attacking nothing.   Here's the ground,
Pistols, and coffee—three in one,
(Alas, O Rabbi Schimeon !)
But never a duellist—no Son,
No Father, and (to please us most)                         740
Decency pleads—no Holy Ghost !
All vanish at the touch of truth,
A cobweb trio—like, in sooth,

That worthy Yankee millionaire,
745 And wealthy nephews, young and fair,
The pleasing Crawfords! Lost! Lost! Lost![78]
"The Holy Spirit, friend! beware!"

Ah! ten days yet to Pentecost!                    The reader
Come that, I promise you—but stay!                may hope.
750 At present 'tis Ascension Day!

At least your faith should be content.            Summary.
I quarrel not with this event.                    Reader dis-
The supernatural element?                          missed to
I deny nothing—at the term                        chapel.
755 It is just Nothing I affirm.
The fool (with whom is wisdom, deem
The Scriptures—rightly!) in his heart
Saith (silent, to himself, apart)
This secret: "אֵין אֱלֹהִים"[79]
760 See the good Psalm! And thus, my friend!
My diatribes approach the end
And find us hardly quarrelling.
And yet—you seem not satisfied?
The literal mistranslated thing
765 Must not by sinners be denied.
Go to your Chapel then to pray!
(I promise Mr. Chesterton[80]
Before the Muse and I have done
A grand ap-pre-ci-a-ti-on
770 Of Brixton on Ascension Day.)

He's gone—his belly filled enough!               Future plans of
This Robert-Browning-manqué stuff!               poet. Jesus
'Twill serve—Mercutio's scratch!—to show         dismissed with
Where God and I are disagreed.                     a jest.
775 There! I have let my feelings go
This once. Again? I deem not so.
Once for my fellow-creature's need!
The rest of life, for self-control,[81]
For liberation of the soul![82]
780 This once, the truth! In future, best
Dismissing Jesus with a jest.

Ah! Christ ascends?[83] Ascension day?            The Jest.
Old wonders bear the bell[84] away?
Santos-Dumont, though! Who can say?

# PENTECOST

TO-DAY thrice halves the lunar week
Since you, indignant, heard me speak
Indignant.   Then I seemed to be
So far from Christianity !
Now, other celebrations fit                                  5
The time, another song shall flit
Reponsive to another tune.
September's shadow falls on June,
But dull November's darkest day
Is lighted by the sun of May.                               10

Here's how I got a better learning.
It's a long lane that has no turning !
Mad as a woman-hunted Urning,
The lie-chased alethephilist : *
Sorcery's maw gulps the beginner :                          15
In Pain's mill neophytes are grist :
Disciples ache upon the rack.
Five years I sought : I miss and lack ;
Agony hounds lagoan twist ;
I peak and struggle and grow thinner,                       20
And get to hate the sight of dinner.
With sacred thirst, I, soul-hydroptic,[1]
Read Levi[2] and the cryptic Coptic ;[3]
With ANET' HER-K UAA EN RA,[4]

And ספרא דצניעותא[5]                                         25
While good MacGregor[5] (who taught freely us)
Bade us investigate Cornelius
Agrippa and the sorceries black
Of grim Honorius and Abramelin ;[6]
While, fertile as the teeming spawn                         30
Of pickled lax or stickleback,
Came ancient rituals,[7] whack ! whack !
Of Rosy Cross and Golden Dawn.[8]

* Truth-lover.

164

My Mahatma.
What price
Kut Humi?

I lived, Elijah-like, Mt. Carmel in :
35      All gave me nothing.   I slid back
To common sense, as reason bids,
And " hence," my friend, " the Pyramids."

At last I met a maniac
With mild eyes full of love, and tresses
40      Blanched in those lonely wildernesses
Where he found wisdom, and long hands
Gentle, pale olive 'gainst the sand's
Amber and gold.   At sight, I knew him ;
Swifter than light I flashed, ran to him,
45      And at his holy feet prostrated
My head ; then, all my being sated
With love, cried " Master !   I must know.
Already I can love."   E'en so.
The sage saluted me राम । राम ।[9]

? ? ? ? ? ? Oh,
how wise
Grampa must
have been,
Bobbie !

50      लमबा पड़ाव की बड़ी दाम ।

ज्ञानी यह सब से मुश्किल काम

है । वाह शाबाश । तुम्हार नाम

सितारों में सोने से लिखा है ।

हमारे पास आव चेले । हम दवाई

55      चिन्ता के वास्ते देंगे ॥   हौ । said I :

" I'm game to work through all eternity,
Your holiness the Guru Swami ! " *   Thus
I studied with him till he told me बस ॥[10]
He taught the A B C of Yoga :
60      I asked किस वास्ते ।[11]  कया होगा ॥[12]
In strange and painful attitude,[13]
I sat, while he was very rude.[14]
With eyes well fixed on my proboscis,[15]
I soon absorbed the Yogi Gnosis.
65      He taught me to steer clear of vices,
The giddy waltz, the tuneful aria,
Those fatal foes of Brahma-charya ; [16]
And said, " How very mild and nice is
One's luck to lop out truth in slices,
70      And chance to chop up cosmic crises ! "

* The correct form of address from a pupil to his teacher.   See Sab-
hapaty Swami's pamphlet on Yoga.

He taught me A, he taught me B,
He stopped my baccy [17] and my tea.
He taught me Y, he taught me Z,
He made strange noises in my head.
He taught me that, he taught me this,                    75
He spoke of knowledge, life, and bliss.
He taught me this, he taught me that,
He grew me mangoes in his hat.[18]
I brought him corn : he made good grist of it :—
And here, my Christian friend, 's the gist of it !      80

The philo-
sophical im-
passe. Practi-
cal advice.
Advice to poet's
fat friend.

First, here's philosophy's despair,
The cynic scorn of self.  I think
At times the search is worth no worry,
And hasten earthward in a hurry,
Close spirit's eyes, or bid them blink,                 85
Go back to Swinburne's [19] counsel rare,
Kissing the universe its rod,
As thus he sings " For this is God ;
Be man with might, at any rate,
In strength of spirit growing straight                  90
And life as light a-living out ! "
So Swinburne doth sublimely state,
And he is right beyond a doubt.
So, I'm a poet or a rhymer ;
A mountaineer or mountain climber.                      95
So much for Crowley's vital primer.
The inward life of soul and heart,
That is a thing occult, apart :
But yet his metier or his kismet
As much as these you have of his met.                   100
So—you be butcher ; you be baker ;
You, Plymouth Brother, and you, Quaker ;
You, Mountebank, you, corset-maker :—
While for you, my big beauty,[20] (Chicago packs pork)
I'll teach you the trick to be hen-of-the-walk.         105
Shriek a music-hall song with a double ong-tong !
Dance a sprightly can-can at Paree or Bolong !
Or the dance of Algiers—try your stomach at that !
It's quite in your line, and would bring down your fat.
You've a very fine voice—could you only control it !    110
And an emerald ring—and I know where you stole it !
But for goodness sake give up attempting Brünnhilde ;
Try a boarding-house cook, or a coster's Matilda !

Still you're young yet, scarce forty—we'll hope at three
    score
115  You'll be more of a singer, and less of a whore.

Each to his trade ! live out your life !
Fondle your child, and buss your wife !
Trust not, fear not, steer straight and strong !
Don't worry, but just get along.
120  I used to envy all my Balti coolies [21]
In an inverse kind of religious hysteria,
Though every one a perfect fool is,
To judge by philosophic criteria,
My Lord Archbishop.   The name of Winchester,
125  Harrow, or Eton [22] makes them not two inches stir.
They know not Trinity, Merton, or Christchurch ;
They worship, but not at your back-pews-high-priced
    Church.
I've seen them at twenty thousand feet
On the ice, in a snow-storm, at night fall, repeat
130  Their prayers [23]—will your Grace do as much for your Three
As they do for their One?   I have seen—may you see !
They sleep and know not what a mat is ;
Seem to enjoy their cold chapaties ; *
Are healthy, strong—and some are old.
135  They do not care a damn [24] for cold,
Behave like children, trust in Allah ;
(Flies in Mohammed's spider-parlour !)
They may not think : at least they dare
Live out their lives, and little care
140  Worries their souls—worse fools they seem
Than even Christians.   Do I dream?
Probing philosophy to marrow,
What thought darts in its poisoned arrow
But this? (my wisdom, even to me,
145  Seems folly) may their folly be
True Wisdom?   O esteemed Tahuti ! [25]
You are, you are, you are a beauty !
If after all these years of worship
You hail Ra [26] his bark or Nuit [27] her ship

Live out thy
life !  Charac-
ter of Balti.
His religious
sincerity.  Re-
lations of poet
and the Egyp-
tian God of
Wisdom.
Crowley dis-
missed with a
jest.

---

* A flat cake of unleavened bread.  As a matter of fact they do not
enjoy and indeed will not eat them, preferring "dok," a paste of coarse
flour and water, wrapped round a hot stone.  It cooks gradually, and
remains warm all day.

And sail—"the waters wild a-wenting                    150
Over your child! The left lamenting"
(Campbell).[28]   The Ibis head,[29] unsuited
To grin, perhaps, yet does its best
To show its strong appreciation
Of the humour of the situation—                    155
In short, dimiss me, jeered and hooted,
Who thought I sported Roland's crest,[30]
With wisdom saddled, spurred, and booted,
(As I my Jesus) with a jest.[31]

**Slowness of Divine Justice. Poet pockets Piety Stakes. National Anthem of Natal.**

So here is my tribute—a jolly good strong 'un—                    160
To the eunuch, the faddist, the fool, and the wrong 'un !
It's fun when you say "A mysterious way [32]
God moves in to fix up his Maskelyne tricks.
He trots on the tides, on the tempest he rides
(Like Cosmo); and as for his pace, we bethought us                    165
Achilles could never catch up with that tortoise !"
No flyer, but very "Who's Griffiths?" *   No jackpot !
I straddle the blind, age ! At hymns I'm a moral ;
In Sankey, your kettle may call me a black pot.
Here's diamond for coke, and pink pearl for pale coral.                    170
Though his mills may grind slowly—what says the old hymn? [33]
Tune, Limerick ! Author? My memory's dim.
The corn said "You sluggard !"
The mill "You may tug hard," (or lug hard, or plug hard ;
I forget the exact Rhyme ; that's a fact)                    175
"If I want to grind slowly I shall,"
A quainter old fable one rarely is able
To drag from its haunt in the—smoke room or stable !
You see (vide supra) I've brought to the test a ton
Of tolerance, broadness. Approve me, friend Chesterton !   180

**But this talk is all indigestion. Now for health.**

So much when philosophy's lacteal river
Turns sour through a trifle of bile on the liver.              s
But now for the sane and the succulent milk
Of truth—may it slip down as smoothly as silk !

**Reasons for undertaking the task.**

"How very hard it is to be" [34]                    185
A Yogi ! Let our spirits see
At least what primal need of thought
This end to its career has brought :

* "Who's Griffiths? The safe man." A well-known advertisement, hence "Who's Griffiths"=safe.

Why, in a word, I seek to gain
190 A different knowledge.  Why retain
The husk of flesh, yet seek to merit
The influx of the Holy Spirit?
And, swift as caddies pat and cap a tee,
Gain the great prize all mortals snap at, he-
195 Roic guerdon of Srotapatti? [35]

With calm and philosophic mind,        Our logical
No fears, no hopes, devotions blind     method.  Clas-
To hamper, soberly we'll state          sical allusion,
The problem, and investigate           demonstrating
200 In purely scientific mood              erudition of
The sheer Ananke of the mind,          poet.
A temper for our steel to find
Whereby those brazen nails subdued
Against our door-posts may in vain
205 Ring.   We'll examine, to be plain,
By logic's intellectual prism
The spiritual Syllogism.

We know what fools (only) call          Whether or
Divine and Supernatural                 not spirit and
                                        matter are dis-
210 And what they name material            tinct, let us in-
Are really one, not two, the line       vestigate the
By which divide they and define         fundamental
Being a shadowy sort of test ;          necessities of
A verbal lusus at the best,             thought.
215 At worst a wicked lie devised
To bind men's thoughts ; but we must work
With our own instruments, nor shirk
Discarding what we erstwhile prized ;
Should we perceive it disagree
220 With the first-born necessity.

I come to tell you why I shun           Impermanence
The sight of men, the life and fun      of the soul.
You know I can enjoy so well,
The Nature that I love as none
225 (I think) before me ever loved.
You know I scorn the fear of Hell,
By worship and all else unmoved.

You know for me the soul is nought [36]
Save a mere phantom in the thought,
That thought itself impermanent,                                    230
Save as a casual element
With such another may combine
To form now water and now wine ;
The element itself may be
Changeless to all eternity,                                          235
But compounds ever fluctuate
With time or space or various state.
(Ask chemists else !)   So I must claim
Spirit and matter are the same [37]
Or else the prey of putrefaction.                                    240
This matters to the present action
Little or nothing.   Here's your theories !
Think if you like :  I find it wearies !

Recapitulation
of principal cos-
mic theories.

It matters little whether we
With Fichte and the Brahmins preach                                  245
That Ego-Atman sole must be ;
With Schelling and the Buddha own
Non-Ego-Skandhas are alone ;
With Hegel and—the Christian? teach
That which completes, includes, absorbs                              250
Both mighty unrevolving orbs
In one informing masterless
Master-idea of consciousness—
All differences as these indeed
Are chess play, conjuring.   " Proceed ! "                           255
Nay !  I'll go back.   The exposition
Above, has points.   But simple fission
Has reproduced a different bliss,
At last a heterogenesis !

Bard check-
mates himself.
Consciousness
and Christi-
anity.
Dhyana and
Hinduism.
Sammasa-
madhi and
Buddhism.

The metaphysics of these verses                                      260
Is perfectly absurd.   My curse is
No sooner in an iron word
I formulate my thought than I
Perceive the same to be absurd
(Tannhäuser).   So for this, Sir, why !                              265
Your metaphysics in your teeth !
Confer A. Crowley, " Berashith."
But hear !   The Christian is a Dualist ;

Such view our normal consciousness !
270    Tells us.   I'll quote you now if you list
From Tennyson.   It isn't much ;
(Skip this and 'twill be even less)
He says : " I am not what I see,[38]
And other than the things I touch." *
275    How lucid is our Alfred T. !
The Hindu, an Advaitist,
Crosses off Maya from the list ;
Believes in one—exactly so,
Dhyana-consciousness, you know !
280    May it not be that one step further
" 'Tis lotused Buddha roaring murther ! " ? [39]
Nibbana is the state above you
Christians and them Hindus—Lord love you !--
Where Nothing is perceived as such.

285    This clever thought doth please me much.      Bard is pleased
                                                    with himself.

But if das Essen ist das Nichts—        Poetee mani-
Ha ! Hegel's window !   Ancient Lichts !    fests a natural
And two is one and one is two—        irritation.
" Bother this nonsense !   Go on, do ! "
290    My wandering thoughts you well recall !
I focus logic's perfect prism :
Lo ! the informing syllogism !

The premiss major.   Life at best       Sabbé pi Duk-
Is but a sorry sort of jest ;            kham ! †
295    At worst, a play of fiends uncouth,
Mocking the soul foredoomed to pain.
In any case, its run must range
Through countless miseries of change.
So far, no farther, gentle youth !
300    The mind can see.   So much, no more.
So runs the premiss major plain ;
Identical, the Noble truth
First of the Buddha's Noble Four !

The premiss minor.   I deplore       Beyond
305    These limitations of the mind.       thought, is
I strain my eyes until they're blind,    there hope?
And cannot pierce the awful veil      Maya again.
                                                    Vision of the

* *In Memoriam.*                  † All is Sorrow.

Visible Image
of the Soul of
Nature, whose
Name is Fat-
ality.

That masks the primal cause of being.
With all respect to Buddha, fleeing
The dreadful problem with the word          310
"Who answers, as who asks, hath erred,"
I must decidedly insist
On asking why these things exist.
My mind refuses to admit
All-Power can be all-Wickedness.             315
—Nay! but it may! What shadows flit
Across the awful veil of mist?
What thoughts invade, insult, impress?
There comes a lightning of my wit
And sees—nor good nor ill address           320
Itself to task, creation's ill,
But a mere law without a will,[40]
Nothing resolved in something, fit
Phantom of dull stupidity,
And evolution's endless stress              325
All the inanity to knit
Thence : such a dark device I see!
Nor lull my soul in the caress
Of Buddha's " Maya fashioned it." [41]
My mind seems ready to agree ;              330
But still my senses worry me.

Futility of all
investigations
of the Mind
into the First
Cause.

Nor can I see what sort of gain
God finds in this creating pain ;
Nor do the Vedas help me here.
Why should the Paramatma cease [42]         335
From its eternity of peace,
Develop this disgusting drear
System of stars, to gather again
Involving, all the realm of pain,
Time, space, to that eternal calm?          340
Blavatsky's Himalayan Balm [43]
Aids us no whit—if to improve
Thus the All-light, All-life, All-love,
By evolution's myrrh and gall,
It would not then have been the All.        345

Faith our only
alternative to
Despair? So
says Mansel.

Thus all conceptions fail and fall.
But see the Cyclopædia-article
On " Metaphysics"; miss no particle

Of thought !   How ends the brave B.D.,
350   Summarising Ontology?
"This talk of 'Real' is a wraith.
Our minds are lost in war of word ;
The whole affair is quite absurd—
Behold ! the righteous claims of Faith !"
355   (He does not rhyme you quite so neatly ;
But that's the sense of it, completely.)

I·do not feel myself inclined,                    The Advaitist
In spite of my irreverent mind,                   position.
So lightly to pass by the schemes
360   Of Fichte, Schelling, Hegel (one,
Small though the apparent unison),
As if they were mere drunken dreams ;
For the first word in India here
From Koromandl to Kashmir
365   Says the same thing these Germans said :
"Ekam Advaita !"⁴⁴ one, not two !
Thus East and West from A to Z
Agree—Alas ! so do not you ?
(It matters nothing—you, I find,
370   Are but a mode of my own mind.)

As far as normal reasoning goes,                  Mind's superior
I must admit my concepts close                    functions.
Exactly where my worthy friend,
Great Mansel, says they ought to end.
375   But here's the whole thing in a word :
Olympus in a nutshell !   I
Have a superior faculty
To reasoning, which makes absurd,
Unthinkable and wicked too,
380   A great deal that I know is true !
In short, the mind is capable,
Besides mere ratiocination,
Of twenty other things as well,
The first of which is concentration !

385   Here most philosophers agree ;                  Does truth
Claim that the truth must so intend,              make itself in-
Explain at once all agony                         stantly appa-
Of doubt, make people comprehend                  rent ?   Not
                                                   reason.

But the results
of concentra-
tion do so.

As by a lightning flash, solve doubt
And turn all Nature inside out :                        390
And, if such potency of might
Hath Truth, once state the truth aright,
Whence came the use for all those pages
Millions together—mighty sages
Whom the least obstacle enrages?                        395
Condemn the mystic if he prove
Thinking less valuable than love?
Well, let them try their various plans !
Do they resolve that doubt of man's?
How many are Hegelians?                                 400
This, though I hold him mostly true.
But, to teach others that same view?
Surely long years develop reason.[45]
After long years, too, in thy season
Bloom, Concentration's midnight flower !                405
After much practice to this end
I gain at last the long sought power
(Which you believe you have this hour,
But certainly have not, my friend !)
Of keeping close the mind to one                        410
Thing at a time -- suppose, the Sun.
I gain this (Reverence to Ganesh' !) [46]
And at that instant comprehend
(The past and future tenses vanish)
What Fichte comprehends.   Division,                    415
Thought, wisdom, drop away.   I see
The absolute identity
Of the beholder and the vision.

Some poetry.

There is a lake * amid the snows
Wherein five glaciers merge and break.                  420
Oh ! the deep brilliance of the lake !
The roar of ice that cracks and goes
Crashing within the water !   Glows
The pale pure water, shakes and slides
The glittering sun through emerald tides,               425
So that faint ripples of young light
Laugh on the green.   Is there a night

---

* This simile for the mind and its impressions, which must be stilled
before the sun of the soul can be reflected, is common in Hindu literature.
The five glaciers are, of course, the senses.

So still and cold, a frost so chill,
That all the glaciers be still ?
430    Yet in its peace no frost.
                                    Arise !
Over the mountains steady stand,
O sun of glory, in the skies
Alone, above, unmoving !   Brand
435    Thy sigil, thy resistless might,
The abundant imminence of light !
Ah !
            O in the silence, in the dark,
In the intangible, unperfumed,
440    Ingust abyss, abide and mark
The mind's magnificence assumed
In the soul's splendour !   Here is peace ;
Here earnest of assured release.
Here is the formless all-pervading
445    Spirit of the World, rising, fading
Into a glory subtler still.
Here the intense abode of Will
Closes its gates. and in the hall
Is solemn sleep of festival.
450    Peace !   Peace !   Silence of peace !
O visionless abode !   Cease !   Cease !
Through the dark veil press on !   The veil
Is rent asunder, the stars pale,
The suns vanish, the moon drops,
455    The chorus of the spirit stops,
But one note swells.   Mightiest souls
Of bard and music maker, rolls
Over your loftiest crowns the wheel
Of that abiding bliss.   Life flees
460    Down corridors of centuries
Pillar by pillar, and is lost.
Life after life in wild appeal
Cries to the master ; he remains
And thinks not.
                        The polluting tides
465    Of sense roll shoreward.   Arid plains
Of wave-swept sea confront me.   Nay !
Looms yet the glory through the grey,
And in the darkest hours of youth
470    I yet perceive the essential truth,

Known as I know my consciousness,
That all division's hosts confess
A master, for I know and see
The absolute identity
Of the beholder and the vision.                    475

How easy to excite derision
In the man's mind !   Why, fool, I think
I am as clever as yourself,
At least as skilled to wake the elf
Of jest and mockery in a wink.                     480
I can dismiss with sneers as cheap
As yours this fabric of my own,
One banner of my mind o'erthrown
Just at my will.   How true and deep
Is Carroll [47] when his Alice cries :             485
" It's nothing but a pack of cards !"
There's the true refuge of the wise;
To overthrow the temple guards,
Deny reality.

And now                        490
(I'll quote you Scripture anyhow)
What did the Sage mean when he wrote
(I am the Devil when I quote)
" The mere terrestrial-minded man
Knows not the Things of God, nor can             495
Their subtle meaning understand ?"
A sage, I say, although he mentions
Perhaps the best of his inventions,
God.

For, at first, this practice leads          500
To holy thoughts (the holy deeds
Precede success) and reverent gaze
Upon the Ancient One of Days,
Beyond which fancy lies the Truth.
To find which I have left my youth,              505
All I held dear, and sit alone
Still meditating, on my throne
Of Kusha-grass,[48] and count my beads,
Murmur my mantra,[49] till recedes
The world of sense and thought—I sink            510

Fact replacing folklore, the Christian sniggers.   Let him beware,

For I speak subtly.

Results of practice.   The poet abandons all to find Truth.

To—what abyss's dizzy brink?
And fall! And I have ceased to think!
That is, have conquered and made still
Mind's lower powers by utter Will.

515
It may be that pure Nought will fail
Quite to assuage the needs of thought ;
But—who can tell me whether Nought
Untried, will or will not avail?

Nothing. The
Apotheosis of
Realism and
Idealism alike.

520
Aum! Let us meditate aright [50]
On that adorable One Light,
Divine Savitri! So may She
Illume our minds! So mote it be!

Gayatri.

I find some folks think me (for one)
So great a fool that I disclaim
525
Indeed Jehovah's hate for shame
That man to-day should not be weaned
Of worshipping so foul a fiend
In presence of the living Sun,
And yet replace him oiled and cleaned
530
By the Egyptian Pantheon,
The same thing by another name.
Thus when of late Egyptian Gods
Evoked ecstatic periods
In verse of mine, you thought I praised
535
Or worshipped them—I stand amazed.
I merely wished to chant in verse
Some aspects of the Universe,
Summed up these subtle forces finely,
And sang of them (I think divinely)
540
In name and form : a fault perhaps—
Reviewers are such funny chaps!
I think that ordinary folk,
Though, understood the things I spoke.
For Gods, and devils too, I find
545
Are merely modes of my own mind !
The poet needs enthusiasm !
Verse-making is a sort of spasm,
Degeneration of the mind,
And things of that unpleasant kind.

Is " The Soul
of Osiris " a
Hymn Book?
How verse is
written.
Prayer.

So to the laws all bards obey 550
I bend, and seek in my own way
By false things to expound the real.
But never think I shall appeal
To Gods.   What folly can compare
With such stupidity as prayer? 555

Some years ago I thought to try
Prayer [51]—test its efficacity.
I fished by a Norwegian lake.
"O God," I prayed, "for Jesus' sake
Grant thy poor servant all his wish! 560
For every prayer produce a fish!"
Nine times the prayer went up the spout,
And eight times—what a thumping trout!
(This is the only true fish-story
I ever heard—give God the glory!) 565
The thing seems cruel now, of course.
Still, it's a grand case of God's force!
But, modern Christians, do you dare
With common prudence to compare
The efficacity of prayer? 570
Who will affirm of Christian sages
That prayer can alter averages?
The individual case allows
Some chance to operate, and thus
Destroys its value quite for us. 575
So that is why I knit my brows
And think—and find no thing to say
Or do, so foolish as to pray.
"So much for this absurd affair [52]
About" validity of prayer. 580
But back!   Let once again address
Our minds to super-consciousness!

You weary me with proof enough
That all this meditation stuff
Is self-hypnosis.   Be it so! 585
Do you suppose I did not know?
Still, to be accurate, I fear
The symptoms are entirely strange.
If I were hard, I'd make it clear
That criticism must arrange 590

An explanation different
For this particular event.
Though surely I may find it queer
That you should talk of self-hypnosis,
595    When your own faith so very close is
To similar experience ;
Lies, in a word, beneath suspicion
To ordinary common sense
And logic's emery attrition.
600    I take, however, as before
Your own opinions, and demand
Some test by which to understand
Huxley's piano-talk,* and find
If my hypnosis may not score
605    A point against the normal mind.
(As you are pleased to term it, though !
I gather that you do not know ;
Merely infer it.)

                    Here's a test !                        A test. The
610    What in your whole life is the best                  artist's concen-
Of all your memories ?  They say                            tration on his
You paint—I think you should one day                        work.
Take me to see your Studio—
Tell me, when all your work goes right,
615    Painted to match some inner light,
What of the outer world you know !
Surely, your best work always finds
Itself sole object of the mind's.
In vain you ply the brush, distracted
620    By something you have heard or acted.
Expect some tedious visitor—
Your eye runs furtive to the door ;
Your hand refuses to obey ;
You throw the useless brush away.
625    I think I hear the Word you say !

I practice then, with conscious power
Watching my mind, each thought controlling,
Hurling to nothingness, while rolling
The thunders after lightning's flower,

---

* See his remarks upon the Rational piano, and the conclusions to whi
the evidence of its senses would lead it.

Destroying passion, feeling, thought,                    630
The very practice you have sought
Unconscious, when you work the best.
I carry on one step firm-pressed
Further than you the path, and you
For all my trouble, comment : "True !                    635
" Auto-hypnosis.   Very quaint ! " [63]
No one supposes me a Saint— [64]
Some Saints to wrath would be inclined
With such a provocation pecked !
But I remember and reflect                    640
That anger makes a person blind,
And my own "Chittam" I'd neglect.
Besides, it's you, and you, I find,
Are but a mode of my own mind.

Objectivity of<br>universe not<br>discussed.

But then you argue, and with sense ;                    645
"I have this worthy evidence
That things are real, since I cease
The painter's ecstasy of peace,
And find them all unchanged."   To-day
I cannot brush that doubt away ;                    650
It leads to tedious argument
Uncertain, in the best event :
Unless, indeed, I should invoke
The fourth dimension, clear the smoke
Psychology still leaves.   This question                    655
Needs a more adequate digestion.
Yet I may answer that the universe
Of meditation suffers less
From time's insufferable stress
Than that of matter.   On, thou puny verse !                    660
Weak tide of rhyme !   Another argument
Will block the railway train of blague you meant
To run me over with.   This world
Or that ?   We'll keep the question furled.

Preferability of
on-

But, surely, (let me corner you !)
*You wish the painter-mood were true !*                    665
To leave the hateful world, and see
Perish the whole Academy ;
So you remain for ever sated,
On your own picture concentrated !                    670

But as for me I have a test
Of better than the very best.
*Respice finem!* Judge the end ;
The man, and not the child, my friend !

675   First ecstasy of Pentecost,
(You now perceive my sermon's text.)
First leap to Sunward flings you vexed
By glory of its own riposte
Back to your mind.   But gathering strength

680   And nerve, you come (ah light !) at length
To dwell awhile in the caress
Of that strange super-consciousness.
After one memory—O abide !
Vivid Savitri lightning-eyed !—

685   Nothing is worth a thought beside.
One hint of Amrita [55] to taste
And all earth's wine may run to waste !
For by this very means Christ gained [56]
His glimpse into that world above

690   Which he denominated " Love."
Indeed I think the man attained
By some such means—I have not strained
Out mind by chance of sense or sex
To find a way less iron-brained

695   Determining direction *x ;* [57]
I know not if these Hindu methods
Be best ('tis no such life and death odds,
Since suffering souls to save or damn
Never existed).   So I fall

700   Confessing : Well, perchance I am
Myself a Christian after all !

So far at least.   I must concede
Christ did attain in every deed ;
Yet, being an illiterate man,

705   Not his to balance or to scan,
To call God stupid or unjust !
He took the universe on trust ;
He reconciled the world below
With that above ; rolled eloquence

710   Steel-tired [58] o'er reason's "why?" and "whence?"
Discarded all proportion just,
And thundered in our ears " I know,"
And bellowed in our brains " ye must."

Fifty years of
Europe worth
a cycle of
Cathay.
Method of
Christ.   The
poet a Chris-
tian.

With reserva-
tions.   Deus in
machinâ.   Pon-
tius Pilate as a
Surrey Magis-
trate.

Mystic mean-
ing of Pente-
cost.

Such reservations—and I class
Myself a Christian : let us pass                    715
Back to the text whose thread we lost,
And see what means this " Pentecost."

Super-con-
sciousness is
the gift of the
Holy Ghost.

This, then, is what I deem occurred
(According to our Saviour's word)
That all the Saints at Pentecost                    720
Received the gift—the Holy Ghost ;
Such gift implying, as I guess,
This very super-consciousness.[50]
Miracles follow as a dower ;
But ah ! they used that fatal power                 725
And lost the Spirit in the act.
This may be fancy or a fact ;
At least it squares with super-sense
Or "spiritual experience."

Poet not a
materialist.
Mohammed's
ideas.

You do not well to swell the list                  730
Of horrid things to me imputed
By calling me "materialist."
At least this thought is better suited
To Western minds than is embalmed
Among the doctrines of Mohammed,                    735
The dogma parthenogenetic *
As told me by a fat ascetic.
He said : " Your worthy friends may lack you late,
But learn how Mary was immaculate ! "
I sat in vague expectant bliss.                     740

Verbatim re-
port of Moslem
account of the
Annunciation.

The story as it runs is this :
(I quote my Eastern friend [41] verbatim !)
*The Virgin, going to the bath,*
*Found a young fellow in her path,*
*And turned, prepared to scold and rate him !*      745
*" How dare you be on me encroaching ? "*
*The beautiful young gentleman,*
*With perfect courtesy approaching,*
*Bowed deeply, and at once began :*
*" Fear nothing, Mary !   All is well !*            750
*I am the angel Gabriel."*
*She bared her right breast* ; (query why ?)
*The angel Gabriel let fly*

* Concerning conception of a virgin.

755
*Out of a silver Tube a Dart*
*Shooting God's Spirit to her heart—*[61]
This beats the orthodox Dove-Suitor !
What explanation could be cuter
Than—Gabriel with a pea-shooter?

760
In such a conflict I stand neuter.
But oh ! mistake not gold for pewter !
The plain fact is : materialise
What spiritual fact you choose,
And all such turn to folly—-lose
765
The subtle splendour, and the wise
Love and dear bliss of truth.   Beware
Lest your lewd laughter set a snare
For any !   Thus and only thus
Will I admit a difference
'Twixt spirit and the things of sense.
770
What is the quarrel between us ?
Why do our thoughts so idly clatter ?
I do not care one jot for matter,
One jot for spirit, while you say
One is pure ether, one pure clay.

Degradation of
symbols.   Es-
sential identity
of all forms of
existence.

775
I've talked too long : you're very good—
I only hope you've understood !
Remember that " conversion " lurks
Nowhere behind my words and works.
Go home and think ! my talk refined
780
To the sheer needs of your own mind.
You cannot bring God in the compass
Of human thought?   Up stick and thump ass !
Let human thought itself expand —
Bright Sun of Knowledge, in me rise !
785
Lead me to those exalted skies
To live and love and understand !
Paying no price, accepting nought—
The Giver and the Gift are one
With the Receiver—O thou Sun
790
Of thought, of bliss transcending thought,
Rise where division dies !   Absorb
In glory of the glowing orb
Self and its shadow !

Practical ad-
vice.

Christian
mystics not
true Christians.
What think ye
of Crowley?
His interlo-
cutor dis-
missed, not
with a jest, but
with a warning.

Now who dares
Call me no Christian? And, who cares?    795
Read; you will find the Master of Balliol,
Discarding Berkeley, Locke, and Paley, 'll
Resume such thoughts and label clear
" My Christianity lies here !"
With such religion who finds fault?    800
Stay, it seems foolish to exalt
Religion to such heights as these,
Refine the actual agonies
To nothings, lest the mystic jeer
" So logic bends its line severe    805
Back to my involuted curve !"
These are my thoughts. I shall not swerve.
Take them, and see what dooms deserve
Their rugged grandeur—heaven or hell?
Mind the dark doorway there ! [62]  Farewell !    810

Poet yawns.

How tedious I always find
That special manner of my mind !

Aum !

Aum ! let us meditate aright
On that adorable One Light,
Divine Savitri ! So may She    815
Illume our minds ! So mote it be !

# NOTES TO ASCENSION DAY AND PENTECOST

"Blind Chesterton is sure to err,
And scan my work in vain;
I am my own interpreter,
And I will make it plain."

## NOTE TO INTRODUCTION

### 1 WILLIAM SHAKESPEARE.

### AN APPRECIATION.

#### BY ALEISTER CROWLEY.*

IT is a lamentable circumstance that so many colossal brains (W. H. Mallock, &c.) have been hitherto thrown away in attacking what is after all a problem of mere academic interest, the authorship of the plays our fathers accepted as those of Shakespeare. To me it seems of immediate and vital importance to do for Shakespeare what Verrall has done so ably for Euripides. The third tabernacle must be filled; Shaw and "the Human" must have their Superhuman companion. (This is not a scale: pithecanthropoid innuendo is to be deprecated.)

Till now—as I write the sun bursts forth suddenly from a cloud, as if heralding the literary somersault of the twentieth century—we have been content to accept Shakespeare as orthodox, with common sense; moral to a fault, with certain Rabelaisian leanings: a healthy tone (we say) pervades his work. Never believe it! The sex problem is his Speciality; a morbid decadence (so-called) is hidden i' th' heart o' th' rose. In other words, the divine William is the morning star to Ibsen's dawn, and Bernard Shaw's effulgence.

The superficial, the cynical, the misanthropic will demand proof of such a statement. Let it be our contemptuous indulgence to afford them what they ask.

May I premise that, mentally obsessed, mono-maniac indeed, as we must now consider Shakespeare to have been on these points, he was yet artful enough to have concealed his

advanced views—an imperative necessity, if we consider the political situation, and the virginal mask under which Queen Bess hid the grotesque and hideous features of a Messaline. Clearly so, since but for this concealment even our Shakespearian scholars would have discovered so patent a fact. In some plays, too, of course, the poet deals with less dangerous topics. These are truly conventional, no doubt; we may pass them by; they are foreign to our purpose; but we will take that stupendous example of literary subterfuge—*King Lear.*

Let me digress to the history of my own conversion.

Syllogistically,—All great men (*e.g.* Shaw) are agnostics and subverters of morals. Shakespeare was a great man. Therefore Shakespeare was an agnostic and a subverter of morals.

*A priori* this is then certain. But—

Who killed Rousseau?
I, said Huxley
(Like Robinson Crusoe),
With arguments true,—so
I killed Rousseau!

Beware of *à priori!* Let us find our facts, guided in the search by *à priori* methods, no doubt; but the result will this time justify us.

Where would a man naturally hide his greatest treasure? In his most perfect treasure-house.

Where shall we look for the truest thought of a great poet? In his greatest poem.

What is Shakespeare's greatest play? *King Lear.*

In *King Lear*, then, we may expect the final statement of the poet's mind. The passage that first put me on the track of the amazing discovery for which the world has to thank me is to be found in Act I. Sc. ii. ll. 132-149:—

"This is the excellent foppery of the world, that, when we are sick in fortune,—often the surfeit of our own behaviour,—we make guilty

* The lamented decease of the above gentleman forbids all hope (save through the courtesy of Sir Oliver Lodge) of the appearance of the companion article.—A. C.

185

of our disasters the sun, the moon, and the stars; as if we were villains by necessity, fools by heavenly compulsion, knaves, thieves, and treachers by spherical predominance, drunkards, liars, and adulterers by an enforced obedience of planetary influence; and all that we are evil in, by a divine thrusting on: an admirable evasion of whoremaster man, to lay his goatish disposition to the charge of a star! My father compounded with my mother under the dragon's tail, and my nativity was under *ursa major;* so that it follows I am rough and lecherous. 'Sfoot! I should have been that I am had the maidenliest star in the firmament twinkled on my bastardizing."

If there is one sound philosophical dictum in the play, it is this. (I am not going to argue with astrologers in the twentieth century.)

It is one we can test. On questions of morality and religion opinions veer; but if Shakespeare was a leader of thought, he saw through the humbug of the star-gazers; if not, he was a credulous fool; not the one man of his time, not a "debauched genius" (for Sir R. Burton in this phrase has in a sense anticipated my discovery) but a mere Elizabethan.

This the greatest poet of all time? Then we must believe that Gloucester was right, and that eclipses caused the fall of Lear! Observe that before this Shakespeare has had a sly dig or two at magic. In *King John,* "My lord, they say five moons were seen to-night" —but there is no eyewitness. So in *Macbeth.* In a host of spiritual suggestion there is always the rational sober explanation alongside to discredit the folly of the supernatural.

Shakespeare is like his own Touchstone; he uses his folly as a stalking-horse, and under the presentation of that he shoots his wit.

Here, however, the mask is thrown off for any but the utterly besotted; Edmund's speech stands up in the face of all time as truth; it challenges the acclamation of the centuries.

Edmund is then the hero; more, he is Shakespeare's own portrait of himself; his ways are dark — (and, alas! his tricks are vain!)—for why? For the fear of the conventional world about him.

He is illegitimate: Shakespeare is no true child of that age, but born in defiance of it and its prejudices.

Having taken this important step, let us slew round the rest of the play to fit it. If it fits, the law of probability comes to our aid; every coincidence multiplies the chance of our correctness in ever increasing proportion. We shall see—and you may look up your Proctor —that if the stars are placed just so by chance not law, then also it may be possible that Shakespeare was the wool-combing, knock-kneed, camel-backed, church-going, plaster-of-Paris, stick-in-the-mud our scholars have always made him.

Edmund being the hero, Regan and Goneril must be the heroines. So nearly equal are their virtues and beauties that our poet cannot make up his mind which shall possess him— besides which, he wishes to drive home his arguments in favour of polygamy.

But the great theme of the play is of course filial duty; on this everything will turn. Here is a test:

*Whenever this question is discussed, let us see who speaks the language of sense, and who that of draggle-tailed emotionalism and tepid melodrama.*

In the first scene the heroines, who do not care for the old fool their father—as how could any sane women? Remember Shakespeare is here about to show the folly of filial love as such—feel compelled, by an act of gracious generosity to a man they despise, yet pity, to say what they think will please the dotard's vanity. Also no doubt the sound commercial instinct was touched by Lear's promise to make acres vary as words, and they determined to make a final effort to get some parsnips buttered after all.

Shakespeare (it is our English boast) was no long-haired squiggle self-yclept bard; but a business man—see Bishop Blougram's appreciation of him as such.

Shall we suppose him to have deliberately blackguarded in another his own best qualities?

Note, too, the simple honesty of the divine sisters! Others, more subtle, would have suspected a trap, arguing that such idiocy as Lear's could not be genuine—Cordelia, the Madame Humbert of the play, does so; her over-cleverness leaves her stranded: yet by a certain sliminess of dissimulation, the oiliness of frankness, the pride that apes humility, she *does* catch the best king going. Yet it avails her little. She is hanged like the foul Vivien she is.*

Cordelia's farewell to her sisters shows up the characters of the three in strong relief. Cordelia—without a scrap of evidence to go on —accuses her sisters of hypocrisy and cruelty. (This could not have previously existed, or Lear would not have been deceived.)

Regan gravely rebukes her; recommends, as it were, a course of Six Easy Lessons in Mind-

---

* I use the word Vivien provisionally, pending the appearance of an essay to prove that Lord Tennyson was in secret an ardent reformer of our lax modern morals. No doubt, there is room for this. Vivien was perfectly right about the "cycle of strumpets and scoundrels whom Mr. Tennyson has set revolving round the figure of his central wittol," and she was the only one with the courage to say so, and the brains to strip off the barbarous glitter from an idiotic and phantom chivalry.

ing Her Own Business; and surely it was unparalleled insolence on the part of a dismissed girl to lecture her more favoured sister on the very point for which she herself was at that moment being punished. It is the spite of baffled dissimulation against triumphant honesty. Goneril adds a word of positive advice. "You," she says in effect, "who prate of duty thus, see you show it to him unto whom you owe it."

That this advice is wasted is clear from Act V. Sc. iii., where the King of France takes the first trivial opportunity * to be free of the vile creature he had so foolishly married.

Cordelia goes, and the sisters talk together. Theirs is the language of quiet sorrow for an old man's failing mind; yet a most righteous determination not to allow the happiness of the English people to depend upon his whims. Bad women would have rejoiced in the banishment of Kent, whom they already knew to be their enemy; these truly good women regret it. "Such unconstant starts are we like to have from him as this of Kent's banishment" (Act I. Sc. i. ll. 304-5).

In Scene ii. Edmund is shown; he feels himself a man, more than Edgar: a clear-headed, brave, honourable man; but with no maggots. The injustice of his situation strikes him; he determines not to submit.†

This is the attitude of a strong man, and a righteous one. Primogeniture is wrong enough; the other shame, no fault of his, would make the blood of any free man boil.

Gloucester enters, and exhibits himself as a prize fool by shouting in disjointed phrases what everybody knew. Great news it is, of course, and on discovering Edmund, he can think of nothing more sensible than to ask for more! "Kent banished thus! And France in choler parted! And the king gone to-night! subscrib'd his power! Confin'd to exhibition! All this done upon the gad! Edmund, how now! what news?" (Act I. Sc. ii. ll. 23-26).

Edmund "forces a card" by the simple device of a prodigious hurry to hide it. Gloucester gives vent to his astrological futilities, and falls to anxiomania in its crudest form,— "We have seen the best of our time: machinations, hollowness, treachery, and all ruinous disorders, follow us disquietly to our graves" (Sc. ii. ll. 125-127).

Edmund, once rid of him, gives us the

* He leaves her in charge of Marshal Le Fer, whom alone he could trust to be impervious to her wiles, he being devoted to another; for, as an invaluable contemporary MS. has it, "Seccotine colle même Le Fer."

† This may be, but I think should not be, used as an argument to prove the poet an illegitimate son of Queen Elizabeth.

plainest sense we are likely to hear for the rest of our lives; then, with the prettiest humour in the world takes the cue of his father's absurdity, and actually plays it on his enemy. Edgar's leg is not so easily pulled—("How long have you been a sectary astronomical?" ll. 169, 170)—and the bastard hero, taking alarm, gets right down to business.

In Scene iii. we find Lear's senile dementia taking the peculiarly loathsome forms familiar to alienists—this part of my subject is so unpleasant that I must skim over it; I only mention it to show how anxious Shakespeare is to show his hidden meaning, otherwise his naturally delicate mind would have avoided the depiction of such phenomena.

All this prepares us for Scene iv., in which we get a glimpse of the way Lear's attendants habitually behave. Oswald, who treats Lear throughout with perfect respect, and only shows honest independence in refusing to obey a man who is not his master, is insulted in language worthier of a bargee than a king; and when he remonstrates in dignified and temperate language is set upon by the ruffianly Kent.

Are decent English people to complain when Goneril insists that this sort of thing shall not occur in a royal house? She does so, in language nobly indignant, yet restrained: Lear, in the hideous, impotent rage of senility, calls her —his own daughter—a bastard (no insult to her, but to himself or his wife, mark ye well!). Albany enters—a simple, orderly-minded man; he must not be confused with Cornwall; he is at the last Lear's dog; yet even he in decent measured speech sides with his wife. Is Lear quieted? No! He utters the most horrible curse, not excepting that of Count Cenci, that a father ever pronounced. Incoherent threats succeed to the boilings-over of the hideous malice of a beastly mind; but a hundred knights are a hundred knights, and a threat is a threat. Goneril had not fulfilled her duty to herself, to her people, had she allowed this monster of mania to go on.

I appeal to the medical profession; if one doctor will answer me that a man using Lear's language should be allowed control of a hundred armed ruffians [in the face of Kent's behaviour we know what weight to attach to Lear's defence: "Detested kite! thou liest" (I. iv. l. 286)], should ever be allowed outside a regularly appointed madhouse, I will cede the point, and retire myself into an asylum.

In fact, Lear is going mad; the tottering intellect, at no time strong ("'Tis the infirmity of age; yet he hath ever but slenderly known himself," I. i. ll. 296-7), is utterly cast down by drink and debauchery: he even sees it himself, and with a pointless bestiality from the Fool, fit companion for the—king—and in that word we see all the concentrated loathing of the true Shakespeare for a despotism, massed in one lurid flame, phantasmagoric horror, the grim First Act rolls down.

## II.

Act II. Sc. i. adds little new to our thesis, save that in line 80 we see Gloucester (ignorant of his own son's handwriting!) accept the forged letter as genuine, as final proof, with not even the intervention of a Bertillon to excuse so palpable a folly, so egregious a crime. What father of to-day would disinherit, would hunt down to death, a beloved son, on such evidence? Or are we to take it that the eclipse gave proof unshakable of a phenomenon so portentous?

In Scene ii. we have another taste of Kent's gentlemanly demeanour; let our conventionalist interpreters defend this unwarrantable bullying if they dare! Another might be so gross, so cowardly; but not our greatest poet! A good portion of this play, as will be shown later, is devoted to a bitter assault upon the essentially English notion that the pugilist is the supreme device of the Creator for furthering human happiness. (See "Cashel Byron's Profession" for a similar, though more logical and better-worded, attack.) Coarse and violent language continues to disgrace Lear's follower; only Gloucester, the unconscionable ass and villain of Scene i., has a word to say in his defence.

In Scene iii. we have a taste of Edgar's quality. Had this despicable youth the consciousness of innocence, or even common courage, he had surely stood to his trial. Not he! He plays the coward's part — and his disguise is not even decent.

In Scene iv. we are shown the heroic sisters in their painful task of restraining, always with the utmost gentleness of word and demeanour, the headstrong passions of the miserable king. Lear, at first quiet in stating his fancied wrongs "*Reg.* 'I am glad to see your highness.' *Lear.* 'Regan, I think you are; I know what reason I have to think so: if thou shouldst not be glad, I would divorce me from thy mother's tomb, Sepulchring an adult'ress. (*To Kent*). O! are you free? Some other time for that. Beloved Regan, Thy sister's naught: O Regan! she hath tied Sharp-tooth'd unkindness, like a vulture, here: (*Points to his heart*). I can scarce speak to thee; thou'lt not believe with how deprav'd a quality—O Regan!' *Reg.* 'I pray you, sir, take patience. I have hope'") (ll. 130–139), an excusable speech, at the first hint that he is not to have it all his own way, falls a-cursing again like the veriest drab or scullion Hamlet ever heard.

Here is a man, deprived on just cause of half a useless company of retainers. Is this wrong (even were it a wrong) such as to justify the horrible curses of ll. 164–168, "All the stor'd vengeances of heaven fall On her ingrateful top! Strike her young bones, You taking airs, with lameness! You nimble lightnings, dart your blinding flames Into her scornful eyes!" With this he makes his age contemptible by the drivel-pathos of ll. 156–158, "Dear daughter, I confess that I am old; Age is unnecessary: on my knees I beg (*Kneeling*) That you'll vouchsafe me raiment, bed, and food," begging what none ever thought to deny him.

Yet such is the patience of Goneril that even when goaded by all this infamous Billingsgate into speech, her rebuke is the temperate and modest ll. 198–200. "Why not by the hand, sir? How have I offended? All's not offence that indiscretion finds And dotage terms so." If we ask a parallel for such meekness under insult, calumny, and foul abuse, we must seek it not in a human story, but a divine.

The heroines see that no half measures will do, and Lear is stripped of all the murderous retinue—what scum they are is shown by the fact that not one of them draws sword for him, or even follows him into the storm—to which his bad heart clings; yet for him—for him in spite of all his loathsomeness, his hatred, his revengefulness—is Regan's gentle and loving,

"For his particular, I'll receive him gladly."

## III.

In Act III. we have another illustration of the morality that passed current with the Tudors, and which only a Shakespeare had the courage to attack. Kent does not stick at treachery—he makes one gulp of treason—straining at the gnat of discipline, he swallows the camel of civil war.

It was then, and is even now, the practice of some—for example, the emigrés of the French Revolution—to invite foreign invasion as a means of securing domestic reaction. The blackguardism implied is beyond language: Shakespeare was perhaps thinking of the proposal, in Mary's reign, to react to Romanism by the aid of Spanish troops. But he will go further than this, will our greatest poet; it were ill that the life of even one child should atone for mere indignity or discomfort to another, were he the greatest in the realm. To-day we all agree; we smile or sneer if any one should differ. "King Lear got caught in the rain—let us go and kill a million men!" is an argument not much understood of Radical Clubs, and even Jingos would pause, did they but take the precaution of indulging in a mild aperient before recording their opinions.

In Scenes iii., vi., and vii., Edmund, disgusted beyond all measure with Gloucester's infamies, honourably and patriotically denounces him.

The other scenes depict the miseries which follow the foolish and the unjust ; and Nemesis falls upon the ill-minded Gloucester. Yet Shakespeare is so appreciative of the virtue of compassion (for Shakespeare was, as I shall hope to prove one day, a Buddhist) that Cornwall, the somewhat cruel instrument of eternal Justice, is killed by his servant. Regan avenges her husband promptly, and I have little doubt that this act of excessive courtesy towards a man she did not love is the moral cause of her unhappy end.

I would note that we should not attempt to draw any opinions as to the author's design from the conversation of the vulgar ; even had we not Coriolanus to show us what he thought.

## IV.

Act IV. develops the plot and is little germane to our matter, save that we catch a glimpse of the unspeakably vile Cordelia, with no pity for her father's serious condition (though no doubt he deserved all he got, he was now harmless, and should have inspired compassion), hanging to him in the hope that he would now reverse his banishment and make her (after a bloody victory) sole heiress of great England.

And were any doubt left in our minds as to who really was the hero of the play, the partizanship of France should settle it. Shakespeare has never any word but ridicule for the French ; never aught but praise of England and love for her : are we to suppose that in his best play he is to stultify all his other work and insult the English for the benefit of the ridiculed and hated Frenchman ?

Moreover, Cordelia reckons without her host. The British bulldogs make short work of the invaders and rebels, doubtless with the connivance of the King of France, who, with great and praiseworthy acuteness, foresees that Cordelia will be hanged, thus liberating him from his "most filthy bargain" : there is but one alarum, and the whole set of scoundrels surrender. Note this well ; it is not by brute force that the battle is won ; for even if we exonerate the King of France, we may easily believe that the moral strength of the sisters cowed the French.

This is the more evident, since in Act V. Shakespeare strikes his final blow at the absurdity of the duel, when Edmund is dishonestly slain by the beast Edgar. Yet the poet's faith is still strong : wound up as his muse is to tragedy, he retains in Edmund the sublime heroism, the simple honesty, of the true Christian ; at the death of his beloved mistresses he cries,

> "I was contracted to them both : all three
> Now marry in an instant——"

At the moment of death his great nature (self-accusatory, as the finest so often are) asserts itself, and he forgives even the vilest of the human race,—"I pant for life : some good I mean to do Despite of mine own nature.[1] Quickly send, Be brief in it, to the castle ; for my writ Is on the life of Lear and on Cordelia. Nay, send in time " (ll. 245-249).

And in that last supreme hour of agony he claims Regan as his wife, as if by accident ; it is not the passionate assertion of a thing doubtful, but the natural reference to a thing well known and indisputable.

And in the moment of his despair ; confronted with the dead bodies of the splendid sisters, the catafalque of all his hopes, he can exclaim in spiritual triumph over material disaster—the victory of a true man's spirit over Fate—

> "Yet Edmund was belov'd."

Edgar is left alive with Albany, alone of all that crew ; and if remorse could touch their brutal and callous souls (for the degeneration of the weakling, well-meaning Albany, is a minor tragedy), what hell could be more horrible than the dragging out of a cancerous existence in the bestial world of hate their hideous hearts had made, now, even for better men, for ever dark and gloomy, robbed of the glory of the glowing Goneril, the royal Regan, and only partially redeemed by the absence of the harlot Cordelia and the monster Lear.

## V.

It may possibly be objected by the censorious, by the effete parasites of a grim conventionalism, that I have proved too much. Even by conventional standards Edmund, Goneril, and Regan appear angels. Even on the moral point, the sisters, instead of settling down to an enlightened and by no means overcrowded polygamy, prefer to employ poison. This is perhaps true, of Goneril at least ; Regan is, if one may distinguish between star and star, somewhat the finer character.

This criticism is perhaps true in part ; but I will not insult the intelligence of my readers. I will leave it to them to take the obvious step and work backwards to the re-exaltation of Lear, Cordelia, Edgar and company, to the heroic fields of their putty Elysium (putty, not

---

[1] This may merely mean "despite the fact that I am dying—though I am almost too weak to speak." If so, the one phrase in the play which seems to refute our theory is disposed of. Execution of such criminals would be a matter of routine at the period of the play.

Putney) in their newly-demonstrated capacity as "unnatural" sons, daughters, fathers, and so on.

But I leave it. I am content—my work will have been well done—if this trifling essay be accepted as a just instalment towards a saner criticism of our holiest writers, a juster appreciation of the glories of our greatest poet, a possibly jejune yet assuredly historic attempt to place for the first time William Shakespeare on his proper pedestal as an early disciple of Mr. George Bernard Shaw; and by consequence to carve myself a little niche in the same temple : the smallest contributions will be thankfully received.

## NOTES TO ASCENSION DAY

1. *I flung out of chapel.*[1]—Browning, *Xmas Eve*, III. last line.

3. *Venus' Bower and Osiris' Tomb.*[2]—Crowley, *Tannhäuser.*

5. *God.*[3]—Hebrew אלהים, Gen. iii. 5.

5. *gods.*[4]—Hebrew אלהים, Gen. iii. 5. The Revisers, seeing this most awkward juxtaposition, have gone yet one step lower and translated both words by "God." In other passages, however, they have been compelled to disclose their own dishonesty and translate אלהים by "gods." For evidence of this the reader may look up such passages as Ex. xviii. 11; Deut. xxxii. 17; Ps. lxxxii. [in particular, where the word occurs twice, as also the word אל. But the revisers twice employ the word "God" and once the word "gods." The A.V. has "mighty" in one case]; Gen. xx. 13, where again the verb is plural; Sam. xxviii. 13, and so on. See the Hebrew Dictionary of Gesenius (trans. Tregelles), Bagster, 1859, *s.v.*, for proof that the Author is on the way to the true interpretation of these conflicting facts, as now established—see Huxley, H. Spencer, Kuenen, Reuss, Lippert, and others—and his orthodox translator's infuriated snarls (in brackets) when he suspects this tendency to accept facts as facts.

6. *Soul went down.*[5]—*The Questions of King Milinda*, 40-45, 48, 67, 86-89, 111, 132.

7. *The metaphysical lotus-eyed.*[6]—Gautama Buddha.

10. *Childe Roland.*[7]—Browning, *Dramatic Romances.*

11. *Two hundred thousand Trees.*[8]—Browning wrote about 200,000 lines.

13. *Your Reverence.*[9]—The imaginary Aunt Sally for the poetic cocoanut.*

16. *"God's right use of it."*[10]—"And many an eel, though no adept In God's right reason for it, kept Gnawing his kidneys half a year."—Shelley, *Peter Bell the Third.*

17. *One tree.*[11]—Note the altered value of

Crowley confuses two common pastoral amusements—throwing wooden balls at cocoanuts and sticks at Aunt Sally.

the metaphor, such elasticity having led Prof. Blümengarten to surmise them to be india-rubber trees.

27. *"Truth, that's the gold."*[12]—*Two Poets of Croisic*, clii. 1, and elsewhere.

28. *"I, you, or Simpkin."*[13]—*Inn Album*, l. 143. "Simpkin" has nothing to do with the foaming grape of Eastern France.

36. *Aischulos.*[14]—See Agamemnon (Browning's translation), Preface.

40. *Aristobulus.*[15]—May be scanned elsehow by pedants. Cf. Swinburne's curious scansion : Arĭstŏphānēs. But the scansion adopted here gives a more creditable rhyme.

42. Βατραχομυομαχια.[16]—Aristophanes Batrachoi.

46. *Mine of so many pounds—pouch even pence of it?*[17]—This line was suggested to me by a large holder of Westralians.

47. *Something easier.*[18]—*Christmas Eve and Easter Day.*

51. *Newton.*[19]—Mathematician and physicist of repute.

51. *Faraday.*[20]—See Dictionary of National Biography.

64. *I, of the Moderns, have alone Greek.*[21]—As far as they would let me. I know some.

74. *Beard.*[22]—" 150. A Barba Senioris Sanctissimi pendet omnis ornatus omnium : & influentia ; nam omnia appellantur ab illa barba, Influentia.

"151. Hic est ornatus omnium ornatuum : Influentie superiores & inferiores omnes respiciunt istam Influentiam.

"152. Ab ista influentia dependet vita omnium.

"153. Ab hac influentia dependent cœli & terra ; pluviæ beneplaciti ; & alimenta omnium.

"154. Ab hac influentia venit providentia omnium. Ab hac influentia dependent omnes exercitus superiores & inferiores.

"155. Tredecim fontes olei magnificentiæ boni, dependent a barba hujus influentiæ gloriosæ ; & omnes emanant in Microprosopum.

"156. Ne dicas omnes ; sed novem ex iis inveniuntur ad inflectenda judicia.

"157. Et quando hæc influentia æqualiter pendet usque ad præcordia omnes Sanctitates Sanctitatum Sanctitatis ab illa dependent.

"158. In istam influentiam extenditur expansio aporrhœæ supernæ, quæ est caput omnium capitum : quod non cognoscitur nec perficitur, quodque non norunt nec superi, nec inferi : propterea omnia ab ista influentia dependent.

"159. In hanc barbam tria capita de quibus diximus, expandantur, & omnia consociantur in hac influentia, & inveniuntur in ea.

"160. Et propterea omnis ornatus ornatuum ab ista influentia dependent.

"161. Istæ literæ, quæ dependent ab hoc Seniore, omnes pendent in ista barba, & consociantur in ista influentia.

"162. Et pendent in ea ad stabiliendas literas alteras.

"163. Nisi enim illæ literæ ascenderent in Seniorem, reliquæ istæ literæ non stabilirentur.

"164. Et propterea dicit Moses cum opus esset : Tetragrammaton, Tetragrammaton bis : & ita ut accentus distinguat utrumque.

"165. Certe enim ab influentia omnia dependent.

"166. Ab ista influentia ad reverentiam adiguntur superna & inferna, & flectuntur coram ea.

"167. Beatus ille, qui ad hanc usque per tingit.

*Idra Suta, seu Synodus minor.* Sectio VI.

"496. *Forehead.*[23]—Frons Cranii est frons ad visitandum : (Al. ad eradicandum) peccatoras.

"497. Et cum ista frons detegitur tunc excitantur Domini Judiciorum, contra illos qui non erubescunt in operibus suis.

"498. Hæc frons ruborem habet roseum. Sed illo tempore, cum frons Senioris erga hanc frontem detegitur, hæc apparet alba ut nix.

"499. Et illa hora vocatur Tempus beneplaciti pro omnibus.

"500. In libro Dissertationis Scholæ Raf Jebha Senis dicitur : Frons est receptaculum frontis Senioris. Sin minus, litera Cheth inter duas reliquas interponitur, juxta illud : (Num. xxiv. 17) ומחץ et confringet angulos Moab.

"501. Et alibi diximus, quod etiam vocetur נצה, literis vicinis permutatis : id est, superatio.

"502. Multæ autem sunt Superationes : ita ut Superatio alia elevata sit in locum alium : & aliæ dentur Superationes quæ extenduntur in totum corpus.

"503. Die Sabbathi autem tempore precum pomeridianarum, ne excitentur judicia, detegitur frons Senioris Sanctissimi.

"504. Et omnia judicia subiguntur ; & quamvis extent, tamen non exercentur. (Al. et sedantur.)

"505. Ab hac fronte dependent viginti quatuor tribunalia, pro omnibus illis, qui protervi sunt in operibus.

"506. Sicut scriptum est : (Ps. lxxiii. 11.) Et dixerunt : quomodo sit Deus ? Et estne scientia in excelso ?

"507. At vero viginti saltem sunt. cur adduntur quatuor ? nimirum respectu suppliciorum, tribunalium inferiorum, quæ a supernis dependent.

"508. Remanent ergo viginti. Et propterea neminem supplicio capitali afficiunt, donec compleverit & ascenderit ad viginti annos ; respectu viginti horum tribunalium.

"509. Sed in thesi nostra arcana docuimus, per ista respici viginti quatuor libros qui continentur in Lege.

*Idra Suta, seu Synodus minor.* Sectio XIIIv
77. *Chains.*[24]—Sakkâha-di*tt*hi, Vi*k*iki*kk*hâ, silabbata-parâmâsa, kâma, patigha, rûparâga, arûparâga, mâno, uddha*kk*a, avi*gg*â.

81. "*Who asks doth err.*"[25]—Arnold, *Light of Asia.*

83. *You.*[26]—You !

86. "*O'erleaps itself and falls on the other.*"[27] —*Macbeth*, I. vii. 27.

92. *English.*[28]— This poem is written in English.

94. *I cannot write.*[29]—This is not quite true. For instance :

This, the opening stanza of my masterly poem on Ladak, reads :—" The way was long, and the wind was cold : the Lama was infirm and advanced in years ; his prayer-wheel, to revolve which was his only pleasure, was carried by a disciple, an orphan."

There is a reminiscence of some previous incarnation about this : European critics may possibly even identify the passage. But at least the Tibetans should be pleased.*

* They were ; thence the pacific character of the British expedition of 1904.—A. C.

97. *While their Buddha I attack.*—Many Buddhists think I fill the bill with the following remarks on—

## PANSIL.[30]

Unwilling as I am to sap the foundations of the Buddhist religion by the introduction of Porphyry's terrible catapult, Allegory, I am yet compelled by the more fearful ballista of Aristotle, Dilemma. This is the two-handed engine spoken of by the prophet Milton ! *
This is the horn of the prophet Zeruiah, and with this am I, though no Syrian, utterly pushed, till I find myself back against the dead wall of Dogma. Only now realising how dead a wall that is, do I turn and try the effect of a hair of the dog that bit me, till the orthodox "literary" † school of Buddhists, as grown at Rangoon, exclaim with Lear : " How sharper than a serpent's tooth it is To have an intellect !" How is this? Listen, and hear !
I find myself confronted with the crux : that, a Buddhist, convinced intellectually and philosophically of the truth of the teaching of Gotama ; a man to whom Buddhism is the equivalent of scientific methods of Thought ; an expert in dialectic, whose logical faculty is bewildered, whose critical admiration is extorted by the subtle vigour of Buddhist reasoning ; I am yet forced to admit that, this being so, the Five Precepts ‡ are mere nonsense. If the Buddha spoke scientifically, not popularly, not rhetorically, then his precepts are not his. We must reject them or we must interpret them. We must inquire : Are they meant to be obeyed ? Or—and this is my theory—are they sarcastic and biting criticisms on existence, illustrations of the First Noble Truth ; *reasons*, as it were, for the apotheosis of annihilation ? I shall show that this is so. Let me consider them "precept upon precept," if the introduction of the Hebrew visionary is not too strong meat for the Little Mary § of a Buddhist audience.

* *Lycidas*, line 130.
† The school whose Buddhism is derived from the Canon, and who ignore the degradation of the professors of the religion, as seen in practice.
‡ The obvious caveat which logicians will enter against these remarks is that Pansil is the Five Virtues rather than Precepts. Etymologically this is so. However, we may regard this as a clause on my side of the argument, not against it ; for in my view these are virtues, and the impossibility of attaining them is the cancer of existence. Indeed, I support the etymology as against the futile bigotry of certain senile Buddhists of to-day. And, since it is the current interpretation of Buddhistic thought that I attack, I but show myself the better Buddhist in the act.—A. C.
§ A catch word for the stomach, from J. M. Barrie's play "Little Mary."

### THE FIRST PRECEPT.

This forbids the taking of life in any form. * What we have to note is the impossibility of performing this ; if we can prove it to be so, either Buddha was a fool, or his command was rhetorical, like those of Yahweh to Job, or of Tannhäuser to himself—

" Go ! seek the stars and count them and explore !
   Go ! sift the sands beyond a starless sea !"

Let us consider what the words can mean. The "Taking of Life" can only mean the reduction of living protoplasm to dead matter : or, in a truer and more psychological sense, the destruction of personality.
Now, in the chemical changes involved in Buddha's speaking this command, living protoplasm was changed into dead matter. Or, on the other horn, the fact (insisted upon most strongly by the Buddha himself, the central and cardinal point of his doctrine, the shrine of that Metaphysic which isolates it absolutely from all other religious metaphysic, which allies it with Agnostic Metaphysic) that the Buddha who had spoken this command was not the same as the Buddha before he had spoken it, lies the proof that the Buddha, by speaking this command, violated it. More, not only did he slay himself ; he breathed in millions of living organisms and slew them. He could nor eat nor drink nor breathe without murder implicit in each act. Huxley cites the " pitiless microscopist" who showed a drop of water to the Brahmin who boasted himself " Ahimsa "—harmless. So among the "rights" of a Bhikkhu is medicine. He who takes quinine does so with the deliberate intention of destroying innumerable living beings ; whether this is done by stimulating the phagocytes, or directly, is morally indifferent.
How such a fiend incarnate, my dear brother Ananda Maitriya, can call him " cruel and cowardly" who only kills a tiger, is a study in the philosophy of the mote and the beam !
Far be it from me to suggest that this is a defence of breathing, eating, and drinking. By no means ; in all these ways we bring suffering and death to others, as to ourselves. But since these are inevitable acts, since suicide would be a still more cruel alternative (especially in case something should subsist below mere Rupa), the command is not to achieve

* Fielding, in "The Soul of a People," has reluctantly to confess that he can find no trace of this idea in Buddha's own work, and calls the superstition the " echo of an older Faith."—A. C.
† The argument that the "animals are our brothers" is merely intended to mislead one who has never been in a Buddhist country. The average Buddhist would, of course, kill his brother for five rupees, or less.—A. C.

the impossible, the already violated in the act of commanding, but a bitter commentary on the foul evil of this aimless, hopeless universe, this compact of misery, meanness, and cruelty. Let us pass on.

### THE SECOND PRECEPT.

The Second Precept is directed against theft. Theft is the appropriation to one's own use of that to which another has a right. Let us see therefore whether or no the Buddha was a thief. The answer of course is in the affirmative. For to issue a command is to attempt to deprive another of his most precious possession—the right to do as he will; that is, unless, with the predestinarians, we hold that action is determined absolutely, in which case, of course, a command is as absurd as it is unavoidable. Excluding this folly, therefore, we may conclude that if the command be obeyed—and those of Buddha have gained a far larger share of obedience than those of any other teacher—the Enlightened One was not only a potential but an actual thief. Further, all voluntary action limits in some degree, however minute, the volition of others. If I breathe, I diminish the stock of oxygen available on the planet. In those far distant ages when Earth shall be as dead as the moon is to-day, my breathing now will have robbed some being then living of the dearest necessity of life.

That the theft is minute, incalculably trifling, is no answer to the moralist, to whom degree is not known; nor to the scientist, who sees the chain of nature miss no link.

If, on the other hand, the store of energy in the universe be indeed constant (whether infinite or no), if personality be indeed delusion, then theft becomes impossible, and to forbid it is absurd. We may argue that even so temporary theft may exist; and that this is so is to my mind no doubt the case. All theft is temporary, since even a millionaire must die; also it is universal, since even a Buddha must breathe.

### THE THIRD PRECEPT.

This precept, against adultery, I shall touch but lightly. Not that I consider the subject unpleasant—far from it!—but since the English section of my readers, having unclean minds, will otherwise find a fulcrum therein for their favourite game of slander. Let it suffice if I say that the Buddha—in spite of the ridiculous membrane legend,* one of those foul follies which idiot devotees invent only too freely—was a confirmed and habitual adulterer. It

* Membrum virile illius in membrana inclusum esse aiunt, ne copulare posset.

would be easy to argue with Hegel-Huxley that he who thinks of an act commits it (cf. Jesus also in this connection, though he only knows the creative value of desire), and that since A and not-A are mutually limiting, therefore interdependent, therefore identical, he who forbids an act commits it; but I feel that this is no place for metaphysical hair-splitting; let us prove what we have to prove in the plainest way.

I would premise in the first place that to commit adultery in the Divorce Court sense is not here in question.

It assumes too much proprietary right of a man over a woman, that root of all abomination!—the whole machinery of inheritance, property, and all the labyrinth of law.

We may more readily suppose that the Buddha was (apparently at least) condemning incontinence.

We know that Buddha had abandoned his home; true, but Nature has to be reckoned with. Volition is no necessary condition of offence. "I didn't mean to" is a poor excuse for an officer failing to obey an order.

Enough of this—in any case a minor question; since even on the lowest moral grounds—and we, I trust, soar higher!—the error in question may be resolved into a mixture of murder, theft, and intoxication. (We consider the last under the Fifth Precept.)

### THE FOURTH PRECEPT.

Here we come to what in a way is the fundamental joke of these precepts. A command is not a lie, of course; possibly cannot be; yet surely an allegorical order is one in essence, and I have no longer a shadow of a doubt that these so-called "precepts" are a species of savage practical joke.

Apart from this there can hardly be much doubt, when critical exegesis has done its damnedest on the Logia of our Lord, that Buddha did at some time commit himself to some statement. "(Something called) Consciousness exists" is, said Huxley, the irreducible minimum of the pseudo-syllogism, false even for an enthymeme, "Cogito, ergo sum!" This proposition he bolsters up by stating that whoso should pretend to doubt it, would thereby but confirm it. Yet might it not be said "(Something called) Consciousness appears to itself to exist," since Consciousness is itself the only witness to that confirmation? Not that even now we can deny some kind of existence to consciousness, but that it should be a more real existence than that of a reflection is doubtful, incredible, even inconceivable. If by consciousness we mean the normal consciousness, it is definitely untrue, since the

Dhyanic consciousness includes it and denies it. No doubt "something called" acts as a kind of caveat to the would-be sceptic, though the phrase is bad, implying a "calling." But we can guess what Huxley means.

No doubt Buddha's scepticism does not openly go quite as far as mine—it must be remembered that "scepticism" is merely the indication of a possible attitude, not a belief, as so many good fool folk think; but Buddha not only denies "Cogito, ergo sum"; but "Cogito, ergo non sum." See *Sabbasava Sutta*, par. 10.*

At any rate Sakkyaditthi, the delusion of personality, is in the very forefront of his doctrines; and it is this delusion that is constantly and inevitably affirmed in all normal consciousness. That Dhyanic thought avoids it is doubtful; even so, Buddha is here represented as giving precepts to ordinary people. And if personality be delusion, a lie is involved in the command of one to another. In short, we all lie all the time; we are compelled to lie by the nature of things themselves — paradoxical as that seems—and the Buddha knew it!

THE FIFTH PRECEPT.

At last we arrive at the end of our weary journey—surely in this weather we may have a drink! East of Suez,† Trombone-Macaulay (as I may surely say, when Browning writes Banjo-Byron ‡) tells us, a man may raise a Thirst. No, shrieks the Blessed One, the Perfected One, the Enlightened One, do not drink! It is like the streets of Paris when they were placarded with rival posters—

> Ne buvez pas de l'Alcool !
> L'Alcool est un poison !

and

> Buvez de l'Alcool !
> L'Alcool est un aliment !

We know now that alcohol is a food up to a certain amount; the precept, good enough for a rough rule as it stands, will not bear close inspection. What Buddha really commands, with that grim humour of his, is : Avoid Intoxication.

But what is intoxication? unless it be the loss of power to use perfectly a truth-telling set of faculties. If I walk unsteadily it is owing to nervous lies—and so for all the phenomena of drunkenness. But a lie involves the assump-

* Quoted below, "Science and Buddhism," note.
† "Ship me somewhere East of Suez, where a man can raise a thirst."—R. KIPLING.
‡ "While as for Quilp Hop o' my Thumb there, Banjo-Byron that twangs the strum-strum there."
—BROWNING, *Pacchiarotto* (said of A. Austin).

tion of some true standard, and this can nowhere be found. A doctor would tell you, moreover, that all food intoxicates: all, here as in all the universe, of every subject and in every predicate, is a matter of degree.

Our faculties never tell us true; our eyes say flat when our fingers say round; our tongue sends a set of impressions to our brain which our hearing declares non-existent—and so on.

What is this delusion of personality but a profound and centrally-seated intoxication of the consciousness? I am intoxicated as I address these words; you are drunk—beastly drunk!—as you read them; Buddha was as drunk as a British officer when he uttered his besotted command. There, my dear children, is the conclusion to which we are brought if you insist that he was serious!

I answer No! Alone among men then living, the Buddha was sober, and saw Truth. He, who was freed from the coils of the great serpent Theli coiled round the universe, he knew how deep the slaver of that snake had entered into us, infecting us, rotting our very bones with poisonous drunkenness. And so his cutting irony—drink no intoxicating drinks !

———

When I go to take Pansil,* it is in no spirit of servile morality; it is with keen sorrow gnawing at my heart. These five causes of sorrow are indeed the heads of the serpent of Desire. Four at least of them snap their fangs on me in and by virtue of my very act of receiving the commands, and of promising to obey them; if there is a little difficulty about the fifth, it is an omission easily rectified — and I think we should all make a point about that; there is great virtue in completeness.

Yes! Do not believe that the Buddha was a fool; that he asked men to perform the impossible or the unwise.† Do not believe that the sorrow of existence is so trivial that easy rules

* To "take Pansil" is to vow obedience to these Precepts.
† I do not propose to dilate on the moral truth which Ibsen has so long laboured to make clear: that no hard and fast rule of life can be universally applicable. Also, as in the famous case of the lady who saved (successively) the lives of her husband, her father, and her brother, the precepts clash. To allow to die is to kill—all this is obvious to the most ordinary thinkers. These precepts are of course excellent general guides for the vulgar and ignorant, but you and I, dear reader, are wise and clever, and know better. Nichtwar?
Excuse my being so buried in "dear Immanuel Kant" (as my friend Miss Br.c.[1] would say) that this biting and pregnant phrase slipped out unaware. As a rule, of course, I hate the introduction of foreign tongues into an English essay.—A. C.

[1] A fast woman who posed as a bluestocking.

easily interpreted (as all Buddhists do interpret the Precepts) can avail against them; do not mop up the Ganges with a duster; nor stop the revolution of the stars with a lever of lath.

Awake, awake only! let there be ever remembrance that Existence is sorrow, sorrow by the inherent necessity of the way it is made; sorrow not by volition, not by malice, not by carelessness, but by nature, by ineradicable tendency, by the incurable disease of Desire, its Creator, is it so, and the way to destroy it is by the uprooting of Desire; nor is a task so formidable accomplished by any threepenny-bit-in-the-plate-on-Sunday morality, the "deceive others and self-deception will take care of itself" uprightness, but by the severe roads of austere self-mastery, of arduous scientific research, which constitute the Noble Eightfold Path.

101-105. *There's one. . . Six Six Six.*[31]— This opinion has been recently (and most opportunely) confirmed by the Rev. Father Simons, Roman Catholic Missionary (and head of the Corner in Kashmir Stamps), Baramulla, Kashmir.

106. *Gallup.*[32] — For information apply to Mr. Sidney Lee.

111. *"It is the number of a Man."*[33]—Rev. xiii. 18.

117. *Fives.*[34]—Dukes.

122. (*Elsewhere.*)[35] — See "Songs of the Spirit" and other works.

128. *The Qabalistic Balm.*[36] — May be studied in "The Kabbalah (*sic*) Unveiled" (Redway). It is much to be wished that some one would undertake the preparation of an English translation of Rabbi Jischak Ben Loria's "De Revolutionibus Animarum," and of the book "Beth Elohim."

139. *Cain.*[37]—Gen. iv. 8.

152. *Hunyadi.*[38]—Hunyadi Janos, a Hungarian table water.

161. *Nadi.*[39]—For this difficult subject refer to the late Swami Vivekananda's "Raja Yoga."

167. *Tom Bond Bishop.*[40]—Founder of the "Children's Scripture Union" (an Association for the Dissemination of Lies among Young People) and otherwise known as a philanthropist. His relationship to the author (that of uncle) has procured him this rather disagreeable immortality. He was, let us hope, no relation to George Archibald Bishop, the remarkable preface to whose dreadfully conventionally psychopathic works is this.

### PREFACE.*

In the fevered days and nights under the Empire that perished in the struggle of 1870,

* To a collection of MSS. illustrating the "Psychopathia Sexualis" of von Kraft-Ebing. The names of the parties have been changed.

that whirling tumult of pleasure, scheming, success, and despair, the minds of men had a trying ordeal to pass through. In Zola's "La Curée" we see how such ordinary and natural characters as those of Saccard, Maxime, and the incestuous heroine, were twisted and distorted from their normal sanity, and sent whirling into the jaws of a hell far more affrayant than the mere cheap and nasty brimstone Sheol which is a Shibboleth for the dissenter, and with which all classes of religious humbug, from the Pope to the Salvation ranter, from the Mormon and the Jesuit to that mongrel mixture of the worst features of both, the Plymouth Brother, have scared their illiterate, since hypocrisy was born, with Abel, and spiritual tyranny, with Jehovah! Society, in the long run, is eminently sane and practical; under the Second Empire it ran mad. If these things are done in the green tree of Society, what shall be done in the dry tree of Bohemianism? Art always has a suspicion to fight against; always some poor mad Max Nordau is handy to call everything outside the kitchen the asylum. Here, however, there is a substratum of truth. Consider the intolerable long roll of names, all tainted with glorious madness. Baudelaire the diabolist, debauchee of sadism, whose dreams are nightmares, and whose waking hours delirium; Rollinat the necrophile, the poet of phthisis, the anxiomaniac; Péladan, the high priest—of nonsense; Mendés, frivolous and scoffing sensualist; besides a host of others, most alike in this, that, below the cloak of madness and depravity, the true heart of genius burns. No more terrible period than this is to be found in literature; so many great minds, of which hardly one comes to fruition; such seeds of genius, such a harvest of—whirlwind! Even a barren waste of sea is less saddening than one strewn with wreckage.

In England such wild song found few followers of any worth or melody. Swinburne stands on his solitary pedestal above the vulgar crowds of priapistic plagiarists; he alone caught the fierce frenzy of Baudelaire's brandied shrieks, and his First Series of Poems and Ballads was the legitimate echo of that not fierier note. But English Art as a whole was unmoved, at any rate not stirred to any depth, by this wave of debauchery. The great thinkers maintained the even keel, and the windy waters lay not for their frailer barks to cross. There is one exception of note, till this day unsuspected, in the person of George Archibald Bishop. In a corner of Paris this young poet (for in his nature the flower of poesy did spring, did even take root and give some promise of a brighter bloom, till stricken and blasted in latter years by the lightning of his own sins) was steadily writing day after day, night after night, often working forty hours at a time, work which he destined to entrance the world. All England should ring with his praises; by-and-by the whole world should know his name. Of these works none of the longer and more ambitious remains. How they were lost, and how those fragments we possess were saved, is best told by relating the romantic and almost incredible story of his life.

The known facts of this life are few, vague, and unsatisfactory; the more definite statements lack corroboration, and almost the only source at the disposal of the biographer is the letters of Mathilde Doriac to Mdme. J. S., who has kindly placed her portfolio at my service. A letter dated October 15, 1866, indicates that our author was born on the 23rd of that month. The father and mother of George were, at least on the surface, of an extraordinary religious turn of mind. Mathilde's version of the story, which has its source in our friend himself, agrees almost word for word with a letter of the Rev. Edw. Turle to Mrs. Cope, recommending the child to her care. The substance of the story is as follows.

The parents of George carried their religious ideas to the point of never consummating their marriage! * This arrangement does not seem to have been greatly appreciated by the wife; at least one fine morning she was found to be enceinte. The foolish father never thought of the hypothesis which commends itself most readily to a man of the world, not to say a man of science, and adopted that of a second Messiah! He took the utmost pains to conceal the birth of the child, treated everybody who came to the house as an emissary of Herod, and finally made up his mind to flee into Egypt! Like most religious maniacs, he never had an idea of his own, but distorted the beautiful and edifying events of the Bible into insane and ridiculous ones, which he proceeded to plagiarise.

On the voyage out the virgin mother became enamoured, as was her wont, of the nearest male, in this case a fellow-traveller. He, being well able to support her in the luxury which she desired, easily persuaded her to leave the boat with him by stealth. A small sailing vessel conveyed them to Malta, where they disappeared. The only trace left in the books of earth records that this fascinating character was accused, four years later, in Vienna, of poisoning her paramour, but thanks to the wealth and influence of her newer lover, she escaped.

The legal father, left by himself with a squalling child to amuse, to appease in his tantrums,

* Will it be believed that a clergyman (turned Plymouth Brother and schoolmaster) actually made an identical confession to a boy of ten years old?

and to bring up in the nurture and admonition of the Lord, was not a little perplexed by the sudden disappearance of his wife. At first he supposed that she had been translated, but, finding that she had not left the traditional mantle behind her, he abandoned this supposition in favour of quite a different, and indeed a more plausible one. He now believed her to be the scarlet woman in the Apocalypse, with variations. On arrival in Egypt he hired an old native nurse, and sailed for Odessa. Once in Russia he could find Gog and Magog, and present to them the child as Antichrist. For he was now persuaded that he himself was the First Beast, and would ask the sceptic to count his seven heads and ten horns. The heads, however, rarely totted up accurately!

At this point the accounts of Mr. Turle and Mathilde diverge slightly. The cleric affirms that he was induced by a Tartar lady, of an honourable and ancient profession, to accompany her to Tibet "to be initiated into the mysteries." He was, of course, robbed and murdered with due punctuality, in the town of Kiev. Mathilde's story is that he travelled to Kiev on the original quest, and died of typhoid or cholera. In any case, he died at Kiev in 1839. This fixes the date of the child's birth at 1837. His faithful nurse conveyed him safely to England, where his relatives provided for his maintenance and education.

With the close of this romantic chapter in his early history we lose all reliable traces for some years. One flash alone illumines the darkness of his boyhood; in 1853, after being prepared for confirmation, he cried out in full assembly, instead of kneeling to receive the blessing of the officiating bishop, "I renounce for ever this idolatrous church;" and was quietly removed.

He told Mathilde Doriac that he had been to Eton and Cambridge—neither institution, however, preserves any record of such admission. The imagination of George, indeed, is tremendously fertile with regard to events in his own life. His own story is that he entered Trinity College, Cambridge, in 1856, and was sent down two years later for an article which he had contributed to some University or College Magazine. No confirmation of any sort is to be found anywhere with regard to these or any other statements of our author. There is however, no doubt that in 1861 he quarrelled with his family; went over to Paris, where he settled down, at first, like every tufthead somewhere in the Quartier Latin; later, with Mathilde Doriac, the noble woman who became his mistress and held to him through all the terrible tragedy of his moral, mental, and physical life, in the Rue du Faubourg-Poissonière. At his house there the frightful scene

)f '68 took place, and it was there too that he
vas apprehended after the murders which he
lescribes so faithfully in "Abysmos." He had
ust finished this poem with a shriek of triumph,
and had read it through to the appalled
Mathilde "avec des yeux de flamme et de
gestes incohérentes," when, foaming at the
mouth, and "hurlant de blasphèmes indi-
cibles," he fell upon her with extraordinary
violence of passion ; the door opened, officers
appeared, the arrest was effected. He was committed to an asylum, for there could be no longer
any doubt of his complete insanity ; for three
weeks he had been raving with absinthe and
satyriasis. He survived his confinement no
long time ; the burning of the asylum with its in-
mates was one of the most terrible events of the
war of 1870. So died one of the most talented
Englishmen of his century, a man who for wide
knowledge of men and things was truly to be
envied, yet one who sold his birthright for a
mess of beastlier pottage than ever Esau
guzzled, who sold soul and body to Satan for
sheer love of sin, whose mere lust of perversion
is so intense that it seems to absorb every other
emotion and interest. Never since God woke
light from chaos has such a tragedy been unrolled before men, step after step toward the
lake of Fire !

At his house all his writings were seized, and,
it is believed, destroyed. The single most
fortunate exception is that of a superbly
jewelled writing-case, now in the possession of
the present editor, in which were found the
MSS. which are here published. Mathilde,
who knew how he treasured its contents, pre-
served it by saying to the officer, "But, sir,
that is mine." On opening this it was found
to contain, besides these MSS., his literary
will. All MSS. were to be published thirty
years after his death, not before. He would
gain no spurious popularity as a reflection of
the age he lived in. "Tennyson," he says,
"will die before sixty years are gone by : if I
am to be beloved of men, it shall be because
my work is for all times and all men, because
it is greater than all the gods of chance and
change, because it has the heart of the human
race beating in every line." This is a patch
of magenta to mauve, undoubtedly ; but — !
The present collection of verses will hardly be
popular ; if the lost works turn up, of course it
may be that there may be found "shelter for
songs that recede." Still, even here, one is, on
the whole, more attracted than repelled ; the
author has enormous power, and he never
scruples to use it, to drive us half mad with
horror, or, as in his earlier most exquisite
works, to move us to the noblest thoughts and
deeds. True, his debt to contemporary writers
is a little obvious here and there ; but these

are small blemishes on a series of poems whose
originality is always striking, and often dreadful, in its broader features.

We cannot leave George Bishop without a
word of inquiry as to what became of the
heroic figure of Mathilde Doriac. It is a bitter
task to have to write in cold blood the dreadful truth about her death. She had the misfortune to contract, in the last few days of her
life with him, the same terrible disease which
he describes in the last poem of his collection.
This shock, coming so soon after, and, as it
were, as an unholy perpetual reminder of the
madness and sequestration of her lover, no
less than of his infidelity, unhinged her mind,
and she shot herself on July 5, 1869. Her
last letter to Madame J—— S—— is one of
the tenderest and most pathetic ever written.
She seems to have been really loved by George,
in his wild, infidel fashion : "All Night" and
"Victory," among others, are obviously inspired by her beauty ; and her devotion to
him, the abasement of soul, the prostitution of
body, she underwent for and with him, is one
of the noblest stories life has known. She
seems to have dived with him, yet ever trying
to raise his soul from the quagmire ; if God is
just at all, she shall stand more near to His
right hand than the vaunted virgins who would
soil no hem of vesture to save their brother
from the worm that dieth not !

The Works of George Archibald Bishop will
speak for themselves ; it would be both impertinent and superfluous in me to point out
in detail their many and varied excellences, or
their obvious faults. The *raison d'être*, though,
of their publication, is worthy of especial notice.
I refer to their psychological sequence, which
agrees with their chronological order. His life-
history, as well as his literary remains, gives
us an idea of the progression of diabolism as
it really is ; not as it is painted. Note also,
(1) the increase of selfishness in pleasure, (2)
the diminution of his sensibility to physical
charms. Pure and sane is his early work ;
then he is carried into the outer current of the
great vortex of Sin, and whirls lazily through
the sleepy waters of mere sensualism ; the pace
quickens, he grows fierce in the mysteries of
Sapphism and the cult of Venus Aversa with
women ; later of the same forms of vice with
men, all mingled with wild talk of religious
dogma and a general exaltation of Priapism
at the expense, in particular, of Christianity,
in which religion, however, he is undoubtedly
a believer till the last (the pious will quote
James ii. 19, and the infidel will observe that
he died in an asylum) ; then the full swing
of the tide catches him, the mysteries of death
become more and more an obsession, and he
is flung headlong into Sadism, Necrophilia,

all the maddest, fiercest vices that the mind of fiends ever brought up from the pit. But always to the very end his power is unexhausted, immense, terrible. His delirium does not amuse; it appals! A man who could conceive as he did must himself have had some glorious chord in his heart vibrating to the eternal principle of Boundless Love. That this love was wrecked is for me, in some sort a relative of his, a real and bitter sorrow. He might have been so great! He missed Heaven! Think kindly of him!

169. *Correctly rhymes.*[41]—Such lines, however noble in sentiment, as: "À bas les Anglais! The Irish up!" will not be admitted to the competition. Irish is accented on the penultimate—bad cess to the bloody Saxons that made it so! The same with Tarshish (see Browning, *Pippa Passes*, II., in the long speech of Bluphocks) and many others.

173. *The liar Copleston.*[42] *—Bishop of Cal-

* Copies were sent to any living persons mentioned in the "Sword of Song," accompanied by the following letter:

Letters and Telegrams: BOLESKINE FOYERS is sufficient address.

Bills, Writs, Summonses, etc.: CAMP XI., THE BALTORO GLACIER, BALTISTAN.

O Millionaire!                My lord Marquis,
Mr. Editor!                   My lord Viscount,
Dear Mrs. Eddy,               My lord Earl,
Your Holiness the Pope!       My lord,
Your Imperial Majesty!        My lord Bishop,
Your Majesty!                 Reverend sir,
Your Royal Highness!          Sir,
Dear Miss Corelli,            Fellow,
Your Serene Highness!         Dog!
My lord Cardinal,             Mr. Congressman,
My lord Archbishop,           Mr. Senator,
My lord Duke,                 Mr. President,
(or the feminine of any of these), as shown
            by underlining it,
Courtesy demands, in view of the
 (a) tribute to your genius
 (b) attack on your (1) political
                    (2) moral
                    (3) social
                    (4) mental
                    (5) physical character
 (c) homage to your grandeur
 (d) reference to your conduct
 (e) appeal to your better feelings
on page —— of my masterpiece, "The Sword of Song," that I should send you a copy, as I do herewith, to give you an opportunity of defending yourself against my monstrous assertions, thanking me for the advertisement, or—— in short, replying as may best seem to you to suit the case.

Your humble, obedient servant,
    ALEISTER CROWLEY.

cutta. While holding the see of Ceylon he wrote a book in which "Buddhism" is described as consisting of "devil-dances." Now, when a man, in a position to know the facts, writes a book of the subscription-cadging type whose value for this purpose depends on the suppression of these facts, I think I am to be commended for my moderation in using the term "liar."

212.—*Ibsen.*[43]—Norwegian dramatist. This and the next sentence have nineteen distinct meanings. As, however, all (with one doubtful exception) are true, and taken together synthetically connote my concept, I have let the passage stand.

219. *I was Lord Roberts, he De Wet.*[44] — *Vide* Sir A. Conan Doyle's masterly fiction, "The Great Boer War."

222. *Hill.*[45]—An archaic phrase signifying kopje.

223. *Ditch.*[46]—Probably an obsolete slang term for spruit.

273. *Some.*[47]—The reader may search modern periodicals for this theory.

282. *The Tmolian.*[48]—Tmolus, who decided the musical contest between Pan and Apollo in favour of the latter.

321. *As masters teach.*[49]—Consult Vivekananda, *op. cit.*, or the *Hathayoga Pradipika.* Unfortunately, I am unable to say where (or even whether) a copy of this latter work exists.

331, 332. *Stand.*—(*Stephen*) *or sit* (*Paul*).[50] Acts vii. 36; Heb. xii. 2.

337. *Samadhi-Dak.*[51]— "Ecstasy-of-meditation mail."

338. *Maha-Meru.*[52]—The "mystic mountain" of the Hindus. See Southey's *Curse of Kehama.*

339. *Gaurisankar.*[53]— Called also Chomokankar, Devadhunga, and Everest.

341. *Chogo.*[54]—The Giant. This is the native name of "K2"; or Mount Godwin-Austen, as Col. Godwin-Austen would call it. It is the second highest known mountain in the world, as Devadhunga is the first.

356. *The history of the West.*[55]—

De Acosta (José)    Natural and Moral History of the Indies.
Alison, Sir A. .    History of Scotland.
Benzoni . . .       History of the New World.
Buckle . . . .      History of Civilisation.
Burton, J. H. .     History of Scotland.
Carlyle . . .       History of Frederick the Great.
Carlyle . . .       Oliver Cromwell.
Carlyle . . .       Past and Present.
Cheruel, A. . .     Dictionnaire historique de la France.
Christian, P . .    Histoire de la Magie

Clarendon, Ld. History of the Great Rebellion.
De Comines, P . Chronicle.
Edwards, Bryan. History of the British Colonies in the W. Indies.
Elton, C . . . Origins of English History.
Erdmann . . . History of Philosophy. Vol. II.
Froude . . . History of England.
Fyffe, C. A. . . History of Modern Europe.
Gardiner, S. R. . History of the Civil War in England.
Gibbon . . . Decline and Fall of the Roman Empire.
Green, J. R. . . A History of the English People.
Guizot . . . . Histoire de la Civilisation.
Hallam, H. . . State of Europe in the Middle Ages.
Hugo, V. . . Napoléon le Petit.
Innes, Prof. C. . Scotland in the Middle Ages.
Kingscote . . History of the War in the Crimea.
Levi, E. . . . Histoire de la Magie.
Macaulay, Ld. . History of England.
McCarthy, J. . A History of our Own Times.
Maistre, Jos. . Œuvres.
Michelet . . . Histoire des Templiers.
Migne, Abbé . Œuvres.
Montalembert . The Monks of the West.
Morley, J. . . Life of Mr. Gladstone.
Motley . . . History of the Dutch Republic.
Napier . . . History of the Peninsular War.
Prescott . . . History of the Conquest of Mexico.
Prescott . . . History of the Conquest of Peru.
Renan . . . . Vie de Jésus.
Robertson, E.W. Historical Essays.
Rosebery, Ld. . Napoleon.
Shakespeare . . Histories.
Society for the Propagation of Religious Truth . . . Transactions, Vols. I.-DCLXVI.
Stevenson, R. L. A Footnote to History.
Thornton, Ethelred, Rev. . . History of the Jesuits.
Waite, A. E. . The Real History of the Rosicrucians.
Wolseley, Ld. . Marlborough.

The above works and many others of less importance were carefully consulted by the Author before passing these lines for the press. Their substantial accuracy is further guaranteed by the Professors of History at Cambridge, Oxford, Berlin, Harvard, Paris, Moscow, and London.

366. *Shot his Chandra.*[56]—Anglicé, shot the moon.
380. *The subtle devilish omission.*[57]—But what are we to say of Christian dialecticians who quote "All things work together for good" out of its context, and call this verse "Christian optimism?" See Caird's "Hegel." Hegel knew how to defend himself, though. As Goethe wrote of him :
"They thought the master too
Inclined to fuss and finick.
The students' anger grew
To frenzy Paganinic. *
They vowed to make him rue
His work in Jena's clinic.
They came, the unholy crew,
The mystic and the cynic:
He had scoffed at God's battue,
The flood for mortal's sin—Icthyosaurian Waterloo !
They eyed the sage askew ;
They searched him through and through
With violet rays actinic.
They asked him ' Wer bist du?'
He answered slowly ' Bin ich?'"
387. *The Fish.*[58]—Because of ἰχθυς, which means Fish, And very aptly symbolises Christ. —*Ring and Book* (The Pope), ll. 89, 90.
395. *Dharma.*[59]—Consult the Tripitaka.
409. *I cannot trace the chain.*[60]—"How vain, indeed, are human calculations !"—*The Autobiography of a Flea*, p. 136.
112. *Table-thing.*[61]—"Ere the stuff grow a ring-thing right to wear."—*The Ring and the Book*, i. 17.
"This pebble-thing, o' the boy-thing." —CALVERLEY, *The Cock and the Bull.*
442. *Caird.*[62]—See his "Hegel."
446. *Says Huxley.*[63]—See "Ethics and Evolution."
459. *Igdrasil.*[64]—The Otz Chiim of the Scandinavians.
467. *Ladies' League.*[65]—Mrs. J. S. Crowley says : "The Ladies' League Was Formed For The Promotion And Defence Of The Reformed Faith Of The Church Of England." (The capitals are hers.) I think we may accept this statement. She probably knows, and has no obvious reasons for misleading.
487. *Sattva.*[66]—The Buddhists, denying an Atman or Soul (an idea of changeless, eternal, knowledge, being, and bliss) represent the fictitious Ego of a man (or a dog) as a temporary agglomeration of particles. Reincarnation only knocks off, as it were, some of the corners of the mass, so that for several births the Ego is constant within limits; hence the possibility of the "magical memory." The "Sattva" is this agglomeration. See my

* Paganini, a famous violinist.

"Science and Buddhism," *infra*, for a full discussion of this point.

518. *And.*[67]—Note the correct stress upon this word. Previously, Mr. W. S. Gilbert has done this in his superb lines:

"Except the plot of freehold land
    That held the cot, and Mary, and—"

But his demonstration is vitiated by the bad iambic "and Ma-"; unless indeed the juxtaposition is intentional, as exposing the sophistries of our official prosodists.

548. *The heathen.*[68]—"The wicked shall be turned into hell, and all the nations that forget God."

580. *Satan and Judas.*[69]—At the moment of passing the final proofs I am informed that the character of Judas has been rehabilitated by Mr. Stead (and rightly: is Mr. Abington * paid with a rope?) and the defence of Satan undertaken by a young society lady authoress —a Miss Corelli—who represents him as an Angel of Light, *i.e.*, one who has been introduced to the Prince of Wales.

But surely there is some one who is the object of universal reprobation amongst Christians! Permit me to offer myself as a candidate. Sink, I beseech you, these sectarian differences, and combine to declare me at least Anathema Maranatha.

602. *Pangs of Death.*[70]—Dr. Maudsley demands a panegyric upon death. It is true that evolution may bring us a moral sense of astonishing delicacy and beauty. But we are not there yet. A talented but debauched Irishman has composed the following, which I can deplore, but not refute, for this type of man is probably more prone to reproduce his species than any other. He called it "Summa Spes."

### I.

Existence being sorrow,
    The cause of it desire,
A merry tune I borrow
    To light upon the lyre:
If death destroy me quite,
    Then, I cannot lament it;
I've lived, kept life alight,
    And—damned if I repent it!

    Let me die in a ditch,
        Damnably drunk,
        Or lipping a punk,
    Or in bed with a bitch!
        I was ever a hog;
    Muck? I am one with it!
    Let me die like a dog;
    Die, and be done with it!

* Famous Adelphi villain.

### II.

As far as reason goes,
    There's hope for mortals yet:
When nothing is that knows,
    What is there to regret?
Our consciousness depends
    On matter'in the brain;
When that rots out, and ends,
    There ends the hour of pain.

### III.

If we can trust to this,
    Why, dance and drink and revel!
Great scarlet mouths to kiss,
    And sorrow to the devil!
If pangs ataxic creep,
    Or gout, or stone, annoy us,
Queen Morphia, grant thy sleep!
    Let worms, the dears, enjoy us!

### IV.

But since a chance remains
    That "I¡" survives the body
(So talk the men whose brains
    Are made of smut and shoddy),
I'll stop it if I can.
    (Ah Jesus, if Thou couldest!)
I'll go to Martaban
    To make myself a Buddhist.

### V.

And yet: the bigger chance
    Lies with annihilation.
Follow the lead of France,
    Freedom's enlightened nation!
Off! sacerdotal stealth
    Of faith and fraud and gnosis!
Come, drink me: Here's thy health,
    Arterio-sclerosis! *

    Let me die in a ditch,
        Damnably drunk,
        Or lipping a punk,
    Or in bed with a bitch!
        I was ever a hog;
    Muck? I am one with it!
    Let me die like a dog;
    Die, and be done with it!

616. *A lizard.*[71]—A short account of the genesis of these poems seems not out of place here. The design of an elaborate parody on

* The hardening of the arteries, which is the predisposing cause of senile decay; thus taken as the one positive assurance of death.

Browning to be called "Ascension Day and Pentecost" was conceived (and resolved upon) on Friday, November 15, 1901. On that day I left Ceylon, where I had been for several months, practising Hindu meditations, and exposing the dishonesty of the Missionaries, in the intervals of big game shooting. The following day I wrote "Ascension Day," and "Pentecost" on the Sunday, sitting outside the dak-bangla at Madura. These original drafts were small as compared to the present poems. Ascension Day consisted of :—

      p. 144, I flung . . .
      p. 146, Pray do . . .
      p. 147, "But why . . .
      p. 149, Here's just . . .
      p. 151, I will . . .
      to p. 160 , . . . but in Hell ! . . .
      p. 161, You see . . .
          to end.

Pentecost consisted of :—

      p. 164, To-day . . .
      p. 168, How very hard . . .
      to p. 170, " Proceed !" . . .
      p. 171, My wandering thoughts . . .
      to p. 172, All-wickedness . . .
      p. 172, Nor lull my soul . . .
      to p. 174, . . . and the vision.
      p. 176, How easy . . .
          to end.

"Berashith" was written at Delhi, March 20 and 21, 1902. Its original title was "Crowleymas Day." It was issued privately in Paris in January 1903. It and "Science and Buddhism" are added to complete the logical sequence from 1898 till now. All, however, has been repeatedly revised. Wherever there seemed a lacuna in the argument an insertion was made, till all appeared a perfect chrysolite. Most of this was done, while the weary hours of the summer (save the mark !) of 1902 rolled over Camp Misery and Camp Despair on the Chogo Ri Glacier, in those rare intervals when one's preoccupation with lice, tinned food, malaria, insoaking water, general soreness, mental misery, and the everlasting snowstorm gave place to a momentary glimmer of any higher form of intelligence than that ever necessarily concentrated on the actual business of camp life. The rest, and the final revision, occupied a good deal of my time during the winter of 1902-1903. The MS. was accepted by the S. P. R. T. in May of this year, and after a post-final revision, rendered necessary by my Irish descent, went to press.

618. *Each life bound ever to the wheel.*[72]—Cf. Whately, " Revelation of a Future State."

652. *This, that, the other atheist's death.*[73]—Their stories are usually untrue ; but let us follow our plan, and grant them all they ask.

709. *A cannibal.*[74]—This word is inept, as it predicates humanity of Christian-hate-Christian.

J'accuse the English language : *anthropophagous* must always remain a comic word.

731. *The Flaming Star.*[75]—Or Pentagram, mystically referred to Jeheshua.

732. *Zohar.*[76]— "Splendour," the three Central Books of the Dogmatic Qabalah.

733. *Pigeon.*[77]—Says an old writer, whom I translate roughly :
" Thou to thy Lamb and Dove devoutly bow,
But leave me, prithee, yet my Hawk and Cow :
And I approve thy Greybeard dotard's smile,
If thou wilt that of Egypt's crocodile."

746. *Lost ! Lost ! Lost !* [78]—See *The Lay of the Last Minstrel.*

759. *Ain Elohim.*[79]—"There is no God !" so our Bible. But this is really the most sublime affirmation of the Qabalist. "Ain is God."
For the meaning of Ain, and of this idea, see "Berashith," *infra.* The "fool" is He of the Tarot, to whom the number O is attached, to make the meaning patent to a child.
"I insult your idol," quoth the good missionary; "he is but of dead stone. He does not avenge himself. He does not punish me." "I insult your god," replied the Hindu ; "he is invisible. He does not avenge himself, nor punish me."
"My God will punish you when you die !"
"So, when you die, will my idol punish you !"
No earnest student of religion or draw poker should fail to commit this anecdote to memory.

767. *Mr. Chesterton.*[80]— I must take this opportunity to protest against the charge brought by Mr. Chesterton against the Englishmen "who write philosophical essays on the splendour of Eastern thought."
If he confines his strictures to the translators of that well-known Eastern work the "Old Testament" I am with him ; any modern Biblical critic will tell him what I mean. It took a long time, too, for the missionaries (and Tommy Atkins) to discover that "Budd" was not a "great Gawd." But then they did not want to, and in any case sympathy and intelligence are not precisely the most salient qualities in either soldiers or missionaries. But nothing is more absurd than to compare men like Sir W. Jones, Sir R. Burton, Von Hammer-Purgstall, Sir E. Arnold, Prof. Max Müller, Me, Prof. Rhys Davids, Lane, and the rest of our illustrious Orientalists to the poor

and ignorant Hindus whose letters occasionally delight the readers of the *Sporting Times*, such letters being usually written by public scribes for a few pice in the native bazaar. As to "Babus" (Babu, I may mention, is the equivalent to our "Mister," and not the name of a savage tribe), Mr. Chesterton, from his Brixton Brahmaloka, may look forth and see that the "Babu" cannot understand Western ideas; but a distinguished civil servant in the Madras Presidency, second wrangler in a very good year, assured me that he had met a native whose mathematical knowledge was superior to that of the average senior wrangler; and that he had met several others who approached that standard. His specific attack on Madame Blavatsky is equally unjust, as many natives, not theosophists, have spoken to me of her in the highest terms. "Honest Hindus" cannot be expected to think as Mr. Chesterton deems likely, as he is unfortunately himself a Western, ahd in the same quagmire of misapprehension as Prof. Max. Müller and the rest. Madame Blavatsky's work was to remind the Hindus of the excellence of their own shastras,* to show that some Westerns held identical ideas, and thus to countermine the dishonest representations of the missionaries. I am sufficiently well known as a bitter opponent of "Theosophy" to risk nothing in making these remarks.

I trust that the sense of public duty which inspires these strictures will not be taken as incompatible with the gratitude I owe to him for his exceedingly sympathetic and dispassionate review of my "Soul of Osiris."

I would counsel him, however, to leave alone the Brixton Chapel, and to "work up from his appreciation of the 'Soul of Osiris' to that loftier and wider work of the human imagination, the appreciation of the *Sporting Times!*"

---

Mr. Chesterton thinks it funny that I should call upon "Shu." Has he forgotten that the Christian God may be most suitably invoked by the name "Yah"? I should be sorry if God were to mistake his religious enthusiasms for the derisive ribaldry of the London "gamin." Similar remarks apply to "El" and other Hebrai-christian deities.

This note is hardly intelligible without the review referred to. I therefore reprint the

---

* Sacred Books.

---

portion thereof which is germane to my matter from the *Daily News*, June 18, 1901 :—

To the side of a mind concerned with idle merriment (*sic!*) there is certainly something a little funny in Mr. Crowley's passionate devotion to deities who bear such names as Mout and Nuit, and Ra and Shu, and Hormakhou. They do not seem to the English mind to lend themselves to pious exhilaration. Mr. Crowley says in the same poem :

The burden is too hard to bear,
    I took too adamant a cross ;
This sackcloth rends my soul to wear,
    My self-denial is as dross.
    O, Shu, that holdest up the sky,
    Hold up thy servant, lest he die !

We have all possible respect for Mr. Crowley's religious symbols, and we do not object to his calling upon Shu at any hour of the night. Only it would be unreasonable of him to complain if his religious exercises were generally mistaken for an effort to drive away cats.

---

Moreover, the poets of Mr. Crowley's school have, among all their merits, some genuine intellectual dangers from this tendency to import religions, this free trade in gods. That all creeds are significant and all gods divine we willingly agree. But this is rather a reason for being content with our own than for attempting to steal other people's. The affectation in many modern mystics of adopting an Oriental civilisation and mode of thought must cause much harmless merriment among the actual Orientals. The notion that a turban and a few vows will make an Englishman a Hindu is quite on a par with the idea that a black hat and an Oxford degree will make a Hindu an Englishman. We wonder whether our Buddhistic philosophers have ever read a florid letter in Baboo English. We suspect that the said type of document is in reality exceedingly like the philosophic essays written by Englishmen about the splendour of Eastern thought. Sometimes European mystics deserve something worse than mere laughter at the hands (*sic!*) of Orientals. If ever was one person whom honest Hindus would have been justified in tearing to pieces it was Madame Blavatsky.

---

That our world-worn men of art should believe for a moment that moral salvation is possible and supremely important is an unmixed benefit. But to believe for a moment that it is to be found by going to particular places or reading particular books or joining particular societies is to make for the thousandth time the mistake that is at once materialism and superstition. If Mr. Crowley and the new mystics think for one moment that an Egyptian desert is more mystic than an English meadow, that a palm tree is more peetic than a Sussex beech, that a broken temple of Osiris is more supernatural than a Baptist chapel in Brixton, then they are sectarians, and only sectarians of no more value to humanity than those who think that the English soil is the only soil worth defending, and the Baptist chapel the only chapel worthy of worship (*sic*). But Mr. Crowley is a strong and genuine poet, and we have little doubt that he will work up from his appreciation of the Temple of Osiris to that loftier and wider work of the human imagination, the appreciation of the Brixton chapel.

G. K. CHESTERTON.

778, 797. *The rest of life, for self-control, For liberation of the soul.*[81]
Who said Rats? Thanks for your advice, Tony Veller, but it came in vain. As the ex-monk * (that shook the bookstall) wrote in confidence to the publisher :

"Existence is mis'ry.
I' th' month Tisri

---

* Joseph McCabe, who became a Rationalist writer. The allusion is to Crowley's marriage and subsequent return to the East.

At th' fu' o' th' moon
I were shot wi' a goon.
[Goon is no Scots,
But Greek, Meester Watts.]
We're awa' tae Burma,
Whaur th' groond be firmer
Tae speer th' Mekong.
Chin Chin ! Sae long.
[Long sald be lang :
She'll no care a whang.]
Ye're Rautional babe,
Aundra McAbe."

Note the curious confusion of personality. This shows Absence of Ego, in Pali Anatta, and will seem to my poor spiritually-minded friends an excuse for a course of action they do not understand, and whose nature is beyond them.

782. *Christ ascends.*[82]—And I tell you frankly that if he does not come back by the time I have finished reading these proofs, I shall give him up.

783. *Bell.*[83]—The folios have "bun."

## NOTES TO PENTECOST

22. *With sacred thirst.*[1]—"He, soul-hydroptic with a sacred thirst." A Grammarian's Funeral.
23. *Levi.*[2]—Ceremonial magic is not quite so silly as it sounds. Witness the following masterly elucidation of its inner quintessence :—

### THE INITIATED INTERPRETATION OF CEREMONIAL MAGIC.*

It is loftily amusing to the student of magical literature who is not quite a fool—and rare is such a combination !—to note the criticism directed by the Philistine against the citadel of his science. Truly, since our childhood has ingrained into us not only literal belief in the Bible, but also substantial belief in Alf Laylah wa Laylah,† and only adolescence can cure us, we are only too liable, in the rush and energy of dawning manhood, to overturn roughly and rashly both these classics, to regard them both on the same level, as interesting documents from the standpoint of folk-lore and anthropology, and as nothing more.

Even when we learn that the Bible, by a

---

* This essay forms the introduction to an edition of the "Goetia" of King Solomon.
† "A Thousand and One Nights," commonly called "Arabian Nights."

profound and minute study of the text, may be forced to yield up Qabalistic arcana of cosmic scope and importance, we are too often slow to apply a similar restorative to the companion volume, even if we are the lucky holders of Burton's veritable edition.

To me, then, it remains to raise the Alf Laylah wa Laylah into its proper place once more.

I am not concerned to deny the objective reality of all "magical" phenomena ; if they are illusions, they are at least as real as many unquestioned facts of daily life ; and, if we follow Herbert Spencer, they are at least evidence of *some* cause.*

Now, this fact is our base. What is the cause of my illusion of seeing a spirit in the triangle of Art?

Every smatterer, every expert in psychology, will answer : " That cause lies in your brain." English children are taught (*pace* the Education Act) that the Universe lies in infinite Space ; Hindu children, in the Akaśa, which is the same thing.

Those Europeans who go a little deeper learn from Fichte, that the phenomenal Universe is the creation of the Ego ; Hindus, or Europeans studying under Hindu Gurus, are

This, incidentally, is perhaps the greatest argument we possess, pushed to its extreme, against the Advaitist theories.—A. C.

told, that by Akaśa is meant the Chitakaśa. The Chitakasa is situated in the "Third Eye," *i.e.*, in the brain. By assuming higher dimensions of space, we can assimilate this fact to Realism; but we have no need to take so much trouble.

This being true for the ordinary Universe, that all sense-impressions are dependent on changes in the brain,* we must include illusions, which are after all sense-impressions as much as "realities" are, in the class of "phenomena dependent on brain-changes."

Magical phenomena, however, come under a special sub-class, since they are willed, and their cause is the series of "real" phenomena called the operations of ceremonial Magic.

These consist of

(1) Sight.
    The circle, square, triangle, vessels, lamps, robes, implements, etc.

(2) Sound.
    The invocations.

(3) Smell.
    The perfumes.

(4) Taste.
    The Sacraments.

(5) Touch.
    As under (1).

(6) Mind.
    The combination of all these and reflection on their significance.

These unusual impressions (1–5) produce unusual brain-changes; hence their summary (6) is of unusual kind. Its projection back into the apparently phenomenal world is therefore unusual.

Herein then consists the reality of the operations and effects of ceremonial magic,† and I conceive that the apology is ample, so far as the "effects" refer only to those phenomena which appear to the magician himself, the appearance of the spirit, his conversation, possible shocks from imprudence, and so on, even to ecstasy on the one hand, and death or madness on the other.

But can any of the effects described in this our book Goetia be obtained, and if so, can you give a rational explanation of the circumstances? Say you so?

I can, and will.

The spirits of the Goetia are portions of the human brain.

Their seals therefore represent (Mr. Spencer's

projected cube) methods of stimulating or regulating those particular spots (through the eye).

The names of God are vibrations calculated to establish:

(*a*) General control of the brain. (Establishment of functions relative to the subtle world.)

(*b*) Control over the brain in detail. (Rank or type of the Spirit.)

(*c*) Control of one special portion. (Name of the Spirit.)

The perfumes aid this through smell. Usually the perfume will only tend to control a large area; but there is an attribution of perfumes to letters of the alphabet enabling one, by a Qabalistic formula, to spell out the Spirit's name.

I need not enter into more particular discussion of these points; the intelligent reader can easily fill in what is lacking.

If, then, I say, with Solomon:

"The Spirit Cimieries teaches logic," what I mean is:

"Those portions of my brain which subserve the logical faculty may be stimulated and developed by following out the processes called 'The Invocation of Cimieries.'"

And this is a purely materialistic rational statement; it is independent of any objective hierarchy at all. Philosophy has nothing to say; and Science can only suspend judgment, pending a proper and methodical investigation of the facts alleged.

Unfortunately, we cannot stop there. Solomon promises us that we can (1) obtain information; (2) destroy our enemies; (3) understand the voices of nature; (4) obtain treasure; (5) heal diseases, etc. I have taken these five powers at random; considerations of space forbid me to explain all.

(1) Brings up facts from sub-consciousness.

(2) Here we come to an interesting fact. It is curious to note the contrast between the noble means and the apparently vile ends of magical rituals. The latter are disguises for sublime truths. "To destroy our enemies" is to realise the illusion of duality, to excite compassion.

(Ah! Mr. Waite,* the world of Magic is a mirror, wherein who sees muck is muck.)

(3) A careful naturalist will understand much from the voices of the animals he has studied long. Even a child knows the difference of a cat's miauling and purring. The faculty may be greatly developed.

(4) Business capacity may be stimulated.

(5) Abnormal states of the body may be

---

* Thought is a secretion of the brain (Weissmann). Consciousness is a function of the brain (Huxley).—A. C.

† Apart from its value in obtaining one-pointedness. On this subject consult בראשית, *infra.*—A. C.

* A poet of great ability. He edited a book called "Of Black Magic and of Pacts," in which he vilifies the same.

corrected, and the involved tissues brought back to tone, in obedience to currents started from the brain.

So for all other phenomena. There is no effect which is truly and necessarily miraculous.

Our Ceremonial Magic fines down, then, to a series of minute, though of course empirical, physiological experiments, and whoso will carry them through intelligently need not fear the result.

I have all the health, and treasure, and logic I need ; I have no time to waste. "There is a lion in the way." For me these practices are useless ; but for the benefit of others less fortunate I give them to the world, together with this explanation of, and apology for, them.

I trust that the explanation will enable many students who have hitherto, by a puerile objectivity in their view of the question, obtained no results, to succeed ; that the apology may impress upon our scornful men of science that the study of the bacillus should give place to that of the baculum, the little to the great—how great one only realises when one identifies the wand with the Mahalingam,* up which Brahma flew at the rate of 84,000 yojanas a second for 84,000 mahakalpas, down which Vishnu flew at the rate of 84,000 crores of yojanas a second for 84,000 crores of mahakalpas—yet neither reached an end.

But I reach an end.

23. *The cryptic Coptic.*[3]—Vide the Papyrus of Bruce.

24. *ANET' AER-K, etc.*[4]—Invocation of Ra. From the Papyrus of Harris.

26. *MacGregor.*[5]—The Mage.

29. *Abramelin.*[6]—The Mage.

32. *Ancient rituals.*[7]—From the Papyrus of MRS. Harris.†

33. *Golden Dawn.*[8]—These rituals were later annexed by Madame Horos,‡ that superior Swami. The earnest seeker is liable to some pretty severe shocks. To see one's "Obligation" printed in the *Daily Mail!!!* Luckily, I have no nerves.

49. राम राम ॥ *etc.*[9]—"Thou, as I, art God (*for this is the esoteric meaning of the common Hindu salutation*). A long road and a heavy price ! To know is always a difficult work . . . Hullo ! Bravo ! Thy name (I have seen) is written in the stars. Come with me, pupil ! I will give thee medicine for the mind."

* The Phallus of Shiva the Destroyer. It is really identical with the Qabalistic "Middle Pillar" of the "Tree of Life."

† An imaginary lady to whom Sairey Gamp in Dickens' " Martin Chuzzlewit " used to appeal.

‡ *Vide* the daily papers of June–July 1901.

Cf. Macbeth : "Canst thou not minister to a mind diseased ? "

58. बस ॥.[10]—Enough.

60. किसवासते ॥.[11]—Why ?

60. कय होग.[1]—What will be ?

61. *Strange and painful attitude.*[13] — Siddhasana.

62. *He was very rude.*[14]—The following is a sample :—

"O Devatas ! behold this yogi ! O Chela ! Accursèd abode of Tamas art thou ! Eater of Beef, guzzling as an Herd of Swine ! Sleeper of a thousand sleeps, as an Harlot heavy with Wine ! Void of Will ! Sensualist ! Enraged Sheep ! Blasphemer of the Names of Shiva and of Devi ! Christian in disguise ! Thou shalt be reborn in the lowest Avitchi ! Fast ! Walk ! Wake ! these are the keys of the Kingdom ! Peace be with thy Beard ! Aum ! "

This sort of talk did me good : I hope it may do as much for you.

63. *With eyes well fixed on my proboscis.*[15]—See Bhagavad-Gita, Atmasamyamyog.

67. *Brahma-charya.*[16]—Right conduct, and in particular, chastity in the highest sense.

72. *Baccy.*[17]—A poisonous plant used by nicotomaniacs in their orgies and debauches. "The filthy tobacco habit," says " Elijah the Restorer " of Zion, late of Sydney and Chicago. That colossal genius-donkey, Shaw, is another of them. But see Calverley.

78. *His hat.*[18]—It may be objected that Western, but never Eastern, magicians turn their headgear into a cornucopia or Pandora's box. But I must submit that the Hat Question is still *sub judice.* Here's a health to Lord Ronald Gower !

86. *Swinburne.*[19]—
" But this thing is God,
To be man with thy might,
To grow straight in the strength of thy spirit,
    and live out thy life as the light."—*Hertha.*

104. *My big beauty.*[20]—Pink on Spot ; Player, Green, in Hand. But I have " starred " since I went down in *that* pocket.

120. *My Balti coolies.*[21]—See my " The Higher the Fewer." *

125. *Eton.*[22]—A school, noted for its breed of cads. The battle of Waterloo (1815) was won on its playing-fields.

128-30. *I've seen them.*[23]—Sir J. Maundevill, " Voiage and Travill," ch. xvi., recounts a similar incident, and, Christian as he is, puts a similar poser.

135. *A—What ?*[24]—I beg your pardon. It was a slip.

146. *Tahuti.*[25]—In Coptic, Thoth.

* Title of a (forthcoming) collection of papers on mountain exploration, etc.

149. *Ra.*[26]—The Sun-God.
149. *Nuit.*[27]—The Star-Goddess.
152. *Campbell.*[28]—" The waters wild went o'er his child, And he was left lamenting."
152. *The Ibis Head.*[29]—Characteristic of Tahuti.
157. *Roland's crest.*[30]—See " Two Poets of Croisic," xci.
159. *A jest.*[31]—See above : Ascension Day.
126. *A mysterious way.*[32]—
" God moves in a mysterious way
    His wonders to perform ;
He plants His footsteps in the sea,
    And rides upon the storm."
Intentional species?
171. *The old hymn.*[33]—This hymn, quoted I fear with some failure of memory—I have not the documents at hand—is attributed to the late Bishop of Natal, though I doubt this, as the consistent and trustful piety of its sentiment is ill-suited to the author of those disastrous criticisms of the Pentateuch. The hymn is still popular in Durban.
Its extraordinary beauty, for a fragment, is only surpassed by Sappho's matchless :

— ◡ — ◡ — ◡ ◡ — ◡
— ◡ — ◡ — ◡ ◡ — ◡
— ◡ — ◡ 'εννεα κ' εξε -
κοντα ◡ — —

185. " *How very hard.*"[34]—
" How very hard it is to be
A Christian !"—*Easter Day*, I. i. 2.
195. *Srotapatti.*[35]—One who has " entered the stream " of Nirvana.
For the advantages of so doing, see the appended Jataka story, which I have just translated from a Cingalese Palm-leaf MS. See Appendix I.
228. *You know for me, etc.*[36]—See Huxley, Hume, 199, 200.
239. *Spirit and matter are the same.*[37]—See Huxley's reply to Lilly.
273. " *I am not what I see.*"[38]—*In Memoriam.* But see H. Spencer, "Principles of Psychology," General Analysis, ch. vi.
281. " *'Tis lotused Buddha.*"[39]—
" Hark ! that sad groan ! Proceed no further ! 'Tis laurelled Martial roaring murther."
—BURNS, *Epigram.*
But Buddha cannot really roar, since he has passed away by that kind of passing away which leaves nothing whatever behind.
322. *A mere law without a will.*[40]—I must not be supposed to take any absurd view of the meaning of the word "law." This passage denies any knowledge of ultimate causes, not asserts it. But it tends to deny benevolent foresight, and *a fortiori* benevolent omnipotence.
Cf. Zoroaster, *Oracles :* " Look not upon the

visible image of the Soul of Nature, for her name is Fatality."
Ambrosius is very clear on this point. I append his famous MS. complete in its English Translation, as it is so rare. How rare will be appreciated when I say that no copy either of original or translation occurs in the British Museum ; the only known copy, that in the Bodleian, is concealed by the pre-Adamite system of cataloguing in vogue at that hoary but unvenerable institution. For convenience the English has been modernised. See Appendix II.
329. *Maya fashioned it.*[41]—Sir E. Arnold, *Light of Asia.*
335. *Why should the Paramatma cease.*[42]—The Universe is represented by orthodox Hindus as alternating between Evolution and Involution. But apparently, in either state, it is the other which appears desirable, since the change is operated by Will, not by Necessity.
341. *Blavatsky's Himalayan Balm.*[43]—See the corkscrew theories of A. P. Sinnett in that masterpiece of confusion of thought — and nomenclature !—" Esoteric Buddhism." Also see the " Voice of the Silence, or, The Butler's Revenge." Not Bp. Butler.
366. *Ekam Advaita.*[44]—Of course I now reject this utterly. But it is, I believe, a stage of thought necessary for many or most of us. The bulk of these poems was written when I was an Advaitist, incredible as the retrospect now appears. My revision has borne Buddhist fruits, but some of the Advaita blossom is left. Look, for example, at the dreadfully Papistical tendency of my celebrated essay :

## AFTER AGNOSTICISM.

Allow me to introduce myself as the original Irishman whose first question on landing at New York was, " Is there a Government in this country?" and on being told "Yes," instantly replied, " Then I'm agin it." For after some years of consistent Agnosticism, being at last asked to contribute to an Agnostic organ, for the life of me I can think of nothing better than to attack my hosts ! Insidious cuckoo! Ungrateful Banyan ! My shame drives me to Semitic analogy, and I sadly reflect that if I had been Balaam, I should not have needed an ass other than myself to tell me to do the precise contrary of what is expected of me.
For this is my position ; while the postulates of Agnosticism are in one sense eternal, I believe that the conclusions of Agnosticism are daily to be pushed back. We know our ignorance ; with that fact we are twitted by those who do not know enough to understand

even what we mean when we say so; but the limits of knowledge, slowly receding, yet never so far as to permit us to unveil the awful and impenetrable adytum of consciousness, or that of matter, must one day be suddenly widened by the forging of a new weapon.

Huxley and Tyndall have prophesied this before I was born; sometimes in vague language, once or twice clearly enough; to me it is a source of the utmost concern that their successors should not always see eye to eye with them in this respect.

Professor Ray Lankester, in crushing the unhappy theists of the recent *Times* controversy, does not hesitate to say that Science *can never* throw any light on certain mysteries.

Even the theist is justified in retorting that Science, if this be so, may as well be discarded; for these are problems which must ever intrude upon the human mind—upon the mind of the scientist most of all.

To dismiss them by an act of will is at once heroic and puerile: courage is as necessary to progress as any quality that we possess; and as courage is in either case required, the courage of ignorance (necessarily sterile, though wanted badly enough while our garden was choked by theological weeds) is less desirable than the courage which embarks on the always desperate philosophical problem.

Time and again, in the history of Science, a period has arrived when, gorged with facts, she has sunk into a lethargy of reflection accompanied by appalling nightmares in the shape of impossible theories. Such a nightmare now rides us; once again philosophy has said its last word, and arrived at a deadlock. Aristotle, in reducing to the fundamental contradictions-in-terms which they involve the figments of the Pythagoreans, the Eleatics, the Platonists, the Pyrrhonists; Kant, in his *reductio ad absurdum* of the Thomists, the Scotists, the Wolffians,—all the warring brood, alike only in the inability to reconcile the ultimate antinomies of a cosmogony only grosser for its pinchbeck spirituality; have, I take it, found their modern parallel in the ghastly laughter of Herbert Spencer, as fleshed upon the corpses of Berkeley and the Idealists from Fichte and Hartmann to Lotze and Trendelenburg he drives the reeking fangs of his imagination into the palpitating vitals of his own grim masterpiece of reconcilement, self-deluded and yet self-conscious of its own delusion.

History affirms that such a deadlock is invariably the prelude to a new enlightenment: by such steps we have advanced, by such we shall advance. The "horror of great darkness" which is scepticism must ever be broken by some heroic master-soul, intolerant of the cosmic agony.

We then await his dawn.

May I go one step further, and lift up my voice and prophesy? I would indicate the direction in which this darkness must break. Evolutionists will remember that nature cannot rest. Nor can society. Still less the brain of man.

" Audax omnia perpeti
Gens humana ruit per vetitum nefas." *

We have destroyed the meaning of vetitum nefas and are in no fear of an imaginary cohort of ills and terrors. Having perfected one weapon, reason, and found it destructive to all falsehood, we have been (some of us) a little apt to go out to fight with no other weapon. "FitzJames's blade was sword and shield," † and that served him against the murderous bludgeon-sword of the ruffianly Highlander he happened to meet; but he would have fared ill had he called a Western Sheriff a liar, or gone off Boer-sticking on Spion Kop.

Reason has done its utmost; theory has glutted us, and the motion of the ship is a little trying; mixed metaphor—excellent in a short essay like this—is no panacea for all mental infirmities; we must seek another guide. All the facts science has so busily collected, varied as they seem to be, are in reality all of the same kind. If we are to have one salient fact, a fact for a real advance, it must be a fact of a different *order*.

Have we such a fact to hand? We have.

First, what do we mean by a fact of a different order? Let me take an example; the most impossible being the best for our purpose. The Spiritualists, let us suppose, go mad and begin to talk sense. (I can only imagine that such would be the result.) All their "facts" are proved. We prove a world of spirits, the existence of God, the immortality of the soul, etc. But, with all that, we are not really one step advanced into the heart of the inquiry which lies at the heart of philosophy, "What *is* anything?"

I see a cat.

Dr. Johnson says it is a cat.

Berkeley says it is a group of sensations.

Cankaracharya says it is an illusion, an incarnation, or God, according to the hat he has got on, and is talking through.

Spencer says it is a mode of the Unknowable.

But none of them seriously doubt the fact that I exist; that a cat exists; that one sees the other. All—bar Johnson—hint—but oh! how dimly!—at what I now know to be—*true?*—no, not necessarily true, but *nearer the truth*. Huxley goes deeper in his demolition of Descartes. With him, "I see a cat," proves "some-

* Horace, *Odes*, I. 3.
† Scott, *The Lady of the Lake*.

thing called consciousness exists." He denies the assertion of duality ; he has no datum to assert the denial of duality. I have.

Consciousness, as we know it, has one essential quality : the opposition of subject and object. Reason has attacked this and secured that complete and barren victory of convincing without producing conviction.* It has one quality apparently not essential, that of exceeding impermanence. If we examine what we call steady thought, we shall find that its rate of change is in reality inconceivably swift. To consider it, to watch it, is bewildering, and to some people becomes intensely terrifying. It is as if the solid earth were suddenly swept away from under one, and there were some dread awakening in outer space amid the rush of incessant meteors—lost in the void.

All this is old knowledge ; but who has taken steps to alter it? The answer is forbidding : truth compels me to say, the mystics of all lands.

Their endeavour has been to slow the rate of change ; their methods perfect quietude of body and mind, produced in varied and too often vicious ways. Regularisation of the breathing is the best known formula. Their results are contemptible, we must admit ; but only so because empirical. An unwarranted reverence has overlaid the watchfulness which science would have enjoined, and the result is muck and misery, the wreck of a noble study.

But what is the one fact on which all agree? The one fact whose knowledge has been since religion began the all-sufficient passport to their doubtfully-desirable company?

This: that "I see a cat" is not only an unwarrantable assumption but a lie ; that the duality of consciousness ceases suddenly, once the rate of change has been sufficiently slowed down, so that, even for a few seconds, the relation of subject and object remains impregnable.

It is a circumstance of little interest to the present essayist that this annihilation of duality is associated with intense and passionless peace and delight ; the fact has been a bribe to the unwary, a bait for the charlatan, a hindrance to the philosopher ; let us discard it.†

* Hume, and Kant in the " Prolegomena," discuss this phenomenon unsatisfactorily.—A. C.
† It is this rapture which has ever been the bond between mystics of all shades ; and the obstacle to any accurate observation of the phenomenon, its true causes, and so on. This must always be a stumbling-block to more impressionable minds ; but there is no doubt as to the fact—it *is* a fact—and its present isolation is to be utterly deplored. May I entreat men ,of Science to conquer the prejudices natural to them when the justly despised ideas of mysticism are mentioned, and to attack the problem *ab initio* on the severely critical and austerely arduous lines which have distinguished their labours in other fields? —A. C.

More, though the establishment of this new estate of consciousness seems to open the door to a new world, a world where the axioms of Euclid may be absurd, and the propositions of Keynes* untenable, let us not fall into the error of the mystics, by supposing that in this world is necessarily a final truth, or even a certain and definite gain of knowledge.

But that a field for research is opened up no sane man may doubt. Nor may one question that the very first fact is of a nature disruptive of difficulty philosophical and reasonable ; since the phenomenon does not invoke the assent of the reasoning faculty. The arguments which reason may bring to bear against it are self-destructive ; reason has given consciousness the lie, but consciousness survives and smiles. Reason is a part of consciousness and can never be greater than its whole ; this Spencer sees ; but reason is not even any part of this new consciousness (which I, and many others, have too rarely achieved) and therefore can never touch it : this I see, and this will I hope be patent to those ardent and spiritually-minded agnostics of whom Huxley and Tyndall are for all history-time the prototypes. Know or doubt ! is the alternative of highwayman Huxley ; " Believe" is not to be admitted ; this is fundamental ; in this agnosticism can never change ; this must ever command our moral as our intellectual assent.

But I assert my strong conviction that ere long we shall have done enough of what is after all the schoolmaster work of correcting the inky and ill-spelt exercises of the theological dunces in that great class-room, the world ; and found a little peace—while they play—in the intimate solitude of the laboratory and the passionless rapture of research—research into those very mysteries which our dunces have solved by rule of thumb ; determining the nature of a bee by stamping on it, and shouting " bee" ; while we patiently set to work with microscopes, and say nothing till we know, nor more than need be when we do.

But I am myself found guilty of this rôle of schoolmaster : I will now therefore shut the doors and retire again into the laboratory where my true life lies.

403, 405. *Reason and concentration.*[45]—The results of reasoning are always assailable : those of concentration are vivid and certain, since they are directly presented to consciousness. And they are more certain than consciousness itself, since one who has experienced them may, with consciousness, doubt consciousness, but can in no state doubt them.

412. *Ganesh.*[46]—The elephant-headed God, son of Shiva and Bhavani. He presides over obstacles.

* Author of a text-book on " Formal Logic."

The prosodist will note the "false quantity" of this word. But this is as it should be, for Ganesha pertains to Shiva, and with Shiva all quantity is false, since, as Parameshvara, he is without quantity or quality.

485. *Carroll.*[47]—See "Alice in Wonderland," Cap. Ult.

508. *Kusha-grass.*[48]—The sacred grass of the Hindus.

509. *Mantra.*[49]—A sacred verse, suitable for constant repetition, with a view to quieting the thought. Any one can see how simple and effective a means this is.

519. *Gayatri.*[50]—This is the translation of the most holy verse of the Hindus. The gender of Savitri has been the subject of much discussion, and I believe grammatically it is masculine. But for mystical reasons I have made it otherwise. Fool!

557. *Prayer.*[51]—This fish-story is literally true. The condition was that the Almighty should have the odds of an unusually long line,—the place was really a swift stream, just debouching into a lake—and of an unusual slowness of drawing in the cast.

But what does any miracle prove? If the Affaire Cana were proved to me, I should merely record the facts: Water may under certain unknown conditions become wine. It is a pity that the owner of the secret remains silent, and entirely lamentable that he should attempt to deduce from his scientific knowledge cosmic theories which have nothing whatever to do with it.

Suppose Edison, having perfected the phonograph, had said, "I alone can make dumb things speak; argal, I am God." What would the world have said if telegraphy had been exploited for miracle-mongering purposes? Are these miracles less or greater than those of the Gospels?

Before we accept Mrs. Piper,* we want to know most exactly the conditions of the experiment, and to have some guarantee of the reliability of the witnesses.

At Cana of Galilee the conditions of the transformation are not stated—save that they give loopholes innumerable for chicanery—and the witnesses are all drunk! (thou hast kept the good wine *till now: i.e.* till men have well drunk—Greek, μεθυσθωσι, *are* well drunk).

And I am to believe this, and a glaring *non sequitur* as to Christ's deity, on the evidence, not even of the inebriated eye-witnesses, but of MSS. of doubtful authorship and date, bearing all the ear-marks of dishonesty. For we must not forget that the absurdities of to-day were most cunning proofs for the poor folk of seventeen centuries ago.

Talking of fish-stories, read John xxi. 1-6,

* A twentieth century medium.

or Luke V. 1-7 (comparisons are odious). But once I met a man by a lake and told him that I had toiled all the morning and had caught nothing, and he advised me to try the other side of the lake; and I caught many fish. But I knew not that it was the Lord.

In Australia they were praying for rain in the churches. The *Sydney Bulletin* very sensibly pointed out how much more reverent and practical it would be, if, instead of constantly worrying the Almighty about trifles, they would pray once and for all for a big range of mountains in Central Australia, which would of course supply rain automatically. No new act of creation would be necessary; faith, we are expressly told, can remove mountains, and there is ice and snow and especially moraine on and about the Baltoro Glacier to build a very fine range; we could well have spared it this last summer.

579. *So much for this absurd affair.*[52]— "About Lieutenant-Colonel Flare."—Gilbert, *Bab Ballads.*

636. *Auto-hypnosis.*[53]—The scientific adversary has more sense than to talk of auto-hypnosis. He bases his objection upon the general danger of the practice, considered as a habit of long standing. In fact,

*Lyre and Lancet.*
  *Recipe for Curried Eggs.*

The physiologist reproaches
Poor Mr. Crowley. "This encroaches
Upon your frail cerebral cortex,
And turns its fairway to a vortex.
Your cerebellum with cockroaches
Is crammed; your lobes that thought they
    caught "X"
Are like mere eggs a person poaches.
But soon from yoga, business worries,
And (frankly I suspect the rubble
Is riddled by specific trouble!)
Will grow like eggs a person curries."
This line, no doubt, requires an answer.

*The Last Ditch.*

First. "Here's a johnny with a cancer;
An operation may be useless,
May even harm his constitution,
Or cause his instant dissolution:
Let the worm die, 'tis but a goose less!"
Not you! You up and take by storm him.
You tie him down and chloroform him.
You do not pray to Thoth or Horus,
But make one dash for his pylorus:—
And if ten years elapse, and he
Complains, "O doctor, pity me!
Your cruel 'ands, for goodness sakes
Gave me such 'orrid stomach-aches.

O

You write him, with a face of flint,
An order for some soda-mint.
So Yoga.   Life's a carcinoma,
Its cause uncertain, not to check.
In vain you cry to Isis : "O ma !
I've got it fairly in the neck."
The surgeon Crowley, with his trocar,
Says you a poor but silly bloke are,
Advises concentration's knife
Quick to the horny growth called life.
"Yoga?   There's danger in the biz !
But, it's the only chance there is !"
(For life, if left alone, is sorrow,
And only fools hope God's to-morrow.)

*Up, Guards, and at 'em !*

Second, your facts are neatly put ;
—Stay !   In that mouth there lurks a foot !
One surgeon saw so many claps
He thought : "One-third per cent., perhaps,
Of mortals 'scape its woes that knock us,
And bilk the wily gonococcus."
So he is but a simple cynic
Who takes the world to match his clinic ;
And he assuredly may err
Who, keeping cats, thinks birds have fur.
You   say :   "There's   Berridge,   Felkin,
    Mathers,
Hysterics, epileptoids, blathers,
Guttersnipe, psychopath, and mattoid,
With ceremonial magic that toyed."
Granted.   Astronomy's no myth,
But it produced Piazzi Smyth.
What crazes actors ?  Why do surgeons
Go mad and cut up men like sturgeons ?
(These questions are the late Chas. Spur-
    geon's.)
Of yogi I could quote you hundreds
In science, law, art, commerce noted.
They fear no lunacy : their one dread's
Not for their noddles doom-devoted.
They are not like black bulls (that shunned
    reds
In vain) that madly charge the goathead
Of rural Pan, because some gay puss
Had smeared with blood his stone Priapus.
They are as sane as politicians
And people who subscribe to missions.
This says but little ; a long way are
Yogi more sane than such as they are.
You have conceived your dreadful bogey,
From seeing many a raving Yogi.
These haunt your clinic ; but the sound
Lurk in an unsuspected ground,
Dine with you, lecture in your schools,
Share your intolerance of fools,
And, while the Yogi you condemn,
Listen, say nothing, barely smile.
O if you but suspected them
Your silence would match theirs awhile !

*A Classical Research.  [Protectionists may ser
if the supply of Hottentots gives out.]*

I took three Hottentots alive.
Their scale was one, two, three, four, five,
Infinity.   To think of men so
I could not bear : a new Colenso
I bought them to assuage their plight,
Also a book by Hall and Knight
On Algebra. . I hired wise men
To teach them six, seven, eight, nine, ten.
One of the Hottentots succeeded.
Few schoolboys know as much as he did !
The others sank beneath the strain :
It broke, not fortified, the brain.

*The Bard a Brainy Beggar.*

Now (higher on the Human Ladder)
Lodge is called mad, and Crowley madder.
(The shafts of Science who may dodge?
I've not a word to say for Lodge.)
Yet may not Crowley be the one
Who safely does what most should shun ?

*Alpine Analogy.*

Take Oscar Eckenstein—he climbs
Alone, unroped, a thousand times.
He scales his peak, he makes his pass ;
He does not fall in a crevasse !
But if the Alpine Club should seek
To follow him on pass or peak—
(Their cowardice, their mental rot,
Are balanced nicely—they will not.)
—I see the Alpine Journal's border
Of black grow broader, broader, broader,
Until the Editor himself
Falls from some broad and easy shelf,
And in his death the Journal dies.
Ah ! bombast, footle, simple lies !
Where would you then appear in type?

*The Poet "retires up."  His attitude undig
nified, his pleasure momentary, the afte.
results quite disproportionate.  He contem
plates his end.*

Therefore poor Crowley lights his pipe,
Maintains : "The small-shot kills the snipe,
But spares the tiger ; " goes on joking,
And goes on smirking, on invoking,
On climbing, meditating,—failing to think
    of a suitable rhyme at a critical juncture
Ah !—goes on working, goes on smoking,
Until he goes right on to Woking.

637.  *No one supposes me a Saint.*[54]—On in
quiry, however, I find that some do.
686.  *Amrita.*[55]—The Elixir of Life : the Dev
of Immortality.

688. *Christ.*[56]—See Shri Parananda, "Comentaries on Matthew and John."

695. *Direction x.*[57]—*Vide supra*, "Ascension ay."

710. *Steel-tired.*[58]—

For Dunlop people did not know
Those nineteen hundred years ago.

723. *Super-consciousness.*[59]—The Christians so claim an ecstasy. But they all admit, and deed boast, that it is the result of long periods of worry and anxiety about the safety of their precious souls : therefore their ecstasy is clearly a diseased process. The Yogic ecstasy requires absolute calm and health of mind and body. It is useless and dangerous under other conditions even to begin the most elementary practices.

742. *My Eastern friend.*[60]—Abdul Hamid, of the Fort, Colombo, on whom be peace.

755. *Heart.*[61]—

Heart is a trifling misquotation :
This poem is for publication.

810. *Mind the dark doorway there !*[62]—This, like so many other (perhaps all) lines in these poems, is pregnant with a host of hidden meanings. Not only is it physical, of saying good-bye to a friend : but mental, of the darkness of metaphysics ; occult, of the mystical darkness of the Threshold of Initiation : and physiological, containing allusions to a whole group of phenomena, which those who have begun meditation will recognise.

Similarly, a single word may be a mnemonic key to an entire line of philosophical argument.

If the reader chooses, in short, he will find the entire mass of Initiated Wisdom between the covers of this unpretending volume.

# AMBROSII MAGI HORTUS ROSARUM *

Translated into English by Christeos Luciftias. Printed by W. Black at the Wheatsheaf in Newgate, and sold at the Three Keys in Nags-Head Court, Gracechurch St.

Opus.

It is fitting that I, Ambrose, called I. A. O., should set down the life of our great Father (who now is not, yet whose name must never be spoken among men), in order that the Brethren may know what journeys he undertook in pursuit of that Knowledge whose attainment is their constant study.

Prima Materia.
A. O.

It was at his 119th year,[1] the Star Suaconch [2] being in the sign of the Lion, that our Father set out from his Castle of Ug [3] to attain the Quinty essence or Philosophical Tincture. The way being dark and the Golden Dawn at hand, he did call forth four servants to keep him in the midst of the way, and the Lion roared before him to bid the opposers beware of his coming. On the Bull he rode, and on his left hand and his right marched the Eagle and the Man. But his back was uncovered, seeing that he would not turn.

Custodes.[4]

Sapiens dom-
inabitur astris.

And the Spirit of the Path met him. It was a young girl of two and twenty years, and she warned him fairly that without the Serpent [5] his ways were but as wool cast into the dyer's vat. Two-and-twenty scales had the Serpent, and every scale was a path, and every path was alike an enemy and a friend. So he set out, and the darkness grew upon him. Yet could he well perceive a young maiden [6] having a necklace of two-and-seventy

S. S. D. D.

---

* It would require many pages to give even a sketch of this remarkable document. The Qabalistic Knowledge is as authentic as it is profound, but there are also allusions to contemporary occult students, and a certain very small amount of mere absence of meaning. The main satire is of course of the "Chymical Marriage of Christian Rosencreutz." A few only of the serious problems are elucidated in footnotes.

---

[1] *I.e.* when 118=change, a ferment, strength. Also=before he was 120, the mystic age of a Rosicrucian.

[2] Her-shell = Herschell, or Uranus, the planet which was ascending (in Leo at Crowley's birth.

[3] Vau and Gimel, the Hierophant and High-Priestess in the Tarot Hence "from his Castle of Ug" means "from his initiation." We cannon in future do more than indicate the allusions.

[4] The Kerubim.

[5] See Table of Correspondences.

[6] The 22nd Key of the Tarot. The other Tarot symbols can be traced by any one who possesses, and to some degree understands, a pack of the cards. The occult views of the nature of these symbols are in some case Crowley's own.

pearls, big and round like the breasts of a sea-nymph ; and they gleamed bound her like moons. She held in leash the four Beasts, but he strode boldly to her, and kissed her full on her full lips. Wherefore she sighed and fell back a space, and he pressed on. Now at the end of the darkness a fire flowed : she would have hindered him : clung she to his neck and wept. *Intellectus.* but the fire grew and the light dazzled her ; so that with a shriek she fell. but the beasts flung themselves against the burning gateway of iron, and it have way. Our Father passed into the fire. Some say that it consumed him utterly and that he died ; howbeit, it is certain that he rose from a *Deus.* harcophagus, and in the skies stood an angel with a trumpet, and on that trumpet he blew so mighty a blast that the dead rose all from their tombs, and our Father among them. "Now away !" he cried. "I would look upon the sun !" And with that the fire hissed like a myriad of serpents and went out suddenly. It was a green sward golden with buttercups ; and in his way lay a high wall. Before it were two children, and with *H. et S. V. A.* abscene gestures they embraced, and laughed aloud, with filthy words and acts unspeakable. Over all of which stood the sun calm and radiant, and was glad to be. Now, think ye well, was our Father perplexed ; and he knew not what he would do. For the children left their foulness and came soliciting with shameless words his acquiescence in their sport ; and he, knowing the law of courtesy and of pity, rebuked them not. But master ever of himself he abode alone, about and above. So saw he his virginity deflowered, and his thoughts were otherwhere. Now loosed they his body ; he bade it leap the wall. The giant flower of ocean bloomed above him ! He had fallen headlong into the great deep. As the green and crimson gloom disparted somewhat before his eyes, he was aware of a Beetle that steadily and earnestly moved across the floor of that Sea *Luna.* inutterable. Him he followed ; "for I wit well," thought the Adept, 'that he goeth not back to the gross sun of earth. And if the sun hath become a beetle, may the beetle transform into a bird." Wherewith he came to land. Night shone by lamp of waning moon upon a misty land- *Quid Umbra-* escape. Two paths led him to two towers ; and jackals howled on either. *tur In Mari.* Now the jackal he knew ; and the tower he knew not yet. Not two would he conquer—that were easy : to victory over one did he aspire. Made he therefore toward the moon. Rough was the hillside and the shadows deep and treacherous ; as he advanced the towers seemed to approach one another closer and closer yet. He drew his sword : with a crash they came together ; and he fell with wrath upon a single fortress. Three windows had the tower ; and against it ten cannons thundered. *Deo Duce* Eleven bricks had fallen dislodged by lightnings : it was no house wherein *Comite Ferro.* our Father might abide. But there he must abide. "To destroy it I am come," he said. And though he passed out therewithal, yet 'twas his home until he had attained. So he came to a river, and sailing to its *Vestigia Nulla* source he found a fair woman all naked, and she filled the river from two *Retrorsum.* vessels of pure water. "She-devil," he cried, "have I gone back one step?" For the Star Venus burned above. And with his sword he clave her from the head to the feet, that she fell clean asunder. Cried the echo : "Ah ! thou hast slain hope now !" Our Father gladdened at that word, and wiping his blade he kissed it and went on, knowing that his luck should now be ill. And ill it was, for a temple was set up in

Adest Rosa Secreta Eros.

his way, and there he saw the grisly Goat enthroned. But he know better than to judge a goat from a goat's head and hoofs. And he abode in that temple awhile therefore, and worshipped ten weeks. And the first week he sacrificed to that goat[1] a crown every day. The second a phallus The third a silver vase of blood. The fourth a royal sceptre. The fifth a sword. The sixth a heart. The seventh a garland of flowers. The eighth a grass-snake. The ninth a sickle. And the tenth week did he daily offer up his own body. Said the goat: "Though I be not an of yet am I a sword." "Masked, O God!" cried the Adept. "Verily, a thou hadst not sacrificed—" There was silence. And under the Goat throne was a rainbow[2] of seven colours: our Father fitted himself as a

Hemaphroditus.

arrow to the string (and the string was waxed well, dipped in a leaden per wherein boiled amber and wine) and shot through stormy heavens. And they that saw him saw a woman wondrous fair[3] robed in flames of hair moon-sandalled, sun-belted, with torch and vase of fire and water. And he trailed comet-clouds of glory upward.

Thus came our Father (Blessed be his name!) to Death, who stood scythe in hand, opposed. And ever and anon he swept round, and me fell before him. "Look," said Death, "my sickle hath a cross-handle See how they grow like flowers!" "Give me salt!" quoth our Father

Mors Janua Vitae.

And with sulphur (that the Goat had given him) and with salt did he bestrew the ground. "I see we shall have ado together," says Death "Aye!" and with that he lops off Death's cross-handle. Now Death was wroth indeed, for he saw that our Father had wit of his designs (and they were right foul!), but he bade him pass forthwith from his dominion And our Father could not at that time stay him: though for himself has he cut off the grip, yet for others—well, let each man take his sword

Adeptus.

The way went through a forest. Now between two trees hung a man be one heel (Love was that tree).[5] Crossed were his legs, and his arms behind his head, that hung ever downwards, the fingers locked. "Who art thou?" quoth our Father. "He that came before thee." "Who am I?" "He that cometh after me." With that worshipped our Father and took a present of a great jewel from him, and went his ways. And he was bitterly a-cold, for that was the great Water he had passed. But our Father's paps glittered with cold, black light, and likewise his navel

Terrae Ultor Anima Terrae.

Wherefore he was comforted. Now came the sudden twittering of heal lest the firmament beneath him were not stable, and lo! he danceth up and down as a very cork on waters of wailing. "Woman," he bad sternly, "be still. Cleave that with thy sword: or that must I we work?" But she cleft the cords, bitter-faced, smiling goddess as she was

[1] The sacrifices are the ten Sephiroth.
[2] See Table.
[3] Ancient form of the Key of ס.
[4] Considered as the agent of resurrection.
[5] In the true Key of מ the tree is shaped like the letter ד = Venus or love The figure of the man forms a cross above a triangle, with apex upwards the sign of redemption.

and he went on. "Leave thine ox-goad,"[1] quoth he, "till I come back an ox!" And she laughed and let him pass. Now is our Father come to the Unstable Lands, 'Od wot, for the Wheel whereon he poised was ever turning. Sworded was the Sphinx, but he out-dared her in riddling: deeper pierced his sword: he cut her into twain: her place was his. But that would he not, my Brethren; to the centre he clomb ever: and having won thither, he vanished. As a hermit ever he travelled and the lamp and wand were his. In his path a lion roared, but to it ran a maiden, strong as a young elephant, and held its cruel jaws. By force he ran to her: he freed the lion—one buffet of his hand dashed her back six paces!—and with another blow smote its head from its body. And he ran to her and by force embraced her. Struggled she and fought him: savagely she bit, but it was of no 'avail: she lay ravished and exhausted on the Lybian plain. Across the mouth he smote her for a kiss, while she cried: "O! thou hast begotten on me twins. And mine also is the Serpent, and thou shalt conquer it and it shall serve thee: and they, they also for a guide!" She ceased; and he, having come to the world's end, prepared his chariot. Foursquare he builded it, and that double: he harnessed the two sphinxes that he had made from one, and sailed, crabfashion, backwards, through the amber skies of even. Wherefore he attained to see his children. Lovers they were and lovely, those twins of rape. One was above them, joining their hands. "That is well," said our Father, and for seven nights he slept in seven starry palaces, and a sword to guard him. Note well also that these children, and those others, are two, being four. And on the sixth day (for the seven days were past) he rose and came into his ancient temple, a temple of our Holy Order, O my Brethren, wherein sat that Hierophant who had initiated him of old. Now read he well the riddle of the Goat (Blessed be his name among us for ever! Nay, not for ever!), and therewith the Teacher made him a Master of the Sixfold Chamber, and an ardent Sufferer toward the Blazing Star. For the Sword, said the Teacher, is but the Star unfurled.[2] And our Father being cunning to place Aleph over Tau read this reverse, and so beheld Eden, even now and in the flesh.

Whence he sojourned far, and came to a great Emperor, by whom he was well received, and from whom he gat great gifts. And the Emperor (who is Solomon) told him of Sheba's Land and of one fairest of women there enthroned. So he journeyed thither, and for four years and seven months abode with her as paramour and light-of-love, for she was gracious to him and showed him those things that the Emperor had hidden; even the cubical stone and the cross beneath the triangle that were his and unrevealed. And on the third day he left her and came to Her who had initiated him before he was initiated; and with her he abode eight days and twenty days:[3] and she gave him gifts.

*Sapientiae Lux Viris Baculum.*

*Femina Rapta Inspirat Gaudium.*

*Pleiades.*

*Dignitates.*

*Amicitia.*

*Amor.*

*Sophia.*

[1] Lamed means ox-goad; Aleph, an ox. Lamed Aleph means No, the denial of Aleph Lamed, El, God.
[2] Read reverse, the Star [=the Will and the Great Work] is to fold up the Sephiroth; *i.e.* to attain Nirvana.
[3] The houses of the Moon. All the gifts are lunar symbols.

The first day, a camel ;
The second day, a kiss ;
The third day, a star-glass ;
The fourth day, a beetle's wing ;
The fifth day, a crab ;
The sixth day, a bow ;
The seventh day, a quiver ;
The eighth day, a stag ;
The ninth day, an horn ;
The tenth day, a sandal of silver ;

Dona Virginis.   The eleventh day, a silver box of white sandal wood ;
The twelfth day, a whisper ;
The thirteenth day, a black cat ;
The fourteenth day, a phial of white gold ;
The fifteenth day, an egg-shell cut in two ;
The sixteenth day, a glance ;
The seventeenth day, an honeycomb ;
The eighteenth day, a dream ;
The nineteenth day, a nightmare ;
The twentieth day, a wolf, black-muzzled ;
The twenty-first day, a sorrow ;
The twenty-second day, a bundle of herbs ;
The twenty-third day, a piece of camphor ;
The twenty-fourth day, a moonstone ;
The twenty-fifth day, a sigh ;
The twenty-sixth day, a refusal ;

Puella Urget
Sophiam Sod-
alibus.

The twenty-seventh day, a consent ; and the last night she gave him all
herself, so that the moon was eclipsed and earth was utterly darkened.   And
the marriage of that virgin was on this wise : She had three arrows, yet
but two flanks, and the wise men said that who knew two was three,[1] should
know three was eight,[2] if the circle were but squared ; and this also one
day shall ye know, my Brethren !   And she gave him the great and perfect
gift of Magic, so that he fared forth right comely and well-provided.   Now

The Sophic
Suggler.

at that great wedding was a Suggler,[3] a riddler : for he said, "Thou hast
beasts : I will give thee weapons one for one."   For the Lion did our
Father win a little fiery wand like a flame, and for his Eagle a cup of ever
flowing water : for his Man the Suggler gave him a golden-hilted dagger (yet
this was the worst of all his bargains, for it could not strike other, but himself only), while for a curious coin he bartered his good Bull.   Alas for our
Father !   Now the Suggler mocks him and cries : "Four fool's bargains
hast thou made, and thou art fit to go forth and meet a fool[4] for thy mate."
But our Father counted thrice seven and cried : "One for the fool," seeing

---

[1] 3, the number of ⊃.   2, the number of the card ⊃.
[2] The equality of three and eight is attributed to Binah, a high grade of
Theurgic attainment.
[3] *Scil.* Juggler, the 1st Key.   The magical weapons correspond to the
Kerubim.
[4] The Key marked O and applied to Aleph, 1.

the Serpent should be his at last. "None for the fool," they laughed
back—nay, even his maiden queen. For she would not any should know
thereof. Yet were all right, both he and they. But truth ran quickly
about; for that was the House of Truth; and Mercury stood far from the *Hammer of*
Sun. Yet the Suggler was ever in the Sign of Sorrow, and the Fig Tree *Thor.*
was not far. So went our Father to the Fool's Paradise of Air. But it is
not lawful that I should write to you, brethren, of what there came to him
at that place and time; nor indeed is it true, if it were written. For alway
doth this Arcanum differ from itself on this wise, that the Not and the *Arcanum.*
Amen,[1] passing, are void either on the one side or the other, and Who shall
tell their ways?

So our Father, having won the Serpent Crown, the Uraeus of Antient
Khem, did bind it upon his head, and rejoiced in that Kingdom for the
space of two hundred and thirty and one days[2] and nights, and turned him
toward the Flaming Sword.[3] Now the Sword governeth ten mighty Kingdoms, and evil, and above them is the ninefold lotus, and a virgin came
forth unto him in the hour of his rejoicing and propounded her riddle.

The first riddle:[4] *Griphus I.*
The maiden is blind.
Our Father: She shall be what she doth not.
And a second virgin came forth to him and said:
The second riddle: Detegitur Yod. *Griphus II.*
Quoth our Father: The moon is full.
So also a third virgin the third riddle: *Griphus III.*
Man and woman: O fountain of the balance!
To whom our Father answered with a swift flash of his sword, so swift
she saw it not.
Came out a fourth virgin, having a fourth riddle: *Griphus IV.*
What egg hath no shell?
And our Father pondered a while and then said:
On a wave of the sea: on a shell of the wave: blessed be her name!
The fifth virgin issued suddenly and said: *Griphus V.*
I have four arms and six sides: red am I, and gold. To whom our Father:
Eli, Eli, lama sabachthani!
(For wit ye well, there be two Arcana therein.)
Then said the sixth virgin openly: *Griphus VI.*
Power lieth in the river of fire.
And our Father laughed aloud and answered: I am come from the
waterfall.
So at that the seventh virgin came forth: and her countenance was *Griphus VII.*
troubled.
The seventh riddle:
The oldest said to the most beautiful: What doest thou here?

---

[1] This is obscure. [2] $0+1+2+ \ldots +21=231$. [3] The Seplinoth.
[4] The maiden (Malkuth) is blind (unredeemed). Answer: She shall be
what she doth not, *i.e.* see. She shall be the sea, *i.e.* "exalted to the throne
of Binah" (the great sea), the Qabalistic phrase to express her redemption.
We leave it to the reader's ingenuity to solve the rest. . Each refers to the
Sephira indicated by the number, but going upward.

Our Father :

And she answered him : I am in the place of the bridge.  Go thou up higher : go thou where these are not.

Griphus VIII.  Thereat was commotion and bitter wailing, and the eighth virgin came forth with rent attire and cried the eighth riddle :

The sea hath conceived.

Our Father raised his head, and there was a great darkness.

Griphus IX.  The ninth virgin, sobbing at his feet, the ninth riddle :

By wisdom.

Then our Father touched his crown and they all rejoiced : but laughing he put them aside and he said : Nay !  By six hundred and twenty[1] do ye exceed !

Griphus X.  Whereat they wept, and the tenth virgin came forth, bearing a royal crown having twelve jewels : and she had but one eye, and from that the eyelid had been torn.  A prodigious beard had she, and all of white : and they wist he would have smitten her with his sword.  But he would not, and she propounded unto him the tenth riddle :

Countenance beheld not countenance.

So thereto he answered : Our Father, blessed be thou !—

Countenance ?

Then they brought him the Sword and bade him smite withal : but he said :

Culpa Urbium Nota Terrae.  If countenance behold not countenance, then let the ten be five.  And they wist that he but mocked them ; for he did bend the sword fivefold and fashioned therefrom a Star, and they all vanished in that light ; yet the lotus abode nine-petalled and he cried, " Before the wheel, the axle." So he chained the Sun,[2] and slew the Bull, and exhausted the Air, breathing it deep into his lungs : then he broke down the ancient tower, that which he had made his home, will he nill he, for so long, and he slew the other Bull, and he broke the arrow in twain ; after that he was silent, for they grew again in sixfold order, so that this latter work was double : but unto the first three he laid not his hand, neither for the first time, nor for the second time, nor for the third time.  So to them he added[3] that spiritual flame (for they were one, and ten, and fifty, thrice, and again) and that was the Beast, the Living One that is Lifan.  Let us be silent, therefore, my brethren, worshipping the holy sixfold Ox[4] that was our Father in his peace that he had won into, and that so hardly.  For of this shall no man speak.

Now therefore let it be spoken of our Father's journeyings in the land of Vo[5] and of his suffering therein, and of the founding of our holy and illustrious Order.

Nechesh.  Our Father, Brethren, having attained the mature age of three hundred

---

[1] Kether adds up to 620.
[2] These are the letters of Ain Soph Aur, the last two of which he destroys, so as to leave only Ain, Not, or Nothing.
[3] To $(1+10+50)$ $3 \times 2$ he adds 300, Shin, the flame of the Spirit$=666$.
[4] $666=6 \times 111$.  $111=$Aleph, the Ox.
[5] His journeys as Initiator.

and fifty and eight years,[1] set forth upon a journey into the Mystic Mountain of the Caves.   He took with him his Son,[2] a Lamb, Life, and   Abiegnus.
Strength, for these four were the Keys of that Mountain.   So by ten
days and fifty days and two hundred days and yet ten days he went forth.
After ten days fell a thunderbolt, whirling through black clouds of rain:
after sixty the road split in two, but he travelled on both at once : after   Mysterium
two hundred and sixty, the sun drove away the rain, and the Star shone   I.N.R.I.
in the day-time, making it night.   After the last day came his Mother,
his Redeemer, and Himself; and joining together they were even as I
am who write unto you.   Seventeen they were, the three Fathers: with
the three Mothers they were thirty-two, and sixfold therein, being as
countenance and countenance.   Yet, being seventeen, they were but
one, and that one none, as before hath been showed.   And this enumera-
tion is a great Mysterium of our art.   Whence a light hidden in a Cross.   Mysterium
Now therefore having brooded upon the ocean, and smitten with the   LVX.
Sword, and the Pyramid being builded in its just proportion, was that
Light fixed even in the Vault of the Caverns.   With one stroke he rent
asunder the Veil ; with one stroke he closed the same.   And entering
the Sarcophagus of that Royal Tomb he laid him down to sleep.   Four   Pastos.
guarded him, and One in the four; Seven enwalled him, and One in
the seven, yet were the seven ten, and One in the ten.   Now therefore
his disciples came unto the Vault of that Mystic Mountain, and with the
Keys they opened the Portal and came to him and woke him.   But
during his long sleep the roses had grown over him, crimson and flaming
with interior fire, so that he could not escape.   Yet they withered at his
glance ; withat he knew what fearful task was before him.   But slaying
his disciples with long Nails, he interred them there, so that they were
right sorrowful in their hearts.   May all we die so !   And what further
befell him ye shall also know, but not at this time.

Going forth of that Mountain he met also the Fool.   Then the discourse
of that Fool, my Brethren ; it shall repay your pains.   They think they   Trinitas.
are a triangle,[3] he said, they think as the Picture-Folk.   Base they are,
and little infinitely.

Ain Elohim.

They think, being many, they are one.[4]   They think as the Rhine-Folk
think.   Many and none.                                                   Unitas.

Ain Elohim.

They think the erect[5] is the twined, and the twined is the coiled, and
the coiled is the twin, and the twins are the stoopers.   They think as the   Serpentes.
Big-Nose-Folk.   Save us, O Lord !

[1] Nechesh the Serpent and Messiach the Redeemer.
[2] Abigenos, Abiagnus, Bigenos, Abiegnus, metatheses of the name of the
Mystic Mountain of Initiation.   The next paragraph has been explained in
the Appendix to Vol. I.
[3] The belief in a Trinity—ignorance of Daath.
[4] Belief in Monism, or rather Advaitism.   Crowley was a Monist only in
the modern scientific sense of that word.
[5] Confusion of the various mystic serpents.   The Big-Nose-Folk = the Jews.
We leave the rest to the insight of the reader.

Ain Elohim.

**Abracadabra.** The Chariot.  Four hundred and eighteen.  Five are one, and six are diverse, five in the midst and three on each side.  The Word of Power, double in the Voice of the Master.

Ain Elohim.

**Amethsh.** Four sounds of four forces.  O the Snake hath a long tail !  Amen

Ain Elohim.

Sudden death : thick darkness : ho ! the ox !

**Ye Fylfat †.** One, and one, and one : Creator, Preserver, Destroyer, ho ! the Redeemer !  Thunder-stone : whirlpool : lotus-flower : ho ! for the gold of the sages !

Ain Elohim.

And he was silent for a great while, and so departed our Father from Him.

**Mysterium Matris.[1]** Forth he went along the dusty desert and met an antient woman bearing a bright crown of gold, studded with gems, one on each knee.  Dressed in rags she was, and squatted clumsily on the sand.  A horn grew from her forehead ; and she spat black foam and froth.  Foul was the hag and evil, yet our Father bowed down flat on his face to the earth.  " Holy Virgin of God," said he, " what dost thou here ?  What wilt thou with thy servant ? "  At that she stank so that the air gasped about her, like a fish brought out of the sea.  So she told him she was gathering simples for **Evocatio.** her daughter that had died to bury her withal.  Now no simples grew in the desert.  Therefore our Father drew with his sword lines of power in the sand, so that a black and terrible demon appeared squeezing up in thin flat plates of flesh along the sword-lines.  So our Father cried : " Simples, O Axcaxrabortharax, for my mother ! "  Then the demon was wroth and shrieked : " Thy mother to black hell !  She is mine ! "  So the old hag confessed straight that she had given her body for love to that fiend of the pit.  But our Father paid no heed thereto and bade the demon **Lucus.** to do his will, so that he brought him herbs many, and good, with which our Father planted a great grove that grew about him (for the sun was now waxen bitter hot) wherein he worshipped, offering in vessels of clay these seven offerings :[2]

The first offering, dust ;

The second offering, ashes ;

The third offering, sand ;

The fourth offering, bay-leaves ;

The fifth offering, gold ;

The sixth offering, dung ;

The seventh offering, poison.

With the dust he gave also a sickle to gather the harvest of that dust.

With the ashes he gave a sceptre, that one might rule them aright.

With the sand he gave a sword, to cut that sand withal.

With the bay-leaves he gave a sun, to wither them.

With the gold he gave also a garland of sores, and that was for luck.

With the dung he gave a Rod of Life to quicken it.

---

[1] This is all obscure.                [2] Refer to the planets.

With the poison he gave also in offering a stag and a maiden.

But about the noon came one shining unto our Father and gave him to drink from a dull and heavy bowl. And this was a liquor potent and heavy, by'r lady! So that our Father sank into deep sleep and dreamed a dream, and in that mirific dream it seemed unto him that the walls of all things slid into and across each other, so that he feared greatly, for the stability of the universe is the great enemy; the unstable being the everlasting, saith Adhou Bin Aram, the Arab. O Elmen Zata, our Sophic Pilaster! Further in the dream there was let down from heaven a mighty tessaract, bounded by eight cubes, whereon sat a mighty dolphin having eight senses. Further, he beheld a cavern full of most ancient bones of men, and therein a lion with a voice of a dog. Then came a voice: "Thirteen [1] are they, who are one. Once is a oneness: twice is the Name: thrice let us say not: by four is the Son: by five is the Sword: by six is the Holy Oil of the most Excellent Beard, and the leaves of the Book are by six: by seven is that great Amen." Then our Father saw one hundred and four horses that drove an ivory car over a sea of pearl, and they received him therein and bade him be comforted. With that he awoke and saw that he would have all his desire. In the morning therefore he arose and went his way into the desert. There he clomb an high rock and called forth the eagles, that their shadow floating over the desert should be as a book that men might read it. The shadows wrote and the sun recorded; and on this wise cometh it to pass, O my Brethren, that by darkness and by sunlight ye will still learn ever these the Arcana of our Science. Lo! who learneth by moonlight, he is the lucky one! So our Father, having thus founded the Order, and our sacred Book being opened, rested awhile and beheld many wonders, the like of which were never yet told. But ever chiefly his study was to reduce unto eight things his many.

And thus, O Brethren of our Venerable Order, he at last succeeded. Those who know not will learn little herein: yet that they may be shamed all shall be put forth at this time clearly before them all, with no obscurity nor obfuscation in the exposition thereof.

Writing this, saith our Father to me, the humblest and oldest of all his disciples, write as the story of my Quintessential Quest, my Spagyric Wandering, my Philosophical Going. Write plainly unto the Brethren, quoth he, for many be little and weak; and thy hard words and much learning may confound them.

Therefore I write thus plainly to you. Mark well that ye read me aright!

Our Father (blessed be his name!) entered the Path on this wise. He cut off three from ten: [2] thus he left seven. He cut and left three: he cut and left one: he cut and became. Thus fourfold. Eightfold. [3] He opened his eyes: he cleansed his heart: he chained his tongue: he fixed

*Marginal notes:*
Somnium Auri Potabilis.

Tredecim Voces.

Ordinis Inceptio.

Vitae.

Viae.

---

[1] Achad, unity, adds to thirteen. There follow attributions of the "thirteen times table."

[2] These are the Buddhist "paths of enlightenment."

[3] The eightfold path. The rest is very obscure.

his flesh: he turned to his trade: he put forth his strength: he drew all to a point: he delighted.

Therefore he is not, having become that which he was not. Mark ye all: it is declared. Now of the last adventure of our Father and of his going into the land of Apes, that is, England, and of what he did there, it is not fitting that I, the poor old fool who loved him, shall now discourse. But it is most necessary that I should speak of his holy death and of his funeral and of the bruit thereof, for that is gone into divers lands as a false and lying report, whereby much harm and ill-luck come to the Brethren. In this place, therefore, will I set down the exact truth of all that happened.

Mirabilia.

In the year of the Great Passing Over were signs and wonders seen of all men, O my Brethren, as it is written, and well known unto this day. And the first sign was of dancing: for every woman that was under the

I. Signum.

moon began to dance and was mad, so that headlong and hot-mouthed she flung herself down, desirous. Whence the second sign, that of

II. Signum.

musical inventions; for in that year, and of Rosewomen, came A and U and M,[1] the mighty musicians! And the third sign likewise, namely, of

III. Signum.

animals: for in that year every sheep had lambs thirteen, and every cart[2] was delivered of a wheel! And other wonders innumerable: they are

Alia Signa.

well known, insomuch that that year is yet held notable.

Now our Father, being very old, came unto the venerable Grove of our August Fraternity and abode there. And so old was he and feeble that he could scarce lift his hands in benediction upon us. And all we waited about him, both by day and night; lest one word should fall, and we not hear the same. But he spake never unto us, though his lips moved and his eyes sought ever that which we could not see. At last, on the day of D., the mother of P.,[3] he straightened himself up and spake. This his final discourse was written down then by the dying lions in their own blood, traced willingly on the desert sands about the Grove of the Illustrious. Also here set down: but who will confirm the same, let him seek it on the sands.

Children of my Will, said our Father, from whose grey eyes fell gentlest tears, it is about the hour. The chariot (Ch.)[4] is not, and the chariot (H.) is at hand. Yet I, who have been car-borne through the blue air by sphinxes, shall never be carried away, not by the whitest horses of the world. To you I have no word to say. All is written in the sacred Book. To that look ye well!

Pater Jubet: Scientiam Scribe.

Ambrose, old friend, he said, turning to me—and I wept ever sore—do thou write for the little ones, the children of my children, for them that understand not easily our high Mysteries; for in thy pen is, as it were, a river of clear water; without vagueness, without ambiguity,

[1] Aum! The sacred word.

[2] Qy. ח (the car) becomes O (a wheel). The commentators who have suspected the horrid blasphemy implied by the explanation "becomes כ, the Wheel of Fortune," are certainly in error.

[3] Demeter and Persephone.

[4] Ch=ח; H=Hades. See the Tarot cards, and classical mythology, for the symbols.

without show of learning, without needless darkening of counsel and word, dost thou ever reveal the sacred Heights of our Mystic Mountain. For, as for him that understandeth not thy writing, and that easily and well, be ye well assured all that he is a vile man and a losel of little worth or worship; a dog, an unclean swine, a worm of filth, a festering sore in the vitals of earth : such an one is liar and murderer, debauched, drunken, sexless, and spatulate ; an ape-dropping, a lousy, flat-backed knave : from such an one keep ye well away! Use hath he little : ornament maketh he nothing : let him be cast out on the dunghills beyond Jordan ; let him pass into the S. P. P., and that utterly ! *Sedes Profunda Paimonis.*

With that our Father sighed deep and laid back his reverend head, and was silent. But from his heart came a subtle voice of tenderest fare-well, so that we knew him well dead. But for seventy days and seventy nights we touched him not, but abode ever about him : and the smile changed not on his face, and the whole grove was filled with sweet and subtle perfumes. Now on the 71st day arose there a great dispute about his body ; for the angels and spirits and demons did contend about it, that they might possess it. But our eldest brother V. N. bade all be still ; and thus he apportioned the sacred relics of our Father. *Oculi Nox Secreta.* *Portae Silentium.* *Partitio.*

To the Angel Agbagal, the fore part of the skull ;
To the demon Ozoz, the back left part of the skull;
To the demon Olcot,[1] the back right part of the skull ;
To ten thousand myriads of spirits of fire, each one hair ;
To ten thousand myriads of spirits of water, each one hair ;
To ten thousand myriads of spirits of earth, each one hair :
To ten thousand myriads of spirits of air, each one hair :
To the archangel Zazelazel, the brain ;
To the angel Usbusolat, the medulla ;
To the demon Ululomis, the right nostril ;
To the angel Opael, the left nostril ;
To the spirit Kuiphiah, the membrane of the nose ;
To the spirit Pugrah, the bridge of the nose ;
To eleven thousand spirits of spirit, the hairs of the nose, one each ;
To the archangel Tuphtuphtuphal,[2] the right eye ;
To the archdevil Upsusph, the left eye ;
The parts thereof in trust to be divided among their servitors ; as the right cornea, to Aphlek ; the left, to Urnbal ;—mighty spirits are they, and bold !
To the archdevil Rama,[3] the right ear and its parts ;
To the archangel Umumatis, the left ear and its parts ;
The teeth to two-and-thirty letters of the sixfold Name : one to the air, and fifteen to the rain and the ram, and ten to the virgin, and six to the Bull ;
The mouth to the archangels Alalal and Bikarak, lip and lip;
The tongue to that devil of all devils Yehowou.[4] Ho, devil ! canst thou speak ?

[1] Col. Olcott, the theosophist.
[2] ? the spirit of motor-cars.
[3] Vishnu, the preserver.
[4] Jehovah.

The pharynx to Mahabonisbash, the great angel ;

To seven-and-thirty myriads of legions of planetary spirits the hairs of the moustache, to each one ;

To ninety and one myriads of the Elohim, the hairs of the beard ; to each thirteen, and the oil to ease the world ;

To Shalach, the archdevil, the chin.

So also with the lesser relics ; of which are notable only : to the Order, the heart of our Father : to the Book of the Law, his venerable lung-space to serve as a shrine thereunto : to the devil Aot, the liver, to be divided : to the angel Exarp and his followers, the great intestine : to Bitom the devil and his crew, the little intestine : to Aub, Aud, and Aur, the venerable Phallus of our Father : to Ash the little bone of the same : to our children K., C., B., C., G., T., N., H., I., and M., his illustrious finger-nails, and the toe-nails to be in trust for their children after them : and so for all the rest ; is it not written in our archives ? As to his magical weapons, all vanished utterly at the moment of that Passing Over. Therefore they carried away our Father's body piece by piece and that with reverence and in order, so that there was not left of all one hair, nor one nerve, nor one little pore of the skin. Thus was there no funeral pomp ; they that say other are liars and blasphemers against a fame untarnished. May the red plague rot their vitals !

Amen.

Thus, O my Brethren, thus and not otherwise was the Passing Over of that Great and Wonderful Magician, our Father and Founder. May the dew of his admirable memory moisten the grass of our minds, that we may bring forth tender shoots of energy in the Great Work of Works. So mote it be !

BENEDICTVS DOMINVS DEVS

NOSTER QVI NOBIS DEDIT

SIGNVM

R. C.

## 1902

# THE THREE CHARACTERISTICS

" LISTEN to the Jataka !" said the Buddha. And all they gave ear. " Long ago, when King Brahmadatta reigned in Benares,[1] it came to pass that there lived under his admirable government a weaver named Suraj Ju[2] and his wife Chandi.[3] And in the fulness of her time did she give birth to a man child, and they called him Perdu' R Abu.[4] Now the child grew, and the tears of the mother fell, and the wrath of the father waxed : for by no means would the boy strive in his trade of weaving. The loom went merrily, but to the rhythm of a mantra ; and the silk slipped through his fingers, but as if one told his beads. Wherefore the work was marred, and the hearts of the parents were woe because of him. But it is written that misfortune knoweth not the hour to cease, and that the seed of sorrow is as the seed of the Banyan Tree. It groweth and is of stature as a mountain, and, ay me ! it shooteth down fresh roots into the aching earth. For the boy grew and became a man ; and his eyes kindled with the lust of life and love ; and the desire stirred him to see the round world and its many marvels. Wherefore he went forth, taking his father's store of gold, laid up for him against that bitter day, and he took fair maidens, and was their servant. And he builded a fine house and dwelt therein. And he took no thought. But he said : Here is a change indeed !

" Now it came to pass that after many years he looked upon his lover, the bride of his heart, the rose of his garden, the jewel of his rosary ; and behold, the olive loveliness of smooth skin was darkened, and the flesh lay loose, and the firm breasts drooped, and the eyes had lost alike the gleam of joy and the sparkle of laughter and the soft glow of love. And he was mindful of his word, and said in sorrow, ' Here is then a change indeed !' And he turned his thought to himself, and saw that in his heart was also a change : so that he cried, ' Who then am I ?' And he saw that all this was sorrow. And he turned his thought without and saw that all things were alike in this ; that nought might escape the threefold misery. ' The soul,' he said, ' the soul, the I, is as all these ; it is impermanent as the ephemeral flower of beauty in the water that is born and shines and dies ere sun be risen and set again.'

" And he humiliated his heart and sang the following verse :

Brahma, and Vishnu, and great Shiva ! Truly
I see the Trinity in all things dwell,
Some rightly tinged of Heaven, others duly
Pitched down the steep and precipice of
  Hell.
Nay, not your glory ye from fable borrow !
These three I see in spirit and in sense,
These three, O miserable seer ! Sorrow,
Absence of ego, and impermanence !

And at the rhythm he swooned, for his old mantra surged up in the long-sealed vessels of sub-conscious memory, and he fell into the calm ocean of a great Meditation.

[1] The common formula for beginning a " Jataka," or story of a previous incarnation of Buddha. Brahmadatta reigned 120,000 years.
[2] The Sun.
[3] The Moon.
[4] Perdurabo. Crowley's motto.

## II.

"Jehjaour[1] was a mighty magician; his soul was dark and evil; and his lust was of life and power and of the wreaking of hatred upon the innocent. And it came to pass that he gazed upon a ball of crystal wherein were shown him all the fears of the time unborn as yet on earth. And by his art he saw Perdu' R Abu, who had been his friend: for do what he would, the crystal showed always that sensual and frivolous youth as a Fear to him: even to him the Mighty One! But the selfish and evil are cowards; they fear shadows, and Jehjaour scorned not his art. 'Roll on in time, thou ball!' he cried. 'Move down the stream of years, timeless and hideous servant of my will! Taph! Tath! Arath!'[2] He sounded the triple summons, the mysterious syllables that bound the spirit to the stone.

"Then suddenly the crystal grew a blank; and thereby the foiled wizard knew that which threatened his power, his very life, was so high and holy that the evil spirit could perceive it not. 'Avaunt!' he shrieked, 'false soul of darkness!' And the crystal flashed up red, the swarthy red of hate in a man's cheek, and darkened utterly.

"Foaming at the mouth the wretched Jehjaour clutched at air and fell prone.

## III.

"To what God should he appeal? His own, Hanuman, was silent. Sacrifice, prayer, all were in vain. So Jehjaour gnashed his teeth, and his whole force went out in a mighty current of hate towards his former friend.

[1] Allan MacGregor Bennett (whose motto in the " Hermetic Order of the Golden Dawn," was Iehi Aour, *i.e.* " Let there be light "), now Ananda Metteya, to whom the volume in which this story was issued is inscribed.
[2] Taphtatharath, the spirit of Mercury.

"Now hate hath power, though not the power of love. So it came about that in his despair he fell into a trance; and in the trance Mara[1] appeared to him. Never before had his spells availed to call so fearful a potency from the abyss of matter. 'Son,' cried the Accursèd One, seven days of hate unmarred by passion milder, seven days without one thought of pity, these avail to call me forth.' 'Slay me my enemy!' howled the wretch. But Mara trembled. 'Enquire of Ganesha concerning him!' faltered at last the fiend.

"Jehjaour awoke.

## IV.

"'Yes!' said Ganesha gloomily, 'the young man has given me up altogether. He tells me I am as mortal as he is, and he doesn't mean to worry about me any more.' 'Alas!' sighed the deceitful Jehjaour, who cared no more for Ganesha and any indignities that might be offered him than his enemy did. 'One of my best devotees too!' muttered, or rather trumpeted, the elephantine anachronism. 'You see,' said the wily wizard, 'I saw Perdu' R Abu the other day, and he said he had become Srotapatti. Now that's pretty serious. In seven births only, if he but pursue the path, will he cease to be reborn. So you have only that time in which to win him back to your worship.' The cunning sorcerer did not mention that within that time also must his own ruin be accomplished. 'What do you advise?' asked the irritated and powerful, but unintelligent deity. 'Time is our friend,' said the enchanter. 'Let your influence be used in the Halls of Birth that each birth may be as long as possible. Now the elephant is the longest lived of all beasts—' 'Done with you!' said Ganesha in great glee, for the idea struck him as ingenious. And he lumbered off to clinch the affair at once.

"And Perdu' R Abu died.

[1] The archdevil of the Buddhists.

## V.

" Now the great elephant strode with lordly footsteps in the forest, and Jehjaour shut himself up with his caldrons and things and felt quite happy, for he knew his danger was not near till the approaching of Perdu' R Abu's Arahatship.   But in spite of the young gently-ambling cows which Ganesha took care to throw in his way, in spite of the tender shoots of green and the soft cocoanuts, this elephant was not as other elephants.  The seasons spoke to him of change—the forest is ever full of sorrow—and nobody need preach to him the absence of an ego, for the brutes have had more sense than ever to imagine there was one. So the tusker was usually to be found, still as a rock, in some secluded place, meditating on the Three Characteristics.  And when Ganesha appeared in all his glory, he found him to his disgust quite free from elephanto-morphism.  In fact, he quietly asked the God to leave him alone.

" Now he was still quite a young elephant when there came into the jungle, tripping merrily along, with a light-hearted song in its nucleolus, no less than a Bacillus.

" And the elephant died.  He was only seventeen years old.

## VI.

" A brief consultation ; and the Srotapatti was reincarnated as a parrot.  For the parrot, said the wicked Jehjaour, may live 500 years and never feel it.

" So a grey wonder of wings flitted into the jungle.  So joyous a bird, thought the God, could not but be influenced by the ordinary passions and yield to such majesty as his own.

" But one day there came into the jungle a strange wild figure.  He was a man dressed in the weird Tibetan fashion.  He had red robes and hat, and thought dark things.  He whirled a prayer-wheel in his hands ; and ever as he went he muttered the mystic words ' Aum Mani Padme Hum.'[1]  The parrot, who had never heard human speech, tried to mimic the old Lama, and was amazed at his success.  Pride first seized the bird, but it was not long before the words had their own effect, and it was in meditation upon the conditions of existence that he eternally repeated the formula.

.*.

" A home at distant Inglistan.  An old lady, and a grey parrot in a cage.  The parrot was still muttering inaudibly the sacred mantra.  Now, now, the moment of Destiny was at hand !  The Four Noble Truths shone out in that parrot's mind ; the Three Characteristics appeared luminous, like three spectres on a murderer's grave : unable to contain himself he recited aloud the mysterious sentence.

" The old lady, whatever may have been her faults, could act promptly.  She rang the bell.  ' Sarah ! ' said she, ' take away that dreadful creature !  Its language is positively awful.'  ' What shall I do with it, mum ? ' asked the ' general.'  ' Aum Mani Padme Hum,' said the parrot.  The old lady stopped her ears.  ' Wring its neck ! ' she said.

" The parrot was only eight years old.

## VII.

" ' You're a muddler and an idiot ! ' said the infuriated God.  ' Why not make him a spiritual thing?  A Nat[2] lives 10,000 years.'  ' Make him a Nat then ! ' said the magician, already beginning to fear that fate would be too strong for him, in spite of all his cunning.  ' There's some one working against us on the physical plane.  We must transcend it.'  No sooner said than done :

[1] " O the Jewel in the Lotus !  Aum ! "  The most famous of the Buddhist formularies.
[2] The Burmese name for an elemental spirit.

a family of Nats in a big tree at Anuradhapura had a little stranger, very welcome to Mamma and Papa Nat.

"Blessed indeed was the family. Five-and-forty feet [1] away stood a most ancient and holy dagoba : and the children of light would gather round it in the cool of the evening, or in the misty glamour of dawn, and turn forth in love and pity towards all mankind—nay, to the smallest grain of dust tossed on the utmost storms of the Sahara !

"Blessed and more blessed ! For one day came a holy Bhikkhu from the land of the Peacock,[2] and would take up his abode in the hollow of their very tree. And little Perdu' R Abu used to keep the mosquitoes away with the gossamer of his wings, so that the good man might be at peace.

"Now the British Government abode in that land, and when it heard that there was a Bhikkhu living in a tree, and that the village folk brought him rice and onions and gramophones, it saw that it must not be.

"And little Perdu' R Abu heard them talk ; and learnt the great secret of Impermanence, and of Sorrow, and the mystery of Unsubstantiality.

"And the Government evicted the Bhikkhu ; and set guard, quite like the end of Genesis iii., and cut down the tree, and all the Nats perished.

"Jehjaour heard and trembled. Perdu' R Abu was only three years old.

### VIII.

"It really seemed as if fate was against him. Poor Jehjaour ! In despair he cried to his partner, 'O Ganesha, in the world of Gods only shall we be safe. Let him be born as a flute-girl before Indra's throne !' 'Difficult is the task,' replied the alarmed deity, 'but I will use all my influence. I

[1] The Government, in the interests of Buddhists themselves, reserves all ground within 50 feet of a dagoba. The incident described in this section actually occurred in 1901.
[2] Siam.

know a thing or two about Indra, for example——'

"It was done. Beautiful was the young girl's face as she sprang mature from the womb of Matter, on her life journey of an hundred thousand years. Of all Indra's flute-girls she played and sang the sweetest. Yet ever some remembrance, dim as a pallid ghost that fleets down the long avenues of deodar and moonlight, stole in her brain ; and her song was ever of love and death and music from beyond.

"And one day as she sang thus the deep truth stole into being and she knew the Noble Truths. So she turned her flute to the new song, when—horror !—there was a mosquito in the flute. 'Tootle ! Tootle !' she began. 'Buzz ! Buzz !' went the mosquito from the very vitals of her delicate tube.

"Indra was not unprovided with a disc.[1] Alas ! Jehjaour, art thou already in the toils ? She had only lived eight months.

### IX.

"'How you bungle !' growled Ganesha. 'Fortunately we are better off this time. Indra has been guillotined for his dastardly murder ; so his place is vacant.' 'Eurekas !' yelled the magus, 'his very virtue will save him from his predecessor's fate.'

"Behold Perdu' R Abu then as Indra ! But oh, dear me ! what a memory he was getting ! 'It seems to me,' he mused, 'that I've been changing about a lot lately. Well, I am virtuous—and I read in Crowley's new translation of the Dhammapada [2] that virtue is the thing to keep one steady. So I think I may look forward to a tenure of my mahakalpa in almost Arcadian simplicity. Lady Bhavani, did you say, boy ? Yes, I am at home. Bring the betel !' 'Jeldi !' he added, with some dim recollection of the

[1] A whirling disc is Indra's symbolic weapon.
[2] He abandoned this. A few fragments are reprinted, supra.

British Government, when he was a baby Nat.

"The Queen of Heaven and the Lord of the Gods chewed betel for quite a long time, conversed of the weather, the crops, the affaire Humbert, and the law in relation to motor-cars, with ease and affability. But far was it from Indra's pious mind to flirt with his distinguished guest! Rather, he thought of the hollow nature of the Safe, the change of money and of position; the sorrow of the too confiding bankers, and above all the absence of an Ego in the Brothers Crawford.

"While he was thus musing, Bhavani got fairly mad at him. The Spretae Injuria Formae gnawed her vitals with pangs unassuageable: so, shaking him quite roughly by the arm, she Put It To Him Straight. 'O Madam!' said Indra.

"This part of the story has been told before—about Joseph; but Bhavani simply lolled her tongue out, opened her mouth, and gulped him down at a swallow.

"Jehjaour simply wallowed. Indra had passed in seven days.

## X.

"'There is only one more birth,' he groaned. 'This time we must win or die.' 'Goetia[1] expects every God to do his duty,' he excitedly lunographed to Swarga.[2] But Ganesha was already on his way.

"The elephant-headed God was in great spirits. 'Never say die!' he cried genially, on beholding the downcast appearance of his fellow-conspirator. 'This'll break the slate. There is no change in the Arupa-Brahma-Loka!'[3] 'Rupe me no rupes!' howled the necromancer. 'Get up, fool!' roared the God. 'I have got Perdu' R Abu elected Maha Brahma.' 'Oh Lord, have you really?' said the wizard, looking a little

[1] The world of black magic.
[2] Heaven.
[3] The highest heaven of the Hindu. "Formless place of Brahma" is its name.

less glum. 'Ay!' cried Ganesha impressively, 'let Aeon follow Aeon down the vaulted and echoing corridors of Eternity: pile Mahakalpa upon Mahakalpa until an Asankhya[1] of Crores[2] have passed away: and Maha Brahma will still sit lone and meditate upon his lotus throne.' 'Good, good!' said the magus, 'though there seems a reminiscence of the Bhagavad-Gita and the Light of Asia somewhere. Surely you don't read Edwin Arnold?' 'I do,' said the God disconsolately, 'we Hindu Gods have to. It's the only way we can get any clear idea of who we really are.'

"Well, here was Perdu' R Abu, after his latest fiasco, installed as a Worthy, Respectable, Perfect, Ancient and Accepted, Just, Regular Mahabrahma. His only business was to meditate, for as long as he did this, the worlds—the whole system of 10,000 worlds—would go on peaceably. Nobody had better read the lesson of the Bible—the horrible results to mankind of ill-timed, though possibly well-intentioned, interference on the part of a deity.

"Well, he curled himself up, which was rather clever for a formless abstraction, and began. There was a grave difficulty in his mind—an obstacle right away from the word 'Jump!' Of course there was really a good deal: he didn't know where the four elements ceased, for example:[3] but his own identity was the real worry. The other questions he could have stilled; but this was too near his pet Chakra.[4] 'Here I am,' he meditated, 'above all change; and yet an hour ago I was Indra; and before that his flute-girl; and then a Nat; and then a parrot; and then a Hathi—"Oh, the Hathis pilin' teak in the sludgy, squdgy creek!" sang Parameshvara. Why, it goes

[1] "Innumerable," the highest unit of the fantastic Hindu arithmetic.
[2] 10,000.
[3] See the witty legend in the Questions of King Milinda.
[4] Meditation may be performed on any of seven "Chakra" (wheels or centres) in the body.

back and back, like a biograph out of order, and there's no sort of connection between one and the other. Hullo, what's that? Why, there's a holy man near that Bo-Tree. He'll tell me what it all means.' Poor silly old Lord of the Universe! Had he carried his memory back one more step he'd have known all about Jehjaour and the conspiracy, and that he was a Srotapatti and had only one more birth; and might well have put in the 311,040,000,000,000 myriads of aeons which would elapse before lunch in rejoicing over his imminent annihilation.

" 'Venerable Sir!' said Mahabrahma, who had assumed the guise of a cowherd, 'I kiss your worshipful Trilbies :[1] I prostrate myself before your estimable respectability.' 'Sir,' said the holy man, none other than Our Lord Himself! 'thou seekest illumination!' Mahabrahma smirked and admitted it. 'From negative to positive,' explained the Thrice-Honoured One, 'though Potential Existence eternally vibrates the Divine Absolute of the Hidden Unity of processional form masked in the Eternal Abyss of the Unknowable, the synthetical hieroglyph of an illimitable, pastless, futureless PRESENT.

" ' To the uttermost bounds of space rushes the voice of Ages unheard of save in the concentrated unity of the thought-formulated Abstract ; and eternally that voice formulates a word which is glyphed in the vast ocean of limitless life.[2] Do I make myself clear?' 'Perfectly. Who would have thought it was all so simple?' The God cleared his throat, and rather diffidently, even shamefacedly, went on :

" ' But what I really wished to know was about my incarnation. How is it I have so suddenly risen from change and death to the unchangeable?'

" 'Child!' answered Gautama, 'your facts are wrong—you can hardly expect to make

[1] Feet.
[2] This astonishing piece of bombastic drivel is verbatim from a note by S. L. Mathers to the " Kabbalah Unveiled."

correct deductions.' 'Yes, you can, if only your logical methods are unsound. That's the Christian way of getting truth.' 'True !' replied the sage, 'but precious little they get. Learn, O Mahabrahma (for I penetrate this disguise), that all existing things, even from thee unto this grain of sand, possess Three Characteristics. These are Mutability, Sorrow, and Unsubstantiality.'

" 'All right for the sand, but how about Me? Why, they *define* me as unchangeable.' 'You can define a quirk as being a two-sided triangle,' retorted the Saviour, 'but that does not prove the actual existence of any such oxymoron.[1] The truth is that you're a very spiritual sort of being and a prey to longevity. Men's lives are so short that yours seems eternal in comparison. But —why, *you're* a nice one to talk! You'll be dead in a week from now.'

" 'I quite appreciate the force of your remarks !' said the seeming cowherd ; 'that about the Characteristics is very clever ; and curiously enough, my perception of this has always just preceded my death for the last six goes.'

" 'Well, so long, old chap,' said Gautama, 'I must really be off. I have an appointment with Brother Mara at the Bo-Tree. He has promised to introduce his charming daughters——'

" 'Good-bye, and don't do anything rash !'

" Rejoice ! our Lord wended unto the Tree !'[2] As blank verse this scans but ill, but it clearly shows what happened.

## XI.

" The ' Nineteenth Mahakalpa ' brough out its April Number. There was a pape by Huxlananda Swami.

" Mahabrahma had never been much mor than an idea. He had only lived si days.

[1] A contradiction in terms.
[2] Arnold, "Light of Asia."

## XII.

" At the hour of the great Initiation," continued the Buddha, in the midst of the Five Hundred Thousand Arahats, "the wicked Jehjaour had joined himself with Mara to prevent the discovery of the truth. And in Mara's fall he fell. At that moment all the currents of his continued and concentrated Hate recoiled upon him and he fell into the Abyss of Being. And in the Halls of Birth he was cast out into the Lowest Hell—he became a clergyman of the Church of England, further than he had ever been before from Truth and Light and Peace and Love ; deeper and deeper enmeshed in the net of Circumstance, bogged in the mire of Tanha [1] and Avigga [2] and all things base and vile. False Vichi-Kichi [3] had caught him at last !

## XIII.

" Aye ! The hour was at hand. Perdu' R Abu was reincarnated as a child of Western parents, ignorant of all his wonderful past. But a strange fate has brought him to this village." The Buddha paused, probably for effect.

A young man there, sole among all them not yet an Arahat, turned pale. He alone was of Western birth in all that multitude.

" Brother Abhavananda, [4] little friend," said the Buddha, " what can we predicate of all existing things ? " " Lord ! " replied the neophyte, " they are unstable, everything is sorrow, in them is no inward Principle, as some pretend, that can avoid, that can hold itself aloof from, the forces of decay."

" And how do you know that, little Brother ? " smiled the Thrice-Honoured One.

" Lord, I perceive this Truth whenever

I consider the Universe. More, its consciousness seems ingrained in my very nature, perhaps through my having known this for many incarnations. I have never thought otherwise."

" Rise, Sir Abhavananda, I dub thee Arahat ! " cried the Buddha, striking the neophyte gently on the back with the flat of his ear. [1]

And he perceived.

When the applause and praise and glory had a little faded, the Buddha, in that golden delight of sunset, explained these marvellous events. " Thou, Abhavananda," he said, " art the Perdu' R Abu of my lengthy tale. The wicked Jehjaour has got something lingering with boiling oil in it, while waiting for his clerical clothes : while, as for me, I myself was the Bacillus in the forest of Lanka : I was the old Lady : I was (he shuddered) the British Government : I was the mosquito that buzzed in the girl's flute : I was Bhavani : I was Huxlananda Swami ; and at the last, at this blessed hour, I am— that I am."

" But, Lord," said the Five Hundred Thousand and One Arahats in a breath, " thou art then guilty of six violent deaths ! Nay, thou hast hounded one soul from death to death through all these incarnations ! What of this First Precept [2] of yours ? "

" Children," answered the Glorious One, " do not be so foolish as to think that death is necessarily an evil. I have not come to found a Hundred Years Club, and to include mosquitoes in the membership. In this case to have kept Perdu' R Abu alive was to have played into the hands of his enemies. My First Precept is merely a general rule. [3] In

[1] Thirst: *i.e.* desire in its evil sense.
[2] Ignorance.
[3] Doubt.
[4] " Bliss-of-non-existence." One of Crowley's eastern names.

[1] The Buddha had such long ears that he could cover the whole of his face with them. Ears are referred to Spirit in Hindu symbolism, so that the legend means that he could conceal the lower elements and dwell in this alone.
[2] Here is the little rift within the lute which alienated Crowley from active work on Buddhist lines ; the orthodox failing to see his attitude.
[3] A more likely idea than the brilliantly logical nonsense of Pansil, *supra*.

the bulk of cases one should certainly abstain from destroying life, that is, wantonly and wilfully : but I cannot drink a glass of water without killing countless myriads of living beings. If you knew as I do, the conditions of existence : struggle deadly and inevitable, every form of life the inherent and immitigable foe of every other form, with few, few exceptions, you would not only cease to talk of the wickedness of causing death, but you would perceive the First Noble Truth, that no existence can be free from sorrow ; the second, that the desire for existence only leads to sorrow ; that the ceasing from existence is the ceasing of sorrow (the third) and you would seek in the fourth the Way the Noble Eightfold Path.

" I know, O Arahats, that you do not need this instruction : but my words will not stay here : they will go forth and illuminate the whole system of ten thousand worlds, where Arahats do not grow on every tree. Little brothers, the night is fallen : it were well to sleep."

## 1902

בראשית

# AN ESSAY IN ONTOLOGY

## WITH SOME REMARKS ON CEREMONIAL MAGIC

בראשית

O Man, of a daring nature, thou subtle production !
Thou wilt not comprehend it, as when understanding some common thing.
ORACLES OF ZOROASTER.

IN presenting this theory of the Universe to
the world, I have but one hope of making
any profound impression, viz.—that my theory
has the merit of explaining the divergences
between three great forms of religion now
existing in the world—Buddhism, Hinduism,
and Christianity, and of adapting them
to ontological science by conclusions not
mystical but mathematical. Of Mohammedanism I shall not now treat, as, in whatever
light we may decide to regard it (and its
esoteric schools are often orthodox), in any
case it must fall under one of the three
heads of Nihilism, Advaitism, and Dvaitism.

Taking the ordinary hypothesis of the
universe, that of its infinity, or at any rate
that of the infinity of God, or of the infinity
of some substance or idea actually existing,
we first come to the question of the possibility of the co-existence of God and man.

The Christians, in the category of the existent, enumerate among other things, whose
consideration we may discard for the purposes of this argument, God, an infinite
being ; man ; Satan and his angels ; man
certainly, Satan presumably, finite beings.
These are not aspects of one being, but
separate and even antagonistic existences.
All are equally real : we cannot accept

mystics of the type of Caird as being orthodox
exponents of the religion of Christ.

The Hindus enumerate Brahm, infinite in
all dimensions and directions—indistinguishable from the Pleroma of the Gnostics—and
Maya, illusion. This is in a sense the ante-
thesis of noumenon and phenomenon, noumenon being negated of all predicates until
it becomes almost extinguished in the Nichts
under the title of the Alles. (Cf. Max Müller
on the metaphysical Nirvana, in his Dhammapada, Introductory Essay.) The Buddhists express no opinion.

Let us consider the force-quality in the
existences conceived of by these two religions
respectively, remembering that the God of
the Christian is infinite, and yet discussing
the alternative if we could suppose him to
be a finite God. In any equilibrated system
of forces, we may sum and represent them as
a triangle or series of triangles which again
resolve into one. In any moving system, if
the resultant motion be applied in a contrary
direction, the equilibrium can also thus be
represented. And if any one of the original
forces in such a system may be considered,
that one is equal to the resultant of the re-
mainder. Let $x$, the purpose of the universe
be the resultant of the forces $G$, $S$, and $M$
(God, Satan, and Man). Then $M$ is also the
resultant of $G$, $S$, and $-x$. So that we can
regard either of our forces as the supreme,
and there is no reason for worshipping one
rather than another. All are finite. This
argument the Christians clearly see : hence
the development of God from the petty

joss of Genesis to the intangible, but self-contradictory spectre of to-day. But if *G* be infinite, the other forces can have no possible effect on it. As Whewell says, in the strange accident by which he anticipates the metre of *In Memoriam* : " No force on earth, however great, can stretch a cord, however fine, into a horizontal line that shall be absolutely straight."

The definition of God as infinite therefore denies man implicitly ; while if he be finite, there is an end of the usual Christian reasons for worship, though I daresay I could myself discover some reasonably good ones. [I hardly expect to be asked, somehow.]

The resulting equilibrium of God and man, destructive of worship, is of course absurd. We must reject it, unless we want to fall into Positivism, Materialism, or something of the sort. But if, then, we call God infinite, how are we to regard man, and Satan ? (the latter, at the very least, surely no integral part of him). The fallacy lies not in my demonstration (which is also that of ortho-doxy) that a finite God is absurd, but in the assumption that man has any real force.[1]

In our mechanical system (as I have hinted above), if one of the forces be infinite, the others, however great, are both relatively and absolutely nothing.

In any category, infinity excludes finity, unless that finity be an identical part of that infinity.

In the category of existing things, space being infinite, for on that hypothesis we are still working, either matter fills or does not fill it. If the former, matter is infinitely great ; if the latter, infinitely small. Whether the matter-universe be $10^{10000}$ light-years in diameter or half a mile makes no difference ; it is infinitely small—in effect, Nothing. The unmathematical illusion that it does exist is what the Hindus call Maya.

If, on the other hand, the matter-universe is infinite, Brahm and God are crowded out, and the possibility of religion is equally excluded.

[1] Lully, Descartes, Spinoza, Schelling. See their works.

We may now shift our objective. The Hindus cannot account intelligibly, though they try hard, for Maya, the cause of all suffering. Their position is radically weak, but at least we may say for them that they have tried to square their religion with their common sense. The Christians, on the other hand, though they saw whither the Manichean Heresy [1] must lead, and crushed it, have not officially admitted the precisely similar con-clusion with regard to man, and denied the existence of the human soul as distinct from the divine soul.

Trismegistus, Iamblicus, Porphyry, Boehme, and the mystics generally have of course substantially done so, though occa-sionally with rather inexplicable reservations, similar to those made in some cases by the Vedantists themselves.

Man then being disproved, God the Person disappears for ever, and becomes Atman, Pleroma, Ain Soph, what name you will, infinite in all directions and in all categories —to deny one is to destroy the entire argu-ment and throw us back on to our old Dvaitistic bases.

I entirely sympathise with my unhappy friend Rev. Mansel, B.D.,[2] in his piteous and pitiful plaints against the logical results of the Advaitist School. But on his basal hypothesis of an infinite God, infinite space, time, and so on, no other conclusion is possible. Dean Mansel is found in the im-possible position of one who will neither give up his premises nor dispute the validity of his logical processes, but who shrinks in horror from the inevitable conclusion ; he supposes there must be something wrong somewhere, and concludes that the sole use of reason is to discover its own inferiority to faith. As Deussen [3] well points out, faith in the Christian sense merely amounts to

[1] The conception of Satan as a positive evil force ; the lower triangle of the Hexagram.
[2] *Encyclopedia Britannica*, Art. Meta-physics.
[3] "The Principles of Metaphysics." Mac-millan.

being convinced on insufficient grounds.[1] This is surely the last refuge of incompetence.

But though, always on the original hypothesis of the infinity of space, &c., the Advaitist position of the Vedantists and the great Germans is unassailable, yet on practical grounds the Dvaitists have all the advantage. Fichte and the others exhaust themselves trying to turn the simple and obvious position that : " If the Ego alone exists, where is any place, not only for morals and religion, which we can very well do without, but for the most essential and continuous acts of life? Why should an infinite Ego fill a non-existent body with imaginary food cooked in thought only over an illusionary fire by a cook who is not there? Why should infinite power use such finite means, and very often fail even then?"

What is the sum total of the Vedantist position? "'I' am an illusion, externally. In reality, the true 'I' am the Infinite, and if the illusionary 'I' could only realise Who 'I' really am, how very happy we should all be!" And here we have Karma, rebirth, all the mighty laws of nature operating nowhere in nothing!

There is no room for worship or for morality in the Advaitist system. All the specious pleas of the Bhagavad-Gita, and the ethical works of Western Advaitist philosophers, are more or less consciously confusion of thought. But no subtlety can turn the practical argument ; the grinning mouths of the Dvaitist guns keep the fort of Ethics, and warn metaphysics to keep off the rather green grass of religion.

That its apologists should have devoted so much time, thought, scholarship, and ingenuity to this question is the best proof of the fatuity of the Advaita position.

There is then a flaw somewhere. I boldly take up the glove against all previous wisdom,

revert to the most elementary ideas of cannibal savages, challenge all the most vital premisses and axiomata that have passed current coin with philosophy for centuries, and present my theory.

I clearly foresee the one difficulty, and will discuss it in advance. If my conclusions on this point are not accepted, we may at once get back to our previous irritable agnosticism, and look for our Messiah elsewhere. But if we can see together on this one point, I think things will go fairly smoothly afterwards.

Consider[1] Darkness ! Can we philosophically or actually regard as different the darkness produced by interference of light and that existing in the mere absence of light?

Is Unity really identical with .9 recurring?

Do we not mean different things when we speak respectively of 2 sine 60° and of $\sqrt{3}$?

Charcoal and diamond are obviously different in the categories of colour, crystallisation, hardness, and so on ; but are they not really so even in that of existence?

The third example is to my mind the best. 2 sine 60° and $\sqrt{3}$ are unreal and therefore never conceivable, at least to the present constitution of our human intelligences. Worked out, neither has meaning ; unworked, both have meaning, and that a different meaning in one case and the other.

We have thus two terms, both unreal, both inconceivable, yet both representing intelligible and diverse ideas to our minds (and this is the point !) though identical in reality and convertible by a process of reason which simulates or replaces that apprehension which we can never (one may suppose) attain to.

Let us apply this idea to the Beginning of all things, about which the Christians lie frankly, the Hindus prevaricate, and the

---

[1] Or as the Sunday-school boy said : " Faith is the power of believing what we know to be untrue." I quote Deussen with the more pleasure, because it is about the only sentence in all his writings with which I am in accord. —A. C.

[1] Ratiocination may perhaps not take us far. But a continuous and attentive study of these quaint points of distinction may give us an intuition, or direct mind-apperception of what we want, one way or the other.—A. C.

Buddhists are discreetly silent, while not contradicting even the gross and ridiculous accounts of the more fantastic Hindu visionaries.

The Qabalists explain the " First Cause " [1] by the phrase : " From 0 to 1, as the circle opening out into the line." The Christian dogma is really identical, for both conceive of a previous and eternally existing God, though the Qabalists hedge by describing this latent Deity as "Not." Later commentators, notably the illustrious [2] Mac-Gregor-Mathers, have explained this Not as " negatively-existing." Profound as is my respect for the intellectual and spiritual attainments of him whom I am proud to have been permitted to call my master,[2] I am bound to express my view that when the Qabalists said Not, they meant Not, and nothing else. In fact, I really claim to have re-discovered the long-lost and central Arcanum of those divine philosophers.

I have no serious objection to a finite god, or gods, distinct from men and things. In fact, personally, I believe in them all, and admit them to possess inconceivable though not infinite power.

The Buddhists admit the existence of Maha-Brahma, but his power and knowledge are limited ; and his agelong day must end. I find evidence everywhere, even in our garbled and mutilated version of the Hebrew Scriptures, that Jehovah's power was limited in all sorts of ways. At the Fall, for instance, Tetragrammaton Elohim has to summon his angels hastily to guard the Tree of Life, lest he should be proved a liar. For had it occurred to Adam to eat of that Tree before their transgression was discovered, or had the Serpent been aware of its properties, Adam would indeed have lived and not died. So that a mere accident saved the remnants of the already besmirched reputation of the Hebrew tribal Fetich.

[1] An expression they carefully avoid using.— A. C.
[2] I retain this sly joke from the first edition.

When Buddha was asked how things came to be, he took refuge in silence, which his disciples very conveniently interpreted as meaning that the question tended not to edification.

I take it that the Buddha (ignorant, doubtless, of algebra) had sufficiently studied philosophy and possessed enough worldly wisdom to be well àware that any system he might promulgate would be instantly attacked and annihilated by the acumen of his numerous and versatile opponents.

Such teaching as he gave on the point may be summed up as follows. " Whence whither, why, we know not ; but we do know that we are here, that we dislike being here, that there is a way out of the whole loathsome affair—let us make haste and take it ! "

I am not so retiring in disposition ; I persist in my inquiries, and at last the appalling question is answered, and the past ceases to intrude its problems upon my mind.

Here you are ! Three shies a penny ! Change all bad arguments.

I ASSERT THE ABSOLUTENESS OF THE QABALISTIC ZERO.

When we say that the Cosmos sprang from 0, what kind of 0 do we mean ? By 0 in the ordinary sense of the term we mean " absence of extension in any of the categories."

When I say " No cat has two tails," I do not mean, as the old fallacy runs, that " Absence-of-cat possesses twò tails " ; but that " In the category of two-tailed things, there is no extension of cat."

Nothingness is that about which no positive proposition is valid. We cannot truly affirm : " Nothingness is green, or heavy, or sweet."

Let us call time, space, being, heaviness, hunger, the categories.[1] If a man be heavy

[1] I cannot here discuss the propriety of representing the categories as dimensions. It will be obvious to any student of the integral calculus, or to any one who appreciates the geometrical significance of the term $x^4$.—A. C.

and hungry, he is extended in all these, besides, of course, many more. But let us suppose that these five are all. Call the man X; his formula is then $X^{t+s+b+h+\lambda}$. If he now eat, he will cease to be extended in hunger; if he be cut off from time and gravitation as well, he will now be represented by the formula $X^{s+b}$ Should he cease to occupy space and to exist, his formula would then be $X^0$. This expression is equal to 1; whatever X may represent, if it be raised to the power of 0 (this meaning mathematically "if it be extended in no dimension or category"), the result is Unity, and the unknown factor X is eliminated.

This is the Advaitist idea of the future of man; his personality, bereft of all its qualities, disappears and is lost, while in its place arises the impersonal Unity, The Pleroma, Parabrahma, or the Allah of the Unity - adoring followers of Mohammed. (To the Musulman fakir, Allah is by no means a personal God.)

Unity is thus unaffected, whether or no it be extended in any of the categories. But we have already agreed to look to 0 for the Uncaused.

Now if there was in truth 0 "before the beginning of years," THAT 0 WAS EXTENDED IN NONE OF THE CATEGORIES, FOR THERE COULD HAVE BEEN NO CATEGORIES IN WHICH IT COULD EXTEND! If our 0 was the ordinary 0 of mathematics, there was not truly absolute 0, for 0 is, as I have shown, dependent on the idea of categories. If these existed, then the whole question is merely thrown back; we must reach a state in which the 0 is absolute. Not only must we get rid of all subjects, but of all predicates. By 0 (in mathematics) we really mean $0^n$, where n is the final term of a natural scale of dimensions, categories, or predicates. Our Cosmic Egg, then, from which the present universe arose, was Nothingness, extended in no categories, or, graphically, $0^0$. This expression is in its present form meaningless. Let us dis-

cover its value by a simple mathematical process!

$$0^0 = 0^{1-1} = \frac{0^1}{0^1} \left[ \text{Multiply by } 1 = \frac{n}{n} \right]$$

$$\text{Then } \frac{0^1}{n} \times \frac{n}{0^1} = 0 \times \infty.$$

Now the multiplying of the infinitely great by the infinitely small results in SOME UNKNOWN FINITE NUMBER EXTENDED IN AN UNKNOWN NUMBER OF CATEGORIES. It happened, when this our Great Inversion took place, from the essence of all nothingness to finity extended in innumerable categories, that an incalculably vast system was produced. Merely by chance, chance in the truest sense of the term, we are found with gods, men, stars, planets, devils, colours, forces, and all the materials of the Cosmos : and with time, space, and causality, the conditions limiting and involving them all.[1]

Remember that it is not true to say that our $0^0$ existed; nor that it did not exist. The idea of existence was just as much unformulated as that of toasted cheese.

But $0^0$ is a finite expression, or has a finite phase, and our universe is a finite universe.; its categories are themselves finite, and the expression "infinite space" is a contradiction in terms. The idea of an absolute and of an infinite [2] God is relegated to the limbo of all similar idle and pernicious perversions of truth. Infinity remains, but only as a mathematical conception as impossible in nature as the square root of $-1$. Against all this mathematical, or semi-mathematical, reasoning, it may doubtless be objected that our

[1] Compare and contrast this doctrine with that of Herbert Spencer ("First Principles," Pt. I.), and see my "Science and Buddhism" for a full discussion of the difference involved. —A. C.

[2] If by "infinitely great" we only mean "indefinitely great," as a mathematician would perhaps tell us, we of course begin at the very point I am aiming at, viz., Ecrasez l'Infini. - A. C.

whole system of numbers, and of manipulating them, is merely a series of conventions When I say that the square root of three is unreal, I know quite well that it is only so in relation to the series 1, 2, 3, &c., and that this series is equally unreal if I make $\sqrt{3}$, $\pi$, $\sqrt[2]{50}$ the members of a ternary scale. But this, theoretically true, is practically absurd. If I mean "the number of a, b, and c," it does not matter if I write 3 or $\sqrt[2]{50}$; the idea is a definite one; and it is the fundamental ideas of consciousness of which we are treating, and to which we are compelled to refer everything, whether proximately or ultimately.

So also my equation, fantastic as it may seem, has a perfect and absolute parallel in logic. Thus: let us convert twice the proposition "some books are on the table." By negativing both terms we get "Absence-of-book is not on the table," which is precisely my equation backwards, and a thinkable thing. To reverse the process, what do I mean when I say "some pigs, but not the black pig, are not in the sty"? I imply that the black pig is in the sty. All I have done is to represent the conversion as a change, rather than as merely another way of expressing the same thing. And "change" is really not my meaning either; for change, to our minds, involves the idea of time. But the whole thing is inconceivable—to ratiocination, though not to thought. Note well too that if I say "Absence-of-books is not on the table," I cannot convert it into "All books are on the table" but only to "some books are on the table." The proposition is an "I" and not an "A" proposition. It is the Advaita blunder to make it so; and many a schoolboy has fed off the mantelpiece for less.

There is yet another proof—the proof by exclusion. I have shown, and metaphysicians practically admit, the falsity alike of Dvaitism and Advaitism. The third, the only remaining theory, *this* theory, must, however antecedently impro-

bable, however difficult to assimilate, be true.[1]

"My friend, my young friend," I think I hear some Christian cleric say, with an air of profound wisdom, not untinged with pity, condescending to pose beardles and brainless impertinence: "where is the *Cause* for this truly remarkable change?"

That is exactly where the theory rears to heaven its stoutest bastion! There is not, and could not be, any cause. Had $0^0$ been extended in causality, no change could have taken place.[2]

Here, then, are we, finite beings in a finite universe, time, space, and causality themselves finite (inconceivable as it may seem) with our individuality, and all the "illusions" of the Advaitists, just as real as they practically are to our normal consciousness.

As Schopenhauer, following Buddha, points out, suffering is a necessary condition of this existence.[3] The war of the contending forces as they grind themselves down to the final resultant must cause endless agony. We may one day be able to transform the categories of emotion as certainly and easily as we now transform the categories of force, so that in a few years Chicago may be importing suffering in the raw state and turning it into tinned salmon: but at present the reverse process is alone practicable.

How, then, shall we escape? Can we expect the entire universe to resolve itself back into the phase of $0^0$? Surely not. In the first place, there is no reason why the whole should do so; $\frac{x}{y}$ is just as convertible as $x$. But worse, the category of causality has been formed, and its inertia is

[1] I may remark that the distinction between this theory and the normal one of the Immanence of the Universe, is trivial, perhaps even verbal only. Its advantage, however, is that, by hypostatising nothing, we avoid the necessity of any explanation. How did nothing come to be? is a question which requires no answer.

[2] See the Questions of King Milinda, vol. ii. p. 103.

[3] See also Huxley, "Evolution and Ethics."

sufficient to oppose a most serious stumbling-block to so gigantic a process.

The task before us is consequently of a terrible nature. It is easy to let things slide, to grin and bear it in fact, until everything is merged in the ultimate unity, which may or may not be decently tolerable. But while we wait?

There now arises the question of freewill. Causality is probably not fully extended in its own category,[1] a circumstance which gives room for a fractional amount of freewill. If this be not so, it matters little; for if I find myself in a good state, that merely proves that my destiny took me there. We are, as Herbert Spencer observes, self-deluded with the idea of freewill; but if this be so, nothing matters at all. If, however, Herbert Spencer is mistaken (unlikely as it must appear), then our reason is valid, and we should seek out the right path and pursue it. The question therefore need not trouble us at all.

Here then we see the use of morals and of religion, and all the rest of the bag of tricks. All these are methods, bad or good, for extricating ourselves from the universe.

Closely connected with this question is that of the will of God. People argue that an Infinite intelligence must have been at work on this cosmos. I reply No! There is no intelligence at work worthy of the name. The Laws of Nature may be generalised in one—the Law of Inertia. Everything moves in the direction determined by the path of least resistance; species arise, develop, and die as their collective inertia determines; to this Law there is no exception but the doubtful one of Free-will; the Law of Destiny itself is formally and really identical with it.[2]

[1] Causality is itself a secondary, and in its limitation as applied to volition, an inconceivable idea. H. Spencer, *op. cit.* This consideration alone should add great weight to the agnostic, and *à fortiori* to the Buddhist, position.
[2] See H. Spencer, "First Principles," "The Knowable," for a fair summary of the facts underlying this generalisation; which indeed he comes within an ace of making in so many words. It may be observed that this law is nearly if not quite axiomatic, its contrary being enormously difficult if not impossible to formulate mentally.

As to an *infinite* intelligence, all philosophers of any standing are agreed that all-love and all-power are incompatible. The existence of the universe is a standing proof of this.

The Deist needs the Optimist to keep him company; over their firesides all goes well, but it is a sad shipwreck they suffer on emerging into the cold world.

This is why those who seek to buttress up religion are so anxious to prove that the universe has no real existence, or only a temporary and relatively unimportant one; the result is of course the usual self-destructive Advaitist muddle.

The precepts of morality and religion are thus of use, of vital use to us, in restraining the more violent forces alike of nature and of man. For unless law and order prevail, we have not the necessary quiet and resources for investigating, and learning to bring under our control, all the divergent phenomena of our prison, a work which we undertake that at last we may be able to break down the walls, and find that freedom which an inconsiderate Inversion has denied.

The mystical precepts of pseudo-Zoroaster, Buddha, Çankaracharya, pseudo-Christ and the rest, are for advanced students only, for direct attack on the problem. Our servants, the soldiers, lawyers, all forms of government, make this our nobler work possible, and it is the gravest possible mistake to sneer at these humble but faithful followers of the great minds of the world.

What, then, are the best, easiest, directest methods to attain our result? And how shall we, in mortal language, convey to the minds of others the nature of a result so beyond language, baffling even imagination eagle-pinioned? It may help us if we endeavour to outline the distinction between the Hindu and Buddhist methods and aims of the Great Work.

The Hindu method is really mystical in the truest sense; for, as I have shown, the Atman is not infinite and eternal: one day it must sink down with the other forces. But by creating in thought an infinite Impersonal Personality, by *defining* it as such, all religions except the Buddhist and, as I believe, the Qabalistic, have sought to annihilate their own personality. The Buddhist aims directly at extinction; the Hindu denies and abolishes his own finity by the creation of an absolute.

As this cannot be done in reality, the process is illusory; yet it is useful in the early stages—as far, at any rate, as the fourth stage of Dhyana, where the Buddha places it, though the Yogis claim to attain to Nirvikalpa-Samadhi, and that Moksha is identical with Nirvana; the former claim I see no reason to deny them; the latter statement I must decline at present to accept.

The task of the Buddhist recluse is roughly as follows. He must plunge every particle of his being into one idea: right views, aspirations, word, deed, life, will-power, meditation, rapture, such are the stages of his liberation, which resolves itself into a struggle against the law of causality. He cannot prevent past causes taking effect, but he can prevent present causes from having any future results. The exoteric Christian and Hindu rather rely on another person to do this for them, and are further blinded by the thirst for life and individual existence, the most formidable obstacle of all, in fact a negation of the very object of all religion. Schopenhauer shows that life is assured to the will-to-live, and unless Christ (or Krishna, as the case may be) destroys these folk by superior power—a task from which almightiness might well recoil baffled!—I much fear that eternal life, and consequently eternal suffering, joy, and change of all kinds, will be their melancholy fate. Such persons are in truth their own real enemies. Many of them, however, believing erroneously that they are being "unselfish," do fill their hearts with devotion for the beloved Saviour, and this process is, in its ultimation, so similar to the earlier stages of the Great

Work itself, that some confusion has, stupidly enough, arisen; but for all that the practice has been the means of bringing some devotees on to the true Path of the Wise, unpromising as such material must sound to intelligent ears.

The esoteric Christian or Hindu adopts a middle path. Having projected the Absolute from his mind, he endeavours to unite his consciousness with that of his Absolute, and of course his personality is destroyed in the process. Yet it is to be feared that such an adept too often starts on the path with the hideous idea of aggrandising his own personality to the utmost. But his method is so near to the true one that this tendency is soon corrected, as it were automatically.

(The mathematical analogue of this process is to procure for yourself the realisation of the nothingness of yourself by keeping the fourth dimension ever present to your mind.)

The illusory nature of this idea of an infinite Atman is well shown by the very proof which that most distinguished Vedantist, the late Swami Vivekananda (no connection with the firm of a similar name[1] across the street), gives of the existence of the infinite. "Think of a circle!" says he. "You will in a moment become conscious of an infinite circle around your original small one." The fallacy is obvious. The big circle is not infinite at all, but is itself limited by the little one. But to take away the little circle, that is the method of the esoteric Christian or the mystic. But the process is never perfect, because however small the little circle becomes, its relation with the big circle is still finite. But even allowing for a moment that the Absolute is really attainable, is the nothingness of the finity related to it really identical with that attained directly by the Buddhist Arahat? This, consistently with

[1] The Swami Vive Ananda, Madame Horos, for whose history consult the Criminal Law Reports.

my former attitude, I feel constrained to deny. The consciousness of the Absolute-wala[1] is really extended infinitely rather than diminished infinitely, as he will himself assure you. True, Hegel says : "Pure being is pure nothing!" and it is true that the infinite heat and cold, joy and sorrow, light and darkness, and all the other pairs of opposites,[2] cancel one another out : yet I feel rather afraid of this Absolute! Maybe its joy and sorrow are represented in phases, just as $0^0$ and finity are phases of an identical expression, and I have an even chance only of being on the right side of the fence!

The Buddhist leaves no chances of this kind ; in all his categories he is infinitely unextended ; though the categories themselves exist ; he is in fact $0^{A+B+C+D+E+..+N}$ and capable of no conceivable change, unless we imagine Nirvana to be incomprehensibly divided by Nirvana, which would (supposing the two Nirvanas to possess identical categories) result in the production of the original $0^0$. But a further change would be necessary even then before serious mischief could result. In short, I think we may dismiss from our minds any alarm in respect of this contingency.

On mature consideration, therefore, I confidently and deliberately take my refuge in the Triple Gem.

Namo Tasso Bhagavato Arahato Sammasambuddhasa![3]

Let there be hereafter no discussion of the classical problems of philosophy and religion! In the light of this exposition the

antitheses of noumenon and phenomenon, unity and multiplicity, and their kind, are all reconciled, and the only question that remains is that of finding the most satisfactory means of attaining Nirvana—extinction of all that exists, knows, or feels ; extinction final and complete, utter and absolute extinction. For by these words only can we indicate Nirvana : a state which transcends thought cannot be described in thought's language. But from the point of view of thought extinction is complete : we have no data for discussing that which is unthinkable, and must decline to do so. This is the answer to those who accuse the Buddha of hurling his Arahats (and himself) from Samma Samadhi to annihilation.

Pray observe in the first place that my solution of the Great Problem permits the co-existence of an indefinite number of means : they need not even be compatible ; Karma, rebirth, Providence, prayer, sacrifice, baptism, there is room for all. On the old and, I hope, now finally discredited hypothesis of an infinite being, the supporters of these various ideas, while explicitly affirming them, implicitly denied. Similarly, note that the Qabalistic idea of a supreme God (and innumerable hierarchies) is quite compatible with this theory, provided that the supreme God is not infinite.

Now as to our weapons. The more advanced Yogis of the East, like the Nonconformists at home, have practically abandoned ceremonial as idle. I have yet to learn, however, by what dissenters have replaced it! I take this to be an error, except in the case of the very advanced Yogi. For there exists a true magical ceremonial, vital and direct, whose purpose has, however, at any rate of recent times, been hopelessly misunderstood.

Nobody any longer supposes that any means but that of meditation is of avail to grasp the immediate causes of our being ; if some person retort that he prefers to rely on a Glorified Redeemer, I simply answer

---

[1] Wala, one whose business is connected with anything. *E.g.* Jangli-wala, one who lives in, or has business with, a jungle, *i.e.* a wild man, or a Forest Conservator.

[2] The Hindus see this as well as any one, and call Atman *Sat-chit-ananda*, these being above the pairs of opposites, rather on the Hegelian lines of the reconciliation (rather than the identity) of opposites in a master-idea. We have dismissed infinity as the figment of a morbid mathematic : but in any case the same disproof applies to it as to God.—A. C.

[3] Hail unto Thee, the Blessed One, the Perfect One, the Enlightened One!

that he is the very nobody to whom I now refer.

Meditation is then the means; but only the supreme means. The agony column of the *Times* is the supreme means of meeting with the gentleman in the brown billycock and frock coat, wearing a green tie and chewing a straw, who was at the soirée of the Carlton Club last Monday night; no doubt! but this means is seldom or never used in the similar contingency of a cow-elephant desiring her bull in the jungles of Ceylon.

Meditation is not within the reach of every one; not all possess the ability; very few indeed (in the West at least) have the opportunity.

In any case what the Easterns call "one-pointedness" is an essential preliminary to even early stages of true meditation. And iron will-power is a still earlier qualification.

By meditation I do not mean merely "thinking about" anything, however profoundly, but the absolute restraint of the mind to the contemplation of a single object, whether gross, fine, or altogether spiritual.

Now true magical ceremonial is entirely directed to attain this end, and forms a magnificent gymnasium for those who are not already finished mental athletes. By act, word, and thought, both in quantity and quality, the one object of the ceremony is being constantly indicated. Every fumigation, purification, banishing, invocation, evocation, is chiefly a reminder of the single purpose, until the supreme moment arrives, and every fibre of the body, every force-channel of the mind, is strained out in one overwhelming rush of the Will in the direction desired. Such is the real purport of all the apparently fantastic directions of Solomon, Abramelin, and other sages of repute. When a man has evoked and mastered such forces as Taphtatharath, Belial, Amaimon, and the great powers of the elements, then he may safely be permitted to begin to try to stop thinking.

For, needless to say, the universe, including the thinker, exists only by virtue of the thinker's thought.[1]

In yet one other way is magic a capital training ground for the Arahat. True symbols do really awake those macrocosmic forces of which they are the eidola, and it is possible in this manner very largely to increase the magical "potential," to borrow a term from electrical science.

Of course, there are bad and invalid processes, which tend rather to disperse or to excite the mind-stuff than to control it; these we must discard. But there is a true magical ceremonial, the central Arcanum alike of Eastern and Western practical transcendentalism. Needless to observe, if I knew it, I should not disclose it.

I therefore definitely affirm the validity of the Qabalistic tradition in its practical part as well as in those exalted regions of thought through which we have so recently, and so hardly, travelled.

Eight are the limbs of Yoga: morality and virtue, control of body, thought, and force, leading to concentration, meditation, and rapture.

Only when the last of these has been attained, and itself refined upon by removing the gross and even the fine objects of its

---

[1] See Berkeley and his expounders, for the Western shape of this Eastern commonplace. Huxley, however, curiously enough, states the fact almost in these words.—A. C.

[2] A possible mystic transfiguration of the Vedanta system has been suggested to me on the lines of the Syllogism—

> God = Being (Patanjali).
> Being = Nothing (Hegel).
> God = Nothing (Buddhism).

Or, in the language of religion:

Every one may admit that monotheism, exalted by the introduction of the ∞ symbol, is equivalent to pantheism. Pantheism and atheism are really identical, as the opponents of both are the first to admit.

If this be really taught, I must tender my apologies, for the reconcilement is of course complete.—A. C.

sphere, can the causes, subtle and coarse, the unborn causes whose seed is hardly sown, of continued existence be grasped and annihilated, so that the Arahat is sure of being abolished in the utter extinction of Nirvana, while even in this world of pain, where he must remain until the ancient causes, those which have already germinated, àre utterly worked out (for even the Buddha himself could not swing back the Wheel of the Law), his certain anticipation of the approach of Nirvana is so intense as to bathe him constantly in the unfathomable ocean of the apprehension of immediate bliss.


AUM MANI PADME HOUM.

# SCIENCE AND BUDDHISM

*(Inscribed to the revered Memory of Thomas Henry Huxley)*

## I.

THE purpose of this essay is to draw a strict comparison between the modern scientific conceptions of Phenomena and their explanation, where such exists, and the ancient ideas of the Buddhists; to show that Buddhism, alike in theory and practice, is a scientific religion; a logical superstructure on a basis of experimentally verifiable truth; and that its method is identical with that of science. We must resolutely exclude the accidental features of both, especially of Buddhism; and unfortunately in both cases we have to deal with dishonest and shameless attempts to foist on either opinions for which neither is willing to stand sponsor. Professor Huxley has dealt with the one in his " Pseudo-Scientific Realism"; Professor Rhys Davids has demolished the other in that one biting comment on " Esoteric Buddhism " that it was "not Esoteric and certainly not Buddhism." But some of the Theosophic mud still sticks to the Buddhist chariot; and there are still people who believe that sane science has at least a friendly greeting for Atheism and Materialism in their grosser and more militant forms.

Let it be understood then, from the outset, that if in Science I include metaphysics, and in Buddhism meditation-practices, I lend myself neither to the whittlers or " reconcilers " on the one hand, nor to the Animistic jugglers on the other. Apart from the Theosophic rubbish, we find Sir Edwin Arnold writing :

" Whoever saith Nirvana is to cease,
Say unto such they lie."

Lie is a strong word and should read " translate correctly." [1]

I suppose it would not scan, nor rhyme : but Sir Edwin is the last person to be deterred by a little thing like that.

Dr. Paul Carus, too, in the " Gospel of Buddha," is pleased to represent Nirvana as a parallel for the Heaven of the Christian It is sufficient if I reiterate the unanimous opinion of competent scholars, that there is no fragment of evidence in any canonical book sufficient to establish such interpretations in the teeth of Buddhist tradition and practice ; and that any person who persists in tuning Buddhism to his own Jew's harp in this way is risking his reputation, either for scholarship or good faith. Scientific men are common enough in the West, if Buddhists are not; and I may safely leave in their hands the task of castigating the sneak-thieves of the Physical area.

## II.

The essential features of Buddhism have been summed up by the Buddha himself. To me, of course, what the Buddha said or did not say is immaterial; a thing is true or not true, whoever said it. We believe Mr. Savage Landor when he affirms that Lhassa is an important town in Tibet Where only probabilities are concerned we are of course influenced by the moral char-

[1] See Childers, Pali Dictionary, *s. v.* Nibbana

acter and mental attainments of the speaker; but here I have nothing to do with the uncertain.[1]

There is an excellent test for the value of any passage in a Buddhist book. We are, I think, justified in discarding stories which are clearly Oriental fiction, just as modern criticism, however secretly Theistic, discards the Story of Hasisadra or of Noah. In justice to Buddhism, let us not charge its Scripture with the Sisyphean task of seriously upholding the literal interpretation of obviously fantastic passages.[2] May our Buddhist zealots be warned by the fate of old-fashioned English orthodoxy! But when Buddhism condescends to be vulgarly scientific; to observe, to classify, to *think*; I conceive we may take the matter seriously, and accord a reasonable investigation to its assertions. Examples of such succinctness and clarity may be found in The Four Noble Truths; The Three Characteristics; The Ten Fetters; and there is clearly a definite theory in the idea of Karma. Such ideas are basic, and are as a thread on which

[1] See Huxley's classical example of the horse, zebra, and centaur.
[2] Similarly, where Buddhist parables are of a mystical nature, where a complicated symbolism of numbers (for example) is intended to shadow a truth, we must discard them. My experience of mysticism is somewhat large; its final dictum is that the parable $x$ may be equated to $a, b, c, d \ldots z$ by six-and-twenty different persons, or by one person in six-and-twenty different moods. Even had we a strong traditional explanation I should maintain my position. The weapons of the Higher Criticism, supplemented by Common Sense, are perfectly valid and inevitably destructive against any such structure. But I am surely in danger of becoming ridiculous in writing thus to the scientific world. What I really wish to show is that one need not look for all the Buddhist fancy dishes to be served at the scientific table to the peril of the scientific digestion. And by a backhanded stroke I wish to impress as deeply as possible upon my Buddhist friends that too much zeal for the accidentals of our religion will surely result in the overwhelming of its essentials in the tide of justly scornful or justly casuistic criticism.—A. C.

the beads of Arabian-Night-Entertainment are strung.[1]

I propose therefore to deal with these and some other minor points of the Buddhist metaphysic, and trace out their scientific analogies, or, as I hope to show, more often identities.

First then let us examine that great Summary of the Buddhist Faith, the Four Noble Truths.

### III.

#### THE FOUR NOBLE TRUTHS.

(1) SORROW.—Existence is Sorrow. This means that "no known form of Existence is separable from Sorrow." This truth is stated by Huxley, almost in so many words, in Evolution and Ethics. "It was no less plain to some of these antique philosophers than to the fathers of modern philosophy that suffering is the badge of all the tribe of sentient things; that it is no accidental accompaniment, but an essential constituent of the Cosmic Process." And in the same essay, though he is disposed to deny more than the rudiments of consciousness to the lower forms of life, he is quite clear that pain varies directly (to put it loosely) with the degree of consciousness. Cf. also "Animal Automatism," pp. 236-237.

(2) SORROW'S CAUSE.—The cause of sorrow is desire. I take desire here to include such a phenomenon as the tendency of two molecules of hydrogen and chlorine to combine under certain conditions. If death be painful to me, it is presumably so to a molecule; if we represent one operation as pleasant, the converse is presumably painful. Though I am not conscious of the individual pain of the countless deaths involved in this my act of writing, it may be there. And what I call "fatigue" may be the echo in my central consciousness of the

[1] See Prof. Rhys Davids on the "Jataka."

shriek of a peripheral anguish. Here we leave the domain of fact ; but at least as far our knowledge extends, all or nearly all the operations of Nature are vanity and vexation of spirit. Consider food, the desire for which periodically arises in all conscious beings.[1]

The existence of these desires, or rather necessities, which I realise to be mine, is unpleasant. It is this desire inherent in me for continued consciousness that is responsible for it all, and this leads us to the Third Noble Truth.

(3) SORROW'S CEASING.—The cessation of desire is the cessation of sorrow. This is a simple logical inference from the second Truth, and needs no comment.

(4) THE NOBLE EIGHTFOLD PATH.— There is a way, to be considered later, of realising the Third Truth. But we must, before we can perceive its possibility on the one hand, or its necessity on the other, form a clear idea of what are the Buddhist tenets with regard to the Cosmos ; and, in particular, to man.[2]

## IV.

### THE THREE CHARACTERISTICS.

The Three Characteristics (which we may predicate of all known existing things) :
(a) Change.    Anikka.
(b) Sorrow.    Dukkha.
(c) Absence of an Ego.    Anatta.

[1] Change is the great enemy, the immediate cause of pain. Unable to arrest it, I slow the process, and render it temporarily painless, by eating. This is a concession to weakness, no doubt, in one sense. Do I eat really in order to check change, or to maintain my ego-consciousness? Change I desire, for my present condition is sorrow. I really desire the impossible ; completely to retain my present egoity with all its conditions reversed.—A. C.
[2] For an able and luminous exposition of "The Four Noble Truths" I refer the reader to the pamphlet bearing that title by my old friend Bhikkhu Ananda Maitriya, published by the Buddhasasana Samagama, 1 Pagoda Road, Rangoon.—A. C.

This is the Buddhist Assertion. What does Science say ?

(a) Huxley, " Evolution and Ethics " :

" As no man fording a swift stream can dip his foot twice into the same water, so no man can, with exactness, affirm of anything in the sensible world that it is. As he utters the words, nay, as he thinks them, the predicate ceases to be applicable ; the present has become the past ; the ' is ' should be ' was.' And the more we learn of the nature of things the more evident is it that what we call rest is only unperceived activity ; that seeming peace is silent but strenuous battle. In every part, at every moment, the state of the cosmos is the expression of a transitory adjustment of contending forces, a scene of strife, in which all the combatants fall in turn. What is true of each part is true of the whole. Natural knowledge tends more and more to the conclusion that " all the choir of heaven and furniture of the earth " are the transitory forms of parcels of cosmic substance wending along the road of evolution, from nebulous potentiality, through endless growths of sun and planet and satellite, through all varieties of matter ; through infinite diversities of life and thought, possibly, through modes of being of which we neither have a conception, nor are competent to form any, back to the indefinable latency from which they arose. Thus the most obvious attribute of the cosmos is its impermanence. It assumes the aspect not so much of a permanent entity as of a changeful process, in which naught endures save the flow of energy and the rational order which pervades it."

This is an admirable summary of the Buddhist doctrine.

(b) See above on the First Noble Truth.

(c) This is the grand position which Buddha carried against the Hindu philosophers. In our own country it is the argument of Hume, following Berkeley to a place where Berkeley certainly never meant to go—a curious parallel fulfilment of Christ's curse against Peter (John xxi.). The Bishop demolishes the idea of a substratum of matter, and

Hume follows by applying an identical process of reasoning to the phenomena of mind.[1]

Let us consider the Hindu theory. They classify the phenomena (whether well or ill matters nothing), but represent them all as pictured in, but not affecting, a certain changeless, omniscient, blissful existence called Atman. Holding to Theism, the existence of evil forces them to the Fichtean position that "the Ego posits the Non-Ego," and we learn that nothing really exists after all but Brahm. They then distinguish between Jivatma, the soul-conditioned; and Paramatma, the soul free; the former being the base of our normal consciousness; the latter of the Nirvikalpa-Samadhi conscious-

[1] The Buddhist position *may* be interpreted as agnostic in this matter, these arguments being directed against, and destructive of, the unwarranted assumptions of the Hindus; but no more. See Sabbasava Sutta, 10. "In him, thus unwisely considering, there springs up one or other of the six (absurd) notions.
"As something real and true he gets the notion, ' I have a self.'
"As something real and true he gets the notion, ' I have not a self.'
"As something real and true he gets the notion, ' By my self, I am conscious of my self.'
"As something real and true he gets the notion, ' By my self, I am conscious of my non-self.'
"Or again, he gets the notion, ' This soul of mine can be perceived, it has experienced the result of good or evil actions committed here and there; now this soul of mine is permanent, lasting, eternal, has the inherent quality of never changing, and will continue for ever and ever ! '
"This, brethren, is called the walking in delusion, the jungle of delusion, the wilderness of delusion, the puppet-show of delusion, the writhing of delusion, the fetter of delusion."
There are, it may be noted, only five (not six) notions mentioned, unless we take the last as double. Or we may consider the sixth as the contrary of the fifth, and correct. The whole passage is highly technical, perhaps untrustworthy; in any case, this is not the place to discuss it. The sun of Agnosticism breaking through the cloud of Anatta is the phenomenon to which I wished to call attention.—A. C.

ness; this being the sole condition on which morals, religion, and fees to priests can continue. For the Deist has only to advance his fundamental idea to be forced round in a vicious circle of absurdities.[1]

The Buddhist makes a clean sweep of all this sort of nonsense. He analyses the phenomena of mind, adopting Berkeley's paradox that "matter is immaterial," in a sane and orderly way. The "common-sense Philosopher," whom I leave to chew the bitter leaves of Professor Huxley's Essay " On Sensation and the Unity of the Structure of Sensiferous Organs," observes, on lifting his arm, "I lift my arm." The Buddhist examines this proposition closely, and begins :

"There is a lifting of an arm."

By this terminology he avoids Teutonic discussions concerning the Ego and Non-ego.[2] But how does he know this proposition to be true? By sensation. The fact is therefore :

"There is a sensation of the lifting of an arm."

But how does he know that ? By perception. Therefore he says :

"There is a perception of a sensation, &c."

And why this perception? From the inherent tendency.

(Note carefully the determinist standpoint involved in the enunciation of this Fourth Skandha; and that it comes lower than Viññanam.)

"There is a tendency to perceive the sensation, &c."

And how does he know there is a tendency? By consciousness. The final analysis reads :

"There is a consciousness of a tendency to perceive the sensation of a lifting of an arm."

He does not, for he cannot, go further back. He will not suppose, on no sort of evidence, the substratum of Atman uniting

[1] As Bishop Butler so conclusively showed.
[2] I may incidentally remark that a very few hours' practice (see Section VIII.) cause "I lift my arm" to be intuitively denied.—A. C.

consciousness to consciousness by its eternity, while it fixes a great gulf between them by its changelessness. He states the knowable, states it accurately, and leaves it there. But there is a practical application of this analysis which I will treat of later. (See VIII. Maha-satipatthana.)

We are told that the memory is a proof of some real "I." But how treacherous is this ground! Did a past event in my life not happen because I have forgotten it? O the analogy of the river water given above is most valid! I who write this am not I who read it over and correct it. Do I desire to play with lead soldiers? Am I the doddering old cripple who must be wheeled about and fed on whisky and bread and milk? And is my difference from them so conspicuously less than from the body lying dead of which those who see it will say, "This was Aleister Crowley"?

What rubbish is it to suppose that an eternal substance, sentient or not, omniscient or not, depends for its information on so absurd a series of bodies as are grouped under that "Crowley"!

Yet the Buddhist meets all arguments of the spiritual order with a simple statement which, if not certain, is at least not improbable. There is, he will tell you, a "spiritual" world, or to avoid any (most unjustifiable) misunderstandings, let us say a world of subtler matter than the visible and tangible, which has its own laws (analogous to, if not identical with, those laws of matter with which we are acquainted) and whose inhabitants change, and die, and are re-born very much as ordinary mortal beings. But as they are of subtler matter, their cycle is less rapid.[1]

As a nominalist, I hope not to be misunderstood when I compare this to the relative mutability of the individual and the species.[2] We have enough examples free

[1] Cf. Huxley, cited *supra*, "possibly, through modes of being of which we neither have a conception, nor are competent to form any. . . ."
[2] Cf. "Evolution and Ethics," note 1.

from such possibility of misinterpretation in our own bodies. Compare the longevity of a bone with that of a corpuscle. But it is this "Substratum" universe, which must not be confounded with the substratum, the arguments for whose existence Berkeley so utterly shattered,[1] which may conserve memory for a period greatly exceeding that of one of its particular avatars. Hence the "Jataka." But the doctrine is not very essential; its chief value is to show what serious difficulties confront us, and to supply a reason for the struggle to some better state. For if nothing

[1] Without an elaborate analysis of the ideas involved in the Ding an sich of Kant, and of H. Spencer's definition of all things as Modes of the Unknowable, I may point out in passing that these hypotheses are as sterile as the "vital principle" in biology, or "phlogiston" in chemistry. They lead literally nowhere. That the phenomenal world is an illusion is all very well; one girds up one's loins to seek reality: but to prove reality unknowable is to shut all avenues to the truth-loving man, to open all to the sensualist. And, if we accept either of the above philosophies, it does not matter. That we feel it does matter is sufficient refutation, for we must obey the sentence awarded on our own testimony, whether we like it or not.

I am aware that this is a somewhat cowardly way of dealing with the question; I prefer to insist that if we once admit that the unknowable (by reason) to consciousness may be known (by concentration) to super-consciousness, the difficulty vanishes.

I think Huxley goes too far in speaking of a man "self-hypnotised into cataleptic trances" without medical evidence of a large number of cases. Edward Carpenter, who has met Yogis, and talked long and learnedly with them, tells a different story.

Even had we a large body of evidence from Anglo-Indian medical men, the proof would still be lacking. They might not be the real men. The Indian native would take intense delight in bringing round the village idiot to be inspected in the character of a holy man by the "Doctor Sahib."

The Anglo-Indian is a fool; a minimum medical education is in most cases insufficient to abate the symptoms to nil, though perhaps it must always diminish them. The Hindu is the Sphinx of civilisation; nearly all that has been written on him is worthless; those who know him best know this fact best.—A. C.

survives death, what does it matter to us? Why are we to be so altruistic as to avoid the reincarnation of a being in all points different from ourselves? As the small boy said, "What has posterity done for me?" But something does persist; something changing, though less slowly. What evidence have we after all that an animal does not remember his man-incarnation? Or, as Levi says, "In the suns they remember, and in the planets they forget." I think it unlikely (may be), but in the total absence of all evidence for or against—at least with regard to the latter hypothesis!—I suspend my judgment, leave the question alone, and proceed to more practical points than are offered by these interesting but not over-useful metaphysical speculations.

## V.

### KARMA.

The law of causation is formally identical with this. Karma means "that which is made," and I think it should be considered with strict etymological accuracy. If I place a stone on the roof of a house, it is sure to fall sooner or later; *i.e.*, as soon as the conditions permit. Also, in its ultimation, the doctrine of Karma is identical with determinism. On this subject much wisdom, with an infinite amount of rubbish, has been written. I therefore dismiss it in these few words, confident that the established identity can never be shaken.

## VI.

### THE TEN FETTERS OR SANYOGANAS.

1. Sakkaya-di*tth*i.    Belief in a "soul."
2. Vi*kiki*k*k*ha.    Doubt.
3. Silabbata-parâmâsa.    Reliance on the efficacy of rites and ceremonies.
4. Kama.    Bodily Desires.

5. Patigha.    Hatred.
6. Ruparaga.    Desire for bodily immortality.
7. Aruparaga.    Desire for spiritual immortality.
8. Mano.    Pride.
9. Udha*kk*a.    Self-righteousness.
10. Avi*gg*a.    Ignorance.

(1) For this is a *petitio principii*.

(2) This, to a scientist, is apparently anathema. But it only means, I think, that if we are not settled in our minds we cannot work. And this is unquestionable. Suppose a chemist to set to work to determine the boiling-point of a new organic substance. Does he stop in the midst, struck by the fear that his thermometer is inaccurate? No! he has, unless he is a fool, tested it previously. We must have our principia fixed before we can do research work.

(3) A scientist hardly requires conviction on this point!

(4) Do you think to combine Newton and Caligula? The passions, allowed to dominate, interfere with the concentration of the mind.

(5) Does brooding on your dislikes help you to accurate observation? I admit that a controversy may stir you up to perform prodigies of work, but while you are actually working you do not suffer the concentration of your mind to be interfered with.

(6 & 7) This Fetter and the next are contingent on your having perceived the suffering of all forms of conscious existence.

(8) Needs no comment. Pride, like humility, is a form of delusion.

(9) Is like unto it, but on the moral plane.

(10) The great enemy. Theists alone have found the infamous audacity to extol the merits of this badge of servitude.

We see, then, that in this classification a scientist will concur. We need not discuss the question whether or no he would find others to add. Buddhism may not be complete, but, as far as it goes, it is accurate.

## VII.

### THE RELATIVE REALITY OF CERTAIN STATES OF CONSCIOUSNESS.

Whether we adopt Herbert Spencer's dictum that the primary testimony of consciousness is to the existence of externality, or no ;[1] whether or no we fly to the extreme idealistic position ; there is no question that, to our normal consciousness, things as they present themselves — apart from obvious illusion, if even we dare to except this—are undisprovable to the immediate apprehension. Whatever our reason may tell us, we act precisely as though Berkeley had never lived, and the herculean Kant had been strangled while yet in his cradle by the twin serpents of his own perversity and terminology.

What criterion shall we apply to the relative realities of normal and dream consciousness? Why do I confidently assert that the dream state is transitory and unreal?

In that state I am equally confident that my normal consciousness is invalid. But as my dreams occupy a relatively small portion of my time, and as the law of causation seems suspended, and as their vividness is less than that of normal consciousness, and above all, as in the great majority of cases I can show a cause, dating from my waking hours, for the dream, I have four strong reasons (the first explanatory to some extent of my reasons for accepting the others) for concluding that the dream is fictitious.

But what of the " dreamless " state? To the dreamer his normal faculties and memories arise at times, and are regarded as fragmentary and absurd, even as the remembrance of a dream is to the waking man. Can we not conceive then of a " dreamless " life, of

[1] Mahasatipa*tth*ana (Sec. VIII.) does admit this perhaps. Yet its very object is to correct consciousness on the lines indicated by reason.

which our dreams are the vague and disturbed transition to normal consciousness ?

The physiological evidence goes literally for nothing. Even were it proved that the recipio-motor apparatus of a " dreamless " sleeper was relatively quiescent, would that supply any valid argument against the theory I have suggested ? Suggested, for I admit that our present position is completely agnostic in respect to it, since we have no evidence which throws light on the matter ; and study of the subject would appear to be mere waste of time.

But the suggestion is valuable as affording us a possibly rational explanation, conformable to the waking man, which the dreamer would indignantly reject.

Suppose, however, a dream so vivid that the whole waking man is abased before its memory, that his consciousness of it appears a thousand times more real than that of the things about him ; suppose that his whole life is moulded to fit the new facts thus revealed to him ; that he would cheerfully renounce years of normal life to obtain minutes of that dream-life ; that his time sense is uprooted as never before, and that these influences are permanent. Then, you will say, delirium tremens (and the intoxication of hashish, in respect more particularly of the time sense) afford us a parallel. But the phenomena of delirium tremens do not occur in the healthy. As for the suggestion of auto-hypnosis, the memory of the " dream " is a sufficient reply. However this may be, the simple fact of the superior apparent reality—a conviction unshakable, *inépuisable* (for the English has no word), is a sufficient test. And if we condescend to argue, it is for pleasure, and aside from the vital fact ; a skirmish, and not a pitched battle.

The " dream " I have thus described is the state called Dhyana by the Hindus and Buddhists. The method of attaining it is sane, healthy, and scientific. I would not take the pains to describe that method, had not illiterate, and too often mystical advocates of the practice obscured the simple grandeur of our edifice by jimcrack pinnacles of stucco — as who should hang the Taj Mahal with fairy lamps and chintz.

It is simple. The mind is compelled to fix its attention on a single thought; while the controlling power is exercised and a profound watchfulness kept up lest the thought should for a moment stray.[1] The latter portion is, to my mind, the essential one. The work is comparable to that of an electrician who should sit for hours with his finger on a delicately adjusted resistance-box and his eye on the spot of light of a galvanometer, charged with the duty of keeping the spot still, at least that it should never move beyond a certain number of degrees, and of recording the more important details of his experiment. Our work is identical in design, though worked with subtler—if less complex—means. For the finger on the resistance-box we substitute the Will; and its control extends but to the Mind; for the eye we substitute the Introspective Faculty with its keen observation of the most minute disturbance, while the spot of light is the Consciousness itself, the central point of the galvanometer scale the predetermined object, and the other figures on the scale, other objects, connected with the primary by order and degree, sometimes obviously, sometimes obscurely, perhaps even untraceably, so that we have no real right to predicate their connection.[2]

[1] Huxley, Essays, V., 136.
[2] This last sentence will be best understood by those who have practised up to a certain point. At first it is easy to trace back by a connected chain of thoughts from the thought which awakes us to the fact that we are wandering to the original thought. Later, and notably as we improve, this becomes first difficult, then impossible. At first sight this fact suggests that we are injuring our brains by the practice, but the explanation is as follows: Suppose we figure the central consciousness as the Sun, intent on seeing that nothing falls into him. First the near planets are carefully arranged, so that no collision can occur; afterwards Jupiter and Saturn, until his whole system is safe. If then any body fall upon the Sun, he knows that it is

How any sane person can describe this process as delusive and unhealthy passes my comprehension; that any scientist should do so implies an ignorance on his part of the facts. I may add that the most rigid necessity exists for perfect health of body and mind before this practice can begin; asceticism is as sternly discouraged as indulgence. How would the electrician do his work after a Guildhall Banquet? The strain of watching would be too much, and he would go off to sleep. So with the meditator. If, on the other hand, he had been without food for twenty-four hours, he might—indeed it has been done often—perform prodigies of work for the necessary period; but a reaction must follow of proportionate severity. Nobody will pretend that the best work is done starving.[1]

Now to such an observer certain phenomena present themselves sooner or later which have the qualities above predicated of our imaginary "dream" preceded by a transition-state very like total loss of consciousness. Are these fatigue phenomena? Is it that this practice for some as yet unknown reason stimulates some special nerve-centre? Perhaps; the subject requires investigation; I am not a physiologist. Whatever physiology may say, it is at least clear that if this state is accompanied with an intense and passionless bliss beyond anything that the normal man can conceive of, and unaccompanied with the slightest prejudice to the mental and physical health, it is most highly desirable. And to the scientist it presents a magnificent field of research.

not from any of those planets with which he is familiar, and, lord of his own system, cannot trace the course or divine the cause of the accident which has disturbed him. And he will accept this ignorance as a proof of how well his own system is going, since he no longer receives shocks from it.—A. C.
[1] Hallucination especially is to be feared. Light-headedness from want of food is quite sufficient explanation for many "Mystic raptures." I do not care to invoke hysteria and epilepsy without positive evidence.—A. C.

Of the metaphysical and religious theories which have been built upon the facts here stated, I have nothing to say in this place. The facts are not at the disposition of all ; from the nature of the subject each man must be his own witness. I was once twitted by some shallow-pated person with the fact that my position cannot be demonstrated in the laboratory, and that therefore (save the mark !) I must be a mystic, an occultist, a theosophist, a mystery-monger, and what not. I am none of these. The above criticism applies to every psychologist that ever wrote, and to the man who makes the criticism by the fact of his making it. I can only say: "You have your own laboratory and apparatus, your mind ; and if the room is dirty and the apparatus ill put together, you have certainly not me to blame for it."

The facts being of individual importance, then, there is little use if I detail the results of my own experience. And the reason for this reticence—for I plead guilty to reticence—that to explain would damage the very apparatus whose use I am advocating. For did I say that such and such a practice leads one to see a blue pig, the suggestion is sufficient to cause one class of people to see a blue pig where none existed, and another to deny or suspect the blue pig when it really appeared, though the latter alternative is unlikely. The consciousness phenomenon, and the bliss, is of so stupendous and well-defined a nature that I cannot imagine any preconceived idea powerful enough to diminish it appreciably. But for the sake of the former class I hold my tongue.[1]

I trust it is now perfectly clear, if my statements are accepted—and I can only

most seriously assure you that honest laborious experiment will be found to verify them in every particular—that whatever arguments are brought forward destructive of the reality of Dhyana, apply with far more force to the normal state, and it is evident that to deny the latter seriously is *ipso facto* to become unserious. Whether the normal testimony may be attacked from above, by insisting on the superior reality of Dhyana—and *à fortiori* of Samadhi, which I have not experienced, and consequently do not treat of, being content to accept the highly probable statements of those who profess to know, and who have so far not deceived me (*i.e.* as to Dhyana), is a question which it is not pertinent to the present argument to discuss.[1] I shall, however, suggest certain ideas in the following section, in which I propose to discuss the most famous of the Buddhist meditations (Mahasatipa*tth*ana), its method, object, and results.

## VIII.

### MAHASATIPA*TTH*ANA.

This meditation differs fundamentally from the usual Hindu methods by the fact that the mind is not restrained to the contemplation of a single object, and there is no interference with the natural functions of the body as there is, *e.g.*, in Pranayama. It is essentially an observation-practice, which later assumes an analytic aspect in regard to the question, "What is it that is really observed?"

The Ego-idea is resolutely excluded from the start, and so far Mr. Herbert Spencer will have nothing to object ("Principles of

[1] On the advisability of so doing I am open to conviction. The scientific mind, I might argue, will not readily fall into that error ; and for the others, they will be useless as a research phalanx, and may as well see blue pigs and be happy as not. In the past, no doubt, research has been choked by the multitude of pseudo-blue-pig-people, from the "T. S." to the "G. D." We must distinguish by methods, not by results.—A. C.

[1] The gravest doubts assail me on further examination of this point. I am now (1906) convinced that the experiences to which I refer constitute Samadhi. The accursed pedantry of the pundits has led to the introduction of a thousand useless subtleties in philosophical terminology, the despair alike of the translator and the investigator, until he realises that it is pedantry, and as worthless as the rest of oriental literature in all matters of exactitude. —A. C.

Psychology," ii. 404). The breathing, motions of walking, &c., are merely observed and recorded ; for instance, one may sit down quietly and say : "There is an indrawing of the breath." "There is an expiration," &c. Or, walking, "There is a raising of the right foot," and so on, just as it happens. The thought is of course not quick enough to note all the movements or their subtle causes. For example, we cannot describe the complicated muscular contractions, &c. ; but this is not necessary. Concentrate on some series of simple movements.

When this through habit becomes intuitive so that the thought is *really* "There is a raising," as opposed to "I raise" (the latter being in reality a complex and adult idea, as philosophers have often shown, ever since Descartes fell into the trap), one may begin to analyse, as explained above, and the second stage is "There is a sensation (Vedana) of a raising, &c." Sensations are further classed as pleasant or unpleasant.

When this is the true intuitive instantaneous testimony of consciousness (so that "There is a raising, &c." is rejected as a palpable lie),[1] we proceed to Sañña, perception.

"There is a perception of a (pleasant or unpleasant) sensation of a raising, &c."

When this has become intuitive—why ! here's a strange result ! The emotions of pain and pleasure have vanished. They are subincluded in the lesser skandha of Vedana, and Sañña is free from them. And to him who can live in this third stage, and live so for ever, there is no more pain ; only an intense interest similar to that which has enabled men of science to watch and note the progress of their own death-agony. Un-

[1] "Why should you expect Vedana to make Rupa appear illusory?" asked a friend of mine, on reading through the MS. of this essay. The reason of my omission to explain is that to me it seemed obvious. The fact had been assimilated. To meditate on anything is to perceive its unreal nature. Notably this is so in concentrating on parts of the body, such as the nose. On this phenomenon the Hindus have based their famous aphorism, "That which can be thought is not true."—A. C.

fortunately the living in such a state is conditional on sound mental health, and terminable by disease or death at any moment. Were it not so, the First Noble Truth would be a lie.

The two further stages Sankhara and Viññanam pursue the analysis to its ultimation, "There is a consciousness of a tendency to perceive the (pleasant or unpleasant) sensation of a raising of a right foot " being the final form. And I suppose no psychologist of any standing will quarrel with this.[1] Reasoning in fact leads us to this analysis ; the Buddhist goes further only so far as he may be said to knock down the scaffolding of reasoning processes, and to assimilate the actual truth of the matter.

It is the difference between the schoolboy who painfully construes "Balbus murum ædificavit," and the Roman who announces that historic fact without a thought of his grammar.

I have called this meditation the most famous of the Buddhist meditations, because it is stated by the Buddha himself that if one practises it honestly and intelligently a result is certain. And he says this of no other.

I have personally not found time to devote myself seriously to this Mahasatipatthana, and the statements here made are those derived from reason and not from experience. But I can say that the unreality of the grosser (rupa) relatively to the subtler Vedana and still more subtle Sañña becomes rapidly apparent, and I can only conclude that with time and trouble the process would continue.

What will occur when one reaches the final stage of Viññanam, and finds no Atman behind it? Surely the Viññanam stage will soon seem as unreal as the former have become. It is idle to speculate ; but if I may escape the imputation of explaining the obscure by the more obscure, I may hint that such a person must be very near the state called Nirvana, whatever may be meant by

[1] I deal with Mr. Spencer and "Transfigured Realism " in a note at the end of this section. —A. C.

this term.   And I am convinced in my own mind that the Ananda (bliss) of Dhyana will surely arise long before one has passed even up to Sankhara.

And for the reality, 'twill be a brave jest, my masters, to fling back on the materialists that terrible gibe of Voltaire's at the mystery-mongers of his day: "Ils nient ce qui est, et expliquent ce qui n'est pas."

### Note to Section VIII.
#### Transfigured Realism.

I will not waste my own time and that of my readers by any lengthy discussion of Mr. Herbert Spencer's "Transfigured Realism." I will not point out in greater detail how he proposes, by a chain of reasoning, to over-throw the conclusions he admits as being those of reason.

But his statement that Idealism is but verbally intelligible is for my purpose the most admirable thing he could have said.

He is wrong in saying that the idealists are bewildered by their own terminology; the fact is that idealist conclusions are pre-sented directly to consciousness, when that consciousness is Dhyanic. (Cf. Section XI.)

Nothing is clearer to my mind than that the great difficulty habitually experienced by the normal mind in the assimilation of meta-physics is due to the actual lack of experi-ence in the mind of the reader of the phenomena discussed.   I will go so far as to say that perhaps Mr. Spencer himself is so bitter because he himself has actual ex-perience of "Transfigured Realism" as a directly presented phenomenon ; for if he supposes that the normal healthy mind can perceive what he perceives, Berkeley's argu-ments must seem to him mere wanton stupidity.

I class the Hindu philosophy with the Idealist ; the Buddhistic with that of Mr. Herbert Spencer ; the great difference be-tween the two being that the Buddhists re-cognise clearly these (or similar) conclusions as phenomena, Mr. Spencer, inconsistently

enough, only as truths verified by a higher and more correct reasoning than that of his opponents.

We recognise, with Berkeley, that reason teaches us that the testimony of conscious-ness is untrue ; it is absurd, with Spencer, to refute reason ; instead we take means to bring consciousness to a sense of its impro-bity.   Now our (empiric) diagnosis is that it is the dissipation of mind that is chiefly re-sponsible for its untruthfulness.   We seek (also by empiric means, alas !) to control it, to con-centrate it, to observe more accurately—has this source of possible error been sufficiently recognised ?—what its testimony really is.

Experience has taught me, so far as I have been able to go, that Reason and Conscious-ness have met together ; Apprehension and Analysis have kissed one another.   The re-conciliation (in fact, remember, and not in words) is at least so nearly perfect that I can confidently predict that a further pursuit of the (empirically-indicated) path will surely lead to a still further and higher unity.

The realisation of the hopes held out by the hypothesis is then of clear evidential value in support of that hypothesis, empiric as it was, and is.   But with the growth and gathering-together, classifying, criticism of our facts, we are well on the way to erect a surer structure on a broader basis.

### IX.
#### AGNOSTICISM.

It should be clearly understood, and well remembered, that throughout all these medi-tations and ideas, there is no necessary way to any orthodox ontology whatever.   As to the way of salvation, we are not to rely on the Buddha ; the vicious lie of vicarious atonement finds no place here.   The Buddha himself does not escape the law of causation ; if this be metaphysics, so far Buddhism is metaphysical, but no further.   While deny-ing obvious lies, it does not set up dogmas ; all its statements are susceptible of proof— a child can assent to all the more important.

And this is Agnosticism. We have a scientific religion. How far would Newton have got if he had stuck to Tycho Brahe as the One Guide? How far the Buddha had he reverenced the Vedas with blind faith? Or how far can we proceed even from partial truth, unless a perfectly open mind be kept regarding it, aware that some new phenomenon may possibly overthrow our most fundamental hypotheses! Give me a reasonable proof of some (intelligent) existence which is not liable to sorrow, and I will throw the First Noble Truth to the dogs without a pang. And, knowing this, how splendid is it to read the grand words uttered more than two thousand years ago: "Therefore, O Ananda, be ye lamps unto yourselves. Be ye a refuge to yourselves. Betake yourselves to no external refuge. Hold fast to the truth as a lamp. Hold fast as a refuge to the truth. Look not for refuge to any one besides yourselves." (Mahaparanibbana Sutta, ii. 33.) And to such seekers only does the Buddha promise "the very topmost Height"—if only they are "anxious to learn." This is the corner-stone of Buddhism; can scientific men deny their assent to these words when they look back on the history of Thought in the West; the torture of Bruno, the shame of Galileo, the obscurantism of the Schoolmen, the "mystery" of the hard-pressed priests, the weapons carnal and spiritual of stake and rack, the labyrinths of lying and vile intrigue by which Science, the child, was deformed, distorted, stunted, in the interest of the contrary proposition?

If you ask me why you should be Buddhists and not indifferentists, as you are now, I tell you that I come, however unworthy, to take up the sword that Huxley wielded; I tell you that the Oppressor of Science in her girlhood is already at work to ravish her virginity; that a moment's hesitation, idleness, security may force us back from the positions so hardly won. Are we never to go forward, moreover? Are our children still to be taught as facts the stupid and indecent fables of the Old Testament, fables that the Archbishop of Canterbury himself would indignantly repudiate? Are minds to be warped early, the scientific method and imagination checked, the logical faculty thwarted—thousands of workers lost each year to Science?

And the way to do this is not only through the negative common-sense of indifference; organise, organise, organise! For a flag we offer you the stainless lotus-banner of the Buddha, in defence of which no drop of blood has ever been, nor ever will be shed, a banner under which you will join forces with five hundred million of your fellow-men. And you will not be privates in the army; for you the highest place, the place of leaders, waits; as far as the triumphs of the intellect are concerned, it is to Western Science that we look. Your achievements have shattered the battle-array of dogma and despotism; your columns roll in triumphant power through the breaches of false metaphysic and baseless logic; you have fought that battle, and the laurels are on your brows. The battle was fought by us more than two thousand years ago; the authority of the Vedas, the restrictions of caste, were shattered by the invulnerable sword of truth in Buddha's hand; we are your brothers. But in the race of intellect we have fallen behind a little; will you take no interest in us, who have been your comrades? To Science Buddhism cries: Lead us, reform us, give us clear ideas of Nature and her laws; give us that basis of irrefragable logic and wide knowledge that we need, and march with us into the Unknown!

The Buddhist faith is not a blind faith; its truths are obvious to all who are not blinded by the spectacles of bibliolatry and deafened by the clamour of priests, presbyters, ministers: whatever name they choose for themselves, we can at least put them aside in one great class, the Thought-stiflers; and these truths are those which we have long accepted and to which you have recently and hardly won.

It is to men of your stamp, men of independent thought, of keen ecstasy of love of knowledge, of practical training, that the Buddhasanana Samagama [1] appeals; it is time that Buddhism reformed itself from within; though its truths be held untarnished (and even this is not everywhere the case), its methods, its organisation, are sadly in need of repair; research must be done, men must be perfected, error must be fought. And if in the West a great Buddhist society is built up of men of intellect, of the men in whose hands the future lies, there is then an awakening, a true redemption, of the weary and forgetful Empires of the East.


X.

### THE NOBLE EIGHTFOLD PATH.

To return from our little digression to the original plan of our essay. It is time to note the "Noble Eightfold Path," referred to, and its consideration deferred, in Section III.

In this Fourth Noble Truth we approach the true *direction* of Buddhism; progress is but another word for change; is it possible to move in a direction whose goal is the changeless? The answer is Yea and Amen! and it is detailed in the Noble Eightfold Path, of which I propose to give a short resumé. First, however, of the goal. It may be readily syllogised :

All existing things are (by nature, inevitably) subject to change.

In Nirvana is no change.

.'. No existing thing is or can be in Nirvana.

Now here is the great difficulty; for this syllogism is perfectly sound, and yet we speak of attaining Nirvana, tasting Nirvana, &c.

[We must distinguish the Hindu Nirvana, which means Cessation of Existence in certain Lokas; never absolute Cessation, as the

[1] Or International Buddhist Society, founded in Rangoon in 1903.

Buddhist tradition, the etymology, and the logical value alike require for the word as applied to the Buddhist goal. See Childers, Pali Dictionary, *sub voce* Nibbana.]

The explanation is really as follows : only by this term Nirvana can we foreshadow to you the reality; for as even the Dawn of Dhyana is indescribable in language, *à fortiori* Nirvana is so. To give an example, for that something of the sort is necessary I freely admit, to defend so apparently mystical a statement, I may give the following from my own experience.

In a certain meditation one day I recorded :

"I was (a) conscious of external things seen behind after my nose had vanished. (b) Conscious that I was *not* conscious of these things. These (a) and (b) were simultaneous."

I subsequently discovered this peculiar state of consciousness classified in the Abhidhamma. That it is a contradiction in terms I am perfectly aware; to assign any meaning to it is frankly beyond me; but I am as certain that such a state once existed in me as I am of anything.

Similarly with Nirvana and its definition. The Arahat knows what it is, and describes it by its accidentals, such as bliss. I must raise, very reluctantly, a protest against the idea of Professor Rhys Davids (if I have understood him aright) that Nirvana is the mental state resulting from the continuous practice of all the virtues and methods of thought characteristic of Buddhism. No; Nirvana is a state belonging to a different plane, to a higher dimension than anything we can at present conceive of. It has perhaps its analogies and correspondences on the normal planes, and so shall we find of the steps as well as of the Goal. Even the simple first step, which every true Buddhist has taken, Sammaditthi, is a very different thing from the point of view of an Arahat. The Buddha stated expressly that none but an Arahat could really comprehend the Dhamma.

And so for all the Eight Stages; as regards their obvious meaning on the moral plane, I can do no better than quote my friend Bhikkhu Ananda Maitriya, in his " Four Noble Truths."

" He who has attained, by force of pure understanding, to the realisation of the Four Noble Truths, who has realised the fact that depends from that understanding, namely that all the constituents of being are by nature endowed with the Three Characteristics of Sorrow, Transitoriness, and Absence of any immortal principle or Atma—such a one is said to be Sammaditthi, to hold right views, and the term has come to mean one of the Buddhist Faith. We may not have taken the other and higher steps on the Noble Eightfold Path; but must have realised those Four Truths and their sequential three Characteristics. He who has attained Sammaditthi has at least entered upon the Holy Way, and, if he but try, there will come to him the power to overcome the other fetters that restrict his progress. But first of all he must abandon all those false hopes and beliefs; and one who has done this is called a Buddhist. And this holding of Right Views, in Pali Sammaditthi, is the first step upon the Noble Eightfold Path.

The second stage is Right Aspiration— Sammasankappo. Having realised the woe and transitoriness and soullessness of all life, there rises in the mind this Right Aspiration. When all things suffer, we at least will not increase their burden, so we aspire to become pitiful and loving, to cherish ill-will toward none, to retire from those pleasures of sense which are the fruitful cause of woe. The will, we all know, is ever readier than the mind, and so, though we aspire to renounce the pleasures of sense, to love and pity all that lives, yet perhaps we often fail in the accomplishment of our aspiration. But if the desire to become pitiful and pure be but honest and earnest, we have gained the Second Step upon the Path—Sammasankappo, Right Aspiration.

He whose motives are pure has no need
VOL. II.

to conceal the Truth—he who truly loves and who has a malice towards none, will ever speak only fair and soft words. By a man's speech do we learn his nature, and that one whose Right Aspirations are bearing fruit attains to the Third Step, Right Speech, Sammavaca. Speaking only the Truth in all things, never speaking harshly or unkindly, in his speech realising the love and pity that is in his heart—that man has attained to Stage the Third.

And because of the great power of a man's thoughts and words to change his being, because by thinking of the pitiful our acts grow full of mercy, therefore is Stage the Fourth called Right Conduct. To him who has gained this Fourth Stage, his intense aspiration, his right understanding, his carefully guarded speech—perhaps for many years of self-control—have at last borne outward fruit, till all his acts are loving, and pure, and done without hope of gain, he has attained the Fourth Step, called Sammakammanto.

And when, growing yet holier, that habit of Right Action grows firm and inalienable, when his whole life is lived for the Faith that is in him, when every act of his daily life, yea, of his sleep also, is set to a holy purpose, when not one thought or deed that is cruel or unpitiful can stain his being— when, not even as a duty, will he inflict pain by deed, word, or thought—then he has gained the Fifth High Path, the Living of the Life that's Right — Samma ajivo. Abstaining from all that can cause pain, he has become blameless, and can live only by such occupations as can bring no sorrow in their train.[1]

To him who has lived so, say the Holy Books, there comes a power which is unknown to ordinary men. Long training and restraint have given him conquest of his mind, he can

[1] From my point of view, this is of course impossible. See Sec. III. If wilful infliction of pain only is meant, our state becomes moral, or even worse!—mystical. I should prefer to cancel this sentence. Cf. Appendix I., *supra.*—A. C.

R

now bring all his powers with tremendous force to bear upon any one object he may have in view, and this ability to so use the energies of his being to put forth a constant and tremendous effort of the will, marks the attainment of the Sixth Stage, Sammávayamo, usually translated Right Effort, but perhaps Right Will-power would come nearer to the meaning, or Right Energy, for effort has been made even to attain to Sammaditthi.[1] And this power being gained by its use he is enabled to concentrate all his thoughts and hold them always upon one object--waking or sleeping, he remembers who he is and what his high aim in life—and this constant recollection and keeping in mind of holy things, is the Seventh Stage, Sammasati. And by the power of this transcendent faculty, rising through the Eight High Trances to the very threshold of Nirvana, he at last, in the Trance called Nirodha Samapatti, attains, even in this life, to the Deathless Shore of Nirvana, by the power of Sammasamadhi, Right Concentration. Such a one has finished the Path—he has destroyed the cause of all his chain of lives, and has become Arahan, a Saint, a Buddha himself."

But none knows better than the venerable Bhikkhu himself, as indeed he makes clear with regard to the steps Sammávayamo and above, that these interpretations are but reflections of those upon a higher plane— the scientific plane. They are (I have little doubt) for those who have attained to them mnemonic keys to whole classes of phenomena of the order anciently denominated magical, phenomena which, since the human mind has had its present constitution, have been translated into language, classified, sought after, always above language, but not beyond a sane and scientific classification, a rigid and satisfactory method, as I most firmly believe. It is to establish such a method ; to record in the language, not of the temple but of the laboratory, its results,

[1] It is of course a specific kind of effort, not mere struggle.

that I make this appeal ; that I seek to enlist genuine, not pseudo-scientific men in the Research ; so that our children may be as far in advance of us in the study of the supernormal phenomena of mind as we are in advance of our fathers in the sciences of the physical world.[1]

Note carefully this practical sense of my intention. I care nothing for the academic meanings of the steps in the Path ; what they meant to the Arahats of old is indifferent to me. " Let the dead past bury its dead ! " What I require is an advance in the Knowledge of the Great Problem, derived no longer from hearsay revelation, from exalted fanaticism, from hysteria and intoxication ; but from method and research.

Shut the temple ; open the laboratory !

## XI.

### THE TWILIGHT OF THE GERMANS.[2]

It is a commonplace of scientific men that metaphysics is mostly moonshine ; that it is largely argument in a circle cannot easily be disputed ; that the advance since Aristotle is principally verbal none may doubt ; that no parallel advance to that of science has been made in the last fifty years is certain.

The reason is obvious.

Philosophy has had two legitimate weapons —introspection and reason ; and introspection is not experiment.

[1] A few weeks after writing these words I came upon the following passage in Tyndall's "Scientific Materialism," which I had not previously read : " Two-thirds of the rays emitted by the sun fail to arouse the sense of vision. The rays exist, but the visual organ requisite for their translation into light does not exist. And so, from this region of darkness and mystery which now surrounds us, rays may now be darting, which require but the development of the proper intellectual organs to translate them into knowledge as far surpassing ours as ours surpasses that of the wallowing reptiles which once held possession of this planet."—A. C.

[2] A Note showing the necessity and scope of the Work in question.

The mind is a machine that reasons: here are its results. Very good; can it do anything else? This is the question not only of the Buddhist; but of the Hindu, of the Mohammedan, of the Mystic. All try their various methods; all attain results of sorts; none have had the genuine training which would have enabled them to record those results in an intelligible, orderly form.

Others deliberately set their face against such an attempt. I am not of them; humanity has grown up; if the knowledge be dangerous in unsuspected ways, what of bacteriology? I have obtained one result; a result striking at the very condition of consciousness; which I may formulate as follows:

"If a single state of consciousness persist unchanged for a period exceeding a very few seconds, its duality is annihilated; its nature is violently overthrown; this phenomenon is accompanied by an indescribable sensation of bliss."

Very well! but I want this formula verified a hundred times, a thousand times, by independent investigators. I want it better stated; its conditions modified, defined exactly. I want it to leave its humble station as my observation, and put into the class of regular phenomena.

But I am verging back towards Hindu philosophy, and it is a reminder well needed at this moment. For this experience of the destruction of duality, this first phenomenon in the series, has, in all its illusory beauty, been seized upon, generalised from, by philosophers, and it is to this basis of partial and therefore deceptive fact that we owe the systems of Vedanta and Idealism, with their grotesque assumptions and muddle-headed " reconcilements " all complete.

One fact, O Sri Cankaracharya, does not make a theory; let us remember your fate, and avoid generalising on insufficient evidence. With this word of warning, I leave the metaphysician to wallow in his mire, and look toward better times for the great problems of philosophy. Remember that when the solution is attained it is not the solution of one learned man for his fellows, but one realised and assimilated by every man in his own consciousness.

And what the solution may be none of us can foreshadow. To hoist the problem on to the horns of a dilemma will avail nothing when A = A may be no longer true; and this by no Hegelian word-juggle; but by direct apperception as clear as the sun at noon.

Therefore; no word more, but—to the work !

## XII.

### THE THREE REFUGES.

Buddham Saranangachami.
Dhammam Saranangachami.
Sangham Saranangachami.
I take my refuge in the Buddha.
I take my refuge in the Dhamma.
I take my refuge in the Sangha.

This formula of adhesion to Buddhism is daily repeated by countless millions of humanity; what does it mean? It is no vain profession of reliance on others; no cowardly shirking of burdens—burdens which cannot be shirked. It is a plain estimate of our auxiliaries in the battle; the cosmic facts on which we may rely, just as a scientist "relies" on the conservation of energy in making an experiment.

Were that principle of uncertain application, the simplest quantitative experiment would break hopelessly down.

So for the Buddhist.

I take my refuge in the Buddha. That there was once a man who found the Way is my encouragement.

I take my refuge in the Dhamma. The Law underlying phenomena and its unchanging certainty; the Law given by the Buddha to show us the Way, the inevitable tendency to Persistence in Motion or Rest—and Persistence, even in Motion, negates change in consciousness—these observed orders of fact are our bases.

I take my refuge in the Sangha.

These are not isolated efforts on my part; although in one sense isolation is eternally perfect and can never be overcome,[1] in another sense associates are possible and desirable. One third of humanity are Buddhists; add men of Science and we form an absolute majority; among Buddhists a very large proportion have deliberately gone out from social life of any kind to tread these paths of Research.

Is the Way very hard? Is the brain tired? The results slow to come? Others are working, failing, struggling, crowned here and there with rare garlands of success. Success for ourselves, success for others; is it not *Compassion* that binds us closer than all earthlier ties? Ay, in joy and in sorrow, in weakness and in strength, do I take my refuge in the Sangha.

## XIII.

### CONCLUSION.

Let me give a rapid resumé of what we have gone through.

(a) We have stripped Science and Buddhism of their accidental garments, and administered a rebuke to those who so swathe them.

(b) We have shown the identity of Science and Buddhism in respect of:

(1) Their fact.
(2) Their theory.
(3) Their method.
(4) Their enemies.

(c) While thus admitting Buddhism to be merely a branch of Science, we have shown it to be a most important branch, since its promise is to break down the wall at which all Science stops.

When Professor Ray Lankester has to write, "The whole order of nature, including living and lifeless matter—man, animal, and gas—is a network of mechanism, the main features and many details of which have been made more or less obvious to the wondering intelligence of mankind by the labour and ingenuity of scientific investigators. But no sane man has ever pretended, since science became a definite body of doctrine, that we know or ever can hope to know or conceive of the possibility of knowing, whence this mechanism has come, why it is there, whither it is going, and what there may or may not be beyond and beside it which our senses are incapable of appreciating. These things are not 'explained' by science, and never can be," he gives a curious example of that quaint scientific pride which knows the limits of its powers, and refuses to entertain the hope of transcending them. Unfortunately, he is as one who, a hundred years ago, should have declared any knowledge of the chemistry of the fixed stars impossible. To invent new methods, and to revolutionise the functions of the senses by training or otherwise is the routine work of to-morrow.[1] But, alas! he goes even further.

"Similarly we seek by the study of cerebral disease to trace the genesis of the phenomena which are supposed by some physicists who have strayed into biological fields to justify them in announcing the 'discovery' of 'Telepathy' and a belief in ghosts."

To talk of cerebral disease as the characteristic of one who merely differs from you (and that because he has more knowledge than yourself) is itself a symptom familiar to alienists. (I may say I hold no brief for Professor Lodge, here attacked. I am not even interested in any of his results, as such of them as I am acquainted with deal with objective and trivial phenomena.)

Of course, as long as what Darwin called variation is called disease by Professor Ray Lankester, we shall (if we accept his views,

---

[1] *i.e.* on normal planes.

[1] See note p. 258.

and it will go hard with us if we do not!) regard all progress in any direction as morbid. So (as with Lombroso) "disease" will become a mere word, like its predecessor "infidelity," and cease to convey any obloquy.

If Science is never to go beyond its present limits; if the barriers which metaphysical speculation shows to exist are never to be transcended, then indeed we are thrown back on faith, and all the rest of the nauseous mess of mediæval superstition, and we may just as well have vital principle and creative power as not, for Science cannot help us. True, if we do not use all the methods at our disposal! But we go beyond. We admit that all mental methods known are singularly liable to illusion and inaccuracy of every sort. So were the early determinations of specific heat. Even biologists have erred. But to the true scientist every failure is a stepping-stone to success; every mistake is the key to a new truth.

And the history of our Science is the history of all Science. If you choose to ape Christendom and put the pioneers of rational investigation into the nature of consciousness on the rack (*i.e.* into lunatic asylums) I doubt not we shall find our Bruno. But it will add an additional pang that persecution should come from the house of our friends.

Let us, however, turn away from the aspect of criticism which an accidental controversy has thus caused me to notice, and so to anticipate the obvious line of attack which the more frivolous type of critic will employ, and return to our proper business, the summary of our own position with regard to Buddhism.

Buddhism is a logical development of observed facts; whoso is with me so far is *Sammaditthi*, and has taken the first step on the Noble Eightfold Path.

Let him aspire to knowledge, and the Second Step is under his feet.

The rest lies with Research.

Aum! I take my refuge holy in the Light and Peace of Buddh.
Aum! I take my refuge, slowly working out His Law of Good.
Aum! I take my refuge lowly in His Pitying Brotherhood.

# THE EXCLUDED MIDDLE; OR, THE SCEPTIC REFUTED

## A DIALOGUE BETWEEN A BRITISH MAN OF SCIENCE AND A CONVERTED HINDU

[This absurdity is a parody upon the serious essay which follows. It is an exceedingly characteristic trait that Crowley himself should have insisted upon this order, and a severe strain upon the devoted hand who try to force themselves to study him. The notes are, of course, Crowley's throughout. To elucidate the allusions would require a note to nearly every phrase. The fact seems to be that any one with universal knowledge at the tips of his fingers can read and enjoy Crowley; but few others.]

## THE EXCLUDED (OR DIVIDED) MIDDLE

*M.* Well,[1] Scepticus,[2] are[3] you[4] restored[5] to[6] health[7]? Our[8] conflict[9] of[11] yesterday[12] was[13] severe.[14]

[1] Plato, *Critias*, 214; Schopenhauer, *Die Welt als Wille und Vorstellung*, xxxii. 76; Haeckel, *Anthropogenie*, II. viii. 24; Aeschylus, *Prom. Vinct.*, 873-6; Hegel, *Logik*, lvi. 3; Robertson, *Pagan Christs*, cvii. 29; Mark ii. 8, iv. 16, x. 21; Tertullian, *Contra Marcionem*, cxv. 33; Cicero, *Pro Varrone*, iv.; *De Amicitia*, xii.; Goethe, *Faust*, I. iv. 18; Crowley, *Opera*, i. 216; R. Ischak ben Loria, *De Revolutionibus Animarum*, cci. 14 (see under קלפות, et seq., *q.v.* p. iii); O. Wilde, *Lord Arthur Savile's Crime*, ed. princ., p. 4; Lev. xvii. Further historical authority may be found in Gibbon and others.

[2] *Punch*, vols. viii., lxvi. *Cf.* Art. "Burnand" in *Dict. Nat. Biog.*, *scil.* Viz. *a-u-c*, xlvii., S. P. Q. R.

[3] From *Encyc. Brit.*, Art. "Existence," and "Buddha," Mahaparinibbana Sutta, to whom the author wishes to express his acknowledgments.

[4] This joke is the old one. Jones asks Smith, "Why are you so late?" Smith wittily answers: "Absurd! I must always come before tea; you can never come till after tea." Here "you" only comes after the "tea" in Scepticus, which shows that Scepticus was a tea-totaller. Mysticus is therefore the drinker; which proves (what Burton and all Eastern scholars affirm) that Omar Khayyam means spiritual wine and not common alcoholic beverages. *Cf.* Burton, *Kasidah: Love and Safety*, ed. princ., p. 45, &c., &c.

[5] This word needs little or no explanation.

[6] Ontogeny can only be misunderstood by thorough study of phylogeny. Crepitation of the bivalves is a concurrent phenomenon. Take away the number you first thought of, and we see that the exostoses of the melanotic pyemata by the river's brim are exostoses and nothing more.

[7] An unpleasant subject—a great comfort to think of—*vide* Wilde, *op. cit.*, and *A Woman of no Importance*. Also Krafft-Ebing, *Psychopathia Sexualis*, xx.; *The Family Doctor*; Quain, *Anatomy of Grey Matter*, cxlv. 24.

[8] The 24th part of a (solar) day.

[9] From French *con;* and Ang. Sax. *flican*, to tickle: hence, a friendly conflict.[10]

[10] See 9, above.

[11] *Vies imaginaires* (Cratès); also *Eaux-de-Vie réelles* (Martel). There is a fine model at the Louvre (Room Z, west wall), and any number of the most agreeable disposition at Julien's or Delacluze's.

[12] Distinguish from to-day and to-morrow, except in the case of Egyptian gods; from to-day and for ever, except in the case of Jesus Christ; from to-day, but not from to-morrow, in the case of the Hindustani word "kal," which may mean either—not either itself, but "to-morrow" or "yesterday," according to the context. Note the comma.

[13] From to be, verb intrans. auxil. mood indic. tense imperf. pers. 3rd.

[14] From French sévère; from Lat. severus-a-um; from Greek σαυρος, a crocodile; from Sanskrit Sar, a king. *Cf.* Persian Sar, a king; also W. African and Kentucky, "sar," master; Lat. Caesar, Germ. Kaiser, Russ. Tsar. *Cf.* Sanskrit Siva, the destroyer, or severe one.

S. Cogitavi,[1] ergo fui. To my breezy nature such a controversy as this of ours on "Tessaracts" was as the ozone-laden discharge from a Brush machine.

M. I was not aware that the termination -ozoon was connected with the allotropic form of oxygen.

S. Little boys should be seen, but not obscene.

M. Seen, no doubt for the Arabic form of Samech ; in Yetzirah Sagittarius, or Temperance in the Tarot of your ridiculous Rosicrucians.

S. No more so than your Semitic Komeike.

M. Semitic?

S. Ike for Isaac, non est dubium—

M. Quin—

S. God save His Majesty![2] but is this Midsummer Night, and are we dreaming ?

M. "There are wetter dreams!"[3] Let us discuss the Divided Middle !

S. Beware of the Water Jump !

M. Hurrah for Taliganj ! I can improve on John Peel's Map of Asia and that ere dawn. I will map you the lucubrations of the (converted) Hindu intellect upon this vital part of the Hegelian logic. Aum Shivaya vashi ![4]

S. Dulce ridentem Mysticum amabo,
    Dulce loquentem.

M. Will you not elide the 'um' ?

S. Then I were left with a bee in my breeches — worse than Plato's in his bonnet.

M. A Scottish sceptic !

S. A Wee Free, Mysticus. A gaelic-speaking Calvinist with three thousand million bawbees in my sporran and a brace of bed-ridden cattle-thieves in my kirk. So I withdraw breeks.

M. And you rely not on Plato ?

S. Verily and Amen. As the French lady exclaimed, O mon Plate !—she would not say Platon, having already got one rhyme in ' mon '—and the Italian took her up that omoplat was indeed good to support the head, wherein are ideas. But to our divided middle !

M. As I should have said before I became a Christian :[1] "O Bhavani ! be pleased graciously to bow down to thy servants : be pleased to construe our prattlings as Japas our prayers as Tapas, our mantras as Rudradarshana, our bead-tellings as Devas ! be pleased moreover to accept our Badli for Sach-bat, our Yupi for Lalitasarira, our subject—O bless our divided middle !—for thine own venerable Yoni. Aum !"

S. I am touched by your eloquence ; but Science has not said its last word on Sabapaty Swami and his application of Pranayama to the aberrations of the evolutionary retrocessions—flexomotor in type, yet sensorial in function—of the Sahasrara-Chakra, as you urged yesterday.

M. I will not press it. But in the so-affected ambulatory vibrations (as I must insist, and you practically agreed) of the lower chakras may yet be found to lie the solution of our primordial dilemma. What is the divided middle ? lest enthymeme ruin our exegesis ere it be fairly started.

S. I will answer you without further circumlocution. The laws of Thought are reducible to three : that of identity, $A$ is $A$ ; that of contradiction, $A$ is not $not$-$A$ ; and

---

[1] See Descartes, *Discours de la Méthode,* i. 1; Huxley, *Des Cartes;* and Mucksley, *Night Carts,* published San. Auth., Bombay 1902. (At this point the damned don who was writing these notes was mercifully struck by lightning. He had intended to annotate every word in this manner in order (as he supposed) to attain a reputation like that of Max Müller *et hoc genus omne.*)

[2] Auberon Quin, King of England, in a novelette called "The Napoleon of Notting Hill."

[3] Wells, "There are better dreams"; but it turns out to mean that the young man is drowned, and at Folkestone too.

[4] *Cf.* Prof. Rice. "The waters of the Hoang-Ho rushing by intoned the Kung."

[1] This is the invariable invocation used by the pious Hindu before any meditation or holy conference.

that of Excluded Middle,[1] *A* and *not-A* taken together constitute the Universe.

*M.* That is a proposition easy to criticise. What of the line of demarcation between *A* and *not-A*? To *A* it is *not-A*, I suppose; to *not-A* it is *A*.

*S.* As in defining the boundaries of nations— Gallia est divisa in partes tres — we may suppose that half the line is of *A*, and half of *not-A*.

*M.* No; for a line cannot be longitudinally split, or bifurcated in a sense parallel with itself. As Patanjali hints in his Kama Linga Sharira—that most delicate of Eastern psychologico - physiologico - philosophical satires—"Bare Sahib ne khansamah-ko bahut rupaiya diya hai."

*S.* The Ethic Dative! But your contention is true, unless we argue with Aristotle ὡκεες στρουθοι περι γας μελαιναs and so on.

*M.* I was sure you would not seriously defend so untenable a position.

*S.* The eleemosynary functions of the— Jigar, I fancy the Vedas have it—

*M.* Yes—

*S.* Forbid.

*M.* Then do you accept the conclusions of the Hegelian logic?

*S.* My logic begins with the Stagyrite and ends with a manual kunt. I shall not surrender without a struggle. I am not an Achilles to be wounded in the heel.

*M.* Then the wound is healed? Forgive me if I trespass on the preserves of Max Beerbohm,[a] and your other ripping cosmopolitan wits!

---

[1] Sir W. Hamilton's proposed quantification of the predicate would serve in this instance. We have to combine the propositions:
All *A* is all *A*.
All *A* is not all *not-A*.
No *A* is not no *not-A*.
Fantastic as it seems, this is the simplest of the eighty-four primary ways of expressing these three laws in a single proposition.
No *not-A* is not no some *not not-A*.
[a] A distinguished author on philosophical and kindred subjects. See his "works." John Lane,[b] 1894.
[b] Lane—a long one, with neither variable-

*S.* No, for I say that the line is, like the Equator, imaginary.

ness nor shadow of turning. Christian name John.[c]

[c] Not to be confused with John, the beloved disciple, who wrote "Caliban [d] on Patmos."[h]

[d] A dwarfish miscreate, celebrated in the works of Browning and Shakespeare (W.).[e]

[e] Dramatic author, flourished A.D. 1600 *circa;* wrote *The Tempest*[f], *Susannah; or, The Two Gentlemen of Veronica's Garden, The Manxman,* and other plays.

[f] A garbled version of this was misbegotten in A.D. 1904 on a London stage; the worst actor of a dreadful crew, in spite of his natural aptitude for the part of Caliban (*q.v. supra, note d*), being one Beerbohm Tree.[g]

[g] Tree, because such a stick. Beerbohm— *vide supra, note a.* I take this opportunity to introduce my system of continuous footnotes, on the analogy of continuous fractions. In this case they are recurring—a great art in itself, though an error in·so far that they fail to subserve the great object of all footnotes, viz. to distract the attention of the reader.

[h] Text appended:—

## CALIBAN ON PATMOS.
*Being the Last Adventure of the Beloved Disciple.*

[COME, kids, lambs, doves, cubs, cuddle! Hear ye John
Pronounce on the primordial protoplast Palingenetic, palæontologic,
And beat that beggar's bleeding בראשית
With truth veracious, aletheiac, true!
John ye hear. Cuddle, cubs, doves, lambs, kids, come!]

First, God made heav'n, earth: Earth gauche, void; deep, dark.
God's Ghost stirred sea. God said 'Light!' 'Twas. 'Saw light,
Good, split off dark, call'd light 'day,' dark 'night.' Eve,
Morn, day I. 'Said, "'Twixt wets be air, split wets!"
'Made air, split wets 'neath air, wets top air; so. Call'd air 'heav'n.' Eve, morn, day II. 'Said, "Low wets,
Cling close, show earth." So. 'Call'd dry 'earth,' wet 'sea.'
Rubbed hands, smacked lips, said 'good.'
[Here John was seized By order of Augustus. He maintained, In spite of the imperial holograph, "My seizer must be Caesar," with a smile: And for persisting in his paradox Was disembowelled: so Genesis got square.]

*M.* But is not imagination to be classed as either *A* or *not-A* ?

*S.* Vae victis ! as Livy says.    I admit it.

*M.* And its products ?

*S.* Me miserum !    I cannot deny it.

*M.* Such as lines ?    Namo Shivaya namaha Aum—to quote our holiest philosopher.

*S.* I am done.    But no !    I can still argue :

  (a) There is no line of demarcation.

  (b) There is a line, but it does not exist.

  (c) There is more than one line—since it is not straight and so cannot enclose a space—and *more than one thing* cannot form part of a universe, since unus implies a whole.

*M.* I should reply :

  (a) It is true that there is no line of demarcation, but that that non-existing line is after all just as much a part of the (non-existing) universe as any other non-existing thing.

   We divide the universe into

    (1) Existing things.

    (2) Non-existing things.

   If *A* exists, the line must be *not-A :* and vice versa.

   Which we know to be false.

  (b) It is true that there is a line, and that it does not exist, but—

*S.* Let us settle (a) first, and return at leisure.    You fail utterly to make the important distinction between mere absence of line and presence of a non-existing line, which is as gross a fallacy as to argue that a man who has gone out to lunch has been annihilated.

*M.* But he *has* been annihilated, from the point of view of the emptiness of his bungalow.

*S.* No ! for the traces of his presence remain and will do so for ever.

*M.* Then a mehta's broom may be as mortal as a femme-de-ménage !

*S.* A trois : πατηρ—ὑιος, the λογος—and πνευμα ἁγιον.

*M.* Then you surrender?    The tripartite anatomy of Tat Sat is granted me ?    Hegel is God, and Zoroaster his prophet ?    " The mind of the Father said ' Into 3 !' and immediately all things w e r e so divided ! " ?

*S.* Arrahmanu arrahimu al maliku al qadusu as salamu—Vete cabron !    Chinga su madre !    I give in on that issue.

*M.* Alhamdolillah !    For there are four letters in Allah الله.    A for Ab—Father, L for Logos—double, for he is both God and man, and H for Holy Ghost.

*S.* The language of your Notariqon is tripartite too !    On point (1) though, 'twas but by a slip.    I fell : I was not pushed. Can you controvert my second defence ?

*M.* It is not a defence at all.    It is a trick to lure me away from the question.    I admit that there is such a line, and that it does not exist—but might it not *negatively subsist,* in the Ain, as it were?    Further, whether it is or is not a concept, a noumenon, a psychosis, an idea — anything !    does not matter.    For since it is a subject with or without predicates and the possibility of predicates, they are themselves predicates [1] which copulate with it even the impossibility of assigning predicates to it, with the exception—you are bound to urge!—of itself.    But this would violate your law of identity, that a predicate should exclude itself from its own category, even were it non-existent, inconceivable, bum.    Consequently, thinkable or unthinkable, our creation of it subjectively has fixed it eternally in the immeasurable void.

*S.* Your argument is as convincing as it is lucid.    But to my third fortress !

*M.* Dorje Vajra Samvritti !    As to your third line of defence, I must admit that my difficulties are considerable.    Yet, Bhavani my aid, I will essay them.    You said, I think—

*S.* There is more than one line, since the line is not straight (otherwise it could not enclose a space).

*M.* I do not see this !

*S.* A curved line is not truly a line, since

[1] *Litera scripta manet.*    Do not steal it, or *tertia poena manet.*

a line must have length without breadth, and a curved line may certainly have breadth, for it need not lie in one plane.[1]

*M.* True.

*S.* Hence we may conclude that the line of demarcation between *A* and *not-A* is many and not one. Now an universe is that which turns to one,[2] when truly considered. Our line does the reverse of this, for it appeared one at first, and split up on examination.

*M.* Exactly ; but that is where I have you in a corner.

*S.* Dollar wheat ! Dollar wheat ! Dollar wheat !

*M.* It is the ' reverse ' which does you.[3] If you turn a man fourth-dimensionally round, his hemispherical ganglia will prove interchangeable ?

*S.* No doubt, for they are symmetrical.

*M.* His polygonal fissures are identical with themselves ?

*S.* I admit it, for they are ambidextrous.

*M.* His hypertrophied constrictor Cunni will feel nothing ?

*S.* No ; it is medial.

*M.* Then how is he changed ?

---

[1] The mathematical proof of this is simple. A surface is composed of an infinite number of parallel straight lines touching each other. Now for parallel straight lines place a single convoluted chortoid with a parabolic direction of $\pi^{n-\theta} + n^{\theta-\pi}$. At all the foci will be ellipses of the form $\dfrac{(n-1)(n+m+1)\sqrt{-1}}{(p+v) \pm \sin^{\theta-1}\cos a}$. Now since $p+v$ is in this case unity and $m=n$, we have—

$$\left\{ \frac{c[\tan\theta - O\cos(\pi+a)\sqrt{-\pi}]c\sin\theta\, e^{i\theta} - e\,\theta^\pi + K}{[c\cos\theta + u\sin\theta][u\tan\theta + t\sec\theta]} \right\}^{-1}$$

If the chortoid lie in one plane this expression $=0$; but if not, it $= \sin\theta^{-1}\cos\theta^{-2}$, $\theta$ being the angle subtended by the common arc of the original curve, by Halley's theorem, or $\sin\dfrac{\theta}{\pi}$, in which case the expression is unreal, and may be neglected.

[2] Two or more things cannot form part of any one thing, in so far as they remain two. Considered in relation to that of which they form part, they become fractions.

[3] *Cf.* A. B. Douglas, *Reminiscences.*

---

*S.* Fourth-dimensionally ; no more.

*M.* Yet his right optic nerve will see through his left eye ?

*S.* Of course.

*M.* Then of an event, an argument, a dialectic euhemerism, protoplasmic or blastodermic ?

*S.* I see what you mean. You would say that duality irresolvable into unity has no parallel in the regions of pure intelligence, seeks no corollary from the intuitive organic reactions of the hyperbolic cells ?[1]

*M.* I would.

*S.* The devil you would !

*M.* I would. Our line becomes single ?

*S.* In the higher sense.

*M.* So that the Mind of the Father riding on the subtle guiders got it right after all ?

*S.* Pretty right.

*M.* And all things are divisible into Three, not into Two ?

*S.* Into *A*, *not-A*, and the dividing line.

*M.* Though the Reason of Man has boggled often enough at this, the intuition of Woman has always perceived it.

*S.* But she has gone too far, placing the importance of that dividing middle above all other things in earth or heaven. We hold the balance fair and firm.

*M.* (*glad*). How blessed is this day, Scepticus !

*S.* (*Conceding the point, and catching the glow*). Let us make a night of it !

*M.* (*Enjoying his triumph*). We will. Do not forget twilight !

*S.* (*In holy rapture*). Into Three, Mysticus, into Three !

*M.* (*Ditto, only more so*). Glory be to the Father, and to the Son, and to the Holy Ghost.

*S.* (*In the trance called Nerodha-Samapatti*). As it was in the beginning, is now, and ever shall be, world without end.

*M.* (*Ditto, after an exhilarating switchback ride through the Eight High Trances*). AMEN.

[1] Both colloid, caudate, and epicycloid, of course.

# TIME *

## A DIALOGUE BETWEEN A BRITISH SCEPTIC AND AN INDIAN MYSTIC

" He (Shelley) used to say that he had lived three times as long as the calendar gave out, which he would prove between jest and earnest by some remarks on Time—
'That would have puzzled that stout Stagyrite.'"
—*Prefix to the " Wandering Jew" in " Fraser's Magazine."*

[The philosophical premises of this and the other essays in this volume should be studied in

Keynes. Formal Logic.
Erdmann. History of Philosophy.
Berkeley. Three Dialogues κ.τ.λ.
Hume. Works.
Kant. Prolegomena: Critique of Pure Reason.
Locke. Human Understanding.
Huxley. Essays (Philosophical).

Patanjali. Aphorisms.
Bhikkhu Ananda Metteya. Essays (principally in the quarterly " Buddhism ").
The Tao Teh King and the Writings of Kwang Tze.
The Sufis, to whom chiefly Crowley is indebted for the foundations of his system of sceptical mysticism.]

## TIME.

A DIALOGUE BETWEEN A BRITISH SCEPTIC AND AN INDIAN MYSTIC.

*Scepticus.* Well, my dear Babu, I trust you have slept well after our fatiguing talk of yesterday.

*Mysticus.* Ah, dear Mister, if you will forgive my adopting what is evidently your idiom, I found it, on the contrary, invigorating. What is it the Psalmist says? That the conversation of the wise is like unto good wine, which intoxicates with delight, while it hurts not the drinker? The balm of your illustrious words, borne like spice upon the zephyr——

*Scept.* Shall we not rather renew our inquiries into the nature of things, than, in unfertile compliment, waste the few hours we snatch awhile from death?

*Myst.* Willingly. But lately you were the " sahib" asking questions concerning Indian Philosophy as a great prince who should condescend to study the habits of horses or dogs —yesterday we changed all that.

*Scept.* I have but one apology to offer— that of Dr. Johnson.[1]

*Myst.* Pray forbear! Yet it may be for a moment instructive to notice the consideration which led you to assume a happier attitude; viz., that such identities of thought (implying such fine parallelisms of brain structure) were discovered, that, in short, you admitted the Indian (as you have been compelled to admit the Gibbon)[2] to classification in your own genus.

*Scept.* You are hard upon my insolence.

*Myst.* Only to make the opportunity of remarking a further parallelism: that the said insolence is matched, maybe surpassed, by my own. A witty Irishman, indeed, observed of the natives of the Tongue of Asia that "the Hindu, with all his faults, was civilised, like the Frenchman: the Musul-

[1] Taunted with having described a horse's "pastern" as his "knee," the great lexicographer pleaded "Ignorance, Madam, pure ignorance."
[2] See Huxley, "Man's Place in Nature," and elsewhere.

* It must not be supposed that the author of this dialogue *necessarily* concurs in the views of either disputant, even where they are agreed.—A. C.

man, with all his virtues, was, like the Englishman, a savage."

And indeed we are too apt to think of you only as red-faced, drunken, beef-eating boors and ruffians, with no soul and less sense, as if you were all soldiers; or as prim, conceited, supercilious, opinionated prigs, as if you were all civilians; or as unspeakable stupidity incarnate in greedy oiliness, as if you were all missionaries. Your highest placed women make virtuous our courtezans by a comparison of costume and manners; if our advices be true, the morality test is still in favour of our light ones. Your law wisely forbids your own venal women to set foot on Indian soil; a rumour is even got about that you have no such women: but political economy is to be thanked, if it be so.[1] Now, though you know that I am aware that India is simply the refuse-heap for your vilest characters and your dullest brains, I see that you so little appreciate the compliment I am trying to pay you, that your foot is already itching to assault my person, and to cause me to remember that your cook never forgets to spit into your honour's soup, were it not that we may find a refuge from difference of caste and race, custom and language, in the supreme unity, that of the ultimate force of which this universe is the expression.

*Scept.* I have listened with patience to what is after all (you must admit) a rather spiteful tirade——

*Myst.* Forgive me if I interrupt. Do me the honour to remember that it was said in self-blame. I tried to give your honour "the giftie" (as one of your worst poets has said) "to see yoursel as ithers see you," the "ithers" in this case being average Hindus, as ignorant of your real character as you confess your untravelled folk to be of ours.

*Scept.* Pray spare me Burns! We are— that is, you and I—on a better understanding now. Let us return, if you will, to the sub-

ject we too lightly touched on yesterday; that of TIME, and the real signification of that mysterious word, which is in the mouths of children, and which to affect not to understand is to stamp oneself, in the opinion of the so-called intellectual classes, as a fantastic.

*Myst.* Yet who of us does understand it? I, at least, am at one with you in declaring its mystery.

*Scept.* You are of the few. Even Huxley, the most luminous of modern philosophers, evidently misunderstands Kant's true though partial dictum that it is subjective, or, in the pre-Kantian jargon, a form of the intellect.

*Myst.* Lest we involve ourselves in controversy, Homeric body-snatchers of Patroclus Kant, let us hastily turn to the question at issue itself. The scholastic method of discussing a point by quotation of Brown's position against Smith may do for the weevilly brain of a University don, but is well known to bring one no nearer to solution, satisfactory or otherwise, of the original problem.

*Scept.* I heartily agree with you so far. We will therefore attack the question *ab initio*: I await you.

*Myst.* As exordium, therefore, may I ask you to recall what we agreed on yesterday with regard to *Tat Sat*, the existent, or real?

*Scept.* That it was one, unknowable, absolute.

*Myst.* Objective?

*Scept.* Without doubt.

*Myst.* Did I not, however, observe that, however that might be, all intuitions, if knowable, were subjective; if objective, unknown?

*Scept.* You did: to which I pointed out that Spencer had well shown how subjectivity, real or no, was a mere proof of objectivity.

*Myst.* And *vice versâ*.[1] Ah! my friend, we shall be tossed about, as the world this 2500 years, if we once enter this vortex. Let us remain where all is smooth in the certainty that the Unknowable is Unreal!

*Scept.* We agreed it to be real!

---

[1] *Cf.* Crowley, *Epigrams* (1550 A.D.)—

" The bawds of the stews be turnèd al out;
But some think they inhabit al England
    throughout."—A. C.

[1] This is not an *ignoratio elenchi*, but a criticism, too extended in scope to introduce here.—A. C.

*Myst.* Oh never ! The word " real " implies to us subjectivity ; a thing is only real *to us* so far as it is known by us ; even its Unknowability is a species of knowledge of it : and, by Savitri ! when I say real *to us*, I say real absolutely, since all things lie to me in the radius of my sensorium. " To others " is a vain phrase,——

*Scept.* True ; for those " others " only exist for you inasmuch as, and in so far as, they are modifications of your own thought-stuff.[1]

*Myst.* Agreed, then ; instead of looking through the glasses of the metaphysician, we will content ourselves with the simpler task of measuring our thoughts by the only standard which is unquestionably valid, *i.e.*, consciousness.

*Scept.* But if that consciousness deceive us ?

*Myst.* We are the more deceived ! But it is after all indifferent ; for it is we who are deceived. Idle to pretend that any other standard can ever be of any use to us, since all others are referred to it !

*Scept.* Ah ! this is equally a branch of the former argument.

*Myst.* That is so. However, we may defer consideration of this problem, though I suspect that it will sooner or later force itself upon our notice.

*Scept.* No doubt. This is very possibly the ultimate unknown and infinite quantity, which lurks unsuspected in all equations, and vitiates our most seeming-certain results.

*Myst.* But, for Heaven's sake, let us postpone it as long as possible, eh ?

*Scept.* Indeed, it is the devil of a subject. But we wander far—By the way, how old are you ? You appear young, but you know much.

*Myst.* You are too polite. I am but an ultimate truth, six world-truths, fourteen grand generalisations, eighty generalisations, sixty-two dilemmas, and the usual odd million impressions.

*Scept.* What is all this? You are surely—

*Myst.* No, most noble Festus.    Put me

[1] The physical basis of thought, as distinguished from its physical mechanism. A Hindu conception. Sanskrit, C h i t t a m.

to the test, and I the matter will reword : which madness would gambol from.[1]    How old may your honour be ?

*Scept.* Forty-five years.

*Myst.* Excuse the ignorance of a " Babu," but as Mr. Chesterton[2] well knows, we do

[1] I am not mad, most noble Festus.    Acts xxvi. 25.    The rest is from *Hamlet*.    There are many other such apt or perverted quotations in the essay.

[2] MR. CROWLEY AND THE CREEDS

AND

THE CREED OF MR. CHESTERTON

WITH A POSTSCRIPT ENTITLED

## A CHILD OF EPHRAIM *

*CHESTERTON'S COLOSSAL COLLAPSE*

————

MR. CROWLEY AND THE CREEDS

BY G. K. CHESTERTON

Mr. Aleister Crowley publishes a work, " The Sword of Song : Called by Christians ' The Book of the Beast,' " and called, I am ashamed to say, " Ye Sword of Song " on the cover, by some singularly uneducated man. Mr. Aleister Crowley has always been, in my opinion, a good poet ; his " Soul of Osiris," written during an Egyptian mood, was better poetry than this Browningesque rhapsody in a Buddhist mood ; but this also, though very affected, is very interesting.    But the main fact about it is that it is the expression of a man who has really found Buddhism more satisfactory than Christianity.

Mr. Crowley begins his poem, I believe, with an earnest intention to explain the beauty of the Buddhist philosophy ; he knows a great deal about it ; he believes in it.    But as he went on writing one thing became stronger and stronger in his soul — the living hatred of Christianity.    Before he has finished he has descended to the babyish " difficulties " of the Hall of Science — things about " the plain words of your sacred books," things about " the panacea of belief "—things, in short, at which any philosophical Hindoo would roll about with laughter.    Does Mr. Crowley suppose that Buddhists do not feel the poetical nature of the books of a religion ?    Does he suppose that they do not realise the immense

* The children of Ephraim, being armed, and carrying bows, turned them back in the day of battle.

not easily grasp Western ideas. What is a "year"?

*Scept.* Hm! Well, ah, the earth moves round——

*Myst.* How long have you been a sectary astronomical?

*Scept.* Er—what?

*Myst.* You are then an astronomer?

importance of believing the truth? But Mr. Crowley has got something into his soul stronger even than the beautiful passion of the man who believes in Buddhism; he has the passion of the man who does not believe in Christianity. He adds one more testimony to the endless series of testimonies to the fascination and vitality of the faith. For some mysterious reason no man can contrive to be agnostic about Christianity. He always tries to prove something about it—that it is unphilosophical or immoral or disastrous—which is not true. He can never say simply that it does not convince him—which is true.

A casual carpenter wandered about a string of villages and suddenly a horde of rich men and sceptics and Sadducees and respectable persons rushed at him and nailed him up like vermin; then people saw that he was a god. He had proved that he was not a common man, for he was murdered. And ever since his creed has proved that it is not a common hypothesis, for it is hated.

Next week I hope to make a fuller study of Mr. Crowley's interpretation of Buddhism, for I have not room for it in this column to-day. Suffice it for the moment to say that if this be indeed a true interpretation of the creed, as it is certainly a capable one, I need go no further than its pages for examples of how a change of abstract belief might break a civilisation to pieces. Under the influence of this book earnest modern philosophers may, I think, begin to perceive the outlines of two vast and mystical philosophies, which if they were subtly and slowly worked out in two continents through many centuries, might possibly, under special circumstances, make the East and West almost as different as they really are.

## THE CREED OF MR. CHESTERTON
### By Aleister Crowley

When a battle is all but lost and won, the victor is sometimes aware of a brilliancy and dash in the last forlorn hope which was lacking in those initial manœuvres which decided the fortune of the day.

Hence comes it that Our Reviewer's apology for Christianity compares so favourably with the methods of ponderous blunder on which people like Paley and Gladstone have relied. But alas! the very vivacity of the attack may leave the column without that support which might enable it, if checked, to retire in good order; and it is with true pity for a gallant opponent—who would be wiser to surrender—that I find myself compelled to despatch half a squadron (no more!) to take him in flank.

Our Author's main argument for the Christian religion is that it is hated. To bring me as a witness to this colossal enthymeme, he has the sublime courage to state that my "Sword of Song" begins with an effort to expound Buddhism, but that my hatred of Christianity overcame me as I went on, and that I end up literally raving. My book is possibly difficult in many ways, but only Mr. Chesterton would have tried to understand it by reading it backward.

Repartee apart, it is surely an ascertainable fact that while the first 29 pages [*] are almost exclusively occupied with an attack on Christianity as bitter and violent as I can make it, the remaining 161 are composed of (a) an attack on materialism, (b) an essay in metaphysics opposing advaitism, (c) an attempt to demonstrate the close analogy between the canonical Buddhist doctrine and that of modern Agnostics. None of these [†] deal with Christianity at all, save for a chance and casual word.

I look forward with pleasure to a new History of England, in which it will be pointed out how the warlike enthusiasm aroused by the Tibetan expedition led to the disastrous plunge into the Boer War; disastrous because the separation of the Transvaal which resulted therefrom left us so weak that we fell an easy prey to William the Conqueror. Our Novelist should really make a strong effort to materialise his creation in "The Napoleon of Notting Hill" of the gentlemen weeping by the graves of their descendants.

Any sound philosophy must be first destructive of previous error, then constructive by harmonising truths into Truth.

Nor can the human mind rest content with negation; I honour him rather whose early emotion is hatred of Christianity, bred of compulsion to it, but who subdues that negative passion, and forces his way to a positive creed, were it but the cult of Kali or Priapus. Here, indeed, modern Agnostics are at fault. They sensibly enough reject error; but they are over-proud of their lofty attitude, and, letting slip the real problems of life, busy themselves with side-issues, or try to satisfy the spiritual part of the brain (which needs food like any other part) with the husks of hate.

[*] Pp. 144–163 in this volume.
[†] Pp. 164–184, 233–243, and 244–261 respectively, in this volume.

*Scept.* I? Goodness gracious bless my soul, no!

*Myst.* Then how do you know all this about the earth?

How few among us can reach the supreme sanity of Dr. Henry Maudsley in such a book as " Life in Mind and Conduct "!

Hence I regard Agnosticism as little more than a basis of new research into spiritual facts, to be conducted by the methods won for us by men of science. I would define myself as an agnostic with a future.

But to the enthymeme itself. A word is enough to expose it.

Other things have been hated before and since Christ lived—if he lived. Slavery was hated. A million men * died about it, and it was cast out of everywhere but the hearts of men.† Euripides hated Greek religion, and he killed the form thereof. Does Our Logician argue from these facts the vitality of slavery or Delphi? Yes, perhaps, when Simon Legree and the Pythoness were actually making money, but to argue their eternal truth, or even their value at that time, is a further and a false step. Does the fact that a cobra is alive prove it to be innocuous?

With the reported murder of Jesus of Nazareth I am not concerned ; but Vespasian's " Ut puto Deus fio " is commonly thought to have been meant as a jest.

Our Romanticist's unique and magnificent dramatisation of the war between the sceptic or lover of truth, and the religious man or lover of life, may be well quoted against me. Though Vespasian did jest, though Christ's " It is finished " were subjectively but the cry of his physical weakness, like Burton's " I am a dead man," it is no less true that millions have regarded it as indeed a cry of triumph. That is so, subjectively for them, but no more, and the one fact does not alter the other.

Surely Our Fid. Def. will find little support in this claim on behalf of death. We all die ; it was the Resurrection and Ascension which stamped Christ as God. Our Philosopher will, I think, fight shy of these events. The two thieves were "nailed up like vermin" on either side of Christ by precisely the same people ; are they also gods? To found a religion on the fact of death, murder though it were, is hardly more than African fetichism. Does death prove more than life? Will Mr. Chesterton never be happy until he is hanged?

These then are the rear-guard actions of his retiring and beaten army.

*Scept.* Astronomers are paid, insufficiently paid, it is true, but still paid, to calculate the movements of the various heavenly bodies. These, being regular, or regularly irregular,

The army itself is pretty well out of sight. There is a puff of artillery from afar to the effect that " no man can contrive to be agnostic about Christianity." This is very blank cartridge. Who is agnostic about the shape of the earth? Who prides himself upon a profound reserve about the colour of a blue pig, or hesitates to maintain that grass is green? Unless under the reservation that both subject and predicate are Unknowable in their essence, and that the copula of identity is but a convention—a form of Agnosticism which after all means nothing in this connection, for the terms of the criticism require the same reservation.

Our Tamburlaine's * subsequent remark that the poor infidel (failing in his desperate attempt to be agnostic) " tries to prove something untrue" is a *petitio principii* which would be a blunder in a schoolboy ; but in a man of Our Dialectician's intelligence can only be impudence.

The main army, as I said, is out of sight. There is, however, a cloud of dust on the horizon which may mark its position. " Does Mr. Crowley suppose that the Buddhists do not feel the poetical nature of the books of religion?" I take this to mean : " You have no business to take the Bible literally ! "

I have dealt with this contention at some length in the " Sword of Song " itself (Ascension Day, lines 216-247): but here I will simply observe that a poem which authorises the Archbishop of Canterbury to convey Dr. Clifford's pet trowels, and makes possible the Gilbertian (in the old sense of pertaining to W. S. Gilbert) position of the Free Kirk to-day, is a poem which had better be burnt, as the most sensible man of his time proposed to do with Homer, or at least left to the collector, as I believe is the case with the publications of the late Isidore Liseux. Immoral is indeed no word for it. It is as criminal as the riddle in " Pericles."

That Our Pantosympatheticist is himself an Agnostic does not excuse him. True, if every one thought as he does there would be no formal religion in the world, but only that individual communion of the consciousness with its self-consciousness which constitutes genuine religion, and should never inflame passion or inspire intolerance, since the non-Ego lies beyond its province.

But he knows as well as I do that there are thousands in this country who would gladly

---

* In the American Civil War, 1861-64. But they were not men, only Americans.
† This is mere rhetoric. Crowley was perfectly familiar with the conditions of "free" wage labour.

---

* Not to confuse with Tambourine or alter into Tamburlesque.

which comes to the same thing, serve us as standards of time.

*Myst.* A strange measure! What is the comparison in one of your poets between "Fifty years of Europe" and "a cycle of Cathay"?

*Scept.* You know our poets well.

* *Myst.* Among my loose tags of thought are several thousand useless quotations. I would give much to have my memory swept and garnished.

*Scept.* Seven other devils wait at the door. But you were saying?

*Myst.* That an astronomer might perhaps justly compute the time during which his eye was actually at the telescope by the motion of the planets, or by the clockwork of his reflector, but that you should do so is absurd.

*Scept.* Yet all men do so and have ever done so.

see him writhing in eternal torture — that physiological impossibility—for his word "a casual carpenter," albeit he wrote it in reverence. That is the kind of Christian I would hang. The Christian who can write as Our Champion of Christendom does about his faith is innocuous and pleasant, though in my heart I am compelled to class him with the bloodless desperadoes of the "Order of the White Rose" and the "moutons enragés" that preach revolution in Hyde Park.

When he says that he will trace "the outlines of two vast and mystical philosophies, which if they were subtly and slowly worked out, &c., &c.," he is simply thrown away on Nonconformity; and I trust I do not go too far, as the humblest member of the Rationalist Press Association, when I suggest that that diabolical body would be delighted to bring out a sixpenny edition of his book. I am not fighting pious opinions. But there are perfectly definite acts which encroach upon the freedom of the individual: indefensible in themselves, they seek apology in the Bible, which is now to be smuggled through as a "poem." If I may borrow my adversary's favourite missile, a poem in this sense is "unhistorical nonsense."

We should, perhaps, fail to appreciate the beauty of the Tantras if the Government (on their authority) enforced the practices of hook-swinging and Sati, and the fact that the cited passages were of doubtful authority, and ambiguous at that, would be small comfort to our grilled widows and lacerated backs.

Yet this is the political condition of England

*Myst.* And all are absurd in doing so, if they really do so, which I doubt. Even the lowest dimly, or perhaps automatically, perceive the folly thereof——

*Scept.* As?

*Myst.* A man will say "Since the Derby was run" more intelligibly than "since May such-and-such a day"; for his memory is of the race, not of a particular item in the ever changing space-relation of the heavens, a relation which he can never know, and of which he can never perceive the significance: nay, which he can never recognise, even by landmarks of catastrophic importance.

*Scept.* One might be humorous on this subject by the hour. Picture to yourself a lawyer cross-examining a farm hand as to the time of an occurrence: "Now, Mr. Noakes, I must warn you to be very careful. Had Herschell occulted α Centauri before you left Farmer Stubbs' field?" while the instructed swain should not blush to reply at this hour. You invoke a "casual camel-driver" to serve your political ends and prevent me having eighteen wives as against four: I prove him an impostor, and you call my attention to the artistic beauty of Ya Sin. I point out that Ya Sin says nothing about four wives, and you say that all moral codes limit the number. I ask you why all this fuss about Mohammed, in that case, and you write all my sentences—and your own—Qabalistically backwards, and it comes out: "Praise be to Allah for the Apostle of Allah, and for the Faith of Islam. And the favour of Allah upon him, and the peace!"

War, I think, if those be the terms.

## POSTSCRIPT

War under certain conditions becomes a question of pace, and I really cannot give my cavalry so much work as Our Brer Rabbit would require. On the appearance of the first part of his article "Mr. Crowley and the Creeds" I signified my intention to reply. It aborted his attack on me, and he has not since been heard of.

*In the midst of the words he was trying to say,*
*In the midst of his laughter and glee,*
*He has softly and suddenly vanished away—*

I suppose I always was a bit of a Boojum!

that Halley's Comet, being the sole measure of time in use on his farm, was 133° S., entering Capricorn, at the very moment of the blow being struck.

*Myst.* I am glad you join me in ridicule of the scheme; but do you quite grasp how serious the situation has become?

*Scept.* I confess I do not see whither you would lead me. Your own computation strikes one as fantastic in the extreme.

*Myst.* Who knows? Think, yourself, of certain abnormal and pathological phenomena, whose consideration might lay down the bases for a possible argument.

*Scept.* There are several things that spring instantly into the mind. First and foremost is the wonderfully suggestive work, misnamed fiction, of our greatest novelist, H. G. Wells. This man, the John Bunyan of modern scientific thought, has repeatedly attacked the problem, or at least indicated the lines on which a successful research might be prosecuted, in many of his wonderful tales. He has (I say it not to rob you of the honour of your discoveries, but in compliment, and I can imagine none higher) put his finger on the very spot whence all research must begin: the illusionary nature of the time-idea. But I will leave you to study his books at your leisure, and try to give a more direct answer to your question. We have cases of brain disorder, where grave local mischief survives the disappearance of general symptoms. One man may forget a year of his life; another the whole of it; while yet another may have odd patches effaced here and there, while the main current flows undisturbed.

*Myst.* He is so much the poorer for such losses?

*Scept.* Certainly.

*Myst.* Did the stars efface their tracks to correspond?

*Scept.* Joshua is dead.

*Myst.* Yama [1] be praised!

*Scept.* Amen.

*Myst.* You have also, I make no doubt,

[1] The Hindu Pluto.

cases where the brain, from infancy, never develops.

*Scept.* True: so that a man of thirty thinks and acts like a child: often like a stupid child. Our social system is indeed devised to provide for these cases; so common are they: the Army, the Cabinet, are reserved for such: in the case of women thus afflicted they are called "advanced" or "intellectual": the advantages of these situations and titles is intended to compensate them for Nature's neglect. Even sadder is it when young men of great parts and talent, flourishing up to a certain age, have their brains gradually spoiled by the preposterous system of education in vogue throughout the more miasmal parts of the country, till they are fit for nothing but "chairs" and "fellowships" at "universities." The schools of philosophy are full of these Pliocene anachronisms, as the responsible government departments are of the congenitally afflicted: in both cases thinking men are disposed to deny (arguing from the absence of human reason and wit, though some of the creatures have a curious faculty resembling the former, shorn of all light-quality) to these unfortunates any conscious life worthy of the name, or the capacity to increase with years in the wisdom or happiness of their more favoured fellow-creatures.

*Myst.* Yet the stars have a regular rate of progression?

*Scept.* I see what you would be at. You would say that of two men born on a day, dying on a day, one may be young, the other old.

*Myst.* Ay! But I would say this to vitiate the standard you somewhat incautiously set up.

*Scept.* Abrogate it then! But where are we?

*Myst.* Here, that we may determine this most vital point; how so to act that we may obtain the most from life; or, if existence, the word of which intuitions are the letters, be, as the Buddhists pretend, misery, how to obtain the least from it.

*Scept.* Let us not speak ill of a noble

religion, though we lament the paradoxical follies of its best modern professors !

*Myst.* A truce to all controversy, then. How shall we obtain the best from life? It is this form of the question that should give you a clue to my goal.

*Scept.* It is so difficult to determine whether Sherlock Holmes [1] is dead or no that I will take no risks. But the answer to your query is obvious. *He lives the longest who remembers most.*

*Myst.* Insufficient. There are lives full of the dreariest incident, like a farmyard novel, or a window in Thrums, or the autobiography of the Master of a College, [2] who lives ninety years and begets sons and daughters, and there is an end of him by-and-by, and the world is nor richer nor poorer, scarce for an anecdote ! Add to your "number of impressions remembered" (and therefore not expunged) the vividness of each impression !

*Scept.* As a coefficient rather. Let us construct a scale of vividness from $a$ to $n$, and we can erect a formula to express all that a Man is. For example he might be : $10a + 33125b + 890c + 800112658e + 992f + \ldots\ldots + \ldots\ldots + \ldots\ldots n$, and, if we can find the ratio of $a : b : c : d : e : f : \ldots\ldots : n$, we can resolve the equation into a single term, and compare man and man.

*Myst.* I catch the idea. Fanciful as it of course is in practice, the theory is sound to the core. You delight me !

*Scept.* Not at all, not at all. Further, I see that since the memory is a storehouse of limited capacity, it follows that he who can remember most is he who can group and generalise most. How easy is it to conjugate your Hindustani verbs ! Because one rule covers a thousand cases. How impossible is it to learn German genders ! Because the gender of each word must be committed arbitrarily to memory.

[1] A detective in sensational fiction of the period.
[2] The gibe is at Butler, Master of Trinity during Crowley's residence.

*Myst.* He then is the longest-lived, and the wisest, and the worthiest of respect, who can sum up all in one great generalisation?

*Scept.* So Spencer defines philosophy : as the art of doing this.

*Myst.* But you leave out this "vividness." He is greater who generalised the data of evolution than he who did the same thing for heraldry : not only because of the number of facts covered, but because of the greater intrinsic value and interest of each fact. Not only, moreover, is the philosopher who can sum up the observations "All men are mortal," "All horses are mortal," "All trees are mortal," and their like, into the one word Anicca, as did Buddha, a wise and great man ; but Aeschylus is also wise and great, who from this universal, but therefore commonplace generalisation, selects and emphasises the particular "Oedipus is mortal."

*Scept.* Your Greek is perhaps hardly equal to your English ; but you are perfectly right, and I do wrong to smile. Since we agree to abandon the mechanical device of the astronomer, all states of consciousness are single units, or time-marks, by which we measure intervals. That some, no longer than others, are more notable, just as the striking of a clock emphasises the hours, though the escapement maintains its rate, is the essential fact in counting.

*Myst.* And what is the test of vividness?

*Scept.* I should say the durability of the memory thereof.

*Myst.* No doubt ; it is then of importance to class these states of "high potential" —— may I borrow the term?

*Scept.* It is a suggestive one, though I must say I am opposed to the practice of Petticoat Lane in philosophical literature. The broad-minded Huxley's aversion to "polarity" is not his least bequest to psychologists. Of course, to begin our classification, all states of normal waking consciousness stand in a class above any other——

*Myst.* I have known dreams——

*Scept.* Wells says : "There are better

dreams !"—and a damned good way to look at death, by heaven !

*Myst.* Yes ! But I meant that some dreams are more vivid than some waking states, even adult states hours long. You remember the " Flying dream," though I daresay you have not experienced it since childhood : it is part of your identity, a shape or defining idea of your mind : but you have forgotten the picnic at—where you will.

*Scept.* There is something to be thankful for in that. Then, there are incidents of sport——

*Myst.* Mysteries of initiation——

*Scept.* Narrow escapes——

*Myst.* The presence of death ——

*Scept.* Shocks——

*Myst.* Some incidents of earliest childhood——

*Scept.* Memories which can be classed, and therefore fall under great headings ; intellectual victories——

*Myst.* Religious emotions——

*Scept.* Ah ! this minute too, for I group them ! All these are intuitions which come near, which touch, which threaten, which alarm, the Ego itself !

*Myst.* Yet in those great ecstasies of love, poetry, and their like ; the Ego is altogether abased, absorbed in the belovèd : the phenomenon is utterly objective.

*Scept.* To be abased is to be exalted. But we are again at metaphysics. The Ego and the Non-Ego are convertible terms. We are agreed that one of the two is a myth ; but we might argue for months and aeons as to which of the two it is.

*Myst.* Here Hindu practice bears out Western speculation, whether we take the shadowy idealism of Berkeley, or the self-refuted [1] Monism of Haeckel. All these men got our results, and interpreted them in the partial light of their varied intellect, their diverse surrounding and education. But the result is the same physiological pheno-

menon, from Plato and Christ to Spinoza and Çankaracharya,[1] from Augustine and Abelard, Boehme and Weigel in their Christian communities to Trismegistus and Porphyry, Mohammed and Paracelsus in their mystic palaces of Wisdom, the doctrine is essentially one : and its essence is that existence is one. But to my experience it is certain that in Dhyana the Ego is rejected.

*Scept.* Before inquiring further of you : What is this Dhyana ? let me say, in view of what you have just urged : How do you know that the Ego is rejected ?

*Myst.* Peccavi. My leanings are Buddhistic, I will confess : indeed, the great majority of Eastern philosophers, arguing *à priori* from the indestructibility of the Ego—a dogma, say I, and no more !—have asserted that in the Dhyanic state the Object is lost in the Ego rather than *vice versâ*, and they support this conclusion by the fact of the glorification of the object.

*Scept.* But this is all *à priori*. For be it supposed that Dhyana is merely a state of more correct perception of the nature of the object than that afforded by normal inspection —and this is a reasonable view !—the argument simply goes to prove that matter, as the Ego, is divine. And this is our old vicious circle !

*Myst.* Also, since the object may be the Infinite. All Dhyana proves is that " things are not what they seem."

*Scept.* Not content with our poets, you seem to have wandered into Longfellow.

*Myst.* Also Tennyson.

*Scept.* I can sympathise : there is a blot on my own scutcheon. You are just, though, in your statement that the glorification of one of two factors——

*Myst.* At the moment of the disappearance of their dividuality——

*Scept.* So ?

*Myst.* Surely. They also themselves disappear, just as carbon, the black solid, and

[1] Haeckel, postulating a unity, is compelled to ascribe to it a tendency to dividuality, thus stultifying his postulate. See the " Riddle of the Universe."

[1] Hindu reformer (about 1000 A.D.), who raised the cult of Shiva from that of a local phallic deity to that of an universal God. The Tamil Isaiah.

chlorine, the green gas, combine to form a limpid and colourless liquid. So it might be absurd to assert either that Subject or Object disappears in Dhyana to the advantage of the other.

*Scept.* But at least this glorification of the consciousness is a proof that reality (as shown in Dhyana) is more glorious than illusion (as shown in consciousness).

*Myst.* Or, that illusion——

*Scept.* Of course ! We are then no further than before.

*Myst.* Indeed we are. Glory, real or false, is desirable. Indeed we are too bold in saying "real or false," by virtue of our previous agreement that the Subjective is the Knowable, and that deeper inquiry is foredoomed futile.

*Scept.* Unless, admitting Physiology,[1] such glory is phantom, poisonous, and your Dhyana a debauch.

*Myst.* You will at least admit, as a basis for the consideration of this and other points that Dhyana is more vivid than any of the normal dualistic states.

*Scept.* I must. I have myself experienced, as I believe, this or a similar condition, and I find it to be so ; intensely so.

*Myst.* I suspected as much.

*Scept.* But pray, lest we talk at cross purposes, define me this Dhyana.

*Myst.* The method is to concentrate the attention on any object (though in Hindu estimation some objects may be far more suitable than others, I believe Science would say any object)——

*Scept.* That was my method.

*Myst.* Suddenly the object disappears: in its stead arises a great glory, characterised by a feeling of calm, yet of intense, of unimaginable bliss.

*Scept.* That was my result. But, more remarkable still, the change was not from the consciousness "I behold a blue pig"—the object I have ever affected—to "I behold

a glory," but to "There is a glory," or "Glory is."

*Myst.* Glory be ! Exactly. That is the test of Dhyana. I am glad to have met you.

*Scept.* Same here. Be good enough to proceed with your exposition !

*Myst.* In a moment. There are other Westerns who study these matters ?

*Scept.* To follow up the line of thought you gave me but just now, we have a great number of philosophers in the West who have enunciated ideas which to the dull minds of the common run of men seem wild and absurd.

*Myst.* You refer to Idealism.

*Scept.* To more ; to nearly all philosophy, save only that self-styled "of common sense," which is merely stupidity glossing ignorance. But Berkeley——

*Myst.* The devout, the angelic——

*Scept.* Hegel——

*Myst.* The splendid recluse ! The lonely and virtuous student who would stand motionless for hours gazing into space, so that his pupils thought him idle or insane——[1]

*Scept.* Spencer——

*Myst.* The noble, ascetic, retired spirit; the single-hearted, the courageous, the holy——

*Scept.* Yes: all these and many others. But what mean your comments ?

*Myst.* That extreme virtue is a necessary condition for one who is desirous of attaining this state of bliss.

*Scept.* There, my friend, you generalise from three. Let me stand fourth (like Ananias) and tell you that after many vain attempts while virtuous, I achieved my first great result only a week after a serious lapse from the condition of a Brahmacharyi.[2]

*Myst.* You ?

*Scept.* The result of despair.

*Myst.* This may serve you as excuse before Shiva.

[1] As represented by Huxley, who, I fancy, spoke from imperfect knowledge of the facts. But *vide infra.*—A. C.

[1] *Cf.* Plato, *Symposium :* Diotima's description of the Vision of absolute Beauty, identical with Hindu doctrine ; and Alcibiades' anecdote of Socrates at Potidæa.—A. C.

[2] Chastity is probably referred to, though Brahmacharya involves many other virtues.

*Scept.* Quit not the scientific ground we walk on !

*Myst.* I regret ; but my astonishment annulled me. On the main point, however, there is no doubt. These Westerns did, more or less, pursue our methods. Why doubt that they attained our results ?.

*Scept.* I never did doubt it. Certain of our philosophers have even imagined that "self-consciousness," as they style it, is the very purpose of the Universe.

*Myst.* They were so enamoured of the Ananda—the bliss——

*Scept.* Presumably. Far be it from me to set myself up against them ; but I may more modestly take the position that "self-consciousness" is a mere phenomenon ; a bye-product, and no more, in the laboratory of life.

*Myst.* Alas ! I can think no better of you for your modesty : whoso would make bricks without straw may as well plan pyramids as hovels.

*Scept.* Your stricture is but too just. Teleology [1] is a science which will make no progress until the most wicked and stupid of men are philosophers, since like is comprehended by like : unless, indeed, we excuse the Creator by saying that, the Universe being a mere mechanism, that it should suffer pain (an emotion He does not feel) is as unintelligible to Him as that a machine should do so is to the engineer. Strain and fatigue are observed by the latter, but not associated by him with the idea of pain : much more so, then, God.

*Myst.* You are bold enough now ! Our philosophers think it not fitting that man should discuss the ways of the inscrutable, the eternal God.

*Scept.* I have you tripping fairly at last ! What do you mean by "eternal"? You who have uprooted my ideas of time, answer me that ?

*Myst.* A woodcock to mine own springe, indeed. I am justly caught with mine own metaphysic.

[1] The science of the Purpose of Things.

*Scept.* Throw metaphysic to the dogs ! I'll none of it. I will resolve it to you, then, on your own principles. The term, so constantly in use, or rather abuse, by your devotees as by ours, is meaningless. All they can mean is a state of consciousness which is never changed—that is, one unit of time, since time is no more than a succession of states of consciousness, and we have no means of measuring the length of one against another : indeed, a " state of consciousness " is atomic, and to measure is really to furnish the means for dissolution of a molecule, and no more. Thus in the New Jerusalem the song must be either a single note, or a phenomenon in time. Length without change is equivalent to an increase in the vividness, as we said before. And after all the Ego can never be happy, for happiness is impersonal, is distinct from the contemplation of happiness. This quite unchanging, this single vivid state, is as near " Eternity " as we can ever get—it is a foolish word.

*Myst.* That state is then impersonal ?

*Scept.* Ah !—Yes, I have described Dhyana.

*Myst.* The heaven of the Christian is then identical with the daily relaxation of the Hindu ?

*Scept.* If we analyse their phrase, yes. But Christians mean " eternal time," a recurring cycle of pleasant states, as when a child wishes that the pantomime "could go on for ever."

*Myst.* Why, do they ever mean anything ? . . . But how does this eternal time differ from ordinary time ? Our guarantee against cessation is the fact that the tendency to change is inherent in all component things.

*Scept.* Our guarantee indeed ! Rather the seal upon the tomb of our hopes ! But to sing, even out of tune, as the Christian does, that " time shall be no more," is, indeed, to cease to mean anything. The dogma of the Trinity itself is not less inane, the only thing that saves it from being blasphemous.

*Myst.* To be intelligible is to be misunderstood.

*Scept.* To be unintelligible is to be found out.

S 2

*Myst.* To be secretive is to be blatant.

*Scept.* To be frank is to be mysterious.

*Myst.* I wish your poet-martyr[1] (I do not refer to Chatterton) could hear us.

*Scept.* To return, I would have you note the paradox that unconsciousness must be reckoned as a form of consciousness, since otherwise the last state of consciousness of a dying person is for him eternity. That this is not so is shown by the phenomena of anæsthesia.

*Myst.* Is it, though? Is the analogy so certain? Is there nothing in the attempt of all religions to secure that a man's last thoughts should be of triumph, peace, joy, and their like?

*Scept.* I have been reading that somewhat mawkish book "The Soul of a People." Disgusted as I was by its ooze of sentimentality, I was yet not unobservant of its cognisance of this fact, and I was even pleased—though this is by the way—to see that the author recognises in the ridiculous First Precept of the Buddhist Faith, or rather in the orthodox travesty of Buddha's meaning, a mere survival of some fetichistic theophagy.

*Myst.* Doesn't it say somewhere that " Long words butter no parsnips "?

*Scept.* It ought to. But pray proceed with your defence of religion—for I presume it is intended as such.

*Myst.* I was saying that if unconsciousness be not reckoned as consciousness, the death-thought is eternal heaven or hell, as it chances to be pleasant or painful. But, on the other hand, if it be so reckoned, if that and that alone has in death no awakening, no change, then is it not certain that there is the Great Peace? Disprove immortality, reincarnation, all survival or revival of the identical——

*Scept.* Identical? Hm !

*Myst.*—of the consciousness which the man calls " I "——

*Scept.* Which Haeckel has pretty effectively done.

*Myst.* And Nirvana is ours for the price of

a packet of arsenic, and a glass of Dutch courage.

*Scept.* In a poem called " Summa Spes," [1] a gifted but debauched Irishman has grossly, yet effectively, stated this view. " Let us eat and drink, for to-morrow we die ! " is the Hebrew for it. But if we survive or revive—

*Myst.* The problem is merely postponed. If " death is a sleep " : why, we know what happens after sleep.

*Scept.* The question resolves itself, therefore, into the other which we both of us anticipated and feared : What is this "identical consciousness " which is the cause of so much confusion of thought. We have in the phenomena of mind ($a$) a set of simple impressions ; ($b$)[2] a machinery for grasping and interpreting these ; of sifting, grouping, organizing, co-ordinating, integrating them ; and ($c$) a " central " consciousness, more or less persistent, that is to say, united to a long series of similar states by the close bond of the emphatic idea, I, which " central " consciousness takes notice of the results presented to it by ($b$). A state which can be summoned at will——

*Myst.* What then is "will"?

*Scept.* You know what I mean. God knows I am bothered enough already without being caught up on a word ! Which can be summoned at will : which in a succession of simple, though highly abstract states, observes the results (forgive the repetition !) presented to it by ($b$). But if we turn the consciousness upon itself, if we add a sixth sense to the futile five ?

*Myst.* It is resolved after all into a simple impression, indistinguishable, so far as I can see, from any other. That is, logically.

*Scept.* An impression, moreover, on what ? It is not the ($c$) that is really examined ; for ($c$) is the examiner : and you have merely formulated a ($d$) expressible by the ratio

---

[1] The reference, presumably ironical, is to the late Oscar Wilde.

[1] See p. 200.

[2] This ($b$) may be divided and subdivided into certain groups ; some, perhaps all of them, liable, in the event of the suppression of ($a$), to become (automatically ?) active, and prevent ($c$) from becoming quiet.—A. C.

$d : c :: c : a$—an infinite process. The final factor is always unknowable—yet it is the one thing known.

*Myst.* And because it is always present, therefore it is unkenned.

*Scept.* We are now nearer Spencer than appeared. For the fact that it must be there, unchanging in function, while consciousness persists, gives the idea of a definite substratum to subserve that function.

*Myst.* I cannot but agree ; and I would further observe that when, in Dhyana, it ceases to examine, and apperceives, the "relative eternity," *i.e.*, the intense vividness of the phenomenon gives us a further argument in favour of its permanence.

*Scept.* But that it should persist after death is a question which we should leave physiology to answer, as much as the obvious question whether sight and taste persist. And the answer is unhesitatingly " No."

*Myst.* Yet the mystic may still reply that the association of consciousness with matter is as incredible as the contrary conception. Cause and effect, he will say, are if anything less likely (*à priori*) than concomitance or casuality. Even occasionalism is no more improbable than that the material should have a manifestly immaterial function.

*Scept.* Yet it is so !

*Myst.* Ah ! would it serve to reply that it is so ! But no ! the materialistic position, fully allowed, is an admission of spirit.[1] They must conceive spirit and matter both as unknowable, as irresolvable, like $x$ and $y$ in a single equation (whose counterpart we seek in Dhyana), so that we may eternally evolve

[1] Maudsley, " Physiology of Mind," asks why it should be more unlikely that consciousness should be a function of matter than that pain should be of nervous tissue.
True. So also Huxley extended the meaning of "nature" to include the "supernatural" in order to deny the supernatural.
So also I (maintaining that darkness only exists) meet the cavil of the people who insist on the separate existence of light by showing that light is, after all, merely a sub-section of one kind of darkness.—A. C. This note is of course ironical.

values for either, but always in terms of the other.

*Scept.* Just so we agreed lately about subject and object.

*Myst.* It is another form of the same Protean problem.

*Scept.* Haeckel even insists upon this in his arrogant way.

*Myst.* Huxley, at once the most and the least sceptical of philosophers, urges it. There is only one method of investigating this matter. Reason is bankrupt ; not only Mansel the Christian but Hume the Agnostic has seen it.

*Scept.* We all see it. The Bank being broken, we do not put what little we have saved into the wildcat stock Faith, as Mansel counsels us ; but add little to little, and hoard it in the old stocking of Science.

*Myst.* Well if no holes !

*Scept.* We expect little, even if we hope for much. We are pretty safe ; 'tis the plodding ass that is Science, and the fat priest rides us still.

*Myst.* We offer you a Bank, where your intellectual coin will breed a thousandfold.

*Scept.* What security do you offer ? Once bit, twice shy ; especially as your business is known to be patronised by some very shady customers.

*Myst.* Do you offer to stop my mouth with security ? We give you all you can wish. Let Science keep the books ! I say it in our own interest ; the slovenly system that has prevailed hitherto has resulted in serious losses to the shareholders. One of our best cashiers, Christ, went off and left mere verbal messages, and those only too vague, as to the business that passed through his hands. Too many of our most brilliant research staff keep their processes secret, and so not only incur the suspicion of quackery, but leave the world no wiser for their work. Others abuse their position as directors to further the ends of other companies not even allied to the parent firm : as when Mohammed, the illuminated of Allah, lent his spiritual force to bolster up the literal sense of the Bible, thus degrading a sublime text-book of mystic lore into the merest nursery, or too often bawdy-house, twaddle and filth. You will alter all this, my friends! Let Science keep the books!

*Scept.* For a cross between a plodding ass and an old stocking, she will do well! And what dividends do you promise?

*Myst.* In the first year. Dhyana; in the second, Samadhi; and in the third, Nirvana.

*Scept.* It is not the first year yet. Is this coin current?

*Myst.* Ah! I remember now your phrase "Dhyana a debauch." You are of course familiar with the name of Maudsley, perhaps the greatest living authority on the brain?

*Scept.* None greater.

*Myst.* By rare good fortune, at the very moment when this aspect of the question was confronting me, and I was (so any one would have imagined) many thousand miles from expert opinion, I had the opportunity of putting the matter before him. Our conversation was pretty much as follows : " What is the cause of the phenomenon I have described?" (I had given just such a sketch as we have drawn above, and added that it was the most cherished possession of all Eastern races. The state was familiar to him.) " Excessive activity of one portion of the brain : relative lethargy of the rest." " Of which portion?" " It is unknown." " Is the phenomenon of pathological significance?" "I cannot say so much : it would be a dangerous habit to acquire : but since recovery is spontaneous, and is apparently complete, it is to be classed as physiological." I obtained the idea, however, that the danger was very serious, perhaps more so than the actual words used would imply. A further inquiry as to whether he could suggest any medical, surgical, or other means, by which this state might be produced at will, led to no result.

*Scept.* This is most interesting : for the very doubts which I did entertain as to the safety of mental methods directed to attaining this result, are dispelled by what is a cautious, if not altogether unfavourable, view

from a naturally-inclined-to-be-unfavourable Western mind. (My mother was of German extraction.) How so? Because my teacher, himself a Western scientific man of no mean attainments, thought no trouble too great, no language too violent (though he is ordinarily a man of unusual mildness and suavity of manner) to be used, to impress upon me the extreme danger of too vigorous attempts to reach the state of concentration. "If you feel the least tired in the course of your daily practice," he never wearied of repeating, "you have done too much, and must absolutely rest for four-and-twenty hours. However fresh you feel, however keen you are to pursue the work, rest you must, or you will but damage the apparatus you are endeavouring to perfect. Rest for longer if you like, never for less." This adjuration recurs with great force to my mind at the present moment. Our Western "Adepts"— if you were a Western I would ask you to forgive the word—know, as the great brain specialist knows, the dangers of the practice ; the dangers of the training, the dangers of success.

*Myst.* Blavatsky's mysteriously - phrased threats were to this effect. Maybe she knew.

*Scept.* Maybe she did. Well, what I wished to point out was that, had you pressed Dr. Maudsley, he might possibly have admitted that scientific precaution, under trained guidance and watching, might diminish the danger greatly, and permit the student to follow out this line of research without incurring the stigma—if it be a stigma—of risking his sanity, or at least his general mental welfare?[1]

[1] Dr. Maudsley, to whom I submitted the MS. of this portion of the dialogue, was good enough to say that it represented very much what he had said, and to add that " the 'ecstasy,' if attained, signifies such a 'standing-out,' ἐκ-στασις, quasi-spasmodic, of a special tract of the brain as, if persisted in, involves the risk of a permanent loss of power, almost in the end a paralysis of the other tracts. —Like other bad habits, it grows by what it feeds on, and may put the fine and complex co-ordinated machinery quite out of gear. The

*Myst.* It may be; in any case I follow knowledge; if my methods be absurd or pernicious, I am but one of millions in the like strait. Nor do I perceive that any other line of action offers even a remote chance of success.

*Scept.* The problem is perennial. It must be attacked on scientific lines, and if the pioneers fall,—well, who expects more from a forlorn hope? Time will show.

*Myst.* We have wandered far from this question of time.

*Scept.* Even from that of consciousness; itself a digression, though a necessary one.

*Myst.* An elusive fellow, this consciousness! Is he continuous, you, who declare him permanent?

*Scept.* Do I, indeed? I gave a possible reason for thinking so; but my adhesion does not follow. The lower consciousnesses, which I called (*a*), are of course rhythmic. The biograph is a sufficient proof of this.

ecstatic attains an illumination (so-called) at the expense of sober reason and solid judgment."

Mysticus would not, I think, wish to contest this view, but rather would argue that if this be the case, it is at least a choice between two evils. Sober reason and solid judgment offer no prize more desirable than death after a number of years, less or greater, while ecstasy can, if the facts stated in this dialogue are accepted, give the joys of all these years in a moment.

But for the sake of argument he would say that there are certainly many men who have practised with success from boyhood, and who still enjoy health and a responsible and difficult position in the world of thinking men. This would suggest the idea that there may be men with special aptitude for, and immunity in greater or less degree against the dangers of, the practice. He would cheerfully admit that the common mystic is an insufferable fool, and that his habits possibly assist the degenerative process. But he would submit that in such cases the brain, such as it is, is not worth protecting. At the same time, it is true, the truest type of Hindu mystic regards the ecstasy as an obstacle, since its occurrence stops his meditation; and as a temptation, since he is liable to mistake the obstacle for the goal.—A. C. (See note 53, p. 209.)

*Myst.* Were one needed. Spencer's generalisation covers this point?

*Scept.* À *priori.* That the higher (*c*) are also rhythmic—for we will have no à *priori* here!—is evident, since the (*a*)s are presented by (*b*) no faster than they come. Even if (*a*), being fivefold, comes always so fast as to overlap, no multitude of impacts can compose a continuity.

*Myst.* But those reasons for permanence were very strong.

*Scept.* Strong, but overcome. Is it not absurd to represent anything as permanent whose function is rhythmic?

*Myst.* Not necessarily. It is surely possible for a continuous pat of butter to be struck rhythmically, for example. That it is inert in the intervals is unproved; but if it were, it might still be continuous. That a higher consciousness exists is certain; that it is unknowable is certain, as shown just now, unless, indeed, we can truly unite (*c*) with itself: *i.e.*, without thereby formulating a (*d*).

*Scept.* But how is that to be done?

*Myst.* Only, if at all, by cutting off (*c*) from (*a*): *i.e.*, by suspending the mechanism (*b*). Prevent sense-impressions from reaching the sensorium, and there will at least be a better chance of examining the interior. You cannot easily investigate a watch while it is going: nor does the reflection of the sun appear in a lake whose surface is constantly ruffled by wind and rain, by hail and thunderbolt, by the diving of birds and the falling of rocks. To do this, thus shown to be essential to even the beginning of the true settlement of the time problem, and the solution of the paradoxes it affords——

*Scept.* How to do this is then a question not to be settled offhand by our irresponsible selves, but one of method and research.

*Myst.* And as such the matter of years.

*Scept.* I have long recognised this. That it should be started on a firm basis by responsible scientific men; that it should be placed on equal terms in all respects with other research : such is the object of my life.

*Myst.* But of mine the research itself.

*Scept.* I applaud you. You are the happy one. I am the martyr. I shall sow, but not reap ; my eyes shall hardly see the first-fruits of my labour ; yet something I shall see. Also, to construct one must clear the ground : to harvest, the plough and harrow are required. First we must rid us of false phrase and lying assumption, of knavery and ignorance, of bigotry and shirking. Let us pull down the church and the Free Library ;[1] with each stone torn thence let us build the humble and practical homes of the true " holy men " of our age, the

[1] The sarcasm is perhaps against the popularity of the worthless novel, as shown in Free Library statistics ; or against the uselessness of any form of reading to a man not otherwise educated.

austere and single-minded labourers in the fields of Physics and Physiology.

*Myst.* Here, moreover, is the foundation of race harmony ; here the possible basis for a genuine brotherhood of man ! He will never be permanently solidarised—excuse the neologism !—by grandiose phrase and transitory emotion ; but in the Freemasonry of the Adepts of Dhyana what temple may not yet be builded ?

*Scept.* Not made with hands — ἐν τοῖς οὐρανοῖς αἰώνιος.

*Myst.* Has not this mystical bond brought you and me together, us diverse, even repugnant in all other ways, yet utterly at one in this great fact ?

*Scept.* We have talked too lightly, friend. Silence is best.

*Myst.* Let us meditate upon the adorable light of that divine Savitri !

*Scept.* May she enlighten our minds !

# EPILOGUE

When the chill of earth black-breasted is
    uplifted at the glance
Of the red sun million-crested, and the forest
    blossoms dance
With the light that stirs and lustres of the
    dawn, and with the bloom
Of the wind's cheek as it clusters from the
    hidden valley's gloom :
Then I walk in woodland spaces, musing on
    the solemn ways
Of the immemorial places shut behind the
    starry rays;
Of the East and all its splendour, of the
    West and all its peace;
And the stubborn lights grow tender, and
    the hard sounds hush and cease.
In the wheel of heaven revolving, mysteries
    of death and birth,
In the womb of time dissolving, shape anew
    a heaven and earth
Ever changing, ever growing, ever dwind-
    ling, ever dear,
Ever worth the passion glowing to distil a
    doubtful tear.
These are with me, these are of me, these
    approve me, these obey,
Choose me, move me, fear me, love me,
    master of the night and day.
These are real, these illusion : I am of them,
    false or frail,
True or lasting, all is fusion in the spirit's
    shadow-veil,
Till the Knowledge-Lotus flowering hides
    the world beneath its stem ;

Neither I, nor God life-showering, find a
    counterpart in them.
As a spirit in a vision shows a countenance
    of fear,
Laughs the looker to derision, only comes
    to disappear,
Gods and mortals, mind and matter, in the
    glowing bud dissever :
Vein from vein they rend and shatter, and
    are nothingness for ever.
In the blessed, the enlightened, perfect eyes
    these visions pass,
Pass and cease, poor shadows frightened,
    leave no stain upon the glass.
One last stroke, O heart-free master, one
    last certain calm of will,
And the maker of Disaster shall be stricken
    and grow still.
Burn thou to the core of matter, to the
    spirit's utmost flame,
Consciousness and sense to shatter, ruin
    sight and form and name !
Shatter, lake-reflected spectre ; lake, rise up
    in mist to sun ;
Sun, dissolve in showers of nectar, and the
    Master's work is done.
Nectar perfume gently stealing, masterful and
    sweet and strong,
Cleanse the world with light of healing in
    the ancient House of Wrong !
Free a million million mortals on the wheel
    of being tossed !
Open wide the mystic portals, and be
    altogether lost !

Photo by René Dupont 5th Av. New York 1906

# THE WORKS

OF

# ALEISTER CROWLEY

*WITH PORTRAITS*

VOLUME III

Martino Publishing
Mansfield Centre, CT
2012

Martino Publishing
P.O. Box 373,
Mansfield Centre, CT 06250 USA

www.martinopublishing.com

ISBN   978-1-61427-279-3

© 2012  Martino Publishing

Cover design by T. Matarazzo

Printed in the United States of America On 100% Acid-Free Paper

# THE WORKS

OF

# ALEISTER CROWLEY

*WITH PORTRAITS*

VOLUME III

FOYERS
SOCIETY FOR THE PROPAGATION OF
RELIGIOUS TRUTH
1907

# CONTENTS OF VOLUME III

# THE STAR AND THE GARTER

## 1904

[The simplicity of this exquisite poem renders all explanations superfluous.]

## ΑΓΝΩΣΤΩ
## ΘΕΩ *

### ARGUMENT.

THE poet, seated with his lady, perceives (i.) that he is in some disgrace, arguing the same (ii.) from a difference in the quality of the subsisting silence. Seeking a cause, he observes (iii.) a lady's garter in one corner of the room. His annoyance is changed (iv.) to joy at the prospect of an argument, and of a better understanding. He will (v.) be frank: no poet truly cares what may happen to him. He sketches (vi.) his argument; but letting fall the word "love" is rapt away into a lyrical transport (vii. and viii.). Further, bidding her (ix.) to fly with him, he points out the value of courage, and its rarity among the bourgeoisie. He calls upon her to awake her own courage, and (x.) bids her embark. His appeal fails, since (xi.) the garter still demands explanation. He then shows (xii.) that mental states are not independent of their physical basis, and casts doubt (xiii.) upon Immortality and Freewill. He asks her (xiv.) to accommodate herself to the facts instead of wasting life upon an Ideal, and to remember that all his acts truly subserve his love for her. He reinforces this (xv.) by a distinction of the important and the unimportant, assures her of his deep passion, and appeals to her. He will (xvi.) show her the picture of the owner of the garter, and gives her (xvii.) the first hint that he does not consider her a rival, any more than dinner is a rival. As (xviii.) she cannot grasp that idea, he states it plainly and describes (xix.) the lady whose forgetfulness has caused the whole trouble. The spell broken, as it were, he describes (xx., xxi.) two other mistresses, a model and an acrobat, and then again flings at her (xxii.) the frank question: Are these rivals in *Love?* He argues that the resemblances are superficial. For (xxiii.) there is no taint of passion in his Love for his Lady. But she (xxiv.) sees that as a fault in her, and offers her person. He refuses it, fearing to destroy Love, and proves (xxv.) that sexual intimacy is no truer than virginal intimacy. He recalls (xxvi.) the hour when their love stood confessed and (xxvii.) that in which the first promptings of passion were caught and smothered in a higher ecstasy. He complains (xxviii.) that he should have needed to voice all this. He urges (xxix.) that the necessary duties of sex should be performed elsewhere. But, should those duties become unnecessary, let them voyage to solitude and peace. Or (xxx.) no! it is well to have the ever-present contrast; let us, however, not despise other folk, but pity them, and for this pity's sake, retire (xxxi.) to meditate, and by this means to achieve the power of redeeming them. He formulates lyrically (xxxii.) this conclusion; and sums up the whole (xxxiii.), insisting finally on the value of the incident as a stepping-stone to the ultimate.

---

* *I.e.,* Eros. The quotation is from Acts xvii. 23, "To the Unknown God."

A

## THE STAR AND THE GARTER.

### I.

WHAT sadness closes in between
Your eyes and mine to-day, my Queen?
In dewfall of our glance hath come
A chill like sunset's in hot lands
Mid iris and chrysanthemum.
Well do I know the shaken sands
Within the surf, the beaten bar
Of coral, the white nenuphar
Of moonrise stealing o'er the bay.
So here's the darkness, and the day
Sinks, and a chill clusters, and I
Wrap close the cloak : then is it so
To-day, you rose-gleam on the snow,
My own true lover? Ardently
I dare not look : I never looked
So : that you know. But insight keen
We (laugh and) call not "love." Now
    crooked
The light swerves somehow. Do you mean—
What? There is coldness and regret
Set like the stinging winter spray
Blown blind back from a waterfall
On Cumbrian moors at Christmas. Wet
The cold cheek numbs itself. A way
Is here to make—an end of all?
What sadness closes in between
Your eyes and mine to-day, my Queen?

### II.

YOU are silent. That we always were.
The racing lustres of your hair
Spelt out its sunny message, though
The room was dusk : a rosy glow
Shed from an antique lamp to fall
On the deep crimson of the wall,
And over all the ancient grace
Of shawls, and ivory, and gems [1]
To cast its glamour, till your face
The eye might fall upon and rest,

  [1] The description is of Crowley's rooms in
the Quartier Montparnasse.

The temperate flower, the tropic stems.
You were silent, and I too. Caressed
The secret flames that curled around
Our subtle intercourse. Profound,
Unmoved, delighting utterly,
So sat, so sit, my love and I.
But not to-day. Your silence stirs
No answering rapture : you are proud,
And love itself checks and deters
The thought to say itself aloud.
Oh ! heart of amber and fine gold
Silverly darting lunar rays !
Oh ! river of sweet passion rolled
Adown invisible waterways !
Speak ! Did I wound you then unguessed ?
What is the sorrow unexpressed
That shadows those ecstatic lids?
A word in season subtly rids
The heart of thoughts unseasonable.
You are silent. Do they speak in hell?

### III.

Is it your glance that told me ? Nay !
I know you would not look that way.
Seeing, you strove to see not. Fool !
I have ruined all in one rash deed.
Learnt I not in discretion's school
The little care that lovers need ?
For see—I bite my lip to blood ;
A stifled word of anguish hisses :—
O the black word that dams thought's
    flood !
O the bad lip that looked for kisses !
O the poor fool that prates of love !
Is it a garter, or a glove ?

### IV.

A FOOL indeed ! For why complain,
Now the last five-barred gate is ope,
Held by a little boy ? I hope
The hour is handy to explain
The final secret. Have I any ?
Yes ! the small boy shall have a penny !

Now you are angry? Be content!
Not fee the assistant accident
That shows our quarry—love—at bay?
My silver-throated queen, away!
Huntress of heaven, by my side,
As moon by meteor, rushing, ride!
Among the stars, ride on! ride on!
(Then, maybe, bid the boy begone!)


### V.

I AM a boy in this. Alas!
Look round on all the world of men!
The boys are oft of genus "ass."
Think yourself lucky, lady, then,
If I at least am boy. You laugh?
Not you! Is this love's epitaph,
God's worm erect on Herod's throne?
" Ah, if I only had not known!"
All wrong, belovèd! Truth be ours,
The one white flower (of all the flowers)
You ever cared for! Ignorance
May set its puppets up to dance;
We know who pulls the strings. No
    sage;
A man unwashed, the bearded brute!
His wife, the mother-prostitute!
Behind the marionetted stage
See the true Punch-and-Judy show,
Turn copper so to silver! Know,
And who can help forgiving? So
Said some French thinker.[1] Here's a
    drench
Of verse unquestionably French
To follow! so, while youth is youth,
And time is time, and I am I,
Too busy with my work to lie,
Or love lie's prize—or work's, forsooth!—
Too strong to care which way may go
The ensuing history of woe,
Though I were jaw, and you were tooth;
So, more concerned with seeking sense
Than worried over consequence,
I'll speak, and you shall hear, the truth.

[1] " Comprendre, c'est pardonner."
            —MME. DE STAEL.

### VI.

TRUTH, like old Gaul, is split in three.[1]
A lesson in anatomy,
A sketch of sociology,
A tale of love to end. But see!
What stirs the electric flame of eyes?
One word—that word. Be destiny's
Inviolate fiat rolled athwart
The clouds and cobwebs of our speech,
And image, integrate of thought,
This ebony anthem, each to each :—
To lie, invulnerable, alone,
Valkyrie and hero, in the zone,
Shielded by lightnings of our wit,
Guarded by fires of intellect
Far on the mountain-top, elect
Of all the hills divinely lit
By rays of moonrise! O the moon!
O the interminable tune
Of whispered kisses! Love exults,
Intolerant of all else than he,
And ecstasy invades, insults,
Outshines the waves of harmony,
Lapped in the sun of day; the tides
Of wonder flow, the shore subsides;
And over all the horizon
Glows the last glimmer of the sun.
Ah! when the moon arises, she
Shall look on nothing but the sea.

### VII.

O LOVE! and were I with thee ever!
Come with me over the round earth,
O'er lake and fountain, sea and river!
Girdle the world with angel girth
Of angel voyage! Shall we roam
In teeming jungles poisonous?
Or make ourselves an eyrie-home
Where the black ice roars ravenous
In glittering avalanche? Or else
Hide in some corrie on the fells
Of heather and bracken, or delight
In grottos built of stalactite?

[1] " Gallia est divisa in tres partes."
        —Cæsar de Bello Gallico, i. 1.

Or be our lonely haunt the sand
Of the Sahara : let us go
Where some oasis, subtly planned
For love, invites the afterglow !
There let us live alone, except
Some bearded horseman, pennoned, ride
Over the waste of ochre, swept
By wind in waves, and sit beside
Our tent a little, bring us news
Of the great world we have lost for—this !
What fool exclaims—"to lose !"?    To
    lose ?
Ay ! earth and heaven for one small kiss !
But he shall sing beside our fire
The epic of the world's desire ;
How Freedom fares, how Art yet revels
Sane in the dance of dogs and devils.
His thunder voice shall climb and crash,
Scourge liars with tongue's lightning lash,
Through ranks of smitten tyrants drive,
Till bosoms heave, and eyes outflash,
And it is good to be alive.
He shall ride off at dawn, and we
Shall look upon our life again ;
You old, and all your beauty be
Broken, and mine a broken brain.
Yet we shall know ; delighting still
In the sole laughter death derides
In vain ; the indomitable will,
Still burning in the spirit, guides
Our hearts to truth ; we see, we know
How foolish were the things he said,
And answer in the afterglow
How good it is that we are dead.
Will you not come ?  Or, where the surf
Beats on the coral, and the palm
Sways slowly in the eternal calm
Of spring, I know a mound of turf
Good for our love to lie on ; good
For breezes, and for sun and shade ;
To hear the murmur of the flood ;
To taste the kava subtly made
To rouse to Bacchic ecstasy,
Since Dionysus silently
Faded from Greece, now only smiles
Amid the soft Hawaian isles ;
Good, above all the good, to keep
Our bodies when we sleep the sleep.

## VIII.

MAKE me a roseleaf with your mouth,
And I will waft it through the air
To some far garden of the South,
The herald of our happening there !

Fragrant, caressing, steals the breeze ;
Curls into kisses on your lips :—
I know interminable seas,
Winged ardour of the stately ships,

Space of incalculable blue
And years enwreathed in one close crown,
And glimmering laughters echoing you
From reverend shades of bard's renown :—

Nature alive and glad to hymn
Your beauty, my delight : her God
Weary, his old eyes sad and dim
In his intolerable abode.

All things that are, unknown and known,
Bending in homage to your eyes ;
We wander wondering, lift alone
The world's grey load of agonies.

Make me a roseleaf with your mouth,
That all the savour steal afar
Unto the sad awaiting South,
Where sits enthroned the answering Star.

## IX.

WILL you not come : the unequal fever
Of Paris hold our lives for ever?
Were it not better to exceed
The avenging thought, the unmeaning deed,
Make one strong act at least ?  How small,
How idiot our lives !  These folk
That think they live—which dares at all
To act ?  The suicide that broke
His chain, and lies so waxen pale
In the Morgue to-day ?  Did he then fail?
Ay, he was beaten.  But to live,
Slink on through what the world can give,

That is a hound's life too. For me,
The suicide stands grand and free
Beside these others. Was it fear
Drove him to stand upon the bank?
The Paris lights shone far and drear;
The mist was down; the night was dank;
The Seine ran easily underneath;
The air was chill: he knew the Seine
By pain would put an end to pain,
And jumped,—and struggled against death,
I doubt not. Ye courageous men
That scorn to flee the world, ye slaves
Of commerce, ye that ply the pen,
That dig, and fill, and loathe your graves!
Ye counter-jumpers, clergy, Jews,
All Paris, smug and good, that use
To point the index scorn, deride
The courage of that suicide—
I ask you not to quit us quite,
But—will you take a bath to-night?
Money might make you. Well: but he,
What was his wage, what was his fee?
Fear fiercer than a mortal fear.
Be silent, cowards, leave him here
Dead in the Morgue, so waxen pale!
He failed: shall ye not also fail?
*Ah! love! the strings are little;*
  *The cords are over strong;*
*The chain of life is brittle;*
  *And keen the sword of song.*
Will you not seize in one firm grip
Now, as I hold you, lip to lip,
The serpent of Event, hold hard
Its slipping coils, its writhe retard,
And snap its spine? Delicate hands
You have: the work is difficult;
Effort that holds and understands
May do it: shall our foes exult,
The daughters of Philistia laugh,
The girls of Askalon rejoice,
Writing for us this epitaph:
"They chose, and were not worth the
  choice"?
You are so pure: I am a man.
I will assume the courage tried
Of yonder luckless suicide,
And you—awaken, if you can,
The courage of the courtezan!

X.

To sea! To sea! The ship is trim;
The breezes bend the sails.
They chant the necromantic hymn,
Arouse Arabian tales.

To sea! Before us leap the waves;
The wild white combers follow.
Invoke, ye melancholy slaves,
The morning of Apollo!

There's phosphorescence in the wake,
And starlight o'er the prow.
One comet, like an angry snake,
Lifts up its hooded brow.

The black grows grey toward the East:
A hint of silver glows.
Gods gather to the mystic feast
On interlunar snows.

The moon is up full-orbed: she glides
Striking a snaky ray
Across the black resounding tides,
The sepulchre of day.

The moon is up: upon the prow
We stand and watch the moon.
A star is lustred on your brow;
Your lips begin a tune,

A long, low tune of love that swells
Little by little, and lights
The overarching miracles
Of love's desire, and Night's.

It swells, it rolls to triumph-song
Through luminous black skies;
Thrills into silence sharp and strong,
Assumes its peace, and dies.

There is the night: it covers close
The lilies folded fair
Of all your beauty, and the rose
Half hidden in your hair.

There is the night : unseen I stand
And look to seaward still :
We would not look upon the land
Again, had I my will.

The ship is trim : to sea ! to sea !
Take life in either hand,
Crush out its wine for you and me,
And drink, and understand !

### XI.

I AM a pretty advocate !
My speech has served me ill.   Perchance
Silence had served : you now look straight
On that clear evidence of France,
The embroidered garter yonder.   Wait !
I had some confidence in fate
Ere I spoke thus.   For while I spoke
The old smile, surely helpless, broke
On your tired lips : the old light woke
In your deep eyes : but silence falls
Blank, blank : the species that appals,
Not our old silence.   I devise
A motto for your miseries :
" There an embroidered garter lies,
And here words—they lie too ? "   I see
Your intuition of the truth
Is still in its—most charming—youth.
You need that physiology !

### XII.[1]

I LOVE you.   That seems simple ?   No !
Hear what the physiologist
Says on the subject.   *To and fro*
*The motor axis of the brain*

[1] In view of the strange uproar which this harmless section created, one person supposing it to testify Crowley's ignorance, another that it was a correct physiological description of the action of the erector penis muscle (! ! !), it should be explained that the speaker wishes to explain that consciousness is a function of the brain, and that, talking to an ignorant girl, he allows himself to talk what is in detail extravagant nonsense.

*Hits on the cerebellum hard,*
*Makes the medulla itch : the bard*
*Twitches his spinal cord again,*
*Excites Rolando's fissure, and*
*Impinges on the Pineal gland.*
*Then Hippocampus major strikes*
*The nerves, and we may say " He likes,"*
*But if the umbilical cord*
*Cut the cerebrum like a sword,*
*And afferent ganglia, sensory bones,*
*Shake in the caecum : then one groans*
*" He likes Miss What's your Name."   And if*
*The appendix vermiformis biff*
*The pericardium, pleura shoves*
*The femur—we may say : " He loves."*
Here is the mechanism strange
(But perfectly correct) to change
My normal calm—seraphic dew !
Into an ardent love for you.

### XIII.

Is there a soul behind the mask ?
What master drives these slaves to task
Thus willing ?   Physiology
Wipes the red scalpel, scorns reply.
My argument to please you swerves,
Becomes a mere defence of nerves.
Why they are thus, why so they act,
We know not, but accept the fact.
How this for my peccation serves ?
Marry, how ?   Tropically !   Pact
I bind with blood to show you use
For this impertinence—and add
A proverb fit to make you mad
About the gander and the goose,[1]
Till you riposte with all your force
A miserable pun on sauce.
The battle when you will !   This truce
I take in vantage, hold my course.
I see mechanic causes reach
Back through eternity, inform
The stellar drift, the solar storm,
The protoplasmic shiver, each

[1] What is sauce for the goose, is sauce for the gander.

Little or great, determinate
In law from Fate, the Ultimate.
If this be meaningless, much more
Vacant your speech and sophic skill
(My feminine and fair Escobar ! [1])
To prove mere circumstance is no bar
Against the freedom of the will.
However this may be, we are
Here and not otherwise, star to star !
Hence then act thou ! Restrain the " Damn !"
Evoked by " I am that I am."
Perpend ! (Hark back to Hamlet !) If
You stand thus poised upon the cliff
Freewill—I await that will ; (One) laughter ;
(Two) the old kiss ; (Three) silence after.
No ? Then vacate the laboratory !
Psychology must crown the event,
And sociology content,
Ethics suffice, the simple story !
(Oh ! that a woman ever went
Through course of science, full and whole,
Without the loss of beauty's scent,
And grace, and subtlety of soul.
Ah God ! this Law maketh hearts ache,
" Who eateth shall not have his cake.")

### XIV.

ACCEPT me as I am ! I give
All you can take. If you dislike
Some fragments of the life I live,
They are not yours : I scorn to strike
One sword-swift pang against your peace.
See ! I'm a mountaineer. Release
That spirit from your bonds : or come
With me upon the mountains, cease
This dull round, this addition sum
Of follies we call France : indeed
Cipher ! And if at times I need
The golden dawn upon the Alps,
The gorges of Himalayan rock,
The grey and ancient hills, the scalps
Of hoary hills, the rattling shock
Of avalanche adown the hills—
Why, what but you, your image, fills

[1] A mediæval logician.

My heart in these ? I want you there.
For whom but you do I ply pen,
Talk with unmentionable men
Of proofs and types—dull things !—for whom
But you am I the lover ? Bloom,
O flower, immortal flower, love, love !
Linger about me and above,
Thou perfumed haze of incense-mist !
The air hath circled me and kissed
Here in this room, on mountains far,
Yonder to seaward, toward yon star,
With your own kisses. Yes ! I see
The roseate embroidery
Yonder—I know : it seems to give
The lie to me in throat and teeth.
That is the surface : underneath
I live in you : in you I live.

### XV.

WILL you not learn to separate
The essential from the accidental,
Love from desire, caprice from fate,
The inmost from the merely mental ?
Our star, the sun, gives life and light :
Let that decay, the æons drown
Sense in stagnation ; death and night
Smite the fallen fragments of the crown
Of spring : but serves the garter so ?
What wandering meteor is this
Across the archipelago
Luminous of our starry bliss ?
Let that be lost : the smile disputes
The forehead's temple with the frown,
When gravitation's arrow shoots,
And stockings happen to slip down.
You are my heart : the central fire
Whereby my being burns and moves,
The mainspring of my life's desire,
The essential engine that approves
The will to live : and these frail friends,
The women I shall draw you, fail
Of more importance to earth's ends
Than to my life a finger-nail.
'Twere pain, no doubt, were torn away
One, a minute distemperature.

I spend a fraction of the day
Plying the art of manicure.
But always beats the heart : the more
I polish, tint, or carve, I ask
Strength from the heart's too generous store
To bend my fingers to the task.
Cease : I am broken : nought remains.
The brain's electric waves are still ;
No blood beats eager in the veins ;
The mind sinks deathward, and the will.
It is no figure of boy's speech,
Lover's enthusiasm, rhyme
Magniloquent of bard, to reach
Truth through the husk of space and time :
No truth is more devout than this :
" In you I live : I live in you."
Had Latmos not known Artemis,
Where were the faint lights of that dew
Of Keats ?  O maiden moon of mine,
Imperial crescent, rise and shine !

### XVI.

I WAS a fool to hide it.   Here
Phantoms arise and disappear,
Obedient to the master's wand.
The incense curls like a pale frond
Of some grey garden glory about
This room ; I take my sceptre out,
My royal crown ; invoke, evoke
These phantoms in the glimmering smoke ;
And you shall see—and take no hurt—
The very limb yon garter girt.

### XVII.

I AM a man.   Consider first
What we may learn, if but we will,
From that small lecture I rehearsed
With very Huxley's strength and skill
And clarity.   What do I mean,
Admitting manhood ?   This : to-day
I fed on oysters, ris-de-veau,
Beefsteak and grapes.   Will you repay
My meal with anger, rosy grow

With shame because instead of you
I went to feed chez Lavenue ?[1]
The habit anthropophagous,
Nice as it is, is not for us.
I love you : will you share my life,
Become my mistress or my wife ?
Agreed : but can your kisses feed me ?
Is it for dinner that you need me ?
But think : it is for you I eat.
Even as the object that I see,
The brain 'tis pictured in ; the beat
Of nerves that mean the picture are
Not like it, but dissimilar.
How can a nervous current be
Like that Velasquez ?  So I find
Dinner a function of the mind,
Not like you, but essential to
(Even it) my honest love of you.
Consider then yon broidered toy
In the same aspect !  Steals no joy
Glittering beneath the sad pale face ?

### XVIII.

STILL grave, my budding Arahat ?
I see the crux of my disgrace
Lies in the mad idea that—that !—
Is not dissimilar, usurps
The very function I have given
Blissful beyond the bliss of heaven—
Aha ! there is a bird that chirps
Another song.   Here's paint and brush
And canvas.   I will paint anon
The limb yon garter once was on ;
Sketch you a nude—my soul—and nude
The very human attitude
We all assume—or else are posers.
Such winners are the surest losers.
I paint her picture, recognise—
Dare you ?—one glimmer of her eyes
Like yours, one shimmer of her skin
Like that your flesh is hidden in,
One laugh upon her lips enough
Like yours for me to recollect,

[1] A famous restaurateur in the Place de
Rennes.

Remind, recall, hint?  Never !  Stuff !
You are, as aye, alone, elect.
Shall we then dive in Paris sewers?
Ay ! but not find you there, nor yet
Your likeness.   Did you then forget
You are my love ?   Arise and shine !
It was your blasphemy, not mine.


### XIX.

A FAINT sweet smell of ether haunts
Yet the remembrance.   Hear the wizard
His lone and melancholy chaunts
Roared in the rain-storm and the blizzard !
The ancient and devoted dizzard !
Appear, thou dream of loveliness !
She wore a rose and amber dress,
With broidery of old gold.   Her hair
Was long and starry, gilded red.
Her face was laughter, shapen fair
By the sweet things she thought and said.
Her whiteness rustled as she walked.
Her hair sang tunes across the air.
She sighed, laughed, whispered, never talked.
She smiled, and loves devout and rare
Flickered about the room.   She stayed
Still in the dusk: her body sang
Out full and clear " O love me ! "   Rang
The silver couplets undismayed,
Bright, bold, convincing.   In her eyes
Glittered enamelled sorceries.
She was a piece of jewel work
Sold by a Christian to a Turk.
She had fed on air that day : the flowers
About her curled, ambrosial bowers
Of some divine perfume : the soul
Of ether made her wise ; control
Of strong distilled delight.   She showered
Wit and soft laughter and desire
About her breasts in bliss embowered,
And subtle and devouring fire
Leapt in live sparks about her limbs.
Her spirit shields me, and bedims
My sight : she needs me : I need her.
She is mine : she calls me : sob and stir
Strange pulses of old passionate
Imperial ecstasies of fate.

Destiny ; manhood ; fear ; delight ;
Desire ; accomplishment ; ere night
Dipped her pale plumes to greet the sun
She was not ; all is past and done.
A dream ?   I wake from blissful sleep,
But is it real ?   Well, I keep
An accidental souvenir
Whence thus to chronicle small beer ;[1]
There is the garter.   Launched our boat,
The stately pinnace once afloat,
You shall hear all ; we will not land
On this or that mediate strand,
Until the voyage be done, and we
Pass from the river to the sea,
And find some isle's secluded nook
More sacred than we first forsook.


### XX.

YES, there are other phases, dear !
Here is a pocket-book, and here
Lies a wee letter.   Floral thyrse ?[2]
Divine-tipped narthex of the pine,[2]
Or morphia's deceitful wine?
The French is ill, the spelling worse !—
But this is horrible !   This, me?
The upholder of propriety,
Who actually proposed to form
A Club to shield us from the swarm
Of common people of no class
Who throng the Quartier Montparnasse !
I wear a collar :[3] loudly shout
That folk are pigs that go without,—
And here you find me up a tree
To make my concierge blush for me !
A girl " uncombed, so badly dressed,
So rudely mannered—and the rest ;
Not at all proper.   Fie ! away !
What would your lady mother say ? "
I tell you, I was put to it
To wake a wonder of my wit

---

[1] See *Othello*, II. i.
[2] The thyrsus and narthex were carried by
the Mænads, the maiden devotees of Bacchus.
[3] The poet libels himself ; he rarely did so.

Winged, to avail me from the scorn
Of my own concierge.  Adorn
The facts I might ; you know them not ;
But that were just the one black blot
On this love's lesson : still, to excuse
Myself to you, who could not choose
But make some weak apology
Before the concierge's eye !
True, you are far too high to accuse—
Perhaps would rather not be told ?
You *shall* hear.   Does a miner lose
If through the quartz he gets to gold ?
Yes : Nina was a thing of nought,
A little laughing lewd gamine,
Idle and vicious, void of thought,
Easy, impertinent, unclean—
Utterly charming !  Yes, my queen !
She had a generous baby soul,
Prattled of love.   Should I control,
Repress perhaps the best instinct
The child had ever had ?   I winked
At foolish neighbours, did not shrink.
Such café Turc I made her drink
As she had never had before ;
Set her where you are sitting ; chatted ;
Found where the fires of laughter lurk ;
Played with her hair, tangled and matted ;
Fell over strict nice conduct's brink,
Gave all she would, and something more.
She was an honest little thing,
Gave of her best, asked no response.
What more could Heaven's immortal king
Censed with innumerous orisons ?
So, by that grace, I recognised
A something somewhere to be prized
Somewhat.   What portress studies song ?
My worthy concierge was wrong.

### XXI.

THEN let not memory shrink abashed,
Once started on this giddy whirl !
Hath not a lightning image flashed
Of my divine boot-button girl ?
She is a dainty acrobat,
Tailor-made from tip to toe ;

A tiniest coquettish hat,
A laughing face alight, aglow
With all the fun of life.   She comes
Often at morning, laughs aloud
At the poor femm' de ménage ; hums
Some dancing tune, invades my cloud
Of idle dreams, sits poised upon
The couch, and with a gay embrace
Cries out " Hullo, my baby ! "   Shone
Such nature in a holier face ?
We are a happy pair at least :
Coffee and rolls are worth a feast,
And laughing as she came she goes !
The dainty little tuberose !
She has a lithe white body, slim
And limber, fairy-like, a snake
Hissing some Babylonian hymn
Tangled in the Assyrian brake.
She stole upon me as I slept :
Who wonders I am nympholept ?
Her face is round and hard and small
And pretty—hence the name I gave her
Of the boot-button girl.   Appal
These words?   Ah, would your spirit save
      her ?
She's right just as she is : so wise
You look through hardly-opened eyes
One would believe you could do better.
Ma foi !  And is your God your debtor ?
So, my true love, I paint you three
Portraits of women that love me.

### XXII.

THESE portraits, darling, are they yours ?
And yet there sticks the vital fact
That these, as you, are women.   Lures
The devil of the inexact
With subtle leasing ?   Nay !  O nay !
I'll catch him with a cord, draw out
By a bent fish-hook through his snout,
Give to my maiden for a play.
You, they, and dinner and—what else ?—
However unlike, coincide
In composition verified
Of final protoplasmic cells.

Shall this avail to stagger thought,
Confuse the reason, bring to nought
The rosebud, in reflecting: Hem !
What beauty hath the flower and stem ?
Carbon we know, and nitrogen,
And oxygen—are these a rose ?
But this though everybody knows,
That this should be the same for men
They know not.   Death may decompose,
Reduce to primal hyle perchance—
I shall not do it in advance !
So let the accidental fact
That these are women, fall away
To black oblivion: be the pact
Concluded firm enough to-day,
Not thus to err.   So you are not
In essence or in function one
With these, the unpardonable blot
On knighthood's shield, the sombre spot
Seen on the photosphere of sun.


### XXIII.

" NAY ! that were nothing," say you now,
Poor baby of the weary brow,
Struggling with metaphysic lore ?
" But these, being women, gave you more :
You spoke of love ! "   Indeed I did,
And you must counter me unbid,
Forgetting how we must define
This floral love of yours and mine.
That love and this are as diverse
As Shelley's poems and my verse.
And now the bright laugh comes in spite
Of all the cruel will can do.
" I take," you say, " a keen delight
In Shelley, but as much in you."
There, you are foolish.   And you know
The thing I meant to say.   O love !
What little lightnings serve to show
Glimpses of all your heart !   Above
All, and beneath all, lies there deep,
Canopied over with young sleep,
Bowered in the lake of nenuphars,
Watched by the countless store of stars,
The abiding love you bear me.   Hear
How perfect love casts flying fear

Forth from its chambers !   Those and this
Are utterly apart.   The bliss
Of this small quarrel far exceeds
That dervish rapture, dancer deeds
Strained for egregious emphasis.
These touch you not !   You sit alone
Passionless upon passion's throne,
And there is love.   Look not below,
Lest aught disturb the silver flow
Of harmonies of love !   Awake !
Awake for love's own solar sake !
Diverse devotion we divide
From the one overflowing tide.
Despise this fact !   So lone and far
Lies the poor garter, that I gaze
Thither ; it casts no vivid rays.
But hither ?   I behold the star !


### XXIV.

NOW your grave eyes are filled with tears;
Your hands are trembling in my own ;
The slow voice falls upon my ears,
An undulating monotone.
Your lips are gathered up to mine ;
Your bosom heaves with fearful breath ;
Your scent is keen as floral wine,
Inviting me, and love, to death.
You, whom I kept, a sacred shrine,
Will fling the portals to the day ;
Where shone the moon the sun shall shine,
Silver in scarlet melt away.
There is yet a pang : they give me this
Who can ; and you who could have failed ?
Is it too late to extend the kiss?
Too late the goddess be unveiled?
O but the generous flower that gives
Her kisses to the violent sun,
Yet none the less in ardour lives
An hour, and then her day is done.
Back from my lips, back from my breast !
I hold you as I always will,
You unprofaned and uncaressed,
Silent, majestical, and still.
Back ! for I love you.   Even yet
Do you not see my deepest fire
Burn through the veils and coverings set
By fatuous phantoms of desire ?

Back !   O I love you evermore.
But, be our bed the bridal sky !
I love you, love you.   Hither, shore
Of far unstained eternity !
There we will rest.   Beware ! Beware !
For I am young, and you are fair.
Nay !   I am old in this, you know !
Ah ! heart of God ! I love you so !

### XXV.

O WHAT pale thoughts like gum exude
From smitten stem of tropic tree !
I talk of veils, who love the nude !
Witness the masterpieces three
Of Rodin that make possible
Life in prosaic Paris, stand
About the room, its chorus swell
From the irritating to the grand.
Shall we, who love the naked form,
The inmost truth, to ourselves fail,
Take shelter from love's lightning-storm
Behind some humbug's hoary veil ?
Ah ! were it so, love, could the flame
Of fast electric fervour flash,
Smite us through husk of form and name,
Leave of the dross a little ash,
One button of pure fusèd gold
Identical—O floral hour !
That were the bliss no eyes behold,
But Christ's delighted bridal dower
Assuming into God the Church.
But—oh ! these nudes of Rodin !   I
Drag one more linnet from its perch
That sang to us, and sang a lie.
Did Rodin strip the clothes, and find
A naked truth fast underneath ?
Never !   Where lurks the soul and mind ?
What is the body but a sheath ?
Did he ply forceps, scalpel, saw,
Tear all the grace of form apart,
Intent to catch some final law
Behind the engine of the heart ?
He tried not ; whoso has, has failed.
So, did I pry beneath the robe,
Till stubborn will availed, nor quailed,
Intimate with the naked probe ?

I know the husks [1] to strip ; name, form,
Sensation, then perception, stress
Of nature thither ; last, the swarm
Of honey-bees called consciousness.
These change and shape a myriad shapes.
Diverse are these, not one at all,
What gain I if my scalpel scrapes,
Turning before some final wall
Of soul?   Not so, nothing is there.
The qualities are all : for this
I stop as I have stopped ; intrude
No science, for I love the fair ;
No wedlock, for I love the kiss ;
No scalpel, for I love the nude.
And we await the deep event,
Whate'er it be, in solitude ;
Silent, with ecstasy bedewed ;
Content, as Rodin is content.

### XXVI.

I WILL not, and you will not.   Stay !
Do you recall that night of June
When from the insufferable day
Edged out the dead volcanic moon
Solemn into the midnight ?   You
Shone your inviolate violet eyes
Into my eyes less sad, and drew
Back from the slender witcheries
Of word and song : and silence knew
What splendour in the silence lies,
The soul drawn back into itself.
It was the deep environing
Wood that then shielded us : the elf
And fairy in an emerald ring,
And hamadryad of the trees,
And naiad of the sleepy lake,
That watched us on the mossy leas
Look on each other's face, and take
The secret of the universe
To sleep with us : you knew, and I,
The purport of the eternal curse,
The ill design of destiny.
You know, and I, O living head
Of love ! the things that were not said.

[1] The Buddhist " Skandhas." See " Science
and Buddhism," vol. ii. p. 244.

## XXVII.

Do you recall ?   Could I forget ?
How once the full moon shone above,
Over the houses, and we let
Loose rein upon the steeds of love ?
How kisses fled to kisses, rain
Of fiery dew upon the soul
Kindled, till ecstasy was pain ;
Desire, delight : and swift control
Leapt from the lightning, as the cloud
Disparted, rended, from us twain,
And we were one : the aerial shroud
Closed on us, shall not lift again
For aught we do : O glamour grown
Inseparable and alone !
And then we knew as now the tune
Our lives were set to, and sang back
Across the sky toward the moon
Into the cloud's dissolving wrack,
Vanished for ever.   And we found
Coprolite less than chrysolite,
Flowers fairer than their food, the ground ;
We knew our destiny, saw how
Man's fate is written on his brow,
And how our love throughout was hewn
And masked and moulded by the moon.

## XXVIII.

AND who is then the moon ?   Bend close,
And clothe me in a silken kiss,
And I will whisper to my rose
The secret name of Artemis.
Words were not needed then : to-day
Must I begin what never I thought
To do : mould flowers in common clay ?
Mud casket of mere words is nought,
When by love's miracle we guess
What either always thinketh.   Yes ?

## XXIX.

So, love, not thus for you and me !
And if I am man, no more, expect
I shall remain so, till, maybe,
The anatomist, old Time, dissect

Me, nerve from flesh, and bone from
    bone,
And raise me spiritual, changed
In all but love for you, my own ;
The little matter rearranged,
The little mind refigured.   This
Alone I hope or think to keep :—
The love I bear you, and the kiss
Too soft to call the breath of sleep.
And, if you are woman, even there
I do decline : we stand above.
I ask not, and will take no share
With you in what mankind call love.
We know each other : you and I
Have nought to do with lesser things.
With them—'tis chance or destiny :
With us, we should but burn our wings.
We love, and keep ourselves apart :
Mouth unto mouth, heart unto heart,
Thus ever, never otherwise.
The soul is out of me, and swings
In desperate and strange surmise
About the inmost heart of things.
This is all strange : but is not life,
Death, all, most strange, not to be told,
Not to be understood by strife
Of brain, nor bought for gleaming gold,
Nor known by aught but love ?   And
    love
Far from resolving soul to sense,
Stands isolated and above
Immaculate, alone, intense,
Concentrate on itself.   But should
The lesser leave me, as it might ;
The lesser never touch you ; would
Your will be one with my delight ?
Leave all the thoughts and miseries !
Invade the glowing fields of sun !
Cross bleak inhospitable seas,
Until this hour be past and done,
And we in some congenial clime
Are then reborn, where danger's nought
To mock the old Parisian time
When fear was still the child of thought !
So we could love, and love, and fate
Never clang brutal on the gong,
And lunch, man-eating tiger, wait
Crouched in the jungles of my song ;

My gaze be steadfast on the star
And never to the garter glide,
And I on rapture's nenuphar
Sit Buddha-like above the tide.


## XXX.

O BLUEBELL of the inmost wood,
Before whose beauty I abase
My head, and bind my burning blood,
And hide within the moss my face,
I would not so—or not for that
Would so : the gods knew well to save
The mountain summit from the flat,
Youth's laughter from its earlier grave.
It is a better love, exists
Only because of these below it :
Mountains loom grander in the mists :
The lover's foolish to the poet.
I know.   Far better strive and earn
The rest you give me than remain
Ever upon the heights that burn
Sunward, and quite forget the plain.
Beauteous and bodiless we are ;
Rapture is our inheritance ;
You shine, an everlasting star,
I, the rough nebula : but whence,
Whither, we know not.   But we know
That if our joy were always so
We might not know it.   Strange indeed
This earth where all is paradox,
Pushed to the truth : what lies succeed
When every truth essential mocks
Its truth in figure of a phrase ?
How should I care for this, and tire
Body by will to sing thy praise,
Who take this lute, throw down the
    lyre
As I have done to-day, to win
No guerdon differing from the toil,
Were that accomplished : pain and sin
Are needed for the counterfoil
Of joy and love : if only so
All men had these in keen excess
Those were forgotten : indigo
Is amber's shadow, but—confess
For all men but ourselves the tint

Of all the earth is dull and black !
Only some glints of love bestow
The knowledge of what meteor wrack
Trails pestilence across the sky.
But we are other—you and I !
So shall we live in deep content,
Unchanging bliss, despise them still
Groping on isle and continent
Wreathed in the mesh of woe and ill?
Ah ! Zeus ! we will not : be the law
Of uttermost compassion ours !
Our snows it shall not come to thaw,
Nor burn the roses from our bowers.


## XXXI.

AY !   There's a law !   For this recede,
Hide with me in the deepest caves
Of some volcanic island ; bleed
Our hearts out by the ambient waves
Of Coromandel ; live alone,
Hermits of love and pity, far
Where tumbled banks of ice are thrown,
Watched by yon solitary star,
Sirius ; there to work together
In sorrow and in joy but one,
In black inhospitable weather,
Or fronting the Numidian sun,
Equally minded ; till the hour
Strike of release, and we obtain
The passionless and holy power,
Making us masters over pain,
And lords of peace : the rays of light
We fling to the awakening globe ;
The cavern of the eremite
Shall glow with inmost fire, a robe
Of diamond energy, shall flash
Even to the confines of wide space ;
Comets their tails in fury lash
To look on our irradiate face.
And we will heal them.   Dragon men
And serpent women, worm and clod,
Shall rise and look upon us then,
And know us to be very God,
Finding a saviour in the sight
Of power attaining unto peace,
And meditation's virgin might
Pregnant with twins—love and release.

Are you not ready ?  Let us leave
This little Paris to its fate !
Our friends a little while may grieve,
And then forget : but we, elate,
Live in a larger air : awake,
Compassion in the Halls of Truth !
Disdain love for love's very sake !
Take all our beauty, strength, and youth,
And melt them in the crucible
To that quintessence at whose gleam
Gold shudders and grows dull ; expel
The final dross by intimate stream
Of glowing truth, our lunar light !
Are you not ready ?  Who would stay ?
Arise, O Queen, O Queen of Night !
Arise, and leave the little day !

## XXXII.

LADY, awake the dread abyss
Of knowledge in impassioned eyes !
Fathom the gulfs of awful bliss
With the poised plummet of a kiss !

Love hath the arcanum of the wise ;
Love is the elixir, love the stone ;
The rosy tincture shall arise
Out of its shadowy cadences.

Love is the Work, and love alone
Rewards the ingenious alchemist.
Chaste fervours chastely overthrown
Awake the infinite monotone.

So, Lady, if thy lips I kissed ;
So, lady, if in eyes of steel
I read the steady secret, wist
Of no gray ghosts moulded of mist ;

I did not bid my purpose kneel,
Nor thine retire : I probe the scar
Of self, the goddess keen and real
Supreme within the naked wheel

Of sun and moon and star and star,
And find her but the ambient coil,
Imagination's avatar,
A Buddha on his nenuphar

Elaborate of Indian toil ;
A mockery of a self ; outrun
Its days and dreams, its strength and spoil,
As runs the conquering counterfoil.

Thou art not ; thou the moon and sun,
Thou the sole star in trackless night,
The unguessed spaces one by one
That mask their Sphinx, the horizon :

Thou, these ; and one above them, light,
Light of the inmost heaven and hell :—
Art changed and fallen and lost to sight,
Who wast as waters of delight.

And I, who am not, know thee well
Who art not : then the chain divides
From love-enlightened limbs, and swell
The choral cries unutterable.

Out of the salt, out of the tides,
The sea, whose drink is death by thirst !
The triumph anthem overrides
The ocean's lamentable sides,

And we are done with life ; accurst
Who linger ; lost who find ; but we
Follow the gold wake of the first
Who found in losing ; who reversed

The dictates of eternity.
Lo ! in steep meditation hearsed,
Coffined in knowledge, fast we flee
Unto the island from the sea.

## XXXIII.

THE note of the silence is changed ; the
    quarrel is over
That rather endeared than estranged : lover
    to lover
Flows in the infinite river of knowledge and
    peace :
Not a ripple or eddy or quiver : the monitors
    cease
That were eager to warn, to awaken : a sleep
    is opposed,
And the leaves of the rose wind-shaken are
    curled and closed,

Gone down in the glare of the sun ; and the twilight perfumes
Steal soft in the wake of the One that abides in the glooms.
Walking he is, and slowly ; thoughtful he seems,
Pure and happy and holy ; as one would who dreams
In the day-time of deep delights no kin to the day,
But a flower new-born of the night's in Hecate's way.
Love is his name, and he bears the ill quiver no more.
He has aged as we all, and despairs ; but the lady who bore
Him, Eros, to ruin the ages, has softened at heart ;
He is tamed by the art of the sages, the magical art.
No longer he burns and blisters, consumes and corrodes ;
He hath Muses nine for sisters ; the holy abodes
Of the maiden are open to him, for his wrath is grown still ;
His eyes with weeping are dim ; he hath changed his will.
We know him ; and Venus sinks, a star in the West ;
A star in the even, that thinks it shall fall into rest.
Let it be so, then ! Arise, O moon of the lyrical spears !
Huntress, O Artemis wise, be upon him who hears !
I have heard thy clear voice in the moon ; I have borne it afar ;
I have tuned it to many a tune ; thou hast showed me a star,
And the star thou hast showed me I follow through uttermost night.

I have shaken my spear at Apollo ; his ruinous might
I have mocked, I have mastered. All hail to the Star of Delight
That is tender and fervid and frail, and avails me aright !
Hail to thee, symbol of love, assurance and promise of peace !
Stand fast in the skies above, till the skies are abolished and cease !

And for me, may I never forget how things came well as they are !
It was long I had wandered yet ere my eyes found out the star.
Be silent, love, and abide ; the wanton strings must go
To the vain tumultuous tide of the spirit's overflow.
I sing and sing to the world ; then silence soon
Be about us clasped and furled in the light of the moon.
Forget not, never forget the terrible song I have sung ;
How the eager fingers fret the lute, and loose the tongue
Tinkles delicate things, faint thoughts of a futile past—
We are past on eagle wings, and the silence is here at last.
The last low wail of the lyre, be it soft with a tear
For the children of earth and fire that have brought us here.
Give praise, O masterful maid, to Nina, and all as they die !
The moon makes blackest of shade ; the star's in the swarthiest sky.
Be silent, O radiant martyr ! Let the world fade slowly afar !
But—had it not been for the Garter, I might never have seen the Star.

ΟΝ ΟΥΝ ΑΓΝΟΩΝ ΕΥΣΕΒΕΙΣ
ΤΟΥΤΟΝ ΕΓΩ ΡΟΔΟΝ¹ ΚΑΤΑΓΓΕΛΛΩ ΣΟΙ

¹ The quotation is altered from Acts xvii. 23, " Whom therefore (*i.e.* because of the poem) thou dost ignorantly worship, him do I Rose declare unto thee." Rose was the name of the poet's wife.

# APPENDIX

## À MADEMOISELLE LE MODELE—DITE JONES

*(To serve as Prelude to a possible Part II.)*

[The humour of this curious poem is partly personal, and Crowley wished to omit it for this reason. But some of the criticism is so apt, and the satire so acute, that we were unwilling to let it drop.]

IN order to avoid the misunderstanding, which I have reason to believe exists,[1] I append this simple personal explanation : let it serve, moreover, as the *hors d'œuvre* to a new feast. For it is not manifest that who wrote so much when all was mystery, should write yet more now all is clear? It is perhaps due to you, the bedrock of my mountains of idealism, that I attained the magical force to make all those dreams come true : for that, then, this.

Further, should Nietzsche play you false, and supply no key to this Joseph confection ; a kid glove and an ortolan are alike to him— and, if this be a haggis, much more is this the case !—you may apply to the only educated man in your neighbourhood, as you applied before in the matter of the Bruce Papyrus (I do not refer to the Bruce Papyrus which all who run may read—all honour to the scribe !), and he will take pleasure in explaining it to you line by line, and letter by letter, if that will serve.

Possess yourself in patience, that is to say, and, should I return from the wilds into which my restless destiny so continually drives me, you may hope for a second part which shall excel the former as realism always must excel idealism.

I have no hope for your brain, and, I am sorry to add, as little for your heart ; but there must be a sound spot in you somewhere [could you not be *natural?*—But no, no !], and that spot may yet be touched and healed by the Homocea[2] of irritable, if never yet by the Lanoline[3] of amoroso-emasculatory, verse. With this, then, farewell !

### I.

There is an eye through which the Kabbalist
  Beholds the Goat.
There is an eye that I have often kissed.
  (That hath a throat.)

[1] A young lady in the Montparnasse Quarter chose to imagine that she was the " Star " itself ; not merely the model for that masterpiece, as was the case.
[2] Latin, Homo, a man ; cea, waxen : hence, an angry man.—A. C.
[3] Tibetan, La, a pass ; English, no, No ! Greek, Linos, a dirge : hence, a temporary pæan.—A. C.

There is an eye that Arab sages say
  Weeps never enough.
There is an eye whose glances make the day
  The day of Love.
There is an eye that is above all eyes,
  That is no eye.
(Stood proud Anatta on the Bridge of Sighs
  And thundered " Why ?")
Which eyes are mine, which thine, poor ape,
    discover,
  And even yet thou hast not lost thy lover.

### II.

Khephra, thou Beetle-headed God !
  Who travellest in thy strength above
The Heaven of Nu, with splendour shod
  Of Thoth, and girt about with Love !
O Sun at midnight ! in thy Bark
  The cynocephali proclaim
Thy effulgent deity, and mark
  The adorations of thy name
In seemly stations one by one,
  As thou encirclest blinder poles
Than Khem or Ammon showed the sun
  In one-eyed sight of secret goals.
So I adore, and sing : for I
  This magic monocle avow,
Distorted from Divinity
  And wrought in subtler fashion now.
An invocation shrined and sealed
  Be this ! The many hear me not,
Though I be vocal, thou revealed.
  I scorn the eye, uphold the—what
Gods call the lotus poppy-hued,
  Brave wound of weeping Isis !—eye
Of Demiourgos, understood
  Of none, O Lily, ladily
Laden with lays of Buddhist bard,
  Maiden with ways and bays of mirth,
And music—is the saying hard ?
  Shall " Cryptic Coptic " block the birth
Of holy ecstasy ? Forbid,
  Ye Gods, forbid ! Posed block, you fail
Of bulging heart by drooping lid.
  Can you not serve as finger-nail ?

B

Ay! God of scissors! barber God!
  My earlier mystery did you learn?
Unshoe the aching pseudopod!
  Mysterious donkey, chew or churn
Your human-kindness-milk to butter!
  I gave you gratis God's advice
(Since God's responsible) to—mutter
  In gutter, pay your tithe to vice
Since virtue kicks you down its stairs.
  So thus I clothed it in strange word
To catch you thinking unawares.
  Think? do you think? Then, thinks a bird.
Read your Descartes! Nietzsche demurred?
To you, who give yourself such airs,
This riddle cannot offer snares!
" Love's mass is holier than wine and wafer.
Thou couldst not beetle be: then, be cock-
    chafer!"
Hence my address, this swoodier Swood
  To Khephra, hence the ambiguous speech,
The alluring analogue, the good,
  The loftiest heaven Art hopes to reach,
The highest goal of man as man;
  The sly Paraprosdokian.
You could not love! You could not serve
  The scouring of Love's scullery! You,
ἴσος θέοισιν? Ha, you swerve
  Back to that subtler meaning! Few
Can guess that miracle of reserve,
  That sacrament of mathematics,
That threescore glee, that three times three,
  That added scream of hydrostatics!
Not I, for one! Be assured, to fail
  With me no arrière-pensée lends.
Fall once the penny, head or tail,
  I care not—all the less my friends!
Faultlessly faulty! Regular
  In ice or fire, tis nullness counts.
So, spring of those Parnassian founts,
  A thousand garters heralded
Thy flawless solitary star:
  A million garters shall bestead
The poet's turn, when, lone and far,
All are dismissed: Some man, low brute,
Cry "Shame, O star that would not shoot,
  And yet went out!" But I, my dear,
(Good-bye!) get neither shriek nor groan:
  Kiss, curse, cat's hiss, I shall not hear,
My dear, for I shall be alone.

### III.

What change of language! Ah, my dear,
  The reason is not far to seek.
You know of old how oft I veer
  From French to Zend, from Jap to Greek.
Teste der titre polyglot
  Del Berashith, καλος kitab!
I trust you take me, do you not?
  But change of thought—ay! there's the barb
To stick and quiver in your heart!
Well, little lady, what of art?

### IV.

All things are branded change. My thought
  Long ran in one delicious groove.
Now newly sits the appointed court
  To try another case, to prove
Another crime. Last week the law
  Dealt with the garter's gross offence.
You were the Judge, enthroned on awe:
  I wove that eloquent defence,
Unwove that Rhadamanthine frown
  Which I had made myself, my star;
For I was counsel for the crown,
  And I the prisoner at the bar.
Did you not see—the sight is sad!—
  How tiny was the part you played,
How little use the poet had
  Even in Maytime for a maid?
Why.! all's a whirl; but I, be sure,
  Am axle, if at all I be;
So you, if yet your light endure,
  Are model, and no more, to me.
So well you sit, though, you shall earn
  Beyond your hourly increment
A knowledge. Are you fit to learn,
  Or will you rather be content
With muddled mighty talk of Teutons
  Evolving from the tangled Skein,
Nietzsche s research compared to Newton's
  In some one's enervated brain.
(Did I say—brain?) I'll talk, and you
  Listen or not, as best beseems
Your lily languor. Irish stew
  Shall float like dewdrops in your dreams.
So shall my new Apocalypse
  Appear to you, my model! Once
You saw a languor on my lips,
  A dawn of many molten suns,
And laughed in springtide of delight;
  But now eclipse inveils your mood
Of me: descends artistic night;
  I see a sun called solitude.
So models kiss, and understand
  So far: the picture moves them not.
By label they approve the grand;
  By critic's candour rave o'er rot.
But, let me hoist you Thornycroft,
  And cry "Behold this Rodin!" bring
Some Poynter, lift the thing aloft,
  Announce a Morice, see you fling
Your soul on knees in fervid praise:—
If so—Off, Lilith! runs the phrase.
  Now, is no barb upon the dart?
  Now, little lady, What of art?

### V.

Moreover (just a word) this chance
  I fling you over space—for luck!
This Scotland yet may catch your France,
  My crow grow germane to your cluck,

See art : see truth as I who see,
  (Am wellnigh fallen in the fight !)
Then the last lie, duality,
  May break before the victor sight.
Then, and then only, That.   Sweet hours
  Of trivial passion deep as death,
Ye are past : I face the solemn powers
  Of sex and soul, of brain and breath.
For you I lift the veil : discover
The actual, for I was your lover.
What should such word imply?  I showed
  Late, in the earlier dithyramb.
But—in yon stone there lurks a toad !—
The Quarter bleats no palinode ;
  Goat it may be, no woolly lamb.
Arithmetic assuage your wrath
Should Cambridge wit write quarter " fourth " !
What said the unctuous slime of art,
  Scrapings of beauty's palette, pimps
Of serious studios, stews or mart
  Of filth, not vice ?   Those painter shrimps !
What did they gloat upon, delight
  To think of better folk than they ?
Hear then their oracle of might,
  The sortes of a Balaam bray.
Through muddy glasses Delphi squints ;
Cowards lack words and glut on hints.

### VI.

Sibyl says nothing—she's a Sphinx !
I wonder, though, what Sibyl thinks.
She argues " he would have her grow
So fell a Trixy—point device !—
His Dante to her Beatrice
Should seem—let music's language show :—
Andante move to Allegro,
Alas for pianissimo ! "
And, in return, suspects I don
One glory more than Solomon :
" Rocks cannot satisfy the coney ;
Lingerie's always worth the money."
In fine, flop, German, from thy throne !
Leave Greek and Papuan alone !
What foreign tongues be worth our own ?
Is Armour jointed unawares ?
Is Canning King, as Carlyle swears ?
This is indeed Cumaean lore—
Ah well, 'tis pity !—say no more !

There's one and twenty for your score,
Ah, how your divination slewed awry,
Ye prurient guttersnipes of prudery !
We know as much, my girl !  We laughed,
And still can laugh at Barbercraft
Plied thus askew.   Then leave them so !
Evoke the ancient afterglow
Rose on our sacramental snow
Of silent love, of mountain grace.
Remember the old tenderness
Even in these bitter words that press
Their ardent breast, their iron face,
Out to expression.   Ay ! remember
  The ancient phantom fire of flowers,
The Druid altars of December,
  The Virgin priestess, the dread hours
Of solemn love.   Then quail before
  The deadly import of my word !
Forget your silly self, and store
  Its vital horror, stabbed and spurred
To fearful pace and torture wild
Deep in your true heart's core, my child !
For though I strip you bare, and run
  My red-hot iron through your flesh,
There is a citadel that none
  May touch—not God !   The rotten rest
Evacuate ;  be seated there.
  Let there be music, and Rome burn !
Then you may climb to be aware
  How well you serve my idle turn,
Yet to yourself avail.   There too
Lies a last doubtful chance for you.
Behold who dare !  (Ay, you are fain !)
  Purblind with prejudice?  No vision.
Palsied with passion ?  Sight in vain.
  Stupid with sense of self?  Division.
Picture, not model?  Then you win.
I painted soul, who saw your skin :—
Be soul !   That saves you.  If you fail,
Why, then, you fail !  Enough of this—
(Read not again Macbeth amiss !)
Give me one customary kiss—
An end of it !  I rend the veil.
The flag falls for the Stakes of Song.
Run, filly, for the odds are long ![1]

[1] [This " possible Part II." is still *in nubibus*
unless we are to suppose from the Greek Dedications
(pp. 1 and 16) that " Rosa Mundi " is to be taken as
such.]

# WHY JESUS WEPT

## A STUDY OF SOCIETY AND OF THE GRACE OF GOD

### 1905

### PERSONS STUDIED.

THE MARQUIS OF GLENSTRAE, K.G,
TYSON, *a farmer.*
SIR PERCIVAL DE PERCIVALE, *Bart.*, K.C.B.
SIR PERCY DE PERCIVALE, *his son.*
JOHN CARRUTHERS, *his friend and steward of his house.*
GREUMOCH, *a Highland gillie.*
ARNOLD, } *household servants.*
RITSON, }
SIR HERPES ZOSTER, M.D., *a celebrated physician.*
SIR GRABSON JOBBS, Q.C., *Solicitor-General.*
Mr. G. K. CHESTERTON.
LORD RONALD GOWER, *as Chorus.*
A Horny-Handed Brother (Plymouth).
A conscientious Chemist.
A Theatre-Goer.
Large but unseen body of retainers.

MAUD, MARCHIONESS OF GLENSTRAE.
ANGELA, LADY BAIRD.
HORTENSE, *her maid.*
MOLLY TYSON, *daughter of Tyson.*
Aged (Plymouth) Sisters, &c., &c.

*The action of the play occupies three years.*

### DEDICATIO MINIMA.

*My dear Christ,*

*A person, purporting to be a friend and disciple of yours, and calling himself John, reports you to have wept. His testimony is now considered by the best authorities to be of a very doubtful order. But if you did weep, this (vide infra) is why. Or if not, surely it would have made you weep, had it met your eye. Excuse the rhyme!*

*You ask me (on dit) to believe you. I shall be willing to do so—merely as a gentleman—till you betray the trust; but at present nobody worthy of serious consideration can give me any clear notion of what you actually assert. I labour under no such disadvantages. So have no diffidence in asking you to believe me. Yours affectionately,*

*ALEISTER CROWLEY.*

### DEDICATIO MINOR.

*My dear Lady S——,*

*I quite agree with your expressed opinion that no true gentleman would (with or without reason) compare any portion of your ladyship's anatomy to a piece of wet chamois leather; the best I can do to repair his rudeness is to acknowledge the notable part your ladyship played in the conception of this masterpiece by the insertion of as much of your name as my lawyers will permit me.*

*I am your ladyship's most humble and obedient servant,*

*ALEISTER CROWLEY.*

### DEDICATIO MAJOR.

*My Friends,*

*To you, Eastern of the Easterns, who have respectively given up all to find Truth; you, Jinawaravansa,[1] who esteemed the Yellow Robe*

---

[1] A Siamese prince who became a Buddhist monk.

more than your Princedom; you, Achiha,[1] by sticking manfully to your Work in the World, yet no more allowing it to touch your Purpose than waters may wet the lotus leaf (to take the oldest and best simile of your oldest and best poets), must I dedicate this strange drama; for, like you, I would abandon all; like you, I see clearly what is of value; or, if not, at least what is worthless; already something! Thus do I wish you and myself the three great boons Sila, Samadhi, and Salam.

### DEDICATIO MAXIMA.

To my unborn child,

Who may learn by the study of this drama to choose the evil and avoid the good — i.e. as judged by Western, or "Christian" standards.

### DEDICATIO EXTRAORDINARIA.

Dear Mr. Chesterton,

Alone among the puerile apologists of your detestable religion you hold a reasonably mystic head above the tides of criticism. You are the last champion of God; with you I choose to measure myself. Others I can despise; you are a force to be reckoned with, as Browning your intellectual father was before you.

Whether we are indeed friends or enemies it is perhaps hard to say: it has sometimes seemed to me that human freedom and happiness are our common goal, but that you found your muddied oafs in Gods, ministers, passive resisters, and all the religious team— the " Brixton Bahinchuts," we might call them; while I, at once a higher mystic and a colder sceptic, found my Messiah in Charles Watts, and the Devil and all his angels. While נחש and משיח alike add to 358, indeed, it is no odds: did you once see this

[1] A metathesis of Crowley's own name; "spelt in full," it adds up to 666; as does Aleister E. Crowley. See the signature to the " Dedicatio Extraordinaria."

[2] Nechesh is the word for serpent used in Genesis iii. Messiach is the expected Redeemer. Their identity is the Vindication of the Serpent and the revelation of Jehovah as the arch-enemy of man. The above doctrine is the most secret of Qabalistic arcana.

you were not far off from the Heart of the Qabalah.

The occasion of this letter is the insertion of a scene equivalent to an "appreciation of the Brixton Chapel" in my masterpiece "Why Jesus Wept." You asked me for it;[1] I promised it;[2] and I hope you will like it. Can I do more than make your Brixton my deus ex machinâ? You see, when I wrote " The Soul of Osiris," Europe was my utmost in travel. To-day, what country of the globe has not shuddered with the joy of my presence? The virgin snows of Chogo Ri, the gloomy jungles of Burma, filled with savage buffaloes and murderous Chins; the peace of Waikiki, the breeding hopeful putrefaction of America, the lonely volcanoes of Mexico, the everlasting furnace sands of Egypt—all these have known me. Travel thou thus far, thou also! Somewhat shalt thou learn! But otherwise; gird on thine armour for thy Christ, O Champion of the dying faith in a man dead!

Arm! arm, and out; for the young warrior of a new religion is upon thee; and his number is the number of a man.

אלהיסמטהדהכדהעולהי

## WHY JESUS WEPT.

In vain I sit by Kandy Lake.
The broad verandah slides to mist.
No tropic rapture strikes awake
The grim soul's candour to insist
The pen reluctant. Beauty's task
Is but to praise the peace of earth;
If Horror's contrast that should ask,
Off from this Paradise of mirth!
Let Kandy Lake, the white soul, mirror
The generalised concept, limn clear
England, a memory clean of error,
A royal reason to be here.
Therefore no reminiscence stirs
My heart of when I lived in Kandy.
Europe's the focus now! that blurs
The picture of my Buddhist dandy,

[1] Vide vol. ii. p. 203, supra.

[2] " I promise Mr. Chesterton | A grand ap-pre-ci-a-ti-on | Of Brixton on Ascension Day."—The Sword of Song.

Allan, who broke his wand of flame,
Discharged his faithful poltergeist,
Gave up attempts to say The Name,[1]
Ananda Maitriya became,
By yellow robes allured, enticed ;
Leaving me all alone to shame
The cunning missionary game ;
And, by bad critics topped and sliced,
Put the ky-bosh on [2] Jesus Christ.

I sing a tale of modern life
(Suited for reading to my wife)
Of how Sir Percy Percivale
Grew from a boy into a man ;
Well ware of every metric plan
A bard may dream, a rhymester scrawl,
Avoiding with deliberate "Damn ! "
(Ut supra) In Memoriam ; [3]
For such suggestion would suffice
To turn your blood to smoke or ice,
Dismissing with a hearty curse
Eunuch psychology, pimp verse.
Moreover, lest my metre move
From year to year in one dull groove,
Invention, hear me !   Strange device
Hatch from this egg a cockatrice
Of novel style, that you who read
The Sword of Song—(your poor, poor head !)
Shall stand amazed (at the new note
Flung faultless from this trembling throat)
That Crowley, ever versatile
And lord of many a new bad style
Should still in's gun have one more cartridge,
And who Ixtaccihuatl's [4] smart ridge
Achieved should still be full of mettle
To go up Popocatapetl. [4]

As song then chills or aches or burns,
The metre shall slew round by turns.

---

[1] The great task of Western occultism is to
" pronounce the name" of Jehovah ; if this be
correctly done, the universe (i.e. of sense) is
annihilated, and the true universe, of spirit, is
made present to the consciousness.
[2] To stop or silence ; to spoil the plans of.
[3] The four lines above are in the metre of
Tennyson's poem "In Memoriam." Its lack
of manliness prompts Crowley's satire.
[4] Mountains in Mexico climbed by Crowley
in 1901.

The gross and bestial demand prose.
(Glance at the page, lass, stop your nose,
And turn to where short lines proclaim
That purity has won the game !)
But stow your prudery, wives and mothers,
You know as much muck as—those others !
Your modest homes are dull ; you need
    me !
Don't let your husbands know ; but—read me !

## SCENE I.

### The Poet inducts his matter.

I draw no picture of the Fates
(Recitativo—rhyming 8s)
Presiding over birth and so on.
I leave the Gods alone, and go on.
Sir Percival de Percivale
Sat in his vast baronial hall
(All unsuspicious of the weird :
" One day a person with a beard
Shall write of thee, and write a lot
Too like the late Sir Walter Scott.") [1]
Sir Percival de Percivale
(Begin again !) was over all
The pangs of death foreseen ; his eye
Sought the high rafter vacantly.
A week, and he would see no more !
His lady long had gone—O Lor' !
I hear " St. Agnes' Eve " [2] suggest
To this 8's better a far best ;
Spenserian solemnitie
Fits this part of my minstrelsie.

Now is the breath of winter in the hall.
The logs die out — the knight would be
    alone !
The brave Sir Percival de Percivale
Sits like an image hewen out of stone.
Ay ! he must die.   The doctors all are
    gòne,

---

[1] Many of Scott's narrative poems are in the
same metre as this passage.
[2] By John Keats, written in Spenserian
stanzas.   What follows is in part a parody
of this style.

And he must follow to the dusk abode,
The solemn place inscrutable, unknown,
Meeting no mortal on that crowded road ;
All swift in the one course, ions to the kathode.[1]

Sir Percival de Percivale was brave.
There doth he sit and little cheer doth get.
He doth not moan or laugh aloud or rave !
The dogs of hell are not upon him yet.
He was the bravest soul man ever met
In court or camp or solitude—then why
Stands his pale forehead in an icy sweat ?
He mutters in his beard this rune awry :
" There lives no soul undrugged that feareth
    not to die."

Lo ! were it otherwise, mere banishment,
I deem he had feared more ! He had an heir.
This was a boy of strength with ardour blent,
High hope embowered in a body fair.
Him had he watched with eager eye, aware
Of misery occult in youth, awake
At the first touch of the diviner air
Of manhood, that could bane and blessing
    make,
The Lord of Life and Death, the secret of
    the Snake.

The snake of Egypt hath a body twin ;
It hath bright wings wherewith it well can fly ;
It is of virtue and of bitter sin ;
It beareth strength and beauty in its eye ;
Beneath its tongue are Hate and Misery ;
Love in its coils is hidden, and its nature
Is double everyway ; dost wonder why
The poet worships every scalèd feature,
And holds him lordliest yet of every kingly
    creature ?[2]

Sir Percival nor moved nor spoke ; awhile
There is black silence in the ancient hall.
Then cometh subtly with well-trainèd smile
The courteous eld, the agèd seneschal.

[1] When an electric current is passed through
water, and many other fluids, a decomposition
is effected, the component atoms finding their
way to one or other pole of the battery. These
atoms are called " ions " and the poles
" anode " and " kathode."
[2] See note *supra* to " Dedicatio Major."

On bended knee " Sir Percy ! " he doth call
To the young boy, and voweth service true.
Whereat he started, spurning at the thrall ;
But then the orphan truth he inward knew,
And on the iron ground his sobbing body
    threw.

It was a weary while before they raised him
Boy as he was, none dare disturb his grief.
And for his grief was strong, they loved and
    praised him
For son's devotion to their dear dead chief.
Long, long he wept, nor bought with tears
    relief.
He knew the loss, the old head wise and grey
Well to assoil him of his spirit's grief,
The twilight dangers of a boy's dim way,
His dragons to confront, his minotaurs to slay.

Yet, when he knew himself the baronet,
He took good order for the house, and bore
Him as beseemed the master ; none may fret
All are as well bestowed as aye before.
His father's eighty was with him fourscore.
His father's old advisers well he groups
Into a closer company ; their lore
He ardently acquires—he loops no loops,[1]
But—Bacon [2]—grapples them to's soul with
    steely hoops !

You, lass, may see here for this Boy's com-
    panions
Virtue and Peace of Mind, Prudence, Respect,
Throwing new roots down like a clump of
    banyans,[3]
Of Early Training Well the just Effect !

[1] A reference to "looping the loop," an acro-
batic feat popular at the time. Hence, to go
a wild and dangerous, as well as an indirect,
course.
[2] A sarcastic reference to the inane theory
that the plays of Shakespeare were written by
Bacon. The misquotation is from *Hamlet*—
" Those friends thou hast, and their adoption
    tried,
Grapple them to thy soul with hoops of
    steel."
[3] The banyan tree puts forth branches which
droop to the earth and take root. A single
tree may thus spread over many acres.

I would applaud thee, camel gracious-necked!
Confirm thee in thy reading of my task,
Were it not foreign to the fact.   Select
Another favour !—this too much to ask.
The boy's exemplar deeds were but an iron
    mask.

(" Ay ! for deception !" Mrs. Sally G—d,
The gawk and dowdy with the long grey teeth,
Jumps to conclusion, instant, out of hand :
" There is some nasty secret underneath !"
None nastier than thy name !  This verse, its
    sheath,
Thou poisonous bitch, is rotten.  Fact, atone !)
Such magic liquors in his veins there seethe
As, would he master, need strong order known
In life's routine, ere he may dare to be alone.

So there alone he was, and like a comet,
Leaps on the utmost ridges of the hills.
Then, like a dog returning to his vomit,
Broods in the hall on all creation's ills !
An idle volume with mere bosh he fills ;
He dreams and dozes, toils and flies afar,
Apace—the body by a thousand wills
Of fire cross-twisted, bruised, is thrust, a spar,
Wreckage of some wild sea, to seas without
    a star.

Listen, O lady, listen, reverend Abbot,
Lord of the Monastery, Fort Augustus ![1]
Hear an awakening spirit's a. b, ab! but
Let not thy mediæval logic thrust us
Into contempt ; nor, lady, can we trust us
Wholly to thy most pardonable failing,
Sentiment ; one will rot, the other rust us.
Let us just listen to the spirit ailing :—
'Tis like a God in bliss, or like a damned soul
    wailing ! [2]

[1] This monastery is chosen because of its
unpleasant proximity to Crowley's home.

[2] (A word to bid you notice with what
    mastery
Of technique that last stanza there was
    written.
I risk a poet's license on one cast, Ery !
(Pet name for thee, Eros !)  The lines are
    smitten
Into due harmony double-rhymed, well-
    knitten.

## SCENE II.[1]

SIR PERCY PERCIVALE (*on a mountain
    summit*).

No higher ?   No higher ?
All hell is my portion.
My mouth is as fire ;
My thought an abortion.
This is the summit ?
Attained is the height.
Down like a plummet
To blackness and night
Hope goes.   Not here,
Not here is Desire,
The ease from fear,
The ice from fire.
Not here—O God !
I would I were dead
Under the sod !
My brain is as lead.
My thoughts are as smoke.
My heart is a fire ;
I know not what fuel
Is feeding its fury !
In vain I invoke
The Lord of Desire !
He is evil and cruel.
The spells of Jewry
Are poured in his ear
In vain : he may hear not.
O would I were dumb !
For the pestilent fever
That bites my blood
Forces like fear
These babblings: I near not
The secret, nor come
To my purpose for ever.

Wherefore, to show I can repeat the effort,
This verse inserted like a playful kitten
To usher in the youth's c. d. e. f., ert
Or inert as may be ; it can't the lucky deaf
    hurt.)—A. C.

[1] These three soliloquies (Scenes II., III.,
and VI.) perhaps represent the self-torture of
the poet's own youth, much of which he spent
in the Lake district.

A turbulent flood
Whispers and yells,
Alight in my breast.
God ! for the spells
That unseal men—a rest !
No higher?   I have climbed
This pinnacled steep.
It mocks me, this heaven
Of thine, Adonai !
Rather be limed
In the dusk, in the deep,
Seven times seven
Thy hells, O Jehovah !
I tune the great Name
To a million vowels :—
It escapes me, the flame !
But deep in my bowels
Growls the deep lust,
The bitter distrust,
The icy fear,
The cruel thought !
O ! I am here—
And here is nought.
I must rave on.
I hate the sun.
Anon !  Anon !
Let us both begone,
Thou fiend that pourest
One by one
These evil words
In my ear, in my heart !
Here on the summit
The air is too thin.
Wild as the winds
Let me ride !  Let me start
Over the plains ;
For here my brain's
Numb, it is dumb, it
Is torn by this passion.
Down !  Eagle-fashion
Drive to the level !
Teeth ! you may gnash on !
My body's anguish
Is help to my soul.
Hail to the revel !
The dance of the devil,
The rhythms that languish,
The rhymes that roll!

Down like the swine
Of the gross Gadarene
In a maddening march
From the snow to the rock,
From the rock to the pine,
From the pine to the larch,
From the tree to the green !
          [*He leaps down, then pauses.*
O Devil !  To mock
With echo the roar
Of a young boy's spirit !
And yet (as before)
I know I inherit
The wit of the mage,
The blood of the king,
The age of the sage !
Ah ! all these sting
Through me—this rage
Is the strength of my blood,
The heat of my body,
The birth of my wit.
To hell with the flood
Of words !  Were I God, he
Had made me as fit
For all things as now,
But added a brow
Cool—O how cool !
Fool ! Fool ! Fool !
          [*With a terrible laugh he springs
          out of sight down the crags.*


## SCENE III.

SIR PERCY PERCIVALE (*in the Hall*).

O the gloom of these distasteful tomes !
The horror of the secrets here discovered !
Awake, ye salamandrines ;[1]  sleep, ye
          gnomes !
Were those  the  sylphs  that  round  me
          hovered
On the mountain, and destroyed my peace ?
O the misery of this world ; the fear
And folly that is unattained desire !
I would be master ; I, the lord of Greece ;

[1] The spirits of fire, air, water, and earth
were respectively named salamanders (fem.
-drines), sylphs, undines, and gnomes.

I the bright Deva[1] of the golden sphere ;
I the swift spirit of the primal fire :—
All these I am, not will be.   O blind ape !
All these are shapeless ; thou art but a shape,
A blind, bad-blooded bat !   Ugh !   Ugh !
   The snake
Wriggling to death amid his burning brake
Is wiser, holier, lordlier.   Open, page
Of the old Rabbi ! [2] tell me of the mage ;
Of him who would ; of him who dared and
   did ;
Of him who feared and failed ; of him who
   fell ;
One peëring lightwards through a coffin-lid,
One aching heavenwards—and achieving
   hell !
O let me do and die as they !   The wand,
The lamp, the sword, come eager to my
   hand ;—
Or, if I wander now upon the moor,
An old red-hatted witch will come, for sure,
And teach me how the dragon deeds are done
Or truck my spirit to the Evil One ;
Or else,—I wot not what.   I am drunk with
   will,
Will toward some destiny most high, most
   holy !
Some of those glories sung with awful skill
By the loud brabble of the monster Crowley,
That poet of the muck-heap !   Oh, enough !
The wind is harsh and vital on the hills.
Forth let me fare !   I am other than the stuff
His dreams are made of !   Aye !   I shall
   endure !
I am destined Lord of many magic wills.
Another Rosencreutz another order
Founds—to a better end than his, be sure !
Away !   away, my lad !   and o'er the border
I shall get myself a buxom bride,
And ride—ride—ride !          [He rises.
Ride to the blacksmith at Gretna Green,
Kiss a fair lady and find her a queen !
O a Queen, for certain !   It is I that ride,
Ride in my youth and pride

With a long sword girt to my waist,
And a strawberry mare sweet-paced,
And a long night with no moon, no star !
I will plunder the traveller from afar ;—
Aye !   and find him an ancient sage,
Learn all his wisdom, marry his daughter,
Become a king and a mage,
Lord of Fire, Earth, Air, and Water !
Ho !   my horse, lads !   Away !   To the
   moor !
Ho !   there's a fox i' the hole, that's sure.
          [Flings swaggering out of the room.


## SCENE IV.

ANGELA, LADY BAIRD (regarding
         herself in a mirror).

I thank you, M. Davenport ! [1]   This smile
Is worth a husband.   Here, one touch of
   pink
Completes a perfect picture—Are these eyes
Dark eno' to look love or sin, and large
(O Atropine ! [2]) to beam forth innocence !
Innocence, a grim jest for sixty years !
Nay, sixty-three ; I lie not to myself ;
Else one sins lying ; thus is virtue mixed,
A bubbling draught that soon lies still and
   flat ;
While my great lust runs deep and dark, nor
   changes
For all that time can do.   What of this
   boy ?
I knew his father ; the man feared me well
For all his open laughter ; would he were
Alive !   I dream one torture writhed about
His heart he'll miss in hell.   I hated him.
This boy of his I saw but yesterday
Ride barehead by me like a madman would,
Is strong and well set—aye ! desirable.
I would be better of his virgin lips :—
          [She puts her lips against the mirror.

---

[1] The Indian generic term for any good
spirit.
[2] Rabbi Schimeon, who first wrote down the
Zohar, the most sacred book of the Qabalah.

[1] A famous dentist in Paris.
[2] The alkaloid of belladonna.   It dilates the
pupil, and is abused to this end by many
foolish women.

(Nay, you are cold ! Like a dead man,
    perhaps !)
I would get gladness of the royal force
Of armed insistence against my restraint.
What is worth while, though, to a woman
    found
Fragrant and fearful to a host of men
Even yet ? they throng me, hunt me ! Why
    should I
Do this unutterable wickedness ?
Because that Moina Marjoribanks grins and
    boasts
She will achieve him ?  Angela, not so !
For its own sweet, most damnable sake,
    say yes !
Look to those cheeks, redress the red-gold
    hair,
Awake the giant wit, the master sin
That is, for an apple's sake, Lord of us all :
These shall despoil her ; these shall ruin
    him.
Yes, I shall clutch him to these sagging
    breasts
Stained, bruised,—enough !—and take his
    life in mine—
Ugh ! pleasure of Hell ! Sir Percy Percivale,[1]
Here is a strumpet.  Ha ! have you a
    sword ?
Enough.  I am dressed.  I am lovely, have
    communed
With my dark heart : I see my way to it :—
Oh joy ! joy ! joy !—Hortense, these candles
    out !
    [*The maid blows out the mirror candles.*
I will go down.  Prepare my scented
    paper,
My rosy wax against my coming here—
When, girl ? I' th' morn, i' th' morn !  When
    else ? I'd write.
        [*She goes out, with a set smile on her
        face, yet a gleam of real laughter
        beneath it.*

[1] Sir Percivale, in *Morte d'Arthur*, being
enamoured of a lady, caused a bed to be prepared.  But laying his sword therein—and in
that sword was a reed cross and the sign of
the crucifix—she was discovered to be the
devil.  See Malory, xiv. 9.

## SCENE V.

*To* CARRUTHERS, *in the Office of* SIR PERCY'S
    *Ancestral Hall, enter* GREUMOCH.

GREUMOCH.

Ay, sir.  The laddie's in the thick o't ! Weel !
She'll be off tae th' muir, a'm thinkin, sin'
    the dee.

CARRUTHERS.

He goes to solitude ?

GREUMOCH.

        Weel, weel, sir, na !
She wadna say the laddie wad gang yon.

CARRUTHERS (*smiling*).

He is ever alone ?

GREUMOCH.

        Oo ay, sir, by his lanes.

CARRUTHERS.

Go now, and tell me ever of his doings.
                [*Exit* GREUMOCH.
The hour is nigh, but when that hour may
    strike
None, not the wisest, may foretell.  I fear
A moment's mischief may destroy these years
Of grave solicitude, their work.  This boy
Thinks his grey father dead.  These words
(*tapping a letter*) shall speak
Even from the tomb.  These words shall be
    obeyed
By force of ancient habit : these give me
Supreme authority to exercise
By stealth, not overt till the hour be come
Should madness seat herself upon the lad,
And he turn serpent on his friends.  But
    no !
There is too strong a discipline of sense,
Too cool a brain, too self-controlled a
    heart :—
Well, we shall see.
            [*Turns to his books.*

## SCENE VI.

SIR PERCY PERCIVALE (on Wastwater).

God, I have rowed !
My hands are one blister ;
My arms are one ache ;
But my brain is a fire,
As erst on the fell,
In the hall ; let me dive
To the under-abode,
Where the sweet-voiced sister
Of the Screes [1] shall forsake
Her home for desire
Of me ! Say the spell !
Down then ! to drive—
　　[He dives.  The waters close over
　　　him.  He rises.
Misery ever !
I dived, and the best
Could dive no deeper.
Did I touch bottom?
Never, O never !
I stand confessed
A footler, a creeper.
These spells—'Od rot 'em !—
Are vain as the world,
As all of the stars.
This mystery's nought.
But for cold !  The lake
Is hot as the curled
Flames at the bars
Of Hell ; it is wrought
Of fire : what shall slake
This terrible thirst,
This torment accurst ?
　　　[He looks into the water.
Yet, in my face
As I gaze on the water
Is something calmer.
What if the king
Of the Screes should see me,
Give me for grace
His beautiful daughter,
Voluptuous charmer ?

[1] The mountain which bounds Wastwater
on the south.

A golden ring
Should bring her to me ;
No marriage dreamy ;
Identity, love !
　　　　　[He looks up.
Stay !  In the wood
By the waterway, stands
A delicate fairy !
　　　[MOLLY TYSON is discovered.
I'll steal from above,
Watch her.  How good !
How sweet of her hands !
How dainty and airy !
How perfect, how kind !
How bright in her thoughts !
How subtle, refined,
The least light of her mind !
Let me approach !
O fear !  O sorrow !
I fear to encroach.
Scree-king, I borrow
Thy frown, thy pride,
Thy magical targe.
To her side I glide,
To the mystical marge
Of this lake enchaunted.
O waters elf-haunted,
Bear me toward her,
A cruel marauder,
A robber of light !
O beauty !  O bright !
How shall I sing thee ?
Nay ! do not fly me !
My bird, why wing thee ?
Be kind !  O be nigh me !
She speaks not.  I'll follow !
[Leaps from boat and wades in to shore.
The world is my bower.
By height and by hollow
I'll seek thee, O flower !
I'll not turn back !
　　　　　[He pursues her.
I'll go on for ever.
The strength of a giant
Is in my limbs —
　　　　　[He reels.
My body is slack ;
My muscles sever ;

My limbs are pliant ;
My eyesight swims.
Come to me ! Come to me !
Thee have I sought !
Thou that wast dumb to me,
Come—I am nought !
[*Striving ever to follow her, he
faints and falls. The girl
stops.*

MOLLY.

Dear me ! The young gentleman's ill
too. What a nice boy it is ! I must go and
help him. Why did he call to me ? (*Goes
back.*) I was afraid—Yes, but I must go.
Something calls me. Is anything the
matter, sir ? (*He does not answer. She lifts
his head to her lap.*) How pale he is ! Poor
boy ! Shall I run to the Hall and get help,
I wonder ? (*Puts him gently down and half
rises. His eyes open.*)

SIR PERCY.

Oh ! I am but a coward. I am not ill,
I was awake. I let you hold me. Forgive
me !

MOLLY.

Forgive you, sir ? I am a poor girl of the
dale.

SIR PERCY.

Your voice is like an empress—no, a
nightingale. You do not speak like a
daleswoman.

MOLLY.

I was at school, sir, at—

SIR PERCY.

O but I love you !
There is none above you,
Not God ! I renounce Thee,
O maker ! Dissolve,
Ye hopes of delusion !
Mage, I will trounce thee !

Sage, to confusion !
Problems to solve ?
Here is my life !
My secret is told—
What is your name,
O fairest of women ?
Bosom of gold !
Faultless your fame !
An aeon were shame
Your beauty to hymn in !
Will you be mine,
Mine and mine only !
Beauty divine,
How I was lonely !
How I was mad !
Say, are you glad,
Glad of me, happy here,
Here in my arms ?
I kiss you, I kiss you !
Say, is it bliss, you
Spirit of holiness ?
Holy I hold you !
Swift as a rapier
Stabbed me your charms,
Broken with lowliness,
Smitten with rapture :—
All is so mixed ;
All is a whirl ;—
(Let me recapture
This lock ; 'tis unfixed.)
Ay, little girl,
Bury my head
In the scent of your hair !
Would I were dead
In your arms ever fair,
Buried and folded
For aye on your breast :—
That were delight,
Eternity moulded
In form of your kiss !
That were the rest
I have sought for, the bliss
I have ached to obtain :—
Ah ! it was pain !

MOLLY.

Ay ! sir, but can you love me ? Me, poor
girl !

SIR PERCY.

Love you? Ah, Christ! I love you so!
Say you love me, love me! Say so! Again!
Again! Aloud! I must hear, or I shall
die.

MOLLY.

I love you. Oh, you hurt me, you do
indeed.

SIR PERCY.

I love you, love you. Yes, you love me!
Love! Christ! Yes, oh! I love you so,
dear heart.

MOLLY.

Dear love, I love you.

SIR PERCY.

Ah, love, love, how I love you. This is
the world! Love! Love! I love you so,
my darling. Oh my white golden heart of
glory!

MOLLY.

I love you, love you so.

SIR PERCY.

Ah, God! I love you! I shall faint
with love. I love you so.

[ANGELA, LADY BAIRD, *is discovered
behind the trees. She suffers the
torments of hell.*

ANGELA (*while the duet continues*).

Ah! if there were a devil to buy souls,
Or if I had not sold mine! Quick bargain,
    God!
Hell catch the jade! Blister her fat red
    cheeks!
Rot her snub nose! Poison devour her guts!
Wither her fresh clean face with old grey
    scabs,
And venomous ulcers gnaw the baby breasts!
Vermin upon her! Infamous drab! Gr!
    Gr!
I would I had her home to torture her.
I would dig out those amorous eyes with
    gimlets,

Break those young teeth and smash that gaby
    grin!
I am utterly wretched! Ah, there is aye
    hope left!—
For see, they part!

SIR PERCY.

Ah, love, at moonrise!

MOLLY.

At my door!

SIR PERCY.

    Hell belch
Its monsters one by one to stop the way!
I would be there.

ANGELA.

Christ! he shall not be there!

MOLLY.

Farewell!

SIR PERCY.

O fairest, fare thee well!

MOLLY.

    Farewell!

[ANGELA *draws nearer, yet remains
concealed.*

SIR PERCY.

O but the moon is laggard!

MOLLY.

    Hard it is!

SIR PERCY.

Time matters not. I am so drunk with love.

MOLLY.

One kiss, one kiss!

SIR PERCY.

    A million! Ay, slack moon,
Dull moon, haste, haste!

MOLLY

    Kiss me again, again!

ANGELA.

Would I had the kissing of her with vitriol !

SIR PERCY.

Your kisses are like young rain.

ANGELA.

The slobbery kisses of virginity.
He shall soon know these calculated, keen,
Intense, important kisses,—mine !    Hell's
    worm !

MOLLY.

Yes, do not leave me.   Let us away now !
No, I must tell them, fetch my—

SIR PERCY.

                    No !  No !  No !
Nothing is necessary unto love,
Not even light.   In chaos love were well.
I love you, love you so, my love, my love.

MOLLY.

How I love you !   Oh, kiss me again !

SIR PERCY.

Yet you were best to go.   This bites like
    Hell's worst agony.

ANGELA.

Amen !

MOLLY.

God be with you !

SIR PERCY.

                    Till we meet again.

MOLLY.

At moonrise.

SIR PERCY.

                    At your door.

ANGELA.

At moonset he shall crawl away from mine.
The dog !   I hate him !   So much the more
    sure

To have him.   Damn them !   Are they cock
    and hen
To make this cackling over their affairs ?
Muck !   Muck !

SIR PERCY.

I love you so, dear heart, dear love.

MOLLY.

Oh yes, I love you !  Percy !

SIR PERCY.

Molly !  Molly !

MOLLY.

Dear boy, how I love you !

SIR PERCY.

And I you, sweetheart.

MOLLY.

Good-bye, then !

SIR PERCY.

Good-bye !   Good-bye !   At moonrise.

MOLLY.

                    At my door.

ANGELA.

Better write it down, and then you won't
forget.

SIR PERCY.

One kiss for good-bye.

MOLLY.

                    Good-bye.
[Slowly  retires,  looking  over  her
    shoulder.   They run back to meet
    each other, and embrace anew for
    some  minutes.    Eventually  SIR
    PERCY  PERCIVALE  tears  himself
    away, MOLLY disappears, and SIR
    PERCY goes sorrowfully back to his
    boat, which he now manœuvres to
    the landing stage.

### ANGELA.

Now let him find it !   This will puzzle him.
When Limburger replaces Patchouli,
Why—moonrise !

[SIR PERCY, *radiant, reaches the landing stage, moors his boat and
mounts.   He sees a pink note on
the wharf.*

### SIR PERCY.

Ah! she has dropped this !
A cruel fool am I ;
I took an honied kiss ;
I revelled in true bliss ;
Yet never thought to try
A keepsake to obtain
To wear my heart upon.
Now God is great and gracious ;
Here's medicine for my pain.
She has left it ; she has gone !
How sweet the air and spacious !
I am happy—let me see !
I guess some verse inspired
By all her soul desired,
Purity, love, well-being—ay ! and me !
[*He opens the note, reads :*—
" To love you, Love, is all my happiness ;
To kill you with my kisses ; to devour
Your whole ripe beauty in the perfect hour
That mingles us in one supreme caress—"[1]
Why, here is love articulate, vital !   I
thought that only poets, not lovers, could
so speak.   And that poets, poor devils,
speaking, could never know.
" So Percy to his Angela's distress—"
Then it is not my Molly that writes this
—who is this Percy ?—not me, at all events,
for there is no Angela that loves me.   (*A
sound of sobbing in the trees.*)   Whom have
we here ?   (*Advances.*)   'Fore God, the most
beautiful woman in the world, except my
Molly !   And her scent !   O she is like some
intimate tropical plant, luring and deadly !

[1] See above, " The Temple of the Holy
Ghost," vol. i. p. 181.

—I am afraid.   (*He discovers* ANGELA,)
Madam, can I aid you ?

### ANGELA.

Leave me !   Leave me !   I am the wretched-
est girl on the wide earth.

### SIR PERCY.

The comeliest, mademoiselle.
(*Aside.*)   I see this is a woman of the
world.   To her with speeches fit for such,
then.

### ANGELA.

I have seen all.   Pity me !   Your flattery
is a sword in my heart !

### SIR PERCY.

Seen ?

### ANGELA.

Your love—you call it so !

### SIR PERCY.

Have you, then—

### ANGELA.

I saw all.   Ah me !   Poor Angela !

### SIR PERCY.

Angela is your name ?

### ANGELA.

My name.

### SIR PERCY.

A lovely name.   No doubt your disposition runs parallel.

### ANGELA.

Meets never ?   You are no courtier, sir !

### SIR PERCY.

Do not say " sir !"

ANGELA.

What shall I say! Oh leave me! I am
ashamed.

SIR PERCY (*very pale*).

Is this your writing?

ANGELA.

Oh shame! shame! shame!
Tell me you have not read it, Sir Percy!

SIR PERCY.

Some I did read—How know you my name?

ANGELA.

I read it in my heart. O but I am
ashamed to speak to you! Or would be
were not that name as a brand to blot out
all feeling from me for evermore.

SIR PERCY (*aside*).

How she speaks! It is indeed an angel
singing.
(*Aloud.*) Indeed, I read too far.

ANGELA.

Pity me!

SIR PERCY.

Dear lady, the joy to know, and so perfectly to express such love is enough.

ANGELA.

You mock me! That girl—do you in
truth love her? She is most beautiful.

SIR PERCY.

O she is my love, my dove, my star, my—
Ah!—I hurt you! (*Aside.*) O beast! What
is this doubt?

ANGELA (*very close to him*).

I hear another anthem in those eyes.
By God, lad, you are wonderful!

SIR PERCY

What would you say?
VOL. III.

ANGELA.

What would I not do? Listen, I am
Angela, Lady Baird. I am rich. That
wealth now for the first time yields me
some pleasure.
The moon rises late, after ten o'clock:
you shall come with me. We are—neighbours, are we not? You shall come to
my castle, I say; there I will prepare all
for you and your young bride: my chaplain
shall marry you at midnight; my name and
power shall shield you from all mischance.

SIR PERCY.

I am my own master.

ANGELA.

You think so? They have kept it from
you, but you have a guardian: ask him if
you may marry a mere country lass--and
you now not yet seventeen.

SIR PERCY.

And you—how old are you?

ANGELA.

That is a rude, rude boy!

SIR PERCY.

Oh, I am so sorry, I forgot.

ANGELA.

I will tell you, though. I am all but twenty-
two!

SIR PERCY.

That is young yet.

ANGELA.

Ah, in your eyes I see sadness—I breathe;
I hope.
Think deeply in yourself, if you love this
girl!
I am older than you, to be sure; but not
so much.
May be you would find my love a better
thing than you think!                          C

Do I perspire now? Do my cheeks run down nasty wet tears? Is my love a monotonous harping on one word? Love, Percy—dare I call you Percy?

SIR PERCY.
If I may call you Angela.

ANGELA.
Love, Percy (*she lays one hand on his shoulder and looks deeply in his eyes*), is wit, and laughter, and wisdom; all of love, and in it; but love without these is a mawkish, moonish distemper of folly—and will pass. I shall not pass, my love!—Ah! you feel my breath upon your face!

SIR PERCY.
Yes—do not!

ANGELA.
I shall do so—you dare not move away from me! I have you? No? Ah, Percy, Percy, will you break a heart that only beats for you?

SIR PERCY.
You woo so well that I think you must have loved before.

ANGELA.
Ay! but not like this. If I have loved it was but to study love, to learn his arts; to make myself the queen I am, that I might have strength to win you — never before has my heart been touched. Now my arts fail me. I am a poor and simple girl; and my eyes are aching with the sight of you, and my lips are mad to kiss you!

SIR PERCY.
Your breath is like a mist of rose-dawn about me.

ANGELA (*aside*).
O true apothecary! Thy drugs are[1] expensive, but well worth the money.

[1] Here and repeatedly below she quotes or alters a well-known passage in Shakespeare.

(*Aloud.*) Nay! but I will go. You have shamed me enough. Go! Go!

SIR PERCY.
Nay! I know better of a sudden. It is you that I love!
[*He would kiss her. She draws away.*

ANGELA.
False, fickle wretch!

SIR PERCY.
I will! I will!

ANGELA.
No! No!

SIR PERCY.
Yes, I was a fool, an ass, a brute. A village girl!

ANGELA.
Blood will have blood, they say.

SIR PERCY.
You are my equal, Angela! You shall be mine, mine, mine!

ANGELA.
If I will not?

SIR PERCY.
You will. You have written more than this.

ANGELA.
If I must—

SIR PERCY.
You must.

ANGELA.
Ah love! (*She yields herself up to him. A long pause.*) Learn my first lesson; at these great moments of life, silence is the best. (*Aside.*) There is a more important one. Had that silly gowk but the wit to lead him—*à fin*—where were I now? Not a drain on his stores, but a—Professor Spooner,[1]

[1] A well-known Oxford Professor, who enjoys the reputation of having invented the blunder of the class "half-warmed fish" for "half-formed wish."

in your next lecture warn the girls to go slow :
it is dangerous as well as cruel to leave a
lover standing.

SIR PERCY.

Oh I have learnt that lesson and a thousand
others.

ANGELA.

You must go now.  The moon—

SIR PERCY.

This love is not of the moon.  To-morrow—

ANGELA.

" And to-morrow and to-morrow."  Speak
not that idle word !

SIR PERCY.

What of this chaplain ?

ANGELA.

What of your guardian ?

SIR PERCY.

Curses of hell !

ANGELA.

Hush ! hush ! sweet words must come from
such sweet lips.

SIR PERCY.

What shall I do ?

ANGELA.

You leave your fate already in my hands ?
Nay, but once married, you'll be master then !

SIR PERCY.

Shame, sweetheart !

ANGELA.

You have the strength of mind to defy convention :  we dine together : we—O love,
how dare you look such looks as these ?—

At moonset ride you back, and none the
wiser.  This always : for did we marry, the
law would have its word to say.

SIR PERCY.

But this you speak of, is it not sin ?  (*She
looks at him.*)  And what if it were ?

ANGELA.

My carriage waits—yonder.

SIR PERCY.

Ah come, come, come !

ANGELA.

Dare I ?

SIR PERCY.

Dare all things !  I will this delight ; it
shall be.  And in five years we can marry,
or my guardian will consent before.

ANGELA.

Come !
(*They go off slowly, closely entwined,
kissing and whispering.*)

SIR PERCY.

You are faint with passion, love.  You
walk heavily.

ANGELA.

Ay, love, it is to feel your strength support
me !  (*Aside.*)  Will the doctors never catch
up with the coiffeurs ?

GREUMOCH (*coming forward, as
he sees them go*).

The de'il an' a' !  The de'il an' a' !  Yon
grimly auld beetch !
Meester Caroothers, Gude guide thee the
nicht !  Y'ere auld bones shall auche sair
wi' sorrow !  Weel, weel, it's an ill warld
after a' !  Greumoch wad be slow wi' sic ill
news, an' she wull maun haste.    Weel,
weel !

[*Exit hastily.*

## SCENE VII.

MOLLY, *outside* TYSON's *Cottage.* *Moonrise.*

### MOLLY TYSON.

O there is edged the waning moon
Out of the hollow of Sty Head Pass ![1]
Gable [1] is grander for the gloom.
Lingmell [1] is silver ! Ah, the bloom
Of the rose of night ; oh, dulcet tune
Of the dew falling on the grass !

I am the veritable Queen
Of Night : my king is hither bound.
A moment and he comes—oh, breast !
Heave if thou wilt !—such stir is rest.
He comes, ah ! steals to me unseen.
The trees are high, the shades profound.

Together over moor and lake !
Together over scaur and fell !
For ever let us travel so ;
To stop so sweet a flight were woe.
Even to stop for love's own sake ;
Save my love did it—Then ? well ! well !

Better to rest together, hard
Hidden in a corner of the ghyll,
Some cavern frosted over close,
Some gully vivid with the rose
Of love ! The frost our years retard !
The rose—perfume our wonder-will !

But while I sing the moon is up.
False moon ! False moon ! So fast to ride.
He is not here ! Sure, he is dead !
O moon, reveal that holiest head !
There is much sorrow in love's cup :
Pleasure goes ever iron-eyed.

Who are these fierce and eager forms
That race across the untrodden moor,
The dark-browed horsemen lashing, crying,
Urging their weary steeds ? Half-dying
The beasts bend bitter to the storm's
Assault : they hunt ? A man, be sure !

[1] A pass, and mountains, in the Lake
district.

These figures touch my soul with fear.
What of my love ? These caitiffs chase him,
May be. Who rides ? I'll catch his bridle,
Plough with his heifer, learn his riddle.
        [*Enter* CARRUTHERS, *riding madly,*
                *crying " Sir Percy ! Sir Percy !"*
You, sir, what makes your honour here !
Sir Percy ? Who then dares to face him ?

### CARRUTHERS.

Let go my bridle, girl, I save a life.

### MOLLY.

You hunt Sir Percy Percivale !

### CARRUTHERS.

                        To save him.

### MOLLY.

God save all honest men from knaves like
        you !
Stay, though, you are his friend ?

### CARRUTHERS.

                        His guardian.

### MOLLY.

And I his promised wife.

### CARRUTHERS.

                        Mad girl, be off !

### MOLLY.

Ay, strike me, coward !

CARRUTHERS (*after thinking a moment*).
                Then, come here, behind me !
Quick, if you love him !

### MOLLY.

                I will see him safe.
What is this danger ?

### CARRUTHERS.

                Danger of your sort.
        [*She mounts.* OLD TYSON *comes out
                into the open.*

### TYSON.

Eh, less, wheer off noo ?

MOLLY.

Father ! Father !

CARRUTHERS.

Now.

[*Spurs on the horse.*

TYSON.

What, ye'll abdooct my darter ?

CARRUTHERS.

Ha ! Ha ! Ha !
[*Gallops off.*


SCENE VIII.

*Dawn.  Outside Castle Baird.  To* CAR-
RUTHERS, GREUMOCH, MOLLY, *and
retainers on horseback enter* LADY BAIRD
*and* SIR PERCY PERCIVALE *on the
battlements.*

CARRUTHERS.

Be a man, Greumoch boy, be a man !

GREUMOCH.

Sir, did she'll no be thinking ye were
greeting yersel', mon, she'll could find it
in her heert to whang ye, whateffer.

ANGELA.

You are early hunting, gentlemen.   Come
in !
My steward shall serve somewhat.
[*Sees* MOLLY.
Ha ! Ha ! Ha !
You bring a lady, then, Carruthers !

CARRUTHERS.

Madam !
Give me that boy !

ANGELA.

You fool, you are too late !
This is a man.

CARRUTHERS.

I warn you, Lady Baird.
The law calls this abduction.

ANGELA.

Pish ! the law !
Go, my dear (*whispers*) husband—ah !
how proud you look !
Come when you will !

CARRUTHERS.

Sir Percy Percivale,
I stand here in your dear dead father's name.

ANGELA.

You stand here, Percy, for yourself—and
me.

CARRUTHERS.

Come down ; I am your guardian.   Know
this !
Without me you do nought, say nought,
spend nought.
Obey me !

SIR PERCY.

Silence, sir, I am your master.
Whatever powers my father may have
given
To you, there's one that I inherit from him :
Namely, to tame the insolent.
[*Turns to* ANGELA.
Dear wife !
I go, as a tooth torn from a jaw.   Expect
I quell this folly in a little while
And come again—to Paris, said you, sweet ?

CARRUTHERS.

Leave your mad chatter with that ghastly
hag !
You fool, the woman is sixty if an hour.

SIR PERCY.

My answer to my promised bride is this.
[*He kisses her.*
So, sir !   To you, this to remember by.
[*He shoots Carruthers in the leg.*

MOLLY.

Oh, Percy, Percy, am I not your love?

SIR PERCY.

I am sorry, heartily, Miss Tyson.

MOLLY.

O !

SIR PERCY.

I did indeed speak foolishly.

ANGELA (aside).

Your purse !

SIR PERCY (aside).

O that were devilish—she's a good girl !

ANGELA.

I hate her.

SIR PERCY.

Buy yourself a pretty hat !
Forget my pretty speeches !
                        [Flings his purse down.

CARRUTHERS.

O Lord Christ !
In one short day—he was a gentleman !
Sir Percival !  Would God I were dead too !
If he had lived—thank God he died !  Sir
    Percy,
Lend me your pistol ; here's a heart to hit !
    [SIR PERCY descends, after taking fare-
    well of ANGELA, and appears again
    on horseback among his men.

SIR PERCY.

Arnold and Ritson, tend the wounded man !
To breakfast, gentlemen !
                        [Looks up.
Farewell !

ANGELA (waves her handkerchief and
    throws a kiss).

Farewell !
    [Exeunt.

ANGELA.

Ah, were such nights thy gift, dear Christ,
    all maids
Were well thy servants.  This is past all
    speaking !
The utmost triumph of a life well spiced
With victory---this beats all.  Hortense !
    Hortense !
Bring me the brandy—pour a double dram !
Here's luck---ah, Satan, give me fifty such !
                    [Drinks off the brandy.
And now to bed again—to sleep, I am tired.
                    [She goes in.

While the scene is being shifted, enter
    GOWER as Chorus.

The figure of the Marquis of Glenstrae
Demands the kind attention of the spot
Of consciousness that readers shift away
In awe of such a high exalted pot,
In England's upper Witenagemot
A figure bright enough to make the sun dun.
Yet common—to conceive him asketh not
Imagination's waistcoat buttons undone !
Any old gentleman in any club in London.

SCENE IX.

Enter the MARQUIS OF GLENSTRAE,
    Outside TYSON'S Cottage.

GLENSTRAE.

Here, then, lives the pretty piece of goods
Angela wrote me of. (MOLLY appears at doorway.)  Ah ! my pretty lass, can you give a
poor old man a glass of milk ?

MOLLY.

Yes, sir, I will fetch you one.  Pray you,
set you down awhile.
                    [He sits down.  She goes.

GLENSTRAE.

Ugh !  Ugh !  This rheumatism at me
again.  I wish I had left the business to
Arthur.—But there, there, one never knows.
(MOLLY comes in with the milk.)  There,
there !  what have you been crying for ?

MOLLY.

O sir !

GLENSTRAE.

I am the Marquis of Glenstrae, my pretty wench. If my name and fortune can serve you—there, there ! I never could bear to see a pretty lass cry.

MOLLY.

O my lord ! I am the most unhappy girl in the world.

GLENSTRAE.

Tell me about it—there, there, don't cry !

MOLLY.

'Twas but yestreen s'ennight.

GLENSTRAE.

A green wound is easiest cured.

MOLLY.

My lord, yestreen s'ennight I was wooed and won, and ere the moonrise he deserted me.

GLENSTRAE.

Dear, dear ! That's bad, bad, bad. There, there, no doubt we shall be able to do something.

MOLLY.

My father thinks it is worse—oh, far worse ! I am to go away into service—oh ! oh !

GLENSTRAE.

And so you shall, my dear, so you shall. Come and live with my wife as her companion, and we will try and find your lover for you. No doubt the arts of this—er— designing female will soon lose their power —there, there, no thanks, I beg ! I never could bear to see a pretty wench cry—there, there !

MOLLY.

O sir, my lord, how can I thank you ?

GLENSTRAE.

Come in, my dear, and let us see your father about it. . . . Can you spare an old man a kiss?

MOLLY.

O my lord !

GLENSTRAE (*kissing her*).

There, there ! Where is your father?
[*They go in.*

## SCENE X.

*Paris.   Night.*   SIR PERCY *and* ANGELA *in bed, the latter asleep.*

SIR PERCY.

O Rose of dawn !   O star of evening !
O glory of the soul of light !
Let my bright spirit speed on urgent wing !
Let me be silent, and my silence sing
Throughout the idle, the luxurious night !
How soft she breathes !   How tender
Her eyes beam down on me !   How slender
Her pale, her golden body lies !
Even asleep the dark long lashes move,
And the eyes see.   She dreams of me, of love,
Of all these bridal ecstasies
That have been ours this month, this month
     of joy.
I am a foolish boy ;
Did not the golden starred Ambassador
Come like a father to me and implore
I would look straight on truth ?
" This is no love-sick youth !"
He cried, " she is nigh sixty years of age ;
Her lovers are a mangled multitude ;
You are one duckling of an infinite brood
This vixen hath up-gobbled !" Am I mage ?
Ay, for I grant the aged diplomat
His truth—the truth for him !   To me she is
The rosy incarnation of a kiss,
The royal rapture of a young delight,
The mazy music of virginity,
Sun of the day, moon of the night,
All, all to me !
Angela, angel !   Thou hast made me man,

And poet over-man !  To thee,
To thee I owe transfiguration, peace,
The wide dominion of the wan
Abyss of air.   I can look out and see
Beyond the stars, black seas
Wherein no star may swim,
Thence, far beyond the vast revolving spheres
Dark, idle, grim,
Full of black joys and shadowy unspoken fears,
Wherein I am master.
There is no place for tears.
Cold adamant disaster
Is lord there, and I overlord.
So flits out, like a sword
Flashed through a duellist's live heart,
My thought ; in all the abodes of sense,
The shrines of love and art,
The adytum of omnipotence,
I am supreme, through thee, sweet Angela !
For all the beauties of the universe,
The glories hidden in the flower's cup,
All, all that wakes the soul to worship, verse,
Ripe verse, all wines, all dreams that the soft
   God lifts up :
All these are eidola,
Mere phantom will o' the wisps, thy love the
   real !
There is no more ideal
For me ; romance hath shot its bolt ;
The badger Jesus skulketh in his holt,
Whence let no dog dare draw him ; let him
   skulk !
All is an empty broken hulk
Floating on waters of derision,
Save for the sole true vision,
Angela, star in chaos !   Breathe, breathe
   deep !
Dear heart of gold, beat slowly in soft sleep !
Her lover watches over Angela.
Angela !   O thou wondrous woman,
Thou chaste pale goddess blooded to the
   human,
Artemis rosy like Hippolyta ! [1]
Ay. my lord, were it true, your liar's lore,
(Oh blasphemy !) were my young love an
   whore,

[1] Possibly the Hippolyta in " Midsummer
Night's Dream."

An hag of sixty ; I were greater so.
He who doth know
And fears and hates,
Is not as he who cares not, but creates
A royal crown from an old bonnet string,
A maiden from a strumpet : that is to be
   like God,
Who from all chaos, from the husks of
   matter,
Crusts shed off putrefaction, shakes a wing
And flies ; bids flowers spring from the dull
   black sod,
Is not the scientist to shatter
Beauty by dint of microscope,
But wakes a wider hope
And turns all to the beautiful ; so I.
Angela, wake !  The midnight hour is nigh :—
Let us renew the vows of love !  appease
These amorous longings with grave ecstasies,
The holy act of uttermost communion,
The sacrament of life !   Awake, awake !
There is a secret in our subtle union
That masters the grey snake.
Ay !  let him lurk !   The Tree of Knowledge
   we
Have fed our fill of ; this is Eden still.
Awake, O Love !  and let me drink my fill
Of thee—and thou of me !
                    [ANGELA *wakes.*

ANGELA.

Ah, Percy, bend you over me !  Bend deep !
Kiss my own eyelids out of tender sleep
Into exasperate love !   Bend close !
Fill me, thy golden rose,
With dew of thy dear kisses !

SIR PERCY.

Ay, again !
Love, love, these raptures are like springtide
   rain
Nestling among green leaves.

ANGELA.

The Lady of Love weaves
Fresh nets of gossamer for thee and me.
O take not back thy lips, even to sing !

SIR PERCY.

Come, rich, come overrolling ecstasy !
I am like to die with joy of everything.

ANGELA.

Die, then, and kiss me dead !

SIR PERCY.
I die ! I die !

ANGELA.

Thy flower-life is shed
Into eternity,
A waveless lake.

SIR PERCY.

Sleep, sleep !                          [*He sleeps.*

ANGELA.

I am awake—
    And being awake I weary somewhat of
these jejune platitudes, these rampant ulula-
tions of preposterous puberty.  These are
the very eructations of gingerbread ; they are
the flatulence of calf-sickness.  I thought I
had taught the boy more sense.  He weakens,
and I weary.  As you will, my Lady Glenstrae !  Hortense !  (HORTENSE *enters with
a glass of brandy.*)    Brandy !

HORTENSE.

Here, milady.

ANGELA.

Not enough, you she-devil.  More !  More !
    [*Exit.*  ANGELA *falls back to sleep.*

SCENE XI.

*Paris.*  ANGELA, LORD *and* LADY GLEN-
STRAE, SIR PERCY DE PERCIVALE.

ANGELA.

You will not believe what I tell you?
These friends will tell you what I mean, and
if I mean it !  You had your dismissal this
morning.   Never dare to address me again !

SIR PERCY.

What !  I have loved you, and you me—
No?—it cannot be so ! and now—I am ill—
you cast me away !  (*Turns his face away.*)
Forgive me, I am very weak.

ANGELA (*goes to him and stands over him*).

You shall have truth, you blind little fool.
I hate you.  From the hour you kissed that
village drab, I hated you.  I wanted your
youth, your strength, your life, your name
on my list, your scalp at my girdle.  Enough !
Do you understand?   These friends will
teach you.  May I never see your pale pasty
face again !
    [*She spits at him and goes.*

SIR PERCY (*half rises and falls back*).

Oh ! oh !  It is impossible.  Lord Marquis, you are a good man.  Tell me, it is a
hideous dream.

GLENSTRAE.

No dream, my boy.  You are the hundredth
she has treated after this fashion.  But cheer
up now.  There !  There !  Women are all
the same.  Eh, Maud ?

LADY GLENSTRAE.

Who calls?   What do you want?   Leave
me alone !

GLENSTRAE.

Ah, nothing !  Nothing, my dear.

LADY GLENSTRAE.

Pull down the blinds.

GLENSTRAE.

Certainly, certainly, my dear, I will ring.
                                    [*Rings.*

SIR PERCY.

I am sick and sane now. God do so to me and more also if I look at a woman again. What a fool I have been !

GLENSTRAE.

Ah, my boy, you will keep clear of the old ones, I know. (*Enter a footman.*) These blinds down ! (*The man obeys.*) But a tasty little morsel like your Molly—your first love. —Eh, my lad ? There ; there, don't be angry !

SIR PERCY.

Pshaw ! You disgust me.
[*The footman turns to go.*

GLENSTRAE (*to footman*).

Wait ! (*To* SIR PERCY.) Would you tell *her* so ?

SIR PERCY.

If I deigned speech.

GLENSTRAE.

Simmons, ask Miss Tyson to step here for a moment. (*Exit servant.*) After which I shall leave you for an hour, my boy. I am to do some business — aha ! some rather pleasant business. There ! there !
[*Enter* MOLLY TYSON.

MOLLY.

O ! Sir Percy ! My lord, could you not have told me of this ?

GLENSTRAE.

Now, your condition !

MOLLY.

Sir Percy, do you, can you love me ? You promised to love me for ever.

SIR PERCY.

Who is this woman ? I am weary of these women.

MOLLY.

Sir, sir, acknowledge me. You know not what hangs on it—my honour even !

GLENSTRAE.

A speech of this breed is not in the bond —but let it pass. There ! there !

MOLLY.

Sir, I beseech you—for an hour—take me away. I am in terrible trouble of body and soul—danger, misery.

SIR PERCY.

O, go ! to the devil for me ! What do I care ? I am tired, I tell you.

GLENSTRAE.

You see, Molly, I told you true.

MOLLY (*turns to the* MARCHIONESS *and kneels by her*).

O, my lady Marchioness ! You are a great lady. Spare me this shame, your lord's shame, your own shame. . . .

LADY GLENSTRAE.

Take her away. Less light !

GLENSTRAE.

Ha ! Ha !

SIR PERCY.

I cannot see your humour, Glenstrae— forgive me so far ! And to tell the truth of it, I can do nothing and care to do less.

GLENSTRAE.

Come, Molly !

MOLLY.

Must I, must I ? Oh, sir, have pity !

GLENSTRAE.

A bargain's a bargain—but there ! there ! —what are you growling at ? A thousand a year and a flat in Mayfair is better than farmer Tyson's butter and eggs.

MOLLY.

Must it be now?

GLENSTRAE.

Much better now. There, there! Wish me good luck, Percy!

SIR PERCY.

I know nothing of your devil's game. Good luck!

GLENSTRAE.

Caste, John Burns.[1]
[*Exeunt* MARQUIS *and* MOLLY.

LADY GLENSTRAE.

Hist! Percy, hither to me. Is no one looking?

SIR PERCY.

No, there is no one here.

LADY GLENSTRAE.

I can cure you. I can make you strong and happy again. O what rapture!

SIR PERCY.

What is it?

LADY GLENSTRAE.

Here, let me give you this medicine. A little prick of pain, and then—pleasure—Oh!
[*She bends caressingly over the arm of*
SIR PERCY DE PERCIVALE, *and*
*stabs it with a needle.*
Get a doctor to give you a prescription like this—they ask a hundred francs—oh! it is a shame! Buy a little syringe; and that is Heaven for all your life.—How do you feel?

SIR PERCY.

Why, I am well at once. I never felt better in my life. The devil take my trouble

1 A demagogue of the period.

now! I shall go out and conquer the whole world. I shall be the great magician, the Lord of the Stars. I have it in me to write poetry. Yes, that, first. (*Goes to table and takes pen and paper.*) In praise of—what is your medicine called, dear Marchioness?

LADY GLENSTRAE.

Who calls me? What is it? Leave me alone!

SIR PERCY.

Tell me, dear Lady—Maud!

LADY GLENSTRAE.

Ah! you are the boy.

SIR PERCY.

Your boy, queen!

LADY GLENSTRAE.

Oh, yes, my boy.

SIR PERCY.

What is this medicine called?

LADY GLENSTRAE.

What medicine? I never take medicine!

SIR PERCY.

But you gave it me—with a needle.

LADY GLENSTRAE.

Oh, that medicine! You like it?

SIR PERCY.

It is heaven, heaven! It is called—

LADY GLENSTRAE.

Morphia.
[*They rest.*

## SCENE XII.

### TWO YEARS LATER.

*Night: The Strand, opposite the Hotel Cecil. A chemist's shop behind. A grey, old, wizened man staggers into the shop.*

**CHEMIST.**

This prescription has been made up before, sir.

**THE MAN.**

Yes, I want it renewed, quickly, quickly.

**CHEMIST.**

I am afraid, sir, it is marked "once only."

**THE MAN.**

You won't? O if you knew what I suffer! I will pay you double.

**CHEMIST.**

I'm afraid not, sir. You may try elsewhere.

**THE MAN.**

O God! O God!

*[Goes out. To him enter on the pavement a bedraggled female.*

**THE WOMAN.**

Come home, ducky, won't you?

**THE MAN.**

O God! O God! I cannot bear it any longer. It is the last I have.

*[He fumbles awhile inside his coat.*

**THE WOMAN** (*catching hold of him*).

Come, stand me a glass of wine, there's a dear.

**THE MAN.**

Ah! that is well. Can I use this woman, I wonder?

**THE WOMAN.**

O God! I am punished. Sir Percy here! What is the matter, dear my love?

**SIR PERCY.**

Never mind love—you are?

**MOLLY.**

O sir, your Molly, that you broke the heart of. See what has come to me!

**SIR PERCY.**

Ah, if you knew. You are the lucky one! I am in grips with a more dread disease Than all your wildest nightmares figure you!

*[A carriage rolls by, as from the theatre. It stops owing to a block in the traffic.*

**MOLLY.**

O sir! I am so sorry for you.

**SIR PERCY.**

And a lot of good that does!

*Enter, on the pavement, the* MARQUIS OF GLENSTRAE, *in his fur coat. The occupant of the carriage,* ANGELA, LADY BAIRD, *recognises him and leans out to greet him.*

**GLENSTRAE.**

Ah, my dear lady, how do you do this cold weather?

**ANGELA.**

Well, very well, thank you—and you?

**GLENSTRAE.**

Well enough—a little rheumatic, perhaps. H'm!

**ANGELA.**

And the dear Marchioness?

**GLENSTRAE.**

Oh, very sad—there—there! She has had to be, ah!—er—under treatment.

ANGELA.

Dear, dear, how very sad! Hullo! Look here on this picture and on that!

[MOLLY *and* SIR PERCY *are discovered.*]

GLENSTRAE.

Oh! Ah! I think I must go on. I have an appointment at the club.

SIR PERCY.

Yet your lordship walks East.

MOLLY.

Oh, I am not revengeful. Give me a fiver, my Lord Marquis, and we'll call it square.

SIR PERCY.

For me, my angel, get this prescription filled.

ANGELA.

Oh, go to the devil, both of you! Marquis, shall we sup at the Carlton?

GLENSTRAE.

With pleasure — ha! a most amusing meeting—ha!

ANGELA.

Where have you been this evening?

GLENSTRAE.

O most dull, indeed! I had to give the Presidential address at St. Martin's Town Hall for the Children's Special Service Mission.

ANGELA.

Yes, your Lordship is indeed a true friend to the little ones. A curious coincidence. I am the new president of the Zenana Mission.

GLENSTRAE.

You!

ANGELA.

Think of the poor heathen women kept in such terrible seclusion!

GLENSTRAE.

Ah! I had not thought your sympathy was genuine; but there, there! There is more real good in human nature than—

ANGELA.

Genuine enough! But what a jest is this!

GLENSTRAE.

A most remarkable coincidence—a very pleasant reminder. Shall we sup?

ANGELA.

Yes; a magnum of Pol Roger, '84 —

GLENSTRAE.

With a dash of brandy in it—

ANGELA.

Will clothe our old loves in a halo of romance again.

GLENSTRAE.

Ha! Ha! We wear well, eh? There, there! (*Opens the carriage door.*) The Carlton. (*Follows and shuts door.*)

[SIR PERCY *and* MOLLY *part. The effect of his last dose is worn off; clutching his prescription, he goes off with set teeth.* MOLLY *goes the other way: to her enter a theatre-goer.*]

MOLLY.

Won't you come with me, ducky?

THEATRE-GOER.

Not to-night. See you some other night.

MOLLY.

Oh, do come, dearie!

THEATRE-GOER.

No, I tell you --try Liverpool Street!

[*Curtain.*

*What follows is strictly by request in the*
*interest of " healthy optimism."*

So far my pen has touched with vivid truth
The constant story of the eternal struggle
Of age and sense with flatulence and youth.
Now—see the venal poet start to juggle !
Young ladies, you desire to see a comedy !
The poet's master pen shall twist the river
Of song into a simple to-and-from eddy,
And you shall laugh where once you feared
      to shiver.
So listen to the happy termination
Of this apparently so sad relation !
'Twill suit your rosy dreams to admiration !
But, be the gatepost witness ! it is rot.
Still, if I hide my face with due decorum
Behind a silken kerchief in the forum,
And laugh aloud—at home—
At the silliness of Rome,
You'll forgive me, will you not ?


SCENE XIII.[1]

The Meeting-House of the Brethren
Gathered Together To The Name Of The
Lord Jesus, sub-section Anti-Ravenite of
the Exclusive section. They are of course
Anti-Stewart, and sound on the Ramsgate
Question, while observing an armed neu-
trality in the matter of Mr. Kelly's action.[2]
In the midst a table with a loaf and a bottle :
also, by their own account, Jesus Christ.
Forms, varnished yellow, around it, them,
and (I suppose) Him. On one of them is a
blackboard with the notice in white paint :

[1] This scene, with the exception of the introduction of Mr. Chesterton, and (of course)
Sir Percy and Molly, is an accurate description
of the "meeting" at Streatham. The incidents and style are authentic.
[2] Themselves must be consulted for elucidation of these historic controversies. Outsiders,
who merely noticed the horripilation of the
Universe, but saw no obvious reason, have
the key in their hands, and may pursue the
research on these lines. Geological papers
please copy.—A. C.

"Those not in fellowship please sit behind
this board." Accepting this dread limitation
are several miserable, well-dressed children
with active minds, who, finding nothing to
interest them in the proceedings, are pointing out to each other the obscene passages
in the Bible ; or, this failing from insufficient
acquaintance with the sacred volume, are
engaged in the Sisyphean task of getting rid
of the form in front by deglutition. There
is also an anæmic and pimply youth with a
sporadic beardlet and a dirty face—if it is a
face—who is vastly interested : one would
say an habitual reader of the *Daily Mail*
watching nobility at lunch.

In front of the board, around the table,
are several dear old ladies and gentlemen,
a beautiful, overdressed, languid woman,
some oilily lousy, lop-eared, leprous, lack-
brained, utterly loathsome tradespeople who
gurgle and grin, and a sprinkling of horny-
handed sons of toil, very shiny.

Above, with an olive-branch in one hand
and a copy of the *Daily News* in the other,
floats Mr. G. K. Chesterton in the position
Padmasana,[1] singing " Beneath the Cross
of Jesus " with one voice, and attempting
" God save the Queen ! " with the other in
a fashion calculated to turn any marine, if
but he be filled with honourable ambition
to excel in the traditional exploits of his
corps, green with envy.

Behind, and for this reason not previously
observed by the vigilant eye of the reader,
are Sir Percy Percivale and Molly Tyson.

Near the " Lord's Table " a brother is
standing and praying ; he intersperses his
prayer with repeated " you know's," like
the Cairene bore in Marryat's novel.


1ST AGED SISTER (*sotto voce*).

Yes ! it's all so blessèd and romantic,
my dear, thank the Lord ! They were both
brought to Jesus on one night, Ascension
Day, as the poor Pagan[2] bodies call it,
through the ministration of Mr. Hogwash,

[1] The " lotus " position, in which Buddha is
commonly represented as sitting.
[2] By Plymouth Brethren all so-called Christian festivals are (rightly, of course, from a
historical standpoint) considered mere aliases
of pagan feasts. —A. C.

the Baptist minister at Brixton (*Mr. Chester-ton executes the cake-walk*), who they say is a good man, and very much blessed of the dear Lord, my dear, in his ministrations, though of course he has not been brought out of sect as yet.[1]

2ND AGED SISTER (*sotto voce*).

Dear! Dear! Very sad! Perhaps the dear Lord will open his eyes.
[*The praying brother sits down sud-denly, satisfied with himself.*

A HORNY-HANDED BROTHER (*who rises grunting, as if the action were painful or unfamiliar*).

Matthew Twenty-fourth and Forty-third and he said unto them: Whither of the twins will ye that I deliver unto you, Barab-bas, or Djeesas that is cawled Croist? Deer Brotheren
[*But let him expound it to himself while we listen to the aged sisters!*

1ST AGED SISTER (*sotto voce*).

So now they're come out of sect, a most marvellous example, my dear, of the wonder-ful workings of the Holy Ghost, don't you think so, my dear? and I hear they're to be received into fellowship next Lord's Day.

2ND AGED SISTER (*do.*).

The young people are interested in one another,[2] are they not?

1ST AGED SISTER (*do.*).

Yes! it's all very dear and blessèd. But hush! how beautifully Mr. Worcester is expounding about Barabbas!

[1] Godly for "become a Plymouth Brother."
—A. C.
[2] Godly for "are in love with one another."
—A. C.

MR. G. K. CHESTERTON (*altogether inaudibly*).

This scene is all description and no drama, and ought to satisfy Mr. Bernard Shaw's idea of a dramatic scene.
[*The beautiful woman gets up and goes. The poet hastily follows her out.*

SCENE XIV.

TEN MONTHS LATER.

SIR PERCY DE PERCIVALE'S *Ancestral Hall.*

SIR HERPES ZOSTER, M.D.
SIR GRABSON JOBHS, Q.C.

SIR HERPES Z.

Yes, indeed, a most fortunate event. The children weigh 46 lbs. between the three of them. All boys!

SIR GRABSON J.

Good! Good! No chance of heirs failing—ha!
But a word in your ear. This morphia?

SIR HERPES Z.

Not a sign of relapse, old friend, and never will be now. Sir Percy is as sound a man as lives in England—I took four other opinions.

SIR GRABSON J.

None as weighty as your own.

SIR HERPES Z.

You are polite, very polite. Where is Carruthers?

SIR GRABSON J.

He is away to Windsor—the King (*they beat their foreheads eighty-seven times upon the ground*) knights him to-day.

SIR HERPES Z.

I knew he had the O.M. and the F.Z.S.; but this knighthood?

SIR GRABSON J.

He has taken up political economy. He will marry a duchess. Greumoch, too, is doing well. After the—ah—event we all deplored so, he entered the Benedictines at Fort Augustus; and to-morrow they instal him as Lord Abbot.

SIR HERPES Z.

What? And he a Highlander?

SIR GRABSON J.

It seems that was a mere disguise; his true name was Johann Schmidt.[1]

SIR HERPES Z.

So? Why the deception?

SIR GRABSON J.

A Jesuit, no doubt! But about Lady Percivale now?

SIR HERPES Z.

Better and better. Old Farmer Tyson, luckily enough, as it turned out, insisted on examination, and no less than twenty-three skilled surgeons—all men of note!—declared her to be *virgo intacta*.

SIR GRABSON J.

Eh? What?

SIR HERPES Z.

You see, Englishmen—ah!

SIR GRABSON J.

Er—ah?

[1] The Abbot of the Fort-Augustus Abbey was at this time a German.

SIR HERPES Z.

Ah!

SIR GRABSON J.

Er—ah! As Whistler said, "You put out your arm, and you hit three"[1]—eh?

SIR HERPES Z.

Probably. At least the anatomical detail is certain. Here is a ph—

SIR GRABSON J.

Tush, tush, old friend, I can take your word for it.

SIR HERPES Z.

You have some good news to announce, I think, as well as I.

SIR GRABSON J.

Sad for the general commonwealth, but of particular joy in this house. The Marquis of Glenstrae had the misfortune yesterday to fall against a circular saw in motion.

SIR HERPES Z.

Dear, dear! and how was that?

SIR GRABSON J.

His lordship was very fond of children, as you may know. It seems he was pursuing

[1] Certain of our little-instructed surgical readers have expressed themselves dissatisfied with the explanation given by Sir G. Jobbs. They argue that it requires to be amplified, since the Marquis of Glenstrae must have had normal habits, otherwise so pure a poet as Crowley would never have introduced him. This is true; but Sir R. Burton has pointed out that the outcry against Greek Art comes chiefly from those who are personally incapable of it.

Englishmen and Virgins are then like Alpine guides and mountains; some can't go, and the rest lose the way.

Hence Mr. Kensit.

*Further Note.*—The silly cavillers now observe that this is no solution of the difficulty, Sir P. Percivale being English. This is absurd: (1) Lady Percivale is just as likely to have remained *virgo intacta* as any other mother. (2) The English law, cognisant of the dilemma set forth above, permits the use of a poker in the relations of man and wife. (3) If God's Grace can break a habit, it can surely rupture a hymen.—AUTHOR.

— it is, I am told, an innocent child's game!—one of the factory hands; and—he stumbled. He was sawn slowly into no less than thirty-eight pieces.

### SIR HERPES Z.

But how does this bear on the case?

### SIR GRABSON J.

Dying without issue, he has left all to Sir Percy here; the King (*cheers from large but unseen body of retainers, who have been eavesdropping*), moreover, unwilling that the Marquisate should die out, will bestow it on the same lucky young fellow.

### SIR HERPES Z.

This is marvellous news!

### SIR GRABSON J.

Again, Lady Baird has just perished in awful agony. Having suffered for twenty years from a hideous and incurable disease, she brought matters to a climax last night by falling into a barrel of boiling sulphuric acid.

### SIR HERPES Z.

How so?

### SIR GRABSON J.

It was her bath-night.

### SIR HERPES Z.

Ah! enamel! But why did it hurt her?

### SIR GRABSON J.

(*Impressively.*) It is the finger of God!

### *The Poet concludes.*

Now I have written four-and-twenty hours
Without a decent rest by Kandy Lake.

I invoke the urgent elemental powers
To bring all to an end for Buddha's sake.
I must bid all ye matrons fond farewell,
Knowing your inmost thoughts; that, had
    ye dared,
Ye would be just as far *en route* for hell
As Angela, the gentle Lady Baird;
And all ye youths, aware that Percy's fall
Is something to be envied of ye all :
And all ye parsons, seeing that ye pray
Your Father for the Luck of Lord Glen-
    strae.

Enough of this ! Insistent Fates
Bid me return to rhyming 8s.
I say what I have seen ill done
In honest clean-lived Albion ;
And if these things the green tree grows,
What price the dry, my lords? Who
    knows?
You say that I exaggerate ;
That " we are not as bad as that."
(Excuse the doubtful tag of verse !)
*Au contraire*, you are vastly worse.
I see the virtuous and the vicious,
The *sans reproche* and the suspicious,
All tarred with the same nasty tar,
Because—I see you as you are.
Permit me to reduce the list
Of optimist and pessimist
By just my name ! I am neither, friends.
I know a stick has got two ends !
Nothing were easier than to show
That Lady Baird avoided woe ;
And Lord Glenstrae, that worthy peer,
Saved whisky by supplying beer.
For what is good, and makes for peace,
What evil, wisdom must increase
Well near omniscience before
One guesses what it all is for.
Still, since *de gustibus non est*—
(My schoolboy readers know the rest !)
I much prefer—that is, mere I—
Solitude to Society.
And that is why I sit and spoil
So much clean paper with such toil
By Kandy Lake in far Ceylon.
I have my old pyjamas on :

I shake my soles from Britain's dust :
I shall not go there till I must ;
And when I must—ah, you suppose
Even I must !—I hold my nose.
Farewell, you filthy-minded people !
I know a stable from a steeple.
Farewell, my decent-minded friends !
I know arc lights from candle-ends.

Farewell ! A poet begs your alms,
Will walk awhile among the palms.
An honest love, a loyal kiss,
Can show him better worlds than this ;
Nor will he come again to yours
While he knows champak-stars [1] from sewers.

[1] The champak, one of the most beautiful
of tropical flowers, has a star-shaped blossom.

# ROSA MUNDI

## AND OTHER LOVE-SONGS

### 1905

#### I

1. ROSE of the World !
Red glory of the secret heart of Love :
Red flame, rose-red, most subtly curled
Into its own infinite flower, all flowers above !
Its flower in its own perfumed passion,
Its faint sweet passion, folded and furled
In flower fashion ;
And my deep spirit taking its pure part
Of that voluptuous heart
Of hidden happiness !

2. Arise, strong bow of the young child Eros !
(While the maddening moonlight, the
memoried caress
Stolen of the scented rose
Stirs me and bids each racing pulse ache,
ache !)
Bend into an agony of art
Whose cry is ever rapture, and whose tears
For their own purity's undivided sake
Are molten dew, as, on the lotus leaves
Silver-coiled in the Sun
Into green-girdled spheres
Purer than all a maiden's dream enweaves,
Lies the unutterable beauty of
The Waters. Yea, arise, divinest dove
Of the Idalian, on your crimson wings
And soft grey plumes, bear me to yon cool
shrine
Of that most softly-spoken one,
Mine Aphrodite ! Touch the imperfect
strings,
Oh thou, immortal, throned above the moon !
Inspire a holy tune
Lighter and lovelier than flowers and wine
Offered in gracious gardens unto Pan
By any soul of man !

3. In vain the solemn stars pour their pale
dews
Upon my trembling spirit ; their caress
Leaves me moon-rapt in waves of loveliness
All thine, O rose, O wrought of many a muse
In Music, O thou strength of ecstasy
Incarnate in a woman-form, create
Of her own rapture, infinite, ultimate,
Not to be seen, not grasped, not even imagi-
nable,
But known of one, by virtue of that spell
Of thy sweet will toward him: thou, unknown,
Untouched, grave mistress of the sunlight
throne
Of thine own nature ; known not even of me,
But of some spark of woven eternity
Immortal in this bosom. Phosphor paled
And in the grey upstarted the dread veiled
Rose light of dawn. Sun-shapen shone thy
spears
Of love forth darting into myriad spheres,
Which I the poet called this light, that
flower,
This knowledge, that illumination, power
This and love that, in vain, in vain, until
Thy beauty dawned, all beauty to distil
Into one drop of utmost dew, one name
Choral as floral, one thin, subtle flame
Fitted to a shaft of love, to pierce, to endue
My trance-rapt spirit with the avenue
Of perfect pleasures, radiating far
Up and up yet to where thy sacred star
Burned in its brilliance : thence the storm
was shed
A passion of great calm about this head,
This head no more a poet's ; since the dream
Of beauty gathered close into a stream

Of tingling light, and, gathering ever force
From thine own love, its unextended source,
Became the magic utterance that makes Me,
Dissolving self into the starless sea
That makes one lake of molten joy, one pond
Steady as light and hard as diamond ;
One drop, one atom of constraint intense,
Of elemental passion scorning sense,
All the concentred music that is I.
O ! hear me not !  I die ;
I am borne away in misery of dumb life
That would in words flash forth the holiest
    heaven
That to the immortal God of Gods is given,
And, tongue-tied, stammers forth—my wife !

4.  I am dumb with rapture of thy loveliness.
All metres match and mingle ; all words tire ;
All lights, all sounds, all perfumes, all gold
    stress
Of the honey-palate, all soft strokes expire
In abject agony of broken sense
To hymn the emotion tense
Of somewhat higher—O ! how highest !—
    than all
Their mystery : fall, O fall,
Ye unavailing eagle-flights of song !
O wife ! these do thee wrong.

5.  Thou knowest how I was blind ;
How for mere minutes thy pure presence
Was nought ; was ill-defined ;
A smudge across the mind,
Drivelling in its brutal essence,
Hog-wallowing in poetry,
Incapable of thee.

6.  Ah ! when the minutes grew to hours,
And yet the beast, the fool, saw flowers
And loved them, watched the moon rise,
    took delight
In perfumes of the summer night,
Caught in the glamour of the sun,
Thought all the woe well won.
How hours were days, and all the misery
Abode, all mine : O thou ! didst thou regret ?
Wast thou asleep as I ?
Didst thou not love me yet ?

For, know ! the moon is not the moon until
She hath the knowledge to fulfil
Her music, till she know herself the moon.
So thou, so I !  The stone unhewn,
Foursquare, the sphere, of human hands
    immune,
Was not yet chosen for the corner-piece
And key-stone of the Royal Arch of Sex ;
Unsolved the ultimate $x$ ;
The virginal breeding breeze
Was yet of either unstirred ;
Unspoken the Great Word.

7.  Then on a sudden, we knew.  From deep
    to deep
Reverberating, lightning unto lightning
Across the sundering brightening
Abyss of sorrow's sleep,
There shone the sword of love, and struck,
    and clove
The intolerable veil,
The woven chain of mail
Prudence self-called, and folly known to who
May know.  Then, O sweet drop of dew,
Thy limpid light rolled over and was lost
In mine, and mine in thine.
Peace, ye who praise ! ye but disturb the
    shrine !
This voice is evil over against the peace
Here in the West, the holiest.  Shaken and
    crossed
The threads Lachesis wove fell from her
    hands.
The pale divided strands
Were taken by thy master-hand, Eros !
Her evil thinkings cease,
Thy miracles begin.
Eros !  Eros !—Be silent !  It is sin
Thus to invoke the oracles of orde.
Their iron gates to unclose.
The gross, inhospitable warder
Of Love's green garden of spice is well
    awake.
Hell hath enough of Her three-headed
    hound ;
But Love's severer bound
Knows for His watcher a more fearful shape,
A formidable ape

Skilled by black art to mock the Gods
    profound
In their abyss of under ground.
Beware! Who hath entered hath no boast
    to make,
And conscious Eden surelier breeds the snake.
Be silent! O! for silence' sake!

8. That asks the impossible. Smite! Smite!
Profaned adytum of pure light,
Smite! but I must sing on.
Nay! can the orison
Of myriad fools provoke the Crowned-with-
    Night
Hidden beyond sound and sight
In the mystery of His own high essence?
Lo, Rose of all the gardens of the world,
Did thy most sacred presence
Not fill the Real, then this voice were
    whirled
Away in the wind of its own folly, thrown
Into forgotten places and unknown.
So I sing on!
            Sister and wife, dear wife,
Light of my love and lady of my life,
Answer if thou canst from the unsullied
    place,
Unveiling for one star-wink thy bright face!
Did we leave then, once cognisant,
Time for some Fear to implant
His poison? Did we hesitate?
Leave but one little chance to Fate?
For one swift second did we wait?
There is no need to answer: God is God,
A jealous God and evil; with His rod
He smiteth fair and foul, and with His
    sword
Divideth tiniest atoms of intangible time,
That men may know he is the Lord.
Then, with that sharp division,
Did He divide our wit sublime?
Our knowledge bring to nought?
We had no need of thought.
We brought His malice in derision.
So thine eternal petals shall enclose
Me, O most wonderful lady of delight,
Immaculate, indivisible circle of night,
Inviolate, invulnerable Rose!

9. The sound of my own voice carries me on.
I am as a ship whose anchors are all gone,
Whose rudder is held by Love the indomi-
    table —
Purposeful helmsman! Were his port high
    Hell,
Who should be fool enough to care? Suppose
Hell's waters wash the memory of this rose
Out of my mind, what misery matters then?
Or, if they leave it, all the woes of men
Are as pale shadows in the glory of
That passionate splendour of Love.

10. Ay! my own voice, my own thoughts.
    These, then, must be
The mutiny of some worm's misery,
Some chained despair knotted into my flesh,
Some chance companion, some soul damned
    afresh
Since my redemption, that is vocal at all,
For I am wrapt away from light and call
In the sweet heart of the red rose.
My spirit only knows
This woman and no more; who would
    know more?
I, I am concentrate
In the unshakable state
Of constant rapture. Who should pour
His ravings in the air for winds to whirl,
Far from the central pearl
Of all the diadem of the universe?
Let God take pen, rehearse
Dull nursery tales; then, not before, O rose,
Red rose! shall the beloved of thee,
Infinite rose! pen puerile poetry
That turns in writing to vile prose.

11. Were this the quintessential plume of
    Keats
And Shelley and Swinburne and Verlaine,
Could I outsoar them, all their lyric feats,
Excel their utterance vain
With one convincing rapture, beat them
    hollow
As an ass's skin; wert thou, Apollo,
Mere slave to me, not Lord—thy fieriest
    flight
And stateliest shaft of light

Thyself thyself surpassing : all were dull,
And thou, O rose, sole, sacred, wonderful,
Single in love and aim,
Double in form and name,
Triple in energy of radiant flame,
Informing all, in all most beautiful,
Circle and sphere, perfect in every part,
High above hope of Art :
Though, be it said ! thou art nowhere now,
Save in the secret chamber of my heart,
Behind the brass of my anonymous brow. [1]

12. Ay ! let the coward and slave who writes
    write on !
He is no more harm to Love than the grey
    snake
Who lurks in the dusk brake
For the bare-legged village-boy, is to the Sun,
The Sire of Life.
The Lover and the Wife,
Immune, intact. ignore. The people hear ;
Then, be the people smitten of grey Fear,
It is no odds !

13. I have seen the eternal Gods
Sit, star-wed, in old Egypt by the Nile ;
The same calm pose, the inscrutable, wan
    smile,
On every lip alike.
Time hath not had his will to strike
At them ; they abide, they pass through all.
Though their most ancient names may fall,
They stir not nor are weary of
Life, for with them, even as with us, Life
    is but Love.
They know, we know ; let, then, the writing go!
That, in the very deed, we do not know.

14. It may be in the centuries of our life
Since we were man and wife
There stirs some incarnation of that love.
Some rosebud in the garden of spices blows,
Some offshoot from the Rose
Of the World, the Rose of all Delight,
The Rose of Dew, the Rose of Love and Night,
The Rose of Silence, covering as with a vesture
The solemn unity of things

[1] This poem was issued under the pseudonym
of H. D. Carr.

Beheld in the mirror of truth;
The Rose indifferent to God's gesture,
The Rose on moonlight wings
That flies to the House of Fire,
The Rose of Honey-in-Youth !
Ah ! No dim mystery of desire
Fathoms this gulf ! No light invades
The mystical musical shades
*Of a faith in the future, a dream of the day*
*When athwart the dim glades*
*Of the forest a ray*
*Of sunlight shall flash and the dew die away !*

15. Let there then be obscurity in this !
There is an after rapture in the kiss.
The fire, flesh, perfume, music, that outpaced
All time, fly off ; they are subtle : there
    abides
A secret and most maiden taste ;
Salt, as of the invisible tides
Of the molten sea of gold
Men may at times behold
In the rayless scarab of the sinking sun :
And out of that is won
Hardly, with labour and pain that are as
    pleasure,
The first flower of the garden, the stored
    treasure
That lies at the heart's heart of eternity.
This treasure is for thee.

16. O ! but shall hope arise in happiness?
That may not be.
My love is like a golden grape, the veins
Peep through the ecstasy
Of the essence of ivory and silk,
Pearl, moonlight, mother-milk
That is her skin ;
Its swift caress
Flits like an angel's kiss in a dream ; remains
The healing virtue ; from all sin,
All ill, one touch sets free.
My love is like a star—oh fool ! oh fool !
Is not thy back yet tender from the rod ?
Is there no learning in the poet's school ?
Wilt thou achieve what were too hard for God?
I call Him to the battle ; ask of me
When the hinds calve ? What of eternity

When he built chaos? Shall Leviathan
Be drawn out with an hook? Enough; I see
This I can answer—or Ernst Haeckel can !
Now, God Almighty, rede this mystery !
What of the love that is the heart of man ?
Take stars and airs, and write it down !
Fill all the interstices of space
With myriad verse——own Thy disgrace !
Diminish Thy renown !
Approve my riddle ! This Thou canst not do.

17. O living Rose ! O dowered with subtle
        dew
Of love, the tiny eternities of time,
Caught between flying seconds, are well filled
With these futilities of fragrant rhyme ;
In Love's retort distilled,
In sunrays of fierce loathing purified,
In moonrays of pure longing tried,
And gathered after many moons of labour
Into the compass of a single day,
And wrought into continuous tune,[1]
One laughter with one languor for its neigh-
        bour.
One thought of winter with one word of June,
Muddled and mixed in mere dismay,
Chiselled with the cunning chisel of despair,
Found wanting, well aware
Of its own fault, even insistent
Thereon ; some fragrance rare
Stolen from my lady's hair
Perchance redeeming now and then the distant
Fugitive tunes.

18.                    Ah ! Love ! the hour is over !
The moon is up, the vigil overpast.
Call me to thee at last,
O Rose, O perfect miracle lover,
Call me ! I hear thee though it be across
The abyss of the whole universe,
Though not a sigh escape, delicious loss !
Though hardly a wish rehearse
The imperfection underlying ever
The perfect happiness.

    [1] It will be noticed in fact that this poem
is in an original metre, no stanza being complete in itself, but one running on into the
next.

Thou knowest that not in flesh
Lies the fair fresh
Delight of Love ; not in mere lips and eyes
The secret of these bridal ecstasies,
Since thou art everywhere,
Rose of the World, Rose of the Uttermost
Abode of Glory, Rose of the High Host
Of Heaven, mystic, rapturous Rose !
The extreme passion glows
Deep in this breast ; thou knowest (and love
        knows)
How every word awakes its own reward
In a thought akin to thee, a shadow of thee ;
And every tune evokes its musical Lord ;
And every rhyme tingles and shakes in me
The filaments of the great web of Love.

19. O Rose all roses far above
In the garden of God's roses,
Sorrowless, thornless, passionate Rose, that
        lies
Full in the flood of its own sympathies
And makes my life one tune that curls and
        closes
On its own self delight ;
A circle, never a line ! Safe from all
        wind,
Secure in its own pleasure-house confined,
Mistress of all its moods,
Matchless, serene, in sacred amplitudes
Of its own royal rapture, deaf and blind
To aught but its own mastery of song
And light, shown ever as silence and deep
        night
Secret as death and final. Let me long
Never again for aught ! This great delight
Involves me, weaves me in its pattern of
        bliss,
Seals me with its own kiss,
Draws me to thee with every dream that
        glows,
Poet, each word ! Maiden, each burden of
        snows
Extending beyond sunset, beyond dawn !
O Rose, inviolate, utterly withdrawn
In the truth : — for this is truth : Love
        knows !
Ah ! Rose of the World ! Rose ! Rose !

## II.

### THE NIGHTMARE.

Up, up, my bride! Away to ride
Upon the nightmare's wings!
The livid lightning's wine we'll drink,
And laugh for joy of life, and think
Unutterable things!

The gallant caught the lady fair
Below the arms that lay
Curling in coils of yellow hair,
And kissed her lips. "Away!"

The lover caught his mistress up
And lifted her to heaven,
Drank from her lips as from the cup
Of poppies drowsed at even.

"Away, away, my lady may!
The wind is fair and free;
Away, away, the glint of day
Is faded from the ghostly grey
That shines beyond the sea."

The lordly bridegroom took the bride
As giants grasp a flower.
"A night of nights, my queen, to ride
Beyond the midnight hour."
The bride still slept; the lonely tide
Of sleep was on the tower.

"Awake, awake! for true love's sake!
The blood is pulsing faster.
My swift veins burn with keen desire
Toward those ebony wings of fire,
The monarchs of disaster!"
The golden bride awoke and sighed
And looked upon her master.

The bride was clad in spider-silk;
The lord was spurred and shod.
Her breasts gleamed bright and white as
milk,
Most like the mother of God;
His heart was shrouded, his face was clouded,
Earth trembled where he trod.

"By thy raven tresses; by those caresses
We changed these five hours past;
By the full red lips and the broad white brow
I charge thee stay; I am weary now;
I would sleep again—at last."

"By thy golden hair; by the laughter rare
Of love's kiss conquering,
By the lips full red and the ivory bed
I charge thee come, I am fain instead
Of the nightmare's lordly wing!"

The bride was sad and spoke no more.
The tower erect and blind
Rocked with the storm that smote it sore,
The thunder of the wind.

Swift to their feet the nightmare[1] drew
And shook its gorgeous mane.
"Who rideth me shall never see
His other life again.

"Who rideth me shall laugh and love
In other ways than these."
"Mount, mount!" the gallant cried, "enough
Of earthly ecstasies!"

The pale bride caught his colour then:
The pale bride laughed aloud,
Fronting red madness in her den:
"The bride-robe be my shroud!

"The bride-robe gave me light and clean
To kisses' nuptial gold.
Now for a draught of madness keen!
The other lips are cold."

They mount the tameless thundering side;
They sweep toward the lea;
The mare is wild; they spur, they ride,
Mad master and hysteric bride,
Along the lone grey sea.

The pebbles flash, the waters shrink!
(So fearful are those wings!)
The lightning stoops to let them drink.
They see each other's eyes, and think
Unutterable things.

[1] Night-mare has of course nothing to do with the horse, etymologically. Mare is from A.S. *mara*, an incubus.—A. C.

And now the sea is loose and loud;
   Tremendous the typhoon
Sweeps from the westward as a shroud,
Wrapping some great god in a cloud,
   Abolishing the moon.

And faster flying and faster still
   They gallop fast and faster.
"Turn, turn thy rein!" she shrieked again,
   "'Tis edged with sore disaster."
He looked her through with sight and will :—
   The pale bride knew her master.

And now the skies are black as ink,
   The nightmare shoreward springs;
The lightning stoops to let them drink.
They hold each other close, and think
   Unutterable things.

The roar of earthquake stuns the ear;
   The powers volcanic rise,
Casting the lava red and sheer
A million miles in ether clear
   Beyond the labouring skies.

Ghastlier faces bend around
   And gristlier fears above.
They see no sight : they hear no sound ;
But look toward the chill profound
   End and abyss of love.

The water and the skies are fallen
   Far beyond sight of them.
All earth and fire gasp and expire :
The night hath lost her starry host,
   Shattered her diadem.

Eternity uplifts its brink
   To bar the wizard wings.
The lightning stoops to let them drink.
They silently espouse, and think
   Unutterable things.

The nightmare neighs! The untravelled
   ways
   Are past on fervid feet.
The limits of the limitless
Flash by like jewels on a dress,
   Or dewdrops fallen in wheat.

"O love! O husband! Did you guess
   I did not wish to go?
And now—what rapture can express
   This?—do you feel and know?"
The girl's arms close in a caress ;
   Her lips are warm aglow ;
She looks upon his loveliness :—
The night has frozen the old stress ;
   His mouth is cold as snow !

But closer to the corpse she links,
   And closer, closer clings.
Her kiss like lightning drops and drinks.
She burns upon his breast, and thinks
   Unutterable things.

Now half a moment stayed the steed;
   And then she thought he sighed ;—
And then flashed forward thrice the old
   speed :—
And then she knew he had died.

But closer to him clings she yet,
   And feeds his corpse with fire,
As if death were not to forget
   And to annul desire.

And therefore as the utter space
   Sped past by hour and hour,
She feeds her face upon his face
   Like a bird upon a flower.

"Awake, awake! for love's own sake!
   I grow so faint and cold ;
I charge thee by the bridal bed,
The violet veins, and the lips full red,
   And the hours of woven gold !"

And colder now the bride's lips grow
   And colder and yet colder,
Until she lies as cold as snow,
   Her head against his shoulder.

The nightmare never checked its pace.
   The lovely pair are gone
Together through the walls of space
   Into oblivion.

## III.

### THE KISS

I BEHOLD in a mist of hair involving
Subtle shadows and shapes of ivory beauty.
Gray blue eyes from the spherèd opal eyelids
Look me through and make me a deep con-
    tentment
Slow dissolving desire.   We sit so silent
Death might sweep over sleep with flowers
    of cypress
(Gathered myriad blossoms, Proserpina's),
Stir us not, nor a whisper steal through love-
    trance.
Still we sit ; and your head lies calm and
    splendid
Shadowed, curve of an arm about it whisper-
    ing.
Still your bosom respires its sighs of silver ;
Still one hand o' me quivers close, caresses,
Touches not.  O a breath of sudden sad-
    ness
Hides your face as a mist grows up a
    mountain !
Mist is over my eyes, and darkness gathers
Deep on violet inset deep of eyepits.
Neither holds in the sight the lovely vision.
Slow the mist is dissolved in the wintry
    sunlight
On the fells, and the heather wakes to
    laughter :—
So sight glimmers across the gulf of sorrow.
You the lily and I the rose redouble,
Bend, soft swayed by a slow spontaneous
    music,
Bend to kiss, are alight, one lamp of moon-
    rays
Caught, held hard in a crystal second.
    Swiftly
Touch, just touch, the appealing floral sisters,
Brush no bloom off the blossom, lift no lip-
    gleam
Off the purple and rose, caressing cressets,
Flames of flickering love.   They draw
    asunder.
Thus, and motionless thus, for ages.  Hither !

## IV.

### ANNIE.

ANEMONES grow in the wood by the stream ;
    And the song of the spring in our garden
Wakes life to the shape of an exquisite dream ;
    And reason of passion asks pardon.

I made up a posy by moonlight, a rose,
    And a violet white from its cranny,
And a bluebell, and stole, on the tips of my
    toes,
    At the dark of the night to my Annie.

Her window was open ; she slept like a child ;
    So I laid the three flowers on her breast,
And stole back alone through the forest deep-
    aisled,
    To dream of the lass I loved best.

And the next night I lay half awake on my bed,
    When—a foot-fall as soft as the breeze !
Oh ! never a word nor a whisper she said
    To disturb the low song of the trees.

But she crept to my side.   Awhile we lay
    close :
    Then : "Have pardon and pity for me !"
She whispered—"your bluebell and violet
    and rose—
    I can give but one flower for three."

## V.

### BRÜNNHILDE.[1]

THE sword that was broken is perfect : the
    hero is here.
Be done with the dwarfs and be done with
    the spirit of fear !

Hark ! the white note of a bird ; and the
    path is declared ;
The sword is girt on, and the dragon is
    summoned and dared.

[1] See Wagner, from whose "Ring of the
Nibelungs" the symbolism of this poem is
taken.

Be done with the dragons !  Awaits for the
    lord of the sword
On the crest of a mountain the maid, the
    availing award.

The spear of the Wanderer shivers, the God
    is exhaust.
Be done with the Gods ! the key of Valhalla
    is lost.

The fires that Loki the liar built up of deceit
Are like roses that cushion the moss for the
    warrior's feet.

Be done with the paltry defences !  She
    sleeps.  O be done
With the mists of the mountain !  Awake to
    the light of the sun !

Awake !  Let the wave of emotions conflict-
    ing retire,
Let fear and despair be engulfed in delight
    and desire.

There is one thing of all that remains : that
    the sword may not bite :
It is love that is true as itself ; and their
    scion, delight.

True flower of the flame of love : true bloom
    of the ray of the sword !
The lady is lost if she wit not the name of
    her lord.

Awaken and hither, O warrior maiden !
    Above
The Man is awaiting.  Be done with the lies !
    It is love.

## VI.

## DORA.

DORA steals across the floor
        Tiptoe ;
Opens then her rosy door,
        Peeps out.
" Nobody !  And where shall I
        Skip to ? "
Dora, diving daintily,
        Creeps out.

" To the woodland !  Shall I find
        Crowtoe,
Violet, jessamine !  I'll bind
        Garlands.
Fancy I'm a princess.   Where
        Go to ?
Persia, China, Finisterre ?
        Far lands ! "

Pity Dora !   Only one
        Daisy
Did she find.   The sulking sun
        Slept still.
Dora stamped her foot.   Aurora
        Lazy
Stirred not.   Hush !  A footstep.   Dora
        Kept still.
What a dreadful monster !   Shoot !
        Mercy !
('Twas a man.)   Suppose the brute
        Ate her ?
By-and-by the ruffian grows
        " Percy."
And she loves him now she knows
        Better.

## VII.

## FATIMA.[1]

FRAUGHT with the glory of a dead despair,
My purple eidola, my purple eidola
March, dance—through hyacinthine spheres
Moaning : they sweep along, attain, aware
How frail is Fatima.
They bathe the Gods with stinging tears.
They weave another thread within the mystic
    veil.
They are drawn up anon in some great hand.
They shudder and murmur in the web of Kama.
They hear no music in the white word Rama.
They rush, colossi, liquid swords of life
Strident with spurious desire and strife.
Mocked !   I am dumb : I await the gray
    command :
I wait for Her :

[1] Written in collaboration with S. M.

Inscrutable darkness through the storm
Loomed out, with broidered features of gold :
    its form
Wing-like lay on the firmaments,
River-like curves in all its movements
Swift from inertia of vast voids rolled, stirred
Gigantic for roar of strepitation : whirred
    The essential All
That was Her veil : her voice I had heard
Had not large sobbing fears surged ; will
    and word
      Fall
Down from the black pearls of the night,
    down, back
    To night's impearléd black ;
Down, from chryselephantine wall
And rose-revolving ball,
Doomed, fierce through Saturn's aeons to
    tear,
Fraught with the glory of a dead despair.


### VIII.

### FLAVIA.

I KISSED the face of Flavia fair,
    In the deep wet dews of dawn,
And the ruddy weight of my lover's hair
Fell over me and held me there
    On the broad Italian lawn.

And the bright Italian moon arose
    And cleft the cypress grove ;
For sadness in all beauty grows,
And sorrow from its master knows
    How to appear like love.

Alas ! that Flavia's gentle kiss,
    And Flavia's cool caress,
And Flavia's flower of utter bliss
Must fade, must cease, must fall and miss
    The height of happiness.

The moon must set, the sun must rise,
    The wind of dawn is chill.
Oh, in this world of miseries
Is one hour's pleasure ill to prize ?
    Is love the means of ill ?

Oh, if there were a God to hear !
    Or Christ had really given
His life ! Or did a Dove appear
Bearing a rosebud, we might fear
    Or hope for hell or heaven.

Alas ! no sign is given.   But short
    Bliss of the earth is ours ;
The kiss that stops the avenging thought ;
The furtive passion shrewdly caught
    Between the summer flowers.

So, Flavia, till the dawn awake
    Cling close, cling close, as this is !
While moonlight lingers on the lake,
Our present happiness we'll take
    And fill the night with kisses !


### IX.

### KATIE CARR.

'TWAS dark when church was out ! the
    moon
    Was low on Rossett Ghyll ;[1]
The organ's melancholy tune
    Grew subtle, far, and still.

All drest in black, her white, white throat
    Like moonlight gleamed ; she moved
Along the road, towards the farm,
    Too happy to be loved.

" O Katie Carr ! how sweet you are !"
    She only hurried faster :
She found an arm about her waist :
    A maiden knows her master.

Through grass and heather we walked to-
    gether ;
    So hard her heart still beat
She thought she saw a ghost, and fast
    Flickered the tiny feet.

" O Katie Carr, there's one stile more !
    For your sweet love I'm dying.
There's no one near ; there's nought to fear."
    The lassie burst out crying.

            [1] A pass in Cumberland.

"From Wastdale Head to Kirkstone Pass
There's ne'er a lass like Kate:"—
The gentle child looked up and smiled
And kissed me frank and straight.

The night was dark, the stars were few :—
Should love need moon or star?
Let him decide who wins a bride
The peer of Katie Carr.


## X.

### NORAH.

NORAH, my wee shy child of wonderment,
  You are sweeter than a swallow-song at
    dusk !
You are braver than a lark that soars and
    fills
  His lofty laughter of love to a hundred
    hills !
You lie like a sweet nut within the husk
  Of my big arms ; and uttermost content
I have of you, my tiny fairy, eh ?
  Do you live in a flower, I wonder, and
    sleep and pray
To the good God to send you dew at dawn
  And rain in rain's soft season, and sun
    betimes,
And all the gladness of the afterglow
  When you come shyly out of the folded
    bud,
Unsheath your dainty soul, bathe it in blood
  Of my heart ?  Do you love me ?  Do you
    know
How I love you ?  Do you love these
    twittering rhymes
I string you ?  Is your tiny life withdrawn
Into its cup for modesty when I sing
  So softly to you and hold you in my hands,
You wild, wee wonder of wisdom ?  Now
    I bring
  My lips to your body and touch you
    reverently,
Knowing as I know what Gabriel under-
    stands
  When he spreads his wings above for
    canopy

When you would sleep, you frail angelic thing
  Like a tiny snowdrop in its own life
    curled—
But oh ! the biggest heart in all the world !


## XI.

### MARY.

MARY, Mary, subtle and softly breathing,
Look once eager out of the eyes upon me,
Draw one sigh, resign and abide in maiden
    Beauty for ever !

Love me, love me, love me as I desire it,
Strong sweet draughts not drawn of a well of
    passion,
Truth's bright crystal, shimmering out of
    sunlight
    Into the moon-dawn.

Closer cling, thou heart of amazèd rapture,
Cords of starlight fashioned about thee net-
    wise,
Tendrils woven of gossamer twist about us !
    These be the binders !

Night winds whirl about the avenger city ;
Darkness rides on desolate miles of moor-
    land ;
Thou and I, disparted a little, part not
    Spirit from spirit.

Strange and sister songs in the middle ether
Grow, divide ; they hover about, above us.
We, the song consummate of love, give music
    Back to the mortal.

Here, my love, a garden of spice and myrtle ;
Sunlight shakes the rivers of love with
    laughter ;
Here, my love, abide, in the amber ages,
    Lapped in the levin.

Linger, linger, light of the blessed moonrise !
Full-orbed sweep immaculate through the
    midnight !
Bend above, O sorrowful sister, kiss me
    Once and for ever !

Let the lake of thought be as still as dark-
    mans [1]
Brooding over magian pools of madness !
Love, the sun, arise and abide above us,
    Mary Mavourneen.

## XII.

### XANTIPPE.

SWEET, do you scold ?  I had rather have
    you scold
    Than from another earn a million kisses.
The tiger rapture on your skin's Greek gold
Is worth a million smiles of sunken cold
And Arctic archangelic passion rolled
    From any other woman.   Heaven misses
The half of God's delight who doth not see
    Some lightning anger dart like love and
      strike
Into the sacred heart its iterant glee
Of scathing tortures worth Hell's agony
To melt—ah, sweet, I know ! in foam and free
Lustre of love redoubled.   Come to me !
    I will avenge that anger, like to like,
With gentle fires of smitten love, will burn
    Into your beauty with the athletic rush
Of conquering godhead ; and your cheek
    shall burn
    From red of wrath to shame's adorable
      blush,
And so in tears and raptures mix the cup
    Of dreadful wine we are wont to drain and
      —well !—
Needs but one glance to lift the liquor up,
    One angry grip to wake me, and to swell
The anguish into rapture—come, to sup
    The liquid lava of the lake of Hell !

## XIII.

### EILEEN.

THE frosty fingers of the wind ; the eyes
Of the melancholy wind : the voice serene
Of the love-moved wind: the exulting secrecies
Of the subtle wind : lament, O harmonies
Of the most musical wind !   Eileen !

[1] Night—an old English canting word.

The peace of the nameless loch : the waiting
    heart
Of the amorous loch : the lights unguessed,
    unseen,
Of the midnight loch ; the winter's sorrow
    apart
Of the ice-bound loch : O majesty of art
Of the most motionless loch ! Eileen !

The gleam of the hills : the stature of the
    hills
Facing the wind and the loch : the cold and
    clean
Sculpture of the stalwart hills ; the iron wills
Of the inscrutable hills ! O strength that
    stills
The cry of the agonised hills ! Eileen !

Come back, O thought, alike from burn and
    ben
And sacred loch and rapture strong and keen
Of the wind of the moor.   A race of little
    men
Lives with the little.   The exalted ken
Knows the synthetic soul.   Eileen !

Close in the silence cling the patient eyes
Of love : the soul accepts her time of teen,
Awaits the answer.   Midnight droops and
    dies,
A floral hour ; what dawn of love shall rise
On a world of sorrow ?   Peace ! Eileen !

Mazed in a Titan world of rock and snow ?
Horsèd among the bearded Bedawin ?
Drowsed on a tropic river in the glow
Of sunset ?  Whither ?  Who shall care or
    know,
When one and all are this ?  Eileen !

## XIV

THE night is void of stars : the moon is full,
Veiling their radiance with her beautiful
Mist of still light.   O slumbrous air !
Wings of the winter, droop to-night ! Behold
The mirror of shuddering silver in the gold
Setting of loose involving hair !

Closer and closer through the dusk of sense
Avails the monotone omnipotence.
Steady, in one crescent tune,
Rises the virgin moon ;
And from the depth of eyes flooded with
love
Shines ecstasy thereof.

Words pass and are not heard.  The ear,
awake
Only for its master's individual sake,
Strains only for three whispered songs,
Hears naught beside, interprets silence so,
Till liquid melodies of music flow
"I love you."   We afford to wait ; who
longs
That knows ?   And we know ; for the moon
is full.

Steals in the ambient aura of delight
That quivering ray intense and cool
Self centred.   Woven of a million lines
There is a curve of light,
A pure, ideal curve, single, that shines
Amid the manifold night
Of all the flowery dreams that build it up.
So from the azure cup
Of heaven inverted is the white wine poured.
Stay, O thou vivid sword
Of soul, and cease, and be not !   Unto me
Through all eternity
Let me be not, and this thing be !

## XV.

O the deep wells and springs of tears !
O the intenser rays of blue,
Fleeting through gray unaltering spheres,
Like skies beholden through the dew !
O pearls of light !   O sombre meres
Wherein a waterwitch is hid,
And chants of sunset rise unbid,
Your eyes, your eyes ! They read me through,
Sphinx ; and your soul, the Pyramid,
Burns upward, and I worship you.

### 2.

But had I moulded beauty's eyes
I had not touched the carving tool
Thus tenderly : my spirit dies
Before you, but my life still lies
Salient, unwounded, and to dule
Wakes : I had rather you were now
Medusa, of the awful brow,
The snaky hair, the face of fear.
So could I shut my eyes ; feel how
Your hair fell back on me and bit,
Your lips descended on my face
In one exenterate kiss : and wit
I should abide a little space—
So little a space !—and solemn rise,
Face the black vaults of the alone,
And, knowing, lift to you mine eyes,
Look on your face, and turn to stone.

## XVI.

THE schoolboy drudges through his Greek ;
Plods to the integral calculus ;
Makes sulphuretted hydrogen ;

And, if the poor dumb thing could speak,
He'd say : Hic labor omnibus
Prodest : vitae verae limen.

Deinde missa juventute
Ave ! cum otio dignitas ![1]
So I : and strove and did not shirk.

But now ?   Confront me life and duty ;
Toil is my daily hap, alas !
And work is still the sire of work.

Shall I repine ?   What joys are hid
In weariness of idleness ?
Rich, young, beloved, shall I recede ?

Enjoy ?   Not I !   I work unbid ;
Book follows book : ideas press
Hurrying over the green mead

[1] This work is good for all men, the threshold of real life.   Then, once youth is past,
Hail !  Ease and dignity.

Of mind : they roll, a rippling stream
Hurrying, hurrying : hour by hour
The brain throbs : shall I never rest ?

Ay ! for a little : peace supreme
Receives my head that lies a flower
Borne on the mountain of thy breast.


## XVII.

Speak, O my sister, O my spouse, speak,
 speak !
 Sigh not, but utter the intense award
Of infinite love ; arise, burn cheek by cheek !
 Dart, eyes of glory ; live, O lambent sword
O' the heart's gold rushing over mount and
 moor
 Of sunlit rapture ! rise all runes above,
Dissolve thyself into one molten lure,
 Invisible core of the visible flame of love ;
Heart of the sun of rapture, whirling ever ;
 Strength of the sight of eagles, pierce the
 foam
Of ecstasy's irremeable river,
 And race the rhythm of laughter to its home
In the heart of the woman, and evoke the
 light
Of love out of the fiery womb of night !


## XVIII.

### FRIENDSHIP.

Better than bliss of floral kiss,
Eternal rapture caught and held ;
Better than rapture's self is this
To which we find ourselves compelled,
The trick of self-analysis.

Thoughts fetter not true love : we weld
No bands by logic : on our lips
The idle metaphysic quibble
Laughs : what portends the late eclipse ?
What oracle of the solar sybil ?

Orion's signal banner dips :
"This is the folly of your youth,
Achieving the exalted aim ;
Because you have gained a higher truth
To call it by a lower name."


## XIX.

Rose on the breast of the world of spring,
 I press my breast against thy bloom,
My subtle life drawn out to thee : to thee
 its moods and meanings cling.
I pass from change and thought to peace,
 woven on love's incredible loom,
Rose on the breast of the world of spring !

How shall the heart dissolved in joy take
 form and harmony and sing ?
How shall the ecstasy of light fall back to
 music's magic gloom ?
O China rose without a tnorn, O honey-bee
 without a sting !

The scent of all thy beauty burns upon the
 wind. The deep perfume
Of our own love is hidden in our hearts,
 the invulnerable ring.
No man shall know. I bear thee down unto
 the tomb, beyond the tomb,
Rose on the breast of the world of spring !


## XX.

Lie still, O love, and let there be delight !
Lie on the soft banks of ambrosial air,
The roseate marble of invisible space.
Secure and silent, O caressing night,
We are in thee ; and thou art everywhere.
Lie still, and read thy soul upon my face.

Swayed slowly by the wind, made crafts-
 men of
The mystery of happiness, we lie
And rock us to and fro, and to and fro.
Shrined in the temple of the world, O love,
We wait self-worshipped through eternity,
Until "to ignore" is equal to "to know."

Lie still, O love, and let me hide my brows
In the deep bosom and the scented vales.
Thy deep drawn breath embrace my hair, resume
My life in thine! Here is an amber house
With gateways of old gold. Far nightingales
Sing like smooth silence through the extreme perfume.

Moving, flying, exulting, on we go,
Borne on blue clouds of glory. On the river,
Over the mountains of the night, above
The stars of the night, above the floral glow
Of the sun dawning now for us for ever
Who rest content in the abode of love!

Lie still, O love, and let the fragrant sleep
Perfume our eyelids with dew-dropping death,
And silence be the witness of the will.
Fall, fall, fall back in the uprolling deep
Wrapt in rose mist of unsuccessive breath
Of love, of love. Lie still, O love, lie still.

## XXI.

UNDER the stars the die was cast to win.
The moonrays stained with pale embroidered bars
The iridescent shimmer of your skin,
        Under the stars.

Great angels drove their pearl-inwoven cars
Through the night's racecourse : silence stood within
The folded cups of passion's nenuphars.

You were my own ; sorrowless, without sin,
That night—this night. Sinks the red eye[1] of Mars ;
The hand of Hermes[1] guides us as we spin
        Under the stars.

[1] Tibetan astrologers give these symbols to the planets Mars and Mercury.

VOL. III.

## XXII.

DROOP the great eyelids purple-veined !
Stand, pure and pale and tremulous !
Dare to believe, O soul unstained,
The truth unguessed and unexplained !

The unquiet air monotonous
Wreathes the sad head in whirring mist.
Hath the delicate will disdained
The delicate lips that would be kissed ?

Like far blue snows by sunrise caught
Love lights the enlightened eyes of blue.
Dare to believe the child-heart's thought,
And wake in wonder ! For I knew
From the first hour that This was true.

## XXIII.

### PROTOPLASM.

ALTHOUGH I cannot leave these bitter leas,
And whisper wiser than the southern breeze,
And mix my master music with the sea's ;

Although I shiver and you smile ; heap coal
And you stand laughing where the long waves roll ;
There is a sympathy of soul to soul.

Not Scylla, not the iron Symplegades
Shall bar that vessel, in delighted ease
Winning her way by stainless sorceries.

Though I be melancholy and thou fair,
And I be dark and thou too high for care ;
Both yet may strive in a serener air,

Clasping the vast, the immeasurable knees ;
Searching the secrets of the calm decrees
Of Hermes gray or gold Musagetes !

Is there another ? Unprofane, aware,
See me secreted, silent, everywhere.
And then consider ! Dost thou dare to dare?

The live sun leaps by invisible degrees ;
The blessèd moon grows slowly through the trees ;
And fire has fire's ingressive agonies.

E

I everywhere abide, and I control
Olympian glories and the Pythian goal.
What isle unfurls yonder life's glimmering
    scroll?

This be thy shrine, and all its splendours
    these !
Awake to dream ! Two desolate nudities
Woven through sculpture into ecstasies.

### XXIV.

Aum ! I unfold the tinted robe,
My love's embroideries one by one,
Unveil her glories, globe on globe,
And find beneath the quivering probe
    A shaking skeleton.

The smile of vermeil lips is past ;
The skull's black grin awhile remains ;
The fallen flesh displays aghast
Ribbed bars of bone : was Venus cast
    For this? What Mars attains?

Where is the poesy that shed
Its dewfall downward through her eyes?
Gaunt sockets stare from bony head.
Moves she? Ah me ! the living dead !
    The poet loves? He lies.

Others perceive thee, peerless maid
Broidered with beauty, starred and gemmed
With purity and light, arrayed
In wit—like moonlight down a glade
    With flowers diademed.

But I remember ; see the form
Serene sink slowly to the dust.
'Tis but a date : the eventful storm
Comes : then or now? What odds? They
    swarm,
    The winds : this breath, one gust.

Ah ! in the spiritual soul
Is there no essence to abide
When flesh and bone alike shall roll
From shape to shape, from goal to goal,
    On time, the envious tide?

All tire, all break, all pass. Beware
False thirst, false trust, false doubts of truth
Whilst thou art young, whilst thou art fair,
Awake and see the sepulchre
    For beauty yawn and youth.

Strive to cessation. Only this
Is the true refuge : this alone
Be implicit in our subtle kiss,
Be master of the imperfect bliss
    We call perfection's throne.

Then, if we strive, not all in vain
This vision of the barrèd bones ;
This knowledge in a poet's brain,
Daring to sing its own deep pain
    In shapeless semitones.

Ah ! if we strive, we attain. In sooth,
The effort is of old begun,
Or I had hardly seen the truth
Beneath thy beauty and thy youth :—
    A mouldering skeleton !

### XXV.

I am so sad and, being alone to-night,
I will not see you. Self-disdain forbids.
I wander through the icy hermitage
Of the populous streets, hoping. O might
Some idle God look through his drowsy lids
And will us happiness ! Serene and sage
Therefore I sit, as if I loved you not,
And train a practised pen, and strive to art ;
Accomplish art, and lose the art therein.
I sit, a bitter Witenagemot,[1]
The saint, the poet, the man : the lover's heart
Pleads at the bar. How should he hope to
    win ?
The saint is silent while the poet strings
These futile follies, gives for bread a stone,
And the man endures. The lover breaks
    the lyre.
Its death-cry, agony, O agony ! rings
One name. The lover sits in hell alone
Fondling the devil that men call desire.

    [1] The ancient parliament of Britain.

## XXVI.

When the wearily falling blossom of mid-
  night
Stirs the face of a sleeper, Mother of Sorrow !
Look thou down in the dawn of heavier
  dewfall.
Tears of widow despair, O mutely lamenting
Crouched in heavenly bowers over the carven
Gateway's ivory flower, tears of revival
Fall, oh fall, to the black abodes of the lonely.
I await, I await, I sing not for sorrow,
Train the fugitive lights of music across me,
Seek by force to avail me, vainly attempting
Song with feather detested, agony futile :
Ply these piteous exercises of cunning,
Hateful—ay ! to myself ! To me it were
  better
Only to woo in the silence, magical silence,
Silence eloquent, wert thou here or afar, love.
Woo thee, nay ! but abide in certain re-
  cession ;
Stilled to the splendid currents fervid of
  passion ;
Float to seas of an unassailable silence
Down the river of love. The words are
  awakened :
Let the soul be asleep. The dawn is upon us.

## XXVII.[1]

Ecstasy, break through poetry's beautiful
  barriers,
Intricate webs, labyrinthine mazes of music !
Leap, love, lightning's self, and, athwart the
  appalling
Evil clouds of an agony bound by existence,
Enter, avail me, exult ! In the masses of
  matter
Nothing avails ; in the splendour spirit is,
  nothing.
Give me love ; I am weary of giants colossal,
Royal, impossible things ; I am fain of a
  bosom
Always breathing sleep, and the symphony,
  silence.
Years are forgotten ; abide, deep love, I am
  happy.
  [1] An acrostic.

## XXVIII.

Could ivory blush with a stain of the sunset
  on highlands
Of snow : could the mind of me span
The tenderness born of the dew in immaculate
  islands
Virgin of maculate man :
Could I mingle the Alps and Hawaii ; Strath
  Ness and A'pura[1] and Baiæ ;
Kashmir and Japan :
Could lilies attain to the life of the Gods :
  could a comet
Attain to the calm of the moon :
I would mingle them all in a kiss, and draw
  from it
The soul of a sensitive tune.
All lovers should hear it and know it : not
  needing the words of a poet
In ebony hewn.
O beam of discovery under the eyelids awaking
The sense of delight ! O assent
Slow dawning through cream into roses ! O
  white bosom shaking
The myrtles of magical scent
In the groves of the heart ! O the pleasure
  that runs over all overmeasure,
The wine of Event !
Overmastered the hurl of the world in the
  hush of our rapture ;
Entangled the bird of success
In the snare of bewildering fancies. We capture
Delight in the toils of a tress
Rough gilded of sunlight and umber with
  virginal shadows of slumber—
Ah ! sorrow, regress !
Till the idle abyss of eternity swoon to our
  pinions
With music of wings as we fly
Through the azure of dreams, and the purple
  of mighty dominions
Exalted, afoam in the sky ;
And to us it were wiser and sweeter to ruin
  the race of the metre,
And song were to die.
  [1] Anuradapura, the ruined sacred city of
Ceylon.

# 1906

## A DRAMATIC VERSION[1] OF

### R. L. STEVENSON'S STORY

# THE SIRE DE MALÉTROIT'S DOOR

(*Written in collaboration with* GERALD KELLY)

## SCENE I.

*The* SIRE DE MALÉTROIT *sitting before the fire. A chime of bells—eleven.*

ALAIN.

'Leven o' th' clock! Plague take these lovers! What? do they make a Malétroit wait? [*Picks up letter from table—reads*] " Mademoiselle " —um, um — " my words might show that love which I cannot declare in writing "—very likely—" nor raise a blush on that alabaster brow "—um! um! ah!— " embrace of the eyes "—is the fellow an octopus?—" Tho' you do not respond to my letters "—ah!—" yet I would not have you leave me "—I daresay not—" Pity me, moon-like queen "—moonlike? um!—" Leave the postern door ajar "—well, it is ajar—" that I may speak with your beauty on the stairs " —um—can't meet him there. Cold! cold! [*Sniffs.*] A pretty letter. [*Throws it aside.*] Andrew! some more logs. [*Enter* ANDREW.] I expect company. [*Chuckles long.*] The old Burgundy, Andrew. [*Exit* ANDREW.] I propose to squeeze Duke Charles' grapes, though fate and my age forbid me a smack at his forces — *neu sinas Medos equitare inultos*—but our good King is no Augustus.

[*Strikes gong. Enter* PRIEST *quietly and quickly.* ALAIN *does not turn round.*

Good evening, father. All is ready?

PRIEST.

All, my lord.

ALAIN.

It is near the time. She has remained in her room?

PRIEST.

All the day.

ALAIN.

Has she attempted no message? eh?

PRIEST.

Sir, she——

ALAIN.

[*Interrupts.*] She has not succeeded, at least?

PRIEST.

I am still Father Jerome.

[*Pause.*

ALAIN.

She is ready dressed as I ordered? And now praying in the Chapel?

[ALAIN *gets up and can now see* PRIEST.

PRIEST.

As you ordered, my lord.

ALAIN.

Content?

[PRIEST *puts out his hands with the gesture " hardly."*

PRIEST.

Young maids are wilful, my lord.

68

ALAIN.

Let her be resigned to the will of Heaven. [*The* PRIEST *smiles subtly.* ALAIN *perceives it.*] And *my* will. [*Strikes gong twice.*] You may retire, father.

> [PRIEST *bows and retires.* Enter CAPTAIN *and stands at salute.*]

Ah, Captain, you have your fifty men in readiness?

CAPTAIN.

Yes, my lord. [*Salutes.*]

ALAIN.

Let them be drawn up behind yon door. When I clap my hands you will raise the arras, but let no man move. And let 'em be silent—the man I hear I hang. [CAPTAIN *salutes.*] You may go. [CAPTAIN *salutes, and exit.* ALAIN *reaches to a tome on the table.*] Now, Flaccus, let us spend this night together as we have spent so many. The crisis of my life—my brother's trust, God rest his soul! [*crosses himself and mutters silently in prayer*]—shall not find Alain de Malétroit unready or disturbed.

SCENE CLOSES.

## SCENE II.[1]

*A narrow dirty street in Paris, fifteenth century. Night pitch black. Passers-by with lanterns.*

FIRST PASSER-BY *stumbles into* SECOND.

SECOND PASSER-BY.

Zounds, man! have a care with thy goings.

FIRST PASSER-BY.

Stand, or I strike. Who but a thief goes lanternless o' nights?

[1] The play may be presented in a single scene, by omitting this Scene, and joining Scenes I. and III. by the noise of a banging door.

SECOND PASSER-BY.

The saints be praised, 'tis my good gossip Peter Halse. What, knowest thou not thy old friend? [FIRST PASSER-BY *lifts his lantern to the other's face.*

FIRST PASSER-BY.

Martin Cloche, by the Mass!

SECOND PASSER-BY.

Ay, Martin Cloche! And his lantern hath gone out, and his heart faileth him somewhat. But these be troublous times.

> [*Enter* FLORIMOND *and waits.*

FIRST PASSER-BY.

The town is full of these drunken English men-at-arms.

SECOND PASSER-BY.

The English be bad, but God save us from the Burgundians! Their own cousin-germans be we, and for that they are but bitterer.

FLORIMOND.

Devil take them! What, will they stand here gossiping all night?

FIRST PASSER-BY.

'Tis a cold night: I would be home.

SECOND PASSER-BY.

Light me, prithee, to my door: it lieth as thou knowest, but a stone's-throw from St. Yniold's.

FIRST PASSER-BY.

Well, let us be going.

> [*Exeunt.*

FLORIMOND.

Now for the moment I have longed for this three months! Blanche! Blanche! I shall see thee, touch thee—who knows what

maiden love may work on maiden modesty?
Ah, fall deeper, ye blessed shadows! Ye
are light enough for Florimond de Champdivers to move toward his bliss!

[*Noise of clashing armour, ribald
laughter, &c. Enter the Watch,
R., drunk.*

#### A WATCHMAN.

Ho, boys! a gay night for thieves.

#### FLORIMOND.

Curse the sots!

[*Crouches back in the shadow.*

#### SECOND WATCHMAN.

(*Sings*)

The soldier's life is short and merry,
His mistress' lips are ripe as a cherry,
Then drink, drink!
The guns roar out and the swords flash clean,
And the soldier sleepeth under the green,
Oh, the soldier's life for me!

But a scurvy night it is, comrades, when the
streets are slippery, and the wine cold in
a man's belly, and never a little white
rabbit of a woman scuttling along in the
dark.

#### THIRD WATCHMAN.

What ho! my lads! Here's a scurvy
Frenchman skulking along. What, will
you make your lass attend you, master?

#### FLORIMOND.

Loose me, knave, I am for England, and
a Captain in your army, or rather that of
Burgundy—if you will be precise.

#### FIRST WATCHMAN.

What do you here, without a lantern,
scaring honest folk?

#### FLORIMOND.

Honesty is no word for to-night. Will
you the loyal man's word?

#### SECOND WATCHMAN.

That's it, my gallant cock! The word!

#### FLORIMOND.

Burgundy and freedom.

#### THIRD WATCHMAN.

So! Give a crown to the poor watchmen
then to drink your Excellency's health, and
luck to your honour's love. Ah! we're
gay when we're young—I've a sweetheart
myself.

#### FLORIMOND.

And now be off!

[*Gives money. Exeunt.*

Cold!—the devil! Ah! but to-night—
at last I shall touch my Blanche. May
Blanche warm me well with a hearty kiss!
The little white cat! Three months! And
I've not so much as exchanged a word.
There must be an end to all that. Faith,
but she makes me think of Biondetta, that
I knew in the Italian campaign. O my
Blanche! One moment, and I am in thine
arms! Blanche! Sweet, sweet Blanche.
O little white-faced rose of France. A
soldier's heart is thine — a soldier's arms
shall be round thee in a moment! 'Tis a
fine thing this love—the strong true abiding
love of a brave man. How like little Florise
her voice is when she sings!

[*By this fool's talk he loses his opportunity. Enter DENYS.*

#### DENYS.

Cold is no word for it. [*Shudders.*]
Where the devil have I got to now? Had
I but vowed St. Denys a candle and put the
same in my pocket, I would not now be in
the dark. Here was a lane, and the folk
had called it Wolf's Throat, and now here's
a door and devil a name to it. Fool I was
to stay winebibbing with Cousin Henri, and
triple knave he to send me forth without
a boy and a light. True! he was under
the table—and seven times fool was I not to
join him there.

FLORIMOND.

O this miserable sot !

[*Crouches again,* DENYS *sees him.*

DENYS.

O thank God ! Here's another poor devil,
a gentleman by his clothes, and a thief by
his manner, and I daresay a good fellow.
[*Goes to* FLORIMOND *and slaps him on the
back.*] Sir, do you know this cursed Paris?
My inn, which I have lost, is the Sign of the
Green Grass—I should say the Field o'
Spring—and 'tis hard by the Church of St.
Anselm, that is hard by the river, and the
hardest of all is that neither church, inn, nor
river can I find this devil of a night.
[*Catches* FLORIMOND *and shakes him
by the shoulder.*

FLORIMOND.

Know you are speaking to a captain in
the army of Duke Charles ! Moderate thy
drunkenness, man, or I will call the watch.

DENYS.

Know me for a captain in the army of His
Majesty King Charles of France, whom God
preserve !

FLORIMOND.

What, traitor?

DENYS.

Traitor in thy teeth ! I have a safe-conduct from your pinchbeck duke. Oh, the
devil ! 'twill serve me but ill these Paris
nights—a fool am I ! Well, sir, I ask your
pardon, and throw myself on your kindness.

FLORIMOND.

Ha ! St. Gris ! Then I have you, my
fine cock. Watch, ho ! A traitor ! I will
pay you your insolence.

[*Calls.*

DENYS.

Oh then, to shut your mouth. [*Draws.*
[FLORIMOND *tries to draw, gets the
flat of* DENYS' *sword on his shoulder,
and runs away. Exit* DENYS
*pursuing and* FLORIMOND *calling
out. Distant shouts. Re-enter*
DENYS, *L.*

DENYS.

Oh, my inn ! my inn ! What a fool am I !
Where can I hide? The air is full of noises.
I would change my safe-conduct for a pair
of wings. I must steal back the way I came,
and St. Denys lend me prudence the next
fool I meet. What a night ! O my God !

*Enter* WATCH, *R., running and shouting.*

Well, for France, then ! My back to the
door, and my sword to the foeman's breast !
[*Puts his back to the door.*] My father's son
could never have died otherwise ! [*Enter*
WATCH.] St. Denys for Beaulieu ! The
door's open. May the luck turn yet !
[*Slides backwards gently through door.*
WATCH *cross stage stumbling, cursing, and crying, "A traitor, a
traitor !"*
[*Stage being clear for a little, suddenly
the door bangs violently.*

DENYS.

[*Inside.*] What the devil was that? The
door !

*Re-enter* FLORIMOND, *R.*

FLORIMOND.

At last ! [*Goes to door and pushes it.*]
The devil take all women ! After all, the
door is shut. Laugh, thou light little fool,
laugh now. One day thou shalt moan upon
the stones, and Florimond de Champdivers
shall shut his door to thee. Damn and damn
and damn ! What served love shall serve
hate : 'tis a poor game that only works one
way. [*Curtain.*

## SCENE III

*The* SIRE DE MALÉTROIT *as in Scene I. He is standing alert and intent, listening. From below are growls and muttered curses ; then a sharp sound like the snapping of a sword.*

ALAIN.

*Amat janua limen!* [*Closes book.*] Now, my friend, whoever you are — for your charming letter does not mention your honourable name—we shall very soon have the pleasure of seeing you. "Embrace of the eyes," eh? You distrust my door already, eh? Why do you knock so? [*Great noise below.*] No honester craftsman ever built a door—you waste time! Why so reluctant to move from the cold night to the "blush of an alabaster brow," and the rest of your accursed troubadour's jargon, to a bliss you little expect. "Gratia cum Nymphis geminisque sororibus audet ducere nuda choros." But your *choros*, Blanche, is but your old uncle, who perhaps loves you better than you think just now. [*A sound of suppressed sobbing from the Chapel.*] Ah! you may weep if you will—but what choice have you left me? And Lord! Lord! what could a loving heart ask more? [*Stumbling on steps, and a muttering,* "*Perdition catch the fool who invented these circular stairs.*"] Ha! He seems a little uncertain of the stair. Hush! [*Enter* DENYS, *who remains behind arras.* ALAIN *sits.*

DENYS.

[*Stumbles and swears.*] O these stairs! They go round and round, or *seem* to go round—faith! I have seen an entire castle do as much—and lead nowhere. [*Pushes against arras and is seen by audience. He hastily withdraws.*] Oh, they do though! Shall I knock? Shall I go in? Shal. I stay here till morning? There are three fools there, and I have a poor choice : to knock is polite, to wait is polite, and to introduce my charming self is the politest of all. [*Peeps in.*] Can't see anybody! It's clearly a gentleman's house—and a fool he is to leave his postern door ajar. Whoever he is, he can hardly blame me for a misadventure—and a curious tale is a passport the world over. Well, let me go in! To go in boldly is to slap Luck the courtezan on the shoulder, and 'tis Venus o' the dice-box to an ace and a deuce but she call me a tall fellow of my hands and bid me sit to supper. Warily now ! . . .
[*Pushes past arras.*

ALAIN.

Good evening, good evening, my dear young friend. Welcome, very welcome! Come to the fire, man, and warm yourself. "Jam satis terris nivis,"—if you know your Horace as you know your Ovid, we shall get along splendidly.
[DENYS *stands stupefied.* ALAIN *waits.*

DENYS.

I fear, sir, I don't know my Ovid. [*With the air of one primed to repeat a lesson.*] I beg a thousand pardons, Monsieur.

ALAIN.

Don't apologise, don't apologise. I've been expecting you all the evening.

DENYS.

Excuse me, sir, there is some mistake— !

ALAIN.

No! No! There is no mistake. Be at ease, my young friend.

DENYS.

[*Shrugs his shoulders.*] But I had no wish to be here—er—er !—Nothing was further from my thoughts than this most unwarrantable intrusion.

ALAIN.

Well, well, that's all right. Here you are, which is the great thing after all, isn't it? Sit down, my dear young friend [DENYS *uncomfortably and slowly takes a chair*], and we shall—er—arrange our little affair. You arrived uninvited, but believe me, most welcome.

DENYS.

Sir, you persist in error. I am a stranger: Denys de Beaulieu is my name, and I am here under a safe-conduct. That you see me in your house is only owing to—your door.

ALAIN.

Ah! my door—a hospitable fancy of mine!

DENYS.

I don't understand. I did not wish . . . oh!

ALAIN.

My dear sir, we old gentlemen expect this reluctance from young bloods. [*With bitter irony.*] We bear it. But [*flaming out*] if the matter touches one's honour—[*rises and looks sternly at* DENYS].

DENYS.

Your *honour?*
[DENYS *is amazed out of all measure.*]

ALAIN.

We try to find some means of overcoming such modesty.

DENYS.

Is this Ovid or Horace?

ALAIN.

To business, then, if you will affect ignorance. [*Strikes gong; enter* PRIEST, *who gives* DENYS *a long keen glance and speaks in an undertone to* ALAIN.] Is she in a better frame of mind?

PRIEST.

She is more resigned, my lord.

ALAIN.

Now a murrain o' these languishing wenches in their green-sickness! By 'r Lady, she is hard to please. A likely stripling, not ill-born, and the one of her own choosing. Why, what more would she have?

PRIEST.

The situation is not usual to a young damsel, and somewhat trying to her blushes.

ALAIN.

She should have thought of that before. This devil's dance is not to my piping, but since she is in it, by 'r Lady, she shall carry it through.
[*Motions* PRIEST *to retire. Exit* PRIEST, *with a low reverence to* ALAIN *and a courteous bow to* DENYS.

DENYS.

[*Rises and clears his throat.*] Sir, let me —explain that——

ALAIN.

Don't explain. May I beg you to be seated, my *dear* young friend. We've been expecting you all night: the lady is ready, though I believe a little tearful: a bride has so much to fear, you know — *et corde et genibus tremit*—eh, my Gaetulian lion?

DENYS.

[*Raises his hand authoritatively to check speech.*] Sir! this misunderstanding, for such I am convinced it is, must go no further. I am a stranger here—

ALAIN.

Well, well, you'll get to know the old place in time. Blanche——

DENYS.

Sir! pray let me speak.    I know you not——

ALAIN.

*We* know *you.*

DENYS.

[*Ironically.*]    I am too honoured.

ALAIN.

Well?

DENYS.

You speak of a lady to me.    You mistake me——

ALAIN.

I hope so.

DENYS.

Do not entrust a stranger with your family secrets, is my advice—as a man of the world.

ALAIN.

But my nephew !—

DENYS.

I do not even know your lordship's honourable nephew.

ALAIN.

I may yet show you a sneaking rascal in his person.

DENYS.

This really cannot go on.    I must beg you, sir, to allow me to go from your house. I came here by an ill chance enough—though it saved my life in sooth.

ALAIN.

And secured you a splendid marriage.

DENYS.

[*Aside.*]    Never, never again will I mix my drinks. [ALAIN *surveys* DENYS *from head to foot, emitting satisfied chuckles at*

*irregular intervals, while* DENYS *clears his throat repeatedly.    This continues long,* DENYS *fidgeting more and more.    DENYS, politely :*] The wind has gone down somewhat.

[ALAIN *falls into a fit of silent laughter.* DENYS *rises and puts on his hat with a flourish.*

DENYS.

Sir, if you are in your wits, I find you insolent : if not, I will not stand here parleying with a madman.

ALAIN.

I must apologise, no doubt, but the circumstances are peculiar.    Is it your custom to steal into the houses of gentlemen after midnight, and accuse the owners of lunacy ? [*Chuckles.*]    Well—let us be polite if we cannot be friendly.

DENYS.

Then, sir, you will permit me to explain my intrusion.

ALAIN.

[*Laughing.*]    Ha! Ha! a fine story, I wager.    'Twill interest me much, i' faith. [DENYS *shows signs of impatience ;* ALAIN *begins to look a little doubtful.    With sudden interest :*] Well, how *did* you come here ?

DENYS.

[*With much quaint lively gesture—his story-telling powers are much in request by his mess, and he is very proud of them.*] Aye, sir ! by 'r Lady, when I think of it, 'tis a curious adventure enough.    [*Pause to collect thoughts.    Then dashes off lively :*] Lost my way in this cursed town—night like hell's mouth—groped about your dirty little black narrow streets—no lantern—quarrelled with an officer—I draw—captain bolts—up run guard—see open door—your door, sir !— in I go ! and then all of a sudden bangs to the door and I am caught like a rat in a trap. I break my sword on the old beast—give it up—up come stairs—ah! stairs come up—I mean *I come*—a murrain on these courtly phrases! and here I stand [*rises and bows*], Denys de Beaulieu, Damoiseau de Beaulieu, in the Province of Normandy, at your lordship's service.

ALAIN.

That is your way of looking after the lady's reputation. Hear mine! Allow me first to introduce myself as Alain de Malétroit, Sire de Malétroit, and Warden of the Marches under his Majesty King Charles—

DENYS.

Whom God preserve!
[*Waves his broken sword.*

ALAIN.

What excellent sentiments, and what an unfortunate omen—dear, dear me! And I have the honour to offer you the hand—I presume you already possess the heart—of the Lady Blanche de Malétroit.

DENYS.

You—what?

ALAIN.

Tut! Tut! The marriage, if you please, will take place in an hour.

DENYS.

[*Aside.*] Oh, he is mad after all! [*Aloud.*] What nightmare is this?

ALAIN.

You are not very polite to the lady—not as polite as your letter.

DENYS.

My letter?
[ALAIN *takes up letter from table and reads.*

ALAIN (*reads*).

"O white-bosomed Blanche! I am pale and wan with suffering for thy love. Pity me, moonlike queen. Leave to-night the postern door"—my postern door—"ajar that I may speak with your beauty on the stairs"—my stairs. "Beware of thy lynx-eyed uncle"—me—ah! yes?

DENYS.

Sir, do you take me for the pernicious idiot that wrote that stuff?

ALAIN.

Sir, I know that there is a lady and a letter and a door and—a marriage.
[*Indicating the appropriate four quarters of the universe.*

DENYS.

And a sword. If it *be* broken—

ALAIN.

*Integer vitæ scel—*

DENYS.

I know *that* tag at least.
[ALAIN *claps his hands, walks toward door behind* DENYS. *The arras swings back and armed men appear.*

ALAIN.

*O maior tandem parcas, insane, minori.*

DENYS.

A truce to all this theatrical folly, Monsieur de Malétroit. Let me do you the honour to take your words seriously. I decline this marriage. I demand free passage from your house.

ALAIN.

I regret infinitely that I cannot comply with Monsieur's most moderate demands—at least [*quickly*] in the sense he means.

DENYS.

I am a prisoner then?

ALAIN.

I state the facts, and leave the inference to Monsieur's indulgence. But before you altogether decline this marriage, it would be perhaps properer did I present you to the lady.

DENYS.

[*Sees that he must humour his strange host; rises and bows in acquiescence with inane smile and phrase.*] Ah, Monsieur, you make me too happy!
> [*This speech is not ironical but conventional and absurd.* ALAIN *strikes the gong. Enter* PRIEST *and bows.*

ALAIN.

Require the presence of the Lady Blanche de Malétroit, if you please, father.

PRIEST (*bows*).

My lord.
> [*Retires. Enter* BLANCHE *in a bridal dress, very shy and ashamed, with downcast eyes.*

DENYS.

[*Aside.*] Ah! but she is beautiful!

ALAIN.

Mademoiselle de Malétroit, allow me to present you to the Damoiseau Denys de Beaulieu. Monsieur Denys, my niece. [BLANCHE *hears the strange name and is shocked, looks up and only sees the back of* DENYS' *head, so low is he bowing. She understands that he has given another name and regains her self-possession.*] Forgive the formality of this introduction, but, after all, your previous acquaintance—[DENYS *stares wildly.*] Under the circumstances, Blanche, I think I should give your little

hand to kiss. [*A pause.*] It is necessary to be polite, my niece.
> [BLANCHE, *tormented beyond endurance, rises up as if to strike her uncle, sees* DENYS, *screams, covers her face with her hands, and sinks on the floor.*

BLANCHE.

That is not the man!—my uncle—that is not the man!

ALAIN.

[*Chuckles.*] So? Of course not. I expected as much. It was so unfortunate you could not remember his name.

BLANCHE.

This is not the man.

ALAIN.

A man, niece. [*Turns airily to* DENYS.] *Tempestiva sequi viro*, Monsieur Denys.

BLANCHE.

Indeed, indeed, I have never seen this person till this moment. [*Turns to* DENYS *imploringly.*] Sir, if you are a gentleman, you will bear me out. Have I seen you—have you ever seen me—before this accursed hour?

DENYS.

I have never had that pleasure. [*Turns to* ALAIN.] This is the first time, my lord, that I have ever met your engaging niece. [*Aside.*] But he doesn't care, he's mad—by 'r Lady, perhaps I'm mad myself.
> [*Goes off into silent laughter.* ALAIN *checks him sternly.*

ALAIN.

Sir, you will find I mean no jest.

DENYS.

Mademoiselle, I ask you a thousand pardons for this scene—none of my making, but of my strange fortune's.

ALAIN.

This gentleman drank a little too much for dinner.

DENYS.

Nay, by St. Denys, not enough, else had I been now along under Cousin Henri's table, and not in this house of maniacs and men-at-arms, and beauties in distress. Oh, pardon me, I am rude. [*With lively gallantry.*] Mademoiselle! I wrong myself when I forget myself: what I would say is that if the arm or brain of Denys de Beaulieu can save you, it is at your disposal [*starts: but serious, struck*]—I mean—[*Aside.*] St. Denys, what a coil is here! Is it possible that I love her?

[*He stands back, aside, amazed. His attitude vibrates between tender pitiful courtesy, lighted with love, and ironical appreciation of his own dilemma.*]

ALAIN.

I will leave you to talk alone.

[*Turns to leave.*

BLANCHE.

[*Jumps up, and flings her arms around him. He repulses her not ungently. She clasps his knees, and he for the first time appears a little awkward and at a loss.*] Uncle, you cannot be in earnest. Why, I'll kill myself first—the heart rises at it—God forbids such marriages. Will you dishonour your white hair?

ALAIN.

Nay, mistress, I will save my brother's memory from shame.

BLANCHE.

O sir, pity me. There is not a woman in the world but would prefer death to such an union. Is it possible [*falters*] that you still think this [*points to* DENYS, *who stands embarrassed and ashamed*] to be the man?

ALAIN.

Frankly, I do. But let me explain to you once for all, Blanche de Malétroit, my way of thinking about this affair. [*Sternly.*] When you took it upon yourself to dishonour my family [BLANCHE *slides to floor and sobs*] and the name I have borne stainless in peace and war for more than threescore years, you forfeited not only the right to question my designs, but that of looking me in the face. I am a tenderer man than your father —he would have spat on you and thrust you from his door. But married you shall be, and that to-night. [*Turns to* DENYS.] And you, Monsieur, will best serve her if you save her. What devil have I saddled your life with that you look at me so black?

[*Turns on his heel and exit. A short silence of embarrassment.*

BLANCHE.

[*Turns on* DENYS *with flashing eyes.*] And what, sir, may be the meaning of all this?

DENYS.

God knows; I am a prisoner in this house, which seems full of mad people. But I understand one thing, [*doubtfully*] I *think:* that you are to be married to me, and that your wishes are to be consulted as little as mine.

BLANCHE.

Monsieur, I blame myself cruelly for the position I have placed you in.

DENYS.

Mademoiselle, I have at least the delicacy to refrain from asking any answer to these riddles. But—

BLANCHE.

O how my head aches! It is only fair to you to tell you—

DENYS.

A moment, of your grace, Mademoiselle. Do not think that I am some obscure fortune-hunter who will jump at the chance so strangely offered him. My name is as noble as your own—ay! were things otherwise, I would still spare you. As it is, I have but to do as my duty and my interest—and yours—demand. We will see if Monsieur de Malétroit can cage me here for ever. [*Looks at sword meditatively.*] That is unfortunate.

BLANCHE.

I am so afraid, sir: I know my uncle well: but—thank you,—thank you!

DENYS.

Is Monsieur de Malétroit at hand?

BLANCHE.

There is a servant within call.
[*Strikes gong thrice.*
[*A pause. Enter* ANDREW.

DENYS.

Ask Monsieur the Sire de Malétroit to honour us with his presence.
[ANDREW *bows and exit.*

BLANCHE.

Monsieur, I don't know what we—you—vill do, but thank you—thank you.

DENYS.

[*Draws himself up.*] Ah! Mademoiselle, trust me, all will be well.
[*Enter* ALAIN *and ironically bows.*

DENYS.

[*Grandly.*] Messire, I suppose that I am to have some say in the matter of this marriage, so let me tell you without further ado, I will be no party to forcing the inclinations of this lady. [ALAIN *smiles*, DENYS *pauses*.] I—er—you understand me, sir? [ALAIN *still smiles*.] Had it been

freely offered to me, I should have been proud to accept her hand, for I perceive she is as good as she is beautiful [ALAIN *still smiles*], but as things are—er—I have the honour, Messire, of refusing [ALAIN *smiles more and more*]—I—er—er—

[ALAIN'S *smile becomes positively insupportable.* BLANCHE *smiles through her tears in gratitude and is secretly tickled at his confusion.* DENYS *gets annoyed, and swings away on his heel with an expression of disgust.*

ALAIN.

I am afraid, Monsieur de Beaulieu, that you do not perfectly understand—the alternative. Follow me, I beseech you, to this window. [*They cross to the window,* DENYS *shrugging his shoulders.*] Look out! [DENYS *looks out into the blackness.* ALAIN *points to just below.*] Here are hooks. Iron hooks. Fastened into the wall. Strong. [*They turn back into room.*] And there [*points*] is the Lady Blanche. And so, Monsieur Denys de Beaulieu, Damoiseau de Beaulieu, in the province of Normandy, I do myself the honour to inform you that unless you are married to my niece in an hour's time, from these hooks you will hang. [BLANCHE *screams aloud, and falls half fainting into a chair.*] I trust your good sense will come to your aid, for of course it is not at all your death that I desire, but my niece's establishment in life. Your family, Monsieur de Beaulieu, is very well in its way, but if you sprang from Charlemagne you should not refuse the hand of a Malétroit with impunity—not if she had been as common as the Paris road, not if she were as hideous as the gargoyles on my roof. Neither my niece, nor you, nor my own private feelings move me in this matter. The honour of my house has been compromised: I believe you to be the guilty person: at least you are now in the secret; and though it will be no satisfaction to me to have your interesting relics kicking their heels from my battlements [*jerks his thumb toward the window*], if I cannot wipe out the dishonour, I shall at least stop the scandal.

DENYS.

Frankly, sir, I think your troubles must have turned your brain; there are other ways of settling such imbroglios among gentlemen.

ALAIN.

Alas, sir! I am old. When I was younger I should have been delighted to honour you; but I am the sole male member of my ancient house. Faithful retainers are the sinews of age, and I were a fool did I not employ the strength I have.

DENYS.

Oh, hang me now, and have done with it!

ALAIN.

No haste. An hour of life is always—an hour. And though one half that time is nigh lapsed already, yet—if you will give me your word of honour to do nothing desperate, and to await my return before you fling yourself from the window,—or, as I guess, —on the pikes of my retainers, I will withdraw myself and them that you may talk in greater privacy with the Lady Blanche. I fought at Arcy, and know what wonders may happen in an hour. [DENYS *turns bitterly, almost savagely, toward* BLANCHE.] You will not disfigure your last hour by want of politeness to a lady?

[DENYS *flushes, accepts the rebuke, bows to both and says simply:*

DENYS.

I give you my word of honour.
[*His decision is not uncoloured by the pathetic petitioning of the mute* BLANCHE.

ALAIN.

I thank you, sir; then I will leave you. [*Turns to go, stops.*] Sir, you are young, you think me a hard man, and perhaps a coward. Remember, pray, that the tears of age are frozen at the heart ere they can spring to the eyes. You may yet think better of the lonely old Sire de Malétroit, and the honour of his house may one day be your own.          [*Exit.*
[BLANCHE *comes over to* DENYS, *who remains leaning heavily on the table.*

BLANCHE.

Oh, sir, how cruelly have I done in my girl's folly, to bring a gallant gentleman to such a pass.

DENYS.

Ah! life is a little thing, fair lady. [*Sighs, gradually getting pleased with himself as a martyr.*] My mother is married again—she needs neither my arm nor my affection; my brother Guichard will inherit my fiefs, and unless I am mistaken, that will console him amply for my death: as for my father— why, I go to join him in an hour. Ay! lady, we are soon forgotten. It is barely ten years since he fell, fighting desperately, with many noble gentlemen around him, and—to-day—I doubt me if the very name of the battle lingers in men's minds! I go to join him in an hour.

BLANCHE.

[*Sighs.*] Ay! sir, you speak sad, but you speak true.

DENYS.

Will there be memory *there?* [DENYS *now fancies himself as a philosopher.*] For I would not marry you—nay! not though I loved you with my soul. In an hour you will be rid of me.

BLANCHE.

Oh, sir, do not be more cruel than our fate itself—to speak as if I could think so.

DENYS.

[*Pities himself.*] You will perhaps sigh once—I hope you will sigh once!—and then you will forget, and laugh, and go back to your old life. Ah! what can I think of all this?

BLANCHE.

I know what you must think, Monsieur de Beaulieu; you dare not say it—but you wrong me. Oh! before God, you wrong me.

DENYS.

[*Distressed.*] Don't! Don't!

BLANCHE.

Do yield: do marry me! Let me tell you how it all came about—you are so brave and young and handsome—I will not have you die.

DENYS.

You seem to think I stand in great fear of death.

BLANCHE.

[*Flushes at this boyish rudeness.*] But *I* will not have you die. I *will* marry you.
[*With determination.*

DENYS.

[*Aside.*] Here is love's language—and Lord knows who's meaning. [*Aloud.*] What you are too generous to refuse I may be too proud to accept.

BLANCHE.

[*Controls her indignation.*] O sir! listen! I have no mother—no father. I am very lonely—how can I tell you? [*Goes over and crouches on chair half-sobbing.*] Three months ago a young man began to stand near me in church. I—I could see I pleased him—and that pleased me; so I listened, when, as I went down the aisle, he whispered me such words as I passed—like poetry, they were so beautiful. I didn't know it was any harm—I let him write me letters, I was so glad that any one should love me. And yesterday he asked me to meet him on the stairs, so that he might tell me with his own voice; but Uncle Alain found the letter, and oh! oh! [*Cries.*]

DENYS.

Poor child! [*Aside.*] By heaven, I do love her. Was ever a man so ill-placed to win a woman?

BLANCHE.

I would not have answered it—oh! Monsieur, I swear to you. I thought no wrong. But uncle shut me up in the chapel, and said I was to be married to-morrow—and—and —set a trap for you.

DENYS.

Mademoiselle, I never thought ill of you, believe me!

BLANCHE.

Then oh, sir! marry me! You shall never see me again, and I will—yes! I will —kill myself, and you shall be free and happy again. It can't hurt you much to say a few words in the chapel with me— and then go back. But pray for me when I am dead.

DENYS.

[*Struggling long with emotion, stops himself from crying and gives a forced laugh.*] Here's romance, if ever there was any. Dog that I am! To laugh when your pale sweet little body is all shaken with weeping. Mademoiselle—Blanche—listen to me, and do not talk such wild nonsense. I will not marry you. I do not love you, or you me. [*Aside.*] Half a lie is better than no truth. [*Aloud.*] I will not ruin your life—and I can commit suicide by merest idleness, a talent I am master of, and one most agreeable to my nature.

BLANCHE.

Oh! Monsieur Denys, but I love you. [*Comes and clings to his knees.*] I do! I do! I will not kill myself, but I will make you love me——

DENYS.

A harder task than you think, little one.

BLANCHE.

Or tolerate me at least. [*Cries.*

DENYS.

O bother! I shall cry too in a minute.

BLANCHE.

You are very unkind. I hate you.

DENYS.

How much of all this is truth? What with pity and drawing-room manners and so on, Truth is the kernel of a devilish hard nut. They say she lives at the bottom of a well—where one is drowned. [*Looks down, craning, as if into a well.*] St. Denys grant I may find her at the end of a rope— where one is hanged. [*With gesture appropriate.*]
[BLANCHE *curls herself up in chair and sobs bitterly.* DENYS *goes to window and looks gloomily out.*]
[*Mimics* ALAIN.] Hooks. Iron hooks. Fastened into the wall. Strong. H'm! and there is the Lady Bl— oh! curséd luck—do you clap me on the shoulder like a good comrade? No! you get round my neck like a lover! Oh! was ever gallant

in such a scrape before? But dawn cannot be far off: I shall—swing myself lightly out of it.

BLANCHE.

[*Sobbing.*] Monsieur Denys! Monsieur Denys!

DENYS.

She has my name pat enough. O poor little girl! If only I didn't love her, with what a good will would I marry her. The nearer one comes to it, the clearer one sees that death is a dark and dusty corner, where a man lies hidden and forgotten till the archangel's — broom. I have few friends now : once I am dead I shall have none.

BLANCHE.

[*Falters.*] You forget Blanche de Malétroit.

DENYS.

You have a sweet nature, Mademoiselle, and you are pleased to estimate a little service far beyond its worth.

BLANCHE.

No, sir, I say more : I recognise in you a spirit that should not give the *pas* to the noblest man in France.

DENYS.

And yet here I die in a mousetrap—with no more noise about it than my own squeaking. [*A pause.*

BLANCHE.

I cannot have my champion think so meanly of himself.

DENYS.

[*Aside.*] Ah! could I forget that I was asked in pity and not in love!
[*Advances, checks himself, swings round and goes to window.*

#### BLANCHE.

I know how you must despise me—oh! you are right. I am too poor a creature to occupy one thought of your mind. Alas! although you must die for me to-morrow—[*She stops short, and waits for him to respond, but* DENYS *is indeed thinking of something else.*] What! You are too proud to link yourself with the dishonoured house of Malétroit? I too have my pride: and now—and now—I would no more marry you than I would marry my uncle's groom.

[*Stamps her foot.* DENYS *turns round and looks at her inquiringly. He has not heard what she has been saying; he becomes again absorbed in his own thoughts.* BLANCHE *gets angrier and angrier, stamps again, and, not attracting his attention, falls into the chair and cries petulantly.*

#### BLANCHE.

It's too hard. To ask and be refused—I, a Malétroit. [DENYS *comes back into the room and faces her. She rises and strikes him across the face with her glove.*] Cowardly boy! [DENYS *turns furiously red, catches her suddenly in his arms and kisses her, flings her away, drops to the floor and groans in an agony of shame and love.*] Double coward! [*She reels away as if he had struck her: comes back to where he crouches, bends over him and strokes his hair.*] Denys! Monsieur Denys! I am so sorry. You are going to die so soon and I am rude to you—when it is all my fault.

[DENYS *rises and stands facing her manfully.*

#### DENYS.

Die! Not I! Blanche, when I kissed you I loved you: I loved you when I saw you in the doorway, and I know you love me now.

#### BLANCHE.

Sir! I do not love you. How dare you speak to me so?

#### DENYS.

You love me. [*Laughing.*] Why, you said so!

#### BLANCHE.

You pass my patience, sir. I was acting, acting for your own safety. I made the most shameful declaration a maid can make for your sake—and you fling it in my teeth.

[DENYS *knows his triumph, and proceeds to enjoy it with laughing speech, as one with a petulant child.*

#### DENYS.

I fail to see that my safety is any the more assured now—without it. Yes, Monsieur de Maladroit, I accept your offer with the best will in the world.

#### BLANCHE.

O you despicable coward! I will kill you at the very altar-steps.

#### DENYS.

Yours is a wonderful strong family for killing, little one.

#### BLÁNCHE.

Mademoiselle de Malétroit is my name.

#### DENYS.

For half-an-hour—nay! barely that.

[BLANCHE *stamps her foot and turns away angry. Breaks down and kneels in chair, crying.* DENYS *follows and stands above her.*

#### DENYS.

O Blanche! Blanche! Do you not see how every tear is like a drop of poisonous dew falling on my heart? You have seen whether I fear death. No love worth Love's name ever yet needed to be asked. And yet—in words! If you care for me at all, do not let me lose my life in a misapprehension! Tho' I would die for you blithely, faith, I had rather live on—in your service. Can you love me a little? Fool! Fool! Ay, there's a pair of us—why do we wait here and let our happiness stand in the cold and knock at our door all night?

BLANCHE.

Don't! Don't make me more miserable and hopeless than I am.
[DENYS *determines to make a general advance.*

DENYS.

[*Tenderly.*] Little fool!
[*He waits. She struggles in herself; and at last rueful and pouting, gets up and stands before him downcast, rubbing her eyes. He takes full advantage of his position.*
[*With mock severity.*] Aren't you ashamed of yourself?

BLANCHE.

[*Sobbing.*] After all you have heard?

DENYS.

[*With double entendre.*] I have heard nothing.
[*He opens his arms to her. She still stands about to sob again, breaks down, but this time flings herself on him and sobs on his breast. Enter* ALAIN *unseen.*
[*Softly.*] My darling!
[BLANCHE *raises her face.* DENYS *goes to kiss her, but she draws back.*

BLANCHE.

The captain's name was Florimond de Champdivers.

DENYS.

I did not hear it. [*A pause.*] Blanche, will you kiss me?
[*They take one long look and then tenderly and very deliberately kiss. They remain so, silently delighting in each other.*

ALAIN.

[*Comes forward with a chuckle.*] Good morning, nephew!
[*They leap up covered with confusion, recover their self-possession, and curtsey and bow respectfully, hand in hand.*

CURTAIN.

# GARGOYLES

## BEING STRANGELY WROUGHT IMAGES OF LIFE AND DEATH

1907

### TO L. BENTROVATA.

Nec tamen illa mihi dextra deducta paterna
Fragrantem Assyrio venit odore domum
Sed furtiva dedit muta munuscula nocte.

Go sunnily through my garden of flowers,
dear maiden o' mine, and once in a while you
shall come upon some grotesque Chinese
dragon with huge and hideous eyes leering
round the delight of the daffodils ; or it may be
some rude Priapus looking over the calm rock-
shadowed beauty of the lake ; or even, hanging amid the glory of elm or beech, an human
skeleton, whose bones shall rattle in the breeze,
and from whose eyeless sockets shall glare I
dare not bid you guess what evil knowledge.

Then, an you be wise, you shall know that
a wise gardener wisely put them there. For
every garden is the world ; and in the world
these are.

So every cathedral is the world, and the
architect of Notre Dame deserved his heaven.

To me life and death have most often
appeared in majesty and beauty, in solemnity
and horror ; in emotions, to be brief, so great
that man had no place therein. But there
are moods, in which the heights are attained
indirectly, and through man's struggle with
the elemental powers.

In these poems you shall hear the laughter
of the gods and of the devils ; understand
their terrors and ecstasies ; live in their
heavens and hells.

But I not only heard and understood and
lived ; I sounded and imposed and begat :
you must also do both, or the universe will
still be a mystery to you as to the others.

## IMAGES OF LIFE

### PROLOGUE.

#### VIA VITÆ.

I.

My head is split. The crashing axe
Of the agony of things shears through
    The stupid skull : out spurt the brains.
The universe revolves, then cracks,
    Then roars in dissolution due ;
        And I am counting up the gains
And losses of a life afire
With dust of thought and dulled desire.

II.

So, all is over. I admit
    Futility the lord of will.
    Life was an episode, for me

As for the meanest monad, knit
    To man by mightier bonds than skill
        Of subtle-souled psychology
May sever. Aim in chaos? None.
The soul rolls senseless as the sun.

III.

Existence, as we know it, spins
    A fatal warp, a woof of woe.
        There is no place for God or soul.
Works, hopes, prayers, sacrifices, sins
    Are jokes. The cosmos happened so :
        Innocent all of guide or goal.
Else, what were man's appointed term ?
To feed God's friend, the coffin-worm !

84

#### IV.

Laugh, thou immortal Lesbian !
  Thy verse runs down the runic ages.
    Where shalt thou be when sun and star,
My sun, my star, the vault that span,
  Rush in their rude, impassive rages
    Down to some centre guessed afar
By mindless Law ?   Their death-embrace
A simple accident of space ?

#### V.

Where is thy fame, when million leagues
  Of flaming gas absorb the roll
    Of many a system ruinous hurled
With infinite pains and dire fatigues
  To build another stupid soul
    For fools to call another world ?
Where then thy fame, O soul sublime ?
Where then thy victory over Time ?

#### VI.

Wilt thou seek deeper than the fact ?
  Take refuge in a city of mind ?
    Build thee an house, and call it heaven ?
Rush on ! there foams the cataract,
  Blind steersman leader of the blind,
    Sole devil herald of the seven
Thy garnished halls should house, O Christ,
Thou being dead, thou sacrificed

#### VII.

Not for atonement, not for bliss ;
  Truly for nothing : so it was.
    Nay, friends, think well !   Renounce
    the dream !
Seek not some mystery in the kiss,
  Some virtue in the chrysopras,
    Some nymph or undine in the stream.
Things as we know them should be enough
To glut our misery and our love.

#### VIII.

Why must despair to madness drive
  The myriad fools that fear to die ?
    God's but a fervid phantom drawn
Out of the hasty-ordered hive
  Of thoughts that battle agony
    In the melancholy hours of dawn.
When vital force at lowest ebbs
Anæmic nerves weave frailest webs.

#### IX.

So, be content !   Should science cleave
  The veil of things and show us peace,
    Well :—but by wild imagining
Think not a golden robe to weave !
  Such moulder.   By fantastic ease
    Ye come not well to anything.
Work and be sober : dotage thinks
By worth of words to slay the Sphinx.

#### X.

Things as they are—of these take hold,
  Their heart of wonder throb to thine !
    All things are matter and force and
    sense,
No two alone.   All's one : the gold
  Of truth is no reward divine
    Of faith, but wage of evidence.
The clod, the God, the spar, the star
Mete in thy measure, as they are !

#### XI.

So lifts the agony of the world
  From this mine head, that bowed awhile
    Before the terror suddenly shown.
The nameless fear for self, far hurled
  By death to dissolution vile,
    Fades as the royal truth is known :
Though change and sorrow range and roll
There is no self—there is no soul !

#### XII.

As man, a primate risen high
  Above his fellows, work thou well
    As man, an incident minute
And dim in time's eternity,
  Work well !   As man, no toy for hell
    And heaven to wrangle for, be mute !
Let empty speculation stir
The idle fool, the craven cur !

#### XIII.

Myself being idle for an hour
  I dare one thing to speculate :
    Namely, that life hath cusps yet higher
On this our curve : a prize, a power
  Lies in our grasp : unthinking Fate
    Shall build a brain to nestle nigher
Unto the ultimate Truth : I burn
To live that later lives may learn.

### XIV.

Simple to say ; to do complex !
　　That we this higher type of man
　　　May surely generate, o' nights
Our lesser brains we vainly vex.
　　Our knowledge lacks ; we miss the plan.
　　　Fools hope our luck will set to rights
Our skill that's baulked.　Yet now we know
At least the way we wish to go.

### XV.

This task assume !　Colossal mind
　　And toil transcending, concentrate
　　　Not on the metaphysic wild ;
Not on the deserts vast and blind
　　Of dark Religion ; not on Fate,
　　　The barren ocean ; but the Child
Shows us a beacon in the night ;
A lens to lure and lend the light.

### XVI.

Wisdom and Love, intenser glow !
　　Beauty and Strength, increase and burn !
　　　Be brothers to the law of life !
Things as they are—their nature know !
　　Act !　Nor for faith nor folly turn !
　　　The hour is nigh when man and wife,
Knowing, shall worship face to face,
Beget and bear the royal race.

### THE WHITE CAT.

HAIL, sweet my sister !　hail, adulterous
　　spouse,
　　Gilded with passionate pomp, and gay with
　　　guilt :
Rioting, rioting in the dreary house
　　With blood and wine and roses splashed
　　　and spilt
About thy dabbling feet, and aching jaws
　　Whose tongue licks mine, twin asps like
　　　moons that curl,
Red moons of blood !　Whose catlike body
　　claws,
　　Like a white swan raping a jet-black girl,

Mine, with hysteric laughter !　O white cat !
　　O windy star blown sideways up the sky !
Twin cat, twin star, 'tis night ; the owl and
　　bat
　　Hoot, scream ; 'tis us they call—to love
　　　or die.
Twin cat, our broomsticks wait : we'll fly
　　afar !
We'll blaze about the unlighted sky, twin
　　star !

### ALI AND HASSAN.

FROM THE ALF LAYLAH WA LAYLAH.

ALI bade Hassan to his house to sup.
They ate, passed round the full forbidden
　　cup,
Till, in an interval of dance and song,
Hassan forgot his manners—loud and long.
Struck with confusion, forth he fares, takes
　　ship
To utmost Ind and far-off Serendip.
Full forty years he there abides : at last,
Rich and respected, he contemns the past :—
" If I declare myself, there's hope, I wot,
Hassan's remembered, and his fault forgot !—"
Determines to revisit home.　Sweet airs
Accomplishing the voyage, he repairs
Unto the barber.　" Tell me of the state !
Haroun still holds the royal Caliphate ? "
" Nay," said the barber, " long ago he passed
Where all delights are 'stinguished at the last,
And all good things forgotten, wallahy !
He died—aha now !—no—yes—let me see !
Ten years, three months, four days, as I'm a
　　sinner,
Since Hassan let the—shame—at Ali's
　　dinner."

### AL MALIK.

A GHAZAL OF AL QAHAR.

AL MALIK the magnificent
Was sitting in his silken tent.

But when he saw the boy Habib
I wis his colour came and went.

Quoth he : By Allah, 'tis a star
Struck from the azure firmament !

Habib : I pour the wine of love
For Al Awaz the excellent.

The king : I envy him thy shape,
Thy voice, thy colour, and thy scent.

Habib : In singing of his slave
Hath Al Awaz grown eminent.

The king : But I, to taste thy lip,
My kingdom willingly had spent.

Habib : Asylum of the World !
My master bade me to present

My loveliness to thee, whose brows
Like to a Scythian bow are bent.

The king accepted him to bear
His cup of wine, and was content.

Let Al Qahar their praises sing :
Three souls, one love, one element.[1]

## SONG.

### I.

DANCE a measure
  Of tiniest whirls !
Shake out your treasure
  Of cinnamon curls !
Tremble with pleasure,
  O wonder of girls !

[1] This poem is very much taboo in Persia, as it is supposed to be little better than a pamphlet in favour of Christianity. The later work of Al Qahar, and especially his master-piece, the Bagh-i-muattar, are, however, if not quite above suspicion, so full of positive piety of the Sufi sort that even the orthodox tolerate what the mystic and the ribald silently or noisily admire.

### II.

Rest is bliss,
  And bliss is rest,
Give me a kiss
  If you love me best !
Hold me like this
  With my head on your breast !

## ANICCA.

HE who desires desires a change.
  Change is the tale of life and death.
Matter and motion rearrange
  Their endless coils ; the Buddha saith :
    "Cease, O my sons, to desire !
    Change is the whole that we see
  By the light of a chaos on fire.
    Cease to desire—you are free !"
Your words, good Gotama, are brave and true ;
Easy to say, but difficult to do !

## TARSHITERING.

### NEPALI LOVE-SONG.[1]

O KISSABLE Tarshitering ! the wild bird calls
    its mate—and I ?
  Come to my tent this night of May, and
    cuddle close and crown me king !
Drink, drink our full of love at last—a little
    while and we shall die,
  O kissable Tarshitering !

Droop the long lashes : close the eyes with
    eyelids like a beetle's wing !
  Light the slow smile, ephemeral as ever a
    painted butterfly,
Certain to close into a kiss, certain to fasten
    on me and sting !

Nay ? Are you coy ? Then I will catch
    your hips and hold you wild and shy
  Until your very struggles set your velvet
    buttocks all a-swing,
Until their music lulls you to unfathomable
    ecstasy,
  O kissable Tarshitering !

[1] Possibly the original of the well-known Hindustani song :—
  "Thora thairo, Tenduk ! thora thairo, tum !
  Thora thairo, thairo thora, thora thairo tum !"
                                    A. C.

## A FRAGMENT.[1]

*In the midst of the desert of Libya, on a mound of sand, lieth a young man alone and naked. Nightfall.*

NIGHT the voluptuous, night the chaste
Spreads her dark limbs, a vaulted splendour,
Above the intolerable waste.
Night the august one, night the tender
Queens it and brides it unto me.
I am the soul serenely free ;
I dare to seek the austere ordeal
That drags the hoodwink of the Real
Back from the Maker's livid eyes
Lustred with hate.   At noon I came
Blind in the desert, saw the sun
Leap o'er the edge, a fury of flame
Shouting for rapture over his prize,
The maiden body of earth.   Outrun
The violent rays ; the dawn is dashed
In one swift moment into dust.
Long lies the land with sunlight splashed,
Brutally violate to his lust.
Alone and naked I watched through
The appalling hours of noon ; I parched ;
I blistered : all the ghastly crew
Of mind's sick horror mocked me ; arched
The flaming vault of hell and pressed
Its passionate murder in my breast.
Seven times I strove to slay me : filled
My mouth with sand to choke my breath.
In vain !   No loftier purpose willed
The iron miracle of death.
So, blind and strangled, I survive.
So, with my skin a single scar,
I hail the night, the night alive
With Hathor for the evening star.
O beauty !   See me broken, burned
Lone on the languorous Lybian plain !
Is there one lesson to be learned
From this my voluntary pain,
My dread initiation, long
Desired and long deferred ?   The Master—
Is he the secret of the song,
Portent of triumph or disaster

[1] Intended as the prologue to a history of an initiate in semi-dramatic form.

The night wind breathes upon the air
Still shimmering from the fearful heat ?
Can I still trust who have learned to dare ?
All others I have known effete,
Bid them await.   Who knows to-day
The purpose of the dread essay ?
Surely I, earlier, further fared !
I knew the deed that closes clay,
Division's sword by sense unbared,
A living lie.   The deep delusion !
Dividuality—confusion !
These I unmasked of yore.   To-day
The hideous blue, the hideous gold
Of sky and sand their wrath unrolled,
Their agony and hate proclaimed.
Is it that night shall kiss to peace
The furious carnival that flamed
Its ruinous ardour from the sun !
Nay, let all light, all things, but cease !
Sense is the seal of double rule.
The million oracles that run
Out of the mouth of God the fool
Are not myself.   To nothing turn !
To nothing look !   Then, then !—discern
Nothing, that one may one remain.
So I am paid the horrible pain
That these my brothers ordered me.
I look upon their brows—I see
Signs many and deep of torture past ;
A star, yon star, true peace at last.

(*There approacheth an aged man, riding upon an ass, with a led ass, and a Nubian servant.*)

*The Adept.* In the name of God, the One, the Great,
Merciful and compassionate,
Acclaim the perfect period
Of ordeal past !
      *The Neophyte.* There is no God !
   *A.* Rise ! in the name of obscure Fate,
Ruthless and uncompassionate.
   *N.* Of endless life, of toil and woe
I am the burned and branded foe.
I came this torture to endure
That I might make my freedom sure.
   *A.* No soul is free.

*N.*                    There is no soul.
See yonder gleams the starry shoal
Of orbs incalculably vast.
They are not present : they are past,
Since the long march of shuddering light
Made years the servants of its might.
There is no soul.
    *A.*               These stars thou seest
Are but the figuring of thy brain.
    *N.* Then of all things the soul were freest.
    *A.* Move then the centre of thy pain !
    *N.* 'Tis done.
    *A.*              A trick to cheat a child.
    *N.* It is the truth that I am nought.
Hear what I have gathered in the wild,
Flowers of imperishable thought
With glory and with rapture clothed.
This being, thinking, loved or loathed,
Hath attributes.   This sand is gold :—
Deem'st thou a gilder lurks within
The atom ?   What should Nature hold
Of aureate save a mind begin
Colour-conception?   Then we win
To think our thought itself a chance
Grafted upon the circumstance
Of cerebrin and lethicin.
    *A.* Ill fares the rifleman that holds
The muzzle to his eye.   Yon gold's
Mental : enough ! the mind is all.
    *N.* No : this is but a slave in thrall
To matter's motion.   We deny
A causeless cause, an entity
Beyond experience, that tricks
Our folly with its idle claim
To be because we feel it.
    *A.*                Sticks
The reason there?
    *N.*             We choose a name
To cover all the host of facts
Comprised in thought.
    *A. (aside)*        The elixir acts.
Then backward work ; the name becomes
With pomp of metaphysic drums
A *causa causans*—God, soul, truth.
So raves the riot, age and youth,
The cart before the horse.   Revered
And reverend master, is your beard
Darwin's survival of some tail ?

Who rants of soul were best to saddle
His face, his arms the ass to straddle,
Since for his voice the part thus bare
Would serve as well to scent the air.
    *A.* Where reverence ceases, ribald jest
Breaks forth, the wise allow the rest.
The perfect master stands confessed.
    *N.* Why ! I supposed your wrath would
        burst ;
My name and number stand accurst
In the great Order of the West !
    *A.* Nay: Buddha smiles; 'twas Jesus wept !
Arise, O brother and adept !
    *N.* Master !
    *A.* The torture-hours are past.
    *N.* The peace of pain is mine at last.
    *A.* Ere the moon rise, the brethren meet.
Come, let us turn toward the South.
    *N.* Lord, I embrace thy holy feet.
    *A.* Nay, let me kiss thee on the mouth.
        *Desunt cetera.*

## THE STUMBLING-BLOCK.

I ALMOST wonder if I ought
    To hymn this height of human pain :
To enter into Jones's thought
    I'd have to work with Jones's brain.

Terrestrial speech is wholly vain
    To carry meaning as it ought :—
    To enter into Jones's thought
I'd have to work with Jones's brain.

This is the High God's cruel sport :
To enter into Jones's thought
    And make its inner meaning plain,
    I'd have to work with Jones's brain.

## WOODCRAFT.

THE poet slept.   His fingers twine
In his wife's hair.   He dreams.   Divine
His dream !   Nay then, I'll tell you it.

He wandered in a forest dim.
A woodcutter encountered him
Where a felled oak required his wit.

This man with a light axe did lop
The little branches at the top.
Then said the poet : " Thus why tax
Your force ? This double-handed axe
Were better laid to the tree-trunk."
" Friend, are you natural, or drunk ? "
Replied the woodsman ; " leaf and twig
Divert the impact of the big
Axe ; chop them first, the trunk is fit
For a fair aim, a certain hit.
How do you work yourself? " He spoke
To empty space—the poet woke ;
And catching up a carving-knife
He slit the weasand of his wife.


### A NUGGET FROM A MINE.

A MINER laboured in a mine.
(The poet dreamed) By coarse and fine
He shovelled dust into a trolley.
" But this " (the poet said) "is folly !
Take up your pick, engage in shock
At the foundation of the rock ! "
The miner swore. " You —— fool !
You clever —— ! go to school
And college and be —— ! Strike you !
There ain't no sense in forty like you !
If I don't clear this muck, the pick
Will foul and jam, slip, swerve, or stick.
Clear off the chips, the blow goes true.
Now, mister, off, my —— to you ! "
The last oath faded in the air.
The poet woke and was aware
Of property and children. Claims
His breech a vesta. Up the flames
Leap ; he stalks forth, free among men,
With just a notebook and a pen.


### AU CAVEAU DES INNOCENTS.

*Oct.* 28, 1904.

NIGHT, like a devil, with lidless eyes,
Stands avenging over the Halls.
Sleep there is none, for day awaits
Tokens of toil ; there is none that dies,

Death being rest ; there is none that calls,
Voice being human ; only the Fates
Rattle the dice at a sombre game,
Game without goal of peace or fame.
Sinister, sombre, horrors and hates
Lurk in the shadows, under the walls.
Light deceives, and the darkness lies.

Love there is none ; he is child of peace :
Joy there is none ; she is bride of force :
Thought there is none ; it is birth :—there
    fell
Ages ago all hope of these.
Lust is awake, and its friend remorse.
Crime we snatch, between spell and spell.
Man is aglare, and is off unheard.
Woman hath speech, of a single word.
Hell may be heaven, for earth is hell !
So do I laugh, and the hideous coarse
Peals like applause re-echo and cease.

Here in the close and noisome cave,
Drunk on the breath of the thieves and
    whores
Close as they cram in the maw of the pit,
Sick with the stench of the kisses that
    rave
Round me, surfeiting sense, in scores ;
Mad with their meaning, I smoke and sit
Rhyming at random through my teeth,
Grey with the mire of the slough beneath,
Deep in the hearts that revel in it,
Drowned in the breath of the hell that
    pours
In the heart of Paris its infamous wave.


Damning the soul of God, I rise,
Stumble among the dissolute bands,
Grope to the steep inadequate stairs
Scrawled with villainous names. My eyes
Loathe the flare of the flickering brands.
Out I climb through the greasy airs
Into the cold and desolate road.
Horror is sure of a safe abode
Here in this heart, too pale for prayers,
While over the Halls avenging stands
Night, like a devil, with lidless eyes.

## ROSA INFERNI.[1]

"Ha ha! John plucketh now at his rose
To rid himself of a sorrow at heart.
Lo,—petal on petal, fierce rays unclose;
Anther on anther, sharp spikes outstart;
And with blood for dew, the bosom boils;
And a gust of sulphur is all its smell:
And lo, he is horribly in the toils
Of a coal-black giant flower of hell!"
—BROWNING, *Heretic's Tragedy*, ix.

### I.

ROSE of the world! Ay, love, in that warm
hour
Wet with your kisses, the bewitching bud
Flamed in the starlight; then our bed your
bower
Heaved like the breast of some alluring flood
Whereon a man might sleep for ever, until
Death should surprise him, kiss his weary will
Into the last repose, profounder power
Than life could compass. Now I tax my
skill
To find another holier name, some flower
Still red, but red with the ecstasy of blood.
Dear love, dear wife, dear mother of the child
Whose fair faint features are a match for
mine,
Lurks there no secret where your body smiled,
No serpent in the generous draught of wine?
Did I guess all, who guessed your life well
given
Up to my kiss? Aha! the veil is riven!
Beneath the smiling mask of a young bride
Languorous, luscious, melancholy-eyed;
Beneath the gentle raptures, hints celestial
Of holy secrets, kisses like soft dew,
Beneath the amorous mystery, I view
The surer shape, a visage grim and bestial,
A purpose sly and deadly, a black shape,
A tiger snarling, or a grinning ape
Resolved by every devilish device
Upon my murder. This I clearly see
Now you are—for an hour—away from me.
I see it once; no need to tell me twice!

### II.

Some Yankee yelled—I tag it to a rime—
"You can't fool all the people all the time."
So he of politics; so I of love.
I am a-many folk (let Buddha prove!)
And many a month you fooled the lot of us—
Your spell is cracked within the ring!
Behold
How Christ with clay worth more than any
gold
Cleared the man's eyes! So the blind
amorous
Is blinded with the horror of the truth
He sees this moment. Foolish prostitute!
You slacked your kiss upon the sodden youth
In some excess of confidence, decay
Of care to hold him—can I tell you which?
Down goes the moon—one sees the howling
bitch!
The salmon you had hooked in fin and gill
You reel unskilfully—he darts away.
Alas! you devil, but vou hold me still!

### III.

O first and fairest of Earth's darling
daughters!
How could I sing you?—you have always
seemed
Unto the saucy driveller as he dreamed
Like a rich sunset seen on tropic waters—
(Your eyes effulgent from a thousand
slaughters
Looked tenderly upon me!) all the red
Raving round you like a glory shed
Upon the excellent wonder of your head;
The blue all massed within your marvellous
eyes;
The gold a curtain of their harmonies
As in a master canvas of de Ryn;[1]
But ever central glowed the royal sun,
A miracle cartouche upon the edge
Of the opalescent waters slantwise seen.
This oval sealed with grave magnificence
Stamped you my queen. Thus looked your
lips to one

[1] Rembrandt.

Who stood a casual on life's slippery ledge,
A blind bat hanging from the tree of sense
Head downward, gorged with sweet banana
      juice,
Indifferent to—incapable of—aught
Beyond these simple reflexes.  Is thought,
Even the highest thought, of any use?


### IV.

We are not discussing metaphysics now.
I see below the beautiful low brow
(Low too for cunning, like enough !) your lips,
A scarlet splash of murder.  From them drips
This heart's blood ; you have fed your fill on
      me.
I am exhaust, a pale, wan phantom floating
Aimless in air, than which I am thinner.  You
I see, more brilliant, of that sanguine hue
(If anything be true that I can see)
Full fed ; you smile, a smile obscenely gloating
On the voluptuous wreck your lust hath
      wrought.
See the loose languor of precipitate thought
These versicles exhale !  How rude the rime !
There is no melody ; the tune and time
Are broken.   Thirteen centuries ago
They would have said, " Alas ! the youth !
      We know
This devil hath from him plucked the im-
      mortal soul."
*I* say : you have dulled my centres of control !


### V.

If you were with me, I were blind to this :
Ready to drain my arteries for your kiss,
Feel your grasp tighten round my ribs until
You crush me in the ecstasies that kill.
Being away and breathing icy air
I am half lover, caring not to care ;
Half-man again—a mere terrestrial ball
Thus breaking up a spiritual thrall—
Eh, my philosophers ?—half-man may yet
      determine
To get back manhood, shake the tree from
      bats :

To change the trope a shade—get rid of
      vermin
By using William Shakespeare's " Rough on
      Rats." [1]

### VI.

Ah, love, dear love, sole queen of my affec-
      tion,
Guess you not yet what wheel of thought is
      spun ?
How out of dawn's tumultuous dejection
And not from noon springs up the splendid
      sun ?
Not till the house is swept and garnished well
Rise seven other devils out of hell.

### VII.

This is the circle ; as the manhood rises
And laughter and rude rhyme engage my pen ;
As I stalk forth, a Man among mere men,
The balance changes ; all my wit surprises
That I who saw the goblins in your face,
That I who cursed you for the murderous
      whore
Licking up life as a cat laps its milk,
Now see you for a dream of youth and grace,
Relume the magic aura that begirt you,
Bless you for purity and life—a store !
An ever-running fountain-head of virtue
To heal my soul and buckler it and harden !
Your body is like ivory and silk !
Your lips are like the poppies in the garden !
Your face is like a wreath of flowers to
      crown me !
Your eyes are wells wherein I long to drown
      me !
Your hair is like a waterfall above me,
A waterfall of sunset !  In your bosom
I hear the racing of a heart to love me.
Your blood is beating like a wind-blown
      blossom
With rapture that you mingle it in mine !
Your breath is fresh as foam and keen as
      wine !
Intoxicating glories are your glances !
Your bodily beauty grips my soul and dances

[1] Meaning that by study of Shakespeare he
would resume higher interests, and baffle the
sensual seductions of this siren.

Its maddening measures in my heart and
    brain !
Is it that so the wheel may whirl again,
That some dull devil in my ear may show
    me :
"For John the Baptist's head—so danced
    Salome !" ?

### VIII.

Then, in God's name forbear ! It does not
    matter.
Life, death, strength, weakness, are but
    idle chatter.
Nothing is lost or gained, we know too well.
For heaven they balance us an equal hell.
We discard both ; an infinite Universe
Remains ; we sum it up—an infinite curse.
So—am I a man ?  I lack my wife's embrace.
Am I outworn ?  I see the harlot's face.
Is the love better and the knowledge worse ?
Shall I seek knowledge and count love dis-
    grace ?
Where is the profit in so idle a strife ?
The love of knowledge is the hate of life.

## DIOGENES.

"ALL things are good" exclaimed the boy.
Who taste the sweetmeat find it cloy.

"All things are ill " the dotard sang.
Who stir the serpent feel the fang.

"All is a dream !" the wise man spake.
Who grasp the bubble find it break.

Aye, to all three the saga saith :
There is no joy in life but death.

There is this limit set to lust :
Ashes to ashes, dust to dust.

O fools and blind that sickly strive
To amass, to glut yourselves, to swive,

To drink, to acquire respect and praise :—
These visions perish as you gaze.

Eternal mockery is the real ;
Eternal falsehood, the ideal.

Choose : nay, abstain from choice of these.
Go, be alone, and be at ease !

Retire : renounce : the hermit's cell
Hath all of earth, and nought of hell.

Renouncing all, keep nought enshrined
A lurking serpent in the mind.

Deem not to catch some goodlier gain
Than these ; the goodliest prize were pain.

Know that the utmost heaven is void
Of aught save star or asteroid !

Or, an it please thee, idly dream
A God therein, a force supreme,

A heart of love, a crown of light,
An infinite music of delight ;—

This, but no more ; let fancy sway
But never fix the transient ray !

All things are lawful, so they be
At most a marshalled imagery.

Dream of Earth's glories higher and higher,
Mounting the minaret, desire ;

Never attaining to the sky,
Realization—lest thou die.

So dream, possessing all ; so dream,
Possessing nothing : I esteem

These twain as one, since dreams they are.
Thus mayst thou journey far and far

And far ! to climes unguessed, to seas
Proud with seignorial argosies,

To mountains strange with golden snows,
To gardens green with many a rose,

To secrets past the sense of sense,
Skies virgin of experience,

Untrodden avenues of mind,
Things far from hurrying humankind.

Thus spins out life its splendid charm :—
Live, love, enjoy, yet do no harm.

No rose of thought may bear or breed
The poisonous thorn of word and deed.

Call " homo sapiens " him who thinks ;
Talkers and doers—missing links !

.　.　.　.　.

Such songs are twilight's, when I stretch
My limbs, and wander down to fetch

My water from the cool cascade,
My wood from the enchanted glade,

My berries from the rustling bough :—
Return, and eat, and sleep.　Allow

For me, the silence and the night ;
Life, peace ; and death, a welcome wight.

### SAID.

THE spears of the night at her onset
Are lords of the day for a while,
The magical green of the sunset,
The magical blue of the Nile.
　　Afloat are the gales
　　In our slumberous sails
On the beautiful breast of the Nile.

We have swooned through the midday, ex-
　　hausted
By the lips—they are whips—of the sun,
The horizon befogged and befrosted
By the haze and the greys and the dun
　　Of the whirlings of sand
　　Let loose on the land
By the wind that is born of the sun.

On the water we stand as a shadow,
A skeleton sombre and thin
Erect on the watery meadow,
As a giant, a lord of the Djinn
　　Set sentinel over
　　Some queen and her lover
Beloved of the Gods and the Djinn.

We saw the moon shudder and sink
In a furnace of tremulous blue ;
We stood on the mystical brink
Of the day as it sprang to us through
　　The veil of the night,
　　And the babe of the light
Was begotten in the caves of the dew.

My lover and I were awake
When the noise of the dawn in our ears
Burst out like a storm or a snake
Or the rush of the Badawi spears.
　　Dawn of desire !
　　But thy kiss was as fire
To thy lovers and princes and peers.

Then the ruin of night we beheld
As the sun stormed the heights of the sky
With his myriad swords, and compelled
The pale tremblers, the planets, to fly.
　　He drave from their place
　　All the stars for a space,
From their bastioned towers in the sky.

Thrilled through to the marrow with heat
We abode (as we glode) on the river.
Every arrow he launched from his seat,
From the white inexhaustible quiver,
　　Smote us right through,
　　Smote us and slew,
As we rode on the rapturous river.

Sweet sleep is perfection of love.
To die into dreams of my lover,
To wake with his mouth like a dove
Kissing me over and over !
　　Better sleep so
　　Than be conscious, and know
How death hath a charm to discover.

Ah ! float in the cool of the gloaming !
Float wide in the lap of the stream
With his mouth ever roving and homing
To the nest where the dove is adream.
　　Better wake so
　　Than be thinking, and know
That at best it is only a dream.

So turn up thy face to the stars !
In their peace be at peace for awhile !
Let us pass in their luminous cars
As a sob, as a sigh, as a smile !
　　Love me and laze
　　Through the languorous days
On the breast of the beautiful Nile !

*May* 1905.

## EPILOGUE.

### PRAYER.

THE light streams stronger through the lamps
      of sense.
        Intelligence
Grows as we go.   Alas : its icy glimmer
      Shows dimmer, dimmer
The awful vaults we traverse.   Were the sun
      Himself the one
Glory of space, he would but illustrate
      The night of Fate.
Are not the hosts of heaven in vain arrayed ?
      Their light dismayed
Before the vast blind spaces of the sky ?
      O galaxy
Of thousands upon thousands closely curled !
      Your golden world
Incalculably small, its closest cluster
      Mere milky lustre
Staining the infinite darkness !  Base and
      blind
        Our minion mind
Seeks a great light, a light sufficient, light
      Insufferably bright,
Hence hidden for an hour : imagining
      This vast vain thing,
We call it God, and Father.   Empty hand
      And prayer unplanned
Stretch fatuous to the void.  Ah ! men my
      friends,
        What fury sends
This folly to intoxicate your hearts ?
      Dread air disparts
Your vital ways from these unsavoury follies,
      Black melancholies
Sit straddled on your bended backs.   The
      throne
        Of the unknown

Is fit for children.   We are too well ware
      How vain is prayer,
How nought is great, since all is immanent,
      The vast content
Of all the universe unalterable.
      We know too well
How no one thing abides awhile at all,
      How all things fall,
Fall from their seat, the lamentable place,
      Before their face,
Weary and pass and are no more.   So we,
      Since hope must be,
Look to the future, to the chance minute
      That life may shoot
Some flower at least to blossom in the night,
      Since vital light
Is sure to fail us on the hideous way.
      What ?   Must we pray ?
Verily, O thou littlest babe, too weak
      To stir or speak,
Capable hardly of a thought, yet seed
      Of word and deed !
To thine assured fruition we may trust
      This weary dust.
We who are old, and palsied, (and so wise !)
      Lift up our eyes
To little children, as the storm-tossed bark
      Hails in the dark
Some hardly visible harbour light ; we hold
      The hours of gold
To our own breasts, whose hours are iron
      and brass :—
        So swift they pass
And grind us down :—we hold the wondrous
      light
        Our scattering sight
Yet sees, the one star in a night of woe.
      We trust, and so
Lift up our voices in the dying day
      Indeed to pray :
*O little hands that are so soft and strong,*
      *Lead us along !*

# IMAGES OF DEATH

## PROLOGUE.

### PATCHOULI.

LIKE memories of love they come,
  My perfumes in the silver vase:
The fragrant root, the odorous gum,
Myrrh, aloes, or olibanum :—
  Anon, like memories of love, they pass !

They pass, and all the wonder-web
Of thought and being is unrolled.
Like sombre tides there flow and ebb
  Wonderful things ! not to be told :
  Beautiful things ! and images of gold.

The touch of brown Habiba's breast,
  The brimming lip, the cheek of down,
The dainty dovelet in its nest :
These fade, as ever a palimpsest
  Like autumn vanishes from gold to brown.

Zuleikha, on whose marble knees
  My bearded head is lazily lain,
Shows like some stirring of the breeze
Fluctuant in the poppied grain,
  No more at all : the vulgar sense is slain.

Of all the world alone abides
  The faint perfume of Patchouli,
That subtle death in love ; it glides
Across the opening dream, derides
  The fetich folly, immortality.

Awake, O dream !  Let distant bells
  And vague muezzins haunt the ear,
Gaunt camels kneel by dusky wells,
  Imagination greyly hear :
  Allahu akbar !  Allahu kabir !

Over inhospitable sands
  Let the simoom its columns spin !
In snowy vales, untrodden lands,
Let there be storm, and bearded bands
  Of robbers pass around the bubbling skin !

Let there be caves of treasure rare
  Deep hidden in sepulchral seas ;
And birds unheard-of darken air
  With royal wings, like argosies
  Sailing beneath magnific promontories !

Let Caliphs mete fantastic law
  And ebon eunuchs swing the sword
So swift, so curved,—let voiceless awe
Sit on the palace dome, to draw
  Some god's destruction on its smiling lord !

May many a maiden comely clad
  Revolve in convoluted curls,
Till from each pliant pose I had
  (By virtue of her wondrous whirls)
  The illusion of a thousand dancing-girls !

Let harlots robed in gold and green
  Sit slowly waving ivory plumes
And wings of palm ; the while their queen
Lurks in some horror-house unseen,
  Damned to be smothered in divine per-
    fumes !

Let there be scenes of blood and pain,
  Some Slav beneath the Cossack knout,
Some mother ripped, some baby slain ;
  Let lust move silently about :—
  Soft laughter hid in all, song whispering
    out !

Then let these things of form decay,
  Some subtler dream dissolve their form,
As I have seen a cloudlet lay
Its forehead on the sea, and pray
  Some idle prayer to sunset, or the storm !

Yea ! as a cloud in worship-trance
  Swoons in invisible delight,
Let slave and king, let death and dance
  Shake off their forms, and clothe their
    light
  In shrouds of sepulchre, the starless night !

Let song and cry leave tune and tone,
  Perish uncried and die unsung !
Nature, the monotonic moan
Roared by the river, thunder alone :—
  The Hoang-Ho, its note, the monstrous
    Kung !¹

Or let Kailasha's² godded peak
  Summon the oread and the gnome
To leave their toils, the word to speak
  That shakes its azure-splitting dome
  With the reverberation—listen !—Aum !

Let olive fail, and mangostin !
  O'erturn the dark forbidden draught !
Give me the taste, the taste unclean
Of human flesh and blood that mean
  Some infinite horror to the light that
    laughed !

So let the scent of lily and rose,
  Of jasmine, taggara,³ pass away !
Let patchouli, patchouli, repose
  My nostrils with your odour grey,
  Dead darlings exquisite in your decay !

So, silk and velvet, fur and skin,
  Your sensuous touch shall quit me quite :
I am at swiving strain with sin—
I'll touch the stars, the blood run thin
  From the torn breast of Night, my mother
    Night.

Nor shall the mind revoke at ease
  These myriad cressets from the sun ;
Constrained in sober destinies
  Thought's river shall its ripples run
  Into the one, the one, the one, the one.

¹ The fundamental tone in Chinese music ;
supposed to be given by the Hoang-Ho river,
according to Professor Rice.
² Sacred mountain in the Himalaya, the
abode of Shiva.
³ An eastern perfume. *Cf.* Max Müller's
Dhammapada.
VOL. III.

Bursting the universe, a grip
  Girds me to God ; aha ! the bliss !
Begone, frail tortures wrung from whip,
Weak joys sucked hard from leman's lip,
  Ye are nought at all, are nought at all, in
    this !

.    .    .    .    .    .

But brown Habiba's fawn-wide gaze
  And white Zuleikha's drowsy glance
Woo me to waking unto day's
  Delight from night's unmeasured trance :—
  To drink, to dally, to desire, to dance.

Ah ! beautiful and firm your hips,
  Habib ! ah ! coolthsome your caress,
Zuleikha ! soft your honey lips—
The tongue of pleasure subtly sips
  The wine that age distils, and calls dis-
    tress.

Enough ! when all is ended, when
  The poppied pleasure purples pain—
Death—shall I laugh or smile ?   Amen !
  I'll wake, one last fond cup to drain,
  And then—to sleep again, to sleep again !

### KALI.¹

THERE is an idol in my house
  By whom the sandal alway steams.
Alone, I make a black carouse
  With her to dominate my dreams.
With skulls and knives she keeps control
  (O Mother Kali !) of my soul.

She is crowned with emeralds like leaves,
  And rubies flame from either eye ;
A rose upon her bosom heaves,
  Turquoise and lapislazuli.
She hath a kirtle like a maid :—
Amethyst, amber, pearl, and jade !

¹ The most popular form, in Bengal, of
Sakti, the Hindu Isis.

G

Her face is fashioned like a moon ;
  Her breasts are tongues of pointed jet ;
Her belly of opal fairly hewn ;
  And round about her neck is set
The holy rosary, skull by skull,
Polished and grim and beautiful !

This jewelled shape of gold and bronze
  Is seated on my bosom's throne ;
She takes my muséd orisons
  To her, to her, to her alone.
Oh Kali, Kali, Kali, quell
This hooded hate, O Queen of Hell !

Her ruby-studded brow is calm ;
  Her eyes shine like some sleepy flood ;
Her breast is oliban and balm ;
  Her tongue lolls out, a-dripping blood ;
She swings my body to and fro ;
She breaks me on the wheel of woe !

To her eternal rapture seems
  Mere nature ; underneath the crown
Of dusky emeralds there streams
  A river of bliss to sluice me down
With blood and tears, to drown my thought,
To bring my being into nought.

The cruel teeth, the steady sneer,
  The marvellous lust of her, I bring
Unto my body bright and clear
  (Dropped poison in a water spring !)
To fill me with the utmost sense
Of some divine experience.

For who but she, the adulterous queen,
  Made earth and heaven with all its stars,
The storm, the hunger epicene,
  The raging at invisible bars,
The hideous cruelty of the whole ?—
These are of Kali, O my soul !

The sterile force of bronze and gold
  Bends to my passion, as it grips
With feverish claws the metal cold,
  And burns upon the brazen lips
That, parted like a poppy bud,
Have gemméd curves like moons of blood.

The mazes of her many arms
  Delude the eye; they seem to shift
As if they spelled mysterious charms
  Whereby some tall grey ship should drift
Out to a windless, tideless sea
Motionless from eternity.

This then I seek, O woman-form !
  O god embowelled in curves of bronze !
The shuddering of a sudden storm
  To mix me with thy minions
The lost, who wait through endless night,
And wait in vain, to see the light.

For I am utterly consumed
  In thee, in thee am broken up.
The life upon my lips that bloomed
  Is crushed into a deadly cup,
Whose devilish spirit squats and gloats
Upon the thirst that rots our throats.

Gape wide, O hideous mouth, and suck
  This heart's blood, drain it down, expunge
This sweltering life of mire and muck !
  Squeeze out my passions as a sponge,
Till nought is left of terrene wine
But somewhat deathless and divine !

Not by a faint and fairy tale
  We shadow forth the immortal way.
No symbols exquisitely pale
  Avail to lure the secrets grey
Of his endeavour who proceeds
By doing to abolish deeds.

Not by the pipings of a bird
  In skies of blue on fields of gold,
But by a fierce and loathly word
  The abomination must be told.
The holy work must twist its spell
From hemp of madness, grown in hell.

Only by energy and strife
  May man attain the eternal rest,
Dissolve the desperate lust of life
  By infinite agony and zest.
Thus, O my Kali, I divine
The golden secret of thy shrine !

Death from the universal force
  Means to the forceless universe
Birth.  I accept the furious course,
  Invoke the all-embracing curse.
Blessing and peace beyond may ie
When I annihilate the " I."

Therefore, O holy mother, gnash
  Thy teeth upon my willing flesh !
Thy chain of skulls wild music clash !
  Thy bosom bruise my own afresh !
Sri Maharani ![1] draw my breath
Into the hollow lungs of death !

There is no light, nor any motion.
  There is no mass, nor any sound.
Still, in the lampless heart of ocean,
  Fasten me down and hold me drowned
Within thy womb, within thy thought,
Where there is nought—where there is
  nought !


### THE JILT.

" WHO is that slinkard moping down the
  street,
  That youth—scarce thirty—bowed like
  sixty ? "  " Oh,
A woman jilted him."  " Absurd ! "  " Conceit !
  Some youths take life—are Puritans, you
  know ! "

I heard it, sitting in the window—glowed,
  Rushed to my wife and kissed her.   Lithe
  and young
The rapture of some ardent madness flowed ;
  And — bye-and-bye — its miracle found
  tongue.

    .   .   .   .   .

Guess, guess the secret why I burn for you
These years so cold to woman as I was !
Guess why your laugh, your kiss, your touch
  run through
  My body, as it were a tunéd glass !

[1] Holy Queen—one of the many thousand
titles of the Goddess.

You cannot guess ?—false devil that you are !
  To Cruelty's add calm's analysis !
You love me ?   Yes—then crown me a
  bearded Sar
  Bull-breasted by my sleek Semiramis ![1]

Did you not hear those men below ?   They
  spoke
Of one I think you have forgotten long ;
Talked of his ruined life—half as a joke—
  But I— But I—it is my whole heart's
  song !

I love you when I think of his pale lips
  Twitching, and all his curls of gold awry;
Your smile of poison as he sighs and sips ;
  Your half-scared laughter as his heart-
  beats die—

Let him creep on, a shattered, ruined thing !
  A ship dismasted on a dreadful sea !
And you—afar—some word of largesse fling
  Pitifully worded for more cruelty !

His death lends savour to our passionate
  life ;
  His is the heart I taste upon your tongue ;
His death-spasms our love-spasms, my wife ;
  His death-songs are the love-songs that
  you sung !

Ah ! Sweet, I love you as I see him stagger
  On with hell's worm a-nuzzling to his
  heart,
With your last letter, like a poisoned dagger,
  Biting his blood, burning his bones apart.

Ah ! Sweet, each kiss I drink from you is
  warm
  With the dear life-blood of a man—a man !
The scent of murder lures me, like a charm
  Tied by some subtlety Canidian.

Ay ! as you suck my life out into bliss,
  Its holier joy is in the deadlier thirst
That drank his life out into the abyss
  Of torture endless, endless and accurst.

[1] Queen of Assyria, famous for glory and
debauchery.  Sar is the royal title.

I know him little ; liking what I know.
  But you—you offer me his flesh and blood.
I taste it—never another vintage owe,
  Nor bid me sup upon another food !

This is our marriage; firmer than the root
  Of love or lust could plant our joy, my
    wife,
We stand in this, the purple-seeded fruit
  Of yon youth's fair and pitiable life.

.   .  .  .  .  .  .

Do I not fear that you may treat me so ?
  One day your passion slake itself some-
    how,
Seek vigour from another murder ? No !
  You harlot, for I mean to kill you—now.


## THE EYES OF PHARAOH.

DEAD Pharaoh's eyes from out the tomb
  Burned like twin planets ruby-red.
Enswathed, enthroned, the halls of gloom
  Echo the agony of the dead.

Silent and stark the Pharaoh sate :
  No breath went whispering, hushed or
    scared.
Only that red incarnate hate
  Through pylon after pylon flared.

As in the blood of murdered things
  The affrighted augur shaking skries
Earthquake and ruinous fate of kings,
  Famine and desperate destinies,

So in the eyes of Pharaoh shone
  The hate and loathing that compel
In death each damnèd minion
  Of Set,[1] the accursed lord of Hell.

Yea ! in those globes of fire there sate
  Some cruel knowledge closely curled
Like serpents in those halls of hate,
  Palaces of the Underworld.

[1] The ass-headed deity of the Egyptians,
slayer of Osiris.

But in the hell-glow of those eyes
  The ashen skull of Pharaoh shone
White as the moonrays that surprise
  The invoking Druse on Lebanon.

Moreover pylon shouldered round
  To pylon an unearthly tune,
Like phantom priests that strike and sound
  Sinister sistrons at the moon.

And death's insufferable perfume
  Beat the black air with golden fans
As Turkis rip a Nubian's womb
  With damascenéd yataghans.

Also the taste of dust long dead
  Of ancient queens corrupt and fair
Struck through the temple, subtly sped
  By demons dominant of the air.

Last, on the flesh there came a touch
  Like sucking mouths and stroking hands
That laid their foul alluring smutch
  Even to the blood's mad sarabands.

So did the neophyte that would gaze
  Into dead Pharaoh's awful eyes
Start from incalculable amaze
  To clutch the initiate's place and prize.

He bore the blistering thought aloft :
  It blazed in battle on his plume :
With sage and warrior enfeoffed,[1]
  He rushed alone through tower and tomb.

The myriad men, the cohorts armed,
  Are shred like husks : the ensanguine
    brand
Leaps like a flame, a flame encharmed
  To fire the pyramid heaven-spanned

Wherein dead Pharaoh sits and stares
  Swathed in the wrappings of the tomb,
With eyes whose horror flits and flares
  Like corpse-lights glimmering in the
    gloom,

[1] Accompanied by those sages and warriors
who owed him feudal service.

Till all's a blaze, one roar of flame,
  Death universal, locked and linked :—
Aha ! one names the awful Name—
  The twin red planets are extinct.


## BANZAI !

THERE leapt upon a breach and laughed
  A royally maniac man.
A bitter craft
Is mine, he saith,
  O soldiers of Japan !
I am the brothel-knave of death,
  The grimly courtesan.

Now who will up and kiss her lips,
  Or grip her breast and bone ?
The subtle life she shears and snips
  Is harder gained than gone ;
The lover's laughter whom she clips
  Is but a dying groan.

She lieth not on a gilded bed
  In the city without the city.[1]
One kiss is hers full rank and red—
Do you sip at her lip? Hell hangs on her
    fangs !
  She loves ; love laughs at pity !

Then who will up to taste her mouth?
  Who on her mount and ride?
Look to the North, the West, the South!
  There is carnage vulture-eyed.
Then who will suck the breath of death,
  The swift and glittering bride?
The bride that clings as a snare with springs
  To the warrior's stricken side?

A shudder struck the hidden men
  As the maniac's mouthings ceased.
Then, kindling, rose a roar :
  " Spread, spread the furtive feast !
The wine of agony pour !
The fruit of valour pluck !
The meat of murder suck !

[1] The prostitutes of Japan live in a city by themselves, whenever they are sufficiently numerous to make this practicable.

Sweet are the songs of her throat !
  Soft are the strokes of her fan !
She hath love by rhyme and rote,
  She is subtle and quick to man !
She danceth ? Say she doth float !
  Rapture is gold in her eyes !
She sigheth honey-sweet sighs
  Of the glory of Japan !
Red are her lips and large,
  The delicate courtesan ! "


Then the officer's voice
  Caught in his throat for joy.
Like birds in spring that rejoice,
  Clearly and softly the boy
Whispered : " Now, let us charge ! "
Then leaping sheer o'er trench and mound,
  They rise as a single man ;
They bound like antelopes over the ground
  For the glory of Japan.

With glittering steel they wheel—they reel ?
  They are steady again and straight !
The dull brute Christians red with the weal
  Of the knout—they will not wait !
The ringing cries of the victors peal
  In, in at the captured gate !

. . . . . . .

Then o'er the field the maniac passed
  And closed the dead men's eyes.
" They are sleeping close with death at last ! "
  The wanton warrior cries.
But he who saw the dead man's jaw
  Grind at the last was aware
That the harlot's kiss was Paradise
  That the soldier tasted there.
And beyond the magnificent joy of death
  Shears through the sky, as a flame
Ripping the air, the lightning breath
  Of the nation's resonant fame.
Hail ! to the Hachiman[1] deed well done !
  To the virile strength of a man !
To the stainless blaze of the Rising Sun
  The glory of Japan !

[1] Japanese God of War.

## LE JOUR DES MORTS.

At Paris upon Dead Man's Day
  I danced into the cemetery.
The air was cool ; the sun was gay ;
The scent of the revolving clay
  Made me most wondrous merry.

Earth, after an agonising bout,
  Had swallowed up a widow clean.
The issue hung for long in doubt :—
—Oh! anybody can make out
  The mystery I mean.

The dead were dancing with the worms ;
  The live were laughing with their lemans ;
The dead-alive were making terms
With God, and notaries, and germs,
  With house-agents and demons.

All Paris keeping sacrament
  Of musing or of melancholy,
Impatient of the next event,
To spend, to barter, to be spent ;—
  I chuckled at the folly.

" I would that I were dead and damned,"
  Thinks every wiser human.
"Corpses have room, and men are jammed ;
Those offer food, and these are crammed :—
  And cheaper, too, is woman ! "

I, being neither God nor ghost,
  A mere caprice of matter,
Hop idly in the hideous host,
Content to chaff the uttermost,
  To cackle and to chatter.

They bring their wreaths to deck the dead,
  As skipping-ropes the devils use them.
One through the immortelles perks his head.
[These sights to ghosties are as bread ;
  The luckless living lose them.]

Grotesque and grim the pageant struts ;
  We sit a-straddle on the crosses.
Our soulless missiles take for butts
The passers' hats, or in their guts
  Disturb their dinner's process.

Thus one man's work is one man's play ;
  The melancholy help the merry.
All tread the ordered stupid way
At Paris, upon Dead Man's Day,
  In Père Lachaise his cemetery.

## AVE MORS.

O virgin ! O my sister ! Hear me, death !
  The tainted kisses of the harlot life
Sicken me ; hers is foul and fevered breath,
  This noisome woman I have made my wife.
She lies asweat, aslime.  O hear me, thou !
  Wash with thy tears this desecrated brow !
With cool chaste kisses cleanse me !  Lay
    me out
    Wrapped in a spotless winding-sheet, and
    soothe
These nerves ill nuzzled by the black swine's
    snout
    With thine eternal anodyne of truth !

The foul beast grunts and snorts ; but hear
    me, death !
  Thy wings are wind-white as her hoofs are
    dunged.
Thy songs are faint and pale with honey
    breath,
  Honey and poppy ! as her mouth hot-
    tongued
Spews out its hideous lust.  O loathéd life !
  Thou nameless horror of the bestial strife
Of love and hate, I straitly charge thee quit
  This bed of nastiness, this putrid sea ;
For not by any amorous tricks of wit
  Shalt thou regain thine empire over me.

O virgin, O my sister ! Hear me, death !
  Thou hast a sleep compelling soul and
    mind.
Thine is the sweet insufferable breath
  That comes like Bessarabia's twilight wind
To bring a quiet coolth from day's long heat,
  Peace to the belly gorged with blood and
    meat,

Stars for the sun that smote, for fire slow
  streams,
For the simoom the zephyr's cooing kiss,
Deep sleep at last from all the evil dreams,
  And rest, the possibility of bliss.


### THE MORIBUND.[1]

#### I.

THE Seven Wise Men of Martaban [2]
Sate round the dying man.

They were so still, one would have said :
If he were dying, they were dead !

The first was agéd ; in his beard
He muttered never a weird.

The next was beautiful and gay :
He had no word to say.

The third was wroth and rusty red,
Yet not a word he said.

The fourth was open and bold :
His silence girt him like fine gold.

The fifth was ruddy and fair of face ;
He held his tongue a space.

The sixth was many-coloured, but
He kept his lips well shut.

The last was like a full great moon ;
He knew, but uttered not, his rune.

#### II.

Now when the time was fully come
The dying man was dumb,

But with his failing hand did make
A sign : my heart doth ache.

[1] A meaning may be found for this poem by
any really profound student of the Qabalah.
[2] Gulf of Martaban, South of Burma.

At that the kingly man, the fourth,
Rose up and spat against the North.

Then made the dying man a sign :
My head is running like strong wine.

The agéd man lifted his mouth
And spat against the South.

He clutched his throat in pang of death,
As if he cried for breath.

Whereat the second beat his breast
And frowned upon the West.

Then the man sighed, as if to say :
The glow of life is gone away.

At this the rusty and wroth released
His eyes against the East.

Then the man touched his navel, as
He felt his life thence pass.

Also he smote his spine ; the base
Of life burnt up apace.

Then rose the many-coloured sage ;
He was right sad with age.

With him arose the ruddy and fair ;
He was right debonair.

They twain to upper air and lower
Advanced the eyes of power.

Ay ! but above the dead man's head
A lotus-flower was spread.

Thence dripped the Amrita, whereby
Life learneth not to die.

The seventh in silence tended it
Against the horror of the pit.

#### III.

Thus in a cage of wisdom lay
The dead man, live as they.

They hold him sacred from the sun,
From death and dissolution.

Within the charméd space is nought
Possible unto thought.

There in their equilibrium
They float—how still, how numb !

There must they rest, there will they stay
Innocent of the judgment day.

Remote from cause, effect retires.
Act slays its dams and sires.

There is no hill, there is no pit.
They have no mark to hit.

It is enough.   Closed is the sphere.
There is no more to hear.

They perish not ; they do not thrive.
They are at rest, alive,

The Seven Wise Men of Martaban ;
And, moribund, the man.


## THE BEAUTY AND THE BHIKKHU :

### A TALE OF THE TENTH IMPURITY.

#### (*From the Pali.*)

#### I.

LISTEN !   The venerable monk pursued
His path with downcast eyes ; his thought
  revolved
Ever in closer coils serenely screwed
About the Tenth Impurity.   **Dissolved**
All vision of his being but of one
Thing only, his sun-whitened skeleton.

#### II.

A dainty lady sick of simple life,
  Chained to the cold couch of some vapid
  man,
Put on her jewels, off the word of wife,
  Resolved to play the painted courtesan,

So  ran  along  the  village  path.   Her
  laughter
  Wooed all the world to follow tumbling
  after.

#### III.

Then when she met the venerable monk
  Her shamelessness desired a leprous
  wreath
Of poisonous flowers, seducing him.   He
  shrunk
  Back from her smile, seeing her close
  white teeth.
Bones ! he exclaimed, and meditating that,
From a mere Bhikkhu grew an Arahat.

#### IV.

Her husband found her gone, in fury followed
  Lashing the pale path with his purple
  feet,
Heedless of stones and serpents.   Hail ! he
  holloaed
  To the new Rahan [1] whom he bowed to
  greet
Kissing the earth : O holy master, say
If a fair female hath passed by this way !

#### V.

The Bhikkhu blessed the irritated man.
  Then the slow sloka [2] serpentine began:
" Friend ! neither man nor woman owns
  This being's high perception, owed
Only to Truth ; nor beams nor stones
  Support the Arahat's abode.
Who grasps one truth, beholds one light,
  Becomes that truth, that light ; discedes
From dark and deliquescent night,
  From futile thoughts and fatuous deeds.
Your girl, your gems, your mournful tones
  Irk not perfection with their goad.
One thing I know—a set of bones
  **Is travelling** on upon this road ! "

[1] Arahat.                    [2] Stanza.

# IMMORTALITY

"From this tale, Callicles, which I have heard and believe, I draw the following inferences:—Death, if I am right, is in the first place the separation from one another of two things, soul and body ; nothing else. And after they are separated they retain their several natures, as in life ; the body keeps the same habit, and the results of treatment or accident are distinctly visible in it : for example, he who by nature or training or both was a tall man while he was alive, will remain as he was, after he is dead ; and the fat man will remain fat ; and so on ; and the dead man who in life had a fancy to have flowing hair, will have flowing hair. And if he was marked with the whip and had the prints of the scourge, or of wounds in him when he was alive, you might see the same in the dead body ; and if his limbs were broken or misshapen when he was alive, the same appearance would be visible in the dead. And in a word, whatever was the habit of the body during life would be distinguishable after death, either perfectly, or in a great measure and for a certain time. And I should imagine that this is equally true of the soul, Callicles ; when a man is stripped of the body, all the natural or acquired affections of the soul are laid open to view."—PLATO, *Gorgias*.

## IMMORTALITY.

### I.

I MOVED. Remote from fear and pain
The white worms revelled in my brain.
Who travelled live may travel dead ;
The soul's no tenant of the head.
They had hanged my body by the neck ;
Bang went the trap. A little speck
Shot idly upon consciousness
Unconscious of the head's distress
When with dropped jaw the body swung
So queer and limp ; the purple tongue
Shooting out swollen and awry.
Men cheered to see the poisoner die.
Not he ! He grinned one visible grin,
The last ; then, muffled in his sin,
He lived and moved unseen of those
Nude souls that masquerade in clothes,
Confuse the form and the sensation,
And have the illusion, incarnation.
I bore myself. Death was so dull.
The dead are strangely beautiful
To the new-comer ; it wears off.

### II.

They told me I was damned. The Shroff[1]
Gave me ten dollars Mex. (For ease
Of English souls the dead Chinese

[1] Money-changer   Mexican dollars were long the sole currency on the Chinese coast.

Are taxed) to pay my way in hell.
On one pound sterling one lives well.
For luxuries are cheaply paid
Since Satan introduced Free Trade ;
And necessaries—woe is me !—
Are furnished to the damned soul free.

### III.

God's hell, Earth's heaven, are not so far.
Dinner brought oysters, caviar,
Anchovies, truffles, curried rabbit
(Bad for the apoplectic habit),
While ancient brandy and champagne
Washed down the dainties. Once again
I seemed to haunt the Continental.[1]
A saucy little elemental
Flitted across ; I heard it sneer ;
"You won't get water, though, I fear."
That's hell all over. Good-bye, greens,
Water, cold mutton, bread, and beans !
They feed us well, like gentlemen,
On chilis, seasoned with cayenne.
Worse, one must finish every course.
'S truth, I had rather eat boiled horse !

### IV.

My first friend was an agéd monk.
He fed on rice and water. Sunk
His cheeks and cold his blood. You see
The fool was a damned soul like me ;

[1] Smart restaurant in London.

He had starved himself on earth in hope
In heaven to banquet with the Pope,
With God and Christ on either hand
And all the angels' choral band
Playing sweet music.  O the fool
To treat earth as a baby's school !
In hell one lives as one is wont.
*Punch* said to would-be bridegrooms:
    Don't !
Might I advise the same to those
Shapeless and senseless embryos
Who seek to live ?  Yes, God is wise
Enough to set a snare for lies
As well as truths.  The soul content
On earth in his own element
Will be content from flesh released.
But he who strives to be a beast
Or strives to be a god ; would gain
Long bliss for a few hours of pain,
Or struggles for no matter what,
Continues.  I would rather not.

### v.

That puzzle's grief I did not share
Because on earth I did not care.
I met a grave philosopher—
'Had sought most nobly not to err
Probing God's Nature.  See his lobes
Swell with hell's torment !  Still he probes
The same fool's problem.  I explain
The simple state of things in vain.
He chose to study God, and die in it.
He made his bed, and he must lie in it.

### vi.

After my dinner I debate
(Urged to the task by habit's Fate)
The project of a poisoning.
In hell one finds that everything
Is easy.  Poison to my hand ;
A cunning potion cool and bland
Fit to administer the draught :—
How like old times !  I nodded, laughed,
Poisoned my neighbour, a young girl
Sent here for marrying an earl.
Of course she did not die.  But then
On earth I never killed my men ;

They only die whom one forgets.
Remember that each action sets
Its mark still deeper in the mind !

### vii.

O piteous lot of humankind
Whose history repeats itself !
Dinner is cleared by gnome and elf;
I pay the bill, take Baal's receipt,
And stroll off smoking.  Soon I meet
The fairest foulest whore that burns.
High feeding pays : desire returns.
She willing (for a copper rin) [1]
For any ecstasy of sin
Gaily embraces me.  A room
Starts up in the half-light, half-gloom,
Perfectly purposed for debauch.
In mirrors shines a wicked nautch,
And on the floor Hawaian belles
Rave in a hula-hula [2]—Hell's !
Fragonard, Rops, had lined the walls
With wild indecent bacchanals,
And bawdy photographs attest
The Devil's taste to be the best.

### viii.

I did not sleep at all : but she :—
O face of deathless agony !
O torture of hell's worm, to wrest
From peace that miserable breast !
Me, me she strikes in mid-delight
Staggered and shattered at the sight,
The moment that she slept.  I laughed
Thereat : the bowl I idly quaffed
Was nectar : she amused me, so.
You see, my friend, I did not know.
I also slept at morn.  Then, then,
A low voice whispered in the den :
"Lucky young fellow !  Brave and clever !
This sort of thing goes on for ever."

### ix.

On earth I dreaded impotence,
Age, death.  You see, I had no sense.
Best be an old man ere you die ;
They wish insensibility,

[1] Japanese coin worth a small portion of a penny.
[2] The indecent dance of the South Seas.

So are their pains the duller. Hell
Is managed infinitely well
From the peculiar standpoint of
A god who says that he is Love.

### X.

That was the poet Crowley's point.
I think *his* nose is out of joint ;
He bet on justice being done ;
And here—it's really rather fun !—
The unlucky devil devil-spurred
Writes, climbs, does Yoga like a bird ;
Just as he was before he " died,"
The ass is never satisfied.
He has only been here forty days,
And has already writ six plays,
Made eight new passes, one new peak,
Is bound to do two more this week,
And as for meditation ! Hard he
Soars from Dhyana to Samadhi ;
Writes wildly sloka after sloka,
Storms the Arupa-Brahma-Loka,
Disdains the mundane need of Khana,[1]
Slogs off, like Buddha, to Nibbana :—
Poor devil !

### XI.

One thing makes me weep.
He was wise one way, and scorned sleep.
Wherefore he sleeps not, does not hear
That still small dreadful voice of fear.
Therefore he realises not
That this is his eternal lot.
Therefore he suffers not at all.

### XII.

Luckier is he than one, a small
Wild girl, whose one desire on earth
Was to—be blunt with it !—give birth
To children. Here she's fairly in it !
Pumps out her fourteen babes a minute ;
Her (under chloroform) the voice
Bids to be gleesome and rejoice :
" No sterile God balks *thine* endeavour.
This sort of thing goes on for ever."

[1] Dinner.

### XIII.

I was a humorous youth enough
On earth ; I laughed when things were
    rough.
Therefore, I take it, now in Hades
The funny side of things—and ladies—
Engages my attention. Well !
You know enough of life in Hell.
I was an altruist, my brothers !
My life one long kind thought for others :
For me six maidens wear the willow :—
Poisoning is a peccadillo.
Hence I'm disposed to give advice
Simple, if possibly not nice ;
Shun life ! an awkward task and deep.
But if you cannot, then—shun sleep !


(Suppose I thus had prophesied,
Gone to my wife to bed, and died !)


## EPILOGUE.

### THE KING-GHOST.

The King-Ghost is abroad. His spectre
    legions
    Sweep from their icy lakes and bleak
    ravines
Unto these weary and untrodden regions
    Where man lies penned among his Might-
    have-beens.
        Keep us in safety, Lord,
        What time the King-Ghost is abroad !


The King-Ghost from his grey malefic
    slumbers
    Awakes the malice of his bloodless brain.
He marshals the innumerable numbers
    Of shrieking shapes on the sepulchral
    plain.
        Keep us, for Jesu's sake,
        What time the King-Ghost is awake !

The King-Ghost wears a crown of hopes
forgotten;
  Dead loves are woven in his ghastly
  robe;
Bewildered wills and faiths grown old and
rotten
And deeds undared his sceptre, sword, and
globe.
    Keep us, O Mary maid,
    What time the King-Ghost goes
    arrayed!

The Hell-Wind whistles through his plume-
less pinions;
  Clanks all that melancholy host of bones;
Fate's principalities and Death's dominions
Echo the drear discord, the tuneless tones.
    Keep us, dear God, from ill,
    What time the Hell-Wind whistles
    shrill.

The King-Ghost hath no music but their
rattling;
  No scent but death's grown faint and
  fugitive;
No light but this their leprous pallor battling
Weakly with night.   Lord, shall these
dry bones live?
    O keep us in the hour
    Wherein the King-Ghost hath his
    power!

The King-Ghost girds me with his gibbering
creatures,
  My dreams of old that never saw the sun.
He shows me, in a mocking glass, their
features,
  The twin fiends " Might-have-been " and
  " Should-have-done."
    Keep us, by Jesu's ruth,
    What time the King-Ghost grins the
    truth!

The King-Ghost boasts eternal usurpature;
  For in this pool of tears his fingers fret
I had imagined, by enduring nature,
  The twin gods " Thus-will-I " and " May-
  be-yet."
    God, keep us most from ill,
    What time the King-Ghost grips the
    will!

Silver and rose and gold what flame resurges?
  What living light pours forth in emerald
  waves?
What inmost Music drowns the clamorous
dirges?
  —Shrieking they fly, the King-Ghost and
  his slaves.
    Lord, let Thy Ghost indwell,
    And keep us from the power of Hell!
                                    Amen.

Kneel down, dear maiden o' mine, and let your eyes
Get knowledge with a soft and glad surprise!
Who would have thought you would have had it in you?
Say nothing!   On the contrary, continue!

# RODIN IN RIME

## 1907

## AUTHOR'S NOTE

### AUGUSTE RODIN AND THE NOMENCLATURE OF HIS WORKS

#### A STUDY IN SPITE

WHEN illegitimate criticism is met with a smart swing on the point of the jaw, and has subsided into an unpleasant and unpitiful heap ; when its high-well-born brother has shaken hands—not without many years of friendly sparring—with the new pugilist, all his family are very disappointed, for Society takes no notice of them in its (to them unseemly) adulation of the rising star. Their unfraternal feeling may even lead them to employ a sandbagger and a dark night to rid them of this dreamer Joseph.

In the case of the success, in the heavy weights, of the Meudon Chicken (M. Rodin will forgive us for the lengths to which we carry our analogy), envy has given up hope even of sandbags, and is now engaged in the ridiculous task of attempting to disconcert the eye of the Fancy Boy by flipping paper pellets at him across the arena. They do not reach him, it is true : but as I, who happen to be sitting in a back row, admiring the clean, scientific sequences of rib-punchers, claret-tappers, &c., &c., recently received one of these missiles in the eye, my attention was called to the disturber. I will now do my part as a law-abiding citizen and take my boot to the offender, as a warning to him and all of his kidney. I shall not mention his name : that he would enjoy : that is perhaps what he hoped. I will merely state that he is one of those unwashen and oleaginous individuals who are a kind of Mérodack-Jauneau without the Mérodack, i.e., without the gleam of intention in their work which to the lay mind redeems even the most grotesque imbecility of technique, and the most fatuous ignorance of all subjects connected or unconnected with art. By philosophy he understands "Science and Health" : by poetry Lake Harris or Eric Mackay : he expects a painting to tell a pretty story or to upset a metaphysical position. His conversation is like that of Planchette : or if William Horton were vocal—— But Heaven forbid !

What he said, though parrot-talk, caught up in some fifth-rate sculptor's studio, no doubt, had so much truth in it, carefully concealed by the lying misinterpretation he had put on it, that, as I said, the pellet hit me. This was what it came to. Rodin's works, it is said, *mean* nothing. He makes a study : people see it in his studio : A. goes up and says to the Master : "Ah, how beautiful," &c., *ad nauseam*—"I suppose it is 'Earth and the Spring.'" B. follows, and suggests "Hercules and Cacus " ; C. thinks "The Birth of a Flower " ; D. calls it "Despair " ; E. varies it with "Moses breaking the Tables of the Law " ; F. cocks his eye warily, and asks if it is not meant for "Mary Magdalene " ; G. votes for "The Beetle-Crusher and his Muse," and so on, day after day, till Z. comes round and recognises it for Balzac. Rodin shakes him warmly by both hands : Balzac it is for all time—and one ceases to wonder that it was rejected !

Now, of course, this paper pellet is in any case very wide of its mark. Rodin can easily sculp himself a tabernacle and go in with Whistler—and even drag in Velasquez ; but here am I illustrating, however feebly, the Works, in Poetry : and poetry cannot, unfortunately, ever be pure technique. I have long wished to write "A Sonnet in W. and P." (with Whip as the keynote) ; a triolet in U. and K. ; an ode in S. Sh. Sw. Sp. and Str.—and so on ; but people would merely say "Nonsense Verses" (so they do now, some of them !). So that my work is liable to the most vital misinterpretation. My best friend tells the utterly false, utterly funny story about me that I wrote one sonnet for "L'Ange déchu " and another for "Icare."

The real heart of the attack is, of course, against Rodin's intention, and it is my object to show what rubbish it is, even granting the literary basis of criticism to be valid. I am given to understand that something of the sort described above does sometimes take place in the naming of a statue (of the allegorical description especially). But that is a question of felicity, of epigram ; never of subject.

In "La Main de Dieu," for example, the meaning is obvious, and not to be wrested or distorted. What does it matter if we call it as at present, or

(a) The Hand of Creation,
(b) The First Lovers,
(c) The Security of Love,
(d) The invisible Guard

—anything in reason ? These are only ways of looking at one idea, and as you are theologian, poet, lover or mystic, so you will choose. And it is the Master's merit, not his fault, if his conception is so broad-based as to admit of different interpretations. The phenomenon is possible because Rodin is the master and not the slave of his colossal technique. The naming of a masterpiece is perhaps harder work than the producing it, and Rodin being a sculptor and not an illicit epigram distiller, is perfectly justified in picking up what he can from the witty and gifted people who throng his studio as much as he will let them.

Let there be an end, then, not to the sordid and snarling jealousy which greatness must inevitably excite, not to the simian tooth-grindings which must always accompany the entrance of a man into the jungle, but to this peculiarly senseless and sidelong attack. One accepts the lion as a worthy antagonist ; one can enjoy playing with a fine dog ; one can sympathise with sincere and honourable labour, though it be in vain ;

one ignores laughingly the attack of tiny and infuriated puppies ; but there are insects so loathsome, so incredibly disgusting, worms whose sight is such an abomination, whose stink is so crapulous and purulent, that, ignoring their malignity, but simply aware of their detestable presence, the heel is ground down in one generous impulse, and the slimy thing is no more. Decomposition, already far advanced, may be trusted speedily to resolve the remains into the ultimate dust of things, mere matter for some new and hopefuller avatar.

Such a worm are you, M. D——, who once, as above described, voided your noxious nastiness in my presence, trusting to conciliate me by the intended compliment that my poems on Rodin were from myself and not from him, and that any other statues would have done as well.

I am as little susceptible to flattery as I am to the venomous dicta of spite and envy, and I resent that when I see it employed as the medium for this. Without your compliment, M. D——, I might have left you to crawl on, lord of your own muck-heap ; with it, I take this opportunity of stamping on you.

NOTE.—I had intended [1] to include reproductions of photographs of those few statues which I have written upon ; but I prefer to pay my readers the compliment of supposing that they possess the originals in either bronze or marble.

---

[1] *I.e.*, in the large first edition, which contains seven of M. Rodin's water-colours. *Vide* Bibliographical Note.

## RODIN IN RIME

### FRONTISPIECE
#### RODIN.

HERE is a man ! For all the world to see
    His work stands, shaming Nature.
    Clutched, combined
In the sole still centre of a master-mind,
The Egyptian force, the Greek simplicity,
The Celtic subtlety. Through suffering free,
    The calm great courage of new art, refined
    In nervous majesty, indwells behind
The beauty of each radiant harmony.

Titan ! the little centuries drop back,
    Back from the contemplation. Stand and span
With one great grip his cup, the Zodiac !
Distil from all time's art his wine, the truth !
Drink, drink the mighty health—an age's youth---
Salut, Auguste Rodin ! Here is a man.

# VARIOUS MEASURES

## THE TOWER OF TOIL.

### (LA TOUR DE TRAVAIL.)

THE old sun rolls; the old earth spins;
Incessant labour bends the stars.
Hath not enough of woes and sins
    Passed? Who shall efface their senseless
    scars?
One makes, one mars. The æons foil
All purpose; rise, O Tower of Toil.

Rise in thy radiance to proclaim
    The agony of the earth alive!
Stand by the sea, a marble flame,
    A lighthouse wedded to an hive!
Still upward strive! O tower, arise
An endless spiral to the skies!

Stand on the weather-beaten coast
    A flaming angel in the noon;
A silver, fascinated ghost
    In midnight's revel with the moon;
In silent swoon be still! the spoil
Of years is thine, O Tower of Toil.

Let day, a glowing vigour, male;
    And night, a virgin bowed and curled,
Stand at the foot; their ardours pale
    Systole and diastole of the world!
With life impearled (their eyes absorb)
They visibly sustain the orb.

Then let the tower in seven tiers
    Rise in its splendour marmorean,
Unite the chill divided years
    In plain perception of the æon.
Cry clear the pæan! Its tunes recoil
About thy flanks, O Tower of Toil.

Below be miners fashioned fair,
    And all that labour in the sea
Sepulchred from the ambient air,
    A fatal weird of dole to dree.
No time to be, no light to live.
Earth's need to these hath hope to give.

Above be various shapes of labour,
    The bodily strength, the manual skill;
They shape the anvil and the sabre,
    The ploughshare and the bolt; they
    fill
The myriad will of brains that boil:
Their fame be thine, O Tower of Toil!

Here set the travailers of land;
    Here the young shepherd, fluteless now;
The mariner with tarry hand;
    The clerk, with pale and foolish brow,
His brain bought cheap for brainless grind:
The bloodless martyr of the mind!

Grow up the grades, O godlike hand,
    Rodin, most rightly named "August"!
Thy splendid sons and daughters stand
    Obedient to the master "must."
The decadent dust thy spells assoil;
Death lives in this, thy Tower of Toil.

Grow up the grades! record the tasks
    These arduous phantoms have achieved!
The growth of mind to mortals asks
    A power not swift to be believed.
What bosoms heaved ere Nature's age
From monkey-man deduced the sage!

So be thy spiral tower the type
    Of higher convolutions drawn
From hunger's woe and murder's gripe
    And lust's revulsion to the dawn
Of days that spawn on holier soil
Thy loftier sons, O Tower of Toil.

There is a flower of native light
    That springs eternal on the earth.
Carve us, O master-hand, aright
    That ecstasy of pain and mirth,
A baby's birth! That prize of fear
Engrave upon the loftiest tier!

Nor in the solitary woe
   (The silent, the unwitting strain)
Forget the miracles that grow
   In the austerely ordered brain!
Darwin and Taine, Descartes and Boyle,
Inscribe thou on the Tower of Toil!

Those who have striven to limn the mind,
   Paint, model, tune, or hymn the light,
Their vision of the world refined
   By mastery of superior sight:
Honour their might! the gain have these
Of all men's woes and ecstasies!

High soul; no benediction seek
   From any spirit but our own!
Crown not the mighty with the weak!
   The Tower be a Tower, and not a Throne!
In man-carved stone the endless coil
Arise untopped, the Tower of Toil!

Deem not that prayer or sacrifice
   Will ever cause the work to end!
Serene, sufficient, let it rise
   Alone; it doth not ask a friend,
Nor shall it bend a fatuous knee
To a fantastic deity.

What crest or chrism were so good
   To work as Art, the crown upon
Work's brow?   Thy will with love endued
   Lift up this loftier Parthenon!
Thine art the consecrative oil
To hallow us the Tower of Toil!


## LA BELLE HEAULMIERE.

AGE and despair, poverty and distress
   Bend down the head that once was blithe
      and fair.
Embattled toward the ancient armouress
   Age and despair!

Where is the force of youth?   The beauty
      where?
   What two-edged memory of some lost
      caress
Lurks in the sorrowful pose and lingers
      there?

O melancholy mother!   Sorceress,
   No more enchantress!   What the harvest
      rare
Sprung from the seed of youth and happiness?
   Age and despair.


## FEMME ACCROUPIE

SWIFT and subtle and thin are the arrows of
      Art:
I strike through the gold of the skin to the
      gold of the heart.
As you sit there mighty in bronze I adore the
      twist
Of the miracle ankle gripped by the miracle
      wrist.
I adore the agony-lipped and the tilted head,
And I pay black orisons to the breasts
      aspread
In multiple mutable motion, whose soul is
      hid.
And the toils of confused emotion the Master
      bid
Lurk in the turn of the torso for poets to see
Is hid from the lesser and dull—hidden from
      me.
She squats, and is void and null; I know her
      not;
As God is above, but more so, she sits, to
      blot
Intelligence out of my brain, conceit from
      my ken;
And I class myself, idle and vain, with the
      newspaper men.


## CARYATIDE

SHALL beauty avail thee, Caryatid, crouched,
      crushed by the weight of a world of woe?
By birthright the burden is thine: on thy
      shoulders the sorrow hath slid
From the hand of the Healer: behold, in
      the steady, continuous throe,
   Shall beauty avail thee, Caryatid?

Thou wast proud of thy beauty : the burden
   of beauty was hid
  From thy eyes: how is't now with thee,
    now ? By the sweat dropping slow
From the brows of thy anguish, we see what
   the weight of it did
  To the patient despair of the brain. Shall
    no God strike a blow ?
Shall no hero be found the unbearable
   burden to rid ?
  And if these be extinct—'tis a fiend that
    laughs eager and low :
  " Shall beauty avail thee, Caryatid ? "

## JEUNE MERE

SURELY the secret whisper of sweet life
Shakes in the shell-ear murmurous memories
Of the old wonder of young ecstasies
In the first hours when the white word of
   wife
She won so hardly out of dark wild strife
And mystery of peace ; thine utter ease,
Abandoned rapture ! Caught and cut by
   seas
Of sudden wisdom, stinging as a knife
Swift struck sets all the blood a-tingle. Woe !
What wakes within ? What holiest intima-
   tion
Of intimate knowledge of the lords of nature ?
She sees her fate smile out on her, doth
   know
Her weird of womanhood, her noble station
Among the stars and ages ; and her stature
Soars o'er the system ; so the scarred mis-
   feature
Of death avails her for the isolation
Of high things ever holy ; this the throe
Of swiftly-comprehended motherhood
Once taught her. Now the whisper of the
   child
Bids her be great, who was supremely good.
For, mark you ! babes are ware of wiser
   things,
And hold more arcane matters in their mild
Cabochon eyes than men are ware of yet.

Therefore have poets, lest they should forget,
Likened the little sages unto kings.
But look ! the baby whispers—hush ! Nay !
   nay !
We shall disturb them loving—come away !

## L'AMOUR QUI PASSE.

LOVE comes to flit, a spark of steel
Struck on the flint of youth and wit ;
Ay, little maid, for woe or weal,
Love comes to flit.

Hermes one whisper thrills. Admit !
Kupris one smile aims—do you feel ?
Eros one arrow—has he hit ?

Why do you sit there immobile ?
A spark extinct is not relit.
Beyond resource, above appeal,
Love comes to flit.

## TETE DE FEMME (MUSEE DU LUXEMBOURG).

IT shall be said, when all is done,
  The last line written, the last mountain
Climbed, the last look upon the sun
  Taken, the last star in the fountain
Shattered, that you and I were one.

What shall they say, who come apace
  After us, heedless, gallant ? Seeing
Our statues, hearing of our race
  Heroic tales, half-doubted, being
So far beyond a rime to trace.

What shall they say ? For secret we
  Have held our love, and holy. Splendour
Of light, and music of the sea
  And eyes and heart serene and tender,
With kisses mingled utterly.

These were our ways. And who shall know ?
  What warrior bard our nuptial glories
Shall sing ? Historic shall we go
  Down through our country's golden stories ?
Shall lovers whisper " Even so

As he loved her do I love you "?
  So much they shall know, surely; never
The truth, how lofty and fresh as dew
  Our love began, abode for ever:
They cannot know us through and through.

We have exceeded all the past.
  The future shall not build another.
This is the climax, first and last.
  We stand upon the summit.   Mother
Of ages, daughter of ages, cast

The fatal die, and turn to death!
  Let evolution turn, involving
As when the gray sun sickeneth—
  Ghostly September! so dissolving
Into the pale eternal breath.

When all is done, shall this be said.
  When all is said, shall this be done,
The æon exhaust and finishéd,
  And slumber steal upon the sun,
My dear, when you and I are dead.

## LA CASQUE D'OR.

### A NINA OLIVIER.

You laughing little light of wickedness, low
  ripples round you love and coils
And twists the Casque of Gold about the
  child-face with a child-caress.
O glory of the tangled net! O subtle vase
  of scented oils!
You laughing little light of wickedness!

Through all the misty wind of light that
  glamours round you, sorceress,
Your face shines out with feline grace, exults,
  a tiger in the toils!
They shall not hold your passion in: fling,
  fling your lips, my murderess,

On mine that I may pass away, a vapour
  that your passion boils,
A rose whose petals flutter down as cruel
  lips and fingers press.
Hear one last careless laugh acclaim my
  corpse the latest of your spoils,
You laughing little light of wickedness.

## LES BOURGEOIS DE CALAIS

PERFECTLY sad and perfectly resolved,
  They are ready, ready to be hanged.
    They go
(Forlorn ones!) against Calais' overthrow;
And all their fate in Calais' is involved
Unto the utmost.   Who will save his folk
  From vengeful ire of the tyrant?   Six are
    these,
  Perfectly sad, and steady, and at ease.
Self-slain, they shall save others from the
    yoke.
  Seven then are these found faithful unto
    death;
  From Calais six; and one from Nazareth.

## REVEIL D'ADONIS.[1]

ADONIS, awake, it is day; it is spring!
It is dawn on the lea, it is light on the lake!
The fawn's in the bush and the bird's on
    the wing!
  Adonis, awake!

Adonis, awake!   We are colour and song
And form, we are Muses most tender to take
Thy life up to Art that was lost over long.
  Adonis, awake!

Adonis, awake! thou hast risen above
The fear in the forest, the brute in the brake.
Thou art sacred to shrines that are higher
    than Love!
  Adonis, awake!

[1] Properly the sequel to Mort d'Adonis on
p. 122.

## LA MAIN DE DIEU

THE Hand.  From mystery that is cloud
  control
The mystery that is emptiness of air,
Purpose and power.  What blossom do
  they bear?
Stability and strength inform—what soul?

*Turn to me, love ! the banks of air are soft.*
  *Turn to me, love ! the skies are blue,*
*Fleeced with the clouds that hang aloft,*
  *Buds that may blossom into dew.*

*Turn to me, love ! lie close and breathe*
  *The smooth waves of the wind !*
*The zephyr in thy locks I'll wreathe,*
  *The breeze entwined.*

*We are so safe ; so happy we :*
  *Our love can never falter ; fate can never*
    *close*
*Hard on the flower of land and sea.*
*Lift, O rose petals of my rose,*
*Toward me, rest, dream on, we are here, we*
    *love.*
*There is no shadow above,*
  *No ghost below : we are here.  Kiss ! Kiss !*
  *For ever.  Who would have believed, have*
    *thought of this ?*

Outside is nothing.  Let what will uproll,
  Within all's certain.  Are we not aware
(Who see the hand) What brain must know
  —and care?
What wisdom formed the racers, find a
  goal?

Careless and confident, let us love on.
Life, one or many, rises from a seed,
  Sprouts, blooms, bears fruit, and then is
    gone—is gone.
Let go the future, ominous and vast !
Loose the bound mind from the unavailing
    past !
  Live, love for ever, now, in every deed !

## DESESPOIR.

INTO the inmost agony of things
  She sees, through glamour of untrusty
    sense,
  The full corruption of omnipotence,
The infinite rage of fishes to have wings,
  The lust of beasts for tentacles ; caught
    thence
Corollary, syllogism, she strides tense
Into the inmost agony of things.

So, fearless, amid gods and evil kings,
  She sits, poor wretch, eternal scientist,
  Straining mild muscles, leaving to its list
The spasm-shaken body.  So she flings
  The teeth-set fate of Fortune's face un
    kissed
Against the fiat : sets her clenchéd fist
In his face : slides spinning with her body's
    twist
Into the inmost agony of things.

## EPERVIER ET COLOMBE.

WHEN, at the awful Judgment-day, God
    stands
Shrunken and shaking at my gaze, before
My hollow seat of agony, it may be
He shall discover me the great excuse
For an ill world ill shapen by ill hands,
For unit joy and misery ten score,
For all his work's complaint ; I think that
    He,
Twitching his fearful fingers, may let loose
This answer : Thus a kiss I brought to being
Which by no other way were possible.
Measure, O man !  Balance with eyes true-
    seeing
If I were right or no to have made Hell !

Then would He stand forgiven — nay !
    acquitted !
I, as I look on this tight coil of bliss,

Swift clasp of Rodin's magical mind love-
    witted,
See all creation fade; abide, one kiss.
Then to my own soul's bow this shaft be
    fitted ;
Thank God for all, seeing that all is this !

## RESURRECTION.

FROM youth and love to sorrow is one stride.
So to the thinker; to the lover's self
Rather it glides or swoons ; the idle elf
That plucks a rose, scatters its petals wide,
Is like the wind, is like the moon-wrought
    tide,
Is most like life : so soft to man, so hard
To the all-gathering brain of a great bard !

Christ answered: Peace to man amid the
    strife !
I am the Resurrection and the Life.
Let the graves open : see the woman grip
Her goodly love, her gainful fellowship !
See the man, hungry, grasp the willing
    bride,
Grope through the dark dawn to her glow-
    ing side !
There is the resurrection trump: confess
The mystery of life is happiness !

Rodin discerned. We see the eagle-eyed
Glory of echoing kisses ; hear the sound
Of glutted raptures break in the profound,
The abyss of time : upsurge the dead. Why
    hide
Thy sorrowful god's brow, O sculptor, mage,
Child of eternity, father of an age ?
Thou hast seen, thou hast showed, that as it
    was on earth
So shall it be in resurrection birth.
The cycle of weariness and passionate pain
Is and was ever and must be again.
There is no death ! Ah ! that is misery !
For this, Lord Christ, is it that thou wouldst
    be,
Thou yesterday, to-day, and thou to-morrow ?
The mystery of this our life is sorrow.

## L'ETERNEL PRINTEMPS.

### I.

THE eternal spring is in the heart of youth.
They are nearest to the secret of the world,
These lovers with their lithe white bodies
    curled
Into the rhythm of a dance ; the truth
Is theirs that feel, not ours that idly see ;
Theirs that inhabit, and not ours that flee
The intimate touch of love and think to
    sleuth
By intellect all the scent of being, whirled
In the wheel of time—roll back, slow years,
    and be
A monument, a memory for me ;
That I may in their passion have a part,
And feel their glory glow within my heart !

### II.

This holy rapture is the eternal spring.
Here in the love that tunes the untrammelled
    feet,
Here in the ardour of the arms that cling,
The alluring amber-touch of sweet to sweet,
The ageless awe of the new love revealed,
The reverence of the new love hovering
    nigh ;
These things are mazes flowery on the field,
Measures to trace a-dancing by-and-by.
Here in the statued pose the rhythm is sealed
That all who are human dance to evermore.
Before this ecstasy all ages yield :
Eternity breaks foamless on time's shore.
And I, because of this delight in me,
Am one in substance with eternity.

## ACROBATES

MY little lady light o' limb
    Twirls on her lover's twisting toes
    Lithe as a lynx, red as a rose,
She spins aloft and laughs at him.
So gay the pose, so quaint the whim,
    One stares and stares : it grows and grows.

So swift the air she seems to skim
  One's senses dazzle ; wonder glows
    Warm in one's veins like love—who
      knows ?
One follows till one's eyes are dim
My little lady light o' limb.


## L'AGE D'AIRAIN.

FRESH in the savage vigour of the time,
The golden youth stands in the golden
  prime,
Erect, acute, astrain.   We look and long
For those bronze lips to blossom into song.
He is silent.   We reflect.   Ourselves grown
  old
Yearn somewhat toward that sensuous glow
  of gold.

All this is folly.   Rodin made him so,
Evoked the strength, the goodliness, the
  glow.
The form is little : in the mind there dwells
Force to avail the childish heart that swells
With aught that is.   The golden prime is
  past—
Aye ! but a nobler gain is ours at last
Who see man weary, but within our span
The perfect promise of the overman.


## FAUNESSE.

THE veil o' th' mist of the quiet wood is
  lifted to the seer's gaze ;
He burns athwart the murky maze beyond
  into beatitude.

A solemn rapture holds the faun : an holy
  joy sucks up the seer
Within its rose-revolving sphere, the orient
  oval of the dawn.

Light's graven old cartouche is sealed upon
  the forest : groves are gray
With filtered glamours of the day, the steely
  ray flung off his shield.

She kneels, yon spirit of the earth ; she
  kneels and looks toward the east.
In her gray eyes awakes the beast from
  slumber into druid mirth.

She is amazed, she eager, she, exotic orchid
  of the glade !
She waits the ripe, exultant blade, life
  tempered by eternity.

And I who witness am possessed by awe
  grown crimson with desire,
Its iron image wrapped in fire and branded
  idly on my breast.

Her face is bronze, her skin is green, as
  woods and suns would have it so.
Her secret wonders grow and glow, limned
  in the luminous patine.

Worship, the sculptor's, clean forgot in
  worship of her body lithe,
And time forgotten with his scythe, and
  thought, the Witenagemot.

Confused in rapture : peace is culled a flower
  from the arboreal root,
The vision dulled, the singer mute, shattered
  the lute, the song annulled.

## SONNETS AND QUATORZAINS

### MADAME RODIN.

HEROIC helpmeet of the silent home !
Shall who sings Art not worship womanhood ?
There is depth of calm beneath the sea's fine
    foam ;
Behind the great there is ever found the good.
Honour and glory to the sacred house
And ark of the covenant of holy trust,
The unseen mother and the secret spouse
Ever availing in the sorrow and dust
That aye avenge the artist's victory won,
That cover up his monuments of fame,
That twist his sight, once steadfast on the
    sun,
To the fear folded in the robes of shame :—
Lest he, to all the world plain victor, find
Himself mere failure to his own white mind.

### LE PENSEUR.

BLIND agony of thought ! Who turns his
    pen
    Or brush or lyre to Art, shall see in this
The symbol of his battle against men
    For men, the picture of the torturing bliss
Of his necessity : sits clutched and closed
    Into himself the adept of wizard thought.
Gripped in his own embrace he sits : keen-
    nosed
    The invisible bloodhounds ache upon the
        slot !
Soon, soon they are on him : soon the fangs
    of hate,
    The sharp teeth of the infinite are in him !
Shall love, or fame, or gold, those pangs
    abate ?
    What siren with smooth voice and breast
        shall win him ?
Never a one, be sure !   In serene awe
The thinker formulates eternal law.

### LA PENSÉE.

EXQUISITE fairy, flower from stone begotten
    Sprung into sudden shape of maidenhood,
Hast thou thy father's anguish all forgotten ?
    Hast thou a balm, who hast hardly under-
        stood ?
Is not thy beauty for his comfort moulded,
    Thy joy and purity his won reward ?
Sweet blush of blood, pale blossom lightly
    folded,
    To thee did he carve his way by right of
        sword ?
Thou who art all delight to all of us,
    Hast thou no special intimate caress
For him whose bloody sweat stood murderous
    On the writhen brow, the bosom of dis-
        tress ?
Ay ! for his anguish thou art gain enough—
One thought, worth all Earth's fame, and
    gold, and love !

### LE BAISER.

INFINITE delicacy in great strength
    Holds the white girl and draws her into
        love.
All her lithe subtlety, her lovely length,
    Is sealed in the embrace about, above
Her visible life.   What mastery of repose,
    Compulsion of motion lurks for us therein
As we gaze back on Greece, as Nature glows,
    Simple and sacred, with no thought of sin,
Yet born to trouble us, to fascinate.
    Here we are, back i' th' springtime of the
        earth ;
God above man ; and above God, dire fate.
    Ancient cosmogony of peace and mirth !
Careless, we careless, do invoke thy rime
Of the ancient rapture of the olden time.

## BOUCHES D'ENFER.

LOOK how it leaps towards the leaper's
    curl
Of vivid ecstasy, life loosed at last
From the long-held leash! The headlong,
    hot-mouthed girl
Upon her sister like a star is cast,
Pallid with death-in-life achieved. O force
Of murder animal in the dead embrace !
The implacable ardour, unavenged remorse
For time's insulting loss, quickens the pace
Unto its prey that gathers, like a storm
Shrouding invisibly the crater's rim
Whence fury yet shall wake, and fire in-
    form
The inane basalt and coruscations dim
Of smouldering infamy. Bow down in awe !
It is enough. The Gods are at feast. With-
    draw !

## LA GUERRE

SHE sits and screams above the folk of peace,
Deafening their quiet ears with hideous
    clamour.
Abhorred and careless she bids order cease.
Her hate resolves the shriek into a stammer
Of inarticulate rage. The wounded man
Twisted in agony beneath her squirms
To hear her raucous blasphemies outspan
The grip of God at this his last of terms.
Yea ! he must die with horror in his ears,
Hate in his heart. The mischief must
    endure.
He hath expiated naught by death. His
    tears,
His thoughts, these strike nor stay her not,
    be sure !
She is Madness, and a fury ; though were
    gone
All life to war, she would scream on—scream
    on.

## W. E. HENLEY.[1]

CLOISTRAL seclusion of the galleried pines
Is mine to-day : these groves are fit for Pan—
O rich with Bacchic frenzy and his wine's
Atonement for the infinite woe of man !
Is there no God of Vital Art to dwell
Serene, enshrined, incensed, adored of us ?
Were not a cemetery His citadel ?
His treasure-house some barred sarcophagus ?
And here his mighty and reverend high-priest
Bade me good cheer, an eager acolyte,
Poured the high wine, unveiled the mystic
    feast ;—
Swooped the plumed anguish of inveterate
    night ;
Devouring torture of insight shot. Night
    hovered ;
Dawn smote. I bowed—O God declared,
    discovered !

## SYRINX AND PAN.

SYRINX is caught upon the Arcadian field.
    The god's grip huddles her girl breasts :
        his grim
And gnarléd lips grin forth the soul of him.
The imprint of his bestial heart is sealed
And stamped armorial on her virgin shield,
    Fame's argent heraldry despoiled. Grows
        dim
For her the universe : supple and slim
She slides in vain. She loathes him—and
    doth yield.

Shame, sorrow, these be sire and dam of
    song.
    Fatality, O Nature, is thy name.
    Along the acccurséd river, stagnant shame,
Eddying woe, from rape and godly wrong,
    Springs the immortal reed : the mortal's cry
    Rises, an angry anthem, to the sky.

[1] Written on a visit to the late W. E. Henley
at Woking some three weeks before his death.
The influence of the man has perhaps over-
shadowed that of the bust of him by Rodin.

## ICARE.[1]

ICARUS cries : " My love is robed in light
And splendour of the summits of the sun.
Wing, O my soul, thy plumed caparison
Through ninety million miles of space beyond
      sight !
Utmost imagination's eagle-flight
Out-soar ! " But he, by his own force un-
      done,
His peacock pinions molten one by one,
Falls to black earth through the impassive
      night.

Lo ! from uprushing earth arises love
Ardent and secret, scented with the night,
Amorous, ready. Sing the awakening bliss
That catches him, from the inane above
Hurled—nay, drawn down ! What utter-
      most delight
Dawns in that death ! Icarus and Gaia kiss.

## LA FORTUNE.

" HAIL, Tyche ! From the Amalthean horn
Pour forth the store of love ! I lowly bend
Before thee : I invoke thee at the end
When other gods are fallen and put to scorn.
Thy foot is to my lips ; my sighs unborn
Rise, touch and curl about thy heart ; they
      spend
Pitiful love. Lovelier pity, descend
And bring me luck who am lonely and for-
lorn."

Fortune sits idle on her throne. The scent
Of honeyed incense wreathes her lips with
      pleasure.
For pure delight of luxury she turns,
Smooth in her goddess rapture. So she
      spurns
And crushes the pale suppliant. Softly bent,
Her body laughs in ecstasy of leisure.

[1] Called " Fille d'Icare " by the distinguished anatomists, priceless idiots, and pragmatical precisians, who see nothing but a block of marble in this most spiritual of Rodin's masterpieces.

## PAOLO ET FRANCESCA

PAOLO ignites, Francesca is consumed.
Loosened she lies, and breathes great gasps
      of love ;
He, like an hunter, hungers, leaps above,
Attains, exults, despairs. This love is
      doomed,
Were there no hell. In granite walls en-
      tombed
Lies the true spirit and the soul thereof.
The body is here—yet is it not enough,
These litanies unchanted, unperfumed ?

Live in the shuddering marble they remain :
Here is the infinite credo of pure pain.
Here let life's agony take hold enough
Of all that lives : let partial tears for them
Wake knowledge, brain-dissolving diadem
Of white-hot woe upon the brows of love !

## LES DEUX GENIES.

GOOD bends and breathes into the rosy
      shell
Of peace and perfume, love in idleness,
Of pure cold raptures, hymns the mystic
      stress,
Imagining's reiterate miracle.

Evil breathes, bending, the reverberate spell
Conjuring ghosts of the insane address
Of agony lurid in the damned caress,
Exulting tortures of the heart of hell.

The maiden sits and listens, smiles. Her
      breath
Is easy ; over her bowed head fall deep
Glowing cascades of hair ; she combs her
      hair

With subtle ecstasy, electric sweep
Of unimaginable joy ; let life and death
Pass ; she will comb, and comb, and will
      not care.

## LA CRUCHE CASSEE.

THE waterpot is broken at the well.
Forth rush the waters, bubbling from the
   brim,
Curling and coiling round the riven rim,
Lost beyond hope; and she, her sighs up-
   swell,
And sorrow shakes her: shame's oblivious
   hell
Burns round her body: in her eyes there
   swim
Tears of deep joy, deep anguish; love's first
   hymn
Is choral in her ear's young miracle.

She knows the utmost now; what waters
   white
She held from heaven's crystal fountains;
   flight
Of what celestial birds struck down :—Ah me!
What god or demigod hath struck remorse
Into that close-crouched, cold, and desolate
   corse,
Wailing her violate virginity?

## LA TENTATION DE SAINT-ANTOINE.

IN mystic dolour wrapt, the ascetic turns
His vague untutored thought to love, and sees
Himself exalted at the amber knees
Of God the Father : his bowed forehead burns
With chastity's white star: no spirit yearns
More keenly from the abyss; yet, God ! are
   these
Subtle star-sparks of spirit chastity's?
These deep-set shiverings saint nor sage
   discerns?

Laughter and love are over him, entice
His life to sweeter scent of sacrifice.
She knows God's will, not he ! Her ardour
   licks
Flowers from the dust. O fool ! that, heavy
   of breath,
Dost rot in worship at the shrine of death !
O mystic rapture of the crucifix !

## EVE.

THE serpent glimmered through the primal
   tree,
Full in the gladness of the afterglow ;
Its royal head warred ever to and fro,
Seeking the knowledge of the doom to be.
Eve, in the naked love and liberty
She had not bartered yet, moved sad and
   slow,
Serene toward the sunset, murmuring low
The tyrant's curse, the hideous decree.

Then she, instructed by the Saviour Snake,
Saw once clear Truth and gave her life, and
   love,
And peace, and favour of the fiend above,
For Knowledge, Knowledge pure for Know-
   ledge' sake.
The full moon rose. Creation's voice was
   dumb
For the first woman's shame, strength,
   martyrdom.

## FEMMES DAMNEES.

KISS me, O sister, kiss me down to death !
The purple of the passionate hour is flaked
With notes of gold : there swim desires un-
   slaked,
Impossible raptures of expostulate breath.
The marble heaves with longing ; hungereth
The mouth half-open for the unawaked
Mouth of the baby blossom, where there
   ached
Never till now the parched sweet song that
   saith :

"Ah ! through the grace of languor and the
   glow
Of form steals sunset flaming on the snow !
Darkness shall follow as love wakeneth
In moonlight, and the flower, chaste love,
   now bloom
First in the bosom, after in the tomb—
Kiss me, O sister, kiss me down to death !"

## NABUCHADNOSOR.

SENSELESS the eyes: the brow bereft of sense.
Hunger is on the throne of pride; and naught
Fills the gray battlefield of ancient thought,
The market places of intelligence,
Save need and greed; whose royal words
    incense
The jealous God of Israel is distraught.
No jewels in the casket nobly wrought.
The shrine is grand; the god is ravished
    thence.

On clawing hands and hardened knees the
    King
Exists, no more; is it a little thing?
King Demos, hear my parable! We pass,
We poets, see you grovel at our feet,
Despise our love, and tender flesh, and
    wheat,
Clamour for lust, and carrion, and grass.

## MORT D'ADONIS.

ADONIS dies. (Imagination hears
The hoarse harsh breathing of the ill-nurtured
    boar)
Venus bends low, half mother and half
    whore,
Whole murderess of boy's budhood. Fall,
    black fears!

Ay! through her widowed, her unwedded
    tears,
The foolish filial appeal, "Restore,
O Father Zeus, this tender life once more!"
Falls the baulked hope of half a million years.

She in her gloom and ignorance will go
Forlorn to Paphos, wrapt in urgent woe,
Her hair funereal swathing her fallen form,
Its wind-swept horror holding him; his white
Torn body blushing through tempestuous
    night.
So breaks the life in hell, the year in storm.

## BALZAC.

GIANT, with iron secrecies ennighted,
Cloaked, Balzac stands and sees. Immense
    disdain,
Egyptian silence, mastery of pain,
Gargantuan laughter, shake or still the
    ignited
Stature of the Master, vivid. Far, affrighted,
The stunned air shudders on the skin. In
    vain
The Master of "La Comédie Humaine"
Shadows the deep-set eyes, genius-lighted.

Epithalamia, birth-songs, epitaphs,
Are written in the mystery of his lips.
Sad wisdom, scornful shame, grand agony
In the coffin-folds of the cloak, scarred
    mountains, lie,
And pity hides i' th' heart. Grim knowledge
    grips
The essential manhood. Balzac stands, and
    laughs.

## LE CYCLOPS SURPREND ACIS ET GALATHEE.

COILED in the hollow of the rock they kiss,
Rolled in one sphere of rapture; looks
    intense
With love, and laughter shapen of innocence!
They cling, and close, and overhang the
    abyss.

But over them! What monster, then, is this
Crouched for his spring, gross muscles nude
    and tense,
Bulged eyeballs ready for the rape, immense
In hate, the imminent spectre? He it is,

The Cyclops. Ay! thought Zeus, and what
    of that?
Were it not well for love, in red rough maw
Swift crunched, to expiate my eldest law?

Better, far better thus. True love lies flat,
A weary plain beyond the single peak.
I then will pity them. I will not speak.

## OCTAVE MIRBEAU.

BRUTAL refinement of deep-seated vice
Carves the coarse features in a sentient
    mould.
The gardens,[1] that were soft with flowers
    and gold
And sickening with murder of lust to entice
The insane to filthier raptures, carrion spice
Of ordure for perfume, bloom there, fixed bold
By the calm of the Master, god-like to behold
The horror with firm chisel and glance of ice.

Ay! and the petty and the sordid soul,
A servile whore's deformed debauchery,[2]
Grins from the image.   Let posterity
From Rodin's art guess Mirbeau's heart, extol
The lethal chamber men ere then will find
For the pimp's pen and the corrupted mind.

  [1] Le jardin des supplices, par Octave
Mirbeau.
  [2] Les mémoires d'une femme de chambre,
par Octave Mirbeau.

## SOCRATE.

### (L'HOMME AU NEZ CASSE.)

CONSUMMATE beauty built of ugliness,
O broken-nose philosopher, is thine.
Diamonds are deepest in the blue-mud mine ;
So is the secret of thy strong success
Dæmonic-glittering through the wear and
    stress
Of tortured feature ; virtue's soul doth shine,
Genius and wisdom in the force divine
That fills thy face ; magnificence ! no less.

Ay! thou shalt drink the hemlock; thou
    shalt suffer
And die for self-respect, for love of others!
To-day are men indissolubly brothers?
Is my life smoother than the Greek's or
    rougher ?
The Greek at least shall stead me in my craft.
Crucify Crowley !   Nay, my friends! the
    draught.

## COLOPHON.

### INCIDENT.

#### (RUE DE L'UNIVERSITE, 182.)

SPELL-BOUND we sat : the vivid violin
Wailed, pleaded, waited, triumphed.   Kingly note
By note imperial from its passionate throat
Vibrates : the shadows fall like pauses in
The workshop of the Master : where there spin
Phrases in marble : fancies fall or float,
Passions exult, despairs abound, loves dote,
Thoughts gallop or abide : and prayer is sin.

Spell-bound we sat : one, young, eagerly moves.
One sits in thought : one listens, dreams, and loves.
One, critical, approves with conscious nod.
But I abode without the spell ; saw these—
Diverse harmonics of identical keys !—
And these were thus : but Rodin heard like God.

# ORPHEUS

## A LYRICAL LEGEND

[The allusions in this poem to classical legend or myth are too numerous to be dealt with by annotation. A good classical dictionary will enable the reader to trace all the allusions.]

## CONTENTS.

## BOOK II.

## BOOK III

Trio: Minos, Eacus, Rhadamanthus—"*Brethren, what need of wonder.*"
Orpheus continues his voyage—"*Ah me! I find ye but ill counsellors.*"
Invokes Hades—"*Now is the gold gone of the year, and gone.*"
Invokes Persephone—"*In Asia, on the Nysian plains, she played.*"
Persephone awakes—"*Ah me! I feel a stirring in my blood.*"
Orpheus pleads with her—"*And therefore, O most beautiful and mild.*"
Persephone invokes Hades -"*Ah me! no fruit for guerdon.*"
Orpheus invokes the Furies—"*In vain, O thou veiled.*"
Septet: The Furies, Orpheus, Hades, Persephone, Echidna—"*Ha! who
      invokes? What horror rages.*"
Orpheus invokes Hermes—"*O Light in Light! O flashing wings of fire!*"
Orpheus' song of triumph—"*The magical task and the labour is ended.*"
Continues to recount his journey—"*So singing I make reverence and retire.*"
Sings his triumph—"*O light of Apollo.*"
Sings, but with misgiving—"*Alas! that ever the dark place.*"

## BOOK IV

Company of Mænads—"*Evoe! Evoe Ho! Iacche! Iacche!*"
    Song—"*Hail, O Dionysus! Hail.*"
    "*Evoe Ho! Give me to drink.*"
    Hymn to Dionysus—"*Hail, child of Semelé.*"
    "*He is here! He is here!*"
Dionysus—"*I bring ye wine from above.*"
Mænads—"*O sweet soul of the waters! Chase me not.*"
Orpheus his spell—"*Unity uttermost showed.*"
    His allocution—"*Worship with due rite, orderly attire.*"
    His hymn to Pan—"*In the spring, in the loud lost places.*"
    His alarm—"*What have I said? What have I done?*"
Lament for Orpheus—Quartet: a Spirit, the River Hebrus, Calliope,
    the Lesbian Shore—"*What is? what chorus swells.*"
Sappho's song—"*Woe is me! the brow of a brazen morning.*"
Duet: Calliope, the Lesbian Shore—"*Silence. I hear a voice.*"
Finale. Nuith—"*Enough. It is ended, the story.*"

---

## WARNING.

MAY I who know so bitterly the tedium of this truly dreadful poem be permitted to warn all but the strongest and most desperate natures from the task of reading or of attempting to read it? I have spent more than three years in fits of alternate enthusiasm for, and disgust of, it. My best friends have turned weeping away when I introduced its name into conversation; my most obsequious sycophants (including myself) were revolted when I approached the subject, even from afar.

I began Book I. in San Francisco one accursed day of May 1901. I was then a Qabalist, deeply involved in ceremonial magic, with a Pantheon of Egypto-Christian colour, in fact, the mere bouillon of which my "Tannhauser" was the froth. The idea was to do the "biggest thing ever done in lyrics." I bound myself by an oath to admit no rhyme unless three times repeated; to average some high percentage of double rhymes—in brief, to perform a gigantic juggle with the unhappy English language. The whole of this first book is technically an ode (! ! !) and was so designed. So colossal an example of human fatuity truly deserves, and shall have, a complete exposure.[1]

Book I. was finished in Hawaii, ere June expired, and Book II. begun.
I had just begun to study the Theosophic writings—their influence, though slight, is apparent. So intent was I on producing a

[1] *Vide* the Contents. Can the Spirit of Perversity attribute the unwieldiness of the structure to its formal symmetry and perfection?

*big* book that the whole of my " Argonauts " was written for the shadow-play by which Orpheus wins Eurydice to an interest in mortal joys and sorrows. Also—believe it!—I had proposed a similar play in Book III., to be called " Heracles " or " Theseus," by performance of which Persephone should be moved, or Hades overwhelmed.

But luckily I was myself overwhelmed first, and it never got a chance at Hades. Book II., then, and its Siamese twin, were written in Hawaii, Japan, China, Ceylon, and South India, where also I began Book III. That also I finished in the Burmese jungle and at Lamma Sayadaw Kyoung at Akyab.

During this period I was studying the Buddhist law ; and its influence on the philosophy of the poem is as apparent as that of Hinduism on Book II.

The summer of 1902 asked another kind of philosophy—the kind that goes with glacier travel in the Mustagh Tagh. Orpheus slept.

Book IV. was begun in Cairo on my way to England, and bears marks of confirmed Buddhism up to the death of Orpheus.

But the more I saw of Buddhism the less I liked it, and the first part of Book IV. is flatly contradicted by its climax.

This is a pitiable sort of confession for a man to make !

What was I to do ? I could not rewrite the whole in order to give it a philosophic unity. Gerald Kelly forcibly prevented me from throwing it into the river at Marlotte, though he admitted quite frankly that he could not read even through Book I. and did not see how any one could. Tell me, he said, conjuring the friendship of years, can *you* read it ? Even a poet should be honest ; I confessed that I could not !

Taking it in sections, with relays and an ambulance, we could see no fault in it, however. It is clumsily built ; it is all feet and face ; but you cannot make a Monster symmetrical by lopping at him.

Still, we cut down every possible excrescence, doctored up the remains so as to look as much like a book as possible (until it is examined), and are about to let it loose on society.

The remaining books all share this fatal lack of Architecture; but they are not so long ; there is some incident, though not much ; and they are proportionately less dull. Further, the scheme is no longer so ambitious, and the failure is therefore less glaring.

I might have done like Burton and his Kasidah, and kept the MS. for twenty years (if I live so long), ever revising it. But (*a*) I should certainly not live twenty years if I had the accursed manuscript in all sorts and sizes of type and colour of ink and pencil to stalk my footsteps, and (*b*) I am literally not the man who wrote it, and, despise him as I may, I have no right to interfere with his work.

But I will not be haunted by the ghost of a Banquo that another man has failed to lay ; and this kind of ghost knows but one exorcism.

One should bury him decently in fine fat type, and erect nice boards over him, and collect the criticisms of an enlightened press, and inscribe them on the tomb.

Then he is buried beyond resurrection ; oblivion takes him, and he will never haunt the author or anybody else again.

Old Man of the Sea, these three years you have drummed your black misshapen heels upon me ; I have had no ease because of you ; I am bepissed and conskited of your beastliness ; and now you are drunk with the idea that you are finished and perfect, I shall roll you off and beat your brains out upon that hardest of flints, the head of the British Public. I am shut of thee. Allah forget thee in the day when he remembereth his friends !

*August* 14, 1904.

## EXORDIUM.

FROM darkness of fugitive thought,
  From problems bewildering the brain,
Deep lights beyond heaven unsought,
  Dead faces seen dimly in rain ;
    From the depths of Mind's caverns, the fire
    Reclaims the old magical lyre ;
The ways of creation are nought,
If only, O mother, O Muse, I may measure
  Thy melodies in me again !

How wayward, how feeble the child
  Three watched from the stars at his birth;
Erato the fierce and the mild ;
  Polymnia grave ; and the girth
    Broad-girdled of gold and desire,
  Melpomene's terrible lyre,
That lifts up her life in the wild,
The star-piercing pæan, and floats in mid-
  ether, and sinks to the earth.

These three of the Muses were mine ;
  They nurtured and knew me and kissed.
Erato was hidden in wine ;
  Polymnia dawned in the mist:
    Melpomene shone in the pyre
    Of terrors that burned in her lyre ;
But all of their passion divine
I lost in the life and the stress of the world
  ere ever the soul of me wist.

But, Orpheus, thy splendider light
  Was the veil of thyself the more splendid.
Thou leapedst as a fountain in flight,
  As a bird in the rainbow descended !
    From the sweet single womb risen
      higher
    Did Calliope string thee her lyre,
Thy mother : and veiled her in night :—
For thyself to Herself art a veil till the veils
  of the Heaven be rended and ended.

Now, single myself as thy soul,
  I pray to Apollo indeed !
Fling forth to the starriest goal
  My spirit, invoking his rede ; [1]
    Care nought for his mercy or ire ;
    Reach impious hands to his lyre.
Determined to die or control
Those strings the immortal at last, though
  the strings of this heart of me bleed.

Come life, or come death ; come disdain
  Or honour from mutable men,
I cry in this passionate pain—
  My blood be poured out in the pen !
    Euterpe ! Espouse me ! inspire
    My life looking up to Thy lyre !
Of thy love, thine alone, am I fain !
Be with me, possess me, reveal me the
  melodies never yet given to men.

The starry and heavenly wheels,
  The earth and her glorious dye,
The light that the darkness reveals,
  The river, the sea, and the sky ;

[1] Counsel.

All nature, or joyful or dire,
  Life, death, let them throng to the lyre,
All sealed with the marvellous seals !
Let them live in my sob, let them love in my
  song, let them even be I !

Let me in most various song
  Be seasons, be rivers that roll,
Be stars, the untameable throng,
  All parts of the ultimate whole;
    All nature in various attire
    Be woven to one tune of the lyre,
One tune where a million belong—
Multitudinous murmur and moan, melodious,
  one soul with my soul !

One soul with the wail of distress
  The ravished Persephone flung ;
One soul with the song of success,
  Demeter's, that found her and sung ;
    One soul with all spirits drawn nigher
    From invisible worlds to the lyre ;—
They throng me and silently press
The strings as I need them, and quicken
  my fingers and loosen my tongue !

And thou, O supreme, O Apollo !
  I have lived in Thy lands for a year,
Under skies, where the azure was hollow,
  The vault of black midnight was clear.
    Think ! I who have borne Thee, nor
      tire—
  May I not lift up on Thy lyre
Most reverent fingers, and follow
Thy path, take Thy reins, drive Thy chariot
  and horses of song without fear ?

Let the lightning be harnessed before me,
  The thunder be chained to my car,
The sea roll asunder that bore me,
  The sky peal my clarion of war !
    As a warrior's my chariot shall gyre !
    As a lord I will sharpen the lyre !
The stars and the moon shall adore me,
Not seeing mean me, but Thyself in the
  glory, the splendidest star.

Around me the planets shall thunder,
  And earth lift her voice to the sea ;
The moon shall be smitten with wonder,
  The starlight look love unto me.
    Comets, meteors, storms shall admire,
    Be mingled in tune to my lyre,
The universe broken in sunder,—
And I—shall I burn, pass away ? Having
  been for a moment the shadow of Thee !

# LIBER PRIMUS VEL CARMINUM

TO

## OSCAR ECKENSTEIN,

WITH WHOM I HAVE WANDERED IN SO MANY SOLITUDES OF
NATURE, AND THEREBY LEARNT THE WORDS AND
SPELLS THAT BIND HER CHILDREN

Τάχα δ' ἐν ταῖς πολυδένδροισιν Ὀλύμπου
Θαλάμαις, ἔνθα ποτ' Ὀρφεὺς κιθαρίζων
ξύναγεν δένδρεα μούσαις, ξύναγεν Θῆρας ἀγρώτας.
                                        —Βακχαι.

Orpheus with his lute made trees,
And the mountain tops that freeze
    Bow themselves when he did sing.
To his music plants and flowers
Ever sprung, as sun and showers
    There had made a lasting spring.

Everything that heard him play,
Even the billows of the sea,
    Hung their heads, and then lay by.
In sweet music is such art,
Killing care and grief of heart—
    Fall asleep, or hearing die.
                    —*Henry VIII.*

. . . vocalem temere insecutæ
    Orphea sylvæ,
Arte materna rapidos morantem
Fluminum lapsus, celeresque ventos,
Blandum et auritas fidibus canoris
    Ducere quercus.
                —*Hor. Carm.*, Lib. I. xii.

## INTRODUCTORY ODE.

CALLIOPE, ORPHEUS.

*Str. a.*

CALLIOPE.

IN the days of the spring of my being,
    When maidenly bent I above
The head of the poet, and, seeing
    Not love, was the lyre of his love;
When laurels I bore to the harper,
    When bays for the lyrist I bore,
My life was diviner and sharper,
    My name in the Muses was more;

When virgin I came to him stainless,
When love was a pleasure and painless!
    What Destiny dreams and discovers
    The fragrance men know for a lover's?
Peace turned into laughter and tears,
Borne down the cold stream of the years!

*Ant. a.*

ORPHEUS.

O mother, O queen many-minded,
    More beauty than beauty may be,
More light than the Sun; I am blinded,
    Sink, tremble, am lost in the sea.

The voice of thy singing descended,
  Rolled round me and wrapped me in mist,
Some sense of thy being, borne splendid ;
  I dreamed, I desired, I was kissed.
Some breath from thy music hath bound me ;
Some tune from thy lyre hath found me.
  Thy words are as rushing of fire ;
  But I know not the lilt of thy lyre :—
Thy voice is as deep as the sea ;
Thy music is darkness to me.

### Str. β.

#### CALLIOPE.

Child of Thracian sire, on me begotten,
  Knowest thou not the laughter and the life ?
Knowest thou not how all things are for-
      gotten,
  Being with a maiden wife ?
How a subtle sense of inmost being
  Wraps thee in, and cuts the world away ;
Sight and sound lose hearing and lose seeing,
  All the night is one with all the day ?
Hearken to her sighing !
Life droops down as dying,
  Melting in the clasp of amorous limbs and
      hair ;
All the darkening world
Round about ye furled—
  Dost thou know, or, knowing, dost thou
      care ?

### Ant. β.

#### ORPHEUS.

Mother, I have lain, half dead, half slumber-
      ing,
  Curtained in Eurydice her hair ;
Clothed in serpent kisses, souls outnumbering
  Dewdrops flung in spray through air.
I have lain and watched the night diminish,
  Fade and fall into the arms of day,
Caring not if earth itself should finish,
  Caring only if my lover stay ;
Listening to her breathing,
Laughing, lover-weaving
  All the silken gold and glory of her head,

Kissing as if time
Forgot its steeps to climb,
  Made eternity's, one with all the dead.

### Str. γ.

#### CALLIOPE.

Listen, then listen, O Thracian !
  Oeager lay on the lea :
I, from my heavenly station ;
I, from my house of creation,
  Stooped, as a mortal to be
Passionate, mother and bride ;
Flashed on wide wing to his side,
  Caught him and drew him to me.
Kisses not mortal I lavished ;
Out of the life of him ravished
  Life for the making of thee.
Son, did I lose in the deed ?
Son, did the breasts of me bleed,
  Bleed for pure love ?  Did I see
Zeus with his face through the thunder
Frowning with fury and wonder ?
  Love in Olympus is free—
I have created a god, not a mortal of mortal
  degree.

### Ant. γ.

#### ORPHEUS.

Hear me, O mother, descended
  To earth, from the sisterly shrine !
Hear me, a mortal unfriended,
Save thou, in thy purity splendid
  Indwell me, invoke the divine !
As sunlight enkindles the ocean,
As moonlight shakes earth with emotion,
  As starlight shoots trembling in wine,
So be thy soul for a man !
Teach my young fingers to span
  That musical lyre of thine !
Passion and music and peace,
Teach me the singing of these !
  Teach me the tune of the vine !
Teach me the stars to resemble,
As tide-stricken sea-cliffs to tremble
  Thy strings, as the wind-shaken pine !
Let these and their fruits and the soul of
  their being be mine, very mine !

## EPODE

### CALLIOPE

As the tides invisible of ocean,
  Sweeping under the dark star-gemmed sea ;
As the frail Caduceus' serpent-motion
  Moves the deep waves of eternity ;
As the star-space lingers and moves on ;
As the comet flashes and is gone ;
As the light, the music, and the thunder
  Of moving worlds retire ;
As the hoarse sounds of the heaven wonder
  When Zeus flings forth his fire ;
As the clang of swords in battle ;
As the low of home-driven cattle ;
As the wail of mothers children-losing ;
  As the clamorous cries of darkening death ;
As the joy-gasp of love's chosen choosing ;
  As the babe's first voluntary breath ;
As the storm and tempest fallen at even ;
As the crack and hissing of the levin ;
As the soft sough of tree-boughs wind-shaken ;
  As the fearful cry of souls in hell,
When past death and blinder life they waken,
  Seeing Styx before their vision swell,
When the bands of earth are broken
As the spirit's spell is spoken
On the vast and barren places
  Where the unburied wander still ;
As the laughter of young faces ;
  As the Word that is the will ;
As the life of wells and fountains,
Of the old deep-seated mountains ;
As the forest's desolate sighing ;
  As the moaning of the earth
Where her seeds are black and dying ;
  As the earthquake's sudden birth ;
As the vast volcano rending
Its own breasts ; as music blending
With young maiden's loving laughter,
  With the joy of fatherhood,
With the cry of Mænads after
  Sacrifice by well or wood ;
As the grave religious throng
Moving silently along,
Leading heifers, snowy-footed,
  Into glades and sacred groves,

Where the altar-stone is suited
  To commemorate the Loves ;
As the choir's most seemly chanting ;
As the women's whispers haunting
Silent woods, or chaster spaces,
  Where the river's water wends ;
As the sound, when the white faces
  Burn from space, and all earth end.
In the presence of the Gods ;
These and all their periods ;
These, and all that of them is,
I bestow on thee, and this
Also, mine eternal kiss !
In one melody of bliss
These and thou and I will mingle,
Till all Nature's pulses tingle,
Hear and follow and obey thee,
  Thee, the lyrist ; thee, the lyre !
These shall hear and not gainsay thee,
  Follow in the extreme desire,
Mingling, tingling, mixed with thee
Even to all Eternity.
These, and all that of them is,
Take from Calliope in this
Single-hearted, many mouthèd, kiss.


## ORPHEUS, SEATED UPON OLYM-
## PUS, TUNES HIS LYRE.

### ORPHEUS.

FIRST word of my song,
  First tune of my lyre,
Muse, loved of me long,
  Be near and inspire !
Bright heart !  Mother strong !
  Sweet sense of desire !
Be near as I lift the first notes impassioned
  of fervour and fire !

Not ever before
  Since Nature began
Hath one cloven her core,
  Found the soul of her span ;
No son that she bore
  Her spirit might scan ;
But I, being born beyond Nature, have known
  her and yet am a man.

Ye fieriest flowers,
    Life-stream of the world,
In passionate bowers
    Of mystery curled,
Come forth ! for the powers
    Of my crying are hurled :—
Come forth ! O ye souls of the fire, where
the sound of my singing is whirled !

    Ye blossoms of lightning,
      Bare boughs of the tree
    Of life, where the brightening
      Abysses of sea
    Reveal ye, the whitening
      Swords kindled of me.
Come forth ! I invoke thee, O lightning, the
flames of the Gods flung free !

### THE LIGHTNING.

The wand of Hermes, the caduceus
    wonder-working,
    Sweeps in mid-æther—
Where we are lurking
    It finds us and gathers.
By our mother the amber
    In her glorious chamber ;
    By the flames that enwreathe her ;
    By the tombs of our fathers ;
Awake ! let us fly, the compeller is nigh.
    Strike ! let us die !

### ORPHEUS.

Ye powers volcanic,
    Cyclopean forces,
Workers Titanic,
    I know your courses.
By fury and panic,
    By Dis and his horses,
Come forth ! I invoke ye, volcanoes, arise
from your cavernous sources !

### THE VOLCANOES.

The Hephæstian hammer on the anvil
    of hell,
    In the hollows accurst,
Falls for the knell
    Of the children of earth.

By the strength of our fires,
The fierce force of our sires,
    Let us roar, let us burst !
By the wrath of our birth,
Up ! and boil over in rivers of lava !
    Uncover ! Uncover !

### ORPHEUS.

Lift up thine amber
    Lithe limber limbs,
Lissome that clamber
    Like god-reaching hymns ;
The flame in its chamber
    Of glory that swims,
The spirit and shape of the fire, mine eyes
with fine dew that bedims !

Exempt from the bond
    All others that binds,
As a flowery frond
    The spark of thee blinds,
Within and beyond
    As a thought of the mind's
In all, and about, and above ! I invoke thee,
my word as the wind's.

### THE FIRE.

I, raging and lowering,
I, flying and cowering,
    I, weaving and woven,
Budding and flowering,
Spiring and showering,
    Cleaving and cloven !
My being encloses
Fountains of roses,
    Lilies, and light !
I wrap and I sunder !
I am lightning and thunder !
The world-souls wonder
    At me and my might !

All-piercing, all-winding,
All-moving, all-blinding,
    All shaken in my hissing ;
My life's light finding
All spirits, and binding
    Their love with my kissing ;

Ruthless, fearless,
Imperial, peerless,
  Creep I or climb.
Nought withstands me,
Bursts me or brands me ;
Nor Heaven commands me,
  Nor Space, nor Time.


Above, the supernal !
Below, the infernal !
  Of all am I master.
On Earth, the diurnal !
In all things eternal !
  Life, love, or disaster !
Abiding unshaken,
I sleep and I waken
  On wonderful wings ;
In depth and in height,
In darkness and light,
In weakness and might,
In blindness and sight,
In mercy and spite,
In day and in night,
Averse or aright,
For dule or delight,
  I am master of things.


ORPHEUS.

O mother, I fear me !
  The might of the lyre !
They tremble to hear me,
  The powers of the fire.
Come near me to cheer me !
  Be near and inspire !
Be strength in my heart and good courage,
  and speed in the single desire !


The fire knows its master !
  They flicker and flare,
Dread dogs of disaster,
  Wild slaves of despair.
Faster and faster—
  My soul is aware
Of a sound that is dimmer and duller, wide
  wings adrift of the air.

Their forces that wander
  No God-voice know they !
Their bridals they squander !
  Unknown is their way !
The sky's heart ? beyond her
  Sweet bosom they stray.
Shall these then obey me and hear ?   Shall
  the tameless ones hear and obey ?


From secretest places
  Whence darkness is drawn,
Where terrible faces
  Enkindle the dawn,
From wordless wide spaces,
  The ultimate lawn,
Come forth ! I invoke thee, O wind, come
  forth to me fleet as a fawn.


THE WINDS.

From fourfold quarters,
  The depth and the height,
We come, the bright daughters
  Of day shed on night ;
The sun and the waters
  Have brought us to light ;
The sound of him slaughters
  Our soul in his sight.
We hear the loud murmur ; we know him ;
  we rest ;
  We breathe in his breast.


ORPHEUS.

By sunlight up-gathered
  As dust of his cars,
By moonlight unfathered,
  Unmothered of stars,
Unpastured, untethered,
  Unstricken of scars,
Come forth ! I invoke ye, O clouds ! ye
  veils ! ye divine avatars !


THE CLOUDS.

Sun's spirit is calling !
  We gather together,
White wreaths, as appalling
  Pale ghosts of dead weather,

The veil of us falling
 On snow-height and heather,
Or hovering and scrawling
 Strange signs in the æther.
We hear the still voice, and we know him
 we come !
 We are sightless and dumb.

ORPHEUS.

More frail than your friends,
 The clouds borne above,
The light of thee blends
 With the moon and her love.
Thy spirit descends
 As a white-throated dove.
Come forth ! I invoke thee, O mist, and
make me a sharer thereof !

THE MIST.

From valleys of violet
 My shadow hath kissed,
From low-lying islet,
 A vision of mist,
The voice of my pilot
 Steals soft to insist.
O azure of sky, let
 Me pass to the tryst !
I hear the low voice of my love ; and I rest
 A maid on his breast.

ORPHEUS.

Thou child of soft wind
 And the luminous air,
Thou, stealing behind
 As a ghost, as a rare
Soft dew, as a blind
 Fierce lion from his lair,
Come forth ! I invoke thee, O rain, look
forth with thy countenance fair !

THE RAIN.

From highland far drifted,
 From river-fed lawn,
From clouds thunder-rifted,
 I leap as a fawn.

The voice is uplifted,
 The lord of my dawn ;
My spirit is shifted,
 My love is withdrawn.
I hear the sweet feet of my God ; I know
 him ; I fall
 In tears at his call.

ORPHEUS.

Cold lips and chaste eyes
 Of frost-fall that leap,
That shake from the skies
 On the earth in her sleep
Kiss nuptial, arise
 As the lyre-strings sweep !
Come forth ! I invoke thee, O frost, the
valleys await thee and weep.

THE FROST.

So silent and wise
 In her cerement clothes,
So secretly lies
 My soul in my snows ;
I awake, I arise,
 For my spirit now knows
The first time in her eyes
 That a voice may unclose
My petals : I hear it ; I come ; I clasp the
warm ground
 In my passion profound.

ORPHEUS.

In valleys heaped high,
 In drifts lying low,
Swift slopes to the sky,
 Come forth to me, snow !
Thy beauty and I
 Are of old even so
As lover and lover.  Come forth ! I invoke
thee ! the hills are aglow.

THE SNOW.

Bright breasts I uncover,
 Heart's heart to thy gaze ;
O lyre of my lover,
 I know thee, thy praise.

Black heavens that hover,
  Blind air that obeys,
I come to thee over
  The mountainous ways
As a bride to the bridegroom : I blush, but
  I come
    And bow to thee dumb.

ORPHEUS.

O blacker than hell,
  O bluer than heaven,
O green as the dell
  Lit of sunlight at even !
O strong as a spell !
  O bright as the levin !
Come forth ! I invoke thee, O ice, by their
  anguish, the rocks thou hast riven !

THE ICE.

My steep-lying masses,
  Mine innermost sheen,
My soundless crevasses,
  My rivers unseen,
My glow that surpasses
  In azure and green
The rocks and the grasses.
  Above, I am queen.
These know thee ; I know thee, O master,
  I hear and obey.
    I follow thy lyrical sway.

ORPHEUS.

O tenderest child
  And phantom of day !
Gleam fitful and wild
  On the flowery way !
Blue skies reconciled
  To the kisses of clay !
Come forth ! I invoke thee, O dew ! The
  maiden must hear and obey.

THE DEW.

Life trembling on leaves,
  Sunrise shed in tears,
Love's arrow that cleaves
  The veil of the years,

Light gathered in sheaves
  Of tenderest fears
As dayspring enweaves
  My soul into spheres—
I hear, and I nestle upon thee, O lyrist
  supreme,
    Light loves in a dream.

ORPHEUS.

Child of sweet rain,
  O fathered of frost !
Bitterest pain
  The birth of thee cost.
Passion is slain
  When wished of thee most.
Come forth ! I invoke thee, O hail, thou lord
  of a terrible host !

THE HAIL.

My father was glad of me
  In places unseen ;
My mother was sad of me,
  Where wind came between ;
Winter is mad of me,
  Earth is my queen ;
Meadows are clad of me,
  Nestled in green.
As pearls in the cloudland I slept ; but I hear
  the loud call ;
    I obey it and fall !

ORPHEUS.

Rain's guerdon and daughter
  By sunlight's spies
Divided in water,
  O light-stream, arise !
Seven petals that slaughter
  The menace of Dis,
Come forth ! I invoke thee, O rainbow ! thou
  maid of the myriad eyes !

THE RAINBOW.

In multiple measure
  The flowers of us fold
The scarlet and azure
  And olive and gold,

Hyperion his treasure
  Of light that is rolled
In music and pleasure
  Unheard and untold.
We are kisses of light and of tears, love's
  triumph on fear.
     We obey : I am here !

### ORPHEUS.

Dim lights shed around me
  In many a form
Like lovers surround me :—
  O tender and warm !
They hunt me, they hound me ;
  They struggle and swarm—
Come forth ! I invoke ye united, the mani-
fold shape of the storm !

### THE TEMPEST.

Wide-winged, many-throated,
  Colossal, sublime,
I come and am coated
  With feathers of Time.
I hear the deep note, head
  My pinions to climb,
The roar of devoted
  Large limbs of the mime
That mocks the loud lords of Olympus ; we
  mingle ; I wake.
  I come with the sound of a snake.

### ORPHEUS.

O storm many-winded,
  O life of the air,
Thou angry and blinded
  Hast sky for thy share.
O mother deep-minded,
  My lyre to my prayer
Responds, and the elements answer or ever
  my soul is aware.

Ye powers of deep water
  And sea-running bays,
Earth's fugitive daughter
  In deep-riven ways,

Enamoured of slaughter,
  A mirage of grays,
Deep blues, and pale greens unbegotten, I
  turn to your lyrical praise.

I tune the loud lyre
  To the haunts of the vale
As a sea-piercing fire
  On the wings of the gale.
I lift my desire,
  I madden, I wail !
Come forth ! I invoke ye, O powers, in the
  waters that purple and pale.

Come forth in your pleasure,
  O fountains and springs !
Come dance me a measure
  Unholpen of wings !
Show, show the deep treasure,
  Unspeakable things !
Come forth ! I invoke ye, O fountains, I
  sweep the invincible strings.

### THE FOUNTAINS.

In the heather deeply hidden,
  From the caverns darkly drawn,
In the woodlands man-forbidden,
  In the gateways of the dawn,
In the glad sweet glades descended,
  On the stark hills gathered high,
Where the snows and trees are blended,
  Kissed at birth by sun and sky ;
We have heard the summons : we are open
  to the day-spring's eye.

### ORPHEUS.

O broad-bosomed lakes
  Whence the mist-tears uprise,
That shed in sweet flakes
  The gleam of the skies,
Whose countenance takes
  The bird as he flies
In kisses, come forth ! I invoke ye, O lakes,
  where the love of me lies !

## THE LAKES.

In the hollow of the mountain,
    In the bosom of the plain,
Fed by river, stream, and fountain,
    Slain by sun, reborn of rain ;
In the desert green-engirded,
    Lying lone in waste and wood,
To my breast the many-herded
    Lowing kine in gracious mood
Come, drink deeply, and are glad of me, my
    pleasant solitude.

## ORPHEUS.

From the breast of the snow
    As a life-swollen stream,
Your love-rivers flow
    Soft hued as a dream,
Adrift and aglow
    With the sunlight supreme.
Come forth ! I invoke ye, O torrents that fall
    in the mazes and gleam !

## THE MOUNTAIN TORRENTS.

Falling fast or lingering love-wise,
    Gathered into mirror-lakes,
Floating sprayed through heaven dove-
    wise,
    Dreaming, dashing ; sunlight shakes
Into million-coloured petals
    All our limpid drops, and wraps
Earth with green, as water settles
    On the rocks and in their gaps,
Mossy rainbow-tinted maidens, flowers and
    fernshoots in their laps.

## ORPHEUS.

Low down in the hollows
    And vales of the earth,
What eagle-sight follows
    Your length and green girth ?
Your light is Apollo's,
    Diana's your mirth !
Come forth ! I invoke ye, O rivers, I have
    watched your mysterious birth !

## THE RIVERS.

In the lowland gently swelling,
    Born and risen out of rain,
Wide the curves and arrowy dwelling
    Where we rest or roll again.
There our calm sides shield the mortal,
    Bears his bark our breast, and we
Follow to the mystic portal
    Where we mingle with the sea.
Every life of earth we list to : should not we
    then answer thee ?

## ORPHEUS.

O see mixt with æther
    In whirls that awake,
Roar skywards and wreathe her
    Bright coils as a snake,
In agony seethe her
    Sad cries for the sake
Of peace—I invoke ye ! Come forth ! O
    spouts in the wave's wild wake !

## THE WATERSPOUTS.

Whirling over miles of ocean,
    Lowering o'er the solemn sea,
Hears our life the deep commotion
    That we know—thy witchery.
Wheeling, hating, fearing ever
    As we thunder o'er the deep,
Death alone our path can sever,
    Death our guerdon if we weep.
We obey thee, we are with thee ! Wilt thou
    never let us sleep ?

## ORPHEUS.

O rolled on the river
    By might of the moon,
Ye tremble and quiver,
    Ye shudder and swoon !
The cities ye shiver :
    The ships know your tune.
Come forth ! I invoke ye, O eagres ! dread
    rivals of shoal and typhoon !

### THE EAGRE.

Flings my single billow spuming
   Into midmost air the world,
As the echo of my booming
   To the furthest star is hurled.
Now I hear the lunar clashing
   That evokes me from the tide,
Now I rise, my fury lashing,
   Rolling where the banks divide—
I obey thee, I am with thee, Lord of Light-
ning, lotus-eyed !

### ORPHEUS.

   In sacred grove,
      In silent wood,
   In calm alcove,
      In mirrored mood,
   What light of love
      Your depth endued?
Come forth ! I invoke ye, O wells, ye
dwellers of dim solitude !

### THE WELLS.

Deep and calm to heaven's mirror
   Through the cedarn grove or ashen,
Willow-woven, or cypress terror,
   To the sky's less serene fashion
Still we look : around our margin
   Holy priestess, longing lover,
Poet musing, vagrant virgin,
   Nor their own mild looks discover,
But the light and glow of that they are
   meditating over.

### ORPHEUS.

   O curves unbeholden,
      Bright glory of bays !
   Deep gulfs grown golden
      With dawn and its ways !
   With sunset enfolden
      In silvery praise !
Come forth ! I invoke ye, O gulfs, where
the sea is as children, and plays.

### THE BAYS.

Where the hills reach to heaven behind us
   A voice is rolled over the steep,
Some godhead whose glory would bind us,
   Reflected far-off on the deep.
We hear the low chant that may blind us,
   The song from the ultimate shore.
We come that our lover may find us
   His bride as he found us before.
We listen, and love ; and his voice is the
   voice of the God we adore.

### ORPHEUS.

   Come forth in your gladness,
      O end of all these !
   O sorrow and madness
      And passion and ease,
   Sharp joy and sweet sadness,
      Deep life and deep peace !
Come forth ! I invoke you, ringed round
earth's girdle, the manifold seas !

### THE SEA.

I hear but one voice in our voices ;
   One tune, multitudinous notes ;
One life that burns low or rejoices,
   One song from the numberless throats.
Where ice on my bosom is piled,
   Where palm-fronded islands begem
My breast, where I rage in the wild
   White storms, where I lap the low
      hem
Of earth's mantle, or war on her crags, I am
   one, and my soul is in them.

I am mother of earth and her daughter ;
   I am father of heaven and his son ;
I am fire in the palace of water ;
   I am God, and my glory is one !
I am bride of the sun and the starlight ;
   The moonlight is bride unto me ;
I am lit of my deeps with a far light,
   My heart and its flame flung free.
I am She, the beginning and end ; I am all,
   and my name is the Sea !

### ORPHEUS.

Then thou, O my mother,
  Hast given to me
The power of another,
  The watery key.
Bright air is my brother,
  My sister the sea ;
I have called, and they answer and come ;
and their song is but glory to thee.

One other is left me,
  The light of the earth.
If Fate had bereft me,
  Oh Muse, of thy birth,
Still I had cleft me
  A way in her girth !
I tune the loud lyre once again to the mother
of men in her mirth.

O mighty and glad
  In spring-time and summer !
O tearful and sad
  When the sun is grown dumber,
When the season is mad,
  And the gods overcome her,
When the sky is fulfilled of the frost and the
fingers of winter numb her !

O marvellous earth
  Of multiple mood
That givest men birth
  And delicate food,
Red wine to make mirth
  Of thine own red blood,
And corn and green grass and sweet flowers
and fruits most heavenly-hued !

Borne skyward in swoon
  By arrowy hours,
Girt round of the moon
  And the girdling flowers,
The sun for a boon,
  Sweet kisses of showers,
O mother, O life, O desire, my soul is a
bird in thy bowers !

My soul is caught up
  In thy green-hearted waves.
I drink at the cup
  Of thy sweet valley graves.
My spirit may sup
  Slow tunes in thy caves.
O hide me, thy child, in thy bosom, that the
heart in me yearns to and craves.

Most virginally sprung
  In the shadow of light,
Eternally young,
  A magical sight,
Wandering among
  Day, twilight, and night,
As a bride in her chamber that dreams many
visions of varied delight.

O how shall my lyre
  Divide thee, dispart
Thy water and fire,
  Thy soul and thy heart,
Thy hills that spring higher,
  Thy flowers that upstart,
How quire thee, my limitless love, with a
lewd and a limited art ?

A fortress, a sphere,
  An arrow of flame ;
Let thy children appear
  At the sound of thy name !
In my silence uprear
  The sweet guerdon of shame !
Be they choral to hymn thee, O mother, thy
magic ineffable fame !

Last birth of the Sun,
  Best gift of the giver,
Thou surely art One !
  As the moon on the river,
Whose star-blossoms run,
  Kiss, tremble, and shiver,
And roll into ultimate space, and are lost to
man's vision for ever.

Come forth to the sound
　　Of the lightning lyre,
Ye valleys profound
　　As a man's desire,
Ye woodlands bound
　　In the hills that are higher
Than even the note of a bird as it wings to
the solar fire !


Ye fruits and corn,
　　Gold, rose, and green,
Vines purple-born,
　　Pearl-hidden sheen,
Trees waving in scorn
　　Of the grass between !
Come forth in your chorus, and chant the
praise of your mother and queen !


Ye trees many-fronded
　　That shake to the wind,
Green leaves that have sounded
　　My harp in your kind,
Light boughs that are rounded,
　　Grey tops that are shrined
In the tears of the heaven as they fall in the
blackening storm grown blind !


Ye fields that are flowered
　　In purple and white,
Embossed and embowered
　　By the love of the light,
Gold-sandalled and showered,
　　Dew-kissed of the night,
Your song is too faint and too joyous for
mortals to hear it aright.


Blue pansies, and roses,
　　And poppies of red,
Pale violets in posies
　　Where Hyacinth bled,
The flower that closes
　　Its dolorous head ;—
What song may be sung, or what tune may
be told, or what word may be said ?


All tropical scent,
　　Blossom-kindled perfume
Love-colours new-lent
　　By the infinite womb,
Gold subtlety blent
　　With the scarlet bloom ;—
Shall ye in my melody live ?  Shall my song
be not rather your tomb ?


Most musical moves
　　The head of the corn ;
Strong glorious loves
　　Of its being are born.
Dim shadows of groves
　　Of Demeter adorn
The waves and the woods of the earth, the
heart of the mother forlorn.


Caves curved of the wind,
　　Deep hollows of earth,
Whence the song of the blind
　　Old prophet had birth,
The caves that confined
　　Deep music of mirth,
Thy caves, O my mother, are these not a
gem in thy virginal girth ?


Ye mountains uplift
　　As an arrow in air ;
Ice-crowned, rock-cliffed,
　　Snow-bosomed bare,
I give ye the gift
　　Of a voice more fair.
Leave echo, and wake, and proclaim that ye
stand against death and despair !


Ye hills where I rested
　　In rapture of life,
From dawn calm-breasted
　　To evening's strife,
Where skies were nested
　　With mist for a wife !
Leave echo, and speak for yourselves : let
your song pierce the heaven as a knife !

Olympus alone
　Of earth's glories is taken
For deity's throne
　Deep-frozen, storm-shaken.
What glories are shown
　When their slumbers awaken !
The avalanche thunders adown, and the gods
　of the gods are forsaken.


To mortals your voices
　Are mighty and glad.
The maiden rejoices :
　The man is grown mad
For love, and his choice is
　The choice of a lad
When a virgin first smiles on his suit, and
　the summer for envy is sad.


Wan grows Aphrodite,
　And Artemis frail ;
Apollo less mighty,
　Red Bacchus too pale.
Dark Hades grows bright, he
　Alone may avail
When the god and the mortal are one, as the
　mountain is one with the gale.


### The Children of Earth.

Our hair deep laden with the scent of earth,
The colour of her rosy body's birth,
　Our mother, lady and life of all that is
　　divine ;
We gather to the sombre sound, as spring
Had whispered, " Follow,' hiding in her
　wing
　Her glorious head and flowing breast of
　　wine.
Though in the hollow of her heart be set
So deep and awful a fire, though the net
　Of all her robes be frail as we are fine,
We gather, listening to the living lyre
Like falling water shot with amber fire,
And blown aloft by winds even to heaven's
　desire.

Deep starry gems set in a silver sea,
Sullen low voices of dark minstrelsy,
　Light whispers of strange loves, of silver
　　woven,
Dumb kisses and wild laughter following :
All these as lives of autumn and of spring
　We are : we follow across the rainbow
　　cloven,
A never-fading path of golden glory,
Whereof the lone Leucadian promontory
　Holds one divinest gate : the other troven
Far, far beyond in interlunar skies,
Where the Himâlayas stir them, and arise
To listen to the song that swells our arteries.

O moving labyrinth sun-crowned, dread maze
Of starry paths, of Zeus-untrodden ways,
　Of mystic vales unfooted of the deep,
Our mother, virgin yet in many places
Unseen of man, beholden of the faces
　Only of elemental shapes of sleep
That are ourselves, her daughters wild and fair
Caught nymphwise in the kisses of the air,
　That flings our songs reverberate from
　　steep to steep,
Songs caught in solar light, we are shed
Even down beyond the valleys of the dead,
And smiled upon in groves ruled by the holy
　head.

Great Pan hath heard us, children of his
　wooing,
Great Pan, that listens to the forest, suing
　Vainly His peace that dwells even in the
　　desolate halls.
The delicately-chiselled flowers nod,
Look to the skies, and see thee for a God,
　O sightless lyre that wails, O viewless voice
　　that calls !
Thy sound is in our death and in her womb,
Far in Spring's milky breast, in Autumn's
　gloom,
　In Summer's feast and song, in Winter's
　　funerals.
In the dead hollow of the hills there rings,
Sharp song, like frost hissing on silver wings,
Or like the swelling tune we listen to for
　Spring's.

We come, we mountains, crowned and in-
cense-bringing,
Robed as white priests, the solemn anthem
singing ;
Or as an organ thundering fiery tunes.
We come, we greener hills, and rend the sky,
With happier chorus and the songs that die
Or mix their subtle joy and being with the
moon's.
We come, we pine-clad steeps, we feathery
slopes,
With footfalls softer than tne antelope's.
We listen and obey : the sacred slumberer
swoons
More tranced than death in this far follow-
ing,
Careless of winter, not invoking spring ;
And all the witless woods company us and
sing.

But not the glades by song of thee unstricken ?
Not they?  Shall they refuse the pulse to
quicken,
Soft smiting the low melody of light ?
Tuned without fingers, the wild woods lift
high
The wordless chant, the murmurous melody,
The song that dwells like moon-enkindled
night.
We draw from low palm groves and cedar
hills,
From stern grey slumbers, for thy music fills
All earth with unimaginable delight.
Have we not brought the leaves dew-
diamonded,
The buds fresh-gleaming, star-blossoms, and
shed
Our scent and colour and song around thy
sacred head ?

We that are flowers are kindled in thy praise,
Even as thy song shed lustre and swift rays,
Darting to brighten and open the folded
flowers.
The violet lifts its head, the lily lightens,
The daisy shakes its dew, the pansy brightens,
All cups of molten light upon the twilight
hours.

The poppy flames anew, the buttercup
Glows with fresh fire, the larkspur rouses up
To be the lark indeed amid the azalea
bowers.
Magnolia and light blooms of roses mute
Rouse them to gather in one golden lute
In fairy light and song into the sky to shoot.

The laughing companies of corn awaken,
Their wind-swept waves by Dædal music taken
Into a golden heaven of festal song.
We shake and glisten in the sun, we see
The very soul and majesty of thee
Thrill in the lyre and leave the lazy long
Notes for crisp magic of sharp rustling sound,
And thy life quickens and thy loves abound,
Listening the answer of our dancing throng.
Joy, sleep, peace, laughter, thought, remem-
brance, came
Even at our prelude, a death-quickening
flame,
And earth rejoiced throughout to hear De-
meter's name.

We come, in bass deep-swelling, rocks and
caves,
A hollow roar across the golden waves
Hidden in islands set deep in the un-
travelled sea.
Across the corn from storm-cleft mountain-
sides
Our voice peals, like the thunder of the tides,
Into the darkling hills that fringe Eternity.
Dire and divine our womb unfruitful bears
Deep music darker than tempestuous airs
When Heaven's anger wakes : when at
our own decree,
With clanging rocks sky-piercing for our tomb,
We call the thunder from our own black
womb,
We hear the voice and we obey—we know
not whom !

We hear thee, who are cliffs and pinnacles
Higher than heaven's base, founded far in
hell's ;
We hear, that sunder the blue skies of
heaven ;

Our voiceless clefts and spires of delicate hue,
Changing and lost in the exultant blue,
  By fire and whirlwind fashioned and then
    riven,
Invoke fresh song, with deep solemnity
In noble notes of mastery answering thee,
  By some young tumult in our old hearts
    driven ;
And this immortal path of splintered rock
Shall lead the wild chant to the sky, and
  mock
The nectared feast of Gods with its im-
  passioned shock.

Deep-mouthed, I, earthquake, wake in
  echoing thunder.
I break my mother's breast ; I tear asunder
  The womb that bore me ; I arise in terror,
Threatening to ruin her, crag, crown, and
  . column,
Reverberate music of that mighty and solemn
  Call of creation, Vulcan's awful mirror.
I rend the sky with clamour terrible,
Shaking the thrones of earth and heaven and
  hell,
  Confound the universe in universal error.
I sound the awful note that summons
  mortals,
As I awake, to pass the dreadful portals
And face the gloom of Dis, the unnameable
  immortals.

Soft our mild music steals through thunder-
  ous pauses,
A phrase made magic by the Second Causes,
  The mighty Ones that dwell beneath the
    empyreàn.
We, vines and fruits and trees with autumn
  laden,
Sing as the bride-song of a married maiden
  Before the god-like vigour of the man
Breaks the frail temple-doors of love asunder,
And wakes the new life's promise in pale
  wonder,
  Shattering the moulded glass, the shape
    Selenian.
Fruits of the earth, our low song joins the
  crowd.

We need not (to be heard) to thunder loud.
Our hearts are lifted up, our heads with love
  low bowed.

The tenderest light, the deepest hidden, is
  shed
Up through dark earth—your home, O happy
  dead !—
  Crusted in darkness lie the secret lights.
Formed in the agony of earth as tears,
Clothed in the crystal mirror of the years,
  We dwell, sweet-hearted nun-like eremites !
Diamond and ruby, topaz and sapphire,
Emerald and amethyst, one clear bright fire,
  We are earth's stars below, as she above
    hath Night's.
Our sweet clean song pierces the cover,
And thin keen notes of music flit and hover
Like spirit-birds upon the lyre of this our
  lover.

We, children of the mountains, lying low
On earth's own bosom, deep, embowered,
  flow
  In wide soft waves of land : upon us sweep
The mightiest rivers : in our hollows lie
Great lakes : our voices hardly rise, but die
  In the cold streams of air : shallow and
    deep :
Leagues by the thousand, dells a minute
  long ;
All we are children of the mighty throng
  That cluster where the mountains fail, and
    sleep
In such cool peace that even thy lyre awakes
Hardly a soul that tenderer music makes.
Yet we arise and listen for our own sweet
  sakes.

THE LIVING CREATURES OF THE EARTH.

The heavy hand is held,
  And the whips leave weary blows.
The mysteries of eld
  Are cancelled and expelled,
  And the miserable throes.

All we are shapen fair
  In many forms of grace,
But change is everywhere,
And time is all our share
  And all the ways of space.

One lives an hour of day;
  One even man's life exceeds;
One loves to chase and slay;
One loves to sing and play;
  Each soul to his own deeds!

A share of joy is ours,
  A double share of grief;
So sum the many hours
In many hopes and powers,
  All powers except the chief.

Emotion fills our souls,
  And love delights us well,
And joy of sense full rolls;
But leads us, and controls
  Life's central citadel.

Whence we were drawn who knows?
  Of law or Gods or chance?
But, as life's river flows,
What Sea shall clasp and close
  Beyond blind circumstance?

Such little power we own
  Of vague experience,
And instinct to enthrone
The life's mere needs alone,
  Nor answer "why" and "whence."

Nor wandering in the night
  Our minds may apprehend
Reflecting in pure light
Of soul, what sound or sight
  May lead us to some end.

We hear the dim sound roll
  From distant mountains drawn,
We follow, but no soul
Guesses that silver goal,
  The sunset or the dawn.

The lyre entices fast
  Our willing feet and wings,
We wonder from the past
What spell is overcast
  From off the sonant strings.

Awhile we deem our mates
  Are calling through the wood;
Awhile the tune creates
These unfamiliar states
  Of thinking solitude.

Awhile we gather clear
  A note of promise swell,
A song of fate and fear,
Assuring us who hear
  Of other shapes to dwell.

A promise vast and grand
  As is the spangled sky!
We dimly understand;
We join the following band
  Of dancing greenery!

We see all Nature bend
  To high Olympus' hill.
Our tunes we choose and send;
We follow to the end,
  O Orpheus, all thy will.

Our little love and hate,
  Our hunger and our fear,
Pass to a solemn state
Pregnant with hope and fate.
  O Orpheus, we are here!


### THE EARTH.

Life hidden in death,
  Life shrined in the soul,
Life bright for his breath,
  Life dark for his goal,
I am Mother, and Burier, and Friend—
Look thou to the end!

I am Light in thy Love,
   I am Love in thy Life.
I am cloistered above
   Where the stars are at strife.
I am life in thy light, and thy death
Is part of my breath.

My voices are many,
   Thy lyre is but one ;
But thou art not as any
   Soul under the sun !
Thou hast power for an hour,
The motherly dower.

One voice of my voices
   Uncalled and unheard,
No song that rejoices
   Of beast or of bird,
No sound of my children sublime,
But the spirit of time.

Fear is his name,
   Nor flickers nor dies
His blackening flame.
   Beware, were thou wise !
Not him shalt thou hail from the dusk with
thy breath ;
   His name—it is Death !

My seasons and years,
   Shalt thou traffic with these ?
Art thou Fate ?  Are her shears
   Asleep or at ease ?
Though Time were no more than the shape
of thy glass—
   Beware ! let him pass !

ORPHEUS.

Not these do I fear,
   O Earth, for their peace.
I cry till they hear
   O'er the desolate seas.
I call ye ! give ear,
   O seasons, to these
Fleet-footed, the strings of the lyre !  Come
   forth ! I invoke ye—and cease.
VOL. III.

O hours of the day,
   And hours of the night,
Pause now while ye may
   In your heavenly flight !
Give answer and say,
   Have I called ye aright ?
Are the strings of my lyre as fire, the voice
   of my singing as light ?

THE HOURS.

Darkness and daylight in divided measure
   Gather as petals of the sunflower,
In many seasons seek the lotus-treasure,
Following as dancing maidens, mute for
   pleasure,
   The fervent flying footsteps of the Hour.

The sun looks over the memorial hills,
   The trampling of his horses heard as wind ;
He leaps and turns, and all his fragrance fills
The shade and silence ; all the rocks and rills
   Ring with the triumph of his steeds behind.

The bright air winnowed by the plumeless
   leapers
   Laughs, and the low light pierces to the
   bed
Where lovers linger, where the smiling
   sleepers
Stir, and the herds unmindful of their keepers
   Low for pure love of morning's dewy head.

The morning shakes its ocean-bathèd tresses,
   The bright sun broadens over all the earth.
The green leaves fall, fall into his caresses,
And all the world's heart leaps, again ad-
   dresses
Its life, and girds it in the golden girth.

Then noon full-fashioned lies upon the steep.
   The large sun sighs and turns his bridle-
   rein,
Thinks of the ocean, turns his heart to sleep,
Laughing no longer, not yet prone to weep,
   Feeling the prelude of the coming pain.

K

The hills and dales are dumb beneath the
    heat,
    And all the world lies tranced or mutely
        dreaming,
Save some low sigh caught up where pulses
    beat
Of warm love waiting in the arboreal seat
    Till the shade lengthen on the lawn light-
        gleaming.

Now all the birds change tune, and all the
    light
    Glows lowlier, musing on departed day.
Strange wings and sombre, heralding the
    night,
Fleet far across the woods; and gleaming
    bright
    The evening star looks from the orient
        way.

Shadow and silence deepen : all the woods
    Take on a tenderer phrase of musical
Breezes: the stream-sought homes and
    solitudes
Murmur a little where the maiden moods
    Are sadder as the evening's kisses fall.

Like silver scales of serpenthood they fall
    Across the blind air of the evening ;
Shadowy ghosts arise funereal
And seek unspeakable things ; and dryads
    call
    The satyr-company to the satyr-king.

And all the light is over; but the sky
    Shudders with blanched light of the un-
        risen moon.
The night-birds mingle their sad minstrelsy
For daylight's requiem : and the sea's reply
    Now stirs across the land's departed tune.

The moon is up : the choral crowd of stars,
    Shapen like strange or unknown animals,
Move in their measure : beyond Æolian bars
The clustering winds, moving as nenuphars,
    Gather and muse before the midnight calls.

The darkness is most deep in hollow dells.
    There, blacker than Cocytus, lurk the
        shades
Darker than death's, more terrible than hell's,
Uttering unwritten words : the silent wells
    Keep their sweet secret till the morning
        maids

Bring their carved pitchers to the moss-
    grown side.
    For now beyond, below the east, appears
A hint as if a band, silvern and wide,
The girdle of some goddess amber-eyed,
    Rose from the solemn company of the
        spheres.

The sky is tinged, as if the amorous flesh
    Of that same queen shone through the
        girdle drawn
By her own kissing fervour through its mesh.
Last, glory of godhead ! flickers, flames the
    fresh
    First faint frail rose and arrow of the dawn.

### SPRING.

Mild glimpses of the quiet moon, let through
    Tall groves of cedar, stain the glade ;
        gleams mild
The kirtle of the unweaned spring, stained
    blue
    From the blue breasts that suckle to the
        child.
        Through the new-leavèd trees
        The hidden stranger sees
The moon's sweet light, the shadows listening
    If a ghost-foot should fall :
    And if a ghost-voice call
Tremble the leaves and light-streaks of the
    spring.
On wavering wing
    The small clouds gallop in the windy sky :
    The hoarse rooks croak and droop them
        to the nest :
One sweet small throat begins to sing,
    Becomes the song, losing identity
    Ere its wail wakes the long low-lying
        crest
    That rears across the west.

Spring, maiden-footed, steals across the
   space,
  Sandalled with tremulous light, with flicker-
    ing hair
Blown o'er the sweet looks of the fair child-
  face,
  Like willows drooping o'er the liquid
    mere,
    Whence timid eyes look far,
    Even where her kisses are
Awaited by the tender mother lips,
    Earth's, that is lonely and old,
    Grown sad, fearful, and cold
With bitter winter and the sun's eclipse ;
So the child slips
  From bough to bough between the weep-
    ing trees,
    And with frail fingers smooths and
    touches them.
They murmur in their sleep : the moonlight
    dips
    And laughs, seeing how young buds catch
    life from these
    Child-kisses on the stem.


The leaves laugh low, and frosty-footed
    Time
Shoulders a lighter burden ; in the dale
Some distant notes of lovely music climb,
  Thrown from the golden-throated night-
    ingale,
    Pale sobs of love and life
    With death and fear at strife,
Fiercely beset and hardly conquering,
  When spring's bright eyes at last
    Flash through the sullen past,
And tune its pain to tears, its peace to
  sing.
The earth's lips cling
  To the child's bosom, and low smiles
    revive ;
    Love is new-born upon the golden
    hour,
And all the life of all the exultant spring
  Breathes in the wind that wakes the world
    alive
    Into the likeness of a flower.

## SUMMER.

Full is the joy of Maidenhood made strong,
  Too proud to bend to swift Apollo's
    kiss ;
Rejoicing in its splendour, and the throng
  Of gaunt hounds leashless before Artemis.
    In strange exulting bliss
The maiden stands, full-grown, with bound-
    ing breasts
    Bared to the noon, and narrow
Keen eyes that glance, dim fires that veil
    their crests
    To flame along the arrow
Aimed at some gallant of ten tines perched
    high
Branching against the sky
  His cedar-spreading horns : erect she
    stands,
  Holding in glimmering hands
    A silver bow across the shining weather,
  While, bound in pearl-wrought bands,
    Her bright hair streams ; she draws the
    quivering feather
Back to the small ear curved : with golden
    zone
Gathering her limbs she stands alone
  Like a young antelope poised upon a spire
    of stone.


What tender lightning flashes in the bosom
  Heaving with vigour of young life ?  What
    storm
Gathers across the brow's broad lotus-
  blossom ?
  What sudden passion fills the fragrant
    form
  With subtle streams of warm
Blood tingling to the finger-tips of rose ?
    Swiftly the maiden closes
The lustre of her look : disdainful glows
    The fire of wreathing roses
In her bright cheeks : she darts away to
  find
    Like some uncovered hind
    Shade in the forest from the stag's pursuit,
    Ere the sun's passion shoot

His ray, strange deeps unknown and feared
    to uncover.
  But now the ancient root
Of some wise oak betrays her to her lover:
  She stumbles and falls prone: the forest
    noon
  Guesses life's law; all nature's tune
  Tells that the hour is come when May
    must grow to June.

Then in the broad glare of the careless sun
  Apollo's light is on her and within;
His shafts of glory pierce her one by one;
  His kisses darken, shivering and keen,
  Swift glories cold and clean
Of that chaste bridal, and the earth gets
    gladness,
  Till the last winter's traces
Fall from the spring's last cold wind—shining
    sadness !—
  And from the frail new faces
Blushing through moss; and all the world is
    light
With the unsufferably bright
  Full joy and guerdon of that sunny season
By Love's sweet trap of treason.
    So the bright girl is now a woman
      brighter;
    And childhood sees a reason
      Beneath the strong stroke of the goodly
        smiter
For all the past: and love at last is hers.
No more the bosom's pride demurs,
While in her womb the first faint pulse of
    motherhood soft stirs.


AUTUMN.

Full amber-breasted light of harvest-moon,
  And sheaves of corn remembering the sun
    Laughing again for love of that caress
When night is fallen, and the sleepy swoon
  Of warm waves lap the shoreland, one by
    one ;
    Forgetful kisses like a dream's possess
All the low-lying land,
  And, statelier than the swaying form
  Of some loud God, lifting the storm

In his disastrous hand,
  Steps the sweet-voiced, the mellow
    motherhood
  Glad of the sun's kiss, full of life, w'
    wooed
  And won and brought to his bed,
Proud of her rhythm in the lusty kiss,
  Triumphant and exulting in the mood
Wherein her being is
  Crowned with a husband's head,
  And left in solitude which is not soli-
    tude.


She strides with mighty steps across the
    glade
  Laughing, her bosom swelling with the
    milk
    Born of a million kisses : leaps her
      womb
Pregnant with fruits, and latter flowers, and
    shade
  Of the great cedar-groves : soft, soft, as
    silk,
    Her skin glows amber, silvered with the
      bloom
Mist-like of the moon's light,
  A slumberous haze of quietude
Shed o'er the hardy limbs, and lustihood,
And boldness, and great might.
  Earth knows her daring daughter, and the
    sea
  Breaks into million-folded mystery
    Of flower-like flashes in the pale moon-
      rise,
Exulting also, now the sun is faded,
  With joy of her supreme fertility
And glowing masteries
    Of autumn summer-shaded,
  The golden fruit of all the blossoming
    sky.


And now the watcher to the bright breasts
    blind
  Loses the seemly shape, the loud swift
    song ;
    Now the moon falls, and all the gold is
      gone,

And round the storm-caught shape hard
    gusts of wind
  Blow, and her leaves are torn, a flying
    throng
    Of orange and purple and red; the
      sombre sun
Shines darkly in her breast
  But wakes no joy therein,
  And all his kisses sharp and keen
Bring only now desire of rest,
  Not their old rapture: the warm violet eyes
  Melt into sweet hot tears; subtler the sighs
    Are interfused of death;
The brave bright looks grow duller,
  And fear is mingled with love's ecstasies
Again, and all her breath
    Fails, and the shape and colour
  Fade, fail, are lost in the sepulchral seas.

### WINTER.

Know ye my children? From the old strong
    breast
  Not weary yet of life's grey change, not
    drawn
Into the utter peace of death, the rest
  Of the dim hour that lingers ere the dawn,
Spring these that laugh upon thee. In the
    snow
    See forests bare and gaunt,
    Where wingèd whispers haunt,
Lighting the dull sky with a slumberous
    glow;
    Hear the strange sounds of winter
      chaunt;
Feel the keen wisdom of the winter thrill
  Young hearts with passionate foretaste
  Of death in some wild waste
Of deserts darkening at some wild god's will,
Of frozen steppes awaiting the repose
  That only death discovers, never sleep.
    My misery is this
That I must wake to childhood gold and
    rose,
  And maidenhood, and wifehood, and still
    keep
    Bound on Life's fatal wheel—revolv-
      ing bliss.

O that worn wisdom and the age of sorrow
  Could learn its bitter lesson, and depart
Into some nightfall guiltless of a morrow,
  Into some cave's unprofitable heart
Beyond this curse of birth! O that dread
    night
    Could come and cover all,
    Even itself to fall
To some abyss past resurrection's might!
    For the old whispers of my old life call
Accursèd hopes, accursèd fears, accursèd
    pleasures.
    Long-suffering of all life!
    Changed consciousness at strife!
  No dancer treads the melancholy measures
Unchanged for one short tune: no dancer
    flags,
    The hateful music luring them to move
    Weary and desolate;
And as the rhyme revolves and shrills and
    drags
    Their limbs insane they smile and call it
      love,
    Or, mocking, call it hatred: it is Fate.

These grey eyes close to the deceitful dream
  Of death that will not take the tired for
    ever.
Again, again, revolves the orb; the stream,
    The dew, the cloud, the ocean, and the
    river.
My magic wand and cup and sword and
    spell
    Languish, forgotten fears.
    The cup is filled with tears;
The sword is red with blood; the pentacle
    Builded of flesh; the wand its snake-
      head rears
Swift energy: my labour is but lost.
    I, who thus thought all things to end,
    Find in the void no friend.
I have but conjured up the fiend that most
I trusted to abolish: all my toil
  Goes to give rest to life, and build anew
    These pinnacles of pain,
Cupola upon cupola; the soil
    To comfort, to avail, to assoil with dew,
    To build the year again.

ORPHEUS.

O hours not of day
    But of æons that roll !
Earth stretches away
    From pole unto pole ;
Four seasons decay,
    Ere one sound of thy soul,
O fervent and following years, springs over
    the solar goal !

Come forth to the sound
    Of the seven sweet strings !
Advance and rebound !
    Be your pomp as a king's !
Girdled around
    With seasons and stings
As a serpent's encompassing Time.   Come
    forth ! on the heavy grey wings !

Ye arbiter lords
    That sit as for doom,
Bright splendour of swords
    Leaps forth in your gloom !
But stronger my chords
    Shall lift in your womb
The love of your passage and time, imme-
    morial ages, your tomb.

Ye linger for long,
    But ye pass and are done:
But I, my sweet song
    Outliveth the sun !
Ye are many and strong ;
    I am stronger, and one !
Come forth ! I invoke ye, O years, in my
    evening orison.

THE YEARS.

Crowned with Eternity, beyond beginning ;
    Sandalled with wings, Eternity's ; the end
Far beyond sight of striving soul or sinning ;
    Ourselves see not, nor know, nor compre-
    hend.
Reeling from chaos, unto Chronos winning,
    Devoured of Him our Father and our
    friend,
This is our life, lead winged or footed golden;
We pass, and each of other is unbeholden.

Ranged in dim spectral order and procession,
    We span man's thought, we limit him in
    time ;
None of the souls of earth have had posses-
    sion
    Of larger loves or passions more sublime.
Where the night-caverns hide our solemn
    session
    The summoning word lifts up our holy
    rhyme.
Even as a mighty river, bend to bend,
We rise in turn and look toward the end.

Also, the Gods arisen from the living
    Lights of the sky, half hidden in the night,
Vast shapes beholden of men unbelieving,
    Staggering the sense and reason with the
    sight,
Manifold, mighty, monstrous, no light giving
    Unto the soul that is not also light ;—
We rise in ghastly power ; we know the
    token,
The speech of silence and the song unspoken.

ORPHEUS.

Come forth to the sound,
    Ye lustres of years
That hide in profound
    Abysses of fears,
Hidden and bound !
    The voice of tears
Implores and impels ye, O lustres, with a
    tune that is strong as a seer's.

THE LUSTRES.

Fivefold the shape sublime that lifts its head
    Uniform, self-repeating, comparable
At last to a man's life: twice seven times
    dead
    Ere the light flickers in that citadel,
Or the great whiteness lure his soul instead
    Of many-coloured earth: ere the strong
    spell
Fail, and the Fates with iron-shapen shears
Cut the frail silver, hide him from the years.

Fivefold: the year that is in darkness hidden,
Being beginning: then the moving year,
All change and tumult; then the quiet un-
chidden
Of deep reflection; then the gladdening
tear
Or saddening smile, the laughter not for-
bidden
And love enfolding the green-woven
sphere:
Lastly, the burning year of flame and fume
That burns men up in fire's sepulchral womb.

Fivefold: the child, the frail, the delicate:
Then the strong laughing mischief: then
the proud
Fight toward manhood and the sense elate,
Creative power and passion: then the loud
Assertion of young will, the quickening rate
And strength in blood, in youth with life
endowed,
And firmness fastening; the last lustre's span
Consolidates and shows the perfect man.

Fivefold: the humour changes as his child
Calls him first "father"; sense of strength
divine
Fills him; then man's work in the world,
and wild
Efforts to fame: then steadier in the shrine
Burns the full flame: then, turning, the years
piled
Seem suddenly a burden; then the fine
Flavour of full maturity is tasted:
The man looks back, and asks if life be
wasted.

Fivefold: delight in woman altering
To joy of sunlight only: love of life
Changing to fear of death: the golden spring
Trembles; he hates the cold, the winter
strife,
Laughs not with lust of combat: feebly cling
His old hands: he has sepultured his wife:
Last, palsied, shaking, drawing tremorous
breath,
He gasps—and stumbles in the pit of death.

ORPHEUS.

O girded and spanned
By the deeds of time,
Rocks shattered and planned
In your depth: where climb
The race and the land,
And the growth sublime
Of worlds—I invoke ye! Come forth, ye
centuries! Come to the rhyme!

THE CENTURIES.

How hardly a man
Though his strength were as spring's
Shall stretch out his span
To the width of my wings!
The years are enfolden
In my bosom golden,
My periods
Are the hours of the Gods.
They have their plan
In my seasons; all things
Are woven in the span
Of the spread of my wings.

My brazen gates cleft
By shafts shed of time,
Are ruined and left
As the Gods sing their rhyme.
Buttress and joist are
Effaced of the cloister.
Fane after fane
We lift us again
To the hoarier transept
Where ages climb,
And ruin is left
Where the Gods said their rhyme.

The deity-year
(Whereof I am an hour)
Shall be born and appear
As the birth of a flower,
Shall fade as they faded,
The flower wreaths braided
In maiden's hair.
The Gods shall fare

As the children of Fear
  In the Fear-God's Power,
And their names disappear
  As the fall of a flower!

The universe-day
  (Whereof I am a second)
Shall fall away
  And be no more reckoned;
Shall fall into ruin.
(Sad garden it grew in!)
Unguessed at, unknown,
Beyond them alone,
Is a space that is grey
  As it caught them, and beckoned,
And lost them—their way
  Is nor counted nor reckoned!

Inconceivable hollow,
  Eternity's womb!
Cataclysmal they follow,
  Tomb hidden in tomb.
Reeled off and unspun,
Time's fashion is done
In the ultimate
Abysses of fate.
Æons they swallow,
  And swamp in the gloom,
Where Eternities follow
  Their biers to their tomb.

ORPHEUS.

O Mother, O hollow
  Sweet heart of the moon!
O matchless Apollo
  That granted the tune!
Time's children follow
  The strings that commune
With Nature well cloven that comes to the
lyre's lilt silver-hewn.

  O bays of the wind,
    And shoreland of Thrace!
  O beaten and blind
    In the light of my face!
  Heaven thunders behind,
    Hell shakes for a space,
As I fling the loud sound to the sky, and the
vaults of the Earth give place.

O mystical tune
  Of a magic litten
Of music, the moon,
  The stars unsmitten,
The sun, the unhewn
  Stones deeply bitten
By runic fingers of time, where decrees of the
Fates are written!

  Time listens, obeys me;
    All Nature replies;
  Nought avoids me, nor stays me,
    Nor checks, nor defies.
  Tribute she pays me
    From seas unto skies.
But Death—shall he heed me or hear? shall
he list to the lyre and arise?

  O thou who art seated,
    Invisible king,
  The never-defeated,
    The shadowy thing!
  What mortal hath greeted
    Thy shrine, but shall sing
Not earthly but tunes of thine own, in the
vaults of Aornos that ring?

  Nor caring nor hearing
    For hearts that be bowed,
  Nor hating nor fearing
    Man's crying aloud,
  Solemnly spearing
    The single, the crowd,
Thou sittest remote and alone, unprofane,
with due silence endowed!

  I call thee by Nature,
    My mother and friend!
  By every creature!
    By life and its end!
  By love, the true teacher,
    My chanting I send,
Invoking thy stature immense, the terrible
form of a fiend!

I hear not a word,
Though my music be rolled
As the song of a bird
Through fields of gold.
Hast thou not heard?
Have I not told
The magic that bridleth the Gods, the Gods
in their houses of old?

Art thou elder than they
In their mountain of light?
Is thy fugitive way
Lost in uttermost night?
Shalt thou not obey,
Or my lyre not affright,
If I call thee by Heaven and Earth with a
God's tumultuous might?

If I curse thee or chide
Shalt thou tremble not, Thou?
Not move thee and hide
From the light of my brow?
Shall my arrows divide
Not the heart of thee now?
Art thou cased in strong iron to mock the
spells that all others avow?

Art thou muffled or hidden
In adamant brass?
Is my music forbidden
In Orcus to pass?
Have I cursed thee and chidden?
My flesh being grass,
I curse not as yet, but command thee; the
names that avail I amass.

No sound? no whisper?
No answer to me?
From dawn-star to Hesper
I call upon thee!
In the hour of vesper
I change the key!
I cry on Apollo to aid, I lift up my lyre on
the sea.

Thou reaper of fear,
Accurst of mankind,
I charge thee to hear,
Deaf horror deep-mined
In hell! O uprear
On the front of the wind!
I curse thee! Thou hearest my hounds of
thunder that mutter behind?

How strange is the dark
And the silence around!
Hardly the spark
Of my silvery sound
Moves, or may mark
The heaven's dim bound.
How strange! I have sought him in vain—
perchance not in vain have I found!

No! Life thrills in me;
Vibrates on the lyre;
The Fates still spin me
Their thread of desire:
Still, woo and win me
Soft eyes, and the dire
Low fervour of sensual phrase, song kin to
the nethermost fire!

In silence I wait
For his voice to roll,
For the coming of Fate,
The strength of my soul.
My words create
One glorious whole
From the fragments divided that seem past a
man's or a god's control.

I, seeing the life
Of the flowers renew,
The victorious strife
Of the spring run through,
The child's birth rife
With loftier dew—
I know the deep truth in myself; see acacia
in cypress and yew.

Death is not at all !
   'Tis a mask or a dream !
The things that befall
   Only slumber or seem !
They fear ; they appal—
   They are not as ye deem !
Death died when I dipped my lyre in the
sweet Heliconian stream !

   Give praise to your lord,
     All souls that draw breath,
   All flowers of the sward !
     For the song of me saith :
   " Sound the loud chord !
     Let love be a wreath !
Death is not for ye any more, for I am the
Master of Death ! "

## PARABASIS.[1]

As I sit in the sound
   Of the wash of the surf,
On the long low ground,
   The trees and the turf ;
In front the profound,
   The warrior seas,
   Upstirred of the breeze,
By the far reef bound—
I know the low music of love, I feel the
sweet murmur in me,
   My soul is in tune with the sea.

   The stars are above me,
   The rocks are below me,
     The sea is around !
   Great Gods that love me
   Lead me, and show me
     Their powers profound.
   Their lightnings move me
   To stir me, to throw me
     As into a swound,
The song of the infinite surf that is beaten
and bound
     As a fierce wolf-hound,
The song that lures me, and lifts me, and
mingles my soul into sound !

[1] The bulk of this Book I. was written at
Waikiki, which is described in this Parabasis.

O Nature, my mother,
   Heart melted on heart
At last ! Not another,
   Not any shall part
   Thy soul from my art.
How should it be otherwise,
   Sister divine,
Lover, my mother wise,
   Wiser than wine ?
Seeing I linger
   Here on the beach—
Let God's own finger
   Here to me reach,
Making me singer
   Each unto each—
Nature and Man made one
In the light and fire of the sun,
   And the sobbing tune
   Of the moon,
Wedded in cyclic bonds,
Where fall the æon-fronds,
   Whose large bed bears a child
   (In its due period)
Not merciful and not severe,
Knowing nor love nor fear,
   But majesty most mild,
   Being indeed a God.

Yea, let the very ray-hand of Apollo
Lead me where none may follow
Save in blind eagle-fury and full flight
Pythian against the light,
Writing in all the sea, the trees, the flowers,
The many-fruited bowers,
The lustred lilies and arboreal scent
And fresh young element
Of blood in every osseous vein of time,
New senses more sublime !
Should it not be that the ill days are past
And my soul lost at last,
Lost in thy bosom who art mother of all
Ere the first was, to fall
After the end. And then, O soul endued
(In this my solitude)
With all the thousand elements of life,
Shall I not call thee wife ?
O Muse long wooed !

Long called to in the forest, on the mountain,
Reached after in the fountain,
Grasped in the slumberous sea,
And yet, ever, aye, ever ! escaping me !

But here where the wise pen
And silver cadences outrunning song,
And clear sweet clean-chiselled English, sharp
    and strong,
Of the one man [1] among the latter men
Who lived with Nature, saw her face to face,
And died not : here in this consummate place,
Immortal now, though the Antarctic sent
Its mightiest coldest wave and rose and rent
The coral and annihilated land,
Or though the swarthy hand
Or foot misshapen of the Hephaestian,
(Hating the air-breathing man,
In such sweet love as dwells, above all other
    places
Here, in our hearts and faces,
Nature's and man's) if his coarse hand or
    foot,
The implacable forceful brute,
Shifted towards the bellows, and one blast
Blew through all the air aghast
And in one vast Titanic war,
Almighty avenging roar,
Oahu flung skywards blown in dust—and
    was no more—
Even then immortal stands
This loveliest of all lands,
Lovelier even than they
Know in Elysian paths, heroic bands
Treading dim gardens brighter than the day,
Even in his voice who is passed, and shall no
    pass away !
Here therefore I know Nature ; I am filled
With dew not earth-distilled
As I have prayed in vain, not vainly willed.
Now all the earth is stilled ;
But ever the monotonous sea
Keeps solemn symphony,
Tuning my lyre to her own melody,
Not understandable in colder lands
Where no man understands

[1] R. L. Stevenson.

More than the mart ; the raucous ironshod
Feet, smashing verses ; the hard heavy hands
Of time : the hateful laugh where whoredom
    trod ;
The savage snarl of man against his friend :—
How should he (such an one) perceive the end,
Or listen to the voice of Nature, know it for
    the voice of God ?

EPODE.

NATURE.

Lo ! in the interstellar space of night,
    Clothed with deep darkness, the majestic
    spaces
Abide the dawn of deity and light,
    Vibrate before the passionless pale faces
Shrined in exceeding glory, eremite.
    The tortoise skies in sombre carapaces
Await the expression and the hour of birth
In silence through the adamantine girth.

I rose in glory, gathered of the foam.
    The sea's flower folded, charioting me risen
Where dawn's rose stole from its pearl-
    glimmering home,
    And heaven laughed, and earth : and mine
    old prison,
The seas that lay beneath the mighty dome,
    Shone with my splendour.  Light did first
    bedizen
Earth with its clusters of fiery dew and spray,
When I looked forth and cried " It is the
    day ! "

The stars are dewdrops on my bosom's space ;
    The sun and moon are glances through my
    lashes,
Long, tender, rays of night ; my subtle face
    Burns through the sky-dusk, lightens, fills,
    and flashes
With solemn joy and laughter of love ; the
    grace
    Of all my body swaying stoops and dashes
Swift to the daisy's dawn of love : and
    swiftest,
O spirit of man, when unto me thou liftest !

Dawn shakes the molten fire of my delight
　　From the fine flower and fragrance of my
　　　　tresses !
Sunset bids darken all my body's light,
　　Mixing its music with the sad caresses
Of the whole world : I wheel in wingless flight
　　Through lampless space, the starless
　　　　wildernesses !
Beyond the universal bounds that roll,
There is the shrine and image of my soul.

Nature my name is called.　O fruitless veil
　　Of the strange self of its own self begotten !
O vision laughterless !　O shadowy tale !
　　O brain that halts before its thought for-
　　　　gotten !
Once all ye knew me—ere the earth grew
　　pale,
　　And Time began, and all its fruit lay
　　　　rotten,
Once, when thou knewest me indeed, and fed
At these strong breasts—Ah ! but the days
　　are dead !

Now, in the dusty corridors of Time,
　　I am forgotten : Gaian [1] language falters
If I would teach thee half an hint sublime
　　Shed of the rayless fire upon my altars.
Vain are the light and laughter of man's
　　rime,
　　Vain the large hymns, and soaring songs
　　　　and psalters !
My face, my breast, no soul of man uncovers,
Nor is my bed made lovely with my lovers !

I long for purple and the holier kiss
　　Of mortal lyrist ; in these arms to gladden ;
To take him to the spring and source of bliss,
　　And in his vast embrace to rouse me,
　　　　madden
Once with the light of passion, not to miss
　　Uttermost rapture till the sweet loves
　　　　sadden
To sweeter peace thrilled with young
　　ecstasy—
Ah ! man's high spirit may not reach to Me !

[1] *I.e.*, terrestrial : from Gaia, a form of γῆ,
the earth.

I am Nature and God : I reign, I am, alone.
　　None other may abide apart : they perish,
Drawn into me, into my being grown.
　　None other bosom is, to bear, to nourish,
To be : the heart of all beneath my zone
　　Of blue and gold is scarlet-bright to cherish
My own's life being, that is, and is not other ;
For I am God and Nature and thy Mother.

I am the thousand-breasted milky spouse,
　　Virginal also : Tartarus and Gaia
Twinned in my womb, and Chaos from my
　　brows
　　Shrank back abashed, my sister dark and
　　　　dire,
Mother of Erebus and Night, that ploughs
　　With starry-sandalled feet the fields of fire ;
My sister shrank and fell, the infernal gloom
Changed to the hot sweet shadow of my
　　womb.

I am : that darkness strange and uterine
　　Is shot with dawn and scented with the
　　　　rose ;
The deep dim prison-house of corn and wine,
　　Flowers, children, stars, with flame far
　　　　subtler glows
Formless, all-piercing, death-defying, divine,
　　A sweet frail lamp whose shadow gleams
　　　　and shows
No darkness, is as light is where its rays
Cross, interweave, and marry with the day's !

I am : the heart that flames from central Me
　　Seeks out all life, and takes again, to
　　　　mingle
Its passion with my might and majesty,
　　Till the vast floods of the man's being tingle
And glow, self-lost within my soul and sea
　　Of love, and sun of utter light, and single
Keen many-veinèd heart : our lips and kisses
Marry and muse on our immortal blisses.

I am : the greatest and the least : the sole
　　And separate life of things.　The mighty
　　　　stresses
Of worlds are my nerves twitching.　Branch
　　and bole
Of forests waving in deep wildernesses

Are hairs upon my body.  Rivers roll
  To make one tear in my superb caresses,
When on myself myself begets a child,
A system of a thousand planets piled !

I am : the least, the greatest : the frail life
  Of some small coral-insect still may tremble
With love for me, and call me queen and wife ;
  The shy plant of the water may dissemble
Its love beneath the fronds ; reply to strife
  With strife, and all its tiny being crumble
Under my rough and warrior husband-kiss,
Whose pain shall burn, and alter, and be bliss !

I am : no word beside that solemn one
  Reigns in sound's kingdom to express my
    station,
Who, clothed and crowned with suns beyond
    the sun,
  Bear on the mighty breast of foam Tha-
    lassian,
Bear on my bosom, jutting plenilune,
  Maiden, the fadeless Rose of the Creation !
The whole flower-life of earth and sky and sea
From me was born, and shall return to me !

I am : for men and beings passionate,
  For mine own self calm as the river-cleaving
Lotus-borne lord of Silence : I create
  Or discreate, both in my bosom heaving :
My lightest look is mother of a Fate :
  My fingers sapphire-ringed with sky are
    weaving
Ever new flowers and lawns of life, designed
Nobler and newer in mine olden mind.

I am : I am not, but all-changing move
  The worlds evolving in a golden ladder
Spiral or helical, fresh gusts of love
  Filling one sphere from the last sphere
    grown gladder ;
All gateways leading far to the above.
  Even as the bright coils of the emerald adder
Climb one by one in glory of sunlight, climb
My children to me up the steep of Time.

I am : before me all the years are dead,
  And all the fiery locks of sunrise woven
Into the gold and scarlet of my head :
  In me all skies and seas are shaken and
    cloven :

All life and light and love about me shed
  Begotten in me, in my moving moven,
Are as my tears : all worlds that ever swam
As dew of kisses on my lips : I am.

But thou, chief lover, in whose golden heart
  The melody and music lifts its pæan,
Whose lyre fulfilled of me, fathered of Art
  And that Sun's song beyond the Empyrèan,
Who art myself, not any more apart,
  Having called my children by the call
    Pandean,
Mellowed with Delphian gold, the Ephesian
  quiver,
To float down Time for ever and for ever ;—

I am thy lyre and thou mine harper : thou
  My music, I thy spirit : thou the lover
And I the bride : the glory of my brow
  Deeper delight, new ardour, to discover
Stoops in thine heart ; my love and light endow
  Thy life with fervour as I bend me over
The starry curve and surface of the sea,
And kiss thy very life out into me.

O central fountain of my yearning veins !
  O mountain single-soaring, thou art blended
Into my heaven : prescient of the pains
  That shall bring forth —what worlds ? my
    heart is rended !
My womb reverberates the solar strains,
  The lyre vibrating in me : sharp and
    splendid
My face glows, gladdens ; nuptial ecstasy
Is all the guerdon and the spoil of me !

I am : the universe grown old must bear
  A scion ere it sink to dædal slumber.
Thou art my strength, and I am only fair.
  Our kisses are as stars ; our loves en-
    cumber
With multitude the fields of space, and where
  Our kisses tune the worlds, their lives out-
    number
The moments of eternity : apart
I am for ever : and, in me, thou art !

EXPLICIT LIBER PRIMUS.

# LIBER SECUNDUS VEL AMORIS

TO

## MARY BEATON

#### WHOM I LAMENT

" The Kabbalists say that when a man falls in love with a female elemental—undine, sylph gnome, or salamandrine, as the case may be—she becomes immortal with him, or otherwise he dies with her. . . . The love of the magus for such beings is insensate, and may destroy him."—*Eliphas Levi.*

"Orpheus for the love he bare to his wife, snatcht, as it were, from him by untimely Death, resolved to go down to Hell with his harp, to try if he might obtain her of the infernal power."—*The Wisdom of the Ancients.*

ORPHEUS, FINDING EURYDICE DEAD, STUNG BY A SERPENT, LAMENTS OVER HER.

COME back, come back, come back, Eurydice !
 Come back to me !
Lie not so quiet, draw some faint sharp breath !
 It is not death :
It cannot, must not be, Eurydice.
 Come back to me !
Let me as yet lament not ! Let me stoop !—
 Those eyelids droop
Not with mere death, but dreams, Eurydice !
 Come back to me !

O you that were my lover and my wife !
 Come back to life !
Come back, breathe softly from the breast of gold
 These arms enfold.
Give me your lips and kiss me once ! O wife,
 Come back to life !
Nay, let the wind but stir the silky hair,
 (God's lesser air,
Not His full blossom of woman's breath !)
 O wife,
 Come back to life !

Stir once, move once, rise once, Eurydice !
 Be good to me !
Rise once.—O sleep not ! Listen ! Is not all
 Nature my thrall ?
Once only : be not dead, Eurydice !
 Be good to me !
I love you—be not dead !—rise up and say
 " I feigned, I lay
Thus so you kissed me "—O Eurydice,
 Be good to me !

There is not one sweet sigh of all the old sighs—
 Open your eyes !
Not one warm breath of the young breast : no sleep
 Could be so deep.
The last pale lotus opens to the skies.
 Open your eyes !
Lift the blue eyelids under the deep lashes
 Till one light flashes !
Wake with one supreme sigh like the old sighs !
 Open your eyes !

I cannot leave you so, Eurydice.
 Come back to me !
Just in the triumph, in love's utmost hour,
 Life's queenliest flower—

All shattered, overblown.  Eurydice,
   Come back to me !
I cannot have you dead, and live : let death
   Strangle my breath
Now as I kiss you still—Eurydice !
   Come back to me !

Fling down the foolish lyre, the witless power!
Cast the dead laurel in the dust !  The flower
   Of all the world is marred, the day's desire
Distorted in the eclipse, the sun's dead hour.

Let me fall down beside thee !  Let me take
The kisses that thou canst not give, and slake
   Despair in purposeless caresses, dire
Shames fang-wise fastened of the eternal
   snake.

Is there no warmth where beauty is so bright ?
No soul still flickering in the lambent light
   Still shed from all the body's excellence ?
No lamp unchidden of the utter night ?

Cannot my life be molten into thee,
Or thy death fall with rosier arms on me,
   Or soul with soul commingle without sense,
As the sun's rays strike deep into the sea ?

O beauty of all beauty—central flower
Of all the blossoms in the summer's bower !
   Fades not all Nature in thy fall ? the sun
Not darken in the miserable hour ?

I hate all Nature's mockery of life.
The laugh is grown a grin ; the gentle strife
   Of birds and waves and winds at play is
     grown
A curse, a cruelty.   My wife ! my wife !

I am broken, I cannot sleep, I cannot die.
Pain, pain for ever !  Nature is a lie,
   The gods a lie.   Myself? but I am found
Sole serious in the hateful comedy.

Blackness, all blackness !  How I hate the
   earth,
The curse that brought my being into birth.
   I, loving more her loveliness, am bound
And broken—thrice more bitter for my
   mirth !

Song, was it song I trusted in ?  Or thou,
Apollo, was it thou didst bind my brow
   With laurel for a poison-wreath of hell
To sear my brain and blast my being now ?

A band of most corroding poison wound
Dissolving with its venom the profound
   Deep of my spirit with its terrible
Sense without speech and horror without
   sound.

A devil intertwining in my heart
Its cold and hideous lust, a twiforked dart
   Even from the fatherly and healing hand—
The double death without a counterpart

In hell's own deepest pit, far, far below
Phlegethon's flame and Styx's stifling flow,
   Far below Tartarus, below the land
Thrust lowest in the devilish vertigo.

If I could weep or slumber or forget !
If love once left me, with his eyelids wet
   With tender memory of his own despair
Or frozen to a statue of regret !

If but the chilling agony, that turns
To bitter fever-heat that stings and burns
   Would freeze me, or destroy me, or impair
My sense, that it should feel not how it
   yearns !

Or if this pain were only pain, and not
A deadness deeper than all pain, a spot
   And central core of agony in me,
One heart-worm, one plague-leprosy, one
   blot

Of death, one anguish deeper than control ?—
Then were I fit to gain the Olympian goal
   And fling forth fiery wailings to the sea,
And tune the sun's ray to my smitten soul !

How should I sing who cannot even see ?
Grope through a mist of changeless misery.
   An age-long pain—no time in wretched.
     ness !—
As of an hammer annihilating me

With swift hard rhythm, the remorseless
  clang ;
Or as a serpent loosening his fang
  To bite more deeply—this inane distress
More than despair or death's detested pang.

I live—that shames me !  I am not a man.
Nothing can I to sharpen or to span
  My throat with iron fingers, or my sword
In my heart's acid where the blood began

Long since to leap, and now drops deadly slow,
Clotted with salt and sulphur and strong woe.
  I shall not die : the first sight of the sward
Stained with the spectral corpse had stung
  me so,

Not stabbed me, since I saw her and survive.
I shall not die—Ah ! shall I be alive ?
  This hath no part in either : bale and bliss
Forget me, careless if I rot or thrive.

Heaven forgot me—or she were not dead !
And Hades— or I should not raise my head
  Now, and look wildly where I used to kiss,
Gaze on the form whence all but form has fled !

I am alone in all the universe,
Changed to the shape and image of a curse,
  Muffled in self-confusion, and my brain
Wakes not nor sleeps : its destiny is worse.

It thinks not, knows not, acts not, nor
  appeals,
But hangs, remembers : it abides and feels
  As if God's vulture clung to it amain,
And furies fixed with fiery darts and wheels

Their horror, thought-exceeding, manifold,
Vertiginous within me—and the cold
  Of Styx splashed on me, making me im-
  mortal,
Invulnerable in its bitter mould ;

Leaving its own ice, penetrating streams,
Grim streaks, and dismal drops, abysmal
  beams
  Thrown from the gulph thorough the place
  and portal,
Each drop o'erladen with a curse that steams

Unnatural in the coldness : let me be
Alone, inviolate of eternity !
  Let all the winds of air leave me, nor fan :
Nor wash me all the waves of all the sea !

Let all the sun's light and the moon's be
  blind,
And all the stars be lampless to my mind,
  Until I see the destiny of man
And span the cruelty that lurks behind

Its beauty, and its glory, and its splendour !—
The girl-babe's face looks up to the mother
  tender,
  Looks for a kiss in dumb desire, and finds
Her jaws closed trap-like to expunge and
  end her !

Let all the life and dream and death be done,
And all the love and hate be woven in one,
  All things be broken of the winter winds,
No soul stand up and look upon the sun !

Save only mine !—that my voice may con-
  found
The universe, and spell the mighty sound
  To shake all heaven and earth, to mingle
  hell
In chaos, in some limitless profound ;

That it may tear Olympus from its place,
Mix it with Hades, change the Ocean space,
  Level the tides of time that sink and swell,
And curse my very father to his face !

O father, father Apollo, did I wrong
Thy chariot and thy horses in my song ?
  Why clove thine arrow the unseated air,
The heaven void of thee, why the thunder-
  thong

Slipped from the tether, and the fatal stone
Sped not to my heart, not to mine alone ?
  Ah why not ? but to hers as she lay sleep-
  ing
By hate, not fate, quelled, fallen, and over-
  thrown ?

She lies so pitiful and pure—and I,
Breast to her breast, mouth to her mouth, I
    lie,
Hand upon hand, and foot on foot, sore
    weeping—
Can she not live again or I not die?

As the old prophet on the child I fall[1]
And breathe—but no breath answers me at
    all.
All of my kisses stir no blush, no sigh ;
She will not hear me ever if I call !


Let the far music of oblivious years
    Sound in the sea beneath !
Are not its waters one with all my tears ?
Hath Atropos no comfort in her shears ?
    No Muse for me one wreath ?

Were I now dead and free to travel far
    Whither I will, ah me !
Not whither I must—were there no avatar
Drawn like my love from some close kindred
    star?
    No shape seen on the sea?

Were I now free of this intense desire,
    By swift magician power
I might fly westward shod with wings of fire
And find my love, and in her arms expire,
    Or wed her for an hour.

(Not for an hour as man, but even as God
    Whose day is like an aeon.
Love hath nor station, stage, nor period :
But is at once in his inane abode
    Beneath the spring Dircean.)

Alas, the will flies ere the power began.
    Lo, in the Idan grove
Invoking Zeus to swell the power of Pan,
The prayer discomfits the demented man !
    Lust lies as still as love.[2]

[1] Referring to the story of Elisha.
[2] This obscure stanza means : that the invocation of high and pure forces cannot be
diverted to low and impure ends ; because the
man becomes identified with what he invokes,
of necessity.
VOL. III.

Therefore in memory only is there life,
    And in sweet shapes of art :
The same thought for the ointment and the
    knife—
Oh lightning ! blast the image of my wife
    Out of my mind and heart !

How can one hour dissolve a year's delight ?
One arrow striking the full eagle-flight
    Drop him so swift, giving no time to die,
No dusk to herald and delay the night?

A serpent stung her sleeping : if the abyss
Know any cell more dolorous than this,
    Were there a sharper tooth to destiny
Than this that strikes me in the dead girl's
    kiss :—

Oh if aught bitterer could be, could know,
If ninefold Styx could gather in its flow
    Cocytus, Phlegethon, and Acheron,
All mixed to one full flood of hate and woe :

And poisoned by all venom like to his
Who kissed Eurydice the traitor-kiss :—
    Then let them sting me fourfold, nor atone
Then for the eightfold misery of this !

Is not some justice somewhere?  Where is
    he
Hateful to God and man, a misery
    To his own vileness by exceeding it,
Who crawls God-cursed throughout eternity

Nay ! sure he lives, and licks his slavered
    lips,
Laughing to think how the sweet morsel
    slips,
    The breast-flower of my bride ; the dainty
    bit
Fit for—ah God ! the pearl-smooth blossom
    drips

Poisonous blood that will not poison me,
Though I drink deep its fierce intensity.
    My lips closed silent on her bosom's light,
The stung blood springs—like pearls beneath
    the sea

Whose moony glimmer hath a purple vein
Hidden—so I athirst of the sad stain
  Drink up her body's life, as if to spite
Its quiet, as if the venom were to drain

Into my life—that hurts me not at all,
Struck by a stronger buffet : let me call
  All deaths ! they come not, seeing I am
    broken
In this one horror where a man may fall.

I am alive, and live not : I am dead,
And die not : on my desolated head
  No dew may drop, no word of God be
    spoken,
None heard, if by some chance some word
  be said.

The wheels of Fate are over me ; quite
    crushed
Lies my pale body where her body blushed,
  Quite dead ! there is no single sob that
    stirs,
No pulse of blood of all that filled and
  flushed

Her cheek and mine, her breast and mine :
    and lo !
How sunset's bloom is faded on the snow !
  There is no laugh of all those laughs of
    hers,
Those tender thrills of laughter I used to
  know.

Nor in all nature weep the careless eyes,
Nor any soul of life may sympathise,
  All I once was in this is torn and rended—
Scorned and forsaken the lone lyre lies.

Hath that not yet some sympathy with me ?
That lyre that was myself, my heart's decree
  And ruler, subtle at the dawn, and splendid
Noonwards, and soft at day's declivity !

I flung it in my anguish to the ground.
I raise it, and its music hath not found
  One string or snapped or loosened, and
    the tune
Is the old triumph garlanded and crowned !

Folly and hate !   Blithe mockery of sorrow !
Shrill me no harsh lies of some sweet to-
    morrow ! [1]
  Soothe me no hateful mysteries of the
    moon,
How one life lends what other lives may
  borrow !

I hate that foolish counterfoil of grief
That one pain to its friend may give relief—
  Eurydice replace Eurydice
Long hence—no separation sharp and brief

But dwelling in the intermediate
Halls between Hades and the house of Fate :
  Atropos cut, and pass to Clotho, and she
Respin the shuttle in some other state.

What shall it boot me now to gather flowers
From this young hope to wile the angry
    hours ?
  That many thousand years shall pass, and
    show
Eurydice again amid her bowers,

Forgetting, and myself again be born,
Clasp her grave beauty in the middle corn,
  Forgetting also : Time as fallen snow
Blotting the mind and memory that adorn

At least our present littleness : nor hope
Of larger excellence, extended scope,
  Shall help me here, forgetting : nothing
    skills
Of this poor truth—to flatter with the trope !

Wooing in mockery !—nothing skills but this
To raise her now, and resuspire the kiss,
  United by the splendour of the will's
Success—to marry, to be made of bliss,

I care not whether here or there : to live
In memory and identity : to give
  No part of self or soul to Lethe's water :
To grapple Nature, interpose an "if"

[1] Follow references to various ancient theories
of immortality, reincarnation, and so on.

In her machinery of conditioned mood ;
Suspending law, suspending amplitude
　Of all Her function ; to espouse her
　　daughter
In forced embrace lasciviously rude,

Indecorous, shameful to the eternal " must " !
Law may be mercy, mercy never just !
　Thus I would alter, and divide her ways,
And let her wheels grind themselves down
　to dust.

One supernatural event—but one !—
Should scale Olympus, shattering the throne
　Of the Ægis-bearing Father : and the days
Of all the Universe be fallen and done.

Well then ?　O sceptred Splendour ! dost
　Thou see
How little means Thy Universe to Me?
　How petty looks Thy will to My desire ?
Hebe and Hera to Eurydice ?

I, knowing all the progress of the earth,
The dim procession, altering death and birth,
　The Seven Stairs, the gusts of life in fire
And Love in Life, and all the serpent girth

Of sevenfold twining worlds and sevenfold
　ways
And nights made sevenfold of the sevenfold
　days
All the vast scheme evolving into man,
And upward, onward, through Olympian haze

Into the crowning spiritual mist,
Where spirit in the spirit may subsist,
　Evolve itself in the amazing plan
Through many planes, as shining amethyst

Melts to the sapphire's sombre indigo,
And lifts, still sapphire, to the ocean glow ;
　Thence into emerald and the golden light,
Till ruby crowns the river's living flow

And glory of colour in the sun's own flame—
Beyond, to colours without sense or name,
　Impossible to man, whose vivid sight
Would blast him with their splendour as they
　came

Flashing through spiritual space, withdrawn
Now, and now flung triumphant in the dawn
　Not of mere sun's rise, but before the birth
Of a new system on the unfolded lawn

Of space beyond the sceptre of the Gods !
I, seeing all this, would foil Time's periods
　For one small woman on this one mean
　　earth,
Would spoil the plan of the inane Abodes,

Throw out of gear all Nature's enginery
For such a grain of tinsel dust as I,
　Reluctant to be mangled in the wheel—
Looks other meanness so contemptibly ?

Yet I persist.　Thou knowest, O most High
　Zeus,
When Hera to thine Io did refuse
　Peace, and the gadfly bit like barbèd steel
Those limbs with dews of love once lying
　loose,

When thy vast body boarded her, wrapped
　round
Her senses with a mist of being profound,
　A flame-like penetration, serpentine,
Twining and leaping without end or bound,

Inevitable as the grasp of Fate :—
Thou, reft of her by envy of thy mate
　Didst shake the heaven with bellowings
　　undivine,
And rooted stars from their primeval state.

Not without law, sayest thou ?　Almighty
　Zeus,
Am I not also mothered of a Muse ?
　Let there be law ! untimely to release
This soul untinctured of the Stygian dews,

Unsprinkled of Lethean lotus-drops !
Life grows so steadily, so sudden stops—
　(Surely no part in Nature's moving peace !)
Thus, when the young, like tempest-stricken
　crops

Unripe, are　blasted　in　the　blossoming
　spring—
This is a miracle, not the other thing !
　Nature insults herself, blasphemes her God,
Thus cutting short the life's hard happening.

Nor would I suffer thus, nor she repine
Had my wife faded (as rose-tinted wine
   Bleached in the sunlight) reached her
     period
And fallen gently in the arms divine,

Caressing arms of pale Persephone,
And bathed her in death's river tenderly,
   Washing the whole bright body, the long
     limbs,
The clothing hair, the face, the witchery

Of all the smiling shape in the dark stream,
As one who gathers the first floral beam
   Of daylight by the water, dives and swims
Deep in cool alleys, softer than a dream :

So, rising to the other bank, aglow
With the bright motion and the stream's
     young flow,
   She might discover the Elysian ground,
And find me waiting, find me sad and slow

Pacing the green flower-lighted turf, and leap
Into my body's kisses, into sleep :—
   Sweeter this latter bridal than we found
The first, now lost in time's eternal deep.

It is not cruel if the ripe fruit fall—
But never an elegy funereal
   Wept for untimely burial, but cried
Aloud against the Fates, forebore to call

In pity or passion on the Gods of peace ;
But cursed, but wailed, nor bade its sharp
     tongue cease
   Until the lightning spat, sharp to divide
Bone from its marrow for their blasphemies !

So I should curse, unless indeed my grief
Be not too great to yield me such relief.
   Methinks a sob must start and mar the
     roar
Of loud harsh laughing bitter unbelief

Scarring the sky with poisonous foam of
     song.
Also, what curse might remedy the wrong?
   Are not all feuds forgotten in a war ?
All stars exhausted in Astræa's throng

When the swift sun leaps skyward ? Let
   me speak
Words rather of wisdom : hate may rage and
     wreak
Vengeance in vain if wisdom smile beyond,
Too high to care, too ultimate to seek.

The bitterest sorrow of all sorrow is this :
I had no time to catch one last long kiss,
   Nor bid farewell, nor lay one lily-frond
Of resurrection for the sign of bliss,

Remembrance of some immortality
Affirmed if not believed : alas for me
   That might not interchange the last sad
     vows,
Nor close the blue eyes clearer than the sea

Before they darkened, and the veil of death
Shrouded their splendour: still there lingereth
   Some sad white lustre on the icy brows,
Some breast-curve surely indicating breath,

Some misty glamour of deep love within
The eye's cold gleam ! some dimple on the
     chin
   Hinting of laughter: even now she seems
A folded rosebud, where the ivory skin

Closes the ripe warm centre flower, the
     mind,
The spirit that was beautifully kind,
   The sense of beauty shadowed in deep
     dreams,
Sent through the horn gates by some sleepy
     wind.

All lingers: all is gone : a little while,
And all the live sweet rapture of the smile
   Of her whole being is discomfited,
The body broken, desolated, vile,

Till nought remains but the memorial urn
Of deep red gold, less golden than did burn
   Once the strong breast : the ash within is
     shed,
Dust given for flowers : what memory shall
     turn

Unto the flowers, think worthy to remember
How the dust scattered from their fading
    ember
  Is their own sign and seal of fatherhood,
Grey seas of sorrow sun-kissed into amber.

Above me hangs the sun : horrid he hangs,
A rayless globe of hell, shooting forth fangs
    Snake-wise to parch and burn my solitude,
Nor leave me quiet lamenting, with these
    pangs

Tearing my liver, more Promethean
Than ever Titan knew—the sunbright span
    Of narrow water mocks me, brightening
Far to the indigo Ionian.

The sun hangs high, as in the Arabian tale
Enchanted palaces defy the gale,
    Perched upon airy mountains, on the wing
Of genii poised, souls suffering and pale

With their long labour : wizard spire and
    dome
That maidens grown magicians had for home,
    Where the charmed sword and graven
    talisman
Held them supremely floating on the foam

Where cloudier seas innavigably roll,
Misty with elemental shape or soul,
    Thin grey essential nebulæ of man,
Caught in the mesh of magical control !

All these are beautiful and shapen so
That every bastion flames a separate glow
    Of changing colour : all detestable,
Abhorrent, since the goodly-seeming show

Is one large lie of cruelty and lust,
Carven from spectral images of dust,
  Founded on visions of the accursed well,
And built of shame and hatred and distrust,

And all things hateful and all lying things—
O song ! where wanderest on forgetful wings?
    Shall these wild numbers help thee to thine
    own,
Or change the winter's gramarye to spring's ?

Rather beguile the tedious mourning hours
With memory of the long-forgotten bowers,
    Where loves resurged from cave and grove
    to throne,
From nuptial banquet to the bed of flowers !

Rather forget the near catastrophe,
And turn my music toward Eurydice,
    Awake in day-dream all the ancient
    days,
When love first blossomed on the springing
    tree !

Let me recall the days beyond regret,
And tune my lyre to love, sharpen and set
    The strings again to the forgotten ways,
That I may tread them over, and forget !

In child-like meditative mood
    I wandered in the dell,
Passed through the quiet glades of the
    wood,
    And sought the haunted well,
Half hopeful that its solitude
    Might work some miracle.

The oaks raised angry hands on high :
    The willows drooped for tears :
The yews held solemn ceremony,
    Magical spells of years.
I saw one cypress melancholy,
    A prince among his peers.

So, turning from the arboreal seat
    And midmost hollow of earth,
I followed Hamadryads' feet
    That made at eve their mirth
To where the streamlet wandered fleet
    To show what time was worth.

I watched the waters wake and laugh
    Running o'er pebbly beaches,
Writing amazement's epitaph
    With freshets, turns, and reaches :—
The only tale too short by half
    That nature ever teaches.

Then growing grander as it swept
  Past bulrushes and ferns,
Gathering the tears that heaven had wept,
  The water glows and burns
In sunlight, where no shadows crept
  Around the lazy turns.

All on a sudden silence came
  Athwart some avenue
Where through the trees arrowed the flame
  From the exultant blue ;
And all the water-way became
  One heart of glittering dew.

The waters narrowed for a space
  Between twin rocks confined,
Carven like Gods for poise and grace,
  Like miracles for mind :
Each fashioned like a kissing face,
  The eyes for joy being blind.

The waters widened in a pool,
  Broad mirror of blue light.
The surface was as still and cool
  As the broad-breasted night.
Engraven of no mortal tool,
  The granite glistened white.

As if to shield from mortal gaze
  A nymph's immortal limbs,
The shadow of the buttress stays
  And dips its head and swims,
While moss engirdles it with grays
  And greens that dew bedims.

Now, at the last, the western end,
  Most miracle of all !
The groves of rock dispart and rend
  Their sacred cincture-wall ;
All tunes of heaven their rapture lend
  To make the waterfall.

There, steaming from the haze and mist
  Where dew is dashed in spray,
Rises a halo sunrise-kissed
  And kissed at close of day
From ruby unto amethyst,
  Within the veil of grey.

And there within the circled light
  I saw a dancing thing,
Most like the tender-leavèd night
  Of moonrise seen in spring,
A shadow luminous and white
  Like a ghost beckoning.

And then dim visions came to me,
  Faint memories of fear :
As when the Argo put on sea
  Such stories we did hear,
Stories to tremble at and flee—
  And others worth a tear.

I thought of how a maiden man
  Might hear a deadly song
And clasp a siren in his span,
  And feel her kiss grow strong
To drag him with caresses wan
  Into the House of Wrong.[1]

Another :[2] how the women grew
  Like vines of tender grape,
And how they laughed as lovers do,
  And took a lover's shape,
And how men sought them, free to woo—
  To leave them, no escape !

Another :[3] how a golden cup
  A golden girl would pour,
And whoso laughed and drank it up
  Grew wise and warrior :
But whoso stayed to smile and sup
  Returned—ah, never more !

And yet again [4]—a river steep,
  A maiden combing light,
Her hair's enchantment—she would weep
  And sing for love's delight,
Until the listener dropped to sleep
  In magic of her night.

[1] See Homer's Odyssey.
[2] See Lucian.
[3] Is this a perversion of the story of Calypso ?
[4] See Goethe's " Lorelei."

And then the maiden smoothed her tresses,
  And led him to the river,
Caught him and kissed with young caresses,
  And then—her cruel smiles quiver!
Beneath the waves his life represses
  For ever and for ever!

I knew the danger of the deed
  The while enrapt I gladdened.
My eyes upon the dancer feed
  As one by daylight saddened
After long night whose slumbers bleed,
  By dreams deceived and maddened!

It might be—the delusive dance,
  The shadowy form I saw,
Apollo's misty quivering lance
  Thrown to elude God's law;
It might be—doth the maid advance,
  Evanish, or withdraw?

So stung by certainty's mistrust,
  Or tranced in dream of sin,
Or blinded by some Panic dust,
  By Dionysian din
Deafened, arose the laughing lust
  To fling my body in!

I stood upon the rock, and cried,
  And held my body high
(Not caring if I lived or died)
  Erect against the sky:
Then plunged into the wheeling tide,
  And vanished utterly.

"O shape half seen of love, and ost
  Beneath time's sightless tide,
What obolus of the vital cost
  Remains, or may abide?
Or what perception memory steal,
Once passed upon the whirling wheel?

"O hope half held of love, and fled
  Beyond the ivory gate,
A dream gone from the hapless head
  By fury of a fate!
What image of the hope returns
But stings with agony that which yearns?

"O face half kissed in faith and fear,
  Eager and beautiful!
Drop for mortality one tear!
  For life one smile recall!
There is no passion made for me—
  Else were my water-well the sea."

Such tune my falling body snapped
  Within the sacred sides,
While the warm waves with laughter lapped,
  And changed their tunèd tides,
And all my being was enwrapped,
  A bridegroom's in a bride's.

Deep in the hollow of the place
  A starry bed I saw,
Gemmed with strange stones in many a space
  Of godlike rune and law.
Such fancies as the fiery face
  Of living Art might draw.

But rising up I lift my head
  Beyond the ripples clean:
My arms with spray dew-diamonded
  Stretched love-wise to my queen
That danced upon the light, and shed
  Her own sweet light between.

But never a mortal joy might know,
  Hold never a mortal lover!
Whose limbs like moonshine glint and glow,
  Throb, palpitate, and hover:—
Pale sunrise woven with the snow
  Athwart a larchen cover!

So danced she in the rainbow mist,
  A fairy frail and chaste,
By moon caressed, by sunlight kissed
  A guerdon vain and waste;
And the misery of her thankless tryst
  Stole on me as she paced.

For never her lips should be caressed
  By love's exulting stings,
Whose starry shape shone in the west,
  Held of the glimmering wings.
Her shadowy soul perceived the jest
  Of man and mortal things.

And there I vowed a solemn oath
    To Aphrodite fair,
Sealing that sacramental troth
    With a long curl of hair,
And the strange prayer's reiterant growth
    Sent shining through the air.

(*Invoking Aphrodite*)

    Daughter of Glory, child
    Of Earth's Dione mild
By the Father of all, the Ægis-bearing King !
    Spouse, daughter, mother of God,
    Queen of the blest abode
In Cyprus' splendour singly glittering.
    Sweet sister unto me,
    I cry aloud to thee!
I laugh upon thee laughing, O dew caught
    up from sea !

    Drawn by sharp sparrow and dove
    And swan's wide plumes of love,
And all the swallow's swifter vehemence,
    And, subtler than the Sphinx,
    The ineffable iynx [1]
Heralds thy splendour swooning into sense,
    When from the bluest bowers
    And greenest-hearted hours
Of Heaven thou smilest toward earth, a
    miracle of flowers !

    Down to the loveless sea
    Where lay Persephone
Violate, where the shade of earth is black,
    Crystalline out of space
    Flames the immortal face !
The glory of the comet-tailèd track
    Blinds all black earth with tears.
    Silence awakes and hears
The music of thy moving come over the
    starry spheres.

    Wrapped in rose, green and gold,
    Blues many and manifold,
A cloud of incense hides thy splendour of
    light ;

[1] An imaginary animal, sacred to Venus.

    Hides from the prayer's distress
    Thy loftier loveliness
Till thy veil's glory shrouds the earth from
    night ;
    And silence speaks indeed,
    Seeing the subtler speed
Of its own thought than speech of the Pan-
    dean reed !

    There no voice may be heard !
    No place for any word !
The heart's whole fervour silently speeds to
    thee,
    Immaculate ! and craves
    Thy kisses or the grave's,
Till, knowing its unworthiness to woo thee,
    Remembers, grows content
    With the old element,
And asks the lowlier grace its earlier music
    meant.

    So, Lady of all power !
    Kindle this firstling flower
The rainbow nymph above the waterfall
    Into a mortal shade
    Of thee, immortal maid,
That in her love I gather and recall
    Some memory mighty and mute
    In love's poor substitute
Of thee, thy Love too high, the impossible
    pursuit !

    Then from the cloud a golden voice
    Great harmonies persuade,
That all the cosmic lawns rejoice
    Like laughter of a maid ;
Till evolution had no choice,
    But heard it, and obeyed.

    " Show by thy magic art
    The hero-story !
Awake the maiden heart
    With tunes of glory !
With mortal joys and tears,
    Keen woes and blisses,
Awake her faiths and fears,
    Her tears and kisses !"

I caught the lavish lyre, and sate
Hard by the waterfall,
Twisting its sweetness intimate
Into the solemn call
Of many dead men that were great,
The plectron's wizard thrall.

Thus as she danced, nor ceased, nor
cared,
I set the sacred throng
Of heroes into acts that fared
In Argo light and long,
The foes they fought, the feats they dared,
In shadow-show and song.

(*The play of Argonautae is shadowed before them by Or-
pheus' magical might.*)

So faded all the dream: so stole
Some fearful fondness in her soul;
Even as a cloud thrilled sharply through
With lightning's temper keen and true,
Splitting the ether: so again
Grew on me the ecstatic pain,
Seeing her tremble in mid-air.
No flower so exquisitely fair
Shakes out its petals at the dawn;
No breath so beautiful is drawn
At even by the listening vale.
For oh! she trembled! Frail and pale,
Her looks surpassing loveliness
Lulled its own light to fond distress,
As if the soul were hardly yet
Fit to remember or forget
New-born! and though the goddess bade
The nymph-bud blossom to a maid,
And soulless immortality
Reach to a soul, at last to die,
For love's own sake, bliss dearly bought
For change's altering coin ill-wrought,
It seemed as though the soul were strange,
Not fledged, not capable to range
At random through the world of sense
Opened so swift and so intense
Unto the being. Thus she stood
Impatient on the patient flood
With wonder waking in her eyes.
Thus the young dove droops wing, and dies,

In wonder why the wingèd thing
Loosed from yon twanging silver string
Should strike, should hurt. But now she
wakes,
Wreathes like a waterfall of snakes
The golden fervour of her hair
About the body brave and bare
Starred in the sunlight by the spray,
And laughed upon me as I lay
Watching the change: First dawn of fire!
First ghost of nightfall's grey desire!
First light of moonrise! Then, as June
Leaps out of May, her lips took tune
To song most soft, a spiral spell,
A siren breathing in a shell.
The notes were clustered round the well
Like angels clustering round a god.
Let memory wake from its abode
Of dim precision lost for long
The grace and grandeur of the song!

Who art thou, love, by what sweet name I
quicken?
By whom, O love, my soul is subtly stricken?
O Love, O Love, I linger
On the dear word and know not any mean-
ing,
Nor why I chant; there is a whisper wean-
ing
My soul from depths I knew to depths I
guess,
Centred in two words only: "Love" and
"Yes."
What lyrist's gentle finger
Strikes out a note, a key, a chord unheard of?
What voice intones a song I know no word of?
Who am I, Love, and where?
What is the wonder of this troublous sing-
ing?
What is the meaning of my spirit's clinging
Still to the two sweet words: repeat, repeat!
"Yes, Love!" and "Yes, Love!" Oh the
murmur sweet!
The fragrance in the air!
I know not, I; amid the choral gladness
Steals an essential tremor as of sadness,
A grace-note to the bosom

Of music's spell that binds me, as in Panic
Dance to some grasp unthinkable, Titanic,
Unto the words fresh flowers that distil
Uttermost fragrance in the mind and will,
    The unsuspected blossom!
What is the change—new birth of spring-
        time kisses
Alone in all these water-wildernesses?
    What change? what loveliness!
Comes this to all? I heard my sisters crying
No tale like this—O! were I only lying
Asleep amid the ferns, my soul would weep
Over and over in its endless sleep;
    "Yes, love!" and "yes!" and "yes!"


So by some spell divinely drawn
She came to me across the dawn,
With open arms to me; and sobbed
"Yes, love!" and "Yes, love!" O how
        throbbed
The giant glory at my heart!
And I? I drew away, apart,
Lest by mere chance to me she came.
But curling as a wind-blown flame
She turned, she found me. As the dew
Melts in the lake's dissolving blue
So to my arms she came. And now,
Now, now I hold her!
                    Broke the brow
Of all wide heaven in thunder! Hear
Tremendous vortices of fear
Swirl in the ether. What new terror
Darkens the blue pool's silver mirror?
How bursts the mountain-chasm asunder?
Whose voice reverberates in thunder
Muttering what curse? The sun dissolves
In anguish; the mad moon revolves
Like a wild thing about its cage;
The stars are shaken in the rage
Of—who but Zeus? Before our gaze,
(My love's in shuddering amaze,
Of birth deceived and death forlorn,
And mine in anger, ay! and scorn!)
He stood--the mighty One! So earth
And heaven proclaimed that fearful birth:
So they grew silent lest he curse.
Dead silence hushed the universe;

And then in clear calm tones he spoke:
"Fools! who have meddled, and awoke
The inmost forces of the world!
One lightning from my hand had hurled
Both to annihilation's brink.
What foolish goddess bade ye think
Ye thus could play with thunder, roll
Your wheels upon the world, control
The stately being of a soul?
Just am I ever! Therefore know
The unrevengeful law of woe
That ye invoke. Thou seekest life,
Child of my water! Thou a wife,
Child of my sun! Draw living breath,
Maiden, and gain the guerdon—death!
Thou take the wife, and risk the fate
Æons could hardly culminate
To lose thy soul! Not two but one
Are ye. Together, as the stone,
The oak, the river, or the sea,
Mere elements of mine be ye,
Or both resolve the dreadful life,
And take death's prize! Take thou the
        wife,
Thou, who didst know. Her ignorance
Resolve itself upon a chance!
She shall decide the double fate.
Be still, my child, and meditate!
This is an hour in heaven." He ceased
And I was silent. She released
Her soul from that tremendous birth
Of fear in gentle-minded mirth.
"Great Sir!" she cried, "the choice is made!
An hour ago I was afraid,
Knew nothing, and loved not. But I
Know now not this you say—to die.
Some doubtful change! An hour ago
I was a nymph. I did not know
This change: but now for death or life
I care not. Am I not his wife?
I love him. Now I would not leave
That joy once tasted; shall not grieve
If even that should ever cease,
So great a pleasure (and a peace!)
I have therein. And by the sense
Of love's intuitive influence
I know he wills me to remain
Woman." "How frivolous and vain,

O Zeus," I cried, " art thou to rise
Out of Olympus' ecstasies !
Omnipotent ! but to control
The first breath of a human soul !—"
The thunder rolled through heaven again,
Void was the spring-delighted plain
Of that gigantic phantasy.
I turned to my Eurydice
Even as she turned.  The faint breath glows,—
The lightning of a living rose.
The bright eyes gleam—night's spotless stars
Glimmering through folded nenuphars.
The red mouth moves, still to the word :
" Yes, love ! " and " yes, love ! "   Then I
      heard
No sound and saw no sight—the world
Folded its mighty wings, and curled
Its passion round us ; bade forget
The joy with which our eyes were wet.
All faded, folded in the bliss ;
Unfolded the first fadeless kiss.


Then my soul woke, not sundering lips,
But winged against the black eclipse
Of sense : my soul on wings did poise
Her glory in the vast turquoise
Of the whole sky : expanded far
Beyond the farthest sun or star,
Beyond all space, all time.  I saw
The very limits of the law
That hath no bounds : beheld the bliss
Of that first wonder of the kiss
In its true self : how very love
Is God, and hath its substance of
Pure light : and how love hath its cause
Beyond religions, worlds, and laws ;
Is in itself the first : and moves
All evolution, and disproves
God in affirming God : all this
In that one rapture of the kiss
I knew, and all creation's pain
Fell into nothing in my brain,
As I, remaining man, involved
All life's true purpose, and dissolved
The phantoms (of itself create)
In a mysterious sweet state,
Wherein some tune began to move
Whose likeness and whose life was love.

Roll, strong life-current of these very veins,
    Into my lover's soul, my soul that is !
Thrill, mighty life of nerves, exultant strains
Triumphant of all music in a kiss !
    Fade ! fade, oh strenuous sense
    Into the soul intense
Of life beyond your weak imagining !
    And, O thou thought, dissever
    Thy airy life for ever
While the bright sounds are lifted up to spring
    Beyond this tide of being,
    Shadows and sense far fleeing
Into a shadow deeper than the Ocean
When passes all the mind's commotion
To a serener sky, a mighty calm emotion !


The whole world fades, folds over its wide
    pinions
Into a darkness deeper than its own.
Silence hath shattered all the dream-
    dominions
    Of life and light : the grey bird's soul is flown
    Into a soundless night,
    Lampless : a vivid flight
Beyond the thrones and stars of heaven down
    hurled,
    Till the great blackness heaves
    An iron breast, and cleaves
The womb of night, another mightier world.
    Lost is my soul, and faded
    The light of life that braided
    Its comet tresses into golden fire.
    Fade, fade, the phantoms of desire !
Speed, speed the song of love upon the living
    lyre !

Lo ! I abide not, and my lover's glory
    Abides not : in the swaying of those tides
Gathers beneath some mighty promontory
    One mightier wave, deep drowns it, and
        abides.
    Save that one wave alone
    Nought in the void is known,
That wave of love, that sole exultant splen·
    dour
        Throned o'er all being, supreme;
        A single-shining beam
    Burning with love, unutterably tender.

Ah! the calm wave retires.
Down all the fearful fires
Go thundering to darkness, so dissever
Their being from pure being, that the
    river
Of love is waveless now, and is pure love for
    ever.

Then mightier than all birth of stars or suns,
    Breaks the vast flood and trembles in its
    tide.
Serene and splendid shine the mystic ones,
    Exult, appal, reiterate, abide.
        Timid and fleet the earth
        Comes rushing back to birth,
Brighter and greener, radiant with gold
        Of a diviner sun,
        An exultation
Of life to life, of light to light untold.
        I?   I remain, and see
        Across eternity
My lover's face, and gaze, and know the
    worth
Of love's life to the glowing earth,
The kiss that wakes all life unto a better
    birth.

So the swoon broke.  I saw the face
(Shining with Love's reverberate grace)
Of my own love across the lawn,
As warm and tender as the dawn
Tinting the snows of heaven-born hills,
Enamelling the mountain rills
With light's chameleon-coloured dyes;
So shone the love-light in grey eyes,
Changing for laughter and for tears,
Changeless for joy of myriad years.
This, this endures; there is no lover,
No loved one ; all the ages cover
These things from sight : but this abides
Floating above the whelming tides
Of time and space : abides for ever
Whether the lovers join or sever.
There is no change : the love exists
Beyond the moment's suns and mists
In me, abiding : and I see
No lover in Eurydice,
Save that her kiss awoke in me

This knowledge, this supreme content,
Annihilation of the event,
The vast eternal element
Of utter being, bliss, and thought,
In dissolution direly wrought
Of sense, identity's eclipse,
The shadow of a lover's lips.
The awful steel of Death divides
The alternation of the tides
Of consciousness, and binds in bliss
The dead man to the girl's live kiss.


So sped my wooing : now I surely think
Suspended here upon the burning brink
    Of this dim agony, invading sense,
That bliss should still abide : but now I
    shrink,


Fall from the crags of memory, and abide
Now in this nature-life, basilisk-eyed,
    And serpent-stinging : yea, I perish thence.
That perishes which was : and I am tied


Unto myself : the "I" springs up again
Bound to the wheel of speedless sense and
    pain,
    None loosing me.    Past is the utter bliss ;
Present the strong fact of the death, the stain


Of the marred lives : I meditate awhile
Not on the mere light of the girl, the smile
    Deepening down to the extremest kiss ;
Not of the long joys of the little isle


Set in Ionian waters, where the years
Passed, one long passion, too divine for tears,
    Too deep for laughter : but on that divine
Sense beyond sense, the shadow of the
    spheres


Lost in the all-pervading light of love :
That bliss all passion and all praise above ;
    Impersonal, that fervour of the shrine
Changed to pure peace that had its substance
    of

Nothing but love : in vain my thoughts evoke
That light amidst the deadly night and smoke
  Of this dread hour : there's nothing serves
    nor skills
Here, since that hateful " I " of me awoke,

Making me separate from the wings of life.
Nothing avails me of the cruel strife
  With my own being : hideous sorrow fills
My heart—O misery ! my wife ! my wife !

Stay ! if I cannot be the Absolute,
Let me be man ! discard the wailing lute
  And wake the lyre : the mightier than me
Drag up the courage in me to dispute

The battle with despair : awake the strings
Stronger than earth, than the immortal kings
  Alike of death and life : invoke the sea
That I may cross her on the viewless wings

Of song, find out the desolating river
That girds the earth, unloose the silver quiver,
  Choosing an arrow of sharp song to run
Down to the waters that lament for ever :—

And cleave them !   That my song's insistent
  spell
Rive the strong gates of iron-builded hell,
  And move the heart of the ill-hearted one.
Yea ! let me break the portals terrible,

And bring her back ! come back, Eurydice !
Come back, pale wanderer to Eternity !
  Come back, my wife, my wife, again to
    love !
Come back, my wife ! come back, come back
    to me !

Enough ! my purpose holds : no feeble
  cries !
No sob shall shake these nerves : no ecstasies
  Of hope, or fear, or love avail to move
Those iron-hearted dooms and destinies.

I will be calm and firm as I were Zeus.
I will descend to Hades and unloose
  My wife : prevail on pale Persephone,
Laving her love-locks with exalted dews

Of stern grey song ; such roseate tunes
  espouse
That all the echoes of that lonely house
  Answer mé sob for sob, that she decree
With love deep-seated in her lofty brows

Forth sparkling : and with Hades inter-
  cede,
So as I stir the judgment-seat, and plead,
  The awful brows may lighten, and decree
My wife's return—a poet's lofty meed !

EXPLICIT LIBER SECUNDUS.

# LIBER TERTIUS VEL LABORIS

TO

THE MEMORY OF

## IEHI AOUR,

WITH WHOM I WALKED THROUGH HELL, AND COMPELLED IT

" Neither were his hopes frustrated : For having appeased them with the melodious sound of his voice and touch, prevailed at length so far, as that they granted him leave to take her away with him ; but on this condition, that she should follow him, and he not to look back upon her, till he came to the light of the upper World; which he (impatient of, out of love and care, and thinking that he was in a manner past all danger) nevertheless violated, insomuch that the Covenant is broken, and she forthwith tumbles back again headlong into Hell."—*The Wisdom of the Ancients.*

" Moody Pluto winks while Orpheus plays."—*Rape of Lucrece.*

## ORPHEUS TRAVELS TO HADES.

As I pass in my flight
  On the awed storm cloud,
    Steeps steeper than sleep,
Depths deeper than night,
  I have furrowed and ploughed
    (Deep calling to deep !)
Through the spaces of light,
  The heads of them bowed
    For the fears that weep,
And the joys that smite,
  And the loves disallowed.
    They are risen ; they leap ;
They wing them in white,
  Crying aloud
    Words widowed that keep
The frost of their fires forgotten and faded
from Memory's steep.

As I pass in my glory
  O'er sea and land,
    I smite the loud tune
From a fervid hand,
  By the promontory,
    The mountainous moon.

Vivid and hoary,
  Twin birds, as I hark,
Take fire, understand
  The ways of the dark,
    As an angel did guide me,
Waving the brand
  Of the dawn's red spark.
My measures mark
The influence fine
Of the voyage divine
Of the airy bark
Wherein I travel
O'er mountain and level,
  The land, and the sea.
And the beings of air,
  And the lives of the land,
And the daughters of fire,
  And the sons of the Ocean,
    Come unto me ;
My chariot bear,
  My tunes understand,
My love desire,
  Share my emotion.
They gather, they gather,
Apollo, O father !
  They gather around ;
  They echo the sound

Of the tune that rejoices,
   The manifold measure
Of feet tuned to voices
   Of terrible pleasure.
We pass in our courses
   Above the grey treasure
Of seas in Earth's forces,
   Her girdle, her splendour.
We bridle the horses
     Of sea as we lend her
   Tunes subtle and tender
To sink in her sources.
     The air's love ?   We rend her !
We pass to the West,
We sink on the breast
Of the Ocean to rest.

As I pass, as I madden
   In fury of flight,
The sea's billows gladden
   Invoking the light.
The depths of her sadden
   Not seeing the sight
Of the glorious one,
Whose steed is the Sun,
   Whose journey is certain,
Who speeds to the gate,
   The visible curtain
Of visible fate.
   My soul takes no hurt in
Their gloom : I await
   The portals to rise
   In the desolate skies.
I trust to my song
Irresistibly strong
   To sunder and shatter
   Those towers of matter.
They rise !  Oh !  They rise,
   The terrible towers
     Of Hades : they lift
Across the white skies
     Those terrible-cliffed
Rocks, where the hours
Beat vainly : where lies
     The horrible rift
Of the earth's green bowers
   Where the wan ships drift,
   And the sun's rays shift,

And the river runs
   Whose banks have no flowers,
Whose waves have no suns.
   Sheer to the terror
Of heaven, the walls
   Strike ; and the mirror
Of water recalls
   No truth, but dim error.
The soul of me falls
   Down to the glamour
Of dream ; and fear
   Beats like a hammer.
Here ! .it is here !
   Lost are my friends ;
The elements shrink
   Where the life-world ends
On the icy brink
   Of the sunless river ;
   Ends, and for ever !

I pass to the portals
   Of death in my flight.
   I sound at the gates.
I call the immortals
   Of death and of night.
   I call on the Fates
By the summons of light.
   The gates are rended ;
The rocks divide ;
   My soul hath descended
Abreast of the tide.
   I, single and splendid,
Death have defied !
I pass by the terrible gates and the guardians
   dragon-eyed.

   I thunder adown
     The vast abyss.
   (The journey's crown
     Is a woman's kiss !),
     What terrors to master !
     What fear and disaster
To gain the renown
   And the fadeless bliss !
I thunder aloud
   On the rocks as I fly,
Borne on a cloud
   In the gloomy sky.

Shaped like a shroud,
    Draped like a pall,
    I shrink not ; I fall
To the blackness below
With my soul aglow.
    No taint of a fear !
For I know, I know
    Eurydice near,
    Eurydice here !
The purpose divine
    Thrills my soul as wine.
Now I pass to the soul of the dark, confront-
ing the innermost shrine.


Hail to ye, warders
That guard the borders
    Of Hades !  All hail to ye, dwellers
        of night !
But I am the soul
In a man's control.
    Ye have nought to do with the dweller
        of light !


Hail to ye, hail
In the hollow vale,
    Your weapons are lifted against me
        in vain.
My lyre shall charm ye,
My voice disarm ye,
    For I am the soul overshadowed of
        pain !


Hail to ye, wardens
Of Death's grey gardens !
    O flowerless and vineless your bower-
        less vale !
But I must alone
To the wonderful throne.
    Let fall the vain spears, shadows !
        Hail to ye !  Hail !


The phantoms diminish,
    The shadows fall back.
        Lost in the vision
In fires that finish
    Stark and black
        With lust and derision ;

And all the illusion
    Is fallen to the ground.
        The warders are beaten
They go in confusion ;
    Their place is not found.
        The air hath eaten
With wide-gaping jaws
    A furious folk.
Lost is the cause
    In Tartarean smoke.
I, through the wall
    Of impassable gloom,
        Apart from the sun,
Pass as a ghost,
    Bearing the lyre.
The sad notes fall
    To the sorrowful womb ;
        One after one
They leap as a host
    With weapons of fire
On a desolate coast,
    Where love is lost
And the bitterness clings of fear, and the
    sadness dogs of desire !


Thrice girded with brass,
    Thrice bound with iron,
        The gate is in three
            Pillars of gold.
But I will pass
    (My heart as a lion,
        My lyre as a key !)
            To the gates of old,
To the place of despair
    And the walls of dread,
        The halls of the doomed,
        The homes of the dead,
The houses where
    The beautiful air
        Is as air entombed.
Nothing can shake
    Those terrible walls.
No man can wake
    With silver calls
The home of the lost and the lone, the gate
    of the Stygian thralls.

But thou, O Titan !
O splendour triform !
Gloomiest dweller
Of uttermost night !
My journey enlighten !
O soul of the storm !
Waker and queller
Of sombre delight,
Hecate ! hearken
The soul of my prayer !
Glitter and darken
Through sulphurous air !
Let the sacrifice move thee to joy, the in-
voker thy glory declare
In words that shall please
Thy terrible peace,
O speedy to save,
In flames of fine fire that bedew the deepest
Tartarean cave !

[*Invoking* HECATE]

O triple form of darkness ! Sombre splen-
dour !
Thou moon unseen of men ! Thou huntress
dread !
Thou crownèd demon of the crownless
dead !
O breasts of blood, too bitter and too tender !
Unseen of gentle spring,
Let me the offering
Bring to thy shrine's sepulchral glittering !
I slay the swart beast ! I bestow the bloom
Sown in the dusk, and gathered in the gloom
Under the waning moon,
At midnight hardly lightening the East ;
And the black lamb from the black ewe's
dead womb
I bring, and stir the slow infernal tune
Fit for thy chosen priest.

Here where the band of Ocean breaks the road
Black-trodden, deeply-stooping, to the
abyss,
I shall salute thee with the nameless kiss
Pronounced toward the uttermost abode
Of thy supreme desire.
I shall illume the fire
Whence thy wild stryges shall obey the lyre,

Whence thy Lemurs shall gather and spring
round,
Girdling me in the sad funereal ground
With faces turnèd back,
My face averted ! I shall consummate
The awful act of worship, O renowned
Fear upon earth, and fear in hell, and
black
Fear in the sky beyond Fate !

I hear the whining of thy wolves ! I hear
The howling of the hounds about thy form,
Who comest in the terror of thy storm,
And night falls faster ere thine eyes appear
Glittering through the mist.
O face of woman unkissed
Save by the dead whose love is taken ere
they wist !
Thee, thee I call ! O dire one ! O divine !
I, the sole mortal, seek thy deadly shrine,
Pour the dark stream of blood,
A sleepy and reluctant river
Even as thou drawest, with thine eyes on
mine,
To me across the sense-bewildering flood
That holds my soul for ever !

The night falls back ;
The shadows give place ;
The threefold form
Appears in the black,
As a direful face
Half seen in the storm.
I worship, I praise
The wonderful ways
Where the smitten rays
Of darkness sunder.
The hand is lifted ;
The gates are rifted ;
The sound is as thunder !
She comes to the summons,
Her face as a woman's,
Her feet as a Fear's,
Turned back on her path
For a sign of wrath :—
She appears, she appears !

I step to the river.
The lyre-strings quiver ;
The limbs of me shudder ;
　So cold is the mist ;
　　So dark is the stream ;
　　　So fearful the boat ;
　So horrid the rudder ;
　　So black is the tryst ;
　　　So frightful the beam ;
　　　So fearing to float ;
　The steersman so dread,
The shadowy shape of a ghost that guides
the bark of the dead !


Agèd and foul,
　His locks wreathe about him.
Horrid his scowl !
　　Haggard his soul !
　My songs control
While they fear him and doubt
　him.
I step in the boat,
　And the waters ache,
　And the old boards shake.
I shall hardly float,
　So heavy the soul
　　Of a living man
　On those waters that roll
Nine times around
　The fatal ground ;
Yet still to my singing we move on the river
Tartarean.


So darker and colder
　The stream as we float :
　　Blacker and bleaker,
　　　The mist on the river !
Stronger the shoulder
　Impels the sad boat.
　　Sadder and weaker
　　　Shudder and quiver
The notes of the lyre.
Quenched is my fire
　In the fog of the air.
Dim my desire
　Cuts through the snare.
The cold confounds me ;

The mist surrounds me ;
　Life trembles and lowers ;
Earth fades from my life.
The love of my wife,
　The light of the flowers,
　Earth's beautiful bowers.
Pass, and are not.
I am awed by the soul of the place, the hope-
less, the desolate spot.


Here is the wharf
　Wearily standing,
Misshapen and dwarf,
　Well fit for such landing !
Darker the bloom
　Of the night-flowers glows,
Shadowing the tomb,
　The indicible woes.
　　Dark and unlovely the cypress
　　　still grows
Deformed and blistered,
　Stunted and blackened,
Where the dead gleams glistered,
　The dusk-lights slackened.
Such is the shore
　Who reacheth may never
　　Return o'er the river !
Here pace evermore
　The terrible ghosts
Malignant of men,
　　Whose airless hosts
　　　In wars unjust
Went down to the den ;
　　Whose fury and lust
Turned poison or steel
　　On their own bad lives.
Here whirls the grim wheel
　Where the dead soul strives
Ever to climb
　To the iron nave,
Find Space and Time,
　Or a God to save,
　Or a way o'er the wave.
The Fate contrives
That he never thrives.
　Revolving anon,
　　The gleam is gone,
And the shadowy smile

Of Hecate darkens.
My sad soul hearkens ;
Moves fearfully on :-
O place of all places discrowned ! Lament-
ing, I linger awhile !

But fronting me tearful,
Me full of lament,
Shoots up the fearful
Den of the hound.
Ages they spent,
Gods, in the graving
That cavern profound,
That temple of hate,
Of horror and craving :—
O who shall abate
The moaning, the raving ?
Dark the dull flame
Of the altar, the flood
Of the black lamb's blood !
But who shall proclaim
That his soul can descry
The depth of that cavern immense where the
guardian of Orcus may lie ?

Sleepest thou, devil ?
Monster of evil !
Spawn of Typhon
By Echidna's lust !
The hateful revel
In blood and dust !
The obscene crone
And the monster's terror !
The hideous thrust
Of an unclean thirst
In the halls of error !
Expunged and accurst,
A lapping of hate,
A bride-bed rotten,
And thou, miscreate
And misbegotten !

O Hecate, hear me !
The terrors awaken,
The cavern is shaken
With horrible groanings.
Cryings and moanings
And howlings draw near me.

I tremble, I fear me !
My lyre is forsaken.
The heart of the hollow
Is helpless to bear
The notes of Apollo
Through Stygian air.

But heavier shrieking
Revolves and resounds
In the ghastly profounds ;
And the voice unspeaking
Of the hound of the damned
Runs eager, and bounds,
Malignantly crammed
In my ears, and the noise
Of infernal joys
In the houses of sin :—
Let me pass to a direr place, to the terrors
unspoken within !

Dead silence succeeds
The sound of the prayer.
Again the loud lyre
Shudders and bleeds
In the desolate air
With a sound as of fire !
The hound recedes ;
But the gates stand there,
Barring desire,
Barring the way
Of the dead unburied,
Unshrived, and unblessed ;
They stand and pray
In legions serried,
Beating the breast,
Tearing the hair,
Rending the raiment.
There is none to care.
No golden paymen
Availeth at all.
There is none to call ;
There is none to pity :
They stand in their pain
At the gate of the city.
There is none to feel
Or give relief;
They are lost ; they are vain ;
They are eaten of grief.

They are sore afraid,
  They are weary with care.
There is none to aid.
    There is none to pity.
They wail in despair
    At the gate of the city.


But I, shall I halt
  At the thrice-barred portal
In the lampless vault,
  I, half an immortal?
By love of my mother,
  By might of my lyre,
    By Nature's assistance,
I, I, not another
  Demand my desire,
    Rebuke your resistance,
By mighty Apollo
  Whose power yet abides,
Though his light may not follow
  Through Stygian tides!
By my power over things
  Both living and dead,
    By my influence splendid
    In heavenly court,
The song of me springs.
  My favour is dread.
    Be your portals rended!
    Your bolts be as nought!
The ethereal kings
  Encompass my head.
    My soul hath transcended
    The limits of thought!
Unbar me the gates!
  Revolve me the hinges!
Mine be the Fate!
  Mine be the springes
Wherein ye have taken
The spirits forsaken!
  But I, shall I quail at a nod?
  Shall I fail for a God?
Is the soul of me shaken?


Darklier winding
  And steeper the way,
Baffling and blinding
  Eyes used to the day.

Rocks cloven by thunder
  And shattered by storm
Awry or asunder
  Rise and reform
In marvellous coils
  Round the adamant road
Whose tangles and toils
  Lead on the abode,
Where dwell in the light
  Of justice infernal
The judges that smite,
That judge men aright,
  Whose laws are eternal!
Those kings that in reigning
For bribing or feigning
  Swerved never an hair
From justice and truth;
  Turned never a care
To wrath or to ruth;
  Did justice, and died.


Thither I haste
  To face the austere
    Faces of peace.
    Shall the lyre cease?
Its music be waste?
    Themselves not hear?
I stride to the presence and sing: and my
  soul is not conquered of fear.


Now the road widens and grows darker still
  As if the shadow of some ancient tower
Cast its deep spell on the reluctant will.


Still tortuous winds the deep descent; the
    hour
  Lies bitterer on my soul: I fear to fail,
To loose in vain the lyre's dissolving power


On the white souls armed in that triple mail
  Of justice, virtue, truth: percipience
Beyond the mute and melancholy veil


That covers from the drowsy eye of sense
  The subtle thought that hides behind the
    mask.
I fear indeed: but now the soul intense

Of truth precedes me and informs the task
 Of the steep ways: I gladden and go on
Ready to sing, to answer, or to ask

As all may happen: now the stern light shone
 Vivid across the blackness, and the rock
Recedes: the narrow stair is changed and
  gone

And the wide air invades: a mighty shock
 To my numbed senses void of vital air
And to my lyre reverberate to mock

With clanging echoes and discordant, where
 The dome reached up, almost to earth, so
  high
Rolled back the pillars and the walls, aglare

With iron justice' frightful symmetry
 Blazoned in blood-like flame, gushing from
  springs
Unseen, unguessed, incredible! There fly

The dreaded banners of the demon kings
 In fearful colours, and the vast inane
Dome catches music from my mouth, and rings

Back iron curses to the blessings vain
 I pour in desperate fervour from the lyre.
So, baffled by the echoes of hell's pain,

Blinded by grisly glamour of hell's fire,
 I take my refuge in the solitude
And grandeur of that irony of ire,

That mockery of mercy: thus I brood
 Apart, alone, upon the cause of Things
And wait those fearful Three. A lifeless
  mood

Stirs my grey being: ay! no passion springs
 In flowerless halls as these: awhile the
  mind
Wanders on void unprofitable wings

No whither: gains new strength at last to find
 Custom breed sight and hearing: in the hall
The sounds grow clear, the black fires fail to
  blind.

I see the mighty buttress of the wall
 Lost in its mighty measure: hear again
The lyre's low notes and light distinctly fall

A gentle influence in the place of pain.
 Oh now the central glory of the place
Falls splendid on the unbewildered brain,

And I am found contemplating a face
 More passionless than mortals': central sits
Throned on pure iron, with brass for cara-
  pace,

Minos: and either side of him befits
 The mighty Rhadamanthus throned on gold
And canopied with silver: sternly knits

His brows the awful Æacus, in cold
 Splendour of justice throned on carven
  lead;
And o'er his head twin dragons bend and
  hold

A cobra's hood made of some metal dread
 Impossible on earth: how calm, how keen
Flash their wise eyes, those judges of the
  dead,

In silent state: how eager, how serene
 Are the broad brows: the heart shrinks up
  and sinks,
Seeing no gallery to slip between

And pass those agèd ones—oft a man thinks
 He faces truth! I know this hour, alas!
That face to face with naked truth he shrinks.

His web of woven fiction may not pass
 (Though he believes it to be truth) with
  them
Who see his mind as though it were a glass

Without a shadow. Yet the ninefold gem
 And million-facet glory of my song
Glittering, made splendid in the diadem

Of flashing music shall assoil the wrong,
 A finer truth interpret. Though the heart
And core of music hold a poisonous throng

Of lies—yet, sing it to sufficient Art,
　　The lie abolishes itself—the tune
Redeems the darkness—the keen flashes start

Of truth availing though the midnight moon
　　Darken, the stars be quenched in utter
　　　　cloud,
And the high sun eclipsed at very noon.

So flash I back the glory calm and proud
　　Irradiating the Three.　So shall my lyre
Sweep the vast courts with acclamation loud

Of splashing music, of exulting fire
　　That revels in its penetrating cover
Of azure life that smites its flickering spire

Of sworded splendour inwards, to discover
　　Not justice, not discernment, not desire,
Not passion, but the sheer will of a lover !

MINOS.

　　Substantial, stern, and strong,
　　Who lifts an alien lyre ?
　　Confounds our echoes dire
　　With strange and stubborn song ?

ÆACUS.

　　Here in the House of Dole
　　Where shadows hardly dare
　　Stand, who doth deem to fare
　　Forth from the outer air
　　Mortal, a strenuous soul ?

RHADAMANTHUS.

　　The large and lordly land
　　Fertile of earth hath sent
　　With dolorous intent
　　Some shape or element.
　　What spell of might hath rent
　　The veil of Hell, and bent
　　Death's purpose to his hand ?

MINOS.

　　What shaft from the bow of Apollo ?

ÆACUS.

　　What quiver of wonder
Hath cleft the black walls of the hollow

RHADAMANTHUS.

　　What terror ?

MINOS.

　　　　What thunder
Hath shaken Hell's gates to the base ?

ÆACUS.

Withstanding the guards to their face ?

RHADAMANTHUS.

　　Hath rent him asunder
The portals of Dis in his wrath ?

MINOS.

　　Hath made for his will
An arrow of light for his path ?

ÆACUS.

　　Left stagnant and chill
The waters of Styx unappeased ?
The keys of our prison hath he seized.

RHADAMANTHUS.

　　A mortal !

MINOS.

　　　　An ill
Most alien to Heaven, by Zeus !

ÆACUS.

　　But impiety's doom,
By Poseidon, shall fill for his use
　　No well-omened tomb.

RHADAMANTHUS.

By Hades, our dogs let us loose !
　　Let death in the gloom
Bring peace to the Hall of the Dead !

MINOS.

A passionate being !
No weal to the light of his head
In the place of the seeing !

ÆACUS.

Awake, wild justice of dread !
Lest shadows be fleeing
In fear of the portent to lurk
In a deeper-detested
Cave, ere we wake to the work.

RHADAMANTHUS.

Black snakes many-crested,
Arise ! lest the calm of the murk
From our places be wrested.

MINOS.

Who art thou ?

ÆACUS.

'Vhat ails thee to irk
From earth tender-breasted
To the milkless dugs of the grave
And the iron breasts of the pit ?

RHADAMANTHUS.

Can a bodily presence save
Against a shadowy wit ?

MINOS.

Thy hope doth dwell, O slave,
Where thy mother fashioned it,
Oh heart of a fool, in thy breast.

ÆACUS.

Away, away to the skies !

RHADAMANTHUS.

That our dead may take their rest.

MINOS.

Arise to the air, arise !

ÆACUS.

Away to the mountain crest !

RHADAMANTHUS.

Veil, veil from the awful eyes !

MINOS.

Endure thy heart as it may,
And steel thine heart,
Thou shalt hear and know and obey
As I say "Depart";
Lest the arrow find its way
And the sternly-shapen dart.

ÆACUS.

A second our justice waits.

RHADAMANTHUS.

It falleth anon.

MINOS.

O fool of hopes and hates
Arise and begone !

ÆACUS.

O toy of the mirthless fates !
Who art thou to con
The mysteries of the dead in the black-souled
bastion ?

MINOS, ÆACUS, RHADAMANTHUS.

Away ! away ! to the light of day !
Now as it may : then as it must.
We are loath to pardon, and loath to slay,
Void of greed and anger and lust,—
But we are iron and thou art clay ;
We are marble and thou but dust.

ORPHEUS.

O iron, bow to silver's piercing note !
O marble, see the shape of ivory !
My justice fountains from a sweeter throat ;
My death is bound beyond eternity.

O wise and just, hear ye the voice of man,
Not seeking to involve in woven spells
Or trickery the decree Tartarean,
By words to blink that justice which is
Hell's !

I came indeed before this awful throne
  To seek a party favour, but I wait
Shuddering and silent, steadfast and alone,
  And change my music at the call of Fate.

For while ye spake in tumult, in this ear
  A music rang from earth's remotest mine,
From star and comet, flaming wheel and
    sphere,
  From Hell's deep vault and from the
    House divine.

A voice diverse, a voice identical
  Called me this hour from bitterest woes
    and black,
Constraining eloquence and mighty thrall
  Of cosmic agony, and wrung me back

From my poor plea to challenge in my song
  The whole domain of deeply-seated law,
Launch thunders not Olympic at the strong
  Bars of the Order backed with strength
    and awe

That men call Will of Zeus : the after scheme
  And primal fate and most primordial plan
Shaped from the earth's first protoplasmic
    dream
  Up to the last great mischief that is man.

All this I challenge : that the suns and stars
  Work in due order and procession meet
Without caprice in viewless, changeless bars,
  Nor self-determinate in their wingless feet.

All nature and all consciousness and thought
  He hath thrown asunder and divided them;
Fixing a gulf of agony athwart,
  Where rolls a tide no soul of man may
    stem.

Himself fixed high, he mocked us with his
    name
  Of "reconciler," and of "one beyond
    all";
And cast his shadow to the deep, to shame
  That oneness in its own division's thrall ;

So that Himself appears in cloud and fire
  Distorted in the world's distorted mirror ;
And dark convulsion and confusion dire
  Stands for his form of error and of terror.

But I perceive, I Orpheus, Lord of Song,
  And every Lord of Song that me shall
    follow
Down steeps of time's own agony and wrong,
  Shall see the lightning bridge the dreadful
    hollow

With jagged flame of master-music, hear
  The blind curse thunder forth against in
    vain
When the swift glory of the rolling sphere
  Of song pours forth its utterance, keen
    with pain,

Mad with delight, and calm beyond woe and
    pleasure.
  Yea, every son of this my soul shall know
In the swift concourse of his music's measure
  One thing impatient of this to and fro

March of hell's dancers.   I perceive a key
  To lock the prison of the world on him
That built the iron walls and made decree
  Long past in æons now grown gray and dim,

Like halls ancestral whence their folk have
    fled,
  The marbles all are broken, and the weeds
Grown o'er the bones of the unquiet dead,
  And time's remorse avails not on its deeds.

I see that time is one : future and past
  Are but one present ; space is one, the
    North
And South and all the sixfold shame holds
    fast
  No more : the poet's fiat hath gone forth

And tamed the masters of division.   Me
  Nor sun can burn, nor moon make mad,
    nor time
Alter : I drown not in the deepest sea,
  Nor choke where icy mountain ridges
    climb

The steeps of heaven : but these, these chil-
  dren, cry
  Their bitter cry for justice.  Mighty Ones,
Lords of the Dusk, incline ye, mercifully,
  Rightly, to misery of all stars and suns

And  planets  and  all  grains  of  dust  that
  sorrow—
  Hark ! from grim Tartarus, most doleful
  bound,
Their throats of anguish notes of triumph
  borrow
  At my loud strain's unprofitable sound.

For who are ye ?  Poor judges of the dead,
  In your stern eyes the sadness is mine own,
Mingled with sense that all your forces dread
  Are vain to take the spirit from one stone.

I would have called to ye in wild strong joy ;
  " Arise, O Lords of Justice, and be girt
With lightnings, and be ardent to destroy
  This Fool's creation and to heal its hurt

With swift annihilation ! "  Ye are vain,
  Alas ! poor powers !  But yet the damned
  rejoice
Hearing the splendour, prophet in my strain,
  And certain comfort in my mighty voice.

For this shall be, that in the utter end
  Shall be an end, that in the vast of time
Shall come a ceasing, and the steel bar bend
  Of the God's will, himself from his sublime

Pinnacled house in heaven headlong cast
  Like his own thunder to the abyss of
  nought
When space and time and being shall be past,
  And the grim thinker perish with his
  thought.

Therefore I leave in hands unshakable
  The destinies of being, and care not
For all the miseries of the damned in hell,
  Or the vain gods' unenviable lot.

I leave the cry of chaos, and recall
  My private pang and woe particular,
One drop of water by mischance let fall
  From some white slave's divinely carven
  jar.

O Lords of Justice, universal woe
  Hath yet its shadows in a singer's soul,
He feels the arrow from a party bow
  Who yet hath strength to struggle with
  the whole.

I love my wife.  The many-coloured throne
  Of Grecian meadows hath nor charm nor
  lure
Now she is gone.  Lamenting and alone
  My dulled heart aches, most that it must
  endure.

Give this decree, O masters !  Few the days
  And light the hours since Heracles de-
  scended
The dusky steep, the intolerable ways,
  And one prey—Theseus—from your prisons
  rended

By might of godhead and the skill of man.
  But now with music from a Muse's breast
Sweetened with milk of tenderness, I scan
  Your eyes with hope, and with a man's
  unrest

And a man's purpose I appeal.  Be just,
  O ye whom greater justice baulks and bars !
Return my lover from the unkind dust
  To the sweet light of the eternal stars !

Be kind, and from the unjust place of fear
  Return by kindness her, the innocent one,
From the grey places to the waters clear
  And meadows fair, and light of moon and
  sun !

Relent.  Reverse the doom.  I see your eyes
  Quiver despite ye : but your hands ye
  wring ;
Little by little bitter tears arise
  Like stubborn water from a frozen spring,

And deep unrest is seated in your limbs.
Ye pity me.  Ye pity.   Mute and weak
With the long trouble of persistent hymns
I bow myself and listen while ye speak.

#### MINOS.

Brethren, what need of wonder
That Hell is burst asunder
Shaken from base to brow, as if with Zeus'
own thunder?
What wonder if our peace
Broke, and our mysteries
Quaked at the prescience of these solemnities?

#### ÆACUS.

Child of the earth and heaven,
Our spirits thou hast riven
With words we must admit, with power of
song—whence given?
Neither of God nor man,
Thy song's amazing span
Hath caused strange joy among the woes
Tartarean.

#### RHADAMANTHUS.

Never in the centuries
Till godlike Heracles
Burst the wild bonds, hath mortal found the
fatal knees;
Nor hath the bitter cry
Of worlds in agony
Answered the groans of those who weep,
and cannot die.

#### MINOS.

Iron of heart and strong,
We also suffer wrong.
We know these words are just.  We avail
not.   Though thy song
Were the sole word of Zeus,
Should that avail to loose
The bands of Being firm, invulnerable dews
Tincturing its bitter brass,
Shielding its vital mass
From every word that cries, "Thus, and thy
day shall pass."

#### ÆACUS.

Typhon !  Typhon !  Typhon !
Heard ye that awful moan
Leap through the blackness from the miser-
able throne?
Vain as each pallid ghost,
Where is thy fatal boast,
Destroyer named of old on Khem's[1] disas-
trous coast?
Old power of evil curled
Below the phantom world,
Canst thou destroy, whose might to misery
is hurled?

#### RHADAMANTHUS.

What god beyond these twain
Abides or may remain
Seated, too strong to quell, exalted over
pain?
Aloof from time and chance,
Fate, will and circumstance,
Canst Thou not wither Life with one in-
dignant glance?
Thy name we know not ; Thine
Is the unbuilded shrine.
We doubt us if Thou be among the powers
divine !

#### MINOS.

Bound by strict line and law,
Fearful with might and awe,
We hold the powerless power
For many an agèd hour.
We move not from our place.
We ask nor give not grace,
Nor change our lordly looks before a sup-
pliant's face.

#### ÆACUS.

Stern in all justice, we
Assent aloud to thee,
We affirm thy cause as right :
We put forth all the might
Of aid : and all is done.
Our utmost power is none
To lift one soul to live and look upon the
sun.

[1] Egypt.

RHADAMANTHUS.

For righteous thought and deed
Apportioning its meed ;
For evil act and mind
Rewarding in its kind ;
So sit we : but our power
Apportions not an hour
To light the dying lamp, revive the faded
flower.

MINOS.

But thou, be strong to sing !

ÆACUS.

Loose arrows from the string !

RHADAMANTHUS.

Bid the wild word take wing !

MINOS.

Hades hath evil fame
To suppliants—bitter shame !—
Inexorable.

ÆACUS.

      Aim
Yet the swift prayer, abide
His word whate'er betide.
What worse ?

RHADAMANTHUS.

      The Gods thy guide !
Go and assail him !

MINOS.

      Stay,
The Queen of Hell !

ÆACUS.

      That way
Leads to the light of day.

RHADAMANTHUS.

A woman's heart may yearn,
To a man's love may turn.

MINOS.

Should she, the ravished, spurn
A man whose love is reft ?

ÆACUS.

Meadows and flowers she left
To Him—O bosom cleft
With a wife's loss !—a wife.

RHADAMANTHUS.

Too doubtful is the strife.

MINOS.

Yet go ! perchance to life.

ÆACUS.

Go ! and the Gods above
Guard thee, O soul of love !

RHADAMANTHUS.

I doubt me much thereof.

ORPHEUS.

Ah me ! I find ye but ill counsellors.
For I will conquer. Have I spent these
    stores
Of will and song for nought ? Hell's heart
    may rend,
But mine endureth even to the end.

Severe and righteous Lords, O fare ye well !
Are not my feet forced forward on a road
Leading to innermost abodes of Hell

Exalted as above the green abode
Of nymphs on broad Olympus, raises high
Its head the kingly snow, gigantic load

Of sombre whiteness cleaving through the
    sky
For gods to dwell in ? So I pass the hall
And seek the gloomy thrones of majesty,

Where I may pledge my last despairing call
Unto the mightiest of the House of Dread,
And loosen Death's inexorable thrall

And bring my lover from among the dead.
Now in the blackness of the rocks that span
The dolorous way I spy a golden thread

Veined in the strength of the obsidian
Flowing and growing, joining vein to vein,
Like fresh blood in the arteries of man,

Up to the very heart. And as I go
Loosen the knees of anguish and grow dim
The shattering flames of pain: the songs
    of woe

Flicker and alter to a solemn hymn
Chanted in slowest measure in deep awe.
Now as a yew-tree sends a mighty limb

Shooting to sunset, the black road's black
    maw
Gapes to the westward; the great trunk
    divides
And all the armies of infernal law

Stand ranked about the venerable sides
Of the black cave: they speak not; dumb
    they stand
And all the frost of all the air abides

Upon them, as a vampire stooped and spanned
The white throat of a maiden and held still
Her powers by virtue of its hate's command,

Somewhat like love's: so all the solemn
    chill
Invades those statued ranks of warriors,
And I pass through, the lightning of my will

A steady stream of flame: high instinct pours
Its limpid light of water on my mind,
So that I range inhospitable shores

Assured of Her I shall most surely find
Ere the end be: awake, O living lyre,
Since in the narrow way and pass confined

I see a darkness infinite as fire,
Clear as all spirit vision, lustrous yet
As ebony shows in caverns rendered dire

By dreadful magic, or as if pure jet
Had taken of itself an inner light,
And its own blackness filled night's coronet

With a new jewel: so I see aright
Where no light is like earth's. The path
    grows broad
And lofty, till the whole hall springs to sight,

And I am standing where the dreaded Lord
And Lady of the region of the lost
Hold awful sway: yet here the flaming sword

Of sight is broken by the deadly frost
That clusters round their thrones: a mist of
    fire
Congealed to vital darkness: yet exhaust

Like a seer's magic glass of air: expire
The dumb black hours in fear: but I am
    ware,
Well ware, by instinct surer still and higher

Than the own sight of soul that they are there,
No mockery of their presence: so even
    hither
My mother's might is on me, on I flare

Into wild war of song: my keen notes wither
The flowers of frost about me and I turn
Ever the strength and mastering frenzy
    thither

With energy of madness: yea, I burn!
My soul burns up upon the lyre! I lend
My whole life's vigour to one song, to earn

Their guerdon of the gods, a god to friend,
And seek through devious ways a single end.

[*Invoking* HADES.

*Str.* I.

Now is the gold gone of the year, and gone
    The glory of the world, and gathered close
The silver of the frost. Far splendid snows
Shine where the bright anemone once shone.
    Ay! for the laughter live
    Of youths and maids that strive

n amorous play, the ancient saws of eld
And wisdom mystical
From bearded lips must fall,
Old eyes behold what young eyes ne'er
beheld :
Namely, the things beyond the triple veil
Of space and time and cause, eternal woof
Of misery overproof :
And aged thoughts assail
The younger hopes, and passion stands
aloof,
And silence takes possession, and the tale
Of earth is told and done.
Then from the Sire of all the Gods, from War
And Love and Wisdom and the eternal Sun
Worship is torn afar :
While unto Thee, O Hades, turn we now,
Awful of breast and brow,
And hear thee in the sea, behold thee in the
Star.

### Ant. 1 [Echo of the Damned].

Ay ! is the earth and upper ether gone,
And all the joy of earth, and gathered close
The darkness and the death-wind and the
snows
On us on whom the sun of air once shone.
What souls are left alive
Vainly lament and strive,
For they shall join the dead of utmost eld ;
The concourse mystical
Who see the seasons fall
Shall soon behold what all we have beheld :—
The accursed stream, the intolerable veil
Of night and death and hell, disastrous
woof
Of anguish overproof
That fruitless wills assail
Ever in vain : good fortune stands aloof
And all kind gods : we, taking up the tale
Of dead men past and done,
Declare that ceaseless is the eternal war,
And victory stedfast set against the Sun.
Yet we perceive afar
Even in Hades, at the end, not now,
Some light upon his brow,
Some comfort in the sea, some refuge in the
Star.

### Str. 2.

O thou ! because thy chariot is golden,
And beautiful thy coursers, and their manes
Flecked with such foam as once upon
the sea
Bore Aphrodite, and thy face is olden,
Worn with dim thought and unsuspected
pains,
And all thy soul fulfilled of majesty ;
Because the silence of thy house is great,
And thy word second spoken after Fate,
And thy light stricken of thine own grim
hand ;
Because thy whisper exceedeth the command
Of Zeus ; thy dim light far outshines his
glory ;
Because, as He the first is, Thou the last :—
Therefore I take up sorrow in my hands,
And ply thine ear with my most doleful story,
Asking a future, who have lost a past :
A guerdon of my singing like the land's
When spring breaks forth from winter, and
the blood
Of the old earth laughs in every new-born
bud.

### Ant. 2 [Echo of the Damned].

O thou ! because thy lyre is keen and golden
And beautiful thy numbers through our
veins
Pouring delight, as on the starry sea
Burn gems of rapture ; though the houses
olden
Relax awhile their unredeeming pains,
And through dead slaves thrill bounteous
majesty ?
Though the strong music of thy soul be
great :—
Shall thy desire avail to alter Fate ?
Or impious hands unloose the awful hand ?
Or futile words reverse the great command ?
Or what availeth ? Though great Hades'
glory
Stoop to thy prayer, and answer thee at
last,
Should Clotho catch the thread in
weaving hands,

Respin what Atropos once cut—that story
  Were vain for thee—that which is past is
    past,
  Nor can Omnipotence avail the land's
Death—Spring's is alien though ancestral
    blood,
And a new birth is current in the bud.

### Str. 3.

Think, then, the deed impossible is done
  Since Theseus fared forth to the ambient
    air !
His thread once cut—was that indeed respun
  Or patched by witchery? a deceit? a
    snare?
I tell ye ; past and future are but one,
  And present—nothing ; shall not Hades
    dare
His own omnipotence against the Sun,
  And let no tittle of his glory share
With all the earth's recuperating wheel,
And every dawn's sure falchion-flash of steel?

### Ant. 3 [Echo of the Damned].

Indeed, a deed impossible was done
  Were the new Theseus heavier than the
    air.
Nay ! but a new thread phantom-frail was
    spun
  And men's blind eyes discovered not the
    snare,
Else were that elder cord and this yet one,
  Cut but in fancy.   Yet, shall mortal dare
To fling a wanton word against the Sun,
  And stand forth candidate for lot and share
Where hangs Prometheus, rolls Ixion's wheel,
And the stone rolls upon the limbs of steel?

### Epode.

These echoes, in my mind foul torturers,
  Present my fears, and image my distrust.
No answer comes, no voice the silence stirs
  With joyful "may" or melancholy "must."
Nor, though the gloom requicken, may I see
  Hades enthroned, my prayers who heedeth
    nought,

Nor glowing tear of bowed Persephone
  Drooped earthward for the ninefold misery
    wrought.
In utter sorrow ever bound she stays,
  Hears not my song, nor heedeth anything,
Whose mind lamenting turns to ancient days
  And Nysian meadows and the hour of
    spring.
Yea, but perchance to touch that secret chord
  Were to awake that sorrow into life ;
Sting, as a wound a deep-envenomed sword,
  The inmost soul of the Aidonean wife.
Listen ! I tune my music to that hour ;
  The careless maidens and the virgin
    laughter,
The bloom of springtide and the fatal flower,
  And all that joy the sorrow echoing after.
So that, dread Hades, thou mayst hear and
    yield,
  Thyself unmastered and inexorable,
The gentle maid as crying in that field,
  Now thy soul's keeper on the throne of
    Hell !
Hail, Hades ! Thou who hearest not my
    song,
  Repealest not the heaven's unjust decree,
Revengest not for me the woe and wrong,
  Shalt glean my sorrow from Persephone.
Hail, Hades ! In the gloom the echoing cry
  Swells, and the chorus darkens as I sing,
And all the fibres of Eternity
  Shake as I loose the loud indignant string.
Hail, Hades ! hear thy wrong proclaimed
    aloud,
  And thou the wronger safe because too
    great.
To like offence harden thy neck, and proud
  Blow thou the dismal challenge unto Fate !

In Asia, on the Nysian plains, she played,
  A slender maid,
With the deep-bosomed Oceanides ;
  Where the tall trees
Girded the meadow with grave walls of green.
  Alone, unseen,
The tender little lady strayed,
  Moving across the breeze.

It was a meadow of soft grass and flowers,
   Where the sweet hours
Lingered and laughed awhile ere noon re-
   poses.
   There were red roses
And crocus, and flag-flowers, and violets,
   And hyacinth, regrets
Of the ill-fortuned God, the quoit-player;
   And soft cool air
Stirred all the field—and there were jessa-
   mines
   And snaky columbines.
So all these maidens played, and gathered
   them
   From sad green stem
Rejoicing blooms with sunlight mixed therein.
   But she, for sin
And iron heart of the ill-minded Zeus,
   Caught up the dews
Deep on her ankles, and went noiselessly
   Toward the laughing sea,
And sought new blossoms—O the traitor,
   Earth,
   That brought to birth
That day, as favouring the desire that
   swelled
   Beneath her heart of eld,
Where dwelt the lonely, the detested one
   Intolerant of the sun,
Hades! But Earth for love of him, for spite
   Of the young girl's delight,
And shame of her own age, brought forth
   that hour
   The fatal flower,
Narcissus—which what soul of man shall
   smell
Goes down to hell,
Caught in the scent of sin—for such a doom
   Demeter's flying loom
Hath woven for revenge and punishment.
   The bright child went
Thither; an hundred heads of blossom sprang;
   The green earth sang,
And the skies laughed, and danced the sea's
   young feet
   For joy of it.
So the child went across that fairest plain
   To pluck, to strain

That blossom of all blossoms to her heart.
   Her long hands dart,
Exceeding delicate and fair, to cull
   That bloom too beautiful,
Eager to gather the fresh floral birth.
   The grim black earth
Gaped; roared athwart the gulf the golden
   car;
   And flaming far
The four white horses with their flashing
   manes!
   The might-resisting reins
Lay in the ghastly hands, the arms of fear
   Of that dread charioteer,
Death; and great Hades armed stood glitter-
   ing,
   Stooped to his spring,
And whirled the child to the beneath
   abode.
   O heavy load!
O bitter harvest of rich-rolling tears!
   What cry who hears?
A shrill shrill cry to father Zeus cried she,
   Forlorn Persephone!
Heard was that agony of grief by none
   Save only by the Sun,
And Her who sat within her awful cave,
   Contemplative and grave,
Hecate, veilèd with a shining veil
   Utterly frail
As the strange web of dainty thoughts she
   wove,
   Somewhat like love.
She heard, and great Apollo: neither
   stayed
Hades, nor stretched to aid
A pitying hand. O pitiful! O grief
   Baffling belief!
The gentle child—the cruel god—Ah me!
   Persephone!
Thus of thy grace, thy sorrow, thy young
   way
   Torn from the day
Of all thy memory of soft shining flowers
   And happy-hearted hours,
Mayst thou be very pitiful to me
   Who aye have pitied thee,
   Persephone!

PERSEPHONE.

Ah me! I feel a stirring in my blood.
Pours through my veins a delicate pale flood
Of memory.   Not the pale and terrible
Goddess whose throne is manifest in Hell
—I am again a child, a playful child.

ORPHEUS.

And therefore, O most beautiful and mild
Sweet mother! art the girl beloved again
Of Hades mighty on the Nysian plain.
And therefore are thine eyes with sorrow dim
For me, and thy word powerful with Him.

PERSEPHONE.

Ah me! no fruit for guerdon,
Who bore the blossom's burden;
There shines no sunlight toward Persephone.
Ravished, O iron-eyed!
From my young sisters' side,
Torn and dragged down below the sundered
        sea,
No joy is mine in all thy bed,
And all thy sorrow shaken on my head.

Cursed above gods be thou
Whose blind unruffled brow
Rules the grim place of unsubstantial things!
Hated, to me thy face
Turns not the glance of grace.
I rule unloved above the infernal kings,
And only thee in all deep Hell
I charm in vain, despair my royal spell.

By might of famine long
And supplication strong
Demeter won the swift Hermetic word:
In bitter days of eld
Thus by great force compelled
The glad earth saw me, careless of my lord,
Rise to her crystal streams and sapphire
        seas,
And Theseus thus owed life to Heracles.

Thou mockest me with power;
Thy sceptre's awful dower
Avails me nothing.   Shall a mortal bring
Such pity wrapped in song
And Echo's choral throng
Of all things live and dead to hear me sing;—
And I by pity moved and love
Have not thy voice to grant him grace
        thereof?

Inexorable Lord!
Accursèd and abhorred
Of men, begin in Hell to show thy grace!
Not to a man's weak life,
Not to thy shuddering wife,
But to the queen's unfathomable face
Dread beyond sorcery and prayer,
And fearful even because it is so fair!

Yea, from the ghastly throne
Unchallenged and unknown
Let the fierce accents roll athwart the skies!
My voice is given, my power
Fares forth to save the flower
Broken but plucked not by these fingers wise.
I love the song—be thou not mute,
But turn a lucky lot towards the suit!

ORPHEUS.

In vain, O thou veiled
        Immutable queen!
Thy strong voice bewailed,
        Thy fair face was seen!
It flushed up and paled;
        The song echoed clean—
But alas! for the veil of the night and the
        fear that is ever between!

Of pity unfilled
        And void of remorse,
He moves unappealed
        In the terrible course.
But the lyre is unchilled:—
        By force unto force
He shall answer me power unto power at the
        source of its source!

Dost thou hear how the weight
Of the earth and the moon
Shudder, as if fate
Were involved in the tune?
The portals of hate
Shake at the rune
Of the magical nature-cry, the song from the
mountains hewn !

To the horrible hollow
In Tartarus steep,
O song of me, follow !
I flee to the deep.
That word of Apollo
Shall shudder and leap ;
That word in the uttermost night shall awake
them who know not of sleep.

Hear, O ye Three,
In the innermost pit
Dwellers that be !
Tartarus, split !
Arise unto me
For I call ye with wit
Of the words that constrain and compel, of
the summons ordered and fit !

O daughter of Earth,
Tisiphone dread,
The ophidian girth,
And the blood-dripping head,
In hideous mirth
Bring living and dead
To torture ! Arise ! I conjure by the might
of the words I have said.

Megæra, thou terror,
O daughter of Night
Whose sight in a mirror
Is death of affright,
Wingèd with error,
I chain thee, and cite
The words that thy soul must obey if a
mortal but say them aright !

Alecto ! I call thee,
My words ring thee round.
My spells enwall thee.
My lyre is crowned
With might to appal thee
With terror profound.
Arise ! O Alecto, arise ! for my song hath
compelled thee and bound.

Ye furies of Hell !
Ye terrors in Heaven !
The strength of the spell
Is as thunder at even
The rocks of the fell
That hath blasted and riven.
Come forth ! I invoke ye, Erinyes, the
charm of the One that is seven.

By the Five that are One,
And the One that is Ten ;
By the snake in the sun
And her mirror in men ;
By the Four that run
And return them again ;
By the fire that is lit in the Lion, the wave
in the Scorpion den !

By the One that is Seven,
The whirling eyes ;
The Two made Eleven,
The dragon's devise ;
The Eight against Heaven,
All crowns of lies ;
Come forth ! I invoke ye, Erinyes, move,
answer, take shape and arise !

By the cross and the wheel
I call ye to hear ;
By the dagger of steel
I command ye, give ear !
By the word that ye feel,
The summons of Fear ;
Come forth ! I invoke ye, Erinyes, move,
answer, arise and appear !

For my purpose is swift,
    And my vengeance strong ;
I shall not shift ;
    I shall cry the wrong.
My voice I uplift
    In terrible song
As your forms take shape before me in the
likeness for which ye long.

    The shape of my passion
        And bitter distress
    Shall clothe ye, and fashion
        An equal dress.
    Ye shall force compassion
        With awful stress
From the soul that hath mocked me, and
turned his heart from my song's excess.

    The ruler of Hell,
        The invisible Lord,
    Hath laughed at my spell,
        Hath slept at my word.
    He hath heard me well—
        Awake, O Sword !
Shall he flout a suppliant thus and no answer
of favour accord ?

    If mercy be sundered
        From splendour and power ;
    If he answer with thunder
        The plaint of a flower ;
    Shall justice wonder
        If Furies devour
So bitter a heart, set a term to his date that
was aye but an hour ?

    Avenge me, ye forces
        Of horror and wrath !
    Clear the dread courses !
        Split open the path !
    With cruel remorse is
        His heart brought to scath.
And a terror is on him at last, the seed of his
hate's aftermath.

#### MEGÆRA.

Ha ! who invokes ?   What horror rages
    Here, to compel our murderous hands to
    smite?

#### ALECTO.

What mortal summons ?   Who his battle
    wages
    So strongly as to call the seed of Night?

#### TISIPHONE.

Ha !   The grim tyrant of despair engages
    Our deadly anguish with his useless might.

#### HADES.

Detested fiends ! avaunt !

#### MEGÆRA.
            He speaks !

#### ALECTO.
            He thunders !

#### TISIPHONE.

His lightnings split the living rock.

#### MEGÆRA.
            Hell sunders
The livid walls and iron-bound prisons of
    death.

#### HADES.

Thus ! to your towers and wail !

#### ALECTO.
            He speaks !

#### TISIPHONE.
            His breath
Is cold as ours.

#### HADES.
            Depart !   Due silence keep,
Lest I enchain ye in a fouler deep
Than aught your horror pictures !

#### MEGÆRA.
            Dost thou hear,
Sister ?

#### ALECTO.

Sweet sister !

TISIPHONE.
                    Dost thou think we fear
Who are all fear? or feel, who are but pain?

MEGÆRA.
Creep round his heart, and cluster in his
    brain,
Ye serpents of my hair!

ALECTO.
                    His blood shall drip
For sweet warm juice on my decaying lip.

TISIPHONE.
My fearful wings enfold him!

ALECTO.
                            My foul eyes
Hold his in terror!

MEGÆRA.
                    All my agonies
Crawl in his vitals!

TISIPHONE.
                    He is mine, mine, mine!
Pour forth of Thebes' abominable wine!
Mine, O thou god, detested and adored!

MEGÆRA.
Mine! he is mine! my lover and my lord!

ALECTO.
Mine!   I am in his shape!

MEGÆRA.
                    Despair! Dispute
Never my passion!

TISIPHONE.
                    Sisters!   Be ye mute!
I am the livid agony that starts
Damp on his brow; the horror in his heart's
Envenomed arteries! and I the fear,
The torment, and the hate!

MEGÆRA.
                    Be of good cheer!
Rend him apart!   Hunger and lust we sate,
Equal in terror on that heart of hate.

ALECTO.
Hell's throne be kingless!

TISIPHONE.
                    Mortal! is it well,
Our vengeance on the impious lord of Hell!

ORPHEUS.
Well! it is well!   And yet my eyes are wet
To see such anguish.

MEGÆRA.
                    Tear the fatal net!

ALECTO.
Bite with strong acid his congealing blood!

TISIPHONE.
Rend out the bowels!

MEGÆRA.
                    Pour the monstrous flood
Of unclean wisdom in his soul!

PERSEPHONE.
                            Desist!

ALECTO.
O face of woman wretched and unkissed,
What hast thou here to do with us?

TISIPHONE.
                            Be quiet!

MEGÆRA.
Quench not the fire of murder!

ALECTO.
                            Loose the riot
Of worms beneath the skull!

TISIPHONE.

              Tear wide apart
The jaws !

MEGÆRA.

Force fear against the inmost heart !

PERSEPHONE.

Mercy ! I plead, sweet sisters !

ORPHEUS.

             And I plead
Vengeance, and help in my extremest need.
Pile up the torture ! Had he not the power,
And silence mocked me ?

MEGÆRA.

          Urge us hour by hour,
Thou couldst not add one particle of pain.

ALECTO.

He speaks not ! Bid his torture speak again !

TISIPHONE.

Speak, murderer !

MEGÆRA.

         Hades ! answer us !

ALECTO.

               Expel
These torments from thy being, us from Hell,
Or Zeus from Heaven !

TISIPHONE.

          Or else obey !

MEGÆRA.

              Obey !

ALECTO.

Obey !

HADES.

    O throne of Hell ! O night ! O day
Of anguish exquisite beyond control,
Fibre and substance of my inmost soul !
There is a power not mine, and yet in me
Burning its cold and cruel agony

With icy flames, its cutting poison fangs
Striking my being with detested pangs.
Alas ! of me and not to be expelled,
Conjured, assuaged, averted. Grey as eld
The juice of blood that stagnates in my veins
Appals their current with avenging pains :—
O pain ! O pitiful and hateful sense
Of agony and grief and impotence !
O misery of the day when Orpheus bore
First his loud lyre across the Stygian shore !
Hath Hell no warders ? Is the threefold gate
Brazen in vain against the foot of Fate ?
Now is but little choice—abase my pride,
Or sink for ever to the gloomy tide
Of fire beneath the utmost reach and span
Of Stygian deeps and walls Tartarean.
Yet I abide.

MEGÆRA.

            Fall ! Fall !

ALECTO.

              Descend the abyss !

TISIPHONE.

Link the lewd fiend with your incestuous
    kiss !

MEGÆRA.

             MEGÆRA.
Hither !

ALECTO.

O hither !

HADES.

           Steams a newer shape
Of threefold terror.

TISIPHONE.

           Shall the god escape
The monstrous wedlock ?

ALECTO

           Let him turn again
His horrid passion to the Nysian plain !

MEGÆRA.

Echidna !

ALECTO.

Mother of the Sphinx and snake
Of Colchus, and the marsh-beast of the lake
Lernean, of Chimaera and Hell's hound—

TISIPHONE.
Answer!

ALECTO.
Arise!

MEGÆRA.
Awake from the profound!

TISIPHONE.

Here is a worthy partner unto thee
To wake thy womb with monstrous progeny,
Yet more detested and detestable
Than all the shapeless brood of hate and Hell.

ECHIDNA.
Ha! rose-lipped lover! Welcome to this
bed!

MEGÆRA.
She plays with words of love!

ALECTO.
Her black eyes shed
Disease for tears.

TISIPHONE.
Her fangs and lips are red
With gouts of putrid blood.

MEGÆRA.
Her guile employs
The sweet soft shape of words of upper joys
More bitterly to rack his soul.

ALECTO.
Ha, sister,
The embrace!

TISIPHONE.
She conquers.

MEGÆRA.
He hath moved.

ALECTO.
He hath kissed her!

TISIPHONE.
Ha! the worse hate of hate in love's white
dress.

MEGÆRA.
And lewdness tricked to look like loveliness.

ALECTO.
Uttermost pain in pleasure's hour supreme.

MEGÆRA.
Hate's nightmare waking love's unreal dream.

ALECTO.
Claws, teeth, and poison!

TISIPHONE.
How she plies her pest!

MEGÆRA.
Strangling she holds him.

ALECTO.
In the inmost breast
Her hands defile him.

TISIPHONE.
In his rotting brain
He teeth, her breath, pass all imagined pain.

MEGÆRA.
Sisters!

ALECTO.
We conquer!

TISIPHONE.
Have we power?

MEGÆRA.
The king
Endures, and is not moved at anything.

ALECTO.
He will not now relent.

TISIPHONE.
He's ours for ever!

HADES.
Ai! Ai!

MEGÆRA.
Hark!

ALECTO.
Listen!

TISIPHONE.
Now he yields—or never!

HADES.
Release! Relent!

ECHIDNA.
Fair lover, let my embrace
Still gladden thee to rapture! let my face
Be like a garden of fresh flowers to cull,
And all thy being and thy body full
As mine of gentle love—then sink to sleep!

MEGÆRA.
Ha! Ha! She mocks him! In the utter
deep,
Her house of evil, sleep is stranger there.

ALECTO.
She sings!

TISIPHONE.
The final misery! Beware!

ECHIDNA.
O tender lover!
My wings still cover
Thy face, and my lips

Are on thine, and my tresses
Like Zephyr's caresses
When the twilight dips.

HADES.
This passes all. Relent. Release! Depart!
I yield: my power is broken, and my heart
Riven, and all my pride ruined, and me
Compelled to earth to loose Eurydice.

ORPHEUS.
Depart!

ERINYES.
Baffled! O misery! Bethink,
Proud Hades, ere thy torture gar thee drink
Humiliation's utmost dregs!

HADES.
I spake.
Depart ye! lest my power regained awake,
And smite ye with a terror more than ye.

MEGÆRA.
We are borne on bitter winds.

ALECTO.
We sink.

TISIPHONE.
We flee!

MEGÆRA.
To the abyss!

ALECTO.
Descend!

TISIPHONE.
Nor hope in vain
The ill-hearted one shall feel our fangs again.

MEGÆRA.
Murder and violation, deafened ear
To suppliants, these our friends are.

ALECTO.

Hate and fear
Leave not for long that bosom.

TISIPHONE.

Now away!
Back from this night more splendid than our
    day!

MEGÆRA.

We may not drag him down this chance.

ALECTO.

Despair
Not, O my sisters!

TISIPHONE.

The next suppliant's prayer
Rejected—

MEGÆRA.

Come, my sisters, we'll be there.

HADES.

Well, be it so.   O wizard, by this strength
Thou hast availed in deepest Hell at length.
I grant thy prayer.   Eurydice be given
To the sweet light and pleasant air of heaven!
Even on this wise.   With Hermes for a
    guide
Up the dread steeps there followeth thee thy
    bride,
And thou before them singing.   If thou yearn
Towards her, if thy purpose change or turn
While in these realms; if thou thy face
    revert;
That shall be hostage unto me for hurt
Of further magic: she shall fade and flee
A phantom frail throughout Eternity,
Driven on my winds, adrift upon my seas!
These are thy favours, and thy duties these.
Invoke thou Hermes, and thy lyre restring!

ORPHEUS.

This I accept and this shall be, O king!

[*Invoking* HERMES.]

O Light in Light! O flashing wings of fire!
    The swiftest of the moments of the sea
                Is unto thee
    Even as some slow-foot Eternity
With limbs that drag and wheels that tire.
O subtle-minded flame of amber gyre,
    It seems a spark of gold
    Grown purple, and behold!
        A flame of gray!
    Then the dark night-wings glow
    With iridescent indigo,
        Shot with some violet ray;
And all the vision flames across the horizon
    The millionth of no time—and when we
        say:
        Hail!—Thou art gone!

The moon is dark beside thy crown; the Sun
    Seems a pale image of thy body bare;
    And for thine hair
    Flash comets lustrous with the dewfall
        rare
Of tears of that most memorable One,
The radiant Queen, the veilèd Paphian.
    The wings of light divine
    Beneath thy body shine;
        The invisible
    Rayed with some tangible flame,
    Seeking to formulate a name,
        A citadel;
And the winged heels are fiery with enormous
        speed,
    One spurning heaven; the other tramp-
        ling hell;
        And thou—recede!

O Hermes! Messenger of inmost thought!
    Descend! Abide! Swift coursing in my
        veins
    Shoot dazzling pains,
The Word of Selfhood integrate of Nought,
The Ineffable Amen! the Wonder wrought.
    Bring death if life exceed!
    Bid thy pale Hermit bleed,
        Yet Life exude;
    And Wisdom and the Word of Him

Drench the mute mind grown dim
  With quietude !
Fix thy sharp lightnings in my night ! My
  spirit free !
  Mix with my breath and life and name thy
    mood
      And self of Thee.

  [HERMES *appears:* ORPHEUS *departs.*

The magical task and the labour is ended ;
  The toils are unwoven, the battle is done ;
My lover comes back to my arms, to the
    splendid
  Abyss of the air and abode of the sun.
The sword be assuaged, and the bow be un-
    bended !
  The labour is past, and the victory won.

The arrows of song through Hell cease to
    hurtle.
  Away to the passionate gardens of Greece,
Where the thrush is awake, and the voice of
    the turtle
  Is soft in the amorous places of peace,
And the tamarisk groves and the olive and
    myrtle
  Stir ever with love and content and release.

O bountiful bowers and O beautiful gardens !
  O isles in the azure Ionian deep !
Ere ripens the sun, ere the spring-wind
    hardens
  Your fruits once again ye shall have me to
    keep.
The sleep-god laments, and the love goddess
    pardons,
  When love at the last sinks unweary to sleep.

The green-hearted hours shall burst into
    flowers.
  The winds shall waft roses from uttermost
    Ind.
Our nuptial dowers shall be birds in our
    bowers,
  Our couches the delicate heaps of the wind,
Where the lily-bloom showers all its light,
    and the powers
  Of earth in our twinning are wedded and
    twinned.

So singing I make reverence and retire ;
Not with high words of worship fairly flung
To that sad monarch from the magic lyre,

And half the triumphs in my heart unsung,
Surpassing, as such triumphs must, all praise
Of golden strings and human-fashioned
    tongue.

But now I follow the uprising ways
By secret paths indubitably drawn
Straight from the centre of the trackless maze

To light of earth and beauty of the dawn,
A sure swift passage taught of wit divine
To the wide ocean, the Achæan lawn.

For, wit ye well, not easy is that shrine
Of access to the mortal, as some tell,
Not knowing : easy and exact the line

Of light to upper air : but awful spell
And dire demand the inward journey needs :
That is the labour, that the work : for Hell

Is not designed for men's aspiring deeds.
The air is fatal, and the fear unspanned,
Even ere the traveller fronts the Stygian
    meads

And utmost edge of the detested land.
Wherefore already doth the light appear
Shaped in the image of a little hand

Far up the rocky cavern : warm and clear
The good air sends its fragrance : glory then
To the great work accomplished even here,

Promise and purpose unto little men
Bound in life's limits : death indeed I sever
By will's efficiency and speechless ken

Of power not God's but man's.  Forget this
    never,
O mortals chained in life's detested den !
I leave this heritage to you for ever.

      O light of Apollo !
        O joy of the sky !
      We see thee, we follow,
      We draw to thee nigh.

We see thee unclouded,
　Whose hearts have been thinned,
Whose souls have been shrouded,
　Whose ears are bedinned
By hell's clamour.　How did
　The strength that has sinned
Avail in the crowded
　Abodes of the wind?


By lightning of rapture
　The soul of my song
My love doth recapture ;
　Lead up to the long
Years in blithe measure
　Of summer and ease ;
Linger at leisure
　For passion and peace.
Sadness and pleasure
　Relent and release :—
A torrent, a treasure,
　A garden of Greece !


Selene, our sister,
・Our lover and friend,
Thy light hath long missed her :
　That hour hath an end.
All æons to squander
　We chance at our will :
We may woo, work or wander
　Through time to our fill,
Hither or yonder
　By fountain or hill,
Each day growing fonder,
　Each night growing still !


Bright Hermes behind me
　Caduceus-armed
Guides : shall he blind me ?
　My spirit be charmed ?
The song shall not swerve her,
　Its glory shall shed
Respite, deserve her
　From gulfs of the dead.
Ah me ! let it nerve her
　These conduits to tread
That lead to the fervour
　Of earth overhead !

Fire, thou dear splendour
　Of uppermost space,
Turn to me tender
　Thine emerald face !
Thy rubies be blended
　With diamond light !
Thy sapphires be splendid,
　Extended to sight !
The portals be rended
　That govern the night,
And the guardians bended
　To magical might !


O air of the glorious
　Garb of the globe,
Don thy victorious
　Glittering robe !
The sun is before us ;
　The moon is above.
Rise and adore us
　Ye dwellers thereof !
The Muses restore us
　To Greece : as we move
Swell the wild chorus
　Of welcome and love !


Alas ! that ever the dark place
　Should from its rocky base
Give up no echo of the god's strong stride,
　And no one whisper steal and thrill
　My heart, dissolve the ill
That gathers close and fears me for my bride.


I were no worse if I were blind.
　I may not look behind
To catch one glimpse of the dear face that
　follows,
　Lest I should gain forbidden lore
　And wisdom's dangerous store
Of the black secrets of those heights and
　hollows.


Alas ! the way is over long,
　And weary of my song
I sing who yearn to catch my love, and hold
　In such ten-thousandfold caress
　As shall annul distress,
And from the iron hours bring the years of
　gold.

Alas ! my soul is filled with fear,
Is the hard conquest here?
Where is Eurydice?  The god hath faded
Back to invisible abodes
And on these rocky roads
Comes no deep perfume of her hair light-
braided.

Alas ! I listen ! and no breath
Assures the walls of death
That life remembers, that their hate is quelled.
My ears, my scent avail me nought ;
My slavish eyes are bought
By the command wherewith I am compelled.

Alas ! my heart sinks momently.
Fear steals and misery.
From faith in faith of Hell my thoughts dis-
sever.
Yet, O my heart ! abide, endure !
Seek not by sight to assure,
Or she is lost to thee and lost for ever !

Now breathes the night-air o'er the deep,
And limb-dissolving sleep
Laps my own country, and the maiden moon
Gleams silver barley from the sea,
And binds it royally
Into a sheaf that waves to the wind's tune.

The rocky portals rise above.
Here I may clasp my love,
Here Hermes shall deliver.  Ah ! how shook
Yon cliff at the wind's ardent kiss !
This is the hour of bliss—
The sea !  The sea ! Eurydice !  Look, Look !

Ai ! but like wind whirled flowers of frost
The flying form is lost !
Cancelled and empty of Eurydice
The black paths where she trod !
Ai ! Ai !  My God !  My God !
Apollo, why hast thou forsaken me ?

EXPLICIT LIBER TERTIUS

## LIBER QUARTUS VEL MORTIS

TO

MY WIFE

LYSANDER (*reads*).

"The riot of the tipsy Bacchanals
Tearing the Thracian singer in their rage."

THESEUS.

That is an old device.
*Midsummer Night's Dream.*

What could the Muse herself that Orpheus bore
  The Muse herself, for her enchanting son
Whom universal Nature did lament
When by the rout that made the hideous roar
  His gory body down the stream was sent
Down the swift Hebrus to the Lesbian shore?
*Lycidas.*

A brighter Hellas rears its mountains
  From waves serener far;
A new Peneus rolls his fountains
  Against the morning star.
Where fairer Tempes bloom, there sleep
Young Cyclads on a sunnier deep.

  .        .        .        .        .

Another Orpheus sings again
And loves, and weeps, and dies.
*Hellas.*

MOUNT IDA.

THE COMPANY OF THE MÆNADS.

MÆNADS.

Evoe! Evoe Ho! Iacche! Iacche!

Hail, O Dionysus! Hail!
  Wingèd Son of Semelé!
Hail, O Hail! The stars are pale.
Hidden the moonlight in the vale;
  Hidden the sunlight in the sea.

Blessed is her happy lot
  Who beholdeth God; who moves
Mighty-souled without a spot,
Mingling in the godly rout
  Of the many mystic loves.

Holy maidens, duly weave
  Dances for the mighty mother!
Bacchanal to Bacchus cleave!
Wave his narthex wand, and leave
  Earthy joys to earth to smother!

Io! Evoe! Sisters, mingle
　In the choir, the dance, the revel!
He divine, the Spirit single,
He in every vein shall tingle.
　Sense and sorrow to the devil!

Mingle in the laughing measure,
　Hand and lip to breast and thigh!
In enthusiastic pleasure
Grasp the solitary treasure!
　Laughs the untiring ecstasy!

Sisters! Sisters! Raise your voices
　In the inspired divine delight!
Now the sun sets; now the choice is
Who rebels or who rejoices,
　Murmuring to the mystic night.

Io! Evoe! Circle splendid!
　Dance, ye maids serene and subtle!
Clotho's task is fairly ended.
Atropos, thy power is rended!
　Ho, Lachesis! ply thy shuttle!

Weave the human dance together
　With the life of rocks and trees!
Let the blue delirious weather
Bind all spirits in one tether,
　Overwhelming ecstasies!

Io Evoe! I faint, I fall,
　Swoon in purple light; the grape
Drowns my spirit in its thrall.
Love me, love me over all,
　Spirit in the spirit shape!

All is one! I murmur.　Distant
　Sounds the shout, Evoe, Evoe!
Evoe, Iacche!　Soft, insistent
Like to echo's voice persistent :—
　Hail! Agave! Autonoe!

AGAVE.

Evoe Ho! Iacche! Hail, O Hail!
Praise him!　What dreams are these?

AUTONOE.
　　　　　Sisters, O sisters!

AGAVE.

Say, are our brethren of the rocks awake?

AUTONOE.

The lion roars.

MÆNADS.
　　　　　O listen to the snake!

AUTONOE.

Evoe Ho! Give me to drink!

AGAVE.
　　　　　　　　Run wild!
Mountain and mountain let us leap upon
Like tigers on their prey!

MÆNADS.
　　　　　Crush, crush the world!

AGAVE.

Tread earth as 'twere a winepress!

AUTONOE.
　　　　　　　Drink its blood,
The sweet red wine!

MÆNADS.
　　　　　Ay, drink the old earth dry!

AGAVE.

Squeeze the last drops out till the frame
　collapse
Like an old wineskin!

AUTONOE.
　　　　　　　So the sooner sup
Among the stars!

AGAVE.

The swift, swift stars!

MÆNADS.
　　　　　　　O night!
Night, night, fall deep and sure!

AUTONOE.

Fall soft and sweet !

AGAVE.

Moaning for love the woods lie.

AUTONOE.

Sad the land
Lies thirsty for our kisses.

MÆNADS.

All wild things
Yearn towards the kiss that ends in blood.

AGAVE.

Blood ! Blood !
Bring wine ! Ha ! Bromius, Bromius !

MÆNADS.

Come, sweet God,
Come forth and lie with us !

AUTONOE.

Us, maidens now
And then and ever afterwards !

AGAVE.

Chaste, chaste !
Our madness hath no touch of bitterness,
No taste of foulness in the morning mouth.

AUTONOE.

O mouth of ripe red sunny grapes ! God !
God !
Evoe ! Dwell ! Abide !

AGAVE.

I feel the wings
Of love, of mystery ; they waft soft streams
Of night air to my heated breast and brow.

MÆNADS.

He comes ! He comes !

AGAVE.

Silence, O girls, and peace !
The God's most holy presence asks the hymn
The solemn hymn, the hymn of agony,
Lest in the air of glory that surrounds
The child of Semelé we lose the earth
And corporal presence of the Zeus-begot.

AUTONOE.

Yea, sisters, raise the chant of riot ! Lift
Your wine-sweet voices, move your wine-
    stained limbs
In joyful invocation !

MÆNADS.

Ay, we sing.

Hail, child of Semelé !
To her as unto thee
Be reverence, be deity, be immortality !

Shame ! treachery of the spouse
Of the Olympian house,
Hera ! thy grim device against the sweet
    carouse !

Lo ! in red roar and flame
Did Zeus descend ! What claim
To feel the immortal fire had then the
    Theban dame !

Caught in that fiery wave
Her love and life she gave
With one last kissing cry the unborn child
    to save.

And thou, O Zeus, the sire
Of Bromius—hunter dire !—
Didst snatch the unborn babe from that
    Olympian fire :

In thine own thigh most holy
That offspring melancholy
Didst hide, didst feed, on light, ambrosia,
    and moly.

Ay ! and with serpent hair
And limbs divinely fair
Didst thou, Dionysus, leap forth to the
nectar air !

Ay ! thus the dreams of fate
We dare commemorate,
Twining in lovesome curls the spoil of mate
and mate.

O Dionysus, hear !
Be close, be quick, be near,
Whispering enchanted words in every curving
ear !

O Dionysus, start
As the Apollonian dart !
Bury thy hornèd head in every bleeding heart !

AGAVE.
He is here ! He is here !

AUTONOE.
Tigers, appear !

AGAVE.
To the clap of my hand
And the whish of my wand,
Obey !

AUTONOE.
I have found
A chariot crowned
With ivy and vine,
And the laurel divine,
And the clustering smell
Of the sage asphodel,
And the Dædal flower
Of the Cretan bower ;
Dittany's force,
And larkspur's love,
And blossoms of gorse
Around and above.

AGAVE.
The tiger and panther
Are here at my cry.
Ho, girls ! Span there
Their sides !

MÆNADS.
Here am I !
And I ! We are ready.

AGAVE.
Strong now and steady !

FIRST MÆNAD.
The tiger is harnessed.

SECOND MÆNAD.
The nightingale urges
Our toil from her far nest.

THIRD MÆNAD.
Ionian surges
Roar back to our chant.

FOURTH MÆNAD.
Aha ! for the taunt
Of Theban sages
Is lost, lost, lost !
The wine that enrages
Our life is enforced.
We dare them and daunt.

AGAVE.
The spirits that haunt
The rocks and the river,
The moors and the woods,
The fields and the floods,
Are with us for ever !

MÆNADS.
Are of us for ever.
Evoe ! Evoe !

AUTONOE.
Agave ! He cometh !

AGAVE.
Cry ho ! Autonoe !

ALL.
Ho ! Ho ! Evoe Ho ! Iacche ! Evoe ! Evoe !

The white air hummeth
With force of the spirit.
We are heirs : we inherit.
Our joys are as theirs ;
Weave with your prayers
The joys of a kiss !
Ho ! for the bliss
Of the cup and the rod.
   He cometh ! O lover !
O friend and O God,
   Cover us, cover
   Our faces, and hover
Above us, within us !
   Daintily shod,
   Daintily robed,
His witcheries spin us
A web of desire.
Subtle as fire
He cometh among us.
   The whole sky globed
      Is on fire with delight,
Delight that hath stung us,
   The passion of night.
Night be our mistress !
That tress and this tress
Weave with thy wind
Into curls deep-vined !
   Passionate bliss !
Rapture on rapture !
Our hymns recapture
The Bromian kiss.
Blessèd our souls !
   Blessèd this even !
We reach to the goals
Of the starriest heaven.
Daphnis, and Atthis, and Chrysis, and Chloe,
Mingle, O maidens ! Evoe ! Evoe !


DIONYSUS.

I bring ye wine from above,
   From the vats of the storied sun ;
For every one of ye love,
   And life for every one.
Ye shall dance on hill and level ;
   Ye shall sing in hollow and height
In the festal mystical revel,
   The rapturous Bacchanal rite !

The rocks and trees are yours,
   And the waters under the hill,
By the might of that which endures,
   The holy heaven of will !
I kindle a flame like a torrent
   To rush from star to star ;
Your hair as a comet's horrent,
   Ye shall see things as they are !
I lift the mask of matter ;
   I open the heart of man ;
For I am of force to shatter
   The cast that hideth—Pan !
Your loves shall lap up slaughter,
   And dabbled with roses of blood
Each desperate darling daughter
   Shall swim in the fervid flood.
I bring ye laughter and tears,
   The kisses that foam and bleed,
The joys of a million years,
   The flowers that bear no seed.
My life is bitter and sterile,
   Its flame is a wandering star.
Ye shall pass in pleasure and peril
   Across the mystical bar
That is set for wrath and weeping
   Against the children of earth ;
But ye in singing and sleeping
   Shall pass in measure and mirth !
I lift my wand and wave you
   Through hill to hill of delight :
My rosy rivers lave you
   In innermost lustral light.
I lead you, lord of the maze,
   In the darkness free of the sun ;
In spite of the spite that is day's
   We are wed, we are wild, we are one !


FIRST MÆNAD.

O sweet soul of the waters ! Chase me not !
What would'st thou ?


A VOICE AS OF RUNNING BROOKS.

Love !


FIRST MÆNAD.

      Love, love, I give, I give.
I yield, I pant, I fall upon thy breast,

O sacred soul of water.   Kiss, ah kiss,
With gentle waves like lips my breast, my
　　two small breasts,
Rose flames on ivory seas !

#### SECOND MÆNAD.

　　　　　　Nay !   Nay !   O soul
Of ivy, clingst thou so for love?

#### A VOICE AS OF THE RUSTLING OF IVY.

　　　　　　　　For love.

#### SECOND MÆNAD.

Cling not so close !   O no !   cling closer then !
Let thy green coolness twine about my limbs
And still the raving blood : or closer yet,
And link about my neck, and kill me so !

#### THIRD MÆNAD.

Soul of the rock !   Dost love me ?

#### A VOICE AS OF FALLING ROCK.

　　　　　　　I love thee.

#### THIRD·MÆNAD.

　　　　　　　Woo me then !
Let all the sharp hard spikes of crystal dart,
Press hard upon my body !   O, I fall,
Fall from thy crags, still clinging, clinging so,
Into the dark.   Oblivion !

#### A DISTANT VOICE.

　　　　　　　Io Evoe !

　　　　　　　　[ORPHEUS enters.

#### CROWD OF MÆNADS.

Evoe !   Evoe !   It is a lion !

#### FOURTH MÆNAD.

　　　　　　　Lion,
O lion, dost thou love me ?

#### FIFTH MÆNAD.

　　　　　　Thee I love,
O tawny king of these deep glades !

#### SIXTH MÆNAD.

　　　　　　　What wood
Were worthy for thy dwelling?

#### CHORUS.

　　　　Come, come, come,
O lion, and revel in our band !

#### ORPHEUS.

　　　　　　　Alas !
I sorrow, seeing ye rejoice.

#### FIRST MÆNAD.

　　　　　　O lion !
That is not kind.

#### ORPHEUS.

　　　Too kind.   Since all is sorrow,
Sorrow implicit in the purest joy,
Sorrow the cause of sorrow ; evil still
Fertile, and sterile love and righteousness.
Eurydice, Eurydice !

#### SECOND MÆNAD.

　　　　　　Drink wine !

#### ORPHEUS.

Ay, mask the grisly head of things that are
By drowning sense.   Such horror as is hid
In life no man dare look upon.   Woe !   Woe !

#### AGAVE.

Call then reproach upon these maiden rites !

#### ORPHEUS.

Nay !   virtue is the devil's name for vice,
And all your righteousness is filthy rags
Wherein ye strut, and hide the one base
　　　thought.
To mask the truth, to worship, to forget ;
These three are one.

#### AGAVE.

What art thou then ?   a man ?

ORPHEUS.

No more.

AGAVE.

No longer?

ORPHEUS.

Nothing.

AGAVE.

What then here
Dost thou amid these sacred woods?

ORPHEUS.

I weep.

AGAVE.

Weep then red wine!

AUTONOE.

Or we will draw thy tears,
Red tears of blood.

AGAVE.

On, girls! this bitter fool
Would stop our revel!

ORPHEUS.

Nay! ye bid me cease
Weeping.

AGAVE.

Then listen! drink this deep full cup,
Or here we tear thee limb from limb!

ORPHEUS.

Do so!
Ay, me! I am Orpheus, poor lost fool of
Fate!
Orpheus, can chaim the wildest to my lyre.
Beasts, rocks, obey—ah, Hades, didst thou
mock,
Alone of all, my songs? Thee I praise not.
[AUTONOE *embraces him.*
Audacious woman!

AGAVE.

Tear the fool in shreds!
Then to the dance!
VOL. III.

ORPHEUS. [1]

The old Egyptian spell!
Stir, then, poor children, if ye can! Ah me!
[*Sings.*
Unity uttermost showed,
I adore the might of thy breath,
Supreme and terrible God
Who makest the Gods and death
To tremble before thee:—
I, I adore thee!

O Hawk of gold with power enwalled,
Whose face is like an emerald;
Whose crown is indigo as night;
Smaragdine snakes about thy brow
Twine, and the disc of flaming light
Is on thee, seated in the prow
Of the Sun's bark, enthroned above
With lapis-lazuli for love
And ruby for enormous force
Chosen to seat thee, thee girt round
With leopard's pell, and golden sound
Of planets choral in their course!
O thou self-formulated sire!
Self-master of thy dam's desire!
Thine eyes blaze forth with fiery light;
Thine heart a secret sun of flame!
I adore the insuperable might:
I bow before the unspoken Name.

For I am Yesterday, and I
To-day, and I to-morrow, born
Now and again, on high, on high
Travelling on Dian's naked horn!
I am the Soul that doth create
The Gods, and all the Kin of Breath.
I come from the sequestered state;
My birth is from the House of Death.

Hail! ye twin hawks high pinnacled
That watch upon the universe!
Ye that the bier of God beheld!
That bore it onwards, ministers
Of peace within the House of Wrath,

[1] Much of the following invocation is a free
rendering of several fine passages in the
Egyptian Book of the Dead.

O

Servants of him that cometh forth
At dawn with many-coloured lights
　　Mounting from underneath the North,
The shrine of the celestial Heights !

He is in me, and I in Him !
　　Mine is the crystal radiance
That filleth æther to the brim
　　Wherein all stars and suns may dance.
I am the beautiful and glad,
　　Rejoicing in the golden day.
I am the spirit silken-clad
　　That fareth on the fiery way.
I have escaped from Him, whose eyes
Are closed at eventide, and wise
To drag thee to the House of Wrong :—
I am armed ! I am armed ! I am strong !
　　I am strong !
I make my way : opposing horns
　　Of secret foemen push their lust
In vain : my song their fury scorns ;
　　They sink, they grovel in the dust.

Hail, self-created Lord of Night !
Inscrutable and infinite !
　　Let Orpheus journey forth to see
　　The Disk in peace and victory !
Let him adore the splendid sight,
　　The radiance of the Heaven of Nu ;
Soar like a bird, laved by the light,
　　To pierce the far eternal blue !

Hail ! Hermes ! thou the wands of ill
　　Hast touched with strength, and they are
　　　shivered !
The way is open unto will !
　　The pregnant Goddess is delivered !

Happy, yea, happy ! happy is he
　　That hath looked forth upon the Bier
　　　That goeth to the House of Rest !
His heart is lit with melody ;
　　Peace in his house is master of fear ;
　　　His holy Name is in the West
When the sun sinks, and royal rays
Of moonrise flash across the day's !

I have risen ! I have risen ! as a mighty
　　hawk of gold !
From the golden egg I gather, and my wings
　　the world enfold.
I alight in mighty splendour from the thronéd
　　boats of light ;
Companies of Spirits follow me ; adore the
　　Lords of Night.
Yea, with gladness did they pæan, bowing
　　low before my car,
In my ears their homage echoed from the
　　sunrise to the star.
I have risen ! I am gathered as a lovely
　　hawk of gold,
I the first-born of the Mother in her ecstasy
　　of old.
Lo ! I come to face the dweller in the sacred
　　snake of Khem ;
Come to face the Babe and Lion, come to
　　measure force with them !
Ah ! these locks flow down, a river, as the
　　earth's before the Sun,
As the earth's before the sunset, and the God
　　and I are One.
I who entered in a Fool, gain the God by
　　clean endeavour ;
I am shaped as men and women, fair for
　　ever and for ever.

(*The* MÆNADS *stand silent and quiet.*)

### ORPHEUS.[1]

Worship with due rite, orderly attire,
The makers of the world, the floating souls
Whence fell these crystals we call earth.
　　Praise Might
The Limitless ; praise Pallas, by whose
　　Wisdom
The One became divided. Praise ye Him,
Chronos, from whom, the third, is form per-
　　ceived.
Praise ye Poseidon, his productive power,
And Juno, secret nature of all things,
On which all things are builded : praise ye
　　Love,

---

[1] The following is paraphrased from one of
the writings (falsely) attributed to Orpheus.

Idalian Aphrodite, strong as fair,
Strong not to loosen Godhead's crown by
   deed
To blind eyes not a God's : and praise pure
   Life,
Apollo in his splendour, whom I praise
Most, being his, and this song his, and his
All my desire and all my life, and all
My love, albeit he hath forsaken me.
These are One God in many : praise ye Him !

#### AGAVE.

We praise indeed who made the choral world
And stars the greatest, and all these the least
Flowers at our feet : but also we may praise
This Dionysus, lord of life and joy,
In whom we may perceive a subtle world
Hidden behind this masquerade of things.
O sisters, thither, thither !

#### ORPHEUS.

          All deceit.
Delusive as this world of shadows is,
That subtler world is more delusive yet,
Involving deeper and still deeper : thought,
Desire of life, in that warm atmosphere
Spring up and blossom new, rank poisonous
   flowers,
The enemies of peace. Nay ! matter's all,
And all is sorrow. Therefore not to be,
Not to think, love, know, contemplate, exist ;
This Not is the one hope.

#### AGAVE.

         Believe it not !
Here is true joy—the woodland revellings,
The smile, the kiss, the laughter leaping up,
And music inward, musings multiform,
Manifold, multitudinous, involved
Each in the deep bliss of the other's love ;—
Ay me ! my sisters. Thither !

#### AUTONOE.

        Wake the dance !

#### MÆNADS.

Pour luscious wine, cool, sweet, strong wine !
   Bring life,
Life overflowing from the cup !

#### ORPHEUS.

         Hush ! Hush !
I hymn the eternal matter, absolute,
Divided, chaos, formless frame of force,
Wheels of the luminous reach of space that
   men
Know by the name of Pan.

#### MÆNADS.

         Hail ! Hail !
Pan ! Son of Hermes ! God of Arcady
And all wild woodlands !

#### ORPHEUS.

     Neither Son, nor Sire,
Nor God : but he is all : all else in him
Is hidden : he the secret and the self
Shrined central in this orb of eyeless Fate,
Phantom, elusive, permanent. In all,
In spirit and in matter immanent,
He also is the all, and all is ill.
Three forms and functions hath the soul ;
   the sea
Murmurs their names repeating : *Maris* call
The soul as it engendereth things below ;
*Neptune* the soul that contemplateth things
Above ; and *Ocean* as itself retracts
Itself into itself : choose ye of these ![1]
But I hymn Pan. Awake, O lyre, awake !
As if it were for the last time, awake !
               [*He sings*.

In the spring, in the loud lost places,
   In the groves of Arcadian green,
There are sounds and shadowy faces
   And strange things dimly seen.
Though the face of the springtide as grace is,
   The sown and the woodland demesne
Have a soul caught up in their spaces,
   Unkenned, and unclean !

[1] Again from pseudo-Orpheus.

It takes up the cry of the wind.
Its eyes with weeping are blind.
A strong hate whirls it behind
 As it flees for ever.
Mad, with the tokens of Fear;
Branded, and sad, without cheer;
Year after ghastly year,
 And it endeth never.

And this is the mystical stranger,
 The subtle Arcadian God
That lurks as for sorrow and danger,
 Yet rules all the earth with his rod.
Abiding in spirit and sense
 Through the manifold changes of man,
This soul is alone and intense
 And one—He is Pan.

More subtle than mass as ye deem it
 He abides in the strife that is dust.
Than spirit more keen as ye dream it,
 He is laughter and loathing and lust.
He is all.   Nature's agonies scream it;
 Her joys quire it clear; in the must
Of the vat is His shape in the steam.   It
 Is Fear, and Disgust.

For the spirit of all that is,
The light in the lover's kiss,
The shame and sorrow and bliss;
 They are all in Pan;
The inmost wheel of the wheels,
The feeling of all that feels,
The God and the knee that kneels,
 And the foolish man.

For Pan is the world above
 And the world that is hidden beneath;
He grins from the mask of love;
 His sword has a jewelled sheath.
What boots it a maiden to gird her?
 Her rape ere the æons began
Was sure; in one roar of red murder
 She breaks: He is Pan.

He is strong to achieve, to forsake her;
 He is death as it clings to desire,
Ah, woe to the Earth!   If he wake her,
 Air, water and spirit and fire

Rush in to uproot her and break her:—
 Yet he is the broken; the pyre,
And the flame and the victim; the maker,
 And master and sire!

And all that is, is force.
A fatal and witless course
It follows without remorse
 With never an aim.
Caught in the net we strive;
We ruin, and think we thrive;
And we die—and remain alive:—
 And Pan is our name!

For the misery catches and winds us
 Deep, deep in the endless coil;
Ourself is the cord that binds us,
 And ours is the selfsame toil.
We are; we are not; yet our date is
 An age, though each life be a span;
And ourself and our state and our fate is
 The Spirit of Pan.

O wild is the maiden that dances
 In the dim waned light of the moon!
Black stars are her myriad glances:
 Blue night is the infinite swoon!
But in other array advances
 The car of the holier tune;
And our one one chance is in mystical
 trances;—
 Thessalian boon!

For swift as the wheels may turn,
And fierce as the flames may burn,
The spirit of man may discern
 In the wheel of Will
A drag on the wheels of Fate,
A water the fires to abate,
A soul the soul to make straight.
 And bid "be still!"

But ye, ye invoke in your city
 And call on his name on the hill
The God who is born without pity,
 The horrible heart that is chill;

The secret corruption of ages
  Ye cling to, and hold as ye can,
And abandon the songs of the sages
  For Passion—and Pan !

O thou heart of hate and inmost terror !
  O thou soul of subtle fear and lust !
Loathsome shape of infamy, thy mirror
  Shown as spirit or displayed as dust !
O thou worm in every soul of matter
  Crawling, feasting, rotting; slime of hell !
Beat and batter ! shear and shatter !
  Break the egg that hides thee well !
Pan ! I call thee ! Pan ! I see thee in thy
  whirling citadel.

I alone of all men may unveil thee,
  Show the ghastly soul of all that is
Unto them, that they themselves may hail
  thee,
  Festering corruption of thy kiss !
Thou the soul of God ! the soul of demon !
  Soul of matter, soul of man !
Show the gross fools, thine, that think them
  freemen,
  What thou art, and what thy heart,
And what they are, that they are thee,
  All creation, whole and part,
Thine and thee, near and far :—
  Come ! I call thee, I who can.
Pan ! I know thee ! Pan ! I show thee !
  Burst thy coffin open, Pan !

What have I said ? What have I done ?

#### MÆNADS.
                  Pan ! Pan !
Evoe, Iacche ! Pan !

#### AGAVE.
        The victim !

#### AUTONOE.
                    Rend
The sole pure thing in this impure gross
  lump,
The shapeless, formless horror that is us
And God—Ah ! rend him limb from limb !

#### ORPHEUS.
                  Apollo !
This is the night. This is the end of all.
No force detains. No power urges on.
I am free ! Alas ! alas !—Eurydice !
    (*He is torn to pieces. A faint
    voice—like his—is still heard,
    ever receding and failing.*)
O night !
Fade, love ! Fade, light !
I pass beyond Life's law.
I melt as snow ; as ice I thaw ;
As mist I dissipate : I am borne, I draw
Through chasms in the mountains : stormy
  gusts
Of ancient sorrows and forgotten lusts
Bear me along : they touch me not : I waste
The memory of long lives interlaced
Fades in my fading. I disintegrate,
Fall into black oblivion of Fate.
My being divides : I have forgot my name.
I am blown out as a thin subtle flame.
I am no more.

#### A SPIRIT.
        What is ? what chorus swells
Through these dark gorges and untrodden
  dells !
What whisper through the forest ? Far
  entwines
The low song with the roses and the vines,
The high song with the mountains and the
  pines,
The inmost song with secret fibre of light,
And in the boiling pools and quorns and
  chasms
Chases the stryges, Death's devote phantasms,
Into a brilliant air wherein they are lost.
Deep in the river moans the choral roar,
Till the deep murmur of the Lesbian shore
Washed of the luminous sea gives answer,
  while
The angry wail of Nature doth beguile
The hours, the wrath of Nature reft of one,
The sole strong spirit that was Nature's sun,
The orb she circled round, the one thing
  clean
From all her gross machinery, obscene

And helpless:—and the lonely mother-cry,
The Muse, her hope down-stricken.   Magically
The full deep chorus stirs the sky ;
Hark ! one voice beyond all
Gives love's own call,
Not hers, Eurydice's,
But thine, thou sweet blood-breasted nightingale
Waking thy choral wail
From Mitylene to remotest seas !

### THE RIVER HEBRUS.

Was e'er a stream before
So sad a burden bore
Rolling a melancholy sorrow down from shore to shore?

### CALLIOPE.

O this is bitterness beyond belief.
Grief beyond grief.
Boots it to weep?  I holp him not with force :
What should avail—remorse?

### RIVER HEBRUS.

Hear upon high the melancholy
Antistrophe
Matching the strophe's agony !
Tides on a terrible sea !

### CALLIOPE.

Bear, bear the laurelled head
Of him I loved, him dead,
O Hebrus, ever downward on thy bosom iron-red !

### RIVER HEBRUS.

All Nature's tunes are dull.
The beautiful,
The harmony of life is null.

### CALLIOPE.

What unto us remains
But in these broken strains
To hymn with voices jarred the jarred world's shriek of woe?

O ! O !

### RIVER HEBRUS.

This discord is an agony
Shuddering harsh in me ;
My waters will empoison the fair fresh-water sea !

### CALLIOPE.

Nay ! all is ended now.
Cover the beaten brow !
Carry the brain of music into the wide Ægean !
No priest pronounce thy pæan
Ever again, Apollo,
Thou false, thou fair, thou hollow !
Die to a groan within a shrine !
Despair thy force divine !
Thou didst achieve this ruin ; let the seas
Roar o'er thy lost name of Musagetes !

### THE LESBIAN SHORE.

Welcome, O holy head !
Welcome, O force not dead !
Reverberating joy of music subtly shed !
Welcome, O glorious, O laurelled one !
Own offspring of the Sun,
The ancient harmony was hardly yet begun.
By thee and by thy life
Arose the Lesbian maiden.
Thou art perished as thy wife ;
My shores with magic loves and songs of life are laden.

### CALLIOPE.

Weep, weep no more !
O loyal Lesbian shore,
I hear a murmur sound more sweet than murmur ever bore.
Not ocean's siren spell
Soft-sounded in a spiral shell
Were quite so exquisite, were all so admirable !

### LESBIAN SHORE.

Nay ! but the agony of the time
Rings in the royal rime !
She hath touched the intimate, and chanced on the sublime.

CALLIOPE.

Ay! Ay! a woman's silky tone
Makes music for eternity her own,
Till all men's victories in song seem a dis-
cordant groan.

LESBIAN SHORE.

Upon my cliffs of green,
Beneath the azure skies,
She stands with looks of fire,
Sappho. Her hands between
Lies the wild world; she flies
From agony to agony of desire.

CALLIOPE.

Him, Orpheus, him she sings;
Loosing the living strings,·
Till music fledged fares forth sunward on
moon-wrought wings.

LESBIAN SHORE.

Yea, by the solar name,
Orpheus her lips acclaim,
The centre and the silence! O! the torrent
of fine flame
Like hair that shooteth forth
To the ensanguine North
Whence ran the drunken crew, Bassarids in
their wrath.

SAPPHO.

Woe is me! the brow of a brazen morning
Breaks in blood on water athirst of Hebrus.
Sanguine horror starts on her hills tenebrous:
Hell hath not heard her!

Dumb and still thy birds, O Apollo, scorning
Song; yells drown them, lecherous anthems
gabbled,
Laughter splashed of Bassarids, blood-be-
dabbled,
Mad with their murder!

O thou many-coloured immortal maiden,
Dawn! O dew, delight of a world! A
sorrow
Hides your holy faces awhile. To-morrow
Comes for your calling?

Still the notes of musical Orpheus, laden
Never now of pain or of failing, follow;
Follow up the height, or adown the hollow
Fairy are falli

O my hopeless misery mind of longing!
O the anguish born in a breast unlovered!
Women, wail the face of a God uncovered,
Brain dead and breath dumb!

Wail the sense of infinite ardours thronging
Fast and fast and faster athwart the heaven,
Keen as light and cruel as fire, as levin
Swift and as death dumb!

Freedom, rapture, victory, fill the chorus,
Dying, ever dying, among the billows;
Whispered, ever whispered among the
willows:—
Pour the libation!

Now springs up a notable age. Adore us
Masters now of music above his magic,
Lords of change, leaps pastoral up to tragic,
Thanks to the Thracian!

Ah, my pain! what desolate female bosoms,
Smitten hearts of delicate males, uncover;
Grip not life for poet or sage or lover,
Feed on derision.

Yea, in these mature me avenger blossoms
Swift as swords to sever the subtle ether,
Lift the earth, see infinite space beneath her,
Swoon at the vision.

This, O Orpheus, this be a golden guerdon
Unto thee for gift of amaze and wonder!
This thy sorrow, sword of a heart asunder,
Beareth a flower.

This the heart of woman—a bitter burden!—
Thou hast filled with seed—O a seed of
madness!
Seed of music! seed of a royal sadness!—
This be our dower!

Ah! the bitter legacy left of lyre-light !
Thou wast Nature's prophet, a wise magician;
Magic fails, and love is a false physician :—
　　Deep our disease is !

Now to us the crouching over the firelight,
Eating out for hunger of love our vitals !
(Eaten out the hollower for respitals
　　Swift as the breeze is.)

Ay ! the golden age is a broken vessel.
All the golden waters exhale, evanish.
Joy of life and laughter of love we banish :
　　Damned is the will dead.

Now with brass and iron we writhe and
　　wrestle.
Now with clay the torrent of fire is tainted.
Life apes death : the lily is curled and
　　painted ;
　　Gold is regilded.

Master, we lament thee, as awful anguish
Seizes on the infinite maze of mortals.
See we love that yearns to the golden portals
　　Bound of the grey god.

Love, thy children, laughter and sunlight,
　　languish.
Aphrodite, miracle of the flashed foam,
Burns with beaten agony in the lashed foam ;
　　Down is the day-god.

Ay ! this first of Lesbian lamentations
Still shall burn from æon to idle æon !
(Chorus, epithalmy, ode, and pæan
　　Dumb or dishevelled !)

Still my songs shall murmur across the
　　nations,
Gain their meed of misery, praise, and
　　yearning,
Smite their stroke on centuries foully burning,
　　Drunk or bedevilled.

Song? No beauty shine in a sphere of music !
Me? my voice be dull, be a void, be toneless !
Match me, sea ! than me thou hast many a
　　moan less,
　　Many a million !

Sun, be broken ! Moon, be eclipsed ; be
　　dew sick !
Ocean flat and poisonous, earth demented !
Living souls go shuddering through the tented
　　Air, his pavilion !

Ay ; the pectis clangs me a soulless discord :—
Let me break my visible heart a-weeping !
Loving? Drinking? Misery. Singing,
　　sleeping
　　Touch not my sorrow.

Orpheus, turn the sorrow-chord to the bliss-
　　chord !
All may rise the easier that the one set.
So our eyes from saddening at the sunset
　　Turn to to-morrow.

CALLIOPE.

Silence. I hear a voice
That biddeth me rejoice.
I know the whole wise plan
Of Fate regarding Man.

THE LESBIAN SHORE.

It is the sun's dark bride
Nuith, the azure-eyed.
No longer Sappho sings her spell ;
His heart divorced, her heart insatiable.
There is deep silence. Earth hath passed
To a new kingdom. In a purpose vast
Her horoscope is cast.

NUITH.

Enough. It is ended, the story
Of magical æons of song ;
The sun is gone down in his glory
　　To the Houses of Hate and of Wrong.
　　Would ye see if he rise?
　　In Hesperian skies
Ye may look for his rising for long.

The magical æon beginneth
Of song in the heart of desire,
That smiteth and striveth and sinneth,
　　But burns up the soul of the lyre :—
　　There is pain in the note :—
　　In the sorcerer's throat
Is a sword, and his brain is afire !

ong after (to men : but a moment
  To me in my mansion of rest)
s a sundawn to blaze what the glow meant
  Seen long after death in the west ;
    A magical æon !
    Nor love-song nor pæan,
  But a flame with a silvery crest.

There shall rise a sweet song of the soul
  Far deeper than love or distress ;
Beyond mortals and gods shall it roll ;
  It shall find me, and crave, and caress.
    Ah ! me it shall capture
    In torrents of rapture ;
  It shall flood me, and fill, and possess.

For brighter from age unto age
  The weary old world shall renew
Its life at the lips of the sage,
  Its love at the lips of the dew.
    With kisses and tears
    The return of the years
  Is sure as the starlight is true.

Yet the drift of the stars is to beauty,
  To strength, and to infinite pleasure.
The toil and the worship and duty
  Shall turn them to laughter and leisure.
    Were the world understood
    Ye would see it was good,
  A dance to a delicate measure.

Ye fools, interweaving in passion
  The lyrical light of the mind !
Go on, in your drivelling fashion !
  Ye shall surely seek long and not find.
    From without ye may see
    All the beauty of me,
  And my lips, that their kisses are kind.

For Eurydice once I lamented ;
  For Orpheus I do not lament :
Ier days were a span, and demented ;
  His days are for aye, and content.
    Mere love is as nought
    To the love that is Thought,
  And idea is more than event.

O lovers ! O poets ! O masters
  Of me, ye may ravish my frown !
Aloof from my shocks and disasters !
  Impatient to kiss me, and crown !
    I am eager to yield.
    In the warrior field
  Ye shall fight me, and fasten me down.

O poets ! O masters ! O lovers !
  Sweet souls of the strength of the sun !
The couch of eternity covers
  Our loves, and our dreams are as done.
    Reality closes
    Our life into roses ;
  We are infinite space : we are one.

There is one[1] that hath sought me and
    found me
  In the heart of the sand and the snow :
He hath caught me, and held me, and
    bound me,
  In the lands where no flower may grow.
    His voice is a spell,
    Hath enchanted me well !
  I am his, did I will it or no.

But I will it, I will it, I will it !
  His speck of a soul in its cars
Shall lift up immensity ! fill it
  With light of his lyrical bars.
    His soul shall concentre
    All space ;. he shall enter
  The beautiful land of the stars.

He shall know me eternally wedded
  To the splendid and subtle of mind ;
For the pious, the arrogant-headed,
  He shall know they nor seek me nor find.
    O afloat in me curled !
    Cry aloud to the world
  That I and my kisses are kind !

O lover ! O poet ! O maiden
  To me in my magical way !
Be thy songs with the wilderness laden !
  Thy lyre be adrift and astray :—
    So to me thou shalt cling !
    So to me thou shalt sing
  Of the beautiful law of the day !

[1] Possibly intended as a reference to the
poet himself.

I forbid thee to weep or to worship;
  I forbid thee to sing or to write!
The Star-Goddess guideth us her ship;
  The sails belly out with the light.
    Beautiful head!
    We will sing on our bed
  Of the beautiful law of the Night!

We are lulled by the whirr of the stars;
  We are fanned by the whisper, the wind;
We are locked in unbreakable bars,
  The love of the spirit and mind.
    The infinite powers
    Of rapture are ours;
  We are one, and our kisses are kind.

EXPLICIT LIBER QUARTUS

# EPILOGUE AND DEDICATION

*November* 18, 1906.

MY DEAR ION,—I address you by the unfamiliar title in giving you, a man self-damned, God knows how unjustly, as the author of the phrase, "I am not an appreciator of poetry, and I have no Keats," these volumes. For the matter thereof is already in great part yours and as such cannot be given. The rest I offer because it is hardly possible to close definitely, as I do now, a period of many years' work, without reflecting upon that period as a whole. And, when I do so, I find you at the beginning like Ladas or Pheidippides of old, running —ready to run until you achieve the goal or your heart burst; but you are among a crowd. I join you. Eight years ago this day you, Hermes, led me blindfold to awake a chosen runner of the course. "In all my wanderings in darkness your light shone before me though I knew it not." To-day (one may almost hope, turning into the straight) you and I are alone. Terrible and joyous! We shall find companions at the End, at the banquet, lissome and cool and garlanded; companions with a Silver Star or maybe a Jewelled Eye mobile and uncertain—as if alive—on their foreheads. We shall be bidden to sit, and they will wreathe us with immortal flowers, and give us to drink of the seemly wine of Iacchus—well! but until then, unless my heart deceives me, no third shall appear to join us. Indeed, may two attain? It seems a thing impossible in nature. May it not be that—near as the resounding roar of the viewless spectators sounds to our dust-dimmed ears—there stands some awful opposer in the way, some fear or some seduction? Why do you grip that bar in your left hand? Does not this loin-cloth irk my limbs? We should have shaved our heads before the race—the curls are moist and heavy! Why did we cumber ourselves with sandals? Long ere now our feet would have grown hard. Well, if my heart bursts, it bursts; you must give these volumes to the young athletes, that they may learn wherefore I failed—wherefore it was given unto me to run thus far. For, if I have put nothing else therein, most surely that is there.

ALEISTER CROWLEY.

# EPILOGUE AND DEDICATION OF

## VOLUMES I., II., III.

### ELEUSIS.

THOSE who are most familiar with the spirit of fair play which pervades our great public schools will have no difficulty, should they observe, in an obscure corner, the savage attack of Jones minor upon Robinson minimus, in deducing that the former has only just got over the "jolly good hiding" that Smith major had so long promised him, the determining factor of the same being Smith's defeat by Brown maximus behind the chapel, after Brown's interview with the Head-Master.

We are most of us aware that cabinet ministers, bishops, and dons resemble each other in the important particular that all are still schoolboys, and their differences but the superficial one produced by greasing, soaping, and withering them respectively; so that it will meet with instant general approval if I open this paper by the remark that Christianity, as long as it flourished, was content to assimilate Paganism, never attacking it until its own life had been sapped by the insidious heresies of Paul.

Time passed by, and they bullied Manes and Cerinthus; history repeated itself until it almost knew itself by heart; finally, at the present day, some hireling parasites of the decaying faith—at once the origin and the product of that decay—endeavour to take advantage of the "Greek movement" or the "Neo-pagan revival" in the vain hope of diverting the public attention from the phalanx of Rationalism—traitorously admitted by Luther, and now sitting crowned and inexpugnable in the very citadel of the faith —to their own dishonest lie that Paganism was a faith whose motto was "Carpe diem,"[1] and whose methods were drink, dance, and Studio Murder.[2] Why is Procopius cleaner than Petronius? Even a Julian could confute this sort of thing; but are we to rest for ever in negation? No: a Robinson minimus ipse will turn, and it is quite time that science was given a chance to measure itself against bulk. I shall not be content with giving Christian apologists the lie direct, but proceed to convict them of the very materialism against which they froth. In a word,

to-day Christianity is the irreligion of the materialist, or if you like, the sensualist; while in Paganism, we may find the expression of that ever-haunting love— nay, necessity!—of the Beyond which tortures and beautifies those of us who are poets.

πάντα καθαρὰ τοῖς καθαροῖς—and, while there is no logical break between the apparently chaste dogma of the Virgin Birth and the horrible grossness of R. P. Sanchez in his De Matrimonio, Lib. ii. Cap. xxi., "Utium Virgo Maria semen emiserit in copulatione cum Spiritu Sancto," so long as we understand an historical Incarnation: the accomplishment of that half of the Magnum Opus which is glyphed in the mystic aphorism " Solve !" enables an Adept of that standing to see nothing but pure symbol and holy counsel in the no grosser legends of the Greeks. This is not a matter of choice: reason forbids us to take the Swan-lover in its literal silliness and obscenity; but, on the other hand, the Bishops will not allow us to attach a pure interpretation to the precisely similar story of the Dove.[1]

So far am I, indeed, from attacking Christian symbolism as such, that I am quite prepared to admit that it is, although or rather because it is the lowest, the best. Most others, especially Hinduism and Buddhism, lose themselves in metaphysical speculations only proper to those who are already Adepts.

The Rosicrucian busies himself with the Next Step, for himself and his pupils; he is no more concerned to discuss Nibbana than a schoolmaster to "settle the doctrine of the enclitic Δή" in the mind of a child who is painfully grappling with the declension of Νεανίας. We can read even orthodox

---

[1] "Gather ye roses!" is the masterpiece of a Christian clergyman.—A. C.
[2] A peculiarly gross case of psychopathic crime which occurred in 1906.

[1] Recently, a certain rash doctor publicly expressed his doubts whether any Bishop of the twentieth century was so filthy-minded a fool. They were, however, soon dispelled by telegrams from a considerable section of the entire Bench, couched in emphatic language.

Christian writers with benefit (such is the revivifying force of our Elixir) by seeking the essence in the First Matter of the Work; and we could commend many of them, notably St. Ignatius and even the rationalising Mansel and Newman, if they would only concentrate upon spiritual truth, instead of insisting on the truth of things, material and therefore immaterial, which only need the touch of a scholar's wand to crumble into the base dust from which their bloodstained towers arose.

Whoso has been crucified with Christ can but laugh when it is proved that Christ was never crucified. The historian understands nothing of what we mean, either by Christ or by crucifixion, and is thus totally incompetent to criticise our position. On the other hand, we are of course equally ill-placed to convert him; but then we do not wish to do so; certainly not *quâ* historian. We leave him alone. Whoso hath ears to hear, let him hear! and the first and last ordeals and rewards of the Adept are comprised in the maxim "Keep silence!"

There should be no possible point of contact between the Church and the world: Paul began the ruin of Christianity, but Constantine completed it. The Church which begins to exteriorise is already lost. To control the ethics of the state is to adopt the ethics of the state: and the first duty of the state will be to expel the rival god Religion. In such a cycle we in England seem to be now revolving, and the new forced freedom of the Church is upon us.

If only the destruction is sufficiently complete, if only all England will turn Atheist, we may perhaps be able to find some Christians here and there. As long as "church" means either a building, an assembly, or even has any meaning at all of a kind to be intelligible to the ordinary man, so long is Christ rejected, and the Pharisee supreme.

Now the materialism which has always been the curse of Christianity was no doubt partly due to the fact that the early disciples were poor men. You cannot bribe a rich man with loaves and fishes: only the overfed long for the Simple Life. True, Christ bought the world by the promise of Fasts and Martyrdoms, glutted as it was by its surfeit of Augustan glories; but the poor were in a vast majority, and snatched greedily at all the gross pleasures and profits of which the educated and wealthy were sick even unto death. Further, the asceticism of surfeit is a false passion, and only lasts until a healthy hunger is attained; so that the change was an entire corruption, without redeeming aspect. Had there been five righteous men in Rome, a Cato, a Brutus, a Curtius, a Scipio, and a Julian, nothing would have occurred; but there was only the last, and he too late. No doubt Maximus, his teacher, was too holy an Adept to mingle in the affairs of the world; one indeed, perhaps, about to pass over to a higher sphere of action: such speculation is idle and impertinent; but the world was ruined, as never before since the fabled destruction of Atlantis, and I trust that I shall take my readers with me when I affirm so proud a belief in the might of the heart whose integrity is unassailable, clean of all crime, that I lay it down as a positive dictum that only by the decay in the mental and moral virility of Rome and not otherwise, was it possible for the slavish greed and anarchy of the Faith of Paul to gain a foothold. This faith was no new current of youth, sweeping away decadence: it was a force of the slime: a force with no single salutary germ of progress inherent therein. Even Mohammedanism, so often accused of materialism, did produce, at once, and in consequence, a revival of learning, a crowd of algebraists, astronomers, philosophers, whose names are still to be revered: but within the fold, from the death of Christ to the Renaissance — a purely pagan movement — we hear no more of art, literature, or philosophy.[1] But we do hear—well, what Gibbon has to say.

There is surely a positive side to all this; we agree that Pagans must have been more spiritual than their successors, if only because themselves openly scoffed at their mythology without in the least abandoning the devout performance of its rites, while the Christian clung to irrelevant historical falsehood as if it were true and important. But it is justifiable —nay, urgent—to inquire how and why? Which having discovered, we are bound to proceed with the problem: " Wherewithal shall a young man cleanse his way ?" receive the answer : " By taking heed thereto accord-

[1] Such philosophy as does exist is entirely vicious, taking its axioms no more from observed fact, but from " Scripture " or from Aristotle. Barring such isolated pagans as M. Aurelius Antoninus, and the neo-Platonists, those glorious decadents * of paganism.

ing to thy word," and interpret "thy word " as " The Works of Aleister Crowley."

But this is to anticipate ; let us answer the first question by returning to our phrase " The Church that exteriorises is already lost." On that hypothesis, the decay of Paganism was accomplished by the very outward and visible sign of its inward and spiritual grace, the raising of massive temples to the Gods in a style and manner to which history seeks in vain a parallel. Security is mortals' chiefest enemy ; so also the perfection of balanced strength which enabled Hwang-sze to force his enemies to build the Great Wall was the mark of the imminent decay of his dynasty and race— truly a terrible " Writing on the Wall." An end to the days of the Nine Sages ; an end to the wisdoms of Lao Tan on his dun cow; an end to the making of classics of history and of odes and of ethics, to the Shu King and the Shih King, and the Li-Ki,

* Decadence marks the period when the adepts, nearing their earthly perfection, become true adepts, not mere men of genius. They disappear, harvested by heaven: and perfect darkness (apparent death) ensues until the youthful forerunners of the next crop begin to shoot in the form of artists. Diagrammatically :

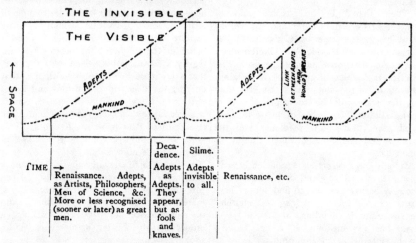

THE INVISIBLE

THE VISIBLE

↑ SPACE

ADEPTS

MANKIND

ADEPTS

LINK (BETWEEN ADEPTS AND WORLD) BREAKS

MANKIND

| TIME → | | Deca-dence. | Slime. | |
|---|---|---|---|---|
| Renaissance. Adepts, as Artists, Philosophers, Men of Science, &c. More or less recognised (sooner or later) as great men. | Adepts as Adepts. | Adepts appear, but as fools and knaves. | Adepts invisible to all. | Renaissance, etc. |

By the Progress of the World we mean that she is always giving adepts to God, and thus losing them ; yet, through their aid, while they are still near enough to humanity to attract it, she reaches each time a higher point. Yet this point is never very high ; so that Aeschylus, though in fact more ignorant than our schoolboys, holds his seat beside Ibsen and Newton in the Republic of the Adepti—a good horse, but not to be run too hard.—A. C.

and the mysterious glories of the holy Yi King itself! Civilisation, decadence, and the slime. Still the Great Wall keeps the Barbarians from China : it is the wall that the Church of Christ set up against science and philosophy, and even to-day its ruins stand, albeit wrapped in the lurid flames of Hell. It is the law of life, this cycle; decadence is perfection, and the perfect soul is assumed into the bosom of Nephthys, so that for a while the world lies fallow. It is in failing to see this constant fume of incense rising from the earth that pessimistic philosophies make their grand fundamental error : in that, and in assuming the very point in dispute, the nature of the laws of other worlds and the prospects of the individual soul. Confess, O subtle author, that thou thyself art even now in the same trap! Willingly, reader; these slips happen when, although one cannot prove to others, one knows.[1] Thou too shalt know, an thou wilt :—ask how, and we come suddenly back to our subject, just as a dreamer may wander through countless nightmares, to find himself in the end on the top of a precipice, whence falling, he shall find himself in bed.

Hear wisdom ! the Lord answered Job out of the whirlwind.

A man is almost obliged to be in communion with God when God is blowing his hat off, drenching him to the skin, whistling through his very bones, scaring him almost to death with a flash of lightning, and so on. When he gets time to think, he thinks just that. In a church all is too clearly the work of man : in the matter of man's comfort man's devices are so obviously superior to God's : so that we compare hats and languidly discuss the preacher.

Religion is alive in Wales, because people have to walk miles to chapel.

[1] Let me run wild for once, I beg; I am tired of emulating Mr. Storer Clouston's Sir Julian Wallingford, " whose reasoning powers were so remarkable that he never committed the slightest action without furnishing a full and adequate explanation of his conduct."—A. C.

Religion is alive among Mohammedans, who pray (as they live) out of doors, and who will fight and die for their ideas ; and among Hindus, whose bloody sacrifices bring them daily face to face with death.

Pan-Islam is possible ; pan-Germany is possible ; but pan-Christendom would be absurd. There were saints in the times of the Crusades, and Crusaders in the times of the Saints : for though the foe was more artificial than real, and the object chimerical, a foe and an aim of whatever sort assist the concentration which alone is life.

So that we need not be surprised to see as we do that religion is dead in London, where it demands no greater sacrifice than that of an hour's leisure in the week, and even offers to repay that with social consideration for the old, and opportunities of flirtation for the young.

The word " dear " has two senses, and these two are one.

Pressing the " out-of-doors " argument, as we may call it, I will challenge each of my readers to a simple experiment.

Go out one night to a distant and lonely heath, if no mountain summit is available : then at midnight repeat the Lord's Prayer, or any invocation with which you happen to be familiar, or one made up by yourself, or one consisting wholly of senseless and barbarous words.[1] Repeat it solemnly and

[1] I am ashamed to say that I have devoted considerable time to the absurd task of finding meanings for, and tracing the corruptions of, the " barbarous names of evocation " which occur in nearly all conjurations, and which Zoroaster warns his pupils not to change, because " they are names divine, having in the sacred rites a power ineffable."

The fact is that many such names are indeed corruptions of divine names. We may trace Eheieh in Eie, Abraxas in Abrae, Tetragrammaton in Jehovah.

But this, an initiate knows, is quite contrary to the true theory.

It is *because* the names are senseless that they are effective. If a man is really praying he cannot bring himself to utter ridiculous things to his God, just as Mark Twain observes that one " cannot pray a lie." So that it is a sublime

aloud, expectant of some great and mysterious result.

I pledge myself, if you have a spark of religion in you, that is, if you are properly a human being, that you will (at the very least) experience a deeper sense of spiritual communion than you have ever obtained by any course of church-going.

After which you will, if you are worth your salt, devote your life to the development of this communion, and to the search for an instructed master who can tell you more than I can.

Now the earlier paganism is simply overflowing with this spirit of communion. The boy goes down to the pool, musing, as boys will ; is it strange that a nymph should reward him, sometimes even with wine from the purple vats of death?

Poor dullards ! in your zeal to extinguish the light upon our altars you have had to drench your own with the bitter waters of most general unbelief. Where are the witches and the fairies and the angels, and the visions of divine St. John? You are annoyed at my mention of angels and witches ; because you know yourselves to be sceptics, and that I have any amount of "scriptural warrant" to throw at your heads, if I deigned ; you are all embarrassed when Maude Adams leans over the footlights with a goo-goo accent so excessive that you die of diabetes in a week, and asks you point-blank : "Do you believe in fairies?" while, for your visions, you do not go to St. John's Island, and share his exile ; but to his Wood, and waste your money.

The early pagan worships Demeter in dim groves : there is silence ; there is no organisation of ritual ; there the worship is spontaneous and individual. In short, the work of religion is thrown upon the religious faculty, instead of being delegated to the quite inferior and irrelevant faculties of mere decorum or even stagecraft. A Christian of the type of Browning understands this perfectly. True, he approves the sincerity which he finds to pervade the otherwise disgusting chapel ; but he cares nothing whatever for the "raree-show of Peter's successor," and though I daresay his ghost will be shocked and annoyed by my mention of the fact, Browning himself does not get his illumination in any human temple, but only when he is out with the universe alone in the storm.

Nor does Browning anywhere draw so perfect and so credible a picture of the intercourse between man and God as the exquisite vision of Pan in "Pheidippides." It is all perfectly natural and therefore miraculous ; there is no straining at the gnats of vestment in the hope of swallowing the camel of Illumination.

In the matter of Pentecost, we hear only, in the way of the "conditions of the experiment," that "they were all with one accord in one place." Now, this being

---

test of faith to utter either a lie or a jest, this with reverence, and that with conviction. Achieve it ; the one becomes the truth, the other a formula of power. Hence the real value of the Egyptian ritual by which the theurgist identified himself with the power he invoked. Modern neophytes should not (we think) use the old conjurations with their barbarous names, because, imperfectly understanding the same, they may superstitiously attribute some real power to them ; we shall rather advise "Jack and Jill went up the hill," "From Greenland's icy mountains," and such, with which it is impossible for the normal mind to associate a feeling of reverence.

What may be the mode of operation of this formula concerns us little ; enough if it succeeds. But one may suggest that it is a case of the will running free, i.e. unchecked, as it normally is, by the hosts of critical larvæ we call reason, habit, sensation, and the like.

But the will freed from these may run straight and swift ; if its habitual goal has been the attainment of Samadhi, it may under such circumstances reach it. It will require a very advanced student to use this type of faith. The Lord's Prayer and the minor exaltation are the certainties for this event.—A. C.

the only instance in the world's history of more than two people in one place being of one accord, it is naturally also the only instance of a miracle which happened in church.

The Quakers, arguing soundly enough that women were such a cause of contention chiefly on account of their tongues, and getting a glimpse of these truths which I have so laboriously been endeavouring to expound, hoped for inspiration from the effects of silence alone, and strove (even by a symbolic silence in costume) to repeat the experiment of Pentecost.

But they lacked the stimulus of Syrian air, and that of the stirring times of the already visible sparks of national revolt: they should have sought to replace these by passing the bottle round in their assemblies, and something would probably have happened, an 'twere only a raid of the police.

Better get forty shillings or a month than live and die as lived and died John Bright !

Better be a Shaker, or a camp-meeting homunculus, or a Chatauqua gurl, or a Keswick week lunatic, or an Evan Roberts revivalist, or even a common maniac, than a smug Evangelical banker's clerk with a greasy wife and three gifted children—to be bank clerks after him !

Better be a flagellant, or one who dances as David danced before the Lord, than a bishop who is universally respected, even by the boys he used to baste when he was headmaster of a great English public school !

That is, if religion is your aim : if you are spiritually minded : if you interpret every phenomenon that is presented to your sensorium as a particular dealing of God with your soul.

But if you come back from the celebration of the Eucharist and say, " Mr. Hogwash was very dull to-day," you will never get to heaven, where the good poets live, and nobody else ; nor to hell, whose inhabitants are exclusively bad poets.

There is more hope for a man who should go to Lord's and say he saw the angels of God ascending and descending upon C. B. Fry.

It is God who sees the possibility of Light in Chaos ; it is the Churches who blaspheme the superb body of Truth which Adepts of old enshrined in the Cross, by degrading the Story of the Crucifixion to a mere paragraph in the *Daily Mail* of the time of Pontius Pilate.

Bill Blake took tea with Ezekiel : Tennyson saw no more in the Arthurian legends than a prophecy of the Prince Consort (though Lancelot has little in common with John Brown), and the result of all is that Tennyson is dead and buried—as shown by the fact that he is still popular —and Blake lives, for poets read and love him.

Now when Paganism became popular, organised, state-regulated, it ceased to be individual : that is to say, it ceased to exist as a religion, and became a social institution little better than the Church which has replaced it. But initiates—men who had themselves seen God face to face, and lived —-preserved the vital essence. They chose men ; they tested them ; they instructed them in methods of invoking the Visible Image of the Invisible. Thus by a living chain religion lived—in the Mysteries of Eleusis.

Further, recognising that the Great Work was henceforth to be secret, a worship of caverns and midnight groves and catacombs, no more of open fields and smiling bowers, they caused to be written in symbols by one of the lesser initiates the whole Mystery of Godliness, so that after the renaissance those who were fitted to the Work might infallibly discover the first matter of the Work and even many of the processes thereof.

Such writings are those of the neo-Platonists, and in modern times the God-illumined Adept Berkeley, Christian though he called himself, is perhaps the most distinguished of those who have understood this truth.[1]

But the orthodox Christian, confronted with this fact, is annoyed; just as the American, knowing himself to be of the filthiest dregs of mankind, pretends that there is no such thing as natural aristocracy, though to be sure he gives himself away badly enough when confronted with either a nigger or a gentleman, since to ape

---

[1] EXTRACTS FROM BERKELEY'S LIFE

[1] "There is a mystery about this visit to Dublin. 'I propose to set out for Dublin about a month hence,' he writes to 'dear Tom,' ' but of this you must not give the least intimation to any one. It is of all things my earnest desire (and for very good reasons) not to have it known I am in Dublin. Speak not, therefore, one syllable of it to any mortal whatsoever. When I formerly desired you to take a place for me near the town, you gave out that you were looking for a retired lodging for a friend of yours; upon which everybody surmised me to be the person. I must beg you not to act in the like manner now—but to take for me an entire house in your own name, and as for yourself; for, all things considered, I am determined upon a whole house, with no mortal in it but a maid of your own getting, who is to look on herself as your servant. Let there be two bedrooms; one for you, another for me, and as you like you may ever and anon lie there.

" ' I would have the house with necessary furniture taken by the month (or otherwise as you can), for I propose staying not beyond that time, and yet perhaps I may.

" ' Take it as soon as possible. . . . Let me entreat you to say nothing of this to anybody, but to do the thing directly. . . . I would of all things have a proper place in a retired situation, where I may have access to fields, and sweet air, provided against the moment I arrive. I am inclined to think one may be better concealed in the outermost skirt of the suburbs, than in the country or within the town. A house quite detached in the country I should have no objections to, provided you judge I shall not be liable to discovery in it. The place called Bermuda I am utterly against. Dear Tom, do this matter cleanly and cleverly, without waiting for further advice. . . . To the person from whom you hire it (whom alone I would have you speak to of it) it will not be strange at this time of the year to be desirous for your own convenience, or health, to have a place in a free and open air ! '

"This mysterious letter was written in April. From April till September Berkeley

EXTRACTS FROM THE BOOK OF THE SACRED MAGIC OF ABRAMELIN THE MAGE

I resolved to absent myself suddenly and go away . . . and lead a solitary life.

I am about here to set down in writing the difficulties, temptations, and hindrances which will be caused him by his own relations . . . beforehand thou shouldest arrange thine affairs in such wise that they can in no way hinder thee, nor bring thee any disquietude.

I took another house at rent . . . and I gave over unto one of my uncles the care of providing the necessaries of life.

"Should you perform this Operation in a town, you should take a house which is not at all overlooked by any one, seeing that in this present day curiosity is so strong that you ought to be upon your guard ; and there ought to be a garden (adjoining the house) wherein you can take exercise."

"Consider then the safety of your person, commencing this operation in a place of safety, whence neither enemies nor any disgrace can drive you out before the end."

" the season of Easter. . . . Then first on the following day . . . I commenced this Holy

dominance is the complement of his natural slavishness. So the blind groveller, Mr. Conformity, and his twin, Mr. Nonconformity, agree to pretend that initiates are always either dupes or impostors; they deny that man can see God and live. Look! There goes John Compromise to church, speculating, like Lot's wife, on the probable slump in sulphur and the gloomy outlook for the Insurance Companies. It will never do for his Christ to be a man of like passions with himself, else people might expect him to aim at a life like Christ's. He wants to wallow and swill, and hope for an impossible heaven.

So that it will be imprudent of you (if you want to be asked out to dinner) to poin out that if you tell the story of the life of Christ, without mentioning names, to a Musulman, he will ask, "What was the name of that great sheikh?" to a Hindu, "Who was this venerable Yogi?" to a Buddhist, "Haven't you made a mistake or two? It wasn't a dove, but an elephant with six tusks: and He died of dysentery."

The fact being that it is within the personal experience of all these persons that men yet live and walk this earth who live in all essentials the life that Christ lived, to whom all His miracles are commonplace, who die His death daily, and partake daily in the Mysteries of His resurrection and ascension.

Whether this is scientifically so or not is of no importance to the argument. I am not addressing the man of science, but the man of intelligence: and the scientist himself will back me when I say that the evidence for the one is just as strong and as weak as

---

again disappears. There is in all-this a curious secretiveness of which one has *repeated examples in his life.*[1] Whether he went to Dublin on that occasion, or why he wanted to go, does not appear."

[2] "I abhor business, and especially to have to do with great persons and great affairs."

[3] "Suddenly, and without the least previous notice of pain, he was removed to the enjoyment of eternal rewards, and although all possible means were instantly used, no symptom of life ever appeared after; nor could the physicians assign any cause for his death."

Operation . . . the period of the Six Moons being expired, the Lord granted unto me His grace . . ."

"a solitary life, which is the source of all good . . . once thou shalt have obtained the sacred science and magic the love for retirement will come to thee of its own accord, and thou wilt voluntarily shun the commerce and conversation of men, &c."

"a good death in His holy Kingdom."

---

It is surely beyond doubt that Berkeley contemplated some operation of a similar character to that of Abramelin. Note the extreme anxiety which he displays. What lesser matter could so have stirred the placid and angelic soul of Berkeley? On what less urgent grounds would he have agreed to the deceptions (harmless enough though they are) that he urges upon his brother?

That he at one time or another achieved success is certain from the universal report of his holiness and from the nature of his writings. The repeated phrase in the Optics, "God is the Father of Lights,"[2] suggests an actual phrase perhaps used as an exclamation at the moment of a Vision to express, however feebly, its nature, rather than the phrase of a reasoner exercising his reason.

This mysterious letter which so puzzles his biographer is in fact the key to his whole character, life, and opinions.

This is no place to labour the point; I have at hand none of the necessary documents; but it might be worth the research of a scholar to trace Berkeley's progress through the grades of the Great Order.—A. C.

---

[1] The italics are ours.—ED.

[2] It occurs in James i. 17.

for the others. God forbid that I should rest this paper on a historical basis! I am talking about the certain results of human psychology: and science can neither help nor hinder me.

True, when Huxley and Tyndall were alive, their miserable intelligences were always feeding us up with the idea that science might one day be able to answer some of the simpler questions which one can put: but that was because of their mystical leanings; they are dead, and have left no successors. To-day we have the certitude, "Science never can tell," of the laborious Ray Lankester

" Whose zeal for knowledge mocks the curfew's call,
And after midnight, to make Lodge look silly,
Studies anatomy—in Piccadilly."

Really, we almost echo his despair. When, only too many years ago, I was learning chemistry, the text-books were content with some three pages on Camphor: to-day, a mere abstract of what is known occupies 400 closely printed pages: but Knowledge is in no wise advanced. It is no doubt more difficult to learn " Paradise Lost " by heart than " We are Seven "; but when you have done it, you are no better at figure-skating.

I am not denying that the vast storehouses of fact do help us to a certain distillation (as it were) of their grain: but I may be allowed to complain with Maudsley that there is nobody competent to do it. Even when a genius does come along, his results will likely be as empirical as the facts they cover. Evolution is no better than creation to explain things, as Spencer showed.

The truth of the matter appears to be that as reason is incompetent to solve the problems of philosophy and religion, *à fortiori* science is incompetent. All that science can do is to present reason with new facts. To such good purpose has it done this, that no modern scientist can hope to do more than know a little about one bud on his pet twig of the particular branch he has chosen to study, as it hangs temptingly from one bough of the Tree of Knowledge.

One of the most brilliant of the younger school of chemists remarks in the course of a stirring discourse upon malt analysis : " Of extremely complex organic bodies the constitution of some 250,000 is known with certainty, and the number grows daily. No one chemist pretends to an intimate acquaintance with more than a few of these . . ." Why not leave it alone, and try to be God?

But even had we Maudsley's committee of geniuses, should we be in any real sense the better? Not while the reason is, as at present, the best guide known to men, not until humanity has developed a mental power of an entirely different kind. For to the philosopher it soon becomes apparent that reason is a weapon inadequate to the task. Hume saw it, and became a sceptic in the widest sense of the term. Mansel saw it, and counsels us to try Faith, as if it was not the very fact that Faith was futile that bade us appeal to reason. Huxley saw it, and, no remedy presenting itself but a vague faith in the possibilities of human evolution, called himself an agnostic: Kant saw it for a moment, but it soon hid itself behind his terminology; Spencer saw it, and tried to gloss it over by smooth talk, and to bury it beneath the ponderous tomes of his unwieldy erudition.

I see it, too, and the way out to Life.

But the labyrinth, if you please, before the clue : the Minotaur before the maiden !

Thank you, madam ; would you care to look at our new line in Minotaurs at 2s. 3d. ? This way, please.

I have taken a good deal of trouble lately to prove the proposition "All arguments are arguments in a circle." Without wearying my readers with the formal proof, which I hope to advance one day in an essay on the syllogism, I will take (as sketchily as you please !) the obvious and important case of the consciousness.

A. The consciousness is made up exclusively of impressions (The tendency to certain impressions is itself a result of impressions on the ancestors of the conscious being). Locke, Hume, &c.

B. Without a consciousness no impression can exist. Berkeley, Fichte, &c.

Both A. and B. have been proved times without number, and quite irrefutably. Yet they are mutually exclusive. The "progress" of philosophy has consisted almost entirely of advances in accuracy of language by rival schools who emphasised A. and B. alternately.

It is easy to see that all propositions can, with a little ingenuity, be reduced to one form or the other.[1]

Thus, if I say that grass is green, I mean that an external thing is an internal thing: for the grass is certainly not in my eye, and the green certainly *is* in it. As all will admit.

So, if you throw a material brick at your wife, and hit her (as may happen to all of us), there is a most serious difficulty in the question, "At what point did your (spiritual) affection for her transform into the (material) brick, and that again into her (spiritual) reformation?"

Similarly, we have Kant's clear proof that in studying the laws of nature we only study the laws of our own minds: since, for one thing, the language in which we announce a law is entirely the product of our mental conceptions.

While, on the other hand, it is clear enough that our minds depend upon the laws of nature, since, for one thing, the apprehension that six savages will rob and murder you is immediately allayed by the passage of a leaden bullet weighing 230 grains, and moving at the rate of 1200 feet per second, through the bodies of two of the ringleaders.

[1] Compare the problems suggested to the logician by the various readings of propositions in connotation, denotation, and comprehension respectively; and the whole question of existential import.—A. C.

It would of course be simple to go on and show that after all we attach no meaning to weight and motion, lead and bullet, but a purely spiritual one: that they are mere phases of our thought, as interpreted by our senses: and on the other that apprehension is only a name for a certain group of chemical changes in certain of the contents of our very material skulls: but enough! the whole controversy is verbal, and no more.

Since therefore philosophy and *à fortiori* science are bankrupt, and the official receiver is highly unlikely to grant either a discharge; since the only aid we get from the Bishops is a friendly counsel to drink Beer —in place of the spiritual wine of Omar Khayyam and Abdullah el Haji (on whom be peace!)—we are compelled to fend for ourselves.

We have heard a good deal of late years about Oriental religions. I am myself the chief of sinners. Still, we may all freely confess that they are in many ways picturesque: and they do lead one to the Vision of God face to face, as one who hath so been led doth here solemnly lift up his voice and testify; but their method is incredibly tedious, and unsuited to most, if not all, Europeans. Let us never forget that no poetry of the higher sort, no art of the higher sort, has ever been produced by any Asiatic race. We are the poets! we are the children of wood and stream, of mist and mountain, of sun and wind! We adore the moon and the stars, and go into the London streets at midnight seeking Their kisses as our birthright. We are the Greeks —and God grant ye all, my brothers, to be as happy in your loves!—and to us the rites of Eleusis should open the doors of Heaven, and we shall enter in and see God face to face! Alas!

" None can read the text, not even I ;
And none can read the comment but myself." [1]

[1] Tennyson must have stolen these lines; they are simple and expressive.

The comment is the Qabalah, and that I have indeed read as deeply as my poor powers allow: but the text is decipherable only under the stars by one who hath drunken of the dew of the moon.

Under the stars will I go forth, my brothers, and drink of that lustral dew: I will return, my brothers, when I have seen God face to face, and read within those eternal eyes the secret that shall make you free.

Then will I choose you and test you and instruct you in the Mysteries of Eleusis, oh ye brave hearts, and cool eyes, and trembling lips! I will put a live coal upon your lips, and flowers upon your eyes, and a sword in your hearts, and ye also shall see God face to face.

Thus shall we give back its youth to the world, for like tongues of triple flame we shall brood upon the Great Deep—Hail unto the Lords of the Groves of Eleusis!

END OF VOL. III.

APPENDICES

# APPENDIX A

## NOTES

### TOWARDS AN OUTLINE OF A BIBLIOGRAPHY OF THE WRITINGS IN PROSE AND VERSE OF ALEISTER CROWLEY *

### EDITIONES PRINCIPES

#### (I)

#### [ACELDAMA: 1898]

Aceldama, | a Place to Bury Strangers in. | a philosophical poem | by | a gentleman of the University of Cambridge. | privately printed. | London : | 1898.

Collation :—Crown 8vo, pp. 29, consisting of Half-title, quotation on reverse from " Songs of the Spirit," p. 13, ll. 1-4 ; Title-page as above, quotation on reverse St. John xii. 24, 25 ; prose Prologue, quotation on reverse Acts i. 18, 19 ; Dedication dated " Midnight, 1897–1898," on reverse "à toi " ; second half-title, quotation on reverse from Swinburne's "The Leper" ; " Poems and Ballads," 1866, pp. 1-10 ; Text, pp. 11-27 ; no headline ; Epilogue p. 28 ; no imprint, but printed by an obscure printer in the Brompton-road, London.

Edition : 2 copies on vellum, numbered 1, 2 ; [1] 10 copies on Japanese vellum, numbered 3-12 ; [2] 88 copies on hand-made paper, numbered 13-100.

Issued in Japanese vellum turned-in wrapper repeating title-page.

#### [THE TALE OF ARCHAIS : 1898]

The | Tale of Archais | a Romance in Verse | by a Gentleman of the University | of Cam-

bridge | London | Kegan Paul, Trench, Trübner & Co. | MDCCCXCVIII.

Collation :—Pott 4to, pp. viii + 89, consisting of Half-title, Title-page in red and black as above (with imprint : " Chiswick Press : —Charles Whittingham & Co. | Tooks Court, Chancery Lane, London." on reverse), pp. iii–iv. ; Dedication " To | The White Maidens of England | this Tale of Greece | is | dedicated " (with blank reverse), pp. v–vi ; continued in verse, pp. vii–viii. ; Prologue in verse, pp. 1 – 5 ; second Half-title, p. 7 ; Text, pp. 8-84 ; Epilogue, pp. 85–89. There are headlines throughout. The imprint — " Chiswick Press :—Charles Whittingham and Co. | Tooks Court, Chancery Lane, London."— is repeated at the foot of the last page.

Edition : 2 copies on Roman vellum, 250 on hand-made paper.

Issued in slate-blue, dull-green, and brick-red boards with white holland backs, and white paper back label. The published price was five shillings.

#### [THE HONOURABLE ADULTERERS : 1899]

The | Honourable Adulterers | a tragedy | by | A. E. C. | 1899.

Collation :—Demy 8vo, cut edges, pp. 8, pagination from 119-126,[1] consisting of Title

---

[1] These large-paper copies measure 7½ × 10, printed on thick vellum, wrapper of Japanese vellum.
[2] These large-paper copies measure 7½ × 10, on thick Japanese vellum, wrapper of thin Japanese vellum.

[1] The pagination is accounted for by the fact that these three pamphlets were printed off from the paged type of *Jephthah and Other Mysteries*, then in the press, and issued separately.

---

* For the bulk of these notes we are indebted to the late Mr. L. C. R. Duncombe-Jewell.

as above; Text, pp. 119–126. Headlines throughout. No imprint.

Edition: 5 copies, on smooth purplish paper.

Issued in blue paper wrapper, repeating title-page.

### [JEPHTHAH AND OTHER MYSTERIES : 1899]

Jephthah | and other mysteries | lyrical and dramatic | by Aleister Crowley | London : Kegan Paul, Trench, | Trübner and Company, Ltd. | 1899 | *all rights reserved.*

Collation :—Demy 8vo, pp. xxii+223, consisting of Half-title, quotation on reverse from *Il Penseroso*; Title-page as above, quotation on reverse from SAPPHO; Quotation from *The Book of the Sacred Magic of Abra-Melin the Mage;* on reverse " The dedication | is to | Algernon Charles Swinburne"; Dedication in verse, pp. vii–xii; Contents, pp. xiii–xiv; Prelude, xv–xxi; second Half-title, "Jephthah, | a tragedy," on reverse quotation from *Hamlet;* second Dedication, "To | Gerald · Kelly, | poet and painter, | I dedicate | this tragedy"; dated "Cambridge, November, 1898." Text, pp. 5–221; Epilogue, pp. 222–223. On reverse, imprint "Chiswick Press :—Charles Whittingham and Co. | Tooks Court, Chancery Lane, London," surmounted by colophon, upon a mound, *a lion rampant, grasping an anchor entwined with a dolphin, the flukes and head in base.* Advertisements at end of book, pp. 8. Headlines throughout.

Editions : 1000 copies on machine-made paper, 6 copies on India paper.

Issued in brick-red boards, linen backs, white paper label, "Crowley | Jephthah | & other | mysteries | lyrical & | dramatic | Kegan Paul, | Trench | Trübner & | Co. Ltd. | 1899 | Price 7s. 6d." The six India-paper copies issued in old gold coloured buckram, lettered on cover " Jephthah " in red.

### [SONGS OF THE SPIRIT : 1898]

Songs of the Spirit | by | Aleister Crowley | "Sublimi feriam sidera vertice" HOR. | London | Kegan Paul, Trench, Trübner & Co. | MDCCCXCVIII.

Collation :—Pott 8vo, pp. x+109. Half-title; on reverse, quotation from *The Tale of*

*Archais ;* Title in red and black as above; reverse, quotation from *Ecclesiastes,*" a fool also is full of words," p. iv. Dedication in verse to J. L. B.,[1] pp. v–vii. Contents, pp. ix–x; Second Half-title; Text, pp. 3–104; Epilogue, pp. 105–109. Imprint on last page,"Chiswick Press:—Charles Whittingham and Co. | Tooks Court, Chancery Lane,London "; surmounted by colophon. No headlines.

Edition: 1 copy on vellum, 50 copies on hand-made paper numbered and signed,[2] 300 copies on machine-made paper.

Issued in Japanese vellum with gold lettering on front of cover "Songs of the Spirit " for copies printed on hand-made paper; and in grey cloth boards, lettered on back "Songs | of the | Spirit | Aleister Crowley | 1898 " in crimson for those printed on machine-made paper. Priced 3s. 6d.

### [THE POEM : 1898]

The Poem | a little drama in four scenes | by | Aleister Crowley | printed privately | London | 1898.

Collation :—Demy 8vo, cut edges, pp. 20, pagination 99–118[*]; consisting of Half-title, "The Poem. | a little drama in four scenes"; Dedication, p. 101; Text, pp. 103–117. Headlines throughout. No imprint.

Edition : 10 copies on smooth paper.

Issued in Japanese vellum wrapper repeating title-page.

### [JEZEBEL : 1898]

Jezebel | and other | Tragic Poems | By Count Vladimir Svareff | Edited, with an Introduction and Epilogue, by | Aleister Crowley | Vignette of Armorial Design of Chiswick Press | London | Privately printed at the Chiswick Press | 1898.

Collation :—Demy 4to, pp. 23, with 8 unnumbered preliminary pages printed from the Caxton fount of antique type; Half-title; Title as above, "Jezebel" and "London" in red; Dedication in verse dated, "Londres, Juin 1898," in French,

---

[1] J. L. Baker, the alchymist.
[2] Carelessly done or not done at all.

"à Gerald"; Contents; Introduction in verse signed "A. C." p. i.; Text, pp. 3–22; Epilogue signed "A. C." p. 23; colophon, printer's mark, *argent, a printer's maul in pale*, the shield surrounded by a scroll; below the imprint, "Chiswick Press: Tooks Court, Chancery Lane, London." No headlines.

Edition: 2 copies on vellum, 10 copies on Japanese vellum, 40 copies on hand-made paper.

Issued in Japanese vellum turned-in wrapper, with legend "Jezebel | and other Tragic Poems" enclosed in ornamental border on front of cover in gold. Unpriced: copies were sold at half-a-guinea.

## [AN APPEAL TO THE AMERICAN REPUBLIC: 1899]

Price Sixpence | An Appeal | to the | American Republic | design of Union Flag and United States Ensign crossed | by | Aleister Crowley | London | Kegan Paul, Trench, Trübner & Co. Ltd. | 1899.

Collation : — Demy 4to, pp. 12. Crimson wrapper and Title-page in one. Text, pp. 1–12. Imprint at foot of last page, "Chiswick Press: Charles Whittingham and Co., Tooks Court, Chancery Lane, London."

Edition: 500 copies on machine-made paper.

## [JEPHTHAH: 1898]

Jephthah | a Tragedy | by | a gentleman of the University of | Cambridge | (Aleister Crowley) | London | 1898 | [not for sale].

Collation :—Demy 8vo, cut edges, pp. 71; consisting of Half-title, "Jephthah | a tragedy," on reverse quotation from *Hamlet ;* Dedication "To | Gerald Kelly, | Poet Painter, | I dedicate | this tragedy; because his friendship was the turquoise, which I had of him before I was a bachelor; and which I would not have given for a wilderness of monkeys."[1] Dated "Cambridge, November 1898";

[1] The reference is to *The Merchant of Venice*, Act III. Scene 1. "Bachelor" refers to the degree of "B.A.," which the Author was expecting to take at the time of writing the Dedication; but which in fact he did not take.

Text, pp. 5–69; "A Note on Jephthah," pp. 70–71. Headlines throughout. No imprint.

Edition: 25 copies on machine-made paper.

Issued in grey paper with an auto-lithograph in black ink, "Aleister Crowley | Jephthah," on cover.

## [THE MOTHER'S TRAGEDY: 1901]

The Mother's | Tragedy | and | Other Poems | by | Aleister Crowley | Privately printed | 1901.

Collation :—Medium 8vo, pp. xii+111; consisting of Half-title; Title as above; Contents, pp. v–vi; Prologue, pp. vii–xii; Text, pp. 1–106; Epilogue, pp. 107–111. No imprint. Headlines throughout.

Edition: 500 copies on machine-made paper.

Issued in blue boards, linen backs, white paper back-label, "Crowley | The | Mother's | Tragedy | and other | Poems." Priced at 5s. 0d.

## [THE SOUL OF OSIRIS: 1901]

The Soul of Osiris | a history | by | Aleister Crowley | London : Kegan Paul, Trench | Trübner and Company, Ltd. | 1901 | *All rights reserved.*

Collation :—Medium 8vo, pp. ix+129; consisting of Half-title; Title as above, on reverse imprint "Chiswick Press: Charles Whittingham and Co. | Tooks Court, Chancery Lane, London"; Contents, pp. v–vi; Prologue, pp. vii–ix; Text, pp. 3–129; Epilogue, "The Epilogue is silence," on reverse imprint of Chiswick Press as before.

Edition: 500 copies on machine-made paper, 6 copies on India paper.

Issued in brick-red boards, linen backs, white paper back-label, "Crowley | The | Soul | of | Osiris | Kegan Paul, Trench | Trübner & | Co. Ltd. Price 5s. 0d.

## [CARMEN SAECULARE: 1901]

Carmen Saeculare | by | St. E. A. of M. and S. | London | Kegan Paul, Trench, Trübner

& Co. Ltd. | Paternoster House, Charing Cross Road | 1901.

Collation:—Demy 4to, pp. 30; consisting of Half-title; Dedication to " The Countess of Glenstrae" ; Title as above ; Prologue, pp. 5–7; Text pp. 9–25; Epilogue, pp. 27–30, dated "s.s. Pennsylvania, July 4, 1900." No headlines.

Edition : 450 copies on machine-made paper, 6 copies on Roman vellum and 50 copies (?) on hand-made paper with title-page, " Carmen Saeculare | by | St. E. A. of M. and S. | Privately issued | London, 1901."

Issued in green paper wrapper repeating title-page with design of shamrock in centre. Price 1s. od.

## [TANNHAUSER: 1902]

Tannhäuser | A story of all time | by | Aleister Crowley | London | Kegan Paul, Trench, Trübet & Co. Ltd. | Paternoster House, Charing Cross Road | 1902.

Collation : — Demy 4to, 142 pp., consisting of Half-title, quotation on reverse from Browning's *Master Hughes of Saxe-Gotha ;* Title-page as above, on reverse " all rights reserved" ; Dedication in verse, pp. 5–7 ; Prose preface, pp. 9–16, dated " Kandy, Ceylon, Sept. 1901." Second Half-title ; Text, pp. 18–142. Imprint at foot, " Turnbull and Spears, Printers, Edinburgh." Two pages of advertisements at end. No headlines.

Edition : 6 copies on Japanese vellum, 500 copies on machine-made paper.

Issued in royal-blue boards, linen backs, white paper back-label, " Crowley | Tannhäuser [1] | a story of | all time | Kegan Paul, | Trench, | Trübner & | Co. Ltd. | 1902. Price 5s. od.

## [NEW YEAR'S CARD, 1903]

New Year, 190

A sonnet printed in gold on fly-sheets of Roman vellum (12) and hand - made paper (50) within a broad scarlet border, size 5⅞ × 6⅞, " from Aleister Crowley, | wishing you a speedy termination of existence." Printed throughout in capital letters.

[1] Note the misprint "aü " for " äu."

## [BERASHITH : 1903]

A.B.   2447, | Paris | בראשׁת | an Essay | in | ontology | with some remarks on ceremonial magic | by | Abhavananda | (Aleister Crowley) | Privately printed for the Sangha of | the West.

Collation :—Size 9 × 7⅜, pp. 24, consisting of Title-page and wrapper in one as above, on reverse, Number of Copy and Errata ; Text, pp. 1–24 ; Imprint at foot of last page, " Clarke & Bishop, Printers, Etc., 338, Rue St. Honoré, Paris." No headlines.

Edition : 200 copies on China paper numbered.

Issued in wrapper and title in one on machine-made paper 10⅝ × 8 ⁸⁄₁₆. Price 5 francs.

## [SUMMA SPES : undated]

Summa | Spes | Aleister | Crowley.

Collation :—Single poem on Japanese vellum 9 × 7½, printed in red with a green ornamental border. Photograph by Haweis and Coles in front, and colophon by T. Spicer Simpson on back.

## [BALZAC : 1903]

Balzac | *Hommage à Auguste Rodin.*

A sonnet which occurs in *Ahab* in a slightly altered form. Was issued in Paris by request, on a single unfolded sheet of Japanese vellum 14⅝ × 9¼ inches : 3 copies printed vertically, and 15 horizontally on the right half of the paper ; also 6 copies on China paper 12⅜ × 9¼ inches printed vertically in the upper moiety of the sheet. No imprint.

## [AHAB : 1903]

Ahab | and other Poems | By Aleister Crowley | with an introduction and Epilogue by | Count Vladimir Svareff | Design of the Chiswick Press, vignette | London. Privately printed at the Chiswick Press | 1903.

Collation :—Demy 4to, pp. 35, and 6 unnumbered preliminary pages, consisting of Half-title ; Title in red and black as above ; Dedication in verse to G. C. J.,[1] dated Paris, December 9, 1902 ; Contents ;

[1] George Cecil Jones, the Theurgist.

Rondel, p. 1 ; Text, pp. 3–33 ; Epilogue, signed "V.S.," p. 35. Printed from the Caxton fount of antique type : no headlines : no imprint.

Edition : 2 copies on vellum, 10 copies on Japanese vellum, 150 copies on handmade paper.

Issued in Japanese vellum turned-in wrapper with legend "Ahab | and other poems " enclosed in ornamental border on front of cover in gold. Price 5s. 0d.

## [ALICE : 1903]

Alice : an | Adultery | privately printed | 1903.

Collation :—Fcp. 8vo, pp. xx+95, consisting of Half-title ; Title as above ; Introduction by the Editor dated " Yokohama, April, 1901," pp. i–xii ; Critical Essay on *Alice* signed " G. K.,"[1] pp. xiii–xx. Prefatory poems, pp. 1–17. Second Half-title ; Text, pp. 21–95. No headlines. No imprint.

Edition : 100 copies on China paper. Price to subscribers, 10s. 6d. ; published price, 21s. 0d.

Issued in green camel-hair, turned-in wrapper lettered on front cover, " Alice," in white.

## [THE GOD-EATER : 1903]

The God-Eater | A Tragedy of Satire | by | Aleister Crowley | Watts & Co. | 17 Johnson's Court, Fleet Street, London, E.C. | 1903.

Collation :—Cr. 4to, pp. 32, consisting of Half-Title, on reverse announcement of works " by the same author" ; Title-page as above ; Dedication ; Text, pp. 7–32. Imprint " R. Clay and Sons, Ltd., Bread St. Hill, E.C., and Bungay, Suffolk," at foot of last page.

Edition : 2 copies on Roman vellum, 300 on machine-made paper.

Issued in green camel-hair wrapper lettered in red, " The | God-eater | A Tragedy | of Satire | By | Aleister Crowley | Watts & Co. | 17 Johnson's Court, Fleet Street, London, E.C. | 1903." Price 2s. 6d.

[1] Gerald Kelly. Both the Introduction and Critical Essay are the result of the collaboration of four men—A. C., G. K., D. J.-F., and I. B.

## [THE STAR AND THE GARTER : 1903]

The Star & | The Garter | By Aleister | Crowley | Watts & Co. | 17 Johnson's Court | London | 1903.

Collation :—Demy 4to, pp. 89, consisting of Half-title ; Title-page as above ; Invocation in Greek ; Text, pp. 7–77 ; Appendix, prose and verse, pp. 79–86 ; Press Notices, pp. 87–89 ; reply to Invocation in Greek, p. 78 ; advertisement one page. Imprint in centre of last page, " printed by Turnbull and Spears, Edinburgh."

Edition : 2 copies on Roman vellum, fifty copies on hand-made paper.

Issued in green camel-hair wrapper, lettered in white on front of cover, " The | Star & | The Garter | by Aleister | Crowley."

## [THE ARGONAUTS : 1904]

The Argonauts | by | Aleister Crowley | Society for the Propagation of Religious Truth | Boleskine, Foyers, Inverness | 1904.

Collation :—Crown 8vo, pp. 102, consisting of Half-title ; Title-page as above ; sub-title, " Jason,"[1] dedication on reverse ; Text of " Jason," pp. 3–17 ; sub-title of " Argo," dedication on reverse ; Text of " Argo," pp. 3–19 ; sub-title " Medea," dedication on reverse ; Text of " Medea," pp. 3–19 ; sub-title " Sirenæ," dedication on reverse ; Text of " Sirenæ," pp. 3–24 ; sub-title " Ares," dedication on reverse ; Text of " Ares," pp. 3–23. Imprint at foot of last page, " Chiswick Press : printed by Charles Whittingham and Co | Tooks Court, Chancery Lane, London." Announcement of works by the same author on reverse. No headlines.

Edition : 2 copies on Roman vellum, 200 copies on machine-made paper.

Issued in green camel's-hair wrapper, lettered in red on front of cover, " The Argonauts | by | Aleister Crowley." Price 5s. 0d.

[1] Each Act is a separate play on the Greek model separately paginated.

238                                  NOTES

[THE SWORD OF SONG : 1904]

The Sword of Song | called by Christians |
The Book of the Beast | Aleister Crowley |
Society for the Propagation of Religious Truth
| Benares | 1904.

Collation :—Post 4to, pp. ix+194, printed in
   red and black, consisting of Half-title,
   parody of passage from *Through the Look-
   ing Glass* on reverse ; Title-page as above,
   Dedication on reverse ; Introductory poem
   *Nothung ;* Half-title ; Prose Introduction to
   " Ascension Day and Pentecost," pp. iii-
   ix ; Text, pp. 1-62 ; Notes, pp, 63-91 ;
   Appendices, pp. 93-121 ; " בראשית | an
   essay | in | ontology | with some remarks
   on | ceremonial magic," pp. 123-148 ;
   " Science and Buddhism," pp. 149-192 ;
   Epilogue in verse, pp. 193-194 ; Index on
   last page, imprint on reverse, " printed | by
   | Philippe Renouard | 19, rue des Saints-
   Pères, 19 | Paris." Headlines throughout.

Editions: 100 copies on a glazed foreign
   paper.[1]

Issued in navy blue wrapper front page lettered
in gold " Ye Sword | of Song," with design in
centre " 666 " thrice repeated on a golden
square (*vide* pp. 4-5 of book), on reverse pub-
lishers' advertisement ; back of cover author's
name in Hebrew characters adding up to " 666,"
in gold ; inside of back page of cover list of
author's works in gold ; back of cover " The
| Sword | of | Song." Price 10s. od.

[GOETIA : 1904]

The Book of the | Goetia | of | Solomon the
King | translated into the English Tongue by a
| Dead Hand | and | adorned with divers other
matters germane | delightful to the wise | the
whole | edited, verified, introduced and com-
mented | by | Aleister Crowley | Society for
the Propagation of Religious Truth | Boles-
kine, Foyers, Inverness | 1904.

Collation :—Demy 4to, pp. ix+65, consisting
   of Half-title, Invocation in Greek on reverse ; Frontispiece ; Title-page as above,
   talisman on reverse ; Prefatory Note, pp.
   v-vi ; Preliminary Invocation, pp. vii-ix ;
   Text, pp. 1-65 ; colophon of Chiswick

[1] There were 10 advance copies issued in a crimson
wrapper repeating title-page, on back " The Sword
of Song " lengthwise, on back outside of cover colophon Louis Seize design, initials of designer " L. M."

Press Mark on reverse of last page. No
headlines. Two illustrations besides
Frontispiece.

Edition : 200 copies on machine-made paper,
1 copy on vellum, 10 copies on Japanese
vellum.

Issued in green camel's-hair wrapper, lettered
in red " Goetia " in centre, surrounded by the
legend " Goetia vel clavicula Salomonis Regis "
frequently repeated. Price 21s. od., raised from
subscription price of 10s. od.
Japanese vellum copies in white and gold.
Japanese vellum turned-in wrapper, same
lettering.

[WHY JESUS WEPT : 1904]

Why | Jesus Wept | a Study of Society | and of
| The Grace of God | by | Aleister Crowley |
Privately Printed | 1904.

Collation :—Post 4to, pp. 16+80. Half-title ; advertisement (of the 21s. edition) ; Title
   as above ; letter from author's mother, 2 pp. ;
   Persons studied ; Quotation from *Times*
   newspaper and John xi. 35. Dedications
   6 pp. to various persons (all these pages
   unnumbered) ; Text, pp. 1-80 ; inset, a slip
   " Note to pp. 75-76 " ; also, loose inset, a
   pamphlet " Mr. Crowley and the Creeds "
   and " The Creed of Mr. Chesterton, &c.
   &c." No imprint, but printed by Philippe
   Rénouard.

Edition : 100 copies on hand-made paper, 20 in
   Japanese vellum ; 1 on Roman vellum.

Issued in turned-in Japanese wrapper ; front,
" Why | Jesus | Wept | Aleister | Crowley | " ;
reverse, colophon of Press ; back, " Why Jesus
Wept."

[ORACLES : THE BIOGRAPHY OF
AN ART : 1905]

Oracles | the biography of an art | unpublished
fragments of the work of Aleister Crowley |
with | explanatory notes by R. P. Lester and |
the Author | 1905 | Society for the Propaga-
tion of Religious Truth | Boleskine, Foyers,
Inverness.

Collation :—Demy 8vo, pp. viii+175+16 advertisements, consisting of Half-title ; Title
   as above ; prefatory note " To Explain " ;
   Contents, pp. vii, viii ; Text, pp. 1-175 ;

Advertisement, pp. 1 - 16.   Headlines throughout.

Edition : 500 copies on machine-made paper.

Issued in green camel-hair paper, on back in large white letters, ORACLES ALEISTER CROWLEY The price was 5s.

## [ORPHEUS : 1905]

Orpheus | a lyrical legend by | Aleister Crowley in two volumes of which | this is volume { one / two } each one crown | *Left.* Society | for the Propagation of | Religious | Truth | *Right.* Boleskine | Foyers | Inverness | 1905.

Printed in Red and Black.

Collation :—Demy 8vo, pp. 156, consisting of Half-title ; Title as above ; Contents, pp. 7–9 ; Warning, pp. 11–14 ; Exordium, pp. 15–19 ; Half-title, Liber Primus vel Carminum, p. 21 ; Dedication " To Oscar Echenstein," &c., p. 23 ; Quotations, p. 24 ; Text, pp. 25–106 ; Half-title, Liber Secundus vel Amoris, p. 107 ; Dedication " To Mary Beaton," &c., 109 ; Quotations, p. 110 ; Text, pp. 111–155 ; Printer's name, p. 156. Headlines throughout.

Volume ii. similarly arranged. Dedications to " The Memory of Jehi Aour," &c., and " To my Wife," p. 148.

Edition : 1 copy on Roman vellum, 500 copies on hand-made paper.

Issued in white boards, linen backs, white label " ORPHEUS | I. (or II.") | Two volumes | Ten Shillings | Boards | CROWLEY.

## [COLLECTED WORKS]

The Works | of | Aleister Crowley | Volume I. | Foyers | Society for the Propagation of | Religious Truth | 1905 | [*All rights reserved*].

Collation :—Extra crown.  In Three Volumes. Vol. I., pp. x+269, consisting of Half-title ; Title as above ; Preface ; Contents, pp. vii–ix ; Text, pp. 1–269 ; Vol. II., pp. viii+283, consisting of Half-title ; Title as above ; Contents, v–vii ; Text, pp. 1–283. Vol. III., pp. vii+230, con-

sisting of Half-title ; Title as above ; Contents, pp. v–vii ; Text, pp. 1+230. Appendices, half-title, and pp. 233–248.

Edition : 1 copy on vellum, 1000 copies on India paper.

Issued in camel-hair paper cover ; on front cover, in large white letters, " The Collected Works of Aleister Crowley."

## [GARGOYLES : 1906]

Gargoyles | being | Strangely Wrought Images | of Life and Death | by | Aleister Crowley | Foyers | Society for the Propagation of Religious Truth | 1906.

Collation :—Pott 8vo, pp. vi+113.  Half-title [reverse ∵ Fifty copies only, &c., on the hand-made copies] ; Title as above in red and black ; Contents, pp. v, vi.

Prose Dedication (" To Lola Bentrovata ") in red and black, pp. 1, 2, and Text, pp. 3–112 ; (presumably) Dedicatory Epilogue, p. 113, printed in red.  Chiswick Press imprint, p. 114.

Edition : 2 copies on Roman vellum, 50 on hand-made paper numbered and signed, 300 copies on machine-made paper.

Issued in facsimile to " Songs of the Spirit." No price, but sold at 3s. 6d. net cash to the trade.

## [ROSA MUNDI : 1905]

Rosa Mundi | a poem | by | H. D. Carr | with an original composition by | Auguste Rodin | prix : vingt francs | price : sixteen shillings net | Paris : Ph-Renouard, rue des Saints Pères | London—of H. D. Carr, care of E. Dennes, 22 Chancery Lane | and through all booksellers | 1905.

Collation :—Foreign glazed paper, measuring 13" × 10" approximately.  Half-title, reverse *tirage ;* 2 copies on vellum, 10 copies on China paper, 488 copies on hand-made paper ; Lithograph by Clot from A. Rodin, woman seated, her arms clasping her knees.  Title as above ; Text, pp. 1–15 ; p. 17, printer's imprint ; Edition as above.

Issued in rose wrappers ; front, Auguste Rodin | Rosa Mundi | H. D. Carr ; reverse, design of curves.

# APPENDIX B

## INDEX OF FIRST LINES TO

### VOLUMES I., II., III.

CPSIA information can be obtained
at www.ICGtesting.com
Printed in the USA
BVHW032312280620
582495BV00001B/1